INTRODUCTION TO THE 2016–2017 EDITION

Highlights of the 2016-2017 Edition of *Intellectual Property Law for Business Lawyers* include:

- **revised and expanded treatment of patent damages case law** (see § § 5:27-5:28, 5:30, and 5:32)
- **up-to-date treatment of patent eligibility** (see § § 5:33 et seq.)
- **new section on the first sale doctrine** (see § 8:25)
- **coverage of the new Defend Trade Secrets Act** (see § § 12:4 and 12:36)

INTRODUCTION TO THE 2016–2017 EDITION

Highlights of the 2016–2017 Edition of Intellectual Property Law for Business Lawyers include:

- revised and expanded treatment of patent damages case law (see §§ 5.27, 5.28, 5.29, and 5.30)
- up-to-date treatment of patent eligibility (see § 5.39 et seq.)
- new section on the first-sale doctrine (see § 3.35)
- coverage of the new Defend Trade Secrets Act (see §§ 12.4 and 12.36).

INTELLECTUAL PROPERTY LAW FOR BUSINESS LAWYERS

2016–2017 EDITION

By

KINNEY & LANGE, P.A.

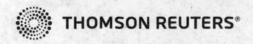

THOMSON REUTERS®

For Customer Assistance Call 1-800-328-4880

Mat #41742164

ABOUT THE AUTHORS

KINNEY & LANGE, P.A. is a full–service intellectual property law
firm founded in 1978 and based in Minneapolis. Our attorneys have a
wide variety of backgrounds in different areas of technology and the
arts. This lends breadth and depth to our practice of patent, trademark,
copyright, unfair competition, and related licensing and litigation. The
firm's clients range from large multinational corporations to small domestic businesses and individuals.

DAVID R. FAIRBAIRN is President and a founding attorney of
Kinney & Lange. Dave is a frequent author and lecturer in the field of
intellectual property. He has also taught "Communications Law" in the
Masters of Business Communication Program of the College of St.
Thomas. Dave served as President of the Minnesota Intellectual Prop-
erty Law Association in 1995–96, is a former member of the Governing
Council of the Hennepin County Bar Association and chaired the Patent
Law committee of the American Intellectual Property Law Association
in 1996–98. He is a member of the Tau Beta Pi and Eta Kappa Nu
Engineering Honors Societies. Dave holds a Bachelor of Electrical
Engineering Degree from the University of Minnesota–Twin Cities (with
distinction) and a Juris Doctor from William Mitchell College of Law
(cum laude). As a tournament fisherman, he qualified for both the 1994
and 1995 MWC World Walleye Championships. Dave also collects
baseball memorabilia.

ALAN M. KOENCK received his Juris Doctor (with high distinction) from the University of Iowa, where he was named to the Order of
the Coif. He received his Bachelor of Science Degree in Electrical
Engineering from Iowa State University. Alan previously worked as an
assistant in the legal department at Norand Corporation, a major
manufacturer of portable data collection and communication systems.
He enjoys sports of all kinds, including golf, tennis and basketball.

LARRIN P. BERGMAN is a native of Jud, North Dakota. Larrin
received a Bachelor of Science degree in Agricultural and Biosystems
Engineering from North Dakota State University, and earned his Juris
Doctor from the University of North Dakota (with distinction). While in
law school, spent a semester studying international comparative law at
the University of Oslo in Oslo, Norway. Prior to law school, Larrin
worked as a design engineer for Beamco in Oslo, Minnesota, where he
developed parts for ATV's, personal watercraft, and snowmobiles.

AUSTEN P. ZUEGE is originally from Central Wisconsin. He
received a Bachelor of Science Degree in Industrial Engineering from
the University of Wisconsin–Madison, and his Juris Doctor (cum laude)
from the University of Illinois College of Law. While at the University of
Wisconsin, he was a member of Professor Barrett Caldwell's Science,
Mathematics, and Engineering Learning Technologies (SMELT)

research team. He was a board member of the Minneapolis Civilian Police Review Authority for four years. Austen enjoys bicycling, music and hiking.

BARRY G. KOEPKE received his Bachelor of Science (with honors) and Master of Science degrees in Metallurgical Engineering from the University of Illinois at Urbana-Champaign and his Ph.D. degree in Metallurgy from Iowa State University. Following graduation, he spent a career at Honeywell and Alliant Techsystems in R&D, Program and Operations Management. During that time he was an Adjunct Professor of Materials Science at the University of Minnesota. He was also, at the request of the National Science Foundation (NSF), and, on leave from Honeywell, Director of the Ceramics Research Program at NSF, Washington, D.C. He has published over 50 papers and is a named inventor on six patents. In his spare time he enjoys weight training and golf. Barry is a non-attorney technical advisor at Kinney & Lange.

MATTHEW J. DE RUYTER graduated from Lawrence University in Appleton, Wisconsin, receiving a Bachelor of Arts degree in Chemistry. After his undergraduate studies, Matt worked as a Research Scientist at CIMA Labs Inc., where his work primarily involved oral dosage drug delivery. Matt received his Juris Doctor (cum laude) from William Mitchell College of Law. While attending law school, Matt interned at Ecolab, Inc. and was a Nationals Qualifier in the Giles Rich Moot Court Competition.

BRIAN T. CRAGGS received his Bachelor of Science in Chemical Engineering from the University of Michigan, and his Juris Doctor from the University of Minnesota Law School. Brian has worked as a Research Assistant at Southwestern University School of Law in Los Angeles, California and as a Student Attorney for the Innocence Project of Minnesota. Prior to attending law school, he worked as an Outage Coordinator and Facility Planner for Great Lakes Gas Transmission Co., in Troy, Michigan, as well as a Laboratory Engineer for Rouge Steel Corporation in Dearborn, Michigan. His interests include bicycling and fantasy sports leagues.

GRANT M. MCNEILLY received his Bachelor of Science Degree in Mechanical Engineering from the University of Wisconsin-Madison. While earning his undergraduate degree, he was a member of the UW Mini-Baja off-road racecar team and twice competed in the UW Innovation Day competition. In addition, Grant was an engineering intern at Orbital Technologies Corporation and GE Healthcare. He received his Juris Doctor from the University of Wisconsin Law School in 2010. In his free time, Grant enjoys travel and outdoor sports.

ERIK A. WRIGHT received his Bachelor of Arts Degree in Physics at Grinnell College in Iowa and his Master of Science Degree in Physics at the University of Illinois, specializing in chaotic systems and physics pedagogy. Erik completed his Juris Doctor (magna cum laude) in 2010 at the University of Minnesota, where he studied patent law and criminal sentencing reform, and served on the Journal of International Law. In his free time, Erik enjoys reading, swimming, and practicing his Swedish and Japanese.

SCOTT C. KRUEGER is originally from Madison, Wisconsin. He received a Bachelor of Science Degree in Computer Engineering from the University of Wisconsin-Madison, and his Juris Doctor from the University of Wisconsin Law School. After receiving his undergraduate degree, Scott worked as a component design engineer for Intel Corp. in Hillsboro, Oregon. While at Intel, he worked as a member of the Core i7 design team focusing extensively on pre-silicon validation. In his free time, Scott enjoys sports of all kinds, coaching and painting.

BOYD B. BLACK received his Bachelor of Science Degree in Mechanical Engineering from Brigham Young University, and his Juris Doctor from the University of Iowa. While earning his undergraduate degree, he interned in the legal department at Novatek Inc., a research and development company specializing in super-materials, down-hole drilling assemblies, and alternative energy solutions. In his free time he enjoys grilling, gardening, and outdoor sports and activities.

RICK W. NELSON graduated summa cum laude from William Mitchell College of Law where he earned his Juris Doctor. Prior to law school, Rick earned his Bachelor of Science in Mathematics from the University of Minnesota. During his time at the U of M, Rick worked as a teaching specialist for a pilot calculus program and helped teach courses in multi-variable calculus and differential equations to science and engineering majors. Rick has over ten years of experience as a software engineer and systems engineer in the aerospace industry. Prior to law school, Rick worked as a senior software engineer, and later as a principal systems engineer at Goodrich Sensors and Integrated Systems in Burnsville, Minnesota. While at Goodrich, he led multi-discipline teams of engineers to design advanced algorithms used in the generation of flight-critical air data. In his free time, Rick enjoys tennis, reading, playing the piano, and spending time with his family.

JESSICA M. ALM THOMAS received her Bachelors of Biomedical Engineering from the University of Minnesota and her Juris Doctor (cum laude) from William Mitchell College of Law. As a part of her undergraduate degree, Jessica worked as a student engineer with a non-profit pediatric medical device company. While in law school, Jessica served as the Managing Editor for *Cybaris®, An Intellectual Property Law Review*, and helped local small businesses protect their trademark rights as part of a trademark internship. In her free time, Jessica enjoys cooking, reading, and playing volleyball.

MICHAEL J. PARISH received his Bachelors of Mechanical Engineering from the University of Minnesota where he graduated with distinction and his Juris Doctor from William Mitchell College of Law. Mike has ten years of experience as a mechanical engineer with experience in the aerospace, electric motor, and generator industries. Prior to and during law school, Mike worked as a senior mechanical engineer at Aero Systems Engineering in Saint Paul, Minnesota. While at Aero Systems, he collaborated with multi-discipline teams of engineers to design wind tunnel and jet engine test cell components. In his free time, Mike enjoys fishing, exercising, cooking, and spending time with his family.

NICHOLAS J. PETERKA received his Bachelors of Science in Civil Engineering from North Dakota State University and his Juris Doctor, summa cum laude, from William Mitchell College of Law. At NDSU, Nick's research in materials science and the development of biomaterials earned him the Barry M. Goldwater Scholarship, a national award given for undergraduate research. While in law school, Nick was an editor of the *William Mitchell Law Review* and a staff member of *Cybaris®, An Intellectual Property Law Review*, a Judicial Intern for Magistrate Judge Franklin L. Noel in the U.S. District Court for the District of Minnesota, and a research assistant for Professor R. Carl Moy. In his free time, Nick enjoys watching and playing sports, cooking, and reading.

THEA E. REILKOFF received her Bachelor of Science Degree in Chemistry from Mayville State University and her Master of Science Degree in Environmental Science and Engineering from Oregon Graduate Institute (now part of Oregon Health & Science University). She received her Juris Doctor from the University of Minnesota (magna cum laude). In law school, Thea served as a Managing Editor of the *Minnesota Law Review*. Prior to attending law school, Thea served as the Director of External Relations for the Yale School of Engineering & Applied Science. Prior to that, she worked as a Research Engineer at the Energy & Environmental Research Center in Grand Forks, North Dakota. In her free time, Thea enjoys spending time with her family and friends, gardening, working on variety of home improvement projects, and reading.

ANDREW R. SWANSON received his Bachelor of Science Degree in Civil Engineering from Iowa State University. He received his Juris Doctor (magna cum laude) from Marquette University Law School. During law school, Andrew was a Judicial Intern in the U.S. District Court for the Eastern District of Wisconsin and for the Honorable Diane S. Sykes of the U.S. Court of Appeals for the Seventh Circuit. Andrew also served as an Articles Editor on the Marquette Law Review. In his free time, Andrew enjoys golfing, traveling, and reading.

ANDREW W. WERNER received his Bachelor of Arts Degree in Applied Physics from Saint John's University and his Juris Doctor, cum laude, from William Mitchell College of Law. During his time at William Mitchell, Andrew served as the Vice President of the Student Intellectual Property Law Association, as a Notes and Comments Editor of *Cybaris®, An Intellectual Property Law Review*, and as a research assistant for Professor R. Carl Moy. Prior to law school, Andrew worked as a Technical Aid in the Patent Liaison Group for 3M in St. Paul, Minnesota and as an Aerospace Engineering Intern for Lake Engineering in Long Lake, Minnesota. In his free time, Andrew enjoys golfing, traveling, and playing Australian Rules Football.

JOHN D. LEIGHTON received his Bachelor of Electrical Engineering, Master of Science in Electrical Engineering, and his Ph.D. in Electrical Engineering from the University of Minnesota. Following graduation, he worked as a device engineer at what is now PolarFab semiconductor fabrication facility. There he analyzed yield issues and designed new fabrication processes for both bipolar and MOSFET integrated circuit processes. John also designed high-speed ASICs circuitry for the disk drive industry, including low-noise sense amplifiers and high-speed inductive drivers. John's process and design career was followed by a stint designing image processing algorithms for Infrared cameras at Fluke Thermography. John was also an Adjunct Professor of Electrical Engineering at St. Thomas University. He is a published author of technical papers and is a named inventor on eighteen patents.

LEA E. WESTMAN received her Bachelors of Science in Chemistry with an emphasis in Biochemistry from Pepperdine University. She received her Juris Doctor, cum laude, from the University of St. Thomas School of Law. After Pepperdine, Lea worked as a chemist researching microbial fuel cells and lithium ion batteries. In law school, Lea won a scholarship to compete in the Federal Bar Association's Thurgood Marshall Moot Court competition, founded the Student Intellectual Property Law Association, and was a research assistant to Prof. Michael Paulsen. Lea was awarded the Minnesota Intellectual Property Law Association Scholarship in 2015. In her free time, Lea teaches youth group at her church and enjoys practicing yoga.

JAIME L. SEKENSKI received her Bachelor of Science in Cell and Molecular Biology from the University of Minnesota Duluth and her Juris Doctor from Mitchell Hamline School of Law. After college, Jaime worked in clinical research on chronic disease studies as a Research Coordinator for HealthPartners Institute for Education and Research. In law school, Jaime was an editor of Cybaris® An Intellectual Property Law Review, the President of the Student Intellectual Property Law Association, a Mitchell Fellow, and a research assistant for Professor R. Carl Moy. In her free time, Jaime enjoys playing hockey, reading, and watching baseball.

BRIAR R. SCHNUCKEL received her Bachelor of Science degree in Biochemistry and Molecular Biology from the University of Minnesota Duluth. She received her Juris Doctor from Mitchell Hamline School of Law, as part of the inaugural graduating class. While in law school, Briar was an associate editor for the Hamline Law Review, the Treasurer of the Student Intellectual Property Law Association, and a research assistant for Professor Sharon Sandeen. Prior to pursuing her bachelor's degree, Briar served for six years in the U.S. Navy. In her spare time, Briar enjoys traveling, exercising, and spending time with her husband.

PREFACE

This book evolved from Kinney & Lange's annual seminar on *Intellectual Property for Business Lawyers*. We first presented the seminar in Minneapolis in 1984, and we gradually expanded our presentation throughout the Upper Midwest. The seminar has always received an enthusiastic response, and thousands of lawyers have attended our presentations over the years. This book is our way of reaching more of you and sharing with you our interest in, and our commitment to, intellectual property law.

In writing this book, our intent was to prepare a book of general interest for attorneys who do not practice regularly in the area, but who encounter intellectual property problems from time to time. Corporate lawyers, commercial litigators and general counsel are our intended audience, but we hope others will find the book useful as well.

We hope you find the book useful. Our goal is to provide business lawyers with a general overview of intellectual property law, enabling them to identify intellectual property issues and understand some basic principles. We did not try to write a law review article or an exhaustive treatise. We did not try to propose or advocate any particular theories. We wanted to write a practical book that business lawyers would refer to again and again.

Intellectual property law is evolving quickly these days. This book was up–to–date when we finished it, but some parts may already be out of date by the time you read it. We point this out to you as a reminder that no book can ever be dispositive. This book is a starting place in analyzing legal problems, not a final stop.

We would like to thank everyone who participated in this project. First, thanks to Thomson Reuters for approaching us with the idea for this book, as well as their continued support. Thanks also to everyone at Kinney & Lange for their support, particularly our editing team, Austen Zuege, David Fairbairn, Larrin Bergman, Alan Koenck, and Matt De Ruyter, without whom this work would never have been completed.

Kinney & Lange, P.A.

May 2016

THOMSON REUTERS PROVIEW™

This title is one of many now available on your tablet as an eBook.

Take your research mobile. Powered by the Thomson Reuters ProView™ app, our eBooks deliver the same trusted content as your print resources, but in a compact, on-the-go format.

ProView eBooks are designed for the way you work. You can add your own notes and highlights to the text, and all of your annotations will transfer electronically to every new edition of your eBook.

You can also instantly verify primary authority with built-in links to WestlawNext® and KeyCite®, so you can be confident that you're accessing the most current and accurate information.

To find out more about ProView eBooks and available discounts, call 1-800-344-5009.

RELATED PRODUCTS

Antitrust

Antitrust Adviser
Irving Scher and Scott Martin

Antitrust and American Business Abroad
Spencer Waller and Andre Fiebig

Antitrust Law Handbook
William C. Holmes and Melissa H. Mangiaracina

Antitrust Law Sourcebook
William C. Holmes and Melissa H. Mangiaracina

Intellectual Property and Antitrust Law
William C. Holmes

International Trade and U.S. Antitrust Law
Spencer Waller and Jeffrey L. Kessler

Materials on Antitrust Compliance
David Steiner

Computer and Related Law

Cloud Computing Legal Deskbook
edited by Gregory Barbee, Christopher Hale, Alexander Major and Melinda Lewis

Computer and Information Law Digest
Kurtis A. Kemper

Computer Software Agreements: Forms and Commentary
John H. Ridley, Peter C. Quittmeyer, and John Matuszeski

Computer Software: Protection, Liability, Law, and Forms
L.J. Kutten

Cybercrime and Security
Pauline C. Reich

Data Security and Privacy Law
Ronald N. Weikers

Global Information Technology Law
Craig J. Blakeley and Jeffrey Matsuura

Information Law
Raymond T. Nimmer

Information Security and Privacy: A Practical Guide to Federal, State and International Law
Andrew Serwin

Internet Law and Practice

Joseph Fazio and International Contributors

Internet Marketing and Consumer Protection
Andrew B. Serwin

Law and Business of Computer Software
Katheryn A. Andresen

Law of Computer Technology
Raymond T. Nimmer

State Computer Law
Virginia V. Shue and James V. Vergari

Thomas on Data Breach
Liisa M. Thomas

Copyright

Copyright Law in Business and Practice
John W. Hazard Jr.

Copyright Litigation Handbook
Raymond J. Dowd

Copyright Registration Practice
James E. Hawes and Bernard C. Dietz

Copyright Throughout the World
edited by Silke von Lewinski

The Law of Copyright
Howard B. Abrams

Patry on Copyright
William F. Patry

Patry on Fair Use
William F. Patry

Entertainment & Sports

Art, Artifact, Architecture & Museum Law
Alexandra Darraby

Cable Television and Other Nonbroadcast Video
Daniel Brenner, Monroe Price, and Michael Meyerson

Entertainment Law
Robert Fremlin and Michael Landau

Entertainment Law: Legal Concepts And Business Practices
Robert Lind et al.

Entertainment, Publishing, and the Arts Handbook
edited by Karen B. Tripp

Film and Multimedia and the Law
James Sammataro

Fundamentals of Sports Law

Walter Champion

Law of Defamation
Rodney A. Smolla

Law of Professional & Amateur Sports
Gary Uberstine

Lindey on Entertainment, Publishing, and the Arts
Alexander Lindey and Michael Landau

Media, Advertising & Entertainment Law Throughout the World
Andrew B. Ulmer and MULTILAW International Contributors

Rights and Liabilities in Media Content: Internet, Broadcast, and Print
Rodney A. Smolla

The Rights of Publicity and Privacy
J. Thomas McCarthy

Smolla and Nimmer on Freedom of Speech
Rodney A. Smolla

General Titles

Assets & Finance: Intellectual Property in Mergers and Acquisitions
David Klein

Calculating Intellectual Property Damages
Richard B. Troxel and William O. Kerr

Callmann on Unfair Competition, Trademarks and Monopolies
Louis Altman and Malla Pollack

Customs Enforcement of Intellectual Property Rights
Timothy P. Trainer and Vicki E. Allums

First Amendment Law Handbook
edited by Rodney A. Smolla

Franchise and Distribution Law and Practice
W. Michael Garner

Intellectual Property: Due Diligence in Corporate Transactions
Lisa M. Brownlee

Intellectual Property in Commerce
Thomas M. Ward and Rita S. Heimes

Intellectual Property Law for Business Lawyers
Kinney & Lange, P.A.

Intellectual Property Law Review
edited by Karen B. Tripp

IP Strategy: Complete Intellectual Property Planning, Access, and Protection
Howard C. Anawalt and Eve Brown

Potato Chips to Computer Chips: The War on Fake Stuff
Timothy P. Trainer

World Intellectual Property Rights and Remedies

Center for International Legal Studies

Licensing

Eckstrom's Licensing in Foreign and Domestic Operations: The Forms and Substance of Licensing
Robert Goldscheider and John Jarosz

Eckstrom's Licensing in Foreign and Domestic Operations: Joint Ventures
Terence F. MacLaren

Eckstrom's Licensing in Foreign and Domestic Operations: Text
David M. Epstein

Forms and Agreements on Intellectual Property and International Licensing
David de Vall and Peter McL. Colley

The Law of Merchandising and Character Licensing: Merchandising Law and Practice
Gregory J. Battersby and Charles W. Grimes

Licensing and the Art of Technology Management
Robert Goldscheider

Licensing Law Handbook
Melvin F. Jager

Modern Licensing Law
Raymond T. Nimmer and Jeff C. Dodd

Multimedia and Technology Licensing Agreements
Gregory J. Battersby and Charles W. Grimes

Patents

The American Invents Act: A Guide to Patent Litigation and Patent Procedure
Edward D. Manzo

Annotated Patent Digest
Robert A. Matthews, Jr.

Biotechnology and the Law
Iver P. Cooper

Designs and Utility Models Throughout the World
International Contributors

Federal Circuit Patent Case Digests
Kevin L. Russell

Generic Pharmaceutical Patent and FDA Law
Shashank Upadhye

Guide to European Patents
Andrew Rudge

Intellectual Property Litigation Guide: Patents & Trade Secrets
Gregory E. Upchurch

Manual of Patent Examining Procedure
from the U.S. Department of Commerce, Patent & Trademark Office

Medical Device Patents
Lawrence M. Sung

Moy's Walker on Patents
R. Carl Moy

Nanotechnology Law
John C. Monica, Jr.

Patent Application Practice
James E. Hawes

Patent Applications Handbook
Stephen A. Becker. Michael E. Fogarty, and Bernard P. Codd

Patent Claim Construction in the Federal Circui
Edward D. Manzo

Patent Claim Interpretation -- Global Edition
Edward D. Manzo

Patent Claims
Ernest Bainbridge Lipscomb III

Patent Damages Law and Practice
John Skenyon, Christopher Marchese, and John Land

Patent Jury Instruction Handbook
Robert A. Matthews, Jr.

Patent Law Basics
John G. Mills III, Donald C. Reiley III, and Robert C. Highley

Patent Law Fundamentals
John G. Mills III, Donald C. Reiley III, and Robert C. Highley

Patent Law Handbook
Lawrence M. Sung and Jeff E. Schwartz

Patent Law Practice Forms
Barry Kramer and Allen D. Brufsky

Patent Law: Legal and Economic Principles
John W. Schlicher

Patent Office Litigation
Sterne, Kessler, Goldstein, and Fox P.L.L.C.

Patent Practice & Policy in the Pacific Rim
Thomas T. Moga

Patents Throughout the World
International Contributors

Pre-litigation Patent Enforcement
Don W. Martens and John B. Sganga, Jr.

Trademarks

International Trademark Dilution

Daniel R. Bereskin and International Contributors

McCarthy on Trademarks and Unfair Competition
J. Thomas McCarthy

Practitioner's Trademark Manual of Examining Procedure
annotated by James E. Hawes and Amanda V. Dwight

Trade Dress Protection
William E. Levin

Trademark Law Practice Forms
Barry Kramer and Allen D. Brufsky

Trademark Manual of Examining Procedure
United States Patent and Trademark Office

Trademark Practice and Forms
Teresa C. Tucker

Trademark Practice Throughout the World
Mary M. Squyres, Nanette Norton and Christopher Dolan

Trademark Registration Practice
James E. Hawes and Amanda V. Dwight

Trademark Trial and Appeal Board Practice and Procedure
Gary D. Krugman

Trademarks Throughout the World
Edward Fennessy and International Contributors

Trade Secrets

Trade Secrets Law
Melvin F. Jager

Trade Secrets Throughout the World
Melvin F. Jager and International Contributors

Unfair Competition

Federal Unfair Competition: Lanham Act § 43(a)
Charles E. McKenney and George F. Long III

Unfair Competition and the ITC: A Treatise on Section 337 Actions
Marcia H. Sundeen, John W. Bateman, T. Cy Walker, and Aimee Soucie

---

Thomson Reuters® thanks you for subscribing to this product. Should you have any questions regarding this product please contact Customer Service at 1-800-328-4880 or by fax at 1-800-340-9378. If you would like to inquire about related publications or place an order, please contact us at 1-800-344-5009.

 **THOMSON REUTERS®**   Thomson Reuters
610 Opperman Drive
Eagan, MN 55123

legalsolutions.thomsonreuters.com

Summary of Contents

Table of Contents

CHAPTER 1. INTRODUCTION

CHAPTER 2. PRINCIPLES OF PATENT LAW

CHAPTER 3.   OBTAINING A PATENT

CHAPTER 4. CORRECTION AND REVIEW OF ISSUED PATENTS

CHAPTER 5. PATENT LITIGATION

CHAPTER 6. PRINCIPLES OF COPYRIGHT LAW

CHAPTER 7. REGISTERING A COPYRIGHT

CHAPTER 8.   COPYRIGHT LITIGATION

CHAPTER 9.   PRINCIPLES OF TRADEMARK LAW

CHAPTER 10. REGISTERING TRADEMARKS

CHAPTER 11. TRADEMARK AND UNFAIR COMPETITION LITIGATION

CHAPTER 12. TRADE SECRETS

CHAPTER 13. THE RIGHT OF PUBLICITY

CHAPTER 14. TRANSFERRING, LICENSING AND SECURING INTELLECTUAL PROPERTY RIGHTS

CHAPTER 15. INTELLECTUAL PROPERTY RIGHTS IN FOREIGN COUNTRIES

CHAPTER 16. EXTRA-TERRITORIAL APPLICATION OF U.S. INTELLECTUAL PROPERTY LAW

CHAPTER 17. ADVISING A BUSINESS ABOUT INTELLECTUAL PROPERTY

APPENDICES

Chapter 1

Introduction

§ 1:1   Origins of U.S. intellectual property law—Origins of
        U.S. patent and copyright law
§ 1:2   —Origins of U.S. trademark law
§ 1:3   The practice of intellectual property law—Patent
        attorneys
§ 1:4   —Professional associations

KeyCite®: Cases and other legal materials listed in KeyCite Scope can be researched through the KeyCite service on Westlaw®. Use KeyCite to check citations for form, parallel references, prior and later history, and comprehensive citator information, including citations to other decisions and secondary materials.

---

§ 1:1   Origins of U.S. intellectual property law—Origins of U.S. patent and copyright law

Research References

West's Key Number Digest, Copyrights and Intellectual Property ⟐1; Patents ⟐1

C.J.S., Copyrights and Intellectual Property §§ 2, 4; Patents §§ 1 to 5, 10 to 12, 15

Most Americans have a negative view of monopolies. The idea that only certain people should have the privilege of engaging in a certain business is contrary to both the democratic notion that all people are equal and the capitalist notion of free enterprise. Yet, most people take for granted monopolies through patents and copyrights.[1]

Upon reflection, monopolies on ideas seem even more offensive

---

[Section 1:1]

[1]The Supreme Court has consistently used the term "monopoly" to describe patents and copyrights, often as "limited monopolies" or "lawful monopolies." *See, e.g.,* Bonito Boats, Inc. v. Thunder Craft Boats, Inc., 489 U.S. 141, 109 S. Ct. 971, 103 L. Ed. 2d 118, 9 U.S.P.Q.2d 1847 (1989)(patents); Feist Publications, Inc. v. Rural Telephone Service Co., Inc., 499 U.S. 340, 111 S. Ct. 1282, 113 L. Ed. 2d 358, 18 Media L. Rep. (BNA) 1889, 18 U.S.P.Q.2d 1275, 121 Pub. Util. Rep. 4th (PUR) 1 (1991) (copyrights). Advocates of intellectual property, however, frequently object to any use of the term "monopoly" due to its negative connotations. For instance, in an early decision by the Court of Appeals for the Federal Circuit, Chief Judge Howard T. Markey argued that a patent is

1

than other kinds of monopolies. Thomas Jefferson believed, "[i]f nature has made any one thing less susceptible than all others to exclusive property, it is the action of the thinking power called an idea."[2] Sharing an idea takes nothing away from the person who shares it. If someone shares his land or his car with someone else, the original owner has less; he cannot farm part of his land or he cannot use his car for some of the time. But a person who shares an idea loses nothing. He or she still has the entire idea; others simply have the same. Jefferson compared an idea to a candle: "[A]s he who lights his taper at mine, receives light without darkening me."[3]

According to Jefferson, a person may exclusively possess an idea only so long as the person keeps it to himself or herself. The moment he or she discloses it to another person, the idea is possessed by everyone. Anyone who hears an idea cannot rid himself or herself of it. Therefore, it should belong to everyone. Jefferson viewed the spread of ideas as a divine right. "That ideas should freely spread from one to another over the globe, for the moral and mutual instruction of man, and improvement of his condition, seems to have been peculiarly and benevolently designed by nature, when she made them, like fire, expansible over all space, without lessening their density in any point, and like the air in which we breathe, move, and have our physical being, incapable of confinement or exclusive appropriation."[4]

Before the Constitution was adopted, some states had granted patents either by special act or by general statute. When the Constitution was adopted, one of the enumerated powers of Congress was a provision for federal patent and copyright laws:[5]

> The Congress shall have Power To * * * promote the Progress of Science and the useful Arts, by securing for limited Times to Authors and Inventors the exclusive Right to their respective Writings and Discoveries.[6]

The constitutional provision is both a grant of power and a limitation. The federal government has the power to grant mo-

---

not a monopoly but a property. "The antitrust laws * * * deal with appropriation of what should belong to others. A valid patent give the public what it did not earlier have." Carl Schenck, A.G. v. Nortron Corp., 713 F.2d 782, 786 n.3, 218 U.S.P.Q. 698, 701 n.3 (Fed. Cir. 1983).

[2]Graham v. John Deere Co. of Kansas City, 383 U.S. 1, 8-9 n.2, 86 S. Ct. 684, 689 n.2, 148 U.S.P.Q. 459, 463 n.2 (1966) (quoting 6 *Writings of* *Thomas Jefferson* at 180–81 (Washington ed.)).

[3]6 *Writings of Thomas Jefferson* at 180–81 (Washington ed.).

[4]6 *Writings of Thomas Jefferson* at 180–81 (Washington ed.).

[5]Sears, Roebuck & Co. v. Stiffel Co., 376 U.S. 225, 228, 84 S. Ct. 784, 787, 140 U.S.P.Q. 524, 527 (1964).

[6]U.S. Const., Art. I, sec. 8, cl. 8.

nopolies to authors and inventors.[7] However, that power is limited to granting monopolies on writings and inventions that advance human knowledge.

This clause was written against the backdrop of the practice of the British Crown in granting monopolies to court favorites. The Crown would grant monopolies not only for innovative products, but for things that had long been in the public domain.[8] "Monopoly was in bad odor by 1776."[9] Therefore, the Founding Fathers were careful to limit rights in intellectual property to creations that added something to the sum of human knowledge. While much of intellectual property law involves trying to determine exactly what the appropriate standard is, the basic idea that only significant inventions and writings should be protected has gone unchanged.

Three theories are usually asserted as the basis of intellectual property rights. The natural law theory claims that creative people have an inherent right to their creations. The natural rights theory is usually connected to a Lockean view that property rights arise from the labor that a person contributes.[10] Thus, creative people have an inherent right to their intellectual property because of the labor they have invested in it.

The Constitution reflects this natural rights theory. Congress is granted the power to "secure" the rights of authors and inventors, rather than grant those rights. The language of this Constitutional clause parallels the language of the Declaration of Independence. The introduction to that document, which reflects Locke's social contract theory of government, begins with the assumption that people have natural rights to life, liberty and the

---

[7]States are prohibited from offering patent-like protection to creations that would not be protected under federal law. The requirements of patentability provide a base line of free competition. Through the creation of patent-like rights, states could essentially redirect inventive efforts away from the careful criteria of patentability developed by Congress over the past 200 years. Bonito Boats, Inc. v. Thunder Craft Boats, Inc., 489 U.S. 141, 155, 109 S. Ct. 971, 980, 9 U.S.P. Q.2d 1847, 1854 (1989).

[8]Graham, 383 U.S. at 5, 86 S. Ct. at 687, 15 L.Ed.2d 545, 148 U.S.P.Q. at 462.

[9]Lawrence M. Friedman, A History of American Law at 255 (2d ed. 1985). Jefferson originally opposed monopolies of any kind, including patents. He urged an amendment to the Constitution (as one of the provisions of the Bill of Rights) that would restrict monopolies. At this time, Jefferson did not accept the argument that limited monopolies serve to encourage ingenuity. "[T]he benefit of even limited monopoly is too doubtful to be opposed to that of their general suppression." Graham, 383 U.S. at 7–8, 86 S. Ct. at 688–89, 15 L.Ed.2d 545, 148 U.S.P.Q. at 463 (quoting 5 Writing of Thomas Jefferson, at 47 (Ford ed. 1895)).

[10]See John Locke, Second Treatise of Government, § 45, in Two Treatises of Government (Peter Laslett ed., Cambridge Univ. Press 1988) (1690).

pursuit of happiness. The purpose of government is "to secure these rights." Similarly, the Constitutional clause implies that the inherent right of creative people to their intellectual property already exists, but Congress is empowered to create a mechanism to "secure" those rights.

This natural rights theory is also reflected in the sole reference to intellectual property in the Federalist Papers:

> The utility of this power will scarcely be questioned. The copyright of authors has been solemnly adjudged, in Great Britain, to be a right at common law. The right to useful inventions seems with equal reason to belong to the inventors. The public good fully coincides in both cases with the claims of individuals.[11]

In contrast to much of U.S. law, French and German law has grounded intellectual property rights in a different conception of natural law, that of "personality" or "moral rights." Derived primarily from the writings of Hegel, this theory contends that the freedom to self-actualize necessarily includes the freedom to define your personality by expressing it as objectively accessible art, writing, or invention.[12] Therefore, a creator owns his or her creation simply because it is part of his or her personality. Because the creator's "moral rights" arise independent of his or her labor, he or she is not necessarily entitled to derivative economic benefits. He or she does, however, have an inalienable right to be publicly credited with creation.[13]

Today, the dominant view of intellectual property rights is the economic incentive theory, and philosophical justifications are rarely mentioned. Legal protection, in the form of a limited monopoly, is granted by society to creative people as an economic incentive to engage in creative efforts. In exchange for disclosing their inventions to the public, inventors are granted a limited monopoly in the form of patents and copyrights. "The economic philosophy behind the clause empowering Congress to grant patents and copyrights is the conviction that encouraging of individual effort by personal gain is the best way to advance public welfare through the talents of authors and inventors in 'science and the useful arts.' "[14] Patents and copyrights encourage innovation by rewarding the creator with the right, limited to a term of

---

[11] *The Federalist* No. 43 (J. Madison), *in The Federalist Papers, available at* http://www.gutenberg.org/cache/epub/18/pg18.html.

[12] Hegel, Philosophy Of Right ¶ 43 (T. M. Knox trans. 1967) (1821).

[13] Justin Hughes, *The Philosophy of Intellectual Property*, 77 Geo. L.J. 287, 350 (1988).

[14] Mazer v. Stein, 347 U.S. 201, 219, 74 S. Ct. 460, 471, 100 U.S.P.Q. 325, 333 (1954).

years, to exclude others from the use of the writing or invention.[15]

But in rewarding the useful invention, the rights and welfare of the community must be dealt with fairly and effectually guarded. Thus, the limited monopoly granted to intellectual property is limited in two ways. First, it is limited in time. Both patents and copyrights expire after a fixed period of time. Once the patent or copyright expires, the monopoly created by it expires too. The right to make the invention or copy the work passes to the public.

Second, the monopoly is limited in scope. While natural rights and moral rights theories focus on the author or inventor, the economic incentive theory focuses on creativity more abstractly. Because the grant of an exclusive right to intellectual property is at odds with the inherent free nature of ideas, only inventions and writings that further human knowledge justify a limited private monopoly. Thus, patent protection is limited to inventions that are new, useful, and not obvious to a skilled artisan.[16] And copyright protection is limited to expressions that are original. No matter how much effort a person puts into a given work, no protection is available unless the works shows at least a minimal level of creativity.[17]

Thus, from their inception in 1790, the federal patent and copyright laws have embodied a balance between the need to promote innovation and the recognition that imitation and refinement through imitation are both necessary to the invention itself and the very life blood of a competitive economy.[18] They embody a carefully crafted bargain for encouraging the creation and disclosure of new, useful and nonobvious advances in technology in exchange for the exclusive right to practice that invention for a period of years.[19]

§ 1:2 Origins of U.S. intellectual property law—Origins of U.S. trademark law

Research References

West's Key Number Digest, Trademarks ⚷1020, 1027

A trademark has no necessary relation to invention or

---

[15]Sears, 376 U.S. at 229-30, 84 S. Ct. at 788, 11 L.Ed.2d 661, 140 U.S.P.Q. at 527.

[16]Graham, 383 U.S. at 8-9, 86 S. Ct. at 689, 15 L.Ed.2d 545, 148 U.S.P.Q. at 465.

[17]Feist Publications, Inc. v. Rural Telephone Service Co., Inc., 499 U.S. 340, 344, 111 S. Ct. 1282, 1287, 18

Media L. Rep. (BNA) 1889, 18 U.S.P. Q.2d 1275, 1283, 121 Pub. Util. Rep. 4th (PUR) 1 (1991).

[18]Bonito Boats, 489 U.S. at 146, 109 S. Ct. at 975, 103 L.Ed.2d 118, 9 U.S.P.Q.2d at 1850.

[19]Bonito Boats, 489 U.S. at 150–51, 109 S. Ct. at 977, 103 L.Ed.2d 118, 9 U.S.P.Q.2d at 1852.

discovery. While patents and copyrights are the fruits of intellectual labor, a trademark is usually nothing more than the adoption of something already in existence as a distinctive symbol of the person using it. It does not depend upon novelty, invention, creativity, or originality. It requires no imagination, no genius, no thought. It is simply founded on priority of appropriation. In fact, trademarks are often the result of accident rather than design. Neither novelty nor originality is in any way essential to the rights conferred by a trademark.[1]

Unlike patents, trademarks do not arise from a government grant. Instead, trademark rights are common law rights that have been recognized for centuries. When the present federal trademark law became effective in 1946, it was the first comprehensive national trademark law in the United States. Thus, the first significant national trademark law was not enacted until more than 150 years after the first patent and copyright laws.

The federal trademark law is usually referred to as the "Lanham Act," in honor of Congressman Fritz G. Lanham (D. Texas, 1919–47), who was instrumental in securing passage of the Act. Congressional power to regulate trademarks is premised on the Commerce Clause,[2] not the patent and copyright clause.[3]

Congress enacted the Lanham Act in 1946 in order to provide national protection of trademarks used in interstate and foreign commerce. Two primary reasons are usually recognized as the impetus behind the Lanham Act. First, the decision in *Erie R.R. v. Tompkins*[4] created great confusion regarding the applicable precedent in trademark cases. Before *Erie*, most trademark cases were litigated in federal court, based upon the diversity of citizenship of the parties. These decisions created a "federal common law" of trademarks, which was implicitly overturned by *Erie*. Second, the Lanham Act was necessitated because of United States obligations under treaties with foreign nations. In particular, the Lanham Act was the first United States trademark law to recognize the registrability of "descriptive" trademarks which had acquired "secondary meaning" in the marketplace.

The Lanham Act did not replace the common law of trademarks,

[Section 1:2]

[1]In re Trade-Mark Cases, 100 U.S. 82, 94, 1879 WL 16583 (1879).

[2]U.S. Const. Art. I, sec. 8, cl. 3.

[3]U.S. Const., Art. I, sec. 8, cl. 8. Congress' first attempt to establish a federal trademark law was held unconstitutional by the Supreme Court. Congress based the Trademark Act of 1870 on the patent clause of the Con-

stitution. The Court held that the patent clause does not extend to trademarks, and that Congress' control over trademarks was limited to its power to regulate commerce. In re Trade-Mark Cases, 100 U.S. 82, 1879 WL 16583 (1879).

[4]Erie R.R. Co. v. Tompkins, 304 U.S. 64, 58 S. Ct. 817, 114 A.L.R. 1487 (1938).

but supplemented and codified the common law at the federal level. Previous federal legislation reflected the view that protection of trademarks was a matter of state concern and that the right to a mark depended solely on common law. Consequently, rights to trademarks were uncertain and subject to variation in different parts of the country. Because trademarks promote competition and the maintenance of product quality, Congress determined that public policy requires that trademarks should receive the greatest protection that can be given.[5]

The Lanham Act explicitly contemplates the continued existence of state law protection. Therefore, the goal of nationwide uniformity, while undoubtedly one of the objectives of the Lanham Act, was not paramount. Instead, the Lanham Act serves the goal of national uniformity by providing a nationwide floor of protection, assuring the public and trademark owners at least a minimum level of protection.

There are two major purposes behind the trademark laws. One is to protect the public so it may be confident that, in purchasing a product bearing a particular trademark which it knows, it will get the product which it asks for and it wants to get. Secondly, where the owner of a trademark has spent energy, time, and money in presenting to the public the product, its investment is protected from misappropriation by others. Therefore, trademark law represents a balancing of the property interests of trademark owners with the public policy of protecting consumers from deceptive practices in the marketplace.

§ 1:3   The practice of intellectual property law—Patent attorneys

Intellectual property lawyers were the first boutique lawyers. Even in the nineteenth century, it was not uncommon for lawyers to specialize in intellectual property law, particularly patent law. This is probably because, as technology became more sophisticated, patent lawyers needed to have backgrounds in technology as well as law. Thus, patent lawyers were among the first attorneys to recognize the need for specialized law firms.

Today, most patent attorneys have a college degree in engineering or one of the hard sciences. This is not only because the training in technology is useful in practice, but an engineering or science degree is required for registration to practice before the U.S. Patent and Trademark Office (USPTO). Admission to practice before the USPTO, however, is not required to represent parties in patent litigation.

---

[5]Park 'N Fly, Inc. v. Dollar Park and Fly, Inc., 469 U.S. 189, 193, 105 S. Ct. 658, 661, 224 U.S.P.Q. 327, 329 (1985).

Patent agents are persons who are registered to practice before the USPTO, but who are not attorneys. At one time, much of the work of preparing patent applications was done by patent agents, many of whom had independent practices. Today, patent agents usually are law clerks who have passed the Patent Bar Exam, but who have not finished law school, or are technical experts working under the direction of an attorney.

Patent attorneys tend to divide themselves into "prosecution attorneys" and "litigation attorneys." Prosecution attorneys prepare and prosecute patent applications before the USPTO, including appeals and patent interferences. Prosecution attorneys also tend to do much of the work in licensing and transferring intellectual property rights.

§ 1:4 The practice of intellectual property law— Professional associations

The major professional organization for intellectual property attorneys is the American Intellectual Property Law Association (AIPLA).[1] The AIPLA is active in lobbying for or against changes in intellectual property statutes, and it commonly files *amicus* briefs in important lawsuits. The AIPLA holds two main meetings each year. The annual meeting is in October in Washington D.C. and is the main national gathering of intellectual property attorneys each year. A Spring meeting rotates through different cities. There is also usually a Mid-Winter Institute in a warm weather location on an alternating coast. The AIPLA publishes two journals, the *AIPLA Quarterly Journal*, a law review-type journal, and the quarterly *Bulletin*, which consists primarily of committee reports and transcripts from AIPLA meetings and seminars.

Another large organization of intellectual property attorneys is the American Bar Association (ABA) Section on Intellectual Property Law. The section tends to be oriented toward patent prosecution attorneys. The ABA Litigation Section has an active intellectual property litigation committee, which is where the intellectual property litigators tend to congregate within the ABA.

Another important organization is the Patent and Trademark Office Society. This is an organization of employees (particularly patent and trademark examiners) of the USPTO. It publishes a monthly journal entitled the *Journal Of The Patent And Trade-*

[Section 1:4]

[1]241 18th Street South, Suite 700, Arlington, VA 22202, (703) 415- 0780. AIPLA's website is found at www.aipla.org.

mark Office Society,[2] which focuses on short, practical articles. At $65 per year, it is the best bargain in intellectual property law.

The International Trademark Association (INTA)[3] is "an international membership organization for the development and protection of trademarks." Its members are largely trademark owners and their attorneys. INTA publishes a bi-monthly journal called *The Trademark Reporter*, a law review-type journal that features exceptionally well-written articles on trademark law.

Yet another large intellectual property organization is the Intellectual Property Owners Association® (IPO), which describes itself as "an international trade association for owners and others interested in patents, trademarks, copyrights, and trade secrets." The association holds an Annual Meeting, typically every September. IPO also offers a variety of publications, and pursues legislative advocacy on behalf of intellectual property owners. Membership is by company or firm rather than on an individual basis.

Another avenue of IP information distribution is the proliferation of IP weblogs or "blogs." Many of them provide a useful source for up-to-the-moment information on cases, legislative changes, practice tips, and other information useful to the practitioner. Some of the more popular blogs include:

- 43(B)log (http://tushnet.blogspot.com)
- Copyright Litigation Blog (http://copyrightlitigation.blogspot.com)
- Intellectual Property Expert Group Blog (http://www.ipeg.com)
- IPKat (http://www.ipkat.com)
- Patently-O Patent Law Blog (http://patentlyo.com)
- The Patent Prospector (http://www.patenthawk.com/blog)
- The TTAB Blog (http://thettablog.blogspot.com)
- USPTO Director's Forum (http://www.uspto.gov/blog)
- IP Watchdog® (http://www.ipwatchdog.com)
- Patent Baristas® (http://www.patentbaristas.com)

---

[2]Patent and Trademark Office Society, P.O. Box 2089, Arlington, VA 22202. PTOS's website is found at www.ptos.org.

[3]655 Third Avenue, 10th Floor, New York, NY 10017–5617. INTA's website is found at www.inta.org.

Chapter 2

Principles of Patent Law

> **KeyCite®:** Cases and other legal materials listed in KeyCite Scope can be researched through the KeyCite service on Westlaw®. Use KeyCite to check citations for form, parallel references, prior and later history, and comprehensive citator information, including citations to other decisions and secondary materials.

§ 2:1 The concept of patents

Research References

West's Key Number Digest, Patents ⬤―1
C.J.S., Patents §§ 1 to 5, 10 to 12, 15

A patent is granted to individuals who invent new and useful inventions. In contrast to a common misconception, a patent is not a right to practice, but a right to exclude. In other words, patents operate as a specialized form of personal property. Like other forms of property, a patent does not give its owner the right to do something that would otherwise be illegal. The patent owner merely has the rights, during the limited term of a valid patent, to exclude others from making, using, selling, offering for sale, or importing the patented invention.

A patent does not give its owner an affirmative right to make, use, sell, offer for sale, or import an invention if he or she does not already possess those rights. If another person has superior rights, for example, through an earlier patent covering a portion of the new invention, the later patent owner may be prohibited from using his or her own invention. This earlier patent does not render the later patent worthless, however, because the right to exclude runs in both directions. The later patent owner may still exclude the earlier patent owner from improving the earlier invention with the additional features claimed in the later patent.

Unlike some other property rights, a patent is not self-enforcing. To protect their rights, patent owners must take positive actions to notify, discourage, and enjoin potential and actual infringers. These actions include marking patented products, demanding that infringement cease, and filing suit for damages and injunctions.

Authority for the U.S. patent system is found in Article I, § 8 of the U.S. Constitution:

> The Congress shall have the Power to * * * promote the Progress of Science and useful Arts, by securing for limited Times to Authors and Inventors the exclusive Right to their respective Writings and Discoveries.

Based on this constitutional provision, George Washington signed the first patent statute on April 10, 1790. That statute provided patent protection for "any useful art, manufacture, engine, machine, or device, or any improvement thereon not before known or used."[1] The statute originally placed the responsibility of granting patents in the hands of the Patent Board, headed by Secretary of State Thomas Jefferson. In 1793, Congress abolished the Patent Board and placed the responsibility for granting patents solely upon the Secretary of State.

In 1836, Congress established the Patent Office. As part of the State Department, the Patent Office was vested with the sole authority to grant patents. The Patent Office moved to the Department of the Interior in 1849 and then to the Department of Commerce in 1926, where it resides today. The name of the Patent Office was changed to the U.S. Patent & Trademark Office ("USPTO") in 1975. The USPTO has its headquarters in Alexandria, VA and satellite offices in Detroit, MI; Dallas, TX; Denver, CO; and Silicon Valley, CA.

Today, U.S. patent law is codified in Title 35 of the U.S. Code. Patent law is entirely governed by federal law, and state laws relating to patents or interfering with federal patent law are preempted.[2] Issues ancillary to patent disputes may be, however, supplemented by state law. For example, while federal law recognizes assignments of patent rights if timely recorded in the USPTO,[3] the substance of assignments and employment agreements requiring assignment of intellectual property rights are typically governed by state law.[4] The rules and regulations promulgated by the Commissioner of Patents for the conduct of proceedings in the USPTO are found in Title 37 of the Code of Federal Regulations.

§ 2:2 Patent attorneys and patent agents

Research References

West's Key Number Digest, Patents ⊙—97
C.J.S., Patents §§ 135 to 138, 145, 178

Patent attorneys are attorneys who are licensed to practice law in one or more states and who are also registered to practice before the USPTO. Patent agents are people who are registered to practice before the USPTO, but who are not licensed to practice law. To become registered to practice before the USPTO, both attorneys and agents must have a college degree or equivalent ex-

[Section 2:1]

[1]Act of April 10, 1790, Ch. 7, 1 Stat. 109.

[2]Bonito Boats, Inc. v. Thunder Craft Boats, Inc., 489 U.S. 141, 167, 109 S. Ct. 971, 986, 9 U.S.P.Q.2d 1847, 1859 (1989).

[3]35 U.S.C.A. § 261.

[4]*But see* Medtronic, Inc. v. White, 526 F.3d 487, 495–497, 87 U.S.P.Q.2d 1017 (9th Cir. 2008).

perience in science or engineering. They must also pass a written examination on patent law and the procedures of the USPTO. Both patent attorneys and patent agents are subject to an ethical code similar to the Professional Rules of Responsibility for attorneys, and may have their licenses revoked for violating that code.[1]

There are only three types of people who are permitted to represent inventors before the USPTO: patent attorneys, patent agents, and the inventors themselves.[2] Although the USPTO allows inventors to represent themselves, it discourages this practice because of the added burden it places on Examiners to ensure that the filing papers are in proper form and that USPTO procedures are followed.

An attorney does not need to be registered to practice before the USPTO to advise clients in various patent-related matters, such as patent litigation or licensing negotiations. Also, nonpatent attorneys may provide opinions on the validity of patents and on the infringement of patents. However, such opinions are typically given less weight than opinions drafted by registered patent counsel. Patent agents may not render validity or infringement opinions since they are not licensed to practice law.

§ 2:3   Patentability opinions

A patentability opinion is a useful tool in determining the possible patent protection available for an invention. The opinion is usually rendered by a patent attorney, although patent agents and general counsel sometimes give such opinions. The opinion is based upon a review of the prior art in view of the invention. It usually includes a description of the attorney or agent's understanding of the invention and his or her understanding of the relevant prior art, and it generally concludes with a statement listing the features of the invention that may be patentable.

In cases where the inventor is new to a field, a patentability opinion can save a great deal of money. Often, the inventor does not realize how much work has been done in a field and therefore has false expectations of the amount of patent protection he or she can obtain. A patentability opinion can give the inventor more realistic expectations before time and money are spent preparing and prosecuting a patent application.

A patentability opinion concluding that patent protection may be available for one or more aspects of an invention is not a guarantee that the USPTO will award a patent. The USPTO

[Section 2:2]   [2]37 C.F.R. § 1.31.
      [1]37 C.F.R. § 10.

does not base its determination of patentability on such opinions, but instead performs its own search and develops its own opinion of patentability based upon the submitted claims.

The first step in preparing a patentability opinion is to conduct a prior art search. There are several databases that provide access to issued U.S. patents and published patent applications. The USPTO provides a free database that allows a searcher to perform basic or advanced searches of either patents or patent applications. Searches can also be performed using the classification system. The USPTO database can be accessed at www.uspto.gov.

Often, keyword searches of the patents are performed. While useful, this type of search is not always reliable. For some technologies, it may be difficult to select words that are unique to a particular class of products without excluding relevant references. For instance, unrelated electrical circuits can be constructed from identical electrical elements if the elements are connected differently in each of the circuits. If a search is performed for the names of the electrical elements, references showing both types of circuits will be identified. In situations where keyword searching may be difficult, a classification search may be more helpful in finding relevant prior art.

Foreign patents or foreign application publications are often included in a search because they can affect the patentability of an invention in the United States. However, the USPTO does not maintain a database of foreign prior art. Some foreign prior art might be found in the examiners' libraries, and copies of some foreign patents can be obtained from the USPTO Technical Library.

To search for foreign prior art, there are several fee-based databases, and some free databases, that allow access to publications of patents and applications from such foreign countries as Germany, France, and Japan. Additionally, these databases usually have access to WIPO (World Intellectual Property Organization) publications of PCT (Patent Cooperation Treaty) applications. Often, the foreign publications will be in English or at least have an English abstract.

A patent search may be commissioned in the appropriate foreign patent office to search for foreign publications. This is done by hiring a patent attorney or professional patent searcher in that country. Because of the difficulty and expense of searching for patents in many different countries, foreign searches like these are generally limited to countries that have very active patent systems and countries that have their patents available on a computer database accessible from the United States.

Once a seemingly relevant foreign abstract has been found, the full text of the patent can be obtained. If the publication is not in English and appears relevant, for a fee, some patent services will translate the patent into English. It is often advisable to look at the patent in its native language before ordering a translation because such translations are very expensive and many patents will be clearly irrelevant upon examination of the drawings.

Searches for nonpatent references may also be performed on computer databases using keyword searching. In addition, technical people who are familiar with the art are invaluable sources of information on the state of the art.

Patentability opinions can be susceptible to "hidden" prior art that could not be discovered at the time of the opinion, such as pending U.S. patent applications. Generally, after eighteen months from the earliest priority date, U.S. patent applications will publish.[1] Prior to an application's publication or issuance (if it did not publish) the application is kept confidential and may be unknown to the public.[2] Once the application publishes or issues, however, it can operate as prior art if the application it is based on was filed prior to the application it is being asserted against.[3] Additional prior art found by the USPTO that did not appear in the search made for the opinion can also prevent patenting of an invention.

§ 2:4 Patent-eligible subject matter

Research References
West's Key Number Digest, Patents ⊕4 to 15
C.J.S., Patents §§ 13 to 14, 16 to 28, 100, 103

To obtain protection under the U.S. patent system, an invention must be more than novel and not obvious. A patentable invention is one that also fits within one of three statutory classes of patent-eligible subject matter. The first class of patent-eligible inventions is processes, machines, manufactures, and compositions of matter.[1] These inventions are protected with utility patents. Examples of the kinds of inventions protected by utility patents include inventions that need to be manufactured, such as electrical circuits, automobile parts, and food additives, as well as methods of producing such items. They also include biological inventions including new bacteria, fungi, some DNA material, and viruses.

The second class of patent-eligible inventions is asexually

[Section 2:3]   [3]35 U.S.C.A. § 102(a)(2).

[1]35 U.S.C.A. § 122(b).   [Section 2:4]

[2]35 U.S.C.A. § 122(a).   [1]35 U.S.C.A. § 101.

reproduced plants. Inventions in this category are protected by plant patents and include new and distinct varieties of spores, mutants, hybrids, and newly found seedlings, other than a tuber propagated plant or a plant found in an uncultivated state.[2] Although the plant must be found on cultivated land, the cultivated land does not have to belong to the patent applicant. To be considered the inventor, the applicant has to be the first to appreciate the plant's distinctiveness and to asexually reproduce the plant. Asexual reproduction involves reproducing the plant through means other than seeds, such as budding, grafting, or rooting of cuttings. Such asexual reproduction gives the "child" plant the exact characteristics of the "parent" plant and thus propagates the plants' specific characteristics that may otherwise be lost through the genetics of sexual reproduction.

The third class of patent-eligible inventions is ornamental designs.[3] These inventions include the nonfunctional aspects of an article of manufacture that set it apart from all other articles of manufacture. Examples include the design of wrought iron fencing, the overall appearance of a piece of exercise equipment, and the shape of a telephone or chair.

Some things are explicitly excluded from patent protection. "Phenomena of nature, though just discovered, mental processes, and abstract intellectual concepts are not patentable, as they are the basic tools of scientific and technological work."[4] For example, the formula describing the gravitational attraction between two objects, or the formula describing the relationship between matter and energy, are not patentable. Additionally, patents relating solely to utilization of nuclear material or atomic energy in atomic weapons are prohibited.[5]

At one time, computer programs were considered non-patent-eligible unless they were claimed as an integral part of some physical process of manufacture. The USPTO now recognizes the patentability of computer programs that are not part of a physical process.[6] As part of that recognition, the USPTO issued guidelines regarding the examination of computer-implemented inventions. Under these guidelines, data structures and computer programs claimed as computer listings are per se not patent eligible.[7] However, according to updated guidelines issued July of 2015, computer programs may be patent eligible if the invention as a whole amounts to "significantly more" than simply

---

[2]35 U.S.C.A. § 161.

[3]35 U.S.C.A. § 171.

[4]Gottschalk v. Benson, 409 U.S. 63, 67, 93 S. Ct. 253, 255, 175 U.S.P.Q. 673, 675 (1972).

[5]42 U.S.C.A. § 2181.

[6]In re Beauregard, 53 F.3d 1583, 1584, 35 U.S.P.Q.2d 1383, 1384 (Fed. Cir. 1995).

[7]M.P.E.P. § 2106(I) (9th ed. 2014).

organizing and comparing data, defined by meaningful limitations that add more than generally linking the use of an abstract idea to the internet or a computer.[8] Nonfunctional information, such as music or photographs, remains unpatentable.

§ 2:5 USPTO publications

Research References

West's Key Number Digest, Patents ⬀97
C.J.S., Patents §§ 135 to 138, 145, 178

When a patent issues it is published by the USPTO. The USPTO also will publish applications that were filed on or after November 29, 2000. Generally, utility and plant patent applications will publish at 18 months from the earliest priority date.[1] However, provisional applications and design patent applications do not publish.[2] An applicant may make a request at the time his or her utility or plant patent application is filed that the application not be published if the applicant certifies that the invention will not be the subject of an application filed in a foreign country.[3] If the applicant changes his or her mind and later decides to file in a foreign country, the applicant has 45 days to notify the USPTO from the date of foreign or international filing, or else the application is deemed abandoned.[4]

Published applications are given a publication number, while patents are given a patent number. As of January 2, 2001, the USPTO began placing kind codes to the right of each of these identifying numbers. The kind code identifies the type of publication. The table below lists the kind codes presently being used on USPTO publications.[5]

Kind Code	Type of Publication
A1	Patent Application Publication
A2	Patent Application Publication (Republication)
A9	Patent Application Publication (Corrected Publication)
B1	Patent (No pregrant publication)

---

[8]USPTO, "July 2015 Update: Subject Matter Eligibility" Appendix 1: Examples (July 2015); *see also* USPTO, "May 2016 Subject Matter Eligibility Update" (May 2015). Additional information about patent eligibility is found in Section 5:33.

[2]35 U.S.C.A. § 122(b)(2)(A).

[3]35 U.S.C.A. § 122(b)(2)(B).

[4]35 U.S.C.A. § 122(b)(2)(B)(iii).

[5]M.P.E.P. § 901.04(a).

[Section 2:5]

[1]35 U.S.C.A. § 122(b)(1).

Kind Code	Type of Publication
B2	Patent (Having a pregrant publication)
C1, C2, C3	Reexamination Certificate
E	Reissue Patent
P1	Plant Patent Publication Application
P2	Plant Patent (No pregrant publication)
P3	Plant Patent (Having a pregrant publication)
P4	Plant Patent Application Publication (Republication)
P9	Plant Patent Application Publication (Corrected Publication)
S	Design Patent

§ 2:6   Example of a utility patent

An example of a Utility Patent is included in Appendix A.

§ 2:7   Example of a utility patent—Cover sheet

Research References
West's Key Number Digest, Patents ⬤⇒98
C.J.S., Patents §§ 137 to 139

The cover sheet is the first sheet of a patent. It includes a summary of the important aspects of the patent, making it easier to perform patent searches. Each item on the cover sheet is found in a separate field which is marked by a number in parentheses (for example, (10)). The numbers are part of an international convention designed to make it possible to identify certain critical information in patents from different countries.

Patent Number. The patent number is located in the upper right hand side of the patent and is marked by (10). U.S. patents have been numbered sequentially as they issued since 1836. Since that time, more than 8,000,000 utility patents have been issued.

Issue Date. The issue date is located just below the patent number and is marked by (45). This date is the official publication date of the patent which marks the beginning of the enforceable patent term and the first date of publication by the USPTO. For patents filed before June 8, 1995, it is also one of the dates used to calculate the end of the patent term, which is the longer of seventeen years from the issue date or twenty years from the filing date.

Reference Name. The reference name is located on the top left of the patent just below the words "United States Patent." The reference name is the last name of the first named inventor in the patent. When there is more than one inventor, the reference name includes the Latin phrase "et al." after the inventor's name, signifying that there is one or more other inventors (for example, Smith et al.). The reference name is often used when referring to a particular patent. For instance, the example patent found in Appendix A is the Jagger et al. Patent. The first inventor named in the declaration associated with the patent is chosen as the reference name.

Patent Title. The patent title is located at the top of the left column below the solid line and is marked by (54). Under current rules, this title must be descriptive of the invention. Older patents may not have descriptive titles because in the past they were not required. Some practitioners purposefully made titles vague to hide their client's technology.

Inventors. The full names of the inventors are listed directly below the patent title and are marked by (75). Listed with their names is the city and state or country, if a non-U.S. inventor, where each inventor resided either at the time they filed their application or at the time the patent issued.

Assignee. The name of the assignee at the time of issuance of the patent is located below the inventors' names in the field marked (73). The city and state or country, if a non-U.S. assignee, where the assignee has a principal place of business is listed next to the assignee's name. The assignee field does not necessarily indicate the current owner of the patent, it only indicates who the owner was at the time the patent was granted. The current owner can be located by ordering an abstract of title from the USPTO or through a reassignment database. Also, the assignment information can be searched on the USPTO website at the following address: www.uspto.gov.

Application Number. The application number is located below the assignee and is marked by (21). The application number is the serial number given to the application while the patent was pending in the USPTO.

Filing Date. The filing date is located below the application number and is marked by (22). The filing date indicates the date an acceptable form of the application was received in the USPTO. Depending on the patent, the filing date is significant for one of several reasons. For all patents filed on or after June 8, 1995, and some filed before that date, the filing date is significant because those patents expire twenty years after their filing date.[1] For patents that do not claim priority from other patents, the filing date establishes a date of priority. The filing date is also sig-

[Section 2:7]
[1]35 U.S.C.A. § 154(a)(2).

nificant because it is generally the earliest date the U.S. patent can be used as prior art against other inventions.[2]

Prior to March 16, 2013, patent applications could be used as prior art as of their publication in a foreign country, or as of their filing date in the United States.[3] For all patents effectively filed on or after March 16, 2013, foreign filings may also be used as prior art as of their effective filing dates.[4] For applications claiming priority to another application, the filing date of the later application is less relevant because the earlier filing date will determine the prior art date. As with applications filed before March 16, 2013, parent applications may also be used to establish an earlier prior art date.

If the issued patent is based on a PCT application, then other fields will be present on the face of the patent giving additional information. The filing date field (22) will instead be the PCT filing date, which is also marked by (22). Below the PCT filing date is the PCT application number and the Section 371(c) filing date marked by (86). Below the PCT application filing information is the PCT application publication number and publication date marked by (87).

Prior Publication. If the application from which the patent issued published, then this publication information is indicated on the face of the patent. The prior publication data is marked by (65) and includes the prior publication number and publication date.

Related U.S. Application Data. If the patent claims priority from one or more prior U.S. applications, then the respective prior application numbers, filing dates, and patent numbers, if known, are also indicated on the cover sheet. If the patent claims priority from a provisional application, then that field is marked by (60). If the patent issues from a divisional of a prior U.S. application, then that field is marked by (62). If the patent issues from a continuation or a continuation-in-part of a prior U.S. application, then that field is marked by (63). If there are no valid U.S. priority claims, then the field is omitted from the face of the patent.

Foreign Application Priority Data. If the patent makes a claim of foreign priority, then this information is marked by (30). The foreign filing date and application number are indicated in this field. If the patent does not make a claim of foreign priority, then this field is omitted from the face of the patent. The foreign filing date is also significant because it is the earliest date the

---

[2]35 U.S.C.A. § 102(a)(2).   [4]35 U.S.C.A. § 102(a)(2).
[3]35 U.S.C.A. § 102(e)(2006).

U.S. patent can be used as prior art against other inventors.[5]

Classes. Classes are listed below the filing date of the patent and are marked by (51) and (52). The classes listed on the cover page categorize the technology disclosed in the patent. There are two separate classification systems listed on the cover page. One is the International Classification System, (51), and the other is the U.S. Classification System, (52). Both systems divide technology into very specific categories and then assign a classification number to each category. One classification number in each system is **bolded** to indicate that the patent is directed largely to the technology found in that classification. The field marked Field of Search, (53), lists the classes of technology searched by the USPTO in examining the application.

References Cited. "References Cited" is located below the field of search and is marked by (56). The References Cited section lists all of the prior art references that were considered by the USPTO during the examination of the patent application. This section may include the categories: U.S. Patent Documents, Foreign Patent Documents, and Other Publications. The U.S. Patent Documents includes both U.S. patents and published U.S. applications. The information included is the patent number or application publication number, issue or publication date, reference name, and principal class considered. For the Foreign Patent Documents, the information given is the foreign country, publication number, and publication date. Bibliographic information about other nonpatent publications that was considered is given for the Other Publications.

Attorney, Agent, or Firm. The name of the attorney, agent, or firm that prosecuted the application, if any, is listed before the Abstract and marked (74).

Abstract. The Abstract is marked by (57) and is intended to be a short summary of the basic inventive aspect of the patent. It is usually between 50 and 150 words, and is often taken directly from the broadest claim in the patent.

Representative Drawing. At the bottom of the cover page is one drawing representative of the invention as a whole. It is selected by the USPTO from the drawings submitted as part of the application.

§ 2:8 Example of a utility patent—Figures

Research References

West's Key Number Digest, Patents ☞100
C.J.S., Patents § 143

---

[5]35 U.S.C.A. § 102(d).

Each figure and each element within a figure is identified by a reference character. Each reference character may refer to only one element, and an element that appears in more than one figure must be identified by the same reference character in each figure. Each reference character that appears in the figures must appear someplace in the written description of the invention, and each reference character in the description must appear in the figures.

With very few exceptions, figures in utility patents must be drawn with black ink on white paper. Color drawings will be accepted, but only after the applicant explains why the color drawings are a necessity. The USPTO discourages color drawings because of the difficulty in reproducing the figures for mass distribution.

§2:9 Example of a utility patent—Specification

Research References

West's Key Number Digest, Patents ☞99
C.J.S., Patents § 139

The specification contains the majority of a patent's text. To fulfill the disclosure requirements necessary for a valid patent, the specification must:

> contain a written description of the invention, and of the manner and process of making and using it, in such full, clear, concise, and exact terms as to enable any person skilled in the art to which it pertains * * * to make and use the same, and shall set forth the best mode contemplated by the inventor or joint inventor of carrying out the invention.[1]

Cross-Reference to Related Applications. If the patent bases its priority date on an earlier filed patent application, the Cross-Reference section lists the earlier patent application or patent and its filing date. Priority claims to related applications may also be included in the Application Data Sheet filed with the application, either in addition to or as an alternative to the Cross-Reference section.

Background of the Invention. The Background section describes the technological field of the invention and the state of the prior art in that field.

Summary of the Invention. The Summary gives a short overview of the invention. It may also point out the utility and advantages of the invention.

Brief Description of the Drawings. The Brief Description

[Section 2:9]

[1]35 U.S.C.A. § 112(a).

lists the figures in the patent and gives a one sentence summary of the contents of each figure.

Detailed Description of the Drawings. The Detailed Description is the heart of the specification. It describes the invention using reference characters to refer to the elements shown in the drawings. It must teach those having ordinary skill in the art how to make and use the invention.[2] It must also disclose the "best mode" of practicing the invention. This is the best mode that the inventor knows of at the time the application is filed.

Claims. Although technically part of the specification, the claims are such an important part of a patent that they are often thought of separately from the rest of the specification. The claims define the scope of patent protection for the invention. In order to infringe the patent, a process or apparatus must include every element of at least one claim in the patent.

Each claim is one sentence, though claims often contain many clauses separated by semicolons. The clauses are usually separated from each other to make them easier to read. Each claim usually begins with the phrase "An apparatus" or "A method" and always ends with a period. Typically, before the first claim is a short introductory clause such as "What I claim is:".

There must be at least one claim, but there is no upper limit to the number of claims that can appear in a patent. However, the USPTO charges an additional fee for every claim over twenty claims and every independent claim over three independent claims that is presented for examination. In addition, the claims cannot be repetitive.

There are two types of claims: independent and dependent. An independent claim stands alone, and its scope can be determined simply by reading it. A dependent claim includes a reference to another claim, such as:

4. The apparatus of claim 3 wherein * * *

The scope of a dependent claim includes not only its own limitations, but all of the limitations of the claim or claims from which it depends. Dependent claims may depend from an independent claim or other dependent claims, and there is no limit to the level of dependency.

Claims may depend on more than one claim in an alternative fashion, such as:

5. The apparatus of claim 4 or claim 3 wherein * * *

---

[2]Process Control Corp. v. HydRe-claim Corp., 190 F.3d 1350, 1359, 52 U.S.P.Q.2d 1029 (Fed. Cir. 1999) (invalid for failure to enable).

These multiple dependent claims are read to have two separate sets of limitations. The first set includes the limitations of the first claim from which it depends, and the second set includes the limitations of the second claim from which it depends. The two sets of limitations are independent of each other. Such a claim would count twice when calculating additional claims fees.[3]

The claims must distinctly point out the subject matter they cover so that those skilled in the art can understand the scope of the claims. If the claims are vague or indefinite about what they cover, they are invalid.[4]

A claim is indefinite if it uses a term or phrase that has no clear definition. For instance, comparative phrases such as "a substantial distance" and "a large aperture" may be indefinite because the terms "substantial" and "large" have no intrinsic meaning. They only have meaning relative to some example of what is "large" or "substantial." An inch is a large distance in micro-chip technology but a small distance in tanker ships. Claims can include such comparative phrases if the phrases are clearly defined within the specification.

Sometimes claims are vague simply because they include grammatical errors. In general, it is grammatically incorrect to refer to an item using a specific article, such as "the," if the item has not been previously identified. When this error appears in a claim, it makes it appear that some specific but unknown item is being claimed instead of simply some generic item. For instance, referring to "the bolt" indicates that a specific bolt should be used, but referring to "a bolt" indicates that any of a number of bolts may be used. A reference to an item using "the" before referring to the item generically with "a" or "an" creates a problem with antecedent basis. Of course, once an item has been identified generically, it can later be referred to specifically as long as it is clear what item is being identified. If two bolts have been previously identified in a claim, a reference to "the bolt" makes the claim vague because it is not clear which bolt is "the" bolt. Similarly, a claim is vague if it uses different terms to refer to a single item. For instance, referring to an item as a "pin" and a "bolt" in the same claim makes the claim confusing and possibly invalid.

§ 2:10 Example of a utility patent application publication

An example of a utility patent application publication is

---

[3]M.P.E.P. § 608.01(n).

[4]See Microprocessor Enhancement Corp. v. Texas Instruments Inc.,

520 F.3d 1367, 86 U.S.P.Q.2d 1225 (Fed. Cir. 2008).

included in Appendix A. Although not included as an example, plant patent applications also publish. Design patent applications and provisional applications do not publish.

§ 2:11 Example of a utility patent application publication—Cover sheet

Research References
West's Key Number Digest, Patents ⚖98
C.J.S., Patents §§ 137 to 139

The cover sheet is the first sheet of a utility patent application publication. It includes a summary of the important aspects of the publication, making it easier to perform searches. Each item on the cover sheet is found in a separate field which is marked by a number in parentheses (for example, (10)). The numbers are part of an international convention designed to make it possible to identify certain critical information in patents from different countries.

Publication Number. The publication number is located in the upper right hand side of the publication and is marked by (10). A U.S. application publication number begins with the year of the publication followed by the sequential number of the publication for that year. After the publication number is the kind code.

Publication Date. The publication date is located just below the publication number and is marked by (43). This date is the official publication date of the application. When an application publication is used as prior art, the publication date establishes the date of the application as a printed publication.

Reference Name. The reference name is located on the top left of the publication just below the words "United States Patent Application Publication." The reference name is the last name of the first named inventor. When there is more than one inventor, the reference name includes the Latin phrase "et al." after the inventor's name, signifying that there is one or more other inventors (for example, Smith et al.). The reference name is often used when referring to an application publication. For instance, the example application publication found in Appendix A is the Jagger et al. application. The first inventor named in the declaration associated with the application is chosen as the reference name.

Application Title. The patent application title is located at the top of the left column below the solid line and is marked by (54). Under current rules, this title must be descriptive of the invention.

Inventors. The full names of the inventors are listed directly below the title and are marked by (76). Listed with their names is the city and state or country, if a non-U.S. inventor, where each inventor resided at the time they filed their application.

Correspondence Address. Listed below the Inventors is the Correspondence Address. This is the address that was given to the USPTO when the application was filed indicating where all correspondence should be sent. This address may be the inventor's address, his or her patent attorney's address, or the assignee's address.

Assignee. The name of the original assignee of the patent application is located below the inventors' names and correspondence address in the field marked (73). The city and state or country, if a non-U.S. assignee, where the assignee has a principal place of business is listed next to the assignee's name. The assignee field does not necessarily indicate the current owner of the application, it only indicates who the owner was at the time the application was filed. Also, if the assignment was not sent to the USPTO at the time of filing, the assignment information generally will not be included on the face of the application publication. The current owner can be located by ordering an abstract of title from the USPTO or through a reassignment database. Also, the assignment information, once the application publishes, can be searched on the USPTO website.

Application Number. The application number is located below the inventor and assignee information and is marked by (21). The application number is the serial number given to the application while it is pending in the USPTO.

Filing Date. The filing date is located below the application number and is marked by (22). The filing date indicates the date an acceptable form of the application was received in the USPTO. Depending on the application, the filing date is significant for one of several reasons. For applications that do not claim priority from other applications, the filing date establishes a date of priority. The filing date is also significant because, barring a claim of foreign priority, it is the earliest date the U.S. application publication can be used as prior art against other inventions.[1]

If the application is based on a PCT application, then other fields will be present on the face of the patent giving additional information. The filing date field (22) will instead be the PCT application filing date, which is also marked by (22). Below the PCT application filing date is the PCT application number marked by (86).

Related U.S. Application Data. If the application claims

[Section 2:11]
   [1]35 U.S.C.A. § 102(a)(2).

priority from one or more prior U.S. applications, then the respective prior application numbers, filing dates, and patent numbers, if known, are also indicated on the cover sheet. If the application claims priority from a provisional application, then that field is marked by (60). If the application is a divisional of a prior U.S. application, then that field is marked by (62). If the application is a continuation or a continuation-in-part of a prior U.S. application, then that field is marked by (63). If there are no valid U.S. priority claims, then the field is omitted from the face of the patent.

Foreign Application Priority Data. If the application makes a claim of foreign priority, then this information is marked (30). The foreign filing date and application number are indicated in this field. If the application does not make a claim of foreign priority, then this field is omitted from the face of the publication. The foreign filing date is also significant because it is the earliest date the U.S. patent can be used as prior art against other inventions.[2]

Publication Classification. Publication Classes of the application are marked by (51) and (52). The classes listed on the cover page categorize the technology disclosed in the application. There are two separate classification systems listed on the cover page. One is the International Classification System, (51), and the other is the U.S. Classification System, (52). Both systems divide technology into very specific categories and then assign a classification number to each category. One classification number in each system is **bolded** to indicate that the application is directed largely to the technology found in that classification.

Abstract. The Abstract is marked by (57) and is intended to be a short summary of the basic inventive aspect of the application. It is usually between 50 and 150 words, and is often taken directly from the broadest claim in the application.

Representative Drawing. At the bottom of the cover page is one drawing representative of the invention as a whole. It is selected by the USPTO from the drawings submitted as part of the application.

§ 2:12   Example of a utility patent application publication—Figures

Research References

West's Key Number Digest, Patents ⬅️100
C.J.S., Patents § 143

The figures and reference characters in an application publica-

---

[2]35 U.S.C.A. § 102(d).

tion are similar to those in a utility patent. The figures published in the application publication are ordinarily the figures that were filed with the application and may not be "formal" drawings. Therefore, these figures may appear different in the patent, if a patent ultimately issues from the application.

§ 2:13 Example of a utility patent application publication—Specification

Research References

West's Key Number Digest, Patents ☞99
C.J.S., Patents § 139

The sections of the specification of the application are similar to those of a utility patent. For the most part, the specification will be identical to the specification of the patent, if a patent ultimately issues from the application, because no new matter may be introduced into the application after it is filed. However, the applicant is allowed to amend the claims. Generally, the claims in the application publication are the claims that were filed with the application. Often times, because of amendments made during prosecution, the claims that may ultimately issue into a patent are different than those claims that were filed.

§ 2:14 Example of a design patent

Research References

West's Key Number Digest, Patents ☞15
C.J.S., Patents §§ 100, 103

An example of a design patent is included in Appendix B.

In a design patent, a "D" is placed before the patent number to designate it as a design patent. The kind code follows the patent number. Design patents are numbered separately from utility patents. The specification and claims are shifted to the cover page because they are very short. The remainder of the patent contains figures that show the ornamental design that is protected by the patent.

The cover page of a design patent is similar to the cover page of a utility patent. In a design patent, there is only one claim and it appears on the cover page. It is often of the form: "The ornamental design for a _____, as shown and described." The only description required in a design patent is a one sentence description of each figure in the patent. The description is usually short enough to appear on the cover page.

The remainder of a design patent is figures. It is important that the figures accurately depict the ornamental design because they are the only description of the invention. In the figures, solid lines define the claimed design, while dashed lines are not part of the claimed design. Photographs may be submitted in the place of figures as long as the ornamental design is the only object in the photographs. Color drawings and color photographs are permitted only in certain cases.

§ 2:15   Example of a plant patent

Research References
West's Key Number Digest, Patents ☞14
C.J.S., Patents § 22

An example of a plant patent is included in Appendix C.

In a plant patent, the first page includes both cover sheet information and a portion of the specification. The cover sheet information and specification are similar to utility patents. Plant patents are numbered separately from utility and design patents. The letters "PP" are placed before the patent number to designate it as a plant patent number. The kind code follows the patent number.

The title of a plant patent is marked (54). Additionally, the Latin name and variety name are marked (50). The general name must use accepted botanical terms and must be descriptive of the plant as a whole and not just its fruit, flower, or seeds. The variety name indicates the kind of plant involved in the patent.

The specification begins with the brief botanical description of the Latin name and variety. A background section includes statements pointing out the distinctive features of the new variety from existing plants. It also states the place and manner in which the plant has been asexually reproduced. Following the background section is a summary of the invention and brief description of the drawings.

The detailed botanical description describes the new variety using terms found in accepted botanical texts. This includes exact descriptions of the colors of the plant using a system of color designations accepted in the botanical art.

There is only one claim in a plant patent. It must claim the entire plant and not just one aspect of the plant. It usually includes the phrase "A new and distinct variety of plant * * * substantially as herein shown and described."

Plant drawings should be artistic and should be in color if the distinctiveness of the plant rests in its color. Photographs are often used in place of drawings because they are easier to produce. The photographs or drawings should show all of the distinctive feature of the plant.

§ 2:16   Ownership of U.S. patents—Original ownership

Research References
West's Key Number Digest, Labor and Employment ☞310; Patents ☞90(1), 195
C.J.S., Patents §§ 120 to 122, 322 to 325

Title in an invention automatically vests in the inventor upon creation. The inventor also automatically owns rights in any patent application and patent on the invention unless an agreement provides otherwise. An example of such an agreement is an employment contract where employees are obligated to assign their inventions to their employer.

§ 2:17 Ownership of U.S. patents—Transfer of ownership

Research References
West's Key Number Digest, Patents ☞193 to 205
C.J.S., Patents §§ 316 to 338, 340 to 341

A patent (or a patent application) is personal property.[1] The owner of the patent may sell, mortgage, or bequeath his or her rights to the patent or application. The patent owner may assign all rights or an undivided interest in the patent. In addition, the patent owner may license others to perform any one of the actions (making, using, selling, offering for sale or importing the invention) that the patent owner could otherwise forbid under the patent grant. However, a patent does not give its owner the right to practice an invention, it only gives him or her the right to exclude others from what is covered in his or her patent. Thus, any license is subject to the rights of third parties.[2]

§ 2:18 Ownership of U.S. patents—Joint ownership

Research References
West's Key Number Digest, Patents ☞92
C.J.S., Patents §§ 126, 134

A patent may have joint owners. Each coinventor owns an undivided interest in the entire patent, regardless of the extent of their inventive contributions.[1] Therefore, unless agreed otherwise, each of the joint owners of a patent may make, use, or sell the patented invention without the consent of and without

---

[Section 2:17]
[1]35 U.S.C.A. § 261.

[2]See § 2:27.

[Section 2:18]
[1]Ethicon, Inc. v. U.S. Surgical Corp., 135 F.3d 1456, 45 U.S.P.Q.2d 1545, 48 Fed. R. Evid. Serv. 1226 (Fed. Cir. 1998).

accounting to the other owners.[2] The only limitations on a joint owner's individual exploitation of the invention are those common to all patent holders: other patents covering some part of their invention; federal, state or local regulation prohibiting exploitation of their invention; or a contract agreeing not to exploit the invention signed by the joint owner. Each joint owner may convey his or her rights to the invention. Once conveyed, the new joint owner enjoys the same rights of exploitation as the conveyor. Despite their general ability to operate independently, all joint owners of a patent must be parties to a suit charging infringement of their patent.[3]

§ 2:19 Priority of inventions—Claiming priority

Research References
West's Key Number Digest, Patents ⊙⇒90, 91
C.J.S., Patents §§ 120 to 126, 131 to 134

"Claiming priority" is a term of art that generally means that the applicant wishes to use the filing date of an earlier application to limit the prior art asserted against a later application. When claiming priority, the later application is said to claim the benefit of the earlier application's filing date.

Prior to implementation of the America Invents Act (AIA) on March 16, 2013, the specific effect of claiming priority depended on the type of application from which priority is claimed. For example, an applicant could claim priority to a U.S. patent application, and the later application would be treated as if it had been filed on the earlier application's filing date. However, a later application that claimed the benefit of a foreign application's filing date did not receive the entire benefit of the foreign application's filing date. In particular, claiming priority from a foreign application did not stop the running of the one year time bar in 35 U.S.C.A. § 102(b) (2006). Thus, if an invention appeared in a printed publication in any country or was on sale or in public use in the United States more than one year before the U.S. application was filed, the application would be barred even it if claimed priority from a foreign application filed less than one year from those events.

Upon implementation of the AIA on March 16, 2013, a later application that claims the benefit of a foreign application's filing date will receive the entire benefit of the foreign application's fil-

---

[2]35 U.S.C.A. § 262.   1093 (11th Cir. 1991).
[3]Devlin v. Ingrum, 928 F.2d 1084,

ing date.[1] Thus, for purposes of the time bars defined under the AIA, which differ from the previous time bars, an applicant may rely on an effective filing date established by the filing of a foreign application to the same extent as he or she would rely on a U.S. application.[2]

§ 2:20 Priority of inventions—Provisional applications

Research References

West's Key Number Digest, Patents ☞97
C.J.S., Patents §§ 135 to 138, 145, 178

A provisional application is only used to secure a filing date for later-filed applications that claim priority from the provisional application. To secure a filing date, the provisional application must provide an enabling disclosure of the invention claimed in the patent. Provisional applications are not examined for patentability and are automatically abandoned one year after their filing date. While provisional applications are not examined when filed, any new disclosures made in a later nonprovisional application claiming priority from the provisional do not receive the benefit of the earlier filing date.

In addition, provisional applications may not claim the benefit of another application's filing date.[1] Therefore, the earliest possible priority date for a provisional application is the date it is actually filed with the USPTO.

§ 2:21 Priority of inventions—Nonprovisional applications

Research References

West's Key Number Digest, Patents ☞97
C.J.S., Patents §§ 135 to 138, 145, 178

A nonprovisional application is examined for patentability and can be used to secure a filing date for other applications. In addition, nonprovisional applications can claim priority from U.S. provisional applications, related U.S. nonprovisional applications, foreign applications, or international applications.

A provisional application may also be converted to a nonprovisional application within twelve months of filing if a written request is submitted, and accompanied by an amendment to include at least one claim and payment of appropriate applica-

---

[Section 2:19]

[1]35 U.S.C.A. § 119(a).
[2]35 U.S.C.A. § 102(b)(1).

[Section 2:20]

[1]35 U.S.C.A. § 111(b)(7).

tion fees. However, the USPTO discourages this practice in favor of filing a new nonprovisional application claiming priority from the provisional. When a provisional application is converted, the patent term is calculated from the filing date of the provisional and not the date of conversion. This approach effectively reduces the available term of protection by up to 12 months.[1]

§ 2:22   Priority of inventions—Divisional applications

Research References

West's Key Number Digest, Patents ⊙97
C.J.S., Patents §§ 135 to 138, 145, 178

A divisional application allows applicants to divide separate inventions into separate applications. If an initial application contains claims to more than one invention, the applicant can divide the inventions by filing a separate divisional application for each of the inventions. When the division is completed, each application only has claims to a single invention. The divisional application must be filed during the pendency of the original application to retain the filing date of that application.[1]

§ 2:23   Priority of inventions—Continuation applications

Research References

West's Key Number Digest, Patents ⊙110
C.J.S., Patents § 156

A continuation application can provide broader protection or protection of a different scope to an invention that is not fully claimed in an earlier application. To claim the benefit of an earlier application's filing date, a continuation application must limit its claims to aspects of the invention that were disclosed in the earlier application. The continuation application must be filed during the pendency of the earlier application to be entitled to the earlier application's filing date.[1]

§ 2:24   Priority of inventions—Continuation-in-part applications

Research References

West's Key Number Digest, Patents ⊙110
C.J.S., Patents § 156

[Section 2:21]
    [1]*See* 37 C.F.R. § 1.53(c)(3).

[Section 2:22]
    [1]35 U.S.C.A. § 121.

[Section 2:23]
    [1]35 U.S.C.A. § 120.

A continuation-in-part application is similar to a continuation application, except that a continuation-in-part application includes information that was not disclosed in the earlier application. An application's disclosure may not be expanded once the application is filed. Therefore, the only way to achieve an expanded disclosure is to file a new application. Continuations-in-part give applicants the opportunity to expand their disclosures without having to forfeit their filing date for the portions of their inventions that were adequately disclosed in the original application.

If the continuation-in-part is filed during the pendency of an earlier application and priority is properly claimed, aspects of an invention that were disclosed in the earlier application receive the benefit of the earlier application's filing date.[1] Aspects that were not fully disclosed in the earlier application receive an effective filing date of the continuation-in-part.

§ 2:25 Nature of U.S. patent rights—Patent term

Research References
West's Key Number Digest, Patents ⬩130 to 133
C.J.S., Patents §§ 233 to 236

From 1861 to 1995, the term of a plant or utility patent issued by the USPTO began on the date that the patent issued and ended 17 years later. As of June 8, 1995, the method of determining a patent's term changed. The current term for plant and utility patents generally ends twenty years after the effective filing date of the patent application, which is the earliest filing date from which the application claims priority.[1] In addition to a U.S. non-provisional filing setting an effective filing date, a U.S. national stage application from an international PCT application would do the same.

Patents in force after June 8, 1995, that issued on applications filed before June 8, 1995, expire either seventeen years from the date of grant, or twenty years from the effective filing date, whichever is later.[2] U.S. design patents continue to have a term of fourteen years from the date of issuance.[3]

The patent term for processes and compositions of matter that are subject to approval by the Food and Drug Administration (F.D.A.) can be extended for F.D.A.-related delays in product

---

[Section 2:24]
[1]35 U.S.C.A. § 120.
[Section 2:25]
[1]35 U.S.C.A. § 154(a)(2).

[2]35 U.S.C.A. § 154(c)(1).
[3]35 U.S.C.A. § 173.

distribution.[4]

The patent term may be extended or adjusted for certain delays in the prosecution of the patent.[5] If there has been a patent term adjustment, the adjustment will be indicated on the cover of the patent.

The term of a utility patent is subject to the payment of maintenance fees.[6] These fees are preferably paid three and one-half years, seven and one-half years, and eleven and one-half years from the date of the original patent grant but may be paid at four, eight, and twelve years from the grant date if a surcharge fee is included. If no fee is received before the four, eight, and twelve year dates, the patent expires as of that date.[7]

Expired patents may be reinstated if the owner of the patent makes a showing that the failure to pay the maintenance fee was unintentional or unavoidable.[8] However, even after the patent is reinstated, anyone who made, purchased, used or imported the invention during the period the patent was expired has an absolute intervening right to sell or continue to use the specific things made, purchased, used or imported while the patent was expired.[9]

§ 2:26   Nature of U.S. patent rights—Exclusionary rights

Research References
West's Key Number Digest, Patents ☞185
C.J.S., Patents §§ 10, 314

The only right provided to the owner of a utility patent or a design patent is the right to exclude others from making, using, selling, offering for sale, or importing the invention covered by the patent.[1] Owners of plant patents have the right to exclude others from asexually reproducing, selling, or using the plant.[2] A patent owner may exclude any product, process, or design that is covered by at least one claim of the patent.

One way that a patent excludes others is by acting as a warning sign. A patent tells the public that the patent owner has the right to exclude others. In this sense, the patent acts as the intellectual property equivalent of a "no-trespassing" sign. A no-trespassing sign does not guarantee that the person who posted the sign has the right to keep others away. Nonetheless, many

---

[4]35 U.S.C.A. §§ 155 and 155A.

[5]35 U.S.C.A. § 154(b); 37 C.F.R. §§ 1.701 et seq.

[6]35 U.S.C.A. § 41(b).

[7]35 U.S.C.A. § 41(b).

[8]35 U.S.C.A. § 41(c)(1).

[9]35 U.S.C.A. § 41(c)(2).

[Section 2:26]

[1]35 U.S.C.A. § 271(a).

[2]35 U.S.C.A. § 163.

people obey the sign and refrain from using the property without investigating whether the person who posted the sign actually has the right to exclude others. Similarly, some people will avoid exploiting an invention simply because a patent seems to indicate that they are excluded from doing so. They will not investigate to see if the patent is valid or if it actually covers all it appears to claim. Instead, they will simply take the patent at face value and not practice the invention that is claimed.

Others, however, will want to test the owner's ability to exclude them from exploiting an item. To exclude these people, the patent owner must usually assert the patent in court.

For those who wish to test a patent, it is often tempting to simply ignore the patent without investigating the patent's validity or scope. However, this raises the potential of liability for willful infringement, which can result in treble damages[3] if the infringer is found to have been "objectively reckless."[4]

§ 2:27 Nature of U.S. patent rights—Patented inventions can infringe other patents

Research References
West's Key Number Digest, Patents ⊸226.10
C.J.S., Patents § 401

Simply because an invention is patented does not mean that a product incorporating the invention cannot infringe another patent. The test for infringement is distinct from the test for patentability. Infringement is found whenever a product or process includes all of the elements of a patent claim.[1] It is usually irrelevant that the product or process has additional elements beyond the claim. If the product or process includes all of the elements of the claim, it infringes the patent. Generally, if a valid patent claims an invention with elements A, B, and C, any subsequently patented product with these elements such as A, B, C, and D will infringe the first patent, even if the subsequent patent is otherwise valid.

Patentability, on the other hand, involves tests of novelty and obviousness. In those tests, additional features beyond what is shown in an existing patent may create an invention that is novel and not obvious and thus create a patentable invention. Because the tests are separate, a patented invention can infringe other

---

[3]35 U.S.C.A. § 284

[4]In re Seagate Tech., LLC, 497 F.3d 1360, 83 U.S.P.Q.2d 1865 (Fed. Cir. 2007), cert. denied, 128 S. Ct. 1445 (2008).

[Section 2:27]

[1]TechSearch, L.L.C. v. Intel Corp., 286 F.3d 1360, 1371, 62 U.S.P.Q.2d 1449 (Fed. Cir. 2002).

patents. Continuing with the previous example, so long as the combination of elements A, B, C, and D is novel and it was not obvious to add element D, a subsequent application claiming A, B, C, and D should be patentable regardless of the fact that the invention infringes the first patent claiming elements A, B, and C.

This distinction must be kept in mind during licensing negotiations. Similar to quit claim deeds in real property, a patent license only gives the licensee the rights the licensor has to give. Since a patent does not give a patent owner the right to make, use, sell or import their invention, the patent owner can not give a licensee the right to take those actions. At most, a patent owner can give a licensee the right to take those actions free of the patent owner's patent. If the product or process is covered by other patents, the licensee may still need to address those patents independently.

§ 2:28 Nature of U.S. patent rights—Patent marking

Research References

West's Key Number Digest, Patents ⊕222

C.J.S., Patents §§ 394 to 395

Once an inventor has filed a U.S. patent application, he or she is permitted to mark his or her products with the phrases "Patent Pending" or "Patent Applied For." However, these markings do not give the applicant a legal right to enforce the patent application. A patent application, by itself, does not give the inventor the right to stop others from making or selling an invention. The fact that the inventor has marked products with the phrase "Patent Pending" does not change this.

The phrase "Patent Pending" is sometimes commercially effective. If a competitor believes that a patent may someday issue on a product, they may be hesitant to invest in equipment to produce the product because once the patent issues the investment could be lost. In fact, marking with the phrase "Patent Pending" is thought to be so commercially effective that U.S. law prohibits such marking unless a patent application has actually been filed and is currently pending. A manufacturer who improperly or falsely uses "Patent Pending" on products can be fined $500 for every offense.[1]

Upon obtaining a patent, a patent owner should, if possible, mark any patent products sold with the word "Patent" or "Pat." along with the patent number. Alternatively, the manufacturer

---

[Section 2:28]

[1]35 U.S.C.A. § 292.

may indicate an Internet address where such patent numbers may be found. Failure to properly mark a patented product may affect the damages the patentee can recover against an infringer.[2]

§ 2:29 Nature of U.S. patent rights—Inventions enter the public domain after a patent expires

Research References
West's Key Number Digest, Patents ⊛131
C.J.S., Patents §§ 233, 236

After a patent expires, the public is free to practice the invention without compensating the inventor. The inventor cannot claim some other separate state right to exclude others from making or using the invention after the patent expires. The federal patent law preempts any equivalent state rights, and patent owners are limited to the rights afforded them by the patent laws.[1] This eventual public dedication of an invention "to promote the Progress of Science and useful Arts" is the price set by the Framers of the Constitution that inventors must pay in exchange for the term of protection.[2]

§ 2:30 Patentability of inventions—The "first to file" patent system

Research References
West's Key Number Digest, Patents ⊛90(1)
C.J.S., Patents §§ 120 to 122

With the passage of the Leahy-Smith America Invents Act (AIA), the United States transitioned from a "first to invent" system to a "first to file system" on March 16, 2013. This is a significant step in harmonizing U.S. patent law with that of most other countries. The most notable difference between the "first to invent" and "first to file" systems is that the date of the invention (*e.g.,* date of conception) is no longer relevant in determining novelty of the invention. Rather, the filing date of the application represents the earliest date the inventor can rely on for establishing novelty. This creates an incentive for inventors to file patent applications quickly.

Under the old "first to invent" system, the first person to conceive of an invention was awarded the patent for that invention, subject to a few exceptions. Although equitable, this system oftentimes created ambiguity about who was actually first to

---

[2]35 U.S.C.A. § 287(a).

[Section 2:29]

[1]Bonito Boats, 489 U.S. at 167,

109 S. Ct. at 986, 103 L.Ed.2d 118, 9 U.S.P.Q.2d at 1859.

[2]U.S. Const. art. I, § 8, cl. 8.

invent and therefore who should receive a patent. In general, the "first to file" system removes ambiguities regarding who should be awarded patent rights, with the first to file the application being awarded rights regardless of who invented first. This may result in an early inventor losing patent rights if another inventor wins the race to the patent office. However, the AIA does provide a remedy to inventors who are beaten to the patent office by a third party that derived or stole the invention from the inventor. This remedy is a derivation proceeding which allows an inventor to challenge whether the third party obtained the subject matter of the invention without authorization from the inventor.[1] For an inventor seeking relief via a derivation proceeding, the proceeding must be filed within one year of issuance of a first patent containing a claim to the allegedly derived invention.[2]

§ 2:31 Patentability of inventions—Inventions must be useful

Research References
West's Key Number Digest, Patents ⚖46 to 49
C.J.S., Patents §§ 59 to 63

To "promote the progress of science and the useful arts," Congress limits utility patent protection to those items that represent a substantial and useful advance beyond the current state of the art.[1] An invention for a utility patent must be useful or "have utility" to be patentable.[2] The test for utility is whether those skilled in the art would recognize a claimed use as legitimate.[3] For process inventions, the product of the process must have utility.[4] Design patents and plant patents need not meet the requirement of utility to be patentable.[5]

Chemical inventions are often susceptible to claims that they lack utility. For example, the well-known unpredictability of chemical reactions can create reasonable doubt as to whether a given chemical will produce a useful result.[6] Perpetual motion machines and other apparently inoperable inventions are also vulnerable to attack for lack of utility if such inventions do not perform their stated functions.

[Section 2:30]

[1]35 U.S.C.A. § 291(a).

[2]35 U.S.C.A. § 291(b).

[Section 2:31]

[1]U.S. Const., art. I, § 8; 35 U.S.C.A. § 101.

[2]35 U.S.C.A. § 101.

[3]In re Brana, 51 F.3d 1560, 1566, 34 U.S.P.Q.2d 1436, 1441 (Fed. Cir. 1995).

[4]Brenner v. Manson, 383 U.S. 519, 534-535, 86 S. Ct. 1033, 1041-42, 148 U.S.P.Q. 689, 695-696 (1966).

[5]35 U.S.C.A. §§ 161, 171.

[6]Application of Marzocchi, 58 C.C.P.A. 1069, 439 F.2d 220, 223, 169 U.S.P.Q. 367, 369-370 (1971).

Although early cases found lack of utility in inventions that promoted immoral behavior (such as gambling), the USPTO has stated that it is not responsible for enforcing moral standards.[7] Nonetheless, inventions useful substantially only for an illegal purpose or inventions only having fraudulent uses would likely be unpatentable for lack of utility.[8]

§ 2:32 Patentability of inventions—Inventions must be novel

Research References
West's Key Number Digest, Patents ☞37
C.J.S., Patents §§ 29 to 30

In nearly every country in the world, an invention must be new, or "novel," to be eligible for patent protection. In most countries, this means that the invention must not be publicly disclosed until a patent application is filed. Public disclosure, in this context, usually includes disclosures in any country, in any language, and by anyone (including the inventor). This rigid requirement is known as an absolute novelty requirement since it bars patentability for inventions that were publicly disclosed.

Prior to passage of the Leahy-Smith America Invents Act (AIA), an invention filed in the United States only needed relative novelty in order to be patentable. Relative novelty allowed some limited disclosure and use of the invention before an application is filed. The limits of the allowed disclosures and uses were previously defined in 35 U.S.C.A. § 102(a) to (g). Any disclosure, use, or sale that exceeded these limits became "prior art" to the invention. Determining whether a particular use or disclosure qualified as prior art was therefore an important task in analyzing whether an invention is entitled to a patent.

Under the AIA, determining whether a particular use or disclosure qualifies as prior art depends on the effective filing date of the application. Any qualifying disclosure made before the effective filing date is prior art, subject to a few exceptions. The AIA defines the effective filing date of the application as the actual filing date of the application or a priority date to which the application is entitled under 35 U.S.C.A. §§ 119, 120, 121, or 365, which includes claims of priority to provisional, continuation,

[7]Ex Parte Murphy, Sagan, Rosenthal, and Ostrowski, 200 U.S.P.Q. 801, 802, 1977 WL 22879 (Pat. & Trademark Office Bd. App. 1977).

[8]R. Carl Moy, *Moy's Walker on Patents* §§ 6:5, 6:15 (4th ed. 2003).

continuations-in-part, divisional, PCT, and foreign applications.[1]

The AIA defines novelty requirements in 35 U.S.C.A. §§ 102(a)(1) to (2), which provides that a person is entitled to a patent unless the claimed invention was patented, described in a printed publication, or in public use, on sale, or otherwise available to the public before the effective filing date of the claimed invention;[2] or the claimed invention was described in a patent or published application having an effective filing date prior to the effective filing date of the claimed invention.[3] The first section provides generally that the claimed invention cannot have been known or available to the public before the effective filing date of the claimed invention. The latter section defines this system as a "first-to-file" system, in which the effective filing date of the claimed invention is compared with the effective filing date of patents or published applications to determine novelty, without reference to who invented first.

With respect to § 102(a)(2), the AIA provides that a prior art reference that claims priority to a parent application has the same effective filing date as the parent application, even if the parent application was filed in another country. This is a change from the "first-to-invent" system, in which a patent or patent application could rely only on the U.S. filing date (or PCT filing date, if designating the United States) for purposes of determining whether the reference qualified as prior art.

With respect to § 102(a)(1), it is worth noting that public use, sale, or availability to the public need not occur in the United States. This is a significant change from the pre-2013 law, in which public uses or offers for sale had to occur in the United States to qualify as prior art. There are unresolved questions as to the meaning of the terms "in public use, on sale, or otherwise available to the public before the effective filing date of the claimed invention." In particular, there is a question as to whether the term "on sale" is the same as or is similar to the on-sale bar defined in the old 35 U.S.C.A. § 102(b), or whether the term "otherwise available to the public" in the current 35 U.S.C.A. § 102(a)(1) modifies the term "on sale" such that only public sales qualify as prior art. Despite the use of the term "on sale" in § 102(a)(1), the legislative history associated with AIA indicates that an offer for sale must be a public offer that makes the invention accessible or available to the public.[4] Under this interpretation, a private or confidential offer for sale would not constitute an "on sale" bar.

[Section 2:32]

[1]35 U.S.C.A. § 100(i)(1).

[2]35 U.S.C.A. § 102(a)(1).

[3]35 U.S.C.A. § 102(a)(2).

[4]157 Cong. Rec. S1370 (daily ed. Mar. 8, 2011).

Under the old statute, the "forfeiture doctrine" judicially developed under § 102 sought to prevent an inventor from commercializing his invention for more than a year prior to the filing of a patent application and then receiving the monopoly benefit of a patent. Secret commercial use of an invention, more than one year prior to filing an application, bars patentability for the commercial user.[5] "Secret commercial use" includes secretly using an inventive process or machine to produce a publicly sold product.[6] Under the old interpretation of the on-sale bar, a private or confidential offer for sale qualified as prior art regardless of whether the private or confidential aspects ever became publicly available.

Under the AIA, the United States has maintained some exceptions to the absolute novelty requirement found in most "first to file" countries, most notably the one-year grace period. In particular, the exceptions provide that a disclosure made one year or less prior to filing a patent application will not qualify as prior art so long as the disclosure was made by the inventor, joint inventor, or by another that obtained the information from the inventor.[7] In addition, a public disclosure (or patent application filing) made by another will not qualify as prior art if, before such disclosure or filing, a disclosure was made by the inventor, joint inventor, or by another that obtained the information from the inventor.[8]

For example, Applicant A provides a public disclosure with respect to an invention on date X. Applicant B files for a patent application on the same invention after date X but before Applicant A has filed for a patent application. Applicant A then files a patent application within one year of date X. Applicant A's public disclosure is not prior art to Applicant A because of the exception provided in § 102(b)(1) that grants a one year grace period for disclosures made by the inventor. In addition, Applicants B filing of a patent application is not prior art to Applicant A because of the exception provided in 35 U.S.C.A. § 102(b)(2) based on the public disclosure made by Applicant A before Applicant B's effective filing date. However, it is important to remember that if Applicant A does not file within one year of his own public disclosure, that disclosure will be prior art to Applicant A's claimed invention, and that any public disclosure prior to filing a

---

[5]*See* Egbert v. Lippmann, 104 U.S. 333, 26 L. Ed. 755, 1881 WL 19820 (1881); *see also* W.L. Gore & Associates, Inc. v. Garlock, Inc., 721 F.2d 1540, 1549–1550, 220 U.S.P.Q. 303, 310 (Fed. Cir. 1983).

[6]Metallizing Engineering Co. v.

Kenyon Bearing & Auto Parts Co., 153 F.2d 516, 68 U.S.P.Q. 54 (C.C.A. 2d Cir. 1946).

[7]35 U.S.C.A. § 102(b)(1).

[8]35 U.S.C.A. § 102(b)(2).

patent application may result in the loss of patent rights in countries that do have an absolute novelty requirement. Thus, it is not recommended to rely on non-patent public disclosures when patent protection is desired.

§ 2:33 Patentability of inventions—Defining novelty

Research References
West's Key Number Digest, Patents ⊶37 to 45
C.J.S., Patents §§ 29 to 30, 34, 101 to 102

This section will address the definitions of novelty in two parts. The definitions under the Leahy-Smith America Invents Act (AIA) will be discussed first, and the pre-AIA law will be discussed afterward. Understanding both sets of law is important, because the definition of novelty has changed significantly after the passage of the AIA, but pre-AIA law will apply to older patents and patent applications.

AIA. An invention lacks novelty if it was described in another U.S. patent application before the effective filing date of the claimed invention.[1] This is only true if the other patent application publishes or is eventually granted. If the application is abandoned before it publishes or issues (where there was no publication), it does not affect the novelty of later inventions.[2]

The second way an invention lacks novelty is if it was patented or described in a printed publication before the effective filing date of the claimed invention. Printed publications also create a time-bar to patentability.[3] This includes publications written in languages other than English and publications distributed outside of the United States. Printed publications include: press releases, sales brochures, catalogs, patents, and technical journals. Internet content can also serve as a printed publication, as long as the content is available to the extent that persons interested and ordinarily skilled in the subject matter or art, exercising reasonable diligence, can locate it.[4]

Although a speech, by itself, wouldn't appear to be a printed publication, the Federal Circuit considered a speech given to 500 people a "printed publication" when a paper related to the speech

---

[Section 2:33]

[1]35 U.S.C.A. § 102(a)(2).

[2]Ex Parte Osmond, Smith, and Waite, 191 U.S.P.Q. 334, 338, 1973 WL 19825 (Pat. & Trademark Office Bd. App. 1973).

[3]35 U.S.C.A. § 102(a)(1).

[4]Voter Verified, Inc. v. Premier Election Solutions, Inc., 698 F.3d 1374, 1380, 104 U.S.P.Q.2d 1553, 1556–1557 (Fed. Cir. 2012), cert. denied, 2013 WL 1467744 (U.S. 2013) and cert. denied, 2013 WL 1467889 (U.S. 2013).

was distributed to six of the 500 people.[5] A publication describing a speech can also be considered a printed publication. Thus, although a speech may not be a printed publication, articles related to the speech may be considered printed publications.

The third way an invention lacks novelty is if it was in public use prior to the effective filing date of the claimed invention.[6] This use can occur anywhere in the world and must be somewhat public. Secret knowledge, such as found in a private, intracorporate communication, does not operate as prior art.[7] Conversely, secret use by the applicant can bar patentability when conducted openly.[8] However, nonsecret use of an invention by others or by the applicant in its natural and intended way in public can operate as prior art.[9]

Public use is generally defined as the use of a product or process "in its natural or intended way," without taking steps to keep the invention secret.[10] There are several policies behind the bar, including:

- Discouraging the removal of inventions that the public reasonably has come to believe are freely available,
- Promoting prompt and widespread disclosure of inventions,
- Allowing inventors reasonable time after sales activities to determine the potential economic value of a patent, and
- Prohibiting inventors from commercially exploiting their inventions for a period greater than the patent term.[11]

An item must be reduced to practice and be operable before using it will destroy novelty.[12] Experimenting with nonfunctional units does not create a prior art use.

Experimental use was once considered an exception to the public use bar, but courts have clarified that public experimentation is not an exception to public use, but merely one factor that may be used to determine whether a public use has occurred. The

---

[5]Massachusetts Institute of Technology v. AB Fortia, 4 Fed. Cir. (T) 8, 774 F.2d 1104, 1108–1109, 7 Int'l Trade Rep. (BNA) 1405, 227 U.S.P.Q. 428, 432 (1985).

[6]35 U.S.C.A. § 102(a)(1).

[7]Continental Oil Co. v. Cole, 634 F.2d 188, 196, 209 U.S.P.Q. 361, 367 (5th Cir. 1981).

[8]TP Laboratories, Inc. v. Professional Positioners, Inc., 724 F.2d 965, 970, 220 U.S.P.Q. 577, 581 (Fed. Cir. 1984).

[9]Marrese v. Richard's Medical Equipment, Inc., 504 F.2d 479, 482–483, 183 U.S.P.Q. 517, 518–519 (7th Cir. 1974).

[10]FMC Corp. v. F. E. Myers & Bro. Co., 384 F.2d 4, 9, 155 U.S.P.Q. 299, 303 (6th Cir. 1967).

[11]Tone Bros., Inc. v. Sysco Corp., 28 F.3d 1192, 1198, 31 U.S.P.Q.2d 1321, 1324–1325 (Fed. Cir. 1994).

[12]Medtronic, Inc. v. Daig Corp., 611 F. Supp. 1498, 1508, 227 U.S.P.Q. 509, 515 (D. Minn. 1985), judgment aff'd, 789 F.2d 903, 229 U.S.P.Q. 664 (Fed. Cir. 1986).

proper test is to consider whether the experimental nature of the use, taken with the circumstances as a whole, produces a use that should bar patentability in light of one or more of the policy reasons for the bar.[13] To make that determination, courts balance the following:

- the length of the test period and number of tests,
- the payments, if any, made by the user for the device,
- the secrecy of the use,
- the extent to which records of the tests were kept, and
- the number of persons, besides the inventor, who witnessed the tests.[14]

Third-party knowledge of the invention only acts as prior art if the knowledge was sufficient enough to permit those skilled in the art to practice the invention.[15] Because it would be easy to falsely assert prior knowledge of an invention, the level of knowledge must be established using some form of corroborating evidence. For example, the text of a speech establishes the level of public knowledge on the date the speech was delivered.[16] If the speech contained enough information to permit those skilled in the art to practice the invention, it could be considered prior art.

For another example, displaying an invention at a trade show is generally, but not always, considered a public use.[17] In those cases that found public uses at trade shows, it did not matter that the invention was hidden. One court found that an invention was in public use if it was used in its "natural and intended way" and open to the public, even though the invention was hidden in a larger machine.[18]

Under pre-AIA § 102, courts created the doctrine of forfeiture that governed secret commercial use of an invention. The changes to the definitions of novelty in the AIA have led to a controversy over whether the doctrine of forfeiture has been superseded by

---

[13]Tone Bros., 28 F.3d at 1198, 31 U.S.P.Q.2d at 1325.

[14]Tone Bros., 28 F.3d at 1200, 31 U.S.P.Q.2d at 1326.

[15]Application of Borst, 52 C.C.P.A. 1398, 345 F.2d 851, 854–855, 145 U.S.P.Q. 554, 557 (1965).

[16]American Standard Inc. v. Pfizer Inc., 722 F. Supp. 86, 129 n.42, 14 U.S.P.Q.2d 1673, 1709 n.42 (D. Del. 1989).

[17]Compare Electro-Nucleonics, Inc. v. Mossinghoff, 593 F. Supp. 125, 127, 224 U.S.P.Q. 435, 436–437 (D.D.C.

1984) (finding public use for trade show display) with Automotive Products PLC v. Tilton Engineering, Inc., 855 F. Supp. 1101, 33 U.S.P.Q.2d 1065, 1085, 1994-1 Trade Cas. (CCH) ¶ 70656 (C.D. Cal. 1994), dismissed, 36 F.3d 1109 (Fed. Cir. 1994) (finding no public use at a trade show).

[18]National Research Development Corp. v. Varian Associates, Inc., 822 F. Supp. 1121, 1131, 28 U.S.P.Q.2d 1436, 1446 (D.N.J. 1993), aff'd in part, vacated in part on other grounds, 17 F.3d 1444, 30 U.S.P.Q.2d 1537 (Fed. Cir. 1994).

statute.[19] In the absence of case law on point, the doctrine of forfeiture is at least something to be aware of. Specifically, the doctrine states that secret commercial use of an invention by the applicant bars patentability for the commercial user.[20] "Secret commercial use" includes secretly using an inventive process or machine to produce a publicly sold product.[21]

The doctrine of forfeiture goes further to state that even if a third party secretly commercially uses the invention, the inventor and his assigns are barred from patenting the invention if they caused the use by giving the third party information about the invention.[22] However, if the third party's use was not precipitated by the inventor or assignee, the inventor is not affected by the use.[23] Thus, if a party secretly made commercial use of an invention for a number of years, a separate inventor could still patent the invention. Such a ruling furthers the policy goal of prompt disclosure by favoring those who promptly file for patent protection over those who commercially exploit the invention in secret.[24]

The fourth way an invention lacks novelty is if the invention is sold or offered for sale before the effective filing date of the claimed invention. Inventions on-sale anywhere in the world prior to the filing of a U.S. patent application are barred from receiving a U.S. patent.[25] The on-sale bar applies when the product is the subject of a commercial offer for sale and the invention is ready for patenting.[26] "On-sale" includes sales by the inventor, people under the inventor's control, and unrelated third parties.[27] The intention to sell must be communicated, but a single offer for sale is enough to bar patentability, even if the offer isn't

---

[19]Elkind, Stephen, Secrets, Secrets Are No Fun! Balancing Patent Law & Trade Secret Law Under the America Invents Act, 22 Fed. Circuit B.J. 431 (2011); Merges, Robert P., Priority and Novelty Under the AIA, 27 Berkeley Tech. L.J. 1023 (2012); Goter, Phillip W., The Commercial Exploitation Continuum, 13 Minn. J.L. Sci. & Tech. 795 (2012).

[20]See Egbert v. Lippmann, 104 U.S. 333, 26 L. Ed. 755, 1881 WL 19820 (1881); see also W.L. Gore & Associates, Inc. v. Garlock, Inc., 721 F.2d 1540, 1549–1550, 220 U.S.P.Q. 303, 310 (Fed. Cir. 1983).

[21]Metallizing Engineering Co. v. Kenyon Bearing & Auto Parts Co., 153 F.2d 516, 68 U.S.P.Q. 54 (C.C.A. 2d Cir. 1946).

[22]Nat'l Research Dev. Corp. v. Varian Assocs., Inc., 17 F.3d at 1446, 30 U.S.P.Q.2d at 1539.

[23]W. L. Gore, 721 F.2d at 1550, 220 U.S.P.Q. at 310.

[24]W. L. Gore, 721 F.2d at 1550, 220 U.S.P.Q. at 310.

[25]35 U.S.C.A. § 102(a)(1).

[26]Pfaff v. Wells Electronics, Inc., 525 U.S. 55, 67, 119 S. Ct. 304, 311–312, 142 L. Ed. 2d 261, 48 U.S.P.Q.2d 1641 (1998).

[27]J.A. LaPorte, Inc. v. Norfolk Dredging Co., 787 F.2d 1577, 1581, 229 U.S.P.Q. 435, 437 (Fed. Cir. 1986).

accepted.[28] However, offers for sale of the invention should be distinguished from mere offers of the rights to the invention. An assignment or sale of rights in an invention or potential patent, without more, does not constitute an offer for sale for purposes of 35 U.S.C.A. § 102(a).[29] This is a very narrow exception. Transactions where an embodiment or enabling disclosure of the invention itself is part of the offer or negotiations can destroy novelty.[30] However, the changes to the definitions of novelty in the AIA have led to a controversy over whether an invention that is secretly on-sale has been disclosed.[31]

There may be a fifth way an invention lacks novelty, and that is if the invention is otherwise available to the public before the effective filing date of the claimed invention.[32] There is some controversy over what this phrase means, due to the lack of judicial construction of the current § 102. One interpretation is that "or otherwise available. . ." is a fifth category of prior art that did not exist before the AIA. The alternative interpretation is that "or otherwise available to the public" is a modifier of the public use and on-sale bars to patentability. The ambiguity of this clause is related to the ambiguity surrounding the doctrine of forfeiture and the on-sale bars discussed above. More specifically, it is unclear as to whether secret activity—such as an applicant's own secret commercial activity—can be used as prior art to a patent application.[33]

There are exceptions to the definition of novelty under the AIA. These provisions effectively preserve the one-year grace period for an inventor's own disclosure that was present in the pre-AIA 35 U.S.C.A. § 102 statute, although the exceptions generally do not extend to disclosures that originate completely independently of the inventor. More specifically, any disclosure made by the inventor or a joint inventor one year or less before the effective filing date of the patent application cannot be prior art to the claimed invention.[34] Furthermore, a disclosure made by a third party is not prior art to a patent application if the subject matter contained therein was previously disclosed by the inventor, a joint inventor, or another who obtained the information from the inventor(s). But again, the patent application must be filed within

---

[28]In re Caveney, 761 F.2d 671, 676, 226 U.S.P.Q. 1, 4 (Fed. Cir. 1985).

[29]Moleculon Research Corp. v. CBS, Inc., 793 F.2d 1261, 1267, 229 U.S.P.Q. 805, 809 (Fed. Cir. 1986).

[30]See, e.g., In re Kollar, 286 F.3d 1326, 1330 n.3, 1330–1331, 62 U.S.P.Q.2d 1425, 1428 n.3, 1428–1429 (Fed. Cir. 2002).

[31]22 Fed. Circuit B.J. 431; 27 Berkeley Tech. L.J. 1023; Morgan, Paul, The Ambiguity in Section 102(A)(1) of the Leahy-Smith America Invents Act, 2011 Patently-O Pat. L.J. 29 (2011).

[32]35 U.S.C.A. § 102(a)(1).

[33]See, e.g., 22 Fed. Circuit B.J. 431; 2011 Patently-O Pat. L.J. 29.

[34]35 U.S.C.A. § 102(b)(1)(A).

one year of the initial disclosure to avoid the prior art.[35] However, the changes to the definitions of novelty in the AIA have led to a controversy over whether the secret sale of an invention is a disclosure that will trigger the start of the one-year grace period.[36]

In addition to these exceptions, the AIA has additional exceptions that apply to disclosures contained in other patents and patent applications, specifically those filed by a different inventor at a time before the effective filing date of the patent application in question.[37] Such a disclosure is not prior art to an inventor's patent application if the subject matter disclosed was obtained from the inventor. In addition, the other patent or patent application is not prior art if the subject matter contained therein was previously disclosed by the inventor, a joint inventor, or another who obtained the information from the inventor(s). Finally, such a patent or patent application is not prior art if both it and the patent application in question were both owned by the same party at the time of filing of the patent in question. This includes situations where single party ownership is not yet established but is secured by an obligation to assign that would transfer ownership to the single party. In addition, joint research agreements between two entities are deemed to satisfy the ownership requirement of this exception if the invention was made within the scope of the joint research agreement.[38]

Pre-AIA. There are many pending applications that were filed and many more patents that issued before the full implementation of the AIA. Therefore, the previous definitions of novelty will apply to any patent or patent application with an effective filing date before March 16th, 2013. While the definitions are mostly the same before and after the AIA, there are key differences between pre-AIA law and the current 35 U.S.C.A. § 102 statute. For example, pre-AIA, the date of invention was an important date for determining the outer boundaries of what was prior art, not the effective filing date. This lead to an additional definition of novelty that stated that an invention lacks novelty if it was invented by another in the United States before the applicant's invention date.[39] Under this section, unlike prior use or prior knowledge, a prior invention does not need to be publicly known. A prior invention will act as prior art as long as it was conserved and reduced to practice, and it was not abandoned, suppressed, or concealed.[40] Note that the prior invention must have been in the United States. Prior inventions in other countries, including

---

[35] 35 U.S.C.A. § 102(b)(1)(B).

[36] 22 Fed. Circuit B.J. 431, 450–59; 27 Berkeley Tech. L.J. 1023, 1034–37, 2011 Patently-O Pat. L.J. 29, 32–35.

[37] 35 U.S.C.A. § 102(b)(2).

[38] 35 U.S.C.A. § 102(c).

[39] 35 U.S.C.A. § 102(a) (2006).

[40] International Glass Co. Inc. v.

NAFTA and WTO countries, did not act as prior art in the United States.

The geographic requirement in pre-AIA 35 U.S.C.A. § 102(a) is also present in other definitions of novelty. For example, the public use and on-sale definitions required the activity to occur in the United States. Therefore, public uses outside of the United States did not create a bar to patentability in the United States.[41] Thus, for example, a newly invented car could have been driven on Germany's Autobahn more than one year before filing for a U.S. patent application. Although, the on-sale bar is even triggered by foreign nationals situated abroad who make offers directed towards persons in the United States.[42] It is also triggered by a sale outside of the United States if substantial sales activity leading to the actual sale took place in the United States.[43]

In addition to the foregoing definitions of novelty, the pre-AIA law had an additional definition. This prior art time-bar is somewhat complicated. If a foreign application is filed by an inventor more than twelve months before he or she files a U.S. application, and the foreign application is granted before the U.S. application is filed, the inventor is barred from patenting the invention in the United States.[44] This time-bar only applies to common inventors filing in a foreign country more than twelve months before filing in the United States. Also, the bar is not activated unless the foreign filing results in a patent that is granted before the U.S. filing date. This means that the bar may not be triggered even though more than one year has passed from the foreign filing date.

As alluded to above, a one-year grace period for certain disclosures existed under the old statute. That one-year grace period was written into the definitions of novelty themselves. In addition, the one-year grace period was broader and applied to disclosures by anyone. More specifically, printed publications, public use, and on-sale activities did not count as prior art if they occurred within one year of the date of application for patent in the United States.[45]

§ 2:34 Patentability of inventions—Inventions must be nonobvious

Research References

U.S., 159 U.S.P.Q. 434, 440, 1968 WL 8418 (Ct. Cl. 1968), report and recommendation adopted, 187 Ct. Cl. 376, 408 F.2d 395, 161 U.S.P.Q. 116 (1969).

[41]35 U.S.C.A. § 102(b) (2006).

[42]In re Caveney, 761 F.2d at 677, 226 U.S.P.Q. at 4.

[43]Robbins Co. v. Lawrence Mfg. Co., 482 F.2d 426, 434, 178 U.S.P.Q. 577, 583, 25 A.L.R. Fed. 473 (9th Cir. 1973).

[44]35 U.S.C.A. § 102(d) (2006).

[45]35 U.S.C.A. § 102(b) (2006).

West's Key Number Digest, Patents ☞16
C.J.S., Patents §§ 68 to 69, 87

An invention cannot be patented if it is only a trivial or obvious modification of the prior art. Recall that it is section 102 that classifies subject matter as being available as prior art. In determining whether an invention is obvious, only that prior art that is available under section 102 may be used to evaluate the state of the art.[1]

An invention is obvious if the differences between the invention and the prior art would have been obvious, at the time the invention was made, to a person having ordinary skill in the art related to the invention.[2] To determine obviousness, courts and the USPTO apply a three-part test that was first articulated by the Supreme Court in Graham v. John Deere: (1) determine the scope and content of the prior art; (2) determine the difference between the art and the claims; and (3) determine the level of ordinary skill in the art.[3] In addition to applying this three-part test, a court or the USPTO may assess secondary considerations in making an obviousness determination.[4] These secondary considerations include, but are not limited to the following: long-felt need for the invention, commercial success of the invention, and competitors' adoption of the invention.

The prior art that may be used in determining obviousness is the same as the prior art used to analyze the novelty of an invention. The prior art for determining obviousness is also limited to analogous art. Analogous art includes art from the same field as the invention and art from other fields that are pertinent to the particular problem solved by the invention.[5] However, in order to be prior art, references outside of the invention's field must be of the type that those skilled in the field would turn to for assistance.

In analyzing obviousness, prior art references are looked at in combination. Each reference may provide one or more piece of the entire invention. To determine patentability, however, the invention must be examined as a whole.[6] The question is not whether any one element in the invention would have been obvious given the existence of the invention's other elements, but whether all of

---

[Section 2:34]

[1]35 U.S.C.A. § 103(a).

[2]35 U.S.C.A. § 103(a).

[3]Graham v. John Deere Co., 383 U.S. 1, 17, 86 S. Ct. 684, 694, 148 U.S.P.Q. 459, 467 (1966).

[4]Graham v. John Deere Co., 383 U.S. at 17-18; Dennison Mfg. Co. v. Panduit Corp., 475 U.S. 809, 810-11, 106 S. Ct. 1578, 1579, 229 U.S.P.Q. 478, 479, 4 Fed. R. Serv. 3d 366 (1986).

[5]Wang Labs., Inc. v. Toshiba Corp., 993 F.2d 858, 864, 26 U.S.P.Q.2d 1767, 1773 (Fed. Cir. 1993).

[6]W.L Gore, 721 F.2d at 1547-48.

the elements together would have been obvious given the prior art. A "combination of familiar elements according to known methods is likely to be obvious when it does no more than yield predictable results."[7]

An expansive and flexible approach can be used when analyzing the obviousness of a claimed invention. In order to find obviousness, it is not required that patents or printed publications contain an explicit teaching, suggestion, or motivation to combine the relevant prior art references. However, prior art references cannot be combined arbitrarily to render a claimed invention obvious, but must rest on some articulated reason having a rational basis. Relevant considerations include any teaching, suggestion, or motivation to combine different teachings found explicitly or implicitly in the prior art, as well as the knowledge of a person of ordinary skill in the art.[8] Again, the interrelated teachings of the prior art as a whole are important, and even an invention composed of elements shown in prior art may be nonobvious if the prior art as a whole teaches away from combining known elements in the manner claimed.

§ 2:35 Patentability of inventions—Inventions must not be previously patented

Research References

West's Key Number Digest, Patents ⊕37, 120
C.J.S., Patents §§ 29 to 30, 210, 213

To promote the progress of science and the useful arts, Congress rewards inventions sufficiently to encourage innovation, but not enough to give inventors the ability to control exploitation of the invention forever. To achieve the proper balance, Congress awards one patent for each invention; it does not allow the same invention to be patented twice.

For instance, if one inventor attempts to obtain two patents for a single invention, only one of the applications is granted. The other is rejected under the doctrine against double patenting. Similarly, if two separate inventors claim the right to patent the same invention, only the first to file[1] (or, in some cases, the first to disclose[2]) is granted the patent. The later inventor's application is rejected for lack of novelty, unless the earlier filer derived the claimed invention from the later filer. This requires the later filer to institute a derivation proceeding to establish ownership of

---

[7]KSR Int'l Co. v. Teleflex Inc., 550 U.S. 398, 127 S. Ct. 1727, 82 U.S.P.Q.2d 1385 (2007).

[8]KSR Int'l Co. v. Teleflex Inc., 550 U.S. 398, 127 S. Ct. 1727, 82

U.S.P.Q.2d 1385 (2007).

[Section 2:35]

[1]35 U.S.C.A. § 102(a).
[2]35 U.S.C.A. § 102(b).

the claimed invention.[3]

The novelty requirement limits the rewards of patent protection to those who truly add to the progress of science and the useful arts, by not rewarding later inventors who add nothing beyond what the first inventors already contributed. The rule against double patenting limits the amount of control an inventor is awarded for their contribution to science. It limits them to one patent grant that may be asserted against others for one patent term. It keeps inventors from asserting multiple patent grants against a single infringer of a single invention, and it keeps inventors from receiving successive patent grants that would permit them to extend their control over an invention beyond the period of a single patent term.

Like the novelty requirement, the rule against double patenting has been extended to include items that are obvious over an inventor's existing patents. Claims in an inventor's patent that are obvious over claims found in one of the same inventor's earlier patents can be rejected or invalidated under double patenting. This type of rejection is referred to as an obviousness-type double patenting rejection. Note that the claims in the later patent must be obvious over the claims of the earlier patent and not the disclosure of the earlier application. An inventor can disclose an invention in one application and still patent the invention in a later application as long as the later claimed invention is not obvious over the claims of the earlier application.

The applicant may partially overcome an obviousness-type double patenting rejection by filing a terminal disclaimer. In the terminal disclaimer, the inventor must dedicate to the public the portion of the later patent's term that extends beyond the earlier patent's term. This removes the possibility that the inventor could extend the term of control beyond the patent term by separately patenting minute variations of the invention. In addition, the terminal disclaimer must include a nonalienation clause that states that the earlier and later patents will always have identical assignees. This helps to prevent inventors from assigning these patents to separate assignees and thus prevents the separate assignees from separately suing an infringer for acts that essentially only relate to a single invention.

§ 2:36 Validity and infringement opinions

Research References

West's Key Number Digest, Patents ⚲227, 319(3), 325.11(2)
C.J.S., Patents §§ 403, 529 to 533, 561 to 562, 569

---

[3]35 U.S.C.A. § 135.

In determining willful infringement for purposes of deciding whether to award enhanced damages and attorneys' fees, a court will decide whether the infringer's conduct meets an "objective recklessness" standard.[1] Though there is no affirmative duty to do so,[2] procurement of a competent validity or infringement opinion remains a strong factor in finding against willfulness.[3] It also follows that such an opinion would likely be deemed more credible coming from patent counsel rather than general counsel, and from independent counsel rather than in-house counsel.[4] Of course, an opinion will only protect those that follow the recommendations of the opinion.[5] The failure to obtain an opinion may not be used to prove willful infringement.[6]

To render a competent validity opinion, an attorney will need to perform a prior art search and review the prosecution history of the patent. The prosecution history, also known as the "file wrapper," includes all of the documents that were filed in the USPTO or issued by the USPTO during the prosecution of the patent application. The prosecution history can be ordered from the USPTO for a fee that is based upon the number of pages in the file wrapper. In addition, file wrappers for more recent applications (generally filed ca. 2002 and later) can be found for free on the USPTO Public Patent Application Information Retrieval (PAIR) website if the application has been published or a patent has issued. Among other things, the prosecution history details what prior art was before the Examiner during the examination and how that prior art was applied against the claims of the patent application. The prosecution history may also indicate whether the applicant mischaracterized the prior art or whether the applicant mischaracterized the invention.

A prior art search is performed as part of a validity study to discover whether all of the prior art was before the Examiner at the time the patent was granted. The search may be limited somewhat because validity opinions are usually given before litigation begins, and the attorney rendering the opinion usually does not have access to discovery tools such as depositions and interrogatories. Without such discovery tools, it is difficult to

---

[Section 2:36]

[1]In re Seagate Tech., LLC, 497 F.3d 1360, 1371, 83 U.S.P.Q.2d 1865 (Fed. Cir. 2007), cert. denied, 128 S. Ct. 1445 (2008).

[2]Seagate Tech., 497 F.3d at 1371.

[3]Spectralytics, Inc. v. Cordis Corp., 649 F.3d 1336, 1348–1349, 99 U.S.P.Q.2d 1012, 1021 (Fed. Cir. 2011).

[4]Underwater Devices Inc. v. Morrison-Knudsen Co., Inc., 717 F.2d 1380, 1390, 219 U.S.P.Q. 569, 576 (Fed. Cir. 1983), overruled on other grounds In re Seagate Tech., LLC, 497 F.3d 1360, 1371, 83 U.S.P.Q.2d 1865 (Fed. Cir. 2007).

[5]Central Soya, 723 F.2d at 1577, 220 U.S.P.Q. at 493.

[6]35 U.S.C.A. § 298.

question the inventor about sales or public uses of the invention that may be prior art to the patent. Thus, the search is usually limited to public documents such as U.S. patents, foreign patents, and technical references.

In rendering a validity opinion, an attorney must take into account the presumption of validity that accompanies all patents issued by the USPTO.[7] In order to invalidate a patent, clear and convincing evidence must be submitted that shows that the patent is invalid.[8] The evidence can be prior art that makes the invention unpatentable or evidence that the USPTO was misled in some way during the prosecution of the patent.

In rendering an infringement opinion, an attorney must determine the scope of each claim in the patent and determine if a particular product or process falls within the scope of one of the claims. To determine the scope of the claims, the attorney reads the language of the claims in light of the entire patent disclosure because the claim language is defined by the disclosure.[9] To determine infringement, the scope of each claim is compared against the accused product. Each separate element of at least one claim of a patent must be found in an accused product before infringement occurs.[10]

For both validity and infringement opinions, an attorney ordinarily needs to review the prosecution history. The prosecution history may be helpful in determining the scope of the claims because it may indicate that the claims are restricted to less than what the claim language would allow. For instance, if the applicant was forced to limit certain claim language to avoid a prior art reference, the claim cannot be interpreted so that it would now include that reference. This form of claim limitation is referred to as prosecution history disclaimer.

---

[7]35 U.S.C.A. § 282.

[8]Microsoft Corp. v. i4i Ltd. P'ship, 564 U.S. __, 131 S.Ct. 2238, 98 U.S.P.Q. 2d 1857 (2011).

[9]Phillips v. AWH Corp., 415 F.3d 1303, 75 U.S.P.Q.2d 1321 (Fed. Cir. 2005) (a term defined narrowly in the specification retains its narrow definition when that term is used in the claims).

[10]Liquid Dynamics Corp. v. Vaughan Co., Inc., 355 F.3d 1361, 1367, 69 U.S.P.Q.2d 1595 (Fed. Cir. 2004); 35 U.S.C.A. § 271.

Chapter 3

Obtaining a Patent

§ 3:33   Maintenance fees

KeyCite®: Cases and other legal materials listed in KeyCite Scope can be researched through the KeyCite service on Westlaw®. Use KeyCite to check citations for form, parallel references, prior and later history, and comprehensive citator information, including citations to other decisions and secondary materials.

---

§ 3:1   Overview

Research References

West's Key Number Digest, Patents ⊘97 to 113
C.J.S., Patents §§ 135 to 175, 178, 180 to 199, 202 to 207

The process of obtaining a patent is similar to a negotiation between the person applying for the patent (the applicant) and the U.S. Patent & Trademark Office (USPTO). The negotiation begins with the applicant making the first offer by submitting an application asserting claims that the applicant believes defines a patentable invention. The USPTO, represented by a patent examiner, either rejects the claims asserted as being too broad and asking for too much patent protection, or accepts the claims as defining the appropriate level of patent protection. Since a patent application typically includes multiple claims of varying scope, this negotiation actually includes a negotiation over each claim so that the USPTO may reject some claims while accepting others. Like most negotiations, several rounds of offers by the applicant and rejections by the USPTO may occur before the applicant receives an acceptance from the USPTO of claims that the applicant believes define an appropriate level of patent protection.

This negotiation is accomplished through a series of Office Actions from the USPTO and responses from the applicant. The Office Actions give detailed reasons for rejecting one or more of the claims, and the applicant's responses amend the claims and/or argue the patentability of the claims in view of previous inventions, referred to as "prior art."

The exchange between the USPTO and the applicant does not continue indefinitely. It ends after the USPTO allows the claims or issues a Final Office Action. A Final Office Action does not immediately terminate the proceedings, because the applicant is usually allowed one response to the Final Office Action. However, if the examiner does not allow the claims after this last response, prosecution of the application is closed. If the applicant still believes that the invention is patentable, he or she may then either file a continuation application to effectively restart the negotiation or appeal the examiner's decision. An appeal is made first to the USPTO's Patent Trial and Appeal Board, and then typically to the Court of Appeals for the Federal Circuit.

§ 3:2 Who may file a patent application—Inventors, guardians, assignees, or any party with sufficient proprietary interest

Research References

West's Key Number Digest, Patents ⚖95 to 98
C.J.S., Patents §§ 129, 135 to 139, 145, 178

Inventors are allowed to draft and file their own patent applications. In addition, legal representatives of deceased or incapacitated inventors and assignees of the invention whose inventor refuses to execute an application may file a patent application on behalf of the inventor, on the same terms and conditions applicable to the inventor.[1] Additionally, any person to whom the inventor has assigned or is under an obligation to assign the invention, or any other person who shows sufficient proprietary interest in the matter, may make an application on behalf of the inventor.[2]

Although they are tolerated, *pro se* applications are discouraged by the USPTO because of the extra burden they place on examiners. For example, few *pro se* applicants have access to or a complete understanding of the current rules of the USPTO and therefore often burden examiners with papers that do not comply with the rules. While many examiners try to be helpful to the *pro se* applicants, they do not have the time to write the patent application for the inventor. Inventors who prosecute their own patent applications are therefore not likely to obtain the broadest patent protection to which they are entitled.

§ 3:3 Who may file a patent application—Patent attorney or patent agent

Research References

West's Key Number Digest, Patents ⚖97
C.J.S., Patents §§ 135 to 138, 145, 178

An applicant for patent may file and prosecute his or her own case, or he or she may be represented by a registered attorney, registered agent, or other individual authorized under 37 C.F.R. §§ 11.8 and 11.9 to practice before the USPTO in patent matters.[1] Patent attorneys are *attorneys* who have been admitted to

---

[Section 3:2]   [Section 3:3]

[1]35 U.S.C.A. §§ 117 to 118.   [1]37 C.F.R. § 1.31.
[2]35 U.S.C.A. § 118.

59

practice before the USPTO upon passing an examination for registration administered by the USPTO. Patent agents are *nonattorneys* who have been admitted to practice before the USPTO upon taking and passing the same examination. To qualify to sit for the registration examination, both attorneys and nonattorneys must demonstrate that they possess the scientific and technical training necessary to enable them to render patent applicants valuable service. Technical competence is generally established by presenting evidence of receipt of a bachelor's degree in a technical subject.

The majority of patent applications filed by patent attorneys are for inventions developed by scientists and engineers at large corporations. As part of their employment contracts, these inventors are usually required to assign their inventions to the corporation. Thus, the patent attorney is usually hired by, and represents, the corporation rather than the inventor.

It is important for a patent attorney to have a good understanding of the invention, including how the invention is made and how it operates. Usually, this is accomplished by the inventor providing the attorney with a written invention disclosure that describes the invention in detail and by meeting with the attorney to explain the invention in detail. Some obstacles to understanding inventions include: language barriers due to differences in nationality; technical language barriers, such as differing use of technical jargon and abbreviations; lack of concreteness in the inventor's conception of the idea; and unfamiliarity with the technical area on the part of the attorney.

In addition to understanding the invention, the attorney should know something about the current state of the art. The current state of the art determines the aspects of the invention that can be protected and thus indicates what features of the invention must be described in the application. In some cases, the patent attorney may know very little about the state of the art and the inventor will have to educate the attorney. Some inventors are hesitant to provide patent counsel with what appears to be damaging prior art because the inventors fear that divulging the prior art will keep them from getting a patent. In cases where the patent attorney depends on the inventor to provide an understanding of the prior art, this secrecy actually hurts the inventor's chances of receiving a valid patent.

As an example of how this can damage an inventor, imagine that an inventor knows of some prior art that is very close to his or her invention, but is not exactly the same as the invention. If the inventor discloses the art to the patent attorney, the attorney may be able to write the application around the prior art by including critical elements that distinguish the invention from the prior art. If, however, the inventor keeps the prior art secret, the attorney may draft a broader application that does not include details about these distinguishing features. If the USPTO discovers the prior art on its own and cites it against the application, the attorney will be in a weaker position to argue around the reference. In fact, the attorney may have to file a new application to include critical matter that distinguishes the invention from the prior art.

Even if the USPTO never finds the undisclosed prior art and issues the patent, the value of the patent is diminished. If the patent is asserted against a competitor, its validity will likely be called into question. The competitor will probably do an extensive search of the prior art and the patent will be weakened by any applicable art that the examiner did not review before issuing the patent. In addition, if the patent is litigated, the accused infringer will be entitled to ask for a copy of all of the prior art in the inventor's possession. If the accused infringer can prove that the inventor had prior art that was not disclosed to the patent office at the time the patent was prosecuted, the accused infringer may be able to establish inequitable conduct in the procurement of the patent. If a court finds there was inequitable conduct, it can invalidate the entire patent. Thus, rather than weakening the inventor's chances for receiving broad patent protection, full disclosure of the prior art to the patent practitioner actually helps to secure the strongest patent protection available.

§ 3:4 Who may file a patent application—Establishing small entity status

Research References

West's Key Number Digest, Patents ⊸103
C.J.S., Patents § 144

In order to give individual inventors and small companies access to the patent system, the United States has developed a three-tiered fee structure that distinguishes between large, small, and micro entities. Smaller entities pay reduced rates for most fees, including application fees. The reduction is substantial: a 50% reduction for small entities, and a 75% reduction for micro entities.[1]

To qualify as a small entity, the applicant must meet one or more of the following criteria:

- the applicant is an individual who has not assigned or licensed any rights in the invention and who is not under a

---

[Section 3:4]   §§ 1.16 to 1.20.

[1]35 U.S.C.A. § 41; 37 C.F.R.

duty to assign rights in their invention to an entity that does not qualify as a small entity,

- the applicant is a small business having no more than 500 employees, and has not assigned or licensed any rights in the invention and who is not under a duty to assign rights in their invention to an entity that does not qualify as a small entity,
- the applicant is a university or other institution of higher education,
- the applicant is a nonprofit organization under § 501(c)(3) and tax exempt under § 501(a) of the Internal Revenue Code, or
- the applicant is a nonprofit scientific or educational organization under a state's nonprofit organization statute.[2]

To qualify as a micro entity for further reduced fees, the applicant must satisfy all the requirements for small entity status, as well as the following additional criteria:

- the applicant has not been named as inventor or more than four previous priority applications in the United States,
- the applicant must have a gross personal income no greater than three times the median household income of the preceding year, and
- no small or large entity may have any license or assignment rights to the invention.

Regardless of these requirements, universities and other institutions of higher education are also entitled to micro entity status under certain circumstances.[3]

Any change in the status of the entity must be taken into account at the time a payment is made. This most often occurs when a company grows above 500 employees.

§ 3:5 Avoiding time bars—Post-AIA

For applications filed on or after March 16, 2013, the standard for novelty is first inventor to file. In determining priority, the effective filing date of the application is the only date which matters. One exception to this general rule is with respect to derivation proceedings. In derivation proceedings, a later applicant may show that an earlier applicant derived the subject matter claimed in his or her application from the later applicant.[1]

Inventors face time limitations (commonly referred to as "time

---

[2]37 C.F.R. § 1.27.   [Section 3:5]

[3]77 Fed. Reg. 75019; 35 U.S.C.A.   [1]35 U.S.C.A. § 135(a).
§ 123.

bars" or "statutory bars") when filing patent applications on their inventions. If the invention was patented, described in a printed publication, on sale, or otherwise publicly available before the effective filing date of the application, patent protection may not be available.[2] Subsequently published patents and patent applications by other inventors can also render an application unpatentable, if such patents or patent applications have earlier effective filing dates.[3]

Certain pre-filing disclosures are permissible and will not bar the applicant from obtaining patent protection. Specifically, disclosures made by any of the inventors one year or less before the effective filing date do not create statutory bars.[4] In fact, where an inventor discloses the claimed subject matter prior to filing a patent application, subsequent disclosures of substantially the same material by any party (even non-inventors) will not create a statutory bar. In this way, an inventor can create a "shield" for up to one year by disclosing the subject matter to be claimed, effectively blocking other applications on the same subject matter and protecting his or her invention from anticipating disclosures by other parties. However, this strategy is generally not advisable, as it prevents the inventor from obtaining patent protection in any foreign jurisdiction that requires absolute novelty. The preferred approach is to file a patent application as early as possible.

§ 3:6 Avoiding time bars—Pre-AIA

Research References

West's Key Number Digest, Patents ⊕75 to 81, 90(1)
C.J.S., Patents §§ 105 to 113, 120 to 122

Prior to implementation of the American Invents Act on March 16, 2013, the United State used a first-to-invent standard to determine priority of invention. This system remains in place today only for applications filed on or before March 15, 2013. Thus, inventors did not have to rush to the USPTO to secure priority. Nevertheless, inventors had time limitations (usually one year) on when they must file for patent protection. Most statutory bars begin running to a disclosure of the inventor by either the inventor or a third party.

A one-year statutory bar began to run if any of the following events occurred:

- the invention was in public use in the United States,
- the invention was on sale in the United States,

---

[2]35 U.S.C.A. § 102(a)(1).   [4]35 U.S.C.A. § 102(b).
[3]35 U.S.C.A. § 102(a)(2).

- the invention was patented or described in a printed publication in any country, or
- a patent application for the invention was filed in another country.[1]

Avoiding these time bars was difficult, especially if neither the inventor nor the attorney knew that one of the triggering events had occurred. Inventors thus did not have to rush to the USPTO to secure priority. Nevertheless, inventors had some time limitations (usually one year) on when they must file for patent protection. Most statutory bars begin running due to a disclosure of the invention, either by the inventor or by a third party.

§ 3:7 Filing the patent application—Filing a provisional patent application

Research References

West's Key Number Digest, Patents ☞97
C.J.S., Patents §§ 135 to 138, 145, 178

Provisional patent applications are never examined for patentability and cannot result in an issued patent.[1] In fact, provisional applications have a statutorily limited life-span of only twelve months.[2] The only purpose of the provisional application is to secure a filing date for a later filed nonprovisional application. The filing date of a patent application is crucial; it both stops the time bars that might prevent an inventor from obtaining a patent and it determines what inventions are considered prior art to the patent application.

There is no established format for provisional applications. They may be of any page length, may be cumulative of earlier provisional applications, and may include multiple inventions. Provisional applications may not be amended after they are filed.[3]

Provisional applications must include certain items in order to secure a filing date for later applications. They must include descriptions of the inventions that are to be claimed in later applications. The descriptions must be in such full, clear, concise, and exact terms as to enable those skilled in the art or science to which the inventions pertain to make and use the inventions.[4] In addition, the descriptions must include the best way the applicant knows of practicing an invention at the time of filing. Additionally, the provisional application must include all drawings neces-

---

[Section 3:6]
  [1]35 U.S.C.A. § 102.

[Section 3:7]
  [1]35 U.S.C.A. § 111(b)(8).

[2]35 U.S.C.A. § 111(b)(5).

[3]37 C.F.R. § 1.53(c).

[4]35 U.S.C.A. § 119(e).

sary to understand the inventions that will be claimed in later applications.[5]

A provisional application that includes all of the above items will be awarded a filing date.[6] However, to keep the filing date, the applicant must submit a filing fee and a cover sheet identifying the application as a provisional application.

Once a provisional application has been awarded a filing date, later filed nonprovisional applications may claim priority from it. By claiming priority, later applications are essentially considered to have been filed on the filing date of the provisional application. In essence, the prior art is "frozen" on the provisional application's filing date, to the extent of what was disclosed in the provisional application. Time bars stop running with respect to subject matter disclosed in the provisional application, and the inventions of others that are publicly disclosed after the filing date cannot affect the novelty of this material. Provisional applications may also be used to secure priority for an application in a foreign country.

As noted above, multiple inventions can be placed in the same provisional application. This has led some patent attorneys to suggest filing periodic provisional applications that include the results of an assortment of current research projects. If it later is determined that some of these results should be patented, a nonprovisional application based on an invention disclosed in a provisional applications can be filed. This strategy is based on the assumption that a provisional application is cheaper and quicker to file than a traditional application, and it is therefore more cost effective to secure a filing date for an invention with a provisional application before assessing its value.

§ 3:8 Filing the patent application—Filing a PCT application

Research References

West's Key Number Digest, Patents ⟲97
C.J.S., Patents §§ 135 to 138, 145, 178

The Patent Cooperation Treaty (PCT) is an international treaty designed to simplify the filing of patent applications in multiple countries for the same invention. The treaty provides for the filing of a single PCT application in all of the designated countries that are signatories of the PCT. This PCT application is often referred to as an "international application."

U.S. patent applicants frequently use a PCT application for filing in foreign countries, because the PCT application can claim

---

[5]35 U.S.C.A. § 111(b)(1)(B).   [6]37 C.F.R. § 1.53(c).

the benefit of the filing date ("claim priority") from a U.S. patent application. For the priority claim to be effective, the PCT application must be filed within twelve months (utility and plant patent applications).

The PCT application process has three distinct stages: (1) filing the application; (2) preliminary searching and examination; and (3) examination in individual countries. In the first stage, the application is typically filed with the inventor's national patent office (e.g., USPTO), and that office, known as the receiving office, reviews the application to make sure it meets basic PCT requirements. The receiving office submits the application to an international searching authority, which performs a search of the prior art and creates a search report containing all of the references it deems relevant to the invention's patentability. The applicant is then given two months to amend the application in light of the search report.

Within nineteen months of the PCT application's priority filing date, the applicant can choose to proceed via either Chapter I or Chapter II of the PCT process. Whether the applicant chooses Chapter I or Chapter II, the deadline for filing national applications is thirty months from the PCT application's priority filing date in most countries. In the Chapter I process, the Examiner issues an international preliminary report on patentability based on the international search report. The selection of Chapter II allows the applicant to conduct a dialogue with the Examiner and make amendments to the application before the search report is established as a written opinion and sent to the designated offices. The examining authority will then issue an international preliminary examination report, which is the examining authority's final position as to whether each claim is novel or involves an inventive step or possesses industrial applicability. The appropriate report is sent to the countries designated in the PCT application.

The international preliminary report on patentability or the international preliminary examination report is not binding on any of the designated countries. It is intended to help the applicant decide if sufficient patent protection is available to make it worthwhile to file applications in one or more of the designated countries. If the invention is clearly not patentable, the report can save an applicant thousands of dollars in application filing fees.

By using the PCT process, an applicant can gain up to thirty months from the priority date in which to evaluate the value of its invention without risking the loss of patent rights. In addition, the PCT process gives the applicant a chance to judge the patentability of its invention without paying filing fees in multiple countries. Accordingly, U.S. applicants frequently use a PCT application that claims priority from a U.S. application to preserve patent rights in foreign countries, while at the same time delaying the expense of foreign national applications until the value of the invention is established.

§ 3:9 Filing the patent application—Filing a nonprovisional application

Research References
West's Key Number Digest, Patents ⊙97
C.J.S., Patents §§ 135 to 138, 145, 178

A nonprovisional application is by far the most common type of patent application. The term "nonprovisional application" includes several different types of U.S. applications: regular applications, divisional applications, continuation applications and continuation-in-part applications. The format for each of these applications is generally the same.[1] A complete nonprovisional application includes a specification, claims, drawings necessary to understand the invention, a declaration or oath made by the inventors and a fee.

Specification. The specification includes several major sections, each playing a unique role. A "Background of the Invention" section describes prior attempts to solve the problem to which the invention is directed. A "Summary of Invention" section briefly summarizes the invention and the major advantages of the invention. A "Brief Description of Drawings" section identifies the nature of each drawing in the application. A "Detailed Description" section is the heart of a nonprovisional application. It describes the invention in sufficient detail to teach those skilled in the art how to make and use the invention. It includes a written description of the invention or discovery and the manner and process of making and using it. The description must be in full, clear, concise and exact terms so as to enable any person skilled in the art or science to which the invention or discovery pertains to make and use the invention. In addition, it must describe at least one specific embodiment of the invention and the "best mode" of the invention contemplated by the inventor.[2] An "Abstract" section briefly describing the invention is included in the application and is provided for placement on the face of a patent issuing from the application.

Claims: The application must include one or more claims that particularly point out and distinctly claim the subject matter

---

[Section 3:9]
[1]37 C.F.R. § 1.77.

[2]35 U.S.C.A. § 112.

which the applicant regards as the invention.[3] The claims define the scope of protection granted by a U.S. patent, and therefore are the central focus during the examination of nonprovisional applications. The terms used in the claims must have clear meaning as defined in the specification. Technically, the claims are part of the specification, though practitioners generally refer to them as being a separate and distinct part of a patent application because of their special legal significance.

Attorneys generally draft a number of claims ranging from the broadest claims possible in view of the prior art to the narrowest claims that the inventor finds acceptable. Drafting a sufficiently broad claim involves stripping the invention to its core elements and then generalizing the invention so that simple changes in form will still be within the scope of the claims. Creating sufficiently broad claims is one of the most creative and difficult aspects of drafting a patent application. If drafted well, such broad claims can add a great amount of value to the patent. However, narrower claims are also important. These narrow claims help to insure that the patent contains claims free from later challenges of invalidity and may be tailored to protect a specific commercial embodiment of an invention.

Some attorneys believe that it is better to file a patent application with some claims that are too broad, than to have all of the claims be too narrow. Patent attorneys generally do not like to have applications allowed when they are first submitted. Such first-action allowances often suggest that the attorney drafted the claims too narrowly and that they could have received more protection for the invention. In fact, some attorneys will try for broader protection for the invention by filing continuation applications if they receive a first-action allowance.

Other patent attorneys attempt to write claims that will be allowed without any rejections. In this way, the patent's file history will not contain any broad claims that were abandoned during prosecution that could be used to limit the interpretation of a claim in litigation.

Drawings. The application must include any drawings that are necessary to understand the invention.[4] The figures are usually drawn in black ink on 8½ × 11 inch or A4 sheets of white paper. Each element claimed in the application must appear in at least one of the drawings and each element described in the specification must be referenced by a number or letter. The USPTO includes very specific requirements for all drawings including margin sizes, lettering sizes, shading, hatching and scale.

---

[3]35 U.S.C.A. § 112.   [4]35 U.S.C.A. § 113.

Oath or Declaration. Although not required to obtain a filing date, an oath or declaration signed by the inventor(s) is required to form a complete application.[5] The USPTO does not begin examination of an application until it has received an oath or declaration. The accuracy and completeness of an oath or declaration is very important in obtaining a valid patent.

The oath or declaration must identify the specification to which it is directed and must state whether the inventor is a sole or joint inventor of the claimed invention.[6] The oath or declaration must be made by all of the actual inventors.[7] This means that all of the actual inventors must sign an oath or declaration for the application. However, if an inventor is dead, incapacitated, cannot be found or simply refuses to sign the oath or declaration, there are procedures for the executor, guardian, or real party in interest to execute the oath or declaration on behalf of the inventor. A person to whom the inventor has assigned or is under an obligation to assign the invention may make an application for patent on the inventor's behalf. Additionally, any person with a sufficient proprietary interest in the patent may file on the inventor's behalf with a showing that such action is appropriate to preserve the rights of the parties.[8]

A declaration or oath must also include a statement that the declarant believes the named inventor or inventors are the original and first inventor or inventors of the subject matter claimed in the patent application.[9] A declarant knowingly and deliberately naming a person as an inventor when in fact that person is not, or knowingly and deliberately omitting a person known to be an inventor, jeopardizes the validity or enforceability of the patent.

The declaration or oath must also include a statement that the inventor or inventors acknowledges the duty to disclose to the USPTO all information known to them to be material to the patentability of their invention.[10] The duty to disclose material information to the USPTO is an ongoing duty that continues until the application is either abandoned or a U.S. patent is granted.

Filing Fee. Although a filing fee is not required to obtain a filing date, it is necessary to form a complete application. Failure to submit the filing fee can cause abandonment of the application if not submitted in response to a notice of missing parts from the USPTO.

---

[5]35 U.S.C.A. § 115; 37 C.F.R. §§ 1.51, 1.53.

[6]37 C.F.R. § 1.63.

[7]37 C.F.R. § 1.64.

[8]35 U.S.C.A. § 118.

[9]37 C.F.R. § 1.63.

[10]37 C.F.R. § 1.63.

§ 3:10 Claiming priority from an earlier application— Claiming priority from a provisional application

Research References

West's Key Number Digest, Patents ⟳110
C.J.S., Patents § 156

There are three types of patent applications that a nonprovisional application can claim priority from: provisional applications, other nonprovisional applications, and foreign or international applications. The rules for claiming such priority are different depending on what type of application forms the basis of priority.

For a nonprovisional application to gain the benefit of a provisional application's filing date, the following requirements must be met:

- the nonprovisional application must be filed within twelve months of the provisional application,
- each invention claimed in the nonprovisional application must comply with the description and "best mode" requirements of 35 U.S.C.A. § 112, and the provisional application's drawings must fulfill the drawing requirements of 35 U.S.C.A. § 113,
- at least one inventor listed in the nonprovisional application must appear in the provisional application, and
- the nonprovisional application must include a reference to the provisional application.[1]

Claiming the benefit of a provisional application's filing date does not affect the term of the nonprovisional application. A nonprovisional patent that claims priority from a provisional application expires twenty years after the filing date of the nonprovisional application.[2]

§ 3:11 Claiming priority from an earlier application— Claiming priority from a nonprovisional U.S. application

Research References

West's Key Number Digest, Patents ⟳110
C.J.S., Patents § 156

To base priority on another nonprovisional U.S. application:

- each invention claimed in the later application must be described in the application providing priority in sufficient

---

[Section 3:10]

[1]35 U.S.C.A. § 119(e).

[2]35 U.S.C.A. § 154(a).

detail to comply with the requirements of 35 U.S.C.A. §§ 112 and 113,

- the applications must have at least one common inventor,
- the later application must be filed before the patenting, abandonment, or termination of proceedings of the application providing priority, and
- the later application must contain a specific reference to the application providing priority.[1]

Unlike basing priority on a provisional or foreign application, basing priority on another nonprovisional application affects the term of the later patent. For a patent claiming priority from a nonprovisional application, the 20-year expiration date is calculated from the filing date of the earliest filed nonprovisional application from which the patent claims priority. For instance, a continuation application filed on January 1, 2004, that bases priority on a regular application filed on January 1, 2003, has an expiration date of January 1, 2023, not January 1, 2024.

§3:12 Claiming priority from an earlier application—Claiming priority from a foreign application

Research References
West's Key Number Digest, Patents ☞90(1)
C.J.S., Patents §§ 120 to 122

To base priority on a foreign application:

- the foreign application must be from a country that permits applications in its country to base priority on earlier filed U.S. applications,
- the U.S. application must be filed within twelve months of the earliest filed application disclosing the invention,
- the U.S. application must be filed within one year of any printed publication describing the claimed invention in any country and within one year of any public use or sale of the claimed invention in the United States,
- the foreign application must adequately disclose the invention claimed in the U.S. application, and
- the foreign application must be filed by the same inventor or assignee.[1]

Among the foreign countries that are recognized for the purposes of claiming priority are the member countries of the Paris Convention. The Paris Convention is a treaty that provides

[Section 3:11]
[1]35 U.S.C.A. § 120.

[Section 3:12]
[1]35 U.S.C.A. § 119.

reciprocal patent rights between its signatories. Member
countries include the United States, Germany, the United
Kingdom, and 171 other countries.

In addition to the requirements listed above, the applicant
must produce a certified copy of the foreign patent application
and make a claim of priority to the USPTO. Failure to make the
claim of priority will result in the USPTO treating the U.S. application as an original U.S. application and not granting the
benefit of the earlier filed foreign application.

§ 3:13   Other requirements of the patent application
process—Information disclosure statements

Research References
West's Key Number Digest, Patents ⚷98
C.J.S., Patents §§ 137 to 139

Inventors, attorneys, and other persons substantially involved
in the preparation or prosecution of the application must disclose
to the USPTO any publication or event they know of that could
affect the patentability of the invention.[1] The requirement is
known as the duty of candor and it is usually fulfilled by filing
one or more Information Disclosure Statements.

An Information Disclosure Statement separately identifies each
reference that is material to the patentability of the invention. In
addition to the Information Disclosure Statement, a copy of each
non-U.S. patent reference listed in the Information Disclosure
Statement must be submitted to the USPTO. For references written in a language other than English, an English translation
must also be submitted if available. If a translation is not available, an English summary of the relevant portions of the references must be submitted.[2]

Material prior art is any document which is art but for which
the patent will issue; in other words, art which would have caused
the patent not to issue had the examiner been aware of its
existence.[3] Material art also includes information that rebuts a
position of patentability taken by the applicant.[4] Prior art that is
cumulative of other material already of record before the USPTO
for a particular application does not need to be submitted by the

---

[Section 3:13]

[1]37 C.F.R. § 1.56.

[2]37 C.F.R. § 1.98.

[3]Therasense, Inc. v. Becton,
Dickinson and Co., 593 F.3d 1289, 93

U.S.P.Q.2d 1489 (Fed. Cir. 2010), reh'g
en banc granted, opinion vacated, 374
Fed. Appx. 35 (Fed. Cir. 2010), opinion
reinstated in part, 649 F.3d 1276, 99
U.S.P.Q.2d 1065 (Fed. Cir. 2011).

[4]37 C.F.R. § 1.56(b).

applicant.[5] Most patent attorneys adopt an expansive view of Information Disclosure Statements. It is usually better to include a reference that may not be relevant than run the risk that the patent might be invalidated in future litigation.

In addition to material prior art, an applicant must disclose the existence of any litigation related to the subject matter of the patent application, any material information that arises from that litigation, and any assertions containing material information made during the litigation that are contradictory to assertions made to the patent examiner.[6]

§ 3:14   Other requirements of the patent application process—Assignment

Research References

West's Key Number Digest, Patents ⬤═196
C.J.S., Patents §§ 326 to 330, 340 to 341

If an inventor assigns his or her invention to someone else, the executed assignment can be recorded at the USPTO upon filing the application. Unless an assignment is recorded in the USPTO within three months from when it is executed or prior to the date of a subsequent purchase or mortgage, it is void against any subsequent purchaser or mortgagee, if the purchaser or mortgagee did not have notice of the assignment.[1] In other words, the patent recording statute is a form of race-notice. By recording the assignment early, the assignee can prevent the inventor from reselling the patent to a third party.

To assign a patent application, the inventor may execute an assignment concurrently with or subsequent to the execution of the application.[2] If the executed assignment is certified by the signature and seal of a Notary Public, the assignment is prima facie evidence that the patent or patent application has been assigned.[3]

It is important that assignments identify the exact corporate name, state of incorporation and address for corporate assignees. Often, inventors or officers of the corporation do not know the legal name of the corporation, so the exact corporate name is obtained from general counsel or from the Secretary of State. The address of the corporation is the address the corporation uses for receiving legal documents.

---

[5]37 C.F.R. § 1.56(b).

[6]Critikon, Inc. v. Becton Dickinson Vascular Access, Inc., 120 F.3d 1253, 43 U.S.P.Q.2d 1666 (Fed. Cir. 1997).

[Section 3:14]

[1]35 U.S.C.A. § 261.

[2]37 C.F.R. § 3.21.

[3]35 U.S.C.A. § 261.

§ 3:15   Other requirements of the patent application process—Power of attorney

Research References
West's Key Number Digest, Patents ⊙97
C.J.S., Patents §§ 135 to 138, 145, 178

When a patent attorney or patent agent signs a paper that is filed with the USPTO, that signature constitutes a representation to the USPTO that he or she is authorized to represent the person that he or she purports to represent.[1] Even so, a power of attorney is routinely filed at the beginning of the application process because it helps to protect the attorney from a later claim that he or she took action on the application without the applicant's consent.

A power of attorney may be revoked at any time. A revocation of power of attorney is effective as soon as the attorney learns of the revocation, and need not be in writing. But, if a change of power of attorney is filed with the USPTO, it is good practice to file a written revocation with the USPTO to revoke any previous power of attorney. An assignment of the application, by itself, does not revoke a power of attorney, so a separate written revocation should be filed with the USPTO if revocation upon assignment is desired.[2]

§ 3:16   Other requirements of the patent application process—Establishing a noninventor's right to prosecute an application

Research References
West's Key Number Digest, Patents ⊙95, 97
C.J.S., Patents §§ 129, 135 to 138, 145, 178

When the assignee of the entire right, title, and interest seeks to take action in a matter before the USPTO with respect to a patent application, the assignee must establish its ownership of the application.[1] Ownership is established using documents or other evidence to show a chain of title from the inventor to the assignee. The evidence can be submitted to the USPTO, or if the evidence was previously recorded on microfilm in the USPTO, the reel and frame number of the microfilm can be specified.[2]

In addition, assignees must sign a statement asserting that they have title to the application. The USPTO will accept the

---

[Section 3:15]
[1]37 C.F.R. § 1.34.
[2]37 C.F.R. § 1.36.

[Section 3:16]
[1]37 C.F.R. § 3.73(b).
[2]37 C.F.R. § 3.73(b).

declaration on behalf of an organization only if the statement is executed by someone having apparent authority to sign on behalf of the organization, such as an officer of the corporation, or if the declaration includes an averment that the person signing is empowered to sign the statement on behalf of the organization.

§ 3:17 Other requirements of the patent application process—Incomplete applications and missing parts

Research References

West's Key Number Digest, Patents ⊕98, 103
C.J.S., Patents §§ 137 to 139, 144

The USPTO issues a Notice of Incomplete Application whenever it receives an application that does not include a complete specification, at least one claim, all necessary drawings, and an application identifier (such as an inventor's name).[1] The application cannot be given a filing date that is earlier than the date on which the missing application elements are filed. In addition, if the missing elements are not filed within two months of the Notice, the USPTO either returns or discards the application. If the application is returned or discarded, the filing fee is refunded less a handling charge.[2]

The USPTO issues a Notice of Missing Parts if the application is filed without a filing fee or an inventor's oath or declaration. The applicant is typically given two months, extendable by payment of extension of time fees, in which to file the missing fee and oath or declaration. Unlike an incomplete application, the filing date is not affected by a later filed oath, declaration, or filing fee. As long as the filing fee and oath or declaration are filed within the specified time period, the filing date is the date the required specification, claims, drawings, and inventors' names were filed. A surcharge fee is, however, assessed for later filed oaths, declarations, or filing fees.

§ 3:18 Other requirements of the patent application process—Filing receipt

Research References

West's Key Number Digest, Patents ⊕104
C.J.S., Patents §§ 145 to 147, 149 to 151, 173 to 175

When the USPTO receives a complete application, including a declaration or oath and filing fee, the USPTO issues a filing

---

[Section 3:17]   [2]37 C.F.R. § 1.53(e).
[1]37 C.F.R. § 1.53(b).

receipt. The filing receipt includes the filing date of the application, the filing fee received by the USPTO, the number of claims and drawings in the application, the inventors' names, and the title of the application. If any of these items is incorrect, a corrected filing receipt can be requested. The filing receipt also includes the following information:

Application Serial Number. The application serial number is used by the USPTO to track correspondence related to the application. Therefore, all correspondence relating to the application must include this serial number.[1]

Group Art Unit. The USPTO Examining Corps is divided into several group art units, each specialized in examining applications directed towards a specific scientific field. Each application received by the USPTO is reviewed to determine which group art unit should examine it. The number of this group art unit is then placed on the filing receipt and the application is transferred to that group art unit. Since that group art unit now has possession of the application, correspondence relating to the application should include the number of the group art unit.[2]

Foreign Filing License Grant. For reasons of national security, the United States requires that inventors secure a license from the U.S. government before filing foreign patent applications on inventions made in the United States.[3] Failure to obtain such a license can bar patentability of the invention in the United States.[4] However, such licenses are routinely granted and often appear on the filing receipt. The license requirement is automatically waived six months after the U.S. filing date.

Preliminary Class. The USPTO classifies inventions based upon the invention's field of technology. This classification is done on a preliminary basis when an application is first received at the USPTO.

§ 3:19   Examination at the USPTO—Patent examiners

Research References
West's Key Number Digest, Patents ☞104
C.J.S., Patents §§ 145 to 147, 149 to 151, 173 to 175

Nearly all of the patent examiners at the USPTO have technical training in one or more specialty areas and generally examine patents in those areas. Patent applications are generally examined by one examiner whose decisions are reviewed by a

---

[Section 3:18]   [3]35 U.S.C.A. § 184.
　[1]37 C.F.R. § 1.5.   [4]35 U.S.C.A. § 185.
　[2]37 C.F.R. § 1.5.

supervisory examiner. Examiners must fulfill quotas for the number of actions they handle within a certain period of time and for the number of cases they dispose of within a time period. The USPTO encourages examiners to advance the examination process as quickly as possible and to come to a determination of patentability or nonpatentability as soon as possible. Examiners are instructed to work with applicants so that patent protection of the proper scope is made available to the applicants for their invention.

To aid the examiner in the examining process, the USPTO issues a *Manual of Patent Examining Procedure* (MPEP). The MPEP is quite large and extensive, covering not only the administrative aspects of examining patent applications, but also the legal criteria for a proper examination. The MPEP is used by patent attorneys and agents, as well as examiners.

When an examiner receives a new application, the examiner performs an independent search of the prior art. Because most examiners specialize within narrow technical fields of invention, they have a strong grasp of the state of the prior art in the field. In addition, the examiner often knows of related fields where relevant prior art may be located. Thus, an examiner's search often turns up art not located by previous searches. When the examiner evaluates art for whether it may be used to support a rejection, the MPEP instructs examiners to give each claim its broadest reasonable interpretation (BRI).[1] Examiners are given broad discretion in interpreting claim terms. In rendering the broadest reasonable interpretation of claims, reviewing courts instruct examiners to read the claim language in light of the specification and teachings in the underlying patent. That is, if the examiner interprets the claim language in a manner that is inconsistent with the specification, then the examiner will have made an unreasonable interpretation.[2]

U.S. patent applications are by default, subject to certain exceptions, published 18 months after the earliest filing date for which benefit is sought under Title 35 U.S.C.A.[3] The application may be published earlier at the request of the applicant.[4] However, the applicant can prevent publication of an application if the applicant makes a nonpublication request upon filing, certifying that the invention disclosed in the application has not and will

---

[Section 3:19]

[1]M.P.E.P. § 2111. The BRI standard is different from the standard applied by courts for issued patents. See Phillips v. AWH Corp., 415 F.3d 1303, 75 U.S.P.Q.2d 1321 (Fed. Cir. 2005).

[2]In re Suitco Surface, Inc., 603 F.3d 1255, 1261, 94 U.S.P.Q.2d 1640 (Fed. Cir. 2010).

[3]35 U.S.C.A. § 122(b); 37 C.F.R. § 1.215.

[4]35 U.S.C.A. § 122(b); 37 C.F.R. § 1.219.

not be the subject of an application filed in another country, or under a multilateral international agreement, that requires publication of applications 18 months after filing.[5] An application that is not published is kept in confidence by the USPTO, and no information concerning it is given out without the authority of the applicant or owner.[6]

Completed applications are ordinarily examined in the order in which they have been filed.[7] Each examiner is instructed to give priority to the application with the oldest effective U.S. filing date.[8] Several mechanisms exist to accelerate patent prosecution, however. In some instances, an applicant can petition to have immediate action taken on the application. This is referred to as a "Petition to Make Special." These petitions are granted without an additional fee if they include a factual showing sufficient to establish that the applicant is in poor health or of advanced age or that the invention will materially (1) enhance the quality of the environment, (2) contribute to the development or conservation of energy resources (3) contribute to countering terrorism, or (4) involve superconductivity. Using the so-called "Patent Prosecution Highway" system, some patents for which at least one claim has already been determined to be patentable may also be eligible for expedited processing, for no additional fee.[9]

Even where the option of a Petition to Make Special would not be available, patent applicants may apply for "Track I" prioritized examination at additional cost.[10] Prioritized examination is only available for utility and plant patent applications with no more than four independent and 30 total claims. Track I prioritized examination ends if and when a final Office Action or notice of allowance is issued, or if the applicant files a notice of appeal, a request for suspension of action, an extension of time, or a request for continued examination.[11] Additional restrictions apply.

Additionally, if the applicant has filed foreign counterpart patent applications, the applicant may be able to accelerate examination of the domestic patent application under the Patent Prosecution Highway (PPH) pilot program. Under the PPH pilot program numerous patent offices across the globe have agreed that when an applicant receives a final decision from a first participating patent office, in which at least one claim has been allowed, the applicant can utilize fast-track examination procedures that are already in place in a second cooperating

---

[5] 35 U.S.C.A. § 122(b)(2)(B).

[6] 35 U.S.C.A. § 122.

[7] 37 C.F.R. § 1.102.

[8] M.P.E.P. § 708.

[9] 75 Fed. Reg. 29312.

[10] Fees are noted in 37 C.F.R. § 1.17. Small and micro entities are entitled to 50% an 75% discounts respectively.

[11] 76 Fed. Reg. 59050.

country. There are no fees associated with participating in the PPH pilot program.

The examiner studies the application and investigates the available prior art including that disclosed in the Information Disclosure Statement to ensure that the application is sufficient in all technical regards, complies with all the rules, complies with all statutes pertaining to patents, is proper in form and contains patentable subject matter.[12] Once the examiner has completed his or her examination of the application, the results are forwarded in written form to the applicant in an "Office Action."

The Office Action notifies the applicant of any rejection, objection, or requirement made by the examiner. The Office Action must state the reasons for any such rejection, objection, or requirement, together with information and references that may assist the applicant in evaluating the propriety of continuing prosecution of the application and of attaining eventual patent protection.[13]

An Office Action typically includes a Notice of References Cited which identifies prior art references that the examiner considers to be pertinent to the application in addition to those references already of record.

If the application contains claims directed to two or more independent or distinct inventions, or contains claims directed to two or more species of an invention, the first Office Action issued by the examiner will typically include an election/restriction requirement. A restriction requirement is a form of objection made by the examiner if the application claims two or more independent and distinct inventions.[14] For example, a product and the process for manufacturing the product may be distinct inventions. If a restriction requirement is received, the applicant must select one invention for examination on the merits. The other invention(s) can be pursued in a divisional application separately filed.

The examiner may object to the form of the specification, drawings or claims. Objections to form may be overcome by simple amendments. An objection differs from a rejection in that an objection may only be reviewed by way of a petition to the Commissioner of Patents and Trademarks, while a rejection may be appealed to the Patent Trial and Appeal Board.

§ 3:20 Examination at the USPTO—Rejection for patent-ineligible subject matter

Research References

---

[12]37 C.F.R. § 1.104.

[13]37 C.F.R. § 104(a)(2).

[14]35 U.S.C.A. § 121.

West's Key Number Digest, Patents ⊛4 to 14, 108
C.J.S., Patents §§ 13 to 14, 16 to 28, 144, 148 to 151

There are two criteria for determining whether an invention is eligible for patent protection, both of which must be satisfied. First, the invention must fall within the boundaries of patentable subject matter, i.e., a new process, machine, manufacture, or composition of matter, or any new and useful improvement thereof.[1] Claims directed to an invention not falling within these boundaries may be rejected by the examiner as being directed to nonstatutory subject matter.[2] Examples of nonpatentable subject matter include: transitory forms of signal transmission (for example, a propagating electrical or electromagnetic signal *per se*), a naturally occurring organism, a human *per se*, a legal contractual agreement between two parties, a game defined as a set of rules, a computer program *per se*, and a company.

Second, assuming the invention does fall within one of the four statutory categories, the invention must not be wholly directed to subject matter encompassing a judicially recognized exception against the patenting of abstract ideas, naturally occurring phenomena, and laws of nature. Determining whether an invention is patent ineligible as encompassing a judicially recognized exception arises most frequently with respect to processes. The Court in *Mayo v. Prometheus* devised a two-part test to analyze claims directed at laws of nature for subject matter eligibility under 35 U.S.C. § 101.[3] The Court in *Alice Corp. v. CLS Bank* clarified that the same test should be applied to abstract ideas and natural phenomena as well.[4] These exclusionary principles seek to prevent patent claims from bestowing a preemptive monopoly that would impede innovation more than promote it, by tying up the basic tools of scientific and technological work.[5] The first step in the analysis is to determine whether a claim is directed to a patent-ineligible concept (laws of nature, natural phenomena and abstract ideas), and second, if so, determine whether any elements in the claim, individually or as an ordered combination, recite an "inventive concept" that amounts to significantly more than the patent-ineligible concept itself, so as to transform the

---

[Section 3:20]

[1]35 U.S.C.A. § 101.

[2]35 U.S.C.A. § 101.

[3]Mayo Collaborative Services v. Prometheus Laboratories, Inc., 132 S. Ct. 1289, 182 L. Ed. 2d 321, 101 U.S.P. Q.2d 1961 (2012).

[4]Alice Corp. Pty. Ltd. v. CLS Bank Intern., 134 S. Ct. 2347, 110 U.S.P.Q.2d 1976 (2014).

[5]Alice Corp. Pty. Ltd. v. CLS Bank Intern., 134 S. Ct. 2347, 110 U.S.P.Q.2d 1976 (2014); *see also* Marchand v. Emken, 132 U.S. 195, 198–200, 10 S. Ct. 65, 33 L. Ed. 332 (1889) (claim to a process that "practically makes all pay tribute who stir the mixture in question by machinery" was too "theoretical and visionary" to be patentable).

claim into a patent-eligible application of the underlying patent-ineligible concept.[6] For a claim to satisfy the second part of the test, it must evidence more than "drafting effort" to limit the ineligible concept to a particular technological environment or by the mere recitation of implementation on a generic computer, and the claimed invention should effect an improvement in a technology or technical field, such as to improve the functioning of a recited computer beyond a mere instruction to implement the underlying concept on a generic, unspecified computer.[7]

§ 3:21 Examination at the USPTO—Rejection for vague or indefinite specification

Research References

West's Key Number Digest, Patents ⊕99, 101(4) to 101(6), 108 C.J.S., Patents §§ 139 to 142, 144, 148 to 151

35 U.S.C.A. § 112 sets forth the requirements for the specification of an application. Section 112(a) requires the specification to contain a written description of the invention and of the manner and process of making and using the invention in such full, clear, concise, and exact terms as to enable any person skilled in the art to which it pertains, or with which it is most nearly connected, to make and use the invention. If the examiner considers the written description of the invention to be unclear or nonenabling, the examiner may reject the specification under § 112(a).

The applicant may overcome a rejection under § 112(a), by amending the specification, while avoiding the addition of new matter, or alternatively by pointing out how the specification does enable persons skilled in the art to make and use the invention. The applicant may additionally overcome assertions by the examiner that the disclosure is insufficient or nonoperable by submitting an affidavit or declaration under 37 C.F.R. § 1.132 in support of the operability of the invention or sufficiency of disclosure.

The second paragraph of § 112 requires that "the specification shall conclude with one or more claims particularly pointing out and distinctly claiming the subject matter which the applicant regards as his invention." The language of § 112(b), provides a basis for several types of rejections not based on prior art. Rejections based upon § 112(b) are usually directed to technical or formal matters regarding the claims and generally may be overcome with minor amendments to the claims.

---

[6]Alice Corp. Pty. Ltd. v. CLS Bank Intern., 134 S. Ct. 2347, 2355, 2357, 110 U.S.P.Q.2d 1976 (2014); *see also infra* § 5:44.

[7]Alice Corp. Pty. Ltd. v. CLS Bank Intern., 134 S. Ct. 2347, 2357–2360 110 U.S.P.Q.2d 1976 (2014).

The applicant may overcome a rejection under § 112(b) by amending the claims to include proper antecedent basis for elements or limitations in the claim, amending the claims to ensure that essential elements, steps, or structural relationships are recited to support any function and by amending the claims to remove unimportant details or elements which tend to hide or obscure the invention.

§ 3:22 Examination at the USPTO—Anticipation rejections

Research References

West's Key Number Digest, Patents ⊘50 to 74, 108
C.J.S., Patents §§ 31 to 58, 101 to 102, 144, 148 to 151

The examiner may reject a claim or claims of a patent application if the claimed invention was patented, described in a printed publication, or in public use, on sale, or otherwise available to the public before the effective filing date of the claimed invention.[1] The examiner makes an anticipation rejection if he or she believes that a single prior art reference discloses every feature of the invention claimed by the applicant.

The examiner may reject the claims based on availability of the invention to the public prior to the effective filing date of the patent application.[2] In particular, the examiner can reject the claims if there is evidence that the invention was patented, described in a printed publication, in public use, or on sale prior to the effective filing date of the patent application.[3] Limited exceptions to the requirements of 35 U.S.C.A. § 102(a) are set forth in § 102(b). For example, an inventor's own disclosures within a year of the effective filing date are disqualified as prior art, as are any substantially identical intervening disclosures of third parties.[4] While 35 U.S.C.A. § 102(a) provides for rejections based on any disclosure which made the invention "otherwise available to the public," no courts have yet determined the meaning of that phrase.[5]

The Leahy–Smith America Invents Act (AIA) was signed into law on September 16, 2011 and central provisions went into effect on March 16, 2013.[6] For pre-AIA applications, the examiner may reject the claims if he or she has evidence that anyone, including the applicant, patented or described the invention in a printed publication in the United States or in a foreign country

---

[Section 3:22]
[1]35 U.S.C.A. § 102(a)(1).
[2]35 U.S.C.A. § 102(a)(1).
[3]35 U.S.C.A. § 102(a)(1).

[4]35 U.S.C.A. § 102(b).
[5]35 U.S.C.A. § 102(a)(1).
[6]Pub. L. No. 112-29.

more than one year prior to the date of application.[7] The examiner may also reject the claims if the examiner has evidence that the invention was in public use or was on sale in the United States more than one year prior to the date of the application.[8]

The applicant may overcome a reference under pre-AIA § 102(b) by persuading the examiner that the claims are distinguishable from the prior art or amending the claims to distinguish them over the prior art. In addition, the applicant may also overcome the rejection based upon a reference under pre-AIA § 102(b) by perfecting a claim to foreign priority under pre-AIA §§ 119(a) to (d) or establishing a priority claim to a provisional application under pre-AIA § 119(e).

However, rejections under the public use or sale provisions of pre-AIA § 102(b) typically cannot be overcome by arguing patentability or amending the claims. These rejections can be overcome if a proper claim to priority under §§ 119 that predates the date of the event is made, or in the case of public use, if one can show that the alleged use was experimental. Practically speaking, the public use and on sale provisions of pre-AIA § 102(b) seldom form the basis for a rejection by an examiner, but these issues frequently arise during litigation involving an issued patent.

§ 3:23 Examination at the USPTO—Obviousness rejections

Research References
West's Key Number Digest, Patents ⊙⊶16, 108
C.J.S., Patents §§ 68 to 69, 87, 144, 148 to 151

Even if the prior art set forth in § 102 does not identically disclose or describe the subject matter of the invention claimed, the examiner may reject the claims as being obvious under 35 U.S.C.A. § 103:

> A patent for a claimed invention may not be obtained, notwithstanding that the claimed invention is not identically disclosed as set forth in section 102, if the differences between the claimed invention and the prior art are such that the claimed invention as a whole would have been obvious before the effective filing date of the claimed invention to a person having ordinary skill in the art to which the claimed invention pertains. Patentability shall not be negated by the manner in which the invention was made.

In analyzing obviousness, one must examine (1) the scope and content of the prior art, (2) the differences between the art and the claims at issue, (3) the level of ordinary skill in the art, and

---

[7]35 U.S.C.A. § 102(b) (2006).   [8]35 U.S.C.A. § 102(b) (2006).

(4) objective evidence.[1] The test for obviousness is extremely factual.

The applicant may overcome an obviousness rejection under § 103 by showing that a *prima facie* case of obviousness has not been established, rebutting the examiner's case for obviousness with objective evidence, or amending the claims if necessary.

For the examiner to establish a *prima facie* case of obviousness, the examiner must establish three things. First, the examiner must provide some suggestion or motivation, either in the references themselves or in the knowledge generally available to one of ordinary skill in the art, to modify the references or to combine the reference teachings. Second, the examiner must provide some reasonable expectation of success. Lastly, the examiner must show that the prior art reference or references when combined teach or suggest all of the claim limitations.[2]

There are several ways in which an applicant can assert that a *prima facie* case of obviousness has not been established. The motivation to modify the reference or to combine reference teachings, as well as the expectation of success, must be found in the prior art and cannot be based on teachings of the application under examination.[3] Absent some reason that would have prompted a person of ordinary skill in the relevant field to combine all prior art elements, the examiner's rejection based on obviousness is improper.[4] Thus, the applicant may overcome the rejection under § 103 by persuasively pointing out that the prior art provides no basis or incentive for combining or modifying the references.

There are a number of additional techniques for overcoming an obviousness rejection. Frist, the applicant may argue that the examiner's proposed modifications to the teachings of the reference would destroy the intent, purpose, or function of the invention disclosed in the reference, thus eliminating motivation for engaging in the modification or change.[5]

Second, the applicant may point to portions of the prior art

[Section 3:23]

[1]Graham v. John Deere Co. of Kansas City, 383 U.S. 1, 2, 86 S. Ct. 684, 686, 148 U.S.P.Q. 459, 467 (1966).

[2]M.P.E.P. § 706.02(j).

[3]In re Vaeck, 947 F.2d 488, 20 U.S.P.Q.2d 1438 (Fed. Cir. 1991).

[4]KSR Int'l Co. v. Teleflex Inc., 550 U.S. 398, 127 S. Ct. 1727, 82 U.S.P.Q.2d 1385 (2007).

[5]In re Gordon, 733 F.2d 900, 221 U.S.P.Q. 1125 (Fed. Cir. 1984). *See also* M.P.E.P. § 2143.01; KSR Intern. Co. v. Teleflex Inc., 550 U.S. 398, 415–421, 127 S. Ct. 1727, 167 L. Ed. 2d 705, 82 U.S.P.Q.2d 1385, 1395–97 (2007); Ball Aerosol and Specialty Container, Inc. v. Limited Brands, Inc., 555 F.3d 984, 89 U.S.P.Q.2d 1870 (Fed. Cir. 2009).

which teach away from the claimed invention.[6]

Third, the applicant may argue that the combined references do not provide a reasonable expectation of success. A prior art suggestion for experimentation is not a case of *prima facie* obviousness.[7] Obviousness does not require absolute predictability, but a reasonable expectation of success is necessary.[8]

Fourth, the applicant may argue that the combined references are from nonanalogous arts, so that a person of ordinary skill in the art would not look to those arts to solve the problem treated by the claimed invention.[9]

Fifth, the applicant may assert that the prior art reference fails to recognize or teach the problem solved by the present invention. As a result, it would not have been obvious to the hypothetical person of ordinary skill in the art to solve the problem, since it was not previously known. Absent recognition of a problem, no teaching suggestion, or motivation exists for such a modification or combination.[10]

Finally, the applicant may argue that the prior art fails to recognize the advantages of the invention. Accidental results, not intended and not appreciated, may not render an invention obvious.[11]

§ 3:24 Examination at the USPTO—Rejection for duplicate claims or double patenting

Research References

West's Key Number Digest, Patents ☞120
C.J.S., Patents §§ 210, 213

The applicant has the right to restate the invention in a reasonable number of ways. However, when two claims in an application are duplicates, or are so close in content that they both cover the same thing, the examiner may reject a claim as being a substantial duplicate of another claim. The applicant may overcome a rejection of a claim based upon the assertion that the claim is a duplicate of another claim in the application by point-

---

[6]U.S. v. Adams, 383 U.S. 39, 86 S. Ct. 708, 15 L. Ed. 2d 572, 148 U.S.P.Q. 479 (1966).

[7]In re Dow Chemical Co., 837 F.2d 469, 473, 5 U.S.P.Q.2d 1529, 1532 (Fed. Cir. 1988).

[8]Application of Clinton, 527 F.2d 1226, 1228, 188 U.S.P.Q. 365, 367 (C.C.P.A. 1976). *See also* In re Fine, 837 F.2d 1071, 5 U.S.P.Q.2d 1596 (Fed. Cir. 1988); In re Geiger, 815 F.2d 686,

688, 2 U.S.P.Q.2d 1276, 1278 (Fed. Cir. 1987).

[9]M.P.E.P. §§ 2141.01, 2141.02.

[10]Application of Sponnoble, 56 C.C.P.A. 823, 405 F.2d 578, 585, 160 U.S.P.Q. 237 (1969).

[11]Tilghman v. Proctor, 102 U.S. 707, 26 L. Ed. 279, 1880 WL 18737 (1880).

ing out differences between the two claims and explaining why the claims are not duplicates.

There are two types of double patenting rejections. In a "same invention" type double patenting rejection, the examiner may reject claims of the application as reciting the same inventive concept as another application or patent under 35 U.S.C.A. § 101. Section 101 has been interpreted as meaning that an inventor may obtain only a single patent for a single invention. Alternatively, under an "obviousness" type double patenting rejection, the examiner may reject claims of the application which recite obvious variations of the same inventive concept as the other application/patent under the judicially created doctrine of "obviousness" type double patenting. The "obviousness" type double patenting rejection is based on public policy and is primarily intended to prevent prolonging the patent term by prohibiting claims of a second patent not patentably distinguishable from claims in a first patent.

A "same invention" type double patenting rejection cannot be overcome while still maintaining the exact claim motivating the rejection. However, the applicant may overcome an "obviousness" type double patenting rejection with one of two strategies. First, the applicant may overcome the "obviousness" type double patenting rejection by timely filing a Terminal Disclaimer if the conflicting application or patent is commonly owned with the application. Second, the applicant may overcome an "obviousness" type double patenting rejection by arguing the differences between the claimed inventions and why the differences are nonobvious.

A Terminal Disclaimer specifies that any patent granted on that application will be enforceable only for and during such period that the patent is commonly owned with the application or patent which forms the basis for the rejection.[1] Equally important, the Terminal Disclaimer shortens the enforceable term of the patent to be granted from the normal term of seventeen years from issue date (for applications filed before June 8, 1995) or twenty years from filing date (for applications filed on or after June 8, 1995) so that the commonly owned patents will expire on the same day. As a result, the filing of a Terminal Disclaimer in an application will prevent a potential extension of monopoly in the last application to be issued as a patent.[2] If two or more pending applications are given a double patenting rejection based upon one another, a Terminal Disclaimer must be filed for each application.[3]

[Section 3:24]
[1]37 C.F.R. §§ 1.321(a), (b).

[2]37 C.F.R. §§ 1.321(a), (b).
[3]M.P.E.P. § 804.02.

§ 3:25 Examination at the USPTO—Restriction and election requirements

Restriction requirements were created to prevent applicants from putting more than one invention in a single patent application. If two or more independent and distinct inventions are claimed in one application, an examiner may require the application to be restricted to one of the inventions.[1] The action of restricting the invention is termed "a requirement for restriction" (also known as "a requirement for division").[2] Generally, a restriction requirement occurs only where there is a need; an examiner versed in one subject area may be unable to understand subject matter outside his or her area of technical expertise. As such, USPTO examiners use restriction requirements to force applicants to split up applications into multiple parts. Because two claims may present different inventions or different technologies, a single examiner may split up the claims, via a restriction requirement, in order to limit the claims examined; this creates less of a burden on the examiner and ensures that examiners do not need to venture into subject matter outside their technical competence.

To respond to restriction requirements, an election (or provisional election) must first be made by the applicant.[3] An applicant must choose to "traverse" or "not traverse" the restriction, meaning that the grounds for restriction are either challenged or not challenged. If an applicant does not distinctly and specifically point out supposed errors in the restriction requirement, the election is treated as non-traversed. If the applicant traverses the requirement for restriction, the applicant may request reconsideration and withdrawal or modification of the requirement.[4] However, traversing a restriction does not relieve the applicant from making a provisional election, which is an election made subject to the grounds of traversal. After a final requirement for restriction, the applicant may petition the Director to review the requirement.[5] Alternatively, the applicant may opt to not traverse the restriction requirement, and instead file a divisional application for the non-elected invention or forego the unelected claims entirely.

Species election is a related but distinct issue. When an ap-

---

[Section 3:25]

[1]37 C.F.R. § 1.141; M.P.E.P. § 802.02.

[2]37 C.F.R. § 1.142; M.P.E.P. § 802.02. Patent Cooperation Treaty (PCT) national phase applications are subject to a different "unity of inven-tion" standard. See M.P.E.P. §§ 823, 1850, 1875, 1893.03(d); 37 C.F.R. § 1.499.

[3]M.P.E.P. § 818.03(b); 37 C.F.R. §§ 1.142, 1.143.

[4]37 C.F.R. § 1.143.

[5]37 C.F.R. § 1.144.

plication contains a generic claim that covers a generic invention (genus) that includes more than one patentably distinct species, examiners may require the applicant to elect a species of his or her invention for examination.[6] When this happens, the applicant must identify which species he or she wishes to have examined, usually by reference to figures of the application or lists of chemical compounds, and identify which claims read on the elected species. Traversal of a species election is generally treated as an admission that the species are not patentably distinct.

When all the claims directed to the elected invention are in condition for allowance, the nonelected invention(s) should be considered for rejoinder.[7] In order to be eligible for rejoinder, a claim to a nonelected invention must "depend from or otherwise require all the limitations of an allowable claim."[8] In order to retain the right to rejoinder, applicant's nonelected invention claims should be amended during prosecution to require the limitations of the elected invention; failure to do so may result in a loss of the right to rejoinder.

§ 3:26   Examination at the USPTO—Examiner interviews

Research References
West's Key Number Digest, Patents ⌘104
C.J.S., Patents §§ 145 to 147, 149 to 151, 173 to 175

A personal interview with the patent examiner can be an invaluable aid in advancing the prosecution of the patent application. Personal interviews with the examiner are permitted at certain times and under certain circumstances. But, an interview with the examiner does not substitute for a formal written response to an Office Action.

Interviews may be conducted by the inventor and/or the inventor's attorney or agent. The attorney or agent must either: (1) have a power of attorney for that application; or (2) be a registered attorney who is known to the examiner to be the local representative of the attorney having actual power in the case; or (3) be a registered agent or attorney who states to the examiner that he or she is the attorney of record or is authorized to represent the applicant or attorney of record.[1]

Interviews merely for the purpose of sounding out the examiner are not permitted. The attorney or agent involved in the interview must have the capacity to reach an agreement on behalf of the

---

[6]M.P.E.P. §§ 808.01 et seq.

[7]M.P.E.P. §§ 821 et seq.

[8]M.P.E.P. § 821.04.

[Section 3:26]

[1]M.P.E.P. § 713.05.

applicant.[2]

After the application is filed, an interview with the examiner will not be permitted until the first Office Action is mailed, unless the examiner initiates the interview. From the mailing date of the first Office Action until the mailing date of the final rejection, the applicant and/or the attorney/agent has a right to an interview with the examiner. After the final rejection has been mailed, one interview is normally permitted, and the purpose of the interview should be presented, preferably in writing, prior to the interview.[3]

Examiner interviews are typically conducted by telephone, although they may also be conducted in person at the USPTO. The attorney or agent must have a power of attorney to conduct a telephone interview. Demonstrations, models, and exhibits are allowed during interviews, but they must be noted in the written description of the interview.[4]

Once an interview is complete, it is the responsibility of the attorney or agent to make the substance of the interview of record, unless the examiner agrees to do so.[5] To make a written description of the interview of record, a written summary of the interview should be filed, either with a response or separately.

§ 3:27   Examination at the USPTO—Response to an office action

Research References

West's Key Number Digest, Patents ☞104, 107 to 109
C.J.S., Patents §§ 144 to 155, 157 to 158, 173 to 175

To avoid abandonment of the application, a Response must be made to any Office Action. The Response may request reconsideration or further examination of the application. Furthermore, the Response may be made with or without an amendment to the application.

Typically, the applicant must respond to an Office Action within six months. This time for response is known as the statutory period, and is calculated from the mailing date of the Office Action.[1] However, the Commissioner of Patents may set a shortened statutory period that is greater than (or equal to) two months.[2] The Response is considered filed as of the day the document arrives at the USPTO, unless the document is filed as Express Mail or is

---

[2]M.P.E.P. § 713.03.   **[Section 3:27]**
[3]M.P.E.P. § 713.09.   [1]35 U.S.C.A. § 133.
[4]M.P.E.P. § 713.08.   [2]37 C.F.R. 1.134.
[5]M.P.E.P. § 713.04.

filed with an appropriate Certificate of Mailing or Certificate of Transmission, in which case the Response is considered filed as of its mailing date or facsimile transmission date. Most responses are now submitted electronically on USPTO's electronic filing system (EFS-web).

The Response or Amendment must distinctly and specifically point out the supposed errors in the Office Action and must respond to every ground of objection, and rejection in the Office Action.[3] Failure to respond to all requirements, objections, and rejections in the Response results in the application becoming abandoned at the end of the allowed time period.[4] However, a request may be made that objections or requirements as to form not necessary for further consideration of the claims be held in abeyance until allowable subject matter is indicated.[5] A general allegation that the claims define a patentable invention without specifically pointing out how the language of the claims patentably distinguishes them from cited references does not constitute a fully responsive Response/Amendment.

In responding to objections or rejections of the Office Action, one may change the application as necessary. This is referred to as an Amendment. It is critical that the Amendment or changes to the application be supported by the original application and contain no new matter. Any Amendment, whether to the specification, drawings, or claims should set forth where in the original application such changes are supported. The application may be amended to add additional claims, or rejected claims may be canceled.

If the claims are amended in response to rejections or objections in the Office Action, the Response must clearly point out the patentable novelty of the amended claims in view of the state-of-the-art cited by the examiner in the Office Action. The Response must also show how the amended claims are distinguishable over the references cited by the examiner.[6]

§ 3:28 Examination at the USPTO—Final office action

Research References
West's Key Number Digest, Patents ⚷104, 108, 109
C.J.S., Patents §§ 144 to 155, 173 to 175

Examination of an application continues until the examiner issues a Final Rejection or Notice of Allowance of the application. If the response to an Office Action fails to place the application in condition for allowance, rejections in the second (or any subse-

---

[3]37 C.F.R. § 1.111.   [5]37 C.F.R. § 1.111.
[4]37 C.F.R. § 1.135.   [6]37 C.F.R. § 1.111(c).

quent) actions on the merits usually will be "made final." However, when the examiner introduces a new ground of rejection not necessitated by an amendment by the applicant, then the subsequent Office Action will not be made final.[1]

When an action is made final, the applicant must either: file a Response/Amendment After Final placing all claims in condition for allowance, abandon the application and possibly file a continuing application, or appeal the rejection before the response period expires.

After a Final Rejection, the ability to amend the application as a matter of right no longer exists.[2] However, an Amendment may be entered when the Amendment: puts the case in condition for allowance or better condition for appeal, complies with any requirement of form or objection made by the examiner, or is accompanied by a showing of good and sufficient reasons why the amendments are necessary and were not earlier presented.[3] Likewise, the examiner may refuse to enter a Response/Amendment After Final if the response raises new issues that require further consideration and/or raises issues of new matter.

An Advisory Office Action may be issued by the examiner in response to a Response/Amendment After Final by the applicant. An Advisory Office Action notifies the applicant as to whether or not the Response or Amendment After Final was entered by the examiner and any reasons supporting the examiner's decision. The applicant receiving an adverse Final Rejection and Advisory Action may file a continuing application or a request for continued examination (RCE), appeal the examiner's decision, or abandon the application.

§ 3:29 Examination at the USPTO—Appeal

Research References

West's Key Number Digest, Patents ⊖111, 113
C.J.S., Patents §§ 180 to 199, 202

An applicant may appeal to the Patent Trial and Appeal Board once any of the claims of the patent application have been rejected twice.[1] Appeals may be used to overcome rejections under 35 U.S.C.A. §§ 101, 102, 103 or 112. Any action or requirement of the examiner that is not appealable may be addressed by filing a petition to the Commissioner of Patents.

The Patent Trial and Appeal Board may affirm or reverse the

[Section 3:28]

[1]37 C.F.R. § 1.113; M.P.E.P. § 706.07(a).

[2]37 C.F.R. § 1.113(a).

[3]37 C.F.R. § 1.116(b)(3).

[Section 3:29]

[1]37 C.F.R. § 41.31.

decision of the examiner in whole or in part on the grounds specified by the examiner, or it may remand the application to the
examiner for further consideration.[2] The Board may also indicate
that a claim would be allowable if amended in a specified manner.[3]
In such a situation, the appellant has the right to amend the
claim in conformity with the statement. A determination by the
Board that a claim as amended is allowable is binding on the
examiner in the absence of new references or grounds of rejection.[4]

In addition, the Board may also reject an appealed claim on a
new ground of rejection.[5] However, a claim rejected on a new
ground is not considered final. In such a case, the Board will
remand the application to the examiner. The appellant has two
options with respect to the new ground of rejection. First, the appellant may submit an appropriate amendment of the claims
and/or showing of facts to the examiner to have the matter
reconsidered by the examiner. The new ground of rejection raised
by the Board will be binding upon the examiner unless an amendment or showing of facts to the examiner overcomes the new
ground of rejection stated in the Board's decision.[6] Second, the
appellant may have the case reconsidered by the Board upon the
same record. This may be done by filing a request for reconsideration that states with particularity the points believed to have
been misapprehended or overlooked.[7]

Lastly, the Board may also recommend rejection of a claim allowed by the examiner and remand the case to the examiner. In
response to the Board's recommendation, the appellant has at
least one month to submit an amendment or argument to the
examiner to overcome the Board's recommended rejection. The
examiner must adopt the Board's recommendation unless he or
she believes that it is overcome by the appellant's amendment or
submission of facts. Should the examiner make the recommended
rejection final, the appellant may once again appeal to the Patent
Trial and Appeal Board.[8]

If the appellant is dissatisfied with the decision of the Board of
Patent Appeals and Interferences, the appellant may appeal to
either the U.S. Court of Appeals for the Federal Circuit[9] or to the
U.S. District Court for the District of Columbia.[10]

The USPTO has implemented a pilot program called the Pre-

---

[2]37 C.F.R. § 41.50(a)(1).   [7]37 C.F.R. § 41.50(b)(2).
[3]37 C.F.R. § 41.50(c).   [8]37 C.F.R. §§ 41.50(b), 41.52, 41.
[4]37 C.F.R. § 41.50(c).   54.
[5]37 C.F.R. § 41.50(b).   [9]37 C.F.R. § 1.301.
[6]37 C.F.R. § 41.50(b)(1).   [10]37 C.F.R. § 1.303.

Appeal Brief Conference Pilot Program.[11] This program offers applicants an avenue to request that a panel of examiners formally review the legal and factual basis of rejections in their application prior to the filing of an appeal brief. The program is intended to spare applicants the added time and expense of preparing an appeal brief if a panel review determines that the examiner's rejections have insufficient basis to warrant an appeal. Procedurally, the request for a preappeal brief conference is filed with a notice of appeal, and if the preappeal brief conference is not successful, then an appeal brief must be filed in order to continue the process of appeal.

§ 3:30 Interferences and derivation proceedings

Research References

West's Key Number Digest, Patents ⚷106
C.J.S., Patents §§ 159 to 172

Depending on the effective filing date of a patent application, conflicts between inventors regarding ownership of an invention may be resolved either through derivation proceedings or interferences. In general, applications filed before March 16, 2013, are subject to 35 U.S.C.A. § 135 (2006) (interference proceedings), and applications filed on or after March 16, 2013, are subject to 35 U.S.C.A. § 135 (2012) (derivation proceedings). However, some applications filed on or after March 16, 2013, may still be subject to interference practice. In particular, continuations, continuations-in-part, PCT applications, and divisional patent applications with an effective filing date prior to March 16, 2013, may still involve interferences.[1]

Derivation proceedings require two applications directed toward the same invention, by different applicants. Within one year after the publication of a claim to the invention, the later applicant may petition for a derivation proceeding. In the petition, the later applicant must allege with particularity the basis for finding that an inventor named in an earlier application derived the claimed invention from an inventor named in the petitioner's application, and further that the earlier application claiming such invention was filed without authorization.[2] The Director of the USPTO then decides whether to institute a derivation proceeding. The Director's determination is final and nonappealable by statute.[3]

In both interferences and derivations, only an applicant for pa-

---

[11]M.P.E.P. § 1204.02.

[Section 3:30]

[1]35 U.S.C.A. § 100(i)(B).

[2]35 U.S.C.A. § 135(a).

[3]35 U.S.C.A. § 135(a).

tent may petition for the proceeding. Where the original inventor disclosed the invention to a second party, the second party may apply for a patent claiming the invention, and the original inventor could not institute a derivation proceeding without applying for a patent on the same invention within the one year period after the second party's application publishes.

In derivation proceedings, the Patent Trial and Appeal Board makes findings regarding the original inventorship of the claimed invention, and may adjust the list of inventors for a given application or patent.[4] The Patent Trial and Appeal Board may also amend inventorship in response to arbitration or settlements between the parties.[5]

An interference is a proceeding instituted before the Patent Trial and Appeal Board between two or more parties claiming the same patentable invention, and is available only for applications with effective filing dates before March 16, 2013.[6] An interference determines the first inventor of the patentable invention. An interference may be declared between two or more pending U.S. patent applications, or between one or more pending applications and one or more unexpired patents of different inventors.[7]

Interferences may be suggested by either an applicant or by the examiner. A patentee is not allowed to suggest an interference, but may alert the examiner of an application claiming interfering subject matter to the possibility of an interference.[8]

Once an interference is initiated, each party submits evidence and arguments in a paper trial setting to determine the first inventor. Generally, the first party to reduce the invention to practice wins the interference unless the first party to reduce the invention to practice suppressed or concealed the invention, derived the invention from its opponent, or the opponent was the first to conceive the invention and was reasonably diligent in reducing the invention to practice.[9]

Reducing an invention to practice usually involves physically constructing or building the invention and proving that the invention serves its intended purpose. Filing a U.S. patent application constitutes a "constructive reduction to practice" and is legally equivalent to an actual reduction to practice if the application meets the requirements of 35 U.S.C.A. § 112. If the U.S. patent application claims priority from an earlier filed foreign patent application, the filing date of the foreign application serves as the date of the constructive reduction to practice of the invention.

---

[4]35 U.S.C.A. § 135(b).

[5]35 U.S.C.A. § 135(e), (f).

[6]37 C.F.R. §§ 41.200 et seq.

[7]37 C.F.R. § 41.202.

[8]37 C.F.R. § 41.202.

[9]35 U.S.C.A. § 102(g).

In proving conception, reduction to practice, and diligence, an inventor cannot merely rely upon his or her own testimony without corroborating documents which are witnessed by others or without corroborating testimony of another who understood the invention at the time it was explained to him or her by the inventor.

To prove conception, the inventor must produce corroborating evidence that shows that the inventor disclosed to another his or her "completed thought expressed in such clear terms as to enable those skilled in the art to make the invention."[10] A party seeking to establish an actual reduction to practice in interference proceeding must satisfy a two prong test: (1) the party constructed an embodiment or performed a process that met every element of the interference count, and (2) the embodiment or process operated for its intended purpose. Thus, for purposes of interference, there is no actual reduction to practice if the constructed embodiment or performed process lacks an element recited in the count or uses an equivalent of that element.[11]

To prove actual reduction to practice, the inventor must show corroborating evidence that he or she built an embodiment of the invention and that the embodiment worked for its intended purpose.[12] One form of corroborating evidence is an inventor's lab notebook. However, to be effective, the notebook must be witnessed by an independent party and must not appear as if it was tampered with after being witnessed. To prove that the notebook was witnessed, the inventor can submit the notebook itself if the witness signed and dated the pages they witnessed, or the inventor may have the witness testify that he or she read and understood the disclosure in the notebook.

§ 3:31 Preissuance third party submissions

Third parties may submit patents and other printed publications to the USPTO for consideration during the prosecution of a patent application.[1] The third party must explain the relevance of each submitted reference.[2] Third party submissions must be made before a notice of allowance on the application at issue is mailed but can otherwise be made at any time before the first rejection of the application at issue by the USPTO, or until six

---

[10]Coleman v. Dines, 754 F.2d 353, 359, 224 U.S.P.Q. 857 (Fed. Cir. 1985).

[11]Eaton v. Evans, 204 F.3d 1094, 53 U.S.P.Q.2d 1696, 1698 (Fed. Cir. 2000).

[12]DSL Dynamic Scis. Ltd. v. Union Switch & Signal, Inc., 928 F.2d 1122, 1125, 18 U.S.P.Q.2d 1152, 1154 (Fed. Cir. 1991).

[Section 3:31]
[1]35 U.S.C.A. § 122(e).
[2]35 U.S.C.A. § 122(e)(2).

months after the application is published, whichever is later.[3] The preissuance submission procedures of 35 U.S.C.A. § 122(e) provide a mechanism for third parties to put relevant documents before the USPTO during patent prosecution but do not allow third parties any continuing involvement in prosecution.

§ 3:32   Allowance and issuance of the patent

Research References
West's Key Number Digest, Patents ☞103, 104, 112, 117
C.J.S., Patents §§ 144 to 147, 149 to 151, 173 to 175, 194, 203 to 207, 209

Once the examiner becomes convinced that the claims are allowable, the examiner notifies the applicant that all the claims are allowed or allowable with a status letter of allowability which may be either a Notice of Allowability or an *Ex Parte Quayle* Action.[1]

Both the Notice of Allowability and *Ex Parte Quayle* Action constitute the first notice to the applicant that all the claims are allowed or allowable. In both actions, prosecution on the merits is closed. The Notice of Allowability states which claims are allowed in the application and sets forth any additional drawing requirements such as the need for drawing corrections or formal drawings. The Notice of Allowability also sets forth that a formal Notice of Allowance and Fee(s) Due is included or will be forthcoming. Typically, the Notice of Allowability is accompanied by additional communications such as an examiner's amendment, an examiner's statement of reasons for allowance, a notification of patent term extension, if any, and the formal Notice of Allowance and Issue Fee Due.

An *Ex Parte Quayle* Action also closes prosecution on the merits. However, an *Ex Parte Quayle* Action also typically requires the applicant to file an appropriate nonsubstantive amendment correcting or meeting any outstanding formal objections or requirements of the examiner. Such corrections typically involve the correction of claimed dependency, the correction of grammatical, typographical or spelling errors, a modification of the title or abstract or the correction of other similar technical formalities.

In lieu of requiring the applicant to correct obvious errors and omissions through an Amendment in response to an *Ex Parte*

---

[3]35 U.S.C.A. § 122(e)(1); 37 CFR § 1.290.

[Section 3:32]

[1]M.P.E.P. § 1302.03, 714.14.

Quayle Action, the examiner may make an Examiner's Amendment. In the Examiner's Amendment, the examiner corrects obvious errors and omissions, and cancels claims previously withdrawn from earlier consideration. Many times the examiner will obtain authorization from the applicant by telephone for such corrections. However, if the Examiner's Amendment is unacceptable to the applicant, the applicant may file an Amendment prior to payment of the issue fee.

If the examiner believes that the record of the prosecution does not make clear the examiner's reasons for allowing a claim or claims, the examiner may issue what is known as an "Examiner's Statement of Reasons for Allowance."[2] Although the Examiner's Statement of Reasons for Allowance may be issued any time during the prosecution of the application, this statement is typically issued with the Notice of Allowability.

If the applicant disagrees or further wishes to comment upon the Examiner's Statement of Reasons for Allowance, the applicant may file a Comment on the Statement of Reasons for Allowance no later than the payment of the issue fee. Failure to file a Comment on the Statement of Reasons for Allowance by applicant, however, does not give rise to any implication that the applicant or patent owner agrees with or acquiesces in the reasoning of the examiner.[3]

Once the examiner determines that the claims are allowed or allowable, the examiner begins preparing the application for formal allowance. In particular, the examiner conducts a final review of the application to ensure the application complies with the rules and regulations of the USPTO. During this process, the examiner checks the application for errors and inconsistencies, renumbers the allowed claims in the sequence in which they will appear in the issued patent, and checks for appropriate cross-referencing notations to earlier applications. In addition, the examiner reviews and collects information which will be printed on the first page of the issued patent, including patent classification information, priority information, patent term extension, and identification of prior art references cited during the course of prosecution. The examiner also designates the most representative figure and the broadest or most representative claim for publication in the Official Gazette on the date of patent issuance.

Once the examiner has concluded that the claims in the application are allowable and that the application meets the formal requirements of the USPTO the examiner will issue a formal No-

---

[2]37 C.F.R. § 1.104(e).
[3]Salazar v. Procter & Gamble Co., 414 F.3d 1342, 1345–47, 75 U.S.P. Q.2d 1369 (Fed. Cir. 2005).

tice of Allowance.[4] At this point in time, jurisdiction over the application is transferred from the examiner to the Patent Issue Division.[5] In addition to "passing the application to issuance," the Notice of Allowance also begins the three month period after the mailing date of the Notice of Allowance in which the applicant must pay the issue fee.

After the Formal Notice of Allowance, no amendment may be made to the application as a matter of right.[6] Although amendments to the application may be requested prior to payment of the issue fee, entry of such amendments is completely within the discretion of the examiner and the USPTO. Entry of amendments that would require the examiner to conduct an additional search of prior art or to perform substantial review of the application are normally refused.

The applicant is required to pay an issue fee within three months from the mailing date of the Notice of Allowance. Failure to pay the issue fee results in the application becoming abandoned, and the patent will not issue.[7] However, late payment of the issue fee may be excused if accompanied by the appropriate petition and fee for delayed payment and a showing that the delay was either unavoidable or unintentional. Before paying the issue fee, the applicant should determine if the issue fee set forth in the Notice of Allowance should be increased or decreased based upon any change in the small entity status of the applicant.

Applications may be withdrawn from issue for further action at the initiative of the USPTO or upon petition by the applicant. A petition by the applicant must include a showing of good and sufficient reasons why withdrawal of the application is necessary. The petition must be accompanied by an appropriate fee. If the application is withdrawn from issue, a new Notice of Allowance will be sent if the application is again allowed. Any amendment accompanying a petition to withdraw an application from issue will be treated as an Amendment After Allowance.

Generally, once the issue fee has been paid, the application will not be withdrawn from issue except for a mistake on the part of the USPTO, noncompliance with the duty to disclose known prior art, illegality of the application, unpatentability of one or more claims, interference purposes, or for abandonment to permit consideration of an Information Disclosure Statement in a continuing application.[8]

If the issue fee is timely paid, the patent will issue in the regular course unless the application is withdrawn from issue or issu-

---

[4] 37 C.F.R. § 1.311.
[5] M.P.E.P. § 1305.
[6] 37 C.F.R. § 1.312.

[7] 37 C.F.R. § 1.316.
[8] 37 C.F.R. § 1.313(b).

ance of the patent is deferred.[9] The formal patent grant is a single page document attached to a bond paper copy of the specification, drawings and claims by a blue ribbon secured under the seal of the USPTO. The date of the patent grant, otherwise known as the issue date, begins the time period in which the patentee may enforce the U.S. patent rights against infringers. In addition, on the issue date, the specification, drawings and the entire file history become available to the public (although portions of the application may have already been available to the public if the application was previously published). After the issue date, continuing applications in the United States claiming priority from the issuing patent may no longer be filed.

Normally, a patent will be issued to the inventors. However, a patent grant may also be issued directly to the inventor's assignee if an assignment is recorded no later than the date upon which the issue fee is paid.[10] If the entire interest of the inventor is assigned to the assignee, the patent will issue to the assignee. If the assignee only holds an undivided part interest, the patent will issue jointly to the inventor and the assignee.[11] On the issue date of the patent, an official copy of the patent will be sent to the patentee unless there is an attorney of record.[12]

§ 3:33 Maintenance fees

Research References

West's Key Number Digest, Patents ⚬103, 133
C.J.S., Patents §§ 144, 234 to 235

To maintain a utility patent in force and effect beyond four years, eight years and twelve years, an appropriate maintenance fee must be submitted to the USPTO within three and one-half years, seven and one-half years, and eleven and one-half years, respectively, from the date of the original patent grant.[1] An additional six month extension may be obtained for each of the periods with payment of a surcharge.[2]

In submitting maintenance fees, the patents for which maintenance fees are being paid must be identified with the patent number and serial number of the U.S. application.[3] Each time a maintenance fee is paid, the patentee must verify the small entity status of the patentee, if applicable, and notify the USPTO of any change in small entity status prior to or concurrent with pay-

---

[9]37 C.F.R. § 1.314.

[10]35 U.S.C.A. § 152; 37 C.F.R. § 3.81.

[11]37 C.F.R. § 3.81.

[12]37 C.F.R. § 1.315.

[Section 3:33]

[1]37 C.F.R. § 1.362(d).

[2]37 C.F.R. § 1.362(e).

[3]37 C.F.R. § 1.366(c).

ment of the maintenance fee.[4]

In addition to the patentee, any person or organization may pay maintenance fees and any necessary surcharges on behalf of the patentee. Authorization from the patentee is not needed to pay maintenance fees and any necessary surcharges on behalf of the patentee.[5]

Failure to pay the required maintenance fee and necessary surcharges will result in the patent expiring at the end of the same date the patent was granted in the fourth, eighth or twelfth year after grant.[6]

An expired patent may be revived by paying the required maintenance fee along with an appropriate surcharge and a petition to the Commissioner of Patents and Trademarks to accept the delayed payment of the maintenance fee. The petition must show that the delay in payment was "unintentional."[7]

During the period in which the patent is temporarily expired, infringement or preparation for infringement by a third party may create "intervening rights" in the third party.[8]

---

[4]37 C.F.R. § 1.366(f).   [7]37 C.F.R. § 1.378.
[5]37 C.F.R. § 1.366(a).   [8]35 U.S.C.A. § 41(c).
[6]37 C.F.R. § 1.362(g).

Chapter 4

Correction and Review of Issued Patents

> **KeyCite®:** Cases and other legal materials listed in KeyCite Scope can be researched through the KeyCite service on Westlaw®. Use KeyCite to check citations for form, parallel references, prior and later history, and comprehensive citator information, including citations to other decisions and secondary materials.

§ 4:1   Overview

Once a patent issues, a range of statutory techniques are available for correcting formal and substantive errors in the issued patent. These statutory techniques include several tools available to patent owners, third parties, or both. Certificates of Correction, reissue applications, supplemental examination, and *ex parte* reexamination can be used by patent holders to correct defects in their own issued patents. Post grant review, *inter partes* review, *ex parte* reexamination, and a temporary transitional program for business method patents can be used by third parties to challenge the validity of patents issued to another. For a side-by-side comparison of these various proceedings, see Appendix D: Comparison of post grant patent proceedings.

The Federal Circuit in *Fresenius v. Baxter* decided that USPTO reexamination decisions trump prior non-final decisions by the district court and the Federal Circuit. The decision applies to patents involved in parallel proceedings in federal court and at the USPTO in which the law gives both entities power to decide the patentability of the patents in question. In *Fresenius*, the court ruled that a USPTO's decision trumps a prior court decision that had not yet been entered and still required findings for damages.[1]

§ 4:2   Certificates of Correction

Research References
West's Key Number Digest, Patents ☞126
C.J.S., Patents §§ 215 to 216

Certificates of Correction are ordinarily used to correct minor, nonsubstantive errors in an issued patent. Certificates of Correction may also be used to rectify errors in inventorship and to perfect claims to foreign or domestic priority. A Certificate of Correction is considered a part of the original patent and typically consists of a single page document providing a notice of mistakes in the original patent and correcting such mistakes if possible. Certificates of Correction are automatically published on the USPTO website and attached to each printed copy of the patent, and are announced in the Official Gazette of the USPTO. Each patent including a Certificate of Correction is to be treated as if the patent had originally issued in such corrected form.

Mistakes incurred through the fault of the USPTO are the subject of Certificates of Correction.[1] A Certificate of Correction of USPTO mistake will not be issued at the request or suggestion of anyone not owning an interest in the patent, nor on motion of the USPTO, without first notifying the patentee (including any assignee of record) and affording the patentee an opportunity to be heard.[2] Because the mistake is incurred through the fault of the Office, the Certificate of Correction of USPTO mistake is issued without expense to the patentee.

Mistakes of minor character such as clerical or typographical mistakes which are not the fault of the USPTO may be corrected with a Certificate of Correction of applicant's mistake. The request for a Certificate of Correction of applicant's mistake must show that the mistake occurred in good faith and must include the appropriate fee. A mistake is not of a minor character if the

---

[Section 4:1]

[1]Fresenius USA, Inc. v. Baxter Intern., Inc., 721 F.3d 1330, 1364–1365, 107 U.S.P.Q.2d 1365 (Fed. Cir. 2013), cert. denied, 134 S. Ct. 2295 (2014).

[Section 4:2]

[1]35 U.S.C.A. § 254; 37 C.F.R. § 1.322.

[2]37 C.F.R. § 1.322.

requested change affects the scope or meaning of the patent.[3]

When a patent incorrectly omits inventors or names persons who are not inventors, correction of the named inventors may be achieved through the use of a Certificate of Correction.[4] The request for a Certificate of Correction to correct inventorship in a patent must include a petition including statements from each inventor being added that the inventorship error occurred without deceptive intention, statements from the current named inventors agreeing to the change or stating they have no disagreement in regard to the requested change, and statements from all assignees agreeing to the requested change.[5]

§ 4:3 Disclaimers

Research References

West's Key Number Digest, Patents ⬌149 to 156
C.J.S., Patents §§ 261 to 269

Disclaimers are used to narrow the scope or limit the term of patents that have received too much protection in the scope of the claims. A disclaimer is a statement filed by an owner of a patent, or of a patent to be granted, in which the owner relinquishes certain legal rights to the patent. To be effective, a disclaimer must be made by every owner of at least a part interest in the patent, or by the owners' attorneys of record. Two types of disclaimers are available—statutory disclaimers and terminal disclaimers. A statutory disclaimer is used to disclaim a specific claim or claims of a patent, while a terminal disclaimer is used to disclaim to the public the entire term, or any portion of the term, of all of the claims of a patent.[1] Terminal disclaimers are often submitted to overcome rejections during prosecution for non-statutory double patenting. Similar to patents including Certificates of Correction, patents including disclaimers are treated as if the patent originally issued without the disclaimed claims or disclaimed portion of the patent term.

§ 4:4 Reissue applications

Research References

West's Key Number Digest, Patents ⬌134 to 148
C.J.S., Patents §§ 237 to 260

A reissue application is an application requesting an existing

---

[3]35 U.S.C.A. § 255; 37 C.F.R. § 1.323.

[4]35 U.S.C.A. § 256; 37 C.F.R. § 1.324.

[5]37 C.F.R. § 1.324.

[Section 4:3]

[1]37 C.F.R. § 1.321.

patent be issued again in corrected form. In contrast to Certificates of Correction which may be used generally to correct only minor errors or errors in inventorship, reissues also have the capability of correcting substantive errors which require active participation of a Patent Examiner. The most common bases for filing a reissue application are: (1) the claims are too narrow or too broad, (2) the disclosure contains inaccuracies, (3) the applicant has failed to or incorrectly claims foreign priority or (4) the applicant has failed to make reference to or incorrectly makes reference to prior co-pending applications. Reissue applications are normally examined by the same examiner who issued the original patent.[1]

A reissue application contains the same parts as an original patent application. In addition to complying with all the rules relating to an original patent application, a reissue application must also comply with requirements relating to reissue applications.[2]

Reissue applications may be filed whenever any issued patent, through error without deceptive intent, is deemed wholly or partly inoperative or invalid by reason of a defective specification or drawing, or by reason of the patentee claiming more or less than he or she had a right to claim in the patent. Accordingly, a reissue application requires an oath or declaration by the applicant for reissue that the applicant believes the original patent to be wholly or partly inoperative or invalid and the reasons why.[3] In particular, in stating the reasons why the applicant believes the original patent to be wholly or partly inoperative or invalid, the applicant must either particularly specify defects in the specification or drawing or specify the excess or insufficiency of the claims.[4] For applications filed prior to September 16, 2012, the applicant must make a statement that the errors arose "without any deceptive intention." The applicant must acknowledge the continuing duty to disclose to the USPTO all information known to be material to patentability. In addition to being signed by the inventor or inventors, the reissue oath must be accompanied by the written consent of every assignee owning an undivided interest in the patent.

The term "defective specification or drawing" has been broadly construed when determining whether a sufficient ground for reissue has been set forth by the reissue applicant.[5] Examples of "a defective specification or drawing" have included: failing to file a

---

[Section 4:4]

[1]M.P.E.P. § 1440.

[2]37 C.F.R. § 1.171.

[3]37 C.F.R. § 1.175.

[4]37 C.F.R. § 1.175.

[5]See also 37 C.F.R. § 1.173 placing additional requirements on the specification and drawings of the reis-

certified copy of the original foreign application to obtain a right of foreign priority, failure to adequately claim priority in an earlier filed co-pending U.S. application, and the misjoinder of inventors. A request for a reissue application on the basis of a defective specification or drawing may be filed anytime during the term of the original patent.

In addition, to correcting errors in the specification or drawings of an application, a reissue application may also correct errors in the scope of the claims. However, if a reissue patent application seeks to enlarge the scope of the claims of the original patent, the reissue patent application must be filed within two years from the date of the original patent.[6] A reissue application filed on the two-year anniversary date of a patent is considered filed within two years.[7] When seeking to enlarge the scope of the claims, the error asserted as justifying the reissue application may be an attorney's failure to appreciate the full scope of the invention.[8]

The reissue application must include an offer to surrender the original patent.[9] Filing a reissue application to correct and possibly improve an issued patent subjects the entire original patent to scrutiny by the examiner. As a result, in addition to the possibility of broadening patent protection or improving the enforceability of the patent, the reissue application may also result in narrower claims. Even unchanged claims from the original patent are once again subject to rejection on all the grounds available against the original application. Furthermore, the reissue examiner may reject the unchanged claims from the original patent as not being supported by an enabling disclosure despite the opposite conclusion of the original application's examiner. Unchanged claims are also subject to being rejected by the reissue examiner on the basis of newly found prior art.

Reissue patents are also subject to the rule against recapture of subject matter which prohibits "recapture" of claimed subject matter surrendered during the prosecution of an application for the original patent.[10] This "prevents a patentee from regaining through reissue the subject matter that he surrendered in an effort to obtain allowance of the original claims."[11] In *North American Container*, the court applied the a three-step analysis to reissue patents:

(1) First, we determine whether, and in what respect, the reis-

---

sue patent application.

[6]35 U.S.C.A. § 251; 37 C.F.R. § 1.173(a).

[7]M.P.E.P. § 1403.

[8]In re Wilder, 736 F.2d 1516, 222 U.S.P.Q. 369 (Fed. Cir. 1984).

[9]37 C.F.R. § 1.178.

[10]M.P.E.P. § 1412.02.

[11]In re Clement, 131 F.3d 1464, 1468, 45 U.S.P.Q.2d 1161 (Fed. Cir. 1997).

sue claims are broader in scope than the original patent claims;

(2) Next, we determine whether the broader aspects of the reissue claims relate to subject matter surrendered in the original prosecution; and

(3) Finally, we determine whether the reissue claims were materially narrowed in other respects, so that the claims may not have been enlarged, and hence avoid the recapture rule.[12]

A reissued patent will be enforceable for the remainder of the patent term of the original patent.[13] However, a broadened reissue patent may be subject to intervening rights. Although infringement actions arising under claims in the original patent which are also included in the reissue patent are unaffected by the reissue process, claims which have changed in scope in the reissue patent are subject to intervening rights. Under the doctrine of intervening rights, an intervening manufacturer or purchaser who has relied upon the scope of the claims in the original patent may either sell or continue using structures which were manufactured before the date of the reissue patent and which were covered only by the claims of the reissue patent.[14]

When a reissue application is filed, the original patent remains in effect until a reissue patent is granted. If the reissue patent is denied or abandoned, the original patent will still be enforceable. The file history of all reissue applications, whether denied, abandoned, or granted, is available to the public.[15]

§ 4:5   Supplemental examination

A patent holder may request supplemental examination of an issued patent to consider, correct, or reconsider information that presents a substantial new question of patentability.[1] In effect, supplemental examination allows patent holders to introduce prior art that could or should have been considered during prosecution but was not disclosed to the USPTO prior to issuance of the patent. A patent cannot be held unenforceable based on the patentee's failure to submit information during prosecution, so long as that information was subsequently disclosed for supplemental examination.[2] Thus, a nondisclosure that could otherwise constitute inequitable conduct before the USPTO can be remedied

---

[12]North American Container, Inc. v. Plastipak Packaging, Inc., 415 F.3d 1335, 1349, 75 U.S.P.Q.2d 1545, 1556 (Fed. Cir. 2005).

[13]35 U.S.C.A. § 252.

[14]35 U.S.C.A. § 252.

[15]See 35 C.F.R. § 1.178.

[Section 4:5]

[1]35 U.S.C.A. § 257(a), (b).

[2]35 U.S.C.A. § 257(c)(1).

by disclosing relevant prior art via supplemental examination after issue.

Prior art considered in supplemental examination is not limited to patents and printed publications and can include up to ten items that present any sort of previously undisclosed information material to patentability.[3] Patent holders can, for instance, correct previous false statements or misrepresentations made during prosecution, or in the patent specification.

Generally, submission of information for supplemental examination cures inequitable conduct with respect to that information even if the USPTO determines that no substantially new question of patentability exists, and foregoes examination.[4] Supplemental examination cannot purge inequitable conduct, however, with respect to a defense raised by an alleged infringer in an infringement action brought by the patent owner before concluding supplemental examination.[5] Supplemental examination is only available to the patent holder, who must provide the USPTO with a summary of the relevance of each new reference presented for supplemental examination.[6]

§ 4:6 *Ex parte* reexamination

Research References

West's Key Number Digest, Patents ⊙–134 to 148
C.J.S., Patents §§ 237 to 260

A request for reexamination may be filed by anyone (i.e. the patent owner or third party) during the period of enforceability of a patent.[1] For purposes of filing a reexamination request, the period of enforceability of a patent is the time period during which the patent may be asserted in infringement litigation.[2] This time period is generally the life of the patent plus six years, but, if an infringement suit is filed within the six-year statute of limitations, reexamination may be requested during the course of that litigation.[3]

The request for reexamination must include a statement pointing out a "substantial new question of patentability" based on prior patents and printed publications. Events other than prior patents and printed publications, such as public use, on sale or fraud considerations should not be included in the request and

---

[3] 35 U.S.C.A. § 257(b); 77 Fed. Reg. 48828.

[4] 35 U.S.C.A. § 257(c)(1).

[5] 35 U.S.C.A. § 257(c)(2)(A).

[6] 37 CFR §§ 1.601 et seq.

[Section 4:6]

[1] 35 U.S.C.A. § 302; 37 C.F.R. § 1.510.

[2] M.P.E.P. § 2211.

[3] M.P.E.P. § 2211.

will not be considered by the examiner if included.[4] The request must set forth the pertinency and manner of applying the printed prior art to each and every claim for which reexamination is requested.[5] The office will generally only examine claims for which reexamination was requested and a substantial new question of patentability was raised.

Once the request accompanied by the appropriate fee is received at the USPTO, abandonment, withdrawal or striking of the request is not permitted.[6] Within three months of receiving the request and the appropriate fee, the USPTO will determine whether the request raises "a substantial new question of patentability" affecting any claim of the patent.[7] If such a new question is found, the USPTO will grant an Order for Reexamination of the patent.

If the reexamination request was submitted by a third party, the patent owner has the opportunity to file a statement or response after the Order for Reexamination is granted. Typically, the Order for Reexamination will set a period of not less than two months from the date of the Order in which the patent owner may file a statement. The statement or response may amend the claims, cancel claims and/or add claims. However, the amendment may not enlarge the scope of the claims and may not introduce new matter. If the request for reexamination was not filed by the patent owner, a copy of the statement will be served on the requestor.[8]

If the patent owner files a statement, the requestor is given a period of two months from the date of service to file a reply.[9] The reply by the requestor must be served upon the patent owner. The reply is not limited to the issues raised in the statement and may include additional prior art patents and printed publications.[10] Because filing a statement allows the requestor an opportunity to submit further prior art and to make additional arguments, the patent owner may elect not to file a statement.

Once *ex parte* reexamination is ordered and the time for submitting any response thereto has expired, no further active participation by anyone other than the patent owner is allowed and all submissions by anyone other than the patent owner will not be acknowledged or considered.[11]

All reexamination proceedings, including any appeals to the Patent Trial and Appeal Board (PTAB), are conducted with

---

[4]M.P.E.P. § 2216.   [8]37 C.F.R. § 1.530.
[5]35 U.S.C.A. § 302.   [9]37 C.F.R. § 1.535.
[6]M.P.E.P. § 2210.   [10]M.P.E.P. § 2251.
[7]35 U.S.C.A. § 303.   [11]37 C.F.R. § 1.550.

special dispatch within the USPTO.[12] As a result, reexamination proceedings are intended to be much more rapid than the prosecution of normal applications or reissue applications, though in actuality this may not be the case, particularly for inter partes re-examination.

The patent claims for which reexamination has been ordered are reexamined on the basis of patents or printed publications. Any issue based upon printed prior art may be raised by the examiner during reexamination, including issues previously addressed by the USPTO during prosecution of the original patent. In addition to relying upon printed prior art cited by the reexamination requestor, the examiner may also rely upon printed prior art of record in the patent file of the original patent or printed prior art newly discovered by the examiner.

Once reexamination is ordered, the reexamination examiner, usually the primary examiner who ordered reexamination, will make a thorough study of the patent and available prior art and will issue a first Office Action.[13] The patent owner then has the opportunity to file a response to the first Office Action requesting reconsideration of the claims with or without amendment to the claims. Additional claims may be added by amendment without any fee provided the total number of claims does not exceed 20 or the number of claims in the original issued patent.[14] Although new and narrower claims may be presented, claims cannot be broadened.[15] Alternatively, pursuant to 37 C.F.R. § 1.132, the applicant can establish additional facts regarding inoperability of the prior art reference or regarding secondary considerations proving nonobviousness of the invention.

Patents undergoing reexamination cannot become abandoned. Furthermore, once an Office Action during the reexamination proceeding is made final, continuation applications are not permitted.

As during ordinary prosecution, adverse decisions by the examiner during a reexamination proceeding may be appealed to the Patent Trial and Appeal Board after a second or final rejection is made of the claims being reexamined. Initiation of the appeal begins by filing a Notice of Appeal with the time specified in the final rejection.[16] Typically, the final rejection specifies a two-month shortened statutory period for reply that can be extended up to six months after the final rejection date. The appeal process with the Patent Trial and Appeal Board follows the same general

---

[12]35 U.S.C.A. § 305.

[13]37 C.F.R. § 1.104.

[14]M.P.E.P. § 2250; 37 C.F.R. § 1.20(c).

[15]M.P.E.P. § 2250; 35 U.S.C.A. § 305.

[16]37 C.F.R. § 41.31(a)(1).

procedure as with regular patent application appeals, although with special dispatch. In an ex parte reexamination proceeding, appeal may only be taken by the dissatisfied applicant/patentee, and not by a dissatisfied third party requestor. Patent holders may appeal only to the Court of Appeals for the Federal Circuit.[17]

Once the time for appeal has expired or any appeal proceeding has terminated in a reexamination proceeding, the USPTO will issue and publish a Reexamination Certificate canceling any claim of the patent finally determined to be unpatentable, confirming any claim of the patent determined to be patentable and incorporating in the patent any proposed amendment or new claim determined to be patentable.[18] The Certificate will be mailed to the patent owner and a copy of the Certificate will be mailed to the reexamination requestor. A copy of the Reexamination Certificate will be stapled to each copy of the patent in the search files.[19]

As with new or amended claims in reissue patents, new or amended claims added during reexamination proceedings and identified on the Certificate of Reexamination may be subject to intervening rights.[20]

§ 4:7 PTAB trials

Trials for *inter partes* review, standard post grant review, and the transitional post grant review process for covered business method patents are heard before a panel of three administrative patent judges from the Patent Trial and Appeal Board, and use simplified trial procedures with limited discovery and a strict timeline.[1] In particular, the trial phase of these proceedings is instituted within six months of filing of an appropriate petition, and by statute can last no more than twelve months. PTAB trials conclude with a written decision by the PTAB, and include short discovery periods: three months for the petitioner, and a total of four months (across two periods) for the patent owner. PTAB trials are intended as an alternative to litigation in Federal courts, and petitioners in these cases are subject to estoppel in subsequent USPTO actions and in Federal court. In practice, however, most PTAB trails involve parallel litigation, and may not entirely displace validity challenges in corresponding district court

---

[17]35 U.S.C.A. § 141(b).

[18]35 U.S.C.A. § 307.

[19]M.P.E.P. § 2292.

[20]35 U.S.C.A. § 307(b).

s-application-process/patent-trial-and-appeal-board/trials for information about PTAB trial timelines and procedures.

[Section 4:7]

[1]See http://www.uspto.gov/patent

proceedings.

In an effort to make post PTAB trial proceedings more efficient, the PTAB in *Liberty Mutual Ins. Co. v. Progressive Casualty Ins. Co.* provided a framework for limiting the number of redundant grounds for unpatentability. Horizontal redundancy exists when multiple prior art references are distinct and separate alternatives to teach the same claim limitation. Vertical redundancy exists when additional prior art references support another ground of unpatentability. In the case of vertical redundancy, a base ground has already been asserted against the claim, and the Petitioner has not explained the relative strengths and weaknesses of each ground of unpatentability.[2] The PTAB provides two methods for handling redundancies. If one ground is "better from all perspectives, Petitioner should assert the stronger ground and not burden the Patent Owner and the Board with the other."[3] When multiple grounds are needed to sustain a single claim, the PTAB requires a "bi-directional explanation" of why each ground is better in some respect than each other ground.[4] In *Liberty Mutual*, the PTAB said, "[o]nly if the Petitioner reasonably articulates why each ground has strength and weakness relative to the other should both grounds be asserted for consideration."[5] Where proceedings were not instituted on some grounds due to redundancy, the PTAB has taken the position that no estoppel attaches.[6] This position has not yet been tested in the courts.

Information submitted in PTAB trials is subject to a strong presumption in favor of public availability.[7] Although the PTAB can seal confidential materials at the request of trial participants, parties seeking nondisclosure must show why requests for nondisclosure are both necessary and narrowly tailored to cover only sensitive or confidential information. The PTAB will not ordinarily allow entire documents to be sealed, where only certain parts of those documents contain sensitive or privileged information.[8]

In actions before the Patent Trial and Appeal Board, a claim "shall be given its broadest reasonable construction in light of the

---

[2]Liberty Mutual Insurance Co. v. Progressive Casualty Insurance Co., 2012 WL 9494791, *7 (U.S. Pat. Tr. & App. Bd. 2012).

[3]Liberty Mutual Ins. Co., 2012 WL 9494791 at *7.

[4]Liberty Mutual Ins. Co., 2012 WL 9494791 at *2.

[5]Liberty Mutual Ins. Co., 2012 WL 9494791 at *7.

[6]See 77 Fed. Reg. 48680, 48689 (Aug. 14, 2012).

[7]See 37 C.F.R. § 42.14.

[8]See, e.g., Purdue Pharma L.P. v. Depomed, Inc., P.T.A.B. Nos. IPR2014-00377, IPR2014-00378, IPR2014-00379 (U.S. Pat. Tr. & App. Bd. 2014).

specification of the patent in which it appears."[9] This is often referred to as the broadest reasonable interpretation (BRI) standard. The BRI standard differs from that of the claim construction applied by federal district courts. District courts apply the *Phillips* standard, which considers how terms are used in context with the language of the claim as well as the language of other claims of the patent to ascertain the meaning of the term.[10] In determining the meaning of claim terms, the *Phillips* standard further considers the written description or specification as an important source for claim construction.[11] Statements made by the Applicant during prosecution regarding the meaning of claim terms are also relevant in the *Phillips* standard.[12] The *Phillips* standard is generally considered narrower than the BRI standard. A split panel of the Federal Circuit upheld the PTAB's use of the BRI standard in an *inter partes* proceeding.[13]

§ 4:8   PTAB trials—Post grant review

Post grant review is a tool for a third party to challenge one or more claims of an issued patent by submitting a petition to the USPTO identifying one or more issued claims sought to be cancelled as unpatentable.[1] The patent owner may not request post grant review. Only patents with an effective filing date on or after March 16, 2013, are eligible for post grant review, and only if the petition is submitted in writing within the first nine months immediately following issue.[2]

A petitioner for post grant review must particularly identify each challenged claim and provide evidentiary grounds for invalidity based on submitted copies of patents and printed publications, affidavits, declarations, or opinions. Invalidity may be asserted based on lack of novelty, non-obviousness, insufficiency of description, or unpatentable subject matter. The petitioner must also identify all real parties in interest.[3] Petitions for post grant review are made publically available,[4] and the owner of the

---

[9]37 C.F.R. §§ 42.100, 42.200, 42. 300.

[10]Phillips v. AWH Corp., 415 F.3d 1303, 75 U.S.P.Q.2d 1321 (Fed. Cir. 2005) (en banc).

[11]*Phillips*, 415 F.3d at 1315, *citing* Vitronics Corp. v. Conceptronic, Inc., 90 F.3d 1576, 1582, 39 U.S.P.Q.2d 1573 (Fed. Cir. 1996)

[12]*Phillips*, 415 F.3d at 1317, *citing* Vitronics, 90 F.3d at 1582.

[13]In re Cuozzo Speed Technologies, LLC, 778 F.3d 1271, 113 U.S.P.

Q.2d 1613 (Fed. Cir. 2015), opinion withdrawn and superseded on reh'g, 793 F.3d 1268, 115 U.S.P.Q.2d 1425 (Fed. Cir. 2015), cert. granted, 136 S. Ct. 890, 193 L. Ed. 2d 783 (2016).

[Section 4:8]

[1]35 U.S.C.A. § 321(a), (b).

[2]35 U.S.C.A. §§ 321(c), 322(a).

[3]35 U.S.C.A. § 322(a).

[4]35 U.S.C.A. § 322(b).

subject patent may file a preliminary response[5] within three months of the request for post grant review.[6] In the preliminary response, the owner is limited to setting out reasons why review should not be granted.[7]

Petitions for post grant review are not automatically granted. The petition must either raise a novel or unsettled legal question important to other patents and patent applications, or demonstrate that at least one of the challenged claims is more likely than not to be found invalid.[8] This determination is made by the Director within three months after: 1) receiving a preliminary response to the petition to post grant review or 2) if a preliminary response is not filed, the last date on which a preliminary response may be filed.[9] Once the Director determines whether to institute post grant review proceedings, the Director's determination is final and not appealable.[10] Post grant review is barred when the petitioner has already challenged the validity of any claim of the patent in a civil action.[11]

Post grant review proceedings are conducted in a litigation-like format with oral hearings and motions. Post grant review proceedings allow for limited discovery, settlement, and protective orders. During the proceeding, the patent holder may file one motion to cancel or narrow the claims. Amendments made during post grant review may not broaden the scope of the claims.[12] The petitioner holds the burden of proving unpatentability by a preponderance of the evidence.[13] The Patent Trial and Appeal Board must issue a final written decision within 12 months of commencement of the proceeding, extendable up to 18 months.[14] This decision may be appealed only to the Court of Appeals for the Federal Circuit,[15] but third party may not appeal without Art. III standing[16]

If a petition for post grant review is accepted, petitioners are estopped from subsequently or simultaneously litigating any grounds that were or could have been raised. Thus, a petitioner may not re-litigate issues of novelty, nonobviousness, sufficiency of description, or patentable subject matter after successfully petitioning for post grant review. Third parties must choose carefully between conventional litigation and the lower costs, lower

---

[5]35 U.S.C.A. § 323.

[6]37 C.F.R. § 42.207(b).

[7]35 U.S.C.A § 323 and 37 C.F.R. § 42.207(a).

[8]35 U.S.C.A. § 324(a), (b).

[9]35 U.S.C.A. § 324(c)(1-2).

[10]35 U.S.C.A. § 324(e).

[11]35 U.S.C.A. § 325(a)(1).

[12]35 U.S.C.A. § 326(d).

[13]35 U.S.C.A. § 326(e)

[14]35 U.S.C.A. § 326(a)(11).

[15]35 U.S.C.A. § 329, 141(c).

[16]Consumer Watchdog v. Wisconsin Alumni Research Foundation, 2014 WL 2490491, *4 (Fed. Cir. 2014).

burden of proof, and accelerated timetable of post grant review.[17] The threat of estoppel attaching to grounds not raised for post grant review in effect forces petitioners to submit every available reference and argument for invalidity when petitioning for post grant review. The PTAB typically institutes post grant review proceedings for only one to three grounds, however, with the remainder left unconsidered as redundant.

§ 4:9 PTAB trials—*Inter partes* review

Inter partes review closely resembles post grant review but only allows third parties to challenge issued patent claims on grounds of novelty and non-obviousness based on patents and printed publications. Third parties may seek *inter partes* review of an issued patent only after nine months have passed since issue, or after the termination of any post grant review proceeding, whichever is later.[1] Thus, no patent will simultaneously undergo both post grant review and *inter partes* review. *Inter partes* review may not be sought by any third party more than one year after being served with notice of infringement of the patent at issue.[2] As with post grant review, *inter partes* review is barred when the petitioner has already challenged the validity of any claim of the patent in a civil action.[3]

Petitions for *inter partes* review must identify all real parties in interest and must demonstrate a reasonable likelihood of success in challenging one or more patent claims based on novelty or nonobviousness.[4] Petitions are published,[5] and the holder of the patent at issue may submit a preliminary response within three months of a notice that a petition for *inter partes* review has received a filing date.[6] In the preliminary response, the Applicant is limited to asserting the reasons for not instituting *inter partes* proceedings.[7] Like post grant review, *inter partes* review is generally structured as litigation, with motions, limited discovery, and the possibility of settlement.[8] Decisions of the Patent Trial and Appeal Board may be appealed only to the Court of Appeals for the Federal Circuit. However, the determination by the Patent Trial and Appeal Board that a request for *inter partes* review is time-barred is not reviewable by the Court of Appeals for the

---

[17]35 U.S.C.A. § 325(e).

[Section 4:9]

[1]35 U.S.C.A. § 311(b), (c).
[2]35 U.S.C.A. § 315(b).
[3]35 U.S.C.A. § 315(a).

[4]35 U.S.C.A. §§ 312(a), 314(a).
[5]35 U.S.C.A. § 312(b).
[6]37 C.F.R. § 42.107(b).
[7]37 U.S.C.A. § 313 and 37 C.F.R. § 42.107(a).
[8]35 U.S.C.A. §§ 316, 317.

Federal Circuit.[9] The third-party requester has the opportunity to comment on any issues raised by the USPTO or the patent owner during the process.[10]

As with post grant review, a successful petition for *inter partes* review estops the petitioner from subsequently or simultaneously litigating any grounds which were or could have been raised during *inter partes* review,[11] although the USPTO has taken the position that grounds for invalidity raised during *inter partes* review but dismissed as redundant are not subject to estoppel.[12] Because *inter partes* review is only available for issues of novelty and nonobviousness, however, *inter partes* petitioners are not estopped from litigating other invalidity issues, such as sufficiency of disclosure, on sale activities, or patentable subject matter.

§ 4:10 PTAB trials—Transitional program for covered business method patents

The Leahy-Smith America Invents Act of 2011 (AIA) introduced a transitional program by which alleged infringers of some business method patents may seek post-grant review of the patents at issue in litigation, without regard to the standard timing rules governing post grant review petitions. Under this transitional program, alleged infringers may challenge claims directed toward non-technological inventions for use in the practice, administration, or management of financial products or services. Claims can generally be challenged on any grounds ordinarily available in post-grant review, but the prior art available to support challenges for obviousness or lack of novelty is limited for patents subject to pre-AIA law.[1]

The transitional program is only available to patents that claim a method or corresponding apparatus for use in the practice, administration, or management of a financial product or service.[2] The program is explicitly unavailable to "technological" inventions, although the USPTO has stated that the phrase "financial product or service" will be interpreted broadly.[3] Petitioners using the transitional program for business method patents are estopped from revisiting invalidity grounds addressed in a final written decision of the PTAB in subsequent USPTO or district

---

[9]Achates Reference Publishing, Inc. v. Apple Inc., 803 F.3d 652, 116 U.S.P.Q.2d 1783 (Fed. Cir. 2015).

[10]35 U.S.C.A. § 316(a)(13).

[11]35 U.S.C.A. § 315(e).

[12]See 77 Fed. Reg. 48680, 48689 (Aug. 14, 2012).

[Section 4:10]

[1]Leahy-Smith America Invents Act, Pub. L. No. 112-29, § 18, 125 Stat. 284, 2011.

[2]37 CFR §§ 42.300 et seq.

[3]77 Fed. Reg. 48756.

court proceedings. In contrast to ordinary post-grant review, however, petitioners are only estopped from revisiting grounds actually raised before the PTAB. Grounds that could reasonably have been raised before the PTAB, but were not, are not subject to estoppel.[4]

_____

[4]Leahy-Smith America Invents   (2011).
Act, Pub. L. No. 112-29, § 18(a)(1)(D)

Chapter 5

Patent Litigation

KeyCite®: Cases and other legal materials listed in KeyCite Scope can be researched through the KeyCite service on Westlaw®. Use KeyCite to check citations for form, parallel references, prior and later history, and comprehensive citator information, including citations to other decisions and secondary materials.

---

§ 5:1 Pre-filing matters—Subject matter jurisdiction

Research References

West's Key Number Digest, Federal Courts ⚭209; Patents ⚭288
C.J.S., Federal Civil Procedure § 339; Federal Courts §§ 99 to 100; Patents §§ 461 to 465

Patent protection in the United States is governed by federal statutory law, and patent infringement disputes have always been decided in federal courts. The exclusive subject matter jurisdiction of the U.S. district courts over patent infringement suits is statutorily mandated by 28 U.S.C.A. § 1338(a). In addition to subject matter jurisdiction, U.S. district courts have original jurisdiction over claims of unfair competition which are joined with a substantial and related claim of patent infringement.[1] Finally, U.S. district courts have supplemental jurisdiction over all other claims that are so related to claims in the action that they form part of the same case or controversy under Article III of the United States Constitution.[2] In patent cases, supplemental claims are typically some sort of business tort, such as interference with contract or interference with prospective business advantage.

[Section 5:1]
[1]28 U.S.C.A. § 1338(b).

[2]28 U.S.C.A. § 1367(a).

Exclusive appellate jurisdiction over patent infringement cases is lodged in the United States Court of Appeals for the Federal Circuit, which was created in 1982 and sits in Washington, D.C.[3] Prior to creation of the Federal Circuit, patent infringement appeals were decided by the regional Circuit Courts of Appeals, and appeals from decisions of the U.S. Patent and Trademark Office (USPTO) were decided by the Court of Customs and Patent Appeals (C.C.P.A.). Patent law interpretation in the various Circuits conflicted on several basic issues, such as: whether patent infringement (and common defenses such as anticipation and obviousness) were questions of law or fact; standards to be met for anticipation and obviousness; the burden of proof on common defenses; and the order of presentation of evidence. As a result of these Circuit conflicts prior to 1982, considerable forum shopping occurred in patent infringement actions. One of the major purposes behind the creation of the Federal Circuit was to alleviate the inconsistencies between the Circuits in deciding basic patent issues and to eliminate the resulting forum shopping.

It may be possible to prohibit the importation of a patented invention through an action with the International Trade Commission. This is discussed in further detail in Chapter 15.

§ 5:2 Pre-filing matters—Personal jurisdiction

Research References
West's Key Number Digest, Patents ☞288
C.J.S., Patents §§ 461 to 465

Personal jurisdiction over a defendant is generally easily satisfied in patent infringement actions. Patent infringement requires an act of making, using, selling, offering for sale, or importing infringing goods in the territories of the United States, and a defendant who has performed one or more of these acts is subject to *in rem* jurisdiction regardless of *in personam* jurisdiction. The exercise of personal jurisdiction over a patent defendant is not dependent upon the regional circuit law of the forum where the case is brought, but rather is decided under Federal Circuit law.[1] The burden of proving jurisdiction rests with the plaintiff.

As with most jurisdictional disputes, the primary jurisdictional issue in patent cases is usually whether the court's exercise of personal jurisdiction would violate the due process clause of the Fourteenth Amendment of the U.S. Constitution. The Federal Circuit has held that analysis of the due process requirement of

---

[3]28 U.S.C.A. § 1295(a).

[Section 5:2]

[1]Beverly Hills Fan Co. v. Royal

Sovereign Corp., 21 F.3d 1558, 1565, 30 U.S.P.Q.2d 1001, 1006, 28 Fed. R. Serv. 3d 435 (Fed. Cir. 1994).

personal jurisdiction related to patent cases is intimately related to substantive patent law. Thus, creation and application of a uniform body of Federal Circuit law is within that court's powers.[2]

In analyzing minimum contacts, a court must focus on "the relationship among the defendant, the forum and the litigation."[3] A court may exercise specific jurisdiction over a nonresident defendant if the defendant has purposefully directed his activities to the forum state *and* the alleged injury to the forum resident arises out of those activities.[4] The nonresident's activities and connection with the forum state must be such that the defendant would "reasonably anticipate being haled into court there."[5]

Usually, the location of injury to a patent owner is where the infringing act takes place.[6] Infringing acts include making, using, selling or offering to sell an infringing product. Thus, personal jurisdiction can usually be obtained anywhere that an infringing product is sold.

Many jurisdictional disputes in patent cases involve a stream of commerce theory. For instance, in a typical jurisdictional dispute, a patent owner sues an infringer in the patent owner's home district, basing jurisdiction on the fact that the defendant's infringing product was available for purchase in that district. The defendant claims that it did not know that its product was for sale in that district and therefore it had no reasonable anticipation of being haled into court in that district.

The Supreme Court has recognized that a stream of commerce theory exists. However, it is divided with respect to the exact parameters of the theory.[7] Justice O'Connor, writing for four Justices in *Asahi Metal Industry Co. v. Superior Court*, believed that merely placing a product in the stream of commerce was insufficient to establish jurisdiction. Instead, there must be action by the defendant that indicates it purposefully directed itself toward the forum state.[8] Examples of such action include, "designing the product for the market in the forum State, advertising in the forum State, establishing channels for providing regular advice to customers in the forum State, or marketing the product

---

[2]Beverly Hills Fan, 21 F.3d at 1564-65, 30 U.S.P.Q.2d at 1006.

[3]Shaffer v. Heitner, 433 U.S. 186, 204, 97 S. Ct. 2569, 2570 (1977).

[4]Burger King Corp. v. Rudzewicz, 471 U.S. 462, 472, 105 S. Ct. 2174, 2182, (1985).

[5]World-Wide Volkswagen Corp. v. Woodson, 444 U.S. 286, 287, 100 S. Ct. 559, 562 (1980).

[6]See Beverly Hills Fan, 21 F.3d at 1570-71, 30 U.S.P.Q.2d at 1004.

[7]See Asahi Metal Industry Co., Ltd. v. Superior Court of California, Solano County, 480 U.S. 102, 107 S. Ct. 1026, Prod. Liab. Rep. (CCH) P 11267 (1987).

[8]Asahi, 480 U.S. at 112, 107 S. Ct. at 1032.

through a distributor who has agreed to serve as the sales agent in the forum State."[9]

But a plurality of four other Justices, led by Justice Brennan, did not consider such a showing of additional conduct to be necessary, as long as the stream of commerce into which the goods were placed was a "regular and anticipated flow of products from manufacturer to distribution to retail sale" and not just "unpredictable currents or eddies" that sweep the products into the forum.[10] The Brennan plurality noted that as long as a participant in the regular and anticipated flow of products is aware that the final product is being marketed in the forum state, the possibility of litigation there will not be a surprise. The Federal Circuit has not decided which version of the stream-of-commerce theory it will apply, electing instead to refrain from taking a position on the right articulation of the stream-of-commerce theory and making personal jurisdiction decisions on an individual basis by assessing whether the facts support such a finding.[11]

§ 5:3   Pre-filing matters—Venue

Research References
West's Key Number Digest, Patents ⊙288
C.J.S., Patents §§ 461 to 465

While forum shopping has been considerably reduced due to the creation of the Federal Circuit, venue remains an important and often hotly-contested question in patent infringement suits. Parties often perceive a "home-court" advantage, largely associated with travel inconvenience for the parties and their counsel at hearings and trial. A home-court advantage may also be perceived based on favoritism of the judge and jury towards a local entity and employer. The existence of declaratory judgment actions for patent infringement often results in a "race to the courthouse" between the plaintiff and the defendant. Therefore, patent owners need to consider venue possibilities before alleging patent infringement in a cease and desist letter. Otherwise, a cease and desist letter may prompt the accused infringer to file a declaratory judgment action in an inconvenient location.

Congress has provided a specific venue statute that covers patent infringement, 28 U.S.C.A. § 1400(b). This statute provides: "Any civil action for patent infringement may be brought in the

---

[9]Asahi, 480 U.S. at 112, 107 S. Ct. at 1032.

[10]Asahi, 480 U.S. at 117, 107 S. Ct. at 1035 (Brennan, White, Marshall & Blackmun, JJ., concurring in part and concurring in the judgment).

[11]See Beverly Hills Fan, 21 F.3d at 1566; AFTG-TG, LLC v. Nuvoton Technology Corp., 689 F.3d 1358, 1362, 104 U.S.P.Q.2d 1217 (Fed. Cir. 2012).

judicial district where the defendant resides, or where the defendant has committed acts of infringement and has a regular and established place of business."

The general venue statute[1] provides a broad definition of "residence" of a corporate defendant: "[A]n entity with the capacity to sue or be sued in its common name . . . shall be deemed to reside, if a defendant, in any judicial district in which such defendant is subject to the court's personal jurisdiction with respect to the civil action in question." In *V.E. Holding Corp. v. Johnson Gas Appliance Co.*,[2] the Federal Circuit held that the general venue statute applies to corporate defendants in patent infringement suits. Since § 1400(b) allows an action for patent infringement to be brought in any judicial district in which the defendant resides, and § 1391(c) defines the place in which a defendant resides as any district in which the court has personal jurisdiction over the defendant, venue and personal jurisdiction have effectively merged in patent infringement cases involving corporate defendants.

§ 5:4 Pre-filing matters—Statute of limitations

Research References

West's Key Number Digest, Patents ☞289
C.J.S., Patents §§ 437 to 438, 466 to 471

The statute of limitations in patent infringement actions only affects damages. A patentee may not recover damages for infringement that occurred more than six years before the complaint was filed, and no action may be brought more than six years after the patent expires.[1] There is no statute of limitations applicable to injunctions. Actions for patent infringement, however, are inherently limited by the term of a patent. No action for injunction may be brought after expiration of the patent, since the patent holder no longer has the right to exclude others. Patent infringement actions more typically involve equitable limitations on actions, such as laches and estoppel.[2]

§ 5:5 Pre-filing matters—Drafting the complaint

Research References

[Section 5:3]

[1]28 U.S.C.A. § 1391(c).

[2]VE Holding Corp. v. Johnson Gas Appliance Co., 917 F.2d 1574, 16 U.S.P.Q.2d 1614 (Fed. Cir. 1990); In re TC Heartland LLC, 2016 WL 1709433 (Fed. Cir. 2016) (reaffirming the holding of *V.E. Holding Corp* and explaining that Congress did not intend to codify any changes to venue rules when Congress passed the 2011 America Invents Act).

[Section 5:4]

[1]35 U.S.C.A. § 286.

[2]*See infra* § 5:44 regarding laches and § 5:45 regarding estoppel.

West's Key Number Digest, Patents ⚬═286, 310.1
C.J.S., Patents §§ 449 to 452, 472, 476 to 491

Statutory standing to bring a patent infringement suit is conferred upon the owner of a patent.[1] An exclusive licensee can, however, bring suit if the license granted "all substantial rights" in the patent, such that the license is akin to an assignment.[2] When the license is written and exclusive, the licensee is treated as a virtual assignee and therefore has sufficient "ownership" interest to gain standing to sue. The license cannot be verbal or implied because it must resemble an assignment in both form and substance.[3] However, the patent owner may be a necessary party under Rule 19 of the Federal Rules of Civil Procedure.

Complaints in patent infringement suits are relatively straightforward. A complaint for patent infringement includes the usual necessary information, such as identification of the parties; an allegation of subject matter jurisdiction under 28 U.S.C.A. §§ 1331 and 1338(a); an allegation of personal jurisdiction; and an allegation of proper venue under 28 U.S.C.A. §§ 1391(c) and 1400. Under Fed. R. Civ. P. 19 and 20, multiple defendants can be joined in a single action if those defendants are necessary parties or the action arises out of common occurrences or transactions. However, by statute, accused infringers cannot be joined in a patent case based solely on allegations of infringement of the same patent or patents.[4]

The plaintiff must show that it has a right to bring the action by alleging that it is the owner of the patent, either by assignment or otherwise. If the patent owner provided the defendant with constructive notice of its patent through marking, or actual notice of infringement charges through an affirmative communication, this should also be alleged. Finally, the complaint must allege that the defendant has committed infringing acts by making, using, selling, offering for sale or importing a product. The complaint does not usually specify exactly how infringement is occurring or which claims of the patent are believed to be infringed. For allegations of inducement or contributory infringement, the complaint must allege an underlying act of direct infringement that, at a minimum, permits an inference that a direct infringer exists.[5] A copy of the patent or patents involved in the suit is typically attached as an exhibit to the complaint. Although

---

[Section 5:5]

[1] 35 U.S.C.A. § 281.

[2] 35 U.S.C.A. § 286.

[3] Enzo APA & Son, Inc. v. Geapag A.G., 134 F.3d 1090, 45 U.S.P.Q.2d

1368 (Fed. Cir. 1998).

[4] 35 U.S.C.A. § 299.

[5] In re Bill of Lading Transmission and Processing System Patent Litigation, 681 F.3d 1323, 1336, 103 U.S.P.Q.2d 1045 (Fed. Cir. 2012).

patent complaints can be fairly general in nature, it may be advisable to draft a more specific complaint in some circumstances.

The complaint may also include allegations of the defendant's knowledge of the patent; allegations of exceptional circumstances, such as bad faith or willful infringement, supporting a request for treble damages and attorney's fees; allegations of irreparable damage to support a preliminary injunction (often a motion for preliminary injunction is filed with the complaint); and allegations of any other supplemental or pendant causes of action, such as unfair competition or other business torts. Of course, the complaint must also include a request for relief, usually including injunctive relief and damages.[6]

Several states have passed legislation designed to curb bad faith assertion of patent rights by non-practicing entities, better known as "patent trolls."[7] Twenty-one states have enacted legislation concerning the bad faith assertion of patent rights, with legislation having been introduced in fourteen more states. While states cannot pass laws that conflict with the federal patent laws, the states are beginning to try to regulate demand letters that assert claims of patent infringement. Under a typical state law, if a person makes a "bad faith assertion" of patent infringement,[8] the target of the assertion or the attorney general of the state may bring an action seeking equitable relief; damages; costs and fees, including attorney's fees; and punitive damages.[9] Vermont was the first state to pass legislation to prevent bad faith assertions of patent infringement, which provides several non-binding factors for finding bad faith, including:

1) if the demand letter lacks, and does not provide upon request, the patent number, the name and address of the patent owner and assignee, and the factual allegations specific to areas covered by the claims;

2) if there is a lack of an analysis comparing the claims to the accused products, or the analysis does not identify which specific products are covered by the claims;

3) a demand for payment of a license fee within an unreasonably short response period;

4) a license offer "not based on a reasonable estimate of the value of the license";

5) the claim is meritless;

6) the claim is deceptive; or

7) if previous suits based on the same or similar claims lacked

---

[6]An example of a complaint for patent infringement is included in Appendix E.

[7]See, e.g., Vt. Stat. Ann. tit. 9, § 4197.

[8]Vt. Stat. Ann. tit. 9, § 4197(a).

[9]Vt. Stat. Ann. tit. 9, § 4199(b).

the required information, or the previous claim was found meritless.[10]

§ 5:6 Drafting the answer

Research References

West's Key Number Digest, Patents ⬤➝310.7
C.J.S., Patents §§ 472, 476 to 491

Pleading the answer is often more difficult than drafting the original complaint. Some defenses are required to be plead in response to a complaint for patent infringement:

The following shall be defenses in any action involving the validity or infringement of a patent and shall be pleaded:

(1) Non-infringement, absence of liability for infringement or unenforceability. * * *

(2) Invalidity of the patent or any claim in suit on any ground specified * * * as a condition for patentability.[1]

The answer usually includes specific or general allegations of any applicable defenses. "Invalidity" covers several potential theories, and the answer often lists sections of the patent statute which are alleged to provide the basis for invalidity. Also, the answer frequently alleges any known equitable defenses, such as laches, estoppel, license, etc. However, failure to disclose the best mode for carrying out the invention is no longer a basis for finding a claim invalid or unenforceable, and therefore cannot be plead as a defense.[2] In addition to the general pleading requirements of § 282, some courts have ruled that the defense of "fraud on the Patent Office" or "inequitable conduct" falls under the special matters provisions of Rule 9(b).[3] "In alleging fraud or mistake, a party must state with particularity the circumstances constituting fraud or mistake."[4]

It is common practice to assert counterclaims of noninfringement and invalidity in an answer to a charge of patent infringement. A counterclaim prevents a court from dismissing a case if no infringement is found, or if the plaintiff withdraws its complaint. If a finding of validity is raised in a declaratory judgment by a lower court, the Federal Circuit must review that find-

---

[10]Vt. Stat. Ann. tit. 9, § 4197(b). The statutes further provide factors that weight against a finding of bad faith (i.e., evidence of good faith). Vt. Stat. Ann. tit. 9, § 4197(c).

[Section 5:6]

[1]35 U.S.C.A. § 282(b).

[2]35 U.S.C.A. § 282(b)(3)(A).

[3]Exergen Corp. v. Wal-Mart Stores, Inc., 575 F.3d 1312, 91 U.S.P. Q.2d 1656 (Fed. Cir. 2009).

[4]Fed. R. Civ. P. 9(b).

ing regardless of the holding on infringement.[5]

§ 5:7 Rule 11 considerations

Research References

West's Key Number Digest, Federal Civil Procedure ⚖2771(8); Patents ⚖325.1

C.J.S., Federal Civil Procedure §§ 1360, 1371, 1374; Patents §§ 529 to 533

Before bringing a complaint for patent infringement, a practitioner should perform an objective evaluation of the claims to be asserted and should verify at least the following facts:

- that the plaintiff has an ownership interest in the patent, either as the inventor, through written assignment, or as an exclusive licensee under 35 U.S.C.A. § 261,

- that the patent has not expired, such as through failure to pay maintenance fees,

- that the named defendant is involved with the product or act complained of,

- that the product or act complained of includes each and every element within at least one claim of the patent, and

- that the defendant does not have permission or authorization under the patent.

Often, the answer needs to include allegations of defenses for which there has not been opportunity for sufficient investigation. These statements should be prefaced by "based on a reasonable opportunity for further investigation or discovery," "based on information and belief," or similar language to avoid the possibility of Rule 11 violations.[1]

Failure to adhere to the requirements of Fed. R. Civ. P. 11 can result in sanctions. Rule 11 sanctions in patent cases are assessed under regional circuit standards[2] and can include expenses and attorney fees.

§ 5:8 Patent office procedures involving issued patents

---

[5]An example of an Answer in a patent infringement case is included in Appendix F.

[Section 5:7]

[1]Fed.R.Civ.P. 11(b).

[2]Eon-Net LP v. Flagstar Bancorp, 653 F.3d 1314, 99 U.S.P.Q.2d 1522 (Fed. Cir. 2011).

Research References
West's Key Number Digest, Patents ⊕134 to 148
C.J.S., Patents §§ 237 to 260

Issued patents may have defects that the patent owner wishes to correct or a third party wishes to challenge. Often the investigation leading up to and surrounding commencement of litigation uncovers such a defect. Additional prior art may be discovered that is more pertinent than the art reviewed during prosecution of the patent. Claims of a patent may have errors in wording that need to be corrected. Reissue, post-grant and inter partes review, reexamination, and supplemental examination proceedings provide an opportunity to address and potentially correct such problems, and should be considered before, or contemporaneously with, filing a complaint or answer.

Reissue proceedings allow the claims of the patent to be substantively amended after issuance of the patent. During the first two years after issuance of the patent, claims may be broadened through a reissue proceeding;[1] however, claim scope that was surrendered during the original prosecution cannot be recaptured.[2] After more than two years, only narrowing amendments are considered in a reissue proceeding.[3] To initiate a reissue, the patentee must file an application for reissue alleging that an error occurred during the prosecution of the patent which renders the patent wholly or partly inoperative or invalid. The USPTO lists initiations of reissue and reexamination proceedings in the Official Gazette.

A reexamination proceeding essentially involves reviewing the patent in light of newly discovered prior art. The reexamination proceeding can be instituted by either the patent holder or a third party.[4] If a third party requests an *ex parte* reexamination based on newly discovered prior art, the third party is entitled to an initial statement of the newly discovered art, but generally is not permitted to further participate in the reexamination proceeding. Courts are not obligated to stay co-pending patent infringement suits during reexamination, but may do so at their own discretion.[5]

Like reexamination, supplemental examination proceedings allow a patent owner to put new information before the patent

---

[Section 5:8]

[1]35 U.S.C.A. § 251.

[2]Medtronic, Inc. v. Guidant Corp., 465 F.3d 1360, 1373, 80 U.S.P.Q.2d 1558 (Fed. Cir. 2006).

[3]35 U.S.C.A. § 251.

[4]35 U.S.C.A. § 302.

[5]Viskase Corp. v. American Nat. Can Co., 261 F.3d 1316, 1328, 59 U.S.P. Q.2d 1823 (Fed. Cir. 2001), *see also* Card Technology Corp. v. DataCard Corp., 2007 WL 2156320 (D. Minn. 2007).

office. Unlike in ex parte reexamination proceedings, this new information need not be limited to patents and printed publications. Supplemental examination proceedings completed prior to filing an infringement suit foreclose inequitable conduct defenses based on any art submitted to the USPTO with the request for supplemental examination.

When the subject matter of a patent in a reissue or reexamination proceeding is simultaneously involved in litigation, the existence of the litigation must be brought to the attention of the USPTO. If the litigation has raised questions of possible prior public use or sales, questions of inventorship, prior art, allegations of fraud, inequitable conduct, or violation of the duty of disclosure, those issues must be brought to the attention of the USPTO as well.[6] "Enough information should be submitted to clearly inform the Office of the nature of these issues so that the Office can intelligently evaluate the need for asking for further materials in the litigation."[7] Litigation relating to a patent is material to the reissue proceedings involving that patent; therefore, it may be appropriate to suspend reissue proceedings until such litigation is resolved.[8] Where reexamination proceedings and litigation are co-pending and the reexamination proceedings become final before there is a final judgment in the litigation, such that all that is left for the district court to do is execute the judgment, then any invalidation of the claims in the reexamination proceedings will be binding on the co-pending litigation.[9]

Third parties seeking to invalidate an issued patent may petition for a post grant review or inter partes review or utilize the transitional program for business method patents. These proceedings are discussed in greater detail in Chapter 3. Post grant review, inter partes review, and the transitional program allow a petitioning third party to participate in litigation-like proceedings with limited discovery and an accelerated timetable. At any time within nine months of issuance, third parties may petition for post grant review of patents with effective filing dates on or after March 16, 2013.[10] After nine months have elapsed, third parties may instead petition for inter partes review. Post grant

---

[6]Manual of Patent Examining Procedure § 2001.06(c) (8th ed., Revised August 2012).

[7]M.P.E.P § 2001.06(c).

[8]Critikon, Inc. v. Becton Dickinson Vascular Access, Inc., 120 F.3d 1253, 43 U.S.P.Q.2d 1666 (Fed. Cir. 1997); but see, Vitronics Corp. v. Conceptronic, Inc., 36 F. Supp. 2d 440, 44 U.S.P.Q.2d 1536 (D.N.H. 1997) (not-

ing that it would be efficient to suspend litigation until reissue proceedings are complete); Speedplay, Inc. v. Bebop, Inc., 211 F.3d 1245, 53 U.S.P. Q.2d 1984 (Fed. Cir. 2000).

[9]Fresenius USA, Inc. v. Baxter Intern., Inc., 721 F.3d 1330, 1339–41, 107 U.S.P.Q.2d 1365 (Fed. Cir. 2013), cert. denied, 134 S. Ct. 2295 (2014).

[10]35 U.S.C.A. §§ 321(c), 322(a).

review and the transitional program may address potential claim invalidity based on the requirements of novelty, non-obviousness, patentable subject matter, and written description, while inter partes review may only address issues of novelty and non-obviousness.[11] Civil actions on a patent by petitioners for post grant or inter partes review are automatically stayed when review proceedings are initiated.[12] Whether a civil action on a patent by petitioners for the transitional program is stayed depends on four factors:

- whether a stay will simplify the issues in question and streamline the trial;
- whether discovery is complete and whether a trial date has been set;
- whether a stay would unduly prejudice the nonmoving party or present a clear tactical advantage for the moving party; and
- whether a stay will reduce the burden of litigation on the parties and on the court.[13]

§ 5:9 Declaratory judgment actions

Research References
West's Key Number Digest, Declaratory Judgment ⊙231, 320
C.J.S., Declaratory Judgments §§ 97 to 101

Declaratory judgment actions often arise in the patent infringement context. The Declaratory Judgment Act[1] provides that in a case of actual controversy, a U.S. court may declare the rights of any interested party seeking declaration. A party charged with patent infringement may bring a declaratory judgment action against the patent holder prior to being sued for infringement, and thereby select the venue for the lawsuit. Conversely, the defendant in a patent infringement suit that has already been filed will often bring declaratory judgment counterclaims of noninfringement, invalidity and unenforceability of the patent. Declaratory judgment actions allow potential competitors to determine whether a market is open to them without requiring them to commit their resources to an activity that could result in

---

[11]35 U.S.C.A. §§ 311(b), 314(a), 322(a).

[12]35 U.S.C.A. §§ 315(a)(2), 325(a)(2).

[13]Leahy-Smith America Invents Act, Pub. L. No. 112-19, § 18(b), 125

Stat. 284, 331 (2011); see also, e.g., Smartflash LLC v. Apple, Inc., 2014 WL 3366661 (E.D. Tex. 2014).

[Section 5:9]

[1]28 U.S.C.A. § 2201.

patent infringement and liability for damages.[2]

A ruling by a district court that a patent is unenforceable may be appealed to the Federal Circuit regardless of infringement.[3] However, the defendant must have filed a declaratory judgment counterclaim in order to provide the Federal Circuit with jurisdiction over an invalidity or unenforceability appeal separate from its jurisdiction over an infringement appeal.

In order for a defendant to initiate a declaratory judgement action, there must be an "actual controversy" between the parties. In the patent context, there must be an actual or implicit charge of infringement and the actual controversy must be present before the declaratory judgment action is ripe for adjudication. There are two prerequisites for establishing the existence of a case of actual controversy between the parties: (1) the patent holder must have engaged in conduct giving rise to a reasonable apprehension on defendant's part that it will face an infringement suit or the threat of one if it commences or continues the activity in question and (2) the defendant must have actually produced the accused device or have actually prepared to produce it.[4]

The defendant has the burden of establishing by a preponderance of the evidence that it has a reasonable apprehension that it will be sued based on the actions of the patent holder. Whether the party's conduct was sufficient to create an actual controversy is a question of law based on the totality of the circumstances.[5]

A patent licensee is not required to breach or terminate a license agreement in order to establish standing for bringing a declaratory judgment action.[6] So long as a licensee continues to make royalty payments to the licensor, the licensor has no reason to seek to enjoin the licensee's sales, and the licensee thus faces no imminent threat of harm. In such a situation, however, the licensee may still bring a declaratory judgment action against the licensor even though the threat of harm to the licensee appears remote.[7] Additionally, even in a declaratory judgment action alleging noninfringement brought by the licensee, the patent holder bears the burden of proving infringement rather than the licensee

---

[2]Akzona Inc. v. E.I. du Pont de Nemours & Co., 662 F. Supp. 603, 609, 9 Int'l Trade Rep. (BNA) 1266, 4 U.S.P. Q.2d 1113, 1116 (D. Del. 1987).

[3]Cardinal Chemical Co. v. Morton Intern., Inc., 508 U.S. 83, 113 S. Ct. 1967, 26 U.S.P.Q.2d 1721 (1993).

[4]Cordis Corp. v. Medtronic, Inc., 835 F.2d 859, 862, 5 U.S.P.Q.2d 1118, 1120, 97 A.L.R. Fed. 683 (Fed. Cir. 1987).

[5]Shell Oil Co. v. Amoco Corp., 970 F.2d 885, 888, 23 U.S.P.Q.2d 1627, 1629 (Fed. Cir. 1992).

[6]MedImmune, Inc. v. Genentech, Inc., 549 U.S. 118, 127 S. Ct. 764, 777, 81 U.S.P.Q.2d 1225, 2007-1 Trade Cas. (CCH) ¶ 75543 (2007).

[7]MedImmune, 127 S.Ct. at 772–773, 777.

bearing the burden of proving noninfringement.[8] Moreover, the case or controversy clause of Article III does not require that a party risk treble damages and a large percentage of its business before seeking a declaration of its legal rights.[9]

Because a patent holder's willingness and capacity to enforce its patent rights is pertinent to the inquiry for declaratory judgement jurisdiction, a patent holder should carefully word any letter that it sends to an accused infringer in order to avoid creating a case or controversy.[10]

§ 5:10   Infringing acts—Direct infringement

Research References

West's Key Number Digest, Patents ☞226 to 226.8
C.J.S., Patents §§ 400, 404, 406 to 407, 413 to 417, 419, 421

A person directly infringes a patent by making, using, offering to sell, selling, or importing into the United States any patented invention without authority during the term of the patent.[1] Prior to December 8, 1995, the acts of offering to sell and importing were not considered to be infringing absent making, using or selling.

A person may directly infringe a patent by impermissibly reconstructing a patented item that has been "spent." However, a purchaser of a patented article is permitted to repair the article during its useful life.[2] The factors to be considered in determining whether the accused infringer has reconstructed an article that has been spent include the nature of the accused infringer's actions, the nature of the device and how it is designed (specifically, whether one component of the patented combination has a shorter useful life than the whole), whether the market has developed to manufacture or service the part at issue, and objective evidence of the patentee's intent.[3] The boundary between "permissible repair" and "impermissible reconstruction" does not turn on the patentee's intent for a component to be disposable in lieu of refilled or repaired, since the purchaser's freedom to repair or modify its own product is overridden under the patent laws only by the patentee's right to exclude a purchaser from making a

---

[8]Medtronic, Inc. v. Mirowski Family Ventures, LLC, 134 S. Ct. 843, 187 L. Ed. 2d 703, 109 U.S.P.Q.2d 1341 (2014).

[9]MedImmune, 127 S. Ct. at 775.

[10]West Interactive Corp. v. First Data Resources, Inc., 972 F.2d 1295, 1298, 23 U.S.P.Q.2d 1927, 1930 (Fed. Cir. 1992).

[Section 5:10]

[1]35 U.S.C.A. § 271(a).

[2]See, e.g., Standard Havens Products, Inc. v. Gencor Industries, Inc., 953 F.2d 1360, 1376, 21 U.S.P. Q.2d 1321, 1333 (Fed. Cir. 1991).

[3]Aktiebolag v. E.J. Co., 121 F.3d 669, 43 U.S.P.Q.2d 1620 (Fed. Cir. 1997).

new patented entity.[4]

A defendant with control over an accused process or product cannot avoid infringement by directing someone else to perform one or more of the acts required for infringement:

> [O]ne may infringe a patent if he employ[s] an agent for that purpose or has the offending articles manufactured for him by an independent contractor. We do not agree that it is necessary that [defendant] himself be a manufacturer of the alleged infringing devices or that he have machinery or manufacturing facilities or employees to make them or a written or an oral contract for supplies for such manufacture.[5]

There can be no direct patent infringement unless a single entity practices every element of at least one valid claim, either literally or under the doctrine of equivalents. This issue is frequently referred to as that of divided infringement or split infringement. Where multiple independent parties practice different parts of an invention, no joint liability for direct infringement arises. Joint liability for direct infringement may arise if the parties are in a principal-agent relationship, a contractual arrangement, or a joint enterprise.[6] Additionally, "when an alleged infringer conditions participation in an activity or receipt of a benefit upon performance of a step or steps of a patented method and establishes the manner or timing of that performance[,]" a third party's actions can be attributed to the alleged infringer such that the alleged infringer "becomes the single actor chargeable with direct infringement."[7] Individually non-infringing actions by multiple parties may give rise to vicarious liability for direct infringement, however, if one entity directs and controls the infringing acts of another.[8]

§ 5:11   Infringing acts—Active inducement of infringement

Research References

---

[4]Hewlett-Packard Co. v. Repeat-O-Type Stencil Mfg. Corp., Inc., 123 F.3d 1445, 43 U.S.P.Q.2d 1650 (Fed. Cir. 1997); Ninestar Technology Co., Ltd. v. International Trade Com'n, 667 F.3d 1373, 33 Int'l Trade Rep. (BNA) 1945, 101 U.S.P.Q.2d 1603 (Fed. Cir. 2012).

[5]Crowell v. Baker Oil Tools, 143 F.2d 1003, 1004, 62 U.S.P.Q. 176 (C.C.A. 9th Cir. 1944).

[6]Akamai Technologies, Inc v. Limelight Networks, Inc., 786 F.3d 899, 114 U.S.P.Q.2d 1749 (Fed. Cir. 2015).

[7]Akamai Techs., Inc. v. Limelight Networks, Inc., Nos. 2009-1372, 2009-1380, 2009-1416, 2009-1417, 2015 WL 4760450, at *5 (Fed. Cir. Aug. 13, 2015) (en banc) (citing Metro-Goldwyn-Mayer Studios Inc. v. Grokster, Ltd., 545 U.S. 913, 930 (2005)).

[8]Muniauction, Inc. v. Thomson Corp., 532 F.3d 1318, 1329, 87 U.S.P. Q.2d 1350 (Fed. Cir. 2008).

West's Key Number Digest, Patents ☞259
C.J.S., Patents §§ 427 to 430

Under 35 U.S.C.A. § 271(b), "[w]hoever actively induces infringement of a patent shall be liable as an infringer." This section of the patent statute protects the patent holder against one who advises, encourages, or otherwise induces others to engage in infringing conduct.[1] This section of the patent statute protects the patent holder against one who aids and abets a direct infringer; the statute's goal is to prevent infringement by imposing liability upon one who intends to infringe by selling a component of a combination patent.[2] However, there can be no liability for active inducement of infringement without at least one act of direct infringement under 35 U.S.C.A. § 271(a).[3]

Establishing active inducement of infringement requires proof that, once the defendants knew of the patent, they actively and knowingly aided and abetted in another's infringement.[4] Mere knowledge of possible infringement is not enough; the inducer must have an affirmative intent to cause infringement.[5] Moreover, inducement requires evidence of culpable conduct, directed to encouraging another's infringement.[6] To show that a defendant knowingly committed an act to induce infringement, a plaintiff must prove that the defendant knew that the invention was both *patented* and *infringed*. A defendant can also be found to have committed induced infringement where the defendant had a good faith belief that the patent was invalid.[7] Even where the defendant lacks actual knowledge that the invention was patented, there can still be liability for induced infringement, but to establish liability the plaintiff must prove that the defendant had more than a "known risk" that the induced acts were infringing, because establishing a "known risk" alone would allow a finding of inducement based on recklessness or negligence.[8] The knowledge requirement for induced infringement is satisfied,

---

[Section 5:11]

[1]Limelight Networks, Inc. v. Akamai Technologies, Inc., 134 S. Ct. 2111, 2118, 110 U.S.P.Q.2d 1681 (2014).

[2]Water Technologies Corp. v. Calco, Ltd., 850 F.2d 660, 668, 7 U.S.P. Q.2d 1097, 1100 (Fed. Cir. 1988); Jones v. Radio Corp. of America, 131 F. Supp. 82, 83, 106 U.S.P.Q. 170, 171 (S.D. N.Y. 1955) (abrogated by, National Presto Industries, Inc. v. West Bend Co., 76 F.3d 1185, 37 U.S.P.Q.2d 1685 (Fed. Cir. 1996)) (*citing* S. Rep. No. 82-1979, 2d Sess. (1952)).

[3]Limelight Networks, Inc., 134 S.Ct. at 2117.

[4]Water Technologies Corp. v. Calco, Ltd., 850 F.2d 660, 668, 7 U.S.P. Q.2d 1097 (Fed. Cir. 1988).

[5]DSU Medical Corp. v. JMS Co., Ltd., 471 F.3d 1293, 1305–06, 81 U.S.P. Q.2d 1238 (Fed. Cir. 2006).

[6]DSU Medical, 471 F.3d at 1306.

[7]Commil USA, LLC v. Cisco Systems, Inc., 135 S. Ct. 1920, 1931, 191 L. Ed. 2d 883, 114 U.S.P.Q.2d 1577 (2015).

[8]Commil USA, LLC v. Cisco

however, where the defendant is willfully blind to the fact that the invention was patented and infringed; in other words, where the defendant deliberately prevents itself from obtaining "clear evidence of critical facts that are strongly suggested by the circumstances."[9] This is the same showing required for the "knowing" element of contributory infringement discussed below.[10]

In addition, corporate officers who actively aid and abet their corporation's infringement may be personally liable for inducing infringement regardless of whether the corporation is the alter ego of the corporate officer. Because officers may be held liable for the acts of the corporation, if the corporation is found to be a willful infringer, then its officers may also be liable as willful infringers.[11]

§ 5:12   Infringing acts—Contributory infringement

Research References
West's Key Number Digest, Patents ⊗259
C.J.S., Patents §§ 427 to 430

Contributory infringement is defined in 35 U.S.C.A. § 271(c):

Whoever offers to sell or sells within the United States or imports into the United States a component of a patented machine, manufacture, combination or composition, or a material or apparatus for use in practicing a patented process, constituting a material part of the invention, knowing the same to be especially made or especially adapted for use in an infringement of such patent, and not a staple article or commodity of commerce suitable for substantial noninfringing use, shall be liable as a contributory infringer.

According to the Supreme Court, the "knowing" element of § 271(c) requires a showing "that the alleged contributory infringer knew that the combination for which his component was especially designed was both *patented* and *infringing*."[1] There

---

Systems, Inc., 720 F.3d 1361, 1366, 107 U.S.P.Q.2d 1290 (Fed. Cir. 2013), petition for certiorari filed, 135 S. Ct. 752, 190 L. Ed. 2d 474 (2014) and judgment vacated, 135 S. Ct. 1920, 191 L. Ed. 2d 883, 114 U.S.P.Q.2d 1577 (2015).

[9]Global-Tech Appliances, Inc. v. SEB S.A., 131 S. Ct. 2060, 2068–2069, 179 L. Ed. 2d 1167, 98 U.S.P.Q.2d 1665 (2011).

[10]Aro Mfg. Co. v. Convertible Top Replacement Co., 377 U.S. 476, 488,

84 S. Ct. 1526, 1552, 141 U.S.P.Q. 681, 700 (1964) ("*Aro II*").

[11]Orthokinetics, Inc. v. Safety Travel Chairs, Inc., 806 F.2d 1565, 1578-79, 1 U.S.P.Q.2d 1081, 1090 (Fed. Cir. 1986).

[Section 5:12]

[1]Aro II, 377 U.S. at 488, 84 S. Ct. at 1552, 12 L.Ed.2d 457, 141 U.S.P.Q. at 687 (emphasis added).

can be no contributory infringement without direct infringement.[2]

In general, it is not an infringing act to make or use a patented product outside of the United States.[3] Section 271(f) addresses contributory infringement for components that originate in the United States, but that are assembled into a patented invention in a foreign country. Section 271(f)(1) states:

> Whoever without authority supplies or causes to be supplied in or from the United States all or a substantial portion of the components of a patented invention, where such components are uncombined in whole or in part, in such manner as to actively induce the combination of such components outside of the United States in a manner that would infringe the patent if such combination occurred within the United States, shall be liable as an infringer.

The Supreme Court has held that when a master version of software is used to generate copies, and the copies, rather than the master, are installed on a foreign manufacturer's computers, the software, in the abstract, is not a component for purposes of § 271(f).[4] On the other hand, a copy of the software, once it is in a tangible medium, is considered a component.[5] But when the copies are made outside of the United States, the component is not supplied from the United States, and thus does not violate § 271(f).[6] The Federal Circuit has further limited the scope of § 271(f) by finding that it does not apply to method or process patents.[7]

A supplier or manufacturer can be found contributorily liable for providing a component that is used in a patented machine or combination.[8] Because there can be no contributory infringement without direct infringement,[9] the component must be supplied to and/or manufactured for a party that is engaging in "impermissible reconstruction" rather than "permissible repair."[10] See Section 5:10 for a discussion on what constitutes direct infringement

---

[2]Deepsouth Packing Co. v. Laitram Corp., 406 U.S. 518, 526, 92 S. Ct. 1700, 1706, 173 U.S.P.Q. 769, 772 (1972); Met-Coil Systems Corp. v. Korners Unlimited, Inc., 803 F.2d 684, 687, 231 U.S.P.Q. 474, 476 (Fed. Cir. 1986).

[3]Deepsouth Packing, 406 U.S. at 527, 92 S. Ct. at 1706.

[4]Microsoft Corp. v. AT & T Corp., 550 U.S. 437, 127 S. Ct. 1746, 82 U.S.P.Q.2d 1400, 33 A.L.R. Fed. 2d 745 (2007).

[5]Microsoft, 127 S. Ct. at 1756.

[6]Microsoft, 127 S. Ct. at 1756–

57.

[7]Cardiac Pacemakers, Inc. v. St. Jude Medical, Inc., 576 F.3d 1348, 1364, 91 U.S.P.Q.2d 1898 (Fed. Cir. 2009), cert. denied, 130 S. Ct. 1088 (2010).

[8]See 35 U.S.C.A. § 271(c).

[9]Deepsouth Packing Co., 406 U.S. at 526; Met-Coil Systems Corp., 803 F.2d at 687.

[10]See Aro II, 377 U.S. at 482–484; see also Kendall Co. v. Progressive Medical Technology, Inc., 85 F.3d 1570, 1576, 38 U.S.P.Q.2d 1917 (Fed. Cir. 1996).

through "impermissible reconstruction."

§ 5:13 Establishing patent infringement—Claim construction

Determining patent infringement is a two-step process. First, the claims must be properly construed to determine their scope and meaning. Second, the claims, as properly construed, must be compared to the accused device.[1]

As a result of the holding in the *Markman* case, claim construction is typically done early in the patent litigation process during a separate claim construction hearing commonly called a *Markman* hearing.[2] Claim construction is a question of law for the court to decide.[3] Because claim construction is a question of law, it is reviewed *de novo* on appeal.[4] However, the underlying determinations of subsidiary factual matters made in the course of claim construction are reviewed under the clearly erroneous standard.[5] The procedures and timeline for *Markman* hearings vary, though some districts may outline procedures in local rules. A *Markman* hearing may take place before discovery closes, often along with a motion for preliminary injunction. A *Markman* hearing may also take place at the end of discovery, often in relation to a motion for summary judgment, or may take place after the trial begins but before jury selection. A *Markman* hearing is not required; the court can approach claim construction in any way it deems best.[6] However, a *Markman* hearing can assist in clearly construing the claims in the context of the accused products, often leading to settlement before parties in a case incur significant expenses due to expert witness and trial costs.

Where the claims are construed in a prior litigation, collateral estoppel may apply to that construction and the patent holder will be bound to that construction.[7] Whether collateral estoppel applies is determined by the law of the regional circuit where the

---

[Section 5:13]

[1]Lantech, Inc. v. Keip Mach. Co., 32 F.3d 542, 546, 31 U.S.P.Q.2d 1666, 1669 (Fed. Cir. 1994).

[2]Markman v. Westview Instruments, Inc., 52 F.3d 967, 970, 34 U.S.P.Q.2d 1321 (Fed. Cir. 1995), aff'd, 517 U.S. 370, 116 S. Ct. 1384, 134 L. Ed. 2d 577, 38 U.S.P.Q.2d 1461 (1996).

[3]Markman, 52 F.3d at 979.

[4]*See* Markman v. Westview Instruments, Inc., 517 U.S. 370, 390,

116 S. Ct. 1384, 1384, 134 L. Ed. 2d 577, 38 U.S.P.Q.2d 1461 (1996).

[5]Teva Pharmaceuticals USA, Inc. v. Sandoz, Inc., 135 S. Ct. 831, 835, 113 U.S.P.Q.2d 1269 (2015).

[6]Ballard Medical Products v. Allegiance Healthcare Corp., 268 F.3d 1352, 1358, 60 U.S.P.Q.2d 1493 (Fed. Cir. 2001).

[7]*See* RF Delaware, Inc. v. Pacific Keystone Technologies, Inc., 326 F.3d 1255, 66 U.S.P.Q.2d 1593 (Fed. Cir. 2003).

subsequent litigation takes place.[8] However, where the district court in the prior litigation merely issues a claim construction without holding an evidentiary hearing to construe the claims, then it is unlikely that that construction will be binding in the subsequent litigation, because the party will not have had a chance to be "fully heard."[9] In addition, collateral estoppel is only operable against a party that was fully heard in a prior litigation; thus, while it may operate to bar the patent holder from arguing a new claim construction, the defendant will almost never be estopped from arguing a new claim construction.

The meaning of some claim language may be apparent on its face, in which case the language is given its plain and ordinary meaning to a person of ordinary skill in the art without need for further interpretation. The meaning of other claim terms may be disputed, however, and may require interpretation by the court to properly construe the claim language. To this end, the Federal Circuit has clarified the guidelines that should be used by courts during claim construction. The purpose of the guidelines is to increase the likelihood that a court will comprehend how a person of ordinary skill in the art would have understood the claim terms in context.[10] Although the guidelines do not provide a step-by-step methodology to proper claim construction, they do outline the relative weight that should be given to each source of evidence, as well as the benefits and detriments of each source.[11]

In determining the scope and meaning of claims at issue, the claims themselves provide "substantial guidance as to the meaning of particular claim terms."[12] For instance, the context of the surrounding words in a claim may provide guidance as to the proper definition of a disputed term.[13] The use of the same term in other claims, as well as differences among the claims, may also be useful in understanding the meaning of a particular claim term.[14] The claims, however, are part of a fully integrated written instrument that includes the written description, making the written description or specification highly relevant to the claim construction process, and typically "the single best guide to the meaning of a disputed [claim] term."[15] The importance of the specification in properly construing claim language is summarized by the following quote from the Federal Circuit:

Ultimately, the interpretation to be given a term can only be

---

[8]RF Delaware, 326 F.3d at 1261.

[9]RF Delaware, 326 F.3d at 1262.

[10]Phillips v. AWH Corp., 415 F.3d 1303, 75 U.S.P.Q.2d 1321 (Fed. Cir. 2005) (en banc).

[11]Phillips, 415 F.3d at 1324.

[12]Phillips, 415 F.3d at 1314.

[13]Phillips, 415 F.3d at 1314.

[14]Phillips, 415 F.3d at 1314.

[15]Phillips, 415 F.3d at 1315, citing Vitronics Corp. v. Conceptronic, Inc., 90 F.3d 1576, 1582, 39 U.S.P.Q.2d 1573 (Fed. Cir. 1996).

determined and confirmed with a full understanding of what the inventors actually invented and intended to envelop with the claim. The construction that stays true to the claim language and most naturally aligns with the patent's description of the invention will be, in the end, the correct construction.[16]

A fine line is drawn between determining the scope and meaning of claim language based on the specification, which is proper, and adding or importing limitations to the claims from the specification, which is improper:

> If everything in the specification were required to be read into the claims, or if structural claims were to be limited to devices operated precisely as the specification-described embodiment is operated, there would be no need for claims. Nor could an applicant, regardless of the prior art, claim more broadly than that embodiment. Nor would a basis remain for the statutory necessity that an applicant conclude his specification with "claims particularly pointing out and distinctly claiming the subject matter which the applicant regards as his invention."[17]

"It is the *claims* that measure the invention."[18] "A limitation may not be read into a claim to avoid infringement," especially when "the limitation sought to be 'read into' a claim already appears in another claim."[19]

In addition to consulting the claims and the specification, the court "should also consider the patent's prosecution history."[20] The prosecution history provides insight into how the patent examiner and the inventor understood the patent.[21] "[T]he prosecution history can often inform the meaning of the claim language by demonstrating how the inventor understood the invention and whether the inventor limited the invention in the course of prosecution, making the claim scope narrower than it would otherwise be."[22] "Prosecution history limits the interpretation of claim terms so as to exclude any interpretation that was disclaimed during

---

[16]Phillips, 415 F.3d at 1316, *citing* Renishaw PLC v. Marposs Societa' per Azioni, 158 F.3d 1243, 1250, 48 U.S.P.Q.2d 1117 (Fed. Cir. 1998).

[17]SRI Intern. v. Matsushita Elec. Corp. of America, 775 F.2d 1107, 1121, 227 U.S.P.Q. 577, 585 (Fed. Cir. 1985) (en banc) (citations omitted) *citing* 35 U.S.C.A. § 112; *see also* Liebel-Flarsheim Co. v. Medrad, Inc., 358 F.3d 898, 904, 69 U.S.P.Q.2d 1801 (Fed. Cir. 2004); Kraft Foods, Inc. v. International Trading Co., 203 F.3d 1362, 1366, 53 U.S.P.Q.2d 1814 (Fed.

Cir. 2000); Anchor Wall Systems, Inc. v. Rockwood Retaining Walls, Inc., 340 F.3d 1298, 1306-1307, 67 U.S.P.Q.2d 1865 (Fed. Cir. 2003).

[18]SRI Int'l, 775 F.2d at 1121.

[19]D.M.I., Inc. v. Deere & Co., 755 F.2d 1570, 1574, 225 U.S.P.Q. 236, 237 (Fed. Cir. 1985).

[20]Phillips, 415 F.3d at 1317, *citing* Vitronics, 90 F.3d at 1582.

[21]Phillips, 415 F.3d at 1317.

[22]Phillips, 415 F.3d at 1317, *citing* Vitronics, 90 F.3d at 1582–83.

prosecution."[23] "Claims may not be construed one way in order to obtain their allowance and in a contrary way against infringers."[24] However, "because the prosecution history represents an ongoing negotiation between the P.T.O. and the applicant, rather than the final product of that negotiation, it often lacks the clarity of the specification and thus is less useful for claim construction purposes."[25]

Although the intrinsic evidence is the most important tool a court has in properly interpreting claim language, the court may also rely on extrinsic evidence, which consists of evidence external to the patent and prosecution history, and includes expert and inventor testimony, dictionaries, and learned treatises.[26] However, although a court is not barred from considering any of the sources discussed above, the court is prohibited from using extrinsic evidence to contradict claim meaning that is unambiguous in light of the intrinsic evidence.[27]

While useful in some circumstances, extrinsic evidence in general is less reliable than the patent and its prosecution history. For instance, one of the problems with extrinsic evidence is that there is "virtually an unbounded universe of potential extrinsic evidence of some marginal relevance that could be brought to bear on any claim construction question."[28] Furthermore, undue or unnecessary reliance on extrinsic evidence "poses the risk that it will be used to change the meaning of claims in derogation of the 'indisputable public records consisting of the claims, the specification and the prosecution history,' thereby undermining the public notice function of patents."[29]

Because claim construction is a question of law for the court, it is reviewed on appeal *de novo*.[30] However, when reviewing subsidiary factual matters made in the course of the court's claim construction, the appellate court must apply the "clearly erroneous" standard of review.[31] Subsidiary factual matters arise when the court uses extrinsic evidence to aid in determining the mean-

---

[23]Southwall Technologies, Inc. v. Cardinal IG Co., 54 F.3d 1570, 1576, 34 U.S.P.Q.2d 1673 (Fed. Cir. 1995).

[24]Tandon Corp. v. U.S. Intern. Trade Com'n, 5 Fed. Cir. (T) 129, 831 F.2d 1017, 1021, 9 Int'l Trade Rep. (BNA) 1330, 4 U.S.P.Q.2d 1283 (1987).

[25]Phillips, 415 F.3d at 1317.

[26]Phillips, 415 F.3d at 1317, *citing* Markman, 52 F.3d at 980, *citing* Seymour v. Osborne, 78 U.S. 516, 20

L. Ed. 33, 1870 WL 12828 (1870); *see also* Vitronics, 90 F.3d at 1583.

[27]Phillips, 415 F.3d at 1318.

[28]Phillips, 415 F.3d at 1318.

[29]Phillips, 415 F.3d at 1319, *citing* Southwall Techs., 54 F.3d at 1578.

[30]Markman, 52 F.3d at 979.

[31]Teva Pharmaceuticals USA, Inc. v. Sandoz, Inc., 135 S. Ct. 831, 831, 113 U.S.P.Q.2d 1269 (2015).

ing of a claim.[32]

§ 5:14 Establishing patent infringement—Literal infringement

Research References

West's Key Number Digest, Patents ⚖157(1), 159, 161, 226.6
C.J.S., Patents §§ 270 to 272, 274, 277 to 279, 282, 285 to 286, 413 to 415, 419, 421

After claim construction is complete, the second step in determining infringement is to decide whether properly interpreted claims encompass the allegedly infringing device.[1] "[T]he accused device must be compared to the claim language as interpreted."[2] To find infringement, each element of a claim (or its substantial equivalent) must be present in the accused device.[3] Each claim of a patent must be considered individually, and infringement of even a single claim requires a finding that the patent is infringed.[4]

Literal infringement may be found if an accused device or method falls entirely within the scope of the asserted claims once properly construed, but there is no literal infringement if any claim limitation is absent from the accused device or method.[5] For a finding of literal infringement, each limitation of the asserted claim must be exactly met by the accused device or method. A deviation of the accused device or method from the claim will preclude a finding of literal infringement.[6]

§ 5:15 Establishing patent infringement—Infringement of a means plus function claim

Research References

West's Key Number Digest, Patents ⚖226.7
C.J.S., Patents §§ 413 to 414, 416 to 417, 419, 421

Certain patent claims are written as "means plus function claims." This special kind of claim is allowed by 35 U.S.C.A.

---

[32]Teva Pharm. USA, 135 S.Ct. at 845–846.

[Section 5:14]

[1]Read Corp. v. Portec, Inc., 970 F.2d 816, 821, 23 U.S.P.Q.2d 1426, 1431 (Fed. Cir. 1992).

[2]Read Corp., 970 F.2d at 821.

[3]Lemelson v. U.S., 752 F.2d 1538, 1551, 224 U.S.P.Q. 526, 533 (Fed. Cir. 1985).

[4]Intervet America, Inc. v. Kee-Vet Laboratories, Inc., 887 F.2d 1050, 1055, 12 U.S.P.Q.2d 1474, 1477 (Fed. Cir. 1989).

[5]Amgen Inc. v. F. Hoffman-La Roche Ltd, 580 F.3d 1340, 1374, 92 U.S.P.Q.2d 1289 (Fed. Cir. 2009).

[6]Lantech, Inc. v. Keip Mach. Co., 32 F.3d 542, 547, 31 U.S.P.Q.2d 1666 (Fed. Cir. 1994), citing Johnston v. IVAC Corp., 885 F.2d 1574, 1577, 12 U.S.P.Q.2d 1382 (Fed. Cir. 1989).

§ 112(f):

An element in a claim for a combination may be expressed as a means or step for performing a specified function without the recital of structure, material, or acts in support thereof, and such claim shall be construed to cover the corresponding structure, material, or acts described in the specification and equivalents thereof.

Despite the literal breadth of the statute, however, means plus function language is not a talisman for limitless protection of the concept that the claim purports to protect. A means plus function claim does not cover every means for performing a specified function.[1]

Instead, far from expanding the scope of a claim, means plus function language actually cuts back on the type of means that can literally satisfy the claim language.[2] Claim elements expressed as a means or step for performing a specified function are construed to cover the corresponding structure, material, or acts described in the specification of the patent and equivalents thereof.[3] One way of looking at means plus function language is that § 112(f) permits means plus function language in a combination claim, but with a "string attached." The attached string limits the applicant to the structure, material or acts in the specification and their equivalents.[4] However, it is important to note that a means plus function claim may be held indefinite for failing to disclose adequate description of the corresponding structure in the specification. To satisfy § 112(b), the corresponding structure of a means plus function limitation should be disclosed in such a manner that one skilled in the art will know and understand what structure corresponds to the means limitation.[5]

Use of the word "means" in a patent claim does not mandate a means plus function interpretation. The word "means" used in a claim triggers a presumption that the inventor intended to use a means plus function clause, as defined under 35 U.S.C.A. § 112(f). However, the means-plus-function clause must identify a means and describe the function that the means performs.

"If the claim recites sufficient structure for performing the

---

[Section 5:15]

[1]Laitram Corp. v. Rexnord, Inc., 939 F.2d 1533, 1536, 19 U.S.P.Q.2d 1367, 1369 (Fed. Cir. 1991).

[2]Williamson v. Citrix Online, LLC, 792 F.3d 1339, 1347–48, 115 U.S.P.Q.2d 1105 (Fed. Cir. 2015).

[3]35 U.S.C.A. § 112(f).

[4]Valmont Industries, Inc. v. Reinke Mfg. Co., Inc., 983 F.2d 1039, 1042, 25 U.S.P.Q.2d 1451, 1454 (Fed. Cir. 1993).

[5]Robert Bosch, LLC v. Snap-On Inc., 769 F.3d 1094, 1101, 112 U.S.P. Q.2d 1617 (Fed. Cir. 2014); Atmel Corp. v. Information Storage Devices, Inc., 198 F.3d 1374, 1382, 53 U.S.P. Q.2d 1225 (Fed. Cir. 1999).

described functions in their entirety," the presumption is overcome and the limitation is not a means-plus-function limitation.[6] "Sufficient structure exists when the claim language specifies the exact structure that performs the functions in question without need to resort to other portions of the specification or extrinsic evidence for an adequate understanding of the structure."[7]

In contrast, a claim can be interpreted as means-plus-function even in the absence of the term "means." If the phrase does not contain the term "means," it is presumptively not subject to § 112(f).[8] However, this presumption may be overcome if it is shown that the claimed phrase fails to recite sufficiently definite structure, or recites function without reciting sufficient structure for performing that function.[9]

In determining whether the scope of a claim that includes a means plus function element encompasses an accused device, the structure in the accused device that performs the claimed function must be compared with the structure in the specification of the patent. For a means plus function claim to be infringed, the accused device must: (1) perform the identical function recited in the means limitation; and (2) perform the function using the structure disclosed in the specification or an equivalent structure.[10]

The test for "equivalents" under § 112(f) is not necessarily the same as the test used in determining infringement under the doctrine of equivalents.[11] Under § 112(f), equivalent means or step function must have existed at the time of patent issuance.[12] The same is not true when applying the doctrine of equivalents for infringement. The "equivalent under the doctrine of equivalents may arise after patent issuance and before the time of

---

[6]TriMed, Inc. v. Stryker Corp., 514 F.3d 1256, 1259–1260, 85 U.S.P. Q.2d 1787 (Fed. Cir. 2008), citing Lighting World, Inc. v. Birchwood Lighting, Inc., 382 F.3d 1354, 1360, 72 U.S.P. Q.2d 1344 (Fed. Cir. 2004).

[7]TriMed, Inc., 514 F.3d at 1259–1260, citing Altiris, Inc. v. Symantec Corp., 318 F.3d 1363, 1376, 65 U.S.P. Q.2d 1865 (Fed. Cir. 2003); see also Envirco Corp. v. Clestra Cleanroom, Inc., 209 F.3d 1360, 1365, 54 U.S.P. Q.2d 1449 (Fed. Cir. 2000).

[8]Massachusetts Institute of Technology and Electronics For

Imaging, Inc. v. Abacus Software, 462 F.3d 1344, 1353, 80 U.S.P.Q.2d 1225 (Fed. Cir. 2006).

[9]Abacus Software, 462 F.3d at 1353.

[10]Valmont, 983 F.2d at 1042, 25 U.S.P.Q.2d at 1454.

[11]Al-Site Corp. v. VSI Intern., Inc., 174 F.3d 1308, 1319-1320, 50 U.S.P.Q.2d 1161 (Fed. Cir. 1999).

[12]Al-Site Corp., 174 F.3d at 1320 citing Warner-Jenkinson Co., Inc. v. Hilton Davis Chemical Co., 520 U.S. 17, 117 S. Ct. 1040, 1053, 41 U.S.P. Q.2d 1865 (1997).

infringement."[13] However, a finding that an accused invention infringes a means-plus-function claim element only under the doctrine of equivalents without a § 112(f) structural equivalents jury instruction leads to the conclusion that the means-plus-function claim element is also literally present in the accused device.[14]

This limitation on construing means plus function elements applies not only to infringement analysis in the courts, but also to validity determinations in the courts and to patentability determinations in the USPTO.[15]

§ 5:16 Establishing patent infringement—Infringement of a design patent

Research References

West's Key Number Digest, Patents ☞252
C.J.S., Patents § 412

The test for infringement of a design patent was set out by the Supreme Court in *Gorham v. White*.[1] "[I]f in the eye of an ordinary observer, giving such attention as a purchaser usually gives, two designs are substantially the same, if the resemblance is such as to deceive such an observer, inducing him to purchase one supposing it to be the other, the first one patented is infringed by the other."[2] An *en banc* Federal Circuit decision in *Egyptian Goddess Inc. v. Swisa Inc.* reestablished the *Gorham* "ordinary observer" test as the sole correct test to use for design patent infringement, stating that "infringement will not be found unless the accused article 'embod[ies] the patented design or any colorable imitation thereof.' "[3] Where a design is composed of functional as well as ornamental features, to prove infringement a patent owner must establish that an ordinary person would be deceived by reason of common ornamental features in the claimed and accused designs.[4] The functional features are not considered. Functional features of

---

[13]Al-Site Corp., 174 F.3d at 1320.

[14]Al-Site Corp., 174 F.3d at 1321.

[15]In re Donaldson Co., Inc., 16 F.3d 1189, 1193, 29 U.S.P.Q.2d 1845, 1849 (Fed. Cir. 1994) (*en banc*). Prior to Donaldson, the P.T.O. had a longstanding practice of not applying 35 U.S.C.A. § 112, paragraph 6 during examination.

[Section 5:16]

[1]Gorham Mfg. Co. v. White, 81 U.S. 511, 1871 WL 14796 (1871).

[2]Gorham, 81 U.S. at 528; see also Crocs, Inc. v. International Trade Com'n, 598 F.3d 1294, 1782, 93 U.S.P.Q.2d 1777, 52 A.L.R. Fed. 2d 655 (Fed. Cir. 2010).

[3]Egyptian Goddess, Inc. v. Swisa, Inc., 543 F.3d 665, 88 U.S.P.Q.2d 1658, 1668 (Fed. Cir. 2008), cert. denied, 129 S. Ct. 1917 (2009) (en banc) (quoting Goodyear Tire & Rubber Co. v. Hercules Tire & Rubber Co., Inc., 162 F.3d 1113, 1116–17 (Fed. Cir. 1998)).

[4]Read Corp. v. Portec, Inc., 970 F.2d 816, 825, 23 U.S.P.Q.2d 1426, 1434 (Fed. Cir. 1992).

a design-patented object do not become less functional simply because the object can be designed without the features.[5] In evaluating a claim of design patent infringement, a trier of fact must consider the ornamental aspects of the design as a whole and not merely isolated portions of the patented design.[6]

The infringement analysis for a design patent is much the same as the analysis of trade dress infringement, in which "likelihood of confusion" is the test. Design patent infringement does not, however, concern itself with the issue of consumer behavior in the actual marketplace—the patentee need not be marketing a product at all.

§ 5:17   Establishing patent infringement—Infringement of a plant patent

Under 35 U.S.C.A. § 161 "[w]hoever invents or discovers and asexually reproduces any distinct and new variety of plant . . . other than a tuber propagated plant or a plant found in an uncultivated state, may obtain a patent therefor." Plant patents may contain only a single claim.[1] A plant patent grants the "right to exclude others from asexually reproducing the plant or selling or using the plant so reproduced."[2]

Due to the requirement that the plant be asexually reproduced, only reproductions of the originally patented plant are protected by a plant patent.[3] The scope of a claim in a plant patent is the asexual progeny of the plant that is shown and described in the patent specification.[4] "[F]or purposes of plant patent infringement, the patentee must prove that the alleged infringing plant is an asexual reproduction, that is, that it is the progeny of the patented plant."[5] It is insufficient to prove that the allegedly infringing plant has the same essential characteristics as the patented plant; instead, the allegedly infringing plant must be "the progeny of the patented plant via 'grafting, budding, cuttings, layering, division and the like, but not by seeds."[6]

---

[5]OddzOn Products, Inc. v. Just Toys, Inc., 122 F.3d 1396, 43 U.S.P.Q.2d 1641 (Fed. Cir. 1997).

[6]Braun Inc. v. Dynamics Corp. of America, 975 F.2d 815, 820, 24 U.S.P.Q.2d 1121, 1125 (Fed. Cir. 1992).

[Section 5:17]

[1]37 C.F.R. § 1.164.

[2]35 U.S.C.A. § 163.

[3]Imazio Nursery, Inc. v. Dania Greenhouses, 69 F.3d 1560, 1566, 36 U.S.P.Q.2d 1673, 135 A.L.R. Fed. 747 (Fed. Cir. 1995).

[4]Imazio Nursery, 69 F.3d at 1569.

[5]Imazio Nursery, Inc. v. Dania Greenhouses, 69 F.3d 1560, 1569, 1566, 36 U.S.P.Q.2d 1673, 135 A.L.R. Fed. 747 (Fed. Cir. 1995).

[6]Imazio Nursery, 69 F.3d at 1569 (quoting S. Rep. No. 315, 71st Cong., 2d Sess. 3 (1930)).

§ 5:18 Establishing patent infringement—Infringement under the doctrine of equivalents

Research References

West's Key Number Digest, Patents ☞230, 237, 245
C.J.S., Patents §§ 408 to 410, 423, 425 to 426

If an accused product does not literally infringe a patent claim, infringement still may be found under a theory known as the doctrine of equivalents. The doctrine of equivalents applies "if, and only if, the differences between the claimed and accused products or processes are insubstantial."[1] Generally speaking, if a device performs substantially the same overall *function* in substantially the same *way* to obtain substantially the same *result* as the claimed invention, then infringement may be found even if the device does not literally infringe each element of a patent claim.[2] Although infringement under the doctrine of equivalents is considered a question of fact, courts are obligated to direct judgment where evidence is such that no reasonable jury could determine two elements to be equivalent.[3] However, the doctrine of equivalents must be applied to each individual element of a claim, not to the invention as a whole.[4] This is known as the "all elements" test, which acts to limit the doctrine of equivalents.

Evidence beyond function, way, and result is also relevant to the doctrine of equivalents. Equivalency is determined in light of the prior art, the patent specification and the prosecution history.[5] " 'An important factor' to be considered, quite apart from function, way, and result 'is whether persons reasonably skilled in the art would have known of the interchangeability of an ingredi-

---

[Section 5:18]

[1]Hilton Davis Chemical Co. v. Warner-Jenkinson Co., Inc., 62 F.3d 1512, 1517, 35 U.S.P.Q.2d 1641, 1644 (Fed. Cir. 1995), opinion supplemented, 64 F.3d 675, 35 U.S.P.Q.2d 1700 (Fed. Cir. 1995) and rev'd on other grounds, 520 U.S. 17, 117 S. Ct. 1040, 41 U.S.P.Q.2d 1865 (1997) and adhered to, 114 F.3d 1161, 43 U.S.P.Q.2d 1152 (Fed. Cir. 1997).

[2]Graver Tank & Mfg. Co. v. Linde Air Products Co., 339 U.S. 605, 608, 70 S. Ct. 854, 856, 85 U.S.P.Q. 328, 330 (1950); Pennwalt, 833 F.2d at 934, 4 U.S.P.Q.2d at 1739; Wilson Sporting Goods Co. v. David Geoffrey & Associates, 904 F.2d 677, 683, 14 U.S.P.Q.2d 1942, 1947 (Fed. Cir. 1990) (disapproved of on other grounds by, Cardinal Chemical Co. v. Morton Intern., Inc., 508 U.S. 83, 113 S. Ct. 1967, 26 U.S.P.Q.2d 1721 (1993)).

[3]Dawn Equipment Co. v. Kentucky Farms Inc., 140 F.3d 1009, 46 U.S.P.Q.2d 1109 (Fed. Cir. 1998).

[4]Warner-Jenkinson Co., Inc. v. Hilton Davis Chemical Co., 520 U.S. 17, 29, 117 S. Ct. 1040, 137 L. Ed. 2d 146, 41 U.S.P.Q.2d 1865 (1997).

[5]*Graver Tank & Mfg. Co.,* 339 U.S. at 609.

ent not contained in the patent with one that was.'"[6] The intent of the accused infringer plays no role in the application of the doctrine of equivalents. Thus, evidence of copying, designing around a patent, or independent development is irrelevant to the issue of infringement.[7] Additionally, the foreseeability of an equivalent at the time of patenting is not a bar to finding infringement under the doctrine of equivalents.[8]

In analyzing infringement under the doctrine of equivalents, it is appropriate (i.e. favored, but not required) to compare the function/way/result of the substitution with the function/way/result of the limitation in the context of the invention; that is, it is appropriate to make a subsidiary analysis of whether a substituted element performs substantially the same overall function or work, in substantially the same way, to obtain substantially the same overall result as the corresponding element of the claim.[9]

Even if the function/way/result test is met, however, there can be no infringement if the asserted scope of equivalency (of what is literally claimed) would encompass the prior art. This is an issue of law.[10] The courts have sometimes characterized claims as being "expanded" or "broadened" under the doctrine of equivalents. Precisely speaking, however, these characterizations are inaccurate:

> To say that the doctrine of equivalents extends or enlarges *the claims* is a contradiction in terms. The claims—i.e., the scope of patent protection *as defined by* the claims—remain the same and application of the doctrine *expands the right to exclude* to "equivalents" of what is claimed.[11]

A patentee may not, under the doctrine of equivalents, obtain coverage that could not have been lawfully obtained from the USPTO by literal claims. To simplify the analysis and bring the issue onto familiar turf, the Federal Circuit suggested visualizing a hypothetical patent claim, sufficient in scope to literally cover the accused product. The pertinent question then becomes whether the hypothetical claim would have been allowed by the

---

[6]Hilton Davis, 62 F.3d at 1518 (quoting Graver Tank, 339 U.S. at 609).

[7]Warner-Jenkinson, 520 U.S. at 17. *But see* Imazio Nursery, Inc. v. Dania Greenhouses, 69 F.3d 1560, 1570, 36 U.S.P.Q.2d 1673, 135 A.L.R. Fed. 747 (Fed. Cir. 1995) (noting that independent creation is a defense to claims of infringement of a plant patent).

[8]Ring & Pinion Service Inc. v. ARB Corp. Ltd., 743 F.3d 831, 834, 109 U.S.P.Q.2d 1779 (Fed. Cir. 2014).

[9]Corning Glass Works v. Sumitomo Elec. U.S.A., Inc., 868 F.2d 1251, 1260, 9 U.S.P.Q.2d 1962, 1967 (Fed. Cir. 1989).

[10]Wilson Sporting Goods, 904 F.2d at 683, 14 U.S.P.Q.2d at 1947.

[11]Wilson Sporting Goods, 904 F.2d at 684, 14 U.S.P.Q.2d at 1948 (emphasis in original).

USPTO over the prior art. If not, then it would be improper to permit the patentee to obtain that coverage in an infringement suit under the doctrine of equivalents.[12] The Federal Circuit has clarified that the hypothetical claim analysis described in *Wilson Sporting Goods* is not obligatory in every doctrine of equivalents determination.[13]

The plaintiff has the burden of proving that the range of equivalents it seeks would not encompass the prior art. This type of analysis has absolutely no effect on the presumed validity of the actual patent claims. The patent claims remain valid whether or not the plaintiff persuades the court that it is entitled to the range of equivalents that it seeks.[14]

Prosecution history estoppel is a defense to infringement under the doctrine of equivalents. During the prosecution of the application, a patent examiner may reject the application based on prior art references. If a patentee, in response to such a rejection, adds a limitation to the claims in an effort to overcome that rejection, the patentee cannot later successfully argue that an accused device, that lacks the additional limitation, infringes the patent. Prosecution history estoppel is not to be confused with prosecution history disclaimer. Prosecution history disclaimer is not based on an applicant's amendments during prosecution, but instead limits the literal scope of the claims based on an applicant's arguments during prosecution. Thus, the literal scope of a claim may be narrowed by prosecution history disclaimer, but the doctrine of equivalents may still be available. However, if an applicant narrows the scope of a claim by amending the claim, equivalents may be surrendered and prosecution history estoppel may apply as well.

Whenever prosecution history estoppel is invoked as a limitation under the doctrine of equivalents, a close examination must be made as to not only what was surrendered, but also the reason for such a surrender. Amendments may be of different types and may serve different functions. Depending on the nature and purpose of an amendment, it may have a limiting effect within a spectrum ranging from great to small to zero.[15] The scope of the estoppel must be determined in light of the prior art that oc-

---

[12]Wilson Sporting Goods, 904 F.2d at 684, 14 U.S.P.Q.2d at 1949.

[13]Key Mfg. Group, Inc. v. Microdot, Inc., 925 F.2d 1444, 1449, 17 U.S.P.Q.2d 1806, 1810 (Fed. Cir. 1991).

[14]Wilson Sporting Goods, 904 F.2d at 685, 14 U.S.P.Q.2d at 1949.

[15]Insta-Foam Products, Inc. v. Universal Foam Systems, Inc., 906 F.2d 698, 703, 15 U.S.P.Q.2d 1295, 1298 (Fed. Cir. 1990) (quoting Hughes Aircraft Co. v. U.S., 717 F.2d 1351, 1363, 219 U.S.P.Q. 473, 481, 31 Cont. Cas. Fed. (CCH) P 71526 (Fed. Cir. 1983) (overruled on other grounds by, 122 S.Ct. 1831; Festo Corp. v. Shoketsu Kinzoku Kogyo Kabushiki Co., Ltd., 234 F.3d 558, 56 U.S.P.Q.2d 1865 (Fed. Cir. 2000)) and reinstated by 122 S.Ct.

casioned the change, as well as the patentee's representations made to the patent examiner as to the reason for the change.[16]

The U.S. Supreme Court has spoken on the application of prosecution history estoppel as applied to the doctrine of equivalents.[17] A "flexible bar" approach is used to determine the estoppel created when an amendment is made to secure the patent and the amendment narrows the patent's scope. Prosecution history estoppel prevents a patentee from attempting to regain subject matter in litigation that has been disavowed before the USPTO to gain patent protection. Therefore, the narrowing amendment must be examined to determine what equivalents were surrendered. Prosecution history estoppel may be created by any amendment made to comply with the Patent Act's requirements, not just those amendments made to avoid the prior art.[18]

Such a narrowing amendment creates a rebuttable presumption that the patentee surrendered the subject matter between the original claim limitations and the amended claim limitations. To rebut this presumption, "the patentee must show that at the time of the amendment one skilled in the art could not reasonably be expected to have drafted a claim that would have literally encompassed the alleged equivalent."[19] There are three ways in which the patentee can rebut the presumption of estoppel, which include showing that: "the equivalent may have been unforeseeable at the time of the application; the rationale underlying the amendment may bear no more than a tangential relation to the equivalent in question; or there may be some other reason suggesting that the patentee could not reasonably be expected to have described the insubstantial substitute in question. In those cases the patentee can overcome the presumption that prosecution history estoppel bars a finding of equivalence."[20]

The Federal Circuit subsequently gave more guidance as to the legal standard that will be applied to each category in determining whether the patentee has rebutted the presumption of surrender. The Federal Circuit also stated "that rebuttal of the presumption of surrender is a question of law to be determined by the court, not a jury."[21]

The Federal Circuit explained that foreseeability requires an objective inquiry into "whether the alleged equivalent would have

---

1831).

[16]Sun Studs, 872 F.2d at 988, 10 U.S.P.Q. at 1345.

[17]Festo Corp. v. Shoketsu Kinzoku Kogyo Kabushiki Co., Ltd., 535 U.S. 722, 122 S. Ct. 1831, 62 U.S.P.Q.2d 1705 (2002).

[18]Festo, 535 U.S. at 736.

[19]Festo, 535 U.S. at 741.

[20]Festo, 535 U.S. at 740–741.

[21]Festo Corp. v. Shoketsu Kinzoku Kogyo Kabushiki Co., Ltd., 344 F.3d 1359, 1367, 68 U.S.P.Q.2d 1321 (Fed. Cir. 2003).

been unforeseeable to one of ordinary skill in the art at the time of the amendment."[22] The Court stated that the objective unforseeability inquiry depends on underlying factual issues, therefore, the district court may take into account expert testimony and other extrinsic evidence.[23]

To determine whether a patentee can rebut the presumption of surrender under the tangential relation to the equivalent standard, the Federal Circuit concluded that the court should focus on the "patentee's objectively apparent reason for the narrowing amendment."[24] The Court further stated that this inquiry should be determined from "the prosecution history record without the introduction of additional evidence, except, when necessary, testimony from those skilled in the art as to the interpretation of that record."[25]

Finally, the Federal Circuit concluded that the "some other reason" category is a narrow category.[26] The Court gave the example that failure to describe an alleged equivalent due to "the shortcomings of language" may qualify as some other reason.[27] The Court also explained that evidence outside of the prosecution history might not be considered in determining whether the patentee met its burden.[28]

§ 5:19 Common discovery and evidentiary issues in patent litigation—Attorney-client privilege

Research References

West's Key Number Digest, Patents ⚷292.1(3), 292.3; Witnesses ⚷197
C.J.S., Patents §§ 494 to 499; Witnesses §§ 316 to 340, 365

The attorney-client privilege, which dates back to the 16th century, is the oldest of the confidential privileges known to the common law.[1] Although created to protect the attorney's honor from the compelled violation of an attorney's oath of secrecy to his or her client, it is now well established that the purpose of the privilege is to encourage the frequent exchange of information between attorney and client, thereby promoting the "broader public interest in the observance of law and administration of justice."[2]

---

[22]Festo, 344 F.3d at 1369.

[23]Festo, 344 F.3d at 1369.

[24]Festo, 344 F.3d at 1369.

[25]Festo, 344 F.3d at 1369-1370.

[26]Festo, 344 F.3d at 1370.

[27]Festo, 344 F.3d at 1370.

[28]Festo, 344 F.3d at 1370.

[Section 5:19]

[1]Union Carbide Corp. v. Dow Chemical Co., 619 F. Supp. 1036, 1046, 229 U.S.P.Q. 401, 406 (D. Del. 1985) (citing 8 J.Wigmore, Evidence, § 2290 (1961)).

[2]Upjohn Co. v. U.S., 1981-1 C.B. 591, 449 U.S. 383, 389, 101 S. Ct. 677,

The widely-accepted definition of the attorney-client privilege was promulgated in *United States v. United Shoe Machinery Corp.*:

> The privilege applies only if (1) the asserted holder of the privilege is or sought to become a client; (2) the person to whom the communication was made (a) is a member of the bar of a court, or his subordinate and (b) in connection with this communication is acting as a lawyer; (3) the communication relates to a fact of which the attorney was informed (a) by his client (b) without the presence of strangers (c) for the purpose of securing primarily either (i) an opinion of law or (ii) legal services or (iii) assistance in some legal proceeding, and not (d) for the purpose of committing a crime or tort; and (4) the privilege has been (a) claimed and (b) not waived by the client.[3]

The burden of proving the existence of the attorney-client or work product privilege rests squarely on the party claiming the privilege.[4] A general allegation of privilege is insufficient. A clear showing must be made which sets forth the items or categories objected to and the reason for that objection.[5]

The application of the privilege in patent litigation presents particular problems. Often patent attorneys perform not only the legal functions of preparing and prosecuting patent applications, but evaluations of the business ramifications of the company's patent position as well. While communications concerning the former enjoy insulation from discovery under the attorney-client privilege, communications with respect to the latter may not.[6]

Communications between a client and a non-attorney patent agent representing that client before the USPTO are protected by a "patent-agent privilege" which functions similarly to the attorney-client privilege.[7] The patent-agent privilege applies only to those communications that fall within the scope of activities

---

682, Fed. Sec. L. Rep. (CCH) P 97817, 1980-81 Trade Cas. (CCH) ¶ 63797, 81-1 U.S. Tax Cas. (CCH) P 9138, 7 Fed. R. Evid. Serv. 785, 30 Fed. R. Serv. 2d 1101, 47 A.F.T.R.2d 81-523 (1981).

[3]U.S. v. United Shoe Machinery Corp., 89 F. Supp. 357, 358–59 (D. Mass. 1950) (rejected by, American Standard Inc. v. Pfizer Inc., 828 F.2d 734, 3 U.S.P.Q.2d 1817 (Fed. Cir. 1987)).

[4]Bulk Lift Intern., Inc. v. Flexcon & Systems, Inc., 122 F.R.D. 482 (W.D. La. 1988), order aff'd, 122 F.R.D. 493, 9 U.S.P.Q.2d 1355 (W.D. La. 1988).

[5]Bulk Lift, 122 F.R.D. at 490, 9 U.S.P.Q. at 1364.

[6]Hercules, Inc. v. Exxon Corp., 434 F. Supp. 136, 147, 196 U.S.P.Q. 401, 406, 24 Fed. R. Serv. 2d 1343 (D. Del. 1977) (rejected by, Advanced Cardiovascular Systems, Inc. v. C.R. Bard, Inc., 144 F.R.D. 372, 25 U.S.P.Q.2d 1354 (N.D. Cal. 1992)).

[7]See In re Queen's University at Kingston, 820 F.3d 1287, 118 U.S.P.Q.2d 1221, 99 Fed. R. Evid. Serv. 1196 (Fed. Cir. 2016) (recognizing the patent-agent privilege). *But see* In re Silver, 2016 WL 4386004 (Tex. App. Dallas 2016) (refusing to recognize the patent-agent privilege in a breach of contract case).

that Congress has authorized patent agents to engage in " 'which are reasonably necessary and incident to the preparation and prosecution of patent applications or other proceeding before the Office involving a patent application or patent in which the practitioner is authorized to participate.' "[8] 37 C.F.R. § 11.5(b)(1) provides guidance as to the scope of activities that Congress has authorized patent agents to engage in; in particular, 37 C.F.R. § 11.5(b)(1) provides that practice before the USPTO includes:

> preparing and prosecuting any patent application, consulting with or giving advice to a client in contemplation of filing a patent application or other document with the Office, drafting the specification or claims of a patent application; drafting an amendment or reply to a communication from the Office that may require written argument to establish the patentability of a claimed invention; drafting a reply to a communication from the Office regarding a patent application; and drafting a communication for a public use, interference, reexamination proceeding, petition, appeal to or any other proceeding before the Patent Trial and Appeal Board, or other proceeding.

Communications with patent agents regarding activities that fall outside the scope of activities authorized by Congress are not afforded protection by the patent-agent privilege, but may instead be protected by the attorney-client privilege. Communications between a non-attorney patent agent and a client may be protected by the attorney-client privilege where the patent agent is employed in the patent department of a corporation or by a law firm, as the patent agent may qualify as a "subordinate" of an attorney, if the agent is working at the direction of, and under the supervision of an attorney.[9] Such a relationship establishes the attorney-client privilege between the non-attorney patent agent and the client.

Certain categories of documents have been held to not be protected by the attorney-client privilege. Information which is subject to a duty of full disclosure to the USPTO does not take on a confidential character merely because it is transmitted through an attorney.[10] Unprotected information may include:

- client authorizations to file applications and take other steps necessary to obtain registration,

- papers submitted to the USPTO and appearing in the file

---

[8]In re Queen's University, at *12, quoting 37 C.F.R. § 11.5(b)(1).

[9]E.g., Gorman v. Polar Electro, Inc., 137 F. Supp. 2d 223, 227-228, 65 U.S.P.Q.2d 1537, 49 Fed. R. Serv. 3d 808 (E.D. N.Y. 2001); Willemijn

Houdstermaatschaapij BV v. Apollo Computer Inc., 707 F. Supp. 1429, 1446, 13 U.S.P.Q.2d 1001 (D. Del. 1989).

[10]Hercules, 434 F. Supp. at 148, 196 U.S.P.Q. at 404.

wrapper of issued patents,

●compendiums of filing fees and requirements in the United States and foreign countries for patent applications,

●lists of patent applications filed and registrations obtained or rejected (including dates and file or registration numbers),

●technical information, such as the results of research, tests, and experiments, communicated to the attorney, but not calling for a legal opinion or interpretation and meant primarily for aid in completing patent applications,

●business advice, such as that related to product marketing,

●communications whose confidentiality has been waived,

●documents written by or obtained from third parties, even though attached to communications seeking or giving legal advice (these will be separated and classified as nonprivileged),

●communications that pass through an attorney who acts only as a conduit for a third party or for a file,

●transmittal letters or acknowledgment of receipt letters, devoid of legal advice or requests for such advice, and disclosing no privileged matter, and

●patent disclosures, draft patent applications, and technical nonlegal material related to the final patent or studies of the prior art.[11]

When the client invoking the attorney-client privilege is a corporation, additional considerations come into play. Communications between employees and corporate counsel must be analyzed on a case-by-case basis to determine whether the communication should be protected.[12] Communications between corporate counsel and individuals outside the corporation will not ordinarily be privileged even if the information is eventually conveyed by the corporate counsel to officers within the corporation. Third party communications do, however, retain a protective shield if the parties have a common legal interest, such as where the parties are co-defendants or are involved in or

---

[11]Duplan Corp. v. Deering Milliken, Inc., 397 F. Supp. 1146, 1168-69, 184 U.S.P.Q. 775, 787 (D.S.C. 1974); Bulk Lift, 122 F.R.D. at 494-95, 9 U.S.P.Q.2d at 1365-66.

[12]Union Carbide, 619 F. Supp. at 1047, 229 U.S.P.Q. at 407 (citing Upjohn, 449 U.S. at 396-97, 101 S. Ct. at 686-87).

anticipate joint litigation.[13]

Additionally, communications with independent contractors may be covered by attorney-client privilege. Courts have found that communications between independent contractors of entities are privileged if the communication was for the purposes of seeking legal advice, was at the direction of the contractor's superior, was within the scope of the representative's duties, and the content was kept among those in the company that needed to know it.[14]

The attorney-client privilege is usually upheld with respect to communications between attorneys and individuals occupying positions of executive responsibility in operating divisions or research departments. For example, in *Hercules Inc. v. Exxon Corp.*, the individuals were kept apprised, on a continuing basis, of specific and general legal developments relevant to the area of their responsibilities, and they had authority to control or substantially participate in decisions to be taken on the advice of the lawyer. Consequently, these employees were considered members of the corporate "control group."[15] Also, communications with senior scientists in the research department were considered covered by the attorney-client privilege. The court reasoned that, while their major contributions were in performing experiments and in relaying technical information upon request to attorneys in the patent department, these scientists were operating at the express or implied direction of control group members to supply the attorneys with the necessary technical information and expertise pursuant to a request for legal advice.[16]

In some circumstances, a joint defense privilege, often referred to as the common interest rule, may extend the attorney-client privilege to communications between two or more parties and/or their respective counsel if they are participating in a joint defense agreement, and if the communications are part of an on-going and joint effort to set up a common defense strategy.[17] A formal agreement should be contemplated between any parties exchanging potentially privileged information where the common interest

---

[13]Leader Technologies, Inc. v. Facebook, Inc., 719 F. Supp. 2d 373, 376 (D. Del. 2010), *citing* Union Carbide Corp. v. Dow Chemical Co., 619 F. Supp. 1036, 1047, 229 U.S.P.Q. 401 (D. Del. 1985).

[14]In re Bieter Co., 16 F.3d 929, R.I.C.O. Bus. Disp. Guide (CCH) P 8490 (8th Cir. 1994).

[15]Hercules, 434 F. Supp. at 145-46, 196 U.S.P.Q. at 406-407.

[16]Hercules, 434 F. Supp. at 146, 196 U.S.P.Q. at 407.

[17]Minebea Co., Ltd. v. Papst, 228 F.R.D. 13, 15 (D.D.C. 2005) (citations omitted); *see also* In re Smirman, 267 F.R.D. 221, 223 (E.D. Mich. 2010); *but see* In re IPCom GmbH & Co., KG, 428 Fed. Appx. 984, 986 (Fed. Cir. 2011) (no common interest when patents and related documents were sold, rather than shared as part of a joint legal claim or defense).

rule may apply.

For the attorney-client privilege to apply, it must not have been waived. Waiver of the privilege often occurs in patent litigation where the "advice of counsel" defense to willful infringement is used. Generally speaking, asserting the advice of counsel defense and disclosing opinions of opinion counsel in a patent case do not constitute waiver of the attorney-client privilege for communications with trial counsel.[18] However, courts have discretion to extend a waiver to trial counsel if the party or its counsel engages in "chicanery."[19]

Although not absolutely required, an opinion of outside counsel, which carefully reviews the patent, the USPTO proceedings related to the patent, the prior art, and the proposed device is usually an important factor to avoid a finding of willful infringement. Obtaining the opinion of outside counsel may be advantageous under most circumstances because asserting the advice of counsel defense and disclosing the opinions of opinion counsel do not constitute waiver of the attorney-client privilege or work product immunity for communications with trial counsel.[20]

If a defendant chooses to invoke the attorney-client privilege, work-product immunity, or both with respect to an opinion or advice received from counsel, the trier of fact is not allowed to draw an adverse inference as to the nature of the advice with respect to willful infringement.[21] Allowing an inference that withheld opinions are adverse to the client's actions could distort the attorney-client relationship, and would be contrary to sound public policy and the administration of justice.[22]

Generally, voluntary waiver by a client of one or more privileged documents passing between a certain attorney and the client discussing a certain subject waives the privilege as to all communications between the same attorney and the same client on the same subject.[23] Therefore, where the advice of counsel has been put in issue, all advisory opinions on the same matter may need to be discoverable to avoid the evils of "opinion shopping" and selective disclosure.[24] If a party were able to make an initial disclosure but shield further discovery with the assertion of privilege, that party might release only the favorable opinion and

---

[18]Seagate, 497 F.3d at 1374.

[19]Seagate, 497 F.3d at 1375.

[20]In re Seagate, 497 F.3d at 1374–76.

[21]Knorr-Bremse Systeme Fuer Nutzfahrzeuge GmbH v. Dana Corp., 383 F.3d 1337, 72 U.S.P.Q.2d 1560, 65 Fed. R. Evid. Serv. 365 (Fed. Cir. 2004).

[22]Knorr-Bremse, 383 F.3d at 1344.

[23]Fort James Corp. v. Solo Cup Co., 412 F.3d 1340, 1349, 75 U.S.P. Q.2d 1257, 67 Fed. R. Evid. Serv. 662 (Fed. Cir. 2005).

[24]In re Seagate, 497 F.3d at 1372.

withhold numerous damaging ones.[25]

Whether a matter is protected by the attorney-client privilege is determined on a case-by-case basis, bearing in mind the purposes of the protection and the need for flexibility and sound judicial discretion. The desire to protect the confidentiality of the attorney-client relationship and to preserve the integrity of the adversarial process must be balanced against the public interest in full and frank disclosure to the USPTO and the liberal spirit of discovery rules.[26]

Communications between an attorney and a client, otherwise protected, which are in furtherance of a fraud are not protected by the attorney-client privilege or work product immunity.[27] Therefore, the attorney-client privilege may be waived if a defendant makes a prima facie showing that the patentee committed fraud in prosecuting its patent. The party seeking discovery bears the burden of showing a prima facie case of fraud, including: a knowing, willful, and intentional act of misrepresentation or omission before the USPTO, that is material and that the USPTO relied upon in deciding to issue the patent.[28] Inequitable conduct before the USPTO by itself is not sufficient to pierce the attorney-client privilege.[29]

The discovering party also must show that the communications or documents sought were made in furtherance of the fraud. Communications after the fact are protected by the attorney-client privilege regardless of the fraud, since one of the primary purposes of the attorney-client privilege is to allow consultation in the interest of establishing a legal defense.[30]

§5:20 Common discovery and evidentiary issues in patent litigation—Attorney work product

Research References

[25]Seagate, 497 F.3d at 1372.

[26]Hercules, 434 F. Supp. at 144, 196 U.S.P.Q. at 405; Howes v. Medical Components, Inc., 698 F. Supp. 574, 581 (E.D. Pa. 1988); See, e.g., Fonar, 227 U.S.P.Q. at 886 (attorney-client privilege waived when defendant's counsel produced two letters written by defendant's in-house counsel); Leybold-Heraeus Technologies, Inc. v. Midwest Instrument Co., Inc., 118 F.R.D. 609, 4 U.S.P.Q.2d 1641 (E.D. Wis. 1987) (attorney-client privilege waived when attorneys were named as witnesses in the case); Board of Trustees of Leland Stanford Jr.

University v. Coulter Corp., 118 F.R.D. 532, 44 Ed. Law Rep. 1178, 4 U.S.P.Q.2d 1652, 9 Fed. R. Serv. 3d 1325 (S.D. Fla. 1987) (attorney-client privileged waived where defendant identified intention to rely on advice of counsel and produced the substance of counsel's opinion in written form).

[27]Bulk Lift, 122 F.R.D. at 494, 9 U.S.P.Q.2d at 1362.

[28]Bulk Lift, 122 F.R.D. at 494, 9 U.S.P.Q.2d at 1362.

[29]Bulk Lift, 122 F.R.D. at 496.

[30]Bulk Lift, 122 F.R.D. at 495.

West's Key Number Digest, Federal Civil Procedure ⚷1600(3); Patents
⚷292.3
C.J.S., Federal Civil Procedure §§ 709, 711, 723; Patents §§ 494 to 499

Rule 26 of the Federal Rules of Civil Procedure allows discovery
"regarding any nonprivileged matter that is relevant to any
party's claim or defense—including the existence, description,
nature, custody, condition, and location of any documents or other
tangible things and the identity and location of persons who know
of any discoverable matter."[1] Rule 26(b)(3) constitutes a restriction on otherwise permitted discovery. It affords qualified protection to "documents and tangible things * * * prepared in
anticipation of litigation or for trial" by a party or the party's
representative. More than the mere possibility of litigation must
be evident before material is protected by work product
immunity.[2]

As in other types of cases, a party seeking discovery of such
documents and tangible things in patent litigation must demonstrate a "substantial need of the materials in the preparation of
the party's case and that the party is unable without undue hard-
ship to obtain the substantial equivalent of the material by other
means."[3] Absolute protection is afforded to "mental impressions,
conclusions, opinions, or legal theories of an attorney or other
representative of a party concerning the litigation."[4]

Work product immunity may be claimed only for documents
prepared by counsel in anticipation of litigation. As with the
attorney-client privilege, the work product protection does not
apply to the underlying facts relevant to litigation, whether or
not they have been reduced to writing or communicated to an
attorney.[5]

§ 5:21 Common discovery and evidentiary issues in patent litigation—Confidential information

Research References
West's Key Number Digest, Patents ⚷292.4
C.J.S., Patents §§ 494, 499

Much of the information which is relevant and discoverable is

---

[Section 5:20]

[1]Fed.R.Civ.P. 26(b)(1).

[2]Bulk Lift Intern. Inc. v. Flexcon
& Systems, Inc., 122 F.R.D. 493, 9
U.S.P.Q.2d 1355, 1364 (W.D. La. 1988).

[3]Fed. R. Civ. P. 26(b)(3)(iii).

[4]Bulk Lift, 122 F.R.D. at 493.

[5]Upjohn Co. v. U.S., 1981-1 C.B.
591, 449 U.S. 383, 395-396, 101 S. Ct.
677, 685-686, Fed. Sec. L. Rep. (CCH)
P 97817, 1980-81 Trade Cas. (CCH) ¶
63797, 81-1 U.S. Tax Cas. (CCH) P
9138, 7 Fed. R. Evid. Serv. 785, 30 Fed.
R. Serv. 2d 1101, 47 A.F.T.R.2d 81-523
(1981).

proprietary information of the parties. Since the parties to patent infringement suits are usually competitors, discovery of technical and financial information is particularly sensitive. A stipulated protective order under Rule 26(c) may be used to allow discovery of confidential information. Many protective orders allow the opposing counsel access to confidential information but prevent opposing counsel from showing or discussing the confidential information with his or her client. Some protective orders provide for two levels of protection, one level of "attorneys eyes only" and the other level allowing access to the client but not allowing open publication. An example of a protective order is included in Appendix G.

§ 5:22 Common discovery and evidentiary issues in patent litigation—E-discovery

Electronic discovery or "e-discovery" is governed by Fed. R. Civ. P. 26, 34, and 45. The scope of e-discovery in patent litigation can be a source of uncertainty, confusion, and significant expense. A discovering party often requests all kinds of electronic information, including metadata, on virtually every electronic device in the possession of the opposing party. This information can include e-mail, electronic files, and more. Producing such information can be an expensive and time-consuming task for even a single personal computer, let alone a number of computers and other devices under the control of a large business. However, Rule 26(b)(2)(B) places some limits on e-discovery for materials "not reasonably accessible because of undue burden or cost." Computer forensics and e-discovery specialists are often used in patent cases to assist attorneys with retrieving and processing electronically-stored information.

When developing a pre-trial discovery plan, patent litigants must discuss "any issues about disclosure or discovery of electronically stored information, including the form or forms in which it should be produced[.]"[1] Parties should consider agreeing to limits on discoverable electronic information and its collection, including limits on the number of custodians, issues, time frame, filters (e.g., search keywords), etc. Some courts have specific e-discovery guidelines. Moreover, the Federal Circuit promulgated a "Model Order Regarding E-Discovery in Patent Cases," that practitioners may wish to consult.[2]

Although in some cases a largely manual electronic document

[Section 5:22]

[1]Fed. R. Civ. P. 26(f)(3)(C).

[2]United Stated Court of Appeals for the Federal Circuit E-Discovery Committee, "An E-Discovery Model Order," at http://www.cafc.uscourts.gov/images/stories/announcements/Ediscovery_Model_Order.pdf (2011).

review (also called "linear review") can be undertaken, use of an automated filtering mechanism may be useful. The two primary filtering mechanisms are the use of search keywords, a list of which may be agreed upon by the parties, and the use of predictive coding or technology-assisted review, which is essentially the use of a computer program that classifies documents in relation to concepts and terms automatically identified from a limited number of sample documents. The use of predictive coding has increased as a means for expediting the document review process and reducing the cost of e-discovery. However, not all predictive coding technology is the same and the quality of the results can vary depending on the data involved and the user's attention to the iterative process required to evaluate accuracy.

§ 5:23 Common discovery and evidentiary issues in patent litigation—Bifurcation

Research References
West's Key Number Digest, Patents ⬤—314(2)
C.J.S., Patents §§ 517 to 522

Due to the complexity of patent infringement cases, bifurcation of trials is sometimes appropriate. Under Rule 42(b):

> The court, in furtherance of convenience or to avoid prejudice, or when separate trials will be conducive to expedition and economy, may order a separate trial of any claim, cross-claim, counterclaim, or third party claim, or of any separate issue or of any number of claims, cross-claims, counterclaims, third-party claims, or issues, always preserving inviolate the right of trial by jury as declared by the Seventh Amendment to the Constitution or as given by a statute of the United States.

The determination of whether or not to bifurcate the trial is within the discretion of the trial court and is rarely overturned.

Parties often seek bifurcation as a method of shortening or avoiding unnecessary portions of trials. For instance, the most common bifurcation in patent cases is separating the liability and damages phases of the trial. The damages trial only occurs if liability is found. Bifurcation also provides an opportunity for settlement between the first and second trial, so that the second set of issues need not be proven. Discovery periods may be bifurcated in accordance with the bifurcated trial schedule, such that discovery of damages, for instance, does not occur until after the trial for liability is concluded. Sometimes, "trifurcation" is appropriate, separating the trial into three phases: infringement, validity and damages. Another type of bifurcation occurs when a trial of issues for the jury is separated from a trial of issues to the judge. Similar to the order of presenting evidence, the decision of whether and how to propose bifurcation to a court is best determined through a combination of experience, analysis and intuition.

§ 5:24 Common discovery and evidentiary issues in patent litigation—Role of expert witnesses

Research References

West's Key Number Digest, Patents ⚷159
C.J.S., Patents §§ 285 to 286

Expert witnesses are often used in patent litigation. Many cases come down to a "battle of the experts" where the trier of fact must determine which expert it finds more credible. Technical experts can provide evidence explaining the technology of the patent and the accused device, explaining the meaning of words within a claim, and explaining how the accused device falls within or outside the claim limitations. For instance, plaintiffs often use an expert witness to "read" the claims onto the accused device. Using an expert witness helps avoid the bias attributed to the patent holder, while at the same time avoiding the antagonistic viewpoint propounded by the opposing party. Expert testimony is particularly helpful in cases where the meaning of disputed terms is not readily apparent from the patent, but requires an understanding of the industry.[1] Expert testimony may also be helpful in establishing objective evidence of nonobviousness such as commercial success and long-felt need in the industry for the inventive aspects of the patent.

Experts in patent law are commonly used to explain the prosecution of a patent and relate the rules applicable to patent practitioners before the USPTO. For instance, patent experts are often used to back-up a claim of inequitable conduct. Legal experts are also often used to explain the underlying legal principles to the jury. However, experts should not be allowed to inject new meaning into terms that are inconsistent with what the inventor clearly sets forth in the patent.[2] Additionally, admission of expert testimony is within the discretion of the trial court, and patent experts can be prevented from testifying if the court so chooses.[3]

Damages experts are usually crucial in determining the amount

[Section 5:24]

[1]Advanced Cardiovascular Systems, Inc. v. Scimed Life Systems, Inc., 887 F.2d 1070, 1073, 12 U.S.P.Q.2d 1539, 1542 (Fed. Cir. 1989).

[2]Bell & Howell Document Management Products Co. v. Altek Systems, 132 F.3d 701, 45 U.S.P.Q.2d 1033 (Fed. Cir. 1997).

[3]Acoustical Design, Inc. v. Control Electronics Co., Inc., 932 F.2d 939, 942, 18 U.S.P.Q.2d 1707, 1709 (Fed. Cir. 1991).

of damages, including a reasonable royalty. These experts often have an accounting background, and their testimony includes a summation of sales and costs.

§ 5:25 Remedies—Injunctions

Research References

West's Key Number Digest, Patents ⚷293, 317
C.J.S., Patents §§ 540 to 541, 543 to 555

"The several courts having jurisdiction of cases under this title may grant injunctions in accordance with the principles of equity to prevent the violation of any right secured by patent, on such terms as the court deems reasonable."[1] Competition in the marketplace usually provides the business justification for initiating a patent infringement suit, and an injunction is often the primary remedy sought. Injunctions are of two types: (1) preliminary injunctions and (2) permanent injunctions. Preliminary injunctions are issued to protect the patent owner's rights during a lawsuit, whereas permanent injunctions are issued after a patent owner prevails on the merits.

As a general proposition, an injunction is an equitable remedy which cannot be granted unless the plaintiff shows that the remedy at law is inadequate.

Patent injunctions should not be overly broad due to the threat of costly contempt proceedings for acts unrelated to those originally judged unlawful. Also, patent injunctions should ordinarily not exceed the term of the patent. A typical injunction would prohibit "the making, using, selling, offering for sale or importing of [specified infringing device], devices no more than colorably different from [specified infringing device], or other devices which infringe [specified U.S. Patent], during the enforceable term of [specified U.S. Patent]."[2] Patent injunctions should be set aside when the legal basis for the injunction ceases to exist. For example, if upon reeaxmaination, the USPTO invalidates a claim providing the legal basis for the injunction, the injunction must be set aside following the final judgment of patent invalidity.[3]

Many patent infringement cases involve a request for a preliminary injunction. The standards applied to the grant of a preliminary injunction are no more or less stringent in patent cases

---

[Section 5:25]

[1]35 U.S.C.A. § 283.

[2]*See* Additive Controls & Measurement Systems, Inc. v. Flowdata, Inc., 986 F.2d 476, 480, 25 U.S.P.Q.2d 1798, 1801 (Fed. Cir. 1993).

[3]ePlus, Inc. v. Lawson Software, Inc., 760 F.3d 1350, 1357-1358, 111 U.S.P.Q.2d 1833 (Fed. Cir. 2014), on reh'g, 2015 WL 3772472 (Fed. Cir. 2015).

than in other areas of the law.[4] In order to obtain a preliminary injunction, the patent owner must establish: reasonable likelihood of success on the merits; irreparable harm; a balance of the hardships tipping in the patent owner's favor; and the issuance of the injunction is in the public interest.[5] These factors, taken individually, are not dispositive; rather, a court must weigh and measure each factor against the other factors and against the form and magnitude of relief requested.[6] For instance, where a showing of the likelihood of success is less forceful, a movant would have to make a stronger showing of irreparable harm in order to tip the balance of equity in the movant's favor.[7]

To show a likelihood of success on the merits, a movant must prove title to the patent and, as a general proposition, must show beyond question that the patent in question is valid and infringed.[8] The grant or denial of a preliminary injunction in a patent case is a matter ultimately committed to the sound discretion of the court.[9] An order granting or denying a motion for a preliminary injunction is appealable as a matter of right.[10]

For the purpose of obtaining a preliminary injunction, validity can be established on the basis of a prior adjudication of the patent-in-suit by the patent owner against another party.[11] Alternatively, validity can be established by demonstrating that the relevant industry has acquiesced to the patent owner's rights.[12] As a general matter, however, public acquiescence, sufficient to be probative of validity, must be long standing.[13]

When a patent owner seeks a permanent injunction, a four-factor test must be satisfied. The plaintiff/patent owner must demonstrate the following:[14]

- that it has suffered an irreparable injury;

---

[4]H.H. Robertson, Co. v. United Steel Deck, Inc., 820 F.2d 384, 387-88, 2 U.S.P.Q.2d 1926, 1927 (Fed. Cir. 1987) (abrogated on other grounds by, Markman v. Westview Instruments, Inc., 52 F.3d 967, 34 U.S.P.Q.2d 1321 (Fed. Cir. 1995)).

[5]T.J. Smith and Nephew Ltd. v. Consolidated Medical Equipment, Inc., 821 F.2d 646, 647, 3 U.S.P.Q.2d 1316, 1317 (Fed. Cir. 1987).

[6]Hybritech Inc. v. Abbott Laboratories, 849 F.2d 1446, 1451, 7 U.S.P.Q.2d 1191, 1195 (Fed. Cir. 1988).

[7]Smith Int'l, Inc. v. Hughes Tool Co., 718 F.2d 1573, 1581 n.7, 219 U.S.P.Q. 686, 693 n.7 (Fed. Cir. 1983).

[8]Smith Int'l, 718 F.2d at 1578, 219 U.S.P.Q. at 690.

[9]Smith Int'l, 718 F.2d at 1578, 219 U.S.P.Q. at 690.

[10]28 U.S.C.A. § 1292(a)(1).

[11]Hybritech, 849 F.2d at 1452, 7 U.S.P.Q.2d at 1197.

[12]Kimberly-Clark Worldwide, Inc. v. First Quality Baby Products, LLC, 900 F. Supp. 2d 903, 917 (E.D. Wis. 2012).

[13]Drexelbrook Controls, Inc. v. Magnetrol Intern., Inc., 720 F. Supp. 397, 401, 12 U.S.P.Q.2d 1608, 1611 (D. Del. 1989), aff'd, 904 F.2d 45, 16 U.S.P.Q.2d 1158 (Fed. Cir. 1990).

[14]eBay Inc. v. MercExchange, L.L.C., 547 U.S. 388, 391, 126 S. Ct. 1837, 1839, 78 U.S.P.Q.2d 1577, 27

- that remedies available by law, such as monetary damages, are inadequate to compensate for that injury;
- that, considering the balance of hardships between the plaintiff and defendant, a remedy in equity is warranted; and
- that the public interest would not be disserved by a permanent injunction.

These are well-established principles of equity and "apply with equal force to disputes arising under the Patent Act."[15] As in other cases governed by these standards, the decision of whether to grant or deny a permanent injunction rests within the equitable discretion of the district courts.[16]

§ 5:26 Remedies—Consent judgments

Research References

West's Key Number Digest, Patents ⊙⃯327(6)
C.J.S., Patents §§ 534 to 538

Consent judgments are a common method of settling patent infringement suits so as to include some sort of injunctive relief in the settlement. The injunctive relief that is the subject of the lawsuit can often be better defined by the parties in a consent judgment than by the court in an injunction. Consent judgments may be used after a finding of liability to craft an injunction workable to both parties.[1]

§ 5:27 Remedies—Lost profits

Research References

West's Key Number Digest, Patents ⊙⃯318
C.J.S., Patents §§ 561 to 562, 564, 566

35 U.S.C.A. § 284 provides that the court should award damages adequate to compensate for the infringement:

Upon finding for the claimant the court shall award the claimant damages adequate to compensate for the infringement, but in no event less than a reasonable royalty for the use made of the invention by the infringer, together with interest and costs as fixed by the court.

Accordingly, patent damages can be calculated based upon:

- lost profits of the patentee,

A.L.R. Fed. 2d 685 (2006).

[15]eBay, 547 U.S. at 391, 126 S. Ct. at 1839.

[16]eBay, 547 U.S. at 391, 126 S. Ct. at 1839.

at 1839.

[Section 5:26]

[1]An example of a consent judgment is included in Appendix H.

- established royalty, or
- reasonable royalty.

To obtain lost profits, a patent holder must demonstrate to a reasonable probability that "but for" the infringement, it would have made the sales the infringer made.[1] Under this standard, liability does not extend to speculative profits, yet causation does not need to be demonstrated with certainty.[2] Additionally, the infringer's liability is limited to lost sales that were or should have been reasonably foreseeable. This foreseeability requirement was introduced by the Federal Circuit in *Rite-Hite Corp. v. Kelley Co., Inc.*, sitting *en banc*, so as to provide full compensation while staying within the traditional limits of proximate cause.[3]

The patent holder must also present evidence sufficient to compute the amount of profits lost.[4] Once this is done, however, any uncertainty as to the amount of the loss is resolved against the infringer.[5] In determining the amount of lost profits, the patentee cannot claim, as its own damages, the lost profits of a related company, such as a subsidiary of the patentee.[6]

In most cases, the patent owner has proved its entitlement to lost profits by satisfying the four-prong test articulated by Judge Markey in *Panduit Corp. v. Stahlin Bros. Fibre Works, Inc.*[7] Under the *Panduit* test, a patent owner must prove:

- demand for the patented product,
- absence of acceptable noninfringing substitutes during the period of infringement,
- manufacturing and marketing capacity to exploit the demand, and
- the amount of profit the patent holder would have made on

[Section 5:27]

[1]Lam, Inc. v. Johns-Manville Corp., 718 F.2d 1056, 1065, 219 U.S.P.Q. 670, 675 (Fed. Cir. 1983); King Instruments Corp. v. Perego, 65 F.3d 941, 952, 36 U.S.P.Q.2d 1129, 1137 (Fed. Cir. 1995).

[2]Del Mar Avionics, Inc. v. Quinton Instrument Co., 836 F.2d 1320, 1327, 5 U.S.P.Q.2d 1255, 1260 (Fed. Cir. 1987).

[3]Rite-Hite Corp. v. Kelley Co., Inc., 56 F.3d 1538, 1546, 35 U.S.P.Q.2d 1065, 1070 (Fed. Cir. 1995) (en banc).

[4]King Instrument Corp. v. Otari Corp., 767 F.2d 853, 863, 226 U.S.P.Q.

402, 409 (Fed. Cir. 1985).

[5]Story Parchment Co. v. Paterson Parchment Paper Co., 282 U.S. 555, 563, 51 S. Ct. 248, 250 (1931); Del Mar Avionics, 836 F.2d at 1327, 5 U.S.P. Q.2d at 1260.

[6]Warsaw Orthopedic, Inc. v. NuVasive, Inc., 778 F.3d 1365, 113 U.S.P.Q.2d 1873 (Fed. Cir. 2015), petition for certiorari filed, 136 S. Ct. 893, 193 L. Ed. 2d 785 (2016).

[7]Panduit Corp. v. Stahlin Bros. Fibre Works, Inc., 575 F.2d 1152, 197 U.S.P.Q. 726 (6th Cir.1978) (Markey, C.J., sitting by designation).

the lost sales.[8]
The first three factors establish causation and the fourth factor
demonstrates the amount of the loss.

The Federal Circuit has adopted the *Panduit* test as a useful
but nonexclusive means for establishing entitlement to lost
profits.[9] Deviations from the application of *Panduit*, however,
have been limited to specific circumstances. In cases where it is
difficult or impossible to establish the absence of noninfringing
substitutes, the Federal Circuit has approved a "market share"
modification of the *Panduit* test.[10] In such cases, the patent holder
may prove its share of the relevant market instead of proving the
second *Panduit* factor. Recovery is then based on the patent
holder's demonstrated share of the market.

Additionally, in two-supplier markets, the Federal Circuit has
stated that lost profits may be inferred without analyzing the
four *Panduit* factors.[11] The two-supplier market analysis is virtually identical to an analysis of the second *Panduit* factor.[12] To get
the benefit of the two-supplier market inference of causation, the
patent holder must prove that the market was indeed a two-
supplier market during the period of infringement.[13] This can be
done by showing that there were no noninfringing substitutes
available and by presenting evidence of a defined relevant
market. If arguably similar products were available, the patent
holder may need to be creative in narrowly defining the relevant
market. After the patent holder establishes the existence of a
two-supplier market, the infringer is then given an opportunity
to rebut the inference that the infringement caused the loss of
profits.[14] The infringer's rebuttal is likely to include evidence
tending to show a lack of demand for the patented feature or the
patent holder's inability to meet the demand. In such a case, the
Panduit factors come in through the back door.

An emerging fact pattern in which lost profits have been

---

[8]Panduit, 575 F.2d at 1156, 197
U.S.P.Q. at 730.

[9]*E.g.*, State Industries, Inc. v.
Mor-Flo Industries, Inc., 883 F.2d
1573, 1577, 12 U.S.P.Q.2d 1026, 1028
(Fed. Cir. 1989); Rite-Hite Corp. v.
Kelley Co., Inc., 56 F.3d at 1548, 35
U.S.P.Q.2d at 1071.

[10]State Industries, 883 F.2d at
1573.

[11]Lam, Inc., 718 F.2d at 1065, 219
U.S.P.Q. at 675; Kaufman Co., Inc. v.
Lantech, Inc., 926 F.2d 1136, 1141, 17
U.S.P.Q.2d 1828, 1833 (Fed. Cir. 1991);
Del Mar Avionics, 836 F.2d at 1327, 5

U.S.P.Q.2d at 1260; Amstar Corp. v.
Envirotech Corp., 823 F.2d 1538, 1543,
3 U.S.P.Q.2d 1412, 1415 (Fed. Cir.
1987).

[12]Micro Chemical, Inc. v. Lextron,
Inc., 318 F.3d 1119, 1124, 65 U.S.P.
Q.2d 1695 (Fed. Cir. 2003).

[13]*See* Water Technologies, 850
F.2d at 673, 7 U.S.P.Q.2d at 1107 (lost
profits improperly awarded where no
evidence was presented to prove a two-
supplier market).

[14]*See* Kaufman, 926 F.2d at 1143,
17 U.S.P.Q.2d at 1833.

awarded is a situation in which the patent holder markets two products that compete in the market with the infringer's product, only one of which is covered by the patent-in-suit. The Federal Circuit, sitting *en banc* in *Rite-Hite Corp. v. Kelley Co. Inc.*,[15] affirmed the district court's award of lost profits due to lost sales of a product that was not covered by the patent-in-suit, but was covered by a second patent owned by plaintiff Rite-Hite. While the infringer argued that the law permitted recovery of lost profits damages only for lost sales of a product covered by the patent-in-suit, the *Rite-Hite* court reasoned that lost profits were appropriate on both products to provide complete compensation for infringement under 35 U.S.C.A. § 284.[16] The *Rite-Hite* court additionally noted that while the *Panduit* test was not the "*sine qua non*" for proving lost profits, *Panduit* was met in this case.[17] The product not covered by the patent-in-suit was not an acceptable noninfringing alternative since it was covered by a second Rite-Hite patent that made it available only to Rite-Hite's customers.[18]

The *Rite-Hite* holding was expanded by a panel of the Federal Circuit in *King Instruments Corp. v. Perego*[19] to provide for recovery of lost profits despite the fact that patent holder King did not make or sell a product that embodied the invention of the patent-in-suit. The Federal Circuit affirmed the district court's award of lost profits on lost sales of a competing product. It is unclear from the record whether King's competing product was covered by any valid patent,[20] but this fact was not critical because King was awarded market share lost profits and thus the second *Panduit* factor (i.e. the absence of noninfringing substitutes) was not at issue.

Another way to approach lost profits is through lost profits due to price erosion. Price erosion damages can be described as "the difference between *actual* costs of goods and *potential* price—the price [the patent holder] could have realized had there been no competition from the infringers."[21] Price erosion lost profits were approved by the Supreme Court over one hundred years ago in

---

[15]Rite-Hite Corp. v. Kelley Co., Inc., 56 F.3d 1538, 35 U.S.P.Q.2d 1065 (Fed. Cir. 1995).

[16]Rite-Hite, 56 F.3d at 1546, 35 U.S.P.Q.2d at 1072.

[17]Rite-Hite, 56 F.3d at 1546, 35 U.S.P.Q.2d at 1072.

[18]Rite-Hite, 56 F.3d at 1546, 35 U.S.P.Q.2d at 1072.

[19]King Instruments Corp. v. Perego, 65 F.3d 941, 36 U.S.P.Q.2d 1129 (Fed. Cir. 1995).

[20]King Instruments, 65 F.3d at 954, 36 U.S.P.Q.2d at 1138 (Nies, J., dissenting).

[21]Matter of Mahurkar Double Lumen Hemodialysis Catheter Patent Litigation, 831 F. Supp. 1354, 1386, 28 U.S.P.Q.2d 1801, 1827 (N.D. Ill. 1993), judgment aff'd, 71 F.3d 1573, 37 U.S.P.Q.2d 1138 (Fed. Cir. 1995) (Easterbrook, C.J., sitting by designation) (emphasis in original).

Yale Lock Mfg. Co. v. Sargent.[22] In that case, the Supreme Court stated: "Reduction of prices, and consequent loss of profits, enforced by infringing competition, is a proper ground for awarding damages. The only question is as to the character and sufficiency of the evidence."[23]

The general standard of proof for an award of price erosion lost profits is the same as that for lost profits due to lost sales: the patent holder must show a reasonable probability that it would have charged higher prices but for the infringement, and it must prove the amount of its loss to a reasonable probability.[24] The usual scenario in which a case of price erosion can be established is where the patent holder can demonstrate that it cut prices to meet the infringer's competition. However, under the proper facts, a patent holder may also recover profits lost from the inability to raise its prices to a level that the market would have sustained absent the infringement.

To prove entitlement to price erosion lost profits, the patent holder generally must present evidence of at least three things: that the infringer's presence in the market caused it to cut prices or prevented it from increasing prices; the price it would have charged in the absence of infringement; and the number of units it would have sold at the higher price. In response, the infringer can try to identify factors other than the infringement that held the patent holder's prices down during the infringement period. Additionally, the infringer can try to show that the patent holder would not have increased its profits by selling at the asserted higher price.

§ 5:28 Remedies—Reasonable royalty

Research References
West's Key Number Digest, Patents ⟨⟩319(1)
C.J.S., Patents §§ 561 to 562, 565, 567 to 568

In many cases, damages in patent infringement are based upon a hypothetical "reasonable royalty." A reasonable royalty is often determined on the "basis of a hypothetical negotiation, occurring between the parties at the time that infringement began."[1] The patentee bears the burden of proving the reasonable royalty,

---

[22]Yale Lock Mfg. Co. v. Sargent, 117 U.S. 536, 6 S. Ct. 934 (1886).

[23]Yale Lock, 117 U.S. at 551, 6 S. Ct. at 942.

[24]Panduit, 575 F.2d at 1157, 197 U.S.P.Q. at 730; Lam, 718 F.2d at

1065, 219 U.S.P.Q. at 675.

[Section 5:28]

[1]Uniloc USA, Inc. v. Microsoft Corp., 632 F.3d 1292, 1312, 98 U.S.P.Q.2d 1203 (Fed. Cir. 2011).

which is often accomplished through expert testimony.[2] To be admissible under *Daubert* and *Kumho*, "expert testimony opining on a reasonable royalty rate must 'carefully tie proof of damages to the claimed invention's footprint in the marketplace.'"[3]

Royalty rates vary widely, and anywhere from 3% to 15% of the manufacturer's selling price (the amount the manufacturer actually receives) is typical. Some commentators and experts have indicated that about 25% of the manufacturer's expected net profit is a suitable measure for a reasonable royalty. The Federal Circuit rejected the idea of the 25% rule, stating that expert testimony relying on the 25% rule fails to tie a reasonable royalty base to the facts of the case at issue and is therefore excluded under *Daubert*.[4] The Federal Circuit has also held that when an expert's testimony relies on royalty rates of prior licenses, the expert's testimony must have a "basis in fact to associate the royalty rates used in prior licenses to the particular hypothetical negotiation at issue in the case."[5]

The Federal Circuit has sanctioned the use of the *Georgia-Pacific* factors to frame the reasonable royalty inquiry, because they "properly tie the reasonable royalty calculation to the facts of the hypothetical negotiation at issue."[6] The *Georgia-Pacific* factors include:

- royalties actually received by the patentee for licensing the patent in suit, proving or tending to prove an established royalty;
- rates paid by the infringer for the use of other patents comparable to the patent-in-suit;
- nature and scope of the license, as exclusive or nonexclusive, or as restricted or nonrestricted in terms of territory or with respect to whom the manufactured product may be sold;
- patentee's established policy and marketing program to maintain his or her patent monopoly by not licensing others to use the invention or by granting licenses under special conditions designed to preserve that monopoly;
- commercial relationship between the patentee and the infringer such as whether they are competitors in the same territory and in the same line of business, or whether they are inventor and promoter;
- effect of selling the patented specialty in promoting sales of other products of the infringer, the existing value of the

---

[2]Uniloc USA, Inc., 632 F.3d at 1315.

[3]Uniloc USA, 632 F.3d at 1317 (quoting ResQet.com, Inc. v. Lansan Inc., 594 F.3d 860, 869 (Fed. Cir. 2010)).

[4]Uniloc USA, 632 F.3d at 1315.

[5]Uniloc USA, 632 F.3d at 1317.

[6]Uniloc USA, 632 F.3d at 1317.

invention to the patentee as a generator of sales of his or her unpatented items, and the extent of such derivative or convoyed sales;

- duration of the patent and the terms of the license;
- established profitability of the product made under the patent, its commercial success, and its current popularity;
- utility and advantages of the patent property over the old modes or devices, if any, that had been used for working out similar results;
- nature of the patented invention, the character of the commercial embodiment of it as owned and produced by the patentee, and the benefits to those who have used the invention;
- extent to which the infringer has made use of the invention, and any evidence probative of the value of that use;
- portion of the profit or of the selling price that may be customary in the particular business or in comparable businesses to allow for the use of the invention or analogous inventions;
- portion of the realizable profit that should be credited to the invention as distinguished from nonpatented elements, the manufacturing process, business risks, or significant features or improvements added by the infringer;
- opinion testimony of qualified experts; and
- amount that a licensor (such as the patentee) and a licensee (such as the infringer) would have agreed upon at the time the infringement began if both had been reasonably and voluntarily trying to reach an agreement, that is, the amount which a prudent licensee—who desired, as a business proposition, to obtain a license to manufacture and sell a particular article embodying the patented invention—would have been willing to pay as a royalty and yet be able to make a reasonable profit and which amount would have been acceptable by a prudent patentee who is willing to grant a license.[7]

"However, evidence purporting to apply to these, and any other factors, must be tied to the relevant facts and circumstances of the particular case at issue and the hypothetical negotiations that would have taken place in light of those facts and circumstances at the relevant time."[8]

Calculation of a reasonable royalty requires the determination

---

[7]Georgia-Pacific Corp. v. U.S. Plywood Corp., 318 F. Supp. 1116, 1120, 166 U.S.P.Q. 235, 238 (S.D. N.Y. 1970), judgment modified on other grounds, 446 F.2d 295, 170 U.S.P.Q. 369 (2d Cir. 1971).

[8]Uniloc USA, 632 F.3d at 1318.

of two separate quantities—a royalty base, or the revenue pool implicated by the infringement, and a royalty rate, the percentage of that revenue pool adequate to compensate the plaintiff for that infringement.[9] These quantities, though related, are distinct.[10] For example, if an infringer has sold 1,000 patented widgets, and each widget was valued at $10, the royalty base would be $10,000. The royalty rate would be the percentage of the $10,000 that would make the patentee whole. If the parties would have hypothetically agreed to a 10% royalty rate, then the patentee would be entitled to a reasonable royalty of $1,000 from the infringer.

Another method of calculating a royalty base involves the entire market value rule. With the entire market value rule, the royalty base encompasses the market for the entire product in which the claimed invention is used, rather than just the market most aligned with the claimed invention.[11] Ideally, the market most aligned with the claimed invention would be the market in which the claimed invention is sold alone. In other words, when the patented invention is used as one of many components in a larger product, and the patentee determines their royalty base on the revenues from the sales of the larger product, the patentee is invoking the entire market value rule to include within the royalty base both infringing and noninfringing elements.[12] Additionally, when the patent covers all aspects of the entire infringing product through the recitation of both "conventional and unconventional elements," the court must still determine the royalty that "account[s] for the relative values of the patentee's invention in comparison to the value of the conventional elements recited in the claim."[13] In such situations, the true question is "how much new value is created by the novel combination, beyond the value conferred by the conventional elements alone."[14]

There is nothing inherently wrong with using the market value of the entire product to establish a royalty base, and sophisticated parties routinely enter into license agreements that base the value of patented inventions as a percentage of the larger commercial product's sales price.[15] However, for a patentee to successfully apply the entire market value rule, the patentee

[9]Cornell University v. Hewlett-Packard Co., 609 F. Supp. 2d 279, 286 (N.D. N.Y. 2009), judgment amended, 2009 WL 1405208 (N.D. N.Y. 2009) (Rader, J., sitting by designation).

[10]Cornell, 609 F. Supp. 2d at 286.

[11]Cornell, 609 F. Supp. 2d at 287.

[12]Cornell, 609 F. Supp. 2d at 286; see also State Industries, Inc. v. Mor-Flo Industries, Inc., 883 F.2d 1573, 1580, 12 U.S.P.Q.2d 1026 (Fed. Cir. 1989).

[13]AstraZeneca AB v. Apotex Corp., 782 F.3d 1324, 1338, 114 U.S.P.Q.2d 1416 (Fed. Cir. 2015).

[14]AstraZeneca, 782 F.3d at 1339.

[15]Lucent Technologies, Inc. v. Gateway, Inc., 580 F.3d 1301, 1339, 92 U.S.P.Q.2d 1555 (Fed. Cir. 2009), cert.

must prove that the patent-related feature is the basis for customer demand.[16]

> The entire market value rule in the context of royalties requires adequate proof of three conditions: (1) the infringing components must be the basis for customer demand for the entire machine including the parts beyond the claimed invention; (2) the individual infringing and noninfringing components must be sold together so that they constitute a functional unit or are parts of a complete machine or single assembly of parts; and (3) the individual infringing and noninfringing components must be analogous to a single functioning unit. It is not enough that the infringing and noninfringing parts are sold together for mere business advantage. Notably, these requirements are additive, not alternative ways to demonstrate eligibility for application of the entire market value rule.[17]

As required by the Federal Circuit, the patentee's proof must use "sound economic and factual predicates" to show some plausible economic connection between the patented feature and the accused operating systems, if the entire market value rule is to apply.[18] This can be done through the use of demand curves, customer surveys, or any other data that indicates that the patentee's invention drove demand amongst consumers for the larger apparatus.[19]

§ 5:29 Remedies—Marking/actual notice

Research References
West's Key Number Digest, Patents ⚿319(1)
C.J.S., Patents §§ 561 to 562, 565, 567 to 568

The availability of damages for patent infringement, whether for lost profits or a royalty, is contingent on either giving constructive notice of the patent through marking patented articles in accordance with 35 U.S.C.A. § 287(a), or on providing actual notice of the infringement. The patent marking statute provides that:

> Patentees, and persons making, offering for sale, or selling within the United States any patented article for or under them, or importing any patented article into the United States, may give notice to the public that the same is patented, either by fixing thereon the word "patent" or the abbreviation "pat.", together with the number

---

denied, 130 S. Ct. 3324, 176 L. Ed. 2d 1240 (2010).

[16]Lucent Technologies, 580 F.3d at 1336.

[17]Cornell, 609 F. Supp. 2d at 286–87.

[18]IP Innovation L.L.C. v. Red Hat, Inc., 705 F. Supp. 2d 687, 689-90 (E.D. Tex. 2010) (quoting Riles v. Shell Exploration and Production Co., 298 F.3d 1302, 1311, 63 U.S.P.Q.2d 1819 (Fed. Cir. 2002)).

[19]Cornell, 609 F. Supp. 2d at 289.

of the patent, or by fixing thereon the word "patent" or the abbreviation "pat." together with an address of a posting on the Internet, accessible to the public without charge for accessing the address, that associates the patented article with the number of the patent, or when, from the character of the article, this can not be done, by fixing to it, or to the package wherein one or more of them is contained, a label containing a like notice.[1]

Use of an Internet website to mark a product is referred to as "virtual marking." Such a website must be freely accessible to the public. Some significant advantages of virtual marking are that many patent numbers can be marked on products that do not provide much space for marking text, and that expiration of patents and issuance of new patents can be easily updated online without changing dies, molds or labels.

In the event of a failure to so mark, a patent owner may not recover damages, except on proof that the infringer was notified of the infringement and continued to infringe thereafter. In such a situation, damages may be recovered only for infringement occurring after such notice. Filing of an action for infringement constitutes actual notice.[2]

The patent owner has the burden of proving notice in compliance with the marking statute.[3] As the statute indicates, the nature of the product sold under the patent must be considered to determine what type of marking is appropriate. With many articles of manufacture, the patent marking can be stamped or molded into the product itself. Such physical marking is not likely to be removed by a subsequent distributor of the product, and is the preferred method of marking.

Additionally, past damages based upon constructive notice are not available unless the marking has been "substantially consistent and continuous."[4] If there was a delay between the date that a patentee began selling its product and the date that the patented product was consistently marked, damages are recoverable only for infringement occurring after full compliance with § 287(a).[5] Full compliance is achieved only when the patented products are consistently marked and unmarked products are no longer being distributed.[6] In some cases, the patent holder may only sell a key component of a patented combination, rather than

[Section 5:29]

[1]35 U.S.C.A. § 287(a).

[2]35 U.S.C.A. § 287.

[3]Motorola, Inc. v. U.S., 729 F.2d 765, 770, 221 U.S.P.Q. 297, 301, 31 Cont. Cas. Fed. (CCH) P 72229 (Fed. Cir. 1984).

[4]American Medical Systems, Inc. v. Medical Engineering Corp., 6 F.3d 1523, 1537, 28 U.S.P.Q.2d 1321, 1331 (Fed. Cir. 1993).

[5]American Medical, 6 F.3d at 1537, 28 U.S.P.Q.2d at 1331.

[6]American Medical, 6 F.3d at 1538, 28 U.S.P.Q.2d at 1332.

the entire patented device. This situation does not obviate the requirement that the patent holder properly mark the product. The component may be marked as "for use under U.S. Patent No. X,XXX,XXX." Alternatively, the patent holder may require its purchasers/implied licensees to mark the entire device under the statute.[7] Written license agreements should impose on the licensee a duty to mark.

If constructive notice is not given, a patentee can recover damages only for infringement occurring after it notified the infringer of the infringement charges. Courts have interpreted the actual notice provision of § 287 to mean written notice of infringement, not merely actual knowledge of the patent. Actual notice requires that the patentee make an "affirmative communication of a specific charge of infringement by a specific accused product or device."[8] Providing a copy of the patent to an infringer without indicating to the infringer that infringement is occurring is insufficient to invoke the notice provisions of the marking statute. Even a direct letter to the infringer advising of the intent to enforce the patent will not suffice unless an allegation of infringement is leveled at a specific device. The filing of an infringement suit constitutes actual notice.[9]

§ 5:30 Remedies—Increased damages

Research References
West's Key Number Digest, Patents ☞319(3)
C.J.S., Patents §§ 561 to 562, 569

After damages are determined, "the court may increase the damages up to three times the amount found or assessed."[1] "Although the statute does not state the basis upon which a district court may increase damages, '[i]t is well settled that enhancement of damages must be premised on willful infringement or bad faith.' "[2] Enhanced damages may be awarded as a penalty for an infringer's increased culpability, namely willful infringement. While a finding of willful infringement is a sufficient basis for increasing damages, the decision to increase damages is within

---

[7]Amsted Industries Inc. v. Buckeye Steel Castings Co., 24 F.3d 178, 185, 30 U.S.P.Q.2d 1462, 1468 (Fed. Cir. 1994).

[8]Amsted, 24 F.3d at 187, 30 U.S.P. Q.2d at 1469.

[9]35 U.S.C.A. § 287.

[Section 5:30]

[1]35 U.S.C.A. § 284.

[2]Beatrice Foods Co. v. New England Printing and Lithographing Co., 923 F.2d 1576, 1578, 17 U.S.P. Q.2d 1553, 1555 (Fed. Cir. 1991) (citation omitted). See S.C. Johnson & Son, Inc. v. Carter-Wallace, Inc., 781 F.2d 198, 200, 228 U.S.P.Q. 367, 368 (Fed. Cir. 1986).

the sound discretion of the trial court.[3]

Enhanced damages are intended to be punitive or vindictive in light of egregious behavior by the infringer.[4] An award of enhanced damages may be warranted if the infringer is found to have infringed with culpable conduct that was wanton, malicious, bad-faith, deliberate, consciously wrongful, flagrant, or otherwise characteristic of a pirate.[5] If an infringer subjectively acted in bad faith at the time of the accused conduct, willful infringement may be found even if a reasonable (though ultimately unsuccessful) defense is later devised or asserted.[6] A finding of enhanced damages follows a preponderance of the evidence standard, and lies in the sound discretion of district courts.[7] However, the district court is limited to awarding enhanced damages only in "egregious cases of misconduct beyond typical infringement."[8]

Failure to obtain advice of counsel, such as an exculpatory opinion, cannot be used to prove willfulness.[9] However, obtaining an opinion from competent and objective counsel still provides numerous benefits, and is recommended whenever a colorable claim of infringement could be raised. If no opinion of counsel is obtained, the mere existence of a substantial defense to infringement is not sufficient to defeat liability for willful infringement.[10] The totality of the circumstances must be examined and weighed by the trier of fact. The existence of a substantial defense to infringement may be weighed by the trier of fact, but there is no per se rule that a substantial defense to infringement will preclude a finding of willful infringement.[11]

Generally, opinions from outside patent counsel are viewed more favorably than those of inside counsel. The issue is the objectivity of the analysis or, conversely, the likelihood of bias on the part of in-house counsel. There is sometimes a feeling that in-house counsel are under pressure to give the opinion that the company wants to hear. Likewise, opinions of a patent attorney are generally viewed more favorably than opinions of a general practice attorney.

Written opinions of counsel should include a detailed discus-

---

[3]Modine Mfg. Co. v. Allen Group, Inc., 917 F.2d 538, 543, 16 U.S.P.Q.2d 1622, 1625 (Fed. Cir. 1990).

[4]Halo Electronics, Inc. v. Pulse Electronics, Inc., 2016 WL 3221515, *7 (U.S. 2016).

[5]Halo Electronics, Inc., 2016 WL 3221515, at *8.

[6]Halo Electronics, Inc., 2016 WL 3221515, at *10–11.

[7]Halo Electronics, Inc., 2016 WL 3221515, at *11–12.

[8]Halo Electronics, Inc., 2016 WL 3221515, at *11.

[9]35 U.S.C.A. § 298.

[10]Knorr-Bremse Systeme Fuer Nutzfahrzeuge GmbH v. Dana Corp., 383 F.3d 1337, 1347, 72 U.S.P.Q.2d 1560, 65 Fed. R. Evid. Serv. 365 (Fed. Cir. 2004) (en banc).

[11]Knorr-Bremse, 383 F.3d at 1347.

sion of infringement and validity (where validity is in question), including discussions of the prior art, the accused device, and the language of each claim at issue. Opinions that are superficial and conclusory in nature, and that include no analysis of specific claims, no interpretation of claim language, no discussion of means-plus-function claim limitations, and no meaningful discussion of the prosecution history, are generally not reliable. However, an opinion that is equivocal is not necessarily incompetent. "An honest opinion is more likely to speak of probabilities than certainties. A good test that the advice given is genuine and not merely self serving is whether the assertive defenses are supported by viable proof during trial . . .."[12]

§ 5:31 Remedies—Attorney's fees

Research References
West's Key Number Digest, Patents ⊙325.11(2)
C.J.S., Patents §§ 529 to 533

Under 35 U.S.C.A § 285, "[t]he court in exceptional cases may award reasonable attorney's fees to the prevailing party." An "exceptional" case is "one that stands out from others with respect to the substantive strength of a party's litigating position (considering both the governing law and the facts of the case) or the unreasonable manner in which the case was litigated."[1] Willful infringement and litigation-related misconduct may be sufficient bases for finding a case exceptional for purposes of awarding attorney's fees, however exceptional cases are not limited to such conduct. A finding that a case is exceptional is one of fact, and must be made by the district court on a case-by-case basis considering the totality of the circumstances. The award of attorney's fees is a two-step process. First, the court must determine if the case is exceptional by a preponderance of the evidence, and second, if an exceptional finding has been made, the court at its discretion determines what amount, if any, should be awarded.

The amount of an "exceptional case" award to an injured party is not necessarily restricted solely to amounts paid by the injured party for purely legal services of lawyers. Rather, determinations of the amount of an award under § 285 are within a court's inherent equitable power and discretion, according to the exceptional-

---

[12]Read Corp. v. Portec, Inc., 970 F.2d 816, 829 n.9, 23 U.S.P.Q.2d 1426 (Fed. Cir. 1992).

[Section 5:31]

[1]Octane Fitness, LLC v. ICON Health & Fitness, Inc., 134 S. Ct.

1749, 1756, 188 L. Ed. 2d 816, 110 U.S.P.Q.2d 1337 (2014).

ity of the particular misconduct.[2] Thus, an injured party also may recover for other legitimate expenses (e.g., expert witness fees in excess of the $30 per day amount specified in 28 U.S.C.A. § 1821(b)) that the injured party was forced to pay in the course of litigating an exceptional case.[3]

§ 5:32 Remedies—Total Profits

35 U.S.C.A. § 289 provides an alternative for the collection of damages for infringement of a design patent:

> Whoever during the term of a patent for a design, without license of the owner, (1) applies the patented design, or any colorable imitation thereof, to any article of manufacture for the purpose of sale, or (2) sells or exposes for sale any article of manufacture to which such design or colorable imitation has been applied shall be liable to the owner to the extent of his total profit, but not less than $250, recoverable in any Untied States district having jurisdiction of the parties.
>
> Nothing in this section shall prevent, lessen, or impeach any other remedy which an owner of an infringed patent has under the provisions of this title, but he shall not twice recover the profit made from the infringement.[1]

If infringement of a design patent is found, a patentee can elect to seek damages equal to the total profits of the infringer, which is the total profits of the infringer realized from sales of products that infringe the design patent,[2] The total profits theory of damages set out in § 289 is different than the lost profits theory set out in 35 U.S.C.A. § 284 in that § 284 damages result from the lost profits of the patentee caused by sales by the infringer.[3] A patentee of a design patent has the option to collect under the remedies available to utility patents, but damages under § 289 are only available for infringement of design patents. However, the patentee can collect damages under only one theory and cannot collect damages for both the total profits of the infringer and its own lost profits.[4] Because damages under § 289 (total profits of the infringer) and § 284 (lost profits of the patentee or a reasonable royalty) are discrete and cannot both be elected in one lawsuit, a patentee who elects to recover damages under § 289

---

[2]Mathis, 857 F.2d at 754, 8 U.S.P.Q. at 1033.

[3]Mathis v. Spears, 857 F.2d 749, 760, 8 U.S.P.Q.2d 1551 (Fed. Cir. 1988).

[Section 5:32]

[1]35 U.S.C.A. § 289.

[2]See Nike, Inc. v. Wal-Mart Stores, Inc., 138 F.3d 1437, 1448, 46

U.S.P.Q.2d 1001 (Fed. Cir. 1998) ("The statute requires the disgorgement of the infringers' profits to the patent holder, such that the infringers retain no profit from their wrong.").

[3]See § 5:27, infra.

[4]Catalina Lighting, Inc. v. Lamps Plus, Inc., 295 F.3d 1277, 63 U.S.P.Q.2d 1545 (Fed. Cir. 2002).

cannot receive enhanced damages as set out in § 284.[5]

§ 5:33 Invalidity and unenforceability defenses—General principles

Research References
West's Key Number Digest, Patents ⚷118, 283(1)
C.J.S., Patents §§ 210 to 211, 214, 436 to 439

An accused infringer has several affirmative defenses which it may assert. These defenses fall into two categories: that one or more of the patent claims being asserted are invalid for failing to comply with the requirements of the patent statutes; or that the entire patent is unenforceable on equitable grounds, such as inequitable conduct, laches, estoppel or patent misuse.

The distinction between validity and enforceability is often overlooked or misunderstood. Validity of a patent is determined for each individual claim. One claim of a patent may be found invalid, while another claim is not. In contrast, enforceability goes to the entire patent. A finding of unenforceability renders all claims of the patent unenforceable. Also, a finding that a patent is invalid applies as to all defendants. In contrast, a patent that is found unenforceable against one defendant may, depending on the basis of the unenforceability, be enforceable against other defendants.

Additionally, it is important to understand the res judicata effect of decisions on validity and enforceability. Once a patent claim is held invalid, subsequent defendants can raise a res judicata defense.[1] However, every defendant is entitled to argue that a patent is invalid and unenforceable, regardless of how many times the validity and enforceability has been previously litigated against other defendants. Thus, while a patent may be found to be invalid or unenforceable, a patent can never be found "valid" and "enforceable." Rather, findings that a patent is not invalid and unenforceable apply only to a particular defendant.

Defenses of patent invalidity essentially cover the same issues as could have been raised by the USPTO during the prosecution of the patent. The alleged infringer is fully entitled to have the trier of fact review the USPTO's decision to grant the patent; but, a patent is presumed valid.[2] In fact, each claim of a patent is

---

[5]*See* § 5:30, *infra*.

[Section 5:33]

[1]Blonder-Tongue Laboratories, Inc. v. University of Illinois Founda-

tion, 402 U.S. 313, 350, 91 S. Ct. 1434, 1453, 169 U.S.P.Q. 513, 527-28, 1971 Trade Cas. (CCH) ¶ 73565 (1971).

[2]35 U.S.C.A. § 282.

presumed valid independently of the validity of other claims.[3] For a claim to be found invalid, the defendant in a patent infringement action must prove by clear and convincing evidence that the claim does not meet the statutory requirements of patentability.[4] The alleged infringer will often present new evidence that was not before the USPTO to support a theory that, in view of all the facts, the patent never should have been issued.

The accused infringer may rely either on the prior art or other evidence that was before the USPTO during prosecution, or on evidence that was not considered by the USPTO. The burden of proof is more difficult to carry when the evidence relied upon consists only of the prior art considered by the examiner.[5] Conversely, a challenger to a patent may more easily carry its burden of proof on the basis of prior art that is more pertinent than that considered by the examiner.[6]

Regardless of whether a challenger to a patent relies on prior art considered by the examiner or prior art not considered by the examiner, the standard of proof for patent invalidity remains clear and convincing evidence.[7] When a challenger to a patent relies on prior art not previously considered by the examiner, the challenger should request a jury instruction instructing the jury to consider that it has heard evidence that the USPTO had no opportunity to evaluate before granting the patent and for the jury to evaluate whether the evidence before it is materially new, and if so, to consider that fact when determining whether an invalidity defense has been proved by clear and convincing evidence.[8]

§ 5:34 Invalidity defenses—Section 101 defenses

Research References

West's Key Number Digest, Patents ⊱46, 120, 283(1)

C.J.S., Patents §§ 59, 210, 213, 436 to 439

Section 101 is a source of three possible invalidity defenses: lack of utility, nonpatentable subject matter and double patenting. All three of these issues commonly arise in the context of prose-

---

[3]35 U.S.C.A. § 282.

[4]Microsoft Corp. v. i4i Ltd. Partnership, 564 U.S. __, 131 S.Ct. 2238, 2243 (2011).

[5]Microsoft, 564 U.S. at __; Hughes Aircraft, 717 F.2d at 1359, 219 U.S.P.Q. at 478 (citations omitted); Fromson v. Advance Offset Plate, Inc., 755 F.2d 1549, 1555, 225 U.S.P.Q. 26, 31 (Fed. Cir. 1985).

[6]Microsoft, 564 U.S. at __; Aktiebolaget Karlstads Mekaniska Werkstad v. U.S. Intern. Trade Com'n, 1 Fed. Cir. (T) 21, 705 F.2d 1565, 1577, 4 Int'l Trade Rep. (BNA) 1769, 217 U.S.P.Q. 865, 873 (1983).

[7]Microsoft Corp. v. i4i Ltd. Partnership, 131 S. Ct. 2238, 98 U.S.P.Q.2d 1857 (2011).

[8]Microsoft Corp. v. i4i Ltd. Partnership, 131 S. Ct. 2238, 98 U.S.P.Q.2d 1857 (2011).

cution before the USPTO[1], but in some cases may arise in litigation.

For an invention to be patentable, it must be useful. The utility argument most often arises in the context of chemical compositions which have been devised, but which have no known uses at the time of filing for patent. A defendant will generally not be able to successfully argue that the device which it is making, using or selling is not useful.

To be eligible for patent protection an invention must fall within one of the four statutory classes defined in 35 U.S.C.A. § 101, which provides patent eligibility to whoever invents any new and useful process, machine, manufacture, or composition of matter. If the invention does not fall within one of these statutory classes, which are informed by constitutional limits, no patent can be granted.[2] In addition, judicially created exceptions to the statutory classes have been developed that make ineligible inventions directed to "laws of nature, physical phenomena, and abstract ideas," as these, the Supreme Court states, "are the basic tools of scientific and technological work" and "monopolization of those tools through the grant of a patent might tend to impede innovation more than it would tend to promote it."[3] Determinations of whether an invention is directed to a judicial exception

---

[Section 5:34]

[1]See May 2016 Update: Memorandum—Formulating a Subject Matter Eligibility Rejection and Evaluating the Applicant's Response to a Subject Matter Eligibility Rejection, USPTO. GOV (May 4, 2016), http://www.uspto.gov/sites/default/files/documents/ieg-may-2016-memo.pdf; May 2016 Update: Subject Matter Eligibility Examples: Life Sciences, USPTO.GOV, http://www.uspto.gov/sites/default/files/documents/ieg-may-2016-ex.pdf (last visited May 20, 2016); May 2016 Update: Index of Eligibility Examples, USPTO.GOV, http://www.uspto.gov/sites/default/files/documents/ieg-may-2016-ex_index.pdf (last visited May 20, 2016); May 2016 Update: Subject Matter Eligibility Court Decisions (Formerly Appendix 3), USPTO.GOV, http://www.uspto.gov/sites/default/files/documents/ieg-may-2016-sme_crt_dec_1.pdf (updated May 17, 2016); May 2016 Update: Memorandum – Recent Subject Matter Eligibility Decisions (Enfish, LLC v. Microsoft

Corp. and TLI Communications LLC v. A.V. Automative, LLC), USPTO. GOV, (May 19, 2016) http://www.uspto.gov/sites/default/files/documents/ieg-may-2016_enfish_memo.pdf; July 2015 Update: Subject Matter Eligibility, USPTO.GOV, http://www.uspto.gov/sites/default/_les/documents/ieg-july-2015-update.pdf (last visited Sept. 18, 2015); 2014 Interim Guidance on Subject Matter Eligibility, USPTO.GOV, http://www.uspto.gov/patent/laws-and-regulations/examination-policy/2014-interim-guidance-subject-matter-eligibility-0 (last visited Sept. 18, 2015).

[2]Bilski v. Kappos, 561 U.S. 593, 649, 130 S. Ct. 3218, 3253, 177 L. Ed. 2d 792, 95 U.S.P.Q.2d 1001, 2010-1 U.S. Tax Cas. (CCH) P 50481 (2010).

[3]Mayo Collaborative Services v. Prometheus Laboratories, Inc., 132 S. Ct. 1289, 1293, 182 L. Ed. 2d 321, 101 U.S.P.Q.2d 1961, 90 A.L.R. Fed. 2d 685 (2012).

(e.g., abstract idea) arise most frequently with respect to inventions directed to processes and biologic materials. Whether a claim is directed to statutory subject matter is a question of law.[4]

While laws of nature, natural phenomena, and abstract ideas are patent ineligible, a specific application of one of those may qualify as patent-eligible subject matter. The court will engage in a two-step process to determine if there is a patent-eligible application of a patent-ineligible judicial exception.[5] First, the court determines whether the claims are directed to a judicial exception, such as an abstract idea.[6] Although the courts have not fully defined the contours of the categories of patent ineligible subject matter, particularly the category of abstract ideas, they have provided some guidance by way of example.[7] The first step of determining whether the claims are directed to a judicial exception is intended to apply a stage-one filter to determine whether the claims, considered in light of the specification, are such that "their character as a whole is directed to excluded subject matter."[8] If the claim is directed to a judicial exception, then the court determines what, if any, recitations provide an "inventive concept" that is sufficient to transform the nature of the claim into a patent-eligible application of that subject matter.[9] This second step involves a determination of whether any elements in the claim, individually or as an ordered combination, recite an "inventive concept" that amounts to significantly more than the patent-ineligible concept itself.[10] Attempting to limit the use of a patent-ineligible concept to a particular technological environment is insufficient to transform that concept into a patent-eligible application.[11] Moreover, when dealing with abstract ideas, the claims must do more "than simply instruct the practitioner to

---

[4]*See* Arrhythmia Research Technology, Inc. v. Corazonix Corp., 958 F.2d 1053, 1055, 22 U.S.P.Q.2d 1033, 1035 (Fed. Cir. 1992).

[5]Alice Corp. Pty. Ltd. v. CLS Bank Intern., 134 S. Ct. 2347, 2355, 110 U.S.P.Q.2d 1976 (2014).

[6]Alice Corp. Pty. Ltd., 134 S. Ct. at 2355.

[7]*See, e.g.,* Alice (finding intermediated settlement an abstract idea); Parker v. Flook (finding a mathematical formula for computing alarm limits an abstract idea); Bilski v. Kappos, 561 U.S. 593, 130 S. Ct. 3218, 177 L. Ed. 2d 792, 95 U.S.P.Q.2d 1001, 2010-1 U.S. Tax Cas. (CCH) P 50481 (2010) (finding a method for hedging against financial risk an abstract idea);

Gottschalk v. Benson, 409 U.S. 63, 93 S. Ct. 253, 34 L. Ed. 2d 273, 175 U.S.P.Q. 673 (1972) (finding an algorithm for converting binary-coded decimal numerals to pure binary form an abstract idea).

[8]Enfish, LLC v. Microsoft Corp., 2016 WL 2756255, *5 (Fed. Cir. 2016) (quoting Internet Patents Corp. v. Active Network, Inc., 790 F.3d 1343, 1346, 115 U.S.P.Q.2d 1414 (Fed. Cir. 2015)).

[9]Alice Corp. Pty. Ltd., 134 S. Ct. at 2355, 2357.

[10]Alice Corp. Pty. Ltd., 134 S. Ct. at 2355, 2357.

[11]Alice Corp. Pty. Ltd., 134 S. Ct. at 2358 (*citing* Bilski, 561 U.S. at 610–611); *see also* Diehr, 450 U.S. at 190

implement the abstract idea of [the claim] on a generic computer."[12] However, the Supreme Court has indicated that a claim may recite patent-eligible subject matter if the claim is directed towards improvements to the computer itself or an improvement in another technology or technical field.[13] The Federal Circuit has elaborated on how the significance of a computer to the underlying concept can be assessed. "To salvage an otherwise patent-ineligible process, a computer must be integral to the claimed invention, facilitating the process in a way that a person making calculations or computations could not."[14] Applying the two-part approach in *Alice Corp. v. CLS Bank*, the Supreme Court ruled that method, computer system and computer-readable medium claims involving the exchange of financial obligations between two parties using a third party intermediary to mitigate settlement risk did not qualify as patent-eligible subject matter where those claims amounted to the mere application of an abstract idea (use of intermediated settlement) by a generic computer mechanism that creates electronic records, etc. to act as the intermediary.[15]

In *Bilksi*, the Supreme Court stated that the "machine-or-transformation" test, long used by the Federal Circuit, can be a useful tool to determine whether an invention is patent eligible, but that it is not the sole test for determining patent eligibility.[16] To satisfy the machine-or-transformation test, a process must be tied to a particular machine or act to transform an article into a different state or thing.[17] The Federal Circuit has attempted to clarify the machine-or-transformation test with respect to signal processing applications.[18] In general, recitation of a machine in a process claim "must impose meaningful limits on the claim's

---

n.14.

[12]Alice Corp. Pty. Ltd., 134 S. Ct. at 2359.

[13]Alice Corp. Pty. Ltd., 134 S. Ct. at 2359–2360.

[14]Bancorp Services, L.L.C. v. Sun Life Assur. Co. of Canada (U.S.), 687 F.3d 1266, 1278, 103 U.S.P.Q.2d 1425 (Fed. Cir. 2012), petition for certiorari filed, 2014 WL 2921725 (U.S. 2014); *see also* SiRF Technology, Inc. v. International Trade Com'n, 601 F.3d 1319, 1377, 94 U.S.P.Q.2d 1607 (Fed. Cir. 2010) ("In order for the addition of a machine to impose a meaningful limit on the scope of a claim [to render the claim patent eligible], it must play a significant part in permitting the claimed method to be performed,

rather than function solely as an obvious mechanism for permitting a solution to be achieved more quickly, i.e., through the utilization of a computer for performing calculations.").

[15]Alice Corp. Pty. Ltd., 134 S. Ct. at 2359–2360.

[16]Bilski, 130 S. Ct. at 3227, 3218.

[17]Diamond v. Diehr, 450 U.S. 175, 183, 101 S. Ct. 1048, 67 L. Ed. 2d 155, 209 U.S.P.Q. 1 (1981).

[18]SiRF Technology, Inc. v. International Trade Com'n, 601 F.3d 1319, 94 U.S.P.Q.2d 1607 (Fed. Cir. 2010) (global positioning signal processing method involving a GPS receiver was patent-eligible subject matter).

scope."[19] "In order for the addition of a machine to impose a meaningful limit on the scope of a claim, it must play a significant part in permitting the claimed method to be performed, rather than function solely as an obvious mechanism for permitting a solution to be achieved more quickly, i.e., through the utilization of a computer for performing calculations."[20] To determine if a system claim offers a meaningful limitation to an abstract method claim, the substantive limitations of the method claim are compared to the substantive limitations of the system claim "to determine what limitations overlap, then identify the system claim's additional limitations."[21] If the system claim and the method claim contain merely minor differences in terminology and require essentially the same process, then the claims "should rise or fall together."[22]

Determining the proper boundaries of patent-eligible subject matter remains a topic of much discussion. There are few, if any, bright-line rules, and patentability often hinges on the manner in which particular claims are drafted. Because guidance from the Supreme Court does not provide a bright-line test, the specifics of patent eligibility tests and the ways in which they are applied for business methods and software-implemented inventions, in particular, remain uncertain in this emerging area of patent law, often leading to panel-specific outcomes on appeal.[23]

The Supreme Court attempted to clarify the boundaries of

---

[19]In re Bilski, 545 F.3d 943, 961, 88 U.S.P.Q.2d 1385, 2008-2 U.S. Tax Cas. (CCH) P 50621 (Fed. Cir. 2008), aff'd but criticized, 130 S. Ct. 3218, 177 L. Ed. 2d 792, 95 U.S.P.Q.2d 1001, 2010-1 U.S. Tax Cas. (CCH) P 50481 (2010).

[20]SiRF Tech., 601 F.3d at 1333.

[21]Accenture Global Servs. v. Guidewire Software, Inc., 728 F.3d 1336, 1342, 108 U.S.P.Q.2d 1173 (Fed. Cir. 2013).

[22]Accenture Global Servs., 728 F.3d at 1344.

[23]See, e.g., DDR Holdings, LLC v. Hotels.com, L.P., 773 F.3d 1245, 113 U.S.P.Q.2d 1097 (Fed. Cir. 2014) (e-commerce system and method that specifies how interactions with the Internet are manipulated to automate the creation of a composite web page by an outsource provider is patent eligible subject matter); Digitech Image Technologies, LLC v. Electronics for Imaging, Inc., 758 F.3d 1344, 111 U.S.P.Q.2d 1717 (Fed. Cir. 2014) (claims to a "device profile" were held to recite mere data in an ethereal, non-physical form outside a statutory category of patent-eligible subject matter, and method claims recited "an ineligible abstract process of gathering and combining data that does not require input from a physical device" and cover any and all use of a "device profile"); buySAFE, Inc. v. Google, Inc., 765 F.3d 1350, 112 U.S.P.Q.2d 1093 (Fed. Cir. 2014) (method of providing a performance guarantee for an online commercial transaction using a computer network is not patent eligible subject matter); buySAFE, Inc. v. Google, Inc., 2014 WL 4337771 (Fed. Cir. 2014) (claims to a "transaction performance guaranty" were squarely about a contractual relationship, with their invocation of computers adding no inventive concept, and therefore were patent-ineligible as a mere attempt to limit the use of the abstract

patentable subject matter with respect to medical procedures in the *Mayo* case.[24] In *Mayo*, a unanimous Court analyzed patentable subject matter as a matter of "preemption," which is a concern about how much future innovation is foreclosed by a given claim relative to the contribution of the inventor. Under the preemption doctrine, claims to patent-eligible subject matter must describe an "inventive concept" that goes beyond merely picking out the relevant audience or reciting well-understood, routine, conventional, or pre-solution activity. The claimed invention in *Mayo* was a test in which a certain metabolite was detected, and, in response to toxicity and efficacy, the dosage of a drug that produces the metabolite was altered. The Supreme Court held the claimed medical treatment was non-patentable because the claims did not recite enough detail to describe a patentable application of natural laws but were instead directed to the natural law itself.[25]

With respect to human genes and gene therapies, improvements in those technologies have allowed for specific nucleotide

---

guarantee idea to a particular technological environment); Ultramercial, Inc. v. Hulu, LLC, 772 F.3d 709, 112 U.S.P.Q.2d 1750 (Fed. Cir. 2014), cert. denied, 2015 WL 2457913 (U.S. 2015) (method of providing advertising when distributing media over the Internet is not patentable subject matter); SAP America v. Versata Dev. Group, Inc., No. CBM2012-00001, 2013 WL 3167735 (PTAB, June 11, 2013) (claims to method and apparatus for pricing products and services were directed to non-patent-eligible subject matter); Dealertrack, Inc. v. Huber, 674 F.3d 1315, 101 U.S.P.Q.2d 1325 (Fed. Cir. 2012) (a software business method involving computer-aided processing of credit applications over electronic networks, is non-patent-eligible subject matter as an abstract idea and was "preemptive of a fundamental concept or idea that would foreclose innovation"); Fort Properties, Inc. v. American Master Lease LLC, 671 F.3d 1317, 101 U.S.P.Q.2d 1785 (Fed. Cir. 2012) (method of creating a real estate investment instrument adapted for performing tax-deferred exchanges not requiring the use of a computer was non-patent-eligible subject matter); CyberSource Corp. v. Retail Decisions, Inc., 654 F.3d 1366, 99 U.S.P.Q.2d 1690 (Fed. Cir. 2011) (detecting fraud

in credit card transaction over the Internet was non-patent-eligible subject matter; and recitation of a software implementation of a purely mental process that could be performed without the use of a computer was still non-patent-eligible); Bilski, 130 S. Ct. 3218 (method of hedging risk for commodities trading in the energy market was non-patent-eligible subject matter); Research Corp. Technologies, Inc. v. Microsoft Corp., 627 F.3d 859, 97 U.S.P.Q.2d 1274 (Fed. Cir. 2010) (method for halftoning gray scale images was patent-eligible subject matter); SiRF Technology, Inc. v. International Trade Com'n, 601 F.3d 1319, 94 U.S.P.Q.2d 1607 (Fed. Cir. 2010) (global positioning signal processing method involving a GPS receiver was patent-eligible subject matter); Enfish, LLC v. Microsoft Corp., 2016 WL 2756255, *5 (Fed. Cir. 2016) (finding that "self-referential table functions" are an improvement on a computer and therefore patent-eligible subject matter).

[24]Mayo Collaborative Servs. v. Prometheus Labs., Inc., 132 S. Ct. 1289, 182 L. Ed. 2d 321, 101 U.S.P.Q.2d 1961 (2012).

[25]Mayo, 132 S.Ct. at 1294.

sequences to be analyzed and isolated. Historically, patents could claim any biological invention with a "distinctive name, character and use."[26] For example, oil-eating microbes that had never existed in nature and had significant utility in cleaning oil spills were held patentable, whereas a mixture of previously-known nitrogen fixators which do not mutually inhibit each other was not patentable, even where the combination of nitrogen fixators was more effective than any on its own.[27] In *Myriad Genetics*, the Supreme Court ruled that a naturally occurring deoxyribonucleic acid (DNA) segment is a mere product of nature and therefore not patent eligible, and it does not become patent eligible merely due to its isolation from a longer, double-helix DNA molecule.[28] However, the Court further held that synthetically created complementary DNA (cDNA) that omits portions of naturally occurring DNA is patent eligible, because the synthetic material is not naturally occurring.[29]

Cases in which patent eligible subject matter is at issue may be invalidated on a motion to dismiss or judgment on the pleadings under Rule 12(b)(6) of the Federal Rules of Civil Procedure, without the benefits of discovery or formal claim construction. Post-*Alice*, district courts have been more inclined to dismiss such cases at the outset or in early stages of litigation. While the Federal Circuit has noted in dictum that Section 101 analysis can be "rife with underlying factual issues" (although ultimately a question of law),[30] it has affirmed such motions to dismiss.[31]

Double patenting is a defense that does arise with some frequency in litigation when a patent holder has two or more patents on the same or similar subject matter. Because the statute refers to obtaining "a patent," "[t]he patent statute by 35 U.S.C. § 101 (1988) precludes a patentee from obtaining more

---

[26]Diamond v. Chakrabarty, 447 U.S. 303, 310, 100 S. Ct. 2204, 65 L. Ed. 2d 144, 206 U.S.P.Q. 193 (1980).

[27]*Compare* Chakrabarty, 447 U.S. 363, *with* Funk Bros. Seed Co. v. Kalo Inoculant Co., 333 U.S. 127, 68 S. Ct. 440, 92 L. Ed. 588, 76 U.S.P.Q. 280 (1948).

[28]Association for Molecular Pathology v. Myriad Genetics, Inc., 133 S. Ct. 2107, 2111, 106 U.S.P.Q.2d 1972 (2013).

[29]Association for Molecular Pathology v. Myriad Genetics, Inc., 133 S. Ct. 2107, 2111, 106 U.S.P.Q.2d 1972 (2013).

[30]Ultramercial, Inc. v. Hulu, LLC,

722 F.3d 1335, 1339, 107 U.S.P.Q.2d 1193 (Fed. Cir. 2013), cert. granted, judgment vacated, 134 S. Ct. 2870, 189 L. Ed. 2d 828 (2014).

[31]*See, e.g.*, Ultramercial, Inc. v. Hulu, LLC, 772 F.3d 709, 112 U.S.P. Q.2d 1750 (Fed. Cir. 2014), petition for certiorari filed, 2015 WL 2457913 (U.S. 2015); Content Extraction and Transmission LLC v. Wells Fargo Bank, Nat. Ass'n, 776 F.3d 1343, 113 U.S.P. Q.2d 1354 (Fed. Cir. 2014) ("Although the determination of patent eligibility requires a full understanding of the basic character of the claimed subject matter, claim construction is not an inviolable prerequisite to a validity determination under § 101.").

than one patent on the same invention."[32] This is referred to as "same invention" type double patenting.

"A good test, and probably the only objective test, for 'same invention,' is whether one of the claims could be literally infringed without literally infringing the other. If it could be, the claims do not define identically the same invention."[33]

The preclusion against same-invention-type double patenting has been extended through the judicially created doctrine of obviousness-type double patenting. Claims in a patent may be held invalid for obviousness-type double patenting if they claim an invention that is not patentably distinct from an earlier patent.

In cases where claims are different, an applicant before the USPTO can use a terminal disclaimer to disclaim a portion of the term of the second patent and overcome rejections on obviousness-type double patenting.[34] A terminal disclaimer requires, *inter alia*, that title of both patents be maintained together in a single entity. Transfer of the second patent without the first will cause the second patent to be invalid. The terminal disclaimer procedure is only available before the USPTO, and generally cannot be used by a patent holder in litigation.

Because the double patenting defense does not affect the first issued patent on any particular subject matter, it may only be a partial defense to allegations of infringement of two or more patents.

§ 5:35 Invalidity defenses—Anticipation

Research References
West's Key Number Digest, Patents ☞50 to 74
C.J.S., Patents §§ 31 to 58, 101 to 102

To be patentable, an invention must be novel.[1] The defense of lack of novelty is known as "anticipation." An invention is anticipated if the same invention, including each and every limitation set forth in the claim of the patent in question and arranged or combined in the same way, is shown in a single prior art reference, such as a patent or publication.[2]

There is no requirement that the anticipatory reference be

---

[32]Ortho Pharmaceutical Corp. v. Smith, 959 F.2d 936, 940, 22 U.S.P.Q.2d 1119, 1122-23 (Fed. Cir. 1992).

[33]Application of Vogel, 57 C.C.P.A. 920, 422 F.2d 438, 441, 164 U.S.P.Q. 619, 622 (1970). *Accord* Manual of Patent Examining Procedure § 804.

[34]Ortho Pharmaceutical, 959 F.2d at 941, 22 U.S.P.Q.2d at 1123.

[Section 5:35]

[1]35 U.S.C.A. § 102.

[2]Net MoneyIN, Inc. v. VeriSign, Inc., 545 F.3d 1359, 1370, 88 U.S.P.

from an analogous field or be intended for the same use as the subject matter of the claim. If each and every claim limitation is shown in the prior art reference, the claim is anticipated, and it is invalid. For prior art to be pertinent, it must be enabling—it must place the public in possession of the invention. The single prior art reference must be explicit enough to enable one skilled in the art to reduce the disclosed invention to practice.[3] "Items which do not sufficiently teach a skilled artisan how to make, use and practice the invention are not prior art to the invention."[4] For a description in a printed publication to render invalid a design patent under 35 U.S.C.A. § 102, "the publication must show the same subject matter as the patent, and must be identical in all material respects."[5]

Prior public use of an invention, either by the patent applicant, by the defendant or by third parties, can invalidate an issued patent. The prior public use bar is set out in § 102 of the patent statutes.[6]

The date of one year prior to filing is referred to as the "critical date" of the patent. Under the public use provisions, pre-critical date actions such as sending samples out to customers and filing a design with a public agency can invalidate a patent.[7] Use of the invention in public by the inventor or by a friend of the inventor before the critical date may similarly invalidate the patent, even if the invention is hidden from public view during such use.[8]

Secret use of a method is only prior art if the secret use was carried out by the inventor. "Where a method is kept secret, and remains secret after a sale of the product of the method, that sale will not, of course, bar another inventor from the grant of a patent on that method."[9]

§ 5:36 Invalidity defenses—On-sale bar

Research References

Q.2d 1751 (Fed. Cir. 2008).

[3]Amgen Inc. v. Hoechst Marion Roussel, Inc., 314 F.3d 1313, 1354, 65 U.S.P.Q.2d 1385 (Fed. Cir. 2003).

[4]Jacobson v. Cox Paving Co., 19 U.S.P.Q.2d 1641, 1647, 1991 WL 328445 (D. Ariz. 1991), aff'd, 949 F.2d 404, 21 U.S.P.Q.2d 2040 (Fed. Cir. 1991).

[5]Hupp v. Siroflex of America, Inc., 122 F.3d 1456, 43 U.S.P.Q.2d 1887 (Fed. Cir. 1997).

[6]35 U.S.C.A. § 102(a)(1).

[7]Milliken Research Corp. v. Dan River, Inc., 739 F.2d 587, 599-600, 222 U.S.P.Q. 571, 580 (Fed. Cir. 1984); Concrete Unlimited Inc. v. Cement-craft, Inc., 776 F.2d 1537, 1538, 227 U.S.P.Q. 784, 785 (Fed. Cir. 1985).

[8]See Egbert v. Lippmann, 104 U.S. 333, 26 L. Ed. 755, 1881 WL 19820 (1881).

[9]D.L. Auld Co. v. Chroma Graphics Corp., 714 F.2d 1144, 1147, 219 U.S.P.Q. 13, 16 (Fed. Cir. 1983). Accord W.L. Gore & Associates, Inc. v. Garlock, Inc., 721 F.2d 1540, 1550, 220 U.S.P.Q. 303, 310 (Fed. Cir. 1983).

West's Key Number Digest, Patents ☞75 to 81
C.J.S., Patents §§ 105 to 113

An invention cannot be patented if it is on sale before the effective filing date of the patent application by the patent owner or anyone else.[1] This requirement is found in 35 U.S.C.A. § 102(a)(1) (2012) and is usually referred to as the "on-sale" bar.

There are four policies underlying the on-sale bar. First, there is a policy against removing inventions from the public which the public has justifiably come to believe are freely available to all as a consequence of prolonged sales activity. Next, there is a policy favoring prompt and widespread disclosure of new inventions to the public. A third policy is to prevent the inventor from commercially exploiting the exclusivity of the invention substantially beyond the patent term. The fourth policy is to give the inventor a reasonable amount of time following sales activity (set by statute as one year) to determine whether a patent is a worthwhile investment.[2]

Disclosures made by the patentee in the year prior to the effective filing date are not considered prior art under 35 U.S.C.A. § 102(a)(1).[3] Under that statute, an on-sale bar exists if the patented invention has been sold or offered for sale more than one year before the filing of the patent application, by the patent owner or anyone else.

Even a single, unrestricted sale brings into operation the § 102(a)(1) bar to patentability. On-sale status may be found from activity by the inventor or the inventor's company in attempting to market the invention. The on-sale bar does not make exceptions for sales made by third parties either innocently or fraudulently. It is also irrelevant that the parties did not know the novel characteristics of the invention on sale.[4] The inventor's loss of rights to a patent flows from the attempt to profit from the invention by commercial exploitation beyond the grace period allowed by Congress.[5] The USPTO has taken a position that for a sale to trigger the on-sale bar as set out in 35 U.S.C.A. § 102 (and amended by the America Invents Act of 2011), the sale must be public. However, the Federal Circuit and Supreme Court have

---

[Section 5:36]

[1]35 U.S.C.A. § 102(a)(1).

[2]UMC Electronics Co. v. U.S., 816 F.2d 647, 652, 2 U.S.P.Q.2d 1465, 1468 (Fed. Cir. 1987).

[3]For patents with an effective filing date prior to March 16, 2013, the on-sale bar is found in 35 U.S.C.A.

§ 102 (2006).

[4]Abbott Laboratories v. Geneva Pharmaceuticals, Inc., 182 F.3d 1315, 1319, 51 U.S.P.Q.2d 1307 (Fed. Cir. 1999).

[5]In re Application of Theis, 610 F.2d 786, 792, 204 U.S.P.Q. 188, 193 (C.C.P.A. 1979).

yet to rule on whether the on-sale bar includes nonpublic sales.[6]

It is not necessary that a sale be consummated for the on-sale bar to operate. Even if no delivery is made prior to the critical date, the existence of a sales contract or the signing of a purchase agreement prior to that date has been held to demonstrate an on-sale status for the invention.[7] Indeed, a firm offer to sell may even be sufficient.[8] The offer must be to a separate entity, as opposed to within a single corporation.[9] A sale made in the context of a research and development contract still gives rise to an on-sale bar.[10] A response by a supplier to the patentee indicating that the supplier is ready to fulfill an order by the patentee for the patented product constitutes a commercial offer for sale, even though it is the supplier offering to sell the product, not the patentee.[11] A mere offer to donate cannot be considered an "offer to sell" under 35 U.S.C.A. § 271(a) if a donation is never made and if such offer includes no hallmarks of a potential commercial transaction, such as price quotation and product description, or communication that the item is available for purchase by the intended donee. The offer must include more than a mere invitation to accept a gift.[12]

The offer for sale need not disclose the invention. Proof that the offered product is in fact the claimed invention (or would render the claimed invention obvious) may be established by any relevant evidence, such as memoranda, drawings, correspondence, and testimony of witnesses.[13] In order to trigger the on-sale bar, it is not necessary to show that all embodiments of the invention were on sale more than one year before the patent application was filed. It is enough to show that one embodiment of the invention was on sale during the one year period.[14] However, the offer for sale must be for the invention, and not for patent or other intellectual property rights to the invention. An agreement

---

[6]One district court, the United States District Court for the District of New Jersey, agreed with the USPTO and has ruled that the sale must be public to trigger the on-sale bar. Helsinn Healthcare S.A. v. Dr. Reddy's Laboratories Ltd., 2016 WL 832089, *51 (D.N.J. 2016).

[7]Buildex Inc. v. Kason Industries, Inc., 849 F.2d 1461, 1464, 7 U.S.P.Q.2d 1325, 1327 (Fed. Cir. 1988).

[8]Buildex, 849 F.2d at 1464, 7 U.S.P.Q.2d at 1327–28.

[9]In re Caveney, 761 F.2d 671, 676, 226 U.S.P.Q. 1, 4 (Fed. Cir. 1985).

[10]Zacharin v. U.S., 213 F.3d 1366,

55 U.S.P.Q.2d 1047 (Fed. Cir. 2000).

[11]Hamilton Beach Brands, Inc. v. Sunbeam Products, Inc., 726 F.3d 1370, 1377, 107 U.S.P.Q.2d 1901 (Fed. Cir. 2013).

[12]HollyAnne Corp. v. TFT, Inc., 199 F.3d 1304, 53 U.S.P.Q.2d 1201, 1205 (Fed. Cir. 1999).

[13]RCA Corp. v. Data General Corp., 887 F.2d 1056, 1060, 12 U.S.P.Q.2d 1449, 1452 (Fed. Cir. 1989).

[14]Scaltech, Inc. v. Retec/Tetra, LLC, 269 F.3d 1321, 60 U.S.P.Q.2d 1687, 45 U.C.C. Rep. Serv. 2d 1036 (Fed. Cir. 2001).

to sell patent rights does not invoke the on-sale bar.[15]

To invoke the on-sale bar, the product or process offered for sale need not include every element of the patented product or process. Sale of a product or process that would render the patented invention "obvious" is sufficient.[16] Consequently, an invention can exist for the purposes of the statutory bar even though it may later be refined or improved.[17] The Supreme Court has concluded that the on-sale bar to patentability applies when two conditions are satisfied before the critical date.[18] First, the product must be the subject of a commercial offer for sale. The court has interpreted the requirement of a "commercial offer for sale" as an offer that meets the requirements of an offer as understood under the well-settled laws of contracts.[19] Second, the invention must be ready for patenting.[20] The second condition may be satisfied in at least two ways: 1) by proof of reduction to practice before the critical date, or 2) by proof that, prior to the critical date, the inventor had prepared drawings or other descriptions of the invention that were sufficiently specific to enable a person skilled in the art to practice the invention.[21]

§ 5:37 Invalidity defenses—Experimental use

Research References
West's Key Number Digest, Patents ⬤➞75 to 81
C.J.S., Patents §§ 105 to 113

In response to a public use or on-sale bar defense, the patent owner may argue that any such use or sale prior to the critical date was an "experimental use." Experimental use is a narrowly construed exception to public use and on-sale bars. Even if there is a bona fide experimental purpose, an inventor may not commercially exploit his or her invention for more than one year prior to filing a patent application on that invention. The experimental use exception applies only if a commercial exploitation is "merely incidental" to the primary purpose of experimentation to

---

[15]Moleculon Research Corp. v. CBS, Inc., 793 F.2d 1261, 1267, 229 U.S.P.Q. 805, 809 (Fed. Cir. 1986).

[16]UMC, 816 F.2d at 656, 2 U.S.P. Q.2d at 1471; RCA, 887 F.2d at 1059, 12 U.S.P.Q.2d at 1454.

[17]Baker Oil Tools, Inc. v. Geo Vann, Inc., 828 F.2d 1558, 1563, 4 U.S.P.Q.2d 1210, 1214 (Fed. Cir. 1987).

[18]Pfaff v. Wells Electronics, Inc., 525 U.S. 55, 119 S. Ct. 304, 48 U.S.P. Q.2d 1641 (1998).

[19]Linear Technology Corp. v. Micrel, Inc., 275 F.3d 1040, 1048, 61 U.S.P.Q.2d 1225, 46 U.C.C. Rep. Serv. 2d 334 (Fed. Cir. 2001).

[20]Pfaff, 525 U.S. at 67.

[21]Pfaff, 525 U.S. at 67–68.

perfect the invention.[1]

In determining whether an on-sale bar exists, the USPTO and the courts must consider the totality of the circumstances relating to the character and extent of commercial activities, along with the character and extent of bona fide experimentation.[2] Such considerations historically applied the standard of whether any public use or sale (or offer to sell) was mainly for the purpose of trade or profit or substantially for the purpose of experimentation.[3]

"Reduction to practice" of the subject invention means that an actual embodiment has been built that includes all elements of the claim.[4] Experimental use, which means perfecting or completing an invention to the point of determining that it will work for its intended purpose, necessarily ends with an actual reduction to practice.[5] Thus, having been reduced to practice, the sale of or offer to sell an invention is no longer justifiable as experimental use.[6] However, the opposite is not true. Reduction to practice is not a requirement of the on-sale bar.[7] Therefore, an offer for sale may invoke the on-sale bar even though the product or process which is offered for sale is still in an "experimental" phase. The test is whether the product or process offered for sale might either "anticipate" the patented invention or render the patented invention "obvious."

§ 5:38 Invalidity defenses—Invention by another

Research References
West's Key Number Digest, Patents ⏧90
C.J.S., Patents §§ 120 to 125

Since March 16, 2013, prior invention by another is not a bar to patentability. However, patents will not be granted where the applicant has derived the invention from another.[1] However, for patent applications with effective filing dates prior to March 16,

[Section 5:37]

[1]Application of Theis, 610 F.2d 786, 793, 204 U.S.P.Q. 188 (C.C.P.A. 1979).

[2]City of Elizabeth v. American Nicholson Pavement Co., 97 U.S. 126, 134–137, 24 L. Ed. 1000, 1877 WL 18449 (1877).

[3]Baker Oil Tools, Inc. v. Geo Vann, Inc., 828 F.2d 1558, 1563, 4 U.S.P.Q.2d 1210 (Fed. Cir. 1987).

[4]RCA Corp. v. Data General Corp., 887 F.2d 1056, 1061, 12 U.S.P. Q.2d 1449, 1453 (Fed. Cir. 1989).

[5]RCA, 887 F.2d at 1061, 12 U.S.P. Q.2d at 1453.

[6]RCA, 887 F.2d at 1061, 12 U.S.P. Q.2d at 1453.

[7]Paragon Podiatry Laboratory, Inc. v. KLM Laboratories, Inc., 984 F.2d 1182, 25 U.S.P.Q.2d 1561 (Fed. Cir. 1993).

[Section 5:38]

[1]35 U.S.C.A. § 291; see supra §§ 3:1 et seq.

2013, prior invention by another is a bar to patentability.

Under 35 U.S.C.A. § 102(g), a person is entitled to a patent unless the invention was made in this country by another who had not abandoned, suppressed, or concealed it. While this section most often comes up in priority battles, it may also provide a defense to a charge of patent infringement. That is, if the alleged infringer itself completed or made an invention before the patentee, or if it can identify someone else who did, the defendant can argue that the patent is invalid, even if the defendant was not the first person to seek patent protection.

§ 5:39 Invalidity defenses—Obviousness

Research References

West's Key Number Digest, Patents ⊙16 to 16.13
C.J.S., Patents §§ 26 to 27, 64 to 65, 68 to 71, 87, 89

A patent is not valid if the claimed invention as a whole would have been obvious before the effective filing date of the claimed invention to a person having ordinary skill in the art to which the claimed invention pertains.[1] Unlike the defense of anticipation, which requires that all of the elements of the invention must be found in a *single* prior art reference, the defense of obviousness allows the defendant to *combine* two or more prior art references to show that the alleged invention would have been obvious to one skilled in the art at the time the invention was made.

Obviousness is a question of law. However, it is based upon several factual inquiries, including:

- the scope and content of the prior art,
- the level of ordinary skill in the art,
- the differences between the claimed invention and the prior art, and
- objective evidence of nonobviousness, such as long-felt need, commercial success, failure of others, copying, or unexpected results.[2]

The disputed facts underlying the legal conclusion of obviousness must be established with clear and convincing evidence. Therefore, the fact finder must decide each of the underlying factual inquiries in the *Graham* test, from which the court

---

[Section 5:39]

[1]35 U.S.C.A. § 103.

[2]Graham v. John Deere Co. of

Kansas City, 383 U.S. 1, 17-18, 86 S. Ct. 684, 694, 148 U.S.P.Q. 459, 467 (1966).

concludes whether the invention was obvious.[3] Alternatively, the Federal Circuit has consistently upheld the practice of submitting the ultimate issue of obviousness to the jury.[4] This holding, however, is based upon the assumption that legal mechanisms (such as the court's power to grant a judgment notwithstanding the verdict) exist which limit the scope of the jury's decision. "There is no question that the judge must remain the ultimate arbiter on the question of obviousness."[5]

The obviousness inquiry is an expansive and flexible analysis; it cannot be confined by a formalistic conception of the words "teaching, suggestion and motivation" to determine whether the teachings of multiple references were properly combined, nor can it be confined by an over-emphasis on the importance of published articles and the explicit content of issued patents.[6] Often, it is necessary to look at the interrelated teachings of multiple patents, the effects of demands known to the design community or marketplace, and the knowledge possessed by a person having ordinary skill in the art, all in order to determine whether there was an apparent reason to combine known elements in the fashion claimed by a given patent.[7] However, the obviousness analysis does not need to seek out precise teachings directed at the specific subject matter of the challenged claim, because a court can take account of the inferences and creative steps that a person of ordinary skill in the art would employ.[8]

The first step in determining validity of a patent is to determine which sources of information are "prior art." Information that is not "prior art" as defined under 35 U.S.C.A. § 102 is not relevant to validity.[9]

Unlike anticipation, prior art can only be applied in an obviousness determination if it is analogous to the field of the invention.[10] Two criteria have evolved for determining whether prior art is analogous:

- whether the art is from the same field of endeavor, regardless of the problem addressed, and
- if the reference is not within the field of the inventor's en-

---

[3]Newell Companies, Inc. v. Kenney Mfg. Co., 864 F.2d 757, 762, 9 U.S.P.Q.2d 1417, 1421 (Fed. Cir. 1988).

[4]Brantingson Fishing Equipment Co. v. Shimano American Corp., 8 U.S.P.Q.2d 1669, 1671, 1988 WL 282154 (Fed. Cir. 1988).

[5]Railroad Dynamics, Inc. v. A. Stucki Co., 727 F.2d 1506, 1515, 220 U.S.P.Q. 929, 938 (Fed. Cir. 1984).

[6]KSR Intern. Co. v. Teleflex Inc.,

550 U.S. 398, 418–20, 127 S. Ct. 1727, 82 U.S.P.Q.2d 1385 (2007).

[7]KSR, 550 U.S. at 418.

[8]KSR, 550 U.S. at 418.

[9]Panduit Corp. v. Dennison Mfg. Co., 810 F.2d 1561, 1568, 1 U.S.P.Q.2d 1593, 1608 (Fed. Cir. 1987).

[10]Finish Engineering Co., Inc. v. Zerpa Industries, Inc., 806 F.2d 1041, 1043, 1 U.S.P.Q.2d 1114, 1116 (Fed. Cir. 1986).

deavor, whether the reference still is reasonably pertinent to the particular problem with which the inventor is involved.[11] In *In re Clay*, the invention was a process for storing refined liquid hydrocarbon product in a storage tank having a "dead volume" by placing a gelatin solution into the dead volume. The claims were rejected as obvious by applying a combination of two references, one of which used a similar gelatin solution to reduce the permeability of hydrocarbon-bearing formations. The Federal Circuit reversed the finding of obviousness, because the reference was not within the field of storage of refined liquid hydrocarbons, and it was not reasonably pertinent to the problem of displacing liquid product from the dead volume of a storage tank.[12]

Whether a reference is analogous may have particular importance in the litigation setting. Because of the exhaustive search that may be conducted in litigation, oftentimes the alleged infringer will argue invalidity based on references which are not directly within the field of the invention.

The prior art must be viewed through the eyes of a person having ordinary skill in the art to which the subject matter pertains.[13] Accordingly, the obviousness inquiry requires a finding of the level of ordinary skill in the art. Factors pertinent to the level of skill element of the *Graham* obviousness analysis include: the education level of the inventor; the type of problems encountered in the art; the prior art solutions to those problems; the rapidity with which innovations are made; the sophistication of the technology; and the educational level of workers active in the field.[14] A person of ordinary skill in the art is "one who thinks along the line of conventional wisdom in the art and is not one who undertakes to innovate."[15]

The crux of the obviousness inquiry is in identifying the differences between the claimed invention and the prior art. While it is the differences which support patentability, the claims must be viewed as a whole. That each element in a claimed invention is old or unpatentable does not determine the nonobviousness of the claimed invention as a whole. Casting an invention as a combination of old elements leads improperly to an analysis of the claimed invention by the parts, not by the whole. The critical inquiry is not whether each element existed in the prior art, but whether

---

[11]In re Clay, 966 F.2d 656, 658-59, 23 U.S.P.Q.2d 1058, 1060 (Fed. Cir. 1992).

[12]In re Clay, 966 F.3d at 659-60.

[13]35 U.S.C.A. § 103.

[14]Environmental Designs, Ltd. v. Union Oil Co. of California, 713 F.2d 693, 696, 218 U.S.P.Q. 865, 868 (Fed. Cir. 1983).

[15]Standard Oil Co. v. American Cyanamid Co., 774 F.2d 448, 454, 227 U.S.P.Q. 293, 298 (Fed. Cir. 1985).

"there is something in the prior art as a whole *to suggest* the desirability, and thus the obviousness, of making the combination."[16]

Objective evidence of nonobviousness can include such factors as commercial success, long-felt need in the industry, and copying of the invention by others.[17] Other secondary considerations include initial expressions of disbelief by experts, failures of others, and licenses taken under the patent within the industry.[18] This objective evidence of nonobviousness should be considered in every case for whatever probative value it has.

For secondary considerations to have probative value, there must be a nexus between the merits of the claimed invention and the secondary considerations. Commercial success attributable to extensive advertising and the patentee's position as a market leader rather than due to the claimed invention in the product does not support a finding of nonobviousness. Evidence showing that persons sought licenses out of a desire to avoid the costs of litigation rather than out of respect for the patent similarly undermines the weight of the objective evidence.[19]

§ 5:40 Invalidity defenses—Lack of enablement

Research References

West's Key Number Digest, Patents ⊕99
C.J.S., Patents § 139

The purpose of the patent system, as set out in the Constitution, is to promote the progress of science and the useful arts.[1] Patents can be held invalid if the specification of the patent document is insufficient to meet these goals. The sufficiency of a patent document is judged by the standards set out in 35 U.S.C.A. § 112, which poses requirements of: enablement, description, best mode and distinct claims. Most patent applications in the United States are prepared by experienced patent attorneys who amply fulfill these requirements, and the majority of challenges to the content and form of a patent application are unsuccessful.

A decision on the issue of enablement requires determination of whether a person skilled in the pertinent art, using the knowledge available to such a person and the disclosure in the patent

---

[16]Custom Accessories, Inc. v. Jeffrey-Allan Industries, Inc., 807 F.2d 955, 959, 1 U.S.P.Q.2d 1196, 1198 (Fed. Cir. 1986) (emphasis in original).

[17]W. L. Gore, 721 F.2d at 1556, 220 U.S.P.Q. at 314-15 (Fed.Cir.1983).

[18]Stratoflex, Inc. v. Aeroquip Corp., 713 F.2d 1530, 1539, 218 U.S.P.Q. 871, 879-880 (Fed. Cir. 1983); EWP Corp. v. Reliance Universal Inc., 755 F.2d 898, 908, 225 U.S.P.Q. 20, 25 (Fed. Cir. 1985).

[19]Pentec, Inc. v. Graphic Controls Corp., 776 F.2d 309, 316, 227 U.S.P.Q. 766, 771 (Fed. Cir. 1985).

[Section 5:40]

[1]U.S. Const., Art. I, § 8, cl. 8.

document, could make and use the full scope of the claimed invention without undue experimentation. However, even routine experimentation is not without bounds and can be determined excessive, particularly if it involves testing for an unreasonable period of time or, as recognized by the Federal Circuit, requires "further iterative research in an unpredictable or poorly understood field."[2] Lack of enablement can additionally be found where claims are over broad and cannot be enabled across the full scope of coverage. The scope of the claims must be reasonably commensurate with the scope of enablement. By preventing over broad claims, the enablement doctrine "ensures that the patent system preserves necessary incentives for follow-on or improvement inventions."[3]

The enablement requirement is met if the description enables any mode of making and using the invention as claimed.[4] The enablement requirement does not require the inventor to set forth, or even know, how or why the invention works or the theory behind the invention. All that is required is that the inventor teach how to achieve the claimed result, even if the theory of operation is not correctly explained or understood.[5]

§ 5:41   Invalidity defenses—Inadequate description of the invention

Research References

West's Key Number Digest, Patents ⬅99
C.J.S., Patents § 139

The specification must also describe the invention sufficiently for those skilled in the art to recognize that the applicant made the invention as claimed.[1] Adequate description of the invention guards against the inventor's overreaching by insisting that the inventor recount the invention in such detail that his or her future claims can be determined to be encompassed within his or her original creation.[2] Compliance with the description requirement is a question of fact reviewable under the clearly erroneous

---

[2]Wyeth and Cordis Corp. v. Abbott Laboratories, 720 F.3d 1380, 1386, 107 U.S.P.Q.2d 1273 (Fed. Cir. 2013).

[3]MagSil Corp. v. Hitachi Global Storage Technologies, Inc., 687 F.3d 1377, 1384, 103 U.S.P.Q.2d 1769 (Fed. Cir. 2012).

[4]Engel Industries, Inc. v. Lockformer Co., 946 F.2d 1528, 1533, 20 U.S.P.Q.2d 1300, 1304 (Fed. Cir. 1991).

[5]Newman v. Quigg, 877 F.2d 1575, 1582, 11 U.S.P.Q.2d 1340, 1345 (Fed. Cir. 1989), judgment modified on other grounds, 886 F.2d 329 (Fed. Cir. 1989).

[Section 5:41]

[1]35 U.S.C.A. § 112.

[2]Vas-Cath Inc. v. Mahurkar, 935 F.2d 1555, 1561, 19 U.S.P.Q.2d 1111, 1115 (Fed. Cir. 1991).

standard.[3] The Federal Circuit has stated that the description requirement is separate and distinct from the enablement requirement described in § 5:39.[4]

The threshold for the description requirement is fairly low, and failure to meet the description requirement is rarely a successful defense to a charge of infringement. Under proper circumstances, drawings alone may provide a written description of an invention as required by § 112. However, proof of reduction to practice, absent an adequate description in the specification of what is reduced to practice, does not serve to describe or identify the invention for the purposes of § 112.[5] The description requirement may arise, for instance, when an applicant is stretching the claims to meet a count of an interference, or when an applicant is relying on a design patent application for priority of a utility patent application.[6] Further, the description requirement may also arise when the claims invoke "means plus function" language as set out in 35 U.S.C.A. § 112(f).[7] When a patent uses "means plus function" language, the patent must have a sufficient description of the means used to accomplish the specific function in the specification. In other words, the specification must disclose sufficient structural details able to accomplish the claimed function. Without such a description, the patent is invalid for failing to adequately describe the invention.[8]

§ 5:42 Invalidity defenses—Indistinct claims

Research References
West's Key Number Digest, Patents ⊙101(6)
C.J.S., Patents §§ 140 to 142

The claims at the end of the patent, measure the scope of protection afforded by the patent. A patent can be ruled invalid if the claims are not sufficiently definite:

The specification shall conclude with one or more claims particularly

---

[3]Ralston Purina Co. v. Far-Mar-Co, Inc., 772 F.2d 1570, 1574, 227 U.S.P.Q. 177, 178 (Fed. Cir. 1985).

[4]Ariad Pharmaceuticals, Inc. v. Eli Lilly and Co., 560 F.3d 1366, 90 U.S.P.Q.2d 1549 (Fed. Cir. 2009), reh'g en banc granted, opinion vacated, 595 F.3d 1329 (Fed. Cir. 2009) and on reh'g en banc, 598 F.3d 1336, 94 U.S.P.Q.2d 1161 (Fed. Cir. 2010).

[5]Enzo Biochem, Inc. v. Gen-Probe Inc., 323 F.3d 956, 63 U.S.P.Q.2d 1609, 1617 (Fed. Cir. 2002), for additional

opinion, see, 63 U.S.P.Q.2d 1618, 2002 WL 32063710 (Fed. Cir. 2002).

[6]Fiers v. Revel, 984 F.2d 1164, 1170, 25 U.S.P.Q.2d 1601, 1605 (Fed. Cir. 1993).

[7]See supra § 5:15.

[8]See Northrop Grumman Corp. v. Intel Corp., 325 F.3d 1346, 1350, 66 U.S.P.Q.2d 1341 (Fed. Cir. 2003); Biomedino, LLC v. Waters Technologies Corp., 490 F.3d 946, 953, 83 U.S.P.Q.2d 1118, 1123 (Fed. Cir. 2007).

pointing out and distinctly claiming the subject matter which the inventor or joint inventor regards as the invention.[1]

Claim definiteness is an issue which is usually resolved before the USPTO during prosecution of the patent, and seldom serves to invalidate a patent which the USPTO has issued.

The amount of detail required to be included in claims depends on the particular invention and the prior art, and is not to be viewed in the abstract but in conjunction with whether the specification is in compliance with § 112(a). Definiteness of claims is generally a question of law.[2] For claims to be definite, the claims must inform a person of ordinary skill in the art of the scope of the invention with reasonable certainty, when the claims are construed in light of the specification and prosecution history of the patent.[3] However, absolute precision is not required, and the claims need only be as precise as the subject-matter allows.[4]

§ 5:43 Unenforceability defenses—Inequitable conduct

Research References

West's Key Number Digest, Patents ⌐97
C.J.S., Patents §§ 135 to 138, 145, 178

Patent infringement defendants also have several affirmative defenses which may result in a finding that all claims of a patent are unenforceable, at least for a period of time and against a particular defendant. The unenforceability defenses are largely equitable in nature and are generally applied at the discretion of the trial court. As a threshold for raising the defense, allegations of inequitable conduct must be pled with specificity and with a particularized factual basis.[1]

"Each individual associated with the filing and prosecution of a patent application has a duty of candor and good faith in dealing with the Office."[2] Intentional failure to fulfill this duty, previously referred to as "fraud on the patent office" and now known as "inequitable conduct," can render a patent unenforceable.

Inequitable conduct can reside in failure to disclose material information, or submission of material misrepresentations, with

---

[Section 5:42]

[1]35 U.S.C.A. § 112(b).

[2]Shatterproof Glass Corp. v. Libbey-Owens Ford Co., 758 F.2d 613, 624, 225 U.S.P.Q. 634, 641 (Fed. Cir. 1985).

[3]Nautilus, Inc. v. Biosig Instruments, Inc., 134 S. Ct. 2120, 110 U.S.P. Q.2d 1688 (2014).

[4]Nautilus, Inc. v. Biosig Instruments, Inc., 134 S. Ct. 2120, 110 U.S.P. Q.2d 1688 (2014).

[Section 5:43]

[1]Exergen Corp. v. Wal-Mart Stores, Inc., 575 F.3d 1312, 1328, 91 U.S.P.Q.2d 1656 (Fed. Cir. 2009).

[2]37 C.F.R. § 1.56(a).

an intent to deceive. Materiality and intent must be proven by clear and convincing evidence.[3] The Federal Circuit has narrowly defined intent and materiality so as to reduce the large number of inequitable conduct claims raised in litigation and the undesirable effects those numerous claims have had on the patent system.[4]

The materiality required to establish inequitable conduct is but-for materiality.[5] Prior art is but-for material when an applicant fails to disclose the prior art to the USPTO, and the USPTO would not have allowed a claim had it been aware of the undisclosed prior art.[6] Hence, in assessing the materiality of a withheld reference, the court must determine whether the USPTO would have allowed the claim if it had been aware of the undisclosed reference.[7] The Federal Circuit has recognized an exception to but-for materiality in cases of affirmative egregious misconduct.[8] When the patentee has engaged in affirmative acts of egregious misconduct, such as the filing of an unmistakably false affidavit, the misconduct is material, and the materiality prong of inequitable conduct is satisfied.[9] The reasoning behind the exception is that a patentee is unlikely to go to great lengths to deceive the USPTO with a falsehood unless it believes that the falsehood will affect issuance of the patent.[10] The Federal Circuit has refused to adopt the USPTO's definition of materiality found in 37 C.F.R. § 1.56.[11]

The intent required to establish inequitable conduct is specific intent on the part of the patentee to deceive the USPTO.[12] In the case where the patentee failed to disclose information to the USPTO, there must be clear and convincing evidence that the patentee made a deliberate decision to withhold a known material reference.[13] "In other words, the accused infringer must prove by clear and convincing evidence that the applicant knew of the reference, knew that it was material, and made a deliberate decision to withhold it."[14] A finding that the patentees misrepresentation or omission amounted to gross negligence or negligence is no longer sufficient to establish the intent prong of inequitable

---

[3]Therasense, Inc. v. Becton, Dickinson and Co., 649 F.3d 1276, 99 U.S.P.Q.2d 1065 (Fed. Cir. 2011); Kingsdown Medical Consultants, Ltd. v. Hollister Inc., 863 F.2d 867, 872, 9 U.S.P.Q.2d 1384, 1389 (Fed. Cir. 1988).

[4]Therasense, Inc. v. Becton, Dickinson and Co., 99 U.S.P.Q.2d 1065, 649 F.3d 1276 (Fed. Cir. 2011).

[5]Therasense, 649 F.3d at 1291.

[6]Therasense, 649 F.3d at 1291.
[7]Therasense, 649 F.3d at 1291.
[8]Therasense, 649 F.3d at 1292.
[9]Therasense, 649 F.3d at 1292.
[10]Therasense, 649 F.3d at 1291.
[11]Therasense, 649 F.3d at 1294.
[12]Therasense, 649 F.3d at 1287.
[13]Therasense, 649 F.3d at 1290.
[14]Therasense, 649 F.3d at 1290.

conduct.[15] Because it is unlikely that the requisite intent can be proven directly—generally no inventor or officer of a corporation will admit under oath that it planned and intended to mislead the USPTO in order to acquire the patent—indirect and circumstantial evidence may be used to infer the requisite specific intent.[16] Though specific intent may be inferred from indirect and circumstantial evidence, the specific intent to deceive must be "the single most reasonable inference able to be drawn from the evidence," and the evidence "must be sufficient to *require* a finding of deceitful intent in the light of all the circumstances."[17] Thus, when multiple reasonable inferences can be drawn from the evidence, intent to deceive cannot be found.[18]

Intent and materiality are separate requirements.[19] A district court should not use a "sliding scale" to establish inequitable conduct, where a weak showing of intent may be found sufficient based on a strong showing of materiality, and vice versa.[20] Additionally, a district court may not infer intent solely from materiality.[21] Instead, a court must weigh the evidence of intent to deceive independent of its analysis of materiality.[22]

§ 5:44 Unenforceability defenses—Laches

Research References
West's Key Number Digest, Patents ⊙289(2)
C.J.S., Patents §§ 437 to 438, 466 to 471

In patent infringement actions, the doctrine of laches holds particular importance. Usually, the defense of laches, if established, results in the withholding of damages for infringement committed prior to the commencement of the suit.[1] However, absent extraordinary circumstances, a finding of laches does not preclude liability for post-filing damages or injunctive relief.[2]

Laches is defined as neglect or delay in bringing suit to remedy an alleged wrong, which taken together with lapse of time and other circumstances, causes prejudice to the adverse party and operates as an equitable bar. Laches assures that old grievances will some day be laid to rest, that litigation will be decided on the

---

[15]Therasense, 649 F.3d at 1290.

[16]Therasense, 649 F.3d at 1290 (emphasis in original).

[17]Therasense, 649 F.3d at 1290.

[18]Therasense, 649 F.3d at 1290.

[19]Therasense, 649 F.3d at 1290.

[20]Therasense, 649 F.3d at 1290.

[21]Therasense, 649 F.3d at 1290.

[22]Therasense, 649 F.3d at 1290.

[Section 5:44]

[1]*See* SCA Hygiene Products Aktiebolag v. First Quality Baby Products, LLC, 807 F.3d 1311, 1332, 116 U.S.P.Q.2d 1541 (Fed. Cir. 2015) (en banc).

[2]*SCA Hygiene Products Aktiebolag,* 807 F.3d at 1333.

basis of evidence that remains reasonably accessible, and that those against whom claims are presented will not be unduly prejudiced by delay in asserting them. Laches was well established as a defense to a claim of patent infringement at the time of recodification of the patent laws in 1952.

To prove the laches defense, a defendant must prove by a preponderance of the evidence two factors: "(1) the plaintiff delayed filing suit for an unreasonable and inexcusable length of time from the time the plaintiff knew or reasonably should have known of its claim against defendant, and (2) the delay operated to the prejudice or injury of the defendant."[3] "[A]pplication of the defense of laches is committed to the sound discretion of the district court."[4] A determination of laches is not made upon the application of mechanical rules, but must have flexibility in its application. "A court must look at all the particular facts and circumstances of each case and weigh the equities of the parties."[5]

"The length of time which is deemed unreasonable has no fixed boundaries, but depends on the circumstances. The period of delay is measured from the date the plaintiff knew or reasonably should have known of defendant's alleged infringing activities to the date of suit."[6] Constructive knowledge of infringement may be imputed to a patentee even where the patentee has no actual knowledge of sales or other conspicuous activities, if these activities are sufficiently prevalent in an inventor's field of endeavor.[7] A rebuttable presumption of laches arises from a six-year delay in filing suit. If the patentee knew or reasonably should have known of the defendant's alleged infringing activity for more than six years prior to bringing suit, prejudice based on the delay is presumed. However, the presumption which arises from a six-year delay in filing suit does not shift the ultimate burden of proof on the laches issue.[8]

Material prejudice to the adverse party may be either economic or evidentiary. Evidentiary prejudice arises by reason of the defendant's inability to present a full and fair defense on the merits, due to loss of records, the death of a witness or the unreliability of memories. Economic prejudice arises where defendant will suffer the loss of monetary investments or incur damages

---

[3]A.C. Aukerman Co. v. R.L. Chaides Const. Co., 960 F.2d 1020, 1032, 22 U.S.P.Q.2d 1321, 35 Fed. R. Evid. Serv. 505 (Fed. Cir. 1992) (en banc).

[4]A.C. Aukerman, 960 F.2d at 1028.

[5]A.C. Aukerman Co. v. R.L. Chaides Const. Co., 960 F.2d 1020,

1032, 22 U.S.P.Q.2d 1321, 35 Fed. R. Evid. Serv. 505 (Fed. Cir. 1992).

[6]A.C. Aukerman Co., 960 F.2d at 1032, 22 U.S.P.Q. at 1327.

[7]Wanlass v. General Elec. Co., 148 F.3d 1334, 46 U.S.P.Q.2d 1915 (Fed. Cir. 1998).

[8]Aukerman, 960 F.2d at 1038, 22 U.S.P.Q. at 1333.

which likely would have been prevented by earlier suit. Such damages or monetary losses are not merely those attributable to a finding of liability for infringement, otherwise economic prejudice would arise in every suit. The courts must look for a change in the economic position of the alleged infringer during the period of delay.

The court must also consider and weigh any justification offered by plaintiff for its delay. Excuses which have been recognized include: other litigation, negotiations with the alleged infringer, wartime conditions, the limited extent of the infringement, and dispute over ownership of the patent. A patentee may also defeat a defense of laches if it shows that the infringer has engaged in particularly egregious conduct, such as conscious copying.

§ 5:45 Unenforceability defenses—Equitable estoppel

Research References
West's Key Number Digest, Patents ☞283(1)
C.J.S., Patents §§ 436 to 439

As with laches, application of equitable estoppel as a defense to patent infringement is in the discretion of the district court and is reviewed under the abuse of discretion standard. Unlike laches, equitable estoppel does not require the passage of an unreasonable period of time in filing suit. No presumption is applicable to the defense of equitable estoppel, regardless of how long the patentee delays in bringing suit. Equitable estoppel bars all relief on a claim, not just pre-filing damages.

An accused infringer must prove three elements to establish equitable estoppel:

- the patentee, through misleading conduct, leads the alleged infringer to reasonably infer that the patentee does not intend to enforce its patent against the alleged infringer. "Conduct" may include specific statements, action, inaction, or silence where there was an obligation to speak,
- the alleged infringer relies on that conduct and
- due to its reliance, the alleged infringer will be materially prejudiced if the patentee is allowed to proceed with its claim.[1]

The first element, that the patentee communicated something in a misleading way, does not require an affirmative act by the patentee. In the vast majority of cases, the "something" is that

---

[Section 5:45]   U.S.P.Q.2d at 1325.
   [1]Aukerman, 960 F.2d at 1028, 22

the patentee did not object to the activities in which the accused infringer was engaged. The patentee's conduct must support an inference by the accused infringer that the patentee did not intend to press an infringement claim against the alleged infringer.

The second element of equitable estoppel is reliance. The accused infringer must show that it relied on the misleading conduct of the patentee in connection with taking some action. Reliance is not the same as prejudice or harm. To show reliance, the infringer must have had a relationship or communication with the patentee which "lulls the infringer into a sense of security in going ahead with [its conduct]."[2]

Finally, the accused infringer must establish that it would be materially prejudiced if the patentee is permitted to proceed with its claim of patent infringement. As with laches, the prejudice may be a change in economic position or a loss of evidence.

Similar to equitable estoppel in that it bars a claim, the *Kessler* doctrine prevents a patent infringement action against a customer of a distributor or seller who has, prior to the lawsuit against the customer, previously prevailed against the patentee in a lawsuit alleging infringement of the product sold to the customer by the distributor or seller.[3]

§ 5:46 Unenforceability defenses—Patent misuse

Research References

West's Key Number Digest, Patents ⊜283(1)

C.J.S., Patents §§ 436 to 439

Patent misuse is an affirmative defense to a claim of infringement which requires the accused infringer to show that the patentee has impermissibly broadened the physical or temporal scope of the patent grant with anticompetitive effect. Claims of patent misuse should be viewed in light of the Patent Misuse Reform Act of 1988, which added two provisions to 35 U.S.C.A. 271(d), as follows:

No patent owner otherwise entitled to relief for infringement or contributory infringement of a patent shall be denied relief or deemed guilty of misuse or illegal extension of the patent right by reason of his having done one or more of the following: * * *

(4) refused to license or use any rights to the patent; or

(5) conditioned the license of any rights to the patent or the sale

---

[2]Aukerman, 960 F.2d at 1043, 22 U.S.P.Q.2d at 1337.

[3]Kessler v. Eldred, 206 U.S. 285, 27 S. Ct. 611, 51 L. Ed. 1065 (1907);

see also Brain Life, LLC v. Elekta Inc., 746 F.3d 1045, 110 U.S.P.Q.2d 1089 (Fed. Cir. 2014).

of the patented product on the acquisition of a license to rights in another patent or purchase of a separate product, unless, in view of the circumstances, the patent owner has market power in the relevant market for the patent or patented product on which the license or sale is conditioned.

Patent misuse may arise in a tying context, wherein a patentee requires purchase of a staple article of commerce as a condition of licensing under the patent. The tying arrangement need not rise to an antitrust violation to render the patent unenforceable. A three-step analysis is appropriate for determining misuse in a tying context:

- determine whether there are two separable items, only one of which is patented,
- determine whether the item allegedly tied to the patented item is a staple or nonstaple item in commerce and
- determine whether the two items are in fact tied.[1]

Patent misuse may also arise in several other contexts, including:

- requiring in a patent license a covenant not to deal in competing goods,[2]
- package licensing schemes, where a patentee refuses to license a patent unless licenses are taken on separate patents,[3]
- contractually obligating licensees to pay royalties for use after expiration of the patent,[4]
- insistence by a patentee on a percentage-of-sales royalty, regardless of use of the patent in those sales,[5] and
- attempts by a patentee to restrain use or disposition of a patented product after a first authorized sale, and other antitrust violations.[6]

All of these types of patent misuse are very fact specific and hinge upon the patentee's intent to expand the patent monopoly beyond the bounds of the patent laws, thereby harming overall

---

[Section 5:46]

[1]Senza-Gel Corp. v. Seiffhart, 803 F.2d 661, 669, 231 U.S.P.Q. 363, 369, 1986-2 Trade Cas. (CCH) ¶ 67307 (Fed. Cir. 1986).

[2]National Lockwasher Co. v. George K. Garrett Co., 137 F.2d 255, 58 U.S.P.Q. 460 (C.C.A. 3d Cir. 1943).

[3]Princo Corp. v. International Trade Com'n, 616 F.3d 1318, 1338, 96 U.S.P.Q.2d 1233, 2010-2 Trade Cas. (CCH) ¶ 77147 (Fed. Cir. 2010), cert. denied, 131 S. Ct. 2480, 179 L. Ed. 2d 1209 (2011) (en banc).

[4]Brulotte v. Thys Co., 379 U.S. 29, 85 S. Ct. 176, 143 U.S.P.Q. 264, 3 A.L.R.3d 761 (1964).

[5]Zenith Radio Corp. v. Hazeltine Research, Inc., 395 U.S. 100, 89 S. Ct. 1562, 161 U.S.P.Q. 577 (1969).

[6]Baldwin-Lima-Hamilton Corp. v. Tatnall Measuring Systems Co., 169 F. Supp. 1, 120 U.S.P.Q. 34 (E.D. Pa. 1958), judgment aff'd, 268 F.2d 395, 121 U.S.P.Q. 363 (3d Cir. 1959).

competition.

§ 5:47 Unenforceability defenses—Patent exhaustion

The judicially created doctrine of patent exhaustion is an affirmative defense to patent infringement. The defense applies in situations where patent owners attempt to control post-sale use of their patented product, for example, by attaching a unilateral notice to the sale that disclaims what uses are and are not permitted. The Supreme Court has explained the doctrine of patent exhaustion by stating: "[t]he authorized sale of an article that substantially embodies a patent exhausts the patent holder's rights and prevents the patentholder from invoking patent law to control post-sale use of the article."[1] While the defense restricts the patentee's rights as to the particular article sold, it does not affect the patentee's ability to prevent a buyer from making new copies of the patented item.[2] A patentee may, however, place reasonable restrictions on the reuse and resale of patented articles.[3] So long as the restriction does not run afoul of some law or policy outside of patent law, such as antitrust law or misuse, parties may contract restrictions on future use of the patented article.[4] Use of the patented article in violation of the restrictions placed during sale thus becomes an infringing act.

More specifically, patent exhaustion arises with method claims when 1) the component sold substantially embodies the system or method claims, and 2) the sale of the component is authorized by the patent holder.[5] In determining whether the authorized sale of an article triggers exhaustion of method claims, the court will ask if the article contains all the inventive aspects of the patented methods and has no reasonable noninfringing use.[6]

Where the manufacture and sale of the patented product takes place abroad, the patent owner's rights are not exhausted and importation into the United States, such as for repair and resale, may still violate patent rights.[7]

One factor that contributes toward satisfying the first element

---

[Section 5:47]

[1]Quanta Computer, Inc. v. LG Electronics, Inc., 128 S. Ct. 2109, 2122, 86 U.S.P.Q.2d 1673 (2008).

[2]Bowman v. Monsanto Co., 133 S. Ct. 1761, 1766, 106 U.S.P.Q.2d 1593 (2013).

[3]Lexmark Int'l, Inc. v. Impression Products, Inc., 816 F.3d 721, 117 U.S.P.Q.2d 1817 (Fed. Cir. 2016).

[4]Lexmark Int'l, Inc., 816 F.3d at 737.

[5]Quanta, 128 S. Ct. at 2111–12.

[6]Helferich Patent Licensing, LLC v. New York Times Co., 778 F.3d 1293, 1308-09, 113 U.S.P.Q.2d 1705 (Fed. Cir. 2015).

[7]Ninestar Technology Co., Ltd. v. Int'l Trade Com'n, 667 F.3d 1373, 33 Int'l Trade Rep. (BNA) 1945, 101 U.S.P.Q.2d 1603 (Fed. Cir. 2012); Lexmark Int'l Inc., 816 F.3d at 754.

identified above, is if "the only step necessary to practice the patent is the application of common processes or the addition of standard parts."[8] A factor that contributes toward satisfying the second element is the breadth of the terms of the license agreement. These terms include the agreement's provisions regarding notice and the licensee manufacturers' authority under the agreement to sell products embodying patent claims.[9]

The doctrine of patent exhaustion can apply across patents, including patent families of continuations and divisionals, and the analysis under the doctrine is not altered by the fact that more than one patent is practiced by the same product. Rather, the analysis under the doctrine should focus on whether the product(s) that partially practice a patent exhaust that particular patent by embodying its essential features.[10]

§ 5:48 Unenforceability defenses—Prior commercial use

35 U.S.C. § 273 provides a defense to infringement based on prior commercial use of a process, machine, manufacture, or composition of matter used in a manufacturing or other commercial process that would otherwise infringe a claimed invention. The prior commercial use does not need to be public use, and, in fact, if the prior commercial use was public, the alleged infringer may be able to raise an invalidity defense. For this reason, establishing the prior commercial use defense does not invalidate the patent. The prior commercial use defense applies only to U.S. patents issued after September 16, 2011. For patents issued prior to this date, the defense is limited to the alleged infringement of business methods.[1] To establish the defense, the alleged infringer must show by clear and convincing evidence that:

- the commercial use was in good faith in the United States;
- the commercial use was either in connection with an internal commercial use or an actual arm's length sale or commercial transfer of a useful end result of such commercial use; and
- the commercial use occurred at least one year before the earlier of (1) the effective filing date of the claimed invention or (2) the date on which the claimed invention was disclosed to the public in a manner that qualified for the exception from prior art under § 102(b).

Section 273 further establishes that commercial uses also include use of subject matter during a period of premarketing regulatory review during which the safety or efficacy of the subject matter is

---

[8]Quanta, 128 S. Ct. at 2120.

[9]Quanta, 128 S. Ct. at 2121–22.

[10]Quanta, 128 S. Ct. at 2120–21.

[Section 5:48]

[1]35 U.S.C.A. § 273 (2006) (amended 2011).

established. Additionally, use of subject matter by a nonprofit laboratory or entity can be a commercial use so long as the public is the intended beneficiary and it is for the continued and noncommercial use by the laboratory or other nonprofit entity.

The prior commercial use defense is personal. It cannot be transferred, licensed, or assigned to a third party except as part of a good faith transfer of the entire business or line of business to which the defense relates and then, the defense is limited to use at the sites where the use occurred prior to the date of transfer or the effective filing date of the claimed invention (whichever is later). The defense cannot be asserted if the subject matter was derived from the patentee or someone in privity with the patentee or for commercial use that was abandoned. Additionally, the defense cannot be asserted against institutions of higher education or associated technology transfer organizations (TTO) if the claimed invention is assigned to or under an obligation to be assigned to the institution or TTO.

The prior commercial use defense does not provide a general license under all claims of the patent at issue, but extends only to the specific subject matter for which prior commercial use has been established. The defense must be established by the heightened standard of clear and convincing evidence. Therefore, businesses that may rely on the defense are encouraged to institute policies to regularly document and retain records of ongoing use of all commercial processes and the development and commercial use of technology not publicly disclosed. There is a risk in asserting the defense if the alleged infringer cannot demonstrate a reasonable basis for doing so. Cases in which there is an unreasonable assertion of the defense will be deemed "exceptional" for the purpose of awarding attorney fees.[2]

§ 5:49 Unenforceability—Experimental use defense and § 271(e)(1)

The common-law experimental use defense provides a very narrow defense for use of a patented invention "for amusement, to satisfy idle curiosity, or for strictly philosophical inquiry" unrelated to the alleged infringer's legitimate business interest or without commercial implication.[1] Under nearly all circumstances, in industry and academic research alike, the alleged infringer will be unsuccessful in establishing the common-law experimental use defense.

---

[2]35 U.S.C.A. § 273(f).

[Section 5:49]

[1]Embrex, Inc. v. Service

Engineering Corp., 216 F.3d 1343, 1349, 55 U.S.P.Q.2d 1161 (Fed. Cir. 2000); Madey v. Duke University, 307 F.3d 1351 (Fed. Cir. 2002).

However, Congress has carved out an exception for certain activities "reasonably related to the development and submission of information" to the Food and Drug Administration (FDA) that would otherwise be infringing. The "safe harbor" provision § 271(e)(1) allows generic drug manufacturers to use a patented drug for the research, development, and testing required for FDA marketing approval before patent expiration. In *Merck KGaA v. Integra Lifesciences I, Ltd.*, the Supreme Court held that the activities can extend to drug compounds for which FDA approval is not ultimately sought, so long as the research on the patented compound "would be appropriate to include in a submission to the [FDA]."[2] In *Eli Lilly and Co. v. Medtronic Inc.*, the Supreme Court interpreted 271(e)(1) to extend to medical devices.[3] The Federal Circuit has held that the safe harbor provision does not extend to research tools or products that are not themselves subject to premarketing regulatory approval or to certain post-approval activities to develop information that may be routinely reported to the FDA.[4]

§ 5:50   Non-Infringement defenses—Repair doctrine

The permissible repair doctrine allows a licensee or owner of a patented product to replace individual unpatented parts of that product, regardless of how essential those parts may be to the patented combination.[1] It is not necessary that the component be spent or broken before it is replaced.[2] It can be difficult to distinguish permissible repair from impermissible reconstruction or determine "how much 'repair' is fair before the device is deemed reconstructed."[3] Although there is not a bright-line test that the courts apply, the Supreme Court has stated that "reconstruction of a patented entity, comprised of unpatented ele-

---

[2]Merck KGaA v. Integra Lifesciences I, Ltd., 545 U.S. 193, 208, 125 S. Ct. 2372, 2384, 162 L. Ed. 2d 160, 74 U.S.P.Q.2d 1801 (2005).

[3]Eli Lilly and Co. v. Medtronic, Inc., 496 U.S. 661, 110 S. Ct. 2683, 110 L. Ed. 2d 605, 15 U.S.P.Q.2d 1121 (1990).

[4]Proveris Scientific Corp. v. Innovasystems, Inc., 536 F.3d 1256, 1265, 87 U.S.P.Q.2d 1602 (Fed. Cir. 2008); Classen Immunotherapies, Inc. v. Biogen IDEC, 659 F.3d 1057, 1070, 100 U.S.P.Q.2d 1492 (Fed. Cir. 2011), cert. denied, 133 S. Ct. 973, 184 L. Ed. 2d 751 (2013).

[Section 5:50]

[1]Aro Mfg. Co. v. Convertible Top Replacement Co., 365 U.S. 336, 345, 81 S. Ct. 599, 5 L. Ed. 2d 592, 128 U.S.P.Q. 354 (1961) (finding "[m]ere replacement of individual unpatented parts, one at a time, whether of the same part repeatedly or different parts successively, is no more than the lawful right of the licensee to repair his property.")

[2]Wilbur-Ellis Co. v. Kuther, 377 U.S. 422, 424-25, 84 S. Ct. 1561, 12 L. Ed. 2d 419, 141 U.S.P.Q. 703 (1964).

[3]Mallinckrodt, Inc. v. Medipart, Inc., 976 F.2d 700, 709, 24 U.S.P.Q.2d 1173 (Fed. Cir. 1992); *see* § 5:10.

ments, is limited to such a true reconstruction of the entity as to 'in fact make a new article,' after the entity, viewed as a whole, has become spent."[4] The licensee of the patented product can replace parts that improve the usefulness of the patented product. However, contractual provisions can alter the basic contours of the repair/reconstruction doctrine. If a single-use license accompanies the product, the patent holder can restrict the licensee's use of the product to a single use without the right to repair.[5] However, if it is an unpatented component of a patented product that is marked disposable or single-use, the licensee can replace the component without infringement. In such case, marking the disposable component for "single use" can be recognized as an instruction or suggestion to replace the disposable component rather than an enforceable license term.[6]

§ 5:51 Non-Infringement defenses—Product made by patented process

Section 271(g) prohibits importation without authority into the United States, or sales within the United States, of a product made by a process patented in the United States.[1] The Federal Circuit has interpreted "product" for the purposes of § 271(g) to include only a "physical and tangible" article manufactured through a production process.[2] It does not include the production or transfer of information even if such activity has a tangible result.[3] If the product at issue falls within the court-defined confines of § 271(g), there are two exemptions, which the accused infringer (importer) may be able to allege as defenses. Specifically, § 271(g) exempts products made a by a patented process that:

- are materially changed by subsequent processes or
- become a trivial and nonessential component of another product.

---

[4]Aro Mfg. Co., 365 U.S. at 346 (citing U.S. v. Aluminum Co. of America, 148 F.2d 416, 425, 65 U.S.P.Q. 6 (C.C.A. 2d Cir. 1945).

[5]See Mallinckrodt Inc., 976 F.2d at 700.

[6]Sage Products, Inc. v. Devon Industries, Inc., 45 F.3d 1575, 33 U.S.P.Q.2d 1765 (Fed. Cir. 1995); Kendall Co. v. Progressive Medical Technology, Inc., 85 F.3d 1570, 1575, 38 U.S.P.Q.2d 1917 (Fed. Cir. 1996).

[Section 5:51]

[1]35 U.S.C.A. § 271(g).

[2]Bayer AG v. Housey Pharmaceuticals, Inc., 340 F.3d 1367, 25 Int'l Trade Rep. (BNA) 1769, 68 U.S.P.Q.2d 1001 (Fed. Cir. 2003); ClearCorrect Operating, LLC v. International Trade Com'n, 810 F.3d 1283, 1293, 37 Int'l Trade Rep. (BNA) 2457, 116 U.S.P.Q.2d 1883 (Fed. Cir. 2015).

[3]NTP, Inc. v. Research In Motion, Ltd., 418 F.3d 1282, 75 U.S.P.Q.2d 1763 (Fed. Cir. 2005).

Chapter 6

Principles of Copyright Law

KeyCite®: Cases and other legal materials listed in KeyCite Scope can be researched through the KeyCite service on Westlaw®. Use KeyCite to check citations for form, parallel references, prior and later history, and comprehensive citator information, including citations to other decisions and secondary materials.

---

§ 6:1   The concept of copyright

Research References

West's Key Number Digest, Copyrights and Intellectual Property ⚷1
C.J.S., Copyrights and Intellectual Property §§ 2, 4

Copyright is founded upon two conflicting principles. First, copyright seeks to protect an author's creativity and expression. At the same time, copyright seeks to encourage authors to give the public access to their works. Like patent law, copyright seeks to balance these two conflicting principles by providing authors with limited protection for a limited number of years.

Copyright laws are predicated upon the U.S. Constitution.[1] Congress enacted the first copyright laws in 1790 and the copyright laws have been revised several times since then. The act currently governing most copyrighted works is the Copyright Act of 1976, which went into effect on January 1, 1978.[2] The Copyright Act of 1976 was a comprehensive revision of the Copyright Act of 1909. The 1909 Act continues to govern pre-1978 copyrighted works.

Prior to the Copyright Act of 1976, a common law copyright existed in unpublished works under state law. Under this scheme, the state common law copyright continued indefinitely until publication (if any), and the federal copyright began if and when the work was published. The 1976 Act preempted common law copyright.[3] Under the 1976 Act, both published and unpublished works of authors are accorded statutory copyright protection.[4] Important amendments to the 1976 Act are the Computer Software Act of 1980, which applies copyright protection to computer software; the Berne Convention Implementation Act of 1988; amendments implementing the General Agreement on Tariffs and Trade (GATT) treaty; and the Digital Millennium Copyright Act of 1998. The Berne amendments took effect on March 1, 1989. They modified several aspects of U.S. copyright law in order to harmonize them with the requirements of the Berne Convention, a treaty for international copyright protection. The GATT amendments began going into effect in December 1994.

§ 6:2 Copyrightable subject matter—Originality

Research References

West's Key Number Digest, Copyrights and Intellectual Property ⚷12
C.J.S., Copyrights and Intellectual Property §§ 19, 92

Copyright protection exists in original works of authorship

[Section 6:1]

[1] U.S. Const., Art. I, sec. 8, cl. 8.

[2] 17 U.S.C.A. §§ 101 et seq.

[3] 17 U.S.C.A. § 301(a).

[4] 17 U.S.C.A. § 104.

fixed in any tangible medium of expression from which they can be perceived, reproduced, or otherwise communicated, either directly or with the aid of a machine or a device.[1]

The originality requirement of the copyright laws means that the work was independently created by the author and possesses some minimal degree of creativity.[2] A work is independently created as long as it was not copied from a pre-existing source. Even if someone creates a work that is identical to a copyrighted work, there is no infringement unless the copyright owner can show that the copyrighted work was actually copied.

However, merely expending effort is not sufficient to meet the test of originality. The Supreme Court has rejected a concept known as the "sweat of the brow" doctrine, which argued that a person is entitled to copyright protection in order to protect the amount of work that he or she did. For example, in *Feist*, the plaintiff had compiled a telephone book. The book included names, addresses and phone numbers of people in a certain geographic region. The names were arranged alphabetically. The court found that the mere alphabetical listing of this information was insufficiently original to constitute a copyrightable work. The plaintiff argued that it was entitled to some protection simply because it went through the effort of compiling the information. The Supreme Court rejected this argument, emphasizing that the Constitution and Copyright Act require that the work be original. Simply gathering facts does not meet the originality requirement.

Notice that the test for "originality" in copyright law does not incorporate a novelty or nonobviousness standard as in patent law. There is no requirement that the work meet certain creative standards. Rather, the level of creativity required is very low. The work satisfies the originality requirement as long as it possesses some creative spark, no matter how crude, humble or obvious.[3] However, copyrightable expression is something that is more than just an idea.

While novelty is not a requirement for copyrightability, it is often important in determining the scope of a copyright. A work that is very different from the works that came before it will be given broader protection than a work that is very similar to pre-existing works. Also, as a practical matter, a copyright owner who can show that his or her work is very different from earlier works is more likely to be able to convince a jury that the defendant copied the work. If a defendant can show that there

---

[Section 6:2]

[1]17 U.S.C.A. § 102(a).

[2]Feist Publ'ns, Inc. v. Rural Tel. Service Co., Inc., 499 U.S. 340, 344,

111 S. Ct. 1282, 1287, 18 Media L. Rep. (BNA) 1889, 18 U.S.P.Q.2d 1275, 121 Pub. Util. Rep. 4th (PUR) 1 (1991).

[3]Feist, 499 U.S. at 344.

were many pre-existing works similar to the copyrighted work, the defendant has a good chance of convincing a jury that the work in question was inspired by other pre-existing works, not the plaintiff's work.

§ 6:3   Copyrightable subject matter—Works of authorship

Research References

West's Key Number Digest, Copyrights and Intellectual Property ⊝3
C.J.S., Copyrights and Intellectual Property §§ 9 to 18, 92, 101

The Copyright Act defines works of authorship by identifying nine categories of copyrightable subject matter. In order to be protected by copyright, the original work that is fixed in some tangible means of expression must fall into at least one of these nine categories.

Literary Works. Literary works are those works, other than audiovisual works, that are expressed in words, numbers or other verbal or numerical symbols.[1] This category includes fiction, nonfiction, poetry, periodicals, textbooks, reference works, directories, catalogs, advertising copy, compilations of data, computer programs and computer databases. The term "literary works" does not refer to any criterion of literary merit or qualitative value; a literary work does not have to be a work of classical literature. For instance, a brochure describing a radio station's promotional contest is copyrightable as a literary work,[2] and so are municipal bond documents.[3] Nor is the particular medium in which the literary work appears important. The medium can be a book, periodical, manuscript, phonorecord, film, tape, disk or card.[4]

The definition of "literary works" includes expression not only in words but also in numbers, or other numerical symbols or indicia, thereby expanding common usage of literary works. Thus, computer programs (whether an object code or source code) are literary works.[5] Also, microcode that is a set of statements or instructions used in a computer to bring about certain results is copyrightable literary work expressed in words, numbers, or other

---

[Section 6:3]

[1]17 U.S.C.A. § 101.

[2]Taft Television and Radio Co., Inc. v. King Broad. Co., 822 F.2d 62, 5 U.S.P.Q.2d 1355 (9th Cir. 1987).

[3]Merritt Forbes & Co. Inc. v. Newman Inv. Sec., Inc., 604 F. Supp. 943, 948, 225 U.S.P.Q. 1179 (S.D. N.Y. 1985).

[4]17 U.S.C.A. § 101.

[5]Computer Assocs. Intern., Inc. v. Altai, Inc., 126 F.3d 365, 44 U.S.P. Q.2d 1281 (2d Cir. 1997); Atari Games Corp. v. Nintendo of America Inc., 975 F.2d 832, 24 U.S.P.Q.2d 1015, 1992-2 Trade Cas. (CCH) ¶ 69969 (Fed. Cir. 1992).

numerical symbols or indicia.[6]

Musical Works. Musical works include musical compositions and any accompanying words. Where the words or lyrics and music have been integrated into a single copyrighted work, the work is protected against unauthorized use of the words alone, the music alone, or any combination of the words, music or adaptations of either.[7] Note that lyrics by themselves without the music are also protectable as literary works, because they constitute poetry, and performance of a musical work is separately protectable as a sound recording.

Dramatic Works. Dramatic works include plays, screenplays, operas, musical comedies, etc. Where there is accompanying music, the work as a whole is registrable as a dramatic work.[8] If the music also exists apart from the dialogue, the music is registrable separately as a musical work.

Pantomime and Choreographic Works. Federal copyright protection for choreography and pantomime was born with the Copyright Act of 1976. Prior to that Act, dance was protectable only if it told a story, developed or characterized an emotion, or otherwise conveyed a dramatic concept or idea.[9] The Copyright Act of 1976 recognized that abstract, nonliterary dance was a worthy form of artistic expression.[10]

The requirement for fixation in a tangible medium can be accomplished by filming, videotaping, diagramming, or reducing pantomime or choreographic work to some form of notation. Fixation can be accomplished by videotaping or still photography. Copyright protection does not extend to social dance steps or simple routines.[11]

Pictorial, Graphic, and Sculptural Works. This category includes two-dimensional and three-dimensional works of fine, graphic and applied art, photographs, prints, art reproductions, maps, globes, charts, technical drawings (including architectural plans), diagrams and models.[12] Works of artistic craftsmanship

---

[6]NEC Corp. v. Intel Corp., 645 F. Supp. 590, 595, 1 U.S.P.Q.2d 1492 (N.D. Cal. 1986).

[7]Shapiro, Bernstein & Co. v. Jerry Vogel Music Co., 161 F.2d 406, 409, 71 U.S.P.Q. 286 (C.C.A. 2d Cir. 1946), *decision clarified*, 73 U.S.P.Q. 5, 1947 WL 43587 (C.C.A. 2d Cir. 1947); *See also* Mills Music, Inc. v. State of Arizona, 187 U.S.P.Q. 22, 1975 WL 21095 (D. Ariz. 1975), *judgment aff'd*, 591 F.2d 1278, 201 U.S.P.Q. 437 (9th Cir. 1979).

[8]*See* April Prods. v. Strand Enters., 79 F. Supp. 515, 77 U.S.P.Q. 155 (S.D. N.Y. 1948).

[9]Horgan v. Macmillan, Inc., 789 F.2d 157, 160, 12 Media L. Rep. (BNA) 2114, 229 U.S.P.Q. 684, 85 A.L.R. Fed. 893 (2d Cir. 1986).

[10]Horgan, 789 F.2d at 160.

[11]Horgan, 789 F.2d at 160.

[12]17 U.S.C.A. § 101; *see also* Mason v. Montgomery Data, Inc., 967 F.2d 135, 23 U.S.P.Q.2d 1676 (5th Cir.

are protectable as to their form, but not as to their mechanical or utilitarian aspects. The design of a useful article is considered a pictorial, graphic, or sculptural work only if, and only to the extent that, the design incorporates features that can be identified separately from, and are capable of existing independently of, the utilitarian aspects of the article.[13]

Commercial labels and packages are also copyrightable.[14] To be copyrightable, however, the print or label must contain an appreciable amount of original text or pictorial material.[15] A label that consists solely of a trademark or a slogan is not copyrightable; the appropriate method of protection is through trademark law.

Examples of copyrightable designs include: the carving on the back of a chair, the design on a flatware handle, designs printed on fabric used to make clothes, taxidermy forms used to mount animal skins,[16] belt buckle designs,[17] a toy airplane,[18] and a sweater design with a pattern of ribbons and bows.[19] Noncopyrightable designs include: face structure of a doll,[20] the overall shape of an outdoor lighting fixture,[21] wire wheel covers for automobiles,[22] and clothing display forms.[23]

Motion Pictures and Other Audio-Visual Works. Motion pictures are audiovisual works consisting of a series of related images which, when shown in succession, impart an impression of motion, together with accompanying sounds, if any.[24] Telecasts of major league baseball games, which are videotaped at the same time as they are broadcast, are independent creations since they reflect creativity in use of camera angles, shot selection, instant replay and split screens. Such telecasts are copyrightable as audio

---

1992) (land ownership maps); Hunt v. Pasternack, 192 F.3d 877, 52 U.S.P. Q.2d 1317 (9th Cir. 1999) (architectural plans).

[13]17 U.S.C.A. § 101; *see* § 6:19.

[14]Drop Dead Co. v. S. C. Johnson & Son, Inc., 326 F.2d 87, 139 U.S.P.Q. 465 (9th Cir. 1963).

[15]Kitchens of Sara Lee, Inc. v. Nifty Foods Corp., 266 F.2d 541, 121 U.S.P.Q. 359 (2d Cir. 1959).

[16]Superior Form Builders v. Dan Chase Taxidermy Supply Co., Inc., 851 F. Supp. 222, 31 U.S.P.Q.2d 1216 (E.D. Va. 1994), *aff'd*, 74 F.3d 488, 37 U.S.P. Q.2d 1571 (4th Cir. 1996).

[17]Kieselstein-Cord v. Accessories by Pearl, Inc., 632 F.2d 989, 208 U.S.P.Q. 1 (2d Cir. 1980).

[18]Gay Toys, Inc. v. Buddy L Corp., 703 F.2d 970, 218 U.S.P.Q. 13 (6th Cir. 1983).

[19]Hukafit Sportswear, Inc. v. Banff, Ltd. (Inc.), 228 U.S.P.Q. 244, 1985 WL 3952 (S.D. N.Y. 1985).

[20]Little Souls, Inc. v. Petits, 789 F. Supp. 56, 22 U.S.P.Q.2d 1755 (D. Mass. 1992).

[21]Esquire, Inc. v. Ringer, 591 F.2d 796, 199 U.S.P.Q. 1 (D.C. Cir. 1978).

[22]Norris Indus., Inc. v. Int'l Tel. & Tel. Corp., 696 F.2d 918, 217 U.S.P.Q. 226 (11th Cir. 1983).

[23]Carol Barnhart Inc. v. Economy Cover Corp., 773 F.2d 411, 228 U.S.P.Q. 385 (2d Cir. 1985).

[24]17 U.S.C.A. § 101.

visual works.[25] Nontextual elements of a television commercial, such as rapid-edit style and use of close-ups, which are separate from script and which represent style, tone, artistic choice and total feel of the commercial are protectable.[26]

Visual displays and accompanying audio sounds of video games produced by computer programs fall within the definition of audiovisual works. They are proper subject matter for copyright protection, even if the computer program that creates them is not copyrightable.[27]

Sound Recordings. Sound recordings are works that result from the fixation of a series of musical, spoken or other sounds regardless of the medium in which they are embodied.[28] Until February 15, 1972, there was no federal protection for sound recordings. Because of the widespread growth of "record pirates," however, state laws prohibiting copying of sound recordings were passed. These laws remain in effect for sound recordings fixed before February 15, 1972.[29] Section 1(f) of the Copyright Act creates a limited copyright in sound recordings and makes unlawful the unauthorized reproduction and sale of copyrighted sound recordings. Congress was concerned with combating extensive pirating of phonograph records and tapes; it did not intend to extend coverage to library uses and home recordings.

The 1971 Sound Recording Amendment extends limited copyright protection to sound recordings fixed after February 15, 1972. Exclusive rights of the owner of a copyright in a sound recording are limited to the rights specified in clauses 1, 2 and 3 of § 106, and do not include any right of performance under § 106(4).[30] A copyright owner acquires exclusive rights to duplicate the recording, but she cannot prevent independent fixation by another of other sounds similar to those copyrighted in the recording.[31]

Architectural Works. An architectural work is the design of a building as embodied in any tangible medium of expression, including a building, architectural plans or drawings. The work includes the overall form as well as the arrangement and composition of spaces and elements in the design, but it does not include individual standard features like common windows, doors and

---

[25]Baltimore Orioles, Inc. v. Major League Baseball Players Ass'n, 805 F.2d 663, 13 Media L. Rep. (BNA) 1625, 231 U.S.P.Q. 673 (7th Cir. 1986).

[26]Chuck Blore & Don Richman Inc. v. 20/20 Advertising Inc., 674 F. Supp. 671, 5 U.S.P.Q.2d 1833 (D. Minn. 1987).

[27]Stern Elecs., Inc. v. Kaufman,

669 F.2d 852, 856, 213 U.S.P.Q. 443 (2d Cir. 1982).

[28]17 U.S.C.A. § 101.

[29]Goldstein v. Cal., 412 U.S. 546, 93 S. Ct. 2303, 178 U.S.P.Q. 129 (1973).

[30]17 U.S.C.A. § 114(a).

[31]U.S. v. Taxe, 540 F.2d 961, 192 U.S.P.Q. 204 (9th Cir. 1976).

other staple building components.[32] Architectural plans may be copyrighted as a "pictorial, graphic and sculptural work" or as an "architectural work," and the building itself may be separately copyrighted as an "architectural work."

The owner of copyrighted architectural plans has the exclusive right to not only the reproduction of those plans but also the exclusive use of those copies to construct the subject matter contained in the plans.[33] A copyright in an architectural work that has been constructed does not include the right to prevent the making, distributing or public display of pictures, paintings, photographs or otherwise pictorial representations of the work, if the building is ordinarily visible from a public place.[34] In addition, the owners of a building embodying an architectural work may alter or destroy the building without the consent of the copyright owner.[35]

Compilations, Collective Works, and Derivative Works. A "compilation" is a work formed by collecting and assembling preexisting materials; or by selecting, coordinating or arranging data in such a way that the resulting work as a whole constitutes an original work of authorship.[36] Copyright protection for a compilation extends only to the material contributed by the author of such work, not to any preexisting material employed in the work.[37] Compilations are protectable because of the selection, coordination and arrangement of the items in the compilation. But the copyright of a factual compilation is "thin." A subsequent compiler is free to use the facts contained in another's publication to aid in preparing a competing work, so long as the competing work does not feature the same selection and arrangement.[38]

A "collective work" is a work, such as an anthology or encyclopedia, in which a number of contributions, constituting separate and independent works in themselves, are assembled into a collective whole.[39] A collective work is a form of compilation in which the materials collected are individually copyrightable. Each contribution to a collective work must be able to stand apart and have separate value. Thus, a photograph of a fashion model wearing designs does not constitute a contribution to a collective work, since if the model were removed from the photograph, then the photograph would be a photograph of empty space in which there

---

[32]17 U.S.C.A. § 101.

[33]Robert R. Jones Assocs., Inc. v. Nino Homes, 858 F.2d 274, 277, 8 U.S.P.Q.2d 1224, 26 Fed. R. Evid. Serv. 1245, 100 A.L.R. Fed. 241 (6th Cir. 1988).

[34]17 U.S.C.A. § 120(a).

[35]17 U.S.C.A. § 120(b).

[36]17 U.S.C.A. § 101.

[37]17 U.S.C.A. § 103(b).

[38]Feist, 499 U.S. at 357, 111 S. Ct. at 1294.

[39]17 U.S.C.A. § 101.

is no separate value.[40]

A "derivative work" is a work based upon one or more preexisting works, such as a translation, musical arrangement, dramatization, fictionalization, motion picture version, sound recording, art reproduction, abridgement, condensation or any other form in which a work may be recast, transformed or adapted. Derivative works include works containing editorial revisions, annotations or elaborations.[41] The resulting derivative work must fall into one of the nine statutory categories of works. The standard for determining whether sufficient matter was added to qualify as a derivative work is whether the author contributed something more than a "nearly trivial" variation.[42]

Creating a different version of a copyrighted work amounts to preparation of a derivative work. For example, removing copyrighted art work prints from a book and mounting the prints on tile constitutes a derivative work because it transforms individual images by incorporating them into the tile-preparing process.[43]

The copyright in a derivative work extends only to the material contributed by the author of such work, as distinguished from the pre-existing material employed in the work. The copyright in a derivative work is independent of the duration, ownership or subsistence of any copyright protection in the pre-existing material.[44] For example, a fabric pattern that added an original design superimposed over a background that was in the public domain is a derivative work, and the scope of the copyright extends only to original additions to the preexisting public domain material.[45]

If an author creates a derivative work without permission of the copyright owner, thus violating the exclusive right to prepare derivative works, then the derivative work as a whole is not entitled to copyright protection.[46] Unlike a compilation work where the compilation author's own work is easily ascertainable

---

[40]Blum v. Kline, 8 U.S.P.Q.2d 1080, 1988 WL 52916 (S.D. N.Y. 1988).

[41]17 U.S.C.A. § 101.

[42]Weissmann v. Freeman, 868 F.2d 1313, 10 U.S.P.Q.2d 1014, 101 A.L.R. Fed. 91 (2d Cir. 1989).

[43]Mirage Editions, Inc. v. Albuquerque A.R.T. Co., 856 F.2d 1341, 1343, 8 U.S.P.Q.2d 1171 (9th Cir. 1988).

[44]17 U.S.C.A. § 103.

[45]Folio Impressions, Inc. v. Byer Cal., 752 F. Supp. 583, 18 U.S.P.Q.2d 1137, 31 Fed. R. Evid. Serv. 1320 (S.D. N.Y. 1990), judgment aff'd, 937 F.2d 759, 19 U.S.P.Q.2d 1418, 33 Fed. R. Evid. Serv. 569 (2d Cir. 1991).

[46]Anderson v. Stallone, 11 U.S.P. Q.2d 1161, 1989 WL 206431 (C.D. Cal. 1989); see also Eden Toys, Inc. v. Florelee Undergarment Co., Inc., 697 F.2d 27, 34-35, 217 U.S.P.Q. 201 (2d Cir. 1982); Gracen v. Bradford Exchange, 698 F.2d 300, 302-303, 217 U.S.P.Q. 1294 (7th Cir. 1983).

and divisible, the author's original contributions to a derivative work are not easily separable from the underlying work. Therefore, no portion of the unauthorized derivative work can gain copyright protection.

Restored Works. A restored work is usually a copyrighted work that has fallen into the public domain due to the noncompliance with formality imposed by U.S. copyright law, such as failure to renew the copyright, lack of proper notice or failure to comply with manufacturing requirements. A copyright that is restored exists for the remainder of the term of copyright that the work would have otherwise been granted in the United States if the work had never entered the public domain.[47]

Government Works. A reference is not in the public domain simply because the government adopts the reference as law and requires its use. When the copyrightability of a reference provides an economic incentive to produce and maintain a work, and the work is readily available to the public, the due process requirement of free access to the law does not justify denying copyright protection. This situation is distinguishable from the situation where the public owns judicial opinions because they pay judges' salaries. Judges' salaries provide adequate economic incentives to produce judicial opinions, and thus judicial opinions would exist regardless of the opportunity for copyright protection.[48]

§ 6:4   Copyrightable subject matter—Fixation

Research References

West's Key Number Digest, Copyrights and Intellectual Property
⚹12(1)

C.J.S., Copyrights and Intellectual Property §§ 19, 92

The Copyright Act protects all works of authorship from the moment they are fixed in a tangible form, whether on film, paper, tape, hard disc, or any other human-or machine-readable format. A work is "fixed" in a tangible medium of expression when it "is sufficiently permanent or stable to permit it to be perceived, reproduced, or otherwise communicated for a period of more than

---

[47]17 U.S.C.A. § 104A; *see also* Golan v. Holder, 132 S. Ct. 873, 181 L. Ed. 2d 835, 33 Int'l Trade Rep. (BNA) 1769, 40 Media L. Rep. (BNA) 1169, 101 U.S.P.Q.2d 1297, 2012-1 Trade Cas. (CCH) ¶ 30184 (2012) (upholding the constitutionality of congressional adjustments to statute governing restored works).

[48]*Compare* Practice Management Information Corp. v. American Medical Ass'n, 121 F.3d 516, 43 U.S.P.Q.2d 1611 (9th Cir. 1997), opinion amended, 133 F.3d 1140, 45 U.S.P.Q.2d 1780 (9th Cir. 1998), *with* Veeck v. Southern Bldg. Code Congress Intern. Inc., 241 F.3d 398, 57 U.S.P.Q.2d 1665 (5th Cir. 2001).

transitory duration."[1] Live broadcasts (such as sporting events, concerts and news programs) meet the fixation requirement if they are simultaneously recorded.[2] The work can be fixed "in any tangible medium of expression, now known or later developed, from which it can be perceived, reproduced or otherwise communicated, either directly or with the aid of a machine or device."[3] The last clause of this provision was added in 1976 to overrule prior decisions requiring that the work be in a human-readable form.

Fixation of computer programs in a "tangible medium" includes storage in memory chips (ROM and RAM), floppy disks and magnetic tape.[4] When a computer technician "loads the [copyrighted] software into the RAM and is then able to view the system error log and diagnose the problem with a computer," the loading of the software can be considered "sufficiently permanent or stable to permit it to be perceived, reproduced, or otherwise communicated for a period of more than a transitory duration."[5]

§ 6:5 Noncopyrightable subject matter

Research References

West's Key Number Digest, Copyrights and Intellectual Property ☞3 to 12

C.J.S., Copyrights and Intellectual Property §§ 9 to 19, 92, 101

Although only a modicum of "creativity" or "originality" is necessary to qualify for copyright protection, certain types of work are not protectable by copyright because they are not sufficiently original. For example, words and short phrases such as names, titles and slogans are not copyrightable.[1] Pepsi's slogan "You got the right one, uh-huh" is not copyrightable.[2] Nor is the title "Loveline" for a radio program,[3] or the phrase "test market

---

[Section 6:4]

[1]17 U.S.C.A. § 101.

[2]17 U.S.C.A. § 101.

[3]17 U.S.C.A. § 102(a).

[4]Apple Computer, Inc. v. Franklin Computer Corp., 714 F.2d 1240, 219 U.S.P.Q. 113, 70 A.L.R. Fed. 153 (3d Cir. 1983).

[5]MAI Sys. Corp. v. Peak Computer, Inc., 991 F.2d 511, 518, 26 U.S.P.Q.2d 1458 (9th Cir. 1993).

[Section 6:5]

[1]Narell v. Freeman, 872 F.2d 907, 911, 16 Media L. Rep. (BNA) 1579, 10 U.S.P.Q.2d 1596 (9th Cir. 1989) (phrases); Trenton v. Infinity Broad. Corp., 865 F. Supp. 1416, 1426, 33 U.S.P.Q.2d 1161 (C.D. Cal. 1994) (titles).

[2]Takeall v. Pepsico, Inc., 14 F.3d 596, 29 U.S.P.Q.2d 1913 (4th Cir. 1993).

[3]Trenton, 865 F. Supp. at 1426.

pricing."[4] However, test statements and testing data for a psychological test are copyrightable even though they are short, simple, declarative sentences since they are neither names, titles, slogans nor merely fragmentary words and phrases.[5]

Typeface designs are not entitled to copyright protection.[6] Typeface has been defined "as a set of letters, numbers, or other symbolic characters, whose forms are related by repeating design elements consistently applied in a notational system and are intended to be embodied in articles, whose intrinsic utilitarian function is for use in composing text or other recognizable combinations of characters."[7] For example, a lettering style emulating a second grader's handwriting does not have the required creativity for copyright protection.[8]

A mere listing of ingredients is not copyrightable, although a more detailed recipe or a compilation is copyrightable. For example, a computer display including a two-column alphabetical listing of twenty items where the user is able to input standard costs for each of the different items was held not to be entitled to copyright protection.[9] However, a beauty products label that went beyond simply a list of ingredients or directions is copyrightable.[10]

Blank forms designed for recording information rather than conveying information are typically not copyrightable.[11] However, a blank form may be eligible for copyright protection if it can be shown to be sufficiently innovative and informative such that the

---

[4]Johnson v. Auto. Ventures, Inc., 890 F. Supp. 507, 36 U.S.P.Q.2d 1385 (W.D. Va. 1995).

[5]Applied Innovations, Inc. v. Regents of the Univ. of Minn., 876 F.2d 626, 635, 54 Ed. Law Rep. 146, 11 U.S.P.Q.2d 1041 (8th Cir. 1989).

[6]37 C.F.R. § 202(1); Eltra Corp. v. Ringer, 579 F.2d 294, 298, 198 U.S.P.Q. 321 (4th Cir. 1978) ("typeface has never been considered entitled to copyright").

[7]H.Rep. 1976 revision 94th Cong., 2d Sess. at 5668.

[8]Murray Hill Publ'ns, Inc. v. ABC Communications, Inc., 264 F.3d 622, 60 U.S.P.Q.2d 1080, 2001 FED App. 0295P (6th Cir. 2001).

[9]Mfrs. Techs., Inc. v. Cams, Inc., 706 F. Supp. 984, 996, 10 U.S.P.Q.2d 1321 (D. Conn. 1989).

[10]The label included text such as:

Hair stays wet-looking as long as you like. Brushes out to full-body dry look. WET is one step-four choice in Sebastian four step program for a healthy scalp and head of hair. WET is not oily, won't flake and keeps hair wet-looking for hours, allowing you to sculpture, contour, wave or curl. It stays looking wet until it's brushed out. When brushed, hair looks and feels thicker, extra full. Try brushing partly, leaving some parts wet for a different look.

Sebastian Int'l, Inc. v. Consumer Contact (PTY) Ltd., 664 F. Supp. 909, 913, 9 Int'l Trade Rep. (BNA) 1426, 3 U.S.P.Q.2d 1401 (D.N.J. 1987), *order vacated*, 847 F.2d 1093, 10 Int'l Trade Rep. (BNA) 1321, 7 U.S.P.Q.2d 1077 (3d Cir. 1988) (court of appeals vacated preliminary injunction on ground that manufacturer was barred by first sale doctrine from establishing infringement through an unauthorized importation).

[11]37 C.F.R. § 202.1(c).

Blank Form Rule (codified in 37 C.F.R. § 202.1(c)) does not apply.[12] Automation of interactive legal forms is not sufficiently original to warrant copyright protection.[13]

In contrast, in *Kregos v. Associated Press*[14] the court found that plaintiff's pitching form was copyrightable. Kregos developed a pitching form involving nine categories of items for recording information. The court determined that if a score card or a blank form contained a group of headings whose selection displayed recognizable creativity, the author's choice of those headings would convey to users the information that this group of categories was something out of the ordinary.[15]

Works consisting entirely of information that is common property containing no original authorship, such as standard calendars, height and weight charts, tape measures and rulers, schedules of sporting events, and lists or tables taken from public documents or common sources are not copyrightable.[16] No one can claim originality in such simple facts and although they may be discovered, they are not created by an act of authorship.[17]

Historical facts are in the public domain and are not copyrightable, even though an overall historical work is protectable. Anyone has a right to avail themselves to the facts contained in a history book and to use such information. An author should not be precluded from saving time and effort by referring to and relying upon prior published facts. The interpretation of historical facts, such as a theory regarding who destroyed the Hindenburg, is not protected by copyright.[18]

Stock or standard literary devices (often referred to as "scenes a faire") such as incidents, characters or settings that are, as a practical matter, indispensable, or at least standard, in the treatment of a given topic, are not copyrightable. Without such standard literary devices, it is virtually impossible to write about a particular historical era or fictional theme. For example, elements such as drunks, prostitutes and vermin are unprotectable "scenes a faire" in a work about police officers in the Bronx.[19] And in a work about Nazi Germany, scenes of the common German

---

[12]ABR Benefits Servs., Inc. v. NCO Group, 52 U.S.P.Q.2d 1119, 1999 WL 695596 (E.D. Pa. 1999).

[13]Ross, Brovins & Oehmke, P.C. v. Lexis Nexis Group, a Div. of Reed Elsevier Group, PLC, 463 F.3d 478, 485, 80 U.S.P.Q.2d 1518, 2006 FED App. 0358P (6th Cir. 2006).

[14]Kregos v. Associated Press, 937 F.2d 700, 19 U.S.P.Q.2d 1161 (2d Cir. 1991).

[15]Kregos, 937 F.2d at 708.

[16]Harper House, Inc. v. Thomas Nelson, Inc., 889 F.2d 197, 206, 12 U.S.P.Q.2d 1779 (9th Cir. 1989).

[17]Feist, 499 U.S. at 347.

[18]Hoehling v. Universal City Studios, Inc., 618 F.2d 972, 979, 6 Media L. Rep. (BNA) 1053, 205 U.S.P.Q. 681 (2d Cir. 1980).

[19]Walker v. Time Life Films, Inc., 784 F.2d 44, 12 Media L. Rep. (BNA)

greeting of the period, "Heil Hitler," or songs such as the German national anthem, are not copyrightable.[20]

No copyright protection is available for any work for the U.S. government, but the U.S. government is not precluded from receiving and holding copyrights transferred to it by assignment, bequest or otherwise.[21] Works of the federal government are not granted copyright protection for three reasons. First, the government publications are often official legal documents which people must have free access to in order for the government to function efficiently. In addition, copyright protection should not give the federal government an unfair competitive advantage in disseminating its work in the marketplace. Finally, the federal government should not be permitted to use copyright as a tool for censoring the publication of embarrassing information appearing in government documents.[22]

§ 6:6 Ownership of a copyright—Initial ownership

Research References
West's Key Number Digest, Copyrights and Intellectual Property ☞41
C.J.S., Copyrights and Intellectual Property §§ 22, 93

Ownership is initially vested in the "author." The "author" for copyright purposes is not always the person who actually created the work. There are three ways to become the author of a copyrighted work:

- Creating the work,
- Having an employee create the work in the course of employment, or
- Hiring a freelancer to create a work for hire under a written agreement.[1]

§ 6:7 Ownership of a copyright—Works made for hire

Research References
West's Key Number Digest, Copyrights and Intellectual Property ☞41(2)
C.J.S., Copyrights and Intellectual Property §§ 22, 93

The employer owns the copyright in a work made for hire. A "work made for hire" is:

(1) a work prepared by an employee within the scope of his or

---

1634, 228 U.S.P.Q. 505 (2d Cir. 1986).
    [20]Hoehling, 618 F. Supp. at 979.
    [21]17 U.S.C.A. § 105.
    [22]Paul Goldstein, *Copyright,*

Principles, Law and Practice § 2.5.2 (1989).

[Section 6:6]
    [1]17 U.S.C.A. § 201.

her employment or

(2) a work specially ordered or commissioned for use as a contribution to a collective work, as a part of a motion picture or other audiovisual work, as a translation, as a supplementary work, as a compilation, as an instructional text, as a test, as answer material for a test, or as an atlas, if the parties expressly agree in a written instrument signed by them that the work shall be considered a work made for hire.[1]

In *Community for Creative Non-Violence v. Reid*,[2] the Supreme Court held that freelancers are almost never "employees" for work for hire purposes. A written work for hire agreement is therefore needed to qualify a freelancer's work as "for hire." The definition of "employee" under § 101 is determined under general agency law. The hiring party's right to control the manner and means by which the work is accomplished is the critical inquiry. Factors relevant to this inquiry include:

- skill required,
- source of tools and instrumentalities,
- location of the work,
- duration of the relationship between the parties,
- method of payment,
- hired party's discretion over when and how long to work,
- regular business of the hiring party,
- employee benefits and
- tax treatment of the hired party.

The several factors set out are balanced to determine employment status: employee or independent contractor. If the person is found to be an independent contractor, then he or she is the owner of the work created and therefore cannot be held liable for copyright infringement.[3]

A sculptor who was commissioned by an organization to produce a work, but who supplied his own tools, worked in his own studio, was retained for less than two months, was paid a specific sum dependent upon completion of the specific job, and received no employment benefits, is an independent contractor for the purposes of a work for hire determination. The sculpture is not a work for hire of the organization even if it directed enough of the sculpture's preparation to oversee that the sculpture met the or-

---

[Section 6:7]

[1]17 U.S.C.A. § 101.

[2]Cmty. for Creative Non-Violence v. Reid, 490 U.S. 730, 109 S. Ct. 2166, 16 Media L. Rep. (BNA) 1769, 10 U.S.P.Q.2d 1985 (1989).

[3]Kirk v. Harter, 188 F.3d 1005, 51 U.S.P.Q.2d 1853 (8th Cir. 1999).

ganization's specifications.[4]

§ 6:8 Ownership of a copyright—Joint ownership

Research References

West's Key Number Digest, Copyrights and Intellectual Property
   ☞41(3)
C.J.S., Copyrights and Intellectual Property §§ 22, 93

The ownership of a copyright initially vests in the author or authors of a work. The authors of a joint work are co-owners of the copyrighted work.[1] A joint work is a work prepared by two or more authors with the intention that their contributions be merged into inseparable or inter-dependent parts of a unitary whole.[2] For example, in *Childress v. Taylor*,[3] Clarice Taylor decided to create a play about Jackie "Moms" Mabley and contacted playwright Alice Childress about writing the play. Taylor had been doing research regarding "Moms." She gave her research to Childress to assist her in the writing of the play. Taylor periodically gave assistance to Childress, and Childress completed the play. The court held that there was no intent of both participants to regard themselves as joint authors. The court emphasized that although in Taylor's mind there was intent for co-authorship, "there was no evidence that Childress ever contemplated, much less would have accepted, crediting the play as 'written by Alice Childress and Clarice Taylor.' " The lack of intent prevented a finding of joint authorship.[4]

Although the law is not completely settled, the Ninth Circuit holds that each co-author must contribute an independently copyrightable portion to the work for them to be considered joint authors. In *Ashton-Tate Corp. v. Ross*,[5] Ross contributed only ideas to the creation of the interface, which are not protectable. Ross argued that the handwritten list of user commands that he gave to help develop the user interface constituted copyrightable expression. However, the court found those arguments meritless, and thus without contributing copyrightable expression, Ross was not a joint author of the work.[6]

Persons accorded joint authorship status enjoy all of the benefits of joint authorship, even if that person's contribution is

---

[4]Cmty. for Creative Non-Violence, 490 U.S. at 752–53.

[Section 6:8]

[1]17 U.S.C.A. § 201(a).

[2]17 U.S.C.A. § 101.

[3]Childress v. Taylor, 945 F.2d

500, 19 Media L. Rep. (BNA) 1321, 20 U.S.P.Q.2d 1191 (2d Cir. 1991).

[4]Childress, 945 F.2d at 509.

[5]Ashton-Tate Corp. v. Ross, 916 F.2d 516, 16 U.S.P.Q.2d 1541 (9th Cir. 1990).

[6]Ashton-Tate, 916 F.2d at 520-21.

relatively minor.[7] The party asserting rights in a joint work must establish the element of authorship of the joint work. Authorship is not the same thing as making a valuable and copyrightable contribution.[8] Moreover, statements of approval, comments, suggestions, or criticism does not amount to authorship.[9]

Factors to be considered in determining whether a party is a co-author of a joint work in the absence of a contract include: whether the party superintended the work by exercising control, whether putative co-authors made objective manifestations of shared intent to be co-authors, and whether the audience appeal of the work turns on the contributions of both putative co-authors, such that share of each in the work's success cannot be appraised. In many cases, control will be the most important factor.[10]

Joint owners of a copyright are tenants-in-common of the copyright in their joint work. This interest entitles each of the co-owners to possess the entire bundle of rights in their copyright. However, they are required to render an accounting to their joint owner for his or her share of any profits earned from the copyrighted work. Each owner also has the right to license or transfer the copyrighted work, but again must render an accounting to the joint owner.

§ 6:9 Ownership of a copyright—Contribution to a collective work

Research References

West's Key Number Digest, Copyrights and Intellectual Property ⊕41(3)

C.J.S., Copyrights and Intellectual Property §§ 22, 93

The copyright in each separate contribution to a collective work is distinct from the copyright in the collective work as a whole. Copyright vests initially in the author of the contribution. In the absence of any express transfer of the copyright, the owner of copyright in the collective work is presumed to have acquired only the privilege of reproducing and distributing the contribution as part of that particular collective work.[1]

---

[7]Bencich v. Hoffman, 84 F. Supp. 2d 1053, 54 U.S.P.Q.2d 1059 (D. Ariz. 2000).

[8]Aalmuhammed v. Lee, 202 F.3d 1227, 1232, 53 U.S.P.Q.2d 1661 (9th Cir. 2000).

[9]Gaylord v. U.S., 595 F.3d 1364, 1376, 94 U.S.P.Q.2d 1116 (Fed. Cir. 2010).

[10]Aalmuhammed, 202 F.3d at 1232.

[Section 6:9]

[1]17 U.S.C.A. § 201(c).

§ 6:10 Ownership of a copyright—Ownership of copyright distinct from ownership of material object

Research References

West's Key Number Digest, Copyrights and Intellectual Property ⊙41.3

C.J.S., Copyrights and Intellectual Property §§ 26, 93

Ownership of a copyright is distinct from ownership of the material object in which the work is embodied.[1] Absent a written assignment, the transfer of the material object embodying the original copyright work (e.g., an original manuscript, photo negative, computer program or documentation) does not transfer any rights in the copyright. Thus, the transfer of the original does not convey with it the written consent to reproduce the work. Likewise, in the absence of a written agreement, the transfer of any rights in the copyright does not convey the property rights in the material object.[2]

As with much of copyright law, this rule makes intuitive sense. If a person buys a copy of *Gone With The Wind*, he or she does not acquire the copyright to the book. He or she may, of course, re-sell the book to a friend or a used book store. But none of these transactions affect the underlying copyright to the book. The person does not have the right to copy the book and sell his or her own edition of *Gone With The Wind*. Only the copyright owner has that right.

§ 6:11 Ownership of a copyright—Assignment of copyrights

Research References

West's Key Number Digest, Copyrights and Intellectual Property ⊙43, 48

C.J.S., Copyrights and Intellectual Property §§ 27, 33, 93

Transfer of copyright ownership must be in writing and signed by the transferor.[1] Transfers are recordable with the Copyright Office.[2] Recordation is constructive notice to the public of the facts stated therein if the document identifies the work and the work is registered.[3]

For example, transfer of ownership of special effects film foot-

---

[Section 6:10]

   [1]17 U.S.C.A. § 202.

   [2]17 U.S.C.A. § 202.

[Section 6:11]

   [1]17 U.S.C.A. § 204.

[2]17 U.S.C.A. § 205.

[3]17 U.S.C.A. § 205(c).

age for use in horror movies must be in writing. In the absence of a writing, evidence showing the footage was shot at the request of the producer, that footage was handed over with intention that it be copied and distributed, and that payment for footage was received, only results in a grant of a nonexclusive license. It was not found sufficient for a transfer of ownership of the work.[4]

Each of the exclusive rights granted to a copyright owner are distinct and severable. For example, it is common that an author will transfer the right to reproduce a copyrighted work, but retain the rights to authorize and prepare derivative works. While a copyright owner may transfer any of the owner's exclusive rights in the copyright, such a transfer neither binds other joint-owners nor limits such joint-owner's rights in the copyright.[5] Thus, while a co-owner may transfer any of the co-owner's exclusive rights, the exclusive rights of any other joint-owners will not be affected by such a transfer. Any transfer of copyright must explicitly include those rights which are transferred.

An assignment of only the right to receive royalties from a copyrighted work does not have to be recorded under 17 U.S.C.A. § 205 in order for that assignment to prevail over a competing transfer of interest. In *Broadcast Music, Inc. v. Hirsch*, the Ninth Circuit held that an assignment of royalties from a copyrighted song has no relationship to the existence, scope, duration, or identification of the copyright, or the rights conferred by the copyright under 17 U.S.C.A. § 106.[6] Accordingly, the rules for recording transfers of interest under the Copyright Act do not apply to assignments of only royalties from a copyrighted work.[7]

A license to use a copyrighted work does not necessarily preclude infringement of the copyright, because the licensee will infringe the owner's copyright if the licensee exceeds the scope of the license. The scope of the license is to be construed in accordance with purposes underlying federal copyright law. State law, to the extent it does not interfere with federal copyright law or policy, can be used for contractual construction.[8] A copyright licensing agreement clause forbidding a licensee to contest validity of a copyright is valid unless shown to violate antitrust laws.[9]

Generally the renewal period of a copyright extinguishes all

---

[4]Effects Associates, Inc. v. Cohen, 908 F.2d 555, 558–559, 15 U.S.P.Q.2d 1559 (9th Cir. 1990).

[5]Corbello v. DeVito, 777 F.3d 1058, 1065, 43 Media L. Rep. (BNA) 1313, 113 U.S.P.Q.2d 1789 (9th Cir. 2015).

[6]Broad. Music, Inc. v. Hirsch, 104 F.3d 1163, 1166, 41 U.S.P.Q.2d 1373,

97-1 U.S. Tax Cas. (CCH) P 50209, 79 A.F.T.R.2d 97-551 (9th Cir. 1997).

[7]Hirsch, 104 F.3d at 1166.

[8]S.O.S., Inc. v. Payday, Inc., 886 F.2d 1081, 12 U.S.P.Q.2d 1241 (9th Cir. 1989).

[9]Saturday Evening Post Co. v. Rumbleseat Press, Inc., 816 F.2d 1191, 2 U.S.P.Q.2d 1499, 1987-1 Trade Cas.

rights, interests and licenses granted under that copyright. However, an author may grant rights in the renewal term previous to renewal if such rights are expressly granted. Still, generally there is a presumption against granting rights in the renewal term. Although a license does not expressly refer to rights granted in the renewal period, the grant of a perpetual and exclusive right to distribute effectively grants distribution rights during the renewal term of a copyright because the term "perpetual" is sufficiently synonymous with forever to rebut the general presumption against conveying rights in the renewal term of a copyrighted work.[10]

A copyright assignment or license that does not expressly describe the period or term of its duration will generally be construed (in absence of contrary evidence) to be effective for the duration of the copyright term.[11]

Regardless of the terms of the agreement, 17 U.S.C.A. § 203 provides that an assignment or license of a copyright can be terminated "at any time during a period of five years beginning at the end of 35 years from the date of execution of the grant." The provision does not establish 35 years as the minimum term of grant.[12] The Eleventh Circuit adopted the same rule stating that if there is a state law allowing termination in less than 35 years for an indefinite duration license, the state law will govern the termination.[13]

§ 6:12 Ownership of a copyright—Mandatory licenses

Research References

West's Key Number Digest, Copyrights and Intellectual Property ⊙48, 48.1

C.J.S., Copyrights and Intellectual Property §§ 27, 33, 86 to 91, 93

One of the special situations that arises under copyright law is that the copyright owner is required to grant a license in certain situations. For example, one type of compulsory license grants the licensee the right to make and distribute phonorecords of a musical work. This compulsory license does not authorize the licensee to make and distribute a sound recording that was not made by the licensee. The compulsory license allows the licensee to record the musical work anew and distribute copies of that

---

(CCH) ¶ 67537 (7th Cir. 1987).

[10]P.C. Films Corp. v. MGM/UA Home Video Inc., 138 F.3d 453, 45 U.S.P.Q.2d 1850 (2d Cir. 1998).

[11]TV Globo Ltda. v. Braz. Up-Date Weekly, Inc., 50 U.S.P.Q.2d 1478, 1999

WL 163378 (S.D. N.Y. 1999).

[12]Walthal v. Rusk, 172 F.3d 481, 50 U.S.P.Q.2d 1311 (7th Cir. 1999).

[13]Korman v. HBC Florida, Inc., 182 F.3d 1291, 51 U.S.P.Q.2d 1672 (11th Cir. 1999).

recording.[1] The compulsory license is limited to distributing the phonorecords to the public for private use.

The jukebox compulsory license is codified in 17 U.S.C.A. § 116. It allows the proprietor of an establishment to perform a nondramatic musical work in public by means of a coin operated phonorecord player. However, this jukebox exemption only applies to establishments that make no direct or indirect charges for admission. Thus, a jukebox located in a tavern that charged an admission or cover charge is not entitled to the jukebox compulsory license, even if not all customers paid the cover charge.[2]

§ 6:13 Exclusive rights—Right to reproduce copies of the work

Research References

West's Key Number Digest, Copyrights and Intellectual Property ⬤⟳36
C.J.S., Copyrights and Intellectual Property §§ 10, 40 to 41, 97

A copyright is a bundle of rights in an original work of authorship. The copyright arises simply from creation of the work; neither registration nor publication are conditions for obtaining a copyright. The owner of a copyrighted work has the exclusive right to:

- reproduce copies of the work,
- prepare derivative works,
- distribute copies of the work,
- perform the work publicly, and
- display the work publicly.[1]

The exclusive right to reproduce copies of the work allows the owner of the copyrighted work to reproduce the work, or to authorize someone else to reproduce the work and copies of phonorecords.[2] "Copies" and "phonorecords" are defined as material objects in which a work is fixed by any method now known or later developed, and from which the work can be perceived, reproduced or otherwise communicated, either directly or with the aid of a machine or device.[3] For example, reproducing a work on an audiotape, videotape, floppy disc, hard drive, or digital media is the exclusive right of the owner because the copy can be perceived with the aid of a tape player, video player, computer, or

---

[Section 6:12]

[1]17 U.S.C.A. § 115.

[2]Chi-Boy Music v. Towne Tavern, Inc., 779 F. Supp. 527, 21 U.S.P.Q.2d 1227 (N.D. Ala. 1991).

[Section 6:13]

[1]17 U.S.C.A. § 106.

[2]17 U.S.C.A. § 106(1).

[3]17 U.S.C.A. § 101.

electronic device.[4]

The owner's right extends to reproduction of the work in media not known at the time of the creation of the work. For example, James Brown granted the right to reproduce a 1964 television performance to the producer of the show, and over twenty-five years later the performance was reproduced on video cassette. The court held that the grant of Brown's right to reproduce encompassed the right to reproduce copies on video cassette even though the video cassette was not in existence in 1964.[5]

§ 6:14 Exclusive rights—Right to prepare derivative works

Research References

West's Key Number Digest, Copyrights and Intellectual Property ⚮38
C.J.S., Copyrights and Intellectual Property §§ 19, 40 to 41, 59, 97

The owner of the copyrighted work has the exclusive right to create, or authorize creation of derivative works. "The protection of derivative rights extends beyond mere protection against unauthorized copying to include the right to make other versions of, perform, or exhibit the work."[1] For example, the preparation of a book concerning the copyrighted television series "Twin Peaks," a derivative work of the television series, is the exclusive right of the owner of "Twin Peaks" teleplays.[2]

The exclusive right to prepare derivative works is limited to the incremental additions of originality contributed by authors of the derivative work.[3] Furthermore, the owner's exclusive right in a derivative work is limited to the original additions that go beyond triviality.[4]

The derivative work exception in § 304(c)(6)(A) allows a licensee to use a derivative work after all rights in a copyright have reverted to the author in the renewal term. However the § 304(c)(6)(A) exception does not cover additional releases of a derivative recording when the grant was limited in scope to cover

---

[4]Paul Goldstein, Copyright, Principles, Law and Practice, § 5.1.

[5]Brown v. Twentieth Century Fox Film Corp., 799 F. Supp. 166, 168-71, 26 U.S.P.Q.2d 1626 (D.D.C. 1992), *judgment aff'd*, 15 F.3d 1159 (D.C. Cir. 1994).

[Section 6:14]

[1]Mirage Editions, 856 F.2d at 1343.

[2]Twin Peaks Prods., Inc. v. Publ'ns Int'l, Ltd., 996 F.2d 1366, 21 Media L. Rep. (BNA) 1545, 27 U.S.P. Q.2d 1001 (2d Cir. 1993).

[3]Silverman v. CBS Inc., 870 F.2d 40, 49, 9 U.S.P.Q.2d 1778 (2d Cir. 1989).

[4]Bates v. Actors Heritage, Inc., 11 U.S.P.Q.2d 1732, 1989 WL 206430 (S.D. N.Y. 1989).

the use of a derivative recording for a specific purpose only.[5]

§ 6:15 Exclusive rights—Right to distribute copies of the work

Research References

West's Key Number Digest, Copyrights and Intellectual Property ⊙⃗36
C.J.S., Copyrights and Intellectual Property §§ 10, 40 to 41, 97

The copyright owner has the exclusive right to distribute copies of the copyrighted work to the public by sale, rental, lease or lending.[1] Distribution of copies of the work is an exclusive right of the copyright owner, even if the distribution is only to one person or the distribution is in the form of a gift.[2]

A state law cannot force upon copyright holders the duty to distribute and make available other copies of their work following the copyright holders' initial decision to publish and distribute copies of their copyrighted work. Such a state law will be preempted by the Copyright Act.[3]

Rental of copyrighted video cassettes is in the exclusive domain of the copyright owner.[4] The owner can prevent others from renting copyrighted works to the public. However, a copyright owner's distribution rights do not exclude others from offering to sell the work when no sale is actually consummated.[5] The copyright owner's exclusive right to distribute copies of the work is limited by the first sale doctrine.[6] The first sale doctrine, as applied to copyright law, generally exhausts the copyright owner's rights in a particular copy of a work upon an authorized or lawful transfer of that copy.[7] Neither the production of, nor the "first sale" of the copy is required to take place within the United States, as long as the copy was lawfully produced or authorized.[8]

§ 6:16 Exclusive rights—Right to perform the work publicly

---

[5]Fred Ahlert Music Corp. v. Warner/Chappell Music, Inc., 155 F.3d 17, 47 U.S.P.Q.2d 1356 (2d Cir. 1998).

[Section 6:15]

[1]17 U.S.C.A. § 106(3).

[2]Ford Motor Co. v. Summit Motor Products, Inc., 930 F.2d 277, 18 U.S.P.Q.2d 1417, R.I.C.O. Bus. Disp. Guide (CCH) P 7731, 19 Fed. R. Serv. 3d 907 (3d Cir. 1991).

[3]Orson, Inc. v. Miramax Film Corp., 189 F.3d 377, 27 Media L. Rep. (BNA) 2322, 51 U.S.P.Q.2d 1818 (3d Cir. 1999).

[4]Paramount Pictures Corp. v. Labus, 16 U.S.P.Q.2d 1142, 1990 WL 120642 (W.D. Wis. 1990).

[5]Paramount, 16 U.S.P.Q.2d at 1142.

[6]17 U.S.C.A. § 109(a).

[7]17 U.S.C.A. § 109(a).

[8]Kirtsaeng v. John Wiley & Sons, Inc., 133 S. Ct. 1351, 185 L. Ed. 2d 392, 35 Int'l Trade Rep. (BNA) 1049, 41 Media L. Rep. (BNA) 1441, 106 U.S.P.Q.2d 1001, 75 A.L.R. Fed. 2d 767 (2013).

Research References
West's Key Number Digest, Copyrights and Intellectual Property ☞36
C.J.S., Copyrights and Intellectual Property §§ 10, 40 to 41, 97

To perform a work means to recite, play, dance or act it, either
directly or by means of any device or process.[1] To perform a work
publicly means (1) to perform it at a place open to the public or at
any place where a substantial number of persons outside of a
normal circle of a family is gathered or (2) to transmit or
otherwise communicate a performance of the work to a place
specified by clause 1 or to the public.[2]

Examples of activities that courts have held to constitute public performance include: performance of a copyrighted musical
composition before twenty-one members and guests at a private
golf club,[3] transmission by cable television programs to cable
system operators of programming containing copyrighted music,[4]
cable network's transmission of sports programming that
included copyrighted musical compositions,[5] and permitting paying customers at a video game arcade to play copyrighted video
games.[6]

§ 6:17 Exclusive rights—Right to display the work publicly

Research References
West's Key Number Digest, Copyrights and Intellectual Property ☞36
C.J.S., Copyrights and Intellectual Property §§ 10, 40 to 41, 97

To display a work means to show a copy of it, either directly or
by means of film, slide, television image or any other device or
process.[1] To display a work publicly means (1) to display it at a
place open to the public or at any place where a substantial
number of persons outside of a normal circle of a family is
gathered or (2) to transmit or otherwise communicate a display of

---

[Section 6:16]

[1]17 U.S.C.A. § 101.

[2]17 U.S.C.A. § 101.

[3]Fermata Int'l Melodies, Inc. v.
Champions Golf Club, Inc., 712 F.
Supp. 1257, 11 U.S.P.Q.2d 1460 (S.D.
Tex. 1989), *decision aff'd*, 915 F.2d
1567 (5th Cir. 1990).

[4]Nat'l Cable Television Ass'n,
Inc. v. Broad. Music, Inc., 772 F. Supp.
614, 20 U.S.P.Q.2d 1481, 1991-2 Trade

Cas. (CCH) ¶ 69541 (D.D.C. 1991).

[5]Coleman v. ESPN, Inc., 764 F.
Supp. 290, 20 U.S.P.Q.2d 1513 (S.D.
N.Y. 1991).

[6]Red Baron-Franklin Park, Inc.
v. Taito Corp., 883 F.2d 275, 11 Int'l
Trade Rep. (BNA) 1520, 11 U.S.P.Q.2d
1548 (4th Cir. 1989).

[Section 6:17]

[1]17 U.S.C.A. § 101.

the work to a place specified by clause 1 or to the public.[2]

Display of copyrighted designs at a trade show that was limited to members of a particular trade organization constitutes a public display.[3] However, use of a copyrighted decoy in a hunt was not a public display.[4]

§ 6:18 Limitations on copyrightable subject matter— Idea-expression dichotomy

Research References
West's Key Number Digest, Copyrights and Intellectual Property ⊙4.5
C.J.S., Copyrights and Intellectual Property §§ 9 to 10

A copyright does not give the author the exclusive right to the idea disclosed. Rather, copyright protection extends only to the expression of the idea.[1] The Copyright Act of 1976 codifies this "idea/expression" dichotomy:

> In no case does copyright protection for an original work of authorship extend to any idea, procedure, process, system, method of operation, concept, principle, or discovery, regardless of the form in which it is described, explained, illustrated, or embodied in such work.[2]

For protection of the underlying idea, procedure, etc., the owner must rely upon the applicable patent or trade secret laws.

A related concept is that of idea/expression unity. Some ideas can only be expressed in a limited number of ways. In these instances the scope of protection for the particular expression is very limited, sometimes to virtually verbatim copying. This is also known as the "merger doctrine," in which the idea and expression are inseparable or merged. Where idea and expression are indistinguishable, a copyright will protect against nothing other than identical copying.

For example, in *Herbert Rosenthal Jewelry Corp. v. Kalpakian*[3] the court held that the plaintiff's jeweled bee pin was not protectable because it was merely an idea that was indistinguishable from the expression of the pin. In other words, since there is only

---

[2]17 U.S.C.A. § 101.

[3]Thomas v. Pansy Ellen Products, Inc., 672 F. Supp. 237, 5 U.S.P.Q.2d 1322 (W.D. N.C. 1987).

[4]Streeter v. Rolfe, 491 F. Supp. 416, 209 U.S.P.Q. 918 (W.D. La. 1980).

[Section 6:18]

[1]*See* Ring v. Estee Lauder, Inc., 874 F.2d 109, 10 U.S.P.Q.2d 1796 (2d Cir. 1989).

[2]17 U.S.C.A. § 102(b).

[3]Herbert Rosenthal Jewelry Corp. v. Kalpakian, 446 F.2d 738, 742, 170 U.S.P.Q. 557 (9th Cir. 1971).

one way to make a jeweled bee pin, plaintiff was not entitled to exclude others from doing so under copyright law. Conferring copyright protection in such an instance would grant a monopoly on the idea to the copyright owner, even though he or she has not gone through the rigorous examination process required to protect an idea under the patent law.[4]

§ 6:19 Limitations on copyrightable subject matter— Utilitarian works

Research References

West's Key Number Digest, Copyrights and Intellectual Property ⚍4
C.J.S., Copyrights and Intellectual Property §§ 9 to 10, 16

The design of a useful article is considered protectable by copyright only if, and to the extent that, it incorporates pictorial, graphic, or sculptural features that can be identified separately from, and are capable of existing independently of, the utilitarian aspects of the article.[1] The determination as to whether artistic aspects of a useful article can be identified separately from, and exist independently of, an article's utilitarian function is necessary only if the article is first determined to be "useful." Thus, a sculptural work whose sole utilitarian function is to portray the article's appearance is not a "useful article," and it remains copyrightable regardless of whether its utilitarian function is separable from the work's sculptural elements.[2]

In other words, works of applied art are protected by copyright, but ornamental designs for useful devices are not. This is because ornamental designs are protectable under the patent laws, which provide only a fifteen year term.[3] Copyrightability of ornamental designs for useful devices would provide a far longer term (at least fifty years) with lower standards for obtaining protection. To obtain a design patent, the design must be ornamental, novel and nonobvious. In contrast, copyright protection requires only originality.

For instance, a mask that is shaped to resemble an animal nose is not a useful article, since the mask has no utility other than that which derives from its appearance. Therefore, the mask is copyrightable as a sculptural work.[4] A toy, like a painting that portrays a real item has no intrinsic utilitarian function other

---

[4]*See also* Kregos, 937 F.2d at 700.

[Section 6:19]

[1]17 U.S.C.A. § 101.

[2]Masquerade Novelty, Inc. v. Unique Indus., Inc., 912 F.2d 663, 15 U.S.P.Q.2d 1881, 17 Fed. R. Serv. 3d

1027 (3d Cir. 1990).

[3]*See* 35 U.S.C.A. § 173 (providing design patents with a "term of 15 years from the date of grant").

[4]Masquerade Novelty, 912 F.2d at 663.

then portrayal of the real item, which suggests that toys are copyrightable. The function of toys are much more similar to that of works of art than to intrinsic utilitarian function of industrial products.[5]

The design of a useful article qualifies as a copyrightable pictorial, graphic, or sculptural work only to the extent that the design incorporates features that can be identified separately from, and are capable of existing independently of, the utilitarian aspects of the article.[6]

In *Brandir Int'l Inc. v. Cascade Pacific*[7] the concept of separability was refined. The court found a bike rack made of bent tubing to be influenced in significant measure by utilitarian concerns. The rack included: widened upper loops to permit parking under and over the rack's curves, straightened vertical elements that allow improved installation and heavy-gauged tubular construction of rust-proof galvanized steel. The court concluded that the bike rack was not copyrightable, since any aesthetic elements of the form of the rack were not conceptually separate from its utilitarian elements. "[I]f design elements reflect a merger of aesthetic and functional considerations, the artistic aspects of a work cannot be said to be conceptually separable from the utilitarian elements. Conversely, where design elements can be identified as reflecting the designer's artistic judgment exercised independently of functional influences, conceptual separability exists."[8]

§ 6:20   Limitations on copyrightable subject matter— Transfer of material objects

Research References

West's Key Number Digest, Copyrights and Intellectual Property ⚭38.5
C.J.S., Copyrights and Intellectual Property §§ 40 to 41, 47, 97

The "first sale" doctrine of § 109(a) protects lawful owners of specific copies of a copyrighted work when they import and sell the copyrighted works. Those who lawfully own copies of a work may import the copies without being liable for copyright infringement because the exclusive rights granted under § 106 are expressly limited by §§ 107 to 120, including § 109(a), which allows a lawful owner of a copy of a copyrighted work to "sell or

---

[5]Gay Toys, Inc. v. Buddy L Corp., 703 F.2d 970, 218 U.S.P.Q. 13 (6th Cir. 1983).

[6]Norris Indus., Inc. v. Int'l Tel. & Tel. Corp., 696 F.2d 918, 217 U.S.P.Q. 226 (11th Cir. 1983); see OddzOn Prods., Inc. v. Oman, 924 F.2d 346, 17

U.S.P.Q.2d 1624 (D.C. Cir. 1991) (tactility of the "Koosh" ball was inseparable from its utilitarian function).

[7]Brandir Int'l Inc. v. Cascade Pacific, 838 F.2d 1202, 5 U.S.P.Q.2d 1089 (2d Cir. 1987).

[8]Brandir, 838 F.2d at 1205.

otherwise dispose of" the work without the authority of the copyright owner.[1] Even though § 109(a) requires the copy be "lawfully made under this title," this clause does not impose a geographic restriction on manufacture or sale of copies.[2] The first sale doctrine can generally be asserted by a lawful owner of a copy, regardless of where the copy was made or first sold, even when acting without permission of the copyright holder. Since the first sale doctrine applies to any lawfully made copy, wherever made, § 109(a) restricts the copyright holder from preventing importation and subsequent resale in the United States.[3]

The first sale doctrine provides that the owner of a particular copy or a phonorecord is entitled to sell or otherwise dispose of the possession of that copy or phonorecord without permission of the copyright owner. After the first sale of a physical object, all subsequent transfers of the object are free from the control of the copyright owner.[4] The first sale doctrine does not transfer the exclusive right to prepare derivative works by the mere sale of the particular copy. Thus, a person may not purchase a book, remove copyrighted art prints and then mount those prints on tiles for resale.[5]

Also, the first sale doctrine is limited by its terms to the right of distribution, and it does not apply to the right of performance. Thus, the first sale doctrine does not apply to a video arcade operator who makes a copyrighted video game available for public use in arcades, because such use violates the exclusive right of performance. Therefore, a video arcade operator must obtain a performance license from the copyright owner to make the work available for public play.[6]

§ 6:21 Limitations on copyrightable subject matter— Computer programs

Research References

West's Key Number Digest, Copyrights and Intellectual Property ☞10.4, 67.3

C.J.S., Copyrights and Intellectual Property §§ 9, 11 to 12, 16, 41, 45, 55, 92, 97, 101

[Section 6:20]

[1]Quality King Distributors, Inc. v. L'anza Research Intern., Inc., 523 U.S. 135, 118 S. Ct. 1125, 140 L. Ed. 2d 254, 26 Media L. Rep. (BNA) 1385, 45 U.S.P.Q.2d 1961 (1998).

[2]Kirtsaeng v. John Wiley & Sons, Inc., 133 S. Ct. 1351, 185 L. Ed. 2d 392, 35 Int'l Trade Rep. (BNA) 1049, 41 Media L. Rep. (BNA) 1441, 106

U.S.P.Q.2d 1001, 75 A.L.R. Fed. 2d 767 (2013).

[3]Kirtsaeng, 133 S.Ct. at 1358.

[4]17 U.S.C.A. § 109(a).

[5]Mirage Editions, 856 F.2d at 1341.

[6]Red Baron-Franklin Park, 883 F.2d at 280.

Copyright infringement requires ownership of a copyrighted work and evidence that the work was copied. Copying can be shown by direct evidence or by showing that "(1) the defendant had access to the plaintiff's copyrighted work and (2) that defendant's work is substantially similar to the plaintiff's copyrightable material." With respect to computer programs, nonliteral similarity of computer programs can constitute infringement if the manner in which certain computer design elements are combined is expressive for purposes of copyright law and the defendant copied this expression.[1]

Two important limitations on copyright protection relate directly to computer programs. It is not an infringement for the owner of a copy of a computer program to make another copy of that program, provided that the new copy is created as an essential step in the utilization of the computer program in conjunction with the machine.[2] This refers to the internal workings of most computers, in which a copy of the program is created in the random access memory in order to utilize the program.

In practice, this rule has been expanded to allow some limited reverse engineering. For example, where the copyright owner develops a software system that prevents a customer from creating a fully functional copy of the program, a defendant may develop a system to defeat the protective function of the copyrighted software. To develop such a system, the defendant had to copy the copyrighted software into the computer memory and analyze the manner in which the program operated. The court recognized that although the defendant used the copyrighted software contrary to its intended purpose, the copy made was created as an essential step in the utilization of the copyrighted program, and therefore such copying was permitted.[3]

The second exception applying to computer programs is the right to make a copy for archival purposes.[4] Computer programs can be stored on a variety of media and the archival copy exception is not limited to copying programs that are subject to destruction or damage by mechanical or electrical failure.[5] The medium of storage does not determine whether the archival exception applies. A copyrighted program can be copied on any medium for any purpose "so long as the owner uses the copy for

---

[Section 6:21]

[1]Softel, Inc. v. Dragon Med. and Scientific Communications, Inc., 118 F.3d 955, 43 U.S.P.Q.2d 1385, 38 Fed. R. Serv. 3d 623 (2d Cir. 1997).

[2]17 U.S.C.A. § 117(a)(1).

[3]Vault Corp. v. Quaid Software Ltd., 847 F.2d 255, 261, 7 U.S.P.Q.2d 1281 (5th Cir. 1988).

[4]17 U.S.C.A. § 117(a)(2).

[5]Vault, 847 F.2d at 265.

archival purposes only and not for unauthorized transfer."[6] However, that archival copy must be deleted if the owner sells or gives away the original program.

The scope of a registered copyright in an earlier version of computer software program extends to protect a later version of the program not separately registered, when the later version incorporates parts of the earlier version.[7]

§ 6:22   Fair use—General rule

Research References

West's Key Number Digest, Copyrights and Intellectual Property ⚖53.2 C.J.S., Copyrights and Intellectual Property §§ 45 to 46, 48

Fair use is a judicially created exception to copyright infringement that is codified in 17 U.S.C.A. § 107. It limits the exclusive rights conferred to the owner of a copyright, by allowing use of a copyrighted work for purposes such as criticism, comment, news reporting, teaching, scholarship or research.[1] Four factors are considered in determining whether the unauthorized use made of a work is a fair use:

- Purpose and character of the use, including whether it is commercial or nonprofit,
- Nature of the work,
- Amount or substantiality of the portion used in relation to the copyrighted work as a whole and
- Effect of the use upon the potential market for or the value of the work.[2]

In evaluating the "purpose and the character" of the fair use, some types of use (such as newspaper reporting) are more justified for protection as fair use. If a use was for a commercial purpose as opposed to a nonprofit purpose, that weighs against a finding of fair use.[3] However, "the crux of the profit/nonprofit distinction is not whether the sole motive of the use is monetary gain but whether the user stands to profit from exploitation of the copyright material without paying the customary price."[4] The intended purpose of the use should also be evaluated for this factor, to ascertain whether the particular use "had not merely the incidental effect but the intended purpose of supplanting the

---

[6]Vault, 847 F.2d at 265.

[7]Montgomery v. Noga, 168 F.3d 1282, 49 U.S.P.Q.2d 1961, 51 Fed. R. Evid. Serv. 752 (11th Cir. 1999).

[Section 6:22]

[1]17 U.S.C.A. § 107.

[2]17 U.S.C.A. § 107.

[3]Harper & Row Publishers, Inc. v. Nation Enters., 471 U.S. 539, 540, 105 S. Ct. 2218, 2220, 11 Media L. Rep. (BNA) 1969, 225 U.S.P.Q. 1073 (1985).

[4]Harper & Row, 471 U.S. at 562.

copyright holder's commercially valuable right of first publication."[5] "Fair use distinguishes between a true scholar and a chiseler who infringes a work for personal profit."[6]

The "nature of the work" inquiry reflects the law's greater need to disseminate factual works than works of fiction or fantasy.[7] Whether a work is unpublished is a critical element of its nature. "The scope of fair use is narrower with respect to unpublished works" because of the copyright holder's interest in confidentiality and creative control of publication.[8]

The "amount and substantiality of the portion used" factor looks at how much of the work was actually copied. This analysis must be performed both on a quantitative and qualitative level. In *Harper & Row*, the Court determined that although in absolute terms the words actually quoted were an insubstantial portion of the copyrighted work, the used portions actually constituted the heart of the copyrighted material. The Court determined that this factor weighed against a finding of fair use in light of the qualitative nature of the taking.[9]

The most important factor of fair use is the "effect of the use upon the potential market for or value" of the copyrighted work.[10] "Fair use when properly applied, is limited to copying by others which does not materially impair the marketability of the work just copied."[11] A showing that if the challenged use should become widespread, it would adversely affect a potential market of the copied work therefore prohibits a finding of fair use. The effect on the potential market must account not only for the original work but also for the market of the derivative works.[12]

§ 6:23 Fair use—Examples of fair use

Research References

West's Key Number Digest, Copyrights and Intellectual Property ☞53.2, 56, 64 to 67.3

C.J.S., Copyrights and Intellectual Property §§ 41, 45 to 46, 48 to 58, 97

One particular kind of fair use involves the right to create a parody of a copyrighted work. In *Campbell v. Acuff-Rose Music, Inc.*,[1] the Supreme Court held that a parody of Roy Orbison's song "Oh, Pretty Woman" by the rap music group 2 Live Crew

---

[5]Harper & Row, 471 U.S. at 540.

[6]Harper & Row, 471 U.S. at 563.

[7]Harper & Row, 471 U.S. at 595.

[8]Harper & Row, 471 U.S. at 540.

[9]Harper & Row, 471 U.S. at 564.

[10]Stewart v. Abend, 495 U.S. 207, 110 S. Ct. 1750, 14 U.S.P.Q.2d 1614

(1990).

[11]Harper & Row, 471 U.S. at 567.

[12]Harper & Row, 471 U.S. at 568.

[Section 6:23]

[1]Campbell v. Acuff-Rose Music, Inc., 510 U.S. 569, 114 S. Ct. 1164, 22 Media L. Rep. (BNA) 1353, 29 U.S.P.

may be a fair use. Although the Court recognized that the parody by 2 Live Crew was a commercial use, the Court refused to adopt a presumption that every commercial use is unfair. "Parody presents a difficult case" because the "parody must be able to 'conjure up' at least enough of that original to make the object of its critical wit recognizable."[2] The Court further remarked that "if quotation of the opening riff and the first line may be said to go to the 'heart' of the original, the heart is also what most readily conjures up the song of parody, and it is the heart at which the parody takes aim. Copying does not become excessive in relation to parodic purpose merely because the portion taken was the original's heart."[3]

Fair use is always a hotly debated topic in copyright law, and advances in technology often test the boundaries of fair use. For instance, the availability of video recorders raised the issue of whether taping a television program constituted copyright infringement. The Supreme Court held that recording a TV program for later viewing in the home was fair use in a contributory infringement action against the manufacturers of home video tape recorders.[4] Video recorders were capable of a substantial noninfringing use and no contributory infringement existed.

One of the more interesting fair use arguments has involved the legal limits of photocopying copyrighted materials. In *Basic Books Inc. v. Kinko's Graphics Corp.*,[5] a group of major publishing houses sued Kinko's for photocopying excerpts from text books, compiling them into "course packets" and selling the course packets to college students. In finding that Kinko's photocopying was not fair use, the court emphasized the commercial nature of Kinko's copying, and that the copying did not add any value to the work, as would a biographer's or critic's use of a copyrighted quote or excerpt. Kinko's was subsequently ordered to pay $510,000 in damages and $1,365,000 in attorneys' fees and costs.

In *American Geophysical Union v. Texaco, Inc.*,[6] a group of publishers filed suit against Texaco for making unauthorized copies of copyrighted articles published in scientific and technical journals. The copies were made for use by the company's research scientists. Despite Texaco's arguments that such copying was reasonable and customary, the court held that this unauthorized

---

Q.2d 1961 (1994).

[2]Campbell, 510 U.S. at 588.

[3]Campbell, 510 U.S. at 588.

[4]Sony Corp. of America v. Universal City Studios, Inc., 464 U.S. 417, 104 S. Ct. 774, 220 U.S.P.Q. 665 (1984).

[5]Basic Books, Inc. v. Kinko's Graphics Corp., 758 F. Supp. 1522, 66 Ed. Law Rep. 983, 18 U.S.P.Q.2d 1437 (S.D. N.Y. 1991).

[6]American Geophysical Union v. Texaco Inc., 60 F.3d 913, 35 U.S.P.Q.2d 1513, 144 A.L.R. Fed. 745 (2d Cir. 1994).

photocopying was not a fair use. The use detracted from the publisher's potential revenues and from the value of their copyrighted works. Additionally, a licensing system was available through the Copyright Clearance Center.

Reverse engineering of a computer program, in order to gain access to and understand the unprotected ideas, processes and methods of operation embodied in the program, may be a fair use.[7] However, in order to invoke the fair use exception, an individual must possess an authorized copy of the program. If a copy of the source code is fraudulently acquired from the Copyright Office, the copying does not qualify as a fair use.[8]

Libraries and archives have a specific right to copy certain materials.[9] A library has the right to reproduce no more than one copy or phono record of a work if: (1) the reproduction is made without any purpose of direct or indirect commercial advantage, (2) the collections or library or archives are open to the public or persons doing research in a specialized field and (3) the reproduction includes a notice of copyright.[10]

These rights also apply to copies made from the collection of a library or archive by a user if: (1) the copy becomes the property of the user and the library or archive has no notice that the copy will be used for any purpose other than private study, scholarship or research and (2) the library or archive displays prominently a warning of copyright.[11]

Furthermore, libraries or archives are generally not liable for copyright infringement for the unsupervised use of reproducing equipment located on its premises, provided that the equipment displays a notice that the making of a copy may be subject to the copyright law.[12] However, a person who uses the reproducing equipment at the library is liable for copyright infringement if it exceeds a fair use of the copyrighted work.[13]

§ 6:24   Digital Millennium Copyright Act of 1998— Overview

Research References

West's Key Number Digest, Copyrights and Intellectual Property ⬥2, 67.3

C.J.S., Copyrights and Intellectual Property §§ 3 to 6, 8, 41, 45, 55, 97

---

[7]Atari, 975 F.2d at 832.

[8]*See also* Sega Enters. Ltd. v. Accolade, Inc., 977 F.2d 1510, 24 U.S.P. Q.2d 1561 (9th Cir. 1992), *as amended*, (Jan. 6, 1993) (Accolade's copying for disassembly purposes was a fair use).

[9]17 U.S.C.A. § 108.

[10]17 U.S.C.A. § 108(a).

[11]17 U.S.C.A. § 108(d).

[12]17 U.S.C.A. § 108(f)(1).

[13]17 U.S.C.A. § 108(f)(2).

The Digital Millennium Copyright Act (DMCA)[1] implemented
two treaties signed at the World Intellectual Property Organization (WIPO) in 1996 and integrated additional related copyright
provisions. The DMCA consists of five titles:

Title I. The "WIPO Copyright and Performances and
Phonograms Treaties Implementation Act of 1998" implemented the terms of the WIPO treaties into the Copyright Act
of 1976.

Title II. The "Online Copyright Infringement Liability
Limitation Act" limited the liability of online service providers
for copyright infringement.

Title III. The "Computer Maintenance Competition Assurance Act" created an exemption to copyright infringement for
making a copy of a computer program for purposes of maintenance or repair.

Title IV. Title IV contains six miscellaneous provisions that
relate to (1) the authority of the Copyright Office to perform
certain policy and international functions, (2) an exemption for
making ephemeral recordings, (3) promoting distance education through digital technologies, (4) exemptions for libraries
and archives, (5) the scope of rights in sound recordings, and
(6) the assumption of contractual obligations related to
transfers of rights in motion pictures.

Title V. The "Vessel Hull Design Protection Act" provided
extended protection for original vessel hull designs.

§ 6:25 Digital Millennium Copyright Act of 1998—
Implementation of WIPO provisions

Research References

West's Key Number Digest, Copyrights and Intellectual Property ⊙2
C.J.S., Copyrights and Intellectual Property §§ 3 to 6, 8

Title I implemented the WIPO Copyright Treaty and the WIPO
Performances and Phonograms Treaty by performing two
functions. First, Title I makes technical amendments to current
U.S. law, so that the laws comply with the provisions of the WIPO
treaties. Under the DMCA, the United States provides copyright
protection to certain works from other member countries that is
at least equivalent to the protection given to domestic works.[1]
Additionally, a preexisting work from a member country that is
not in the public domain in its country of origin, but that is in the
public domain in the United States due to a failure to comply
with formalities or due to a lack of treaty relations, must be

---

[Section 6:24]

[1]Pub. L. No. 105-304, 112 Stat.
2860 (Oct. 28, 1998).

[Section 6:25]

[1]17 U.S.C.A. §§ 104(b), (d).

restored.[2] Lastly, registration of a foreign work in the Copyright Office is not a prerequisite to initiating a lawsuit.[3]

Second, Title I implemented two provisions in chapter 12 of the Copyright Act that are directed toward maintaining the integrity of copyright protection systems and copyright management information. The first provision, § 1201, prohibits circumvention of technological measures that are designed to protect copyrighted works. Technical measures are divided into two areas: measures that prevent unauthorized access to a copyrighted work and measures that prevent unauthorized copying of a copyrighted work. Devices or services that (1) are designed or produced primarily to circumvent, (2) have only a limited commercially significant purpose other than to circumvent, or (3) are marketed for use in circumventing, are prohibited. There are numerous exceptions to § 1201, including: a nonprofit library, archive, and educational institution exception; a law enforcement, intelligence, and other governmental activities exception; reverse engineering; encryption research; protection of minors; personal privacy; and security testing.[4] The broadest exception to § 1201 establishes an administrative rule-making procedure that evaluates the impact of the prohibition.[5]

Pursuant to this rule-making procedure, the Librarian of Congress may exempt certain classes of copyrighted works whose users are, or are likely to be, adversely affected in their ability to make non-infringing uses due to the prohibition on circumvention.[6] Exempted works include computer programs that allow the "unlocking" of cell phones, tablets, and mobile hotspots, as well as computer programs that permit the "jailbreaking" of cell phones, smart TV's, and automobiles.[7]

The second provision, § 1202, generally prohibits tampering with copyright management information.[8] § 1202 prohibits a person from knowingly providing or distributing false copyright management information and prohibiting a person from knowingly removing, altering, or distributing copyright management information without the authority of the copyright owner. § 1202 is subject to certain exceptions, including a law enforcement, intelligence, and other governmental activities exception, and

---

[2]17 U.S.C.A. § 104A(h).

[3]17 U.S.C.A. § 411(a).

[4]17 U.S.C.A. §§ 1201(d) to (j).

[5]17 U.S.C.A. §§ 1201(a)(1)(B) to (E).

[6]17 U.S.C.A. § 1201(a)(1).

[7]Exemption to Prohibition on Circumvention of Copyright Protection Systems for Access Control Technologies, 80 Fed. Reg. 65,944 (October 28, 2015) (to be codified at 37 C.F.R. pt. 201).

[8]17 U.S.C.A. § 1202.

providing limited liability for broadcast and cable systems.[9]

Any person injured by a § 1201 or 1202 violation can seek a civil remedy in Federal court.[10] § 1204 of the Copyright Act also makes it a criminal offense to willfully violate § 1201 or 1202 for the purposes of commercial advantage or private financial gain.

§ 6:26 Digital Millennium Copyright Act of 1998— Limitations on online infringement liability

Research References

West's Key Number Digest, Copyrights and Intellectual Property ⬤─67.3
C.J.S., Copyrights and Intellectual Property §§ 41, 45, 55, 97

Title II of the DMCA added four limitations on the liability of online service providers for copyright infringement, set out in § 512 of the Copyright Act.[1] The limitations are based on the conduct of the service provider and are divided into four categories: (1) transitory digital network communications; (2) system caching; (3) information residing on systems or networks at direction of users; and (4) information location tools.

All of the limitations in § 512 provide a complete bar on monetary relief and restrict injunctive relief.[2] In order to be eligible for the limited liability provisions set out in § 512, a party must be a "service provider." In terms of the first limitation, a service provider is defined as "an entity offering the transmission, routing, or providing of connections for digital online communications, between or among points specified by a user, of material of the user's choosing, without modification to the content of the material as sent or received."[3] For purposes of the last three limitations, a service provider is defined as "a provider of online services or network access, or the operator of facilities therefor."[4] Additionally, a service provider must adopt, reasonably implement, and inform subscribers and account holders of a policy terminating the accounts of subscribers who are repeat infringers. A service provider must also accommodate and not interfere with standard technical measures.[5]

Section 512(a) limits the liability of service providers for transitory communications. Service providers have limited liability when they act merely as a data conduit that transmits digital information on a network at another's request. Acts of transmitting

---

[9]17 U.S.C.A. §§ 1202(d) to (e).

[10]17 U.S.C.A. § 1203.

[Section 6:26]

[1]17 U.S.C.A. § 512.

[2]17 U.S.C.A. § 512(a) to (d) and (j).

[3]17 U.S.C.A. § 512(k)(1)(A).

[4]17 U.S.C.A. § 512(k)(1)(B).

[5]Digital Millennium Copyright Act, Pub. L. No. 105-304, § 512(i), 112 Stat. 2860 (1998).

digital information include transmitting, routing, or providing connections for information.[6] In order for a service provider to be eligible for this limitation, the transmission must be initiated by someone other than the provider and must be carried out by an automatic process. The service provider must not determine the recipients of the information, must not make intermediate copies available to anyone other than the intended recipients, and must not modify the transmitted material.[7]

Under § 512(b), service providers have limited liability for system caching, meaning that service providers can for a limited time retain copies of material that someone else has made available online and transmits to a subscriber. This limitation is subject to numerous requirements. The intermediate or temporary storage by the service provider must be carried out through an automatic process and the material must not be modified. The service provider must also comply with certain rules regarding replacing copied material with material from the original location, limit access to the material, and remove or block any information posted without the copyright owner's authorization. In addition, the service provider must not interfere with technology informing a person who posts information how many "hits" were received.[8]

Under § 512(c), service providers also have limited liability for storing information on systems or networks at the direction of users.[9] Under this limitation, service providers have limited liability for posting infringing material on websites hosted on their systems. For service providers to qualify for this limitation, the provider must not have knowledge of the infringing activity. If the service provider has the right and ability to control the infringing activity, the provider must not receive any financial benefit from the activity, and the provider must promptly take down or block access to any material once informed that the material is infringing. Lastly, the service provider is required to designate an agent who will receive notifications of alleged infringement.

To qualify for the safe harbor provision of § 512(c), a service provider must not have actual knowledge of infringing material. Section 512(c) sets out two ways a service provider may be put on notice that there is infringing material in its system. The first is by notice from the rightful copyright owner to the service

---

[6]17 U.S.C.A. § 512(a).

[7]17 U.S.C.A. § 512(a)(1) to (4).

[8]17 U.S.C.A. § 512(b). *See also* Viacom Intern. Inc. v. YouTube, Inc.,

718 F.Supp.2d 514 (S.D.N.Y.), aff'd in part, rev'd in part, 676 F.3d 19, 102 U.S.P.Q.2d 1283 (2d Cir. 2012).

[9]17 U.S.C.A. § 512(c).

provider's designated agent.[10] Upon receipt of a notice of infringement, the service provider must expeditiously take down the material and notify the alleged infringer that the material has been
taken down.[11] The alleged infringer then has the opportunity to
file a counter-notice claiming that it is not infringing.[12] If a
counter-notice is filed, then the service provider must tell the
copyright holder.[13] The copyright holder then has 10-14 business
days to file a lawsuit against the alleged infringer. If a lawsuit is
not filed, the service provider must repost the removed material.[14]
This process is generally referred to as the takedown process.

The second way a service provider may be put on notice is
through "red flags." Section 512(c) requires that service providers
not be "aware of facts or circumstances from which infringing
activity is apparent."[15] A service provider will not fall into the
§ 512(c) safe harbor if it can be shown that there were "red flags"
that the service provider should have been aware of that pointed
to infringing activity.

Section 512(d) limits the liability of service providers referring
or linking users by use of information location tools to a site
containing infringing material. Information location tools include
hyperlinks, online directories, and search engines. In order to
limit their liability, service providers must not have knowledge
that the site contains infringing material. Additionally, if the service provider has the right and ability to control the infringing
activity, the provider must not receive any financial benefit from
the activity and the provider must promptly take down or block
access to any material upon information that the material is
infringing.[16]

§ 6:27 Digital Millennium Copyright Act of 1998—The making available right

The WIPO Copyright Treaty and WIPO Performances and
Phonograms Treaty collectively extend to authors, performers,
and phonogram producers, the exclusive right to authorize the
communication of their works to the public. This right includes
the "making available to the public of their works in such a way
that members of the public may access these works from a place
and at a time individually chosen by them."[1] Infringement of this
exclusive right occurs, for example, when someone uploads a

---

[10]17 U.S.C.A. § 512(c)(1)(A)(3).

[11]17 U.S.C.A. § 512(c)(1)(C),
(g)(2)(A).

[12]17 U.S.C.A. § 512(g)(3).

[13]17 U.S.C.A. § 512(g)(2)(B).

[14]17 U.S.C.A. § 512(g)(2)(C).

[15]17 U.S.C.A. § 512(c)(1)(A)(ii);
but see Perfect 10, Inc. v. CCBill LLC,
488 F.3d 1102 (9th Cir. 2007).

[16]17 U.S.C.A. § 512(d).

[Section 6:27]

[1]WIPO Copyright Treaty art. 8,

work to a public file-sharing network without authorization.[2] The right applies to any current or future technology that allows or will allow a work to be digitally communicated.

When adopting and implementing the DMCA, Congress did not expressly incorporate the making available right, nor did it amend the exclusive rights enumerated in § 106 of the copyright statutes. Instead, it found that § 106 sufficiently supported and gave effect to the substance of the making available right. Specifically, offers to communicate to the public in the form of a download implicate the right of distribution. Offers made via streaming content or the display of an image implicate the right of public performance or public display.[3]

§ 6:28 Moral rights

Research References

West's Key Number Digest, Copyrights and Intellectual Property ⚷6
C.J.S., Copyrights and Intellectual Property §§ 9, 16

Regardless of the exclusive rights granted by the copyright laws, the author of the work of visual art has the right to claim authorship of that work and to prevent the use of his or her name as the author of any work of visual art which he or she did not create. The author also has the right to prevent the use of his or her name as the author of a work of visual art in the event of a distortion, mutilation or other modification of the work that would be prejudicial to his or her honor or reputation.[1] Unauthorized insertion of advertisements into video recordings of a motion picture without any other showing that the act significantly altered or distorted the copyrighted motion picture does not violate any moral rights of the artist.[2] There are certain exceptions to the author's rights of attribution and integrity, particularly modifications which result from the inherent nature of the materials or the passage of time, or modifications resulting from attempts to preserve the work.[3]

An author of a work of visual art also has the right to prevent any intentional distortion, mutilation or other modification of

---

Dec. 20, 1996, 36 I.L.M. 65 (1997); WIPO Performances and Phonograms Treaty arts. 10, 14, Dec. 20, 1996, 36 I.L.M. 76 (1997).

[2]U.S. Copyright Office, The Making Available Right in the United States: A Report of the Register of Copyrights 1-2 (Feb. 23, 2016).

[3]U.S. Copyright Office, The Making Available Right in the United States: A Report of the Register of Copyrights 74 (Feb. 23, 2016).

[Section 6:28]

[1]17 U.S.C.A. § 106A(a)(2).

[2]Paramount Pictures Corp. v. Video Broad. Sys., Inc., 724 F. Supp. 808, 12 U.S.P.Q.2d 1862 (D. Kan. 1989).

[3]17 U.S.C.A. § 106A(c).

that work that would be prejudicial to his or her honor or reputation, and to prevent the destruction of a work of recognized stature.[4] This right is limited in instances in which the work of visual art has been incorporated or made part of a building. In those circumstances, these rights do not apply when removing the work would cause the destruction or mutilation of the work. If the owner of a building wishes to remove a work of visual art that is part of the building, and it can be removed without destroying the work, then the author's moral rights do apply.[5]

For example, in *Carter v. Helmsley-Spear Inc.*[6] the court held that it would be prejudicial to the plaintiff's honor and reputation and would destroy the recognized stature of a work of art if Helmsley-Spear were allowed to alter or remove an uncompleted art work incorporated into the lobby of a New York building. The art work, containing several sculptural and other elements incorporated into the lobby, was a work in progress when Helmsley-Spear ordered the plaintiffs out of the building and expressed an intent to alter or remove the art work.

Assignment of a copyright to a third party does not entitle that third party to assert claims preserved strictly for the author. Moral rights are inalienable and unassignable, and as such may only be asserted by the author/composer, or that person's heirs.[7]

---

[4]17 U.S.C.A. § 106A(a)(3).

[5]17 U.S.C.A. § 113(d).

[6]Carter v. Helmsley-Spear, Inc., 71 F.3d 77, 37 U.S.P.Q.2d 1020, 138 A.L.R. Fed. 711 (2d Cir. 1995).

[7]Boosey & Hawkes Music Publishers, Ltd. v. Walt Disney Co., 28 Media L. Rep. (BNA) 1478, 53 U.S.P.Q.2d 2021, 2000 WL 204524 (S.D. N.Y. 2000).

Chapter 7

Registering a Copyright

KeyCite®: Cases and other legal materials listed in KeyCite Scope can be researched through the KeyCite service on Westlaw®. Use KeyCite to check citations for form, parallel references, prior and later history, and comprehensive citator information, including citations to other decisions and secondary materials.

---

§ 7:1   Registration is not mandatory

Research References

West's Key Number Digest, Copyrights and Intellectual Property
  ⊜50.16
C.J.S., Copyrights and Intellectual Property §§ 39, 71, 96

For works created on or after January 1, 1978, protection under

249

the copyright laws is automatic from the moment of creation.[1] The author may then seek registration with the U.S. Copyright Office at any time during the life of the copyright. Such registration is not a condition of copyright protection.[2]

Even though copyright protection exists regardless of whether the copyright is registered with the Copyright Office, a copyright registration serves several important purposes. A registration (or preregistration) is a prerequisite for filing a civil copyright infringement action based on a work of United States origin.[3] Registration is also a prerequisite to recovery of statutory damages and of attorneys' fees in an infringement action.[4] Registration issued within the first five years of the copyright holder's first publication of the work further provides prima facie evidence of the validity of the copyright and of the facts stated in the certificate, such as ownership.[5] The copyright holder has the burden of showing that the alleged infringing work was derived or copied from the copyright holder's work.[6]

In addition, copyright registration is useful in establishing a public record for the copyright claim. This may prove important in litigation. Finally, registration allows the owner of the copyright to record the registration with the U.S. Customs Service for protection against the importation of infringing copies.[7] Recording copyright registrations with the U.S. Customs Service can be a relatively inexpensive, yet effective, tool for suppressing infringing activity, without the expense of federal court litigation.[8]

As will be covered in detail below, registration is generally a fairly simple process and is relatively inexpensive. Consequently, registering a work is almost always the recommended course of action.

§ 7:2 Publication—Definition of publication

Research References

West's Key Number Digest, Copyrights and Intellectual Property ☞31
C.J.S., Copyrights and Intellectual Property §§ 31, 35

Publication is the distribution of copies or phonorecords of a work to the public by sale or other transfer of ownership, or by

---

[Section 7:1]

[1]17 U.S.C.A. § 102(a).

[2]17 U.S.C.A. § 408(a).

[3]17 U.S.C.A. § 410(c).

[4]17 U.S.C.A. § 412.

[5]17 U.S.C.A. § 410(c).

[6]Sandberg & Sikorski Corp. v.
Andin Int'l Inc., 51 U.S.P.Q.2d 1574, 1999 WL 628076 (S.D. N.Y. 1999).

[7]19 C.F.R. § 133.31(a).

[8]For additional information on recordation of intellectual property rights with the Commissioner of U.S. Customs and Border Protection, visit http://www.cbp.gov/.

rental, lease, or lending. The offering to distribute copies or phonorecords to a group of persons for purposes of further distribution, public performance, or public display, constitutes
publication. However, a public performance or display of a work
does not of itself constitute publication.[1]

For the distribution of copies or phonorecords to constitute
publication, they must be available to the public. Essentially, in
order for distribution to be considered available to the public, the
persons to whom distribution is made must be under no implied
or expressed restriction with respect to disclosure of the work's
content.[2] Thus, if the person to whom distribution of the work is
made is free to disclose the work to others, the work is considered
to be published.

When a work is available in a public library, the Copyright Office will register the work as published under the assumption
that the public has full access to the work. However, if the Copyright Office is informed that there is restricted access to the work,
registration as a published work may be denied.[3]

In addition to the actual distribution of a work, publication
may also occur through an offering to distribute a work. However,
the offer to distribute must be for multiple copies that are in current existence. The offer to distribute works that are still in progress and not yet completed will not be considered by the Copyright Office to constitute publication.[4]

An application for copyright registration must include the date
and nation of first publication if the work has been published.[5] In
addition, works published in the United States must be deposited
in the Copyright Office for the use or disposition of the Library of
Congress.[6] Finally, deposit requirements for registration of
published works differ from those for registration of unpublished
works. Consequently, an initial determination of whether the
work has been published should be made when seeking copyright
registration. At first glance, this determination may seem fairly
straight forward. However, an applicant should be aware that
determining whether a work has been published is not always as
easy as it seems.

The current Copyright Act went into effect on January 1, 1978.
Before that time, copyright was generally obtained by publishing

---

[Section 7:2]

[1]17 U.S.C.A. § 101.

[2]See H.R. Rep. 94-1476, 94th
Cong., 2d Sess. 138 (1976); Moore v.
Columbia Pictures Indus., Inc., 17
U.S.P.Q.2d 1226, 1990 WL 120679 (D.
Minn. 1990).

[3]See Compendium of Copyright
Office Practices, § 1905.1 (3d ed.2014)
[hereinafter Compendium III].

[4]See Compendium III, § 1906.

[5]17 U.S.C.A. § 409(8).

[6]17 U.S.C.A. § 407(b).

the work and giving notice of copyright. Thus, it was critical that the published work included a copyright notice, and that the notice was of proper form and location. Copyright could also be obtained by a registration process before January 1, 1978.

§ 7:3 Publication—Copyright Office policy on publication

Research References

West's Key Number Digest, Copyrights and Intellectual Property ☞31
C.J.S., Copyrights and Intellectual Property §§ 31, 35

Generally, a designation of whether or not a work has been published will be left to the discretion of the applicant. The Copyright Office ordinarily will not attempt to decide whether publication has occurred. Nor will the Copyright Office attempt to make a factual investigation to determine whether publication has occurred.[1] Thus, it is up to the applicant to carefully consider and determine the proper designation.

In practice, where the applicant provides the Copyright Office with sufficient facts to support the conclusion that publication has occurred, the Copyright Office will accept such a designation.[2] However, where the facts stated by the applicant present inconsistencies or otherwise indicate that the work has not in fact been published despite the designation as such, the Copyright Office will communicate with the applicant and may not accept the applicant's designation of a work as published.[3] Similarly, if an application does not indicate that a work has been published, but contains information which suggests that the work has been published, the Copyright Office will usually contact the applicant to determine whether the publication date was inadvertently left out of the application.[4]

When there is only one copy of a work, and that single copy is transferred by sale, rental, lease, lending, etc., such a transfer is not considered a publication under the Copyright Act. However, when multiple copies of the work are transferred by sale, rental, lease, lending, etc., this will generally be sufficient for registration to be made as a published work.[5]

§ 7:4 Publication—Copyright Office policy on date of first publication

Research References

West's Key Number Digest, Copyrights and Intellectual Property ☞31

[Section 7:3]

[1]*See* Compendium III, § 1904.1.

[2]*See* Compendium III, § 1904.2.

[3]*See* Compendium III, § 1904.3.

[4]*See* Compendium III, § 1904.3.

[5]*See* Compendium III, § 1905.1.

C.J.S., Copyrights and Intellectual Property §§ 31, 35

In the same way that the Copyright Office will generally accept an applicant's designation of whether a work has been published, the Copyright Office will also generally accept, without question, an applicant's designation of the date of first publication. Only where a statement made by the applicant clearly shows that the first publication did not occur on that date will the Copyright Office reject the applicant's statement. In the event that an applicant's statement is inconsistent with the basis given, the Copyright Office will generally contact the applicant.[1]

§ 7:5 Publication—Copyright Office policy on nation of first publication

Research References

West's Key Number Digest, Copyrights and Intellectual Property ⬤⇌31
C.J.S., Copyrights and Intellectual Property §§ 31, 35

When an applicant provides a publication date, the nation of first publication should also be provided.[1] However, an application will not fail, nor will its status as published fail, when the nation of publication is not provided in the application. Generally, the Copyright Office will contact the applicant to determine the nation of first publication. Also, the Copyright Office will generally accept the statement of the applicant regarding the nation of first publication, unless it is inconsistent with the basis stated by the applicant.[2]

§ 7:6 Who may register a copyright

Research References

West's Key Number Digest, Copyrights and Intellectual Property ⬤⇌50.16
C.J.S., Copyrights and Intellectual Property §§ 39, 71, 96

Essentially, any owner of a copyright may apply to register the work. The owner of a copyright, the owner of any exclusive right thereunder, or the duly authorized agent of such owner is legally entitled to submit an application for registration of the copyright.[1]

Ownership of the copyright of a work initially vests in the author or authors of the work, that is, in the person or persons

---

[Section 7:4]
    [1]See Compendium III, § 612.7.
[Section 7:5]
    [1]17 U.S.C.A. § 409(8).

[2]See Compendium III, § 612.7.
[Section 7:6]
    [1]17 U.S.C.A. § 408(a).

who created the work.[2] Only a human or humans can be an author or authors of a copyrightable work, thus a work authored by an animal (such as a monkey or an elephant), a force of nature (such as the appearance of cuts marks defects in natural stone), a machine that operates randomly or automatically, or is asserted to be inspired by a supernatural force or being is ineligible for copyright protection and cannot be registered.[3] If the work was made for hire, the employer for whom the work was prepared is considered the author, and therefore, the owner of the work.[4] Any of these owners would be authorized to apply for registration of the copyright.

A copyright claimant may also apply for copyright registration. In addition to the author of the work, a copyright claimant may be a person that has obtained ownership of all the rights initially belonging to the author.[5] Thus, if the original author of copyright transferred the copyright, via any number of legal conveyances, to a second party, that second party would be the copyright claimant and would be able to apply for copyright registration.

The owner of any of the exclusive rights making up the copyright, that is, the right to reproduce, to prepare derivative works, to distribute copies, to perform the work publicly, or to display the copyrighted work publicly, may also apply to register the work.

Finally, any authorized agent of any of the aforementioned authors, claimants, or owners of exclusive rights, may apply to register a copyright so long as they are duly authorized to act on behalf of the author, claimant, or owner.

§ 7:7 Preparing the registration—Requirements of registration

Research References

West's Key Number Digest, Copyrights and Intellectual Property
⁂50.10 to 50.20
C.J.S., Copyrights and Intellectual Property §§ 38 to 39, 71, 96

Registration involves the filing of three essential items: (1) an application,[1] (2) an appropriate filing fee, and (3) the deposit of nonreturnable copies[2] with the Copyright Office. The Copyright Office prefers each of these items to be in the same envelope or package and sent to:

---

[2]17 U.S.C.A. § 201(a).   **[Section 7:7]**
[3]*See* Compendium III, § 313.2.   [1]17 U.S.C.A. § 409.
[4]17 U.S.C.A. § 201(b).   [2]17 U.S.C.A. § 407.
[5]37 C.F.R. § 202.3(a)(3)(ii).

Library of Congress Copyright Office
101 Independence Avenue SE
Washington, D.C. 20559-6000

Typically, when an application is received with less than the required three elements, the Copyright Office will return the application to the sender unprocessed, with instructions for proper registration.

The Copyright Office also offers online registration for basic claims to copyright for literary works, visual arts works, and performing arts works including motion pictures, sound recordings and single serials. Basic claims include: (1) a single work, (2) multiple unpublished works if they are by the same author(s) and owned by the same claimant, and (3) multiple published works if they are all first published together in the same publication on the same date and owned by the same claimant. Benefits of filing an electronic copyright claim through the electronic Copyright Office (eCO) include:

- a lower filing fee than traditional registration;
- a faster processing time;
- an earlier effective date of registration;
- the availability of online status tracking;
- the availability of secure payment by credit or debit card, electronic check or Copyright Office deposit account; and
- the ability to upload certain categories of deposits directly into the eCO as electronic files.

§ 7:8 Preparing the registration—Application fee for registration

Research References

West's Key Number Digest, Copyrights and Intellectual Property ⚭50.20

C.J.S., Copyrights and Intellectual Property §§ 39, 71, 96

The Copyright Office will accept remittance in the form of checks, money orders, or bank drafts, but not cash. The current registration fee is $35 for electronically-filed registrations for single authors, $55 for all other electronically-filed registrations, and $85 for basic registrations using the other paper forms (PA, SR, TX, VA, and SE).[1] The Copyright Office has the authority to adjust fees at three year intervals. The most recent adjustment

---

[Section 7:8]
[1]37 C.F.R. § 201.3.

was in May 2014.

§ 7:9   Preparing the registration—Application forms for registration

Research References

West's Key Number Digest, Copyrights and Intellectual Property
☞50.20
C.J.S., Copyrights and Intellectual Property §§ 39, 71, 96

A copyright application is made on a form provided by the Copyright Office.[1] Traditional registration required an applicant to select a paper form (Form TX, Form SE, Form VA, Form SR, or Form PA) corresponding to the type of work the applicant was seeking to register. If unable to register electronically, the Copyright Office encourages applicants to use electronically-editable PDF format forms for the following categories of work: (1) literary works; (2) performing arts works; (3) visual arts works; (4) motion picture/audiovisual works; (5) sound recordings; and (6) single serial issues. These forms are available on the Copyright Office Website, www.copyright.gov. The forms allow applicants to complete the form from their personal computer, print the completed form, and mail it along with a check or money-order and deposit to the Copyright Office.

A sample of Form TX for literary works is included in Appendix I.

Regardless of the type of work and corresponding form, there is certain information that is required for every application submitted to the Copyright Office. Every application must include:

- the name and address of the copyright claimant,
- in the case of a work other than an anonymous or pseudonymous work, the name and nationality or domicile of the author or authors, and, if one or more of the authors is dead, the dates of their deaths,
- if the work is anonymous or pseudonymous, the nationality or domicile of the author or authors,
- in the case of a work made for hire, a statement to this effect,
- if the copyright claimant is not the author, a brief statement of how the claimant obtained ownership of the copyright,
- the title of the work, together with any previous or alternative titles under which the work can be identified,
- the year in which creation of the work was completed,

[Section 7:9]
[1]17 U.S.C.A § 409.

- if the work has been published, the date and nation of its first publication,
- in the case of a compilation or derivative work, an identification of any preexisting work or works that it is based on or incorporates, and a brief, general statement of the additional material covered by the copyright claim being registered,
- in the case of a published work containing material of which copies are required by section 601 [of the Copyright Act] to be manufactured in the United States, the names of the persons or organizations who performed the processes specified by the subsection (c) of section 601 with respect to that material, and the places where those processes were performed, and
- any other information regarded by the Register of Copyrights as bearing upon the preparation or identification of the work or the existence, ownership, or duration of the copyright.[2]

For current copyright registration forms, go to www.copyright.gov or call the Forms and Publications Hotline at (202) 707-9100. The phone number for general information is (202) 707-3000.

§ 7:10 Preparing the registration—Deposit copies required for registration

Research References

West's Key Number Digest, Copyrights and Intellectual Property ⚭50.10

C.J.S., Copyrights and Intellectual Property §§ 38 to 39

The third requirement for a proper application is the deposit of nonreturnable copies with the Copyright Office.[1] The required deposit for copyright registration varies depending upon whether the work has been published, whether the work was first published outside the United States, or whether the work is a collective work.

For unpublished works, the applicant should deposit one complete copy or phonorecord.[2] For published works, the applicant should deposit two complete copies or phonorecords of the best edition.[3] In the case of a work first published outside of the U.S., only one copy is required for deposit.[4] Finally, in the case of a collective work, the applicant should deposit one copy or phonorec-

---

[2]17 U.S.C.A. §§ 409(1) to (11).

[Section 7:10]

[1]17 U.S.C.A. § 408(b).

[2]17 U.S.C.A. § 408(b)(1).

[3]17 U.S.C.A. § 408(b)(2).

[4]17 U.S.C.A. § 408(b)(3).

ord of the best edition of the collective work.[5]

For an unpublished work, a complete copy or phonorecord of a work is a copy or phonorecord representing the entire copyrightable content of the work for which registration is sought.[6] For a published work, a complete copy or phonorecord of a work includes all elements comprising the applicable unit of publication of the work, including elements that, if considered separately, would not be copyrightable subject matter.[7]

There are a number of exceptions to the requirement of two complete copies or phonorecords for published works. For example, the deposit of one complete copy or phonorecord will suffice for the following:

- published three dimensional cartographic representations of area (such as globes),
- published diagrams illustrating scientific or technical works or formulating scientific or technical information in linear or other two-dimensional form,
- published greeting cards, picture postcards, and stationery,
- individually published lectures, sermons, speeches, and addresses,
- published contributions to a collective work,
- musical compositions published in copies only or in both copies and phonorecords,
- published multimedia kits which are prepared for use in systematic instructional activities,
- works consisting of multiple parts that are packaged and published in a flat-sided box or similar container, and
- motion pictures.[8]

§ 7:11 Preparing the registration—Other deposit considerations

Research References

West's Key Number Digest, Copyrights and Intellectual Property ⊚50.10

C.J.S., Copyrights and Intellectual Property §§ 38 to 39

It is important to recognize that although copyright registration is not required, § 407 of the Copyright Act requires the deposit of copies or phonorecords in the Copyright Office for all works published in the United States. The deposit must be made within three months of the publication and must be made regardless of whether or not the owner of copyright or of the exclusive

---

[5]17 U.S.C.A. § 408(b)(4).   [7]37 C.F.R. § 202.2(b)(2)(ii).

[6]37 C.F.R. § 202.20(b)(2)(i).   [8]37 C.F.R. § 202.20(c)(2)(i).

right of publication in the work desires to register the work.[1]

The failure to deposit copies or phonorecords in the Copyright Office does not affect copyright in the work, but may result in fines and other penalties. The Register of Copyrights may make a deposit demand on any persons obligated to make a deposit under the Copyright Act. If a deposit is not made within three months of the demand, the persons upon whom the demand is made are liable: (1) to a fine of not more than $250 for each work; (2) to pay into a specially designed fund in the Library of Congress the total retail price of the copies or phonorecords demanded, or, if no retail price has been fixed, the reasonable cost of the Library of Congress of acquiring them; and (3) to pay a fine of $2,500, in addition to any other above-identified fine, if such person willfully or repeatedly fails or refuses to comply with such a demand.[2]

§ 7:12   Duration of copyright registrations—Works created on or after January 1, 1978

Research References

West's Key Number Digest, Copyrights and Intellectual Property ⬦33
C.J.S., Copyrights and Intellectual Property §§ 31 to 33, 94

Copyright in a work created on or after January 1, 1978, or created before January 1, 1978, with existing rights subsisting in a renewal term provided by the Copyright Act of 1976, exists from the date of creation and, for the most part, the basic term of the copyright is seventy years beyond the life of the author.[1] In the case of a joint work, the copyright term is seventy years beyond the life of the last surviving author.[2] In the case of an anonymous work, a pseudonymous work, or a work made for hire, the term of the copyright is ninety-five years from the date of first publication or one hundred twenty years from the date of creation, whichever comes first.[3] Since the basic term of copyrighted work created on or after January 1, 1978, is seventy years beyond the life of the author,[4] an important initial determination in any question of copyright duration is when the work was "created" and when the author died.

A work is created when it is fixed in a copy or phonorecord for the first time. Where a work is prepared over a period of time, a portion of it that has been fixed at any particular time consti-

---

[Section 7:11]

  [1]17 U.S.C.A. § 407(a).

  [2]17 U.S.C.A. § 407(d).

[Section 7:12]

  [1]17 U.S.C.A. § 302(a).

[2]17 U.S.C.A. § 302(b).

[3]17 U.S.C.A. § 302(c).

[4]17 U.S.C.A. § 302(a).

tutes the work as of that time. Where the work has been prepared in different versions, each version constitutes a separate work.[5]

Consequently, a work is not created until it is "fixed." A work is fixed, under the statute, when its embodiment in a copy or phonorecord, by the authority of the author, is sufficiently permanent or stable to permit it to be perceived, reproduced, or otherwise communicated for a period of more than transitory duration. A work consisting of sounds, images, or both, that are being transmitted, is fixed for the purposes of the Copyright Act if a fixation of the work is made simultaneously with its transmission.[6]

Thus, when a work is sufficiently permanent to be perceived for a significant period of time, by the authority of the author, for the first time on or after January 1, 1978, the term of copyright is seventy years beyond the life of the author.

Since the basic term of a copyright is seventy years beyond the life of the author, the date of the death of the author is critical to determining the duration of the copyright. To that end, the Register of Copyrights maintains current records of information relating to the deaths of authors of copyrighted works based on recorded statements. Any person having an interest in a copyright may at any time record in the Copyright Office a statement of the date of death of the author of the copyrighted work. Further, any such person may also record a statement that the author is still living on a particular date.[7]

Under certain circumstances, the benefits of a presumption that the author has been dead for at least seventy years may be obtained. After a period of ninety-five years from the year of first publication of a work, or a period of one hundred twenty years from the year of its creation, whichever expires first, any person who obtains a certified report from the Copyright Office that the records provided by the Register of Copyrights disclose nothing to indicate that the author of the work is living, or died less than seventy years before, is entitled to the benefits of a presumption that the author has been dead for at least seventy years. Reliance in good faith upon this presumption is a complete defense to any action for infringement under the Copyright Act.[8]

§ 7:13 Duration of copyright registrations—Works created before January 1, 1978

Research References

---

[5]17 U.S.C.A. § 101.   [7]17 U.S.C.A. § 302(d).
[6]17 U.S.C.A. § 101.   [8]17 U.S.C.A. § 302(e).

West's Key Number Digest, Copyrights and Intellectual Property ⊶33
C.J.S., Copyrights and Intellectual Property §§ 31 to 33, 94

Works that were not in the public domain, that is, not published or copyrighted before January 1, 1978, are now specifically provided for under § 303 of the Copyright Act. Under that section, the term provided by § 302 will control. Consequently, the duration of copyright in works created, but not published or registered, before January 1, 1978, will be essentially the same as works created on or after January 1, 1978. That is, the basic term of a copyright is seventy years beyond the life of the author; in the case of a joint work, the copyright term is seventy years beyond the life of the last surviving author; and in the case of an anonymous work, a pseudonymous work, or a work made for hire, the term of the copyright is ninety-five years from the date of first publication or one hundred twenty years from the date of creation, whichever comes first.[1]

In addition, the term of copyright in works created but not published or copyrighted before January 1, 1978, in every case, will not expire before December 31, 2002. Further, if the work is published on or before December 31, 2002, the term of the copyright will not expire before December 31, 2047.[2]

Before January 1, 1978, works that were neither published nor copyrighted were protected by common law copyright. As described above, those works are now provided for under § 303 of the Copyright Act. For those works that were either published or copyrighted before January 1, 1978, copyright was secured either on the date the work was published or on the date of registration if the work was registered. In either case, the works are protected for an initial term of copyright of twenty-eight years, beginning upon the date the copyright was originally secured.[3] During the last year of the first term (i.e., the twenty-eighth year), the copyright may be renewed for an additional sixty-seven years.

In the case of a posthumous work or of any periodical, encyclopedia, or other composite work upon which copyright was originally secured or any work copyrighted by a corporate body, the proprietor of such copyright is entitled to a renewal and extension of the copyright for sixty-seven years. In the case of any other copyrighted work, including a contribution by an individual author to a periodical or encyclopedia or other composite work, the author of such work, the widow or widower, the author's executors, or the author's next of kin is entitled to an extension

---

[Section 7:13]
[1]17 U.S.C.A. § 302(c).

[2]17 U.S.C.A. § 303(a).
[3]17 U.S.C.A. § 304.

of the copyright in such work for an additional sixty-seven years.[4]

Renewal registration is optional. A copyright owner is not required to make the renewal filing in order to extend the original twenty-eight year copyright term to the full ninety-five years.

§ 7:14 Copyright notice—Form of notice

Research References

West's Key Number Digest, Copyrights and Intellectual Property
⬤50.1(2)
C.J.S., Copyrights and Intellectual Property §§ 35, 95

Before March 1, 1989, the use of a copyright notice was mandatory on all published works. Any work published before that date which did not include notice risked loss of copyright protection. Since March 1, 1989, use of a copyright notice for works is optional. However, using a copyright notice is almost always good practice. It is not necessary to obtain permission from the Copyright Office to use a copyright notice. The use of a copyright notice is the responsibility of the copyright owner.

Copyright notice should include at least:

- The word "copyright" or the symbol ©,
- Year of first publication of the work, and
- Name of the copyright owner(s).

When the work is a compilation work or a derivative of a previously published work, it is sufficient to include the year the compilation or derivative work was published. Also, an abbreviation by which the name of the owner can be recognized is sufficient for the name of the owner.

For example, proper notice may include the following:[1]

Copyright 2015 Kinney & Lange, P.A.

or

© 2015 Austen Zuege

The symbol (c) (the letter "c" in parenthesis) is technically not proper notice. Although it may suffice, it should only be used with one of the other proper forms, e.g., (c) Copyright 2015 Kinney & Lange, P.A.[2]

§ 7:15 Copyright notice—Method of affixing notice

---

[4]17 U.S.C.A. §§ 304(a)(1)(B) and (C).

[Section 7:14]

[1]17 U.S.C.A. § 401(b)

[2]*See* Forry, Inc. v. Neundorfer, Inc., 837 F.2d 259, 5 U.S.P.Q.2d 1510, 113, 113 A.L.R. Fed. 857 (6th Cir. 1988).

Research References

West's Key Number Digest, Copyrights and Intellectual Property
$\Longleftrightarrow$50.1(2)

C.J.S., Copyrights and Intellectual Property §§ 35, 95

The notice must be affixed to the copies in a manner and location that give reasonable notice of the claim of copyright.[1]

For computer programs, notice should be affixed to ROM, magnetic disk, or other medium in which it is embodied and distributed. Documentation should include the copyright notice and a statement that the notice covers the program. If the program generates a visual display, notice should also be displayed for a short time on the screen.

For phonorecords of sound recordings, "℗" replaces "©."[2] The notice on the phonorecord may appear on the surface of the phonorecord or on the phonorecord label or container, provided the manner of placement and location give reasonable notice of the claim.[3]

The year and date may be omitted where a pictorial, graphic or sculptural work is reproduced in or on greeting cards, postcards, stationery, jewelry, dolls, toys, or any useful articles.[4]

In general, a copyright notice on a collective work covers all of the separate contributions it contains. However, an advertisement inserted on behalf of persons other than the owner of the copyright in the collective work (e.g., an advertisement in a newspaper or magazine) must carry a separate copyright notice.[5]

§ 7:16 Omission of copyright notice—Works published before January 1, 1978

Research References

West's Key Number Digest, Copyrights and Intellectual Property
$\Longleftrightarrow$50.1(4)

C.J.S., Copyrights and Intellectual Property §§ 35, 95

Copyright notice has never been required on unpublished works, and notice is not required currently on published works. For published works, however, former law required notice. Therefore, the effect of omitting copyright notice on published works depends on the date of publication.

Prior to January 1, 1978 (the effective date of the Copyright Act of 1976), omission of copyright notice on a work published with the copyright owner's authority resulted in a loss of the

---

[Section 7:15]

[1]17 U.S.C.A. § 401(c).

[2]17 U.S.C.A. § 402(b).

[3]17 U.S.C.A. § 402(c).

[4]17 U.S.C.A. § 401(b)(2).

[5]17 U.S.C.A. § 404(a).

copyright. Current copyright law does not provide for retroactive protection of such works. So, if a work was published without notice before January 1, 1978, the copyright is permanently lost.

A work published in a foreign country before January 1, 1978, without a copyright notice does not preclude subsequent U.S. copyright protection for work. Under the 1909 Copyright Act, publication of a work without a copyright notice in a foreign country did not put work in the public domain in the United States, provided the publication did not cause the work to fall into the public domain in that foreign country.[1]

§ 7:17 Omission of copyright notice—Works first published between January 1, 1978 and March 1, 1989

Research References
West's Key Number Digest, Copyrights and Intellectual Property
    ⊕50.1(4)
C.J.S., Copyrights and Intellectual Property §§ 35, 95

The 1976 Act provided that the omission of notice did not invalidate a copyright if:

[N]otice has been omitted from no more than a relatively small number of copies or phonorecords distributed to the public; or

[R]egistration for the work has been made before or is made within five years after publication without notice, and a reasonable effort is made to add notice to all copies or phonorecords that are distributed to the public in the United States after the omission has been discovered; or

[N]otice has been omitted in violation of an express written requirement that, as a condition of the copyright owner's authorization of the public distribution of copies or phonorecords, they bear the prescribed notice.[1]

Thus, for works first published between January 1, 1978, and March 1, 1989, it may be possible to rectify the omission of notice.

An innocent infringer who can prove that he or she was misled by the omission of the copyright notice from a work which was publicly distributed by authority of the copyright owner before March 1, 1989, incurs no liability for actual or statutory damages for any infringing acts before receiving actual notice of a copyright registration.[2]

[Section 7:16]
[1]Twin Books Corp. v. Walt Disney Co., 83 F.3d 1162, 38 U.S.P.Q.2d 1847 (9th Cir. 1996).

[Section 7:17]
[1]17 U.S.C.A. § 405(a).
[2]17 U.S.C.A. § 405(b).

§ 7:18 Omission of copyright notice—Works first published after March 1, 1989

Research References

West's Key Number Digest, Copyrights and Intellectual Property
⊙50.1(4)
C.J.S., Copyrights and Intellectual Property §§ 35, 95

The Berne Convention Implementation Act amended the copyright law to make use of copyright notice optional for any work first published after March 1, 1989. Omission of notice, however, may enable infringers to prove that their infringement was "innocent," thus reducing actual or statutory damages.[1] Consequently, a copyright notice should be applied to all published works even though it is not required under current law.

§ 7:19 Omission of copyright notice—Notice removed without authorization

Research References

West's Key Number Digest, Copyrights and Intellectual Property
⊙50.1(4)
C.J.S., Copyrights and Intellectual Property §§ 35, 95

Copyright protection is not affected by removal, destruction, or obliteration of the copyright notice, without authorization of the copyright owner, from any publicly distributed copies or phonorecords.[1]

§ 7:20 Omission of copyright notice—Notice on unpublished works

Research References

West's Key Number Digest, Copyrights and Intellectual Property
⊙50.1(2)
C.J.S., Copyrights and Intellectual Property §§ 35, 95

As stated above, notice has never been required on unpublished works. It is good practice, however, to place a copyright notice on copies that leave the owners control because it is sometimes difficult to distinguish a preliminary distribution from actual publication. An appropriate notice for unpublished works is:

Unpublished work © 2015 Kinney & Lange, P.A.

[Section 7:18]
    [1]17 U.S.C.A. §§ 401(d), 402(d), 504(c).

[Section 7:19]
    [1]17 U.S.C.A. § 405(c).

The date used should be the date of creation.

If the unpublished work contains trade secrets, applying a copyright notice creates somewhat of a dilemma—especially where copies of the work are distributed with some form of confidentiality agreement. If copyright notice is placed on the work, this is arguably an admission that the work is "published" and is therefore no longer a trade secret. If, however, the copyright notice is omitted and it is later determined that the work has been published by virtue of distribution of copies, "innocent infringement" claims may be alleged to reduce damages.

Accordingly, the following statement is recommended for unpublished works. Again, the date used should be the date of creation:

> This unpublished work is protected by trade secret, copyright and other laws. In the event of publication, the following notice shall apply:

Unpublished work © 2015 Kinney & Lange, P.A.

§ 7:21 Certificate of registration
Research References
West's Key Number Digest, Copyrights and Intellectual Property
 ⊙50.25
C.J.S., Copyrights and Intellectual Property §§ 39, 71, 96

The Register of Copyrights will issue a certificate of registration under seal of the Copyright Office to an applicant when the Register determines that the formal and legal requirements of the Copyright Act have been met. The certificate contains the information given in the application, as well as the number and effective date of the registration.[1]

The effective date of copyright registration is the day on which an application, deposit, and fee have all been received in the Copyright Office. In order to establish the effective date, the Register of Copyrights or a court of competent jurisdiction must determine that the application, deposit, and fee are acceptable for registration.[2] If less than all the requirements have been met in an application, the effective date of registration is the date when the necessary information is finally provided.[3]

The certificate of registration performs an important function

---

[Section 7:21]   [2]17 U.S.C.A. § 410(d).
 [1]17 U.S.C.A. § 410(a).   [3]*See* Compendium III, § 1802.

in any judicial proceeding that is brought based on the copyright. First, an action for copyright infringement may not be instituted until pre-registration or registration of the copyright claim has been made in accordance with the Copyright Act.[4] However, an applicant is also entitled to institute an action for civil copyright infringement if the deposit, application, and fee required for registration have been delivered to the Copyright Office in proper form and registration has been refused.[5] Circuit courts are split on whether mere delivery of all the necessary documents to the Copyright Office is enough to satisfy this requirement or if actual refusal of the registration is also required.[6] Notice of the infringement action, with a copy of the complaint, must be served on the Register of Copyrights.[7]

Second, the certificate of registration is prima facie evidence of the validity of the copyright in any judicial proceedings where the certificate of a registration is made before, or within five years after, the date of first publication of the work.[8] Further, the registration is prima facie evidence of the facts stated in the certificate. Each court retains its own discretion as to the evidentiary weight accorded the certificate of registration.[9] Consequently, given the relative ease of procurement, as well as the low cost, of copyright registration, registration should be sought as soon as possible for each work of suitable subject matter.

---

[4]17 U.S.C.A. § 411(a).

[5]17 U.S.C.A. § 411(a).

[6]*Compare* La Resolana Architects, PA v. Clay Realtors Angel Fire, 416 F.3d 1195, 1205, 75 U.S.P.Q.2d 1496 (10th Cir. 2005) (rejecting the proposition that § 411 confers federal jurisdiction for an infringement action upon mere submission of a copyright application), *with* Apple Barrel Prods., Inc. v. Beard, 730 F.2d 384, 386–87, 222 U.S.P.Q. 956 (5th Cir. 1984) (requiring only proof of payment of the required fee, deposit of the work in question, and receipt by the Copyright Office of the registration application).

[7]17 U.S.C.A. § 410(c).

[8]17 U.S.C.A. § 410(c).

[9]17 U.S.C.A. § 410(c).

Chapter 8

Copyright Litigation

KeyCite®: Cases and other legal materials listed in KeyCite Scope can be researched through the KeyCite service on Westlaw®. Use KeyCite to check citations for form, parallel references, prior and later history, and comprehensive citator information, including citations to other decisions and secondary materials.

§ 8:1 Pre-filing matters—Subject matter jurisdiction

Research References

West's Key Number Digest, Copyrights and Intellectual Property ⟨⟩79; Federal Courts ⟨⟩213
C.J.S., Copyrights and Intellectual Property §§ 8, 67, 98; Federal Civil Procedure § 340; Federal Courts § 101

Federal district courts have original jurisdiction over all civil actions arising under any federal copyright statute.[1] The federal courts' subject matter jurisdiction is exclusive.[2] There is no common law copyright. The current copyright law explicitly pre-empts all "legal or equitable rights that are equivalent to any of the exclusive rights" of the federal copyright law.[3] Therefore, like patent infringement cases, copyright infringement cases must be brought in federal court. Unlike trademark infringement cases, state courts do not have concurrent jurisdiction over copyright infringement cases. No action for copyright infringement may be brought until the work that is subject to such action has first been registered in the Copyright Office, or at least an attempt to register has been made and refused by the Copyright Office.[4] The registration requirement contained in 17 U.S.C.A. § 411(a) establishes a precondition to filing a copyright infringement claim, however, the requirement "does not restrict a federal court's subject-matter jurisdiction."[5]

One situation that arises repeatedly in copyright cases is when a plaintiff tries to bring a breach of contract case in federal court by pleading a copyright infringement case. For example, many copyrights are subject to licensing agreements or some other contract. If one party violates the terms of the agreement, such as failing to pay the royalty or license fee, or printing more copies of the work than was authorized by the contract, the plaintiff often seeks to obtain federal subject matter jurisdiction by pleading both a copyright infringement claim and a breach of contract claim. The copyright infringement claim is predicated upon the

---

[Section 8:1]
[1]28 U.S.C.A. § 1338(a).

[2]28 U.S.C.A. § 1338(b).

[3]17 U.S.C.A. § 301(a).

[4]17 U.S.C.A. § 411(a); Goebel v.

Manis, 39 F. Supp. 2d 1318, 50 U.S.P. Q.2d 1537 (D. Kan. 1999).

[5]Reed Elsevier, Inc. v. Muchnick, 559 U.S. 154, 157, 130 S. Ct. 1237, 176 L. Ed. 2d 18, 38 Media L. Rep. (BNA) 1321, 93 U.S.P.Q.2d 1719 (2010).

breach of contract. For instance, plaintiff will claim that defendant made copies of the copyrighted work and, because defendant failed to pay the agreed license fee, the copies were unauthorized. Federal courts view these kinds of cases with suspicion, and will often dismiss them because they are primarily contract cases in which the alleged copyright infringement is incidental.

Whether the case is a copyright or a contract case turns on whether the licensing provisions help define the scope of the license. The license will be construed to make this determination. Only after the copyright holder has established that the disputed terms between the parties are limitations on the scope of the license, rather than independent contractual provisions, will the copyright holder gain the benefits of copyright enforcement. The copyright holder must establish that the rights claimed as violated are copyrights, not contractual rights, to presume irreparable harm under copyright laws.[6] Once an assignment or license has expired, the copyright owner may hold the former licensee/grantee liable for infringement for subsequent use of the work giving rise to a federal claim under the Copyright Act.[7]

As with trademark infringement cases, appeals from copyright infringement cases are decided by the regional circuit courts. The Court of Appeals for the Federal Circuit does not have appellate jurisdiction over copyright infringement cases, unless they are joined with a patent infringement claim.

§ 8:2 Pre-filing matters—Personal jurisdiction

Research References

West's Key Number Digest, Copyrights and Intellectual Property ⊙79
C.J.S., Copyrights and Intellectual Property §§ 8, 67, 98

Personal jurisdiction in copyright cases is analyzed in the same way as other questions of personal jurisdiction. The case must be brought in a jurisdiction in which defendant has sufficient minimum contacts to satisfy the due process requirements of the U.S. Constitution.

Copyright infringement is a commercial tort that is considered to take place at the point of consumer purchase. An actual sale is not necessary to establish personal jurisdiction and the tort may

---

[6]Sun Microsystems, Inc. v. Microsoft Corp., 188 F.3d 1115, 1122, 51 U.S.P.Q.2d 1825 (9th Cir. 1999).

[7]Kamakazi Music Corp. v. Robbins Music Corp., 684 F.2d 228, 230 (2d Cir. 1982); Gerig v. Krause Publications, Inc., 58 F. Supp. 2d 1261, 1268, 51 U.S.P.Q.2d 1936 (D. Kan. 1999).

be performed either directly by defendant or through a retailer.[1] Thus, sale of an infringing work within a particular district is generally sufficient to establish personal jurisdiction.

For example, a defendant who made 0.8% of its total sales in a district was subject to personal jurisdiction.[2] Similarly, a person who advertised his business in at least one magazine of national circulation, received a small number of inquiries from prospective customers in the jurisdiction, and who delivered one of the infringing works into the jurisdiction was subject to jurisdiction in that state.[3]

When applying legal principles to situations involving the Internet, the applicability of traditional minimum contacts analysis remains unclear. Because websites are accessible to Internet users around the world, personal jurisdiction becomes a major concern for potential defendants who may be haled into court in distant forums.

Courts typically use a sliding scale for determining purposeful availment in relation to Internet contacts, where "the likelihood that personal jurisdiction can be constitutionally exercised is directly proportionate to the nature and quality of commercial activity that an entity conducts over the Internet."[4] At one end of the spectrum are so-called active websites.[5] Personal jurisdiction is proper with active websites where a defendant clearly does business over the Internet and, for example, enters into contracts with residents of foreign jurisdictions that involve "the knowing and repeated transmission of computer files over the Internet."[6] At the other end of the spectrum are so-called passive websites.[7] Personal jurisdiction is not found in "situations where a defendant has simply posted information on an Internet Website which is accessible to users in foreign jurisdictions . . . [and] does little

---

[Section 8:2]

[1] Bus. Trends Analysts v. Freedonia Group, Inc., 650 F. Supp. 1452, 1455-56 (S.D. N.Y. 1987).

[2] Fox-Rich Textiles, Inc. v. Malden Mills Indus., Inc., 14 U.S.P.Q.2d 1843, 1845, 1989 WL 140246 (S.D. N.Y. 1989).

[3] Blue Compass Corp. v. Polish Masters of Am., 777 F. Supp. 4, 5, 21 U.S.P.Q.2d 1399 (D. Vt. 1991).

[4] Zippo Mfg. Co. v. Zippo Dot Com, Inc., 952 F. Supp. 1119, 1124, 42 U.S.P. Q.2d 1062 (W.D. Pa. 1997).

[5] See, e.g., Panavision Int'l., L.P. v. Toeppen, 141 F.3d 1316, 46 U.S.P.

Q.2d 1511 (9th Cir. 1998) holding modified by Yahoo! Inc. v. La Ligue Contre Le Racisme Et L'Antisemitisme, 433 F.3d 1199 (9th Cir. 2006); Blumenthal v. Drudge, 992 F. Supp. 44, 26 Media L. Rep. (BNA) 1717 (D.D.C. 1998).

[6] Zippo, 952 F. Supp. at 1124.

[7] See, e.g., Millennium Enters., Inc. v. Millennium Music, LP, 33 F. Supp. 2d 907, 49 U.S.P.Q.2d 1878, 81 A.L.R.5th 697 (D. Or. 1999); Bensusan Rest. Corp. v. King, 126 F.3d 25, 44 U.S.P.Q.2d 1051 (2d Cir. 1997); Maritz, Inc. v. Cybergold, Inc., 947 F. Supp. 1328, 40 U.S.P.Q.2d 1729 (E.D. Mo. 1996).

more than make information available to those who are interested in it . . . ."[8] The middle ground between active and passive websites is analyzed by looking to "the level of interactivity and commercial nature of the exchange of information that occurs on the Web site."[9]

This framework, or an equivalent test, has been adopted by a majority of the circuit courts.[10] Those circuits are more likely to rely upon this framework in assessing specific jurisdiction issues, and less likely to extend it to assess general jurisdiction issues.[11] However, other courts have questioned the foundation of this analytical framework.[12]

§ 8:3 Pre-filing matters—Venue

Research References
West's Key Number Digest, Copyrights and Intellectual Property ⚖79
C.J.S., Copyrights and Intellectual Property §§ 8, 67, 98

In a copyright case, venue is proper in any district in which the defendant "resides or may be found."[1] The defendant may be found in any district in which the defendant is subject to personal jurisdiction.[2] Thus, in copyright infringement cases, personal jurisdiction and venue have merged. If a court has personal jurisdiction over a defendant, then venue is proper.

While a party may be found in any district in which it is amenable to personal jurisdiction, remember that jurisdiction must be analyzed in the context of federal districts, not simply states.

---

[8]Zippo, 952 F. Supp. at 1124.

[9]Zippo, 952 F. Supp. at 1124.

[10]E.g., Toys "R" Us, Inc. v. Step Two, S.A., 318 F.3d 446, 452–54, 65 U.S.P.Q.2d 1628, 55 Fed. R. Serv. 3d 591 (3d Cir. 2003); ALS Scan, Inc. v. Digital Serv. Consultants, Inc., 293 F.3d 707, 713, 63 U.S.P.Q.2d 1389, 52 Fed. R. Serv. 3d 1121 (4th Cir. 2002); Mink v. AAAA Dev. LLC, 190 F.3d 333, 336, 52 U.S.P.Q.2d 1218 (5th Cir. 1999); Neogen Corp. v. Neo Gen Screening, Inc., 282 F.3d 883, 890, 61 U.S.P.Q.2d 1845, 2002 FED App. 0080P (6th Cir. 2002); Lakin v. Prudential Sec., Inc., 348 F.3d 704, 711 (8th Cir. 2003); Cybersell, Inc. v. Cybersell, Inc., 130 F.3d 414, 419, 44 U.S.P.Q.2d 1928 (9th Cir. 1997); Soma Med. Int'l. v. Standard Chartered Bank, 196 F.3d 1292, 1296-97 (10th Cir. 1999); Gorman v. Ameritrade Holding Corp., 293 F.3d

506, 513, 52 Fed. R. Serv. 3d 869 (D.C. Cir. 2002).

[11]See Lakin, 348 F.3d at 712; Revell v. Lidov, 317 F.3d 467, 471, 173 Ed. Law Rep. 403, 31 Media L. Rep. (BNA) 1521 (5th Cir. 2002); see also Soma Med., 196 F.3d at 1296-97; Bell v. Imperial Palace Hotel/Casino, Inc., 200 F. Supp. 2d 1082, 1091 (E.D. Mo. 2001).

[12]Hy Cite Corp. v. Badbusinessbureau.com, L.L.C., 297 F. Supp. 2d 1154, 70 U.S.P.Q.2d 1266 (W.D. Wis. 2004).

[Section 8:3]

[1]28 U.S.C.A. § 1400(a).

[2]Lipton v. Nature Co., 781 F. Supp. 1032, 1035, 21 U.S.P.Q.2d 1944 (S.D.N.Y. 1992), aff'd, 71 F.3d 464, 37 U.S.P.Q.2d 1012 (2d Cir. 1995).

Thus, where a defendant's only contacts with Wisconsin were delivering the allegedly infringing product to cities in western Wisconsin, it would not be subject to personal jurisdiction in the Eastern District of Wisconsin.[3]

§ 8:4 Pre-filing matters—Drafting the complaint

Research References

West's Key Number Digest, Copyrights and Intellectual Property ⊶82
C.J.S., Copyrights and Intellectual Property §§ 8, 70, 98

Copyright infringement complaints are relatively simple, and a complaint that follows the structure of Form 19 of the Federal Rules of Civil Procedure is acceptable. Plaintiff must assert that it is the owner of a copyrighted work that has been registered with the Copyright Office, and that defendant has violated one of plaintiff's exclusive rights under 17 U.S.C.A. § 106. An example of a complaint for copyright infringement is included in Appendix K.

No special forms of pleading are required. A general allegation that defendant infringed a copyrighted work, which is alleged to be an original compilation or other work, is sufficient to state a claim for copyright infringement. Furthermore, a copyright owner may prevail on a claim for declaratory judgment of infringement without a showing of entitlement to monetary relief, because the existence of damages suffered is not an essential element of a claim for copyright infringement.[1] Since the element of copyrightable originality is often subtle, plaintiff is not held to a particularity requirement akin to Federal Rule of Civil Procedure 9(b).[2]

One important thing to remember is that a copyright must be registered with the Copyright Office before a suit can be filed.[3] The copyright itself comes into existence at the moment that the work is created. However, the federal registration is required before the law will allow the copyright owner access to the courts. This is one of the benefits offered to copyright owners in order to encourage registration. If a work has not been registered, the owner must obtain registration before filing the complaint.

§ 8:5 Pre-filing matters—Pre-emption of state law claims

Research References

---

[3]Milwaukee Concrete Studios, Ltd. v. Field Mfg. Co., Inc., 8 F.3d 441, 447, 28 U.S.P.Q.2d 1594, 27 Fed. R. Serv. 3d 335 (7th Cir. 1993).

[Section 8:4]

[1]On Davis v. The Gap, Inc., 246 F.3d 152, 158 (2d Cir. 2001), as amended, (May 15, 2001).

[2]Mid Am. Title Co. v. Kirk, 991 F.2d 417, 422, 26 U.S.P.Q.2d 1538, 25 Fed. R. Serv. 3d 572 (7th Cir. 1993).

[3]17 U.S.C.A. § 411.

West's Key Number Digest, Copyrights and Intellectual Property ⬤109; States ⬤18.87

C.J.S., Copyrights and Intellectual Property §§ 8, 103, 108; Monopolies § 20

The Copyright Act of 1976 specifically pre-empts state laws that are equivalent to the exclusive rights protected by the federal copyright laws.[1] The Copyright Act establishes a two-part test for pre-emption. First, the copyright owner's work must "come within the subject matter of copyright" as defined by 17 U.S.C.A. § 102 and § 103. Second, the rights granted under state law must be "equivalent to" the exclusive rights within the general scope of the Copyright Act.[2]

Under the first element of the test, the work need only fall within the general scope of copyright. It does not require the copyright to be enforceable, and it certainly does not mean that the copyright infringement claim must be successful. If, for example, the copyright is rendered invalid, or if the accused work is not substantially similar to the copyrighted work, state law claims may not be used simply as fall-back positions.

Most disputes involve the second element of the pre-emption test. To meet this part of the test (that the state law claim is "equivalent to" the copyright claim) the state law claim must be one which arises from the same act which gives rise to the copyright claim—reproduction, performance, distribution or display. To properly plead a state law claim, the right under state law must have an "extra element" that changes the nature of the action so that it is qualitatively different from a copyright infringement claim. If the plaintiff cannot set forth an "extra element" to support its state law claim, but merely relies on the same facts (i.e., reproduction, distribution or display of the allegedly infringing work) to support its state law claims as it relies upon to support its copyright claim, then the state law claim is pre-empted.

Thus, when considering whether to add state law counts to a copyright infringement complaint, plaintiff should analyze potential state law claims to determine whether the claim may be pre-empted. The most common "extra element" that has survived § 301 is a state law claim arising from the disclosure of confidential information. If a confidential relationship existed between the parties, and the "copyright infringement" arose from

---

[Section 8:5]

[1]17 U.S.C.A. § 301.

[2]Harper & Row, Publishers, Inc. v. Nation Enters., 501 F. Supp. 848, 850, 6 Media L. Rep. (BNA) 2204, 212 U.S.P.Q. 274 (S.D. N.Y. 1980), *order*

aff'd, 723 F.2d 195, 9 Media L. Rep. (BNA) 2489, 220 U.S.P.Q. 321 (2d Cir. 1983), *judgment rev'd on other grounds*, 471 U.S. 539, 105 S. Ct. 2218, 11 Media L. Rep. (BNA) 1969, 225 U.S.P.Q. 1073 (1985).

defendant's use of information received pursuant to that confidential relationship, then the state law claim is qualitatively different from a copyright infringement claim, and the state law claim is not pre-empted.

§ 8:6   Pre-filing matters—Right to a jury

Research References

West's Key Number Digest, Jury ☞14(1.1)
C.J.S., Juries §§ 50, 53 to 57, 61 to 68, 71 to 75, 79, 99, 126 to 127

Parties to a copyright infringement case have a right to trial by jury. This is true even in cases where plaintiff seeks only statutory damages. The Seventh Amendment provides the right to a jury trial on all issues relating to a statutory damages award, including the amount of those damages.[1]

§ 8:7   Liability for copyright infringement—Direct infringement

Research References

West's Key Number Digest, Copyrights and Intellectual Property ☞77
C.J.S., Copyrights and Intellectual Property §§ 8, 64, 98

Copyright infringement occurs whenever one of the copyright owner's exclusive rights listed in 17 U.S.C.A. § 106 is violated.[1] Thus, a direct infringer is anyone who reproduces the copyrighted work; prepares a derivative work; sells or otherwise distributes unauthorized copies; performs a literary, musical, dramatic, choreographic, pantomime, motion picture or audiovisual work; or displays a literary, musical, dramatic, choreographic, pantomime, or pictorial, graphic or sculptural work.

Although infringement outside the U.S. does not violate U.S. copyright law, a plaintiff can recover damages from overseas exploitation of its copyrighted work if the defendant's infringing act of copying took place in the United States.[2]

§ 8:8   Liability for copyright infringement—Contributory infringement

---

[Section 8:6]

[1]Feltner v. Columbia Pictures Television, Inc., 523 U.S. 340, 353, 118 S. Ct. 1279, 140 L. Ed. 2d 438, 26 Media L. Rep. (BNA) 1513, 46 U.S.P. Q.2d 1161, 163 A.L.R. Fed. 721 (1998).

[Section 8:7]

[1]17 U.S.C.A. § 501(a).

[2]Los Angeles News Service v. Reuters Television Intern., Ltd., 149 F.3d 987, 992, 26 Media L. Rep. (BNA) 2001, 47 U.S.P.Q.2d 1349 (9th Cir. 1998), as amended on denial of reh'g and reh'g en banc, (Aug. 25, 1998).

Research References

West's Key Number Digest, Copyrights and Intellectual Property ⏁77
C.J.S., Copyrights and Intellectual Property §§ 8, 64, 98

A contributory infringer is one who, with actual constructive knowledge of the infringing activity, induces, causes or materially contributes to the infringing conduct of another.[1] Willful blindness to the infringing conduct of another also equates to knowledge.[2] In order to be liable for contributory infringement, the infringing activity must be substantial.[3] As with contributory patent infringement, there can be no contributory infringement without direct infringement of a copyright.[4]

A foreign defendant can be liable for contributory infringement if the foreign defendant knowingly ships the infringing product to the U.S. defendant. In this situation, if the foreign defendant should have known that the U.S. defendant would sell the infringing product, then the foreign defendant is liable.[5]

While intent to infringe may not be imputed solely from the design or distribution of a product capable of substantial lawful use, the accused infringer's intent is relevant in determining contributory infringement. Thus, where a company provided software for the purpose of downloading and copying copyrighted music over the internet, the fact that the software could be used for legal copying of public domain music or non-copyrighted documents was not sufficient to avoid liability for copyright infringement given the evidence of the infringer's actions and statements promoting illegal copying.[6] "[O]ne who distributes a device with the object of promoting its use to infringe copyright, as shown by clear expression or other affirmative steps taken to foster infringement, is liable for the resulting acts of infringement by third parties."[7]

§ 8:9 Liability for copyright infringement—Inducement of infringement

[Section 8:8]

[1]Gershwin Publ'g Corp. v. Columbia Artists Mgmt., Inc., 443 F.2d 1159, 1162, 170 U.S.P.Q. 182, 14 A.L.R. Fed. 819 (2d Cir. 1971).

[2]BMG Rights Management (US) LLC v. Cox Communications, Inc., 117 U.S.P.Q.2d 1359, 2015 WL 7756130 (E.D. Va. 2015).

[3]Demetriades v. Kaufmann, 690 F. Supp. 289, 294, 8 U.S.P.Q.2d 1130 (S.D. N.Y. 1988).

[4]R&R Recreation Products, Inc. v. Joan Cook Inc., 25 U.S.P.Q.2d 1781, 1784, 1992 WL 88171 (S.D. N.Y. 1992).

[5]Blue Ribbon Pet Products, Inc. v. Rolf C. Hagen (USA) Corp., 66 F. Supp. 2d 454, 52 U.S.P.Q.2d 1837 (E.D. N.Y. 1999).

[6]Metro-Goldwyn-Mayer Studios Inc. v. Grokster, Ltd., 545 U.S. 913, 918-21, 125 S. Ct. 2764, 162 L. Ed. 2d 781, 33 Media L. Rep. (BNA) 1865, 75 U.S.P.Q.2d 1001 (2005).

[7]Grokster, 545 U.S. at 919.

Research References

West's Key Number Digest, Copyrights and Intellectual Property ☞77
C.J.S., Copyrights and Intellectual Property §§ 8, 64, 98

Under common law, one who actively aids or induces an infringer may be held liable for the direct infringing acts of a third party.[1] As a result of the *Grokster* case, whoever "distributes a device with the object of promoting its use to infringe copyright, as shown by clear expression or other affirmative steps taken to foster infringement, is liable for the resulting acts of infringement by third parties."[2] This doctrine was adopted directly from the doctrine of active inducement of infringement under patent law.[3]

The elements required to build a case of inducement are the following: intent to bring about the infringement, distribution of a device suitable for infringing use, and actual infringement by the recipient of the device.[4] The latter two elements are easily proven. Any device that can duplicate copyrighted material will probably be sufficient, as the peer-to-peer file sharing software at issue in *Grokster* fulfilled that requirement. Actual infringement is shown by demonstrating a recipient of the device duplicated copyrighted material with the device or demonstrating other modes of direct infringement.[5]

Intent to bring about the infringement can be found from evidence of the device manufacturer's statements or actions that show their objective was to induce infringement.[6] Primarily, this can be shown by an advertisement or message disseminated to the users of the device encouraging them to infringe copyrights.[7] Additionally, this can be demonstrated by evidence of encouraging use of a known infringing device, by not implementing filters designed to limit infringing activity. Intent can also be shown indirectly by evidence that increased infringing activity leads to increased revenue.[8]

§ 8:10 Liability for copyright infringement—Vicarious liability

Research References

[Section 8:9]

[1]*See Grokster*, 545 U.S. at 936–937.

[2]*See Grokster*, 545 U.S. at 936–937.

[3]*See Grokster*, 545 U.S. at 936–37; 35 U.S.C.A. § 271(b); *see* supra § 4:11 for more detailed information regarding active inducement of patent infringement.

[4]*See Grokster*, 545 U.S. at 939–941.

[5]*See* supra § 8:7 for more detailed information regarding direct infringement.

[6]*See Grokster*, 545 U.S. at 939–941.

[7]*See Grokster*, 545 U.S. at 939.

[8]*See Grokster*, 545 U.S. at 939.

West's Key Number Digest, Copyrights and Intellectual Property ☞77
C.J.S., Copyrights and Intellectual Property §§ 8, 64, 98

Vicarious liability for copyright infringement exists where a party has the right and ability to supervise infringing activity and an obvious and direct financial interest in exploitation of the copyrighted material.[1] For instance, a president and sole shareholder of a company who personally approved an infringing sale, who approved the price to be charged for copies, and who had a financial interest in the sale of the infringing work is vicariously liable for infringement.[2] Similarly, an independent agent who worked on behalf of the company that made the infringing work, who initiated the process of selling the book, and who received commission for those sales is also vicariously liable.[3]

A parent corporation cannot be held vicariously liable for its subsidiaries' infringing actions unless there is a substantial and continuing connection between them with respect to those actions. The parent must have a direct financial interest in the infringing activity and the right and ability to supervise the subsidiary.[4] However, an employer is liable for willful copyright infringement of its employee who, acting within the scope of her employment, deliberately copies a copyrighted work.[5]

In order to be vicariously liable, the person must have some active involvement in the infringing act. A newspaper publisher who had a large financial interest in the newspaper, but who had no real authority, was not vicariously liable for the newspaper's copyright infringement.[6] Neither was a trade show organizer who did not have the right or ability to supervise or control the actions of the show's exhibitors.[7]

§ 8:11   Liability for copyright infringement—Liability of states

Research References

[Section 8:10]

[1]Broadcast Music, Inc. v. Metro Program Network, Inc., 21 U.S.P.Q.2d 1713, 1715, 1991 WL 323414 (N.D. Iowa 1991).

[2]Pinkham v. Sara Lee Corp., 983 F.2d 824, 834, 25 U.S.P.Q.2d 1336 (8th Cir. 1992).

[3]Sara Lee Corp., 983 F.2d at 834.

[4]Banff Ltd. v. Ltd., Inc., 869 F. Supp. 1103, 1110, 33 U.S.P.Q.2d 1896 (S.D. N.Y. 1994).

[5]Spectravest, Inc. v. Fleet Street, Ltd., 13 U.S.P.Q.2d 1457, 1460, 1989 WL 135386 (N.D. Cal. 1989).

[6]Brunswick Beacon, Inc. v. Schock-Hopchas Publ'g; Co., 810 F.2d 410, 414, 13 Media L. Rep. (BNA) 2030, 1 U.S.P.Q.2d 1701 (4th Cir. 1987), rejected by Cmty. for Creative Non-Violence v. Reid, 490 U.S. 730, 109 S. Ct. 2166, 16 Media L. Rep. (BNA) 1769, 10 U.S.P.Q.2d 1985 (1989).

[7]Artists Music, Inc. v. Reed Publ'g (USA), Inc., 31 U.S.P.Q.2d 1623, 1994 WL 191643 (S.D. N.Y. 1994).

West's Key Number Digest, Federal Courts ☞265
C.J.S., Federal Courts §§ 126 to 127, 129

The Eleventh Amendment of the U.S. Constitution bars copyright infringement actions against a state. However, in 1990, Congress attempted to abrogate state sovereign immunity by passing the Copyright Remedy Clarification Act.[1] Under this statute, no state, instrumentality of a state, or any officer or employee of a state or instrumentality who is acting in his or her official capacity, is immune from copyright infringement under the Eleventh Amendment or any other doctrine of sovereign immunity. States, instrumentalities of states, and officers and employees of states and instrumentalities are specifically identified as persons who may commit copyright infringement under 17 U.S.C.A. § 501(a).

Abrogation of a state's Eleventh Amendment immunity turns on an express statement of intent by Congress to do so, coupled with a valid exercise of power under the Constitution. When Congress amended the Copyright Act, it met the express statement requirement by explicitly requiring states to submit to suit in federal court for violations of the Act's provisions. However, Congress did not have the authority to abrogate state sovereign immunity. Congress was not responding to the kind of massive constitutional violations that have prompted proper remedial legislation, did not consider the adequacy of state remedies that might have provided the required due process of law, and did not seek to limit the coverage to arguably constitutional violations. As such, the Copyright Remedy Clarification Act is an improper exercise of Congressional legislative power. Therefore, states enjoy immunity from unconsented-to suits in federal court under the Eleventh Amendment.[2]

§ 8:12 Establishing copyright infringement—Exclusive rights of the copyright owner

Research References
West's Key Number Digest, Copyrights and Intellectual Property ☞51
C.J.S., Copyrights and Intellectual Property §§ 41, 71

17 U.S.C.A. § 106 defines the five exclusive rights conferred to the owner of a copyright. The "bundle of rights" includes the exclusive right to do and to authorize:

[Section 8:11]
[1]17 U.S.C.A. § 511.
[2]Chavez v. Arte Publico Press,

204 F.3d 601, 608, 142 Ed. Law Rep. 36, 53 U.S.P.Q.2d 2009 (5th Cir. 2000).

Reproduction: to reproduce the work in copies or phonorecords,

Derivation: to prepare derivative works based on the copyrighted work,

Distribution: to distribute copies or phonorecords of the copyrighted work to the public by sale or other transfer of ownership, or by rental, lease or lending,

Performance: in the case of literary, musical, dramatic, and choreographic works, pantomimes, and motion pictures and other audiovisual works, to perform the work publicly and

Display: in the case of literary, musical, dramatic, and choreographic works, pantomimes, and pictorial, graphic or sculptural works, including the individual images of a motion picture or other audiovisual work, to display the copyrighted work publicly.[1]

Infringement occurs when any of these exclusive rights are violated.[2] To establish copyright infringement, plaintiff must prove ownership of the copyright and copying by defendant.[3]

A copyright does not grant the right to exclude others from use of an idea. Copyright protects only a particular embodiment of an idea. Therefore, if someone independently creates a work that is similar, or even identical to, the copyrighted work, no infringement occurs. Copyright infringement requires actual copying.[4]

§ 8:13 Establishing copyright infringement—Ownership of the copyright

Research References

West's Key Number Digest, Copyrights and Intellectual Property ⊕51
C.J.S., Copyrights and Intellectual Property §§ 41, 71

Ownership of a copyright is initially vested in the "author." The author is either the creator of the work, the creator's employer, if the work was created in the regular course of employ-

---

[Section 8:12]

[1]17 U.S.C.A. § 106.

[2]17 U.S.C.A. § 501(a).

[3]Sid & Marty Krofft Television Prods., Inc. v. McDonald's Corp., 562 F.2d 1157, 1162, 196 U.S.P.Q. 97 (9th

Cir. 1977).

[4]Feist Publ'ns, Inc. v. Rural Telephone Serv. Co., Inc., 499 U.S. 340, 346, 111 S. Ct. 1282, 1288, 18 Media L. Rep. (BNA) 1889, 18 U.S.P.Q.2d 1275, 121 Pub. Util. Rep. 4th (PUR) 1 (1991).

ment, or the person who commissions the work, if a written agreement so provides.[1]

A copyright must be registered with the Copyright Office before an infringement action may be brought.[2] A copyright registration certificate is prima facie evidence of copyright ownership.[3]

§ 8:14　Establishing copyright infringement—Access

Research References

West's Key Number Digest, Copyrights and Intellectual Property ☞53(1)

C.J.S., Copyrights and Intellectual Property §§ 10, 41, 61, 71

Because direct evidence of copying is usually unavailable, plaintiff may establish copying indirectly by proving that:

- defendant had "access" to the copyrighted work, and
- the accused work is "substantially similar" to the copyrighted work.[1]

To prove "access" plaintiff must establish that defendant "had a reasonable opportunity to view or [an] opportunity to copy the allegedly infringed work."[2] However, "[a]ccess must be more than a bare possibility and may not be inferred through speculation and conjecture."[3]

One case ruling on the "access" issue involved a previously relatively unknown Brazilian singer, Morris Kaiserman (professionally known as Morris Albert), who gained fame by composing and recording the hit record "Feelings." Following Kaiserman's success, he was sued for copyright infringement by the composer of an obscure French song "Pour Toi," which was written and recorded by Louis Gaste seventeen years earlier. Gaste contended that Kaiserman had gained access to Gaste's virtually unknown song through Kaiserman's publisher, Enrique Lebendiger.[4]

The court, relying on testimony that a recording of Gaste's

[Section 8:13]

[1]17 U.S.C.A. § 201.

[2]17 U.S.C.A. § 411.

[3]17 U.S.C.A. § 410(c).

[Section 8:14]

[1]Krofft, 562 F.2d at 1162.

[2]La Resolana Architects, PA v. Reno, Inc., 555 F.3d 1171, 1178, 89 U.S.P.Q.2d 1721 (10th Cir. 2009) (citing Autoskill Inc. v. Nat'l Educ. Support Sys., Inc., 994 F.2d 1476, 1490, 24 Bankr. Ct. Dec. (CRR) 495, 26 U.S.P.

Q.2d 1828, 25 Fed. R. Serv. 3d 838 (10th Cir. 1993) (internal quotation marks omitted)).

[3]Gaste v. Kaiserman, 863 F.2d 1061, 1066, 9 U.S.P.Q.2d 1300 (2d Cir. 1988); see also La Resolana Architects, PA, 555 F.3d at 1178; Mag Jewelry Co., Inc. v. Cherokee, Inc., 496 F.3d 108, 117, 83 U.S.P.Q.2d 1812, 30 A.L.R. Fed. 2d 851 (1st Cir. 2007); Armour v. Knowles, 512 F.3d 147, 153, 85 U.S.P. Q.2d 1292 (5th Cir. 2007).

[4]Gaste, 863 F.2d at 1063.

"Pour Toi" was sent to Lebendiger seventeen years before Kaiserman recorded "Feelings," stated:

> Although Gaste's theory of access relies on a somewhat attenuated chain of events extending over a long period of time and distance, we cannot say as a matter of law that the jury could not reasonably conclude that Kaiserman had access to the song through Lebendiger. Access through third parties connected to both a plaintiff and a defendant may be sufficient to prove a defendant's access to a plaintiff's work.[5]

Consequently, access is determined by a relatively low standard. Generally, access is proven whenever defendant at least had a chance to see the plaintiff's work.

Absent direct evidence, copying may be inferred from a showing that the defendant had access to the plaintiff's work prior to the creation of the defendant's work, and there is a substantial similarity between the works. Similarity alone typically cannot lead to a finding of copying, without evidence of access prior to the allegedly offending work's creation.[6]

Where a plaintiff cannot demonstrate access he may establish copying by demonstrating that his copyrighted work and the allegedly infringing work are strikingly similar. Striking similarity exists where the proof of similarity in appearance is so striking that the possibilities of independent creation, coincidence and prior common source are precluded.[7]

§ 8:15 Establishing copyright infringement—Substantial similarity

Research References

West's Key Number Digest, Copyrights and Intellectual Property ☞53(1)

C.J.S., Copyrights and Intellectual Property §§ 10, 41, 61, 71

In most copyright cases, the most important issue is substantial similarity.[1] To prove that two works are "substantially similar," plaintiff must demonstrate similarity in both idea and expression.

---

[5]Gaste, 863 F.2d at 1067.

[6]Grubb v. KMS Patriots, L.P., 88 F.3d 1, 39 U.S.P.Q.2d 1187 (1st Cir. 1996).

[7]Corwin v. Walt Disney Co., 468 F.3d 1329, 1343-44, 80 U.S.P.Q.2d 1597, 71 Fed. R. Evid. Serv. 828 (11th Cir. 2006), *opinion vacated and superseded on reconsideration*, 475 F.3d 1239, 81 U.S.P.Q.2d 1496 (11th Cir. 2007).

[Section 8:15]

[1]*See, e.g.*, Brown Bag Software v. Symantec Corp., 960 F.2d 1465, 1472, 22 U.S.P.Q.2d 1429, 22 Fed. R. Serv. 3d 771 (9th Cir. 1992) (because Symantec concedes that ownership and access are not at issue, the defendant's motion for summary judgment focused on Brown Bag's allegations of substantial similarity); Shaw v. Lindheim, 908 F.2d 531, 534, 15 U.S.P.Q.2d 1516 (9th

The courts have developed a two-step test for determining substantial similarity.[2] The test permits a finding of infringement only if plaintiff proves both substantial similarity of general ideas under the "extrinsic" (or "objective") test and substantial similarity of the protectable expression of those ideas under the "intrinsic" (or "subjective") test.[3] Although the approach varies slightly among the Circuits, this two-step approach is generally the test for substantial similarity.

The extrinsic test is used to determine whether the ideas of the two works are substantially similar. This is an objective test for which analytic dissection and expert testimony are appropriate. In applying the extrinsic test, the court must consider criteria such as the type of work involved, the materials involved, the subject matter and the setting for the subject.[4]

In *Sid & Marty Krofft Television Productions, Inc. v. McDonald's Corp.*,[5] plaintiffs (the creators of H. R. Pufnstuf) alleged that the use of certain characters in McDonald's advertisements infringed plaintiff's copyrighted characters.[6] It was in deciding this copyright issue that the *Krofft* court established and utilized the intrinsic/extrinsic test.[7] The court first determined whether there was a substantial similarity in "general ideas" between the two works.[8] This issue is determined by the trier of fact, but it does not depend on the responses of the trier of fact. It depends on specific criteria that can be listed and analyzed.

If the ideas are found to be similar or identical, the second step is the intrinsic test, which determines whether there is similarity

---

Cir. 1990), *opinion amended and superseded*, 919 F.2d 1353 (9th Cir. 1990) (defendants conceded Shaw's ownership of the original script and their access to the script, thus the only issue before the court on the copyright claim was whether defendants' script is substantially similar to Shaw's script).

[2]Data E. USA, Inc. v. Epyx, Inc., 862 F.2d 204, 208, 9 U.S.P.Q.2d 1322 (9th Cir. 1988).

[3]Olson v. National Broadcasting Co., Inc., 855 F.2d 1446, 1448–49, 8 U.S.P.Q.2d 1231 (9th Cir. 1988); Kroft, 562 F.2d at 1164.

[4]Sid & Marty Krofft Television Productions, Inc. v. McDonald's Corp., 562 F.2d 1157, 1164, 196 U.S.P.Q. 97 (9th Cir. 1977). Although *Krofft* is generally regarded as having introduced the "idea-expression" dichotomy with

its extrinsic and intrinsic tests, a bifurcated approach to analysis of copyright infringement can be traced back to Arnstein v. Porter, 154 F.2d 464, 68 U.S.P.Q. 288 (C.C.A. 2d Cir. 1946). Under the first step, the *Arnstein* court determines whether the two works are substantially similar. Analysis and dissection of the works, and the testimony of experts are appropriate in this step. Arnstein, 154 F.2d at 469. Under the second step, the test becomes the response of the ordinary observer. Analysis, dissection and expert testimony are irrelevant to this determination. Arnstein, 154 F.2d at 468.

[5]Krofft, 562 F.2d at 1160.

[6]Krofft, 562 at 1162.

[7]Krofft, 562 F.2d at 1165.

[8]Krofft, 562 F.2d at 1164.

of expression. The intrinsic test is a subjective test, depending upon the response of an ordinary, reasonable person.[9] The intrinsic test is satisfied if an ordinary, reasonable person would conclude that defendant unlawfully appropriated the plaintiff's protectable expression by taking material of substance and value.[10]

Under the intrinsic test, the trier of fact should consider similarity in the "total concept and feel" of the two works.[11] Analytic dissection of the dissimilarities is not appropriate under this test because it distracts a reasonable observer from a comparison of the total concept and feel.[12] In applying the test, however, it must be taken into account that the copyright laws preclude appropriation of only those elements of the work that are protected by the copyright (i.e., expression of an idea, not the idea itself).[13] Furthermore, scènes à faire, or situations in which there is essentially no other way to express a particular idea except by using certain elements, are not protectable.[14] For example, "[g]eneral plot ideas are not protected by copyright law; they remain forever the common property of artistic mankind."[15] Thus, the court will filter out and disregard these and other non-protectable elements when making a substantial similarity determination.[16]

The Ninth Circuit eventually revisited its own analysis in Krofft and slightly altered the intrinsic test in order to allow a more objective comparison, but it retained the fundamental bifurcation

---

[9]Narell v. Freeman, 872 F.2d 907, 913, 16 Media L. Rep. (BNA) 1579, 10 U.S.P.Q.2d 1596 (9th Cir. 1989).

[10]Atari, Inc. v. North American Philips Consumer Electronics Corp., 672 F.2d 607, 614, 214 U.S.P.Q. 33 (7th Cir. 1982), superseded by statute on other grounds as stated in Scandia Down Corp. v. Euroquilt, Inc., 772 F.2d 1423, 1429, 227 U.S.P.Q. 138, 3 Fed. R. Serv. 3d 195 (7th Cir. 1985).

[11]Data East, 862 F.2d at 208.

[12]Aliotti v. R. Dakin & Co., 831 F.2d 898, 901, 4 U.S.P.Q.2d 1869 (9th Cir. 1987); but see Bridgeport Music, Inc. v. UMG Recordings, Inc., 585 F.3d 267, 275, 92 U.S.P.Q.2d 1526 (6th Cir. 2009) ("[I]t is appropriate to modify [the substantial similarity test] for situations in which a smaller fragment of a work has been copied literally, but

not the overall theme or concept—an approach referred to in the literature as 'fragmented literal similarity.' " In those situations, "the copying of a relatively small but qualitatively important or crucial element can be an appropriate basis upon which to find substantial similarity.").

[13]Atari, 672 F.2d at 614.

[14]Funky Films, Inc. v. Time Warner Entm't Co., L.P., 462 F.3d 1072, 1077, 34 Media L. Rep. (BNA) 2345, 80 U.S.P.Q.2d 1052 (9th Cir. 2006) (relying on Metcalf v. Bochco, 294 F.3d 1069, 1074, 63 U.S.P.Q.2d 1412 (9th Cir. 2002)).

[15]Berkic v. Crichton, 761 F.2d 1289, 1293, 11 Media L. Rep. (BNA) 2450, 226 U.S.P.Q. 787 (9th Cir. 1985).

[16]Funky Films, 462 F.3d at 1077.

on the finding of substantial similarity.[17] The Ninth Circuit found that lower courts had been including "a lengthy list of concrete elements under the extrinsic test."[18] Many of these concrete elements were outside the scope of the extrinsic test; they were not limited to similarities in ideas. Nonetheless, these elements were helpful in determining similarities between the works. Thus, the Ninth Circuit concluded that "[b]ecause the criteria incorporated into the extrinsic test encompass all objective manifestations of creativity, the two tests are more sensibly described as objective and subjective analysis of *expression*, having strayed from *Krofft's* division between expression and ideas."[19]

In support of the objective/subjective standard, the Ninth Circuit noted that in many copyright decisions a judicial determination under the intrinsic test is virtually devoid of analysis. In fact, the intrinsic test essentially is a mere subjective judgment as to whether two literary works are or are not similar.[20]

More comparison of the two works in a framework of "objective" analysis, where expert testimony and dissection are entirely appropriate, should be included in the analysis. However, the fundamental aspect that has pervaded the Ninth Circuit's framework of copyright infringement still remains. The test still requires a two-part finding of substantial similarity, one which allows the use of dissection and expert testimony and one which requires the fact finder to determine the response of the ordinary reasonable person without the aid of either dissection or expert testimony.

A further interpretation of the test for substantial similarity is the so-called "ordinary observer test," which inquires "whether an average lay observer would recognize the alleged copy as having been appropriated from a copyrighted work."[21] Similarly, a "discerning observer" test is used to determine substantial similarity when the accused infringing work contains both protectable and unprotectable elements, excluding the unprotectable elements in the comparison. A copyrighted work and accused infringing work were found to be substantially similar because a discerning person would find substantial similarity in shape, layout, overall appearance, and particular expression of concepts.[22]

Another analysis of the substantial similarity test was detailed

---

[17]Shaw, 908 F.2d at 533–35.

[18]Shaw, 908 F.2d at 534.

[19]Shaw, 908 F.2d at 535 (emphasis in original).

[20]Shaw, 908 F.2d at 535.

[21]Sandberg & Sikorski Corp. v.

Andin Int'l, Inc., 50 U.S.P.Q.2d 1699, 1999 WL 199070 (S.D. N.Y. 1999), *judgment entered*, 51 U.S.P.Q.2d 1574, 1999 WL 628076 (S.D. N.Y. 1999).

[22]Blue Ribbon Pet Products, Inc. v. Rolf C. Hagen (USA) Corp., 66 F. Supp. 2d 454, 461, 52 U.S.P.Q.2d 1837

by the Court of Appeals for the Fourth Circuit in *Dawson v. Hinshaw Music Inc.*[23] In this case, application of the ordinary observer test was limited. An "intended audience" standard was instituted.[24]

If the intended audience is more narrow than the lay observer, in that it possesses a more specialized expertise, then the intrinsic test should focus on whether a member of the intended audience would find the works substantially similar. The court concluded that such an inquiry would necessarily require the admission of testimony from members of the intended audience or those who are experts on such audiences.[25]

This variation of the intrinsic test allows admission of testimony from members of the intended audience or from those who possess expertise with respect to the tastes and perceptions of that audience. In this way, expert testimony on the intrinsic test is allowed.

§ 8:16 Establishing copyright infringement—Computer software

Research References

West's Key Number Digest, Copyrights and Intellectual Property ⊕67.3
C.J.S., Copyrights and Intellectual Property §§ 41, 45, 55, 97

See also § 5:21 Computer Programs and § 7:19 Fair Use of Computer Programs.

Copyright infringement related to computer software is unique enough to require special attention. Courts have found the traditional test of substantial similarity to be inadequate for infringement of software. "As scientific knowledge advances, courts endeavor to keep pace, and sometimes—as in the area of computer technology—they are required to venture into less than familiar waters."[1] Therefore, courts have modified the traditional test for substantial similarity in copyright infringement cases involving computer software.

One of the earliest formulations of a test for substantial similarity of computer software was adopted by the Third Circuit in *Whelan Associates, Inc. v. Jaslow Dental Laboratory, Inc.*[2] *Whelan* articulated the "single-idea" rule for separating copyrightable expression from uncopyrightable ideas. "[T]he purpose or

(E.D. N.Y. 1999).

[23]Dawson v. Hinshaw Music Inc., 905 F.2d 731, 736, 15 U.S.P.Q.2d 1132 (4th Cir. 1990).

[24]Dawson, 905 F.2d at 735.

[25]Dawson, 905 F.2d at 735.

[Section 8:16]

[1]Computer Assocs. Int'l, Inc. v. Altai, Inc., 982 F.2d 693, 696, 37 Fed. R. Evid. Serv. 348, 119 A.L.R. Fed. 741 (2d Cir. 1992).

[2]Whelan Assocs., Inc. v. Jaslow

function of . . . [the] work [is] the work's idea, and everything that is not necessary to that purpose or function [is] part of the expression of the idea."[3]

Whelan was criticized for assuming that only one idea underlies any computer program, and that once a separable idea can be identified, everything else must be expression. This criticism recognizes the reality of the structural design of computer programs. Typically, the ultimate function of a computer program is the composite result of interacting subroutines. Since each subroutine is itself a program, and thus, may be said to have its own idea, the single-idea general formulation that a program's overall purpose equates with the program's idea is inadequate in most cases.[4]

Currently, the leading test for analyzing computer copyright infringement is the "abstraction-filtration-comparison" test. This test views the program as a combination of constituent structural parts and examines each part, as opposed to the program as a whole, to separate protectable expressions from unprotectable ideas. Under either the "single-idea" rule or the "abstractions" test, the protectable elements of the programs at issue are compared to determine whether there is substantial similarity.[5]

The first step of the abstraction-filtration-comparison test is to use the concept of levels of abstractions to test the similarity of the works. Essentially, the levels of abstraction theory recognizes that as more and more of an incident is left out of any work, patterns of increasing generality will fit the work equally well. The last, or "highest," level may be no more than the most general statement of what the work is about. For example, in the context of literature, at the highest level of abstraction a book may be a science fiction novel. Obviously, this is the point in the series of abstractions where copyright protection no longer exists, because the author would be attempting to protect the use of his or her ideas.[6] No one can claim copyright on the idea of a science fiction novel.

In the context of a computer program, the lowest level of abstraction is the program as a set of individual instructions organized into a hierarchy of modules or subroutines. At the higher levels of abstraction are the ultimate functions of the

---

Dental Lab., Inc., 797 F.2d 1222, 230 U.S.P.Q. 481, 21 Fed. R. Evid. Serv. 571 (3d Cir. 1986), *rejected by* CMAX/Cleveland, Inc. v. UCR, Inc., 804 F. Supp. 337, 26 U.S.P.Q.2d 1001 (M.D. Ga. 1992).

[3]Whelan, 797 F.2d at 1236.

[4]Altai, 982 F.2d at 705 (*citing* 3 Melville F. Nimmer and David Nimmer, *Nimmer on Copyright* § 13.03(F)).

[5]Altai, 982 F.2d at 706.

[6]Altai, 982 F.2d at 705.

program.[7] As the *Altai* court stated:

> Initially, in a manner that resembles reverse engineering on a the-
> oretical plane, a court should dissect the allegedly copied program's
> structure and isolate each level of abstraction contained within it.
> This process begins with the code and ends with an articulation of
> the program's ultimate function. Along the way, it is necessary es-
> sentially to retrace and map each of the designer's steps—in the op-
> posite order in which they were taken during the program's
> creation.[8]

The next step in the abstraction-filtration-comparison test is to
engage in a filtration process whereby protectable expression is
separated from non-protectable material. "This process entails
examining the structural components at each level of abstraction
to determine whether their particular inclusion at that level was
'idea' or was dictated by considerations of efficiency . . .; required
by factors external to the program itself; or taken from the public
domain . . . ."[9]

Once a court has sifted out all of the elements of the allegedly
infringed program that are "ideas," the final step in the
abstraction-filtration-comparison test is to compare the remaining core of protectable expression. At this point, the court's
substantial similarity inquiry focuses on whether defendant copied any aspect of this protected expression, as well as an assessment of the copied portion's relative importance with respect to
the plaintiff's overall program.[10]

In the area of copyright infringement of computer software, the
test for infringement, and specifically for substantial similarity,
is one which is likely to remain dynamic, as the technology
continues to explode. "[C]omputer technology is a dynamic field
which can quickly outpace judicial decision-making. Thus, in
cases where the technology in question does not allow for a literal
application of the . . . [abstraction-filtration-comparison test],
district courts . . . [should not be foreclosed] from utilizing a
modified version."[11] For example, the scope of a registered copyright in an earlier version of computer software program extends
to protect a later version of the program not separately registered,
when the later version incorporates parts of the earlier version.[12]

Most computer cases involve allegations of copying the text of
the computer code. Some of the more difficult cases involve allegations of copying some form of the computer's display, rather

---

[7]Altai, 982 F.2d at 707.

[8]Altai, 982 F.2d at 707.

[9]Altai, 982 F.2d at 707.

[10]Altai, 982 F.2d at 710.

[11]Altai, 982 F.2d at 706.

[12]Montgomery v. Noga, 168 F.3d
1282, 1292, 49 U.S.P.Q.2d 1961, 51, 51
Fed. R. Evid. Serv. 752 (11th Cir.
1999).

than the program that creates that display. The threshold issue in most screen display cases is whether plaintiff's work is copyrightable in the first place. *Lotus Development Corp. v. Borland International, Inc.*,[13] involved the copyrightability of the "Lotus 1-2-3" spreadsheet program. Borland did not dispute that it factually copied the words and arrangement of the Lotus menu command hierarchy, but argued that the command hierarchy is not copyrightable because it is a system, method of operation, process, or procedure foreclosed from protection by 17 U.S.C.A. § 102(b).[14] The First Circuit agreed with Borland that the Lotus menu command hierarchy is uncopyrightable. An equally divided U.S. Supreme Court affirmed the First Circuit in a two-sentence opinion.[15]

The *Lotus* court, relying on 17 U.S.C.A. § 102(b),[16] found that the Lotus menu hierarchy is a method of operation, and thus, uncopyrightable. The court explained that the command hierarchy provides the means by which users control and operate the system. Without the menu command hierarchy, users would not be able to access, control or make use of the Lotus program.[17]

The court analogized the Lotus menu command hierarchy to the buttons that control a video cassette recorder:

> Users operate VCRs by pressing a series of buttons that are typically labelled "Record, Play, Reverse, Fast Forward, Pause, Stop/ Eject." That the buttons are arranged and labeled does not make them a "literary work," nor does it make them an "expression" of the abstract "method of operating" a VCR via a set of labeled buttons. Instead, the buttons are themselves the "method of operating" the VCR.[18]

§ 8:17 Establishing copyright infringement—Role of expert witnesses

Research References

West's Key Number Digest, Copyrights and Intellectual Property ☞83(2) to 83(7)

C.J.S., Copyrights and Intellectual Property §§ 8, 71, 98

The role of the expert witness in copyright infringement ac-

---

[13]Lotus Development Corp. v. Borland Intern., Inc., 49 F.3d 807, 818, 34 U.S.P.Q.2d 1014 (1st Cir. 1995), *judgment aff'd,* 516 U.S. 233, 116 S. Ct. 804 (1996).

[14]Lotus, 49 F.3d at 818.

[15]Lotus Development Corp. v. Borland Intern., Inc., 516 U.S. 233, 116 S. Ct. 804, 133 L. Ed. 2d 610 (1996).

[16]"In no case does copyright protection for an original work of authorship extend to an idea, procedure, process, system, method of operation, concept, principle, or discovery, regardless of the form in which it is described, explained, illustrated, or embodied in such work." 17 U.S.C.A. § 102(b).

[17]Lotus, 49 F.3d at 815.

[18]Lotus, 49 F.3d at 817.

tions is limited to the objective analysis of ideas and expression. Initially, the line had been drawn between comparing ideas embodied in the subject works and comparing the respective expressions of common ideas in the works. In comparing ideas, expert testimony was entirely appropriate; in comparing the respective expressions of those ideas expert testimony was not allowed.[1] However, the standard now recognizes that the line is more properly drawn between objective and subjective analyses of expression.[2] As such, expert opinion is relevant not only to the analysis of ideas behind two works but also to the objective analysis of expression.[3]

With respect to computer programs, the role of the expert witness appears to be further expanded. In the context of computer programs, courts have held that the trier of fact need not be limited by its own lay perspective. The district court has discretion to decide to what extent, if any, expert opinion, regarding the highly technical nature of computer programs, is warranted in a given case. The traditional role of lay observers in judging substantial similarity in copyright cases that involve the aesthetic arts, such as music, visual works or literature is not altered.[4]

§ 8:18 Defenses—Fair use

Research References

West's Key Number Digest, Copyrights and Intellectual Property ⬅53.2, 56, 64 to 67.2

C.J.S., Copyrights and Intellectual Property §§ 41, 45 to 46, 48 to 54, 56 to 58

Fair use has long been recognized as an affirmative defense to copyright infringement. It originated as a judicially-created doctrine, notwithstanding the fact that the phrase "fair use" was not referred to in the initial Copyright Statute.[1] The gist of the fair use defense is to "look to the nature and objects of the selections made, the quantity and value of the materials used, and the degree in which the use may prejudice the sale, or diminish the profits, or supersede the objects, of the original work."[2]

[Section 8:17]

[1]Brown Bag Software v. Symantec Corp., 960 F.2d 1465, 1474, 22 U.S.P.Q.2d 1429, 22 Fed. R. Serv. 3d 771 (9th Cir. 1992).

[2]Shaw, 919 F.2d at 1357.

[3]Brown Bag, 960 F.2d at 1474.

[4]Altai, 982 F.2d at 713–14.

[Section 8:18]

[1]Campbell v. Acuff-Rose Music, Inc., 510 U.S. 569, 577, 114 S. Ct. 1164, 22, 127 L. Ed. 2d 500, 22 Media L. Rep. (BNA) 1353, 29 U.S.P.Q.2d 1961 (1994).

[2]Folsom v. Marsh, 9 F. Cas. 342, 348, No. 4901 (C.C.D. Mass. 1841).

Fair use allows the accused infringer to use copyrighted material in a reasonable manner without the consent of the copyright owner.[3] Fair use defense tempers the protection of copyright ownership by allowing the use of a limited amount of copyrighted material under some circumstances.[4] Since fair use is an affirmative defense to copyright infringement, the party claiming that its use of the copyrighted work constitutes fair use carries the burden of proof.[5]

The fair use defense was codified in the Copyright Act of 1976:

[T]he fair use of a copyrighted work . . . for purposes such as criticism, comment, news reporting, teaching (including multiple copies for classroom use), scholarship, or research, is not an infringement of copyright. In determining whether the use made of a work in any particular case is a fair use, courts consider—

(1) the purpose and character of the use, including whether such use is of a commercial nature or is for nonprofit educational purposes,

(2) the nature of the copyrighted work,

(3) the amount and substantiality of the portion used in relation to the copyrighted work as a whole and

(4) the effect of the use upon the potential market for or value of the copyrighted work.[6]

By codifying the fair use defense, Congress intended to "restate the present judicial doctrine of fair use, not change, narrow, or enlarge it in any way."[7]

As evidenced by the language of the statute, the fair use defense does not entail a bright line test.[8] Fair use is a mixed question of law and fact.[9] The factors listed in § 107 are not exclusive. All are to be explored and the results weighed together.[10] However, if the use of the copyrighted work does not fall within any of the categories listed in § 107, the use of the work will be subject to more scrutiny. In evaluating whether a use is a "fair use," the primary factor is the effect the use has on the market for the underlying work.[11]

Purpose And Character Of Use. The first factor listed in

---

[3]Harper & Row Publishers, Inc. v. Nation Enters., 471 U.S. 539, 549, 105 S. Ct. 2218, 2224, 11 Media L. Rep. (BNA) 1969, 225 U.S.P.Q. 1073 (1985).

[4]Twin Peaks Prods., Inc. v. Publ'ns Int'l, Ltd., 996 F.2d 1366, 1373, 21 Media L. Rep. (BNA) 1545, 27 U.S.P.Q.2d 1001 (2d Cir. 1993).

[5]Am. Geophysical Union v. Texaco Inc., 60 F.3d 913, 918, 35 U.S.P.Q.2d 1513, 144 A.L.R. Fed. 745 (2d Cir. 1994).

[6]17 U.S.C.A. § 107.

[7]H.R.Rep.No. 94-1476, p. 66 (1976); S.Rep.No. 94-473, p. 62 (1975).

[8]Campbell, 510 U.S. at 577.

[9]Harper & Row, 471 U.S. at 560.

[10]Campbell, 510 U.S. at 577.

[11]Stewart v. Abend, 495 U.S. 207, 238, 110 S. Ct. 1750, 1770, 14 U.S.P.

§ 107 is "the purpose and character of the use, including whether such use is of a commercial nature or is for nonprofit educational purposes."[12] This is not to say, however, that the mere fact that a use is educational and not for profit insulates the use from a finding of infringement, nor that a commercial use bars a finding of fair use.[13] The Supreme Court has interpreted this language to mean that the fact that a publication is commercial, as opposed to nonprofit, is a separate factor that tends to weigh against a finding of fair use.[14] In fact, cases involving plainly "commercial" uses have been found to be fair use.[15] Similarly, nonprofit, educational uses have been found to be unfair.[16] Likewise, private news reporting is not a presumptively fair use.[17]

In an effort to aid courts in interpreting the first factor, the Supreme Court has held that "transformative use" is central to a proper analysis of fair use.[18] A transformative use means the transformation the second user has given or produced from the original, copyrighted article. The transformative use concept is useful because it assesses the "value" generated by the second use and also the means by which this value is generated. For example, where the second use is merely an untransformed duplication, there is little value generated. No contribution of new "intellectual value" or fostering the advancement of the arts and sciences is made, thereby providing limited justification for a finding of fair use.[19] Conversely, where the secondary use adds something different or new and/or has a further purpose, the value generated goes beyond that of the original, thus promoting science and the arts.[20] Courts have recognized that the preferred uses listed in § 107 generally involve transformation of an original work.[21] For instance, Google's display of thumbnail photographs in its search engine is transformative and likely to be a fair use, so a preliminary injunction is not appropriate.[22] An artist's use of a copyrighted photograph from a magazine in a col-

---

Q.2d 1614 (1990).

[12]Patry on Copyright §§ 10:13 to 10:137.50 (2012).

[13]Campbell, 510 U.S. at 584.

[14]Harper & Row, 471 U.S. at 562.

[15]Warner Bros. Inc. v. Am. Broad. Companies, Inc., 720 F.2d 231, 242, 222 U.S.P.Q. 101 (2d Cir. 1983); A.V. ex rel. Vanderhye v. iParadigms, LLC, 562 F.3d 630, 638, 90 U.S.P.Q.2d 1513 (4th Cir. 2009).

[16]Marcus v. Rowley, 695 F.2d 1171, 1174–75, 8 Ed. Law Rep. 258, 217 U.S.P.Q. 691 (9th Cir. 1983).

[17]L.A. News Serv. v. Tullo, 973 F.2d 791, 797, 20 Media L. Rep. (BNA) 1626, 24 U.S.P.Q.2d 1026 (9th Cir. 1992) (citing Harper & Row, 471 U.S. at 561).

[18]Campbell, 510 U.S. at 581–83.

[19]Texaco, 60 F.3d at 923.

[20]Campbell, 510 U.S. at 579.

[21]Texaco, 60 F.3d at 923.

[22]Perfect 10, Inc. v. Amazon.com, Inc., 487 F.3d 701, 721, 82 U.S.P.Q.2d 1609 (9th Cir. 2007), opinion amended and superseded on reh'g, 508 F.3d 1146, 99 U.S.P.Q.2d 1746 (9th Cir.

lage painting is also a fair use.[23] Likewise, the rock band Green Day's use of copyrighted street art in a background montage during their touring show was held to be a fair use of copyrighted material.[24] However, a work that does not reflect any "further purpose" than the original work is not sufficiently transformative.[25] For example, a postage stamp of copyrighted soldier sculptures constituting part of the Korean War Veterans Memorial shared a common purpose with the soldier sculptures themselves, namely honoring Veterans of the Korean War, and thus was not a transformative work.[26]

Nature Of The Copyrighted Work. The second factor analyzed in review of the fair use defense is the nature of the copyrighted work. Under this factor, greater protection is provided to creative works.[27] In this vein, courts generally recognize fictional work as being more "creative" then a factual work.[28] With respect to factual works, "the law generally recognizes a greater need to disseminate factual works than works of fiction or fantasy."[29]

In addition to reviewing the "creativity" of the copyrighted work, the inquiry is normally made into the status of the work as either published or unpublished. The original Senate report to the 1976 Copyright Act stated "the applicability of the fair use defense to unpublished works is narrowly limited since, although the work is unavailable, this is the result of a deliberate choice on the part of the copyright owner."[30] In 1992, Congress amended § 107 to add "[t]he fact that a work is unpublished shall not itself bar a finding of fair use if such finding is made upon consideration of all the above factors." Thus, where the copyrighted work is unpublished, the second factor is key, and tends to negate fair use.[31] The concern is that the author of an unpublished work should have the right to control the first public dissemination of his or her work, and that this right outweighs any claim of fair use.[32] Thus, courts will be more likely to find fair use when the

---

2007).

[23]Blanch v. Koons, 467 F.3d 244, 259, 80 U.S.P.Q.2d 1545 (2d Cir. 2006).

[24]Seltzer v. Green Day, Inc., 725 F.3d 1170, 1180, 107 U.S.P.Q.2d 1803 (9th Cir. 2013).

[25]Gaylord v. U.S., 595 F.3d 1364, 1376, 94 U.S.P.Q.2d 1116 (Fed. Cir. 2010).

[26]Gaylord, 595 F.3d at 1373.

[27]Suntrust Bank v. Houghton

Mifflin Co., 268 F.3d 1257, 1271, 60 U.S.P.Q.2d 1225 (11th Cir. 2001); Peter Letterese & Assocs., Inc. v. World Inst. of Scientology Enters., 533 F.3d 1287, 1312, 87 U.S.P.Q.2d 1563 (11th Cir. 2008).

[28]Twin Peaks, 996 F.2d at 1376.

[29]Harper & Row, 471 U.S. at 563.

[30]S.Rep.No. 94-473, p. 64 (1975).

[31]Harper & Row, 471 U.S. at 555.

[32]Harper & Row, 471 U.S. at 555.

copyrighted material has been published.[33]

Amount And Substantiality Of The Portion Used. The third factor entails a review of the amount and substantiality of the portion used in relation to the copyrighted work as a whole.[34] As this language indicates, the court looks at the quantity of the material used, along with the value of that material. Notably, the amount and substantiality of the portion used is not based upon a "percentage" of the copied work with respect to the allegedly infringing work; it is done with respect to the copyrighted work itself.[35] "There are no absolute rules as to how much of a copyrighted work may be copied and still be considered a fair use."[36]

Courts often engage in a "word count" or "percentage" comparison. The court will literally count the number of words copied and compare that to the total number of words contained in the copyrighted material. Courts will usually find that a use is not fair when the copied material forms a "substantial percentage" of the copyrighted work.[37] Obviously, where defendant copied the entirety of the copyrighted work, this factor will weigh against fair use.[38]

Fair use is unavailable to a defendant who, while only copying what is otherwise a "minuscule" amount of the copyrighted work, copies the "heart" of the copyrighted work. For example, in *Harper & Row*, defendant, a magazine publisher, had taken some 300 words out of President Ford's soon-to-be-published memoirs. While the 300 words were only a small amount of the overall copyrighted work, the Supreme Court held that the third factor weighed against a finding of fair use as the importance of words taken amounted to the "heart of the book."[39]

Effect On The Market For The Copyrighted Work. The fourth factor, market effect, has been widely held as the "single most important element of fair use."[40] In evaluating this factor, a court must consider not only the primary market for the copyrighted work, but the current and potential market for derivative works.[41] Notably, however, the "importance" of this fourth factor may have been lessened by the Supreme Court decision in

---

[33]New Era Publ'ns Int'l, ApS v. Carol Publ'g Group, 904 F.2d 152, 158, 17 Media L. Rep. (BNA) 1913, 14 U.S.P.Q.2d 2030 (2d Cir. 1990).

[34]*See generally* Patry on Copyright §§ 10:141 to 10:144 (2012).

[35]Harper & Row, 471 U.S. at 564-65.

[36]Maxtone-Graham v. Burtchaell, 803 F.2d 1253, 1263, 13 Media L. Rep.

(BNA) 1513, 231 U.S.P.Q. 534, 5 Fed. R. Serv. 3d 849 (2d Cir. 1986).

[37]New Era, 904 F.2d at 158.

[38]Texaco, 60 F.3d at 921.

[39]Harper & Row, 471 U.S. at 566.

[40]Harper & Row, 471 U.S. at 566.

[41]Lewis Galoob Toys, Inc. v. Nintendo of Am., Inc., 964 F.2d 965, 971, 22 U.S.P.Q.2d 1857 (9th Cir. 1992), *as amended*, (Aug. 5, 1992).

Campbell v. Acuff-Rose Music, Inc.[42] *Campbell's* discussion of the fourth factor omits the previous statement that the market effect is the most important element. "Apparently abandoning the idea that any factor enjoys primacy, *Campbell* instructs that '[a]ll [four factors] are to be explored, and the results weighed together, in light of the purposes of copyright.' "[43]

With respect to the fourth factor, the focus is on whether the allegedly infringing use tends to interfere with the sales of the copyrighted article.[44] Thus, where a defendant's work is sold in a market that the plaintiff has no interest in occupying, the fourth factor will weigh in favor of fair use.[45] Notably, actual present harm is not the required showing. Instead, the copyright owner need only show that if the use becomes widespread, the potential market for the copyrighted work would be adversely affected.[46]

Courts have generally reviewed the market effect factor by determining whether the purpose or character of the alleged use is commercial.[47] However, this narrow focus is not entirely correct. The Supreme Court has stated that commercial use of copyrighted material is presumptively unfair and a likelihood of future harm is presumed.[48] Subsequently, however, the Supreme Court expounded upon this presumption. The court limited the presumption or inference of market harm to cases involving mere duplication of the copyrighted work for commercial purposes. The court went on to explain that when a secondary use is transformative, market substitution is less certain so that market harm cannot be presumed.[49]

In the context of the DMCA, copyright owners must consider fair use before sending a takedown notification under § 512(c). One element of a proper notification is "[a] statement that the complaining party has a good faith belief that use of the material in the manner complained of is not authorized by the copyright owner, its agent, or the law."[50] In *Lenz v. Universal Music Corp.*, the Ninth Circuit held that fair use is a non-infringing use authorized by law, and therefore, one cannot send a proper takedown

---

[42]Campbell, 114 S. Ct. at 1164.

[43]Texaco, 60 F.3d at 926 (quoting Campbell, 114 S. Ct. at 1171).

[44]Hustler Magazine Inc. v. Moral Majority Inc., 796 F.2d 1148, 1155, 13 Media L. Rep. (BNA) 1151, 230 U.S.P.Q. 646 (9th Cir. 1986).

[45]Twin Peaks, 996 F.2d at 1377.

[46]Amsinck v. Columbia Pictures Industries, Inc., 862 F. Supp. 1044, 1048-1049, 33 U.S.P.Q.2d 1131 (S.D. N.Y. 1994).

[47]Nat'l Rifle Ass'n of Am. v. Handgun Control Fed'n of Ohio, 15 F.3d 559, 561, 22 Media L. Rep. (BNA) 1252, 29 U.S.P.Q.2d 1634, 1994 FED App. 0028P (6th Cir. 1994).

[48]Sony Corp. of Am. v. Universal City Studios, Inc., 464 U.S. 417, 451, 104 S. Ct. 774, 793, 220 U.S.P.Q. 665 (1984).

[49]Campbell, 114 S. Ct. at 1117.

[50]17 U.S.C.A. § 512(c)(3)(A)(v).

notification without considering fair use.[51] A complaining party who fails to consider fair use prior to sending a takedown notice may be liable for damages for misrepresentation under § 512(f).

§ 8:19   Defenses—Fair use of computer programs

Research References

West's Key Number Digest, Copyrights and Intellectual Property ⬥67.3
C.J.S., Copyrights and Intellectual Property §§ 41, 45, 55, 97

As it does in other areas of copyright law, computer software presents some unique fair use situations. For instance, the fair use defense has been asserted by defendants who reverse engineer a copyrighted computer program to gain access to the program's source code. This reverse engineering, or translation, into source code entails copying of the copyrighted object code. The argument becomes, then, that this copying is a fair use because one cannot get access to the unprotectable source code without copying the protected object code.

The Ninth Circuit addressed this issue in *Sega Enterprises Ltd. v. Accolade, Inc.*[1] Accolade, via reverse engineering, copied Sega's interface specifications for its GENESIS game console. The interface specification permitted Accolade to make game cartridges that were compatible with the GENESIS game console. The Ninth Circuit held that Accolade's copying of the object code was a fair use. "[A]lthough Accolade's ultimate purpose was the release of Genesis-compatible games for sale, its direct purpose in copying Sega's code, and thus its direct use of the copyrighted material, was simply to study the functional requirements for the Genesis compatibility so that it could modify existing games and make them usable with Genesis console."[2] A similar decision was reached in the case of *Atari Games Corp. v. Nintendo of America, Inc.*[3]

§ 8:20   Defenses—Lack of notice

Research References

West's Key Number Digest, Copyrights and Intellectual Property ⬥50.1(4), 75
C.J.S., Copyrights and Intellectual Property §§ 8, 35, 43, 62, 95, 98

---

[51]Lenz v. Universal Music Corp., 801 F.3d 1126, 43 Media L. Rep. (BNA) 2305, 115 U.S.P.Q.2d 1965 (9th Cir. 2015).

[Section 8:19]

[1]Sega Enters. Ltd. v. Accolade, Inc., 977 F.2d 1510, 24 U.S.P.Q.2d 1561 (9th Cir. 1992), *as amended*, (Jan. 6, 1993).

[2]Sega, 977 F.2d at 1522.

[3]Atari Games Corp. v. Nintendo of Am. Inc., 975 F.2d 832, 24 U.S.P.Q.2d 1015, 1992-2 Trade Cas. (CCH) ¶ 69969 (Fed. Cir. 1992).

Copyright notice has never been required on unpublished works, and notice is no longer required on published works. However, for works published before March 1, 1989, the law requires notice. Therefore, the effect of omitting copyright notice on published works depends on the date of publication. In particular, the defense of lack of notice or "innocent infringement" can have a bearing on recoverable damages depending upon the distribution date of the work in question.

The Copyright Act provides an exception for lack of notice:

> Any person who innocently infringes a copyright, in reliance upon an authorized copy or phonorecord from which the copyright notice has been omitted and which was publicly distributed by authority of the copyright owner before the effective date of the Berne Convention Implementation Act of 1988, incurs no liability for actual or statutory damages under § 504 for any infringing act committed before receiving actual notice that registration for the work has been made under § 408, if such person proves that he or she was mislead by the omission of notice.[1]

Thus, lack of notice may be a viable defense against allegations of infringement of a copyrighted work publicly distributed before March 1, 1989.

Importantly, the exception provided under § 405(b) is not available for works publicly distributed after March 1, 1989, because the notice requirement is no longer in effect. Further, it has been held that an infringer's reliance upon an unauthorized copy or phonorecord from which the copyright notice has been omitted cannot rely upon § 405(b) which contains the explicit requirement of an "authorized" copy.[2]

§ 8:21 Defenses—Fraud

Research References

West's Key Number Digest, Copyrights and Intellectual Property ☞50.20

C.J.S., Copyrights and Intellectual Property §§ 39, 71, 96

A registered copyright can be invalidated where proof of deliberate fraud on the Copyright Office is shown. The acts of "fraud" can appear in different forms. However, whatever the form, the act must be deliberate.[1]

For example, intentional failure to mention a public domain

[Section 8:20]

[1]17 U.S.C.A. § 405(b).

[2]Dolori Fabrics, Inc. v. Limited, Inc., 662 F. Supp. 1347, 1354-55, 3 U.S.P.Q.2d 1753, 4 U.C.C. Rep. Serv.

2d 393 (S.D. N.Y. 1987).

[Section 8:21]

[1]Donald Frederick Evans and Associates, Inc. v. Continental Homes, Inc., 785 F.2d 897, 904, 229 U.S.P.Q.

work which is almost indistinguishable from the application can result in a showing of fraud.[2] In this vein, it has been consistently held that an applicant's failure to advise the Copyright Office of facts which might otherwise have led to rejection of the application will constitute grounds for holding the registration invalid.[3] In one case, plaintiff desired to copyright various costumes. However, in its copyright application, plaintiff failed to designate the work as "costume" and instead referred to it as a "soft sculpture." As noted by the court, the Copyright Office consistently rejects applications to register costumes. Plaintiff admitted knowledge of this fact, and its knowing failure to advise the Copyright Office that its work was a "costume" resulted in a finding of fraud.[4] Determination of whether a fraud has been committed on the Copyright Office is a mixture of law and fact.[5]

It should be emphasized, however, that fraud requires an intentional act or omission. Where an applicant's omissions in a copyright application are inadvertent and innocent, copyright registration will not be overcome due to fraud.[6] Similarly, unintentional inaccuracies in a copyright registration will not bar an action for infringement.[7] Thus, where an applicant unintentionally omits reference to an unpublished underlying work, and later corrects this mistake, a showing of fraud cannot be made.[8] Normally, then, an inadvertent omission which has no material affect on a defendant will not suffice to invalidate a copyright for fraud.[9]

§ 8:22 Defenses—Misuse

Research References

West's Key Number Digest, Copyrights and Intellectual Property ⚖75; Equity ⚖65

C.J.S., Copyrights and Intellectual Property §§ 8, 43, 62, 98; Equity §§ 102 to 114

The defense of copyright misuse arises from the equitable doc-

---

321 (11th Cir. 1986) (failure to list preexisting work on registration application does not invalidate registration unless "intentional or purposeful").

[2]Russ Berrie & Co., Inc. v. Jerry Elsner Co., Inc., 482 F. Supp. 980, 205 U.S.P.Q. 320 (S.D. N.Y. 1980).

[3]Whimsicality, Inc. v. Rubie's Costume Co., Inc., 891 F.2d 452, 456, 13 U.S.P.Q.2d 1296 (2d Cir. 1989).

[4]Whimsicality, 891 F.2d at 456.

[5]Whimsicality, 891 F.2d at 455.

[6]Eckes v. Card Prices Update, 736 F.2d 859, 861, 222 U.S.P.Q. 762 (2d Cir. 1984).

[7]Harris v. Emus Records Corp., 734 F.2d 1329, 1335, 222 U.S.P.Q. 466 (9th Cir. 1984).

[8]S.O.S., Inc. v. Payday, Inc., 886 F.2d 1081, 12 U.S.P.Q.2d 1241 (9th Cir. 1989).

[9]Masquerade Novelty, Inc. v. Unique Indus., Inc., 912 F.2d 663, 668, 15 U.S.P.Q.2d 1881, 17 Fed. R. Serv. 3d 1027 (3d Cir. 1990).

trine of unclean hands. An accused infringer may avoid liability for infringement by showing that the copyright owner has acted inequitably in obtaining or enforcing his or her copyright. Generally, the inequitable conduct involves violating a rule of practice in registering the copyright or violating the antitrust laws. The anticompetitive conduct must relate directly to the claim of copyright infringement.

To prevail on an enforcement-type misuse defense, the accused infringer need only prove that the copyright is being used in a manner that violates the public policy embodied in the grant of a copyright; it does not need to prove any kind of antitrust violation.[1] Courts have also held that providing copyrighted open-source software, such as Linux, under the GNU General Public License ("GPL") does not violate the federal antitrust laws.[2]

It is not improper to affix a copyright symbol to a work that contains both copyrighted and non-copyrightable elements, and it is acceptable to affix a copyright notice to a derivative work for both original and new material in a work. As such, neither action would lead to a finding of misuse.[3]

As an equitable defense, copyright misuse arguably bars only equitable (injunctive) relief. However, the general rule is that copyright misuse will render the copyright completely unenforceable against all infringers.

§ 8:23 Defenses—Statute of limitations

Research References

West's Key Number Digest, Copyrights and Intellectual Property ⟐80
C.J.S., Copyrights and Intellectual Property §§ 8, 68, 98

A three-year statute of limitations applies to civil actions for copyright infringement.[1] A cause of action for copyright infringement accrues when the copyright owner has actual knowledge of a violation, or is chargeable with such knowledge.[2] While this statement appears on its face to be straightforward, it is applied in different ways in different circuits. The majority rule is that when acts of infringement occur more than three years prior to the filing of the lawsuit, the plaintiff may not recover for those

---

[Section 8:22]

[1]Lasercomb Am., Inc. v. Reynolds, 911 F.2d 970, 977, 15 U.S.P.Q.2d 1846, 1990-2 Trade Cas. (CCH) ¶ 69145, 18 Fed. R. Serv. 3d 130 (4th Cir. 1990).

[2]Wallace v. Int'l Bus. Machs. Corp., 467 F.3d 1104, 1108, 80 U.S.P.Q.2d 1956, 2006-2 Trade Cas. (CCH)

¶ 75480 (7th Cir. 2006).

[3]Janel Russell Designs, Inc. v. Mendelson & Associates, Inc., 114 F. Supp. 2d 856, 866, 56 U.S.P.Q.2d 1604 (D. Minn. 2000).

[Section 8:23]

[1]17 U.S.C.A. § 507(b).

[2]Wallace, 467 F.3d at 1108.

acts.[3] However, in a case of continuing copyright infringement, damages may be recovered for all acts that occurred within the three years preceding the filing of the lawsuit.[4] This view has been followed in the Second,[5] Fifth[6] and Sixth[7] Circuits.

In contrast, the Seventh Circuit applies a continuing tort theory. That court held that an initial copying by defendant was not a separate or completed wrong, but instead was the first step in a course of conduct which continued until the final infringing copy was sold by defendant.[8] Therefore, the statute of limitations will not begin to accrue until the last act of infringement has occurred.

In the absence of actual knowledge of an infringement, a plaintiff may nonetheless be charged with inquiry notice under the so-called discovery rule.[9] Under this rule, the statue of limitations starts to run from when a reasonably diligent person in the plaintiff's shoes would have acquired an awareness of the putative infringement. Typically, a court will not charge a plaintiff with inquiry notice unless some sort of triggering event or series of events comes to the attention of the plaintiff that fairly suggests a reason to investigate whether he may have suffered an injury at the hands of a putative infringer.

Once a claim for copyright infringement is barred by the statute of limitations, plaintiff has the burden to demonstrate that, for some equitable reason, the statute should be tolled.[10] For example, the statute of limitations will be tolled where defendant fraudulently conceals the cause of action.[11] However, such a tolling is not indefinite. It will last only so long as the fraud is effective. In other words, fraudulent concealment will not lessen plaintiff's duty of diligence to learn of the facts giving rise to a

---

[3]Kregos v. Associated Press, 3 F.3d 656, 662, 27 U.S.P.Q.2d 1881 (2d Cir. 1993); Roley v. New World Pictures, Ltd., 19 F.3d 479, 481, 30 U.S.P.Q.2d 1654, 140 A.L.R. Fed. 813 (9th Cir. 1994).

[4]Stone v. Williams, 970 F.2d 1043, 23 U.S.P.Q.2d 1492 (2d Cir. 1992).

Roley v. New World Pictures, Ltd., 19 F.3d 479, 30 U.S.P.Q.2d 1654, 140 A.L.R. Fed. 813 (9th Cir. 1994).

[5]Stone, 970 F.2d at 1049-1050.

[6]Makedwde Pub. Co. v. Johnson, 37 F.3d 180, 182, 32 U.S.P.Q.2d 1635 (5th Cir. 1994).

[7]Hoste v. Radio Corp. of Am., 654 F.2d 11, 212 U.S.P.Q. 153 (6th Cir. 1981).

[8]Taylor v. Meirick, 712 F.2d 1112, 1119, 219 U.S.P.Q. 420 (7th Cir. 1983), rejected by McCool v. Strata Oil Co., 972 F.2d 1452, R.I.C.O. Bus. Disp. Guide (CCH) P 8066, R.I.C.O. Bus. Disp. Guide (CCH) P 8243 (7th Cir. 1992).

[9]Warren Freedenfeld Assocs., Inc. v. McTigue, 531 F.3d 38, 44, 87 U.S.P.Q.2d 1301 (1st Cir. 2008).

[10]Makedwde, 37 F.3d at 182 n. 4 (citing Prather v. Neva Paperbacks, Inc., 446 F.2d 338, 170 U.S.P.Q. 378, 13 A.L.R. Fed. 916 (5th Cir. 1971)).

[11]Prather, 446 F.2d at 341.

cause of action.[12]

§ 8:24   Defenses—Laches

Research References

West's Key Number Digest, Copyrights and Intellectual Property ⚷80
C.J.S., Copyrights and Intellectual Property §§ 8, 68, 98

As one would expect, the equitable defense of laches is available to bar plaintiff's claim in the copyright context. As with other areas of the law, a defendant who suffers prejudice as the result of plaintiff's unreasonable and inexcusable delay in bringing a copyright action can invoke the defense of laches.[1] Unlike the statute of limitations defense, a claim of laches is premised upon a showing of prejudice. Laches cannot be used to bar a timely claim for legal damages. In extraordinary circumstances, however, laches can be used to bar a claim for equitable relief brought within the statute of limitations period. Even if laches cannot be used to bar a claim for legal damages or equitable relief, courts may still consider Plaintiff's delay in filing suit at the remedial stage when considering the amount of damages to award or whether to grant equitable relief.[2] "Even where such extraordinary circumstances exist, however, laches serves as a bar only to the recovery of retrospective damages, not to prospective relief."[3] While defendant may believe that he or she was "prejudiced" by some delay on the part of plaintiff, requiring the plaintiff to have engaged in unwarranted and unnecessary investigation will not suffice to establish laches.[4]

Plaintiff's knowledge that infringement would likely occur in the future, without more, is insufficient to start the laches period for any such future infringement claims. Someone who is not the obvious owner of a copyright need not file an action for a declaration of copyright ownership whenever an ownership dispute arises in order to avoid exposure to a laches defense in a subsequent infringement action. The period of delay for laches in an infringement action runs only from the time that a plaintiff knew or should have known about the actual or impending infringement,

---

[12]Stone v. Williams, 970 F.2d 1043, 23 U.S.P.Q.2d 1492 (2d Cir. 1992).

[Section 8:24]

[1]New Era Publ'ns Int'l, ApS v. Henry Holt & Co., Inc., 873 F.2d 576, 16 Media L. Rep. (BNA) 1559, 10 U.S.P.Q.2d 1561 (2d Cir. 1989).

[2]Petrella v. Metro-Goldwyn-Mayer, Inc., 134 S. Ct. 1962, 110 U.S.P.Q.2d 1605 (2014).

[3]Peter Letterese, 533 F.3d at 1321.

[4]MacLean Associates, Inc. v. Wm. M. Mercer-Meidinger-Hansen, Inc., 952 F.2d 769, 780–781, 21 U.S.P.Q.2d 1345 (3d Cir. 1991).

not from the time of an adverse claim of ownership.[5]

§ 8:25 Defenses—First sale doctrine

The first sale doctrine may be asserted as a defense to infringement of the exclusive distribution right. As discussed in § 6:15, the doctrine essentially provides that a copyright owner divests him or herself of the right to control the distribution of a work once he or she transfers title to a lawfully made copy of a work to another.[1] The defense is limited in several respects. Only the owner of a copy may raise the first sale defense, as the doctrine does not apply to anyone who acquires a copy "by rental, lease, or loan."[2] Further, the doctrine does not apply to the infringement of exclusive rights beyond the distribution right. Therefore, a defendant who makes unauthorized copies of an otherwise lawfully-obtained copy of a work may not raise the first sale doctrine as a defense to infringement of the right of reproduction.

The Ninth Circuit addressed the issue of burden of proof with respect to the first sale defense in *Adobe Systems Inc. v. Christenson*.[3] The court held that, as an affirmative defense, the party asserting the first sale defense bears the burden of "show[ing] ownership through lawful acquisition."[4] Thereafter, the burden shifts to the copyright owner to prove the absence of a first sale.[5]

Disputes over digital content, such as in *Adobe*, present another issue, because most digital content is licensed, and not sold to customers. Generally, the protection of the first sale doctrine is not available to a licensee, because he or she is not the owner of a lawfully made copy.[6] In cases where the plaintiff claims to have licensed the digital content to the defendant, the plaintiff bears the burden of establishing the existence of a license. Some licensing agreements operate as a *de facto* sale, so even where a license exists, a court may examine its terms to determine whether or not the plaintiff has actually sold the content to the customer.

§ 8:26 Defenses—License defense

Research References

---

[5]Kling v. Hallmark Cards Inc., 225 F.3d 1030, 1041, 56 U.S.P.Q.2d 1025 (9th Cir. 2000).

[Section 8:25]

[1]17 U.S.C.A. § 109(a).

[2]17 U.S.C.A. § 109(d).

[3]Adobe Systems Inc. v. Christenson, 809 F.3d 1071, 117 U.S.P.Q.2d 1257 (9th Cir. 2015).

[4]Adobe, 809 F.3d at 1079.

[5]Adobe, 809 F.3d at 1079.

[6]Quality King Distributors, Inc. v. L'anza Research Intern., Inc., 523 U.S. 135, 146–147, 118 S. Ct. 1125, 140 L. Ed. 2d 254, 26 Media L. Rep. (BNA) 1385, 45 U.S.P.Q.2d 1961 (1998).

West's Key Number Digest, Copyrights and Intellectual Property ☞75
C.J.S., Copyrights and Intellectual Property §§ 8, 43, 62, 98

Failure to obtain a compulsory license within the proper time frame before manufacturing and distributing the copyrighted work makes one accountable for copyright infringement. Furthermore, if there is a dispute on whether a license exists, the burden is on the alleged infringer to prove its existence. The copyright owner bears the burden of proving the alleged infringer's copying was unauthorized if the scope of the license is disputed.[1]

§ 8:27 Remedies—Injunctions

Research References

West's Key Number Digest, Copyrights and Intellectual Property ☞85, 86
C.J.S., Copyrights and Intellectual Property §§ 8, 75, 79, 98

An injunction is fairly routine in copyright cases. Courts have authority to grant injunctions in copyright cases under 17 U.S.C.A. § 502(a). Courts have wide latitude in granting and framing injunctions. Injunctions may be granted "on such terms as [the court] may deem reasonable to prevent or restrain infringement of a copyright."[1] Injunctions against copyright infringement cover the entire United States, and they are enforceable in any federal court having personal jurisdiction over the enjoined party.[2]

Courts may grant a preliminary injunction at the outset of litigation if circumstances warrant it. A preliminary injunction is viewed as a rather extreme remedy and requires balancing of four factors to decide whether to grant the injunction. The four factors include: Plaintiff's likelihood of success on the merits of the case; irreparable harm to Plaintiff if an injunction is not issued; balance of equities between the parties; and the public interest. In an extreme case, a court found Plaintiff would suffer irreparable harm if a preliminary injunction was not issued because she received death threats when her likeness was used in an anti-Islamic film that was posted on www.YouTube.com. Plaintiff appeared in an independent film and had a copyright in her performance. The creators of the anti-Islamic film used her likeness and dubbed her voice without her permission, thus

---

[Section 8:26]

[1]Tasini v. N.Y. Times Co., Inc., 206 F.3d 161, 28 Media L. Rep. (BNA) 1748, 54 U.S.P.Q.2d 1032 (2d Cir. 2000), judgment aff'd, 533 U.S. 483, 121 S. Ct. 2381, 29 Media L. Rep. (BNA) 1865, 59 U.S.P.Q.2d 1001, 5 A.L.R. Fed. 2d 623 (2001).

[Section 8:27]

[1]17 U.S.C.A. § 502(a).
[2]17 U.S.C.A. § 502(b).

infringing her copyright. The court granted a preliminary injunction ordering Google, the parent organization of YouTube, to remove the video.[3]

A permanent injunction is warranted if liability has been established and the threat of infringement exists. In fact, the court may even enter a permanent injunction prohibiting sale of an infringing work, even though defendant ceases infringing activity before the plaintiff filed suit.[4]

The court may also permanently enjoin future infringement of copyrighted works that are owned by plaintiff, but were not alleged to be infringed in the suit. Such an injunction is proper if defendant has been found guilty of infringement, if there is a history of continuing infringement and if a significant threat of future infringement remains.[5]

§8:28 Remedies—Impoundment

Research References

West's Key Number Digest, Copyrights and Intellectual Property ⬤→71
C.J.S., Copyrights and Intellectual Property §§60 to 61, 76, 79, 97 to 98

In addition to enjoining future infringement, the court may prevent future infringement by impounding any infringing works that already exist. Impoundment may include not only the infringing works, but any plates, molds, master tapes, photograph negatives or any other articles that are used to make the copies.[1] The impoundment may take place at any time during the case. Often, if a preliminary injunction is granted, any existing copies of the allegedly infringing works are impounded by the court.

If a final judgment of infringement is entered, the court has the same authority to impound any existing infringing works. The court has broad discretion in determining whether impoundment is appropriate, and it has the authority to order "other reasonable disposition" of any infringing works.[2]

As a practical matter, disposition of the infringing works depends in large part upon the judge's preference, the willfulness of the infringement and the nature of the infringing works. Some judges are very strict about having the infringing works impounded. Others allow existing inventory to be sold, with any profits going to plaintiff.

---

[3]Garcia v. Google, Inc., 743 F.3d 1258, 1264, 42 Media L. Rep. (BNA) 1309, 109 U.S.P.Q.2d 1799 (9th Cir. 2014).

[4]Walt Disney Co. v. Powell, 897 F.2d 565, 568, 14 U.S.P.Q.2d 1160 (D.C. Cir. 1990).

[5]Walt Disney, 897 F.2d at 568.

[Section 8:28]

[1]17 U.S.C.A. §503.

[2]17 U.S.C.A. §503.

§ 8:29   Remedies—Actual damages and infringer's profits

Research References

West's Key Number Digest, Copyrights and Intellectual Property ⊸87
C.J.S., Copyrights and Intellectual Property §§ 8, 77 to 79, 98 to 100

In a copyright case, the plaintiff may elect between two different kinds of damages. Plaintiff may choose to receive either its actual damages and any additional profits of the infringer or statutory damages. The election available to plaintiff by § 504 may be made "at any time before final judgment is rendered."[1] However, once the plaintiff makes an election, it gives up its right to seek any other type of damages.[2]

Plaintiff is entitled to its actual damages and any additional profits of defendant that were not already taken into account in computing actual damages. The remedies are not cumulative. Plaintiff is not entitled to its actual damages and the infringer's profits. Another way of looking at this measure of damages is that the plaintiff is entitled to either its actual damages or defendant's profits, whichever is greater. A jury in a copyright action can return a verdict for both actual damages and lost profits.[3]

In proving defendant's profits, the plaintiff only needs to prove defendant's gross revenue. Upon plaintiff's demonstration of the infringer's revenues, the burden shifts to the infringer to show what portion of its revenue did not result from infringement.[4] The infringer has the burden of proving that certain elements of its profits are attributable to factors other than the copyrighted work and the method of apportionment must clearly take into account the value to infringer of plaintiff's work and should only compensate plaintiff for profits due to infringement.[5]

In awarding plaintiff an award based upon the infringer's profits, the court must make a finding as to what portion, if any, of such profits resulted from sales by the infringer that were not taken into account when plaintiff's actual damages were calculated. This ensures that any sales by the infringer which resulted in lost opportunities for sales by the plaintiff were not considered as part of the infringer's profits.[6]

Finally, willful infringers may not be denied all overhead

[Section 8:29]

[1] 17 U.S.C.A. § 504(c)(1).

[2] Twin Peaks, 996 F.2d at 1380.

[3] Kleier Adver., Inc. v. Premier Pontiac, Inc., 698 F. Supp. 851, 852, 8 U.S.P.Q.2d 1175 (N.D. Okla. 1988), aff'd in part, rev'd in part, 921 F.2d 1036, 18 Media L. Rep. (BNA) 1529, 17 U.S.P.Q.2d 1200 (10th Cir. 1990).

[4] Konor Enters., Inc. v. Eagle Publ'ns, Inc., 878 F.2d 138, 141, 11 U.S.P.Q.2d 1307 (4th Cir. 1989).

[5] Jarvis v. A & M Records, 827 F. Supp. 282, 295, 27 U.S.P.Q.2d 1812 (D.N.J. 1993).

[6] U.S. Payphone, Inc. v. Execu-

deductions. Rather, if willful infringement is found, the Court must give extra scrutiny in evaluating the overhead expenses claimed by the infringer. Overhead expenses are not included in the total amount of profit the infringer gained through the sale and production of the infringing product. The infringer has the burden of showing that there is a nexus between the expense claimed and the sale of the infringing product.[7]

§8:30 Remedies—Statutory damages

Research References

West's Key Number Digest, Copyrights and Intellectual Property ☞87(3)

C.J.S., Copyrights and Intellectual Property §§ 8, 77 to 79, 98 to 100

Statutory damages may be awarded for any sum between $750 and $30,000, as the court considers just.[1] If the infringement was willful, the court has the discretion to increase the award of statutory damages to $150,000. If defendant has no reason to know that it was infringing a copyright, the court has the discretion to decrease the award of statutory damages to $200.

A court is not required to follow any rigid formula in awarding statutory damages, but enjoys wide discretion in such an award.[2] In awarding damages, the court should consider both the willfulness of defendant's conduct and the deterrent value of sanctions that are imposed. The parties may submit all of their supporting evidence to the court.[3] Awards of three or four times defendant's profit is not unjust in order to deter future infringement.[4]

Statutory damages are calculated according to the number of works infringed, rather than the number of infringements, and therefore only one penalty may be accessed for multiple infringements of the same work.[5] For example, if defendant is found to have made 20,000 copies of plaintiff's copyrighted novel, this is considered one infringement of one work. The range of statutory damages is $750 to $30,000. If defendant is found to have made one copy each of plaintiff's ten copyrighted photographs, then ten works have been infringed, and the range of statutory damages is

---

tives Unlimited of Durham, Inc., 931 F.2d 888, 18 U.S.P.Q.2d 2049 (4th Cir. 1991) (unpublished).

[7]Hamil America Inc. v. GFI, 193 F.3d 92, 105, 52 U.S.P.Q.2d 1225 (2d Cir. 1999).

[Section 8:30]

[1]17 U.S.C.A. § 504(c).

[2]Chi-Boy Music v. Charlie Club, Inc., 930 F.2d 1224, 1229, 18 U.S.P.Q.2d 1713 (7th Cir. 1991).

[3]Cable/Home Communication Corp. v. Network Prods., Inc., 902 F.2d 829, 853, 15 U.S.P.Q.2d 1001 (11th Cir. 1990).

[4]Kamar Int'l. v. Russ Berrie & Co., Inc., 829 F.2d 783, 786, 4 U.S.P.Q.2d 1373 (9th Cir. 1987).

[5]Walt Disney, 897 F.2d at 569.

$7500 to $300,000.

The current copyright statute (in contrast to the Copyright Act of 1909) shifts the unit of damages inquiry for statutory damages from the number of infringements to the number of works. Thus, for example, the author of eight scripts for eight television episodes is not limited to one award of statutory damages just because the eight works continue a plot line from one episode to the next.[6]

§ 8:31   Remedies—Willful infringement

Research References

West's Key Number Digest, Copyrights and Intellectual Property ⊸52
C.J.S., Copyrights and Intellectual Property § 43

Copyright infringement is willful if the defendant knows that its actions constitute infringement. Such knowledge may be actual or constructive, and may be inferred from the defendant's conduct or proven directly. Reckless disregard of a copyholder's rights, as well as actual knowledge of infringement, is sufficient for an award of enhanced damages under 17 U.S.C.A. § 504(c)(2).[1] A history of prior copyright actions against a party can be used as evidence of willful infringement.[2]

Enhanced or punitive damages are not subject to the same absolute cap as statutory damages, but when the ratio of punitive damages to compensatory damages becomes too great, courts may find that the punitive damages amount is unconstitutionally excessive and in violation of due process.[3] In determining what amounts to a constitutional award of punitive damages, the court will look at the following "guideposts": (1) the reprehensibility of defendant's conduct, (2) the disparity between plaintiff's harm and the award, and (3) a comparison of the award and civil penalties in comparable cases.[4] In determining an acceptable ratio between punitive and compensatory damages, the Supreme Court has repeatedly rejected the use of bright-line rules, but has noted that "an award of more than four times the amount of compensatory damages might be close to the line of constitutional

---

[6]Twin Peaks, 996 F.2d at 1381.

[Section 8:31]

[1]N.A.S. Imp. Corp. v. Chenson Enters., Inc., 968 F.2d 250, 252, 23 U.S.P.Q.2d 1387 (2d Cir. 1992).

[2]Twin Peaks, 996 F.2d at 1382.

[3]Bridgeport Music, Inc. v. Justin Combs Publ'g, 507 F.3d 470, 486, 84 U.S.P.Q.2d 1449 (6th Cir. 2007), cert.

denied, 129 S. Ct. 85 (2008).

[4]Bridgeport Music, 507 F.3d at 486 (relying on State Farm Mut. Auto. Ins. Co. v. Campbell, 538 U.S. 408, 418, 123 S. Ct. 1513, Prod. Liab. Rep. (CCH) P 16805, 60 Fed. R. Evid. Serv. 1349, 1 A.L.R. Fed. 2d 739 (2003); BMW of N. Am., Inc. v. Gore, 517 U.S. 559, 575, 116 S. Ct. 1589 (1996)).

impropriety."[5]

§ 8:32 Remedies—Attorney's fees

Research References

West's Key Number Digest, Copyrights and Intellectual Property
⟐90(2)

C.J.S., Copyrights and Intellectual Property §§ 79, 82, 98

The court has discretion to award attorney's fees and costs to the prevailing party in any copyright infringement action.[1] The term "prevailing party" refers to either the plaintiff or defendant. Thus, under the copyright damages statute, prevailing plaintiffs and prevailing defendants are to be treated alike, but the award of attorney's fees is not automatic. An award of fees remains within the court's equitable discretion.[2] Attorney's fees are not available for any infringement of either an unpublished or published work commenced before registration of the work unless the registration is made within three months after the first publication of the work.[3]

The court may take into account frivolousness, motivation, objective unreasonableness, and the need to advance considerations of compensation and deterrence when determining awards for attorney's fees. However, application of these factors must be faithful to the purposes of the Copyright Act and are applied to prevailing plaintiffs and defendants in an evenhanded manner. The principle of evenhandedness states that the court should begin the consideration of an attorney's fees award in a copyright action with an evenly balanced scale without regard to whether the plaintiff or defendant prevails, and thereafter determine entitlement without weighting the scales in advance. An award of attorney's fees to a prevailing defendant that furthers the underlying purposes of the Copyright Act is reposed in sound discretion of the district courts, and such discretion is not cabined by a requirement of culpability on the part of the losing party. A court's discretion may be influenced by the plaintiff's culpability in bringing or pursuing the action, but blameworthiness is not a prerequisite to awarding fees to a prevailing defendant.

Additionally, an award of attorney's fees incurred by the defendant in defending the plaintiff's appeal from an award of attorney's fees by a federal district court is warranted under 17 U.S.C.A. § 505, since it served the purpose of the Copyright Act

---

[5]State Farm, 538 U.S. at 408.

[Section 8:32]

[1]17 U.S.C.A. § 505.

[2]Fogerty v. Fantasy, Inc., 510

U.S. 517, 534, 114 S. Ct. 1023, 127 L. Ed. 2d 455, 29 U.S.P.Q.2d 1881 (1994).

[3]17 U.S.C.A. § 412.

for defendant to defend the appeal.[4] "[I]f . . . the claim or defense was frivolous and the prevailing party obtained no relief at all, the case for awarding attorneys' fees is compelling."[5] "[A]s a consequence of the successful defense of an infringement suit the defendant is entitled to a "very strong" presumption in favor of receiving attorneys' fees, in order to ensure that an infringement defendant does not abandon a meritorious defense in situations in which "the cost of vindication exceeds the private benefit to the party."[6]

---

[4]Fantasy, Inc. v. Fogerty, 94 F.3d 553, 561, 39 U.S.P.Q.2d 1933 (9th Cir. 1996).

[5]Klinger v. Conan Doyle Estate, Ltd., 761 F.3d 789, 791 (7th Cir. 2014) (citations omitted).

[6]Klinger v. Conan Doyle Estate, Ltd., 761 F.3d at 791 (explaining a declaratory judgment plaintiff in a copyright case is in effect a defendant permitted to precipitate the infringement suit).

Chapter 9

Principles of Trademark Law

KeyCite®: Cases and other legal materials listed in KeyCite Scope can be researched through the KeyCite service on Westlaw®. Use KeyCite to check citations for form, parallel references, prior and later history, and comprehensive citator information, including citations to other decisions and secondary materials.

§ 9:1 The concept of trademarks—Definitions

Research References
West's Key Number Digest, Trademarks ☞1021, 1026

A "trademark" is a designation that indicates the source or origin of goods and that distinguishes those goods from the goods of others. A "service mark" is just like a trademark, except that it identifies the source or origin of services rather than goods. Unless otherwise indicated, statements about trademarks are generally applicable to service marks, and references to trademarked "goods" also include services. Trademarks and service marks are also called "marks."

The Lanham Act, which governs federal registration of trademarks, defines a trademark as "any word, name, symbol or device, or any combination thereof."[1] Although the most common forms of trademarks are words and designs, almost anything capable of identifying the source of goods may serve as a trademark.[2]

A "trade name" is the name under which a business entity conducts its business. In some cases, the same word functions as both a trademark and a trade name, depending on the context. For example, the sentence "This is a HONEYWELL thermostat" is a trademark usage, and the sentence "At Honeywell, we are proud of our products" is a trade name usage. Note that the trademark functions as an adjective, and the tradename functions as a noun. The tradename/trademark distinction is important because trade names are accorded less protection than trademarks, and trade names cannot be federally registered.

The definition of "trade dress" has expanded over time from referring to the total image and overall appearance of a product to now include a product's design, product packaging, color or other distinctive features related to a product that distinguishes those goods from goods of another. Trade dress is thus capable of functioning as a trademark and is entitled to protection as a

---

[Section 9:1]

[1]15 U.S.C.A. § 1127.

[2]See Qualitex Co. v. Jacobson Products Co., Inc., 514 U.S. 159, 115 S. Ct. 1300, 34 U.S.P.Q.2d 1161 (1995).

trademark to the extent that the trade dress is distinctive and nonfunctional.

§ 9:2 The concept of trademarks—Duration of rights

Research References

West's Key Number Digest, Trademarks ☞1151 to 1155

Trademark rights have an indefinite duration and potentially can last forever. This indefinite duration contrasts markedly with the limited duration of patents and copyrights, which expire after a fixed number of years. As a consequence, trademarks may be a company's most valuable intellectual property right.

The duration of a trademark hinges on use of the mark by its owner and by others. If the owner fails to use the mark, this failure may constitute abandonment of the mark. Moreover, to avoid abandonment and dedication to the public, the owner must not only use the mark properly, but must also ensure that others use the mark properly. Improper use of the mark may result in the mark's abandonment or cause it to become generic. In either case, the owner loses rights to the mark and the mark returns to the public domain. Loss of trademark rights is discussed further in §§ 9:24 to 9:26.

§ 9:3 The concept of trademarks—Purpose of trademarks

Research References

West's Key Number Digest, Trademarks ☞1027

Trademarks serve several important functions. A trademark's principal functions are: to distinguish goods and identify their source, to assure consistent quality of goods, and to advertise and promote products.

To function as a trademark or service mark, a word, symbol, or other designation must indicate the source of goods or services and distinguish them from the goods and services of competitors.[1] Although the source may be a single anonymous entity with exclusive rights to the mark, or multiple entities with rights to the mark under a license or franchise agreement, the mark indicates that a single source ultimately controls all products sold under the mark.

When a trademark fails to indicate a single source, such as when suppliers use similar marks, the failure may cause confusion among consumers. Consumers presented with two

---

[Section 9:3]
[1]15 U.S.C.A. § 1127.

313

confusingly-similar marks may mistake one mark for the other or form the mistaken belief that the same entity owns both trademarks. This confusion may affect the consumer's ultimate purchasing decision, because the consumer may believe that products with certain marks have the goodwill of a producer they know and trust.[2] In other words, consumers rely on marks to reduce their costs of shopping and making purchases.[3] Thus, to protect the ability of marks to indicate a single source and to reduce consumer confusion the first, (or senior) user of a mark has the right to exclude use of confusingly similar marks by a later (or junior) user.

A trademark also functions to indicate consistent quality of the goods or services sold under the mark. Goods and services sold under a trademark may be any quality level, high or low, so long as the quality is consistent for the goods and services under the mark.

Trademarks and service marks also play a key role in advertising and promoting goods and services. Advertisements, in fact, often feature the trademark more prominently than the product, imbuing the mark with status or cachet. In addition, the trademark is often the only point-of-sale advertising for a product and forms the basis of purchasing decisions for brand-conscious consumers. For instance, a particular consumer may buy only LEVI jeans, NIKE shoes, or CHAMPION sweatshirts.

§ 9:4 The concept of trademarks—Policy behind trademark law

Research References
West's Key Number Digest, Trademarks ☞1020, 1080

The primary motivation of trademark law is to protect consumers from confusion. Trademark laws discourage or prevent the use of confusingly similar marks for the benefit of both consumers and trademark owners. "Likelihood of confusion" is, therefore, the touchstone of trademark infringement law. A senior trademark user may bring a civil lawsuit against a junior user of a mark that is likely to cause confusion with the senior user's mark. Likelihood of confusion is a multi-factor inquiry that considers such factors as the similarity of the marks in sight, sound and appearance, the goods on which the marks are used, and the channels of trade in which the products are marketed and sold. The inquiry further considers such factors as the sophistication

---

[2]Thomas & Betts Corp. v. Panduit Corp., 65 F.3d 654, 657, 36 U.S.P.Q.2d 1065, 1067 (7th Cir. 1995).

[3]Qualitex, 514 U.S. at 163-164, 115 S. Ct. at 1303, 131 L.Ed.2d 248, 34 U.S.P.Q.2d at 1163.

of typical consumers of the product, the level of care typically used by purchasers of the product, and whether any other similar marks are used by third parties. The likelihood of confusion analysis is discussed in detail in § 11:9.

Another purpose served by trademark law is preservation of the trademark owner's investment. Trademark laws protect the trademark owner from:

- diversion of sales,
- disparagement of the owner's name, and
- dilution.

Diversion of sales occurs where consumers are led to the mistaken belief that goods sold under one mark come from the same source as goods sold under another more senior mark. If two confusingly similar marks are used on the same goods, consumers may purchase goods from one source believing that they originate from the other. This is known as "passing off." Trademark laws protect trademark owners from diversion of sales by making actionable the use in commerce of any mark that is likely to be confused with the trademark owner's mark.

Disparagement of a trademark owner's name may occur where a junior user sells inferior goods or provides inferior services under a mark confusingly similar to a senior user's mark. Consumers may believe that the trademark owner was the source of the inferior goods. This disparagement may ultimately lead to loss of sales. Trademark laws help to assure that a producer will reap the rewards associated with selling a desirable product.

Dilution of a trademark may occur where a competitor sells products under a mark that is not necessarily confusing to consumers, but nonetheless causes a trademark owner's mark to lose distinctiveness in consumers' eyes. A federal anti-dilution statute was passed in January 1996 and subsequently revised in October 2006.[1] Prior to the passage of that statute, trademark dilution was a cause of action only in states that recognized common law trademark dilution or that had adopted state dilution statutes.

Trademark laws further the quality assurance function of trademarks in that trademark rights may be lost if the quality of a product does not remain consistent. If the quality of a trademarked product is suddenly changed or is not maintained at a consistent level, the mark may be deemed abandoned.[2]

Additionally, trademark laws protect the marketplace and com-

---

[Section 9:4]

[1]15 U.S.C.A. § 1125(c); Trademark Dilution Revision Act, Pub. L.

No. 109-312, 120 Stat. 1730 (Oct. 6, 2006).

[2]See infra § 8:26.

petition by preserving honesty and fair dealing. Federal law provides a cause of action against anyone who uses a counterfeit or imitation of a registered trademark.[3] Federal law also provides a cause of action for any false or misleading representation in connection with goods or services that is likely to cause confusion with a senior user's mark, regardless of whether the senior user's mark is registered.[4] A federal cause of action was also created to extend protection to an owner of a mark against domain name registrations that are identical or confusingly similar to the mark and registered in bad faith with an intent to profit from that mark.[5] Unfair competition is also a cause of action under statutes and common law of the various states.

§ 9:5 Distinctiveness of marks—The distinctiveness continuum

Research References

West's Key Number Digest, Trademarks ⚷1029

Marks are categorized along a continuum according to their distinctiveness. To be protectable, a trademark must be capable of distinguishing goods from the goods of others. In legal terms, a trademark must be "distinctive." Trademarks, however, vary in distinctiveness. The most distinct marks receive the greatest breadth of protection, and less distinctive marks receive more narrow protection. From strongest to weakest, marks can be "fanciful," "arbitrary," "suggestive," "descriptive," or "generic."[1] Fanciful, arbitrary and suggestive marks are considered inherently distinctive.[2] Descriptive marks, on the other hand, are not protectable as trademarks unless the trademark owner can show that the descriptive mark has become distinctive by acquiring secondary meaning.[3] The generic name for a product cannot serve as a trademark and is not protectable at all.[4]

The classification of a mark is an issue of fact.[5] It is sometimes

---

[3]15 U.S.C.A. § 1114.

[4]15 U.S.C.A. § 1125.

[5]15 U.S.C.A. § 1125(d), see also § 10:34.

[Section 9:5]

[1]Abercrombie & Fitch Co. v. Hunting World, Inc., 537 F.2d 4, 8, 189 U.S.P.Q. 769 (2d Cir. 1976).

[2]Two Pesos, Inc. v. Taco Cabana, Inc., 505 U.S. 763, 766, 112 S. Ct. 2753, 2757, 23 U.S.P.Q.2d 1081, 1085 (1992).

[3]Two Pesos, 505 U.S. at 766, 112 S. Ct. at 2757, 120 L.Ed.2d 615, 23 U.S.P.Q.2d at 1083; Rockland Mortg. Corp. v. Shareholders Funding, Inc., 835 F. Supp. 182, 189, 30 U.S.P.Q.2d 1270, 1275 (D. Del. 1993).

[4]Official Airline Guides, Inc. v. Goss, 6 F.3d 1385, 1391, 28 U.S.P.Q.2d 1641, 1645 (9th Cir. 1993).

[5]Ford Motor Co. v. Summit Motor Products, Inc., 930 F.2d 277, 292 n.18, 18 U.S.P.Q.2d 1417, 1429 n.18, R.I.C.O. Bus. Disp. Guide (CCH) P 7731, 19

difficult to determine what category a particular mark falls within.[6] The distinction between suggestive and descriptive terms is particularly blurred. Additionally, a mark may be in one category for a particular product, but another category for a different product. For example, APPLE as applied to computers is arbitrary, but it would be generic when used to describe the forbidden fruit.

In classifying a mark, the intent of the trademark owner in choosing the mark is not controlling.[7] The impact of the mark on prospective consumers of the product is what matters.[8] For example, a court acting as fact finder found the mark ROCKLAND MORTGAGE CORP. for a mortgage company is arbitrary in the minds of potential mortgage purchasers, even though the trademark owner argued that the mark was adopted because it was suggestive of the mortgage business.[9]

§ 9:6 Distinctiveness of marks—Fanciful marks

Research References

West's Key Number Digest, Trademarks ☞1039

Fanciful marks are coined or "made up" words, invented solely to function as trademarks.[1] Because fanciful marks do not exist as words in the English language before they are used as trademarks, consumers associate these marks with nothing other than the goods sold under them. These marks are therefore given the greatest realm of protection from infringement. Examples of fanciful marks are KODAK film[2], EXXON oil[3] and SANKA decaffeinated coffee.[4]

§ 9:7 Distinctiveness of marks—Arbitrary marks

Research References

Fed. R. Serv. 3d 907 (3d Cir. 1991).

[6]Abercrombie & Fitch, 537 F.2d at 8, 189 U.S.P.Q. at 764; Investacorp, Inc. v. Arabian Inv. Banking Corp. (Investcorp) E.C., 931 F.2d 1519, 1522, 19 U.S.P.Q.2d 1056, 1058 (11th Cir. 1991).

[7]Rockland Mortgage, 835 F. Supp. at 189, 30 U.S.P.Q.2d at 1274.

[8]Rockland Mortgage, 835 F. Supp. at 189, 30 U.S.P.Q.2d at 1274-75.

[9]Rockland Mortgage, 835 F. Supp. at 189, 30 U.S.P.Q.2d at 1275.

[Section 9:6]

[1]Official Airline Guides, 6 F.3d at 1390, 28 U.S.P.Q.2d at 1644.

[2]Eastman Kodak Co. v. Rakow, 739 F. Supp. 116, 15 U.S.P.Q.2d 1631 (W.D. N.Y. 1989) ("[t]he Kodak trademark is perhaps one of the strongest and most distinctive trademarks . . . in the world"). Legend has it that KODAK was coined because it sounded to George Eastman like the clicking made by a camera shutter. Marshall La Cour and Irvin T. Lathrop, *Photo Technology* at 5 (2d ed.1942).

[3]U.S. Trademark Registration No. 902,044.

[4]U.S. Trademark Registration No. 175,372.

West's Key Number Digest, Trademarks ⊚1039

Arbitrary marks consist of real words arranged in such a way that is nondescriptive of any quality of the goods or services that they designate.[1] Because they have no relationship to the goods they designate other than as trademarks, arbitrary marks can be very distinctive. Therefore, they receive strong legal protection. CAMEL cigarettes[2], SHELL gasoline service stations[3], APPLE computers[4] and ARROW shirts[5] are examples.

§ 9:8   Distinctiveness of marks—Suggestive marks

Research References
West's Key Number Digest, Trademarks ⊚1038

Suggestive marks are marks that call to mind some aspect of the products they designate, but require "imagination, thought and perception to reach a conclusion as to the nature of the goods."[1] While suggestive marks are not as strong as fanciful or arbitrary marks, they nonetheless are treated as inherently distinctive marks and in fact can be very effective trademarks. Suggestive marks are popular with business owners because less advertising is needed to gain a consumer association between the mark and the goods than with fanciful or arbitrary marks. LONDON FOG raincoats[2] and COPPERTONE suntan oil[3] are examples of suggestive marks that are very valuable and effective.

§ 9:9   Distinctiveness of marks—Descriptive marks

Research References
West's Key Number Digest, Trademarks ⊚1035

A descriptive term is one that immediately describes an ingredient, quality, characteristic or feature of the goods or services on which it is used, or that directly conveys information regarding

---

[Section 9:7]

[1]Official Airline Guides, 6 F.3d at 1390, 28 U.S.P.Q.2d at 1644.

[2]U.S. Trademark Registration No. 126,760.

[3]U.S. Trademark Registration No. 1,760,294.

[4]U.S. Trademark Registration No. 1,078,312.

[5]E.g., U.S. Trademark Registra-

tion Nos. 340,809 and 107,962.

[Section 9:8]

[1]Stix Products, Inc. v. United Merchants & Mfrs., Inc., 295 F. Supp. 479, 488, 160 U.S.P.Q. 777, 785 (S.D. N.Y. 1968).

[2]U.S. Trademark Registration No. 603,047.

[3]U.S. Trademark Registration Nos. 601,438 and 917,825.

the nature, function, purpose or use of the goods or services.[1] Whether a term is descriptive must be determined in relation to the goods or services for which it is used, the context in which it is used, and the possible significance the term would have to the average purchaser.[2]

A mark that is merely descriptive is not protectable as a trademark unless it has acquired distinctiveness or "secondary meaning" through use.[3] This requirement of acquired secondary meaning is based on the dual rationale that a descriptive term does not serve as an indicator of source unless the public has been educated to associate it with a single source through use, and that one manufacturer should not be allowed to monopolize the use of such a term.[4]

Even after a descriptive term has achieved trademark status, however, third parties have a right to make "fair use" of the term. Use of a descriptive trademark is fair use when it is used other than as a mark, in good faith, and in its descriptive sense.[5] For example, it was held that advertising CANADA DRY fruit-flavored ginger ale as "Your New Main Squeeze" was not an infringement of the mark MAIN SQUEEZE for fruit juices.[6] Fair use is discussed in more detail in § 11:17.

Determining whether a mark is descriptive or suggestive is not easy, and is usually subjective. However, this characterization is often critical, since unlike descriptive terms, which are not protectable until they acquire secondary meaning, a suggestive mark is protectable immediately upon use. For example, the mark "L.A." for light or low alcohol beer was found by one court to be merely descriptive and hence not protectable as a trademark because there was no sufficient showing of secondary meaning.[7] Another court classified the same mark for the identical goods as suggestive and thus entitled to trademark protection.[8]

A mark comprised of a descriptive term combined with an inherently distinctive component is considered inherently distinc-

---

[Section 9:9]

[1]In re Pennzoil Products Co., 20 U.S.P.Q.2d 1753, 1755, 1991 WL 326581 (T.T.A.B. 1991).

[2]Pennzoil Products, 20 U.S.P. Q.2d at 1755.

[3]Investacorp, 931 F.2d at 1522, 19 U.S.P.Q.2d at 1058.

[4]PaperCutter, Inc. v. Fay's Drug Co., Inc., 900 F.2d 558, 562, 14 U.S.P. Q.2d 1450, 1453 (2d Cir. 1990).

[5]15 U.S.C.A. § 1115(b)(4); KP Permanent Make-Up, Inc. v. Lasting

Impression I, Inc., 543 U.S. 111, 125 S. Ct. 542, 160 L. Ed. 2d 440, 72 U.S.P. Q.2d 1833 (2004).

[6]Citrus Group, Inc. v. Cadbury Beverages, Inc., 781 F. Supp. 386, 391, 21 U.S.P.Q.2d 1031, 1035 (D. Md. 1991).

[7]G. Heileman Brewing Co., Inc. v. Anheuser-Busch, Inc., 873 F.2d 985, 10 U.S.P.Q.2d 1801 (7th Cir. 1989).

[8]Anheuser-Busch Inc. v. Stroh Brewery Co., 750 F.2d 631, 224 U.S.P.Q. 657 (8th Cir. 1984).

tive and protectable regardless of whether it has secondary meaning.[9] A combination of multiple descriptive terms does not, however, result in an inherently distinctive trademark unless the combination creates a new and different commercial impression from that of the individual components.[10] Applying this rule, it was held that the combination mark DJDJ for disc jockey services remained descriptive.[11] In contrast, while it was admitted that the words "sugar" and "spice" are descriptive of bakery products, it was held that the mark SUGAR & SPICE was suggestive and hence inherently distinctive of bakery products because it connoted the nursery rhyme "sugar and spice and everything nice."[12] Additionally, translations of otherwise descriptive terms into a foreign language does not avoid the terms' descriptive classification unless the foreign language is considered dead or obscure.[13] Also, the use of ".com" or another top level domain, "Inc." "Co." or "Corp." typically does not add any source-identifying significance to a descriptive mark.[14] The meaning of a mark to prospective purchasers remains the issue when determining the descriptive nature of the mark.

Examples of descriptive marks include MULTI-VIS for multiple viscosity motor oil,[15] and DOUBLE CERTIFIED ORGANIC for pasta that was independently certified organic as to both its forming and processing.[16] Famous descriptive marks include WHEATIES cereal[17] and BUFFERIN buffered aspirin.[18]

§ 9:10   Distinctiveness of marks—Generic terms

Research References

---

[9]In re Disc Jockeys Inc., 23 U.S.P.Q.2d 1715, 1716, 1992 WL 205047 (T.T.A.B. 1992).

[10]Disc Jockeys, 23 U.S.P.Q.2d at 1716.

[11]Disc Jockeys, 23 U.S.P.Q.2d at 1716.

[12]Application of Colonial Stores, Inc., 55 C.C.P.A. 1049, 394 F.2d 549, 157 U.S.P.Q. 382 (1968).

[13]*Compare* In re Oriental Daily News, Inc., 230 U.S.P.Q. 637, 1986 WL 83605 (T.T.A.B. 1986) (Chinese characters that translate as ORIENTAL DAILY NEWS held merely descriptive of newspaper), *with* General Cigar Co., Inc. v. G.D.M. Inc., 988 F. Supp. 647, 45 U.S.P.Q.2d 1481 (S.D. N.Y. 1997) (translation of COHIBA in Taino Indian language to tobacco did not bar registration of mark for cigars as descriptive because prospective purchasers of COHIBA cigars were not likely to make association between the mark and a word in a language spoken by indigenous population of the Dominican Republic).

[14]In re Oppedahl & Larson LLP, 373 F.3d 1171, 71 U.S.P.Q.2d 1370 (Fed. Cir. 2004).

[15]Pennzoil Products, 20 U.S.P.Q.2d 1753, 1991 WL 326581.

[16]In re Eden Foods Inc., 24 U.S.P.Q.2d 1757, 1992 WL 355505 (T.T.A.B. 1992).

[17]U.S. Trademark Registration No. 199,448.

[18]U.S. Trademark Registration No. 1,785,176.

West's Key Number Digest, Trademarks ☞1034

Generic terms are not trademarks at all. A generic term is one that is the common name for a class or genus of goods.[1] A generic term is incapable of functioning as a trademark because the common product name by definition identifies a type of goods rather than the source of the goods.[2] An entity would obtain an unfair advantage over its competitors if it were allowed to obtain trademark rights to a generic term and remove that term from use in the public domain in association with that product. Competitors cannot be deprived of the right to call a product by its name in advertising and sales of their goods.[3] Trademark laws are not intended to give this sort of monopoly to the first user.

The test for determining whether a mark is generic is its primary significance to the relevant public.[4] The Lanham Act codifies the test first articulated by Judge Learned Hand as "[w]hat do buyers understand by the word for whose use the parties are contending?" The "relevant public" refers to the consumers that may purchase the product in the marketplace.[5] For example, the relevant public for a surgical device may be limited to medical professionals, but the relevant public for an automobile washing service encompasses all automobile owners and operators.[6] If the relevant public understands a term as describing the genus of the goods in question, the term is generic.[7] Evidence of the public's understanding of a term may be obtained from any competent source, such as dictionaries, newspaper and magazine articles, consumer surveys and purchaser testimony.[8]

Despite the inability of a generic term to function as a trademark, a generic term may be protectable as part of a mark that comprises a generic term in combination with a protectable feature. Additionally, it is possible that a combination of generic terms may form a distinctive protectable composite mark.[9] The composite must create a commercial impression that is new and

---

[Section 9:10]

[1]Park 'N Fly, Inc. v. Dollar Park and Fly, Inc., 469 U.S. 189, 193, 105 S. Ct. 658, 661, 224 U.S.P.Q. 327, 329 (1985).

[2]In re Gould Paper Corp., 834 F.2d 1017, 1018, 5 U.S.P.Q.2d 1110, 1111 (Fed. Cir. 1987).

[3]Abercrombie & Fitch, 537 F.2d at 9, 189 U.S.P.Q. at 764.

[4]15 U.S.C.A. § 1064(3).

[5]15 U.S.C.A. § 1064(3).

[6]Magic Wand, Inc. v. RDB, Inc., 940 F.2d 638, 641, 19 U.S.P.Q.2d 1551, 1553-54 (Fed. Cir. 1991).

[7]In re Advanced Spine Fixation Systems Inc., 25 U.S.P.Q.2d 1363, 1364, 1992 WL 421452 (T.T.A.B. 1992).

[8]Advanced Spine Fixation Systems, 25 U.S.P.Q.2d at 1364, 1992 WL 421452.

[9]Association of Co-op. Members, Inc. v. Farmland Industries, Inc., 684 F.2d 1134, 1140, 216 U.S.P.Q. 361, 366 (5th Cir. 1982).

different from the sum of its parts.[10] The addition of ".com" or another top-level domain typically does not add any source-identifying significance to a generic mark.[11] However, registering a term on the Supplemental Register is not evidence that the term is not generic.[12] Supplemental registration is only prima facie evidence that a registration was issued and does not provide any statutory presumption that the term is a trademark.[13]

Examples of marks that have been held generic include SCREENWIPES for television and computer screen cleaning wipes,[14] ALL NEWS CHANNEL for a twenty-four hour television news channel[15] and HAND HAMMERED WOK for woks that had been hammered into shape by hand.[16]

§ 9:11 Secondary meaning

Research References

West's Key Number Digest, Trademarks ☞1028, 1032

As mentioned above, fanciful, arbitrary and suggestive marks are considered inherently distinctive and function as trademarks immediately upon use. Alternatively, descriptive marks are protectable only upon proof that the mark has acquired distinctiveness over time. Acquired distinctiveness is called "secondary meaning." Marks that are descriptive and thus require proof of secondary meaning include geographically descriptive marks, surnames, noninherently distinctive designs, noninherently distinctive product configurations, and noninherently distinctive trade dress.

A mark has secondary meaning if it has come to be uniquely associated with a specific source.[1] The existence of secondary meaning is a question of fact.[2] To establish secondary meaning, it

---

[10]See Texas Pig Stands, Inc. v. Hard Rock Cafe Intern., Inc., 951 F.2d 684, 21 U.S.P.Q.2d 1641 (5th Cir. 1992) (PIG SANDWICH for a menu item consisting of barbecued pig meat on a bun was not generic).

[11]In re Steelbuilding.com, 415 F.3d 1293, 75 U.S.P.Q.2d 1420 (Fed. Cir. 2005).

[12]See §§ 9:1 et seq. for a discussion of the Supplemental Register.

[13]Novartis Consumer Health, Inc. v. McNeil-PPC, Inc., 53 U.S.P.Q.2d 1406, 1999 WL 707721 (D.N.J. 1999).

[14]Gould Paper, 834 F.2d 1017, 5 U.S.P.Q.2d 1110.

[15]In re Conus Communications Co., 23 U.S.P.Q.2d 1717, 1992 WL 205048 (T.T.A.B. 1992).

[16]In re Westminster International Co. Inc., 23 U.S.P.Q.2d 1958, 1992 WL 233380 (T.T.A.B. 1992).

[Section 9:11]

[1]Two Pesos, 505 U.S. at 766 n. 4, 112 S. Ct. at 2756 n.4, 120 L.Ed.2d 615, 23 U.S.P.Q.2d at 1082 n.4.

[2]PaperCutter, Inc. v. Fay's Drug Co., 900 F.2d 558, 564, 14 U.S.P.Q.2d 1450, 1454 (2d Cir. 1990). See also 815 Tonawanda Street Corp. v. Fay's Drug Co., 842 F.2d 643, 647–648, 6 U.S.P.Q.2d 1284 (2d Cir. 1988).

must be proven that the primary significance of a mark in the minds of the public is to identify the source of the product, rather than the product itself.[3]

Secondary meaning for a mark must also be shown apart from the mark's combination with any other mark.[4] For example, the mark COCOA BUTTER FORMULA was found not to have secondary meaning despite 20 years of advertising and sales growth of the mark PALMER'S COCOA BUTTER FORMULA because the mark was never used separately from the house mark of PALMER'S.[5]

While a long period of substantially exclusive use of a descriptive mark is evidence of distinctiveness, there is no legal minimum length of time that a mark must be in use before it can attain secondary meaning.[6] In registering a mark, however, federal law provides that five years of exclusive and continuous use prior to the date a claim of distinctiveness is made may be accepted as prima facie evidence that the mark has acquired secondary meaning.[7] Present day advanced channels of communication, including television, radio, magazines, newspapers and the Internet, allow a trademark to be presented to a great number of people with much greater speed than was possible in the past. Older cases that contemplate achievement of secondary meaning only after a period of years should thus be viewed with the changed marketplace in mind. Secondary meaning can exist where the source is anonymous, so long as there is a single source to which the public links a product.[8]

§9:12 Things that function as marks—Common kinds of trademarks

Research References

West's Key Number Digest, Trademarks ⊛1022

Most any designation may serve as a trademark or service mark, so long as it is distinctive and it functions to distinguish the source of particular goods or services. The following are examples of various types of trademarks and service marks.

---

[3]Inwood Laboratories, Inc. v. Ives Laboratories, Inc., 456 U.S. 844, 851 n.11, 102 S. Ct. 2182, 2187 n.11, 214 U.S.P.Q. 1, 9 n.11, 34 Fed. R. Serv. 2d 1101 (1982).

[4]E.T. Browne Drug Co. v. Cococare Products, Inc., 538 F.3d 185, 87 U.S.P.Q.2d 1655 (3d Cir. 2008).

[5]E.T. Browne Drug, 538 F.3d 185, 87 U.S.P.Q.2d 1655.

[6]Jackson v. Universal Intern. Pictures, 36 Cal. 2d 116, 222 P.2d 433, 435, 87 U.S.P.Q. 131, 134 (Sup. Ct. Cal. 1950).

[7]15 U.S.C.A. § 1052(f).

[8]Sunbeam Corp. v. Equity Industries Corp., 635 F. Supp. 625, 629, 229 U.S.P.Q. 865, 866 (E.D. Va. 1986), aff'd, 811 F.2d 1505, 1 U.S.P.Q.2d 1752 (4th Cir. 1987).

Word marks may be comprised of a single word or a word string. A word mark may be either inherently distinctive or descriptive.

Single   **PLAYSKOOL** for toys[1]
Word

                PILLSBURY for cake mixes[2]

Word   **BEN & JERRY'S** for ice cream[3]
String

                3 MINUTE MIRACLE for hair
                conditioners[4]

Additionally, a word mark may be written in a stylized form, which particular style may be protectable as a trademark.

Stylized Word—**CAMPBELL'S** in script writing
                for soup[5]

A group of letters or even a single letter can function as a trademark. Likewise, one or more numbers can function as a trademark. Examples are:

Number   **501** for jeans[6]

Letters   **IBM** for computers[7]

Virtually any type of design may function as a trademark. Design marks vary greatly in distinctiveness. Some designs are deemed inherently distinctive, while others are protectable only upon attaining secondary meaning.

[Section 9:12]

[1]U.S. Trademark Registration No. 513,311.

[2]U.S. Trademark Registration No. 698,691.

[3]U.S. Trademark Registration No. 1,303,989.

[4]U.S. Trademark Registration No. 1,780,994.

[5]U.S. Trademark Registration No. 804,371.

[6]U.S. Trademark Registration No. 1,552,985.

[7]U.S. Trademark Registration No. 1,058,803.

Drawing   **Gerber baby face** for baby foods[8]

Symbol   A stylized design of an **Ankh-like Symbol** for sound recordings originating from Paisley Park Enterprises[9]

Sign   **Golden arches** for drive-in restaurant services[10]

A slogan, like any other string of words, may function as a trademark provided that it is used in such a way as to distinguish the source of goods or services. Many slogans, however, function only as advertising copy that is not likely to be perceived as identifying the source, in which case they do not function as trademarks.[11] Examples of slogans that have achieved trademark significance are WHERE THERE'S LIFE * * * THERE'S BUD for Budweiser beer,[12] I'M LOVIN' IT for McDonald's,[13] and GREAT TASTE . . . LESS FILLING for Miller Lite beer.[14]

In determining whether a slogan functions as a trademark, the slogan is examined in the context in which it is used. A slogan should be emphasized or set apart in the text, otherwise consumers are not likely to recognize it as a trademark.[15] For example, it was held that "NATUR-ALL-IZE YOUR HAIR COLORING" did not function as a trademark where it was used only as part of the phrase "NATUR-ALL-IZE YOUR HAIR COLORING WITH ANOTHER NEW SERVICE" in advertising copy.[16] Slogans that are popular slang expressions, such as "Come on Strong" may function as trademarks but are given a narrow scope of protection.[17] The trademark owner cannot prevent others from using the expression in a nontrademark sense.[18] In general, the longer the slogan, the less likely consumers would perceive it as a trademark. Examples of slogans that were found incapable of

---

[8]U.S. Trademark Registration Nos. 313,879; 658,323 and 765,611.

[9]U.S. Trademark Registration No. 1,822,461 (this symbol is also the name of the artist formerly and again known as Prince).

[10]U.S. Trademark Registration No. 764,838.

[11]In re Morganroth, 208 U.S.P.Q. 284, 287, 1980 WL 30167 (T.T.A.B. 1980).

[12]Chemical Corp. of America v. Anheuser-Busch, Inc., 306 F.2d 433, 436, 134 U.S.P.Q. 524, 526, 2 A.L.R.3d 739 (5th Cir. 1962).

[13]U.S. Trademark Registration No. 2,978,889.

[14]U.S. Trademark Registration No. 1,564,927.

[15]Morganroth, 208 U.S.P.Q. at 288.

[16]Morganroth, 208 U.S.P.Q. at 288.

[17]See B & L Sales Associates v. H. Daroff & Sons, Inc., 421 F.2d 352, 353, 165 U.S.P.Q. 353, 354 (2d Cir. 1970).

[18]See B & L Sales Associates, 421 F.2d at 353, 165 U.S.P.Q. at 354.

functioning as trademarks include THE BABY BOOTIE SOCK THAT WILL NOT KICK OFF for socks,[19] and the phrase BLACKER THE COLLEGE, SWEETER THE KNOWLEDGE for T-shirts.[20]

A trademark that consists of a single color is registrable and protectable as a trademark under the Lanham Act. For several years, there was a split in the Circuits as to whether a single color alone could function as a trademark. In 1995, the Supreme Court resolved this split in favor of trademark protection.[21]

The Supreme Court held that three requirements must be met for a color alone to be registrable as a trademark. A color can be registered provided that:

- the color has become distinctive of the applicant's goods in commerce (i.e. it has acquired secondary meaning),
- there is no competitive need for colors to remain available in the industry, and
- the color is not functional.[22]

A color is functional, and cannot serve as a trademark, if it is essential to the use or purpose of the article, if it affects the cost or quality of the article, or if exclusive use of the feature would put competitors at a significant disadvantage, unrelated to the reputation of the product.[23]

Other types of designations, while rare, may also function as a trademark if used in a manner that indicates source. For example, NBC received a trademark registration for the sound of its three chimes for broadcast services.[24] A fragrance may function as a trademark if it is used in a manner that consumers would perceive as an indication of origin.[25] Factors that indicate a fragrance serves as a source indicator for a product include:

- the fragrance is an optional addition to the product rather than an inherent characteristic,
- the scented nature of the product is promoted in advertising, and
- consumers have come to recognize the scent as identifying the particular source of the product (i.e. the fragrance has

---

[19]In re Sanda Hosiery Mills, 154 U.S.P.Q. 631, 1967 WL 11667 (T.T.A.B. 1967).

[20]In re Pro-Line Corp., 28 U.S.P. Q.2d 1141, 1993 WL 398575 (T.T.A.B. 1993).

[21]Qualitex Co. v. Jacobson Products Co., Inc., 514 U.S. 159, 115 S. Ct. 1300, 34 U.S.P.Q.2d 1161 (1995).

[22]Qualitex, 514 U.S. at 166, 115 S. Ct. at 1304, 131 L.Ed.2d 248, 34 U.S.P.Q.2d at 1164.

[23]Inwood, 456 U.S. at 851 n.10, 102 S. Ct. at 2187 n.10, 72 L.Ed.2d 606, 214 U.S.P.Q. at 4 n.10.

[24]U.S. Trademark Registration Nos. 523,616 and 916,522.

[25]In re Clarke, 17 U.S.P.Q.2d 1238, 1990 WL 354572 (T.T.A.B. 1990).

acquired secondary meaning).[26]
An example of a fragrance that functions as a trademark is a "high impact, fresh, floral fragrance reminiscent of Plumeria blossoms" on sewing threads.[27] In contrast, the fragrance of products that are inherently scented (e.g. perfume) or to which a scent is typically added (e.g. household cleaning products) are product features and therefore do not function as trademarks.[28]

§9:13 Things that function as marks—Combination marks

Research References

West's Key Number Digest, Trademarks ☞1058

A combination mark is a mark comprised of multiple types of designations. A common type of combination mark is a mark comprised of both words and a design. An example is the word "GERBER" displayed with the Gerber baby face.[1]

The term "combination mark" is also used to describe a word mark comprised of words from two or more different categories along the distinctiveness continuum. The combination might be, for example, a suggestive term combined with a generic term, or a descriptive term combined with a fanciful term. The resulting combination is then classified along the continuum in the class of its most distinctive term. So, a descriptive term combined with a fanciful term forms a fanciful mark, and a suggestive term combined with a generic term forms a suggestive mark.

A combination mark is protectable as a trademark in its entirety. An element of a combination mark may also be individually protectable as a trademark provided that it is distinctive of the goods by itself.[2] Trademark owners frequently obtain trademark registrations for each element of a combination mark as well as for the combination itself. This is recommended, to achieve maximum trademark protection.

§9:14 Things that function as marks—House marks

Research References

West's Key Number Digest, Trademarks ☞1060

---

[26]Clarke, 17 U.S.P.Q.2d at 1239.

[27]Clarke, 17 U.S.P.Q.2d at 1238.

[28]Clarke, 17 U.S.P.Q.2d at 1239 n.4.

[Section 9:13]

[1]U.S. Trademark Registration Nos. 405,310 and 655,920.

[2]Igloo Products Corp. v. Brantex, Inc., 202 F.3d 814, 53 U.S.P.Q.2d 1753 (5th Cir. 2000).

A house mark is a trademark that is the primary mark used by a company to designate the entire range of goods or services provided by that company. Secondary marks are typically used with the house mark as a designation of specific goods sold by that company. An example is Kraft Foods. The house mark for Kraft Foods is KRAFT.[1] Secondary marks used by Kraft include PHILADELPHIA for cream cheese[2] and CHEEZ WHIZ for processed cheese spread.[3] House marks can be very effective in establishing consumer brand recognition.

§ 9:15 Things that function as marks—Family of marks

Research References

West's Key Number Digest, Trademarks ⬤1060

A family of trademarks is "a group of marks having a recognizable common characteristic, wherein the marks are composed and used in such a way that the public associates not only the individual marks, but the common characteristic of the family, with the trademark owner."[1] A family of marks may include a plurality of marks with a common word, prefix, suffix or syllable.[2] Famous trademark families include McDonald's restaurants' families of "MC" and "MAC" marks[3] and the "R US" family that includes TOYS "R" US and KIDS "R" US.[4]

The importance of trademark families is that families of marks receive a greater breadth of protection than do individual marks. Where a family of marks exists, the trademark owner may demonstrate a likelihood of confusion with either an individual mark in its family of marks or with the family as a whole. For example, it was held that confusion was likely between McDonald's family of marks and the terms "McTEDDY" for teddy bears,[5] "McSLEEP"

[Section 9:14]

[1]E.g., U.S. Trademark Registration Nos. 554,187, 670,330, 801,424 and 1,052,526 for a variety of foods.

[2]U.S. Trademark Registration No. 1,659,932.

[3]U.S. Trademark Registration No. 795,650.

[Section 9:15]

[1]J & J Snack Foods Corp. v. McDonald's Corp., 932 F.2d 1460, 1462, 18 U.S.P.Q.2d 1889, 1891 (Fed. Cir. 1991).

[2]J. Thomas McCarthy, Trademarks and Unfair Competition § 23:61

(4th ed. 2014).

[3]E.g., McDonald's Corp. v. McBagel's, Inc., 649 F. Supp. 1268, 1 U.S.P.Q.2d 1761, 95 A.L.R. Fed. 1 (S.D. N.Y. 1986); Quality Inns Intern., Inc. v. McDonald's Corp., 695 F. Supp. 198, 8 U.S.P.Q.2d 1633 (D. Md. 1988); and McDonald's Corp. v. McKinley, 13 U.S.P.Q.2d 1895, 1989 WL 274414 (T.T.A.B. 1989).

[4]Geoffrey Inc. v. Stratton, 16 U.S.P.Q.2d 1691, 1990 WL 10072476 (C.D. Cal. 1990), aff'd, 951 F.2d 359 (9th Cir. 1991).

[5]McDonald's Corp. v. McKinley, 13 U.S.P.Q.2d 1895, 1989 WL 274414 (T.T.A.B. 1989).

for lodging,[6] "McBAGELS" for bagels,[7] and "McPRETZEL" for pretzels,[8] even though those marks were not confusingly similar to any particular mark in the family.

The existence of a family of marks is a question of fact, based on the extent of the use, advertisement and promotion of the family, and the distinctiveness of the common element.[9] The use, advertisement and distinctiveness of the marks are evaluated to determine the existence of a family.[10] A family of marks can be shown by evidence that the common element of the marks has been so extensively advertised and used that consumers would associate a mark that includes that element with the source of the family.[11] Consumers must recognize that the common characteristic indicates a common origin.[12] Non-distinctive characteristics cannot achieve family significance. For example, it was found that there was no family of "ETTE" marks in CREAMETTES, KIDETTES, SALADETTES, etc.[13] A descriptive term may, however, become the basis for a family if secondary meaning is established.[14]

§9:16 Things that function as marks—Trade dress

Research References
West's Key Number Digest, Trademarks ☞1061

Historically, trade dress referred primarily to the shape of a product or the overall appearance of a product's packaging. More recently, it has evolved into a seemingly limitless concept that includes anything that might make any impression on a consumer. Now, any product feature that relates to the overall image of a product may be part of the product's trade dress.[1] Trade dress includes such things as product configuration, the packaging and labeling of a product, including any drawings and

---

[6]Quality Inns, 695 F. Supp. 198, 8 U.S.P.Q.2d 1633.

[7]McDonald's Corp., 649 F. Supp. at 1269, 1 U.S.P.Q.2d at 1762, 95 A.L.R. Fed. at 2.

[8]J & J Snack Foods, 932 F.2d at 1461, 18 U.S.P.Q.2d at 1990.

[9]McDonald's Corp., 649 F. Supp. at 1271, 1 U.S.P.Q.2d at 1764, 95 A.L.R. Fed. at 4.

[10]J & J Snack Foods, 932 F.2d at 1462, 18 U.S.P.Q.2d at 1991.

[11]Geoffrey Inc., 16 U.S.P.Q.2d at 1694.

[12]J & J Snack Foods, 932 F.2d at 1462, 18 U.S.P.Q.2d at 1891.

[13]Creamette Co. v. Merlino, 299 F.2d 55, 132 U.S.P.Q. 381 (9th Cir. 1962).

[14]The Norwich Pharmacal Company v. Salsbury Laboratories, 168 U.S.P.Q. 250, 255, 1970 WL 9971 (T.T.A.B. 1970).

[Section 9:16]

[1]Two Pesos, Inc. v. Taco Cabana, Inc., 505 U.S. 763, 112 S. Ct. 2753, 23 U.S.P.Q.2d 1081 (1992).

colors used and the style and layout of lettering.[2] More specifically, trade dress may include features such as size, shape, color
or color combinations, texture, graphics or slogans. Trade dress
may also include marketing strategies and even the distinctive
layout of a restaurant.[3]

The registrability of trade dress requires consideration of two
issues, functionality and distinctiveness. In order to be entitled to
registration, the trade dress must be nonfunctional and
distinctive.

Trade dress features can serve as trademarks to the extent
that those features are nonfunctional. The "functionality doctrine" prevents trademark law from encroaching into the province of patent law by allowing a single producer to control a useful product feature.[4] Patent law encourages invention by granting
inventors the right to exclude others from using their invention
for a limited period of time, in exchange for disclosure to the public of that invention. Because trademarks may be continued in
perpetuity, if a product's functional features could be protected as
trademarks "a monopoly over such features could be obtained
without regard to whether they qualify as patents."[5] The purpose
of trademark protection is not to prevent others from competing,
but to allow manufacturers to place identifying symbols on their
products so that consumers may easily determine the source of a
product.[6] Functional features of a product are only protectable
under the patent laws, if at all. A product feature is functional "if
it is essential to the use or purpose of the article or if it affects
the cost or quality of the article."[7]

With regard to distinctiveness, certain trade dress features,
such as product packaging may be either inherently distinctive or
descriptive. However, many trade dress features such as color or
product design, have been held to lack the ability to be inherently
distinctive. Thus, they require a showing of secondary meaning
in order to be protectable trade dress and function as a
trademark.[8] The Supreme Court has noted that the distinction
between product packaging and product design may be difficult

---

[2]Two Pesos, 505 U.S. 763.

[3]Two Pesos, 505 U.S. 763 (holding that the atmosphere of a Mexican
restaurant, including its festive interior and exterior areas, its menus and
servers' uniforms, was protected trade
dress).

[4]Qualitex, 514 U.S. at 164, 115
S. Ct. at 1304, 131 L. Ed. 2d 248, 34
U.S.P.Q.2d at 1163.

[5]Qualitex, 514 U.S. at 164-165,

115 S. Ct. at 1304, 131 L.Ed.2d 248,
34 U.S.P.Q.2d at 1163.

[6]Brunswick Corp. v. Spirit Reel
Co., 832 F.2d 513, 519, 4 U.S.P.Q.2d
1497, 1500, 23 Fed. R. Evid. Serv. 1272
(10th Cir. 1987).

[7]Inwood Laboratories, 456 U.S.
at 850 n.10, 102 S. Ct. at 2186 n.10,
214 U.S.P.Q. at 8 n.10, 34 Fed. R. Serv.
2d 1101.

[8]Wal-Mart Stores, Inc. v. Samara

to discern and accordingly instructed courts to err on the side of caution and require the one seeking trade dress protection to make a showing of secondary meaning.[9] However, evidence of direct copying may establish a prima facie case of secondary meaning.[10] Thus, while it is possible to register trade dress features as trademarks, as a practical matter, they are difficult to obtain.

Product Configuration	Frozen water beads for Dippin' Dots Ice Cream[11]
Package Configuration	The geometric pattern and colors of Red Bull[12]

Legally, there is really no difference between a trademark and trade dress. The latter term is simply a specific species of trademark. However, most lawyers and judges refer to cases involving the shape of a product or the design of a package as "trade dress" cases.

Trade dress that is not registered is also protectable under the Lanham Act, provided the necessary showing of distinctiveness and nonfunctionality are shown.[13] The legal basis for an unregistered trade dress claim is 15 U.S.C.A. § 1125(a), commonly referred to as § 43(a) of the Lanham Act. Section 43(a) provides:

(a) Any person who, on or in connection with any goods or services, or any container for goods, uses in commerce any word, term, name, symbol, or device, or any combination thereof, or any false designation of origin, false or misleading description of fact, or false or misleading representation of fact, which

(1) is likely to cause confusion, or to cause mistake, or to deceive as to the affiliation, connection, or association of such person with another person, or as to the origin, sponsorship, or approval of his or her goods, services, or commercial activities by another person, or

(2) in commercial advertising or promotion, misrepresents

Bros., Inc., 529 U.S. 205, 120 S. Ct. 1339, 54 U.S.P.Q.2d 1065, 1068-69 (2000).

Wal-Mart Stores, 529 U.S. 205, 120 S. Ct. 1339, 54 U.S.P.Q.2d at 1068–69.

[10]Leviton Mfg. Co., Inc. v. Universal Sec. Instruments, Inc., 304 F. Supp. 2d 726 (D. Md. 2004).

[11]U.S. Trademark Registration No. 2,756,102.

[12]U.S. Trademark Registration No. 4,130,437.

[13]15 U.S.C.A. § 1125(a)(3).

the nature, characteristics, qualities, or geographic origin of his or her or another person's goods, services, or commercial activities,

shall be liable in a civil action by any person who believes that he or she is or is likely to be damaged by such act.[14]

The primary purpose of § 43(a) is to protect the consumer benefit of being able to quickly recognize the source of a product or service. The easiest way for consumers to recognize the source of a product is through its packaging or labeling. Confusion caused by packaging and labeling of a product constitutes the most basic form of trade dress infringement.

An early case protecting the shape of a product as trade dress under § 43(a) was *Truck Equipment Service Co. v. Fruehauf Corp.*[15] In protecting the exterior design of a cornhusker truck body, the court stressed the competition aspect of trade dress protection. "Full and fair competition requires that those who invest time, money and energy into the development of goodwill and a favorable reputation be allowed to reap the advantages of their investment."[16] The distinctive shape of other products has been similarly protected.[17]

In *Sears, Roebuck & Co. v. Stiffel Co.*[18] and *Compco Corp. v. Day-Brite Lighting, Inc.*,[19] (the *Sears-Compco cases*), the Supreme Court held that federal patent laws preempt those state laws that effectively prohibit copying of patentable subject matter. Despite the fact that the state laws in *Sears-Compco* involved consumer confusion over product configurations, courts have regularly held that § 43(a) protection for product configurations is not preempted by federal patent laws. Recent cases have reasoned that § 43(a) is a federal statute and that *Sears-Compco* preempted only state laws. In addition, many courts reason that, if only the nonfunctional features of the product are protected under § 43(a), "the careful balance struck in the patent laws be-

---

[14]15 U.S.C.A. § 1125(a).

[15]Truck Equipment Service Co. v. Fruehauf Corp., 536 F.2d 1210, 191 U.S.P.Q. 79 (8th Cir.1976).

[16]Truck Equipment Service Co., 536 F.2d at 1215, 191 U.S.P.Q. at 83.

[17]Nabisco Brands, Inc. v. Conusa Corp., 722 F. Supp. 1287, 11 U.S.P.Q.2d 1788 (M.D. N.C. 1989), aff'd, 892 F.2d 74, 14 U.S.P.Q.2d 1324 (4th Cir. 1989) (shape of Lifesavers candies protected); Car-Freshner Corp. v. Scentex, Inc., 12 U.S.P.Q.2d 1361, 1989 WL 47373 (N.D. N.Y. 1989), aff'd,

927 F.2d 594 (2d Cir. 1991) (two-dimensional pine tree shaped air freshener protected); Chemlawn Services Corp. v. GNC Pumps, Inc., 690 F. Supp. 1560, 6 U.S.P.Q.2d 1348 (S.D. Tex. 1988), order aff'd, 856 F.2d 202 (Fed. Cir. 1988) (shape of lawn care spray gun protected).

[18]Sears, Roebuck & Co. v. Stiffel Co., 376 U.S. 225, 84 S. Ct. 784, 140 U.S.P.Q. 524 (1964).

[19]Compco Corp. v. Day-Brite Lighting, Inc., 376 U.S. 234, 84 S. Ct. 779, 140 U.S.P.Q. 528 (1964).

tween society's desire to encourage new ideas and its desire to promote competition" will not be disturbed.[20] As further explained by the Supreme Court, where an expired utility patent claimed certain features, one who seeks to establish trade dress protection bears the heavy burden of showing that the features are nonfunctional, for instance by showing that it is merely an ornamental, incidental, or arbitrary aspect of the device.[21] However, trade dress protection may be available for features that are not the "central advance" of the utility patent.[22]

Therefore, in trade dress cases, the issue is whether a product feature's primary significance to consumers is as an identifier of source or as an element which contributes to the inherent appeal of the product. It is not enough that the consumer associates the form of a product with a particular producer; consumers must desire the product with the particular feature because it signifies that producer.[23]

Examples of trade dress that has been held inherently distinctive are the overall package design of WERTHER'S ORIGINAL TOFFEE[24] and the overall shape and color striping of PORTA-SHADE and GAZEBO portable shade structures.[25] Trade dress that was held nondistinctive includes the appearance of a troll doll having most of its features in common with a troll doll that had been in the public domain for twenty-five years and the remaining characteristics copied from the SMURFS dolls,[26] and the configuration of a square refuse bin that was novel enough to merit a design patent.[27]

§ 9:17   Special kinds of marks—Surnames

Research References

West's Key Number Digest, Trademarks ☞1042

---

[20]Artemide SpA v. Grandlite Design and Mfg. Co., Ltd., 672 F. Supp. 698, 4 U.S.P.Q.2d 1915 (S.D. N.Y. 1987).

[21]TrafFix Devices, Inc. v. Marketing Displays, Inc., 532 U.S. 23, 121 S. Ct. 1255, 149 L. Ed. 2d 164, 58 U.S.P. Q.2d 1001 (2001); Kellogg Co. v. National Biscuit Co., 305 U.S. 111, 119–120, 59 S. Ct. 109, 83 L. Ed. 73, 39 U.S.P.Q. 296 (1938).

[22]Leviton Mfg. Co., 304 F. Supp. 2d at 736.

[23]Thomas & Betts Corp. v. Panduit Corp., 65 F.3d 654, 658-59, 36 U.S.P. Q.2d 1065, 1069 (7th Cir. 1995).

[24]Storck USA, L.P. v. Farley Candy Co., Inc., 797 F. Supp. 1399, 25 U.S.P. Q.2d 1927 (N.D. Ill. 1992).

[25]Gale Group Inc. v. King City Indus. Co. Ltd., 23 U.S.P.Q.2d 1208, 1992 WL 163595 (M.D. Fla. 1992).

[26]EFS Marketing, Inc. v. Russ Berrie & Co., Inc., 836 F. Supp. 128, 29 U.S.P.Q.2d 1436 (S.D. N.Y. 1993), aff'd in part, vacated in part, rev'd in part on other grounds, 76 F.3d 487, 37 U.S.P.Q.2d 1646, 1996-1, 1996-1 Trade Cas. (CCH) ¶ 71299 (2d Cir. 1996).

[27]Rubbermaid Commercial Products, Inc. v. Contico Intern., Inc., 836 F. Supp. 1247, 29 U.S.P.Q.2d 1574 (W.D. Va. 1993).

Trademark law treats surnames similar to descriptive terms.[1] A mark that is primarily a surname is protectable as a trademark only if it has acquired distinctiveness, or in other words, attained secondary meaning distinctive of the goods.[2] Secondary meaning, or acquired distinctiveness, is generally shown by evidence of long and exclusive use which changes the significance of the mark in the mind of consumers of the product from a surname identifying an individual to an identification of the source of the particular goods or services.[3]

By the requirement of distinctiveness, the law delays the appropriation of exclusive rights in a name which is shared by more than one individual, each of whom have an interest in using their surname in business.[4] Once an individual's name has acquired secondary meaning in the marketplace, a later competitor who seeks to use the same or similar name must take "reasonable precautions to prevent mistake."[5] Under the Lanham Act, a mark that is "primarily merely a surname" is not registrable on the Principal Register without proof of secondary meaning.[6] The common law has since adopted the "primarily merely a surname" terminology in analysis of unregistered marks.

A mark may have an ordinary language meaning in addition to its surname significance. In such a case, the ordinary language meaning is likely to be the primary meaning to the public.[7] If, however, the ordinary language meaning is obscure, the primary significance of the mark may indeed be that of a surname.[8] Similarly, a mark may have a suggestive significance when used in connection with the specified goods that overrides the surname significance of the mark.[9]

A term may also have a geographical significance that is more

---

[Section 9:17]

[1]815 Tonawanda Street Corp. v. Fay's Drug Co., Inc., 842 F.2d 643, 648, 6 U.S.P.Q.2d 1284, 1288 (2d Cir. 1988).

[2]Conagra, Inc. v. Singleton, 743 F.2d 1508, 1513, 224 U.S.P.Q. 552, 555 (11th Cir. 1984).

[3]In re Etablissements Darty Et Fils, 759 F.2d 15, 17, 225 U.S.P.Q. 652, 653 (Fed. Cir. 1985).

[4]Darty, 759 F.2d at 17, 225 U.S.P.Q. at 653.

[5]L.E. Waterman Co. v. Modern Pen Co., 235 U.S. 88, 94, 35 S. Ct. 91, 92 (1914).

[6]15 U.S.C.A. § 1052 (e)(3), (f).

[7]Darty, 759 F.2d at 17, 225 U.S.P.Q. at 653; Fisher Radio Corporation v. Bird Electronic Corporation, 162 U.S.P.Q. 265, 1969 WL 9101 (T.T.A.B. 1969) (finding that while BIRD has surname significance, it is not primarily merely a surname).

[8]In re Nelson Souto Major Piquet, 5 U.S.P.Q.2d 1367, 1368, 1987 WL 123866 (T.T.A.B. 1987) (holding that N. PIQUET was primarily merely a surname even though there existed a card game called "Piquet").

[9]In re Bdh Two Inc., 26 U.S.P.Q.2d 1556, 1558, 1993 WL 156484 (T.T.A.B. 1993) (finding that the surname significance of GRAINGERS loses out to the suggestive significance of GRAINGERS when that term is used in connection with grain-based

dominant than its surname significance, in which case it is not primarily merely a surname.[10] But, if the geographical significance of a term is weak, that does not dissipate its significance as a surname.[11]

Ordinarily, the presence of an initial before a term having surname significance reinforces the significance of the term as a surname.[12] In some cases, however, an initial preceding the term having surname significance may be perceived as indicating two given names.[13]

The primary significance of a mark may be to identify a famous person or place, in which case it is not primarily merely a surname. For example, the mark DA VINCI was found to primarily connote artist Leonardo DaVinci and was not primarily merely a surname.[14] In contrast, it was found that the term WILTSE for medical equipment used by orthopaedic surgeons was primarily merely a surname despite the fact that a Dr. Wiltse had published a number of articles relating to devices used in spinal treatment.[15]

A rare surname may or may not be primarily merely a surname, depending upon whether it looks like a surname.[16] The mark PIRELLI was held primarily merely a surname on this basis.[17] Conversely, the mark GARAN, while found to be a rare surname, was held not primarily merely a surname as used on hosiery because the average person would not perceive it as one.[18]

In the case of a surname, secondary meaning is established in a name when "a significant quantity of the consuming public understand the name as referring exclusively to the appropriate

products).

[10]In re Colt Industries Operating Corp., 195 U.S.P.Q. 75, 78, 1977 WL 22526 (T.T.A.B. 1977) (holding that the primary significance of FAIRBANKS was not that of a surname, because its significance as a well-known Alaskan city was just as dominant as its surname significance).

[11]In re Hamilton Pharmaceuticals Ltd., 27 U.S.P.Q.2d 1939, 1943, 1993 WL 368803 (T.T.A.B. 1993) (finding that while there are several cities named "Hamilton," the primary significance of the term HAMILTON is not geographical).

[12]In re S. Oliver Bernd Freier Gmbh & Co. Kg, 20 U.S.P.Q.2d 1878, 1991 WL 326588 (T.T.A.B. 1991).

[13]In re S. Oliver Bernd Freier Gmbh & Co. Kg, 20 U.S.P.Q.2d 1878, 1991 WL 326588 (T.T.A.B. 1991) (holding that while "Oliver" is a surname, the mark S. OLIVER is not primarily merely a surname because it may be a usage of Oliver as a middle name).

[14]Lucien Piccard Watch Corp. v. 1868 Crescent Corp., 314 F. Supp. 329, 331, 165 U.S.P.Q. 459 (S.D. N.Y. 1970).

[15]In re Advanced Spine Fixation Systems Inc., 25 U.S.P.Q.2d 1363, 1367, 1992 WL 421452 (T.T.A.B. 1992).

[16]In re Industrie Pirelli Societa Per Azioni, 9 U.S.P.Q.2d 1564, 1566, 1988 WL 252329 (T.T.A.B. 1988).

[17]Industrie Pirelli, 9 U.S.P.Q.2d at 1566.

[18]In re Garan Inc., 3 U.S.P.Q.2d 1537, 1987 WL 124291 (T.T.A.B. 1987).

party."[19] As with other descriptive terms, a term that is primarily merely a surname may lose its surname significance when used as part of a combination mark. Such a combination mark must be evaluated to determine the commercial impression created by the mark as a whole.[20] If the combination is distinctive, the mark is protectable without having to establish secondary meaning.

For example, a surname combined with a design loses its surname significance if the design is distinctive.[21] If, however, a design is nondistinctive, such as a stylization of the lettering of a surname, the mark remains primarily merely a surname.[22] The surname significance of a mark comprised of a surname combined with wording depends on whether the wording by itself is capable of functioning as a mark. If the wording is capable of functioning as a mark (that is, if it is fanciful, arbitrary or suggestive), then the combination mark is registrable without proving secondary meaning. But, if the wording is the generic or descriptive name of goods or services sold under the mark, the combination mark remains primarily merely a surname.[23]

§ 9:18   Special kinds of marks—Geographic terms

Research References

West's Key Number Digest, Trademarks ☞1045

Geographic terms are protectable as trademarks only if they acquire secondary meaning.[1] There are two basic reasons for this rule. First, prior to attaining secondary meaning, a geographic term is likely to be perceived by the public as an indication of the geographic origin of the product rather than as a source

---

[19]President and Trustees of Colby College v. Colby College-New Hampshire, 508 F.2d 804, 807, 185 U.S.P.Q. 65, 66 (1st Cir. 1975).

[20]Ex Parte Norquist Products, Inc., 109 U.S.P.Q. 399, 400, 1956 WL 8063 (Comm'r Pat. & Trademarks 1956).

[21]Norquist, 109 U.S.P.Q. at 400 (holding that the mark NORQUIST CORONET appearing with a distinctive design is not primarily merely a surname).

[22]See In re Pickett Hotel Company, 229 U.S.P.Q. 760, 763, 1986 WL 83680 (T.T.A.B. 1986) (PICKETT SUITE HOTEL in stylized lettering was primar-

ily merely a surname since the stylization was not so distinctive as to create a separate commercial impression).

[23]In re E. Martinoni Company, 189 U.S.P.Q. 589, 590, 1975 WL 20966 (T.T.A.B. 1975) (the mark LIQUEUR MARTINONI is primarily merely a surname as used on liqueur).

[Section 9:18]

[1]A further discussion of geographic terms is found in § 9:31. Since the inception of the Lanham Act, the law regarding geographic terms has developed mainly in connection with trademark registration. Investacorp, 931 F.2d at 1522, 19 U.S.P.Q.2d at 1058.

designation.[2] Such a term does not serve a trademark function. Second, no one seller in a particular area should be given a monopoly on the right to indicate the geographic origin of a product; at least not until the public begins to associate the geographic term with that seller.[3]

Secondary meaning is established in a geographically descriptive mark "where the mark no longer causes the public to associate the goods with a particular place, but to associate the goods with a particular source."[4] Thus, it was held that the marks BOSTON and BOSTON BEER had not acquired secondary meaning where a consumer survey demonstrated a product-place association rather than a product-source association.[5]

As with other combination marks, a combination mark that includes geographic terms must be viewed as a whole to determine whether it is protectable.[6] The combination mark may take on a different commercial impression, allowing protection of the geographic term as part of the combination.[7]

A geographic term may also be used in an arbitrary sense, in which case the geographic term may form an inherently distinctive mark.[8] A three-step inquiry can be used in determining if a geographic term is used arbitrarily:

- Is the mark the name of a place or region where the product is produced?
- Is the geographic term likely to denote to reasonable buyers that the goods come from the place named?
- Is the place noted for these particular goods?[9]

Applying this test, it was found that PHILADELPHIA was a geographic term being used arbitrarily to identify KRAFT cream cheese.[10]

§ 9:19 Special kinds of marks—Abbreviations, misspellings and foreign words

Research References

[2]In re Pebble Beach Co., 19 U.S.P.Q.2d 1687, 1688, 1991 WL 326557 (T.T.A.B. 1991).

[3]Pebble Beach, 19 U.S.P.Q.2d at 1688.

[4]Boston Beer Co. Ltd. Partnership v. Slesar Bros. Brewing Co., Inc., 9 F.3d 175, 181, 28 U.S.P.Q.2d 1778, 1783 (1st Cir. 1993).

[5]Boston Beer, 9 F.3d at 181, 28 U.S.P.Q.2d at 1783.

[6]California Cooler, Inc. v. Loretto Winery, Ltd., 774 F.2d 1451, 1455, 227 U.S.P.Q. 808, 810–811 (9th Cir. 1985).

[7]California Cooler, 774 F.2d at 1455, 227 U.S.P.Q. at 811.

[8]Kraft General Foods, Inc. v. BC-USA, Inc., 840 F. Supp. 344, 349, 29 U.S.P.Q.2d 1919, 1923 (E.D. Pa. 1993).

[9]Kraft General Foods, 840 F. Supp. at 349, 29 U.S.P.Q.2d at 1923.

[10]Kraft General Foods, Inc., 840 F. Supp. at 346.

West's Key Number Digest, Trademarks ⚙1052, 1054

The treatment of an abbreviation depends on whether consumers would readily recognize the mark as an abbreviation. If it is apparent that the mark is an abbreviation of some word or initials representing a series of words, then the mark is treated like the term it abbreviates.[1] It is generally presumed that the public perceives an abbreviation as representing the phrase from which it is derived.[2] It is possible, however, that the public will not make the connection between initials used in connection with a product and the words from which the initials were derived.[3] In such a case, the abbreviation may be treated as a fanciful or arbitrary mark.

Consumer surveys may be used to demonstrate whether consumers make such a connection.[4] Survey evidence was introduced in one case to demonstrate that a majority of prospective customers recognize that the term L.A. stands for and describes low alcohol, as applied to beer.[5]

A misspelling of a descriptive term is treated as a descriptive term.[6] If, however, the word is misspelled beyond recognition, it may be treated as an arbitrary or fanciful mark.[7] Likewise, a misspelling of a generic word is treated as a generic word, so long as the misspelling does not change the consumer perception of the word as the common term for the product it represents.[8]

Foreign words are translated into English and then tested for distinctiveness.[9] The English translation of a foreign mark is used to determine similarity of meaning, and the foreign mark is used in examining similarities in sight and sound.[10]

§ 9:20 Acquiring trademark rights—Common law rights

Research References

[Section 9:19]

[1]*See* G. Heileman Brewing Co., Inc. v. Anheuser-Busch, Inc., 873 F.2d 985, 992, 10 U.S.P.Q.2d 1801, 1808 (7th Cir. 1989).

[2]G. Heileman, 873 F.2d at 992, 10 U.S.P.Q.2d at 1808.

[3]G. Heileman, 873 F.2d at 992, 10 U.S.P.Q.2d at 1808.

[4]G. Heileman, 873 F.2d at 993, 10 U.S.P.Q.2d at 1809-10.

[5]G. Heileman, 873 F.2d at 996, 10 U.S.P.Q.2d at 1810.

[6]In re State Chemical Manufacturing Co., 225 U.S.P.Q. 687, 1985 WL 72012 (T.T.A.B. 1985).

[7]Venetianaire Corp. of America v. A & P Import Co., 429 F.2d 1079, 167 U.S.P.Q. 481 (2d Cir.1970).

[8]Miller Brewing Co. v. G. Heileman Brewing Co., Inc., 561 F.2d 75, 195 U.S.P.Q. 281 (7th Cir. 1977) (holding that LITE was generic for light beer).

[9]Menendez v. Holt, 128 U.S. 514, 520, 9 S. Ct. 143, 144 (1888).

[10]Horn's, Inc. v. Sanofi Beaute, Inc., 963 F. Supp. 318, 322, 43 U.S.P.Q.2d 1008 (S.D. N.Y. 1997).

West's Key Number Digest, Trademarks ⊕1132

Trademark rights are acquired and maintained by use of a mark.[1] The first person to use a mark ("the senior user"), has priority over subsequent or "junior" users of the mark. Common law rights in trademarks are acquired by use of the mark in connection with sales of goods or services. Protection accorded to marks at common law basically parallels that which is given to federally registered marks.

A mark must be used in connection with goods or services. This requirement is based upon the definition of a trademark as a designation that indicates the source or origin of goods or services and distinguishes those goods or services from the goods or services of others. Trademark rights must then be viewed in conjunction with the particular goods or services on which the mark is used. For example, use of a mark on a breakfast cereal provides the trademark owner with rights in the mark as to breakfast cereals. While the trademark owner may be able to prevent others from using its mark on goods that are closely related to breakfast cereals, such as breakfast bars, use of the mark for breakfast cereals accrues no rights in the mark as to different lines of goods, such as shampoo or television sets. However, a trademark owner may have a claim for dilution against junior users who are using a similar mark on noncompeting products.[2]

Trademarks that are inherently distinctive (i.e., fanciful, arbitrary and suggestive marks), are immediately protectable upon adoption and first use in trade. However, rights do not accrue in marks that require secondary meaning to be protectable (i.e., descriptive marks) until secondary meaning is acquired. Once a mark has been used, rights in the mark may arise under federal statutory law, state statutory law or state common law.

§ 9:21 Acquiring trademark rights—Federal registration

Research References

West's Key Number Digest, Trademarks ⊕1239 to 1242

Federal registration is available to marks that have been used in commerce. "Commerce" is defined as all commerce that may

---

[Section 9:20]

[1]Major League Baseball Properties, Inc. v. Sed Non Olet Denarius, Ltd., 817 F. Supp. 1103, 1126, 26 U.S.P.Q.2d 1731, 1747 (S.D. N.Y. 1993),

vacated pursuant to settlement, 859 F. Supp. 80 (S.D. N.Y. 1994).

[2]See §§ 10:22 et seq. for a discussion of trademark dilution.

lawfully be regulated by Congress.[1] Registration is obtained by filing an application with the U.S. Patent and Trademark Office (USPTO). While a mark cannot be registered until it is used in commerce, an application may be based upon either actual use of the mark or an intention to use the mark.

Filing a federal application confers a nationwide right of priority in the mark, contingent upon eventual registration of the mark.[2] This nationwide right of priority provides the registrant with prior rights against any user that adopts the mark after the filing date of the application that resulted in registration, regardless of the actual geographic area in which the registrant uses the mark. The registrant does not, however, have the right to stop use of the mark by others who had been using it prior to the registrant's filing date. The registrant can, nevertheless, limit the prior user to the geographic area in which they were selling prior to the filing date.[3]

In the case of a trademark, "use" requires that the mark be placed on the goods, on the containers for the goods, or on tags or labels affixed to the goods.[4] If the nature of the goods is such that it is impracticable to place the mark on the goods, their containers, or their tags or labels, placing the mark on documents associated with the goods or their sale satisfies this requirement.[5] In the case of a service mark, there are no goods to which the mark can be affixed. Use of a service mark, therefore, includes the use or display of the mark in the sale or advertising of the services in interstate commerce.[6]

"Use" of a mark to support registration must be "bona fide" use of the mark in the ordinary course of trade.[7] "Bona fide" means that a sale of products bearing the mark must serve some business purpose other than to acquire trademark rights. Under prior law (before adoption of the intent-to-use provisions in 1989), mere "token use" of a mark was adequate so as to satisfy the "use" requirements of federal registration. "Token use" refers to the practice of affixing a mark to a limited number of products and selling those products to a prearranged buyer or buyers across state lines for the purpose of establishing trademark rights in the mark. The buyer was often a related entity to the seller. Token use of a trademark no longer satisfies the use requirements. The rationale for the statute's stricter use requirement is that there is no longer any need to engage in the token use fiction. If there has been no bona fide use of a mark, an intent-

---

[Section 9:21]

[1]15 U.S.C.A. § 1127.

[2]15 U.S.C.A. § 1057(c).

[3]See § 10:19.

[4]15 U.S.C.A. § 1127.

[5]15 U.S.C.A. § 1127.

[6]15 U.S.C.A. § 1127.

[7]15 U.S.C.A. § 1127.

to-use application may be filed to reserve rights in the mark.

§ 9:22 Acquiring trademark rights—State registration

Research References
West's Key Number Digest, Trademarks ☞1256

All fifty states have statutes that provide for state registration of trademarks. Most of these state statutes are patterned after the Lanham Act. As with federal registrations, use of the mark in commerce is a prerequisite for state registrations.

Typically, applications for state registration are given only a cursory examination. Accordingly, state registrations generally are obtained much quicker than federal registrations, sometimes in as little as a couple weeks. While state registrations are simple, cheap and easy to obtain, they also are not very valuable. A state registration provides rights only within the territory of the state in which it is registered. A federal registration may, for example, issue for a mark previously registered in a state by another party.

It is important to note that registration of a corporate name or an assumed name with a Secretary of State is not the same thing as registration of the term as a trademark. Nor does it afford the registrant any trademark rights. The approval of a corporate name does not give the corporation the right to infringe another's trademark.[1] The same is true of registration of domain names on the Internet.

The tests applied for approving corporate names are not the same as the test used for trademark registration. The Secretary of State bases corporate name availability on whether or not the corporate name is "deceptively similar" to another name. Only the names of various firms are compared; there is no evaluation as to the businesses or products of the two corporations. Nor does the Secretary of State compare the proposed corporate name against federal trademark registrations, state trademark registrations in other states, or common law usage.

§ 9:23 Acquiring trademark rights—Protection of unregistered marks under § 43(a)

Research References
West's Key Number Digest, Trademarks ☞1425

Federal trademark rights are provided under § 43(a) of the

[Section 9:22]
[1]Little League Baseball, Inc. v. Daytona Beach Little League, Inc., 193

U.S.P.Q. 611, 614, 1977 WL 22777 (M.D. Fla. 1977).

Lanham Act for any trademark that is used in commerce, regardless of whether it is federally registered.[1] Section 43(a) provides a civil cause of action for infringement of an unregistered trademark under what are commonly referred to as unfair competition causes of action. An infringement action under § 43(a) lies where: (1) the plaintiff is the senior user of the mark and has attained market penetration in a relevant area; (2) the mark is inherently distinctive or has obtained secondary meaning in the relevant market place; and (3) the defendant's use of the mark is likely to cause confusion. Section 43(a) is the only means of protecting an unregistered trademark under federal law. There is no federal common law for unregistered marks.

§ 9:24 Loss of trademark rights—Abandonment through nonuse

Research References

West's Key Number Digest, Trademarks ⊙1153

Trademark rights may be lost through abandonment of the mark. Abandonment is failure to use a mark with an intent not to resume use.[1] When a mark has been abandoned, it returns to the public domain. Another party can adopt the mark as its own and become the new owner of the mark.

Any acts that tend to show an intent not to resume use are evidence of abandonment. Significantly, an intent not to resume use is not necessarily equivalent to an intent to abandon. A trademark owner may well have no intent to use a mark again, without forming an intent to abandon it.[2] Additionally, nonuse for three consecutive years is prima facie evidence of abandonment of a federally registered trademark.[3] This shifts the burden of production (but not of proof) to the owner of the discontinued mark to show an intent to resume the mark's use.[4] The presumption for abandonment of registered marks has also been applied in cases involving common law marks.[5] Abandonment by nonuse can also result from a change in the goods that are sold under

---

[Section 9:23]

[1]15 U.S.C.A. § 1125(a).

[Section 9:24]

[1]15 U.S.C.A. § 1127.

[2]Exxon Corp. v. Humble Exploration Co., Inc., 695 F.2d 96, 101, 217 U.S.P.Q. 1200, 1204-05, 83 A.L.R. Fed. 281 (5th Cir. 1983).

[3]15 U.S.C.A. § 1127. Until recently, a registered mark was pre-

sumed abandoned after only a two year period of nonuse. The statute was amended to implement a provision of the GATT treaty.

[4]Crash Dummy Movie, LLC v. Mattel, Inc., 601 F.3d 1387, 1391, 94 U.S.P.Q.2d 1315, 81 Fed. R. Evid. Serv. 1261 (Fed. Cir. 2010).

[5]Miller Brewing Co. v. Oland's Breweries (1971) Ltd., 548 F.2d 349, 192 U.S.P.Q. 266 (C.C.P.A. 1976).

the mark. Similarly, if the mark continues to be used for some types of goods but not for others, the mark may be abandoned as to those goods for which the mark is no longer used.

§ 9:25 Loss of trademark rights—Abandonment through affirmative acts of owner

Research References

West's Key Number Digest, Trademarks ⚲1201

A mark may be abandoned inadvertently through one of several affirmative acts of the trademark owner. These acts include improper assignment of the mark, failure to adequately control the quality of the goods sold under the mark, and making changes to the mark itself.

Transfer of a trademark without the goodwill of the business symbolized by the mark can result in abandonment of the mark. Such a transfer is sometimes termed a "naked" or "in gross" assignment.[1] Such a transfer is an improper assignment, because trademark rights exist only "as a right appurtenant to an established business or trade in connection with which the mark is employed."[2] Physical assets do not need to accompany the trademark to have a valid transfer.[3] Transfer of the trademark must be accompanied only by the goodwill of the business represented by the trademark.[4] A mere recitation that the goodwill is being transferred with the mark, however, does not guarantee that the assignment will be valid. If, for example, the nature of the assignee's goods are too different, a court may find that no significant goodwill passed with the mark. This was the case where the assignor used its mark for women's pixie boots, and the assignee used the mark for men's shoes and hiking boots.[5]

Licensing a trademark without adequate quality control by the licensor can also result in abandonment of the mark.[6] This is termed a "naked" license. For example, a mark licensed to third parties without control of the activities and standards of those parties can be deemed abandoned.[7] Similarly, a substantial change in the quality of goods sold under a mark can result in an

---

[Section 9:25]

[1]Sands, Taylor & Wood Co. v. Quaker Oats Co., 978 F.2d 947, 956, 24 U.S.P.Q.2d 1001, 1009 (7th Cir. 1992).

[2]United Drug Co. v. Theodore Rectanus Co., 248 U.S. 90, 97, 39 S. Ct. 48, 51, (1918).

[3]Sands, Taylor & Wood, 978 F.2d at 956, 24 U.S.P.Q.2d at 1009.

[4]Sands, Taylor & Wood, 978 F.2d at 956, 24 U.S.P.Q.2d at 1009.

[5]Clark & Freeman Corp. v. Heartland Co. Ltd., 811 F. Supp. 137 (S.D. N.Y. 1993).

[6]Dawn Donut Co. v. Hart's Food Stores, Inc., 267 F.2d 358, 121 U.S.P.Q. 430 (2d Cir.1959).

[7]Movie Mania Metro, Inc. v. GZ DVD's Inc., 306 Mich. App. 594, 857

abandonment of the mark.[8] Legal protection of trademarks is based upon the premise that consumers can rely upon trademarks to guarantee consistent quality. If goods sold under a single trademark vary in quality, the mark is not serving its intended role as a quality indicator.

Abandonment may also result from altering the mark itself. Trademark owners sometimes make changes to a mark to update the look of the mark or to modify the feel of the mark. For example, General Mills has updated Betty Crocker's look several times over the past decades to reflect changing hair and clothing styles as well as the changing role of women in our society.[9] So long as the old and the new versions of the mark create the same overall commercial impression on buyers, the mark is not abandoned.[10] This determination of creating the same, continuing commercial impression is referred to as "tacking" and is an inquiry that "operates from the perspective of an ordinary purchaser or consumer."[11] As such, whether two trademarks may be tacked in order to determine priority is a question of fact.[12] But, if the new form of the mark has a different commercial impression than the old form of the mark, the old form is deemed abandoned.[13] The effect of this abandonment is twofold: (1) the new mark cannot rely upon the old form to claim priority, and (2) the old form reenters the public domain.

§ 9:26 Loss of trademark rights—Genericide

Research References

West's Key Number Digest, Trademarks ☞1166

Trademark rights are lost if a mark becomes generic. "Genericide" occurs when a once legitimate mark evolves into the common or "generic" name for the product sold under it. Because it depends upon acceptance by the consuming public, genericide generally occurs only after a mark has achieved widespread recognition. A manufacturer's own marketing efforts may con-

---

N.W.2d 677, 112 U.S.P.Q.2d 1661 (2014).

[8]Independent Baking Powder Co. v. Boorman, 175 F. 448 (C.C.D. N.J. 1910).

[9]See U.S. Trademark Registration Nos. 1,508,102; 1,647,768 and 2,457,103.

[10]Sands, Taylor & Wood, 978 F.2d at 955, 24 U.S.P.Q.2d at 1008 (no abandonment of mark changed from

THIRST-AID, FIRST AID FOR YOUR THIRST to THIRST-AID).

[11]Hana Financial, Inc. v. Hana Bank, 135 S. Ct. 907, 190 L. Ed. 2d 800, 113 U.S.P.Q.2d 1365 (2015).

[12]Hana Financial, Inc. v. Hana Bank, 135 S. Ct. 907, 190 L. Ed. 2d 800, 113 U.S.P.Q.2d 1365 (2015).

[13]See Hess's of Allentown, Inc. v. National Bellas Hess, Inc. 169 U.S.P.Q. 673 (T.T.A.B. 1971).

tribute to this.[1] Thus, the owner of a highly successful mark must be particularly careful to guard against generic usage of the mark.

Terms that once were protectable trademarks but now are generic include THERMOS,[2] ESCALATOR,[3] ASPIRIN,[4] YO-YO,[5] CELLOPHANE,[6] TRAMPOLINE,[7] and CUBE STEAK.[8]

If a mark that is federally registered becomes generic, the registration may be canceled.[9] The test for genericness under the Lanham Act is the "primary significance of the registered mark to the purchasing public."[10] A mark that has become generic for only some of the products or services for which it is registered will be canceled only as to those.[11] For example, "Murphy" has been held to be a generic term for a genus of fold-out wall beds.[12] Hypothetically, however, the Murphy Bed Company might be able to retain trademark protection for related products such as "Murphy sheet sets" or "Murphy lounge chairs" assuming the term was not also generic for those products.

A trademark registration for a product configuration may also be canceled if the product configuration becomes generic. The term "generic name" as used in 15 U.S.C.A. § 1064(3) must be read expansively to encompass anything that has the potential, but fails to serve as an indicator of source, such as names, words, symbols, devices, or trade dress. Any narrower interpretation of "generic name" would allow incontestible trademarks, other than names that become generic, to retain incontestible status despite their inability to serve as source designators. Such a proposition would contravene the purposes of the Lanham Act.[13]

It is possible (although difficult) to reclaim a generic term from the public domain by educating consumers to use the term as a

---

[Section 9:26]

[1]Abercrombie & Fitch, 537 F.2d at 9, 189 U.S.P.Q. at 775.

[2]King-Seeley Thermos Co. v. Aladdin Industries, Inc., 321 F.2d 577, 138 U.S.P.Q. 349 (2d Cir. 1963).

[3]Haughton Elevator Company v. Seeberger (Otis Elevator Company Substituted), 85 U.S.P.Q. 80, 1950 WL 4178 (Dec. Comm'r Pat. 1950).

[4]Bayer Co. v. United Drug Co., 272 F. 505 (S.D. N.Y. 1921).

[5]Donald F. Duncan, Inc. v. Royal Tops Mfg. Co., 343 F.2d 655, 144 U.S.P.Q. 617 (7th Cir.1965).

[6]DuPont Cellophane Co. v. Waxed Products Co., 85 F.2d 75, 30 U.S.P.Q. 332 (2d Cir. 1936).

[7]Nissen Trampoline Co. v. American Trampoline Co., 193 F. Supp. 745, 129 U.S.P.Q. 210 (S.D. Iowa 1961).

[8]Spang v. Watson, 205 F.2d 703, 97 U.S.P.Q. 290 (D.C. Cir. 1953).

[9]15 U.S.C.A. § 1064(3).

[10]15 U.S.C.A. § 1064(3).

[11]15 U.S.C.A. § 1064(3).

[12]Murphy Door Bed Co., Inc. v. Interior Sleep Systems, Inc., 874 F.2d 95, 10 U.S.P.Q.2d 1748 (2d Cir. 1989).

[13]Sunrise Jewelry Mfg. Corp. v. Fred S.A., 175 F.3d 1322, 50 U.S.P.Q.2d 1532 (Fed. Cir. 1999).

trademark rather than a generic term.[14] Singer Manufacturing Co. did this with its SINGER trademark. In 1896, the Supreme Court found that the mark had become a generic term for sewing machines.[15] After a period of continuous, extensive advertising designed to educate consumers to associate the mark solely with sewing machines made by Singer, a circuit court found that the mark was recaptured by Singer.[16]

§ 9:27 Preserving trademark rights—Trademark owner's duty to preserve mark

Research References

West's Key Number Digest, Trademarks ☞1152

A trademark owner should take measures to ensure that its trademark rights are not lost. Loss of trademark rights may occur through abandonment or genericide. To prevent a mark from becoming a generic term, the trademark owner should do the following:

- properly designate and use the mark as a trademark,
- distinguish the mark in written text,
- use the mark as an adjective, and
- police third-party usage of the mark.

To prevent unintentional abandonment of the mark, the trademark owner should monitor dates of use. While abandonment requires no set period of nonuse, it should be kept in mind that there is a three-year presumption of abandonment for federally registered marks.[1]

Also, before making any changes to the mark or to the trademarked goods, the owner should determine whether the change would have any negative effect on priority rights in the mark. If the types of goods sold under a mark changes, the trademark owner may not be able to rely upon prior use of the mark for priority purposes. Likewise, if the mark is modified in some manner, such as to update its look, the updated mark could be viewed as an entirely new mark. In such a case, the old version would be deemed abandoned. Consequently, the trademark owner could not "tack on" use of the old version of the mark to its new mark in establishing a date of first use.

---

[14]*See* Singer Mfg. Co. v. Briley, 207 F.2d 519, 99 U.S.P.Q. 303 (5th Cir. 1953).

[15]Singer Mfg. Co. v. June Mfg. Co., 163 U.S. 169, 16 S. Ct. 1002 (1896).

[16]Singer Mfg. Co., 207 F.2d at 520, 99 U.S.P.Q. at 304.

[Section 9:27]

[1]15 U.S.C.A. § 1127.

§ 9:28 Preserving trademark rights—Proper designation of mark

Research References

West's Key Number Digest, Trademarks ⚖1142

The manner in which a mark should be designated depends upon whether or not the mark is registered with the USPTO, and if it is not, the proper designation depends also upon whether the mark is a trademark or a service mark.

The Lanham Act provides that a federally registered mark may be designated by any one of the following notations:

"Registered in U.S. Patent and Trademark Office,"

"Reg. U.S. Pat. & Tm. Off.," or

The letter "R" enclosed within a circle—®.[1]

A trademark, service mark, certification mark or collective mark that is federally registered should be accompanied by one of these designations each time it is displayed. The "R within a circle" symbol is the most commonly used federal designation, since it can easily be integrated into the display of most marks without detracting from the mark's aesthetic appeal.

A mark that is not federally registered should be designated using the notation "TM" for a trademark or "SM" for a service mark. The designation is the same regardless of whether there is a state registration for the mark.

The trademark designation need not be placed in any specific position in relation to a mark. A designation may appear anywhere near the mark, so long as an observer can readily determine what is being designated as a mark.

Properly designating a mark alerts others that the owner is asserting trademark rights in the mark. The trademark designation can also aid a trademark owner in defending against a claim of abandonment. It is evidence of the trademark owner's intent to use and not to abandon the mark.

For federally registered marks, the symbol of registration additionally provides constructive notice of the registration. In the absence of such constructive notice, damages and profits recoverable in a trademark infringement suit are recoverable only for that period of time after the infringer had actual notice of the trademark.[2]

[Section 9:28]

[1]15 U.S.C.A. § 1111.

[2]15 U.S.C.A. § 1111.

§ 9:29   Preserving trademark rights—Distinguishing the mark

Research References

West's Key Number Digest, Trademarks ☞1142

A printed trademark should not only be accompanied by the appropriate designation, it should also be distinguished from other text in some other manner. Some ways of distinguishing a mark are to:

- capitalize the letters of the   ACME
  mark:
- use a special type size or   **Acme**
  typeface:
- set off the mark in quotes: "Acme"

Distinguishing a mark from other text is necessary to show precisely what characters comprise the claimed mark. It also promotes brand recognition by heightening consumer awareness of the mark. The more well-known a mark becomes, the more valuable it is as an advertising tool. Further, a famous mark receives greater protection from infringement. And, if the mark is a descriptive term, consumer awareness can create secondary meaning in the mark so as to support registration on the Principal Register.

§ 9:30   Preserving trademark rights—Using the mark as an adjective

Research References

West's Key Number Digest, Trademarks ☞1154

To prevent a trademark from becoming generic, the mark should always be used as an adjective, never a noun. The word "brand" can be effective in accomplishing this—"JELL-O Brand gelatin," not "JELL-O." When a mark begins to be used as a noun in referring to the goods, it is on its way to becoming generic. The mark should not be used in plural or possessive form, as this implies that it is a noun. Trademarks are easily misused in advertising copy, so in many cases a trademark owner is its own worst enemy. Advertisements and promotional materials should all be reviewed for proper usage of the mark as an adjective.

If the product sold under a mark is a new product for which there is no common name, the trademark owner must coin a common name for it. This coined name must be different from the trademark, so that the trademark has a generic noun to modify. In other words, the trademark owner must be able to answer the question "what is your product called?" without using the trademark. Otherwise, the trademark is destined to become the generic term for the product. The trademark owner may have to embark on an advertising campaign to educate the public that its trademark is not a generic name. Sometimes, despite taking all reasonable steps to prevent it, the public adopts the trademark as the common name for a product. In such a case, an effort can be made to reclaim the mark from generic use. But, this generally takes an expensive advertising campaign, and there is no guarantee that it will be successful.

§ 9:31 Preserving trademark rights—Policing third-party use

Research References
West's Key Number Digest, Trademarks ☜1165

To maintain all of its trademark rights, a trademark owner must be vigilant in policing third-party use of its trademark. The trademark owner must watch for two things: third-party usage of its trademark as a generic term and infringement of the mark.

As discussed above, a trademark should be used as an adjective rather than as a noun. Many trademark owners advertise to promote correct usage of their marks. Many also send "press-kits" to media copy editors instructing them on correct usage of the term. Marks may also be listed with the International Trademark Association (INTA), which maintains a glossary of commonly misused marks for reference by the media. A trademark owner should spot-check print media that is likely to contain references to its mark to ascertain whether the mark is being used correctly. Anytime an incorrect usage is found, the user should be contacted and instructed on how to properly use the mark.

Likewise, a trademark owner should take measures to stop or prevent others from infringing its mark. Infringement occurs where a junior user adopts a mark that is likely to be confused with a senior user's mark. Anytime a trademark owner becomes aware of a use that it believes infringes its trademark, the owner should put the third party on notice of the owner's trademark rights. The notice should include a demand that the third party immediately cease and desist use of the mark. The trademark owner should attempt to get a written statement from the infringer agreeing to discontinue use. If the infringer insists on continuing its use, the trademark owner should consider the necessity of bringing an infringement suit. Policing unauthorized use in this manner preserves the maximum remedies and damages for infringement under federal and state law. Additionally, a trademark is given a greater breadth of protection under the law if similar marks are not in use by third parties.[1]

It is advisable to monitor the Official Gazette of the USPTO for publication of similar marks that third parties are attempting to register. If it is believed that a published mark is likely to cause confusion with the trademark owner's mark, an opposition should be filed.[2] Similarly, if the trademark owner discovers that a mark likely to be confused with its own has registered, a petition for cancellation should be filed.[3]

§ 9:32 Selecting a trademark—Conduct a trademark clearance search

Research References

West's Key Number Digest, Trademarks ☞1131

A trademark should be carefully selected so as to avoid infringement of existing marks. This can be done by conducting a trademark clearance search prior to adopting a mark. Other considerations in adopting a trademark should include the realm of legal protection it would be given, and whether the mark comprises subject matter that is federally registrable.

A trademark clearance search should be conducted before a mark is adopted. Failure to perform a trademark search to determine whether a proposed mark is available before making a significant investment in signs, advertising, packaging, and point-of-sale material can be extremely expensive. Neither cost nor time considerations are an excuse for failing to perform at least some form of trademark searching. It is far better to find out at the front end that a proposed mark is already in use by someone else. Adopting a mark already used by someone else constitutes trademark infringement.

Also, before making any proposed change to a mark or to the goods on which it is used, a trademark owner should consider whether the change would create a likelihood of confusion with another party's mark. Particularly, before applying a mark to a radically different type of goods, a trademark clearance search should be conducted.

Preliminary searches can be completed in hours. With the

[Section 9:31]

[1]Andy Warhol Enterprises, Inc. v. Time Inc., 700 F. Supp. 760, 764, 9 U.S.P.Q.2d 1454, 1460 (S.D. N.Y. 1988).

[2]See discussion of oppositions in § 9:38.

[3]See discussion of cancellations in § 9:39.

development of computerized databases for trademark searching, trademark practitioners are often able to provide same-day reports on whether a particular mark or corporate name will face a trademark infringement problem. A relatively large number of marks initially selected by clients turn out to be unavailable because of existing federal registrations or applications that show up in a computer trademark search.

A more complete or full search can also be performed. A full search covers not only federal registrations, but also state registrations, and common law usages found in trade directories, and lists of company names. Once again, the cost of a full search is insignificant compared to possible infringement charges, wasted production time and wasted materials bearing an unusable mark.

Even before a trademark search is performed, there are several other simple, yet easily overlooked, ways of detecting a potential trademark problem. One easy way is to perform an Internet search to see whether there are any companies with similar names. Such listings may include foreign corporations not registered to do business in the state. However, they can still represent potential trademark problems. Also, perform an Internet search for the particular types of goods or services intended to be provided under the mark. Finally, an inquiry to the Secretary of State can be made to ascertain whether any corporate names or trademark registrations appear to conflict with the proposed mark.

If any of these simple and quick checks or a full search turns up a questionable situation, alternative marks should be considered. It is far better to be flexible at the early stages, before significant investments are made. Business owners tend to become very inflexible about their chosen marks once they become emotionally (as well as financially) committed to them.

§ 9:33 Selecting a trademark—Consider strength of mark

Research References

West's Key Number Digest, Trademarks ⬥1029

The strength of a potential trademark is an important consideration in selecting a mark. A mark is strong if it has a distinct tendency to identify the goods or services sold under it as emanating from a particular source. The strength of a newly adopted mark depends upon where it falls along the distinctiveness continuum. Fanciful marks are the strongest, followed by arbitrary, suggestive and descriptive marks. Generic terms are not marks at all.

Stronger marks receive greater protection from infringement.

Additionally, fanciful, arbitrary and suggestive marks are considered inherently distinctive and are protectable immediately upon use in a trademark sense. Descriptive marks are not protectable until they become distinctive by acquiring "secondary meaning" to the purchasing public, which typically takes a period of years. A would-be trademark owner should thus give serious thought to adopting a mark that is either fanciful, arbitrary or suggestive.

§ 9:34   Selecting a trademark—Avoid unregistrable subject matter

Research References
West's Key Number Digest, Trademarks ⊂⟩1072

Subject matter that is not registrable on the federal register should be avoided if maximum trademark protection is desired. Unregistrable subject matter includes such things as immoral or scandalous matter, disparaging matter, insignia of the United States or foreign nations, Olympic symbols, and the portrait or signature of a living person without consent. A detailed discussion of unregisterable subject matter can be found in §§ 10:24 to 10:32. A potential mark should be evaluated for any subject matter that may preclude federal registration. If the potential mark contains any subject matter that is even arguably unregistrable, adoption of a different mark should be considered. It can be costly to pursue or defend a registration that contains arguably unregistrable subject matter. Additionally, state statutes and common law generally follow federal trademark law as to proscribed subject matter, so a mark that is not registerable on the federal register may not be protectable as a trademark at all.

Chapter 10

Registering Trademarks

KeyCite®: Cases and other legal materials listed in KeyCite Scope can be researched through the KeyCite service on Westlaw®. Use KeyCite to check citations for form, parallel references, prior and later history, and comprehensive citator information, including citations to other decisions and secondary materials.

§ 10:1 Advantages of federal trademark registration

Research References

West's Key Number Digest, Trademarks ⟹1350 to 1357

Although trademark rights are available under common law and under state statutes, registering a trademark under federal law provides a number of advantages.

Registering a mark on the principal register gives nationwide constructive notice to others of a registrant's claim to own the mark.[1] Those adopting the mark after the date of application to register the mark cannot use the mark in good faith.[2]

Registration on the Principal Register serves as prima facie evidence of the registrant's exclusive right to use the mark.[3] The registrant also benefits from a presumption that the date of first use cited on the registration certificate is the actual first date of use.[4]

The right to use a mark registered on the Principal Register in continuous use for five consecutive years after the registration date becomes "incontestable."[5] To trigger the incontestable status, the registrant must file an affidavit (known as a § 15 affidavit)

[Section 10:1]

[1]15 U.S.C.A. § 1072.

[2]15 U.S.C.A. § 1072; Dawn Donut Co. v. Hart's Food Stores, Inc., 267 F.2d 358, 121 U.S.P.Q. 430 (2d Cir. 1959).

[3]15 U.S.C.A. § 1057(b).

[4]Zazu Designs v. L'Oreal, S.A., 979 F.2d 499, 24 U.S.P.Q.2d 1828 (7th Cir. 1992) (*citing* Rolley, Inc. v. Younghusband, 204 F.2d 209, 97 U.S.P.Q. 252 (9th Cir. 1953)).

[5]15 U.S.C.A. § 1065.

attesting to five years of consecutive use.[6] Incontestability may be challenged only if the mark is later abandoned, if the registration was obtained fraudulently, if the mark is being used to misrepresent the source of the goods or services in connection with which it is used, or if the mark becomes generic.[7]

Federal registration also allows registrants to display the circle-R registration symbol "®" or the words "Registered in the U.S. Patent and Trademark Office" or "Reg. U.S. Pat. & Tm. Off." with the registered mark.[8] Failing to use this symbol or to provide another form of actual notice precludes recovery of infringement damages under federal law.[9]

Registering a mark further gives the registrant the right to record the mark with the Bureau of Customs to stop importation of goods bearing infringing marks.[10]

§ 10:2   Trademark examination within the USPTO— Sources of law

Research References

West's Key Number Digest, Trademarks ⟜1287

The Federal Trademark Act of 1946 (the "Lanham Act") is a comprehensive act governing the registration and protection of trademarks used in commerce. Although codified at 15 U.S.C.A. §§ 1051 et seq., references to the Lanham Act often recite its original section numbers (§§ 1 et seq.).

Title 37 of the Code of Federal Regulations (37 C.F.R.) lists the rules of practice in patent and trademark cases. These rules, made by the Commissioner of Patents and Trademarks, have binding legal authority to the extent they are not inconsistent with the trademark statutes.

The Trademark Manual of Examining Procedure (T.M.E.P.), which is published by the Patent and Trademark Office (USPTO), contains the guidelines and procedures for the USPTO's trademark examination practices. The T.M.E.P. reflects the USPTO's interpretations of current trademark law and thus provides only persuasive legal authority. USPTO trademark examiners, also called examining attorneys, follow the procedures outlined in the T.M.E.P. for examining trademark applications. The T.M.E.P., however, is also intended to assist the applicant.

---

[6]15 U.S.C.A. § 1065.

[7]15 U.S.C.A. § 1065; Park 'N Fly, Inc. v. Dollar Park and Fly, Inc., 469 U.S. 189, 105 S. Ct. 658, 224 U.S.P.Q. 327 (1985).

[8]15 U.S.C.A. § 1111.

[9]15 U.S.C.A. § 1111.

[10]15 U.S.C.A. § 1124.

§ 10:3 Trademark examination within the USPTO—Basic registration scheme

Research References

West's Key Number Digest, Trademarks ☞1061 to 1067

The Lanham Act provides for federal registration of four types of marks: trademarks, service marks, collective marks and certification marks. Trademarks and service marks are more common than collective and certification marks. In this text (and elsewhere), the term "trademark" or "mark" generally refers to trademarks and service marks, unless otherwise indicated.

The Lanham Act defines a "trademark" as a word, name, symbol, device or combination thereof used not only to identify and distinguish marked goods from those manufactured or sold by others, but also to indicate the source of the marked goods.[1] This definition, which has been interpreted broadly, encompasses virtually any designation capable of distinguishing the source of goods.[2] Registrable forms of trademarks include words, numbers, letters, designs, slogans, product and package configurations, colors, sounds, and fragrances.

A "service mark" is a word, name, symbol, device, or combination thereof used to identify and distinguish the services of one person from the services of others and to indicate the source of the services.[3] A service mark registration can be obtained even if the applicant provides services solely to its own members.[4] Service marks are just trademarks used to identify services rather than goods. Like trademarks, service marks may assume any form capable of distinguishing goods. In this text, "trademarks" should be understood to include service marks, and "goods" should be understood to include services, unless otherwise indicated.

A "collective mark" is a trademark or service mark that denotes the goods or services of members of a collective group, such as a cooperative or an association, and a collective membership mark is a mark that denotes membership in a collective group, such as a union, association, or other organization.[5] A collective mark is owned by the collective, or parent organization, which controls use of the mark by its members and which may itself use the mark as a trademark or a service mark.[6] With permission of the collective, each member of the collective may apply the collective

---

[Section 10:3]

[1]15 U.S.C.A. § 1127.

[2]Qualitex Co. v. Jacobson Products Co., Inc., 514 U.S. 159, 115 S. Ct. 1300, 34 U.S.P.Q.2d 1161 (1995).

[3]15 U.S.C.A. § 1127.

[4]Capital Speakers Inc. v. Capital Speakers Club of Washington D.C. Inc., 41 U.S.P.Q.2d 1030, 1996 WL 754043 (T.T.A.B. 1996).

[5]15 U.S.C.A. § 1127.

[6]T.M.E.P. § 1304.

mark to its own goods or services. In the case of a collective membership mark, each group member may use the membership mark to show its membership in the group.

A "certification mark" is a word, name, symbol, device, or any combination thereof, used by a person other than its owner to certify some characteristic of goods or services sold under the mark.[7] Characteristics commonly certified include standards of safety and quality, place of origin, mode of manufacture, and material of manufacture. The mark may also certify that members of a union or other organization made the goods or rendered the services.[8] Unlike collective marks, certification marks are not trademarks because they do not indicate the source of goods or services.

§ 10:4   Trademark examination within the USPTO—Principal and supplemental registers

Research References

West's Key Number Digest, Trademarks ☞1240, 1245, 1246

The USPTO maintains both a Principal Register and a Supplemental Register of trademarks. The Principal Register includes marks that are unique or distinctive indicators of a single source of goods and services, while the Supplemental Register includes marks that, while capable of serving as an indicator of a single source of goods and services, fail to indicate a single source at the present time.[1] Marks that are ineligible for the Principal Register are often eligible for registration on the Supplemental Register. For instance, a mark such as STICKY STUFF which is descriptive of its associated goods, glue, is ineligible for the Principal Register unless the mark has acquired a secondary meaning identifying a single source. A descriptive mark, however, is registrable on the Supplemental Register without proving secondary meaning.

Marks on the Principal Register have full benefit of the trademark laws, whereas marks on the Supplemental Register have only partial benefit. For example, an owner of a mark on the Supplemental Register cannot enlist the Bureau of Customs to stop the importation of goods bearing infringing marks.[2] Therefore, if a mark is eligible, an application to register the mark should request registration on the Principal Register.

---

[7] 15 U.S.C.A. § 1127.

[8] 15 U.S.C.A. § 1127.

[2] 15 U.S.C.A. § 1096.

[Section 10:4]

[1] 15 U.S.C.A. §§ 1052 and 1091.

However, a mark on the Supplemental Register may later attain secondary meaning and qualify for registration on the Principal Register.[3] In such a case, the owner may file a new application to register the mark on the Principal Register. Generally, five years of continuous use is required to re-register a mark from the Supplemental Register onto the Principal Register.

§ 10:5   Trademark examination within the USPTO— Classification system

Research References

West's Key Number Digest, Trademarks ⟜1287

To facilitate trademark searches and examinations, the USPTO uses numerical classification schedules to organize marks according to their associated goods and services.[1] The USPTO uses two numerical classification schedules: a primary International Classification schedule and a secondary U.S. Classification schedule used for registrations stemming from applications filed before adoption of the International schedule.[2] Although the International schedule is the primary schedule, the USPTO refers to both schedules in its trademark searches and thus assigns both U.S. and International class numbers to trademark applications and registrations.

The current International Classification schedule has 45 classes, including 34 classes of goods and 11 classes of services.[3] Each International Class has an unofficial descriptive name, such as "Vehicles" for class 12 and "Games and Playthings" for class 28, to help identify the class. The U.S. schedule includes 52 classes of goods and 8 service classes.[4] Certification marks are divided between two classes, one for goods and the other for services, and collective membership marks have their own class.[5]

In addition to facilitating searches, the classification schedule is the basis for trademark application filing fees. The filing fees depend on the number of classes of goods and services indicated in the application. A single trademark may be registered in a number of classes, provided its associated goods or services qualify for each separate class. In some cases, a mark for a single product may be registered in several classes, based on the multiple uses of the product.[6] For example, the mark WARTHOG for armored tanks may be registered in International Classes 12

---

[3]15 U.S.C.A. § 1052(f).

[Section 10:5]

[1]15 U.S.C.A. § 1112; 37 C.F.R. § 2.85.

[2]37 C.F.R. § 2.85.

[3]37 C.F.R. § 6.1.

[4]37 C.F.R. § 6.2.

[5]37 C.F.R. §§ 6.3, 6.4.

[6]T.M.E.P. § 1401.07.

for vehicles and 13 for firearms.

§ 10:6 Trademark examination within the USPTO— Priority between multiple users

Research References

West's Key Number Digest, Trademarks ⇔1137, 1288

Sometimes more than one applicant attempts to register the same mark or a substantially similar mark. In these cases, the applicant whose application has the earliest filing date gains the right to have its mark published for opposition in the Official Gazette or registered on the Supplemental Register.[1] If the applicants have the same filing date, the application with the earliest date of execution receives priority.[2] Applications that lose the battle for priority are suspended until the priority mark is registered or abandoned.[3] The only way for the later filed mark to become registered is with a successful opposition or cancellation of the prior filed mark or with a concurrent use registration, which is most commonly achieved by agreement of the parties involved.

§ 10:7 Types of applications for trademark registration— Use-based applications

Research References

West's Key Number Digest, Trademarks ⇔1287

A use-based application, also called an application under § 1(a), is an application to register a mark based on actual use in commerce.[1] The use-based application must assert that the applicant has adopted and is commercially using the mark as shown in the application's drawing.[2] "Use in commerce," or commercial use, means a bona fide, legal use in the ordinary course of trade.[3] Using a mark merely to reserve trademark rights is not a "bona fide" use.[4] The term "commerce" includes any commerce that Congress can regulate, i.e., interstate commerce.[5]

Using a trademark in commerce requires using the mark on the goods, containers for the goods, tags or labels affixed to the

---

[Section 10:6]
[1]37 C.F.R. § 2.83(a).
[2]37 C.F.R. § 2.83(b).
[3]37 C.F.R. § 2.83(c); T.M.E.P. § 907.

[Section 10:7]
[1]15 U.S.C.A. § 1051(a).

[2]37 C.F.R. § 2.33(b)(1).
[3]15 U.S.C.A. § 1127.
[4]15 U.S.C.A. § 1127.
[5]15 U.S.C.A. § 1127.

goods, or displays associated with the goods. If placing the mark on the goods is impractical, use in commerce requires including the mark on documents associated with the goods or their sale.[6] A web page displaying a product and also providing a means of ordering the product can qualify as a "document" associated with the goods, as long as the mark appears on the web page in a manner that associates the mark with the product.[7] Using a trademark in commerce also requires actually selling or transporting the goods in commerce.[8] Using a service mark, on the other hand, requires using or displaying the mark in the selling or advertising of services and in performing the services in commerce.[9] Alternatively, one may establish use of a service mark by performing the services commercially in more than one state or in the United States and a foreign country.[10]

A use-based application must identify the date of applicant's first use of the mark in commerce, or the date of the first use of the mark in commerce which inures to the applicant's benefit.[11] The date of first use in commerce is the date on which the goods were first sold or transported, or the date on which the services were first rendered, under the mark in a type of commerce that may be lawfully regulated by Congress if such use is bona fide and in the ordinary course of trade.[12]

The applicant may not file an application on the basis of use of a mark in commerce if such use has been discontinued.[13]

If incorrect dates of use have been specified for any reason, an amendment of dates must be supported by an affidavit or declaration under 37 C.F.R. § 2.20. Applicants are not permitted to amend a date of first use that is later than the filing date of the application.[14]

In specifying the dates of first use, the applicant should give dates that are as definite as possible.[15] If the applicant provides a date that is not specific, the examining attorney will take the last date that falls within the applicant's identification.[16] Thus, for example, "October 2003" is interpreted as "October 31, 2003."

An applicant is not required to specify the type of commerce in which the mark is in use. The USPTO presumes that an applicant who states that the mark is in use in commerce is stating that the mark is in use in a type of commerce that Congress can

---

[6]15 U.S.C.A. § 1127.

[7]In re Dell Inc., 71 U.S.P.Q.2d 1725, 1727, 2004 WL 1942043 (T.T.A.B. 2004).

[8]Dell, 71 U.S.P.Q.2d at 1727.

[9]Dell, 71 U.S.P.Q.2d at 1727.

[10]Dell, 71 U.S.P.Q.2d at 1727.

[11]37 C.F.R. § 2.34(a)(1).

[12]T.M.E.P. § 903.02.

[13]T.M.E.P. § 903.02.

[14]37 C.F.R. § 2.71(c).

[15]T.M.E.P. § 903.06.

[16]T.M.E.P. § 903.06.

regulate, such as interstate, territorial and commerce between the United States and a foreign country.[17]

A purely intrastate use is insufficient to establish the federal jurisdiction basis for an application to register. However, if an intrastate sale directly affects a type of commerce that may lawfully be regulated by Congress, this may be sufficient "use in commerce" to support the application.[18] An applicant whose claimed use in commerce is intrastate in nature must submit a verified statement that "the mark is in use in commerce that can be regulated by Congress," or amend the basis of the application to an intent-to-use application.[19]

§ 10:8   Types of applications for trademark registration— Intent-to-use applications

Research References
West's Key Number Digest, Trademarks ☞1141

An intent-to-use (ITU) application, also called an application under § 1(b), is an application to register a mark based on a bona fide intent to use the mark in commerce.[1] ITU applications allow the applicant to reserve marks before actual use in commerce. However, the USPTO only registers marks after actual use in commerce has taken place. Thus, even though an ITU application reserves the mark, actual registration hinges on actual use of the mark.

The ability to reserve, or hold, a mark until actual use adds greater certainty to business and market planning. In particular, it gives prospective registrants some assurance that the marks they desire for products under development will be available when the products finally reach the market. Before the 1988 debut of ITU applications, businesses risked enormous sums developing and refining products for market only to lose their desired marks to others who actually used the marks before they did.

"Use" of a mark must be "bona fide" use of the mark in the ordinary course of trade.[2] "Bona fide" means that sales of marked goods must be part of an ongoing program to exploit the mark commercially, and not just an attempt to establish trademark

---

[17]T.M.E.P. § 901.03.

[18]*See* Larry Harmon Pictures Corp. v. Williams Restaurant Corp., 929 F.2d 662, 18 U.S.P.Q.2d 1292 (Fed. Cir. 1991).

[19]T.M.E.P. § 901.04.

[Section 10:8]
[1]15 U.S.C.A. § 1051(b).
[2]15 U.S.C.A. § 1127.

rights.[3] Token uses, such as affixing a mark to a few products and selling those products to a prearranged buyer across state lines, will not provide an acceptable "bona fide" use of a mark.

§ 10:9 Types of applications for trademark registration—Applications based on foreign applications

Research References
West's Key Number Digest, Trademarks ⚿1266

A § 44(d) application is an application based on a foreign trademark application combined with actual use or intent to use.[1] Section 44(d) grants filing-date priority to the applicant who has previously filed applications to register its marks in a treaty country. A treaty country is a country that has signed a treaty governing trademark relations between it and the United States.[2] If a qualified applicant files its U.S. application within six months of filing its first application to register the mark in the applicant's home country, and the home country is a treaty country, the USPTO treats its U.S. application as if it were filed on the filing date of that foreign application.[3] In other words, the U.S. application has an effective filing date earlier than its actual U.S. filing date. This procedure is known as giving the applicant its priority date. A similar procedure is available to U.S. applicants filing in treaty countries.

The filing date is significant because it constitutes a constructive date of first use in the United States for purposes of determining priority of publication under 37 C.F.R. § 2.83. Thus, the § 44(d) application receives priority over any other application that might otherwise pose a possible bar to registration because of likelihood of confusion, provided that the other application has a filing date later than the § 44(d) applicant's priority filing date.[4]

Any foreign application used to gain an earlier priority date must be the applicant's first application in a treaty country for the same mark and for the same goods or services. If the relevant application was not the first filed, the examining attorney must refuse registration on the grounds the application was void as

---

[3]La Societe Anonyme des Parfums le Galion v. Jean Patou, Inc., 495 F.2d 1265, 1272, 181 U.S.P.Q. 545, 549 (2d Cir. 1974).

[Section 10:9]
[1]15 U.S.C.A. § 1126(d) (also known as § 44(d) of the Lanham Act).

[2]15 U.S.C.A. § 1126(b).

[3]15 U.S.C.A. § 1126(d).

[4]37 C.F.R. § 2.83; T.M.E.P. § 1003.05.

filed.[5] Therefore, it is important to determine not only whether the foreign application is the first application for the mark, but also whether it was filed within six months of filing the U.S. application.

An application filed in the United States under § 44(d) will be treated as if it were filed in the United States on the same date as the filing in the foreign country for the purpose of determining priority for publication under 37 C.F.R. § 2.83.

The foreign application, standing alone, does not provide a basis for registration. The applicant must have a separate basis for registration in the United States. Thus, the earlier foreign application must be combined with actual use in commerce, an intent to use in commerce, an actual foreign registration or the final grant of the foreign registration upon which the § 44(d) application was based.[6] The § 44(d) application must also include a statement indicating the filing date of the foreign application, the foreign country where it was filed, the serial number of the foreign application, and a statement claiming priority from the foreign application.[7]

If the applicant fails to file the U.S. application within six months of the foreign application, the applicant may not apply in the United States until it actually uses the mark, establishes a bona fide intent to use the mark, or provides a certification or certified copy of a foreign registration for the mark. Thus, failing to apply within the six month period may significantly delay the applicant's ability to file in the United States.[8]

§ 10:10 Types of applications for trademark registration—Applications based on foreign registrations

Research References

West's Key Number Digest, Trademarks ⬤1266

A § 44(e) application is an application based on a foreign trademark registration.[1] An application relying on a foreign registration must include a certification or certified copy of the

---

[5]T.M.E.P. § 1003.01.

[6]T.M.E.P. § 1003.

[7]37 C.F.R. § 2.34(a)(4).

[8]T.M.E.P. § 1003.02.

[Section 10:10]

[1]15 U.S.C.A. § 1126(e) (also

known as § 44(e) of the Lanham Act). A § 44(e) application is not based on a Madrid Protocol registration. Rather, an application based on a Madrid Protocol registration is known as a § 66(a) application and is discussed in § 9:12, *infra*.

foreign registration and an English translation of it.[2] The application must also include a statement of a bona fide intention to use the mark in commerce.[3] In order to be registered on the Principal Register, the application must still meet the registration requirements of the Lanham Act, 15 U.S.C.A. § 1052.[4]

The foreign registration must be in force when the United States issues a registration based on the foreign registration. If the foreign registration could expire before the United States registration issues, the applicant should submit certification showing that the foreign registration has been renewed and will be in effect when the U.S. registration issues.[5]

The § 44(e) applicant in the United States must be the owner of the foreign registration relied upon in the United States on the date of filing.[6] If the foreign registration identifies a party other than the applicant in the United States as the owner, the Office will accept the application, grant a filing date, and will require the applicant to establish that the United States applicant was the owner of the foreign registration on the date of filing in the United States. Failure to do so will make the application void as filed.[7]

If the foreign registration is not in English, the applicant must also provide a translation of the foreign registration with the certification or certified copy of the foreign registration.[8] The translator should sign the translation but need not swear to the translation.[9] This translation may be submitted after filing the application. If the foreign registration becomes abandoned some time during the prosecution of the United States application, the applicant should notify the examining attorney. In such an instance, the examining attorney will advise the applicant that the United States application is void unless the applicant has another basis for registration at the time of filing in the United States.[10]

§ 10:11 Types of applications for trademark registration—The Madrid Protocol and international registration of marks

Research References
West's Key Number Digest, Trademarks ⬮1261

---

[2]37 C.F.R. § 2.34(a)(3)(ii).

[3]37 C.F.R. § 2.34(a)(3)(i).

[4]In re Rath, 402 F.3d 1207, 1212, 74 U.S.P.Q.2d 1174 (Fed. Cir. 2005).

[5]37 C.F.R. § 2.34(a)(3)(iii); T.M.E.P. § 1004.01(a).

[6]T.M.E.P. § 1005; In re De Luxe, N.V., 990 F.2d 607, 26 U.S.P.Q.2d 1475 (Fed. Cir. 1993).

[7]T.M.E.P. § 1005.

[8]37 C.F.R. § 2.34(a)(3)(iii).

[9]T.M.E.P. § 1004.01(b).

[10]T.M.E.P. § 1004.01(a).

The Protocol Relating to the Madrid Agreement Concerning the International Registration of Marks ("Madrid Protocol") is an international treaty that allows a trademark owner the possibility to protect its mark in any of the Madrid Protocol countries by filing a single application.[1] In November 2003, the Madrid Protocol went into effect in the United States.[2] As of February 2013, the Madrid Protocol has 88 member countries.

A United States trademark owner can submit an "international application" to the USPTO to seek registration of the mark in any of the countries that have joined the Madrid Protocol.[3] The United States trademark owner must have an application filed in or a registration issued by the USPTO.[4] In addition, the trademark owner must be a national of the United States, have a domicile in the United States, or have a real and effective industrial or commercial establishment in the United States.[5]

The requirements for an international application originating in the United States are: (1) a basic application or a basic registration in the United States; (2) the same mark, owner and description of the mark as the mark, owner and description of the mark of the basic application or registration; (3) a color claim if appropriate; (4) an indication of the type of mark if the mark in the basic application and/or registration is a three-dimensional mark, a sound mark, a collective mark or a certification mark; (5) a list of the goods and/or services that is identical to or narrower than the list of goods and/or services in each claimed basic application or registration; (6) a list of designated Contracting Parties (i.e., countries the applicant would like the mark registered in); (7) the certification fee, the international application fees for all classes, and the fees for all designated Contracting Parties; (8) a statement that the applicant is entitled to file an international application in the USPTO; and (9) an e-mail address for receipt of correspondence.[6]

Once the international application meets the filing requirements, the USPTO certifies that certain information in the international application based on a United States basic applica-

---

[Section 10:11]

[1]Madrid Protocol, June 27, 1989, I.P.L.T. MT 3-007, *available at* http://www.wipo.int/madrid/en/legal_texts/pdf/madrid_protocol.pdf; *see also* Common Regulations Under the Protocol Relating to the Madrid Agreement Concerning the International Registration of Marks And Protocol Relating to That Agreement ("Common Regulations"), ch. 2 (April 1, 2004), *available at* http://www.wipo.int/madrid/en/legal_text s/pdf/common_regulations.pdf.

[2]Madrid Protocol Implementation Act of 2002, Pub.L. 107-273, 116 Stat. 1758, 1913 to 1921 ("MPIA").

[3]Madrid Protocol, art. 2.

[4]37 C.F.R. § 7.11, T.M.E.P. § 1901.

[5]37 C.F.R. § 7.11, T.M.E.P. § 1901.

[6]37 C.F.R. § 7.11, T.M.E.P. § 1902.02.

tion or registration is the same as the information contained in the basic application or registration.[7] The USPTO then forwards the international application to the International Bureau.[8]

The International Bureau reviews the international application to determine whether the Madrid Protocol filing requirements have been met.[9] If the requirements are met and the fees paid, the International Bureau will register the mark, publish it in the *WIPO Gazette of International Marks* ("WIPO Gazette"), send a certificate to the international applicant, and notify the Offices of the Contracting Parties designated in the international application.[10] The applicant may designate additional Contracting Parties in a subsequent designation.[11]

Each of the designated Contracting Parties examines the request for an extension of protection (or territorial extension) to that country and examines the mark the same as it would a national application under its laws.[12] If the international application meets the requirements for registration for that country, the Contracting Party will grant protection of the mark in its country.[13] A Contracting Party must refuse to grant an extension of protection in 18 months and notify the International Bureau of such refusal, or the holder of the international registration is automatically granted protection of its mark in that country.[14] An international registration has a 10-year term from the date of registration and may be renewed for additional 10-year periods with payment of a renewal fee to the International Bureau.[15]

§ 10:12 Types of applications for trademark registration—Applications based on an international registration under the Madrid Protocol

A § 66(a) application finds its basis in an international application or registration under the Madrid Protocol.[1] Specifically, a § 66(a) application refers to a request by the trademark holder for extension of protection of the international registration to the

---

[7]37 C.F.R. § 7.13, T.M.E.P. § 1902.03.

[8]37 C.F.R. § 7.13, T.M.E.P. § 1902.03.

[9]*See* Madrid Protocol, arts. 3 and 11; *see also* Common Regulations, ch. 2 rule 11.

[10]Common Regulations, ch. 3 rule 14.

[11]37 C.F.R. § 7.21.

[12]Madrid Protocol, arts. 3ter and 4, T.M.E.P. § 1901.

[13]Madrid Protocol, art. 4, T.M.E.P. § 1901.

[14]Madrid Protocol, art. 5, T.M.E.P. § 1901.

[15]Madrid Protocol, arts. 6 and 7, T.M.E.P. § 1905.

[Section 10:12]

[1]T.M.E.P. § 1201.

United States under the Madrid Protocol.[2] After the request is made, the International Bureau forwards the necessary application papers and fees to the USPTO.

The request for extension of protection to the United States may be included in the international application, or in a subsequent designation made after the International Bureau registers the mark.[3] The filing date of the § 66(a) application is the international registration date, or if the request for extension of protection to the United States is made in a subsequent designation, the filing date is the date the subsequent designation was recorded by the International Bureau.[4] If the International Bureau receives the international application within two months of the date of receipt in the Office of Origin, the date of the international registration is the date of receipt in the Office of Origin. Otherwise, the date of the international registration is the date the international application was received by the International Bureau.[5]

The USPTO examines the § 66(a) application under the same standards as any other application for registration on the Principal Register.[6] If the proposed mark is not registrable on the Principal Register, the USPTO must refuse the extension of protection.[7] While actual use is not required, a § 66(a) application must include a declaration that the applicant has a bona fide intention to use the mark in commerce that can be controlled by Congress.[8] The international classification of goods/services in a § 66(a) application cannot be changed from the classification given to the goods/services by the International Bureau.[9]

The USPTO will issue a certificate of extension of protection after the USPTO finds the mark meets the standards for registration, and the mark is not opposed, or survives all oppositions filed.[10] A registered extension of protection always remains part of and dependent upon the international registration.[11] If the international registration becomes abandoned, the USPTO will cancel the certificate of extension of protection. In this respect, a registered extension of protection differs from a § 44 registration,

[2]37 C.F.R. § 7.25(b); 15 U.S.C.A. § 1141e(a). The request for extension of protection to the United States may not be based on a U.S.P.T.O. basic application or registration. T.M.E.P. § 1904.01(h).

[3]37 C.F.R. § 7.25(b); T.M.E.P. § 1904.01.

[4]15 U.S.C.A. § 1141f(b); 37 C.F.R. § 7.26.

[5]T.M.E.P. § 1901.

[6]T.M.E.P. § 1904.02(a).

[7]15 U.S.C.A. § 1141h(a)(4); 37 C.F.R. §§ 2.47(c) and 2.75(c).

[8]15 U.S.C.A. § 1141f(a); T.M.E.P. §§ 1904.01(c), 1902.05.

[9]T.M.E.P. § 1904.02(b).

[10]15 U.S.C.A. § 1141i(a); T.M.E.P. § 1904.05.

[11]15 U.S.C.A. § 1141i(a); T.M.E.P. § 1904.05.

which is independent from the underlying foreign registration. If the certificate of extension is canceled, the holder of the international registration may "transform" the cancelled registered extension of protection (or request for extension of protection) into an application under § 1 or § 44 of the Lanham Act.[12]

If the mark does not meet the standards for registration, the USPTO must send a notification of refusal of the request for extension of protection to the International Bureau within 18 months of receiving the request. After that time, the request for extension of protection cannot be refused.[13]

§ 10:13 Requirements of the application

Research References

West's Key Number Digest, Trademarks ⟐1287

In general, applying to register a mark requires filing a drawing of the mark, filing a fee for each class of goods or services actually used or intended for use with the mark, and filing a written application.[1] The application, written in English, includes several elements: (1) the name of the applicant, (2) the name and address to be used for communications, (3) a drawing of the mark, (4) identification of the goods, (5) basis for registration (including at least one specimen in use-based applications), and (6) the filing fee for at least one class of goods.[2]

The United States now accepts trademark applications on-line through its Trademark Electronic Application System ("TEAS") accessible from the USPTO website at www.uspto.gov. An on-line application is available at the website and requires similar obligations to a traditional paper application.[3] There are two main differences with the on-line application: a drawing of the mark (if the mark consists of stylized wording or a design) and a specimen of use are both submitted as *.JPG image files or *.PDF files to the USPTO,[4] and the filing fees for an on-line application are less.

§ 10:14 Requirements of the application—Information about the mark and its owner

Research References

West's Key Number Digest, Trademarks ⟐1287

---

[12]15 U.S.C.A. § 1141j; T.M.E.P. § 1904.09.

[13]T.M.E.P. § 1904.03(a).

[Section 10:13]

[1]37 C.F.R. §§ 2.21 and 2.32; (4).

T.M.E.P. § 818.

[2]37 C.F.R. §§ 2.21(a) and 2.32.

[3]37 C.F.R. § 2.32.

[4]37 C.F.R. §§ 2.53(c) and 2.56(d)

Applications to register a mark must identify the applicant of the mark. The applicant must be a natural or legal person, such as a firm, corporation, union, association, or other organization capable of suing and being sued in a court of law.[1]

Only the owner of a mark can apply to register the mark.[2] The owner is typically the entity that applies the mark to its goods or uses the mark for its services.[3] In the case of intent-to-use applications, the applicant must be entitled to use the mark and must have a bona fide intention to use it in commerce.[4] If the applicant is not the owner of a mark at the time of filing the application, the application is void.[5] Moreover, such an application cannot be salvaged by amending it to specify the true owner, since this action is tantamount to allowing the original applicant to assign its nonexistent rights to the true owner.[6]

To identify the applicant, the application should include the correct legal form of the applicant's name. A corporate applicant, for example, should be identified by its name as set forth in its Articles of Incorporation. If the applicant's legal name includes an assumed name under which it does business, an assumed name designation, such as "d.b.a." for doing business as, or "t.a." for trading as, should connect the actual name to the assumed name.[7] To avoid ambiguities, the applicant's name throughout the application should be consistent with the name as shown in the signature block of the application.

The application should also identify the applicant's form of business or legal entity, such as partnership, joint venture, corporation, or association, immediately after the applicant's name.[8] The test of correctness for entity status is the applicant's status in its state of domicile. For instance, "company" is indefinite when designating the legal entity of the U.S. applicant, but it may be acceptable for the applicant domiciled in a country where it identifies a legal entity.[9] As with the applicant's name, the applicant's legal status should be consistent throughout the application to avoid raising questions.

The application must also identify the applicant's citizenship or its state or nation of organization.[10] For example, if the applicant is a corporation, the application should identify its state or country of incorporation. For joint applicants or joint ventures,

---

[Section 10:14]

[1]15 U.S.C.A. § 1127.

[2]15 U.S.C.A. § 1051; T.M.E.P. § 803.01.

[3]T.M.E.P. § 803.01.

[4]T.M.E.P. §§ 804.02 and 806.01(b)

[5]T.M.E.P. § 803.01.

[6]T.M.E.P. § 803.06; 37 C.F.R. § 2.71(d).

[7]T.M.E.P. § 803.02.

[8]T.M.E.P. § 803.03.

[9]T.M.E.P. § 803.03.

[10]37 C.F.R. § 2.33(a)(3)(i); T.M.E.P. § 803.04.

the application should identify the citizenship or state or foreign country of organization of each party.[11] In the case of a partnership, the application must set forth the state or foreign country under the laws of which the partnership is organized, and, in the case of domestic partnerships or domestic joint ventures, the citizenship information for each general partner in the partnership or active member in the joint venture.[12]

The application must also specify the address of the applicant.[13] The address should include a U.S. zip code or its foreign equivalent.[14]

§ 10:15 Requirements of the application—Description of goods and services

Research References
West's Key Number Digest, Trademarks ☞1287

The application must identify the goods and services that the applicant actually uses with the mark, or that the applicant intends to use with the mark.[1] The identification of the goods or services should use common, generally-understood names for the goods and services and should be clear, accurate, and as precise as possible to identify the goods with reasonable certainty.[2] The identification should also be consistent with the goods or services indicated by the specimens and be specific enough to determine appropriate classification of the goods and services.[3] To gauge compliance with these identification standards, examining attorneys and practitioners may consult the Acceptable Identification of Goods and Services Manual. This manual provides an extensive, though inexhaustive, list of acceptable language for identifying goods and services of various types.[4]

Because of restrictions against expanding the identification of goods and services after filing the application, practitioners should carefully describe the goods and services, using broader rather than narrower terms. If the scope of the goods and services becomes an issue during the examination, it can be narrowed or clarified, but never expanded.[5] Moreover, failure to

---

[11]T.M.E.P. § 803.04.

[12]T.M.E.P. § 803.04.

[13]37 C.F.R. § 2.32(a)(4)(iii).

[14]T.M.E.P. § 803.05.

[Section 10:15]

[1]37 C.F.R. § 2.32(a)(6)(v).

[2]T.M.E.P. §§ 805 and 1402.03; In re Societe Generale Des Eaux Minera-

les De Vittel S.A., 824 F.2d 957, 3 U.S.P.Q.2d 1450 (Fed. Cir. 1987); The Procter & Gamble Company v. Economics Laboratory, Inc., 175 U.S.P.Q. 505, 1972 WL 17812 (T.T.A.B. 1972).

[3]T.M.E.P. § 1402.05.

[4]T.M.E.P. § 1402.04.

[5]37 C.F.R. § 2.71(a); T.M.E.P. § 1402.06.

properly identify the goods and services at the time of filing may cause loss of the filing date.[6]

If known, the application should also designate the international class number or numbers corresponding to the identification of goods and services, and the number of filing fees required for the application.[7] If the application fails to designate class numbers, or designates incorrect class numbers, the examining attorney will designate correct class numbers.[8] If the number of filing fees fails to support the number of classes designated in the application, or the number of classes encompassed by the identification of goods and services, the examining attorney may require the applicant to limit the scope of the goods and services or to submit additional filing fees.[9] Applications designating more than one class of goods or services are called combination applications.[10]

§ 10:16 Requirements of the application—Filing basis

Research References

West's Key Number Digest, Trademarks ☞1287

The application must assert a basis for filing the application.[1] The application may be based on actual use of a mark in commerce, an intention to use the mark in commerce, a foreign application combined with use or an intention to use, a foreign registration combined with use or an intention to use, or an extension of protection of an international registration to the United States, under 15 U.S.C.A. § 1141f(a).[2] The application cannot assert both actual use and an intention to use. Particular requirements that must be fulfilled for each filing basis are discussed above in §§ 9:7 to 9:12.

The applicant may assert different bases for different classes, and may also assert different bases as to different goods or services within a class. T.M.E.P. § 806.02(a). However, in an application based on an extension of protection of an international registration, the applicant cannot claim more than one basis.[3]

§ 10:17 Requirements of the application—Drawings

Research References

---

[6]37 C.F.R. § 2.21(a)(4).

[7]37 C.F.R. §§ 2.21(a)(5) and 2.32.

[8]T.M.E.P. § 1401.03(b).

[9]T.M.E.P. § 1401.04.

[10]T.M.E.P. § 1401.04; T.M.E.P. § 1401.04(b).

[Section 10:16]

[1]37 C.F.R. § 2.32(a); T.M.E.P. § 806.

[2]15 U.S.C.A. §§ 1051 and 1126; 37 C.F.R. § 2.34; T.M.E.P. § 806.

[3]37 C.F.R. § 2.34(b)(3); T.M.E.P. § 806.02(a).

West's Key Number Digest, Trademarks ☞1287

The application must also include a drawing representing the constituent elements of the mark as used or intended for use.[1] The drawing requirements are strictly enforced. An application must include a drawing that conforms to the rules or it will not be accorded a filing date. Additionally, there may not be more than one mark in the drawing since an application must be limited to one mark. Otherwise, the application will be denied a filing date.[2]

The drawing of the mark must be a substantially exact representation of the mark as used on or in connection with the goods and services as shown by the specimens. If the application is an intent-to-use application, the drawing of the mark must be a substantially exact representation of the mark as intended to be used, and as ultimately actually used on or in connection with the goods or services as shown by the specimens included with an Amendment to Allege Use under 37 C.F.R. § 2.76 or a Statement of Use under 37 C.F.R. § 2.88.[3]

There are two forms of drawings, known as special form drawings and standard character drawings. Special form drawings are for marks that are comprised in whole or in part of special characteristics such as elements of design or color, styles of lettering or unusual forms of punctuation. This type of drawing is required to be made with black ink in a process that will reproduce satisfactorily unless the mark includes color.[4] Standard character drawings are not actually drawn at all. They are referred to as drawings because they perform the function of a drawing. In a standard character drawing, the mark should be in black on a white background, although examining attorneys have discretion to accept a drawing that shows the mark in white on a black background if this will more accurately depict the mark.[5] A standard character drawing is a drawing including words, letters, numbers, or any combination thereof without claim to any particular font style, size, or color.[6] There are trademark rules concerning the type of paper to be used for drawings, the size of

---

[Section 10:17]

[1] 15 U.S.C.A. §§ 1051(a)(2) and (b)(2).

[2] 37 C.F.R. § 2.21(a)(3); T.M.E.P. § 807.010.

[3] 37 C.F.R. § 2.51.

[4] 37 C.F.R. § 2.52(b); T.M.E.P. § 807.04.

[5] 37 C.F.R. § 2.52(a); T.M.E.P. § 807.03. A standard character set that lists letters, numerals, punctuation marks, and diacritical marks that may be used in a standard character drawing can be found at: http://www.uspto.gov/teas/StandardCharacterSet.html.

[6] 37 C.F.R. § 2.52(a); T.M.E.P. § 807.03. A standard character set that lists letters, numerals, punctuation marks, and diacritical marks that may be used in a standard character drawing can be found at: http://www.uspto.

drawings, headings on the drawings, and drawings which show placement of the mark on the goods. There are also rules concerning drawings filed through TEAS, including specifications for the file format and size of a digitized image.[7] The T.M.E.P. should be consulted before submitting drawings to be sure that they comply with the standards, since they are strictly enforced and a filing date will be refused if the drawing is not in proper form.[8]

§ 10:18   Requirements of the application—Specimens of use[1]

Research References

West's Key Number Digest, Trademarks ⊛1287

An application based on actual use must include one specimen of use for each class of goods identified in the application. Specimens are not required at the time of filing an intent-to-use application. However, the specimen is required prior to actual registration of the mark.[2] Applications based on foreign applications or foreign registrations do not require specimens.[3]

Specimens can consist either of samples of the material used for labeling the goods in trade, or photographs of the labeled goods in the trade channel. The type of material that is submitted as a specimen will vary depending on the particular circumstances of each application. Specimens provide part of the basis for examination because they show the manner in which the mark is seen by the public, including matter which appears in association with the mark in trade. Specimens also provide supporting evidence of facts recited in the application.[4]

There are two forms of physical specimens, electronically filed specimens and paper specimens.[5] For electronically filed specimens, a digitized image of the specimen must be submitted in a.jpg or.pdf format and a sound specimen must be submitted in a.wav, .wmv, .wma, .mp3, .mpg, or.avi format.[6]

The basic requirements for the paper specimens are that they be made of material suitable for being placed inside a legal-sized file wrapper, that they be capable of being arranged flat (e.g., by being folded), and that they be of a size not exceeding 8½ inches wide and 11 inches long fully extended or when folded. If a speci-

---

gov/teas/StandardCharacterSet.html.

[7]37 C.F.R. § 2.52(c); T.M.E.P. § 807.05.

[8]*See, generally,* 37 C.F.R. § 2.52; T.M.E.P. § 807.

[Section 10:18]

[1]37 C.F.R. § 2.56; T.M.E.P. § 904.

[2]*See, generally,* 37 C.F.R. § 2.56(a); T.M.E.P. § 904.

[3]T.M.E.P. § 904.

[4]T.M.E.P. § 904.

[5]T.M.E.P. § 904.02.

[6]37 C.F.R. § 2.56(d)(4); T.M.E.P. §§ 904.03(d), 1202.15.

men that does not conform to these size requirements is submitted, the USPTO will create a facsimile meeting the requirements, and the original will be destroyed.[7] Specimens should include color if color is a feature of the mark.[8] The trademark rules specify that a specimen shall be a label, tag or container for the goods, or a display associated with the goods.

Specimens that bear the trademark registration symbol ® are not acceptable because the mark is not in fact registered.[9] Improper use of a federal registration symbol that is done deliberately with the intention to deceive or mislead the public or the USPTO is fraud.[10]

Advertising materials are not generally acceptable as specimens for goods. Any materials that function merely to tell the prospective purchaser about the goods or promote the sale of the goods are unacceptable to support trademark use. However, an instruction sheet may be acceptable to show trademark use.[11] The following types of items are generally considered to be merely advertising and thus, unless they comprise point of sale material, are not acceptable as specimens of use on goods: advertising circulars and brochures, price lists, announcements, publicity releases, listings in trade directories, and business cards.

Moreover, materials that are used by the applicant in conducting its internal business are unacceptable as specimens of use for goods. These materials include all documents whose sole function is to carry out the applicant's business dealings, such as invoices, billheads, waybills, and business stationery.[12] Likewise, bags or other packaging materials bearing the name of a retail store and used by the store merely for packaging the items of sold merchandise are not acceptable to show trademark use of the store name for the product sold by the store.[13]

§ 10:19 Requirements of the application—Declaration or oath

Research References

West's Key Number Digest, Trademarks ⚷1287

The application may be signed by the applicant with verification by oath (notarized in the United States) or with an un-

---

[7]37 C.F.R. § 2.56(d)(2); T.M.E.P. § 904.02(b).

[8]T.M.E.P. § 904.02(c)(ii).

[9]T.M.E.P. § 906.

[10]Copelands' Enterprises, Inc. v. CNV, Inc., 945 F.2d 1563, 20 U.S.P.Q.2d 1295 (Fed. Cir. 1991); T.M.E.P. § 906.02.

[11]T.M.E.P. § 904.04(b).

[12]In re Chicago Rawhide Mfg. Co., 455 F.2d 563, 173 USPQ 8 (C.C.P.A. 1972).

[13]T.M.E.P. § 904.04(b).

notarized declaration.[1] The application must include an averment by the person making the application that he or she believes the applicant to be the owner of the mark sought to be registered or to be entitled to use the mark in commerce. Use-based applications must also include an averment that the mark is used in commerce, specifying the nature of the use in commerce, while I.T.U applications must include averment that the application has a bona fide intention to use the mark in commerce.[2] The application must contain an averment that, to the best of the applicant's knowledge, no other person, firm, corporation or association has the right to use such mark in commerce, either in identical form thereof or in such near resemblance thereto as to be likely, when used on or in connection with the goods of a person, to cause confusion or to cause mistake or to deceive.[3] If the applicant signs by declaration, the declaration must contain a warning to the declarant that willful false statements and the like are punishable by fine or imprisonment or both.[4]

§ 10:20 Requirements of the application—Fee

Research References

West's Key Number Digest, Trademarks ☞1287

The application must also include a filing fee for each class of goods and/or services designated within the application.[1] Each class is regarded as a separate application for fee purposes. For a single class application only one filing fee is required. For an application that contains more than one class, only one filing fee is required to obtain a filing date, but a filing fee for each class is required before the application will be approved for publication or registration.

§ 10:21 Requirements of the application—Foreign registration certificate

Research References

West's Key Number Digest, Trademarks ☞1287

Applications based on § 44(e) should include a certified copy of

---

[Section 10:19]

[1]37 C.F.R. § 2.32(b); T.M.E.P. § 804.01.

[2]37 C.F.R. § 2.33(b).

[3]37 C.F.R. § 2.33(b).

[4]37 C.F.R. § 2.20; Nationstar Mortgage LLC v. Mujahid Ahmad, 112 U.S.P.Q.2d 1361, 2014 WL 6480655 (T.T.A.B. 2014); citing Herbaceuticals, Inc. v. Xel Herbaceuticals, Inc., 86 U.S.P.Q.2d 1572, 2008 WL 618623 (T.T.A.B. 2008).

[Section 10:20]

[1]15 U.S.C.A. §§ 1051(a)(1) and (b)(1); 37 C.F.R. § 2.21(a)(5).

the foreign registration certificate from the applicant's country of origin, or a certification from the agency that issued such registration indicating the applicant's ownership of the registration.[1] Additionally, when a foreign registration issues in an application based on § 44(d), a certified copy or a certificate of the registration certificate must be filed.

§ 10:22 Requirements of the application—Designation of domestic representative by foreign applicant

Research References
West's Key Number Digest, Trademarks ☞1287

If the applicant is not domiciled in the United States, then the application should include a designation of a domestic representative who can receive notices or participate in proceedings affecting the mark.[1] This practice is encouraged, but not mandatory.[2]

§ 10:23 Requirements of the application—Allegations of use in ITU applications

Research References
West's Key Number Digest, Trademarks ☞1287

Before an application based on an intention to use the mark may register, the applicant must file an allegation of use of the mark in commerce. The form of the allegation of use may be either an Amendment to Allege Use pursuant to § 1(c) of the Act (15 U.S.C.A. § 1051(c)) or a Statement of Use pursuant to § 1(d) of the Act (15 U.S.C.A. § 1051(d)).

An Amendment to Allege Use may be filed at any time between the filing of the application and the date that the examining attorney approves the mark for publication or the date of expiration of the six-month response after issuing a final action. The application is thereafter treated like a use-based application. Amendments to Allege Use filed after approval of the mark for publication are refused and returned to the applicant.[1] A complete Amendment to Allege Use requires (1) a verified statement that the applicant is believed to be the owner of the mark sought to be registered, that the mark is in use in commerce, the date of first

---

[Section 10:21]
  [1]37 C.F.R. § 2.34(a)(3).
[Section 10:22]
  [1]37 C.F.R. § 2.24.
  [2]T.M.E.P. § 604.

[Section 10:23]
  [1]37 C.F.R. § 2.76(a).

use of the mark and the date of first use of the mark in commerce, (2) one specimen of the mark, and (3) a fee for each class in which the applicant seeks registration.[2]

A Statement of Use can be filed only after the mark has been published and the examiner indicates that the application is registrable by issuing a notice of allowance. The Statement of Use must be filed within six months after the notice of allowance is issued, or within an extension of time granted by the Commissioner.[3] The first six-month extension is automatically granted. Further six-month extensions are granted only for good cause. No extension is granted beyond 36 months after issuance of the notice of allowance.[4] The Statement of Use must include a verified statement that the applicant is believed to be the owner of the mark sought to be registered and that the mark is in use in commerce. Further, it must specify a date of the applicant's first use of the mark, the date of first use of the mark in commerce, and a description of the goods and services which have been sold or provided under the mark.[5] It must also include one specimen of the mark and a fee for each class. If use has not occurred for all of the goods or services, the applicant may file simultaneously with the Statement of Use a request to divide the application, and pay a second filing fee. Registration then proceeds on the goods having use and the balance of the goods continue as an intent-to-use application.[6]

§10:24 Grounds for refusal to register—Proposed mark does not function as a trademark

Research References

West's Key Number Digest, Trademarks ☞1022 to 1026

During examination of a trademark application, an examining attorney will evaluate the proposed trademark to determine whether it meets the requirements for registration. A number of grounds exist for refusing to register a mark. Registration will be refused on statutory grounds if the proposed trademark is likely to be confused with a previously used mark, if it contains unregistrable subject matter, or if it is merely descriptive or deceptively misdescriptive of the goods on which it is used.[1]

The Trademark Act distinguishes trade names from trademarks by definition. While a trademark is used for identifying goods and distinguishing a trademark owner's goods from those

---

[2]37 C.F.R. § 2.76(b).

[3]15 U.S.C.A. § 1051(d).

[4]T.M.E.P. § 1108.03.

[5]37 C.F.R. § 2.88(b).

[6]37 C.F.R. § 2.87.

[Section 10:24]

[1]15 U.S.C.A. § 1052.

manufactured and sold by others, trade names and commercial names are names used by a person to identify his or her business or vocation.[2] The Lanham Act does not provide for registration of trade names on either the Principal or Supplemental Register. Trade names, however, often dually serve as trademarks, in which case they are registrable as trademarks.

The question of whether the applicant's trade name is also used as a trademark is decided on a case-by-case basis. Whether a trade name also performs the function of a trademark depends on the manner in which it is used and the probable impact of such use on customers.[3] If the subject presented for registration is a trade name or part of a trade name, the examining attorney determines whether it is also used as a trademark or service mark by examining the specimens and other evidence of record in the application.

§ 10:25 Grounds for refusal to register—Confusing similarity to registered mark

Research References

West's Key Number Digest, Trademarks ⟠1080 to 1098

Registration of a proposed trademark will be refused if the examiner finds that the mark so resembles a registered mark or a previously used trademark or trade name so as to be likely to cause confusion, to cause mistake or to deceive.[1]

After a trademark application is filed, a trademark examiner conducts a search of registered marks to determine whether the proposed mark is likely to be confused with any previously registered mark. If the examiner determines that there is a likelihood of confusion, registration of the mark is rejected in an Office Action. The applicant may submit a response to the Office Action and attempt to persuade the examiner that confusion is not likely. If the examiner accepts the applicant's reasoning, the examiner may withdraw the rejection, and the mark may proceed to publication.

Registration of a proposed mark may also be refused based upon a likelihood of confusion with a trade name or an unregistered mark previously used by another and not abandoned. However, because of the difficulty in searching for unregistered marks and trade names, likelihood of confusion rejections are usually based upon registered marks.

---

[2]15 U.S.C.A. § 1127.

[3]In re Unclaimed Salvage & Freight Company, Inc., 192 U.S.P.Q. 165, 1976 WL 21118 (T.T.A.B. 1976).

[Section 10:25]

[1]15 U.S.C.A. § 1052(d).

In the initial examination, while the trademark examiner may consider all of the likelihood of confusion factors,[2] the initial examination is typically based upon the similarity of the marks (in appearance, sound, and connotation) and the similarity of the goods. Other factors, such as established channels of trade, fame of the prior mark, and the extent of any actual confusion, require an evaluation of evidence provided by the applicant and/or the owner of the prior mark. Such factors are therefore not generally raised by the examiner.

§ 10:26   Grounds for refusal to register—Scandalous or immoral subject matter

Research References
West's Key Number Digest, Trademarks ⊙1072

The Lanham Act sets forth several categories of subject matter that cannot be registered as a trademark or part of a trademark. For instance, a mark comprised of scandalous or immoral subject matter is not registrable.[1] The terms "scandalous" and "immoral" are not defined in the Lanham Act. The meaning of these terms has been established by reference to dictionary definitions and judicial decisions.[2] "Scandalous" has been alternatively defined as shocking to the sense of propriety, offensive to the conscience or moral feelings, or calling out condemnation.[3] Generally, courts have found it unnecessary to consider whether a mark is immoral, finding it sufficient to determine whether the mark is scandalous.[4] Presumably, it is thought that anything "immoral" would also be "scandalous."

Whether a mark consists of scandalous matter is determined from the standpoint of a substantial composite of the general public (although not necessarily a majority) in the context of the changing social morals and sensitivities of contemporary attitudes.[5]

Recent examples of marks that have been deemed scandalous include the mark DICK HEADS for restaurant and bar services positioned directly underneath a caricature of a human head composed primarily of graphic and readily recognizable represen-

---

[2]*See* § 10:9.

[Section 10:26]

[1]15 U.S.C.A. § 1052(a).

[2]In re McGinley, 660 F.2d 481, 485, 211 U.S.P.Q. 668, 673 (C.C.P.A. 1981); In re Mavety Media Group Ltd., 33 F.3d 1367, 31 U.S.P.Q.2d 1923 (Fed.

Cir. 1994).

[3]McGinley, 660 F.2d at 486, 211 U.S.P.Q. at 673.

[4]McGinley, 660 F.2d at 485 n.6, 211 U.S.P.Q. at 672 n.6.

[5]Mavety Media Group, 33 F.3d at 1367, 31 U.S.P.Q.2d at 1923.

tation of male genitalia,[6] a mark for shirts including a silhouette of a defecating dog and its feces,[7] and the mark JACK-OFF for entertainment in the nature of adult-oriented conversations by telephone.[8] Marks determined not to be scandalous include BIG PECKER brand for T-shirts,[9] the mark BLACK TAIL for an adult entertainment magazine,[10] and the mark OLD GLORY CONDOM CORP. and flag design for use on condoms.[11]

§ 10:27 Grounds for refusal to register—Deceptive matter

Research References
West's Key Number Digest, Trademarks ☞1073

Deceptive matter is not registrable on either the Principal or the Supplemental Register.[1] The Federal Circuit has articulated a three-part inquiry for determining whether a mark consists of deceptive matter:

- Is the mark misdescriptive of the character, function, composition or use of the goods?
- If so, are prospective purchasers likely to believe that the misdescription actually describes the goods?
- If so, is the misdescription likely to affect the decision to purchase?[2]

A careful distinction must be made between marks comprising deceptive matter, which are unregistrable, and marks comprising "deceptively misdescriptive" or "primarily geographically misdescriptive" matter, which may be registrable under § 2(e) with a showing of secondary meaning. If a misdescription is not material to the purchasing decision, the mark falls within § 2(e) and is potentially registrable. But, if a misdescription is material, the mark is comprised of deceptive matter and is not registrable even if it has acquired secondary meaning. For instance, in the case of a mark comprised of a geographic term, it is appropriate to first determine whether the mark is primarily geographically deceptively misdescriptive under § 2(e)(2). If so, the mark may be

---

[6]In re Wilcher Corp., 40 U.S.P. Q.2d 1929, 1996 WL 725479 (T.T.A.B. 1996).

[7]Greyhound Corp. v. Both Worlds Inc., 6 U.S.P.Q.2d 1635, 1988 WL 252489 (T.T.A.B. 1988).

[8]In re Boulevard Entertainment, Inc., 334 F.3d 1336, 67 U.S.P.Q.2d 1475 (Fed. Cir. 2003).

[9]In re Hershey, 6 U.S.P.Q.2d 1470, 1988 WL 252485 (T.T.A.B. 1988).

[10]Mavety Media Group, 33 F.3d at 1367, 31 U.S.P.Q.2d at 1923.

[11]In re Old Glory Condom Corp., 26 U.S.P.Q.2d 1216, 1993 WL 114384 (T.T.A.B. 1993).

[Section 10:27]

[1]15 U.S.C.A. § 1052(a).

[2]In re Budge Mfg. Co., Inc., 857 F.2d 773, 8 U.S.P.Q.2d 1259 (Fed. Cir. 1988).

established as a geographically deceptive mark under § 2(a) by additionally showing that the misrepresentation is material to the purchasing decision.[3]

For example, the mark SUPER SILK for clothing, namely dress shirts and sport shirts made of silk-like fabric was found to be deceptive,[4] the mark LONDON LONDON and related design for sportswear was found to be geographically deceptive,[5] and the mark PARIS BEACH CLUB for T-shirts and sweatshirts was found not geographically deceptively misdescriptive or geographically deceptive.[6]

§ 10:28   Grounds for refusal to register—Disparaging matter

Research References

West's Key Number Digest, Trademarks ⊙1073

Section 2(a) bars registration of a mark that disparages, falsely suggests a connection with, or brings into contempt or disrepute institutions, living or dead persons, beliefs or national symbols.[1] Symbols of foreign countries, along with those of the United States, are protected as national symbols.[2] The Federal Circuit Court of Appeals has held that the disparaging provision of § 2(a) of the Lanham act is unconstitutional.[3]

At least one court has characterized the disparagement analysis as a two-step process where the first inquiry relates to "the meaning of the matter in question, as it appears in the marks and as those marks are used in connection with the services identified in the registrations . . . ," and the second relates to whether the meaning is one that disparages the person or group

---

[3]Institut Nat. Des Appellations D'Origine v. Vintners Intern. Co., Inc., 958 F.2d 1574, 22 U.S.P.Q.2d 1190 (Fed. Cir. 1992).

[4]In re Phillips-Van Heusen Corp., 63 U.S.P.Q.2d 1047, 2002 WL 523343 (T.T.A.B. 2002).

[5]In re Juleigh Jeans Sportswear Inc., 24 U.S.P.Q.2d 1694, 1992 WL 340751 (T.T.A.B. 1992) (because the primary significance of "London" is a geographic location, the public was likely to associate clothing with the city of London, and because London has a reputation for fashion, that renders the misdescription material to the purchasing decision).

[6]In re Sharky's Drygoods Co., 23 U.S.P.Q.2d 1061, 1992 WL 147883 (T.T.A.B. 1992) (because consumers would recognize the humorous and incongruous nature of the mark, they would not expect that the goods originated from Paris).

[Section 10:28]

[1]15 U.S.C.A. § 1052(a).

[2]In re Anti-Communist World Freedom Congress, Inc., 161 U.S.P.Q. 304, 1969 WL 9040 (T.T.A.B. 1969).

[3]In re Tam, 808 F.3d 1321, 1357-58, 44 Media L. Rep. (BNA) 1037, 117 U.S.P.Q.2d 1001 (Fed. Cir. 2015).

implicated by the mark.[4] That court also noted that the ultimate question as to whether a mark "may disparage" a particular person or group is a question of fact.[5]

A mark is disparaging if it would reasonably be understood as referring to a specific person, institution, belief or national symbol, and it would be considered offensive or objectionable by a reasonable person of ordinary sensibilities.[6] The determination of whether the mark would be considered offensive should be taken from the viewpoint of the person or group implicated by the mark.[7] Whether the mark is disparaging to the person or group is judged as of the time the mark was registered.[8] However, if a mark is determined to be disparaging it is only the statutory right to registration that is unavailable, not the right to use the mark.[9]

A party bringing a disparagement suit shall not be required to conduct a survey, but the party must still show that the mark containing or comprising disparaging matter relates to the allegedly disparaged group's views concerning the mark.[10] Articles in newspapers and magazines are probative evidence as to whether a mark is disparaging. Dictionary definitions are also probative. A dictionary definition may, for example, provide evidence that a particular word or phrase used in a mark has more than one meaning, and therefore would not necessarily be understood as referring to a particular person or group.[11] However, perceptions of the general public are irrelevant to the determination of whether the mark is disparaging to the particular person or group.[12] An example of a mark rejected for registration on the basis that it may be disparaging is the mark KHORAN for "alcoholic beverages, namely, wines." The Board found the mark gave the commercial impression of referring to the holy text of Islam, which prohibits the consumption of alcohol, making the use of KHORAN for wine disparaging to the religion and beliefs of

---

[4]Pro-Football, Inc. v. Harjo, 284 F. Supp. 2d 96, 68 U.S.P.Q.2d 1225 (D.D.C. 2003).

[5]Pro-Football, Inc., 284 F. Supp. 2d at 96, 68 U.S.P.Q.2d at 1225.

[6]Greyhound, 6 U.S.P.Q.2d at 1639.

[7]In re Hines, 32 U.S.P.Q.2d 1376, 1994 WL 587037 (T.T.A.B. 1994).

[8]Amanda Black horse, Marcus Briggs-Cloud, Philip Gover, Jillian Pappan, and Courtney Tsotigh v. Pro-Football, INC., 2014 WL 2757516 (T.T.A.B. 2014).

[9]Amanda Black horse, Marcus Briggs-Cloud, Philip Gover, Jillian Pappan, and Courtney Tsotigh v. Pro-Football, INC., 2014 WL 2757516 (T.T.A.B. 2014).

[10]Boswell v. Mavety Media Group Ltd., 52 U.S.P.Q.2d 1600, 1999 WL 1040108 (T.T.A.B. 1999).

[11]In re in Over Our Heads Inc., 16 U.S.P.Q.2d 1653, 1990 WL 354546 (T.T.A.B. 1990).

[12]Pro-Football, 284 F. Supp. 2d at 96, 68 U.S.P.Q.2d at 1225.

Muslim Americans.[13]

Where there is any doubt as to whether a mark is disparaging, the trend in the USPTO is to pass a mark along for publication. The theory behind this practice is that a person or group that believes it is disparaged by the mark has standing to bring an opposition proceeding against registration of the mark.[14]

§ 10:29   Grounds for refusal to register—Other kinds of unregistrable subject matter

Research References

West's Key Number Digest, Trademarks ☞1068 to 1070

A mark comprised of a flag, a coat of arms, or other insignia of the United States, any state or municipality, or any foreign nation is not registrable.[1] This provision has been construed narrowly to include only insignia that are akin to a flag or a coat of arms. Thus, for example, the Statue of Liberty is not an insignia of the United States.[2] Further, registration of a mark containing individual features of, or a distorted representation of, a flag or other insignia is not barred.[3]

Some names and symbols of the U.S. government, as well as some national and international organizations, are protected by statute. Some of these statutes impose criminal penalties for misuse of the protected insignia, while others provide for civil enforcement. Criminal penalties are imposed, for example, for unauthorized use of the name or sign of the Red Cross,[4] decorations or medals of the Armed Forces,[5] and the Coat of Arms of the Swiss Confederation.[6] Civil penalties are provided for unauthorized use of Olympic symbols,[7] the Little League name and emblem,[8] and insignia of the Girl Scouts of America,[9] to name a few. The USPTO will refuse registration of such insignia, absent a showing that the applicant is an authorized user.

A mark that is a name, portrait, or signature of a living indi-

---

[13]In re Lebanese Arak Corporation, 94 U.S.P.Q.2d 1215, 2010 WL 766488 (T.T.A.B. 2010).

[14]See, e.g., Over Our Heads, 16 U.S.P.Q.2d at 1653 (allowing the mark MOONIES and design for dolls that drop their pants to be published for possible opposition by followers of the Reverend Moon).

[Section 10:29]

[1]15 U.S.C.A. § 1052(b).

[2]Liberty Mut. Ins. Co. v. Liberty Ins. Co. of Tex., 185 F. Supp. 895, 127

U.S.P.Q. 312 (E.D. Ark. 1960).

[3]Knorr-Nahrmittel Aktiengesellschaft v. Havland International, Inc., 206 U.S.P.Q. 827, 1980 WL 30123 (T.T.A.B. 1980).

[4]18 U.S.C.A. § 706.

[5]18 U.S.C.A. § 704.

[6]18 U.S.C.A. § 708.

[7]36 U.S.C.A. § 220506.

[8]36 U.S.C.A. § 130506.

[9]36 U.S.C.A. § 80305.

vidual is not registrable unless that person's consent is on record.[10] Additionally, a mark comprising the name, portrait, or signature of a deceased U.S. president during the life of the president's widow is not registrable, except by written consent of the widow.[11] Registration of a name is barred by this section regardless of whether it is a full name, surname, shortened name or nickname, so long as a particular living person is identified by the name.[12] A name is considered to identify a particular person if the public would associate the mark as used on the specified goods with the individual having the name in question.[13]

The person identified by a mark must give consent in writing, and must explicitly provide consent to register the mark.[14] Written consent to use a mark is not sufficient.[15]

§ 10:30   Grounds for refusal to register—Merely descriptive or deceptively misdescriptive mark

Research References

West's Key Number Digest, Trademarks ☞1035

If a proposed mark consists of a term that is merely descriptive or deceptively misdescriptive of goods, registration will be refused unless the applicant shows that the mark has become distinctive of the applicant's goods.[1] A mark is "merely descriptive" if it conveys information about a quality, ingredient, function, characteristic or purpose of the goods or services on which it is used.[2] A mark is "deceptively misdescriptive" if: (1) the mark misdescribes a characteristic, quality, function, composition or use of the goods or services for which it is used, and, if this is answered in the affirmative, (2) prospective purchasers are likely to believe that the misdescription actually describes the goods or services.[3]

A merely descriptive or deceptively misdescriptive mark becomes distinctive after it has been used in association with the

---

[10]15 U.S.C.A. § 1052(c).

[11]15 U.S.C.A. § 1052(c).

[12]In re Sauer, 27 U.S.P.Q.2d 1073, 1074, 1993 WL 236534 (T.T.A.B. 1993), aff'd, 26 F.3d 140 (Fed. Cir. 1994).

[13]Sauer, 27 U.S.P.Q.2d at 1075 (registration of the mark BO BALL for an oblong white leather ball with red stitching refused on the grounds that consumers would associate the mark with Bo Jackson).

[14]T.M.E.P. § 1206.04(a).

[15]T.M.E.P. § 1206.04(a).

[Section 10:30]

[1]15 U.S.C.A. § 1052(e)(1), (f).

[2]In re Disc Jockeys Inc., 23 U.S.P. Q.2d 1715, 1992 WL 205047 (T.T.A.B. 1992).

[3]In re Berman Bros. Harlem Furniture Inc., 26 U.S.P.Q.2d 1514, 1515, 1993 WL 156481 (T.T.A.B. 1993) (holding that the mark FURNITURE MAKERS for retail furniture stores services not including the manufacture of furniture was deceptively misdescriptive).

goods so as to create "secondary meaning" in the eyes of consumers. Thus, to register such a mark the applicant must show that it has acquired "secondary meaning." Exclusive and continuous use of the mark in commerce for the five years preceding the date on which a claim of distinctiveness is made may be accepted by the USPTO as prima facie evidence of distinctiveness.[4]

A mark may be registered on the Supplemental Register regardless of whether it is merely descriptive or deceptively misdescriptive of the goods. If a mark registered on the Supplemental Register acquires distinctiveness, a trademark owner may file a new application and submit proof of secondary meaning. If that proof is accepted by a trademark examiner, the mark may be registered on the Principal Register.

§ 10:31 Grounds for refusal to register—Geographically descriptive or misdescriptive marks

Research References
West's Key Number Digest, Trademarks ⟐1047

Under § 2(e), a mark that is primarily geographically descriptive when used in connection with the applicant's goods is not registrable on the Principal Register unless it has become distinctive of the goods under § 2(f).[1] A geographically descriptive mark is, however, registrable on the Supplemental Register without establishing secondary meaning.

A mark that is primarily geographically deceptively misdescriptive of the applicant's goods is per se not registrable on either the Principal Register or the Supplemental Register under § 2(e), unless it became distinctive of the goods before December 8, 1993, the date that amendments mandated by the North American Free Trade Agreement (NAFTA) were enacted.[2] The NAFTA amendments to the Lanham Act preclude registration of primarily geographically deceptively misdescriptive marks even if they have acquired secondary meaning or disclaimed the primarily geographically deceptively misdescriptive terms.[3] This prohibition against registering geographically deceptively misdescriptive marks is in effect a false advertising statute. However, the NAFTA amendments "grandfather" in marks that acquired distinctiveness before December 8, 1993.

To determine whether a mark including a geographic term is

---

[4]15 U.S.C.A. § 1052(f).

[Section 10:31]

  [1]15 U.S.C.A. § 1052(e)(2), (f).

[2]15 U.S.C.A. § 1052(e)(2), (f).

[3]In re Wada, 194 F.3d 1297, 52 U.S.P.Q.2d 1539 (Fed. Cir. 1999).

primarily geographically descriptive, the threshold issue is whether the primary significance of the term is geographic. A term is primarily geographic if it is the name of a generally known geographic place.[4] The geographic term may be the full name of a geographic location, an abbreviation or nickname for a geographic location, or a map or outline of a geographic area so long as purchasers would be likely to perceive it as a geographic location.[5] A mark that is descriptive of a geographic location that is owned by the user is not a geographic term within the meaning of § 2(e)(2), and is therefore registrable.[6] For example, the mark 17-MILE DRIVE is not primarily geographically descriptive of goods sold by Pebble Beach Company because the Pebble Beach Company owns the area known as the 17-Mile Drive.[7]

If the place described in a primarily geographic mark is not the origin of the user's goods or services, the mark is potentially geographically deceptively misdescriptive. Alternatively, if the geographic location described in the mark is the origin of the user's goods or services, the mark is potentially geographically descriptive. In either case, registrability turns on whether there is a goods-place (or services-place) association between the applicant's goods and the geographic location. A goods-place association will be found if purchasers are likely to believe that the goods or services originate in the location identified by the mark.[8]

To reject a mark as geographically descriptive or misdescriptive, an examiner must have a reasonable basis for believing that the public would make this association.[9] Newspaper and magazine articles are frequent sources of evidence that a goods-place association would be made. For example, an association between the New England area and bread was established from excerpts from news stories in which the word "bread" was written in close proximity to the term "New England."[10]

It is not dispositive that a geographic term used in a mark is

[4]See In re Nantucket, Inc., 677 F.2d 95, 213 U.S.P.Q. 889 (C.C.P.A. 1982).

[5]In re Canada Dry Ginger Ale, 24 C.C.P.A. 804, 86 F.2d 830, 32 U.S.P.Q. 49 (1936) (map of Canada conveys same idea as word "Canada").

[6]In re Pebble Beach Co., 19 U.S.P. Q.2d 1687, 1991 WL 326557 (T.T.A.B. 1991).

[7]Pebble Beach, 19 U.S.P.Q.2d at 1688.

[8]In re Loew's Theatres, Inc., 769 F.2d 764, 226 U.S.P.Q. 865 (Fed. Cir. 1985); see also In re California Innova-

tions, Inc., 329 F.3d 1334, 66 U.S.P. Q.2d 1853 (Fed. Cir. 2003) ("§ 1052 no longer treats geographically deceptively misdescriptive marks differently than geographically deceptive marks.").

[9]Loew's Theatres, 769 F.2d at 764, 226 U.S.P.Q.2d at 865; see also In re California Innovations, Inc., 329 F.3d 1334, 66 U.S.P.Q.2d 1853 (Fed. Cir. 2003) ("§ 1052 no longer treats geographically deceptive misdescriptive marks differently than geographically deceptive marks.").

[10]In re Pan-O-Gold Baking Co., 20 U.S.P.Q.2d 1761, 1991 WL 326589

the name of more than one place, so long as the mark as used on the applicant's goods would likely elicit a connection with one particular place.[11] For instance, a goods-place association was shown for the mark DURANGO (Mexico) on chewing tobacco because tobacco is a principal crop of the Durango region of Mexico, even though there is a Durango, Texas.[12]

If consumers are not likely to make an association between a geographic term and the applicant's goods, the mark is not geographically descriptive or deceptively misdescriptive, and registration on the Principal Register is not prohibited by § 2(e). In such a case, the mark is treated as an arbitrary designation.[13]

If a goods-place association is found for a geographically misdescriptive mark, the mark must be barred from registration under § 2(a) as a deceptive mark.[14] If a misdescription is material to the purchasing decision, the mark is deceptive and registration is barred (regardless of whether the mark acquired secondary meaning prior to NAFTA). Thus, in any analysis of a geographically misdescriptive term, registrability must be analyzed under both § 2(a) and § 2(e)(3).

In the case of a certification mark, the mark may properly certify the geographic origin of goods.[15] A certification mark comprising a descriptive geographic term is therefore registrable without proving secondary meaning.

§ 10:32 Grounds for refusal to register—Primarily merely a surname

Research References

West's Key Number Digest, Trademarks ⊂⇒1042

A mark consisting of a word that is primarily merely a surname is not registrable on the Principal Register unless it has acquired secondary meaning.[1] A mark is primarily merely a surname if its primary significance to the purchasing public is that of a surname.[2]

Even though a mark is a surname, it may not be primarily merely a surname. The test for determining whether a mark is

---

(T.T.A.B. 1991).

[11]Loew's, 769 F.2d at 767-768, 226 U.S.P.Q. at 868.

[12]Loew's, 769 F.2d at 767-768, 226 U.S.P.Q. at 868.

[13]Conagra Inc. v. Saavedra, 4 U.S.P.Q.2d 1245, 1987 WL 123843 (T.T.A.B. 1987).

[14]Institut Nat. Des Appellations D'Origine, 958 F.2d at 1580, 22 U.S.P. Q.2d at 1195.

[15]15 U.S.C.A. § 1127.

[Section 10:32]

[1]15 U.S.C.A. § 1052(e)(4), (f).

[2]In re Hamilton Pharmaceuticals Ltd., 27 U.S.P.Q.2d 1939, 1940, 1993 WL 368803 (T.T.A.B. 1993).

primarily merely a surname is the primary significance of the mark as a whole to the purchasing public.[3] A term that is used as a surname, but that has another meaning that exceeds its significance as a surname, is not considered primarily merely a surname. If this is the case, the mark will fall on the descriptiveness continuum according to the nonsurname meaning and be treated accordingly. However, the fact that other meanings for a term having surname significance exist does not necessarily mean that the primary significance of the term to the purchasing public would be other than that of its surname significance.[4]

To support a rejection as primarily merely a surname, the trademark examiner must establish a prima facie case.[5] The burden then shifts to the applicant to rebut the showing made by the examiner.[6] To establish a prima facie case, the examiner generally will look for surname usage of a term in telephone directories or computerized research databases. Evidence of record may also indicate surname significance. The manner in which a mark is used on a specimen may suggest surname significance, for instance if the mark is depicted with the portrait or signature of an individual. Additionally, the fact that the mark is the surname of someone related to the applicant is evidence that the mark is primarily merely a surname. The applicant may rebut the prima facie case by presenting evidence that the mark has some other significance that exceeds its surname significance, or that the addition of other matter to the mark removes it from the category of primarily merely a surname.

§ 10:33   Proving secondary meaning

Research References
West's Key Number Digest, Trademarks ⬤1628

Proving secondary meaning, or acquired distinctiveness, is sometimes necessary to prove that a mark is in fact a mark, i.e. that the mark distinctly identifies a single source of goods or services in commerce.[1] Marks requiring this kind of evidentiary support are those that lack inherent distinctiveness.

To register these marks on the Principal Register, the applicant

---

[3]In re Hutchinson Technology Inc., 852 F.2d 552, 7 U.S.P.Q.2d 1490 (Fed. Cir. 1988).

[4]Hamilton Pharmaceuticals, 27 U.S.P.Q.2d at 1942.

[5]Hamilton Pharmaceuticals, 27 U.S.P.Q.2d at 1942.

[6]Hamilton Pharmaceuticals, 27 U.S.P.Q.2d at 1942.

[Section 10:33]

[1]See 15 U.S.C.A. § 1052(f); Loew's, 769 F.2d at 769, 226 U.S.P.Q. at 869 (stating that whether acquired distinctiveness has been established is a question of fact).

must show that the mark in question has acquired distinctiveness for the goods or services identified in the application.[2] In general, the applicant may present any competent evidence to establish distinctiveness.[3] Although the amount of evidence hinges on the particular circumstances of each application, more descriptive marks require more evidence of distinctiveness than do less descriptive marks.[4]

There are three basic ways to show acquired distinctiveness. First, the applicant may present a claim that it has used or has benefitted from five years of continuous and substantially exclusive use of the mark.[5] Second, the applicant may present a claim of ownership of one or more prior registrations of the same mark on the Principal Register for the same or related goods or services.[6] The prior registrations must be in full force and effect.[7] Third, the applicant may submit actual evidence of acquired distinctiveness.[8] Actual evidence may include long use of the mark, advertising expenditures supporting the mark, affidavits or declarations asserting recognition of the mark as an indicator of source, survey evidence, and studies relating to market research and consumer reaction.[9]

§ 10:34 Examination of applications—Initial examination and office actions

Research References

West's Key Number Digest, Trademarks ☞1287

Upon filing an application and payment of the prescribed filing fee, the Patent and Trademark Commissioner must refer the application to the examiner in charge of trademark registration who in turn will direct examination of the application for compliance.[1] Examining attorneys generally examine applications in the order they are received.[2] However, under extraordinary circumstances, the applicant may successfully petition the Commissioner for special status to accelerate examination.[3]

In addition to inspecting the application, the drawing and the

---

[2]T.M.E.P. § 1212; Yamaha Intern. Corp. v. Hoshino Gakki Co., Ltd., 840 F.2d 1572, 6 U.S.P.Q.2d 1001 (Fed. Cir. 1988).

[3]T.M.E.P. § 1212.01.

[4]T.M.E.P. § 1212.01.

[5]15 U.S.C.A. § 1052(f); T.M.E.P. § 1212.05.

[6]37 C.F.R. § 2.41(b); T.M.E.P. § 1212.04.

[7]T.M.E.P. § 1212.04(d).

[8]37 C.F.R. § 2.41(a); T.M.E.P. § 1212.06. See also In re Owens-Corning Fiberglas Corp., 774 F.2d 1116, 227 U.S.P.Q. 417 (Fed. Cir. 1985).

[9]T.M.E.P. § 1212.06(a) to (d).

[Section 10:34]

[1]15 U.S.C.A. § 1062.

[2]T.M.E.P. § 702.01.

[3]T.M.E.P. § 702.02.

specimens, examining a trademark application includes conducting a search for marks that are confusingly similar to the mark
under examination.[4] The Trademark Search Library, which is
open to the public, and the on-line Trademark Electronic Search
System (TESS) include copies of all marks that have been
registered as well as copies of pending and abandoned marks.[5]
These searches are typically not limited to the classes of goods or
services designated in the application. The marks resulting from
the search are called references.

After examining the application, the examining attorney issues
an Office Action, indicating his or her assessment of the application's compliance with the statutory requirements for
registration. The Office Action, which typically includes results of
the trademark search, advises the applicant whether its mark is
registrable.[6] If the mark is not registrable, the Office Action
should inform the applicant of every deficiency or defect making
the mark ineligible for registration.[7] The Office Action may also
request additional information the examining attorney believes
will be useful in evaluating the application.[8] After receiving the
Office Action, the applicant has six months from the date of mailing to respond.[9]

§ 10:35 Examination of applications—Responses to an office action

Research References
West's Key Number Digest, Trademarks ⚷1287

In response to an Office Action refusing to register a mark, the
applicant may file a response addressing the issues raised in the
Action. The response may amend the application, provide
requested information, or rebut assertions in the Action. The response should also request reexamination of the application in
light of the response.

During pendency of an application, the applicant may amend
the drawings of the mark to agree with the specimens or to
comply with formal requirements, or sometimes even to add or
delete features.[1] The standard of acceptability for changes to a
mark is whether the changes constitute a material alteration of

---

[4]T.M.E.P. § 704.01

[5]T.M.E.P. § 104.

[6]15 U.S.C.A. § 1062(b); T.M.E.P. § 705.

[7]15 U.S.C.A. § 1062(b); T.M.E.P. § 704.01.

[8]37 C.F.R. § 2.61(b); T.M.E.P. § 814.

[9]15 U.S.C.A. § 1062(b).

[Section 10:35]

[1]37 C.F.R. § 2.72.

the mark.[2] It is also possible to amend a mark after registration.[3]

The applicant may either voluntarily or involuntarily disclaim an unregistrable component of a mark that is otherwise registrable.[4] Disclaimers serve the purpose of allowing the registration of marks which are registrable as a whole but include matter that would not be registrable standing alone.[5] They also help prevent false impressions regarding the extent of a registrant's rights in a mark.[6] Disclaimers do not prejudice the applicant's capacity to reclaim any disclaimed features in a new application if those features later become distinctive of the applicant's goods or services.[7] For example, the applicant for Kentucky Fried Chicken in stylized red lettering might disclaim the words "fried chicken," and later reclaim them in another application when the words of the whole phrase "Kentucky Fried Chicken" acquired distinctiveness over a long period of use with extensive advertising.

The identification of goods or services may only be amended to clarify or limit its scope.[8] The scope of the goods or services cannot be expanded by amendment. For example, consider "men's and women's sleeping apparel" as an identification of goods for a registrable mark. It would be permissible to amend the identification by limiting the goods to women's sleeping apparel, since this reduces the scope of the initial description. However, it would be impermissible to delete "sleeping" from the description, since this would expand the scope to any type of men's or women's apparel. In general, qualifying language may not be deleted from the identification of goods and services.[9]

It is generally possible to amend an application after publication, provided the amendment is proper. An amendment after publication is an amendment filed after the time when the USPTO is able to withdraw the mark from its scheduled publication in the Official Gazette.[10] Generally, the USPTO can withdraw a mark from publication, if it receives the amendment at least 20 days before the scheduled publication date.[11] Amendments after publication are contingent on USPTO approval.[12] Amendments after publication may require re-publication.

---

[2] 37 C.F.R. § 2.72(a); T.M.E.P. § 807.14.

[3] 37 C.F.R. § 2.173; T.M.E.P. § 1609.02.

[4] 15 U.S.C.A. § 1056(a); T.M.E.P. § 1213.

[5] T.M.E.P. § 1213.

[6] T.M.E.P. § 1213.

[7] 15 U.S.C.A. § 1056(b).

[8] 37 C.F.R. § 2.71(a); T.M.E.P. § 1402.06.

[9] T.M.E.P. § 1402.06(a).

[10] T.M.E.P. § 1505.

[11] T.M.E.P. § 1505.

[12] T.M.E.P. § 1505.01.

§ 10:36 Examination of applications—Appeal to Trademark Trial and Appeal Board

Research References

West's Key Number Digest, Trademarks ☞1313

The applicant may appeal any final decision of the examiner to the Trademark Trial and Appeal Board (TTAB).[1] A second refusal to register is considered a final decision for purposes of appeal, even if the examiner does not make the decision final.[2] If the final decision concerns compliance with a technical provision of the rules, rather than a matter of substance, the applicant may petition the Director to review an Examining Attorney's formal requirements instead of appealing to the TTAB.[3] Common matters of substance include those pertaining to 15 U.S.C.A. §§ 1052 to 1056 and 1091 (e.g., whether a mark is immoral, deceptive, or scandalous; whether marks are confusingly similar; and whether a mark is merely descriptive).

Applicants typically initiate the appeal by filing a notice of appeal, identifying the substance of the appeal, and including the prescribed fee. The notice must be filed within six months of the final decision.[4] After filing the notice of appeal, the applicant must submit an appeal brief, and the examining attorney will answer applicant's brief with the examining attorney's appeal brief.[5] Applicant may rebut the examining attorney's brief with a reply brief.[6] The TTAB considers the briefs and an oral argument (if the applicant has requested one) in deciding the issue.

§ 10:37 Examination of applications—Publication

Research References

West's Key Number Digest, Trademarks ☞1287, 1293

When an application for registration on the Principal Register has been examined and appears to be registrable, it will be published for public inspection and potential opposition.[1] The USPTO publishes trademarks in a weekly publication called the *Official Gazette*. This publication includes a depiction of each mark, its claimed date of first use, the name of the applicant, a list of the goods or services applied for, and the filing date and se-

---

[Section 10:36]

[1]15 U.S.C.A. § 1070.

[2]37 C.F.R. § 2.141.

[3]37 C.F.R. § 2.146(a); T.M.E.P. § 1702.

[4]37 C.F.R. § 2.142(a).

[5]37 C.F.R. § 2.142(b); T.M.E.P. § 1501.02.

[6]37 C.F.R. § 2.142(b); T.M.E.P. § 1501.02(a).

[Section 10:37]

[1]37 C.F.R. § 2.80; T.M.E.P. § 1502.

rial number of the application. After publication, any entity believing that it would be damaged by registration of the mark may file an opposition to the registration.[2] The opposition must be filed within 30 days of the publication date or within an extended period granted by the TTAB. During the time between the date of publication and the notice of allowance or registration, the USPTO refers to the application as "published."

Applications for registration on the Supplemental Register are not published for opposition. The marks are, however, published in the *Official Gazette* upon registration, and anyone who believes that it is or will be damaged by the registration may petition to cancel the mark.[3]

§ 10:38 Inter partes proceedings before the TTAB—Oppositions

Research References
West's Key Number Digest, Trademarks ⟂1290

An opposition is an administrative proceeding conducted before the T.T.A.B. It is an "inter partes" proceeding, in which an "opposer" files an opposition to registration of another's trademark application. Any person "who believes that [it] would be damaged" by registration of a mark on the Principal Register may contest registration of that mark by bringing an opposition.[1]

An opposition is commenced by filing a notice of opposition.[2] The opposition must be brought within 30 days after the mark is published in the Official Gazette.[3] Extensions of time in which to oppose, however, are available upon written request filed prior to the expiration of the 30-day period.

It is common to file requests for extensions of time to oppose. A 30-day extension of time in which to oppose is given as a matter of right, and further extensions of time may be granted for good cause.[4] The requests for extension are filed with the USPTO, and the USPTO sends a copy of each extension to the applicant. Extensions of time to file an opposition aggregating more than 120 days from the date of publication are granted only upon the consent of the applicant or upon a showing of "extraordinary circumstances."[5]

Requesting an extension of time allows the potential opposer to

---

[2]15 U.S.C.A. § 1063; *see also* § 9:38 below.

[3]15 U.S.C.A. § 1092; T.M.E.P. § 1503.01.

[Section 10:38]

[1]15 U.S.C.A. § 1063.

[2]37 C.F.R. § 2.101(a).

[3]15 U.S.C.A. § 1063; 37 C.F.R. § 2.101(c).

[4]37 C.F.R. § 2.102(c).

[5]37 C.F.R. § 2.102(c).

evaluate the merits of a possible opposition proceeding, and to prepare a notice of opposition. Typically, a potential opposer will want to have some information about the applicant, such as the nature of its business, the channels of trade in which the applicant sells its goods, and the size of the applicant's business. This information helps a potential opposer to assess the likelihood of success in an opposition, and to determine whether it would truly be damaged by registration of the applicant's mark.

The notice of opposition must "set forth a short and plain statement showing why the opposer believes it would be damaged by the registration of the opposed mark and state the grounds for opposition."[6] A notice of opposition is the equivalent of a complaint, and should be pleaded in the same manner as a complaint. The starting point to determine whether a party has standing to oppose the registration of a trademark is § 13 of the Lanham Act. In addition to § 13, an opposer must satisfy two judicially-created requirements to have standing. First, the opposer must have a "real interest" in the proceedings. Second, the opposer must have a direct and personal stake in the outcome of the proceedings.[7]

The grounds for opposition may be any legal defect or deficiency in the application.[8] The opposer usually raises one or more of the bars to registration set forth in § 2 of the Lanham Act. Misuse by the applicant of the "®" notice is also a ground for opposition.[9] Most commonly, the opposition is based upon a likelihood of confusion with a trademark or trademarks owned by the opposer. The opposer's mark may be either a registered mark or a common law mark. For a common law mark, the opposer must prove that it functions as a trademark for the opposer's goods or services and that the opposer has priority in the mark as against the applicant. For a registered mark, however, the opposer receives the benefit of the presumptions of ownership of the mark and use of the mark from the filing date of the registration.[10] Additional evidence must be presented only if the opposer wants to rely upon a first use date that is earlier than the filing date.

The opposition may also be based upon other grounds, such that the proposed mark disparages or falsely suggests a connection with the opposer,[11] or that the proposed mark is merely descriptive, if primarily geographically descriptive or misdescriptive, or is generic. Another basis for an opposition is likelihood of

---

[6]37 C.F.R. § 2.104(a).

[7]Ritchie v. Simpson, 170 F.3d 1092, 50 U.S.P.Q.2d 1023 (Fed. Cir. 1999).

[8]J. Thomas McCarthy, *Trademarks and Unfair Competition* § 20:13 (4th ed. 2003).

[9]Copelands' Enterprises, 945 F.2d at 1563, 20 U.S.P.Q.2d at 1295.

[10]15 U.S.C.A. § 1115(a),(b).

[11]University of Notre Dame Du Lac v. J.C. Gourmet Food Imports Co., Inc., 703 F.2d 1372, 10 Ed. Law Rep. 88, 217 U.S.P.Q. 505 (Fed. Cir. 1983).

dilution of a famous mark.[12] In order to have standing to oppose based upon descriptiveness, the opposer must plead and prove that it has a competitive right to use the mark descriptively in its business.[13] The opposer bears the burden of proof to establish that the mark opposed should not be allowed to register.[14]

After a notice of opposition has been filed, jurisdiction over the proceeding is transferred from the USPTO to the TTAB. The TTAB sends a written notification of the opposition to the attorneys for each party (or to the parties themselves if unrepresented).[15] The notice specifies the time in which the applicant has to file an answer. This time period is typically 40 days from the mailing date of the notification.

The answer must admit or deny the allegations of the notice of opposition, in the same manner that an answer in a civil action must admit or deny allegations of a complaint.[16] The answer should also contain any defenses to the opposer's claims, including the equitable defenses of unclean hands, laches, estoppel, acquiescence, fraud, mistake, or a prior judgment.[17] A defense attacking the validity of any registration relied upon in the notice of opposition is a compulsory counterclaim, if the grounds for such a counterclaim are known to the applicant at the time the answer is filed.[18] If the applicant makes a counterclaim, the opposer has 30 days in which to answer the counterclaim.[19]

§ 10:39 Inter partes proceedings before the TTAB—Cancellations

Research References

West's Key Number Digest, Trademarks ⊕1297

Even if no opposition to a registration of a mark is sustained and the mark passes to registration, the registration may be canceled by a person "who believes that [it] is or will be damaged by the registration."[1] Cancellations are brought by a "petitioner" who petitions for cancellation of a registered trademark. A cancellation proceeding may be brought against marks on the Supplemental Register as well as on the Principal Register.[2] A cancella-

---

[12]15 U.S.C.A. §§ 1063(a) and 1125(c).

[13]Binney & Smith Inc. v. Magic Marker Industries, Inc., 222 U.S.P.Q. 1003, 1984 WL 63077 (T.T.A.B. 1984).

[14]Sanyo Watch Co., Inc. v. Sanyo Elec. Co., Ltd., 691 F.2d 1019, 1022, 215 U.S.P.Q. 833, 834 (Fed. Cir. 1982).

[15]37 C.F.R. § 2.105.

[16]37 C.F.R. § 2.106(b).

[17]37 C.F.R. § 2.106(b)(1).

[18]37 C.F.R. § 2.106(b)(2)(i).

[19]37 C.F.R. § 2.106(b)(2)(iii).

[Section 10:39]

[1]15 U.S.C.A. § 1064.

[2]15 U.S.C.A. § 1092.

tion proceeding is commenced by filing a petition for cancellation and the required fee.[3] The petition for cancellation must "set forth a short and plain statement showing why the petitioner believes that it is or will be damaged by the registration and state the grounds for cancellation."[4]

After receiving the petition, the TTAB notifies the party in the position of defendant, referred to as the "registrant," that a cancellation proceeding has been commenced and that an answer is due within 40 days. As in an opposition proceeding, the answer must admit or deny the allegations of the petition.[5] The answer should also allege any defenses that are available.[6] A defense attacking the validity of any registration relied upon in the petition for cancellation is a compulsory counterclaim.[7]

For marks that have been registered on the Principal Register for less than five years, a cancellation may be based upon any of the grounds that could have been raised in an opposition. That is, on any ground that would have prevented registration in the first place. As with oppositions, likelihood of confusion is the most common ground for bringing a cancellation proceeding. Another basis for cancellation is likelihood of dilution of a famous mark.[8]

For marks that have been registered on the Principal Register for more than five years and have attained incontestability status, however, the cancellation may be based only upon the specific grounds in 15 U.S.C.A. § 1064, which are set out below.

- The mark has become the generic name for the goods or services for which it is registered, or a portion thereof,
- The mark has been abandoned,
- The registration was obtained fraudulently or contrary to the statutory bars of §§ 2(a), 2(b), 2(c), or 4 and
- The mark is being used by or with the permission of the registrant, so as to misrepresent the source of the goods or services in connection with which the mark is used.

Fraud made in declarations under §§ 8 and 15, as well as fraud in the original application papers, all relate to fraudulently obtaining a registration.[9]

A mark on the Supplemental Register may be canceled on the grounds that the registrant is not entitled to registration or the mark has been abandoned, and the mark may be canceled at any

---

[3]37 C.F.R. § 2.111(a).

[4]37 C.F.R. § 2.112.

[5]37 C.F.R. § 2.114(b)(1).

[6]37 C.F.R. § 2.114(b)(1).

[7]37 C.F.R. § 2.114(b)(2)(i).

[8]15 U.S.C.A. §§ 1064 and 1125(c).

[9]*See* Volkswagenwerk Aktiengesellschaft v. Advance Welding and Mfg. Corp., 184 U.S.P.Q. 367, 1974 WL 20103 (T.T.A.B. 1974).

time.[10]

A mark may be canceled in whole or in part.[11] In other words, a mark may be canceled as to all of the goods or as to only some of the goods.

Like the opposer in an opposition proceeding, the petitioner bears the burden of proof by a preponderance of the evidence.[12] If the petitioner prevails and a mark is canceled from the Principal or Supplemental Register, this does not affect other rights in the mark that do not flow from federal registration. Common law rights, state registrations, and rights under § 43(a) of the Lanham Act remain unaffected.

§ 10:40 Inter partes proceedings before the TTAB— Procedures in inter partes proceedings

Research References

West's Key Number Digest, Trademarks ☞1296, 1303

Inter partes proceedings are conducted much like federal district court actions. The opposer in an opposition proceeding and the petitioner in a cancellation proceeding are the party in the position of plaintiff.[1] Similarly, the applicant in an opposition proceeding and the respondent in a cancellation proceeding are in the position of defendant.[2] The primary difference between inter partes proceedings before the TTAB and a court proceeding is that trial testimony in TTAB proceedings is taken and presented to the Board only by deposition.[3]

Oppositions and cancellations are governed by the Federal Rules of Civil Procedure except where specifically superseded by procedures outlined in 37 C.F.R. §§ 2.101 to 2.145.[4] The TTAB Manual of Procedure ("T.B.M.P."), a publication of the USPTO, further details procedures to be followed in inter partes proceedings. The Board sets testimony periods which correspond to setting a case for trial in court proceedings.[5] Trial testimony is taken only by deposition, and is submitted to the Board in transcript form. These testimonial depositions are conducted similarly to discovery depositions. The proceedings conclude with a final hearing, for which the parties submit briefs and may

---

[10]15 U.S.C.A. § 1092.

[11]15 U.S.C.A. § 1068.

[12]Massey Junior College, Inc. v. Fashion Institute of Technology, 492 F.2d 1399, 181 U.S.P.Q. 272 (C.C.P.A. 1974).

[Section 10:40]

[1]37 C.F.R. § 2.116(b).
[2]37 C.F.R. § 2.116(b).
[3]37 C.F.R. § 2.116(e).
[4]37 C.F.R. § 2.116(a).
[5]37 C.F.R. § 2.116(d).

optionally request an oral argument.[6]

Few oppositions make it as far as a final hearing. Most settle fairly early in the discovery process, after each party has an opportunity to assess its case in light of discovered information. Oppositions and cancellations can be quite expensive if taken all the way to final hearing.

Most motions available in federal court proceedings are applicable to TTAB inter partes proceedings. Motions in inter partes proceedings must be made in writing and be accompanied by a brief.[7] An oral hearing is not held on motions except on order by the Board.[8] If a dispositive motion is filed, the Board will suspend the proceeding with respect to all matters not pertinent to the motion.[9] Because the filing of a motion stays the proceeding, the party in the position of defendant sometimes uses motion practice as a stalling technique. The Board does not typically rule on a motion for a period of at least several months, although there is an ongoing effort to eliminate backlog so that decisions can be rendered more quickly.

It is fairly common in a cancellation or opposition proceeding for one of the parties to bring a motion for summary judgment. A summary judgment motion may be filed at any time prior to the opening of the plaintiff's testimony.[10] While the issues in these proceedings are typically heavily fact-intensive (e.g., the multiple factual inquiries of the *du Pont* factors), summary judgment may be granted in the absence of material factual disputes and on the issue of likelihood of confusion.[11]

For less contentious cases in which the parties stipulate to most facts, the parties can agree to use the Accelerated Case Resolution (ACR) procedure to avoid the cost and delay of a full opposition proceeding.[12] Often compared to summary judgement motions, the ACR procedure empowers the TTAB to decide key factual issues before making a final determination in the case. Although the ACR procedure can be requested at a later time in an opposition proceeding, the greatest cost and time savings is achieved when the parties request the ACR procedure at the pretrial conference or early in the discovery process.

Any party to an inter partes proceeding who is dissatisfied with the decision of the TTAB may appeal to the U.S. Court of

---

[6]37 C.F.R. §§ 2.128 and 2.129.

[7]37 C.F.R. § 2.127(a).

[8]37 C.F.R. § 2.127(a).

[9]37 C.F.R. § 2.127(d).

[10]37 C.F.R. § 2.127(e)(1).

[11]Sweats Fashions, Inc. v. Pannill Knitting Co., Inc., 833 F.2d 1560, 4 U.S.P.Q.2d 1793 (Fed. Cir. 1987).

[12]See TBMP § 702.04.

Appeals for the Federal Circuit.[13] Alternatively, if no appeal is taken, the party may file an action in a United States District Court.[14] However, issues appearing in subsequent actions that are materially the same as the issues decided by the TTAB are subject to issue preclusion.[15] The appeal or civil action must be commenced within two months of the date of the TTAB decision.[16]

§ 10:41 Duration and renewal of registrations

Research References

West's Key Number Digest, Trademarks ⊚1304

The duration of trademark registrations has varied over the years, depending upon the trademark act under which the registration issued. The Lanham Act of 1946, which is the current trademark act, originally specified that a trademark registration would remain in force for 20 years and that registrations were renewable for 20-year periods. A revision to the Lanham Act that took effect on November 16, 1989, however, reduced both the term of registration and the term of renewal from 20 to 10 years. So, trademarks registered on or after November 16, 1989 have a 10-year term, renewable for 10-year periods. Registrations issued under the Lanham Act prior to November 16, 1989, had a duration of 20 years, but are now renewable for periods of only 10 years.[1]

While trademark registrations under the Lanham Act have a term of 10 or 20 years, obtaining registration for the full 10- or 20-year term is contingent upon filing an affidavit during the sixth year after the date of registration.[2] Such an affidavit is mandated in § 8 of the Lanham Act and is referred to as a "§ 8 affidavit." A § 8 affidavit must set forth those goods or services recited in the registration for which the mark is still in use. A specimen showing use of the mark must be attached to the affidavit, or, if the mark is not in use at the time of filing the affidavit, the applicant must show that the nonuse is due to special circumstances and not to any intention to abandon the mark. If a registrant fails to file a § 8 affidavit, the Commissioner will cancel the registration.[3] The purpose of requiring registrants to file a § 8 affidavit is so that those marks which are no longer being used in

---

[13]35 U.S.C.A. § 1071(a).

[14]35 U.S.C.A. § 1071(b).

[15]B & B Hardware, Inc. v. Hargis Industries, Inc., 135 S. Ct. 1293, 191 L. Ed. 2d 222, 113 U.S.P.Q.2d 2045 (2015).

[16]37 C.F.R. § 2.145(d).

[Section 10:41]

[1]15 U.S.C.A. § 1058; 37 C.F.R. § 2.181(a).

[2]15 U.S.C.A. § 1058; T.M.E.P. § 1604.01.

[3]15 U.S.C.A. § 1058.

commerce will be removed from the register.[4]

To renew a registration, the applicant must file an application for renewal within one year before the expiration of the term or renewal term of the registration, or within six months after expiration upon payment of an additional fee.[5] The renewal registration must include a request for renewal of the registration and a fee for each class. If the renewal application covers less than all the goods and services listed in the registration, a list of the goods and services to be renewed must be included.[6]

---

[4]T.M.E.P. § 1604.   [6]37 C.F.R. § 2.183.
[5]15 U.S.C.A. § 1059.

Chapter 11

Trademark and Unfair Competition Litigation

KeyCite®: Cases and other legal materials listed in KeyCite Scope can be researched through the KeyCite service on Westlaw®. Use KeyCite to check citations for form, parallel references, prior and later history, and comprehensive citator information, including citations to other decisions and secondary materials.

---

§ 11:1 Pre-filing matters—Subject matter jurisdiction

Research References

West's Key Number Digest, Trademarks ⟜1557

Trademark litigation differs from many other intellectual property disputes governed by federal law because state and federal courts have concurrent jurisdiction. That is, a trademark suit may be brought in any state court or U.S. district court that has personal jurisdiction over the defendant. 28 U.S.C.A. § 1338(a) grants U.S. district courts subject matter jurisdiction over patent, plant variety protection, trademark and copyright cases, and "[s]uch jurisdiction shall be exclusive of the courts of the states in patent, plant variety protection and copyright cases." Thus, by negative implication, federal subject matter jurisdiction is nonexclusive over trademark cases.

One limitation on concurrent jurisdiction over trademark disputes is the fact that the federal courts have jurisdiction only over trademark disputes that involve a "use in commerce."[1] Generally, use of a mark is deemed to be "in commerce" when it is placed on or accompanies goods transported in commerce, or when the mark is used in conjunction with sale, advertising, or rendering of services in commerce. "Use in commerce" also extends to using the instrumentalities of commerce, including telephone and Internet services. For example, Internet users can use interstate telephone lines to access websites, therefore establishment of an Internet website meets the threshold of "use in commerce" for

---

[Section 11:1]

[1]15 U.S.C.A. § 1114(1).

purposes of subject matter jurisdiction.[2]

As a practical matter, few trademark cases are litigated in state courts. One likely explanation is that many trademark litigators practice primarily in federal courts and are simply more familiar with federal court practice. Also, since many trademark litigators prefer to try cases in federal court, federal court judges have a greater proportion of trademark and other intellectual property cases on their dockets and thus tend to be more knowledgeable about trademark law than their state court counterparts. Assuming there are no extenuating circumstances, their own experience with federal rules and practice, combined with the likelihood of having a knowledgeable judge, will incline attorneys to choose federal courts over state courts.

If, however, unique factors around a particular trademark case tend to favor bringing it in state court, the attorney should be careful in drafting the complaint to ensure it remains in state court. If the complaint includes a cause of action concerning validity, dilution, or infringement of a federally registered mark, the case is still eligible for federal court jurisdiction. Even if filed in state court, the defendant will have the option of removing such a case to federal court. Thus, if the attorney wants to make sure that a case stays in a state court, then the complaint should only include state causes of action not involving a federally registered mark, such as common law trademark infringement, trademark infringement or dilution under a state statute, as well as other unfair competition claims available under state law. By not pleading any federal causes of action or litigating a federally registered mark, such a complaint will not raise an issue or question of federal law. Without a federal question, a defendant will only be able to remove the case to federal court by showing the allegations in the complaint satisfy the complete diversity and amount in controversy requirements for diversity jurisdiction.

§ 11:2 Pre-filing matters—Personal jurisdiction

Research References

West's Key Number Digest, Trademarks ⚷1558

As in most cases, the test for personal jurisdiction over a defendant in a trademark case involves a two step inquiry. First, the court must determine whether a state's long arm statute authorizes the exercise of jurisdiction over the defendant. If so, the court must next decide whether the court's exercise of personal jurisdiction according to the long arm statute would

---

[2]Planned Parenthood Federation of America, Inc. v. Bucci, 42 U.S.P.Q.2d 1430, 1997 WL 133313 (S.D. N.Y.1997), aff'd, 152 F.3d 920 (2d Cir.1998).

violate the due process clause of the Fourteenth Amendment of the U.S. Constitution.[1]

State long arm statutes vary, but most contain some sort of requirement that the defendant commit an act in the state causing injury or property damage or commit an act outside of the state causing injury or property damage in the state.[2] Therefore, even when the defendant could constitutionally be subject to specific or general jurisdiction in a particular forum, it is often important at the outset for the complainant to determine the location of injury to ensure a court can properly exercise personal jurisdiction in a trademark dispute in accordance with the state's long arm statute. The general rule is that the harm caused by trademark infringement is the likelihood of confusion between plaintiff's goods and defendant's goods. Thus, a court will have personal jurisdiction so long as the allegedly infringing goods were sold in that jurisdiction.

For example, the South Dakota long arm statute provides jurisdiction over any person involved in "[t]he commission of any act which results in accrual within this state of a tort action."[3] This statute has been interpreted by the South Dakota Supreme Court to mean long arm jurisdiction is appropriate if the injury has occurred in the state, even if the events leading to the injury took place outside of the state.[4]

In trademark infringement actions, some courts have held that the claim arises at the place of the "passing off," which is "where the deceived customer buys the defendant's products in the belief that he is buying the plaintiff's."[5] However, other courts have identified the site of injury as being the place where the plaintiff suffers the economic impact.[6] In one Eighth Circuit case, the court did not have to choose between these two locations because the court found that both tests were satisfied in the forum state.[7] The defendant had sold infringing products in South Dakota, while the plaintiff suffered economic injury as its principal place of business was in South Dakota.[8]

Trademark infringement does not require an actual sale of the product bearing the infringing mark. Circulating printed materi-

---

[Section 11:2]

[1]See, e.g., Dakota Industries, Inc. v. Dakota Sportswear, Inc., 946 F.2d 1384, 1387-1388, 20 U.S.P.Q.2d 1450 (8th Cir. 1991).

[2]See, e.g., Minn. Stat. § 543.19, subd. 1.

[3]SDCL 15-7-2(2).

[4]Dakota, 946 F.2d at 1388.

[5]Dakota, 946 F.2d at 1388 (quoting Vanity Fair Mills, Inc. v. T. Eaton Co., 234 F.2d 633, 639, 109 U.S.P.Q. 438 (2d Cir. 1956)).

[6]Dakota, 946 F.2d at 1388 (citing Acrison, Inc. v. Control and Metering Ltd., 730 F. Supp. 1445, 1448, 14 U.S.P.Q.2d 1833 (N.D. Ill. 1990)).

[7]Dakota, 946 F.2d at 1388–89.

[8]Dakota, 946 F.2d at 1388-89.

als bearing the allegedly infringing mark is itself a tortious act for purposes of the long arm statute.[9] However, to satisfy due process requirements, the advertising must be directed at the forum state. Absent additional contacts purposefully directed at the forum in question, advertising in nationally circulated magazines reaching the forum jurisdiction is usually insufficient to exercise personal jurisdiction over the advertiser. At the same time, such advertising may still be considered as one element among several in analyzing a defendant's overall contacts with the forum.[10]

For example, in *Sidco Industries, Inc. v. Wimar Tahoe Corp.*,[11] the court held that defendant's publishing advertisements in national publications, combined with sending direct mail brochures to travel agents in Oregon, was sufficient to establish personal jurisdiction. In *Sidco*, plaintiff was the owner of a hotel in Oregon which operated under the federally registered service mark of "Horizon Motor Inn." Defendant was a Nevada corporation which operated a casino/resort at Lake Tahoe, Nevada, known as the "Lake Tahoe Horizon Casino/Resort."

Defendant owned no property in the state of Oregon, had no offices, employees, agents or bank accounts in Oregon. Defendant advertised in various national magazines, none of which were specifically directed at Oregon. In addition, defendant had advertised to travel agencies in the "hotel and travel index" which was distributed to every travel agent in Oregon. Also, defendant advertised its resort through direct mail brochures, some of which had been sent to Oregon.

In analyzing personal jurisdiction, the court noted that placing advertisements in national publications circulated in the forum state is not sufficient to grant the state personal jurisdiction over the defendant. However, such advertisements may be considered in analyzing the entirety of defendant's contacts with the state. In addition to advertising in nationally circulated magazines, defendant also sent direct mail brochures to travel agents in the state. Also, defendant's contacts with the state directly related to the service mark at issue in the suit. The mailing of these brochures was a degree of purposeful interjection into Oregon which was different in kind from the mere fortuitous contacts

---

[9]Whelen Engineering Co., Inc. v. Tomar Electronics, Inc., 672 F. Supp. 659, 663 (D. Conn. 1987).

[10]Land-O-Nod Co. v. Bassett Furniture Industries, Inc., 708 F.2d 1338, 1341, 219 U.S.P.Q. 281 (8th Cir. 1983), *but see* Akro Corp. v. Luker, 45 F.3d 1541, 1548, 33 U.S.P.Q.2d 1505 (Fed. Cir. 1995).

[11]Sidco Industries Inc. v. Wimar Tahoe Corp., 768 F. Supp. 1343, 1349, 19 U.S.P.Q.2d 1850 (D. Or. 1991).

through national publications.[12]

While there are few cases specifically addressing personal jurisdiction in dilution cases, a similar analysis would likely be appropriate. Generally, dilution involves blurring or tarnishing a trademark by associating the mark with unrelated or substandard goods or services. Therefore, personal jurisdiction in a dilution action will frequently be proper where the unrelated or substandard goods are offered for sale. Personal jurisdiction in dilution cases would analogously be proper in jurisdictions that recognize the injury caused to the trademark owner at the location of its principal place of business.

International access to the Internet can lead to situations where potentially infringing or dilutive use of marks occurs simultaneously online and offline. This raises particularly important personal jurisdiction issues when a trademark owner attempts to hale a foreign defendant into a court in the United States.[13]

Trademark cases involving the Internet typically raise specific jurisdiction issues,[14] as opposed to general jurisdiction issues. The case of *Zippo Mfg. Co. v. Zippo Dot Com, Inc.* established the majority view in assessing specific jurisdiction when the Internet is involved.[15] Under *Zippo*, "the likelihood that personal jurisdiction can be constitutionally exercised is directly proportionate to the nature and quality of commercial activity that an entity conducts over the Internet."[16] However, not all courts subscribe to the Zippo analysis, recognizing that the interactivity, functions and purposes of websites vary greatly and do not fall along a

---

[12]Sidco, 768 F. Supp. at 1348-49; see also Wells Fargo & Co. v. Wells Fargo Exp. Co., 556 F.2d 406, 194 U.S.P.Q. 10 (9th Cir. 1977) (Defendant negotiated and consummated a loan in the forum state, which gave rise to the cause of action. "Plaintiffs would seem to have a claim for trademark infringement and unfair competition growing out of this loan. Any activity of making the loan may, in this case, be characterized as either the transaction of business or the commission of a tortious act in Nevada for purposes of [Nevada's long-arm statute]").

[13]See § 7:2 for more detailed information regarding cyberlaw jurisdiction issues.

[14]E.g., Toys "R" Us, Inc. v. Step

Two, S.A., 318 F.3d 446, 65 U.S.P.Q.2d 1628, 55 Fed. R. Serv. 3d 591 (3d Cir. 2003) (specific jurisdiction in trademark infringement case); ALS Scan, Inc. v. Digital Service Consultants, Inc., 293 F.3d 707, 63 U.S.P.Q.2d 1389, 52 Fed. R. Serv. 3d 1121 (4th Cir. 2002) (same); Bensusan Restaurant Corp. v. King, 126 F.3d 25, 44 U.S.P.Q.2d 1051 (2d Cir. 1997) (same); Cybersell, Inc. v. Cybersell, Inc., 130 F.3d 414, 44 U.S.P.Q.2d 1928 (9th Cir. 1997) (same); CompuServe, Inc. v. Patterson, 89 F.3d 1257, 24 Media L. Rep. (BNA) 2100, 39 U.S.P.Q.2d 1502, 1996 FED App. 0228P (6th Cir. 1996) (same).

[15]952 F. Supp. 1119 (W.D. Pa. 1997).

[16]Zippo, 952 F. Supp. at 1124.

single continuum.[17]

Cases are in disagreement as to whether the mere sending of advertising related to an allegedly infringing mark, such as advertising on the Internet, is sufficient to establish personal jurisdiction in a particular state. However, the majority of cases hold that a defendant's advertising over the Internet is not sufficient to establish personal jurisdiction absent an indication that the advertising was being intentionally directed toward the selected forum.[18]

Personal jurisdiction in cybersquatting cases is assessed under a different set of criteria. "[S]imply registering someone else's trademark as a domain name and posting a website on the Internet is not sufficient to subject a party domiciled in one state to jurisdiction in another . . ., there must be 'something more' to demonstrate that the defendant directed his activity toward the forum state."[19]

§ 11:3 Pre-filing matters—Venue

Research References
West's Key Number Digest, Trademarks ⚯1561

In federal court practice, proper venue depends on the type of defendant and is defined by statute. Venue and personal jurisdiction have effectively merged for corporate defendants:

[A] defendant that is a corporation shall be deemed to reside in any judicial district in which it is subject to personal jurisdiction at the time the action is commenced.[1]

If a court has personal jurisdiction over the corporate defendant, venue will also be proper.

With respect to individual defendants, 28 U.S.C.A. § 1391(b)(2) controls venue:

A civil action may be brought in

* * *

(2) a judicial district in which a substantial part of the

---

[17]*See, e.g.,* Trintec Industries, Inc. v. Pedre Promotional Products, Inc., 395 F.3d 1275, 1281, 73 U.S.P.Q.2d 1587 (Fed. Cir. 2005).

[18]McCarthy on Trademarks and Unfair Competition §§ 32:41 and 32:45.50 (4th ed.); *but see* Rescuecom Corp. v. Google Inc., 562 F.3d 123, 90 U.S.P.Q.2d 1287 (2d Cir. 2009) (keyword advertising did constitute use in

commerce).

[19]Panavision Intern., L.P. v. Toeppen, 141 F.3d 1316, 1322, 46 U.S.P.Q.2d 1511 (9th Cir. 1998) (holding modified on other grounds by, Yahoo! Inc. v. La Ligue Contre Le Racisme Et L'Antisemitisme, 433 F.3d 1199 (9th Cir. 2006)).

[Section 11:3]
[1]28 U.S.C.A. § 1391(d).

events or omissions giving rise to the claim occurred * * *

In at least one trademark infringement case, the above language has been interpreted to mean that venue is proper in a district in which the accused infringer caused confusion and diminution of the value of the plaintiff's mark, or in the jurisdiction in which the plaintiff resided, since any impact on the plaintiff's business was likely to occur there. Therefore, a substantial part of the acts or omissions giving rise to the claim occurred in that venue.[2]

§ 11:4 Pre-filing matters—Statute of limitations

Research References
West's Key Number Digest, Trademarks ⊙⇒1562

There are no explicit statutes of limitations for trademark infringement or dilution. They are continuing torts, so the tort is taking place as long as the accused infringer continues to use the accused mark. However, the equitable doctrine of laches may limit the relief available to trademark owners who do not timely assert their rights.[1]

§ 11:5 Pre-filing matters—Drafting the complaint

Research References
West's Key Number Digest, Trademarks ⊙⇒1583

A trademark owner has the option of choosing from one or more causes of action when drafting a complaint. Depending on the law in the jurisdiction and the particular facts of a case, the complaint can potentially allege causes of action under federal trademark law, state statutes covering dilution and deceptive trade practices, as well as trademark infringement under state common law.

Trademark infringement complaints often contain several counts. If the mark is federally registered, there will be a count for infringement of a registered mark under § 32 of the Lanham Act.[1] A mark registered under state law would include a count under a corresponding state statute. In addition, most attorneys will also plead a cause of action for common law trademark infringement, in case the trademark registrations are invalidated because of some procedural defect. A cause of action for common

---

[2]Sidco, 768 F. Supp. at 1349.   **[Section 11:5]**

[Section 11:4]   [1]15 U.S.C.A. § 1114(1).

[1]See § 10:21.

law trademark infringement of unregistered marks exists in most states, as well as a federal cause of action for common law trademark infringement under § 43(a) of the Lanham Act.[2] In addition, many states have adopted a version of the Uniform Deceptive Trade Practices Act.[3] This provides trademark owners with a statutory cause of action under state law for infringement of a registered or common law mark.

To properly state a cause of action for trademark infringement, a complaint must allege sufficient facts to support two major elements. First, the plaintiff must assert ownership of rights in one or more trademarks being improperly used by the defendant. For federally registered marks, the plaintiff merely needs to identify the registration of the mark (by registration number) and allege that the registration was issued or assigned to the plaintiff. In cases involving common law marks or trade dress, the plaintiff needs to show that (1) it has used the common law mark or trade dress, and (2) the common law mark or trade dress is inherently distinctive or has acquired secondary meaning in the market. To satisfy the second element of an infringement suit, the plaintiff must allege that defendant's use of a mark causes a likelihood of confusion in the relevant market.

In addition to infringement, a plaintiff can frequently allege dilution of its marks or its trade dress. A federal cause of action for dilution exists under § 43(c) of the Lanham Act, and many states have adopted antidilution statutes. For a dilution claim, the plaintiff generally will need to allege facts supporting ownership of the mark as described relative to an infringement action. Plaintiff also must assert in the complaint that the defendant's use of one or more marks has caused dilution of the strength, and thus the value, of plaintiff's mark by tarnishment or blurring. However, additional and more detailed allegations may be required to properly assert a cause of action for dilution, depending on the statute applicable to a particular jurisdiction. For example, the federal antidilution statute also requires the court to determine whether and when the plaintiff's mark became famous relative to the introduction and use of the defendant's mark.[4]

Whether the plaintiff is claiming infringement, dilution, or both, simple assertions of the above factors are usually sufficient in jurisdictions with lenient notice pleading rules. However, for at least those cases being heard in federal court, the plaintiff may wish to consider specifically pleading some of the applicable likelihood of confusion or dilution factors found in the Lanham

---

[2]215 U.S.C.A. § 1125(a).

[3]Unif. Deceptive Trade Practices

Act, 7A U.L.A. 265 (1966).

[4]15 U.S.C.A. § 1125(c)(2)(A).

Act to reduce the risk of the complaint being dismissed. A district court has the discretion to dismiss a complaint with prejudice if it finds the claims are not "plausible" or the complaint merely contains a "legal conclusion couched as a factual allegation."[5] Conclusory allegations do not count for purposes of determining whether a claim is well pled.[6] Further, in federal and state jurisdictions requiring initial discovery disclosures, specific pleadings may also be helpful in avoiding discovery disputes.[7]

§ 11:6 Pre-filing matters—Rule 11 considerations

Research References

West's Key Number Digest, Federal Civil Procedure ☞2771(4)
C.J.S., Federal Civil Procedure §§ 1360, 1371, 1374

Though problems associated with Rule 11 of the Federal Rules of Civil Procedure are rare in trademark cases, there are a few key issues an attorney should consider before filing suit. Counsel should make sure the plaintiff is the actual owner of the asserted trademark. Counsel should also obtain samples of the allegedly infringing mark, either by way of the actual product or an advertisement showing use of the mark.

The attorney should also investigate the length of defendant's use of the allegedly infringing mark to try to ensure the client's use of the mark is senior to the defendant's use. One surprisingly common scenario in trademark cases is that plaintiff's counsel sends out a cease and desist letter (or, even worse, files a complaint) alleging that defendant's use of a mark is likely to cause confusion with plaintiff's mark. Defendant responds by agreeing that there is a likelihood of confusion, but points out that defendant's use of the mark pre-dates plaintiff's use of its mark. In other words, plaintiff is infringing defendant's mark! If a trademark owner finds that another person has used a mark longer than the trademark owner, the trademark owner will want to either change his or her own mark, or take the position that there is no likelihood of confusion between the marks.

§ 11:7 Liability for trademark infringement

Research References

West's Key Number Digest, Federal Courts ☞265; Trademarks ☞1564
C.J.S., Federal Courts §§ 126 to 127, 129

---

[5]Ashcroft v. Iqbal, 129 S. Ct. 1937, 1953, 173 L. Ed. 2d 868, 2009-2 Trade Cas. (CCH) ¶ 76785, 73 Fed. R. Serv. 3d 837 (2009) (aff'ing Bell Atlantic Corp. v. Twombly, 550 U.S. 544, 127 S. Ct. 1955 (2007).

[6]Ashcroft, 129 S. Ct. at 1954.

[7]See, e.g., Fed. R. Civ. P. 26(a)(1).

Liability for trademark infringement arises from unauthorized use of a valid and protectable mark in commerce.[1] Thus, any member of the distribution chain can be held liable for trademark infringement.[2] It is no excuse that someone else created the mark, or made the product bearing the mark. If someone sells a product bearing the infringing mark, then he or she is liable for trademark infringement.[3]

As a practical matter, most trademark infringement cases only name the manufacturer as the defendant. In part, this is because one of the easiest ways to stop infringement is to cut it off at the root. Also, retailers often sell the trademark owner's products as well as the accused products. Therefore, most trademark owners are reluctant to sue their retailers out of respect for that business relationship. It is, however, possible to sue distributors who apply a trademark to repackaged or reconfigured goods, such that the trademark is being applied to goods that are materially different from those produced by the trademark holder.[4]

A corporate officer can be held personally liable for trademark infringement and unfair competition if the officer "directs, controls, ratifies, participates in, or is the moving force behind

---

[Section 11:7]

[1] 15 U.S.C.A. §§ 1114(1)(a) and 1125(1). But see 1-800 Contacts, Inc. v. WhenU.Com, Inc., 414 F.3d 400, 75 U.S.P.Q.2d 1161 (2d Cir. 2005) (use of a mark to generate "pop-up" ads is not trademark "use" as required for a finding of infringement); Bosley Medical Institute, Inc. v. Kremer, 403 F.3d 672, 674, 679–80, 74 U.S.P.Q.2d 1280 (9th Cir. 2005) ("noncommercial use of a trademark as the domain name of a website—the subject of which is consumer commentary about the products and services represented by the mark—does not constitute infringement"); Playboy Enterprises, Inc. v. Netscape Communications Corp., 55 F. Supp. 2d 1070, 1073, 52 U.S.P.Q.2d 1162 (C.D. Cal. 1999), aff'd, 202 F.3d 278 (9th Cir. 1999) (sales of Internet banner advertisements responding to the search terms "playboy" and "playmate" did not constitute use of the trademarks PLAYBOY and PLAYMATE in commerce).

[2] Stabilisierungsfonds Fur Wein v. Kaiser Stuhl Wine Distributors Pty. Ltd., 647 F.2d 200, 207, 209 U.S.P.Q. 633, 31 Fed. R. Serv. 2d 325 (D.C. Cir. 1981).

[3] McCarthy § 25:19; see also Boston Professional Hockey Ass'n, Inc. v. Dallas Cap & Emblem Mfg., Inc., 510 F.2d 1004, 1010, 185 U.S.P.Q. 364, 1975-1, 1975-1 Trade Cas. (CCH) ¶ 60258 (5th Cir. 1975) (rejected by, International Order of Job's Daughters v. Lindeburg and Co., 633 F.2d 912, 208 U.S.P.Q. 718 (9th Cir. 1980)) and (disapproved of on other grounds by, University of Pittsburgh v. Champion Products, Inc., 566 F. Supp. 711, 219 U.S.P.Q. 834 (W.D. Pa. 1983)) and (rejected by, Ford Motor Co. v. Greatdomains.Com, Inc., 177 F. Supp. 2d 635, 177 A.L.R. Fed. 637 (E.D. Mich. 2001)) (holding that trademark law protects the trademark itself, even when not attached to separate goods and services).

[4] See Prestonettes, Inc., v. Coty, 264 U.S. 359, 44 S. Ct. 350 (1924) (Holmes J.); but see Champion Spark Plug Co. v. Sanders, 331 U.S. 125, 67 S. Ct. 1136, 73 U.S.P.Q. 133 (1947) (Douglas, J.). This is commonly referred to as the doctrine of "genuine goods."

the infringing activity."[5] Liability is independent of whether the officer knows that his or her acts will result in infringement.[6]

However, states have sovereign immunity protection that may shield them from suit. For example, a state university is immune under the Constitution's Eleventh Amendment from suit for damages in federal court brought under the Lanham Act and the Copyright Act despite provisions under both acts purporting to abrogate state sovereign immunity. Provisions explicitly requiring states to consent to suits in federal court where they are accused of copyright or trademark infringement are outside Congressional power granted under the Constitution.[7] Because Lanham Act claims may be brought in state court, common law sovereign immunity rather than Eleventh Amendment sovereign immunity applies to actions brought against a state in its own courts.[8] Despite limits on suits for damages, prospective injunctive or declaratory relief may be obtained in federal court against named state officers acting beyond their authority to prevent violations of federal law in the future.[9]

§ 11:8   Establishing trademark infringement—Ownership of the mark

Research References

West's Key Number Digest, Trademarks ⌖1360

A Certificate of Registration of the federally registered trademark provides *prima facie* evidence of the validity of the mark, the registration of the mark, the registrant's ownership of the mark, and the registrant's exclusive right to use the mark in commerce.[1] Inclusion on the Principal Register, maintained by the USPTO, also serves as constructive notice of these property rights to everyone living, working, or doing business in the United

---

[5]Babbit Electronics, Inc. v. Dynascan Corp., 38 F.3d 1161, 1183–1184, 33 U.S.P.Q.2d 1001 (11th Cir. 1994).

[6]Bambu Sales, Inc. v. Sultana Crackers, Inc., 683 F. Supp. 899, 913, 7 U.S.P.Q.2d 1177 (E.D. N.Y. 1988) (*citing* Polo Fashions, Inc. v. Branded Apparel Merchandising, Inc., 592 F. Supp. 648, 225 U.S.P.Q. 480 (D. Mass. 1984)).

[7]Chavez v. Arte Publico Press, 204 F.3d 601, 142 Ed. Law Rep. 36, 53 U.S.P.Q.2d 2009 (5th Cir. 2000) (vacated and remanded with instructions to dismiss; finding the Copyright Clause (Art. I, § 8, cl. 8) does not abrogate state immunity and Congress exceeded its remedial authority under the Due Process clause (Am. XIV, § 5)).

[8]Alden v. Maine, 527 U.S. 706, 709, 119 S. Ct. 2240, 5 Wage & Hour Cas. 2d (BNA) 609, 138 Lab. Cas. (CCH) P 33890 (1999) ("a sovereign's immunity in its own courts has always been understood to be within the sole control of the sovereign itself.").

[9]*See* Ex parte Young, 209 U.S. 123, 28 S. Ct. 441 (1908).

[Section 11:8]

[1]15 U.S.C.A. § 1057(b).

States. Once granted, the only way for someone with a potentially senior mark to overcome these presumptions without getting a court judgment is to contest the registration before the Trademark Trial and Appeal Board, operated under the authority of the USPTO.

In addition, a mark that has been registered for five years may become "incontestable" pursuant to 15 U.S.C.A. § 1065. The incontestability provision of the Lanham Act provides means for the registrant to quiet title in the ownership of his or her mark.[2] The registration of an incontestable mark is conclusive evidence of the validity of the mark, the registration of the mark, the registrant's ownership of the mark, and the registrant's exclusive right to use the mark in commerce.[3] However, incontestability does not speak to the relative strength of a mark beyond meeting the minimum statutory requirements for validity.

In order to establish ownership rights to a common law mark, a plaintiff must prove that (1) it used the mark and (2) the mark meets the requirements of being a trademark.[4] Proving use of the mark is usually very simple. The plaintiff need only show that the mark was used in commerce in connection with some goods or services.

However, since a common law mark has not been examined by the USPTO, the plaintiff must also prove that the word or symbol that it uses rises to the level of a trademark. This is done in court in the same way that it is done before the USPTO. The plaintiff must either prove that its mark is inherently distinctive, and therefore can function as a trademark, or it must show that its mark is descriptive and has acquired secondary meaning in the market.[5]

To establish ownership of trade dress, a plaintiff must prove that the trade dress has either acquired secondary meaning or is inherently distinctive and that the trade dress is nonfunctional.[6] The element of nonfunctionality makes trade dress cases different than trademark cases involving word-marks. The practice of

---

[2]Park 'N Fly, Inc. v. Dollar Park and Fly, Inc., 469 U.S. 189, 198, 105 S. Ct. 658, 224 U.S.P.Q. 327 (1985).

[3]15 U.S.C.A. § 1115(b).

[4]Loegering Mfg., Inc. v. Grouser Products, Inc., 330 F. Supp. 2d 1057, 1072 (D.N.D. 2004).

[5]First Bank v. First Bank System, Inc., 84 F.3d 1040, 1045, 38 U.S.P.Q.2d 1837 (8th Cir. 1996).

[6]TrafFix Devices, Inc. v. Marketing Displays, Inc., 532 U.S. 23, 29, 121 S. Ct. 1255, 1259, 58 U.S.P.Q.2d 1001 (2001); Two Pesos, Inc. v. Taco Cabana, Inc., 505 U.S. 763, 769, 112 S. Ct. 2753, 23 U.S.P.Q.2d 1081 (1992); I.P. Lund Trading ApS v. Kohler Co., 163 F.3d 27, 37-38, 49 U.S.P.Q.2d 1225 (1st Cir. 1998); First Brands Corp. v. Fred Meyer, Inc., 809 F.2d 1378, 1381, 1 U.S.P.Q.2d 1779, 87 A.L.R. Fed. 1 (9th Cir. 1987); LeSportsac, Inc. v. K Mart Corp., 754 F.2d 71, 75, 225 U.S.P.Q. 654, 78 A.L.R. Fed. 695 (2d Cir. 1985).

protecting only the nonfunctional aspects of the product under § 43(a) "strikes an appropriate balance between the goal of the functionality defense on the one hand, which is to encourage competition and the broadest dissemination of useful design features, and the Lanham Act's purpose on the other, which is to prevent confusion as to source."[7]

A product configuration is functional if its design is essentially dictated by its utility or purpose.[8] "Functionality is determined in light of utility, which is determined in light of superiority of design, and rests upon the foundation essential to effective competition."[9] The effect upon competition is really the crux of the matter.[10] "[A] product feature is functional if it is essential to the use or the purpose of the article or if it affects the cost or quality of the article."[11]

In determining the functionality of trade dress, courts focus on whether protection of the dress hinders competition or prohibits others, like the defendant, from competing effectively in the sales of goods.[12] Thus, "functional" does not mean simply that the feature serves a function, but it means that the feature is necessary to afford competitors means to compete effectively.[13]

Trade dress law recognizes the fact that virtually every product is a combination of functional and nonfunctional features. Trade dress is not "functional" simply because the design or feature serves any function at all. Protection is not lost merely because a shape or feature serves a useful purpose.[14] A particular trade dress made up of functional features will still be protected

---

[7]Artemide SpA v. Grandlite Design and Mfg. Co., Ltd., 672 F. Supp. 698, 708, 4 U.S.P.Q.2d 1915 (S.D. N.Y. 1987).

[8]In re Morton-Norwich Products, Inc., 671 F.2d 1332, 213 U.S.P.Q. 9 (C.C.P.A. 1982) (holding the shape of a spray container nonfunctional and thus registrable as a configuration mark).

[9]Morton-Norwich, 671 F.2d at 1340.

[10]Black & Decker, Inc. v. Hoover Service Center, 886 F.2d 1285, 12 U.S.P.Q.2d 1250 (Fed. Cir. 1989) (abrogated by, 122 S.Ct. 1831; Festo Corp. v. Shoketsu Kinzoku Kogyo Kabushiki Co., Ltd., 234 F.3d 558, 56 U.S.P.Q.2d 1865 (Fed. Cir. 2000)) and reinstated by 122 S.Ct. 1831 and (abrogated on other grounds by, Festo

Corp. v. Shoketsu Kinzoku Kogyo Kabushiki Co., Ltd., 234 F.3d 558, 56 U.S.P.Q.2d 1865 (Fed. Cir. 2000), judgment vacated, 535 U.S. 722, 122 S. Ct. 1831, 62 U.S.P.Q.2d 1705 (2002)) (holding DUSTBUSTER wedge-shaped bowl functional).

[11]Inwood Laboratories, Inc. v. Ives Laboratories, Inc., 456 U.S. 844, 850 n.10, 102 S. Ct. 2182, 214 U.S.P.Q. 1, 34 Fed. R. Serv. 2d 1101 (1982).

[12]Woodsmith Pub. Co. v. Meredith Corp., 904 F.2d 1244, 1244 n.6, 15 U.S.P.Q.2d 1053 (8th Cir. 1990).

[13]Schwinn Bicycle Co. v. Ross Bicycles, Inc., 870 F.2d 1176, 1188, 10 U.S.P.Q.2d 1001 (7th Cir. 1989).

[14]Truck Equipment Service Co. v. Fruehauf Corp., 536 F.2d 1210, 1218, 191 U.S.P.Q. 79 (8th Cir. 1976).

so long as the overall design itself is not proven to be functional.[15] Therefore, breaking a plaintiff's trade dress into individual elements and then attacking certain of those elements as being functional is improper, because it misconceives the scope of the appropriate functionality test.[16]

Evidence which is useful to demonstrate that a particular design is functional includes: a utility patent that discloses the utilitarian advantages of the design, advertising materials in which the originator of the design touts its utilitarian advantages, facts tending to establish the unavailability to competitors of alternative designs and facts indicating that the design results from a comparatively simple or cheap method of manufacturing the product or container.[17]

In contrast, the existence of alternative designs that are equally suitable to perform the utilitarian tasks of plaintiff's product is evidence that trade dress is not functional.[18] The existence of actual or potential alternative designs that work equally well strongly suggests that the particular design used by the plaintiff is neither functional nor needed by competitors to effectively compete on the merits.[19] The importance of alternative designs cannot be over emphasized and is a key factor in determining that a trade dress is nonfunctional.[20]

In determining functionality, courts should perform not only a feature-by-feature analysis of the shape of the article, but should assess also the totality of features or overall appearance of the article. The overall appearance of the product is protectable even if the product includes functional features.[21]

One particular type of functionality, which has been embraced by the Supreme Court, is referred to as "aesthetic functionality." A design is aesthetically functional if a design's aesthetic value

---

[15]Taco Cabana Intern., Inc. v. Two Pesos, Inc., 932 F.2d 1113, 19 U.S.P.Q.2d 1253 (5th Cir. 1991), judgment aff'd, 505 U.S. 763, 112 S. Ct. 2753, 120 L. Ed. 2d 615, 23 U.S.P.Q.2d 1081 (1992); AmBrit, Inc. v. Kraft, Inc., 812 F.2d 1531, 1538, 1 U.S.P.Q.2d 1161 (11th Cir. 1986).

[16]Hartford House, Ltd. v. Hallmark Cards, Inc., 846 F.2d 1268, 1272, 6 U.S.P.Q.2d 2038 (10th Cir. 1988); Le Sportsac, 754 F.2d at 76.

[17]In re Weber-Stephen Products Co., 3 U.S.P.Q.2d 1659, 1987 WL 124298 (T.T.A.B. 1987); Dentsply Intern., Inc. v. Kerr Mfg. Co., 732 F. Supp. 482, 15 U.S.P.Q.2d 1289 (D. Del.

1990).

[18]Morton-Norwich, 671 F.2d at 1341; Hartford House, 846 F.2d at 1273.

[19]In re Honeywell Inc., 8 U.S.P.Q.2d 1600, 1603, 1988 WL 252417 (T.T.A.B. 1988).

[20]Hartford House, 846 F.2d at 1273.

[21]American Greetings Corp. v. Dan-Dee Imports, Inc., 807 F.2d 1136, 1 U.S.P.Q.2d 1001 (3d Cir. 1986) (holding that overall appearance of "Care Bears" was nonfunctional despite functionality of "tummy graphics" as important feature).

lies in its ability to "confe[r] a significant benefit that cannot practically be duplicated by the use of alternative designs."[22] It is arguable that aesthetic functionality should be appropriately limited to cases in which a market for replacement products depends upon aesthetically matching products already sold.[23]

§ 11:9   Establishing trademark infringement—Likelihood of confusion

Research References

West's Key Number Digest, Trademarks ⊕1081

Full and fair competition requires that those who invest money and energy into the development of good will and a favorable reputation be allowed to reap the advantages of their investment.[1] As a major part of this investment, trademarks and trade dress will identify one seller's goods to consumers and will further distinguish them from goods sold by others.[2] The direct result of consumer trademark identification is that where a consumer has had a good experience with a product, he or she will simply look for the same trademark when making any future purchases.[3] Trademark and unfair competition law protects this commercial activity.

Another important feature of trademark law is the protection of consumers against confusion when purchasing a product.[4] The basic purpose of trademark protection is that no one should sell goods in such a way as to make it appear that they come from

---

[22]Restatement (Third) of Unfair Competition § 17, cmt. c (quoted in Qualitex Co. v. Jacobson Products Co., Inc., 514 U.S. 159, 170, 115 S. Ct. 1300, 34 U.S.P.Q.2d 1161 (1995)); see also Wallace Intern. Silversmiths, Inc. v. Godinger Silver Art Co., Inc., 916 F.2d 76, 81, 16 U.S.P.Q.2d 1555 (2d Cir. 1990).

[23]See Meadowcraft, Inc. v. B.I. Industries, Inc., 226 U.S.P.Q. 244, 1985 WL 72661 (N.D. Ala. 1985) (finding floral design stamped on patio furniture aesthetically functional where customers benefit in having new pieces match existing pieces); Deere & Co. v. Farmhand, Inc., 560 F. Supp. 85, 97–99, 217 U.S.P.Q. 252 (S.D. Iowa 1982), judgment aff'd, 721 F.2d 253 (8th Cir. 1983) (finding color

of new farm implements, painted a unique green color to match green tractors, aesthetically functional); Keene Corp. v. Paraflex Industries, Inc., 653 F.2d 822, 211 U.S.P.Q. 201 (3d Cir. 1981) (finding outdoor building lamps aesthetically functional where there were only a limited number of configurations or designs for a lamp that were architecturally compatible with the types of structures on which they were placed).

[Section 11:9]

[1]Fruehauf, 536 F.2d at 1215.

[2]McCarthy § 3:1.

[3]Schwinn, 870 F.2d at 1182.

[4]Inwood Laboratories, 456 U.S. at 854 n.14.

some other source.[5] Because of this recognized policy against consumer confusion, a new seller entering a market has a duty to properly dress his or her product so as to avoid a likelihood of consumers confusing it with the products of a first manufacturer.[6]

However, a trademark is not a monopoly on the use of a name or phrase. Rather, the legal relevance of a trademark is to show the source, identity, sponsorship or origin of the product.[7] Therefore, the principal focus in analyzing a trademark infringement action is often whether the consuming public is likely to be confused as to the source, identity, sponsorship, or origin of the goods.[8] The mere possibility of confusion is not enough. Rather, "there must be a substantial likelihood that the public will be confused."[9]

Courts frequently look to a multitude of factors in determining whether actions of an accused infringer rise to the level of causing a likelihood of confusion. Various versions of these tests involving multiple factors, sometimes known as "digits of confusion," were adopted by most federal circuit courts in the 1960s or 1970s. Over time, each circuit has developed its own list of factors. The test for a particular jurisdiction is usually referred to by the case in which the court adopted the approach. Thus, trademark attorneys will often refer to the Second Circuit's "Polaroid Test" or the Federal Circuit's "DuPont test" when discussing the likelihood of confusion in those circuits.[10]

Likelihood of confusion must be determined in light of the total effect of defendant's product and package in the eye and mind of the ordinary purchaser.[11] The test of consumer confusion is based upon whether the products create the same general overall impression, not whether they can be differentiated when subjected to a side-by-side comparison.[12] A reasonable consumer need not think that, in buying defendant's product, he or she is

[5]Chevron Chemical Co. v. Voluntary Purchasing Groups, Inc., 659 F.2d 695, 701, 212 U.S.P.Q. 904 (5th Cir. 1981).

[6]Mobil Oil Corp. v. Pegasus Petroleum Corp., 818 F.2d 254, 259, 2 U.S.P.Q.2d 1677 (2d Cir. 1987).

[7]Calvin Klein Cosmetics Corp. v. Lenox Laboratories, Inc., 815 F.2d 500, 503, 2 U.S.P.Q.2d 1285 (8th Cir. 1987).

[8]Vitek Systems, Inc. v. Abbott Laboratories, 675 F.2d 190, 192, 216 U.S.P.Q. 476, 10 Fed. R. Evid. Serv. 1195 (8th Cir. 1982).

[9]Fisher Stoves, Inc. v. All Nighter Stove Works, Inc., 626 F.2d 193, 194, 206 U.S.P.Q. 961 (1st Cir. 1980).

[10]See Polaroid Corp. v. Polarad Elecs. Corp., 287 F.2d 492, 128 U.S.P.Q. 411, 4 Fed. R. Serv. 2d 81 (2d Cir. 1961); Application of E. I. DuPont DeNemours & Co., 476 F.2d 1357, 177 U.S.P.Q. 563 (C.C.P.A. 1973).

[11]Vision Sports, Inc. v. Melville Corp., 888 F.2d 609, 616, 12 U.S.P.Q.2d 1740 (9th Cir. 1989).

[12]Direct Marketing of Virginia, Inc. v. E. Mishan & Sons, Inc., 753 F. Supp. 100, 106, 17 U.S.P.Q.2d 1683 (S.D. N.Y. 1990); Harold F. Ritchie, Inc. v. Chesebrough-Pond's, Inc., 281 F.2d 755, 762, 126 U.S.P.Q. 310 (2d Cir. 1960).

actually buying from plaintiff. If a reasonable consumer believes that defendant's product is licensed by plaintiff, or made by plaintiff and sold by defendant under its own brand name, a likelihood of confusion exists.[13] For example, with respect to trade dress, it is the overall impression given by plaintiff's trade dress which is important, not the differences in detail between it and defendant's product.[14]

Since each jurisdiction has a slightly different test for likelihood of confusion, it is important to examine the precedent in whatever jurisdiction a trademark case is venued. The *DuPont* test is an illustrative example with a number of factors that a court may rely on to determine whether an accused mark presents a likelihood of confusion:

- The similarity or dissimilarity of the marks in their entireties as to the appearance, sound, connotation and commercial impression;
- the similarity or dissimilarity and nature of the goods or services as described in an application or registration or in connection with which a prior mark is in use;
- the similarity or dissimilarity of established, likely-to-continue trade channels;
- the conditions under which buyers to whom sales are made, i.e., "impulse" versus careful, sophisticated purchasing;
- the fame of the prior mark (sales, advertising, length of use);
- the number and nature of similar marks in use on similar goods;
- the nature and extent of any actual confusion;
- the length of time during and conditions under which there has been concurrent use without evidence of actual confusion;
- the variety of goods on which a mark is or is not used (house mark, family of marks, product mark);
- the market interface between plaintiff and the owner of a prior mark;
- a mere "consent" to register or use;
- agreement provisions designed to preclude confusion, i.e., limitations on continued use of the marks by each party;
- assignment of the mark, application, registration and goodwill of the related business; and
- laches and estoppel attributable to the owner of a prior mark and indicative of lack of confusion;

---

[13]First Brands, 809 F.2d at 1384.
[14]St. Ives Laboratories, Inc. v.
Nature's Own Laboratories, 529 F. Supp. 347, 350 (C.D. Cal. 1981).

- the extent to which plaintiff has a right to exclude others from use of its mark on its goods;
- the extent of potential confusion, i.e., whether *de minimis* or substantial; and
- any other established fact probative of the effect of use.[15]

The *DuPont* factors are not elements a plaintiff must prove. Rather, they list the kinds of evidence that might be relevant in any given trademark infringement case. None of these factors is determinative of a finding of likelihood of confusion, and all factors should be considered as a whole.[16] A determination of likelihood of confusion is made by balancing the relevant factors in a particular case, keeping in mind that the factors are not listed in an order of merit and that each may, from case to case, play either a major or a minor role.[17] No single factor is controlling, and not all of the factors are relevant or of a similar weight in every case.[18]

As a practical matter, some of these factors are more important than others. In most trademark cases the strength of the plaintiff's mark, the similarity of the marks, and the similarity of the goods are typically the most important factors. Other factors may or may not be important. It is not uncommon that some of the factors are simply not applicable to a given case.

For example, the existence of actual confusion can be highly effective in showing the likelihood of consumer confusion if there has been sufficient time and opportunity for consumer confusion to occur. However, if a mark has not yet appeared commercially on the market, then there has likely been insufficient opportunity for consumer confusion to manifest itself, and few inferences can be drawn from the lack of actual confusion.[19]

As another example, the most important factors to consider in a likelihood of confusion analysis in the context of the World Wide Web are the similarities of the parties' marks, relatedness of the goods and services, and simultaneous use of the Web as a marketing channel.[20]

Also of significant importance in infringement cases is the

---

[15]DuPont, 476 F.2d at 1361.

[16]SquirtCo. v. Seven-Up Co., 628 F.2d 1086, 1091, 207 U.S.P.Q. 897 (8th Cir. 1980).

[17]DuPont, 476 F.2d at 1361.

[18]Opryland USA Inc. v. Great American Music Show, Inc., 970 F.2d 847, 850, 23 U.S.P.Q.2d 1471 (Fed. Cir. 1992).

[19]Nabisco, Inc. v. PF Brands, Inc., 191 F.3d 208, 228, 51 U.S.P.Q.2d 1882 (2d Cir. 1999) (abrogated on other grounds by, Moseley v. V Secret Catalogue, Inc., 537 U.S. 418, 123 S. Ct. 1115, 65 U.S.P.Q.2d 1801 (2003)).

[20]GoTo.com, Inc. v. Walt Disney Co., 202 F.3d 1199, 1205, 53 U.S.P.Q.2d 1652 (9th Cir. 2000) (*citing* Brookfield Communications, Inc. v. West Coast Entertainment Corp., 174 F.3d 1036, 1055 n.16, 50 U.S.P.Q.2d 1545

degree of protection afforded a mark. The degree of protection afforded a mark is partly a function of the strength of the mark; the weaker the mark, the less protection it will be afforded.[21] Strength of the mark refers to where on the spectrum of distinctiveness the mark lies. That is, an arbitrary or fanciful mark is very strong, while a descriptive mark is usually much weaker. However, the fact that a mark is descriptive does not mean it is weak. If a descriptive mark has acquired significant secondary meaning, it may become extremely strong. Registration of a trademark is *prima facie* evidence of the validity and ownership of the mark and is the basis for protection of an exclusive right to use the mark. However, registration does not guarantee the ability to exclude the defendant in the context of any particular infringement action.[22] The plaintiff is still required to show a likelihood of confusion.[23] Nor does the incontestability of a plaintiff's registration signify that the mark is strong.[24]

§ 11:10   Common discovery and evidentiary issues in trademark litigation—Proving secondary meaning

Research References

West's Key Number Digest, Trademarks ⬦1628

Strength is very important to the degree of protection afforded to a mark in an infringement or dilution action. Generally, the strength of a mark is related in large part to its distinctiveness. Certain types of marks, such as fanciful, arbitrary, or suggestive marks, are considered inherently distinctive and are enforceable without additional showings of distinctiveness. Descriptive marks can also be considered distinctive, but courts, as well as the USPTO, require additional proof the descriptive mark has acquired secondary meaning.

In trademark litigation, secondary meaning is shown in the same way as it is shown in registering a descriptive mark. A trademark or trade dress acquires secondary meaning when consumers associate the product with a single, perhaps anonymous source.[1] The concepts of secondary meaning and distinctiveness that are applicable to trademark law in general are also ap-

---

(9th Cir. 1999)).

[21]Scott v. Mego Intern., Inc., 519 F. Supp. 1118, 1129, 213 U.S.P.Q. 824 (D. Minn. 1981).

[22]Davis v. Walt Disney Co., 430 F.3d 901, 903, 77 U.S.P.Q.2d 1309, 35 Envtl. L. Rep. 20253 (8th Cir. 2005).

[23]Tana v. Dantanna's, 611 F.3d 767, 96 U.S.P.Q.2d 1001 (11th Cir. 2010).

[24]Munters Corp. v. Matsui America, Inc., 909 F.2d 250, 252, 15 U.S.P.Q.2d 1666 (7th Cir. 1990).

[Section 11:10]

[1]PAF S.r.l. v. Lisa Lighting Co., Ltd., 712 F. Supp. 394, 402, 12 U.S.P.

plicable to trade dress cases under § 43(a) of the Lanham Act. "If the features of the trade dress sought to be protected are arbitrary and serve no function either to describe the product or assist in its effective packaging, there is no reason to require a plaintiff to show consumer connotations associated with such arbitrarily selected features."[2]

Two primary ways of showing secondary meaning are by demonstrating extensive advertising, which presumably results in broad recognition, or by conducting a survey. Secondary meaning is usually proven by evidence that a substantial segment of the relevant market has associated the trademark with a source. In determining whether secondary meaning has been established, courts may consider the amount and nature of advertising using the trademark, the length of time and manner in which the trademark has been used, the exclusivity of the use, the amount of goods and services sold under the mark, unsolicited media coverage of the product, consumer surveys, direct consumer testimony, the number of customers and proof of intentional copying of the product.[3] Secondary meaning is an issue of fact.[4]

A plaintiff is not required to prove the existence of each and every one of these elements; they are guidelines in determining whether secondary meaning exists.[5] In fact, a strong showing of even a single factor may be enough to prove that the trademark comes from a single source.[6] For example, extensive advertising by a trademark owner can establish the requisite recognition of the product by purchasers.[7]

In determining whether a trademark or trade dress has obtained secondary meaning, the relevant market or consumer group must be defined. The relevant consumer group is generally defined as the class of people who would normally consider

---

Q.2d 1161 (S.D. N.Y. 1989); Centaur Communications, Ltd. v. A/S/M Communications, Inc., 830 F.2d 1217, 1221-22, 4 U.S.P.Q.2d 1541 (2d Cir. 1987).

[2]Chevron, 659 F.2d at 702.

[3]U.S. Gold & Silver Investments, Inc. v. Director, U.S. Mint, 682 F. Supp. 484, 488, 5 U.S.P.Q.2d 1213 (D. Or. 1987), judgment aff'd, 885 F.2d 620, 12 U.S.P.Q.2d 1237 (9th Cir. 1989); Bloomfield Industries, Div. of Specialty Equipment Companies, Inc. v. Stewart Sandwiches, Inc., 716 F. Supp. 380, 385, 12 U.S.P.Q.2d 1626 (N.D. Ind. 1989); see also In re Steelbuilding.com, 415 F.3d 1293,

1300, 75 U.S.P.Q.2d 1420 (Fed. Cir. 2005).

[4]Japan Telecom, Inc. v. Japan Telecom America Inc., 287 F.3d 866, 873, 62 U.S.P.Q.2d 1593 (9th Cir. 2002).

[5]Thompson Medical Co., Inc. v. Pfizer Inc., 753 F.2d 208, 217, 225 U.S.P.Q. 124 (2d Cir. 1985).

[6]M. Kramer Mfg. Co., Inc. v. Andrews, 783 F.2d 421, 449, 228 U.S.P.Q. 705 (4th Cir. 1986).

[7]Burke-Parsons-Bowlby Corp. v. Appalachian Log Homes, Inc., 871 F.2d 590, 596, 10 U.S.P.Q.2d 1443 (6th Cir. 1989).

purchasing the product.[8]

The most common way of showing secondary meaning is to show extensive advertising and commercial success.[9] In addition, however, a plaintiff must establish a nexus between its trademark or trade dress and its evidence of secondary meaning. Evidence of commercial success of a product does not establish secondary meaning in the appearance of the product unless there is proof that the trademark or trade dress is responsible for that commercial success; something else (particularly, the nature of the product itself) may be responsible.[10] Strong market demand for a product usually signifies desirability of the product, not secondary meaning in its trade dress.[11]

Evidence of deliberate copying can also lead to an inference of secondary meaning. At the same time, a contrary inference can be drawn where the accused infringer is simply attempting to satisfy market demand for a particular product and makes reasonable efforts to distinguish its goods from those of the plaintiff by using its own trademarks.[12]

Consumer surveys are yet another type of evidence that can be used to support an inference of secondary meaning.[13] Despite some flaws in methodology, surveys are generally admissible on this point because the law recognizes that no survey will be perfect.[14] The proper approach is to view survey evidence with some understanding of the difficulty in devising and running a survey and to use any technical defects in the methodology to lessen evidentiary weight but not to reject the results out of hand.[15]

---

[8]PAF S.r.l. v. Lisa Lighting Co., Ltd., 712 F. Supp. 394, 12 U.S.P.Q.2d 1161 (S.D. N.Y. 1989) (a relevant consumer group consisted of those persons interested in home and office design); Remcraft Lighting Products, Inc. v. Maxim Lighting, Inc., 706 F. Supp. 855, 11 U.S.P.Q.2d 1808 (S.D. Fla. 1989) (the relevant buyer group was made up of wholesale customers); National Shoe Stores Co. v. National Shoes of N.Y., Inc., 213 Md. 328, 131 A.2d 909, 913, 113 U.S.P.Q. 380 (1957) (relevant consumer group framed by geography).

[9]But see OBX-Stock, Inc. v. Bicast, Inc., 558 F.3d 334, 89 U.S.P.Q.2d 1928 (4th Cir. 2009) (even though plaintiff spent a substantial amount of money on advertising, consumers only associated "OBX" with a geographical region leaving "OBX" with no secondary meaning).

[10]Aromatique, Inc. v. Gold Seal, Inc., 28 F.3d 863, 873, 31 U.S.P.Q.2d 1481 (8th Cir. 1994).

[11]Braun Inc. v. Dynamics Corp. of America, 975 F.2d 815, 827, 24 U.S.P.Q.2d 1121 (Fed. Cir. 1992).

[12]Aromatique, 28 F.3d at 871.

[13]Centaur Communications, 830 F.2d at 1223.

[14]See McCarthy on Trademarks and Unfair Competition § 32:190.

[15]SquirtCo. v. Seven-Up Co., 628 F.2d 1086, 1091, 207 U.S.P.Q. 897 (8th Cir. 1980).

§ 11:11 Common discovery and evidentiary issues in trademark litigation—Proving likelihood of confusion

Research References

West's Key Number Digest, Trademarks ⌐1629

As noted previously, likelihood of confusion is based upon a balancing of many different factors. In any particular case, different factors may be applicable. However, in most cases, the most important factors are strength of the mark, similarity of the marks and similarity of the goods. Also, evidence of intentional infringement and actual confusion are usually sought by a trademark owner because of the powerful effect of those sorts of evidence.

The strength or distinctiveness of a mark is measured by its tendency to identify the goods or services sold under the mark as emanating from a particular, although possibly anonymous, source.[1] Generally the strength of a mark depends on two factors: (1) the distinctiveness of the mark; and (2) the extent to which the mark is recognized by the relevant consuming class.[2] Strength of a trademark is typically shown by factors like: the degree and manner of plaintiff's advertising; the length and manner of plaintiff's use of the trademark; and whether plaintiff's use of the trademark has been exclusive.[3]

Some marks may be so strong that they become "famous." The fame of the trademark or trade dress plays a dominant role in cases featuring a famous or strong trademark or trade dress. Famous marks enjoy a wide latitude of legal protection, because a mark with extensive public recognition and renown deserves more protection than an obscure or weak mark.[4] As one example, antidilution statutes were initially established in part to protect this fame and goodwill from being eroded over time by the acts of others. As the legal concept of dilution has been refined, several jurisdictions have statutes also providing protection to merely strong or inherently distinctive marks.

Similarity of the marks is based on an examination of the

[Section 11:11]

[1]Beer Nuts, Inc. v. Clover Club Foods Co., 711 F.2d 934, 939, 221 U.S.P.Q. 209 (10th Cir. 1983).

[2]Woodroast Systems, Inc. v. Restaurants Unlimited, Inc., 793 F. Supp. 906, 911, 24 U.S.P.Q.2d 1748 (D. Minn. 1992), aff'd, 994 F.2d 844 (8th Cir. 1993); Aveda Corp. v. Evita Market-ing, Inc., 706 F. Supp. 1419, 1428, 12 U.S.P.Q.2d 1091 (D. Minn. 1989).

[3]Clamp Mfg. Co., Inc. v. Enco Mfg. Co., Inc., 870 F.2d 512, 517, 10 U.S.P.Q.2d 1226 (9th Cir. 1989).

[4]Kenner Parker Toys Inc. v. Rose Art Industries, Inc., 963 F.2d 350, 352, 22 U.S.P.Q.2d 1453 (Fed. Cir. 1992).

marks as a whole, including visual impression and sound.[5] The use of identical words, or even dominant words in common, does not automatically mean that two marks are similar. Rather, in analyzing the similarities of sight, sound and meaning between two marks, a court must look to the overall impression created by the marks and not merely compare individual features. Further, although similarity is measured by the trademarks as entities, similarities weigh more heavily than differences.[6] Exact duplication of a mark is not required. The two marks need not be identical to be similar.[7] Minor differences between the products will not avoid confusion. For example, comparison of the respective color schemes, lettering styles and package designs should be made to determine whether the two marks, as used in the marketplace, are different enough to avoid consumer confusion.[8] The fact that an allegedly infringing mark is not identical to a plaintiff's mark does not prevent a likelihood of confusion between the marks. As one court said:

> Of course few would be stupid enough to make exact copies of an-
> other's mark or symbol. It has been well said that the most success-
> ful form of copying is to employ enough points of similarity to
> confuse the public with enough points of difference to confuse the
> courts.[9]

Because § 43(a) of the Lanham Act defines trade dress infringement in terms of consumer confusion, there is no set standard for the degree of similarity in packaging and labeling that constitutes actionable trade dress infringement. Consumers commonly identify a product's source by considering the size, font, color, and location of wording on a package or label.[10] The arrangement of background colors, photographs, and drawings used in packaging and labeling also may serve as source identifiers to consumers.[11] Packaging of a product can include the sale environment such as display advertisements or the shape of a building

---

[5]SquirtCo. v. Seven-Up Co., 628 F.2d 1086, 1091, 207 U.S.P.Q. 897 (8th Cir. 1980).

[6]Vitek, 675 F.2d at 192.

[7]David Sherman Corp. v. Heublein, Inc., 340 F.2d 377, 380, 144 U.S.P.Q. 249 (8th Cir. 1965).

[8]General Mills, Inc. v. Kellogg Co., 824 F.2d 622, 627, 3 U.S.P.Q.2d 1442 (8th Cir. 1987).

[9]Baker v. Master Printers Union of New Jersey, 34 F. Supp. 808, 811, 47 U.S.P.Q. 69 (D.N.J. 1940).

[10]Time Inc. Magazine Co. v. Globe Communications Corp., 712 F. Supp. 1103, 16 Media L. Rep. (BNA) 1746, 10 U.S.P.Q.2d 1915 (S.D. N.Y. 1989) (holding that cover format of People Magazine, including condensed weight lettering, display of logo with contrasting colored border, and secondary cover photograph in the upper right hand corner was protectable trade dress).

[11]Chevron Chemical Co. v. Voluntary Purchasing Groups, Inc., 659 F.2d 695, 212 U.S.P.Q. 904 (5th Cir. 1981) (finding labeling on bottles of lawn and garden chemicals violates § 43(a)).

wherein the product is sold.[12] Trade dress can extend to marketing strategies and slogans.[13] Trade dress can also extend to the distinctive decor of a restaurant.[14]

Similarity of the goods, sometimes called "competitive proximity" or the "degree of competition," refers to whether the products compete with each other or are substantially different so that no reasonable consumer would think that they come from the same source. A number of factors are considered in determining the degree of competition between goods, including:

- the manner in which the competing goods are advertised, displayed or sold,
- the place where they are sold, and
- the class of customers for whom they are designed and to whom they are sold.[15]

Similarity in the advertising campaigns used for the products may also be considered.[16] Thus, where products are in direct competition, the degree of similarity required to prove a likelihood of confusion is less than situations where the products do not compete directly against each other.[17]

Although these three factors are usually the most important, other factors, if present, are very helpful in proving likelihood of confusion. Likelihood of confusion is bolstered by finding that a defendant adopted a trademark with the intent of deriving benefit from the reputation of the trademark owner.[18] A newcomer to a market has a duty to avoid trademarks that may be confusingly similar to the well-known trademark of a competitor. "One who adopts a mark similar to another already established in the marketplace does so at his peril, because the court presumes that he can accomplish his purpose: that is, that the public will be

---

[12]Commerce Foods, Inc. v. PLC Commerce Corp., 504 F. Supp. 190, 212 U.S.P.Q. 137 (S.D. N.Y. 1980); Clayton v. Howard Johnson Franchise Systems, Inc., 730 F. Supp. 1553 (M.D. Fla. 1988).

[13]Original Appalachian Artworks, Inc. v. Toy Loft, Inc., 684 F.2d 821, 215 U.S.P.Q. 745 (11th Cir. 1982) (enjoining use of adoption papers and a birth certificate in the sale of dolls); Chemical Corp. of America v. Anheuser-Busch, Inc., 306 F.2d 433, 134 U.S.P.Q. 524, 2 A.L.R.3d 739 (5th Cir. 1962).

[14]Two Pesos, Inc. v. Taco Cabana, Inc., 505 U.S. 763, 112 S. Ct. 2753, 23 U.S.P.Q.2d 1081 (1992).

[15]Morningside Group Ltd. v. Morningside Capital Group, L.L.C., 182 F.3d 133, 139, 51 U.S.P.Q.2d 1183 (2d Cir. 1999); McGregor-Doniger Inc. v. Drizzle Inc., 599 F.2d 1126, 1134-35, 202 U.S.P.Q. 81, 5 Fed. R. Evid. Serv. 521 (2d Cir. 1979).

[16]John H. Harland Co. v. Clarke Checks, Inc., 711 F.2d 966, 976, 219 U.S.P.Q. 515 (11th Cir. 1983).

[17]SquirtCo., 628 F.2d at 1091.

[18]John H. Harland, 711 F.2d at 977.

deceived."[19] A wrongful intent can be inferred where an alleged infringer knew of the plaintiff's dress, had freedom to choose any trademark, and "just happened" to choose a trademark confusingly similar to plaintiff's.[20] Any doubt as to whether confusion, deception or mistake is likely must be resolved against the newcomer.[21]

Courts look at multiple factors in assessing likelihood of confusion, including evidence of actual confusion. Any evidence of actual confusion is strong proof of the fact of a likelihood of confusion.[22] While helpful, actual confusion is not necessary to finding likelihood of confusion.[23] The "statutory test is likelihood of confusion, not actual confusion." Evidence of actual confusion is rare but, if it exists, can be very helpful in proving likelihood of confusion.[24] Evidence of an actual buyer communicating with the wrong source of the product is an important factor in proving the likelihood of confusion because even with a single instance of actual confusion, the confused buyer is precisely the one for whom confusion is most significant.[25] An example of this can be found in *WWP, Inc. v. Wounded Warriors Family Support*.[26] The court affirmed the damages award after relying on the testimony that a donator donated to the wrong organization based upon misleading information on the infringer's website.[27] The donator decided to stop donations because they never received a thank you from the organization they thought they were donating to.[28] Actual consumer confusion may also be shown indirectly by circumstantial evidence, such as consumer surveys.[29] Conversely, in some circuits, "it is certainly proper for the trial judge to infer from the absence of actual confusion that there was no likelihood of confusion."[30]

Confusion is more likely when the goods involved are relatively inexpensive. Purchasers typically exercise less care in the selection of inexpensive items that they purchase on impulse. This is

---

[19]Beer Nuts, 711 F.2d at 941.

[20]Dreyfus Fund, Inc. v. Royal Bank of Canada, 525 F. Supp. 1108, 1121, 213 U.S.P.Q. 872 (S.D. N.Y. 1981).

[21]Soft Sheen Products, Inc. v. Revlon, Inc., 675 F. Supp. 408, 416, 4 U.S.P.Q.2d 1519 (N.D. Ill. 1987).

[22]David Sherman, 340 F.2d at 380.

[23]Amstar Corp. v. Domino's Pizza, Inc., 615 F.2d 252, 263, 205 U.S.P.Q. 969, 29 Fed. R. Serv. 2d 1528 (5th Cir. 1980).

[24]Wella Corp. v. California Concept

Corp., 558 F.2d 1019, 1023, 194 U.S.P.Q. 419 (C.C.P.A. 1977).

[25]Brunswick Corp. v. Spinit Reel Co., 832 F.2d 513, 522, 4 U.S.P.Q.2d 1497, 23 Fed. R. Evid. Serv. 1272 (10th Cir. 1987).

[26]WWP, Inc. v. Wounded Warriors Family Support, Inc., 628 F.3d 1032, 97 U.S.P.Q.2d 1688 (8th Cir. 2011).

[27]WWP, 628 F.3d at 1044.

[28]WWP, 628 F.3d at 1044.

[29]Brunswick, 832 F.2d at 522.

[30]McGregor-Doniger, 599 F.2d at 1136.

especially true for goods which are staple, relatively inexpensive, and subject to frequent replacement.[31] "Purchasers of such products have long been held to a lesser standard of purchasing care."[32]

An approach to establishing likelihood of confusion that is particularly relevant to the Internet is a theory called initial interest confusion. "Initial interest confusion occurs when the defendant uses the plaintiff's trademark 'in a manner calculated' to capture initial consumer attention, even though no actual sale is finally completed as a result of the confusion."[33] One court noted that "[a]lthough [initial customer confusion is] dispelled before an actual sale occurs, initial interest confusion impermissibly capitalizes on the goodwill associated with a mark and is therefore actionable trademark infringement."[34] Initial interest confusion can also result when a website uses another's trademark in a metatag, which is encoded in web pages but not ordinarily visible to users surfing the Web. One court explained initial interest confusion, in the context of embedded metatags, as follows:

> Using another's trademark in one's metatags is much like posting a sign with another's trademark in front of one's store. Suppose West Coast's competitor (let's call it "Blockbuster") puts up a billboard on a highway reading—"West Coast Video: 2 miles ahead at Exit 7"— where West Coast is really located at Exit 8 but Blockbuster is located at Exit 7. Customers looking for West Coast's store will pull off at Exit 7 and drive around looking for it. Unable to locate West Coast, but seeing the Blockbuster store right by the highway entrance, they may simply rent there. Even consumers who prefer West Coast may find it not worth the trouble to continue searching for West Coast since there is a Blockbuster right there. Customers are not confused in the narrow sense: they are fully aware that they are purchasing from Blockbuster and they have no reason to believe that Blockbuster is related to, or in any way sponsored by, West Coast. Nevertheless, the fact that there is only initial consumer confusion does not alter the fact that Blockbuster would be misappropriating West Coast's acquired goodwill.[35]

The doctrine of initial interest confusion has not been followed by

---

[31]In re Martin's Famous Pastry Shoppe, Inc., 748 F.2d 1565, 1567, 223 U.S.P.Q. 1289 (Fed. Cir. 1984).

[32]In re Martin's, 748 F.2d at 1567.

[33]Interstellar Starship Services, Ltd. v. Epix, Inc., 304 F.3d 936, 941, 64 U.S.P.Q.2d 1514 (9th Cir. 2002) (quoting Brookfield Communications, Inc. v. West Coast Entertainment Corp.,

174 F.3d 1036, 1062, 50 U.S.P.Q.2d 1545 (9th Cir. 1999)).

[34]Playboy Enterprises, Inc. v. Netscape Communications Corp., 354 F.3d 1020, 1025, 69 U.S.P.Q.2d 1417 (9th Cir. 2004).

[35]Brookfield Communications, 174 F.3d at 1064.

some courts.[36] Nonetheless, it remains a significant means of potentially establishing liability beyond the traditional bounds of the likelihood of confusion analysis for trademark infringement.

§ 11:12   Common discovery and evidentiary issues in trademark litigation—Third party uses

Research References

West's Key Number Digest, Trademarks ⊱1529, 1566

Defendants in trademark infringement cases often argue that the trademark owner has no trademark rights because there are many third parties using similar marks. As a general rule, an accused infringer may not claim that it must be excused from infringement because others are guilty of the same wrong.[1]

The Court of Appeals for the Ninth Circuit addressed just this issue in *Sealy, Inc. v. Easy Living, Inc.*[2] The Ninth Circuit found that it was proper to exclude evidence which tended to show that plaintiff Sealy allowed some third parties to use its mark, but refused to allow defendant to do so.[3] The court held that "whether Sealy, under different circumstances, objected to sale of its mattresses with non-Sealy foundations in east coast markets is ultimately irrelevant to whether [defendants] intended that [their] foundations would be passed off as Sealy products."[4]

An increasingly common tactic for a trademark infringement defendant is to present a computer search showing a large number of "hits" of the allegedly infringing mark. However, this sort of evidence is usually of minimal weight. Evidence of third party use is of no probative value in the absence of actual use of those marks:

The same is true of the references in the LEXIS/NEXIS excerpts. Their appearance in these articles does not prove that they are in use. But, in addition, with regard to the latter, it is not clear how

---

[36]*E.g.,* Holiday Inns, Inc. v. 800 Reservation, Inc., 86 F.3d 619, 39 U.S.P.Q.2d 1181, 1996 FED App. 0179P (6th Cir. 1996) (use of the phone number "1-800-H(zero)LIDAY" was not a use of the mark 1-800-HOLIDAY nor did it create customer confusion with respect to that mark).

[Section 11:12]

[1]National Lead Co. v. Wolfe, 223 F.2d 195, 204, 105 U.S.P.Q. 462 (9th Cir. 1955); Playboy Enterprises, Inc. v. Chuckleberry Pub., Inc., 486 F. Supp. 414, 423 n.9, 206 U.S.P.Q. 70 (S.D.

N.Y. 1980); Century 21 Real Estate Corp. v. Sandlin, 846 F.2d 1175, 1181, 6 U.S.P.Q.2d 2034 (9th Cir. 1988) (discovery regarding other infringers is irrelevant to the issue of likelihood of confusion).

[2]Sealy, Inc. v. Easy Living, Inc., 743 F.2d 1378, 224 U.S.P.Q. 364, 1984-2, 1984-2 Trade Cas. (CCH) ¶ 66320, 16 Fed. R. Evid. Serv. 1061 (9th Cir. 1984).

[3]Sealy, 743 F.2d at 1382.

[4]Sealy, 743 F.2d at 1382.

these terms are being presented, that is, whether they're intended to be trademarks, trade names or other.[5]

Although third-party use is not relevant on the issue of infringement, courts look to these activities when evaluating the strength of the mark. For example, in *Andy Warhol Enterprises, Inc. v. Time Inc.*,[6] the court found "that third-party use or infringement cannot be raised by an alleged infringer as a defense or excuse, but may be considered in determining the likelihood of confusion." The court concluded that they would "consider third-party uses in evaluating the strength of the mark."[7]

§ 11:13 Common discovery and evidentiary issues in trademark litigation—Surveys

Research References

West's Key Number Digest, Trademarks ⊘1629(4)

A survey showing the state of mind of prospective purchasers can be used to show the existence of a likelihood of confusion.[1] Of course, no survey will be perfect.[2] While no definitive percentage exists above which actual consumer confusion has undoubtedly taken place, 19% is a significant level of consumer confusion.[3] Cases with a 7.7% level of confusion have been determined to be strong evidence of likelihood of confusion.[4]

§ 11:14 Remedies—Injunctions

Research References

West's Key Number Digest, Trademarks ⊘1700

The owner of a federally registered trademark is entitled to an injunction in order to prevent the use of an infringing mark:

The several courts * * * shall have power to grant injunctions, according to the principles of equity and upon such terms as the court

---

[5]Charrette Corp. v. Bowater Communication Papers Inc., 13 U.S.P.Q.2d 2040, 2043, 1989 WL 274417 (T.T.A.B. 1989); see also In re Merrill Lynch, Pierce, Fenner, and Smith, Inc., 828 F.2d 1567, 1571, 4 U.S.P.Q.2d 1141 (Fed. Cir. 1987).

[6]Andy Warhol Enterprises, Inc. v. Time Inc., 700 F. Supp. 760, 764, 9 U.S.P.Q.2d 1454 (S.D. N.Y. 1988).

[7]Warhol, 700 F. Supp. at 765.

[Section 11:13]

[1]La Maur, Inc. v. Revlon, Inc., 245 F. Supp. 839, 842-43, 146 U.S.P.Q. 654 (D. Minn. 1965).

[2]See McCarthy § 32:190.

[3]National Football League v. Governor of State of Del., 435 F. Supp. 1372, 195 U.S.P.Q. 803 (D. Del. 1977).

[4]Grotrian, Helfferich, Schulz, Th. Steinweg Nachf. v. Steinway and Sons, 365 F. Supp. 707, 717, 180 U.S.P.Q. 506 (S.D. N.Y. 1973), judgment modified on other grounds, 523 F.2d 1331, 186 U.S.P.Q. 436 (2d Cir. 1975).

may deem reasonable, to prevent the violation of any right of the registrant of a mark registered in the Patent and Trademark Office.[1]

Because the injury caused by confusion is by its nature irreparable, injunctive relief is routine in trademark and trade dress cases. Irreparable harm necessary for preliminary injunctive relief may be presumed where there is a high probability of confusion as to sponsorship.[2]

An injunction must be specific in its terms and appropriately protect plaintiff's interests. An injunction generally includes the elimination of confusion on all of defendant's future sales, but may not require elimination of the confusion caused by defendant's past sales.[3] Temporary restraining orders are also available under appropriate circumstances. Infringing articles may be impounded or destroyed under § 36 of the Lanham Act (15 U.S.C.A. § 1118).

Obtaining an injunction under § 43(a) may be easier than obtaining monetary relief. Injunctive relief is generally granted upon a showing of a "likelihood of confusion," but monetary relief may be denied absent either proof of actual confusion or proof of intent or willfulness. Factual proof of damage may require a higher level of proof than proof of amount of damage.

§ 11:15 Remedies—Damages

Research References

West's Key Number Digest, Trademarks ☞1650

In trademark and trade dress cases, a successful plaintiff is entitled, subject to the principles of equity, to recover:

- defendant's profits,
- any damages sustained by the plaintiff, and
- the costs of the action.[1]

In addition,

the court may enter judgment, . . . for any sum above the amount found as actual damages, not exceeding three times such amount. * * * The court in exceptional cases may award reasonable at-

---

[Section 11:14]

[1]15 U.S.C.A. § 1116(a).

[2]Sunward Electronics, Inc. v. McDonald, 362 F.3d 17, 26, 69 U.S.P.Q.2d 2002 (2d Cir. 2004) (*citing* Church of Scientology Intern. v. Elmira Mission of the Church of Scientology, 794 F.2d 38, 41, 230 U.S.P.Q. 325 (2d Cir. 1986)).

[3]PAF S.r.l. v. Lisa Lighting Co., Ltd., 712 F. Supp. 394, 12 U.S.P.Q.2d 1161 (S.D. N.Y. 1989) (holding that recall of 1500 desk lamps was not appropriate).

[Section 11:15]

[1]15 U.S.C.A. § 1117(a); *see also* Restatement (Third) of Unfair Competition §§ 36 to 37 (1995).

torney fees to the prevailing party.[2]

While damages are available upon a finding of infringement, typical trademark and trade dress cases do not result in large monetary awards. The principal remedy for trademark and trade dress infringement is an injunction. Parties bringing an infringement action should generally not enter litigation with the expectation of receiving significant monetary damages.

To recover monetary damages under § 35 of the Lanham Act, courts have required the plaintiff to prove damage by actual consumer confusion or deception resulting from the violation, rather than a mere likelihood of confusion. A finding of actual confusion requires some evidence from the marketplace, rather than a mere comparison of marks by the fact finder. "Actual consumer confusion may be shown by direct evidence, a diversion of sales or direct testimony from the public, or by circumstantial evidence such as consumer surveys."[3] In certain circumstances, plaintiffs have not been required to prove actual confusion for an award of damages.[4]

There are several manners by which monetary damages may be measured under the theories of recovery authorized by statute, including:

- defendant's profits from the infringing sales;
- plaintiff's actual business losses;
- plaintiff's loss of profits;
- costs of litigation;
- multiplied damages under the trebling provision of § 35;
- punitive damages in certain situations;
- attorney's fees incurred during prosecution;
- attorney litigation fees for the exceptional case; and
- pre-judgment interest.

Any accounting period for measuring damages should be co-extensive with the period of infringement.

The most common theories of recovery used to support a judgment for damages include disgorgement of defendant's profits and awarding lost profits and/or actual business losses incurred by the plaintiff due to the infringing activities. Those two

---

[2]15 U.S.C.A. § 1117(a).

[3]Brunswick, 832 F.2d at 525.

[4]Resource Developers, Inc. v. Statue of Liberty-Ellis Island Foundation, Inc., 926 F.2d 134, 17 U.S.P.Q.2d 1842 (2d Cir. 1991) (holding that proof of intent or willful infringement shifts burden to defendant to prove absence of confusion); Getty Petroleum Corp. v. Island Transp. Corp., 878 F.2d 650, 11 U.S.P.Q.2d 1334 (2d Cir. 1989) (holding that evidence of actual confusion was not necessary for situations in which the purchaser could not discover the falsity of the advertisement at the time of sale, such as for record albums and gasoline).

principal theories of recovery may be cumulative.[5] However, where double recovery would occur, such as where the parties engage in direct competition and relevant customer sales would overlap, then cumulative recovery under those two theories is generally *not* allowed.[6]

An award of defendant's profits from infringing sales can be justified under an "unjust enrichment" rationale or as an indirect method of measuring "plaintiff's loss." However, courts generally only grant an accounting of the defendant's profits where there has been willful infringement or palming off.[7] Under either rationale, in assessing the defendant's profits, the plaintiff need only prove the amount of defendant's sales.[8] Once the plaintiff makes a *prima facie* showing of the defendant's gross sales, the burden shifts to the defendant to prove any deductions.[9]

Possible deductions which the defendant may prove to reduce the award include costs of producing the article, overhead costs and advertising costs. In order to lower the amount of the plaintiff's recovery, the defendant must prove all expenses, costs or deductions which it claims to have incurred in selling its product.[10] In this regard, the defendant must supply specific corroborating evidence of any deduction claimed.[11]

In addition to deductions claimed by the defendant, an award of defendant's profits may be limited by the plaintiff's capabilities. A damage award may be reduced if the plaintiff could not have manufactured enough goods or could not have sold the goods in the geographic locations where the defendant's sales occurred.[12] The award may be reduced further if the court apportions sales according to the percentage of defendant's consumers who were

---

[5]George Basch Co., Inc. v. Blue Coral, Inc., 968 F.2d 1532, 1537, 23 U.S.P.Q.2d 1351 (2d Cir. 1992); Merriam-Webster, Inc. v. Random House, Inc., 815 F. Supp. 691, 701, 26 U.S.P.Q.2d 1161 (S.D. N.Y. 1993), on reconsideration in part, 1993 WL 205043 (S.D. N.Y. 1993) and vacated, 35 F.3d 65, 32 U.S.P.Q.2d 1010 (2d Cir. 1994) (On appeal, the court vacated the injunction and dismissed the complaint holding that, as a matter of law, no confusion or likelihood of confusion existed, and there was no dilution under New York law of either Merriam-Webster's trademarks or trade dress).

[6]*McCarthy*, § 30:73.

[7]*See, e.g.*, Champion Spark Plug Co. v. Sanders, 331 U.S. 125, 67 S. Ct. 1136, 91 L. Ed. 1386, 73 U.S.P.Q. 133 (1947) (Douglas, J.); George Basch Co., Inc. v. Blue Coral, Inc., 968 F.2d 1532, 23 U.S.P.Q.2d 1351 (2d Cir. 1992); Restatement Third, Unfair Competition § 37.

[8]15 U.S.C.A. § 1117(a).

[9]Mishawaka Rubber & Woolen Mfg. Co. v. S.S. Kresge Co., 316 U.S. 203, 205-206, 62 S. Ct. 1022, 86 L. Ed. 1381, 53 U.S.P.Q. 323 (1942).

[10]15 U.S.C.A. § 1117(a).

[11]Maltina Corp. v. Cawy Bottling Co., Inc., 613 F.2d 582, 205 U.S.P.Q. 489 (5th Cir. 1980).

[12]Truck Equipment Service Co. v. Fruehauf Corp., 536 F.2d 1210, 191 U.S.P.Q. 79 (8th Cir. 1976).

confused (based on survey evidence).

Awarding infringement damages according to a plaintiff's lost profits is consistent with the basic tort theory of attempting to put the plaintiff into a position absent the infringing acts of the tortfeasor. Generally, plaintiff's damages are measured as the volume of defendant's infringing sales multiplied by plaintiff's profit per additional sale.[13] The plaintiff's damages may also be measured under a price erosion theory, which measures the extent to which the plaintiff's profits in the goods dropped during the period of infringement. The plaintiff need only make a *prima facie* showing of reasonably forecasted profits (including pre-infringement "base" profits), whereupon the defendant has the burden of proving that the plaintiff's losses were caused by something other than the defendant's own wrongful conduct.

Plaintiff's damages may also be assessed based upon the plaintiff's actual business losses, without having to forecast income the plaintiff would have made if not for the defendant's infringement. The plaintiff's actual business losses may include:

- loss of sales due to actual confusion;
- damage to the plaintiff's business good will;
- loss of income resulting from a reduction in the price of goods due to the infringing competition;
- expenses, such as remedial advertising actually incurred in preventing purchasers from being deceived by the infringer's wrongful product; and
- loss of a reasonable royalty that would have accrued from licensing the mark to the defendant.

Loss of sales due to actual confusion includes documented instances of lost sales. Damage to the plaintiff's good will may also be quantified as an actual business loss. Expenses incurred to avoid customer confusion are a classic form of compensatory damages. Actual damages for the loss of a reasonable royalty generally result in a relatively low award, but may be an attractive option to plaintiffs where other measures of damages are difficult to prove.

At some point during an infringement trial, the judge typically requires the plaintiff to choose between a defendant's profits or a plaintiff's damages theory of recovery. Awards under a defendant's profits theory tend to be smaller because the defendant has the ability to prove up significant deductions that reduce the ultimate award. However, it is common for plaintiffs to ultimately

---

[13]Celebrity Service Intern. Inc. v. Celebrity World Inc., 9 U.S.P.Q.2d 1673, 1988 WL 1091944 (S.D. N.Y. 1988); Aalba-Dent, Inc. v. Certified Alloy Products, Inc., 203 U.S.P.Q. 326, 1979 WL 25004 (N.D. Cal. 1979).

choose a theory based upon defendant's profits, because the burden of discovery then falls substantially upon the defendant to produce business records relating to the infringing activities. Under either theory, expert testimony is needed to quantify and support the parties' damage calculations.

Other possible damage recoveries include the costs of litigation, multiplied damages under the trebling provision of § 35, punitive damages in certain situations, and attorney's fees incurred during prosecution. As with any award of damages, pre-judgment interest is available. While § 35 gives courts discretion to increase damages and award punitive damages and litigation costs, such awards are unlikely in the absence of willful or intentional infringement.[14]

In addition to recovery for profits or damages, reasonable attorney's fees may be awarded to the prevailing party in "exceptional cases."[15] The test for whether a case qualifies as exceptional varies from jurisdiction to jurisdiction and depends on whether the prevailing party is the plaintiff or the defendant.[16]

It is also worth noting that liability and damages are distinguishable issues. In § 43(a) actions, evidence on the issue of damages is often distinct from evidence on the issue of liability such as secondary meaning and consumer confusion. Therefore, the trial for damages may be appropriately bifurcated from the trial for liability.[17]

§ 11:16 Defenses—Abandonment

Research References

West's Key Number Digest, Trademarks ⚖1169

Because trademark and trade dress law protects against consumer confusion, trademark rights are not automatically abandoned when manufacturing stops. Trademark rights continue as long as the trademark serves as a source identifier for the public. Thus, a competitor may not appropriate a mark simply

---

[14]*Cf.* 15 U.S.C.A. § 1117(e) (establishing a presumption of willfulness for providing false domain name registration information).

[15]15 U.S.C.A. § 1117(a).

[16]Nightingale Home Healthcare, Inc. v. Anodyne Therapy, LLC, 626 F.3d 958, 96 U.S.P.Q.2d 2017 (7th Cir. 2010) (providing in dictum that the appropriate test is stated differently depending on which party is the losing party, e.g., if the losing party is the plaintiff, the test is whether the plaintiff was guilty of abuse of process in suing; if the losing party is the defendant, the test is whether the defendant had no defense yet persisted in the trademark infringement or false advertising).

[17]Roulo v. Russ Berrie & Co., Inc., 886 F.2d 931, 12 U.S.P.Q.2d 1423 (7th Cir. 1989); Giro Sport Design Inc. v. Pro-Tec Inc., 10 U.S.P.Q.2d 1863, 1989 WL 418774 (N.D. Cal. 1989).

because of a short period of nonuse.[1] It may also be possible for infringement to occur many years after manufacturing has stopped when products bearing the mark at issue remain in active use in the market. For instance, Ferrari successfully sued for trade dress infringement of its DAYTONA SPYDER some fifteen years after it had discontinued production, because Ferrari was still receiving beneficial association with this distinctive trade dress.[2]

However, § 1064 of the trademark statutes provides for the cancellation of any mark that has been abandoned. An action for cancellation of a registration may be brought in court or as an administrative action before the Trademark Trial and Appeal Board (T.T.A.B.). A mark is deemed "abandoned":

> when its use has been discontinued with intent not to resume such use. Intent not to resume may be inferred from circumstances. Nonuse for three consecutive years shall be prima facie evidence of abandonment. "Use" of a mark means bona fide use of that mark made in the ordinary course of trade, and not made merely to reserve a right in a mark.[3]

Under the Lanham Act, proof of nonuse for three years creates a presumption that the mark has been abandoned. Once a *prima facie* case of abandonment is made by the challenger's evidence of nonuse for more than three years, the burden shifts to the owner to rebut it.[4]

Because a trademark owner's certificate of registration is *prima facie* evidence of validity of the registration and continued use of the registered mark, the burden of proof is placed upon those who seek cancellation.[5] The level of proof needed when abandonment is asserted as an affirmative defense in a court action is different than the level of proof needed in a cancellation proceeding before the T.T.A.B. As an affirmative defense, the burden on the party asserting that defense is one of strict proof of the elements of abandonment.[6] However, in a cancellation proceeding, the petitioner only needs to prove abandonment by a preponderance

---

[Section 11:16]

[1]Beech-Nut Packing Co. v. P. Lorillard Co., 273 U.S. 629, 47 S. Ct. 481 (1927) (Holmes, J.).

[2]Ferrari S.p.A. Esercizio Fabbriche Automobili e Corse v. McBurnie, 11 U.S.P.Q.2d 1843, 1989 WL 298658 (S.D. Cal. 1989); *see also* Esercizio v. Roberts, 944 F.2d 1235, 20 U.S.P.Q.2d 1001 (6th Cir. 1991).

[3]15 U.S.C.A. § 1127 ("abandoned").

[4]Saratoga Vichy Spring Co., Inc. v. Lehman, 625 F.2d 1037, 208 U.S.P.Q. 175 (2d Cir. 1980).

[5]15 U.S.C.A. § 1057(b); Cerveceria Centroamericana, S.A. v. Cerveceria India, Inc., 892 F.2d 1021, 13 U.S.P.Q.2d 1307 (Fed. Cir. 1989).

[6]U. S. Jaycees v. Philadelphia Jaycees, 639 F.2d 134, 209 U.S.P.Q. 457 (3d Cir. 1981).

of the evidence.[7]

Once the party moving for abandonment has shown a period of at least three years of nonuse, it creates a rebuttable presumption that the trademark has been abandoned. This presumption shifts the burden of production to the nonmoving party. As such, the nonmoving party must come forward with evidence showing intent to resume meaningful commercial use of the mark.[8] If it does not, the mark will be found to have been abandoned. Specifically, the registrant must put forth evidence showing what activities it engaged in during the nonuse period, or what outside events occurred which would allow one to infer that they had intent to resume use.[9]

The ultimate burden of persuasion always remains with the party moving for a finding of abandonment. Thus, even when the burden of production shifts, once the nonmoving party raises at least a question of fact regarding intent to resume use, the party moving for abandonment must prove intent with a prescribed level of certainty. Courts have generally held that defendants asserting an abandonment defense face a "stringent," "heavy," or "strict burden of proof."[10] Some courts have characterized such a burden of proof as a preponderance standard,[11] while other courts have considered it a clear and convincing standard.[12] As described above, in a cancellation proceeding the party moving for abandonment must prove nonuse and intent not to resume use by a preponderance of the evidence.[13]

The plaintiff can rebut the presumption of abandonment by showing its intent to resume meaningful commercial use of the mark. The presumption of abandonment is rebuttable by showing reasonable grounds for the suspension of use by the mark owner and plans to resume use in the reasonably foreseeable future when conditions causing the suspension of use subside.[14] A number of courts have found that retaining the ability to produce the product which is associated with the mark shows an intent to

---

[7]Cerveceria, 892 F.2d at 1023.

[8]AmBrit, Inc. v. Kraft, Inc., 812 F.2d 1531, 1 U.S.P.Q.2d 1161 (11th Cir. 1986).

[9]Imperial Tobacco Ltd., Assignee of Imperial Group PLC v. Philip Morris, Inc., 899 F.2d 1575, 1581, 14 U.S.P.Q.2d 1390 (Fed. Cir. 1990).

[10]Cumulus Media, Inc. v. Clear Channel Communications, Inc., 304 F.3d 1167, 1175, 64 U.S.P.Q.2d 1353, 53 Fed. R. Serv. 3d 823 (11th Cir. 2002).

[11]E.g., Cerveceria Centroamericana, S.A. v. Cerveceria India, Inc., 892 F.2d 1021, 13 U.S.P.Q.2d 1307 (Fed. Cir. 1989).

[12]E.g., Emmpresa Cubana Del Tabaco v. Culbro Corp., 213 F. Supp. 2d 247 (S.D. N.Y. 2002).

[13]Cerveceria, 892 F.2d at 1021.

[14]Silverman v. CBS Inc., 870 F.2d 40, 9 U.S.P.Q.2d 1778 (2d Cir. 1989).

resume use of the mark.[15]

However, courts have placed limits on the types of showings that will rebut the presumption of abandonment. For example, subsequent use does not necessarily prove an earlier intent to resume use of the mark.[16] The Commissioner of Patents and Trademarks has also found that decreased demand for a product which results in an intentional decision to discontinue the product does not excuse nonuse of the mark.[17] Moreover, sales of remaining inventory do not show an intent to resume use of a trademark.[18]

Use of a mark must be bona fide in order to avoid a finding of abandonment.[19] In *La Societe*, the court found that eighty-nine sales in twenty years was a "meager trickle of business" that did not constitute the kind of bona fide use intended to afford a basis for trademark protection.[20] Similarly, the T.T.A.B. found that the sale of $20 worth of cat food a year for fourteen years was merely annual token use.[21] The court found that the sales were only nominal use of the trademark and were therefore insufficient to rebut a *prima facie* case of abandonment.[22]

The trademark owner's testimony that he had no intent to abandon the mark does not show an intent to resume use. "If all the party had to do to avoid a holding of abandonment was to testify that he never had any intent to abandon the mark, then no mark would ever be held abandoned."[23] "A party's testimony that he had some vague and nebulous intention to resume use of the mark at some indeterminate date may be outweighed by his actions, which may speak louder than his words: '[The] purely subjective intention in the abandoner's mind to reengage in a former enterprise at some indefinite future time is not sufficient to avoid abandonment where an objective analysis of the situation

---

[15]Sterling Brewers, Inc. v. Schenley Industries, Inc., 58 C.C.P.A. 1172, 441 F.2d 675, 169 U.S.P.Q. 590 (1971) (disapproved of by, Roulo v. Russ Berrie & Co., Inc., 886 F.2d 931, 12 U.S.P.Q.2d 1423 (7th Cir. 1989)); Koppers Co., Inc. v. Krupp-Koppers GmbH, 517 F. Supp. 836, 853-854, 210 U.S.P.Q. 711 (W.D. Pa. 1981); Sands, Taylor & Wood Co. v. Quaker Oats Co., 978 F.2d 947, 24 U.S.P.Q.2d 1001 (7th Cir. 1992).

[16]AmBrit, 81 F.2d at 1551.

[17]In re Moorman Manufacturing Company, 203 U.S.P.Q. 712, 713, 1979 WL 24864 (Comm'r Pat. & Trademarks 1979); *see also* Lipton Industries, Inc. v. Ralston Purina Co., 670 F.2d 1024,

213 U.S.P.Q. 185 (C.C.P.A. 1982).

[18]Uncas Mfg. Co. v. Clark & Coombs Co., 309 F.2d 818, 820, 135 U.S.P.Q. 282 (1st Cir. 1962); Oshman's Sporting Goods Inc. v. Highland Import Corp., 16 U.S.P.Q.2d 1395, 1397, 1990 WL 354531 (T.T.A.B. 1990).

[19]15 U.S.C.A. § 1127 ("abandoned").

[20]La Societe, 495 F.2d at 1272.

[21]Continental Grain Co. v. Strongheart Products Inc., 9 U.S.P.Q.2d 1238, 1240, 1988 WL 252323 (T.T.A.B. 1988).

[22]Continental Grain, 9 U.S.P.Q.2d at 1240.

[23]*McCarthy*, § 17:13.

furnishes ample evidence to warrant the inference of abandonment.' "[24]

Lastly, sporadic, casual, and nominal shipments of goods after a period of nonuse are not by themselves indicative of intent to resume use. While sporadic and casual use in conjunction with a trademark maintenance program may be conclusive of an intent not to abandon a mark, it does not necessarily establish an intent to resume use.[25] Since intent is a very subjective element, it is difficult to clearly define what will and will not show intent to resume use. However, at least one court recognized the difference between an intent not to abandon and an intent to resume use by stating that "an owner may not wish to abandon its mark but have no intent to resume its use."[26] An intent not to abandon standard would allow owners to warehouse marks with neither commercial use nor plans to resume commercial use, which is not permitted by the Lanham Act.[27]

§ 11:17 Defenses—Descriptive use of a mark

Research References
West's Key Number Digest, Trademarks ☞1521

A party will not be liable for infringement if a use qualifies as a "fair use." "A fair use is a descriptive use of a name to indicate nature, quality, and purpose of the goods themselves, the name of the manufacturer or the distributor of the goods."[1] Fair use is a statutory defense to infringement of an incontestable mark.[2]

The fair use defense prevents the trademark rights of one party from being extended to preclude another party from describing its product to the public. When a person chooses a mark with descriptive qualities, the fair use doctrine recognizes that he or she cannot exclude some kinds of competing uses, particularly those which use words in their primary descriptive and nontrade-

---

[24]McCarthy, § 17:13 (quoting Culbro, 585 F. Supp. at 22).

[25]Exxon Corp. v. Humble Exploration Co., Inc., 695 F.2d 96, 100-101, 217 U.S.P.Q. 1200, 83 A.L.R. Fed. 281 (5th Cir. 1983).

[26]Exxon, 695 F.2d at 99, 102; accord Hiland Potato Chip Co. v. Culbro Snack Foods, Inc., 720 F.2d 981, 222 U.S.P.Q. 790 (8th Cir. 1983).

[27]Exxon, 695 F.2d at 99; see also Intrawest Financial Corp. v. Western Nat. Bank of Denver, 610 F. Supp. 950,

958, 227 U.S.P.Q. 27 (D. Colo. 1985) (sham use designed to prevent others from using a mark is not bona fide use; "Mere warehousing of marks, is impermissible under the Lanham Act").

[Section 11:17]

[1]Burger King Corp. v. Pilgrim's Pride Corp., 705 F. Supp. 1522, 1529, 12 U.S.P.Q.2d 1526 (S.D. Fla. 1988), judgment aff'd, 894 F.2d 412 (11th Cir. 1990).

[2]15 U.S.C.A. § 1115(b)(4).

mark sense.[3] The fair use defense thus prevents a trademark registrant from appropriating a descriptive term for its own use to the exclusion of others, who may be prevented thereby from accurately describing their own goods.[4] The holder of a protectable descriptive mark has no legal claim to an exclusive right in the primary, descriptive meaning of the term; consequently, anyone is free to use the term in its primary descriptive sense.[5] Parties asserting a fair use defense often frame the issue in terms of the limits on trademark protection imposed by the First Amendment.

As an affirmative defense, defendant bears the burden of proving each and every element of the fair use defense. The defendant must show that its use was: not as a trademark; done fairly and in good faith; and only to describe to users its goods.[6]

The first element of the fair use defense requires that defendant's use is "otherwise than as a mark," meaning a nontrademark use.[7] Some questions that are considered in determining whether a use is a trademark use or a nontrademark use include:

- Is the use of the term meant to attract public attention?
- Is the term a prominent element on the package?
- What size is the lettering?
- How different is the type style?
- Is the term set off?
- Does a subordinate phrase actually describe the product being sold?[8]

The size and prominence of the alleged infringing use is usually the most important factor. For example, in *United States Shoe Corp. v. Brown Group, Inc.*,[9] plaintiff advertised a line of "comfortable women's dress pumps" using the slogan "Looks like a pump, feels like a sneaker." Plaintiff spent more than $9 million on advertising which included that slogan over a period of two years.

---

[3]Herman Miller, Inc. v. Palazzetti Imports and Exports, Inc., 270 F.3d 298, 319, 60 U.S.P.Q.2d 1633, 2001-2, 2001-2 Trade Cas. (CCH) ¶ 73489 (6th Cir. 2001).

[4]*E.g.,* Sunmark, Inc. v. Ocean Spray Cranberries, Inc., 64 F.3d 1055, 36 U.S.P.Q.2d 1046 (7th Cir. 1995) (preliminary injunction denied where the defendant used the words "sweet-tart" to describe a juice drink).

[5]Zatarains, 698 F.2d at 791.

[6]Burger King, 705 F. Supp. at 1529 (S.D.Fla.1988); Service Merchandise Co. v. Service Jewelry Stores, Inc., 737 F. Supp. 983, 993, 14 U.S.P.Q.2d 1164 (S.D. Tex. 1990) (SERVICE JEWELRY STORE is not a fair use of plaintiff's incontestable registration for SERVICE MERCHANDISE).

[7]*See* 15 U.S.C.A. § 1115(b)(4).

[8]Tree Tavern Products, Inc. v. Conagra, Inc., 640 F. Supp. 1263, 1269, 231 U.S.P.Q. 260 (D. Del. 1986).

[9]U.S. Shoe Corp. v. Brown Group, Inc., 740 F. Supp. 196, 15 U.S.P.Q.2d 1138 (S.D. N.Y. 1990), decision aff'd, 923 F.2d 844 (2d Cir. 1990).

The defendant used a print advertisement which featured a photograph of a woman's pump with the headline "Think of it as a sneaker with no strings attached." The text of the ad included the phrase "And when we say it feels like a sneaker we're not just stringing you along." The defendant's print advertisement also included defendant's logo and slogan. The plaintiff contended that the statement "And when we say it feels like a sneaker" was deliberately meant to mislead consumers into believing the defendant's product was the same as the shoe which was previously advertised with the slogan "Looks like a pump, feels like a sneaker."

The court held that the defendant's use of the words "feels like a sneaker" falls squarely within the fair use defense of 15 U.S.C.A. § 1115(b)(4). The court found that the defendant did not use the phrase as an identifier or trademark to indicate origin or source. The defendant's use of the words "feels like a sneaker" was not as a caption or slogan, but was used simply as a fragment of a sentence in small print. Also, the print advertisement used by defendant prominently displayed defendant's own logo and slogan.

Of secondary importance is the use of a generic descriptor to identify the product. For example, in *Burger King Corp. v. Pilgrim's Pride Corp.*,[10] defendant unsuccessfully argued that its use of the terms CHICKEN TENDERS and CHICKEN BREAST TENDERS was a fair use of plaintiff's mark CHICKEN TENDERS. Among other factors considered in denying the fair use defense, the court found it important that a generic description of the product followed the words CHICKEN TENDERS on defendant's package.

The fact that defendant conducted a trademark search can often be used to establish a trademark use, rather than a fair use. In *Burger King*, there was also testimony that defendant had conducted a trademark search on the term and wanted to adopt the term as a trademark. There was also evidence that defendant knew of plaintiff's registered mark, and that defendant had switched from the mark CHICKEN NUGGETS to CHICKEN TENDERS. The court used these facts to help reach its finding that defendant was improperly using CHICKEN TENDERS as a trademark.[11]

Good faith is one of the least litigated, but potentially most

---

[10]Burger King Corp. v. Pilgrim's Pride Corp., 705 F. Supp. 1522, 12 U.S.P.Q.2d 1526 (S.D. Fla. 1988), judgment aff'd, 894 F.2d 412 (11th Cir. 1990).

[11]*Cf.* Zatarains, Inc. v. Oak Grove Smokehouse, Inc., 698 F.2d 786, 796, 217 U.S.P.Q. 988 (5th Cir. 1983) (court relied upon defendant's testimony that it did not intend to use the term in a trademark sense and never attempted to register the words as a trademark).

dangerous elements, for a defendant. Remember that the burden is on defendant to show its good faith, so defendant must present evidence on this element. However, since it is usually impractical to prove a negative, defendant must usually, as a practical matter, overcome whatever evidence plaintiff has to show bad faith.

Sometimes, mere knowledge of plaintiff's mark is sufficient to show bad faith. For example, in *Ringling Brothers-Barnum and Bailey Combined Shows, Inc. v. Celozzi-Ettelson Chevrolet, Inc.*,[12] plaintiff owned the trademark THE GREATEST SHOW ON EARTH. Defendant argued that its mark, THE GREATEST USED CAR SHOW ON EARTH was a fair use of plaintiff's registered mark. The court, noting that the fair use defense requires good faith, held that bad faith may be found where defendant was aware of plaintiff's mark before it began its infringement.[13]

Internal memoranda and paper trails generated by larger companies can be very dangerous. In *Burger King*, there were a series of memoranda from defendant to its advertising agency which showed that defendant knew about plaintiff's prior use of the mark CHICKEN TENDERS. The evidence demonstrated that defendant had decided to switch from NUGGETS to TENDERS and subsequently produced advertising and packaging strikingly similar to plaintiff.[14]

An acknowledgment by defendant as to plaintiff's trademark rights may also be used to negate defendant's good faith. In *Institute for Scientific Information, Inc. v. Gordon and Breach, Science Publishers, Inc.*,[15] defendant asserted the fair use defense with respect to its use of the term CURRENT CONTENTS. In finding that a genuine issue of material fact existed as to defendant's good faith use of the term, the court focused on the fact that plaintiff and defendant had previously negotiated an agreement in which defendant promised not to use CURRENT CONTENTS. Defendant had abided to the terms of the agreement for three and one half years before breaching it.

The court held that in making that agreement, defendant had made a business judgement to contract away its legal right to make fair use of plaintiff's CURRENT CONTENTS trademark.

---

[12]Ringling Bros.-Barnum & Bailey Combined Shows, Inc. v. Celozzi-Ettelson Chevrolet, Inc., 855 F.2d 480, 8 U.S.P.Q.2d 1072 (7th Cir. 1988).

[13]Ringling Brothers, 855 F.2d at 4842; *see also* Frito-Lay, Inc. v. Bachman Co., 704 F. Supp. 432, 437, 14 U.S.P.Q.2d 1027 (S.D. N.Y. 1989) ("Awareness of the pre-existing use of a trademark gives rise to an inference of bad faith").

[14]Burger King, 705 F. Supp. at 1530.

[15]Institute for Scientific Information, Inc. v. Gordon and Breach, Science Publishers, Inc., 931 F.2d 1002, 18 U.S.P.Q.2d 1527 (3d Cir. 1991).

In the context of a summary judgment motion, plaintiff's allegation suggested that defendant intentionally breached the agreement, and under those circumstances an adverse inference of bad
faith may be drawn.

Determination of whether a term is used descriptively requires
careful examination of the context in which the term is used. For
example, in *United States Shoe*,[16] the court held that defendant's
use of the words "feels like a sneaker" fell squarely within the
fair use defense of 15 U.S.C.A. § 1115(b)(4). Defendant used the
phrase "feels like a sneaker" in a descriptive sense, claiming a
virtue of the product. The court held that defendant was essentially restating a key selling claim for its product—that
defendant's shoe was designed specifically to incorporate the
comfort of athletic shoes.

Similarly, in *Team Central Inc. v. Xerox Corp.*,[17] plaintiff Team
Central sued Xerox for using the mark TEAM XEROX. Plaintiff
was the owner of federal registrations for the marks TEAM and
TEAM ELECTRONICS. The court held that "Team Central's
rights to the marks TEAM and TEAM ELECTRONICS do not
prevent others from using the word 'team' in its primary or generic sense."[18] The court found that Xerox was using "TEAM" in
its generic sense because its advertisement referred to a team of
Xerox employees and the fundamental concept of teamwork.[19]

Dictionary definitions may also be useful in proving a use was
descriptive. In *Munters Corp. v. Matsui America, Inc.*,[20] plaintiff
owned a registered trademark in "HONEYCOMB" for a dehumidi-
fying apparatus. The court held that defendant's description of
its dehumidifier as "honeycomb-shaped" was a fair use by relying
on a definition for "honeycomb" found in the dictionary. The court
found that defendant used the term "honeycomb" to directly describe the configuration of its product, which resembled "a tissue
of holes separated by thin walls or partitions."

The alleged descriptive use must in fact be descriptive. In
Burger King, the evidence showed that the term CHICKEN
TENDERS did not describe the product. The product contained
other things besides chicken tenderloin, which represented only
about 23% of the total product. The ingredients list of the product

---

[16]U.S. Shoe Corp. v. Brown Group,
Inc., 740 F. Supp. 196, 15 U.S.P.Q.2d
1138 (S.D. N.Y. 1990), decision aff'd,
923 F.2d 844 (2d Cir. 1990).

[17]Team Cent. Inc. v. Xerox Corp.,
606 F. Supp. 1408, 226 U.S.P.Q. 929
(D. Minn. 1985).

[18]Team Central, 606 F. Supp. at

1413.

[19]Team Central, 606 F. Supp. at
1414.

[20]Munters Corp. v. Matsui
America, Inc., 730 F. Supp. 790, 14
U.S.P.Q.2d 1993 (N.D. Ill. 1989),
judgment aff'd, 909 F.2d 250, 15 U.S.P.
Q.2d 1666 (7th Cir. 1990).

did not include the word "tenderloin" or "tender."[21]

Similarly, in *Ringling Brothers*, the court found that defendant's use of THE GREATEST USED CAR SHOW ON EARTH was not descriptive:

> If Celozzi-Ettelson had used the slogan "The Greatest Used Car Showroom on Earth" it might have had a plausible argument that its slogan was laudatory and descriptive; but it used the word "Show," not "Showroom" and, unlike the circus, the used car business is not literally a show. The slogan is therefore not descriptive of the cars it sells or the retail services it offers.[22]

Fair use involves descriptive marks, and a trademark owner who chooses a descriptive mark must accept that some consumer confusion is possible. A party raising the fair use defense is not obligated to prove that its use is unlikely to cause consumer confusion. The burden of proving likelihood of confusion always resides with the trademark owner and "the defendant has no independent burden to negate the likelihood of any confusion in raising the affirmative defense that a term is used descriptively, not as a mark, fairly, and in good faith."[23] Importantly, there is no rule in trademark infringement that all consumer confusion must be avoided; "some possibility of consumer confusion must be compatible with fair use."[24]

The fair use defense has been extended to include a nominative fair use defense where a defendant uses a mark to identify the goods or services of the owner of the mark. In the Ninth Circuit, to assert nominative fair use three requirements must be met: first, the product or service in question must be one not readily identifiable without use of the trademark; second, only so much of the mark or marks may be used as is reasonably necessary to identify the product or service; and third, the user must do nothing that would, in conjunction with the mark, suggest sponsorship or endorsement by the trademark holder.[25]

The Third Circuit has established its own interpretation of this

---

[21]Burger King, 705 F. Supp. at 1529.

[22]Ringling Brothers, 855 F.2d at 484.

[23]KP Permanent Make-Up, Inc. v. Lasting Impression I, Inc., 543 U.S. 111, 124, 125 S. Ct. 542, 551, 72 U.S.P.Q.2d 1833 (2004).

[24]543 U.S. at 121, 125 S. Ct. at 550.

[25]New Kids on the Block v. News America Pub., Inc., 971 F.2d 302, 308-09, 20 Media L. Rep. (BNA) 1468,

23 U.S.P.Q.2d 1534 (9th Cir. 1992) (footnote omitted) (it is irrelevant whether a use that does not imply sponsorship or endorsement is carried on for profit and in competition with the trademark holder's business); *see also* Toyota Motor Sales, U.S.A., Inc. v. Tabari, 610 F.3d 1171, 95 U.S.P.Q.2d 1702 (9th Cir. 2010) (finding nominative fair use in defendant's use of the LEXUS trademark in their domain name "buy-a-lexus.com" because use of the LEXUS mark was necessary to convey their specialty in brokering LEXUS cars and because a clear dis-

three-pronged nominative fair use test aimed at addressing the "lack of clarity" resulting from the Ninth Circuit test.[26] Thus, the Third Circuit applies a slightly different set of elements: first, is the use of plaintiff's mark necessary to describe plaintiff's product or service and defendant's product or service; second, is only so much of the plaintiff's mark used as is necessary to describe the products or services; and third, does the defendant's conduct or language reflect the true and accurate relationship between plaintiff and defendant's products or services.[27]

§ 11:18 Defenses—Parody

Research References
West's Key Number Digest, Trademarks ⊕1524(2)

Using justifications similar to those raised by the fair use defense, many accused infringers have successfully argued that they are not liable for infringement because they used another's trademark as a parody within their rights under the First Amendment. While generally responsive to such arguments, some courts do not consider parody to be an affirmative defense so much as evidence that is probative of whether defendant's use caused a likelihood of confusion. Parody is "merely a way of phrasing the traditional response that customers are not likely to be confused as to the source, sponsorship, or approval."[1] As long as advertisers continue to sell products with humor and satire, courts will be faced with many more creative assertions of the parody defense.

When a plaintiff's trademark is used in parody, the critical question remains whether the use has created a likelihood of confusion. Because parody is a form of expression protected by the First Amendment, the likelihood of confusion determination takes on added complexity for parody uses.[2] One court explained that:

A parody must convey two simultaneous—and contradictory— messages: that it is the original, but also that it is *not* the original

---

claimer was provided on the landing page of the website disclaiming affiliation with Toyota).

[26]Century 21 Real Estate Corp. v. Lendingtree, Inc., 425 F.3d 211, 228, 76 U.S.P.Q.2d 1769 (3d Cir. 2005).

[27]425 F.3d at 228.

[Section 11:18]

[1]Dr. Seuss Enterprises, L.P. v. Penguin Books USA, Inc., 109 F.3d

1394, 1405, 25 Media L. Rep. (BNA) 1641, 42 U.S.P.Q.2d 1184 (9th Cir. 1997).

[2]In this regard, it is often helpful to consider similarities to parody defenses in copyright cases. *See* § 7:18.

and is instead a parody. To the extent that it does only the former but not the latter, it is not only a poor parody but also vulnerable under trademark law, since the customer will be confused.[3]

Courts must strike a balance between the competing goals of free expression and preventing consumer confusion. Successful use of the parody defense is highly unpredictable. Some courts have been reluctant to accept a defendant's parody argument, even when it is obvious.[4] Perhaps this is because some courts appear to consider whether the parody is in "good taste" or because of narrower interpretations of First Amendment protection for certain subject matter. Other courts have been more open to the parody defense.[5] Since *Campbell v. Acuff-Rose Music, Inc.*, where the Supreme Court affirmed parody as a fair use in copyright, parody defenses to trademark infringement have succeeded more and more.[6]

The parody defense is not well settled across the circuit courts, but certain principles can help distinguish between legitimate parody and improper infringement. The real distinction in parody cases seems to come down to what the court considers to be the main purpose of trademark law. Those courts that emphasize the trademark owner's property interest in the mark tend to be hostile to the parody defense. Conversely, courts that believe that the main purpose of trademark law is to avoid confusion are more likely to find in favor of a parodist.

Chemical Corp. of America v. Anheuser-Busch, Inc.,[7] is usually recognized as the first parody case, although the concept was too new to be invoked by name. Plaintiff, owner of the slogan "Where there's life, there's Bud," received an injunction against defen-

---

[3]Cliffs Notes, Inc. v. Bantam Doubleday Dell Pub. Group, Inc., 886 F.2d 490, 494, 16 Media L. Rep. (BNA) 2289, 12 U.S.P.Q.2d 1289 (2d Cir. 1989) (emphasis in original).

[4]*See* Mutual of Omaha Ins. Co. v. Novak, 836 F.2d 397, 5 U.S.P.Q.2d 1314, 98 A.L.R. Fed. 1 (8th Cir. 1987) (rejected by, Westchester Media v. PRL USA Holdings, Inc., 214 F.3d 658, 55 U.S.P.Q.2d 1225 (5th Cir. 2000)) (enjoining the printing of "Mutant of Omaha" and "Nuclear Holocaust Insurance" on T-shirts, caps, buttons, and coffee mugs); Dallas Cowboys Cheerleaders, Inc. v. Pussycat Cinema, Ltd., 604 F.2d 200, 5 Media L. Rep. (BNA) 1814, 203 U.S.P.Q. 161 (2d Cir. 1979) (enjoining distribution and exhibition of X-rated movie of women in outfits similar to those of the Dallas Cowboy cheerleaders).

[5]*See, e.g.,* Mattel, Inc. v. MCA Records, Inc., 296 F.3d 894, 63 U.S.P.Q.2d 1715 (9th Cir. 2002) (finding use of the mark BARBIE in a song was a parody and a fair use).

[6]McGeveran, The Imaginary Trademark Parody Crisis (And the Real One), 90 Wash. L. Rev. 713, 715 (2015) (discussing the increasing success of parody defenses in trademark infringement cases since *Campbell*); *see* Campbell v. Acuff-Rose Music, Inc., 510 U.S. 569, 578, 114 S. Ct. 1164, 127 L. Ed. 2d 500, 22 Media L. Rep. (BNA) 1353, 29 U.S.P.Q.2d 1961 (1994).

[7]Chemical Corp. of America v. Anheuser-Busch, Inc., 306 F.2d 433, 134 U.S.P.Q. 524, 2 A.L.R.3d 739 (5th Cir. 1962).

dant's use of the slogan "Where there is life, there's bugs" in conjunction with insecticides. The court of appeals affirmed the injunction, stating "[t]he gist of this action is that the plaintiff has a property interest in the slogan, built up at great expense, and that it and its products are favorably known as a result of its use of this property right * * * ."[8]

Another early parody case was *Girl Scouts v. Personality Posters Mfg. Co.*[9] Plaintiff sought a preliminary injunction enjoining defendant from selling a poster consisting of a smiling girl dressed in the well-known green uniform of the Junior Girl Scouts, "with her hands clasped above her protruding, clearly pregnant abdomen" and the caveat "BE PREPARED" appearing next to her hands. The court denied the injunction, holding that plaintiff had "failed utterly to establish the requisite element of customer confusion."[10]

In *Coca-Cola Co. v. Gemini Rising, Inc.*,[11] plaintiff successfully obtained a preliminary injunction enjoining the defendant from selling a poster which used the famous red and white Coca-Cola logo with the term "Enjoy Cocaine" substituted for "Enjoy Coca-Cola." "[The] trademark belongs to and is uniquely identified with Plaintiff and its products. Plaintiff's property right in its mark clearly extends to its reproduction and publication in advertising and for other promotional uses regarding its products."[12]

In *Dallas Cowboys Cheerleaders, Inc. v. Pussycat Cinema, Ltd.*,[13] the plaintiff sought a preliminary injunction against defendant's adult film *Debbie Does Dallas*, which featured women wearing cheerleader costumes consisting of white boots, white shorts, blue blouse, and white star-studded vest and belt. The court granted the motion, emphasizing that "the trademark laws are designed not only to prevent consumer confusion but also to protect the synonymous right of a trademark owner to control his product's reputation."[14]

In *L.L. Bean, Inc. v. Drake Publishers, Inc.*,[15] the plaintiff, publisher of the famous L.L. Bean catalog, sued the publishers of

---

[8]Chemical Corp., 306 F.2d at 437.

[9]Girl Scouts of U. S. of America v. Personality Posters Mfg. Co., 304 F. Supp. 1228, 163 U.S.P.Q. 505 (S.D. N.Y. 1969).

[10]Girl Scouts, 304 F. Supp. at 1231.

[11]Coca-Cola Co. v. Gemini Rising, Inc., 346 F. Supp. 1183, 175 U.S.P.Q. 56 (E.D. N.Y. 1972).

[12]Coca-Cola, 346 F. Supp. at 1188.

[13]Dallas Cowboys Cheerleaders, Inc. v. Pussycat Cinema, Ltd., 604 F.2d 200, 5 Media L. Rep. (BNA) 1814, 203 U.S.P.Q. 161 (2d Cir. 1979).

[14]Dallas Cowboys, 604 F.2d at 205 (quoting James Burrough Ltd. v. Sign of Beefeater, Inc., 540 F.2d 266, 274, 192 U.S.P.Q. 555 (7th Cir. 1976)).

[15]L.L. Bean, Inc. v. Drake Publishers, Inc., 811 F.2d 26, 13 Media L. Rep. (BNA) 2009, 1 U.S.P.Q.2d 1753 (1st Cir. 1987) (rejected by, United We

an adult magazine for trademark infringement and trademark dilution for publishing a two page article entitled "L.L. Beam's Back-To-School-Sex-Catalog." The article featured plaintiff's trademark and featured nude models using products which were described in a "crudely humorous fashion."[16]

The court of appeals reversed the district court's finding of infringement. "[A] trademark is not property in the ordinary sense but only a word or symbol indicating the origin of a commercial product. The owner of a mark acquires the right to prevent the goods to which the mark is applied from being confused with those of others and to prevent his own trade from being diverted to competitors through their use of misleading marks."[17] Therefore, "[t]rademark rights do not entitle the owner to quash an unauthorized use of the mark by another who is communicating ideas or expressing points of view * * * 'When the common law developed the doctrine of trademarks and tradenames, it was not creating a property in advertisements more absolute than it would have allowed the author of *Paradise Lost*.' "[18]

The owner of the JORDACHE trademark which was used on blue jeans, filed suit against defendant's use of the mark LARDASHE on blue jeans in *Jordache Enterprises, Inc. v. Hogg Wyld, Ltd.*[19] The court found that there was no likelihood of confusion between the products. Most interesting was the court's observation on the elements of intent. Noting that deliberate adoption of a similar mark may lead to an inference of intent to pass off goods as those of another, the court recognized that "[t]he proper focus is whether defendant had the intent to derive benefit from the reputation or goodwill of plaintiff."[20] Where a party chooses a mark as a parody of an existing mark, the intent is not necessarily to confuse the public, but to amuse:

> In one sense, a parody is an attempt to derive benefit from the reputation of the owner of a mark, if only because no parody could be made without the initial mark. The benefit to the one making the parody, however, arises from the humorous association, not from public confusion as to the source of the marks. A parody relies upon a difference from the original mark, presumably a humorous differ-

Stand America, Inc. v. United We Stand, America New York, Inc., 128 F.3d 86, 44 U.S.P.Q.2d 1351, 39 Fed. R. Serv. 3d 88 (2d Cir. 1997)).

[16]L.L. Bean, 811 F.2d at 27.

[17]L.L. Bean, 811 F.2d at 29 (quoting Power Test Petroleum Distributors, Inc. v. Calcu Gas, Inc., 754 F.2d 91, 97, 225 U.S.P.Q. 368, 1985-1, 1985-1 Trade Cas. (CCH) ¶ 66409 (2d Cir.

1985)).

[18]L.L. Bean, 811 F.2d at 29 (quoting Chadwick v. Covell, 151 Mass. 190, 193, 23 N.E. 1068, 1069 (1890)).

[19]Jordache Enterprises, Inc. v. Hogg Wyld, Ltd., 828 F.2d 1482, 4 U.S.P.Q.2d 1216, 92 A.L.R. Fed. 1 (10th Cir. 1987).

[20]Jordache, 828 F.2d at 1485.

ence, in order to produce its desired effect.[21]

The court also emphasized the inherent risk in society that someone may play a joke on you. "No one likes to be the butt of a joke, not even a trademark. But the requirement of trademark law is that a likely confusion of source, sponsorship or affiliation must be proven, which is not the same thing as a right not to be made fun of."[22] In addition, as the court succinctly concluded, "An intent to parody is not an intent to confuse the public."[23]

Not all parodies are created equal. The Eighth Circuit gave substantial weight to certain commercial uses of a mark that could otherwise be considered a parody. For instance, in *Mutual of Omaha Ins. Co. v. Novak*,[24] plaintiff sought an injunction against the defendant's sale of T-shirts depicting a feather-bonneted, emaciated human head with the logo "Mutant of Omaha" and the caption "Nuclear Holocaust Insurance." In rejecting the parody defense, the court relied heavily on the findings of a survey commissioned by the plaintiff. It also rejected defendant's First Amendment claim, emphasizing that "Mutual's trademarks are a form of property."[25] Because trademarks were viewed as property, plaintiff's rights superseded defendant's First Amendment rights where adequate alternative avenues of communication, such as books, magazines and films, existed.

In *Cliffs Notes, Inc. v. Bantam Doubleday Dell Publishing Group*,[26] the plaintiff sought a preliminary injunction against the defendant's "Spy Notes," a parody of plaintiff's famous Cliffs Notes study aids. Defendant readily admitted that it copied the prominent features of Cliffs Notes in order to make its "Spy Notes" parody effective. Defendant's cover replicated the distinctive yellow color, black diagonal strips and black lettering of Cliffs Notes. The court noted that the principle issue in parody cases is "how to strike a balance between the two competing considerations of allowing artistic expression and preventing consumer confusion."[27] The court believed that this balancing test should take into account the ultimate test in trademark law whether there is a likelihood of confusion between the plaintiff's and the defendant's products. At the same time, a balancing ap-

---

[21]Jordache, 828 F.2d at 1486.

[22]Jordache, 828 F.2d at 1486 (quoting 2 J. Thomas McCarthy, *Trademarks and Unfair Competition* § 31:38 (2d ed.1984)).

[23]Jordache, 828 F.2d at 1487.

[24]Mutual of Omaha Ins. Co. v. Novak, 836 F.2d 397, 5 U.S.P.Q.2d 1314, 98 A.L.R. Fed. 1 (8th Cir. 1987) (rejected by, Westchester Media v. PRL USA Holdings, Inc., 214 F.3d 658, 55 U.S.P.Q.2d 1225 (5th Cir. 2000)).

[25]Mutual of Omaha, 836 F.2d at 402.

[26]Cliffs Notes, Inc. v. Bantam Doubleday Dell Pub. Group, Inc., 886 F.2d 490, 16 Media L. Rep. (BNA) 2289, 12 U.S.P.Q.2d 1289 (2d Cir. 1989).

[27]Cliffs Notes, 886 F.2d at 494.

proach provides greater latitude for work such as parodies, in which expression, and not commercial exploitation of another's trademark, is a primary intent, and in which there is a need to evoke the original work being parodied.[28] Relying on the differences between the Spy Notes and Cliffs Notes, the court held that there was no likelihood of confusion.

Plaintiff sought an injunction against defendant's sale of T-shirts that parodied the famous Budweiser beer logo in *Anheuser-Busch, Inc. v. L & L Wings, Inc.*[29] The design depicted on the defendant's T-shirt showed a red, white and blue label of a beer can. However, the words on the can did not refer to beer, but instead referred to Myrtle Beach, South Carolina. The appellate court found that a reasonable jury could find that the defendant's T-shirt was a parody. The appellate court rejected plaintiff's argument that the T-shirt design was not a parody because its purpose was to make money, not to make a commentary about Budweiser beer. The appellate court found that the T-shirt fit the conventional definition of trademark parody—"a simple form of entertainment conveyed by juxtaposing the irreverent representation of the trademark with the idealized image created by the mark's owner."[30] The defendant's T-shirt design mimicked the characteristic turns of phrase on the Budweiser label by applying them to the beach. The court of appeals found that the district court, in granting judgment notwithstanding the verdict in favor of infringement, erred by ignoring the issue of parody in applying the multi-factored likelihood of confusion test, which "is at best awkward in the context of parody."[31] For example, intentional similarities between the trademark and defendant's product cannot lead to a presumption of likelihood of confusion in the parody context. In parody cases, intentional similarity is unavoidable. The appellate court reinstated a jury verdict finding no violation of the Lanham Act.[32]

The parody defense was applied to baseball cards which provided humorous commentary on the players. The cards did not cause public confusion as to the source of the cards, and therefore did not infringe the Lanham Act. However, they did violate the Major League Baseball Players Association (MLBPA) right of publicity as embodied in Okla. Stat. tit. 12, § 1449(A). The court went on to say that the First Amendment rights of the card manufacturer outweighed the publicity rights of the MLBPA.

---

[28]Cliffs Notes, 886 F.2d at 495.

[29]Anheuser-Busch, Inc. v. L. & L. Wings, Inc., 962 F.2d 316, 22 U.S.P. Q.2d 1502, 22 Fed. R. Serv. 3d 575 (4th Cir. 1992).

[30]Anheuser-Busch, 962 F.2d at 321.

[31]Anheuser-Busch, 962 F.2d at 321.

[32]Anheuser-Busch, 962 F.2d at 323.

Application of this statute violated the First Amendment right of free speech even though the cards were humorous and not serious commentary, since the cards provide social commentary on public figures. Also, there was no distinction due to the fact that this was commercial merchandise, because the cards were not mere advertisements. Indeed, the cards did "not merely lampoon a celebrity, but exposes[d] the weaknesses of an idea or value the celebrity stands for in society."[33]

In another case, a likelihood of confusion existed between the plaintiff's ELVIS PRESLEY marks and the defendant's service mark THE VELVET ELVIS for nightclubs. Successful parody weighs against a likelihood of confusion, but the parody must mimic the original mark and the justification for mimicry wanes when the mark is not the target of the parody. The plaintiff prevailed because the defendant was parodying the "faddish, eclectic bars of the 60's" rather than Elvis.[34]

People for the Ethical Treatment of Animals (PETA) sued Defendant for trademark infringement for his use of "peta.org" for a website called "People Eating Tasty Animals." Defendant claims he created the website as a parody of PETA. The court stated that Defendant's use of the "PETA" mark does not qualify as a parody because Defendant's domain name simply copies PETA's mark, conveying the message that defendant is related to PETA. Also, it is not a parody because the website does not simultaneously convey that defendant's website is a parody of Plaintiff's mark and that Defendant is not related to PETA, thus creating a likelihood of confusion.[35]

However, a Subsequent Fourth Circuit decision effectively limited the *PETA* case to its particular facts. In a later case, an individual registered and operated a website with a domain name containing a common misspelling of the name of a well-known religious figure.[36] The court agreed that the figure's name had achieved secondary meaning and could be used as a valid common law trademark. However, neither the domain name "fallwell.com" nor the content of the website itself was found likely to cause consumer confusion despite the similarity of spelling of Reverend Falwell's name.[37] While there may have been some initial interest confusion based on the domain name, the

---

[33]Cardtoons, L.C. v. Major League Baseball Players Ass'n, 95 F.3d 959, 24 Media L. Rep. (BNA) 2281, 39 U.S.P.Q.2d 1865 (10th Cir. 1996).

[34]Elvis Presley Enterprises, Inc. v. Capece, 141 F.3d 188, 46 U.S.P.Q.2d 1737, 40 Fed. R. Serv. 3d 1021 (5th Cir. 1998).

[35]People for Ethical Treatment of Animals v. Doughney, 263 F.3d 359, 60 U.S.P.Q.2d 1109 (4th Cir. 2001).

[36]Lamparello v. Falwell, 420 F.3d 309, 310, 76 U.S.P.Q.2d 1024 (4th Cir. 2005).

[37]Lamparello, 420 F.3d at 314.

court decided that it was immediately apparent upon visiting the website that the operator was using the accused mark for criticism and comment. The accused website included several disclaimers and articles dedicated to criticism of the trademark owner's frequent public statements on sensitive political and religious topics. The court emphasized that, "[n]o one would believe that Reverend Falwell sponsored a site criticizing himself, his positions, and his interpretations of the Bible."[38]

In *Anheuser-Busch, Inc. v. Balducci Publications*, the defendant included, on the back cover of a parody magazine, a mock advertisement utilizing plaintiff's MICHELOB mark.[39] The Plaintiff presented survey evidence showing actual confusion, and the court did not give weight to the defendant's objections to shortcomings in the methodology of the survey and classification of the responses, which were not supported by expert testimony or other survey evidence.[40] In essence, the court largely relied upon the survey evidence of actual confusion to find a likelihood of confusion, without engaging in significant review of the methodology used to produce the survey results.

In *Mattel, Inc. v. MCA Records, Inc.*, the plaintiff brought a trademark infringement claim against a record company that releases a pop song, "Barbie Girl," that purported to parody a popular toy doll.[41] The Ninth Circuit affirmed summary judgment of noninfringement. Whenever trademarks transcend their source-identifying function, "the trademark owner does not have the right to control public discourse whenever the public imbues his mark with a meaning beyond its source-identifying function."[42] Here, the defendant's use was a nominative fair use, as the song did "not rely on the BARBIE mark to poke fun at another subject but targets Barbie herself."[43]

As illustrated in these cases, courts will often look to whether the primary purpose of the parody is commercial or merely critical in nature. While commercial exploitation of a parody is not completely prohibited, a court is more likely to view the competing marks from a property perspective when the accused infringer primarily created the parody to take advantage of the existing goodwill of the original mark. Those courts which focus on trademarks as *property* are likely to find that plaintiff's trademark rights have been violated and that parody is not a defense

---

[38]Lamparello, 420 F.3d at 315.

[39]Anheuser-Busch, Inc. v. Balducci Publications, 28 F.3d 769, 22 Media L. Rep. (BNA) 2001, 31 U.S.P.Q.2d 1296 (8th Cir. 1994).

[40]Balducci, 28 F.3d at 772 n.2, 775 n.4.

[41]Mattel, Inc. v. MCA Records, Inc., 296 F.3d 894, 63 U.S.P.Q.2d 1715 (9th Cir. 2002).

[42]Mattel, 296 F.3d at 900.

[43]Mattel, 296 F.3d at 901.

to infringement.[44] On the other hand, courts which focus on trademarks as a mechanism for avoiding confusion are likely to favor a parody defense. Parodies generally focus on very strong or famous marks. If the parody is sufficiently "heavy-handed" to be a good parody, and the court is not enamored with protecting the investment of the trademark owner, then the parody defense is likely to succeed.[45]

Also important is the manner in which the court applies the likelihood of confusion test. Each Circuit has adopted a multi-factored test for determining likelihood of confusion. If the court blindly applies the various factors, looking at things like the similarities between the marks and the intent to appropriate the mark, without considering the fact that the defendant's use is a parody, then a finding of infringement is almost certain. If, on the other hand, the court correctly uses the multi-factor test for likelihood of confusion as a guide, and considers the context of the use, then a parody defense may prevail.[46]

§ 11:19 Defenses—Limited geographic use

Research References

West's Key Number Digest, Trademarks ⊕1104

Trademark rights depend upon actual use of the mark in commerce. A common situation arises in which two users independently create and use the same trademark in different geographic areas. If those users eventually expand into the same geographic area, a dispute arises as to who has rights to the mark.

The general rule is that whoever uses a mark in a certain geographic area has trademark rights in that area only. These situations are usually referred to as *"Dawn Donut"* cases, referring to the leading case on the issue, *Dawn Donut Co. v. Hart's*

---

[44]*See, e.g.,* Coca-Cola Co. v. Gemini Rising, Inc., 346 F. Supp. 1183, 175 U.S.P.Q. 56 (E.D. N.Y. 1972); Mutual of Omaha Ins. Co. v. Novak, 836 F.2d 397, 5 U.S.P.Q.2d 1314, 98 A.L.R. Fed. 1 (8th Cir. 1987) (rejected by, Westchester Media v. PRL USA Holdings, Inc., 214 F.3d 658, 55 U.S.P.Q.2d 1225 (5th Cir. 2000)).

[45]*See, e.g.,* Cliffs Notes, Inc. v. Bantam Doubleday Dell Pub. Group, Inc., 886 F.2d 490, 16 Media L. Rep. (BNA) 2289, 12 U.S.P.Q.2d 1289 (2d Cir. 1989); Eveready Battery Co., Inc. v. Adolph Coors Co., 765 F. Supp. 440,

19 U.S.P.Q.2d 1265 (N.D. Ill. 1991); Anheuser-Busch, Inc. v. L. & L. Wings, Inc., 962 F.2d 316, 22 U.S.P.Q.2d 1502, 22 Fed. R. Serv. 3d 575 (4th Cir. 1992).

[46]*Compare* Mutual of Omaha Ins. Co. v. Novak, 836 F.2d 397, 5 U.S.P.Q.2d 1314, 98 A.L.R. Fed. 1 (8th Cir. 1987) (rejected by, Westchester Media v. PRL USA Holdings, Inc., 214 F.3d 658, 55 U.S.P.Q.2d 1225 (5th Cir. 2000)) *with* Anheuser-Busch, Inc. v. L. & L. Wings, Inc., 962 F.2d 316, 22 U.S.P.Q.2d 1502, 22 Fed. R. Serv. 3d 575 (4th Cir. 1992).

Food Stores, Inc.[1]

For example, suppose a California company begins using the mark ACME on widgets in 1962. Its sales are modest and limited to California and adjoining states. In 1988, a New York company begins using the same mark on the same goods. The New York company is successful and gradually expands its business westward. In 1996, it begins selling ACME brand widgets in Arizona and first learns about the older California company.

The California company has rights to the ACME mark for widgets in California and adjoining states. The New York company may not use ACME on widgets in those states. However, the New York company has priority in all of the other states. Thus, if the California company tries to expand outside of its traditional market, it will not be able to use the ACME mark.

A different situation arises with federally registered marks. Assume the facts of our hypothetical are the same, except that the California company registered its ACME mark sometime before 1988. The federal registration provides nationwide constructive notice that the California company owns the ACME mark for widgets. When the parties meet each other in 1996, the California company has rights not only in its traditional market, but throughout the entire country. The California company can seek an injunction for trademark infringement not only in California, but in any other state that it expands into.

It is important to note, however, that the first user can only seek an injunction in those jurisdictions in which it is actually using the mark. Where an unauthorized use of a conflicting mark is confined to a distinct and geographically separate market by the junior user, there is no present likelihood of confusion.[2] In such a situation, the registrant is not entitled to enjoin the junior user's use of the trademark.[3]

A registrant's remedies are thus limited. It has no presently enforceable rights in an area in which there is no presently provable probability of expansion of the registrant's services or repu-

---

[Section 11:19]

[1]Dawn Donut Co. v. Hart's Food Stores, Inc., 267 F.2d 358, 121 U.S.P.Q. 430 (2d Cir. 1959); *see also* Burger King of Fla., Inc. v. Hoots, 403 F.2d 904, 159 U.S.P.Q. 706 (7th Cir. 1968) (the plaintiff's federal registration of a mark gave them exclusive rights to the mark in Illinois except for the market area where the defendants, without knowledge of the plaintiff's prior use, actually used the mark in commerce prior to the plaintiff's registration); *but cf.* Weiner King, Inc. v. Wiener King Corp., 615 F.2d 512, 204 U.S.P.Q. 820 (C.C.P.A. 1980) (junior user awarded national registration when senior user had no intention of expansion beyond local market).

[2]John R. Thompson Co. v. Holloway, 366 F.2d 108, 114, 150 U.S.P.Q. 728 (5th Cir. 1966).

[3]Dawn Donut, 267 F.2d at 364.

tation that will create a likelihood of confusion.[4] However, once the federal registrant actually commences business in the junior user's territory, the federal registrant is entitled to an immediate injunction. The Ninth Circuit has stated:

> We hold that where a federal registrant has expanded its business to the point that the use of the conflicting similar marks by the registrant and the unauthorized user are no longer confined to separate and distinct market areas and there is established a likelihood of public confusion, the federal registrant is entitled under the authority of the Lanham Act to injunctive relief.[5]

However, a junior user may not acquire any substantive trademark rights against the registrant. The language of the Lanham Act, as well as its legislative history, shows an intent to provide nationwide protection for expanding businesses.[6] Under 15 U.S.C.A. § 1115(b), the owner of an incontestable trademark registration has the exclusive right to use its mark in commerce to the exclusion of all conflicting marks. Furthermore, 15 U.S.C.A. § 1072 makes registration of a mark on the principal register constructive notice of the registrant's claim of ownership. By eliminating the defense of good faith and lack of knowledge on the part of the junior user, §§ 1072 and 1115 afford a registrant nationwide protection for its registered marks, regardless of the geographic area in which the registrant actually uses his mark. Because of §§ 1072 and 1115, the junior user is not entitled to exclude the plaintiff from using the mark in the junior user's area or to use that mark concurrently once the plaintiff exploits the mark in connection with sales in that area.

A corollary of the *Dawn Donut* rule is that there can be no abandonment of a registered trademark in a limited geographic area. 15 U.S.C.A. § 1127, which provides for abandonment in certain cases of nonuse, applies only when the registrant fails to use his mark, within the meaning of § 1127, anywhere in the nation. Since the Lanham Act affords a registrant nationwide protection, a contrary holding would create an insoluble problem of measuring the geographical extent of the abandonment.[7]

The holding in *Dawn Donut* is limited. If the use of the marks by the registrant and the unauthorized user are confined to two sufficiently distinct and geographically separate markets, with no likelihood that the registrant will expand its use into the junior user's market, so that no public confusion is possible, then the registrant is not entitled to enjoin the junior user's use of the

---

[4]John R. Thompson, 366 F.2d at 114.

[5]Mister Donut of America, Inc. v. Mr. Donut, Inc., 418 F.2d 838, 844, 164 U.S.P.Q. 67 (9th Cir. 1969).

[6]John R. Thompson, 366 F.2d at 114-15.

[7]Dawn Donut, 267 F.2d at 363.

mark.[8] To sustain a claim for injunctive relief, the plaintiff need not show that the marks are actually being used concurrently in the same trading area. It is enough that expansion by the registrant into the junior user's market is likely in the normal course of its business.[9]

Not all courts follow the Dawn Donut rule. For example, in *Circuit City Stores, Inc. v. CarMax, Inc.*, the Sixth Circuit noted it employs a multifactor test for determining infringement liability.[10] A concurring judge added that the *Dawn Donut* rule may have outlived its usefulness in light of the increasing mobility of contemporary society, particularly in light of technological innovations such as the Internet.[11] More and more businesses now operate in a global market, due to the efficient means now available to reach consumers in far away regions. For many types of goods and services, it may be increasingly difficult to identify businesses limited to a distinct geographic area.

§ 11:20 Defenses—Labeling and use of disclaimers

Research References

West's Key Number Digest, Trademarks ⟢1436

One of the most common ways in which a defendant seeks to avoid liability for infringement is for the defendant to use its own trademark on its packaging. For instance, in *Bristol-Myers Squibb Co. v. McNeil-P.P.C. Inc.*,[1] the makers of EXCEDRIN P.M. sued the makers of TYLENOL P.M. for trade dress infringement because the TYLENOL P.M. carton was very similar to the EXCEDRIN P.M. carton. The only difference in the cartons were the color of the background and the trade names proceeding the P.M. designator. The court said that the presence and prominence of markings tending to dispel confusion as to origin, sponsorship or approval of goods in question is highly relevant to an inquiry concerning the similarity of the two trade dresses.[2] The court found that the presence and prominence of the trade names EXCEDRIN and TYLENOL on the packages eliminated any confusion, and thus held that there was no trade dress

---

[8]Dawn Donut, 267 F.2d at 364.

[9]Dawn Donut, 267 F.2d at 364 n.4.

[10]Circuit City Stores, Inc. v. CarMax, Inc., 165 F.3d 1047, 49 U.S.P.Q.2d 1507, 1999 FED App. 0026P (6th Cir. 1999).

[11]Circuit City, 165 F.3d at 1057 (Jones, J. concurring).

[Section 11:20]

[1]Bristol-Myers Squibb Co. v. McNeil-P.P.C., Inc., 973 F.2d 1033, 24 U.S.P.Q.2d 1161 (2d Cir. 1992).

[2]Bristol-Myers Squibb, 973 F.2d at 1046.

infringement.[3] Except in cases where consumers exercise virtually no care in selecting products, clarity of labeling and packaging will suffice to preclude almost all possibility of consumer confusion.[4]

However, a defendant's labeling of its product with its own trademark and selling the product through its own channels of distribution will not necessarily avoid a finding of likelihood of confusion.[5] In fact, some cases have held that a manufacturer cannot eliminate a likelihood of confusion simply by applying its own name to a product where the product which it resembles has already been found to have secondary meaning.[6] Other courts have held that adding a housemark or other label does not preclude a likelihood of confusion.[7] "[A] purchaser could well think plaintiff had licensed defendant as a second user and the addition is thus 'an aggravation, and not a justification.' "[8]

Another common way to avoid likelihood of confusion is by use of disclaimers. As one example, a company, Ace Co., might seek to avoid confusion between its mark and that of a competitor, Acme Corp., by including a disclaimer that reads: "ACME is a registered trademark of the ACME Corp. This product is not affiliated with the ACME corporation in any way." Such a disclaimer may be helpful, for example, where the marks are used in different markets or when the marks are used in comparative advertising. However, if the disclaimer or trademark is inadequately displayed such that the overall impression of the product is still confusing, infringement may still be found.[9]

§ 11:21 Defenses—Laches and acquiescence

Research References

West's Key Number Digest, Trademarks ⚷1533

In situations where a defendant has been using the allegedly infringing mark for a long period of time, an affirmative defense of laches may be available. In situations where a trademark

---

[3]*See also* Conopco, Inc. v. May Dept. Stores Co., 46 F.3d 1556, 1568, 32 U.S.P.Q.2d 1225 (Fed. Cir. 1994); Bristol-Myers, 973 F.2d at 1046–47; L.A. Gear, Inc. v. Thom McAn Shoe Co., 988 F.2d 1117, 1134, 25 U.S.P.Q.2d 1913 (Fed. Cir. 1993).

[4]Versa Products Co., Inc. v. Bifold Co. (Mfg.) Ltd., 50 F.3d 189, 203, 33 U.S.P.Q.2d 1801 (3d Cir. 1995).

[5]Fruehauf, 536 F.2d at 1221.

[6]Fruehauf, 536 F.2d at 1220-21;

A. T. Cross Co. v. Jonathan Bradley Pens, Inc., 470 F.2d 689, 692, 176 U.S.P.Q. 15 (2d Cir. 1972).

[7]Schwinn, 870 F.2d at 1187.

[8]A.T. Cross, 470 F.2d at 692 (quoting Menendez v. Holt, 128 U.S. 514, 521, 9 S. Ct. 143 (1888)).

[9]Artemide SpA v. Grandlite Design and Mfg. Co., Ltd., 672 F. Supp. 698, 4 U.S.P.Q.2d 1915 (S.D. N.Y. 1987).

owner has implicitly given a defendant consent to use a mark, an affirmative defense of acquiescence may be available.

Laches is an equitable doctrine based on the theory "that equity aids the vigilant and not those who slumber on their rights."[1] Laches has two required elements: (1) a trademark owner's unreasonable delay in bringing suit; and (2) prejudice to the accused infringer.[2] Some courts have further broken the first element into two parts: delay and legally inadequate excuse for delay.[3]

The period of delay on the part of the trademark owner begins at the time the owner knew or should have known of the defendant's use.[4] The factors to be considered in the assessment of laches include (1) progressive encroachment (where the defendant did not originally use the mark or trade dress in competition with the plaintiff, but then gradually directs its marketing or manufacturing efforts such that it is placed more squarely in competition with the plaintiff), (2) damage the plaintiff was suffering, and (3) likelihood of confusion at the time the plaintiff sued.[5] There is no exact length of time which equates to an unreasonable delay. Two years has generally been determined not to constitute an unreasonable delay.[6] Some courts have utilized an analogous statute such as tortious injury to property in determining whether an unreasonable delay has occurred.[7] Settlement attempts via negotiations may excuse a trademark owner's

---

[Section 11:21]

[1]N.A.A.C.P. v. N.A.A.C.P. Legal Defense & Educational Fund, Inc., 753 F.2d 131, 137, 225 U.S.P.Q. 264 (D.C. Cir. 1985).

[2]Brunswick Corp. v. Spinit Reel Co., 832 F.2d 513, 523, 4 U.S.P.Q.2d 1497, 23 Fed. R. Evid. Serv. 1272 (10th Cir. 1987).

[3]E.g., Brittingham v. Jenkins, 914 F.2d 447, 456, 16 U.S.P.Q.2d 1121, 116 A.L.R. Fed. 863 (4th Cir. 1990); AmBrit, 812 F.2d at 1545 (11th Cir. 1986); N.A.A.C.P., 753 F.2d at 131.

[4]E.g., Armco, Inc. v. Armco Burglar Alarm Co., Inc., 693 F.2d 1155, 1161, 217 U.S.P.Q. 145, 35 Fed. R. Serv. 2d 753 (5th Cir. 1982) (not explicitly deciding whether inquiry is into subjective knowledge or an objective standard, noting other courts adoption of an objective standard); Safeway Stores, Inc. v. Safeway Quality Foods, Inc., 433 F.2d 99, 103, 166 U.S.P.Q. 112 (7th Cir. 1970) ("Plaintiff is chargeable with the information it might have received had due inquiry been made."). But cf. Georgia-Pacific Corp. v. Great Plains Bag Co., 614 F.2d 757, 759, 204 U.S.P.Q. 697 (C.C.P.A. 1980) (to prove defense of laches the party asserting defense must show that the party against whom the defense is asserted either had actual knowledge of the accused trademark use or at least show that it would have been inconceivable for the party to be unaware of such use).

[5]Kason Industries, Inc. v. Component Hardware Group, Inc., 120 F.3d 1199, 43 U.S.P.Q.2d 1831 (11th Cir. 1997).

[6]AmBrit, 812 F.2d at 1546; Piper Aircraft Corp. v. Wag-Aero, Inc., 741 F.2d 925, 933, 223 U.S.P.Q. 202, 16 Fed. R. Evid. Serv. 86 (7th Cir. 1984).

[7]Hot Wax, Inc. v. Turtle Wax, Inc., 191 F.3d 813, 52 U.S.P.Q.2d 1065, 1999-2 Trade Cas. (CCH) ¶ 72651 (7th

delay in filing an action.[8]

The length of delay may also affect the relief available to the trademark owner. A proven laches defense will bar monetary damages,[9] but may not bar an injunction against further infringement or damages for post-suit action.[10] "By reason of laches, a plaintiff in a trademark infringement action may lose the right to recover damages or wrongfully derived profits during the period prior to the filing of suit. Upon a showing of infringement, however, the plaintiff may still be entitled to injunctive relief, * * * and to damages and profits for the period subsequent to the filing of suit."[11] The two-tier approach used by some courts differentiates between mere unreasonable, prejudicial delay barring pre-suit monetary damages, and egregious delay or affirmative acquiescence barring all relief. Other courts balance each party's interests and equities, weighing various factors.[12]

The last element is prejudice on the part of the accused infringer. Expenditure of substantial capital does not necessarily equate to prejudice, especially if expenditures are made while asserting a legal right to do so after notice of the owner's claim.[13] Egregious bad faith conduct by the accused infringer may also preclude a laches defense.[14] However, "a defendant's mere awareness of a plaintiff's claim to the same mark * * * [does not establish] the bad intent necessary to preclude the availability of the laches defense."[15]

Acquiescence is an equitable defense based upon affirmative actions or representations by the trademark owner that give implied consent to the accused infringer's actions.[16] While some cases use the terms acquiescence and laches synonymously to

---

Cir. 1999); Tandy Corp. v. Malone & Hyde, Inc., 769 F.2d 362, 366, 226 U.S.P.Q. 703 (6th Cir. 1985) ("Only rarely should laches bar a case before the analogous statute has run.").

[8]N.A.A.C.P., 753 F.2d at 137 n.59.

[9]Brittingham, 914 F.2d at 456.

[10]James Burrough Ltd. v. Sign of Beefeater, Inc., 572 F.2d 574, 197 U.S.P.Q. 277 (7th Cir. 1978).

[11]James Burrough Ltd. v. Sign of Beefeater, Inc., 572 F.2d 574, 197 U.S.P.Q. 277 (7th Cir. 1978).

[12]E.g., Tustin Community Hospital, Inc. v. Santa Ana Community Hospital Assn., 89 Cal. App. 3d 889, 153 Cal. Rptr. 76, 86-87, 205 U.S.P.Q. 83 (4th Dist. 1979); Carl Zeiss Stiftung v. V. E. B. Carl Zeiss, Jena, 293 F.

Supp. 892, 917, 160 U.S.P.Q. 97 (S.D. N.Y. 1968), judgment aff'd as modified, 433 F.2d 686, 167 U.S.P.Q. 641, 1971, 1971 Trade Cas. (CCH) ¶ 73407 (2d Cir. 1970).

[13]AmBrit, 812 F.2d at 1546-47; Tandy Corp. v. Malone & Hyde, Inc., 777 F.2d 1130, 1131, 228 U.S.P.Q. 621 (6th Cir. 1985).

[14]N.A.A.C.P., 753 F.2d at 137 (listing conscious fraud or bad faith by defendant as factor negating invocation of laches defense).

[15]Conan Properties, Inc. v. Conans Pizza, Inc., 752 F.2d 145, 150, 225 U.S.P.Q. 379 (5th Cir. 1985).

[16]E.g., Kellogg Co. v. Exxon Corp., 209 F.3d 562, 54 U.S.P.Q.2d 1413, 2000 FED App. 0123P (6th Cir. 2000).

denote a single type of affirmative defense, the better view is to distinguish use of the two terms.[17] The difference between laches and acquiescence is that laches denotes passive consent while acquiescence denotes affirmative action.[18] In other words,"[l]aches is a negligent and unintentional failure to protect one's rights while acquiescence is intentional."[19]

Establishing a defense of acquiescence requires proof of three elements: "(1) That petitioner actively represented that it would not assert a right or a claim; (2) that the delay between the active representation and assertion of the right or claim was not excusable; and (3) that the delay caused the registrant undue prejudice."[20] Thus, the acquiescence defense is distinguishable from a laches defense in that "[a]cquiescence requires 'a finding of conduct on the plaintiff's part that amounted to an assurance to the defendant, express or implied, that plaintiff would not assert his trademark rights against the defendant."[21]

§ 11:22   Defining trademark dilution

Research References

West's Key Number Digest, Trademarks ⊕1458

An action for trademark dilution can be a powerful complement or alternative to traditional trademark infringement suits. Trademark infringement looks at the consumer's response to an allegedly infringing mark, asking whether there is a likelihood the consumer will be confused. In contrast, trademark dilution looks at the response of the trademark owner, asking whether the value of the mark will be diminished by someone else using a mark similar to the first mark.

As a matter of policy, traditional trademark infringement seeks to protect the public from being confused by similar trademarks. As a secondary matter, trademark infringement seeks to protect a trademark owner's investment in his or her mark by preventing those confusingly similar uses. Trademark dilution, on the other hand, disregards the confusion issue. The primary purpose of trademark dilution is to protect the investment of the

---

[17]See McCarthy § 31:41.

[18]Coach House Restaurant, Inc. v. Coach and Six Restaurants, Inc., 934 F.2d 1551, 1558, 19 U.S.P.Q.2d 1401 (11th Cir. 1991).

[19]Elvis Presley Enterprises, Inc. v. Elvisly Yours, Inc., 936 F.2d 889, 894, 19 U.S.P.Q.2d 1377, 19 Fed. R. Serv. 3d 1397 (6th Cir. 1991).

[20]Coach House, 934 F.2d at 1558.

[21]Elvis Presley Enters., 936 F.2d at 894 (quoting Sweetheart Plastics, Inc. v. Detroit Forming, Inc., 743 F.2d 1039, 1046, 223 U.S.P.Q. 1291, 81 A.L.R. Fed. 659 (4th Cir. 1984)); see also Johnny's Fine Foods, Inc. v. Johnny's Inc., 286 F. Supp. 2d 876, 880-81, 68 U.S.P.Q.2d 1505 (M.D. Tenn. 2003).

trademark owner, and maintain the integrity and distinctiveness of the trademark.

What exactly is dilution? If you read the cases on dilution, you will quickly come to the conclusion that no one really knows what it is. General definitions, however, are plentiful, such as:

- Dilution is when a second user waters down the effectiveness of a first user's mark.[1]
- Dilution is an infection which, if allowed to spread, will inevitably destroy the advertising value of the mark.[2]
- Dilution is the gradual erosion of the strength of a trademark by another trademark.[3]
- Dilution is the gradual whittling away of the trademark's distinctiveness through use by third parties on nonconfusing, noncompeting products.[4]
- Dilution statutes protect strong, well-recognized marks even in the absence of a likelihood of confusion, if defendant's use is such as to tarnish, degrade or dilute the distinctive quality of a mark.[5]
- Dilution statutes protect the selling power that a distinctive mark has engendered for a product in the mind of the consuming public.[6]

Perhaps the best definition of dilution comes from Judge Kozinski of the Ninth Circuit:

> What differentiates dilution from trademark infringement and unfair competition is that it dispenses with the need to show likelihood of confusion. The dilution statute protects against an injury less immediate than the loss of sales due to purchaser confusion; it protects against what is frequently termed "the gradual diminution or whittling away of the value of a trademark, resulting from use by another * * *." Dilution thus refers to copying which, while not sufficiently confusing to divert sales in the short run, will tend to divert them in the long run by weakening the instantaneous favor-

---

[Section 11:22]

[1]Munters Corp. v. Matsui America, Inc., 730 F. Supp. 790, 796, 14 U.S.P.Q.2d 1993, 2003 (N.D. Ill. 1989), judgment aff'd, 909 F.2d 250, 15 U.S.P.Q.2d 1666 (7th Cir. 1990).

[2]Polaroid Corp. v. Polaraid, Inc., 319 F.2d 830, 836, 138 U.S.P.Q. 265, 270 (7th Cir. 1963).

[3]Hyatt Corp. v. Hyatt Legal Services, 736 F.2d 1153, 1158, 222 U.S.P.Q. 669, 671 (7th Cir. 1984).

[4]Ringling Bros.-Barnum & Bailey

Combined Shows, Inc. v. Celozzi-Ettelson Chevrolet, Inc., 855 F.2d 480, 482, 8 U.S.P.Q.2d 1072, 1074 (7th Cir. 1988).

[5]Toho Co., Ltd. v. Sears, Roebuck & Co., 645 F.2d 788, 793, 3 Int'l Trade Rep. (BNA) 1063, 210 U.S.P.Q. 547, 552 (9th Cir. 1981) (quoting 2 J. Thomas McCarthy, *Trademarks & Unfair Competition* § 24.13 at 155 (1973)).

[6]Sally Gee, Inc. v. Myra Hogan, Inc., 699 F.2d 621, 624, 217 U.S.P.Q. 658, 661 (2d Cir. 1983).

able associations the public makes with highly regarded products.[7]

While these definitions of dilution may be interesting from a jurisprudential standpoint, they do not help practitioners determine when a mark is or is not being diluted.

Before one can understand what dilution is, it is helpful to understand where it came from. Unlike most of trademark law, which was developed by common law courts to address changing market conditions, dilution was developed by academics and practitioners to protect the interests of trademark owners. Thus, while most trademark principles developed from the grass-roots to remedy situations that judges and juries thought were unfair, dilution was bestowed by the legislatures.

§ 11:23 History of dilution—Trademark law in the nineteenth century

Research References
West's Key Number Digest, Trademarks ⊸1450

There is an underlying dynamic equilibrium in trademark law between those people who believe that the purpose of trademark law is to prevent confusion in the marketplace and those people who believe that trademark rights are identical to other kinds of property, like patents or real estate.

When trademark infringement cases first appeared in the United States in the 1840s, courts looked to the common law for an analogous cause of action. Two possible theories were proffered as the basis of trademark infringement based upon these two different theories of trademark law: the torts of *deceit* and *trespass*.[1]

Under the deceit theory, a trademark owner was allowed to obtain relief when customers were deceived or confused into believing that the infringing products actually originated from the trademark owner. This kind of action was commonly referred to as "passing off," and, historically, required evidence of actual confusion.

The trespass theory of trademark infringement was based on an analogy between trademarks and two other types of intel-

---

[7]Plasticolor Molded Products v. Ford Motor Co., 713 F. Supp. 1329, 1342, 11 U.S.P.Q.2d 1023, 1034 (C.D. Cal. 1989), opinion vacated, 767 F. Supp. 1036, 18 U.S.P.Q.2d 1975 (C.D. Cal. 1991) (citations omitted) (J. Kozinski sitting by designation) (vacated in favor of consent judgment).

[Section 11:23]

[1]*See* Milton W. Handler, Are the State Antidilution Laws Compatible with the National Protection of Trademarks?, 75 Trademark Rep. 269 (1985).

lectual property, patents and copyrights. As property, proponents of the trespass theory argued, a trademark was infringed whenever another person used the same or a similar mark, because this use harmed the trademark owner's property right in the trademark.

Both the courts and Congress adopted the deceit theory as the test of trademark infringement. The Supreme Court explicitly rejected the trespass theory as early as 1880, and it has reaffirmed its support of the deceit theory as recently as 1988.

The Court recognized that the law of unfair competition has its roots in the common law tort of deceit, and that the purpose of unfair competition law is to protect consumers from confusion as to source. While that concern may result in the creation of "quasi-property rights" in marks, the focus of the law remains on the protection of consumers, not (like patent and copyright law) on the protection of producers as an incentive to innovation.[2]

> The plaintiff has the right not to lose his customers through false representations that those are his wares which in fact are not, but he may not monopolize any design or pattern, however trifling. The defendant, on the other hand, may copy plaintiff's goods slavishly down to the minutest detail count; but he may not represent himself as the plaintiff in their sale.[3]

Similarly, when Congress passed the Lanham Act in 1946, it was predicated on the concept of likelihood of confusion, thereby coming down squarely for the idea that trademark infringement is founded on deceit, not trespass. In contrast, trademark dilution picks up on the theory of trespass as the basis for asserting violation of trademark rights.

Since Congress and the federal courts had rejected the trespass theory of trademark infringement, proponents of this theory went to the states. Since the 1950s, about two thirds of the states have passed anti-dilution statutes. The original idea behind dilution was to provide added protection for owners of very strong (or "famous") trademarks. Usually, a trademark owner will only be able to stop an infringer if the marks are similar and the marks are used on similar goods. If the accused infringer uses the same or similar mark on very different goods, there is no trademark infringement.

Dilution was intended to be an alternative form of relief for owners of very strong trademarks which were used on unrelated

---

[2]Bonito Boats, Inc. v. Thunder Craft Boats, Inc., 489 U.S. 141, 157, 109 S. Ct. 971, 981, 9 U.S.P.Q.2d 1847, 1855 (1989).

[3]Bonito Boats, 489 U.S. at 157,

109 S. Ct. at 981, 103 L.Ed.2d 118, 9 U.S.P.Q.2d at 1855 (quoting Crescent Tool Co. v. Kilborn & Bishop Co., 247 F. 299, 301 (C.C.A. 2d Cir. 1917)).

products. If the trademark owner could show that its mark was extremely strong or well-known, or "famous," and the accused infringer was using that famous mark on goods that are very different from those of the trademark owner, then the mark was being diluted.

§ 11:24 History of dilution—A rational basis for trademark protection

Research References

West's Key Number Digest, Trademarks ⟜1450

Dilution arose because of perceived bad results in trademark infringement cases and the law's inability to keep pace with changes in marketing. The 1880s saw an explosion of trademarks. Many of the most recognizable and powerful marks in the world appeared in a few short years, as America created the idea of mass-marketing.

In the early part of this century, most courts applied a rigid test in trademark infringement cases, which only found trademark infringement in situations where the marks were used on identical goods. These are the kind of cases we would now think of as trademark counterfeiting, rather than simple infringement. This strict interpretation lead to a very narrow interpretation of trademark rights which was inconsistent with commercial reality.

In 1927, a famous law review article by Professor Frank Schecter proposed the idea of trademark dilution.[1] Schecter did not actually create the concept of trademark dilution. He found the idea in decisions by European courts, particularly German courts, which held that a trademark owner had "the utmost interest in seeing that its mark is not diluted [verwassert]."[2]

In his article, Schecter pointed out the need to protect strong trademarks from being whittled away by their use on noncompeting goods. Schecter proposed re-interpreting trademark law to emphasize a trademark owner's property rights, rather than confusion among consumers.

However, Schecter placed some important limitations on the concept of dilution. Schecter thought that dilution should only apply to coined or "fanciful" trademarks, when the identical mark was used by someone who did not compete with the trademark owner.

In the meantime, a slow evolution was taking place in the

[Section 11:24]

[1]Frank I. Schecter, *A Rational Basis For Trademark Protection*, 40

Harv.L.Rev. 813 (1927).

[2]Schecter, 40 Harv. L. Rev. at 832.

federal courts. Interpreting the concept of likelihood of confusion, the federal courts developed the concept of "related goods" which greatly expanded the reach of trademark infringement. Courts also fashioned the multi-factor approach to analyzing likelihood of confusion. Instead of simply using a side-by-side comparison, courts looked to the totality of the marketing situation to determine whether there was a likelihood of confusion as to source, sponsorship, affiliation or connection.[3]

However, proponents of the property theory of trademarks, apparently not satisfied with the slow evolution of the law in the courts, went to state legislatures to create the state system of protecting trademarks from dilution.

Even after state dilution statutes became fairly common, it was the conventional wisdom among trademark attorneys that courts were reluctant to enforce dilution statutes, and judges tended to ignore the statutes. This is probably because judges, viewing trademark law more objectively than most trademark practitioners, saw the alarming breadth of dilution statutes:

> [I]f dilution were treated simply as unfair competition minus the need to show likelihood of confusion, the doctrine would effectively render unfair competition and trademark loss superfluous for redressing claims of trade name copying.[4]

Therefore, dilution was usually limited by the courts so that only the most distinctive marks were eligible for protection. "So limited, dilution coexists peaceably with unfair competition as an adjunct doctrine providing a greater measure of protection for the most distinctive trade names."[5]

§ 11:25   Dilution statutes—State dilution statutes

Research References
West's Key Number Digest, Trademarks ⟜1451

Trademark dilution is almost entirely a creature of statute. Until the first federal antidilution statute was passed on January 16, 1996, dilution was governed entirely on a state-by-state basis. As of 2010, at least 37 states had passed antidilution statutes in one form or another, while Ohio is the only state to have recognized dilution as a common law cause of action.[1]

Over the years, the International Trademark Association

---

[3]*See* § 10:9, *supra*.

[4]Plasticolor, 713 F. Supp. at 1342, 11 U.S.P.Q.2d at 1034.

[5]Plasticolor, 713 F. Supp. at 1342, 11 U.S.P.Q.2d at 1035.

[Section 11:25]

[1]Ameritech, Inc. v. American Information Technologies Corp., 811 F.2d 960, 965, 1 U.S.P.Q.2d 1861, 1865 (6th Cir. 1987) (*citing* National City

(INTA) has drafted and published many revisions to its Model State Trademark Bill ("MSTB"). As of 2010, four states have passed laws encompassing the concepts of the 2007 MSTB, which attempts to coordinate state law with the last major change to federal dilution law in 2006.[2] Many other states have previously codified variations on the 1992 or 1996 versions of the MSTB.[3] Other states with antidilution statutes require a finding of actual dilution, a much higher standard for the plaintiff to meet.[4] The remaining state statutes[5] have language similar to the following INTA 1992 Revised Model State Bill,

> The owner of a mark which is famous in this state shall be entitled, subject to the principles of equity and upon such terms as the court deems reasonable, to an injunction against another person's commercial use of a mark or trade name, if such use begins after the mark has become famous and causes dilution of the distinctive quality of the mark, and to obtain such other relief as is provided in this section. In determining whether a mark is distinctive and famous, a court may consider factors such as, but not limited to:
>
> A. the degree of inherent or acquired distinctiveness of the mark in this state;
>
> B. the duration and extent of use of the mark in connection with the goods and services with which the mark is used;
>
> C. the duration and extent of advertising and publicity of the mark in this state;
>
> D. the geographical extent of the trading area in which the mark is used;
>
> E. the channels of trade for the goods or services with which the mark is used;
>
> F. the degree of recognition of the mark in the trading areas and channels of trade in this state used by the mark's owner and the person against whom the injunction is sought;
>
> G. the nature and extent of use of the same or similar mark by third parties; and
>
> H. whether the mark is the subject of a state registration in this state, or a federal registration under the Act of March 3, 1881, or under the Act of February 20, 1905, or on the principal register.

In an action brought under this section, the owner of a famous

---

Bank of Cleveland v. National City Window Cleaning Co., 19 Ohio Op. 2d 448, 88 Ohio L. Abs. 445, 180 N.E.2d 20, 134 U.S.P.Q. 54 (Ct. App. 8th Dist. Cuyahoga County 1962)).

[2]See, e.g., Ala. Code § 8-12-17, Cal. Bus. & Prof. Code § 14247.

[3]See, e.g., Fla. Stat. Ann. § 495.151, 765 ILCS 1036.

[4]See, e.g., Nev. Rev. Stat. § 600.435.

[5]Alaska, Arizona, Arkansas, Connecticut, Hawaii, Idaho, Illinois, Iowa, Kansas, Minnesota, Montana, Nebraska, Nevada, New Jersey, New Mexico, Pennsylvania, South Carolina, Tennessee, Utah, Washington, West Virginia, and Wyoming.

mark shall be entitled only to injunctive relief in this state, unless
the person against whom the injunctive relief is sought willfully
intended to trade on the owner's reputation or to cause dilution of
the famous mark. If such willful intent is proven, the owner shall
also be entitled to the remedies set forth in this chapter, subject to
the discretion of the court and the principles of equity. The following shall not be actionable under this section:

A. Fair use of a famous mark by another person in comparative
    commercial advertising or promotion to identify the compet-
    ing goods or services of the owner of the famous mark.

B. Noncommercial use of the mark.

C. All forms of news reporting and news commentary.

§ 11:26 Dilution statutes—Federal dilution statute

Research References
West's Key Number Digest, Trademarks ☞1451, 1457

Within a few years of passage, the original 1996 Federal
Trademark Dilution Act ("FTDA") was litigated up to the U.S.
Supreme Court. The Court interpreted the FTDA as requiring
proof of "actual dilution" before such an action could be successfully brought.[1] After this decision, Congress passed the Trademark Dilution Revision Act ("TDRA") of 2006. Among the many
revisions to federal dilution law the TDRA brought into effect
was lowering and clarifying the standards for a finding of "likelihood of dilution."

Federal law recognizes a cause of action for dilution when there
is a likelihood of "dilution by blurring" or "dilution by tarnishment" of a famous mark.[2] Dilution itself is defined as "the lessening of the capacity of a famous mark to identify and distinguish
goods or services, regardless of the presence or absence of (1)
competition between the owner of the famous mark and other
parties, or (2) likelihood of confusion, mistake, or deception."[3] The
statute defines dilution by blurring as:

association arising from the similarity between a mark or trade
name and a famous mark that impairs the distinctiveness of the
famous mark. In determining whether a mark or trade name is
likely to cause dilution by blurring, the court may consider all relevant factors, including the following:
(i) The degree of similarity between the mark or trade name and
the famous mark.
(ii) The degree of inherent or acquired distinctiveness of the famous
mark.

[Section 11:26]

[1]Moseley v. V Secret Catalogue,
Inc., 537 U.S. 418, 123 S. Ct. 1115, 155

L. Ed. 2d 1, 65 U.S.P.Q.2d 1801 (2003).
[2]15 U.S.C.A. § 1125(c)(1).
[3]15 U.S.C.A. § 1127.

(iii) The extent to which the owner of the famous mark is engaging in substantially exclusive use of the mark.

(iv) The degree of recognition of the famous mark.

(v) Whether the user of the mark or trade name intended to create an association with the famous mark.

(vi) Any actual association between the mark or trade name and the famous mark.[4]

Dilution by tarnishment is "association arising from the similarity between a mark or a trade name and a famous mark that harms the reputation of the famous mark."[5]

Similar to many of the state statutes, the federal statute is explicitly limited to famous marks. The federal statute also provides a list of factors for courts to examine in determining whether a mark is famous, such as the degree of distinctiveness of the mark, the length of use of the mark, the extent of advertising, the geographic scope of use, and the extent of use of similar marks by third parties.

Like the rest of federal trademark law, the federal dilution statute does not replace or preempt state trademark law. As a practical matter, dilution cases often include both state and federal law claims, particularly because some state statutes provide more protection than the federal statute. While not preempting state law entirely, the federal antidilution statute does provide a "safe harbor" from state statutes. Ownership of a federally registered trademark acts as a complete bar to a claim of dilution under state law. This provides yet another incentive for trademark owners to register their marks.

One significant difference between the federal and some state dilution statutes is that money damages are available under the federal statute. If the accused diluter "willfully intended to trade on the registrant's reputation or to cause dilution of the registrant's mark," the trademark owner is entitled to the same damages that are available for trademark and trade dress infringement. Further, "the availability of money damages may possibly trigger the Seventh Amendment" and mandate the right to a jury trial.[6] For cases involving only injunctive relief, the federal dilution statute does not provide for a jury trial.[7]

The Federal Trademark Dilution Act is presumptively inapplicable to conduct occurring and completed prior to enactment of

---

[4]15 U.S.C.A. § 1125(c)(2)(B).

[5]15 U.S.C.A. § 1125(c)(2)(C).

[6]Ringling Brothers-Barnum & Bailey Combined Shows, Inc. v. Utah Div. of Travel Development, 955 F. Supp. 598, 41 U.S.P.Q.2d 1924 (E.D. Va. 1997), disagreed with on other grounds by Moseley v. V Secret Catalogue, Inc., 537 U.S. 418, 123 S. Ct. 1115, 65 U.S.P.Q.2d 1801 (2003).

[7]Ringling Brothers, 955 F. Supp. at 598, 41 U.S.P.Q.2d at 1924.

the Act.[8] However, prospective injunctive relief may be available when the original violation occurred before the effective date of the Act, and the violation is ongoing.[9]

The federal dilution statute explicitly provides for noncommercial use and fair use defenses.[10] Claims under the federal dilution statute are limited to those seeking relief against commercial, trademark uses of a mark. "Although the boundary between commercial and noncommercial speech has yet to be clearly delineated, the core notion of commercial speech is that it does no more than propose a commercial transaction. If speech is not purely commercial—that is, if it does more than propose a commercial transaction—then it is entitled to full First Amendment protection."[11] Thus, this provision of the federal statute prevents trademark owners from acquiring "word monopolies" on their marks and prevents them from prohibiting the use of marks in satires, editorials, criticism, and political discussions.

§ 11:27 Analyzing a dilution case

Research References
West's Key Number Digest, Trademarks ⊸1458

A claim for dilution under the Federal Trademark Dilution Act requires proof that (i) the senior mark is famous; (ii) the senior mark is distinctive; (iii) the junior use is a commercial use in commerce; (iv) the junior use began after the senior mark had become famous;[1] and (v) the junior use is likely to cause dilution. Although the language in the case does not include the "is likely to cause" language in element (v), the 2006 revision to the federal dilution statute makes clear Congress' intent to change the standard of proof to a likelihood of dilution instead of actual dilution. Elements (i)—(iv) as written are still very likely good law[2] on the distinctive quality of the senior mark.[3]

---

[8]Resorts of Pinehurst, Inc. v. Pinehurst Nat. Development Corp., 973 F. Supp. 552, 43 U.S.P.Q.2d 1746 (M.D. N.C. 1997).

[9]Viacom Inc. v. Ingram Enterprises, Inc., 141 F.3d 886, 889-890, 46 U.S.P.Q.2d 1473, 1475 (8th Cir. 1998).

[10]15 U.S.C.A. § 1125(c)(3).

[11]Mattel, Inc. v. MCA Records, Inc., 296 F.3d 894, 906-907, 63 U.S.P. Q.2d 1715, 1722 (9th Cir. 2002) (internal quotation marks and citations omitted).

[Section 11:27]

[1]Rosetta Stone Ltd. v. Google, Inc., 676 F.3d 144, 171, 102 U.S.P.Q.2d 1473 (4th Cir. 2012).

[2]See 15 U.S.C.A. § 1125(c).

[3]Perkins School for the Blind v. Maxi-Aids, Inc., 274 F. Supp. 2d 319, 325, 69 U.S.P.Q.2d 1932 (E.D. N.Y. 2003), citing Nabisco, Inc. v. PF Brands, Inc., 191 F.3d 208, 215, 51 U.S.P.Q.2d 1882 (2d Cir. 1999) (abrogated by, Moseley v. V Secret Catalogue, Inc., 537 U.S. 418, 123 S. Ct. 1115, 155 L. Ed. 2d 1, 65 U.S.P.Q.2d 1801 (2003)).

In most states,[4] in order to maintain a cause of action for dilution, a plaintiff must prove two elements:

- an extremely strong mark, either because of the mark's distinctive quality or because it has acquired secondary meaning and
- a likelihood of dilution.[5]

An injunction may be obtained under a dilution statute if the prior user can show that the mark is distinctive and that the subsequent user's use dilutes that distinctiveness. Neither competition between the users nor confusion need be shown.[6] The focus is on damage to the mark's inherent value as a symbol rather than on whether consumers may be misled as to the origin or sponsorship of a product.[7]

§ 11:28 Dilution—Famous marks

Research References

West's Key Number Digest, Trademarks ⚖1468

"[V]alue judgments about the strength of a mark sufficient to be diluted, are difficult to make."[1] The federal dilution statute refers to "famous" trademarks, while most state dilution statutes refer to either "distinctive" or "famous" trademarks. The original notion of dilution was that there was a special category of extremely strong or "famous" trademarks[2] that was entitled to special protection. These marks are so well-known and powerful that their owners should be entitled to prevent others from using the marks even in situations that would not be likely to confuse

---

[4]An obvious problem in discussing dilution at a general level is that dilution is a statutory claim, and not every state has the same statute. This chapter discusses general principles of dilution that are applicable in most jurisdictions. Obviously, a lawyer faced with an actual case will carefully read the applicable statute and cases that interpret it.

[5]Sally Gee, 699 F.2d at 625–26, 217 U.S.P.Q. at 661; Pignons S.A. de Mecanique de Precision v. Polaroid Corp., 657 F.2d 482, 493, 212 U.S.P.Q. 246, 255 (1st Cir. 1981); Deere & Co. v. MTD Products, Inc., 41 F.3d 39, 42, 32 U.S.P.Q.2d 1936, 1938 (2d Cir. 1994); Hasbro, Inc. v. Clue Computing, Inc., 66 F. Supp. 2d 117, 137, 52 U.S.P.

Q.2d 1402, 1418 (D. Mass. 1999), aff'd, 232 F.3d 1, 56 U.S.P.Q.2d 1766 (1st Cir. 2000).

[6]Hyatt, 736 F.2d at 1157, 222 U.S.P.Q. at 671–72.

[7]Toho Co., Ltd. v. Sears, Roebuck & Co., 645 F.2d 788, 793, 3 Int'l Trade Rep. (BNA) 1063, 210 U.S.P.Q. 547 (9th Cir. 1981).

[Section 11:28]

[1]J. Thomas McCarthy, *Trademarks and Unfair Competition* § 24.14 (3d ed.1993).

[2]One commentator suggests that marks capable of being diluted be called "SuperMarks."

any consumers.[3]

Dilution was intended to prevent the appearance of DUPONT shoes, BUICK aspirin tablets, SCHLITZ varnish, KODAK pianos, and BULOVA gowns.[4] According to dilution proponents, it would be unfair to allow third parties to use these well-known marks on goods that are different from the trademark owner's goods, with no fear of recrimination.

However, most cases interpreting dilution statutes have wandered far away from the original notion of famous marks, and the concept of fame is given only lip-service, if it is recognized at all. According to many courts, in order to be protected, a mark need not be famous or celebrated, but it must be an extremely strong mark either because of its inherently distinctive quality or the fact that it has acquired secondary meaning.[5] Some courts will now protect almost any mark. In New York[6] and other states[7], a mark is sufficiently distinctive to be protected by dilution statutes if the mark has acquired secondary meaning. Thus, any trademark can be diluted.

The federal dilution statue lists four nonexclusive factors to examine in determining whether a mark possesses the requisite degree of recognition to be considered famous within the meaning of the statute:

- The duration, extent, and geographic reach of advertising and publicity of the mark, whether advertised or publicized by the owner or third parties,
- The amount, volume, and geographic extent of sales of goods or services offered under the mark,
- The extent of actual recognition of the mark, and
- Whether the mark was registered under the Act of March 3, 1881, or the Act of February 20, 1905, or on the principal register.

This list is much the same as a list of factors considered in analyzing the strength of a trademark.

Distinctiveness for dilution purposes often has been equated

[3]Dilution applies to trade dress as well as trademarks. Merriam-Webster, Inc. v. Random House, Inc., 35 F.3d 65, 73, 32 U.S.P.Q.2d 1010, 1016 (2d Cir. 1994).

[4]Sally Gee, 699 F.2d at 625, 217 U.S.P.Q. at 662.

[5]Kraft General Foods, Inc. v. Allied Old English, Inc., 831 F. Supp.

123, 134, 31 U.S.P.Q.2d 1094, 1102 (S.D. N.Y. 1993).

[6]Deere & Co., 41 F.3d at 42, 32 U.S.P.Q.2d at 1938.

[7]Such as Arkansas, Champions Golf Club, Inc. v. Sunrise Land Corp., 846 F. Supp. 742, 758, 32 U.S.P.Q.2d 1419, 1428 (W.D. Ark. 1994).

with the strength of a mark for infringement purposes.[8] That is, courts will look at the same factors in analyzing whether a mark is strong enough to be diluted as it looks at in determining whether a mark is "strong" for purposes of infringement.

For instance, the length of time the mark is used, the scope of advertising and promotions, the nature and extent of the business and scope of the first user's reputation are also important factors that must be considered in determining the distinctiveness of a mark.[9]

Even though use of a mark may be reasonably common, and the mark is not coined or invented, the mark may still be diluted. The fact that a mark is coined or invented may make distinctiveness easier to show, but it is neither necessary nor sufficient to establish distinctiveness.[10]

A mark's strength is measured by its inherent distinctiveness, as well as its distinctiveness in the marketplace. For instance, the mark MIRACLE-GRO is a suggestive mark that is conceptually distinct due to the unique combination of terms, along with the misspelling of "grow."[11] However, distinctiveness has also been defined simply as a mark that has acquired secondary meaning.[12] A presumption of inherent distinctiveness may also arise under the federal dilution statute by virtue of a mark's incontestable status.[13]

Other factors are also involved in determining whether a mark is sufficiently strong to be diluted. Use of the mark by many third parties will prevent the mark from being sufficiently distinctive to merit protection under the dilution statute. Also, concurrent use of the marks for several years will effectively preclude a finding that the mark could be diluted.

A showing that a trademark or trade dress is famous in a niche market is not enough to establish dilution if the plaintiff and the defendant are using marks in separate markets.[14] However, a mark that is not famous to the general public may still be entitled

---

[8]Mead Data Cent., Inc. v. Toyota Motor Sales, U.S.A., Inc., 875 F.2d 1026, 1030, 10 U.S.P.Q.2d 1961, 1965 (2d Cir. 1989).

[9]Ringling Bros. v. Celozzi-Ettelson Chevrolet, 855 F.2d at 483, 8 U.S.P.Q.2d at 1075.

[10]Hyatt, 736 F.2d at 1158, 222 U.S.P.Q. at 672.

[11]Stern's Miracle-Gro Products, Inc. v. Shark Products, Inc., 823 F. Supp. 1077, 1091, 27 U.S.P.Q.2d 1267, 1276 (S.D. N.Y. 1993).

[12]Stern's Miracle-Gro Products, 823 F. Supp. at 1091, 27 U.S.P.Q.2d at 1276.

[13]Savin Corp. v. Savin Group, 391 F.3d 439, 451, 73 U.S.P.Q.2d 1273, 1278 (2d Cir. 2004).

[14]Mead Data, 875 F.2d at 1031, 10 U.S.P.Q.2d at 1965; Times Mirror Magazines, Inc. v. Las Vegas Sports News, L.L.C., 212 F.3d 157, 54 U.S.P.Q.2d 1577, 1581, 165 A.L.R. Fed. 783 (3d Cir. 2000).

to dilution protection where both parties are operating in the same or related niche markets, so long as the asserted mark possesses a high degree of fame in that niche market.[15]

Also, the fair use defense of the Lanham Act[16] to claims of trademark infringement does not apply to either federal or state dilution statutes. Whether a mark is adopted in good faith, and is thus a fair use under the Lanham Act, is not a defense to charges of dilution in those states.[17] Of course, the fair use defense would have limited application, because it only applies to descriptive marks. Thus, it would probably only be a defense in jurisdictions such as New York, where weak or descriptive marks may be diluted, provided they acquired secondary meaning.

Often, the easiest way to develop an understanding of a legal definition is to look at the results of some cases. Here is a (nonexhaustive) list of marks that were determined to be strong enough to be diluted:

STRONG ENOUGH TO BE DILUTED

501[18]

AMERICAN EXPRESS[19]

AMERICAN UNITED LIFE INSURANCE[20]

ARRT[21]

BLUE BOOK[22]

BULL'S EYE[23]

---

[15]Times Mirror Magazines, Inc. v. Las Vegas Sports News, L.L.C., 212 F.3d 157, 54 U.S.P.Q.2d 1577, 1581, 165 A.L.R. Fed. 783 (3d Cir. 2000).

[16]15 U.S.C.A. § 1115(b)(4); see discussion in § 10:17. The fair use defense of § 1115(b)(4) to claims of trademark infringement differs from the fair use defense of 15 U.S.C.A. § 1125(c)(4)(A) to claims of trademark dilution.

[17]Ringling Bros. v. Celozzi-Ettelson Chevrolet, 855 F.2d at 483, 8 U.S.P.Q.2d at 1075.

[18]Jordache Enterprises, Inc. v. Levi Strauss & Co., 841 F. Supp. 506, 30 U.S.P.Q.2d 1721 (S.D. N.Y. 1993).

[19]American Exp. Co. v. American Exp. Limousine Service Ltd., 772 F. Supp. 729, 21 U.S.P.Q.2d 1009 (E.D. N.Y. 1991).

[20]American United Life Ins. Co. v. American United Ins. Co., 731 F. Supp. 480, 15 U.S.P.Q.2d 1873 (S.D. Fla. 1990).

[21]American Registry of Radiologic Technologists v. McClellan, 2004 WL 377054 (N.D. Tex. 2004), aff'd, 155 Fed. Appx. 744 (5th Cir. 2005).

[22]Kelley Blue Book v. Car-Smarts, Inc., 802 F. Supp. 278, 24 U.S.P.Q.2d 1481 (C.D. Cal. 1992).

[23]Kraft, 831 F. Supp. at 123, 31 U.S.P.Q.2d at 1094.

CENTURY 21[24]

CHAMPIONS[25]

CHICKEN TENDERS[26]

Shape of COCA-COLA Bottle[27]

DON'T LEAVE HOME WITHOUT IT[28]

ENERGIZER BUNNY[29]

FORD[30]

GALLO[31]

GOLDEN ARCHES[32]

THE GREATEST SHOW ON EARTH[33]

HOOVER[34]

HOULIHAN'S[35]

JAGUAR[36]

---

[24]Century 21 Real Estate Corp. v. Sandlin, 846 F.2d 1175, 6 U.S.P.Q.2d 2034 (9th Cir.1988).

[25]Champions Golf Club, 846 F. Supp. at 742, 32 U.S.P.Q.2d at 1419.

[26]Burger King Corp. v. Pilgrim's Pride Corp., 705 F. Supp. 1522, 12 U.S.P.Q.2d 1526 (S.D. Fla. 1988), judgment aff'd, 894 F.2d 412 (11th Cir. 1990).

[27]Coca-Cola Co. v. Alma-Leo U.S.A., Inc., 719 F. Supp. 725, 12 U.S.P.Q.2d 1487 (N.D. Ill. 1989).

[28]American Exp. Co. v. Vibra Approved Laboratories Corp., 10 U.S.P.Q.2d 2006, 1989 WL 39679 (S.D. N.Y. 1989).

[29]Eveready Battery Co., Inc. v. Adolph Coors Co., 765 F. Supp. 440, 19 U.S.P.Q.2d 1265 (N.D. Ill. 1991).

[30]Plasticolor, 713 F. Supp. at 1342, 11 U.S.P.Q.2d at 1034.

[31]E. & J. Gallo Winery v. Consorzio del Gallo Nero, 782 F. Supp. 457, 20 U.S.P.Q.2d 1579 (N.D. Cal. 1991).

[32]McDonald's Corp. v. Arche Technologies, 17 U.S.P.Q.2d 1557, 1990 WL 10072486 (N.D. Cal. 1990), judgment entered, 1990 WL 10556830 (N.D. Cal. 1990).

[33]Ringling Bros. - Barnum & Bailey Combined Shows Inc. v. Celozzi-Ettleson Chevrolet Inc., 6 U.S.P.Q.2d 1300, 1987 WL 149721 (N.D. Ill. 1987), adopted, 1987 WL 17127 (N.D. Ill. 1987), judgment aff'd, 855 F.2d 480, 8 U.S.P.Q.2d 1072 (7th Cir. 1988) and aff'd, 855 F.2d 480, 8 U.S.P.Q.2d 1072 (7th Cir. 1988).

[34]Hoover Co. v. Citicorp Venture Capital Ltd., 674 F. Supp. 460, 6 U.S.P.Q.2d 1396 (S.D. N.Y. 1987).

[35]Gilbert/Robinson, Inc. v. Carrie Beverage-Missouri, Inc., 758 F. Supp. 512, 19 U.S.P.Q.2d 1481 (E.D. Mo. 1991), judgment aff'd, 989 F.2d 985, 26 U.S.P.Q.2d 1378 (8th Cir. 1993).

[36]Jaguar Cars Ltd. v. Skandrani, 771 F. Supp. 1178, 18 U.S.P.Q.2d 1626 (S.D. Fla. 1991).

KIRBY[37]

KODAK[38]

"Mc" Family of McDonald's marks[39]

MICHELOB[40]

MIDWEST RESEARCH INSTITUTE[41]

MIRACLE-GRO[42]

NEXXUS[43]

NUGGET[44]

The OSCAR Statuette[45]

PERL[46]

ROADWAY MOTOR PLAZA[47]

SPORTSTRAP[48]

THE FIVE SATINS[49]

---

[37]Scott Fetzer Co. v. Gehring, 288 F. Supp. 2d 696, 701 (E.D. Pa. 2003).

[38]Eastman Kodak Co. v. Rakow, 739 F. Supp. 116, 15 U.S.P.Q.2d 1631 (W.D. N.Y. 1989).

[39]McDonald's Corp. v. McBagel's, Inc., 649 F. Supp. 1268, 1 U.S.P.Q.2d 1761, 95 A.L.R. Fed. 1 (S.D. N.Y. 1986).

[40]Anheuser-Busch, Inc. v. Balducci Publications, 28 F.3d 769, 22 Media L. Rep. (BNA) 2001, 31 U.S.P.Q.2d 1296 (8th Cir. 1994).

[41]Midwest Research Institute v. S & B Promotions, Inc., 677 F. Supp. 1007, 6 U.S.P.Q.2d 1269 (W.D. Mo. 1988).

[42]Stern's Miracle-Gro Products, Inc. v. Shark Products, Inc., 823 F. Supp. 1077, 27 U.S.P.Q.2d 1267 (S.D. N.Y. 1993).

[43]NEXxUS Products Co. v. Gentle Concepts, Inc., 28 U.S.P.Q.2d 1257, 1993 WL 496824 (M.D. Fla. 1993).

[44]Nugget Distributors Co-op. of America, Inc. v. Mr. Nugget, Inc., 776 F. Supp. 1012, 20 U.S.P.Q.2d 1263 (E.D. Pa. 1991).

[45]Academy of Motion Picture Arts and Sciences v. Creative House Promotions, Inc., 944 F.2d 1446, 19 U.S.P.Q.2d 1491 (9th Cir.1991).

[46]Perl Brand Foods Corp. v. Deli Direct From Perl, Inc., 14 U.S.P.Q.2d 1569, 1989 WL 418445 (N.D. Ill. 1989).

[47]Roadway Exp., Inc. v. Roadway Motor Plazas, Inc., 17 U.S.P.Q.2d 1131, 1990 WL 120945 (N.D. N.Y. 1990).

[48]Regal Industries, Inc. v. Genal Strap, Inc., 33 U.S.P.Q.2d 1289, 1994 WL 161374 (E.D. Pa. 1994), opinion amended on reconsideration, 1994 WL 388686 (E.D. Pa. 1994), judgment aff'd in part, appeal dismissed in part, 68 F.3d 457 (3d Cir. 1995) (amendment unrelated to findings of dilution).

[49]Baker v. Parris, 777 F. Supp. 299, 22 U.S.P.Q.2d 1611, 115 A.L.R. Fed. 669 (S.D. N.Y. 1991).

VUITTON[50]

WING-DINGS[51]

And here is a sample of marks that were not strong enough to be diluted:

NOT STRONG ENOUGH TO BE DILUTED

ACCURIDE[52]

AGATHA[53]

BABY TALK[54]

DAYTONA[55]

DENTIST'S CHOICE[56]

ESSENCE[57]

(EXCEDRIN) PM[58]

FIRST SOUTHERN BANK[59]

FRUIT (OF THE LOOM)[60]

HEARTWISE[61]

IMS[62]

---

[50]Louis Vuitton, S.A. v. After Dark Boutique, 680 F. Supp. 1507, 6 U.S.P. Q.2d 1641 (N.D. Fla. 1988).

[51]Hester Industries, Inc. v. Tyson Foods, Inc., 16 U.S.P.Q.2d 1275, 1990 WL 88645 (N.D. N.Y. 1990).

[52]Accuride Intern., Inc. v. Accuride Corp., 871 F.2d 1531, 10 U.S.P.Q.2d 1589 (9th Cir. 1989).

[53]Brown v. Quiniou, 744 F. Supp. 463, 16 U.S.P.Q.2d 1161 (S.D. N.Y. 1990).

[54]Parenting Unlimited Inc. v. Columbia Pictures Television Inc., 743 F. Supp. 221, 16 U.S.P.Q.2d 1171 (S.D. N.Y. 1990).

[55]HBP, Inc. v. American Marine Holdings, Inc., 290 F. Supp. 2d 1320, 1338, 68 U.S.P.Q.2d 1798, 1810 (M.D. Fla. 2003), aff'd, 129 Fed. Appx. 601 (11th Cir. 2005).

[56]Wonder Labs, Inc. v. Procter & Gamble Co., 728 F. Supp. 1058, 14 U.S.P.Q.2d 1645 (S.D. N.Y. 1990).

[57]Essence Communications, Inc. v. Singh Industries, Inc., 703 F. Supp. 261, 10 U.S.P.Q.2d 1036 (S.D. N.Y. 1988).

[58]Bristol-Myers Squibb Co. v. McNeil-P.P.C., Inc., 973 F.2d 1033, 24 U.S.P.Q.2d 1161 (2d Cir.1992).

[59]Great Southern Bank v. First Southern Bank, 625 So. 2d 463, 30 U.S.P.Q.2d 1522 (Fla. 1993).

[60]Fruit of the Loom, Inc. v. Girouard, 994 F.2d 1359, 26 U.S.P. Q.2d 1782 (9th Cir.1993).

[61]Worthington Foods, Inc. v. Kellogg Co., 732 F. Supp. 1417, 14 U.S.P.Q.2d 1577 (S.D. Ohio 1990).

[62]IMS Ltd. v. International Medical Systems, Inc., 1 U.S.P.Q.2d 1268, 1986 WL 9692 (E.D. N.Y. 1986).

INTERVIEW[63]

JBJ[64]

LEXIS[65]

MAID TO ORDER[66]

MDT[67]

TELEVISION CITY[68]

TOWER RECORDS[69]

WE TREAT YOU RIGHT[70]

Some courts have been more reluctant than others to grant trademark owners sweeping rights. For example, in *Fruit of the Loom, Inc. v. Girouard*,[71] the court refused to protect the mark FRUIT against defendant's use of the mark FRUIT FLOPS on thongs. The court did not think that the mark FRUIT by itself was sufficiently strong to merit protection against dilution. Moreover, the court was concerned that if FRUIT was protected by itself, plaintiff would be able to assert that mark against noncompetitors as well as competitors. Since the mark is used by a large number of people, Fruit of the Loom would be able to effectively exclude all use of the word FRUIT by noncompetitors. Third, the court held that "whittling away will not occur unless there is at least some subliminal connection in a buyer's mind between the two parties' uses of the marks. Such a connection is not the same as likelihood of confusion, but it does require a threshold showing of some mental association between the protected mark and the alleged diluter."[72]

Thus, some courts are clinging to the belief that "[t]he dilution

---

[63]Andy Warhol Enterprises, Inc. v. Time Inc., 700 F. Supp. 760, 9 U.S.P. Q.2d 1454 (S.D. N.Y. 1988).

[64]Oxford Industries, Inc. v. JBJ Fabrics, Inc., 6 U.S.P.Q.2d 1756, 1988 WL 9959 (S.D. N.Y. 1988).

[65]Mead Data, 875 F.2d at 1026, 10 U.S.P.Q.2d at 1961.

[66]Kern v. WKQX Radio, 175 Ill. App. 3d 624, 125 Ill. Dec. 73, 529 N.E.2d 1149, 9 U.S.P.Q.2d 1131 (1st Dist. 1988).

[67]MDT Corp. v. New York Stock Exchange, Inc., 858 F. Supp. 1028, 30 U.S.P.Q.2d 1849 (C.D. Cal. 1994).

[68]CBS Inc. v. Liederman, 866 F. Supp. 763, 33 U.S.P.Q.2d 1333 (S.D. N.Y. 1994), aff'd, 44 F.3d 174, 33 U.S.P. Q.2d 1640 (2d Cir. 1995).

[69]Tower Publications, Inc. v. MTS Inc., 21 U.S.P.Q.2d 1303, 1991 WL 222265 (N.D. Ill. 1991).

[70]American Dairy Queen Corp. v. RTO, Inc., 16 U.S.P.Q.2d 1077, 1990 WL 103649 (N.D. Ill. 1990).

[71]Fruit of the Loom, 994 F.2d at 1359, 26 U.S.P.Q.2d at 1782.

[72]Fruit of the Loom, 994 F.2d at 1363, 26 U.S.P.Q.2d at 1785.

doctrine" is only available to protect distinctive marks as exemplified by such famous names as TIFFANY, POLAROID, ROLLS ROYCE and KODAK.[73] Others are excluding weak, nondistinct, descriptive trademarks, regardless of fame or acquired secondary meaning, from protection under the dilution statutes.[74]

§ 11:29 Dilution—Theories of dilution

Research References

West's Key Number Digest, Trademarks ⬦1461 to 1467

While success of a trademark infringement case depends in significant part on the strength of the mark, antidilution laws are intended in many ways to help trademark owners preserve that strength. The very nature of dilution is to gnaw away insidiously at the value of a trademark.[1] Thus, dilution is an act which threatens two separate, but related, components of a mark's value: junior users may blur a mark's product identification or they may tarnish the affirmative associations that a mark conveys.[2]

As a result, courts usually look at two possible theories in analyzing whether a mark is likely to be diluted:

- diminution in the uniqueness and individuality of the mark ("blurring"); or

- injury resulting from use of a mark in a manner that tarnishes or appropriates the goodwill and reputation associated with plaintiff's mark ("tarnishment").[3]

One court has identified four different kinds of dilution:

- protecting the mark against association with something

---

[73]Sykes Laboratory, Inc. v. Kalvin, 610 F. Supp. 849, 858 (C.D. Cal. 1985).

[74]TCPIP Holding Co., Inc. v. Haar Communications, Inc., 244 F.3d 88, 97, 57 U.S.P.Q.2d 1969, 1977 (2d Cir. 2001); Avery Dennison Corp. v. Sumpton, 189 F.3d 868, 875, 51 U.S.P.Q.2d 1801, 1807-08 (9th Cir. 1999).

[Section 11:29]

[1]Hyatt, 736 F.2d at 1158, 222 U.S.P.Q. at 672.

[2]Sally Gee, 699 F.2d at 625, 217 U.S.P.Q. at 662.

[3]Mead Data, 875 F.2d at 1031, 10 U.S.P.Q.2d at 1969 (J. Sweet, concurring); Anheuser-Busch, 28 F.3d at 777, 22 Media L. Rep. (BNA) 2001, 31 U.S.P.Q.2d at 1302. Some courts add a third possible kind of dilution: injury to the value of a mark caused by actual or potential confusion. L.L. Bean, Inc. v. Drake Publishers, Inc., 811 F.2d 26, 30, 13 Media L. Rep. (BNA) 2009, 1 U.S.P.Q.2d 1753, 1756 (1st Cir. 1987) (rejected by, United We Stand America, Inc. v. United We Stand, America New York, Inc., 128 F.3d 86, 44 U.S.P.Q.2d 1351, 39 Fed. R. Serv. 3d 88 (2d Cir. 1997)). "It is abundantly clear that a plaintiff demonstrates a likelihood of dilution where the products operate in the same markets and the names are similar enough to cause confusion among the purchasing public." Kraft, 831 F. Supp. At 134, 31 U.S. P.Q.2d at 1103. How this differs from trademark infringement is far from clear.

unsavory or degrading;

- protecting against tarnishing of the mark, and resulting injury to business reputation, caused by association with poorly manufactured products;
- protecting against "genericide," the tendency of a widely used product name to become the generic term for a product; and
- protecting against the gradual impairment of a trademark when it is used to identify unaffiliated products, a practice that tends to diffuse the public's immediate association of the mark with the source.[4]

"Blurring" occurs where the uniqueness of a mark is gradually whittled away by another's use:

> The evil which the Legislature sought to remedy was not public confusion caused by similar products or services sold by competitors, but a cancer-like growth of dissimilar products or services which feeds upon the business reputation of an established distinctive trademark * * * The harm that [dilution] is designed to prevent is the gradual whittling away of a firm's distinctive trademark.[5]

Thus, dilution by blurring may occur where the defendant uses the plaintiff's trademark to identify the defendant's goods and services, raising the possibility that the mark will lose its ability to serve as a unique identifier of the plaintiff's product.[6]

The federal dilution statute defines dilution by blurring as an "association arising from the similarity between a mark or trade name and a famous mark that impairs the distinctiveness of the famous mark."[7] The statute goes on to provide six nonexclusive relevant factors for the courts to consider when determining whether a mark is likely to cause dilution by blurring:

- the degree of similarity between the mark or trade name and the famous mark;
- the degree of inherent or acquired distinctiveness of the famous mark;
- the extent to which the owner of the famous mark is engaging in substantially exclusive use of the mark;
- the degree of recognition of the famous mark;
- whether the user of the mark or trade name intended to create an association with the famous mark; and
- any actual association between the mark or trade name and

---

[4]Plasticolor, 713 F. Supp. at 1343–44, 11 U.S.P.Q.2d at 1036.

[5]Allied Maintenance Corp. v. Allied Mechanical Trades, Inc., 42 N.Y.2d 538, 399 N.Y.S.2d 628, 631–32, 369 N.E.2d 1162, 1165–66, 198 U.S.P.Q. 418, 422 (1977).

[6]Deere & Co., 41 F.3d at 43, 32 U.S.P.Q.2d at 1938.

[7]15 U.S.C.A. § 1125(c)(2)(B).

the famous mark.

"Tarnishment arises when the plaintiff's trademark is linked to products of shoddy quality or is portrayed in an unwholesome or unsavory context likely to evoke unflattering thoughts about the owner's products.[8] In these sorts of cases, the trademark's reputation and commercial value might be diminished because the public will associate the lack of quality or lack of prestige in the defendant's goods with the plaintiff's unrelated goods, or because the defendant's use reduces the trademark's reputation and standing in the eyes of consumers as a wholesome identifier of the owner's products or services.[9] Tarnishment is usually found where a distinctive mark is depicted in the contents of sexual activity, obscenity or illegal activities.[10]

The federal dilution statute defines dilution by tarnishment as an "association arising from the similarity between a mark or trade name and a famous mark that harms the reputation of the famous mark."[11] Unlike blurring, however, Congress chose not to provide any factors for consideration by the courts; this could be because Congress is satisfied with allowing the current case law to flesh out the tarnishment cause of action.

Although dilution statutes can help prevent "genericide" of a mark, a mark that has ceased to be source-designating and has become generic cannot be revived by these dilution statutes because the mark is no longer distinctive as required by the statutes.[12]

§ 11:30 Dilution—Proving dilution

Research References
West's Key Number Digest, Trademarks ⊙1605

The Federal Trademark Dilution Act specifies that "the owner of a famous mark that is distinctive . . . shall be entitled to an injunction against another person who . . . commences use of a mark or trade name in commerce that is likely to cause dilution

---

[8]Deere & Co., 41 F.3d at 43, 32 U.S.P.Q.2d at 1939.

[9]Deere & Co., 41 F.3d at 43, 32 U.S.P.Q.2d at 1939.

[10]See, e.g., Coca-Cola Co. v. Gemini Rising, Inc., 346 F. Supp. 1183, 1191, 175 U.S.P.Q. 56, 59 (E.D. N.Y. 1972); Pillsbury Co. v. Milky Way Productions, Inc., 8 Media L. Rep. (BNA) 1016, 215 U.S.P.Q. 124, 135, 1981 WL 1402 (N.D. Ga. 1981); Chemical Corp. of America v. Anheuser-Busch, Inc., 306 F.2d 433, 134 U.S.P.Q. 524, 2 A.L.R.3d 739 (5th Cir. 1962).

[11]15 U.S.C.A. § 1125(c)(2)(C).

[12]Illinois High School Ass'n v. GTE Vantage Inc., 99 F.3d 244, 247, 113 Ed. Law Rep. 1103, 40 U.S.P.Q.2d 1633, 1636 (7th Cir. 1996), as amended, (Dec. 3, 1996).

by blurring or dilution by tarnishment of the famous mark . . .."[1]

The Supreme Court had previously held, under the older version, that the dilution statute's language "unambiguously requires a showing of actual dilution, rather than a likelihood of dilution."[2] Congress responded to this decision by passing the TDRA in 2006, overruling the Supreme Court's interpretation and lowering the standard of proof to a likelihood of dilution. Recall that several states also subscribe to a likelihood of dilution standard.[3]

Some courts have approached analyzing "likelihood of dilution" in very much the same way they analyze likelihood of confusion, by using a multi-factor test that examines:

- similarity of the marks,
- similarity of the products,
- sophistication of the consumers,
- predatory intent,
- renown of the senior user's mark, and
- renown of the junior user's mark.[4]

How similar do the marks need to be in order to find dilution? The courts have not been clear. The short answer is that the second user's mark must be similar enough so that it is likely to dilute the first user's mark. A dilution claim requires a higher degree of similarity than an infringement claim.[5]

It is clear that marks do not need to be identical. "[T]he use of obvious simulations or markedly similar marks might have the same diluting effect as would an appropriation of the original mark, [so that] the concept of exact identity has been broadened into that of substantial similarity."[6] However, it appears that marks must be more similar in a dilution case than in a traditional trademark infringement case. The marks must be "very" or "substantially" similar, or a viable claim for dilution will not lie.[7] However, the similarity requirement may be less stringent in circumstances in which the senior mark is highly distinctive and the junior mark is being used for a closely related

---

[Section 11:30]

[1]15 U.S.C.A. § 1125(c)(1).

[2]Moseley v. V Secret Catalogue, Inc., 537 U.S. 418, 433, 123 S. Ct. 1115, 1124, 65 U.S.P.Q.2d 1801 (2003).

[3]*See* § 10:25.

[4]Mead Data, 875 F.2d at 1035, 10 U.S.P.Q.2d at 1963.

[5]AutoZone, Inc. v. Tandy Corp., 373 F.3d 786, 806, 71 U.S.P.Q.2d 1385, 1399, 2004 FED App. 0200P (6th Cir. 2004).

[6]Mead Data, 875 F.2d at 1029, 10 U.S.P.Q.2d at 1963.

[7]Mead Data, 875 F.2d at 1029, 10 U.S.P.Q.2d at 1964.

product.[8]

Some courts look at similarity of the marks in light of the way that the marks are encountered and used in the marketplace.[9] Marks encountered primarily through the Internet have been deemed substantially similar based on the similarity of their text,[10] whereas marks that are similar in text, but are likely to be encountered in other venues where text and strings of words are not as important as packaging and logos, such as at a store, have been deemed not substantially similar.[11]

Some factors that may be considered in alleviating a claim of dilution or likelihood of dilution include prominent display of dissimilar source identifiers (such as housemarks) and different logos or trade dress.[12]

§ 11:31 Dilution—Remedies

Research References

West's Key Number Digest, Trademarks ☞1704(6), 1714(4)

Another difference between trademark infringement and trademark dilution is the remedies that are available. If a defendant is found liable for trademark infringement, he or she may be enjoined from future infringement and may also be liable for damages. The trademark owner may seek damages based upon its own actual monetary damages or the infringer's unjust enrichment.[1]

In contrast, the federal and state dilution laws primarily provide injunctive relief for the owner of a famous trademark

---

[8]Perfumebay.com Inc. v. EBAY, Inc., 506 F.3d 1165, 1180, 84 U.S.P.Q.2d 1865 (9th Cir. 2007).

[9]Perfumebay.com, 506 F.3d at 1165.

[10]Perfumebay.com, 506 F.3d at 1165. The court found that the use of Perfumebay, which encompassed all of the "eBay" trademark, created confusion as both used the Internet as a marketing and advertising facility which exacerbates the likelihood of confusion due to the importance of text over logos when utilizing such things as Internet search engines.

[11]Starbucks Corp. v. Wolfe's Borough Coffee, Inc., 559 F. Supp. 2d 472, 88 U.S.P.Q.2d 1268 (S.D. N.Y. 2008). The court found that while the core terms were similar, Mr. Char-

bucks, as used in commerce, was not substantially similar to Starbucks due to the dissimilar packaging and the non-use of Charbucks as a standalone term in products and marketing that the customer was likely to encounter.

[12]Merriam-Webster, 35 F.3d at 73, 32 U.S.P.Q.2d at 1016; Playtex Products, Inc. v. Georgia-Pacific Inc., 67 U.S.P.Q.2d 1923, 1931, 2003 WL 21939706 (S.D. N.Y. 2003), judgment aff'd, 390 F.3d 158, 73 U.S.P.Q.2d 1127 (2d Cir. 2004) (the WET ONES and QUILTED NORTHERN MOIST ONES trademarks "are not sufficiently similar to support a claim for dilution under either the federal or state statute.").

[Section 11:31]

[1]15 U.S.C.A. § 1117.

against another who engages in commercial activities that tend to dilute the distinctive quality of the owner's famous mark. The federal dilution statute, and many of the state dilution states, provide for monetary damages only when the person against whom the injunction is sought willfully intended to trade on the owner's reputation or to cause dilution of the famous mark.[2] The remaining state statutes only provide for injunctive relief.

This distinction, however, is largely academic. As a practical matter, trademark infringement cases are about injunctions. While the statute provides for damages, courts are reluctant to award any monetary damages unless the trademark owner can prove the "extra element" of actual confusion or intentional infringement.[3] Therefore, for the practitioner who is trying to decide between pursuing an infringement theory or a dilution theory, this is usually not a major issue, unless the practitioner thinks he or she has a good chance of showing actual confusion.

An issue which may arise with respect to injunctive relief under the state anti-dilution statutes is the scope of the injunction. If dilution is shown only under state law, but not under the Federal Trademark Dilution Act, it is reasonable to argue that the scope of any injunction should be limited to that state alone. Many states have not passed anti-dilution statutes, and it does not seem fair that someone be enjoined nationwide from doing something that is not illegal in many states. A particular injustice can be seen in the case of a nonresident defendant, whose state of residence does not have an anti-dilution statute, who is sued under the forum state's anti-dilution statute. Subsequently, the defendant could be enjoined by an out-of-state judge from doing something in his home state that is not illegal.[4]

The scope of an injunction under a state anti-dilution statute has not been discussed in any cases. Most state dilution cases are venued in federal court, either as diversity cases or as supplemental state law claims to a federal trademark infringement and/or dilution action. Federal judges are used to granting nationwide injunctions under federal trademark laws, and they do not seem reluctant to grant broad injunctions in state dilution cases. Of course, this may also result from the fact that trademark lawyers are also used to dealing with nationwide injunctions, so they do not commonly argue this point. Another possibility is that the ac-

---

[2]15 U.S.C.A. § 1117(e).

[3]*See* §§ 10:14, 10:15.

[4]Another potential issue (which has never been addressed in any dilution case) is the choice of law under an appropriate conflicts of laws analysis.

The law of the forum state has always been applied in dilution cases. However, this may be because most trademark lawyers are used to dealing with federal law, and they do not necessarily think about raising the choice of law issue.

cused infringers do not care about the scope of the injunction because they need to use consistent packaging and marks throughout the country, so if they are enjoined in one place, they need to modify all of their packaging.

§ 11:32 Dilution by competing goods

Research References
West's Key Number Digest, Trademarks ⚖1461

Originally, dilution was intended to apply to situations in which a trademark was used on noncompeting goods and a cause of action for traditional trademark infringement was not available.[1] However, the language of many early statutes was not clear, stating that dilution applied "notwithstanding the absence of competition between the parties."[2] This language has been interpreted to mean that dilution applied to both competitors and noncompetitors in some states[3], while in other states the same language was held to mean that dilution applied only to noncompetitors[4]; a competitor's remedy lay in trademark infringement, not dilution.

The language of later dilution statutes was clarified to apply to both competitors and noncompetitors. In these later statutes, dilution applies regardless of the presence or the absence of competition between the parties.[5] The Federal Trademark Dilution Act also applies regardless of competition.[6]

§ 11:33 Dilution—Using another person's trademark

[Section 11:32]

[1]See § 10:9.

[2]This language continues to exist in the Alabama, California, Delaware, Florida, Georgia, Louisiana, Maine, Massachusetts, Missouri, New Hampshire, New York, Oregon, and Rhode Island dilution statutes.

[3]Plasticolor, 713 F. Supp. at 1329, 11 U.S.P.Q.2d at 1023; Nikon Inc. v. Ikon Corp., 987 F.2d 91, 96, 25 U.S.P. Q.2d 2021, 2026 (2d Cir. 1993) (New York dilution "statute is applicable to competitors as well as noncompetitors.").

[4]E.R. Squibb & Sons, Inc. v. Princeton Pharmaceutical, Inc., 17 U.S.P.Q.2d 1447, 1454, 1990 WL 272707 (S.D. Fla. 1990); Harley-Davidson Motor Co. v. Iron Eagle of Cent. Florida, Inc., 973 F. Supp. 1421, 1426 (M.D. Fla. 1997); Soloflex, Inc. v. NordicTrack, Inc., 31 U.S.P.Q.2d 1721, 1731, 1994 WL 568401 (D. Or. 1994);

[5]Arizona, Arkansas, Connecticut, Hawaii, Idaho, Illinois, Iowa, Kansas, Minnesota, Mississippi, Montana, Nebraska, Nevada, New Jersey, New Mexico, Pennsylvania, South Carolina, Tennessee, Utah, Washington, West Virginia, and Wyoming. The Texas anti-dilution statute applies "regardless of whether there is competition between the parties." Tex. Bus. & Com. Code Ann. § 16.29; Pebble Beach Co. v. Tour 18 I, Ltd., 942 F. Supp. 1513, 1564 (S.D. Tex. 1996), judgment aff'd as modified, 155 F.3d 526, 48 U.S.P.Q.2d 1065 (5th Cir. 1998).

[6]15 U.S.C.A. § 1125(c)(1).

Research References
West's Key Number Digest, Trademarks ⬦1465, 1524

A particular kind of case that often arises under the guise of dilution is the use of another person's trademark, either in comparative advertising, advertisements poking fun at a competitor, or parody and satire.

In general, simply using a competitor's mark in conducting truthful comparative advertising is not dilution.[1] However, altering a competitor's mark in order to poke fun at the competitor may constitute a violation of a dilution statute. For instance, in *Deere & Co. v. MTD Products, Inc.*,[2] the court granted a preliminary injunction against a competitor's television advertisement that featured an animated version of John Deere's "leaping stag" mark. Deere's trademark came to life in the commercial, leaping off of a Deere lawn mower and running in fear from the competitor's lawn mower.

The court held that a competitor's use of an altered form of the plaintiff's trademark constituted dilution under New York law. The court distinguished situations in which the defendant had not altered the plaintiff's trademark. "As long as the mark is not altered, such use serves the beneficial purpose of imparting factual information about the relative merits of competing products and imposes no risk of diluting the selling power of the competitor's mark."[3]

Sellers of commercial products may wish to attract attention to their commercials or products by poking fun at widely recognized marks of noncompeting products, such as the Energizer Bunny.[4] In cases such as this, there is a risk that the mark will be diluted. Other cases have involved the use by a noncompetitor of a humorous variation of the trademark.[5] The most difficult cases are those in which the use of the mark parodied has the dual purpose

---

[Section 11:33]

[1]Diversified Marketing, Inc. v. Estee Lauder, Inc., 705 F. Supp. 128, 9 U.S.P.Q.2d 1882 (S.D. N.Y. 1988).

[2]Deere & Co., 41 F.3d at 41, 32 U.S.P.Q.2d at 1937.

[3]Deere & Co., 41 F.3d at 44, 32 U.S.P.Q.2d at 1940. *See also* Wendy's Intern., Inc. v. Big Bite, Inc., 576 F. Supp. 816, 223 U.S.P.Q. 35 (S.D. Ohio 1983).

[4]Eveready Battery Co., Inc. v. Adolph Coors Co., 765 F. Supp. 440, 19 U.S.P.Q.2d 1265 (N.D. Ill. 1991) (denying preliminary injunction

against beer commercial spoofing the Energizer Bunny).

[5]Louis Vuitton Malletier S.A. v. Haute Diggity Dog, LLC, 507 F.3d 252, 84 U.S.P.Q.2d 1969 (4th Cir. 2007) (holding that the sale of "Chewy Vuiton" products did not result in dilution of "LOUIS VUITTON" trademark); McDonald's Corp., 649 F. Supp. at 1268, 1 U.S.P.Q.2d at 1761. (finding that the use of the name "McBAGEL'S" resulted in dilution under state law); Universal City Studios, Inc. v. T-Shirt Gallery, Ltd., 634 F. Supp. 1468, 230 U.S.P.Q. 23 (S.D. N.Y. 1986) (holding that "Miami Mice" t-shirts do

of making a satiric comment and selling a competing product.[6]

Satirists who are selling no product, apart from the publication or other medium that contains their expression, may wish to parody a mark to make a point of social commentary.[7] In cases of satire, the risk of some dilution of the identifying power of the mark is tolerated in the interest of maintaining broad opportunities for expression.[8]

Another case that often arises is where a person registers a domain name that includes another's trademark. Whether such use is dilutive turns on whether the use is commercial in nature. In order to constitute an actionable dilution claim under the federal statute, the use of another's trademark must be commercial in nature.[9] "Commercial use" has been interpreted to be roughly analogous to the "in connection with a sale of goods or services" requirement for a trademark infringement analysis.[10]

If a person registers a domain name that includes another's trademark and the website contains information that is critical of the trademark owner's goods or services, the trademark owner probably does not have an actionable federal dilution claim because such use is not commercial.[11] However, some state courts have found that under state dilution statutes, registering a domain name that contains another's trademark constitutes a

---

not dilute "MIAMI VICE" trademark); Coca-Cola Co. v. Gemini Rising, 346 F. Supp. at 1183, 175 U.S.P.Q. at 56 (enjoining print, distribution, and sale of "Enjoy Cocaine" posters).

[6]Yankee Pub. Inc. v. News America Pub. Inc., 809 F. Supp. 267, 21 Media L. Rep. (BNA) 1033, 25 U.S.P.Q.2d 1752 (S.D. N.Y. 1992) (holding that New York Magazine's "very recognizable takeoff on the pictorial elements of the Farmer's Almanac's well-known traditional cover design" did not dilute Plaintiff's trademark).

[7]L.L. Bean, 811 F.2d at 26, 13 Media L. Rep. (BNA) 2009, 1 U.S.P.Q. at 1753; Smith v. Wal-Mart Stores, Inc., 537 F. Supp. 2d 1302, 86 U.S.P. Q.2d 1835 (N.D. Ga. 2008); Girl Scouts of U. S. of America v. Personality Posters Mfg. Co., 304 F. Supp. 1228, 1233, 163 U.S.P.Q. 505, 509 (S.D. N.Y. 1969); Stop the Olympic Prison v. U.S. Olympic Committee, 489 F. Supp. 1112, 1123, 207 U.S.P.Q. 237, 245 (S.D. N.Y. 1980).

[8]But see Anheuser-Busch, 28 F.3d

at 778, 31 U.S.P.Q.2d at 1303 (parody on the back cover of a humor magazine diluted MICHELOB mark because "the casual viewer might fail to appreciate its editorial purpose").

[9]15 U.S.C.A. § 1125(c)(1); Bosley Medical Institute, Inc. v. Kremer, 403 F.3d 672, 676, 74 U.S.P.Q.2d 1280, 1283 (9th Cir. 2005). The noncommercial use exemption is designed to prevent courts from issuing injunctions that interfere with the First Amendment. Nissan Motor Co. v. Nissan Computer Corp., 378 F.3d 1002, 1016-17, 72 U.S.P.Q.2d 1078 (9th Cir. 2004).

[10]Bosley Medical Institute, 403 F.2d at 676, 74 U.S.P.Q.2d at 1283.

[11]Bosley Medical Institute, 403 F.2d at 672, 74 U.S.P.Q.2d at 1280. See also Nissan Motor Co. v. Nissan Computer Corp., 378 F.3d 1002, 1017, 72 U.S.P.Q.2d 1078 (9th Cir. 2004) ("Negative commentary about Nissan Motor does more than propose a commercial transaction and is, therefore, non-commercial.").

likelihood of dilution because it lessens that mark's ability to identify the true owner's goods or services.[12]

§ 11:34 Cybersquatting

Research References

West's Key Number Digest, Trademarks ☜1490

Alphanumeric domain names (e.g., "kinney.com") make it possible for Internet users to easily locate content stored on a network of interconnected computers around the globe over the World Wide Web. The Internet Corporation for Assigned Names and Numbers (ICANN) oversees administration of the domain name system (DNS), which is the system under which alphanumeric domain names are matched with Internet Protocol (IP) addresses (e.g., "123.45.6.789") that uniquely identify every computer on the Internet. ICANN accredits institutions and corporations to serve as domain name "registrars," who are generally responsible for registering domain names on a first-come first-served basis.

Domain names always include a top level domain (TLD). This top level domain is one such as ".com", ".biz", ".tv", or ".edu". TLDs are classified as either generic TLDs (gTLDs) or two-letter country code TLDs (ccTLDs). Domain names also include a second level domain name (SLD). SLDs are words or terms that precede the TLD, such as the "kinney" of "kinney.com". SLDs are acquired through registry with ICANN-approved registrars. Domain names (the combination of a SLD and TLD) are assigned to one, and only one, entity.

Prior to March 2013, ICANN had only permitted the existence of 22 gTLDs. Beginning in March 2013, ICANN started approving the creation and use of new gTLDs, which can include non-Latin characters (such as Chinese, Japanese, Cyrillic, and Arabic). The creation of new gTLDs is significant to trademark holders because it dramatically increases the number of possible gTLD and SLD combinations that could be identical or confusingly similar to their own trademarks. For example, some of the new domain name combinations could include: "www.kinney.lange," "www.home.kinney," "www.kinney&lange.home," "www.kinney&lange.iplaw," or "www.kinney.lange.firm."

ICANN has created the Trademark Clearing House to help trademark holders monitor and protect their rights as the number of domain names expand. The Trademark Clearing House

---

[12]Horseshoe Bay Resort Sales Co. v. Lake Lyndon B. Johnson Imp. Corp.,   53 S.W.3d 799, 812 (Tex. App. Austin 2001).

includes a central trademark repository, and the Trademark Clearing House attempts to protect the rights of trademark holders who have registered their information with the central trademark repository through two services: the Sunrise Service and the Trademark Claims Service. As each new gTLD is approved by ICANN, the new gTLD goes through a 30 day "Sunrise period" where the trademark holders that have submitted and validated their information through the central repository will have the option to pre-register their domain name with the new gTLD before it is offered to the public. The Sunrise service will not apply to new gTLDs that will belong exclusively to specific organizations and other closed groups. The Trademark Claim Service is a notification service that will notify both trademark holders that have registered with the service and domain name registrants of possible infringements.

The Anticybersquatting Consumer Protection Act (ACPA) amended the Lanham Act to create a cause of action for trademark owners who wish to prevent another party from using a domain name that is identical or confusingly similar to a distinctive or famous mark. The ACPA creates a cause of action for cybersquatting that is separate and distinct from a trademark infringement action. Use of a domain name as an Internet address is not necessarily use as a trademark. Therefore, it is important to consider both causes of action.

Many cybersquatting actions are brought as *in personam* actions against the owner, operator, or registrant of the disputed website. However, if those parties cannot be found after diligent effort by the plaintiff, the ACPA also authorizes *in rem* actions against the domain name itself.[1] For *in rem* actions, the situs of a domain name is the judicial district in which either the domain name authority (i.e., the registrar) is located or a judicial district in which domain name registration documents are deposited with the court (i.e., the registration authorities deposit the disputed intangible property, not unlike interpleader).[2] A trademark owner must establish that *in personam* jurisdiction is unavailable before an *in rem* action may proceed under the ACPA.[3]

Actions under the ACPA follow a two part inquiry. The court must determine (1) if the alleged cybersquatter had a bad faith intent to profit from use of the mark and (2) whether the alleged cybersquatter registers, traffics in, or uses a domain name that, in the case of a mark that is distinctive at the time of registra-

---

[Section 11:34]

[1]15 U.S.C.A. § 1125(d)(2).

[2]15 U.S.C.A. § 1125(d)(2)(C); *see also, e.g.*, Mattel, Inc. v. Barbie-Club. com, 310 F.3d 293, 64 U.S.P.Q.2d 1879 (2d Cir. 2002).

[3]Porsche Cars North America, Inc. v. Porsche.net, 302 F.3d 248, 255, 64 U.S.P.Q.2d 1248 (4th Cir. 2002).

tion of the domain name, is identical or confusingly similar to
that mark, or, in the case of a famous mark that is famous at the
time of registration of the domain name, is identical or confusingly similar to or dilutive of that mark.[4]

The ACPA defines a nonexclusive list of factors for assessing
bad faith.[5] These factors address a number of concerns, including
whether the defendant had a reasonable basis for registering the
domain name, and whether certain factors are present that tend
to indicate bad faith.[6]

The ACPA further contains a safe harbor provision that states:
bad faith intent "shall not be found in any case in which the
court determines that the person believed and had reasonable
grounds to believe that the use of the domain name was fair use
or otherwise lawful."[7]

An intent to profit need not be a traditional commercial use,
such as operating a website under the registered domain name.
Making a statement to the press and posting the statement on a
website asking another party to "settle" or "make an offer" are
sufficient to constitute an intent to profit from registration of a
domain name.[8] However, a legitimate offer to settle a cybersquatting case after the commencement of litigation will not convert
good faith in registration to bad faith under the ACPA.[9]

In the context of contributory infringement, a domain registration proxy service (also called "privacy" or "anonymity" services)
may be liable for the wrongful use of a mark by its licensee of a
registered domain name.[10] "A Registered Name Holder licensing
use of a Registered Name according to this provision shall accept
liability for harm caused by wrongful use of the Registered Name,
unless it promptly discloses the identity of the licensee to a party
providing the Registered Name Holder reasonable evidence of actionable harm."[11] The mere receipt of a demand from a registered
mark owner will not generally suffice to provide notice of the illegitimate use of a domain name so as to justify contributory

---

[4]15 U.S.C.A. § 1125(d)(1)(A).

[5]15 U.S.C.A. § 1125(d)(1)(B).

[6]Lucas Nursery and Landscap-
ing, Inc. v. Grosse, 359 F.3d 806, 809,
70 U.S.P.Q.2d 1149, 2004 FED App.
0071P (6th Cir. 2004).

[7]15 U.S.C.A. § 1225(d)(1)(B)(ii);
see also Coca-Cola Co. v. Purdy, 382
F.3d 774, 785, 790–91, 72 U.S.P.Q.2d
1305 (8th Cir. 2004); People for Ethical
Treatment of Animals v. Doughney,
263 F.3d 359, 369, 60 U.S.P.Q.2d 1109
(4th Cir. 2001).

[8]Doughney, 263 F.3d at 368.

[9]Interstellar Starship Services,
Ltd. v. Epix, Inc., 304 F.3d 936, 947,
64 U.S.P.Q.2d 1514 (9th Cir. 2002).

[10]Solid Host, NL v. Namecheap,
Inc., 652 F. Supp. 2d 1092 (C.D. Cal.
2009).

[11]ICANN Registrar Accreditation
Agreement ¶ 3.7.7.3 at https://www.ica
nn.org/resources/pages/approved-with-
specs-2013-09-17-en#whois; see also
Solid Host, NL v. Namecheap, Inc., 652
F. Supp. 2d 1092 (C.D. Cal. 2009).

liability.[12] The demand must be accompanied by sufficient evidence of a violation in order to impose a duty on the defendant to investigate the matter further.[13]

Remedies available under the ACPA include "the forfeiture or cancellation of the domain name or the transfer of the domain name to the owner of the mark,"[14] or damages.[15]

A leading case on the application of the ACPA is *Sporty's Farm L.L.C. v. Sportsman's Market, Inc.*[16] Sportsman's Market was a mail order catalog company selling products primarily in the aviation market, and registered the mark SPORTY'S in 1985.[17] The court held the SPORTY'S mark was inherently distinctive, the domain name was confusingly similar to the mark, and there was a bad faith intent to profit by the defendant, Sporty's Farm.[18] Sporty's Farm also planned to enter into direct competition in the aviation products market, and Sporty's Farm's explanation that the name was a variant of the name of the owner's dog was "more amusing than credible."[19] The court affirmed the grant of an injunction, which required Sporty's Farm to relinquish the "sportys.com" domain name.[20]

ICANN has established a Uniform Domain Name Dispute Resolution Policy (UDRP) for resolving domain name disputes, including cybersquatting. Any party wishing to register a domain name with an accredited domain-name registrar, for all gTLDs like ".com", ".net", and ".org", must assent to the UDRP. The UDRP has also been adopted by managers of certain ccTLDs (e.g., ".nu", ".tv", and ".ws").[21]

The UDRP provides for a mandatory administrative hearing, through an approved dispute-resolution service provider, only for domain name disputes that meet the following cumulative requirements:

- the domain name registered by the domain name registrant is identical or confusingly similar to a trademark or service mark in which the complaintant has rights;
- the domain name registrant has no rights or legitimate interests in respect to the domain name in question; and
- the domain name has been registered and is being used in

---

[12]Solid Host, 652 F. Supp.2d at 1116.

[13]Solid Host, 652 F. Supp.2d at 1116.

[14]15 U.S.C.A. § 1125(d)(1)(C).

[15]15 U.S.C.A. § 1117.

[16]Sporty's Farm L.L.C. v. Sportsman's Market, Inc., 202 F.3d 489, 53 U.S.P.Q.2d 1570 (2d Cir. 2000).

[17]Sporty's Farm, 202 F.3d at 493-94.

[18]Sporty's Farm, 202 F.3d at 497-99.

[19]Sporty's Farm, 202 F.3d at 499.

[20]Sporty's Farm, 202 F.3d at 492.

[21]*See, generally*, ICANN, Uniform Domain-Name Dispute-Resolution Policy at https://www.icann.org/resources/pages/help/dndr/udrp-en.

bad faith.[22]

Administrative proceedings under the UDRP are not arbitration proceedings subject to the Federal Arbitration Act.[23] The results of UDRP are not binding on courts, as courts may undertake an independent determination of the rights of the respective parties.[24]

In addition to the UDRP, ICANN has also established the Uniform Rapid Suspension (URS) system. The URS is intended to provide rapid relief to trademark holders for clear-cut cases of infringement, offering cheaper and faster responses than under the UDRP.[25] The same dispute requirements listed above with respect to the UDRP are necessary.[26] The entire URS process generally lasts between about 20 and 25 days compared to about two months for a single-panel decision under the UDRP. The URS process can also be less expensive than the UDRP. However, the only remedy allowed under the URS is suspension of the domain name.[27] Additionally, the domain name is only temporarily suspended, the complainant is unable to obtain use or possession of the domain name, and once the suspension period expires, anyone can re-register the domain name and use it, potentially requiring additional URS actions.[28] Thus, depending on the particular facts of a situation, a complainant should weigh whether to proceed under the UDRP or URS process.

A trademark owner must choose a forum in which to bring a cybersquatting action. A trademark owner may choose to bring an administrative action under the UDRP, which typically involves relatively small filing fees and a relatively short turnaround. On the other hand, a trademark owner can sue in court under the ACPA in the first instance. A number of considerations are relevant to choosing a forum. Under the ACPA, courts can award damages, which are not available under the UDRP. Also, the UDRP and ACPA standards differ in that a mark need not be distinctive or famous under the UDRP. However, a defendant who loses in a UDRP proceeding can later have the administrative decision independently reviewed in a court under the ACPA.

Some defensive measures are available to domain name

---

[22]WIPO, Uniform Domain Name Dispute Resolution Policy ¶ 4(a) at https://www.icann.org/resources/pages/policy-2012-02-25-en (hereinafter UDRP).

[23]Parisi v. Netlearning, Inc., 139 F. Supp. 2d 745, 751-52, 59 U.S.P.Q.2d 1051 (E.D. Va. 2001); see also 9 U.S.C.A. §§ 1 et seq.

[24]See UDRP ¶ 4(k).

[25]See, generally, ICANN, Uniform Rapid Suspension System at http://newgtlds.icann.org/en/applicants/urs (hereinafter URS).

[26]See URS ¶ 1.2.6.

[27]See URS ¶ 10.

[28]See URS ¶ 10.4.

registrants in cybersquatting cases. The UDRP provides protections against "reverse domain name hijacking."[29] Reverse domain name hijacking is an illegitimate use of the UDRP administrative process, and "usually involves big businesses threatening to sue legitimate domain registrants who do not give up the right to the registration."[30] Likewise, under the ACPA, domain name registrants who are subject to reverse domain name hijacking may obtain injunctive relief against overreaching trademark owners.[31]

§ 11:35 Advertising law—Section 43(a) of the Lanham Act—Prohibits false representations

Research References

West's Key Number Digest, Antitrust and Trade Regulation ⚗163

In many markets, advertisers and advertising agencies often engage in highly competitive and aggressive business practices. As part of these aggressive business strategies, disputes involving competitors and their advertising agencies are more likely to be resolved in court rather than through more informal means. In addition, their legal representatives frequently invoke § 43(a) of the Lanham Act as a tool to redress injuries arising out of advertising by a competitor in the private sector.[1]

If a competitor objects to an advertisement made by another company, a variety of avenues may be available to enjoin future running of the advertisement and/or to recover damages based on prior running of the advertisement. The theory of recovery chosen will largely depend upon the type of injury sustained by the competitor. The largest body of case law in this area occurs under violations of the federal trademark laws,[2] collectively referred to as the "Lanham Act."

Section 43(a) prohibits commercial activities that tend to

---

[29]UDRP ¶ 1.

[30]MAHA Maschinenbau Haldenwang GmbH & Co. KG v. Deepak Rajani WIPO Case No. D2000-1816 (March 2, 2001) available at http://www.wipo.int/amc/en/domains/decisions/html/2000/d2000-1816.html (to show reverse domain name hijacking, "Respondent must show knowledge on the part of the Complainant of Respondent's right or legitimate interest in the disputed domain name and evidence of similar conduct by the Complainant in the face of such knowledge."); see also, Mess Enterprises v. Scott Enterprises Ltd., 74 U.S.P.Q.2d 1289, 2005 WL 914448 (W.I.P.O.A.M.C. 2005).

[31]Barcelona.com, Incorporated v. Excelentisimo Ayuntamiento De Barcelona, 330 F.3d 617, 625, 67 U.S.P.Q.2d 1025 (4th Cir. 2003).

[Section 11:35]

[1]However, states and arms of a state have Eleventh Amendment sovereign immunity from suits under § 43(a) of the Lanham Act. College Sav. Bank v. Florida Prepaid Postsecondary Educ. Expense Bd., 527 U.S. 666, 119 S. Ct. 2219, 144 L. Ed. 2d 605, 135 Ed. Law Rep. 362, 51 U.S.P.Q.2d 1065, 1999-1 Trade Cas. (CCH) ¶ 72551 (1999).

[2]15 U.S.C.A. §§ 1051 et seq.

mislead the consuming public. Among the litany of commercial sins which have regularly been held redressable under § 43(a) are trade dress infringement, false indications of sponsorship or endorsement, false descriptions of goods or services, false comparative advertisements, and infringement of unregistered trademarks.

The variety of wrongs redressed by § 43(a) appear to be quite diverse. An analysis of the case law shows, however, that a common thread of reasoning exists. A violation of § 43(a) is usually found when a likelihood of consumer confusion exists as to source, sponsorship or affiliation. Rulings under § 43(a) are often justified under one of two general theories: (1) it is fundamentally unfair to trade upon goodwill which has been developed through the labor and cost of another; and (2) the public has a right not to be deceived.

Section 43(a) provides:

(1) Any person who, on or in connection with any goods or services, or any container for goods, uses in commerce any word, term, name, symbol, or device, or any combination thereof, or any false designation of origin, false or misleading description of fact, or false or misleading representation of fact, which

(A) is likely to cause confusion, or to cause mistake, or to deceive as to the affiliation, connection, or association of such person with another person, or as to the origin, sponsorship, or approval of his or her goods, services, or commercial activities by another person, or

(B) in commercial advertising or promotion, misrepresents the nature, characteristics, qualities, or geographic origin of his or her or another person's goods, services, or commercial activities,

shall be liable in a civil action by any person who believes that he or she is or is likely to be damaged by such act.[3]

The Lanham Act is silent regarding whether a failure to disclose facts or information relating to a product in advertisements violates § 43(a). This allows the courts to further develop and interpret § 43(a) as it pertains to failure to disclose in advertising.[4] Courts have since noted that failure to disclose material facts is actionable,[5] such as where the failure to disclose renders affirmative representations false or misleading.

---

[3]15 U.S.C.A. § 1125(a).

[4]Senate Judiciary Committee, 100th Cong., 2d Sess., Report on S. 1883 (September 15, 1988) (Statement of Senator Biden).

[5]*E.g.*, U.S. Healthcare, Inc. v. Blue Cross of Greater Philadelphia, 898 F.2d 914, 921, 17 Media L. Rep.

§ 11:36 Advertising law—Section 43(a) of the Lanham Act—Use of celebrities or fictional characters

Research References
West's Key Number Digest, Torts ⊚⇒384

Section 43(a) has been broadly construed to protect against confusion regarding sponsorship or endorsement of a product. Section 43(a) has been used to extend a "right of publicity" to famous people or fictitious characters. Section 43(a) has also been used to protect against the false attribution of editorial credit. Despite the broad protection afforded under § 43(a) for sponsorship, parody use of a well-known personality may not be viewed as confusing the public regarding sponsorship. Sponsorship rights have been the subject of § 43(a) actions regarding many celebrities, including Woody Allen, Rosa Parks, Tom Waits, Elvis Presley, and Bette Midler. Confusion over celebrity sponsorship may arise in several different ways, including use of look-a-likes, use of sound-a-likes, and unauthorized use of pictures and statements of the actual celebrity.

For instance, in *Allen v. National Video, Inc.*,[1] a picture of a Woody Allen look-a-like was used to promote a video rental company in magazine advertisements. This picture was found to create a likelihood of consumer confusion as to whether Woody Allen endorsed the advertisement. A small disclaimer included in some of the advertisements, "Celebrity double provided by Ron Smith Look-Alike's, Los Angeles, California," was found to be insufficient to dispel confusion, both in size and content.[2]

Similar to the § 43(a) right of publicity afforded to pictures of celebrities, unauthorized use of a celebrity's voice, which creates confusion on whether the celebrity endorses a product, also may be actionable.[3] "[W]hen a distinctive voice of a professional singer is widely known and is deliberately imitated in order to sell a

---

(BNA) 1681, 14 U.S.P.Q.2d 1257, 1993-2 Trade Cas. (CCH) ¶ 70466 (3d Cir. 1990); Santana Products, Inc. v. Bobrick Washroom Equipment, Inc., 249 F. Supp. 2d 463, 521, 2003-1 Trade Cas. (CCH) ¶ 73997 (M.D. Pa. 2003), aff'd in part, vacated in part, remanded, 401 F.3d 123, 73 U.S.P.Q.2d 1769, 2005-1 Trade Cas. (CCH) ¶ 74688 (3d Cir. 2005) (court of appeals vacated order on basis of laches).

[Section 11:36]

[1]Allen v. National Video, Inc.,
610 F. Supp. 612, 226 U.S.P.Q. 483 (S.D. N.Y. 1985).

[2]*See also* Allen v. Men's World Outlet, Inc., 679 F. Supp. 360, 15 Media L. Rep. (BNA) 1001, 5 U.S.P. Q.2d 1850 (S.D. N.Y. 1988) (finding a newspaper photograph of Woody Allen look-a-like Phil Boroff with a clarinet to infringe Allen's § 43(a) rights).

[3]Midler v. Ford Motor Co., 849 F.2d 460, 15 Media L. Rep. (BNA) 1620, 7 U.S.P.Q.2d 1398 (9th Cir. 1988).

product, the sellers have appropriated what is not theirs."[4]

Unauthorized use of pictures or statements of a celebrity may be actionable under § 43(a) if the use is found to be misleading. In *Cher v. Forum Int'l, Ltd.*,[5] Forum magazine was found to have violated Cher's right of publicity by publishing an interview Cher gave to Us magazine. The court found that Forum's advertising confused consumers into believing that Cher read and endorsed Forum magazine. Unauthorized and unprivileged printing of the names, trademarks and/or likenesses of various rock stars and musical groups on T-shirts similarly violates the § 43(a) right of publicity.[6]

Fictional characters are generally treated the same way as well-known personalities under § 43(a). Therefore, if there is a likelihood of confusion as to source, sponsorship or affiliation, those holding the rights in the fictitious character can maintain an action under § 43(a).[7] Because the confusion concerns sponsorship rather than source of the product, clear statements as to who manufactured the product will not alleviate the confusion, and direct competition is not required to find infringement.

A right of publicity for organizations is similarly protected under § 43(a). Again the confusion concerns sponsorship, not source of the product. In *Dallas Cowboys Cheerleaders, Inc. v. Pussycat Cinema, Ltd.*,[8] the defendant falsely advertised that the movie starred an "ex-Dallas Cowboys Cheerleader." Finding the requisite confusion as to sponsorship likely, the court stated "[I]t is hard to believe that anyone who had seen defendants' sexually depraved film could ever thereafter disassociate it from plaintiff's

---

[4]Midler, 849 F.2d at 463. *See also* Waits v. Frito-Lay, Inc., 20 Media L. Rep. (BNA) 1585, 23 U.S.P.Q.2d 1721, 1992 WL 183781 (9th Cir. 1992), opinion amended and superseded on denial of reh'g, 978 F.2d 1093 (9th Cir. 1992) (rejected on other grounds by, Conte Bros. Automotive, Inc. v. Quaker State-Slick 50, Inc., 165 F.3d 221, 49 U.S.P.Q.2d 1321, 1999-1 Trade Cas. (CCH) ¶ 72383 (3d Cir. 1998)) (reaffirms *Midler*, and protects the voice of Tom Waits); Lahr v. Adell Chemical Co., 300 F.2d 256, 132 U.S.P.Q. 662 (1st Cir. 1962) (voice of Daffy Duck protected); Sinatra v. Goodyear Tire & Rubber Co., 435 F.2d 711, 168 U.S.P.Q. 12 (9th Cir. 1970) (voice of Nancy Sinatra not protected); Booth v. Colgate-Palmolive Co., 362 F. Supp. 343, 179 U.S.P.Q. 819 (S.D. N.Y. 1973) (voice of Shirley Booth not protected).

[5]Cher v. Forum Intern., Ltd., 7 Media L. Rep. (BNA) 2593, 213 U.S.P.Q. 96, 1982 WL 916836 (C.D. Cal. 1982), aff'd in part, modified in part and rev'd in part on other grounds, 692 F.2d 634, 8 Media L. Rep. (BNA) 2484, 217 U.S.P.Q. 407 (9th Cir. 1982).

[6]Winterland Concessions Co. v. Sileo, 528 F. Supp. 1201, 213 U.S.P.Q. 813 (N.D. Ill. 1981), judgment aff'd, 830 F.2d 195 (7th Cir. 1987).

[7]Major League Baseball Promotion Corp. v. Colour-Tex, Inc., 729 F. Supp. 1035, 14 U.S.P.Q.2d 1177 (D.N.J. 1990).

[8]Dallas Cowboys Cheerleaders, Inc. v. Pussycat Cinema, Ltd., 604 F.2d 200, 5 Media L. Rep. (BNA) 1814, 203 U.S.P.Q. 161 (2d Cir. 1979).

cheerleaders."[9] In enjoining the distribution and exhibition of the X-rated movie *Debbie Does Dallas*, the court explained:

> In order to be confused, a consumer need not believe that the owner of the mark actually produced the item and placed it on the market. The public's belief that the mark's owner sponsored or otherwise approved the use of the trademark satisfies the confusion requirement.[10]

However, in a number of cases the courts have recognized limits on the right of publicity. In *ETW Corp. v. Jireh Pub., Inc.*,[11] the Sixth Circuit denied a claim under § 43(a) brought by professional golfer Tiger Woods against an artist who used his likeness in a painting. Tiger Woods had sought to protect any use of his likeness, rather than a particular representation consistently used as a trademark. The court held that sweeping claims to trademark rights in each and every photograph and image of a celebrity must fail, because, "as a general rule, a person's image or likeness cannot function as a trademark."[12]

In weighing the public interest in free expression against the right of publicity for use of a celebrity's name in the title of an expressive work, the "balance will normally not support application of [§ 43(a) of the Lanham Act] unless the title has no artistic relevance to the underlying work whatsoever . . . ."[13] If the title has some artistic relevance to the underlying work, then § 43(a) will normally not be applied "unless the title explicitly misleads as to the source or the content of the work."[14] With some expressive uses of a celebrity's name or image, the First Amendment may wholly bar application of the Lanham Act. For example, in *Parks v. LaFace Records*, the hip-hop group OutKast titled a popular song "Rosa Parks," and were accused of violating a right of publicity under § 43(a) held by Rosa Parks, the civil rights activist.[15] The court held that the song's composers did not intend the song to be about the civil rights activist and the lyrics were in fact not about her.[16] Summary judgment was improper because reasonable persons could have found that there was an artistic

---

[9]Pussycat Cinema, 604 F.2d at 205.

[10]604 F.2d at 205 (citations omitted).

[11]ETW Corp. v. Jireh Pub., Inc., 332 F.3d 915, 67 U.S.P.Q.2d 1065, 2003 FED App. 0207P (6th Cir. 2003).

[12]ETW, 332 F.3d at 922.

[13]Rogers v. Grimaldi, 875 F.2d 994, 999, 16 Media L. Rep. (BNA) 1648, 10 U.S.P.Q.2d 1825 (2d Cir. 1989) (footnote omitted) (summary judgment

granted, dismissing Lanham Act claims regarding the film "Ginger and Fred" by renowned Italian director Federico Fellini).

[14]Grimaldi, 875 F.2d at 999 (footnote omitted).

[15]Parks v. LaFace Records, 329 F.3d 437, 31 Media L. Rep. (BNA) 1897, 66 U.S.P.Q.2d 1735, 2003 FED App. 0137P (6th Cir. 2003).

[16]Parks v. LaFace Records, 329 F.3d 437, 31 Media L. Rep. (BNA) 1897, 66 U.S.P.Q.2d 1735, 2003 FED

relationship between the civil rights activist's name and the content of the song as well as that the title was not misleading.[17]

However in other instances, the First Amendment may not bar application of the Lanham Act. For example, in *Dillinger v. Electronic Arts*, Electronic Arts used the name "Dillinger" on a tommy gun in the video games *"The Godfather"* and *"The Godfather II."*[18] The plaintiff, who owns the trademark on the name "Dillinger," brought an action to prevent Electronic Arts from placing the "Dillinger" name on a gun which appears in the game but does not appear anywhere in Electronic Art's advertising or promotions.[19] In such a case the plaintiff is required to show that the use of the mark has no artistic relevance and that the use of the mark explicitly misleads the public as to the source or content of the work. Here the court stated that the "Dillinger" name is closely associated with the tommy gun and therefore was artistically relevant.[20] The court also stated that since Electronic Art's use of the name "Dillinger" was "a single text-line used to identify one of many weapons within a visually complex video game comprised of many countless elements," that there was no explicit misleading of the general public.[21] Summary judgment was proper in favor of defendant Electronic Arts because no issue of fact existed as to whether the Dillinger name was relevant to the content of *The Godfather* Games, or as to whether the use of the name explicitly misled consumers.[22]

When considering bringing a right of publicity claim under § 43(a), practitioners should be mindful of trends in various circuits. Recent cases have shown that courts in California tend to more strongly protect celebrities' property interests in their public image, whereas courts elsewhere, particularly in New York, tend to more strongly protect the public's interests in free expression. In addition, courts have been slow to protect new forms of expression. For instance, courts have cited Andy Warhol's paintings of celebrities as an example of artistic expression that is shielded from Lanham Act claims by the First Amendment. This recognition, however, came only after paintings by the internationally renowned Warhol had been in the public consciousness for over four decades, and long after the

---

App. 0137P (6th Cir. 2003).

[17]Parks v. LaFace Records, 329 F.3d 437, 31 Media L. Rep. (BNA) 1897, 66 U.S.P.Q.2d 1735, 2003 FED App. 0137P (6th Cir. 2003).

[18]Dillinger, LLC v. Electronic Arts Inc., 101 U.S.P.Q.2d 1612, 2011 WL 2457678 (S.D. Ind. 2011).

[19]Dillinger, LLC v. Electronic Arts Inc., 101 U.S.P.Q.2d 1612, 2011 WL

2457678 (S.D. Ind. 2011).

[20]Dillinger, LLC v. Electronic Arts Inc., 101 U.S.P.Q.2d 1612, 2011 WL 2457678 (S.D. Ind. 2011).

[21]Dillinger, LLC v. Electronic Arts Inc., 101 U.S.P.Q.2d 1612, 2011 WL 2457678 (S.D. Ind. 2011).

[22]Dillinger, LLC v. Electronic Arts Inc., 101 U.S.P.Q.2d 1612, 2011 WL 2457678 (S.D. Ind. 2011).

artist's death.

Another consideration is that most states recognize rights of publicity and privacy either under statutory or common law.[23] For instance, the following types of invasion of privacy or publicity may be actionable: (1) an unreasonable intrusion upon the seclusion of another; (2) the appropriation of another's name or likeness; (3) unreasonable publicity given to another's private life; and (4) publicity that unreasonably places the other in a false light before the public.[24] It is common for a plaintiff to bring an action alleging a right of publicity or privacy claim in addition to a Lanham Act claim under § 43(a).

§ 11:37   Advertising law—Section 43(a) of the Lanham Act—False attribution of credit

Research References

West's Key Number Digest, Antitrust and Trade Regulation ☞167

Section 43(a) protects against false attribution of authorship or editorial credit as part of the protections offered regarding sponsorship of products. For instance, an actor or actress is protected under § 43(a) against having his or her name removed from credits and advertisements for a movie, and against having a different name substituted for his or her name in the credits and advertisements.[1] The rationale for protecting rights of authorship such as acting credit is that those who invest time, money and energy into the development of a product and its accompanying goodwill should be allowed to reap the advantages of their investment.

Failure to give appropriate authorship credit is actionable under § 43(a). In *R.H. Donnelley Corp. v. Illinois Bell Telephone Co.*,[2] Illinois Bell began publishing Yellow Page directories that had previously been published as a joint effort between R. H. Donnelly and Illinois Bell. Illinois Bell was enjoined from

---

[23]*See* §§ 12:1 et seq.

[24]Dodrill v. Arkansas Democrat Co., 265 Ark. 628, 590 S.W.2d 840, 5 Media L. Rep. (BNA) 1385 (1979); *see also* Onassis v. Christian Dior-New York, Inc., 122 Misc. 2d 603, 472 N.Y.S.2d 254, 10 Media L. Rep. (BNA) 1859 (Sup 1984), judgment aff'd, 110 A.D.2d 1095, 488 N.Y.S.2d 943 (1st Dep't 1985) (use of a look-alike model in a manner designed to create the impression that the actual person appeared in the ad constituted an unauthorized display of a "portrait or picture" of the plaintiff in violation of New York's privacy statute).

[Section 11:37]

[1]Smith v. Montoro, 648 F.2d 602, 211 U.S.P.Q. 775 (9th Cir. 1981) (rejected by, Conte Bros. Automotive, Inc. v. Quaker State-Slick 50, Inc., 165 F.3d 221, 49 U.S.P.Q.2d 1321, 1999-1 Trade Cas. (CCH) ¶ 72383 (3d Cir. 1998)).

[2]R.H. Donnelley Corp. v. Illinois Bell Telephone Co., 595 F. Supp. 1202, 225 U.S.P.Q. 402 (N.D. Ill. 1984).

advertising regarding the Yellow Pages without mentioning R. H. Donnelly's previous contributions.[3] An accurate acknowledgement of plaintiff's contribution at the front of a book may defeat an action for false attribution of editorial credit under § 43(a).[4]

If an author's contribution to a work has been materially altered so as to damage the author's reputation, § 43(a) protects against false attribution that solely lists the original author as creator of the work. Thus § 43(a) has been interpreted to extend a type of "moral rights" to authors, if a distortion, alteration or mutilation of a work engenders consumer confusion.[5] Courts have found that attributions of an author's name to distortions, alterations and mutilations of a work that engender customer confusion are actionable under § 43(a).[6]

§ 11:38 Advertising law—Section 43(a) of the Lanham Act—False advertising

Research References

West's Key Number Digest, Antitrust and Trade Regulation ☞163

Section 43(a) seeks to allow maximum information dissemination to consumers so long as the information disseminated is not false or misleading. Because neither competitor can make false or misleading statements about either its own or the other competitors' products or services, the competitors compete on an even playing field. The public interest of limiting consumer confusion is served by making it possible for competitors to require truthfulness from each other. Competitors are hardly burdened because they remain free to completely and truthfully inform the public of

---

[3]R.H. Donnelley Corp. v. Illinois Bell Telephone Co., 595 F. Supp. 1202, 225 U.S.P.Q. 402 (N.D. Ill. 1984); see also Dodd v. Fort Smith Special School Dist. No. 100, 666 F. Supp. 1278, 41 Ed. Law Rep. 624, 4 U.S.P.Q.2d 1395 (W.D. Ark. 1987) (holding that students must be given appropriate credit for contributions to historical biography).

[4]Feerick v. Arthur Young & Co., 715 F. Supp. 1234, 12 U.S.P.Q.2d 2021 (S.D. N.Y. 1989).

[5]Cf. 17 U.S.C.A. § 106A (moral rights for visual artists protected under the copyright laws).

[6]Gilliam v. American Broadcasting Companies, Inc., 538 F.2d 14, 24–25, 192 U.S.P.Q. 1 (2d Cir. 1976)

(finding that ABC's editing of "Monty Python's Flying Circus," which omitted over one quarter of the original, was actionable under § 43(a) for distortion, saying: "the truncated version at times omitted the climax of the skits to which appellant's rare brand of humor was leading and at other times deleted essential elements in the schematic development of a story line."); see also Benson v. Paul Winley Record Sales Corp., 452 F. Supp. 516, 204 U.S.P.Q. 498 (S.D. N.Y. 1978) (finding alteration of recording of George Benson's guitar music to be violation of § 43(a)); Jaeger v. American Intern. Pictures, Inc., 330 F. Supp. 274, 169 U.S.P.Q. 668 (S.D. N.Y. 1971) (finding mutilation of motion picture actionable under § 43(a)).

any facts regarding their products or services.

A claim for false description of goods or services or false advertising under § 43(a) involves the following elements:

- Defendant made a false statement of fact in its advertising;
- Those advertisements actually deceived or have a tendency to deceive a substantial segment of their audience;
- Such deception is material in that it is likely to influence the purchasing decision of consumers;
- The statement concerns goods or services in interstate commerce; and
- The plaintiff has been, or is likely to be injured as a result of the false advertising, either because of diversion of sales or because of loss of good will.[1]

Comparative advertising decisions have adopted the same standard as used in analyzing false statements about one's own products or services.[2] Statements about a competitor's products or services are generally more dangerous than statements about your own products or services. Less information is known about a competitor's goods, and the competitor can change the underlying facts to lead to a claim of false advertising. Specific mention of a competitor in an advertisement is apt to catch the competitor's attention; you should expect that the named competitor will critically examine the advertisement for anything that could be construed as being false. Comparison statements about a present condition (present pricing, product line capabilities, etc.) are particularly dangerous, as the condition can change immediately.

In false advertising claims under the Lanham Act, cases consistently distinguish between two types of comparative advertising claims: "My product is better than yours," versus "Tests prove that my product is better than yours." To succeed on the first type of claim, a plaintiff must prove that defendant's claim of superiority is false. However, to successfully challenge the second type of claim, a plaintiff must only prove that the test relied upon by the defendant was not sufficiently reliable to conclude with reasonable certainty that it establishes the proposition for which it was cited.[3]

The first element of a false advertising claim is that defendant made a false statement "of fact." Statements which are reason-

[Section 11:38]

[1]Skil Corp. v. Rockwell Intern. Corp., 375 F. Supp. 777, 782, 183 U.S.P.Q. 157 (N.D. Ill. 1974).

[2]See, e.g., U.S. Healthcare, Inc. v. Blue Cross of Greater Philadelphia, 898 F.2d 914, 17 Media L. Rep. (BNA) 1681, 14 U.S.P.Q.2d 1257, 1993-2 Trade Cas. (CCH) ¶ 70466 (3d Cir. 1990).

[3]Rhone-Poulenc Rorer Pharmaceuticals, Inc. v. Marion Merrell Dow, Inc., 93 F.3d 511, 39 U.S.P.Q.2d 1832, 1996-2 Trade Cas. (CCH) ¶ 71531 (8th Cir. 1996).

ably viewed as opinions are not actionable under § 43(a). Statements of opinion, boasting, or generalized statements that exaggerate the quality of a product are considered to be merely "puffing" the attributes of a product and are known as "puffery." Under the theory that consumers do not rely on such subjective generalized statements, § 43(a) does not prohibit puffery. Whether a statement is mere puffery has been held to be a question of law.[4] The line between statements which are puffery and statements which may bring on consumer reliance is difficult to draw, and it appears that the puffery exception is narrowly construed.[5]

Material omissions may also be actionable. In certain circumstances, material omissions of fact may be actionable if they lead to consumer confusion. An example of this is omission of the country of origin on foreign made goods.[6]

A photograph may be a statement of fact. Photographs used in advertising often have been the basis for § 43(a) liability. Because photographs can convey such a large array of meanings ("a picture is worth a thousand words"), a photograph which is false or inaccurate in any respect may serve as the false statement of fact necessary under § 43(a). For instance, a picture which is out of date may convey false information as to the good or service sold under the advertisement.[7] Similarly, if an advertisement depicts attachments that are not sold with the product, the advertisement may be enjoined.[8]

Use of a photograph of a competitor's goods in advertising may result in liability under § 43(a), if the advertising implies that

---

[4]Cook, Perkiss and Liehe, Inc. v. Northern California Collection Service Inc., 911 F.2d 242, 246, 15 U.S.P.Q.2d 1894 (9th Cir. 1990) (holding the statement "the low cost commercial collection experts" to be puffery).

[5]Performance Industries, Inc. v. Koos, Inc., 18 U.S.P.Q.2d 1767, 1990 WL 161253 (E.D. Pa. 1990) (holding statement that product "goes twice as far" found actionable rather than mere puffery); American Home Products Corp. v. Abbott Laboratories, 522 F. Supp. 1035, 214 U.S.P.Q. 351 (S.D. N.Y. 1981) (enjoining advertisement for medication as "new two-step treatment" or "new medication" when medication had been in use for more than twenty years under different name).

[6]Bohsei Enterprises Co., U.S.A. v. Porteous Fastener Co., 441 F. Supp. 162, 200 U.S.P.Q. 719 (C.D. Cal. 1977).

[7]CBS, Inc. v. Gusto Records, Inc., 403 F. Supp. 447, 448, 189 U.S.P.Q. 615 (M.D. Tenn. 1974) (finding that recent picture of Charley Rich on album cover was a false statement of fact because the album contained songs recorded ten to fifteen years earlier).

[8]Tripledge Products, Inc. v. Whitney Resources, Ltd., 735 F. Supp. 1154, 15 U.S.P.Q.2d 1434 (E.D. N.Y. 1990) (enjoining advertisements depicting complete windshield wipers when only rubber blades were offered for sale).

the photograph is of one's own goods.[9] A picture of a competitor's product is particularly objectionable if the product sold is inferior to the product in the photograph.[10] Even if a product is intended to be identical to a competitor's, an advertised photograph may serve as the basis for liability if the product has not yet been manufactured by the defendant and consumers could be confused as to who manufactured the product in the photograph.[11]

While some manipulation of pictures (such as to improve the clarity of the pictures) used in comparative advertising may be allowable, any manipulation of pictures which tends to mislead a consumer will be found actionable. Advertisements of a competitor's prices are especially vulnerable to § 43(a) liability because prices are so easily and often changed.[12] Statements implying that comparative testing has been done must be based on actual testing results.[13]

The second element of a false advertising claim is that the advertisements actually deceive or have a tendency to deceive consumers. Generally, the truth or falsity of advertising is judged with reference to consumer reaction surveys, the court's own independent reaction, and the direct testimony of consumers. In determining whether a statement is misleading, the court must consider first its literal meaning. When advertising or label statements are "facially" or "blatantly" false, consumer confusion is presumed without consumer reaction evidence.[14]

Section 43(a) covers more than literal falsehoods. After reviewing the statement's literal meaning, the court then considers whether the statement conveys any implied message to the particular audience at which it was directed. When the challenged advertisement is implicitly rather than explicitly false, its tendency to violate the Lanham Act by misleading, confusing or

---

[9]L'Aiglon Apparel v. Lana Lobell, Inc., 214 F.2d 649, 102 U.S.P.Q. 94 (3d Cir. 1954).

[10]Accurate Leather & Novelty Co., Inc. v. LTD Commodities Inc., 18 U.S.P.Q.2d 1327, 1990 WL 205865 (N.D. Ill. 1990) (enjoining use of photograph of plaintiff's purse which contained thicker leather and higher quality metal fixtures).

[11]National Presto Industries, Inc. v. Hamilton Beach, Inc., 18 U.S.P.Q.2d 1993, 1990 WL 51663 (N.D. Ill. 1990).

[12]U-Haul Intern., Inc. v. Jartran, Inc., 601 F. Supp. 1140, 225 U.S.P.Q. 306 (D. Ariz. 1984), aff'd in part, modified in part and rev'd in part, 793 F.2d 1034, 230 U.S.P.Q. 343 (9th Cir. 1986) (finding altered pictures and comparative pricing statements misleading).

[13]Stiffel Co. v. Westwood Lighting Group, 658 F. Supp. 1103 (D.N.J. 1987).

[14]Coca-Cola Co. v. Tropicana Products, Inc., 690 F.2d 312, 318, 216 U.S.P.Q. 272 (2d Cir. 1982) (finding statement that orange juice is packaged "as it comes from the orange" blatantly false for pasteurized juice).

deceiving should be tested by public reaction.[15]

Actual misstatements, partially correct statements, or failures to disclose which tend to deceive may also be actionable.[16] Stated in broad terms, § 43(a) also covers "clever use of innuendo, indirect intimations, and ambiguous suggestions."[17] If § 43(a) were construed differently, such misleading techniques "could shield the advertisement from scrutiny precisely when protection against such sophisticated deception is most needed."[18]

In cases where advertisements are attacked, not because they are literally false, but because they have a tendency to deceive for some other reason, such as the nature of the presentation, the role of the court is more limited. A court's subjective reaction to the advertisement is "at best not determinative and at worst irrelevant."[19] Rather, it is the reaction of the group to which the advertisement is directed that is dispositive.[20]

Courts have recognized that broad restrictions on advertising do not necessarily further the public interest in avoiding misleading, confusing or deceiving consumers. For example, interpreting "misleading" to include factual propositions that are susceptible to misunderstanding would make consumers worse off by suppressing truthful statements that will help many of them find superior products. A "misunderstood" statement is not the same as one designed to mislead.[21]

When a statement of fact involves a complex issue such as scientific results, the court may not be in a position to judge the ultimate truth or falsity of the statement. In these circumstances, the court will judge whether reasonable testing was done that supported the claim.[22] Literal falsehoods which are true in context are allowed. If a defendant's statements, though literally false, do

---

[15]Princeton Graphics Operating, L.P. v. NEC Home Electronics (U.S.A.), Inc., 732 F. Supp. 1258, 1265 (S.D. N.Y. 1990) (finding that the computer video monitor industry understood a particular standard for "compatibility," and that defendants' product, although compatible in some contexts, did not support "compatibility" so as to meet the industry standard).

[16]Ragold, Inc. v. Ferrero, U.S.A., Inc., 506 F. Supp. 117, 124, 209 U.S.P.Q. 835 (N.D. Ill. 1980).

[17]American Home Products Corp. v. Johnson and Johnson, 577 F.2d 160, 165, 198 U.S.P.Q. 132 (2d Cir. 1978).

[18]American Home Products, 577 F.2d at 165.

[19]American Home Products, 577 F.2d at 172.

[20]American Home Products, 577 F.2d at 166.

[21]Mead Johnson & Co. v. Abbott Laboratories, 201 F.3d 883, 886, 53 U.S.P.Q.2d 1367, 2000-1 Trade Cas. (CCH) ¶ 72743 (7th Cir. 2000), opinion amended on denial of reh'g, 209 F.3d 1032, 54 U.S.P.Q.2d 1509, 2000-1 Trade Cas. (CCH) ¶ 72877 (7th Cir. 2000) (the statement "1st Choice of Doctors" on packaging was not misleading because "1st" can denote a plurality rather than a majority, or "1st" can be meaningless puffery).

[22]Alpo Petfoods, Inc. v. Ralston Purina Co., 720 F. Supp. 194, 12 U.S.P.

not have a tendency to deceive when read in context with the advertisement, no § 43(a) claim will lie.[23]

The third element of a false advertising claim is that a defendant made a false statement "of fact." The statutory language which prohibits false statements "of fact" has also been judicially interpreted as requiring the statement to be material in the purchasing decisions of consumers. Statements which indicate the result of testing are generally found to be material in consumers purchasing decisions. Therefore, a defendant who has made such a statement will bear the burden of proving that reasonable testing has been conducted to support the statement.[24]

Claims under § 43(a) frequently arise with respect to advertising claims that are based upon tests and surveys. While ad claims based on objective data are usually easy to verify or refute, ads based on subjective tests or surveys ("More people prefer Brand A to Brand B" or "Brand A is as good as Brand B but costs less") are harder to verify. The type of questions, order of questions, subject selection procedures, sample sizes, tabulation of results and language used in reporting results can all affect the validity of the ad claim and the determination of whether sufficient research supports the ad claim.[25]

The fourth element of a § 43(a) false advertising claim requires that the defendant's statement be used "in commerce." Such use "in commerce" must be "on or in connection with any goods or services, or any container for goods."[26] This language, similar to the Commerce Clause of the Constitution, has been read broadly to cover virtually all promotional advertising. Furthermore, the

---

Q.2d 1178 (D.D.C. 1989), decision aff'd in part, rev'd in part on other grounds, 913 F.2d 958, 16 U.S.P.Q.2d 1081, 1993-2 Trade Cas. (CCH) ¶ 70461 (D.C. Cir. 1990) and order modified, 1991 WL 25793 (D.D.C. 1991) (enjoining unproven advertising that dog food lessens the severity of canine hip dysplasia).

[23]Avis Rent A Car System, Inc. v. Hertz Corp., 782 F.2d 381, 386, 228 U.S.P.Q. 849 (2d Cir. 1986) (holding that defendant's statements that "Hertz has more new cars than Avis has cars," while literally false as to car ownership, was true in context as to cars available for rent).

[24]Tripledge Products, Inc. v. Whitney Resources, Ltd., 735 F. Supp. 1154, 15 U.S.P.Q.2d 1434 (E.D. N.Y. 1990) (enjoining statements, made without testing, that windshield wiper

rubber resists "heat, cold, chemicals and distortion far better than ordinary wiper blades"); Vidal Sassoon, Inc. v. Bristol-Myers Co., 661 F.2d 272, 213 U.S.P.Q. 24 (2d Cir. 1981) (requiring testing on adult women, not teenagers, to support statements that tests were conducted with "over 900 women like" fashion model Christina Ferrare).

[25]See, e.g., Castrol, Inc. v. Quaker State Corp., 977 F.2d 57, 24 U.S.P.Q.2d 1838, 1993-2 Trade Cas. (CCH) ¶ 70459 (2d Cir. 1992); Coors Brewing Co. v. Anheuser-Busch Companies, Inc., 802 F. Supp. 965, 26 U.S.P.Q.2d 1117, 1994-1 Trade Cas. (CCH) ¶ 70556 (S.D. N.Y. 1992); W.L. Gore & Associates, Inc. v. Totes Inc., 788 F. Supp. 800, 23 U.S.P.Q.2d 1091 (D. Del. 1992).

[26]15 U.S.C.A. § 1125(a)(1).

commercial aspect of the speech has been held to alleviate any First Amendment problems with regulation of false or misleading speech. Statements that specifically refer to a product and are motivated by a desire for revenue are commercial in nature and thus regulated under § 43(a) without violation of the First Amendment.[27] Commercial speech has been defined as "expressions related solely to the economic interests of the speaker and its audience. Speech may be classified as commercial, however, even when, in addition to having a business purpose, it has an informational or a social purpose."[28]

Statements of consumer advocates are outside § 43(a). Section 43(a) cannot be used to stifle criticism of goods or services by one who is not engaged in marketing or promoting a product or service because such statements are not considered commercial speech and thus are entitled to higher degrees of constitutional protection:

> [S]ection 43(a) should not be read in any way to limit political speech, consumer or editorial comment, parodies, satires, or other constitutionally protected material * * * The section is narrowly drafted to encompass only clearly false and misleading commercial speech.[29]

The fifth element of a false advertising claim requires the plaintiff to show that he or she is or is likely to be injured by the defendant's statements. The "likely" injury requirement has been read broadly, so that virtually any party with a commercial interest can bring a suit under § 43(a).[30] Mere consumers generally have no standing.[31]

If a defendant can convince the court that marketplace confusion has actually benefitted plaintiff because of defendant's "well-known positive reputation," then a likely injury has not been shown and the § 43(a) claim must be dismissed.[32] In a suit for damages (rather than merely injunctive relief) under § 43(a), evi-

---

[27]U.S. Healthcare, Inc., 898 F.2d at 934 (3d Cir.1990).

[28]National Artists Management Co., Inc. v. Weaving, 769 F. Supp. 1224, 1232, 20 U.S.P.Q.2d 1113 (S.D. N.Y. 1991) (holding that telephone conversations with a number of friends, acquaintances and colleagues about the reason for leaving her employer were "in commerce" for § 43(a) purposes).

[29]Wojnarowicz v. American Family Ass'n, 745 F. Supp. 130, 142, 17 U.S.P. Q.2d 1337 (S.D. N.Y. 1990) (quoting

legislative history of 1988 Amendment).

[30]See Johnson & Johnson v. Carter-Wallace, Inc., 631 F.2d 186, 208 U.S.P.Q. 169 (2d Cir. 1980).

[31]Boule v. Hutton, 70 F. Supp. 2d 378, 52 U.S.P.Q.2d 1808, 1999-2 Trade Cas. (CCH) ¶ 72690 (S.D. N.Y. 1999), aff'd, 328 F.3d 84, 31 Media L. Rep. (BNA) 1793, 66 U.S.P.Q.2d 1659, 2003-2 Trade Cas. (CCH) ¶ 74095 (2d Cir. 2003).

[32]Branch v. Ogilvy & Mather, Inc., 16 U.S.P.Q.2d 1179, 1186, 1990 WL

dence of some actual injury resulting from the deception has been held to be an essential element of the plaintiff's case.[33]

As discussed above with respect to trademark infringement and dilution, a defense of laches may also be available to a defendant accused of false advertising. Because the Lanham Act establishes no time limitation for claims alleging unfair competition or false advertising, and because there is no corresponding federal statute of limitations, courts often look to the most analogous state statute of limitations in analyzing a defense of laches. The six year statute of limitations on fraud claims is most analogous to an unfair competition claim, rather than the three year statute of limitations for injury to property. The language of the Lanham Act makes clear that there is an intimate relationship between fraud and injury, because the Lanham Act applies to deceptive business practices that attempt to induce a consumer to purchase a product by falsely passing it off as the same as, or better than, a competitor's product.[34]

§ 11:39 Advertising law—State advertising law—Uniform Deceptive Trade Practices Acts

Research References

West's Key Number Digest, Antitrust and Trade Regulation ⌾160

Many of the cases under state advertising law causes of action arose before use of § 43(a) of the Lanham Act became popular. Today these state law actions are often pleaded in addition to a § 43(a) claim.[1] Nonetheless, most states provide substantial remedies, under statutory or common law, to redress advertising practices.[2] Those remedies are typically found either under a deceptive trade practices act or under a consumer protection act. Many states allow double or treble damages and attorney's fees to a successful plaintiff.[3]

Depending upon the jurisdiction, a competitor may bring a cause of action to address advertising under the Uniform Decep-

---

74540 (S.D. N.Y. 1990).

[33]Harper House, Inc. v. Thomas Nelson, Inc., 889 F.2d 197, 209, 12 U.S.P.Q.2d 1779 (9th Cir. 1989).

[34]Conopco, Inc. v. Campbell Soup Co., 95 F.3d 187, 40 U.S.P.Q.2d 1042, 1996-2 Trade Cas. (CCH) ¶ 71551 (2d Cir. 1996).

[Section 11:39]

[1]See, e.g., American Home

Products Corp. v. Johnson and Johnson, 436 F. Supp. 785, 3 Media L. Rep. (BNA) 1097, 196 U.S.P.Q. 484 (S.D. N.Y. 1977), judgment aff'd, 577 F.2d 160, 198 U.S.P.Q. 132 (2d Cir. 1978).

[2]See, e.g., Kukui Nuts of Hawaii Inc. v. R. Baird & Co., Inc., 7 Haw. App. 598, 789 P.2d 501 (1990) (construing Haw. Rev. Stat. § 480-2 (1985)).

[3]E.g., Ala. Code § 8-19-10(a) (2004).

tive Trade Practices Act ("U.D.T.P.A.").[4] The teeth of the
U.D.T.P.A. is in § 2(a), which broadly defines "deceptive trade
practice." A person engages in a deceptive trade practice when, in
the course of his business, vocation, or occupation, he:

- passes off goods or services as those of another;
- causes likelihood of confusion or of misunderstanding as to
  the source, sponsorship, approval, or certification of goods or
  services;
- causes likelihood of confusion or of misunderstanding as to
  affiliation, connection, or association with, or certification
  by, another;
- uses deceptive representation or designation of geographic
  origin in connection with goods or services;
- represents that goods or services have sponsorship, approval,
  characteristics, ingredients, uses, benefits, or quantities that
  they do not have or that a person has a sponsorship, approval, status, affiliation, or connection that he does not
  have;
- represents that goods are original or new if they are deterio-
  rated, altered, reconditioned, reclaimed, used, or secondhand;
- represents that goods or services are of a particular standard, quality, or grade, or that goods are of a particular
  style or model, if they are of another;
- disparages the goods, services, or business of another by
  false or misleading representation of fact;
- advertises goods or services with intent not to sell them as
  advertised;
- advertises goods or services with intent not to supply reasonably expectable public demand, unless the advertisement
  discloses a limitation of quantity;
- makes false or misleading statements of fact concerning the
  reasons for, existence of, or amounts of price reductions; or
- engages in any other conduct which similarly creates a likelihood of confusion or of misunderstanding.[5]

Through this broad definition of "deceptive trade practice," the
U.D.T.P.A. codifies the major ways in which statements have
been found false and material under § 43(a) of the Lanham Act.
Any person likely to be damaged by a deceptive trade practice
has standing under the U.D.T.P.A. No proof of actual damage or
intent is required for injunctive relief, but monetary damages are
not available under the U.D.T.P.A. unless provided for by other
statutes or common law.

The U.D.T.P.A. was designed to bring state law up to date by

---

[4]Unif. Deceptive Trade Practices
Act, 7A U.L.A. 265 (1966).

[5]Unif. Deceptive Trade Practices
Act, 7A U.L.A. 265 (1966).

removing undue restriction on the common law action for deceptive trade practices. Most of the older legislation is characterized by seldom enforced criminal sanctions, and has not been a widely used weapon against misleading advertising. The relief provided by the U.D.T.P.A. is in addition to previously existing remedies.

§11:40 Advertising law—State advertising law—Defamation and commercial torts

Research References

West's Key Number Digest, Antitrust and Trade Regulation ⚲163; Libel and Slander ⚲130

When an advertisement denigrates or impugns the products or services of another company, claims can be made for business defamation, commercial disparagement and trade libel. The availability of a claim for any of these three torts depends on the particular jurisdiction. Whether such a claim is brought under state statutory or common law will also depend on the particular jurisdiction. In some states, such as Alabama and Texas, claims for "trade libel" or similar business advertising torts are technically not recognized. However, state law claims for libel of either a specific entity or individual have been upheld for advertising statements made in a business context.[1]

The three torts of business defamation, commercial disparagement and trade libel are quite similar. All three torts require pleading and proof of a statement which is false and unprivileged. Courts have held that cases for disparagement alone must prove pecuniary loss directly related to the statements as an element of liability, while cases of defamation or libel must only prove pecuniary loss as an element of damages.

In general, courts have found for the plaintiff under defamation or libel theories when the advertising statement reflects upon the character or integrity of the other company or individual. Unsubstantiated advertising statements which impute fraud, deceit, dishonesty or reprehensible conduct in business can be grounds for recovery.[2]

On the other hand, advertising statements which merely state superiority of one product or service over another are generally not found actionable. Every competitor in the marketplace is

---

[Section 11:40]

[1]*See, e.g.*, Jetco Electronic Industries v. Gardiner, 325 F. Supp. 80 (S.D. Tex. 1971); Newspapers, Inc. v. Matthews, 161 Tex. 284, 339 S.W.2d 890, 100 A.L.R.2d 218 (1960).

[2]Zerpol Corp. v. DMP Corp., 561 F. Supp. 404, 409, 9 Media L. Rep. (BNA) 1802, 218 U.S.P.Q. 459, 1983-1 Trade Cas. (CCH) ¶ 65370 (E.D. Pa. 1983).

expected to sing a little of the tune "Anything Theirs Can Do, Ours Can Do Better." So long as statements are not found to be specifically directed to verifiable facts, no action for business defamation or disparagement will lie.[3] This is essentially the same "puffery" defense found in cases dealing with § 43(a) of the Lanham Act.

The plaintiff does not necessarily have to be specifically named in the advertisement. Advertising statements have been found actionable, even though no one was specifically named in the advertisement, when extrinsic evidence clearly indicated that the advertisement was directed at a specific competitor. Statements of fact which are directed to the industry as a whole can also be found actionable to competitors in the industry.

§ 11:41 Advertising law—State advertising law— Warranties and product liability

Research References

West's Key Number Digest, Antitrust and Trade Regulation ⌖163; Products Liability ⌖7
C.J.S., Products Liability § 10

Numerous cases have held that representations in advertising constitute express or implied warranties of product performance capabilities, tolerances or acceptably safe methods of use. State and federal statutes may apply to very specific advertising practices, products, services and industries. For example, legislation in some jurisdictions particularly addresses "sale"[1] pricing advertisements, making specific requirements for "wholesale"[2] price, "—percent off"[3] or "going out of business"[4] advertising statements.

Most jurisdictions also have legislation making "bait and switch" tactics illegal.[5] "Bait and switch" laws address the practice of advertising a particular product at a particular price to attract customers, followed by salespeople denigrating the advertised product with an intent to coerce the customer into

---

[3]Sims v. Mack Truck Corp., 488 F. Supp. 592, 605, 206 U.S.P.Q. 11, 1980-1 Trade Cas. (CCH) ¶ 63238 (E.D. Pa. 1980) (rejected by, SI Handling Systems, Inc. v. Heisley, 753 F.2d 1244, 225 U.S.P.Q. 441 (3d Cir. 1985)); Ringling Bros.-Barnum & Bailey Combined Shows, Inc. v. Chandris America Lines, Inc., 321 F. Supp. 707, 169 U.S.P.Q. 290 (S.D. N.Y. 1971).

[Section 11:41]

[1]*See, e.g.,* Or. Rev. Stat. § 646.885(1).

[2]*See, e.g.,* Fla. Stat. Ann. § 817.41.

[3]*See, e.g.,* Ala. Code § 8-13-1.

[4]*See, e.g.,* Or. Rev. Stat. § 646.885(2).

[5]*See, e.g.,* Ga. Code Ann. § 26-2-152(b).

purchasing a (generally more expensive) competing brand.

Many states have advertising statutes directed at specific professions, such as certified public accountants, attorneys, chiropractors, dentists, optometrists, physical therapists, podiatrists, and real estate brokers. Considerably more industries have specific advertising legislation than can be included here. For instance, the following industries have specific advertising requirements or limitations, imposed either federally or by many states: alcoholic beverages; firearms and other weapons; fishing; health maintenance organizations; hearing aids; heating and air conditioning; hotels and lodging; insecticide, fungicide, and rodenticides; insurance; lotteries and games of chance; motor vehicles; oleomargarine, butter and dairy products; telephone solicitation; tobacco products; travel and vacation timeshares; and weights, measure, and labeling.

Chapter 12

Trade Secrets

§ 12:35   —Attorneys' fees
§ 12:36   Federal trade secrets actions
§ 12:37   Criminalization of trade secret law

KeyCite®: Cases and other legal materials listed in KeyCite Scope can be researched through the KeyCite service on Westlaw®. Use KeyCite to check citations for form, parallel references, prior and later history, and comprehensive citator information, including citations to other decisions and secondary materials.

---

§ 12:1 Importance of trade secrets

Research References

West's Key Number Digest, Antitrust and Trade Regulation ☞410

Trade secret law provides an avenue for intellectual property protection distinct from that provided by patent or copyright law. Often, a business or individual will have competitively significant information that does not meet the requirements for U.S. patent protection.[1] Similarly, copyright protection may be unavailable because copyright law only protects the expression of an idea, and not the idea itself.[2] Alternatively, the information may be of a type that the creator does not want to make available to competitors, as otherwise required for either patent or copyright protection. In these situations, trade secret protection is the best, if not only, available option for protecting valuable information.

In addition to encompassing a broader area of subject matter than either patent or copyright, trade secret law offers the possibility of protection for an extended period of time. In fact, so long as the trade secret owner takes proper steps, a trade secret can be preserved indefinitely.[3] Thus, the holder of a properly maintained trade secret can enjoy a competitive advantage for longer than the 20 years (from filing) of protection provided by a United States utility patent or the life plus 70 years of protection provided by a United States copyright registration.[4] A good example of this is the long-lived "secret formula" for the Coca-Cola brand soft drink.[5]

An additional advantage to trade secret protection is the relative ease with which trade secret rights are established. In some cases, information can be accorded trade secret status as soon as

---

[Section 12:1]

[1]35 U.S.C.A. §§ 101 to 103.

[2]17 U.S.C.A. § 102(b).

[3]Restatement (First) of Torts § 757 cmt. a (1939).

[4]35 U.S.C.A. § 154; 17 U.S.C.A. §§ 302 to 304.

[5]James Pooley, Trade Secrets § 501(1)(b) (1997).

it is created.[6] Perhaps even more valuable to the potential owner is the fact that trade secret protection does not require completion of application forms or other paperwork and filing fees normally associated with patents and copyrights.[7]

Trade secret law provides a business or individual with a system to protect confidential information. Without trade secret law, important confidential information not otherwise protectable by a patent or copyright could be stolen by an unscrupulous competitor, leaving the creator with no legal recourse for protecting the investment of time and money in developing that information.[8]

Trade secret law provides protection for "commercial intangibles," while encouraging innovation and maintaining standards of commercial ethics.[9] Balanced against this goal of protection is the policy of free and open competition.[10] While an understandable desire exists to acknowledge ownership of an alleged trade secret when it appears that another has copied it, unpatented information is prevalent, and courts have recognized that competition may not always be fair. As one court noted, "competition is ruthless, unprincipled, uncharitable, unforgiving and a boon to society."[11] Therefore, a party seeking to protect information as a trade secret must remain cognizant of these policies which underly trade secret law.

The theory of trade secret protection evolved under both common law tort and contract theories.[12] Early trade secret decisions varied from state to state, with only moderate uniformity in interpretation. However, in 1939 the Restatement (First) of Torts was published by the American Law Institute. Section 757 of this document was the first attempt to set forth a nationally accepted definition of trade secrets, requirements for protection, and reme-

---

[6]Restatement (Third) of Unfair Competition § 39 cmt. d (1995).

[7]Restatement (Third) of Unfair Competition § 39 cmt. c (1995).

[8]Restatement Third, Unfair Competition § 38, comment a (1995). *See* Computer Associates Intern., Inc. v. Altai, Inc., 982 F.2d 693, 717, 37 Fed. R. Evid. Serv. 348, 119 A.L.R. Fed. 741 (2d Cir. 1992) (noting that trade secret protection is a " 'uniquely valuable' weapon in the defensive arsenal of computer programs" because trade secret doctrine protects the discovery of ideas, processes, and systems which are explicitly precluded from coverage under copyright law).

[9]Salsbury Laboratories, Inc. v. Merieux Laboratories, Inc., 908 F.2d 706, 710, 15 U.S.P.Q.2d 1489 (11th Cir. 1990); Kewanee Oil Co. v. Bicron Corp., 416 U.S. 470, 481, 94 S. Ct. 1879, 1886, 181 U.S.P.Q. 673 (1974).

[10]PepsiCo, Inc. v. Redmond, 54 F.3d 1262, 1267, 10 I.E.R. Cas. (BNA) 1089, 35 U.S.P.Q.2d 1010 (7th Cir. 1995).

[11]Composite Marine Propellers, Inc. v. Van Der Woude, 962 F.2d 1263, 1268, 22 U.S.P.Q.2d 1568 (7th Cir. 1992).

[12]Restatement (Third) of Unfair Competition § 39 cmt. h (1995).

dies for misappropriation.[13] The Restatement (Second) of Torts (1978) purposefully omitted numerous sections of the original Restatement, including those relating to trade secrets. However, in the Restatement (Third) of Unfair Competition, approved in 1995, the American Law Institute presented a revised statement of trade secret law. The Restatement (Third) of Unfair Competition is to be applicable to actions under common law unless specifically noted otherwise.[14] However, the definitions provided by § 757 of the Restatement (First) of Torts continue to be applied in a number of states, and because of this, where appropriate, will be used throughout this chapter.

While the Restatement (First) of Torts § 757 provided some guidance and uniformity to trade secret law, confusion remained.[15] In 1979, the National Conference of Commissioners on Uniform State Laws approved a Uniform Trade Secrets Act (UTSA). The UTSA was designed to provide:

> unitary definitions of trade secret and trade secret misappropriation and a single statute of limitations for the various property, quasi-contractual and violation of fiduciary relationship theories of noncontractual liability used at common law.[16]

The UTSA has been adopted, with varying modifications, by 48 states, the District of Columbia, Puerto Rico, and the U.S. Virgin Islands.[17] Although entirely exclusive, the UTSA has been interpreted as applying the principles set forth in § 757 of the

---

[13]Restatement (First) of Torts § 757 (1939).

[14]Restatement (Third) of Unfair Competition § 39 cmt. b (1995).

[15]U.T.S.A. Prefatory Note (1985).

[16]U.T.S.A. Prefatory Note (1985).

[17]Adoptions of 1985 U.T.S.A.: Arkansas, Ark. Code Ann. §§ 4-75-601 to 4-75-607; California, Cal. Civ. Code §§ 3426 to 3426.11; Connecticut, Conn. Gen. Stat. §§ 35-50 to 35-58; Indiana, Ind. Code §§ 24-2-3-1 to 24-2-3-8; Louisiana, La. Rev. Stat. Ann. §§ 51:1431 to 51:1439; Rhode Island, R.I. Gen. Laws §§ 6-41-1 to 6-41-11; Washington, Wash. Rev. Code §§ 19.108.010 to 19.108.940. Adoptions with 1985 Amendments: Alabama, Ala. Code §§ 8-27-1 to 8-27-6; Alaska, Alaska Stat. §§ 45.50.910 to 45.50.945; Arizona, Ariz. Rev. Stat. §§ 44-401 to 44-407; Colorado, Colo. Rev. Stat. §§ 7-74-101 to 7-74-110; Delaware, Del. Code Ann. tit. 6, §§ 2001 to 2009; District of Columbia, D.C. Code §§ 36-401 to 36-410; Florida, Fla. Stat. ch. 688.001 to 688.009; Georgia, Ga. Code Ann. §§ 10-1-760 to 10-1-767; Hawaii, Haw. Rev. Stat. §§ 482B-1 to 482B-9; Idaho, Idaho Code Ann. §§ 48-801 to 48-807; Illinois, 765 Ill. Comp. Stat. 1065/1 to 1065/9; Iowa, Iowa Code Ann. §§ 550.1 to 550.8; Kansas, Kan. Stat. Ann. §§ 60-3320 to 60-3330; Kentucky, Ky. Rev. Stat. Ann. §§ 365.880 to 365.900; Maine, Me. Rev. Stat. Ann. tit. 10, §§ 1541 to 1548; Maryland, Md. Code Ann., Com. Law §§ 11-1201 to 11-1209; Michigan, Mich. Comp. Laws Ann. §§ 445. 1901 to 445.1910; Minnesota, Minn. Stat. §§ 325C.01 to 325C.08; Mississippi, Miss. Code Ann. §§ 75-26-1 to 75-26-19; Missouri, Mo. Rev. Stat. §§ 417.450 to 417.467; Montana, Mont. Code Ann. §§ 30-14-401 to 30-14-409; Nebraska, Neb. Rev. Stat. §§ 87-501 to 87-507; Nevada, Nev. Rev. Stat. §§ 600A.010 to 600A.100; New Hampshire, N.H. Rev. Stat. Ann. §§ 350-B:1 to 350-B:9; New Jersey, N.J.

Restatement (First) of Torts.[18] Similarly, it has been recited that the Restatement (First) of Torts was the basic source for the UTSA's definition of trade secret.[19] Other courts view the UTSA as merely displacing conflicting tort, restitutionary and other laws regarding civil liability for misappropriation.[20] While some states have varied the language of the UTSA, and other states have not adopted the UTSA, it is the leading framework for trade secret protection. The Restatement (Third) of Unfair Competition also follows the UTSA, including an adoption of the UTSA definition of a trade secret.[21] In addition to its straightforward language, the UTSA has developed a large body of interpretive case law. Because of this, language from the UTSA will be cited where appropriate throughout this chapter.

§ 12:2 Defining trade secrets—Restatement (First) of Torts

Research References

West's Key Number Digest, Antitrust and Trade Regulation ⊸413

Analysis of trade secret protection must begin by identifying what is meant by "trade secret." According to comment (b) of § 757 of the Restatement (First) of Torts, a "trade secret" is:

[A]ny formula, pattern, device or compilation of information which is used in one's business, and which gives him an opportunity to obtain an advantage over competitors who do not know or use it. It may be a formula for a chemical compound, a process of manufacturing, treating or preserving materials, a pattern for a machine or

---

Stat. Ann. 56:15-1 to 56:15-9; New Mexico, N.M. Stat. Ann. §§ 57-3A-1 to 57-3A-7; North Carolina, N.C. Gen. Stat. Ann. §§ 66-152 to 66-157; North Dakota, N.D. Cent. Code §§ 47-25.1-01 to 47-25.1-08; Ohio, Ohio Rev. Code Ann. §§ 1333.61 to 1333.69; Oklahoma, Okla. Stat. tit. 78, §§ 85 to 94; Oregon, Or. Rev. Stat. Ann. §§ 646.461 to 646.475; Pennsylvania, 12 Pa. Cons. Stat. §§ 5301 to 5308; P.R. Laws Ann. tit. 10 §§ 4131 to 4141; South Carolina, S.C. Code Ann. §§ 39-8-10 to 39-8-130; South Dakota, S.D. Codified Laws §§ 37-29-1 to 37-29-11; Tennessee, Tenn. Code Ann. §§ 47-25-1701 to 47-25-1709; Texas, Tex. Civ. Prac. & Rem. Code Ann. §§ 134.001 to 134.007; Utah, Utah Code Ann. §§ 13-24-1 to 13-24-9; Vermont, Vt. Stat. Ann. tit. 9, §§ 4601 to 4609 tit. 12, § 523; Virgin Islands, V.I. Code Ann. tit. 11, §§ 1001 to 1010; Virginia, Va. Code Ann. §§ 59. 1-336 to 59. 1-343; West Virginia, W. Va. Code Ann. §§ 47-22-1 to 47-22-10; Wisconsin, Wis. Stat. § 134.90; Wyoming, Wyo. Stat. Ann. §§ 40-24-101 to 40-24-110. Not adopted: Massachusetts (introduced 2013), and New York (introduced 2007).

[18]Electro-Craft Corp. v. Controlled Motion, Inc., 332 N.W.2d 890, 898, 220 U.S.P.Q. 811 (Minn. 1983).

[19]Minuteman, Inc. v. Alexander, 147 Wis. 2d 842, 434 N.W.2d 773, 777 (1989).

[20]Boeing Co. v. Sierracin Corp., 108 Wash. 2d 38, 738 P.2d 665, 673, 4 U.S.P.Q.2d 1417, 1987-1 Trade Cas. (CCH) ¶ 67572 (1987) (interpreting Washington's version of the U.T.S.A.).

[21]Restatement (Third) of Unfair Competition § 39 cmt. b (1995).

other device, or a list of customers.

The Restatement (First) of Torts further defined a "trade secret" as being something more than simply information regarding a single or ephemeral event, but is instead a process or device for continuous use in the operation of a business. The Restatement (First) of Torts provided a number of other examples of protectable information, such as a machine or formula for the production of goods, operations of a business, or methods of office management.

In addition to describing the types of information that may qualify for trade secret protection, § 757 of the Restatement (First) of Torts detailed something that is obviously implied by the term "trade secret," namely that the information *must be kept secret*.[1] Information of general knowledge in an industry or of public knowledge cannot be maintained by a single entity as its own secret.[2] In the same vein, matters or information which are fully disclosed by the goods which one markets cannot be claimed as secret.[3] It should be noted that complete secrecy is not required. However, a substantial element of secrecy must exist so that it will be difficult for others to acquire the same information.[4]

The Restatement (First) of Torts set forth a number of factors to be considered in determining whether information is a trade secret:

- the extent to which the information is known outside of the owner's business,
- the extent to which the information is known by employees and others involved in the owner's business,
- the extent of measures taken by the owner to guard the secrecy of the information,
- the value of the information to the owner and to his competitors,
- the amount of effort or money expended by the owner in developing the information, and
- the ease or difficulty with which the information could be properly acquired or duplicated by others.[5]

A final aspect of the Restatement's definition of "trade secret" is the level of novelty associated with the information. Unlike an invention claimed by a patent, a trade secret need not meet a

---

[Section 12:2]

[1]Restatement (First) of Torts § 757 cmt. a (1939).

[2]Restatement (First) of Torts § 757 cmt. b (1939).

[3]Restatement (First) of Torts § 757 cmt. b (1939).

[4]Restatement (Third) of Unfair Competition § 39 cmt. f (1995).

[5]Restatement (First) of Torts § 757 cmt. b (1939).

statutory level of "novelty" to be protected.[6] In distinguishing trade secret from patent law, the Restatement (First) of Torts recognized that the policies underlying patent protection and trade secret protection are different:

> The patent monopoly is a reward to the inventor but such is not the case with a trade secret. Its protection is not based on a policy of rewarding or otherwise encouraging the development of secret processes or devices. The protection is merely against breach of faith and reprehensible means of learning another's secret. For this limited protection it is not appropriate to require also the kind of novelty and invention which is a requisite of patentability.[7]

§ 12:3 Defining trade secrets—Uniform Trade Secrets Act

Research References

West's Key Number Digest, Antitrust and Trade Regulation ☞411

The UTSA defines "trade secret" in a more concise manner than the Restatement (First) of Torts:

> "Trade secret" means information, including a formula, pattern, compilation, program, device, method, technique or process, that:
> (i)   derives independent economic value, actual or potential, from not being generally known to, and not being readily ascertainable by proper means by, other persons who can obtain economic value from the disclosure or use, and
> (ii) is the subject of efforts that are reasonable under the circumstances to maintain its secrecy.[1]

This definition is meant to be broader than the one presented by the Restatement (First) of Torts. The limitation that a trade secret be "continually used in one's business" is left out for the purpose of covering information that has commercial value from a negative viewpoint, such as the results of research proving certain processes will not work.[2] Further, information categorized as a trade secret under the UTSA does not lose its protected status simply because it has been committed to memory rather than written down. The Act does not distinguish between written and memorized information.[3]

§ 12:4 Defining trade secrets—Economic Espionage Act/ Defend Trade Secrets Act

---

[6]Restatement (First) of Torts § 757 cmt. b (1939).

[7]Restatement (First) of Torts § 757 cmt. b (1939).

[Section 12:3]

[1]U.T.S.A. § 1(4) (1985).

[2]U.T.S.A. § 1 cmt. (1985).

[3]Ed Nowogroski Ins., Inc. v. Rucker, 137 Wash. 2d 427, 971 P.2d 936, 946, 16 I.E.R. Cas. (BNA) 82, 50 U.S.P.Q.2d 1268 (1999).

18 U.S.C.A. § 1839(3) defines a trade secret as:

all forms and types of financial, business, scientific, technical, economic, or engineering information, including patterns, plans, compilations, program devices, formulas, designs, prototypes, methods, techniques, processes, procedures, programs, or codes, whether tangible or intangible, and whether or how stored, compiled, or memorialized physically, electronically, graphically, photographically, or in writing if—

(A) the owner thereof has taken reasonable measures to keep such information secret; and

(B) the information derives independent economic value, actual or potential, from not being generally known to, and not being readily ascertainable through proper means by, the public;

This definition is applicable to federal civil (private) trade secret misappropriation claims under the Defend Trade Secrets Act, and also to criminal trade secret misappropriation under the Economic Espionage Act.

§ 12:5 Defining trade secrets—Other definitions of trade secrets

Research References

West's Key Number Digest, Antitrust and Trade Regulation ☜413

Section 39 of the Restatement (Third) of Unfair Competition defines a trade secret as:

[A]ny information that can be used in the operation of a business or other enterprise and that is sufficiently valuable and secret to afford an actual or potential economic advantage over others.

This definition is meant to be consistent with the definition set forth by the UTSA[1]

The Federal Courts have also defined "trade secrets" in different contexts. Specifically, for the purposes of the Freedom of Information Act (FOIA), a trade secret is defined as "a secret, commercially valuable plan, formula, process, or device that is used for making, preparing, compounding, or processing of trade commodities and that can be said to be the end product of either innovation or substantial effort."[2] This is a more narrow definition than that advanced by the Restatements or UTSA.

As evidenced by the varying definitions, a "trade secret" can encompass a wide variety of proprietary information. There are, however, common elements the information must satisfy before

---

[Section 12:5]

[1]U.T.S.A. § 1(4) (1985).

[2]Herrick v. Garvey, 298 F.3d 1184, 63 U.S.P.Q.2d 1748, 59 Fed. R. Evid.

Serv. 472 (10th Cir. 2002); American Family Mut. Ins. Co. v. Roth, 485 F.3d 930, 933, 25 I.E.R. Cas. (BNA) 1771, 82 U.S.P.Q.2d 1701 (7th Cir. 2007).

legal protection will be recognized.[3] Further, the manner in which the owner treats the information also affects the legal protection it receives.[4]

Before delving into these elements, one caveat must be made. It is impossible to precisely say what a trade secret is or is not.[5] In one case, a particular piece of information may qualify for trade secret protection, while in another, it may not.[6] It is important for the practitioner to recognize this difficulty when advising a client regarding trade secret issues. The broad definitions provided by the Restatement (First) of Torts and the UTSA, along with relevant case law, should be used as a guide when researching the facts of each case before rendering any type of opinion.

§ 12:6 Elements of a trade secret—Novelty

Research References

West's Key Number Digest, Antitrust and Trade Regulation ☞413

The Restatement (First) of Torts of Torts explicitly provides that trade secret information need not reach the level of inventiveness or novelty which is required for a patent.[1] In the same breath, however, the Restatement states that the nature of the information is an important factor in determining the relief available. That is to say, the information must have some value in order to be protected.[2]

In contrast to the Restatement (First) of Torts, the language of the UTSA does not allude to a requisite level of novelty or inventiveness. Inferentially, however, there is a level of inventiveness that must be established under the UTSA The UTSA requires that the information have independent economic value and not be readily ascertainable by proper means.[3] Taken together, these two elements effectively require a certain level of inventiveness or novelty. In other words, where certain information has no value and/or is known by virtually everyone in a particular industry, it likewise is not novel. In contrast, information

---

[3]Restatement (First) of Torts § 757 cmt. b (1939).

[4]Restatement (First) of Torts § 757 cmt. b (1939).

[5]Restatement (Third) of Unfair Competition § 39 cmt. d (1995).

[6]Xpert Automation Systems, Corp. v. Vibromatic Co., Inc., 569 N.E.2d 351, 356 (Ind. Ct. App. 1991); Ed Nowogroski Ins., 971 P.2d at 948; Western Medical Consultants, Inc. v. Johnson, 80 F.3d 1331, 1337, 11 I.E.R.

Cas. (BNA) 1005, 38 U.S.P.Q.2d 1426 (9th Cir. 1996) (discussing cases where customer list information is afforded or denied trade secret coverage).

[Section 12:6]

[1]Restatement (First) of Torts § 757 cmt. b (1939).

[2]Restatement (First) of Torts § 757 cmt. b (1939).

[3]U.T.S.A. § 1(4)(i) (1985).

is novel when it has value and no one else knows about it.[4]

Courts have held that at least some novelty is required before protection will be afforded.[5] Several jurisdictions continue to list novelty as a prerequisite to trade secret protection.[6] When analyzing this novelty requirement, the courts generally incorporate a factual inquiry into whether or not the idea is original or is not a matter of public knowledge.[7] In this regard, a trade secret may be no more than a slight mechanical advance over common knowledge and the practice in the art.[8] Further, a trade secret can exist in a combination of characteristics and components each of which, by itself, is in the public domain, but the unified process and operation of which is unique.[9]

Beyond a much less stringent level of novelty, trade secret law has an additional distinction from patent law. With patents, an invention is only novel to the first person who invents it.[10] All others are then precluded from claiming patent rights in the invention, even though they may independently create the same invention at some later point in time.[11] This is not true with trade secrets. The unique nature of trade secrets allows more than one individual or entity to claim ownership rights in the same independently developed information, regardless of who developed it first, so long as that information is not readily available to others and is maintained in secrecy by the various owners.[12]

For a process, device, or compilation of information to qualify as a trade secret, the individual elements of the process, device, or compilation need not be novel or original; the novelty requirement only demands that the combination of elements be novel.[13] For example, the structure, sequence and organization of a com-

---

[4]Murray v. Bank One, 99 Ohio App. 3d 89, 98, 649 N.E.2d 1307, 1313 (10th Dist. Franklin County 1994).

[5]Electro-Craft Corp. v. Controlled Motion, Inc., 332 N.W.2d 890, 899, 220 U.S.P.Q. 811 (Minn. 1983).

[6]See Arco Industries Corp. v. Chemcast Corp., 633 F.2d 435, 441–42, 208 U.S.P.Q. 190 (6th Cir. 1980) (applying Michigan law); Salsbury Lab., 908 F.2d at 711 (applying Georgia law); Investors Guaranty Fund, Ltd. v. Morgan Stanley & Co., Inc., 50 U.S.P.Q.2d 1523, 1998 WL 906577 (S.D. N.Y. 1998), aff'd, 199 F.3d 1322 (2d Cir. 1999).

[7]Murray, 582 N.E.2d at 1129.

[8]SI Handling Systems, Inc. v. Heisley, 753 F.2d 1244, 1255, 225 U.S.P.Q. 441 (3d Cir. 1985) (citing Anaconda Co. v. Metric Tool & Die Co., 485 F. Supp. 410, 422, 205 U.S.P.Q. 723 (E.D. Pa. 1980)).

[9]Q-Co Industries, Inc. v. Hoffman, 625 F. Supp. 608, 617, 228 U.S.P.Q. 554 (S.D. N.Y. 1985).

[10]See §§ 2:19 to 2:24, infra.

[11]See §§ 2:19 to 2:24, infra.

[12]Surgidev Corp. v. Eye Technology, Inc., 648 F. Supp. 661, 688 (D. Minn. 1986), order aff'd, 828 F.2d 452, 4 U.S.P.Q.2d 1090 (8th Cir. 1987).

[13]Softel, Inc. v. Dragon Medical and Scientific Communications, Inc., 118 F.3d 955, 968, 43 U.S.P.Q.2d 1385, 38 Fed. R. Serv. 3d 623 (2d Cir. 1997).

puter code may qualify as a trade secret, even though the code's author freely discussed the use of menus, English language commands, functional modules, and external files.[14] Similarly, no rule exists that proposals for new products cannot as a matter of law constitute trade secrets. Even if the marketing product ideas could not constitute trade secret information, the results of the research aimed at developing the product could be protected as trade secrets.[15]

§ 12:7 Elements of a trade secret—Economic value

Research References

West's Key Number Digest, Antitrust and Trade Regulation ⚖413

Trade secrets embody a potentially endless list of information. The UTSA constrains these possibilities by specifically requiring that the information provide the owner with some commercial advantage or economic value.[1] The Restatement (First) of Torts makes similar reference to this requirement by including factors useful for determining whether given information is a trade secret: "the value of the information to [the owner] and to his competitors, and the amount of effort or money expended by [the owner] in developing the information."[2]

The term "economic value" refers to the value of the information to either the owner or a competitor, including information that would be useful to a competitor and would require cost, time and effort to duplicate.[3] In other words, where a competitor would materially benefit from knowing the information and would have to spend time and money to create the same information independently, the information does in fact have economic value.[4]

Beyond this somewhat ambiguous definition, courts have found economic value to have been established in a variety of situations. For example, proof of commercial or economic value may be established circumstantially through proof of a defendant's intent to use or actual use of the information.[5] Alternatively, proof of independent economic value can be established through a showing of the time and money expended in developing the information in

---

[14]Softel, 118 F.3d at 968.

[15]Bausch & Lomb Inc. v. Alcon Laboratories, Inc., 64 F. Supp. 2d 233, 247-48, 52 U.S.P.Q.2d 1385 (W.D. N.Y. 1999).

[Section 12:7]

[1]U.T.S.A. § 1(4)(i) (1985); *see also* U.T.S.A. § 2(a) (1985).

[2]Restatement (First) of Torts § 757 (1939).

[3]US West Communications, Inc. v. Office of Consumer Advocate, 498 N.W.2d 711, 714 (Iowa 1993).

[4]Surgidev, 648 F. Supp. at 687–88.

[5]Surgidev, 648 F. Supp. at 692.

question.[6]

Where information, such as a poem or screenplay, derives economic value only from broad dissemination, there is likely no independent economic value.[7]

§ 12:8   Elements of a trade secret—Not generally known or readily ascertainable

Research References

West's Key Number Digest, Antitrust and Trade Regulation ☞417

The UTSA requires that to be accorded trade secret status, the information in question must not be capable of being readily ascertained by proper means.[1] That is, if others can discover the allegedly proprietary information by merely examining an existing product which is publicly available and which incorporates the trade secret, the information will not be protected as a trade secret.[2] The reason for this view is simple. It would be unfair to allow one company to obtain legal protection (other than patent or copyright) for a product or information that is available to the public.[3]

Whether information is readily accessible or easily discoverable by proper means is a question of fact.[4] Some inquiries which assist in making this factual determination are the time and money taken to develop the information; the time and money required for a competitor to independently develop the information; and how difficult it would be to reverse engineer the product to obtain the information.[5]

Publication of the trade secret information destroys its status as a trade secret, regardless of whether the publication occurs in industry trade journals, reference books, or advertising.[6] However, general reference to a trade secret in an advertisement or in an article is not likely to make the information readily ascertainable. The disclosure must be sufficient to "translate into

---

[6]Electro-Craft, 332 N.W.2d at 901.

[7]Stromback v. New Line Cinema, 384 F.3d 283, 305, 72 U.S.P.Q.2d 1545, Fed. Sec. L. Rep. (CCH) P 28878, 2004 FED App. 0314P (6th Cir. 2004).

[Section 12:8]

[1]U.T.S.A. § 1(4)(i) (1985).

[2]U.T.S.A. § 1 cmt. (1985) (describing reverse engineering).

[3]Bonito Boats, Inc. v. Thunder Craft Boats, Inc., 489 U.S. 141, 160, 109 S. Ct. 971, 982, 9 U.S.P.Q.2d 1847 (1989); Restatement (Third) of Unfair Competition § 39 cmt. c (1995).

[4]See § 12:30, supra.

[5]Electro-Craft, 332 N.W.2d at 899.

[6]Picker Intern., Inc. v. Parten, 935 F.2d 257, 264, 1991-1 Trade Cas. (CCH) ¶ 69495 (11th Cir. 1991).

practical application the theoretical concepts described."[7] Much like published literature, public use or display of a product or machine embodying the trade secret information in a manner sufficient to disclose the trade secret obliterates any potential trade secret status.[8]

One must be careful in analyzing whether public use of a product makes the alleged trade secret readily ascertainable. If the trade secret is defined as the overall product itself, then public use of the product makes it readily ascertainable.[9] However, where the trade secret is hidden in the product (for example the secret formula of Coca-Cola brand soft drink or a computer language encoded into a computer program), simple use of the product does not make the trade secret readily ascertainable.[10] Thus, it is important to accurately define the alleged trade secret.

The ability to reverse engineer the trade secret may also provide an indication whether it is readily ascertainable. Reverse engineering is the process of starting with a publicly available product and working backwards by examining the product to find out how it was developed or what it comprises, and thereby discovering whatever secret information is embodied in the product.[11] With respect to the readily ascertainable element of trade secrets, the time it takes to reverse engineer a product is an accepted factor for determining whether information is readily ascertainable.[12] Further, even where reverse engineering could uncover the information in question, it has been held that the information is still not readily ascertainable unless reverse engineering quickly reveals the information.[13] In this regard, the more complex and detailed the trade secret information is, the less likely it will be classified as readily ascertainable. While reverse engineering a product may reveal, for example, certain dimensional attributes, it likely cannot uncover tolerances or

---

[7]Jostens, Inc. v. National Computer Systems, Inc., 318 N.W.2d 691, 700, 214 U.S.P.Q. 918, 33 U.C.C. Rep. Serv. 1642, 30 A.L.R.4th 1229 (Minn. 1982).

[8]Motorola, Inc. v. Fairchild Camera & Instrument Corp., 366 F. Supp. 1173, 1189, 177 U.S.P.Q. 614, 1973-1 Trade Cas. (CCH) ¶ 74402 (D. Ariz. 1973).

[9]Restatement (Third) of Unfair Competition § 39 cmt. f (1995); see, e.g., Medinol Ltd. v. Boston Scientific Corp., 346 F. Supp. 2d 575, R.I.C.O. Bus. Disp. Guide (CCH) ¶ 10813 (S.D. N.Y. 2004) (stent and its blueprint were not protectable trade secrets under New York law because the product was already public).

[10]Celeritas Technologies, Ltd. v. Rockwell Intern. Corp., 150 F.3d 1354, 1358, 47 U.S.P.Q.2d 1516 (Fed. Cir. 1998) (information contained in a modem is nonetheless a protectable trade secret because it is not readily ascertainable on inspection).

[11]U.T.S.A. § 1(4)(i) (1985).

[12]ILG Industries, Inc. v. Scott, 49 Ill. 2d 88, 94, 273 N.E.2d 393, 396, 171 U.S.P.Q. 371 (1971).

[13]Electro-Craft, 332 N.W.2d at 899-900.

manufacturing techniques.[14] Therefore, by defining the trade secret as dimensional tolerances or manufacturing techniques as opposed to actual dimensions, the trade secret destroying effects of reverse engineering can be avoided.

§ 12:9   Elements of a trade secret—Reasonable efforts to maintain secrecy

Research References

West's Key Number Digest, Antitrust and Trade Regulation ⊙⇒417

The final element for trade secret protection requires the owner to establish that reasonable efforts were employed to maintain the secrecy of the information. Fundamental to the existence of the trade secret is that it be, in fact, secret.[1] This entails a number of factual inquiries. As a starting point, this factor does not require the owner to maintain absolute secrecy over its information; only partial secrecy or qualified secrecy is required.[2] Furthermore, a trade secret is not lost by being confidentially disclosed to agents or employees without whose assistance the information could not be made of any value.[3]

Whether a person or company has employed reasonable steps to maintain secrecy varies in each case. Some factors, however, appear on a relatively consistent basis:

- having a practice of keeping secret documents in locked files,[4]
- providing guarded entrances to a plant,[5]
- restricting visitors and requiring badges for all employees,[6]
- using nondisclosure agreements with sub-contractors,[7] and
- incorporating a system of passwords to protect secrecy of software code.[8]

Importantly, the owner of an asserted trade secret must actually enforce its secrecy steps. It is not enough to have only a subjective intent to treat something as secret.[9]

When reviewing these secrecy steps, the precautions taken

---

[14]SI Handling Sys., 753 F.2d at 1256.

[Section 12:9]

[1]Kewanee Oil, 416 U.S. at 475.

[2]Electro-Craft, 332 N.W.2d at 901.

[3]Surgidev, 648 F. Supp. at 692.

[4]Surgidev, 648 F. Supp. at 693.

[5]Electro-Craft, 332 N.W.2d at 902.

[6]Sigma Chemical Co. v. Harris, 794 F.2d 371, 374, 230 U.S.P.Q. 322 (8th Cir. 1986).

[7]Pioneer Hi-Bred Intern. v. Holden Foundation Seeds, Inc., 35 F.3d 1226, 1236, 31 U.S.P.Q.2d 1385, 39 Fed. R. Evid. Serv. 993 (8th Cir. 1994).

[8]Trandes Corp. v. Guy F. Atkinson Co., 996 F.2d 655, 27 U.S.P.Q.2d 1014 (4th Cir. 1993).

[9]Arco Indus., 633 F.2d at 443.

must be reasonable under the circumstances.[10] Companies need not "guard against the unanticipated, the undetectable, or the unpreventable methods of espionage now available" or create an "impenetrable fortress."[11] For example, in one instance, a defendant used an aerial reconnaissance flight to view the plaintiff's confidential plant design during construction of the plant. The court held that "reasonable precautions" did not require the trade secret owner to provide security against such actions.[12]

§ 12:10   Confidentiality agreements—Employee agreements

Research References

West's Key Number Digest, Contracts ⊙118; Labor and Employment ⊙304
C.J.S., Contracts §§ 249 to 254, 257 to 260, 267 to 268

Trade secret misappropriation cases are decidedly fact specific. Certain types of information, such as customer lists, may be protectable in one case, but not in another.[1] Similarly, a defendant's actions in one case may constitute misappropriation, whereas those same actions will not impose liability in another.[2] In light of this, owners of trade secrets must take steps to maximize their ability to protect their trade secrets, including security measures, document handling policies, and specific identification of trade secrets.[3] Another important procedure is the regular use of confidentiality, or nondisclosure, agreements.

One area such agreements are often used is in the employer-employee context. Employers often require employees to sign a confidentiality agreement as a condition of employment. Confidentiality agreements serve several purposes. First, confidentiality agreements put the employee on notice of what information the employer considers a trade secret.[4] Further, signed confidentiality agreements are evidence of reasonable steps to maintain

---

[10]Pioneer, 35 F.3d at 1235-36 (8th Cir. 1994).

[11]E. I. duPont deNemours & Co. v. Christopher, 431 F.2d 1012, 1016-17, 166 U.S.P.Q. 421 (5th Cir. 1970).

[12]E.I. duPont deNemours & Co., 431 F.2d at 1017.

[Section 12:10]

[1]Telerate Systems, Inc. v. Caro, 689 F. Supp. 221, 231, 8 U.S.P.Q.2d 1740 (S.D. N.Y. 1988).

[2]Restatement (Third) of Unfair Competition § 38 cmt. b (1995).

[3]U.T.S.A. § 1 cmt. a (1985); Restatement (Third) of Unfair Competition § 39 cmt. g (1995).

[4]Aries Information Systems, Inc. v. Pacific Management Systems Corp., 366 N.W.2d 366, 369, 226 U.S.P.Q. 440, 53 A.L.R.4th 1037 (Minn. Ct. App. 1985).

secrecy.[5] Finally, confidentiality agreements provide the employer with a breach of contract claim, in addition to a trade secret misappropriation claim.[6] Proof of a legally protectable trade secret is not required for a breach of contract claim.[7] Thus, a confidentiality agreement may protect information revealed to an employee during the course of his or her employment that does not otherwise constitute a trade secret.[8]

Of course, any breach of contract claim is limited by the language of the contract. If the confidentiality agreement prohibits an employee from disclosing an employer's "trade secrets," and the term "trade secrets" is left undefined, courts will look to previous decisions regarding how a "trade secret" is legally defined.[9]

Different states have different rules with respect to construction requirements for confidentiality agreements. In general, a promise of at-will employment is adequate consideration for an employee's agreement to keep an employer's information confidential.[10] The majority of courts recognize that a confidentiality agreement which is unlimited as to time and geography is enforceable.[11] Because trade secrets can exist indefinitely, so long as they are kept secret,[12] a confidentiality agreement through which the owner maintains that secrecy must also be indefinite.

From a trade secret owner's perspective, a confidentiality clause should be drafted broadly. In other words, the confidentiality clause should not be limited to "trade secrets" as defined by the Restatement (First) of Torts § 757 or the UTSA. Parties are entitled to enter into contracts by which they agree not to use or disclose confidential information, even though the information may not qualify as a trade secret.[13] Thus, a confidentiality clause should purport to prevent the disclosure of any "confidential information" as so defined by the information's owner.

---

[5]Restatement (Third) of Unfair Competition § 39 cmt. g (1995).

[6]Restatement (First) of Torts § 757 cmt. b (1939).

[7]E. I. Du Pont De Nemours Powder Co. v. Masland, 244 U.S. 100, 102, 37 S. Ct. 575, 576 (1917).

[8]AMP Inc. v. Fleischhacker, 823 F.2d 1199, 1201, 3 I.E.R. Cas. (BNA) 73, 3 U.S.P.Q.2d 1421, 8 Fed. R. Serv. 3d 600 (7th Cir. 1987).

[9]Cherne Indus., Inc. v. Grounds & Associates, Inc., 278 N.W.2d 81, 89-90, 205 U.S.P.Q. 854 (Minn. 1979); Uniroyal Goodrich Tire Co. v. Hudson, 873 F. Supp. 1037, 1040 (E.D. Mich.

1994), judgment aff'd, 97 F.3d 1452 (6th Cir. 1996).

[10]Ackerman v. Kimball Intern., Inc., 652 N.E.2d 507, 509, 11 I.E.R. Cas. (BNA) 153 (Ind. 1995); PepsiCo, Inc. v. Redmond, 54 F.3d 1262, 1271, 10 I.E.R. Cas. (BNA) 1089, 35 U.S.P. Q.2d 1010 (7th Cir. 1995).

[11]Larx Co. v. Nicol, 224 Minn. 1, 28 N.W.2d 705, 711, 71 U.S.P.Q. 115 (1946).

[12]See § 12:1, infra.

[13]Concept, Inc. v. Thermotemp, Inc., 553 So. 2d 1325, 1327 (Fla. Dist. Ct. App. 2d Dist. 1989).

Many employment contracts will contain a noncompete clause in addition to the confidentiality clause. Unless specifically worded otherwise, the confidentiality clause will be read independently of the noncompete clause.[14] The obligations imposed by each clause are separate and distinct. Thus, a noncompete clause which incorporates geographic and/or time limitations should not be read into the confidentiality clause, which can and should be indefinite in duration.[15] Conversely, a court may choose not to enforce a noncompete agreement if the court finds that the agreement is overbroad and unduly infringes on the employee's ability to pursue work in his or her chosen field.[16]

When dealing with independent contractors, all employees of the independent contractor should be subject to a confidentiality agreement.[17] A confidentiality agreement by which the independent contractor agrees not to disclose confidential information, may not bind the independent contractor's employees. At least one case has held that an independent contractor's employees are free to use confidential information disclosed to their company without violating the confidentiality clause signed by the independent contractor.[18]

§ 12:11 Confidentiality agreements—Implied duty of confidentiality

Research References

West's Key Number Digest, Labor and Employment ⟨⟩304 to 308

A written contract provides the best evidence of a confidentiality agreement.[1] However, in the employer-employee context, a duty of confidentiality has been held to be an implied term of employment.[2] Even though an employment contract contains no express covenant not to disclose, employees have, in any event, an implied duty not to disclose.[3]

In addition to the employer-employee relationship, other circumstances may create a relationship of trust and confidence

---

[14]Uniroyal Goodrich Tire, 873 F. Supp. at 1044.

[15]Uniroyal Goodrich Tire, 873 F. Supp. at 1044.

[16]NanoMech, Inc. v. Suresh, 777 F.3d 1020, 39 I.E.R. Cas. (BNA) 1317, 113 U.S.P.Q.2d 1699, 165 Lab. Cas. (CCH) P 61563 (8th Cir. 2015).

[17]Composite Marine Propellers, 962 F.2d at 1265.

[18]Composite Marine Propellers, 962 F.2d at 1265.

[Section 12:11]

[1]Extrin Foods, Inc. v. Leighton, 202 Misc. 592, 598, 115 N.Y.S.2d 429, 434, 93 U.S.P.Q. 457 (Sup 1952).

[2]Extrin Foods, 115 N.Y.S.2d at 434.

[3]Extrin Foods, 115 N.Y.S.2d at 434.

from which an implied duty of confidentiality will arise.[4] For example, where an inventor discloses an invention to a company and informs that company that the information is confidential, a duty to maintain that confidentiality may arise.[5] When a manufacturer actively solicits disclosure from an inventor, an implied duty may arise.[6] Similarly, where the inventor makes clear that the disclosure is part of a course of negotiations aimed at creating a licensing agreement or entering into a similar business transaction, a duty may be implied.[7] Simple disclosure, however, without any of these circumstances, will not create an implied duty of confidentiality.[8]

An implied duty of confidentiality may also arise where one party loans a product containing trade secret information to another solely for purposes of testing or evaluation.[9] When the product, and thus the confidential information, is disclosed in this manner, an implied duty to preserve the confidentiality will arise.[10] Similarly, when trade secrets are disclosed during commercial negotiations for purchase of a business, a duty of confidentiality may be implied by law.[11]

§ 12:12   Ownership of a trade secret—Employee work and submissions

Research References

West's Key Number Digest, Labor and Employment ⬤304 to 308, 311, 312

A company's trade secret and/or confidential information is ultimately developed by its employees. The vast majority of inventors in the United States today are employed with an obligation to assign.[1] It is now generally accepted that work performed by that employee, and thus any and all resulting "confidential infor-

---

[4]Julie Research Laboratories, Inc. v. Select Photographic Engineering, Inc., 810 F. Supp. 513, 520 (S.D. N.Y. 1992), judgment aff'd in part, vacated in part, 998 F.2d 65, 27 U.S.P. Q.2d 1394 (2d Cir. 1993).

[5]Phillips v. Avis, Inc., 1995 WL 417587 (N.D. Ill. 1995); Goldberg v. Medtronic, Inc., 686 F.2d 1219, 1226, 216 U.S.P.Q. 89 (7th Cir. 1982).

[6]Smith v. Dravo Corp., 203 F.2d 369, 376, 97 U.S.P.Q. 98 (7th Cir. 1953).

[7]Smith v. Snap-On Tools Corp., 833 F.2d 578, 580, 5 U.S.P.Q.2d 1122

(5th Cir. 1987).

[8]Snap-On Tools, 833 F.2d at 580.

[9]Mineral Deposits Ltd. v. Zigan, 773 P.2d 606, 608 (Colo. App. 1988).

[10]Mineral Deposits, 773 P.2d at 608.

[11]Dravo, 203 F.2d at 376 (applying Pennsylvania law).

[Section 12:12]

[1]*See* Ingersoll-Rand Co. v. Ciavatta, 110 N.J. 609, 624, 542 A.2d 879, 886, 3 I.E.R. Cas. (BNA) 1285, 8 U.S.P.Q.2d 1537 (1988).

mation" is owned by the employer.[2] Thus, an employee is normally not free to use trade secret information he or she developed for an employer after the employment relationship has ended.

For example, in *Dionne v. Southeast Foam Converting & Packaging, Inc.*,[3] the plaintiff filed suit to enjoin the defendant, a former employee, from using confidential information allegedly owned by the plaintiff. The defendant denied liability for misappropriation, stating that he had personally developed the information in question and was therefore free to use it. The court rejected this argument.[4] The defendant had developed the trade secret information while employed by the plaintiff and therefore the plaintiff-employer was the owner of the trade secret information. The court noted that the defendant had signed a confidentiality agreement, placing him on notice of the confidential nature of information developed.[5]

Under the common law of trade secrets, where an employer pays an employee to create an invention, the employer owns that invention or ideas which meet the definition of a trade secret.[6] Where an employee creates exactly what he or she was employed to create, ownership of what is created is with the employer.[7] However, questions do arise where an employee invents something on his or her own time, which the common law regards as property of the employee who conceived, developed and perfected it.[8]

As an alternative to giving an employer outright ownership of trade secret information developed by an employee, some courts instead create "shop rights" to the information. The shop rights doctrine has its origin in patent law.[9] Where an employee during his or her hours of employment, working with his or her employer's materials and equipment, conceives and perfects an invention for which he or she obtains a patent, he or she must accord the employer a nonexclusive right to practice the invention.[10] The shop right is based on the employer's presumed contribution

---

[2]Ingersoll-Rand, 542 A.2d at 886.

[3]Dionne v. Southeast Foam Converting & Packaging, Inc., 240 Va. 297, 397 S.E.2d 110, 17 U.S.P.Q.2d 1565 (1990).

[4]Dionne, 397 S.E.2d at 113.

[5]Dionne, 397 S.E.2d at 114.

[6]Computer Associates Intern., Inc. v. American Fundware, Inc., 831 F. Supp. 1516, 1524, 1993-2 Trade Cas. (CCH) ¶ 70477 (D. Colo. 1993).

[7]United Centrifugal Pumps v. Cusimano, 9 U.S.P.Q.2d 1171, 1988 WL 1091936 (W.D. Ark. 1988) (*citing* Solomons v. U.S., 26 Ct. Cl. 620, 137 U.S. 342, 11 S. Ct. 88 (1890)).

[8]Ingersoll-Rand, 542 A.2d at 885.

[9]Ingersoll-Rand, 542 A.2d at 886.

[10]U.S. v. Dubilier Condenser Corporation, 289 U.S. 178, 188, 53 S. Ct. 554, 558, 17 U.S.P.Q. 154, 85 A.L.R. 1488 (1933), decision amended, 289 U.S. 706, 53 S. Ct. 687 (1933) (deleting one paragraph concerning lack of validity of assignments to United States government).

to the invention through materials, time and equipment.[11]

Some courts have used this shop right approach to provide employers the right to use trade secret information developed by an employee after that employee has left the employer.[12] In determining whether an employer has outright ownership of trade secret information or simply a shop right to use that information, courts have looked at the purposes of employment.[13] Where an employee is hired for the express purpose of creating specific inventions or is directed to devote his or her talents to development of inventions, the resulting inventions are owned by the employer. Conversely, if employment is on general terms, a court is more likely to invoke the shop right approach.[14] In this regard, employment contracts are normally quite helpful in establishing employer ownership of employee creations.

Because the common law doctrines are somewhat vague in defining the rights of employers and employees to an employee's invention, most employers use written contracts to allocate invention rights.[15] Several states have adopted statues which essentially restrict the instances in which an employer can compel assignment of an employee's invention, effectuating a balance between the interests of the parties involved. For example, Minnesota Statutes § 181.78 provides:

> Any provision in an employment agreement which provides that an employee shall assign or offer to assign any of the employee's rights in an invention to the employer shall not apply to an invention for which no equipment, supplies, facility or trade secret information of the employer was used and which was developed entirely on the employee's own time, and (1) which does not relate (a) directly to the business of the employer or (b) to the employer's actual or demonstrably anticipated research or development, or (2) which does not result from any work performed by the employee for the employer. Any provision which purports to apply to such an invention is to that extent against the public policy of this state and is to that extent void and unenforceable.[16]

Other states have adopted similar rules.[17] Notably, these statutes are directed toward assignment of inventions for patent

---

[11]California Eastern Laboratories, Inc. v. Gould, 896 F.2d 400, 402, 13 U.S.P.Q.2d 1984, 1990-1 Trade Cas. (CCH) ¶ 68923 (9th Cir. 1990).

[12]Ingersoll-Rand, 542 A.2d at 885–892 (discussing "holdover agreement" validity).

[13]Pursche v. Atlas Scraper & Engineering Co., 300 F.2d 467, 484, 132 U.S.P.Q. 104, 5 Fed. R. Serv. 2d 275 (9th Cir. 1961).

[14]Pursche, 300 F.2d at 485.

[15]Jamesbury Corp. v. Worcester Valve Co., 443 F.2d 205, 214, 170 U.S.P.Q. 177 (1st Cir. 1971).

[16]Minn. Stat. § 181.78(1).

[17]California (Cal. Lab. Code § 2870); Delaware (19 Del. C. § 805); Illinois (765 Ill. Comp. Stat. § 1060/2); Kansas (K.S.A. § 44-130); North Carolina (N.C. Gen. Stat. § 66-57.1); and Washington (Wash. Rev. Code Ann.

purposes, but can be applied to a trade secret analysis.[18] Other courts have expressed doubt as to whether the shop right doctrine applies to trade secrets.[19]

§ 12:13 Ownership of a trade secret—Non-employee submissions

Research References

West's Key Number Digest, Antitrust and Trade Regulation ⊗420

To develop new materials, products and/or manufacturing techniques, most companies rely upon their own employees. Companies often invest heavily in research and development for new products or improvements of existing products. However, even with this investment, not every useful idea can be conceived or developed by a company. Individuals, unassociated with a particular company, will invent or think of new products or improvements to existing products. Normally, these individuals do not have the manufacturing or monetary resources to develop their ideas, and instead submit them to an applicable company for use. When the individual, for whatever reason, does not have patent protection for the invention, questions as to ownership will arise depending upon how this submission is made.

For example, an independent mechanic may come up with a new design for a hand tool. Unable to manufacture this new tool on his or her own, the inventor may approach a large tool company with the idea. If the inventor submits the idea without any nondisclosure or confidentiality agreements, his or her trade secret rights to the invention may be lost. However, the inventor can preserve his or her trade secret rights by requiring the manufacturer to execute a confidentiality agreement of some type. These agreements normally provide that the manufacturer can not disclose and/or use the trade secret information submitted by the inventor without consent.

The risks associated with submitting an idea without a confidentiality agreement are exemplified in *Bank Travel Bank v. McCoy*.[1] There, the plaintiff developed what he believed to be a unique idea for combining the services of a bank and travel agency in arranging and financing vacation travel. The plaintiff

§ 49.44.140).

[18]Eaton Corp. v. Giere, 971 F.2d 136, 7 I.E.R. Cas. (BNA) 1077, 23 U.S.P.Q.2d 1705 (8th Cir. 1992) (applying Minnesota statute in context of trade secret).

[19]United Centrifugal Pumps v. Cusimano, 9 U.S.P.Q.2d 1171, 1988 WL 1091936 (W.D. Ark. 1988).

[Section 12:13]

[1]Bank Travel Bank v. McCoy, 802 F. Supp. 1358 (E.D. N.C. 1992), order aff'd, 4 F.3d 984 (4th Cir. 1993).

submitted this idea to the defendant. This submission did not contain a confidentiality requirement and in fact explicitly waived any "cost or obligation" on the defendant's part. The court rejected the plaintiff's claim of trade secret misappropriation because a disclosure, without any attempt to insure the information's confidentiality, voids any claim to trade secret protection.[2]

When submitting an idea to a company, a confidential agreement must be used. Notably, the inventor should have the agreement executed prior to submitting the invention. As a practical matter, companies are hesitant to sign confidentiality agreements and, in many cases, to receive invention submissions. The reason for this reluctance is relatively straight forward. Often times, a company's own engineers are working on inventions similar to the one submitted. When that product comes out on the market, the company will want to avoid a lawsuit related to misappropriation for an invention it had created on its own.

§ 12:14　Ownership of a trade secret—Termination of employment

Research References

West's Key Number Digest, Contracts ⊂⟩118; Labor and Employment ⊂⟩304

C.J.S., Contracts §§ 249 to 254, 257 to 260, 267 to 268

Skills developed by an employee during a term of employment are not "owned" by the employer. Therefore, while an employer's technical information is protectable, the general skills and knowledge acquired by an employee during the course of employment are not.[1] The right of an employee to take general skills and knowledge with him or her is the result of a balancing between employee's rights and employer's rights.[2] Public policy recognizes that employees should be free to move from employer to employer as part of vigorous business competition.[3] Therefore, the concept of trade secret will not cover a person's aptitude, skill, dexterity, manual and mental ability, and such other subjective knowledge obtained while in the course of employment.[4]

While the rule that an employee is free to use general skills and knowledge is, for the most part, straight forward, it does present some problems in application. For example, in *Stampede Tool Warehouse, Inc. v. May*, the court examined whether a

---

[2]Bank Travel, 802 F. Supp. at 1360.

[Section 12:14]

[1]Salsbury Lab., 908 F.2d at 713.

[2]AMP, 823 F.2d at 1205.

[3]Morlife, Inc. v. Perry, 56 Cal. App. 4th 1514, 66 Cal. Rptr. 2d 731, 735, 13 I.E.R. Cas. (BNA) 291, 45 U.S.P.Q.2d 1741 (1st Dist. 1997).

[4]SI Handling Sys., 753 F.2d at 1255.

customer list constituted a protectable trade secret.[5] The defendant, a former employee, took the plaintiff's customer list prior to leaving employment. The court noted that while general knowledge cannot be a trade secret, the general knowledge in this case was the method the employees used in finding perspective customers, not the actual customer list. Therefore, while the ex-employee was free to "take" his knowledge of how to create a customer list, the customer list itself was protected.[6]

Thus, skills and knowledge acquired by an employee during employment cannot be left behind, so long as those things exist within the mind of the employee.[7] All that knowledge, skill and information, except separate trade secrets specifically designated by the employer, become a part of the employee's equipment for the transaction of any business subsequent to leaving employment.[8]

§12:15 Losing trade secret rights through public disclosure—Sale of products incorporating secret information

Research References

West's Key Number Digest, Antitrust and Trade Regulation ⊶419

Public use or sale of a product alleged to be a trade secret "totally precludes" a plaintiff's claim for trade secret protection.[1] Similarly, where a trade secret defendant purchases a product from the plaintiff, trade secret law cannot prevent that same defendant from reverse engineering or dissecting that product to ascertain allegedly trade secret information.[2] The reason for this rule is that to allow an individual or company to sell an unpatented product to the public, but then to later claim trade secret protection for that product, would improperly permit state law to circumvent the U.S. patent law.[3] A converse holding would essentially prohibit reverse engineering whereby a party starts with the known product and works backwards to discern the process by which it was manufactured or its constituent parts.[4]

Where a misappropriation claim is premised on a violation of

[5]272 Ill.App.3d 580, 209 Ill.Dec. 281, 651 N.E.2d 209 (Ill. App. 1995).

[6]Stampede, 651 N.E.2d at 217.

[7]Curtis 1000, Inc. v. Pierce, 905 F. Supp. 898, 901-02 (D. Kan. 1995).

[8]Curtis 1000, 905 F. Supp. at 901–02.

[Section 12:15]

[1]Ring v. Estee Lauder, Inc., 874 F.2d 109, 110, 10 U.S.P.Q.2d 1796 (2d Cir. 1989).

[2]Roboserve, Ltd. v. Tom's Foods, Inc., 940 F.2d 1441, 1445, 20 U.S.P.Q.2d 1321, 16 U.C.C. Rep. Serv. 2d 987 (11th Cir. 1991).

[3]Bonito Boats, 489 U.S. at 160.

[4]Bonito Boats, 489 U.S. at 160.

confidence, a public disclosure does not necessarily preclude protection. For example, where a defendant is supplied confidential information regarding a plaintiff's product from the plaintiff under circumstances whereby the defendant knew of the confidential nature, subsequent sales of the product by the plaintiff will not hinder the plaintiff's claim for a breach of fiduciary duty.[5]

§ 12:16   Losing trade secret rights through public disclosure—Disclosure in patent or copyrights

Research References

West's Key Number Digest, Antitrust and Trade Regulation ☞419

Anything that is disclosed in a patent is public knowledge and cannot be claimed as a trade secret.[1] Thus, a general principle exists that trade secret rights terminate upon the issuance of a patent which reveals the information upon which a trade secret is allegedly established.[2] A party may obtain patent protection for a particular product, and then prevent others from making, using or selling that product. However, the specification associated with that product patent will disclose the manner and process of making that particular product.[3] When the patent application publishes or the patent issues, this method of manufacturing as disclosed in the specification is then in the public domain, and can no longer be claimed as a trade secret.[4] After the patent expires, the method of manufacturing is free for all to use.[5] However, a trade secret claim for a pending application is extinguished only when the patent application publishes or the patent issues. Therefore, a party may be liable for trade secret misappropriation for the period of time before the patent application publishes or the patent issues, and for patent infringement after the patent issues.[6]

In a related context, trade secret protection appears to be unavailable for copyrighted materials. Copyright protection requires one to deposit the material with the Library of Congress.[7] These deposits are subject to public inspection, and therefore are in the

---

[5]Classic Instruments, Inc. v. VDO-Argo Instruments, Inc., 73 Or. App. 732, 753, 700 P.2d 677, 694, 226 U.S.P.Q. 894 (1985).

[Section 12:16]

[1]Coenco, Inc. v. Coenco Sales, Inc., 940 F.2d 1176, 1179 n.3 (8th Cir. 1991); Rototron Corp. v. Lake Shore Burial Vault Co., Inc., 712 F.2d 1214, 1215, 220 U.S.P.Q. 169 (7th Cir. 1983).

[2]Stutz Motor Car of America, Inc. v. Reebok Intern., Ltd., 909 F. Supp.

1353, 1359, 38 U.S.P.Q.2d 1253 (C.D. Cal. 1995), decision aff'd, 113 F.3d 1258 (Fed. Cir. 1997).

[3]35 U.S.C.A. § 112.

[4]35 U.S.C.A. § 112.

[5]Arco Indus., 633 F.2d at 443.

[6]Stutz Motor Car of America, 909 F. Supp. at 1360.

[7]17 U.S.C.A. § 407.

public domain.[8] However, at least one court has held that copyright protection, or more particularly an application for copyright, does not preclude trade secret protection absent evidence that anyone in the public ever reviewed or inspected the documents deposited by the plaintiff.[9] This is likely an exception rather than the rule. However, trade secrets in computer software have been found to coexist with copyright registrations in a few cases, because software often has its own category of treatment and is exempted from complete disclosure under the Copyright Act.[10]

§ 12:17 Losing trade secret rights through public disclosure—Other forms of disclosure

Research References

West's Key Number Digest, Antitrust and Trade Regulation ☞419

Disclosing a product incorporating trade secret information to the government without any requirement of confidentiality will result in loss of trade secret rights.[1] However, where the disclosure is required and the government maintains the information in confidence from the general public, trade secret rights are not lost.[2] If information is claimed to be a trade secret but required to be disclosed by a regulatory law, the loss of secrecy may result in a finding that the regulatory law is a taking under the Fifth Amendment of the United States Constitution.[3] As with other forms of property, specific laws cannot destroy property interests. A law requiring that the owner disclose the trade secret to the government, which is in turn required to disclose the information to the public upon request, destroys the secrecy, and thus the value of the trade secret. In such a case, an analysis must be conducted to determine if a regulatory law results in a taking.[4]

In addition to purposeful sale of a product, the mere inadvertent or accidental disclosure of trade secret information results in loss of protection.[5] But not all states have expressly adopted this rule. For example, the court in *B.C. Ziegler and Co. v. Ehren*

---

[8]17 U.S.C.A. § 705.

[9]Murray, 582 N.E.2d at 1130.

[10]Tedder Boat Ramp Systems, Inc. v. Hillsborough County, Fla., 54 F. Supp. 2d 1300, 1303, 51 U.S.P.Q.2d 1683 (M.D. Fla. 1999).

[Section 12:17]

[1]Secure Services Technology, Inc. v. Time and Space Processing Inc., 722

F. Supp. 1354, 1361, 12 U.S.P.Q.2d 1617, 36 Cont. Cas. Fed. (CCH) P 75764 (E.D. Va. 1989).

[2]Boeing, 738 P.2d at 675.

[3]Philip Morris, Inc. v. Reilly, 312 F.3d 24, 47, 65 U.S.P.Q.2d 1065 (1st Cir. 2002).

[4]Philip Morris, 312 F.3d at 47.

[5]Julie Research Lab., 810 F. Supp. at 520.

decided that accidental disclosure did not negate trade secret protection under Wisconsin law. There, the defendant misappropriated the plaintiff's trade secret customer list by reconstructing shredded papers discarded by the plaintiff. This inadvertent disclosure by the plaintiff did not recuse the defendant from the claim of misappropriation of trade secrets.[6]

Finally, where a third party other than the plaintiff also has the information upon which the trade secret claim is based, trade secret protection can be lost.[7] To maintain the trade secret claim, the plaintiff must keep that information secret.[8] However, if the third party does not protect the information as confidential, and instead discloses it freely, trade secret protection is lost.[9]

§ 12:18   Misappropriation of trade secrets—Elements of a misappropriation claim

Research References

West's Key Number Digest, Antitrust and Trade Regulation ☞410

The Restatement (First) of Torts does not explicitly state that improper acquisition of a trade secret is actionable. Instead, the Restatement (First) of Torts focuses upon disclosure or use of another's trade secret:

> one who discloses or uses another's trade secret, without a privilege to do so, is liable to the other if * * *
>
> (b) his disclosure or use constitutes a breach of confidence reposed in him by the other in disclosing the secret to him, or
>
> (c) he learned the secret from a third person with notice of the facts that it was a secret and * * * that the third person's disclosure of it was otherwise a breach of his duty to the other * * * *[1]

The Restatement (Third) of Unfair Competition enhances this definition of misappropriation. Section 40 of the Restatement (Third) of Unfair Competition divides misappropriation of trade secrets into two areas. First, one is subject to liability for misappropriation of another's trade secret if that person acquires information, that he or she knows or should know is the other's trade secret, by means that are improper.[2] Second, a person is subject to liability for the misappropriation of another's trade secret if he

---

[6]B.C. Ziegler and Co. v. Ehren, 141 Wis. 2d 19, 414 N.W.2d 48, 53 (Ct. App. 1987).

[7]SI Handling Sys., 753 F.2d at 1259.

[8]SI Handling Sys., 753 F.2d at 1259.

[9]SI Handling Sys., 753 F.2d at 1259.

[Section 12:18]

[1]Restatement (First) of Torts § 757 (1939).

[2]Restatement (Third) of Unfair Competition § 40(a) (1995).

or she improperly uses or discloses the other's trade secret without the other's consent, when the trade secret was brought to his or her attention through a confidential relationship, was acquired by improper means, was acquired from another who was in breach of a confidential relationship, or was disclosed by accident or mistake.[3]

The UTSA's definition of trade secret misappropriation is quite similar to that of the Restatement (Third) of Unfair Competition.[4] The UTSA defines improper acquisition, disclosure or use as acts of misappropriation. Misappropriation includes:

(i) Acquisition of a trade secret of another by a person who knows or has a reason to know that the trade secret was acquired by improper means; or

(ii) Disclosure or use of a trade secret of another without express or implied consent by a person who

(A) Used improper means to acquire knowledge of the trade secret; or

(B) At the time of disclosure or use, knew or had reason to know that his knowledge of the trade secret was

(I) Derived from or through a person who had utilized improper means to acquire it;

(II) Acquired under circumstances giving rise to a duty to maintain its secrecy or limit its use; or

(III) Derived from or through a person who owed a duty to the person seeking relief to maintain its secrecy or limit its use; or

(C) Before a material change of his position, knew or had reason to know that it was a trade secret and that knowledge of it had been acquired by accident or mistake.[5]

In this regard "improper means" is defined to include theft, bribery, misrepresentation, breach or inducement of a breach of a duty to maintain secrecy, or espionage through electronic or other means.[6]

In cases of misappropriation by a foreign entity, the International Trade Commission (ITC) is authorized to exclude imports where it finds "[u]nfair methods of competition and unfair acts in

---

[3]Restatement (Third) of Unfair Competition § 40(b) (1995).

[4]Restatement (Third) of Unfair Competition § 39 cmt. b (1995) The similarity between the Restatement (Third) of Unfair Competition and

U.T.S.A. is not surprising given the Restatement (Third) of Unfair Competition was drafted with the U.T.S.A. in mind.

[5]U.T.S.A. § 1(2) (1985).

[6]U.T.S.A. § 1(1) (1985).

the importation of articles . . . into the United States."[7] The ITC
outlines four elements of misappropriation of trade secrets:

> (1) the existence of a process that is protectable as a trade secret
> (*e.g.*, that is (a) of economic value, (b) not generally known or read-
> ily ascertainable, and (c) that the complainant has taken reason-
> able precautions to maintain its secrecy); (2) that the complainant
> is the owner of the trade secret; (3) that the complainant disclosed
> the trade secret to respondent while in a confidential relationship
> or that the respondent wrongfully took the trade secret by unfair
> means; and (4) that the respondent has used or disclosed the trade
> secret causing injury to the complainant.[8]

A trade secret may be misappropriated even if the defendant's
product is not identical to the product made with the alleged
trade secret. For example, under Minnesota law, if a trade secret
is sufficiently unique, emergence of similar, slightly altered product gives rise to inference of misappropriation.[9] Unlike in a patent case, the plaintiff need not prove that the defendant copied
or used each and every element of the trade secret.[10] Trade secret
misappropriation may be shown if the defendant created a new
product that the defendant could not have made without use of
the plaintiff's trade secret.[11] Further, a user of another's trade secret is liable for trade secret misappropriation, even though the
user modified or improved the trade secreted process, product, or
information, if the substance of the user's modified or improved
process, product, or information is derived from the trade secret.[12]

At least with respect to computer programs, claims of misappropriation of trade secrets that are based solely upon copying
may be found qualitatively equivalent to copyright infringement,
and are preempted by the Copyright Act.[13]

In general, the owner of a trade secret is not entitled to prevent
others from using public information to replicate his product, nor
may the owner prevent others from making similar products that

---

[7]19 U.S.C.A. § 1337.

[8]In the Matter of Certain Rubber
Resins & Processes for Mfg. Same
Comm'n Opinion, U.S.I.T.C. Inv. No.
337-TA-849, 2014 WL 7497801 (Int'l
Trade Comm'n 2014).

[9]Minn. Stat. § 325C.01, subd. 3;
Wyeth v. Natural Biologics, Inc., 395
F.3d 897, 900, 74 U.S.P.Q.2d 1852 (8th
Cir. 2005).

[10]Mangren Research and Development Corp. v. National Chemical Co.,
Inc., 87 F.3d 937, 944, 39 U.S.P.Q.2d

1339 (7th Cir. 1996).

[11]Mangren Research & Dev., 87
F.3d at 944.

[12]Reingold v. Swiftships, Inc., 126
F.3d 645, 651, 44 U.S.P.Q.2d 1481 (5th
Cir. 1997).

[13]Huckshold v. HSSL, L.L.C., 344
F. Supp. 2d 1203, 1209 (E.D. Mo. 2004)
(*citing* Dun & Bradstreet Software
Services, Inc. v. Grace Consulting, Inc.,
307 F.3d 197, 218, 64 U.S.P.Q.2d 1705
(3d Cir. 2002)).

are not derived from the trade secret.[14]

§ 12:19 Misappropriation of trade secrets—Acquisition by improper means

Research References

West's Key Number Digest, Antitrust and Trade Regulation ☞413

The key element in establishing misappropriation is that the trade secret was acquired through "improper means."[1] No bright-line test exists for determining whether means are improper under the UTSA Further, the Restatement (First) of Torts admits that "a complete catalog of improper means is not possible."[2] Generally, there are two main categories of improper means.[3] The first category is criminal acts, such as theft, fraud, breaking and entering, trespass, bribing and swindling.[4]

The second category includes acts which are taken to overcome measures put in place to maintain secrecy of the trade secret information, such as fraud, interference with contractual obligations, and breach of a contract in obtaining or using the trade secret.[5] The latter has been interpreted to include more than simply a breach of a past or present employment agreement. Breach of an implied contract, based upon unjust enrichment, has been held to be improper means.[6] Also, breach of an implied contract based on the fact that the trade secret information was taken and used under the knowledge that compensation was expected for the information has been held to constitute improper means.[7]

Improper means can also include conduct which is otherwise lawful, but is improper under the circumstances.[8] Companies devise elaborate schemes for discovering their competitor's trade secrets, which on their face are legal, but remain industrial espionage which will not be condoned by the courts.[9] For example, the act of bribing a patent draftsman to reproduce detailed draw-

---

[14]MicroStrategy Inc. v. Li, 268 Va. 249, 262, 601 S.E.2d 580, 588 (2004).

[Section 12:19]

[1]Restatement (First) of Torts § 757(a) (1939); U.T.S.A. § 1(2) (1985).

[2]Restatement (First) of Torts § 757 cmt. f (1939).

[3]Restatement (Third) of Unfair Competition § 43 cmt. c (1995).

[4]Restatement (Third) of Unfair Competition § 43 cmt. c (1995).

[5]Restatement (Third) of Unfair

Competition § 43 cmt. c (1995).

[6]Mitchell Novelty Co. v. United Mfg. Co., 199 F.2d 462, 465, 95 U.S.P.Q. 120 (7th Cir. 1952).

[7]Landsberg v. Scrabble Crossword Game Players, Inc., 802 F.2d 1193, 1196, 231 U.S.P.Q. 658 (9th Cir. 1986).

[8]U.T.S.A. § 1 cmt. (1985).

[9]See Tennant Co. v. Advance Mach. Co., Inc., 355 N.W.2d 720, 726 (Minn. Ct. App. 1984).

ings prepared for a competitor has been characterized as improper means.[10] Similarly, an airplane overflight used as aerial reconnaissance to determine a competitor's plant layout during construction of the plant was found to be improper.[11] In this vein, trade secret protection serves the purpose of maintaining commercial morality.[12]

§ 12:20 Misappropriation of trade secrets—Reverse engineering

Research References

West's Key Number Digest, Antitrust and Trade Regulation ⊙413

While the list of "improper means" is virtually endless, one particular method has been specifically identified as acceptable. Reverse engineering, that is, starting with a known product and working backward to define the process which aided in its developmental manufacture, is a proper means of acquiring another's trade secret information.[1] In fact, the Restatement (Third) of Unfair Competition specifically states that "independent discovery and analysis of publicly available products or information are not improper means of acquisition."[2]

There are two primary effects that reverse engineering has on trade secrets. First, if reverse engineering of a product can quickly reveal the alleged trade secrets, then that information is readily ascertainable and is not entitled to trade secret protection.[3] Conversely, if the trade secret cannot be revealed in a "reasonable period of time" by reverse engineering, then trade secret protection is possible.[4] However, even in the latter case, if the reverse engineering party eventually is able to ascertain the trade secret, it is not liable for misappropriation because reverse engineering is not an improper means of acquiring the trade secret.[5]

The fact that a party could eventually reverse engineer a trade secret will not preclude a finding of trade secret misappropriation

---

[10]A. H. Emery Co. v. Marcan Products Corp., 389 F.2d 11, 15, 156 U.S.P.Q. 529, 11 Fed. R. Serv. 2d 377 (2d Cir. 1968).

[11]E.I. duPont deNemours & Co., 431 F.2d at 1017.

[12]Pioneer, 35 F.3d at 1239.

[Section 12:20]

[1]Kewanee Oil, 416 U.S. at 477.

[2]Restatement (Third) of Unfair Competition § 43 (1995).

[3]Electro-Craft, 332 N.W.2d at 900 (holding that features which are not readily ascertainable by reverse engineering are protectable as a trade secret).

[4]U.T.S.A. § 1 cmt. (2007); Thermodyne Food Service Products, Inc. v. McDonald's Corp., 940 F. Supp. 1300, 1307, 40 U.S.P.Q.2d 1801 (N.D. Ill. 1996).

[5]U.T.S.A. § 1 cmt. (1985); Thermodyne Food Serv. Products, 940 F. Supp. at 1307.

if the trade secret is actually obtained using improper means.[6] Protection will be accorded to a trade secret holder against the disclosure or unauthorized use gained by improper means, even if others might have discovered the trade secret by reverse engineering.[7]

§ 12:21 Misappropriation of trade secrets—Disclosure or use without consent

Research References

West's Key Number Digest, Antitrust and Trade Regulation ⊙413

Under either the UTSA or § 757 of the Restatement (First) of Torts, disclosure or use of another's trade secret is actionable as misappropriation. Misappropriation by disclosure or use without consent often arises in situations where a confidential relationship of some type has been established, such as employer-employee or licensor-licensee.[1] In these situations, the party receiving trade secrets has a duty to maintain the confidentiality of that information.[2] When that same party instead discloses the trade secret information to another without consent of the trade secret owner, a misappropriation has occurred. For example, a former employee misappropriates his former employer's trade secret by disclosing technical trade secret data of his former employer.[3] Similarly, an insurance agency may enjoin a former employee from disclosing policy holder information.[4] It is not necessary that the defendant have physically taken a document on which the trade secret information is recorded. Misappropriation can occur where an employee memorizes a customer list and uses his or her memory of that list in competition with his or her ex-employer.[5]

"Use" of a trade secret is in no way limited to directly copying another's trade secret in the manufacture of a product. For example, where a company alters a competitor's trade secret, which it has wrongly obtained, that company will still be found to

---

[6]Reingold, 126 F.3d at 651.

[7]Reingold, 126 F.3d at 651.

[Section 12:21]

[1]Hyde Corp. v. Huffines, 158 Tex. 566, 576, 314 S.W.2d 763, 769, 117 U.S.P.Q. 44 (1958); Restatement (Third) of Unfair Competition § 41 cmt. b (1995).

[2]Restatement (Third) of Unfair Competition § 41 cmt. b, § 42 (1995).

[3]Syntex Ophthalmics, Inc. v. Novicky, 591 F. Supp. 28, 37, 221 U.S.P.Q. 860 (N.D. Ill. 1983), judgment aff'd, 745 F.2d 1423, 223 U.S.P.Q. 695 (Fed. Cir. 1984), cert. granted, judgment vacated on other grounds, 470 U.S. 1047, 105 S. Ct. 1740, 225 U.S.P.Q. 792 (1985).

[4]Prudential Ins. Co. of America v. Pochiro, 153 Ariz. 368, 371, 736 P.2d 1180, 1183 (Ct. App. Div. 2 1987).

[5]Stampede, 651 N.E.2d at 217.

have "used" another's trade secret.[6] A slight alteration of a competitor's protected secret implicates the same concerns as cases of outright misappropriation.[7]

Furthermore, "use" occurs when a party uses a competitor's trade secret information as a starting point for producing its own, competing product.[8] This point is important and often forms the basis of a misappropriation claim. The common scenario arises where a defendant utilizes a plaintiff's trade secret blue-prints or other design drawings to come up with an end product or process which is, on its face, different from the plaintiff's. While the end product or process may not, at first glance, embody any of the plaintiff's trade secret information, a use or misappropriation has nonetheless occurred.[9] For example, even though trade secret technology is never "incorporated" into defendant's product, a defendant who develops technology more quickly than would otherwise have been possible by using the technology will be guilty of trade secret misappropriation.[10] By starting from the plaintiff's information, the defendant has been able to the save time and expense endured by the plaintiff in arriving at a final design or process.[11] These savings are normally in the form of trial-and-error, where various parameters were tried and rejected by the trade secret creator, for different reasons. By skipping past these development steps, undertaken and essentially paid for by the plaintiff, the defendant will have gained an unfair advantage, thus constituting a use or misappropriation.[12]

Where a person discovered information or developed a procedure after sifting through vast quantities of potentially ineffective possibilities, a court will prevent competitors from even seeing the area from which the successful result was obtained. This type of analysis has been analogized to playing "Where's Waldo?"[13] In some cases, even an indication of the general portion of the puzzle area can greatly reduce the competitor's time to locate the results independently. In fact, even indicating that the competitor should be looking for "Waldo" might reveal too much information. It is unfair to permit someone to misappropriate the results of years of research and development.[14]

---

[6]Superior Flux & Mfg. Co. v. H&S Industries, Inc., 210 U.S.P.Q. 669, 670, 1980 WL 30229 (N.D. Ohio 1980).

[7]Pioneer, 35 F.3d at 1239.

[8]Salsbury Lab., 908 F.2d at 713.

[9]Pioneer, 35 F.3d at 1239.

[10]Foster-Miller, Inc. v. Babcock & Wilcox Canada, 210 F.3d 1, 12, 54

U.S.P.Q.2d 1193, 54 Fed. R. Evid. Serv. 453 (1st Cir. 2000).

[11]Murray, 582 N.E.2d at 1130.

[12]Murray, 582 N.E.2d at 1130.

[13]Alk Associates, Inc. v. Multimodal Applied Systems, Inc., 276 N.J. Super. 310, 647 A.2d 1359, 1363 (App. Div. 1994).

[14]Alk Assoc., 647 A.2d at 1363.

§ 12:22 Preparing to bring a trade secret misappropriation suit—Statute of limitations

Research References

West's Key Number Digest, Limitation of Actions ⚷32(1), 55(6), 95(7)

C.J.S., Limitations of Actions §§ 164, 176 to 179

Under the UTSA, an action for misappropriation of trade secrets must be brought within three years after the misappropriation is discovered, or within three years of when the misappropriation should have been discovered through the exercise of reasonable diligence. A continuing misappropriation constitutes a single claim.[1] One of the principal contributions of the UTSA is to establish a single statute of limitations for the various property, quasi-contractual, and violation of fiduciary relationship theories of noncontractual liability utilized in common law.[2] In adopting the UTSA, several states have modified the three-year limitation. Georgia, Illinois, and Missouri have adopted a five-year statute of limitations.[3] Maine, Nebraska and Ohio have adopted a four-year statute of limitations.[4]

When interpreting a statute of limitations issue, it must be remembered that misappropriation occurs when the potential defendant acquires trade secret information by improper means.[5] Therefore, a plaintiff should not wait to bring an action until after the defendant begins using or disclosing the trade secret. The statute of limitations may have already run.[6] In the case of disclosure of confidential information constituting a trade secret, a claim for misappropriation of trade secrets arises when the trade secret information is disclosed without the consent of its owner; however, the statute of limitations in a misappropriation suit does not begin to toll until the owner of the trade secret is made aware of the disclosure.[7] However, mere apprehension that a misappropriation is occurring is not enough to start the clock on the statute of limitations; it begins to run when the trade secret holder has knowledge of misuse.[8]

Prior to passage of the UTSA, there was conflicting authority as to whether trade secret misappropriation was a continuing

---

[Section 12:22]

[1]U.T.S.A. § 6 (1985).

[2]U.T.S.A. Prefatory Note (1985).

[3]Ga Code Ann. § 10-1-766; Il. St. Ch. 765 §§ 1065/7; Mo. St. 417.461.

[4]ME Stat. T. 10 § 1547; Neb. Rev. Stat. § 87-506; Ohio Rev. Code Ann. § 1333.66.

[5]See §§ 12:18 to 12:21, infra.

[6]AVCO Corp. v. Precision Air Parts, Inc., 676 F.2d 494, 497, 216 U.S.P.Q. 1086 (11th Cir. 1982).

[7]McLeod v. Northwest Alloys, Inc., 90 Wash. App. 30, 969 P.2d 1066, 1067, 46 U.S.P.Q.2d 1296 (Div. 3 1998).

[8]Sokol Crystal Products, Inc. v. DSC Communications Corp., 15 F.3d 1427, 1430, 29 U.S.P.Q.2d 1756 (7th Cir. 1994) (applying Wisconsin law).

wrong. For example, *Monolith Portland Midwest Co. v. Kaiser Aluminum & Chemical Corp.*,[9] found misappropriation not to be a continuing wrong under California law, with the statute of limitations beginning upon initial misappropriation. In contrast, *Underwater Storage, Inc. v. U.S. Rubber Co.*,[10] viewed trade secret misappropriation as a continuing wrong under general principles. The UTSA rejects the continuing wrong approach to the statute of limitations, but delays commencement of the limitation until the aggrieved party discovers or should reasonably have discovered the existence of the misappropriation.[11]

The issue of whether or not trade secret misappropriation is a continuing tort is an important distinction. Where misappropriation constitutes a continuing tort, the statute of limitations time period is effectively extended. Each new instance of misappropriation restarts the limitations period.[12] Where the continuing tort theory is not applied, the statute of limitations begins to run when the misappropriation first takes place or is first discovered.[13] It does not restart with subsequent acts of misappropriation.

The continuing tort or continuing harm theory has been extended to situations where the statute of limitations bars an action against a given defendant who misappropriates a party's trade secret outside of the limitations period, and then later misappropriates other trade secrets of that same party within the limitations period.[14]

Whether misappropriation constitutes a continuing wrong depends upon one's view of trade secrets. If trade secret law is viewed by a court as being premised upon the protection of confidential relationships, rather than protection of trade secrets as "property," then misappropriation is not a continuing harm. With the "confidential relationship" theory, parties who are victimized by breaches of confidential relationships are provided with a remedy.[15] When viewed in this manner, any misappropriation is a breach of that relationship, thus accruing the sole cause of action, regardless of what takes place between the parties

---

[9]Monolith Portland Midwest Co. v. Kaiser Aluminum & Chemical Corp., 407 F.2d 288, 160 U.S.P.Q. 577 (9th Cir. 1969).

[10]Underwater Storage, Inc. v. U.S. Rubber Co., 371 F.2d 950, 151 U.S.P.Q. 90 (D.C. Cir. 1966).

[11]U.T.S.A. § 6 cmt. (1985).

[12]Underwater Storage, 371 F.2d at 955.

[13]*See, e.g.,* U.T.S.A. § 6 cmt. (1985).

[14]Telex Corp. v. International Business Machines Corp., 367 F. Supp. 258, 360, 179 U.S.P.Q. 777, 1973-2 Trade Cas. (CCH) ¶ 74774 (N.D. Okla. 1973), judgment rev'd on other grounds, 510 F.2d 894, 184 U.S.P.Q. 521, 1975-1 Trade Cas. (CCH) ¶ 60127 (10th Cir. 1975).

[15]Monolith Portland Midwest Co. v. Kaiser Aluminum & Chemical Corp., 407 F.2d 288, 160 U.S.P.Q. 577 (9th Cir. 1969).

later in time.[16] A relatively obvious question with this theory arises in the context where no confidential relationship ever existed between the parties, such as where a company exercises "unethical" measures to steal a competitor's trade secrets.

In contrast, where trade secrets are viewed as property, the continuing tort theory prevails. Under the "trade secret as property" approach, a party could define a number of individual trade secrets or property items. Each time any one of these trade secrets or property items is stolen, a new cause of action would arise. The UTSA has explicitly rejected this approach, at least in terms of decreeing that the "continuing tort" approach will not apply. The UTSA apparently adopts a middle ground by starting the statute of limitations period only after the trade secret owner has discovered, or reasonably should have discovered, the misappropriation.[17]

New York state court decisions have developed their own interpretation of the continuing tort rule. When a defendant misappropriates and discloses a trade secret, he or she becomes liable upon disclosure. However, when the defendant keeps the secret confidential but uses the information to his or her commercial advantage, each successive use constitutes a new, actionable tort for the purpose of the running of the statute of limitations.[18] Thus, when a defendant publicly discloses another's confidential information, the cause of action accrues upon the date of that public disclosure. Similarly, the plaintiff may start the limitations period by openly marketing the product. The point, according to New York case law, is that once the information is no longer secret or confidential, there is no property to protect.[19]

§ 12:23 Preparing to bring a trade secret misappropriation suit—Pleadings

Research References

West's Key Number Digest, Antitrust and Trade Regulation ⚿428

The level of specificity required for pleadings depends on whether the jurisdiction uses "fact" pleading or "notice" pleading. When suing in a "fact pleading" jurisdiction, the trade secret

---

[16]Intermedics, Inc. v. Ventritex, Inc., 822 F. Supp. 634, 651, 27 U.S.P.Q.2d 1641 (N.D. Cal. 1993).

[17]U.T.S.A. § 6 cmt. (1985).

[18]Lemelson v. Carolina Enterprises, Inc., 541 F. Supp. 645, 659, 216 U.S.P.Q. 249 (S.D. N.Y. 1982).

[19]Construction Technology, Inc. v. Lockformer Co., Inc., 704 F. Supp. 1212, 1225, 10 U.S.P.Q.2d 1401, R.I.C.O. Bus. Disp. Guide (CCH) P 7115 (S.D. N.Y. 1989) (abrogated by, Conopco, Inc. v. Campbell Soup Co., 95 F.3d 187, 40 U.S.P.Q.2d 1042, 1996-2 Trade Cas. (CCH) ¶ 71551 (2d Cir. 1996)).

plaintiff must take care to allege more than a legal conclusion of ownership of a secret process or confidential information. Some courts may require the plaintiff to be clear about what information is protectable, rather than burdening the court with "sifting through technical data to distill out a trade secret."[1]

For example, in *Diodes, Inc. v. H. D. Franzen*,[2] the plaintiff's trade secret complaint was dismissed for failing to allege facts sufficient to show the existence of a trade secret process. The plaintiff's complaint alleged the existence of a secret process, but did not state the subject matter of this process other then to hint that it had something to do with the manufacture of diodes. The court was unimpressed with this pleading. In dismissing the complaint, the court recognized that a trade secret owner does not have to spell out the details of the trade secret to avoid dismissal of a complaint, but must nevertheless allege the ultimate facts showing the existence of a trade secret or other confidential data to state a sufficient cause of action.[3] While the result in *Diodes* is questionable because of California's change to notice pleading, the possible results from failing to adequately define and/or disclose the trade secrets involved is nevertheless real. This is especially true considering that California still requires an identification with reasonable particularity of trade secrets to commence discovery in a misappropriation case.[4]

Since most jurisdictions use notice pleading, a more general pleading as to the nature of an alleged trade secret was traditionally sufficient. However, in *Bell Atlantic Corp. v. Twombly*, the U.S. Supreme Court held that a notice pleading complaint must allege "enough facts to state a claim to relief that is plausible on its face."[5] A plaintiff must "plead factual content that allows the court to draw the reasonable inference that the defendant is liable for the misconduct alleged."[6] Conclusory allegations do not count for purposes of determining whether a claim is well pled.[7]

This heightened standard for pleading can be troublesome for parties bringing a trade secret action. On one hand, a plaintiff will want to describe the trade secret well enough to survive a motion to dismiss. On the other hand, a plaintiff will want to be

---

[Section 12:23]

[1]TouchPoint Solutions, Inc. v. Eastman Kodak Co., 345 F. Supp. 2d 23, 28 (D. Mass. 2004).

[2]Diodes, Inc. v. Franzen, 260 Cal. App. 2d 244, 67 Cal. Rptr. 19 (2d Dist. 1968).

[3]Diodes, 260 Cal.App.2d at 252, 67 Cal.Rptr. at 24.

[4]Cal. Civ. Pro. Code § 2019(d).

[5]Bell Atlantic Corp. v. Twombly, 550 U.S. 544, 570, 127 S. Ct. 1955, 167 L. Ed. 2d 929, 2007-1 Trade Cas. (CCH) ¶ 75709, 68 Fed. R. Serv. 3d 661 (2007).

[6]Ashcroft v. Iqbal, 129 S. Ct. 1937, 1949, 173 L. Ed. 2d 868, 2009-2 Trade Cas. (CCH) ¶ 76785, 73 Fed. R. Serv. 3d 837 (2009).

[7]Iqbal, 129 S. Ct. at 1954.

careful not to describe a trade secret so specifically that the "secret" is no longer secret. Since the Twombly and Iqbal decisions, courts have dismissed trade secret claims that did not specifically identify the trade secret.[8] At least in some cases, however, the requisite level of specificity is not especially high.[9]

In addition to alleging the trade secret, the plaintiff must also sufficiently assert the use of precautionary measures to preserve the secrecy of the confidential information in question. That is, the complaint must allege that the plaintiff employed precautionary measures to preserve the allegedly exclusive knowledge of the information at issue so as to actually render it a trade secret.[10]

Another requirement of a trade secret complaint is improper use.[11] In the case where the defendant is actually using trade secret information with a process or product, this allegation will be easy to plead. However, where the plaintiff is a company which sues an ex-employee who is working for a competitor, this actual threat of use is not so apparent.[12] It is not sufficient to allege that a defendant could misuse a plaintiff's trade secrets, or that plaintiff fears that the defendant might use those secrets. There must be an allegation that the defendants have in fact threatened to use the plaintiff's trade secrets or that they will inevitably do so.[13]

§ 12:24   Preparing to bring a trade secret misappropriation suit—Pre-emption

Research References

West's Key Number Digest, Antitrust and Trade Regulation ⟜416;

[8]Medafor, Inc. v. Starch Medical Inc., 2009 WL 2163580 at *1 (D. Minn. 2009) (dismissing complaint alleging the trade secret as "business methodologies, formulas, devices, and compilations of information, including suppliers and customers"); American Petroleum Institute v. Technomedia Intern., Inc., 2010 WL 1233496 at *3 (D.D.C. 2010) (dismissing complaint alleging trade secret as "trade secrets consist[ing] of information, including compilations, programs, methods, techniques, and processes").

[9]Zep, Inc. v. First Aid Corp., 2010 WL 1195094 at *10 (N.D. Ill. 2010) (denying motion to dismiss trade secret identified as "confidential information and trade secrets includ[ing], but . . . not limited to, names and identities of customers, knowledge of customer needs, knowledge of customer buying history and patterns, customer contact lists, supply lists, competitive pricing information and training provided to sales representatives"); ACS Partners, LLC v. Americon Group, Inc., 2010 WL 883663 at *10 (W.D. N.C. 2010) (denying motion to dismiss trade secret identified as "pricing methodology").

[10]Precision Concepts, Inc. v. Bonsanti, 172 A.D.2d 737, 738, 569 N.Y.S.2d 124, 125 (2d Dep't 1991).

[11]See § 12:21, infra.

[12]Teradyne, Inc. v. Clear Communications Corp., 707 F. Supp. 353, 356-57, 11 U.S.P.Q.2d 1368 (N.D. Ill. 1989).

[13]Teradyne, 707 F. Supp. at 356-57.

States ☞18.84
C.J.S., Monopolies § 20

Two types of pre-emption issues arise in trade secret misappropriation cases. First, there is the issue of whether trade secret claims under a state statute pre-empt common law torts. The UTSA addresses the pre-emption issue:

(a) Except as provided subsection (b), this [Act] displaces conflicting tort, restitutionary, and other law of this State providing civil remedies for misappropriation of a trade secret.

(b) This [Act] does not affect:

(1) Contractual remedies, whether or not based upon misappropriation of a trade secret;

(2) Other civil remedies that are not based upon misappropriation of a trade secret; or

(3) Criminal remedies, whether or not based upon misappropriation of a trade secret.[1]

Perhaps a more important question is whether state trade secret laws are pre-empted by federal law. The normal context in which a claim of pre-emption arises is with respect to the Copyright Act. Any state's legal or equitable right equivalent to the Copyright Act is pre-empted by federal law.[2] Section 301 of the Copyright Act pre-empts claims which are equivalent to a copyright claim.[3] While courts have not reached unanimity on the pre-emption issue, the vast weight of the authority holds that state trade secret claims are not pre-empted unless they assert nothing more than a copyright claim.[4]

It has been expressly determined that the patent statute does not pre-empt state trade secret laws.[5] However, trade secret law cannot be used to protect patented subject matter. Issuance of a patent publicly discloses the subject matter of the patent.[6] A patent provides the patent owner with the right to prevent others from making, using or selling a product and discerning its makeup, but the same protection cannot be provided by state trade secret law.[7] Therefore, one cannot use a trade secret claim to protect any unpatented part or combination of parts in a machine that is sold to another.[8]

[Section 12:24]

[1]U.T.S.A. § 7 (1985).

[2]Boeing, 738 P.2d at 674.

[3]17 U.S.C.A. § 301.

[4]Restatement (Third) of Unfair Competition § 39 cmt. c (1995).

[5]Kewanee Oil, 416 U.S. at 493.

[6]Restatement (Third) of Unfair Competition § 39 cmt. c (1995).

[7]Bonito Boats, 489 U.S. at 160.

[8]Roboserve, 940 F.2d at 1445.

§ 12:25 Preparing to bring a trade secret misappropriation suit—Protection of trade secret during litigation

Research References

West's Key Number Digest, Federal Civil Procedure ⊙1416, 1516, 1600(1); Pretrial Procedure ⊙41, 183.1, 285.1, 356.1

C.J.S., Discovery §§ 12, 29, 47, 82 to 85; Federal Civil Procedure §§ 688, 709

Trade secret litigation often presents a true predicament for the prospective plaintiff. After alleging ownership of trade secrets, it is likely that the defendant will attempt to learn of the exact contents or makeup of any and all trade secrets during discovery. Where the plaintiff and defendant are competitors, the plaintiff will understandably not want the competitor-defendant to learn of its trade secrets. For example, where the plaintiff alleges that the defendant stole a portion of a protected customer list, the plaintiff will not want to be forced to disclose the entire list to the defendant during discovery. Further, as court proceedings and documents are available to the public, the plaintiff faces a real risk of public disclosure of its trade secret, thus possibly destroying the trade secrets.[1]

A trade secret defendant faces a similar quandary during litigation. A common defense to a claim of trade secret misappropriation is that the defendant independently came up with its own competing device, process, list, etc.[2] In order to prove this defense, the defendant will be forced to disclose the steps used to create its own information, along with the final results. The defendant, in this instance, will likely view this information as being its own trade secret, and will not want to disclose the information to the competitor-plaintiff. The same concerns regarding public disclosure during trial also hold true for a trade secret defendant.

The UTSA recognizes these concerns and provides an explicit command to the court when dealing with a trade secret's action:

> [A] court shall preserve the secrecy of an alleged trade secret by reasonable means, which may include granting protective orders in connection with discovery proceedings, holding in-camera hearings, sealing the records of the action, and ordering any person involved

---

[Section 12:25]

[1]Restatement (Third) of Unfair Competition § 43 cmt. b (1995) ("A person may also acquire a trade secret through an analysis of published materials . . . that are in public view or otherwise accessible").

[2]U.T.S.A. Prefatory Note (2007); Miller v. Owens-Illinois, Inc., 187 U.S.P.Q. 47, 48, 1975 WL 21097 (D. Md. 1975).

in the litigation not to disclose an alleged trade secret without prior court approval.[3]

The drafters of the UTSA stated that reasonable assurances of secrecy must be provided to prevent chilling of otherwise meritorious trade secret litigation.[4] The drafters recognize that a balancing must be achieved in which a respondent is provided sufficient information to present a defense, while the trier of fact has sufficient information to resolve the merits.[5] In addition to the suggested methods for protecting secrecy, the drafters went on to add that secrecy can be protected by restricting disclosure to a party's counsel and his or her assistants and by appointing a disinterested expert as a special master to hear secret information and report conclusions to the court.[6]

Protective orders are a common means of protecting trade secret information during litigation. Rule 26(c) of the Federal Rules of Civil Procedure specifically provides a court with the authority to protect trade secrets, such as confidential research, development or commercial information, so that it is not revealed or revealed only in a designated way during discovery. However, "there is no absolute privilege for trade secrets and similar confidential information."[7]

A trial judge has the authority to limit discovery, via a protective order, so that only the party's attorneys and experts can review the information.[8] In cases involving misappropriation of trade secrets, a protective order will restrict disclosure of designated trade secret information to certain persons. For example, disclosure may be limited solely to the parties' attorneys and experts who must agree to make no further disclosure, including disclosure to their clients, without an appropriate court order.[9] In jurisdictions where the UTSA has not been adopted, the same approach to protective orders has been approved.[10] A protective order should include:

- a definition of what material may be designated as proprietary, trade secret or confidential,
- a procedure for designating the confidential material (e.g., whether the documents will be stamped or otherwise marked prior to production),

---

[3]U.T.S.A. § 5 (1985).

[4]U.T.S.A. § 5 cmt. (1985).

[5]U.T.S.A. § 5 cmt. (1985).

[6]U.T.S.A. § 5 cmt. (1985).

[7]Federal Open Market Committee of the Federal Reserve System v. Merrill, 443 U.S. 340, 362, 99 S. Ct. 2800, 2813, 5 Media L. Rep. (BNA) 1221 (1979) (quoting 8 C. Wright and

A. Miller, *Federal Practice and Procedure*, § 2043 (1970)).

[8]Alk Associates, Inc. v. Multimodal Applied Systems, Inc., 276 N.J. Super. 310, 647 A.2d 1359, 1362 (App. Div. 1994).

[9]U.T.S.A. § 5 cmt. (1985).

[10]Alk, 647 A.2d at 1362.

- a method for challenging the designation of "confidential material,"
- a description of how the confidential material may be used in connection with the litigation,
- an identification of who may receive the confidential materials,
- an attached agreement that any third party that is allowed to review information stamped as confidential will adhere to the terms of the protective order,
- a description of how confidential information shall be presented to the court (such as a cover sheet stating: "This Document is Subject to a Protective Order Issued by the Court and May Not Be Examined or Copied Except in Compliance with that Order"),
- provisions regarding the return of confidential information following the end of the litigation and
- a procedure for designating confidential information disclosed at depositions.

An example of a protective order is included in Appendix G.

§ 12:26 Proving trade secret misappropriation—Burden of proof

Research References

West's Key Number Digest, Antitrust and Trade Regulation ⚖=431

In a trade secret misappropriation case, the owner of the alleged trade secret has the burden of proof to show possession of a valid trade secret.[1] This requires proof by a preponderance of the evidence.[2] The prevailing view in most jurisdictions is that the determination of the existence of a trade secret is a question of fact.[3] However, some jurisdictions refer to the existence of a trade secret as a conclusion of law.[4] This approach likely stems from

---

[Section 12:26]

[1]Electro-Craft, 332 N.W.2d at 898; Julie Research Lab., 810 F. Supp. at 517; Baxter Intern., Inc. v. Morris, 976 F.2d 1189, 1194, 7 I.E.R. Cas. (BNA) 1377, 24 U.S.P.Q.2d 1429 (8th Cir. 1992); Basic Chemicals, Inc. v. Benson, 251 N.W.2d 220, 226, 195 U.S.P.Q. 197 (Iowa 1977).

[2]Surgidev, 648 F. Supp. at 680.

[3]See, e.g., Wilson v. Barton & Ludwig, Inc., 163 Ga. App. 721, 296 S.E.2d 74, 78, 220 U.S.P.Q. 375 (1982);

Surgidev, 648 F. Supp. at 692 n.15; Integrated Cash Management Services, Inc. v. Digital Transactions, Inc., 920 F.2d 171, 174, 17 U.S.P.Q.2d 1054 (2d Cir. 1990); Network Telecommunications, Inc. v. Boor-Crepeau, 790 P.2d 901, 902 (Colo. App 1990); SI Handling Sys., 753 F.2d at 1257 (3d Cir. 1985).

[4]Trandes Corp. v. Guy F. Atkinson Co., 996 F.2d 655, 27 U.S.P.Q.2d 1014 (4th Cir. 1993); American Express Financial Advisors, Inc. v. Yantis, 358 F. Supp. 2d 818 (N.D. Iowa 2005).

the view that trade secret misappropriation is a statutory interpretation of the UTSA (or that particular state's adaption).[5]
However, even in these minority courts, this "conclusion of law"
is based upon applicable facts or is a mixed question of law and
fact.[6]

These findings of fact are based on the various elements
required to establish the validity of a trade secret, such as economic value, whether the information is not generally known,
and the sufficiency of the measures used to maintain secrecy.[7] As
previously described, the elements required to show a valid trade
secret vary from state to state, normally depending upon whether
the UTSA is used or whether the Restatement (First) of Torts is
applicable.

§ 12:27 Proving trade secret misappropriation—Proving economic value

Research References

West's Key Number Digest, Antitrust and Trade Regulation ☞432

There is no standard set of "facts" that conclusively show independent economic value.[1] One common approach, however, is for
the trade secret owner to provide evidence of the time and dollars
spent in creating the alleged trade secret information.[2] Other
types of evidence include showing that the trade secret information is unavailable in the marketplace.[3] Notably, "independent
economic value" does not require a showing that no one else in
the industry has the information alleged to be a trade secret.[4]

The fact that an idea is developed by others may make it less
valuable in the market, yet the information may still give a commercial advantage, and therefore, value over competitors.[5] For
the most part, the requirements for a showing of "economic value"
are relatively low. Even a slight competitive edge will satisfy the

---

[5]Minuteman, Inc. v. Alexander,
147 Wis. 2d 842, 434 N.W.2d 773, 778
(1989).

[6]Trandes, 996 F.2d at 661.

[7]Economy Roofing & Insulating
Co. v. Zumaris, 538 N.W.2d 641, 649
(Iowa 1995).

[Section 12:27]

[1]Restatement (Third) of Unfair
Competition § 39 cmt. e (1995).

[2]Electro-Craft, 332 N.W.2d at

901 n.12.

[3]Avtec Systems, Inc. v. Peiffer,
805 F. Supp. 1312, 1320 (E.D. Va.
1992), aff'd in part, vacated in part on
other grounds, 21 F.3d 568, 9 I.E.R.
Cas. (BNA) 532, 30 U.S.P.Q.2d 1365
(4th Cir. 1994).

[4]Electro-Craft, 332 N.W.2d at
900.

[5]Classic Instruments, 700 P.2d
at 694.

economic value requirement of trade secret protection.[6] Investment of time is a showing of value.[7] However, whatever this limited proof may be, it still, nonetheless, must be shown.[8]

§ 12:28 Proving trade secret misappropriation—Proving novelty

Research References

West's Key Number Digest, Antitrust and Trade Regulation ☞432

A specific showing of "novelty" is not an element under the UTSA, but many states continue to require a showing of novelty or originality.[1] Further, while not specifically identified, the UTSA's requirement of "not generally known to others" carries forward many of the same analyses utilized for novelty. As a general rule, novelty is a question of fact. However, at least one court has held that the determination of whether a trade secret is novel or original is a mixed question of fact and law.[2]

The usual evidence submitted to show that a particular piece of information is novel or not generally known will normally come from the plaintiff, one if its officers or an expert witness testifying that the claimed information is not generally known in the industry. Beyond this, it is normally up to the defendant to refute this testimony by providing evidence of use or knowledge of the trade secret by others in the industry. Pointedly, courts have recognized that this "element" of the trade secret definition may properly be characterized as an affirmative defense.[3] Where there is a dispute as to whether or not information is "generally known," a showing that a particular product which embodies alleged trade secrets had no competition for several years is proof of being generally unknown.[4]

From the trade secret defendant's perspective, the phrase "not generally known" is not an all encompassing term. In other words, it means something less than "is not available to the general public." The defendant need only show that persons in the relevant industry have knowledge of the alleged trade secret

---

[6]Telerate Sys., 689 F. Supp. at 232.

[7]ISC-Bunker Ramo Corp. v. Altech, Inc., 765 F. Supp. 1310, 1319 (N.D. Ill. 1990).

[8]Composite Marine Propellers, 962 F.2d at 1267.

[Section 12:28]

[1]See e.g. Buffets, Inc. v. Klinke, 73 F.3d 965, 968, 37 U.S.P.Q.2d 1449

(9th Cir. 1996) (stating Washington's version of UTSA requires novelty).

[2]Phillips v. Avis, Inc., 1995 WL 417587 (N.D. Ill. 1995).

[3]Surgidev, 648 F. Supp. at 688.

[4]Salsbury Lab., 908 F.2d at 711.

information. The drafters' comment to the UTSA expressly supports this position:

> A method of casting metal, for example, may be unknown to the general public but readily known within the foundry industry.[5]

In such a case, the information is "generally known" (or not novel) and therefore cannot be protected.

A special problem in establishing "not generally known or readily ascertainable" or "novelty" arises in the context of customer lists or related items of information. Quite frequently, companies establish a list of their customers and/or potential customers. From this point, the additional information contained on the customer list can become very detailed. For example, the list might include a contact person's name and number, customer preferences, product preferences, etc. For most companies, the customer list and the additional information is quite valuable and is the source of great concern when an employee leaves the company with the customer list in hand. If this happens, the company will likely sue the ex-employee and/or his or her new employer for trade secret misappropriation, claiming that trade secrets are embodied in the customer list.

One of the many interesting questions presented in this scenario is whether a list of customers is "not generally known" when, more than likely, the customers are listed in a standard telephone book. As a general rule, customer lists can be classified as trade secrets, but only under appropriate circumstances.[6] However, where the information contained in the customer list is readily discoverable by other means, for example where the industry in question has a relatively small number of potential customers, names of those customers will not be protected under trade secret law.[7] Generally speaking, where the trade secret plaintiff can show that the customer list contains additional information, or that specific customer names are more difficult to obtain due to the type of industry involved, trade secret protection will normally be provided.

§ 12:29 Proving trade secret misappropriation—Proving secrecy

Research References

West's Key Number Digest, Antitrust and Trade Regulation ⚷432

---

[5]U.T.S.A. § 1 cmt. (1985).

[6]Michels v. Dyna-Kote Industries, Inc., 497 N.E.2d 586, 589 (Ind. Ct. App. 1986).

[7]Xpert Automation Sys., 569 N.E.2d at 356; Surgidev, 648 F. Supp. at 691.

Proof of secrecy is a question of fact.[1] In the usual case, the trade secret plaintiff will present facts regarding the various procedures used by the plaintiff to maintain the secrecy of the information in question. Often a company will have an established secrecy program designed to protect all of its confidential information. A company in this situation will present evidence of this overall policy and how it is enforced to show that adequate measures were taken to protect the secrecy of the specific information in question. For example, a company will show restricting visitor access to the company's manufacturing facilities,[2] apprising employees of the secret nature of various information via an employee manual or handbook,[3] or placing a proprietary notice on confidential blueprints or other documents.[4]

In response to the plaintiff's evidence of secrecy, a defendant may attack the secrecy policies and procedures as being insufficient.[5] This can be done by presenting evidence of additional secrecy steps or policies normally used in the industry.[6] Alternatively, the defendant may attack the plaintiff's secrecy procedures by putting into evidence instances or possibilities of disclosure despite the steps taken.[7]

Also, a defendant may point to disclosures of the alleged trade secret information by the plaintiff to others that occurred in spite of the security precautions.[8] When presenting this argument, however, the defendant must be certain that the disclosure(s) in question can be classified as a "public" disclosure. In other words, if the disclosure was made in confidence or to someone who owed the trade secret owner a duty of confidence, the reasonable steps to maintain secrecy will not be obviated. For example, a trade secret owner will not abandon or lose its trade secret by a limited public publication for a restricted purpose.[9] When the trade secret is disclosed as part of licensing negotiations or as part of a

[Section 12:29]

[1]Lehman v. Dow Jones & Co., Inc., 783 F.2d 285, 298 (2d Cir. 1986); Trandes Corp. v. Guy F. Atkinson Co., 996 F.2d 655, 27 U.S.P.Q.2d 1014 (4th Cir. 1993).

[2]Surgidev, 828 F.2d at 455.

[3]Saunders v. Florence Enameling Co., Inc., 540 So. 2d 651, 655, 9 U.S.P.Q.2d 1066 (Ala. 1988).

[4]Aries Info. Sys., 366 N.W.2d at 368; ISC-Bunker Ramo Corp. v. Altech, Inc., 765 F. Supp. 1310, 1322 (N.D. Ill. 1990).

[5]Pioneer, 35 F.3d at 1236; Business Trends Analysts, Inc. v.

Freedonia Group, Inc., 700 F. Supp. 1213, 1236, 10 U.S.P.Q.2d 1481 (S.D. N.Y. 1988), aff'd in part, rev'd in part on other grounds, 887 F.2d 399, 12 U.S.P.Q.2d 1457 (2d Cir. 1989).

[6]Pioneer, 35 F.3d at 1236; Bus. Trends Analysts, 700 F. Supp. at 1236.

[7]Arco Indus., 633 F.2d at 443 (noting failure to restrict areas of plaintiff's plant or screen visitors).

[8]United Wild Rice, Inc. v. Nelson, 313 N.W.2d 628, 634 (Minn. 1982); Fishing Concepts, Inc. v. Ross, 226 U.S.P.Q. 692, 695, 1985 WL 1549 (D. Minn. 1985).

[9]Space Aero Products Co. v. R. E. Darling Co., 238 Md. 93, 112, 208 A.2d

sale, the trade secret status is not lost.[10] Where a confidentiality agreement exists between the trade secret owner and the person or persons to whom the information was disclosed, this fact is further proof of reasonable steps to maintain secrecy.[11]

§ 12:30 Proving trade secret misappropriation—Proving improper use

Research References

West's Key Number Digest, Antitrust and Trade Regulation ⚷432

Misappropriation is, in most jurisdictions, a question of fact.[1] The burden of establishing misappropriation is on the party asserting rights in a trade secret.[2] Some courts have expressed a position that once the plaintiff proves that a defendant obtained and used a trade secret, the burden shifts to the defendant to prove that it lawfully acquired the information in question.[3] These cases normally involve breach of a confidential relationship. It has been held that where the defendant actively pursued a plaintiff's secrets, discarded highly relevant information of its own development, consistently denied obtaining the protected materials through any means, and possessed secrets shown to have probably been derived from plaintiff's secrets, the burden-shifting analysis may be appropriate.[4]

As defined by the UTSA, "misappropriation" can be either "improper use" or "improper acquisition."[5] With these two types of misappropriation in mind, trade secret misappropriation cases can be broken down into two general categories. First, where the defendant allegedly breached some type of confidential relationship with the plaintiff to improperly use or disclose the trade secret in question. Second, where the defendant did not have a confidential relationship with the plaintiff, but instead employed industrial espionage or some other form of improper means to acquire and/or use the information in question.

Generally, the trade secret plaintiff may establish a requisite confidential relationship by proof of an express contractual agree-

---

74, 83, 145 U.S.P.Q. 356 (1965).

[10]Speedry Chemical Products, Inc. v. Carter's Ink Co., 306 F.2d 328, 332, 134 U.S.P.Q. 88 (2d Cir. 1962); Hoeltke v. C.M. Kemp Mfg. Co., 80 F.2d 912, 923, 26 U.S.P.Q. 114 (C.C.A. 4th Cir. 1935), opinion after grant of reh'g, 28 U.S.P.Q. 176, 1936 WL 25411 (C.C.A. 4th Cir. 1936).

[11]Pioneer, 35 F.3d at 1237.

[Section 12:30]

[1]See, e.g., Curtis 1000, 905 F. Supp. at 902.

[2]Pioneer, 35 F.3d at 1239.

[3]Garter-Bare Co. v. Munsingwear Inc., 723 F.2d 707, 714-15, 221 U.S.P.Q. 751 (9th Cir. 1984).

[4]Pioneer, 35 F.3d at 1240-41.

[5]U.T.S.A. § 1 (1985).

ment or agreements between it and the defendant.[6] However, the confidential relationship need not be so formalistic. A confidential relationship arises where one party places its trust in a second party and the second party knows of the trust reposed in it.[7]

The most common situation in which a confidential relationship is breached occurs in the employer/employee context. When an employee leaves his or her employer and enters into competition with the employer, use of trade secret information of the former employer constitutes a disclosure or use and therefore misappropriation.[8] Confidential relationships can also be established between contractors and vendors.[9] The key with respect to the alleged confidential relationship is that the relationship, and the plaintiff's actions in light of that relationship, must have put the defendant on notice as to the confidentiality of the information in question.[10] In fact, even in the employer-employee scenario, where the employer fails to put its employees on notice of what information is to be held confidential, a claim for misappropriation will not be recognized.[11]

An important distinction with respect to the confidential relationship scenario should be noted. According to the UTSA, misappropriation can occur through improper acquisition or improper disclosure or use.[12] In the confidential relationship scenario, the initial acquisition of trade secret information is normally not actionable as the trade secret owner freely gave the information to the defendant under the guise of the confidential relationship. The actual misappropriation takes place when the confidant later improperly discloses or uses this information.[13] This is a relatively subtle distinction, but should be remembered by the trade secret owner when presenting evidence as part of its case.

For example, where an employer sues a former employee for misappropriation of trade secrets that were disclosed to the employee during the term of his or her employment, the proper claim is for improper disclosure or use and not for improper acquisition.[14] However, if that same ex-employee, following termination of employment, later returns to the ex-employer's plant and steals trade secret information, a claim of misappropriation exists for improper acquisition.[15] In contrast, the ex-employee's new employer can be held to have misappropriated

---

[6]Surgidev, 648 F. Supp. at 694.

[7]Surgidev, 648 F. Supp. at 695.

[8]U.T.S.A. § 1(2)(ii)(B)(II) (1985).

[9]U.T.S.A. § 1(2) (1985).

[10]Aries, 366 N.W.2d at 369.

[11]Electro-Craft, 332 N.W.2d at 903.

[12]U.T.S.A. § 1(2)(i) and (ii) (1985).

[13]Restatement (Third) of Unfair Competition § 42 cmt. b (1995).

[14]Restatement (Third) of Unfair Competition § 42 cmt. b (1995).

[15]Restatement (Third) of Unfair Competition § 40 (1995).

the trade secret by hiring the ex-employee and thereby acquiring trade secrets by an improper means, such as by inducement of a breach of a duty to maintain secrecy.[16]

§ 12:31 Proving trade secret misappropriation—Proving inevitable disclosure

Research References

West's Key Number Digest, Antitrust and Trade Regulation ☞432

A more specific misappropriation issue arising in the confidential relationship context is a claim of inevitable disclosure.[1] In this situation, the employer sues an ex-employee for misappropriation of alleged trade secrets. As is the case with other employer/ex-employee cases, the ex-employee has gone to work with a competitor. The former employer believes that the ex-employee will disclose and/or use trade secret information in his or her new position. The difference from the normal cases arises where the ex-employee has only recently left the employer, and has not likely had an opportunity to actually disclose or use the trade secret information. However, the former employer believes that the ex-employee's new position will inevitably require him or her to disclose and/or use the employer's trade secret information. With this scenario, the employer brings an action to prevent the ex-employee from assuming the new position on the basis of this inevitable disclosure.[2]

Courts have recognized that a plaintiff may prove a claim of trade secret misappropriation by demonstrating the defendant's new employment will inevitably lead him or her to rely on the plaintiff's trade secrets.[3] To succeed under the inevitable disclosure doctrine, the plaintiff should present evidence that the ex-employee possesses extensive and intimate knowledge of trade secret information and that the ex-employee will necessarily be making decisions in his or her new position which require reliance upon those trade secrets. For example, in *PepsiCo, Inc. v. Redmond*,[4] the defendant Redmond was a high level manager for the plaintiff in the area of sports drinks. Redmond left PepsiCo to work for a competitor in that same industry. PepsiCo presented evidence that Redmond had extensive and intimate knowledge

---

[16]Restatement (Third) of Unfair Competition § 40 (1995).

[Section 12:31]

[1]*See, e.g.,* AMP Inc. v. Fleischhacker, 823 F.2d 1199, 1207, 3 I.E.R. Cas. (BNA) 73, 3 U.S.P.Q.2d 1421, 8 Fed. R. Serv. 3d 600 (7th Cir. 1987).

[2]*See, e.g.,* Fleischhacker, 823 F.2d at 1207.

[3]Fleischhacker, 823 F.2d at 1207; Teradyne, 707 F. Supp. at 356.

[4]PepsiCo, Inc. v. Redmond, 54 F.3d 1262, 10 I.E.R. Cas. (BNA) 1089, 35 U.S.P.Q.2d 1010 (7th Cir. 1995).

about strategic goals for PepsiCo in the upcoming year. It was further shown that Redmond would be making decisions about his new employer's sports drinks and new age drinks by relying upon his knowledge of PepsiCo's trade secrets.[5] The court believed that the trade secrets in question would enable Redmond's new employer to achieve a substantial advantage by knowing exactly how PepsiCo would price, distribute, and market its sports drinks and new age drinks and be able to respond strategically. Further, the court was unimpressed with the veracity of Redmond's assertion that he did not intend to use PepsiCo's trade secrets based upon inconsistent statements made during a preliminary hearing.[6]

The veracity of the ex-employee's promise to not disclose trade secret information to his or her new employer is an important aspect of the inevitable disclosure doctrine. The court in *FMC Corp. v. Cyprus Foote Mineral Co.*,[7] interpreted North Carolina's case law to indicate that its "courts would refuse to enjoin an employee from working for its former employer's competitor under the doctrine of 'inevitable discovery' absent some showing of bad faith, underhanded dealing, or employment by an entity so plainly lacking comparable technology that misappropriation can be inferred."[8]

A claim of inevitable disclosure must amount to more than mere speculation. For example, the new fact that a former employee had access to secret information regarding James Bond films while working at MGM/United Artists, and then went to work at Sony Corporation, was not sufficient to demonstrate improper acquisition, disclosure, or use of the trade secret information.[9]

§ 12:32 Proving trade secret misappropriation—Proving improper acquisition

Research References

---

[5]PepsiCo, 54 F.3d at 1269.

[6]PepsiCo, 54 F.3d at 1271.

[7]FMC Corp. v. Cyprus Foote Mineral Co., 899 F. Supp. 1477 (W.D. N.C. 1995).

[8]FMC Corp., 899 F. Supp. at 1483. *See also* Campbell Soup Co. v. Giles, 47 F.3d 467, 472, 33 U.S.P.Q.2d 1916 (1st Cir. 1995) (finding that the trial court's record contained no indication that the defendant was dishonest or would be inclined to breach his confidentiality agreement with the

plaintiff as supporting conclusion that plaintiff was unlikely to suffer irreparable harm in inevitable disclosure claim).

[9]Danjaq LLC v. Sony Corp., 50 U.S.P.Q.2d 1638, 1999 WL 317629 (C.D. Cal. 1999) (noting that at summary judgement, the nonmoving party seeking to rely on inferences drawn from certain facts must demonstrate genuine issues material not only to the underlying facts, but also to proposed inferences).

West's Key Number Digest, Antitrust and Trade Regulation ⊜432

The other category of trade secret cases involves situations where the defendant used methods other than breach of a confidential relationship to acquire trade secret information and those methods are allegedly improper. The obvious and most cited example is the use of an aircraft to view partially-completed, guarded buildings of a competitor.[1] However, courts recognize that direct evidence of industrial espionage is rarely available and not required.[2] Similarly, it has been held that the UTSA does not require a plaintiff to prove actual theft or conversion of physical documents containing trade secret information to prove misappropriation.[3]

The circumstantial evidence normally used by plaintiffs to infer an improper acquisition include repeated attempts by the defendant to acquire the trade secret information and failure of the defendant to present adequate explanation for its own development of a competing technology.[4] Courts are often convinced by a plaintiff who describes years of work and expenditures to develop a certain trade secret, while the defendant is unexplainably able to develop the same information in a relatively short period of time.[5] An important point to note is that even if improper means are used, an action for misappropriation will not be recognized when the plaintiff is unable to establish a valid trade secret. Also, as emphasized by the above discussion, misappropriation in the area of industrial espionage does not require a showing of actual disclosure or use. Instead, it need only be shown that the trade secret information was acquired by improper means.[6]

§ 12:33 Remedies—Injunctive relief

Research References
West's Key Number Digest, Injunction ⊜56, 138.33
C.J.S., Injunctions §§ 116 to 118, 120, 267 to 275

The UTSA provides for injunctive relief from trade secret misappropriation:

(a) Actual or threatened misappropriation may be enjoined. Upon application to the court, an injunction shall be terminated when the trade secret has ceased to exist, but the injunction

---

[Section 12:32]

[1]E.I. duPont deNemours, 431 F.2d at 1015.
[2]Pioneer, 35 F.3d at 1239.
[3]Ed Nowogroski Ins., 971 P.2d at 946.
[4]Pioneer, 35 F.3d at 1239-40.
[5]SI Handling Sys., 753 F.2d at 1259.
[6]Minuteman, 434 N.W.2d at 778.

may be continued for an additional reasonable period of time in order to eliminate commercial advantage that otherwise would be derived from the misappropriation.

(b) In exceptional circumstances, an injunction may condition future use upon payment of a reasonable royalty for no longer than the period of time for which use could have been prohibited. Exceptional circumstances include, but are not limited to, a material and prejudicial change of position prior to acquiring knowledge or reason to know of misappropriation that renders a prohibitive injunction inequitable.

(c) In appropriate circumstances, affirmative acts to protect a trade secret may be compelled by court order.[1]

The comments to the UTSA provide:

Injunctions restraining future use and disclosure of misappropriated trade secrets are frequently sought. Although punitive perpetual injunctions have been granted, § 2(a) of this Act adopts the position of the trend of authority limiting the duration of injunctive relief to the extent of the temporal advantage over good-faith competitors gained by misappropriation.

The general principle of § 2(a) and (b) is that an injunction should last for as long as is necessary, but no longer than is necessary, to eliminate the commercial advantage or "lead time" with respect to good faith competitors that a person has obtained through misappropriation. Subject to any additional period of restraint necessary to negate lead time, an injunction accordingly should terminate when a former trade secret becomes either generally known to good-faith competitors or generally knowable to them because of the lawful availability of products that can be reverse engineered to reveal a trade secret.[2]

As with other areas of law, injunctive relief in the trade secret context can be in the form of a temporary restraining order, preliminary injunction or permanent injunction.[3] Basically, a motion for injunctive relief requires a court to carefully weigh four factors: whether the movant has shown a likelihood of a reasonable probability of success on the merits; whether the movant will be irreparably injured by denial of such relief; whether granting preliminary relief will result in even greater harm to the nonmoving party; and whether granting preliminary relief will be in the public interest.[4] Notably, while some courts have assumed irreparable harm in trade secret cases, it has been held that the

---

[Section 12:33]

[1]U.T.S.A. § 2 (1985).

[2]U.T.S.A. § 2 cmt. (1985).

[3]*See, e.g.*, Integrated Cash Management Services, Inc. v. Digital Transactions, Inc., 920 F.2d 171, 175, 17 U.S.P.Q.2d 1054 (2d Cir. 1990); Restatement (Third) of Unfair Competition § 44(3) (1995).

[4]SI Handling Sys., 753 F.2d at 1254.

UTSA provision that injunctions could be granted on such equitable terms as a court deems reasonable, does not create an exception from the general statutory requirement that injunctions can be granted only upon a showing of irreparable harm.[5]

Injunctive relief should not go beyond the need to protect the legitimate interests of a trade secret owner and should not unduly burden the defendant.[6] In the normal case, a successful trade secret plaintiff will receive permanent injunctive relief that prevents the defendant from disclosing or using trade secrets for a certain amount of time. The duration and scope of an injunction are decided upon the facts of each case, at the trial court's discretion.[7] Any information which the defendant is prevented from using or disclosing pursuant to the injunction cannot be publicly available, such as through a patent or other public disclosure of the trade secret owner.[8] Further, the injunction cannot prevent use of trade secret information once those trade secrets are publicly disclosed.[9]

Generally, an injunction should last for a period of time that would be reasonably required for independent development of the trade secret information.[10] The plaintiff will normally describe the length of time it took to develop the information, whereas the defendant will attempt to show that it could develop the information more quickly.[11] The duration of injunction can range from a few months, to a few years,[12] to perpetual.[13] With a perpetual or "permanent" injunction, the court normally maintains jurisdiction to modify or revoke the injunction as circumstances dictate.[14]

§ 12:34 Remedies—Damages

Research References

West's Key Number Digest, Antitrust and Trade Regulation ⚬=437

In addition to injunctive relief, monetary damages and attorney's fees are also available to a successful trade secret plaintiff. Several different methods are available for calculating

---

[5]Bishop & Co. v. Cuomo, 799 P.2d 444, 446 (Colo. App 1990); see also eBay Inc. v. MercExchange, L.L.C., 547 U.S. 388, 391, 126 S. Ct. 1837, 164 L. Ed. 2d 641, 78 U.S.P.Q.2d 1577, 27 A.L.R. Fed. 2d 685 (2006).

[6]Stampede, 651 N.E.2d at 217.

[7]Boeing, 738 P.2d at 681.

[8]Scharmer v. Carrollton Mfg. Co., 525 F.2d 95, 99, 187 U.S.P.Q. 736, 1975-2 Trade Cas. (CCH) ¶ 60562 (6th Cir. 1975).

[9]SI Handling Sys., 753 F.2d at 1266 (citing Kewanee Oil, 416 U.S. at 473–74).

[10]Restatement (Third) of Unfair Competition § 44 cmt. f (1995).

[11]Restatement (Third) of Unfair Competition § 44 cmt. f (1995).

[12]Baxter, 976 F.2d at 1195.

[13]Integrated Cash, 920 F.2d at 175.

[14]Wolfe v. Tuthill Corp., Full-Rite Div., 532 N.E.2d 1, 3 (Ind. 1988).

the amount of damages a plaintiff should recover. The UTSA provides:

(a) Except to the extent that a material and prejudicial change of position prior to acquiring knowledge or reason to know of misappropriation renders a monetary recovery inequitable, a complainant is entitled to recover damages for misappropriation. Damages can include both the actual loss caused by misappropriation and the unjust enrichment caused by misappropriation that is not taken into account in computing actual loss. In lieu of damages measured by any other methods, the damages caused by misappropriation may be measured by imposition of liability for a reasonable royalty for a misappropriator's unauthorized disclosure or use of a trade secret.

(b) If willful and malicious misappropriation exists, the court may award exemplary damages in an amount not exceeding twice any award made under subsection (a).[1]

The same theories of recovery (i.e. plaintiff's loss and defendant's unjust enrichment, or a reasonable royalty) have been recognized by other jurisdictions which have not adopted the UTSA[2]

While the UTSA and common law provide at least three methods for calculating damages due to misappropriation of trade secrets, computing damages in a trade secret's case is "not cut and dry."[3] When interpreting Virginia's version of the UTSA, the *American Sales* court held that the UTSA dictates that plaintiff's loss plus defendant's unjust enrichment is the appropriate measure unless it would provide an inadequate sum; otherwise it should be a reasonable royalty exclusively.[4] Other courts have repeated the same theme, requiring that in choosing among competing damage recovery theories, courts should select the measure "which affords the plaintiff the greatest recovery."[5]

The determination and definition of what a reasonable royalty is has been analogized to the determination of damages in a patent infringement case.[6] Basically, this entails the court approximating the actual value of the infringed secret to the

---

[Section 12:34]

[1]U.T.S.A. § 3 (1985).

[2]Softel, 891 F. Supp. at 942; University Computing Co. v. Lykes-Youngstown Corp., 504 F.2d 518, 536, 183 U.S.P.Q. 705 (5th Cir. 1974) (applying GA law under the Restatement (First) of Torts; GA has now adopted the U.T.S.A.).

[3]American Sales Corp. v. Adventure Travel, Inc., 862 F. Supp. 1476, 1479 (E.D. Va. 1994), on reconsideration in part, 867 F. Supp. 378 (E.D. Va. 1994) (reconsidering award of attorney's fees).

[4]American Sales, 862 F. Supp. at 1479.

[5]Pioneer, 35 F.3d at 1244.

[6]University Computing, 504 F.2d at 535.

defendant based upon a fictional negotiation between the plaintiff and defendant for a license to be granted at the time of the beginning of the infringement, assuming both parties are reasonably trying to reach an agreement.[7] Because of this, the reasonable royalty approach has been held to be most appropriate when the parties actually had or contemplated a royalty arrangement.[8] The *Pioneer* court also noted that the reasonable royalty approach is most appropriate when other theories would result in no recovery for the plaintiff, similar to what is provided in the UTSA[9]

The theory of lost profits has been widely accepted as a method of determining damages in a trade secret misappropriation case.[10] The plaintiff's lost profits are the most useful measure where the defendant disclosed or published the plaintiff's secret and seriously injured its business.[11] Much like the reasonable royalty calculation, the lost profits approach in a trade secret case has been analogized to that used for patent cases.[12] The *Pioneer* case, which resulted in a $46,700,000 award based upon the plaintiff's lost profits, affirmed the trial court's calculation which was based upon the defendant's actual sales figures, the capacity of plaintiff's production lines, plaintiff's profitability history and a reasonable estimate of the plaintiff's lost share in the affected market. From this total value, the court reduced the amount by two-thirds based upon its determination that the plaintiff could not have obtained the full market penetration achieved by the defendant.[13] Whatever factors are utilized to calculate the plaintiff's lost profits, a plaintiff must still establish a pecuniary loss as a result of the misappropriation of its trade secrets.[14]

Under the UTSA § 3(a), a plaintiff can recover both its lost profits and the unjust enrichment to the defendant caused by the misappropriation. However, this does not allow a plaintiff to recover a double counting. In fact, the UTSA adopts an express prohibition upon the counting of the same item as both a loss to a complainant and an unjust benefit to the misappropriator.[15]

The UTSA provides for the recovery of punitive damages where, if willful and malicious misappropriation exists, the court may award exemplary damages in an amount not exceeding twice any

---

[7]University Computing, 504 F.2d at 537.

[8]Pioneer, 35 F.3d at 1244.

[9]Pioneer, 35 F.3d at 1243.

[10]Pioneer, 35 F.3d at 1244.

[11]American Sales, 862 F. Supp. at 1479.

[12]Pioneer, 35 F.3d at 1245.

[13]Pioneer, 35 F.3d at 1245.

[14]Aerosonic Corp. v. Trodyne Corp., 402 F.2d 223, 230, 160 U.S.P.Q. 166, 38 A.L.R.3d 560 (5th Cir. 1968) (reversal of district court's award of $15,000 because plaintiff failed to establish how it had been damaged by defendant's misappropriation).

[15]U.T.S.A. § 3 (1985).

award otherwise made under subsection (a).[16] The determination of the amount of a punitive damage award is left to the discretion of the trial court and will not be reversed unless clearly erroneous.[17] In states which have not adopted the UTSA, there is no formula by which the finder of fact must determine punitive damages. In those states, the amount fixed need not bear a particular relationship to the amount awarded as compensatory damages.[18]

§ 12:35 Remedies—Attorneys' fees

Research References

West's Key Number Digest, Antitrust and Trade Regulation ⚲438

The UTSA provides for an award of attorney's fees:

> If (i) a claim of misappropriation is made in bad faith, (ii) a motion to terminate an injunction is made or resisted in bad faith, or (iii) willful and malicious misappropriation exists, the court may award reasonable attorneys' fees to the prevailing party.[1]

Much like an award of punitive damages, the award of attorney's fees is discretionary with the trial court, and will be overturned only for manifest abuse.[2] In fact, the same showing of willful and malicious misappropriation is the standard. The provision for the award of attorney's fees against a party who maintained a proceeding in bad faith is not intended to penalize a party and/or counsel for asserting a colorable claim or defense.[3]

§ 12:36 Federal trade secrets actions

The Defend Trade Secrets Act provides a federal, private civil cause of action for trade secret misappropriation, if the trade secret is related to a product or service used in, or intended for use in, interstate or foreign commerce.[1] This cause of action allows trade secret owners to pursue trade secret misappropriation claims in federal court, but does not eliminate state trade secret

---

[16]U.T.S.A. § 3(b) (1985); Micro Data Base Systems, Inc. v. Dharma Systems, Inc., 148 F.3d 649, 654, 46 U.S.P.Q.2d 1922, 35 U.C.C. Rep. Serv. 2d 747 (7th Cir. 1998) (applying New Hampshire's version of the U.T.S.A.).

[17]Boeing, 738 P.2d at 680.

[18]Softel, 891 F. Supp. at 945 (reconsidering amount of punitive damages but still not applying a formula).

[Section 12:35]

[1]U.T.S.A. § 4 (1985).

[2]Boeing, 738 P.2d at 682; nClosures Inc. v. Block and Co., Inc., 770 F.3d 598, 605, 112 U.S.P.Q.2d 1774 (7th Cir. 2014).

[3]Optic Graphics, Inc. v. Agee, 87 Md. App. 770, 591 A.2d 578, 590 (1991).

[Section 12:36]

[1]18 U.S.C.A. §§ 1831 to 1839.

misappropriation causes of action.

The Defend Trade Secrets Act defines misappropriation of a trade secret as

(A) acquisition of a trade secret of another by a person who knows or has reason to know that the trade secret was acquired by improper means; or (B) disclosure or use of a trade secret of another without express or implied consent by a person who (i) used improper means to acquire knowledge of the trade secret; (ii) at the time of disclosure or use, knew or had reason to know that the knowledge of the trade secret was (I) derived from or through a person who had used improper means to acquire the trade secret; (II) acquired under circumstances giving rise to a duty to maintain the secrecy of the trade secret or limit the use of the trade secret; or (III) derived from or through a person who owed a duty to the person seeking relief to maintain the secrecy of the trade secret or limit the use of the trade secret; or (iii) before a material change of the position of the person, knew or had reason to know that (I) the trade secret was a trade secret; and (II) knowledge of the trade secret had been acquired by accident or mistake.[2]

The term "improper means" in the Act is defined such that it "(A) includes theft, bribery, misrepresentation, breach or inducement of a breach of a duty to maintain secrecy, or espionage through electronic or other means; and (B) does not include reverse engineering, independent derivation, or any other lawful means of acquisition."[3]

In a federal trade secrets misappropriation claim, various remedies available under proper circumstances include seizure of property (in extraordinary cases where warranted to prevent irreparable injury due to dissemination of the misappropriated trade secrets), injunctive relief, and damages.[4] Damages may be calculated based on (i) actual loss and any unjust enrichment not addressed in computing damages for actual loss, or (ii) a reasonable royalty for the unauthorized disclosure or use of the trade secret.[5] Furthermore, if the trade secret is willfully and maliciously misappropriated, exemplary damages may be further awarded in an amount not more than two times the amount of the underlying damages. Attorney's fees can also be awarded to a prevailing party if a claim of misappropriation is made in bad faith (which may be established by circumstantial evidence), a motion to terminate an injunction is made or opposed in bad faith, or the trade secret was willfully and maliciously misappropriated.

Pursuant to the Defend Trade Secrets Act, 18 U.S.C.A.

---

[2]18 U.S.C.A. § 1839(5).

[3]18 U.S.C.A. § 1839(6).

[4]18 U.S.C.A. § 1836(b)(2) and (b)(3).

[5]18 U.S.C.A. § 1836(b)(3).

§ 1833(b)(1) provides a whistleblower protection provision that states

> An individual shall not be held criminally or civilly liable under any Federal or State trade secret law for the disclosure of a trade secret that (A) is made (i) in confidence to a Federal, State, or local government official, either directly or indirectly, or to an attorney; and (ii) solely for the purpose of reporting or investigating a suspected violation of law; or (B) is made in a complaint or other document filed in a lawsuit or other proceeding, if such filing is made under seal.

Moreover, 18 U.S.C.A. § 1833(b)(2) states

> An individual who files a lawsuit for retaliation by an employer for reporting a suspected violation of law may disclose the trade secret to the attorney of the individual and use the trade secret information in the court proceeding, if the individual (A) files any document containing the trade secret under seal; and (B) does not disclose the trade secret, except pursuant to court order.

Importantly, employers are required to provide notice to employees of this whistleblower protection, for any contracts or agreements governing the use of a trade secret or other confidential information that are entered into or updated after enactment of the Defend Trade Secrets Act on May 11, 2016; failure to provide such a notice makes exemplary damages (up to two times the damages for actual loss and unjust enrichment or a reasonable royalty) unavailable in any suit against an employee who failed to receive the notice.[6]

§ 12:37 Criminalization of trade secret law

Research References
West's Key Number Digest, Larceny ⊙1
C.J.S., Larceny §§ 1 to 2, 50 to 51

The misappropriation of trade secrets has also been criminalized by a number of jurisdictions. Congress has extended federal protection of intellectual property by passing The Economic Espionage Act.[1] Similarly, a growing number of states are criminalizing the theft of trade secrets to compliment the civil remedies already in place.[2]

Misappropriation of trade secrets, or "economic espionage," is now a federal crime under 18 U.S.C.A. §§ 1831 to 1832. The statutes distinguish between two types of criminal trade secret

---

[6]18 U.S.C.A. § 1833(b)(3).

[Section 12:37]

[1]U.T.S.A. § 4 (1985).

[2]Restatement (Third) of Unfair Competition § 39 cmt. b (1995); *See e.g.*, Rev. Code Wash. 9A.56.010(6); Ga. Code Ann. § 16-8-13.

misappropriation. Section 1831 covers misappropriation by foreign governments or their agents, which is punishable by fines of up to $5 million or imprisonment of up to 15 years. Offending organizations may be subject to fines of up to the greater of $10 million "or 3 times the value of the stolen trade secret to the organization, including expenses for research and design and other costs of reproducing the trade secret that the organization thereby avoided."[3] Section 1832 covers misappropriation that is intended to benefit individuals and corporations. Under § 1832, individuals are subject to fines and up to 10 years of imprisonment, while organizations are subject to fines of up to $5 million.[4]

The wording of the Economic Espionage Act of 1996 is not unconstitutionally vague. Particularly, the wording of the Act is not unconstitutionally vague when applied to the conduct of a criminal defendant who has been charged with the inchoate offenses of attempt and conspiracy.

---

[3]Foreign and Economic Espionage Penalty Enhancement Act of 2012, Pub. L. No. 112-269, § 2, 126 Stat. 2442 (Jan. 14, 2013).

[4]U.S. v. Hsu, 40 F. Supp. 2d 623,

630, 50 U.S.P.Q.2d 1659 (E.D. Pa. 1999).

(Thus far, no court has found the wording of the Economic Espionage Act of 1996 to be unconstitutionally vague.).

Chapter 13

The Right of Publicity

KeyCite®: Cases and other legal materials listed in KeyCite Scope can be researched through the KeyCite service on Westlaw®. Use KeyCite to check citations for form, parallel references, prior and later history, and comprehensive citator information, including citations to other decisions and secondary materials.

---

§ 13:1 Evolution of the right of publicity—The right of privacy

Research References

West's Key Number Digest, Torts ⟜325

The right of publicity provides a party with the right to protect the commercial value of that individual's identity. The right of publicity grew out of the common law right of privacy. The connection between the right of publicity and the right of privacy has created significant confusion at times. Courts have tended to commingle the right of publicity with various privacy rights, but the right of publicity is now generally regarded as a separate and distinct right.[1] To understand the right of publicity, and to distinguish it from other closely related rights, it is necessary to briefly explore the origin of the right of privacy, and how the right of publicity emerged as a distinct tort.

The beginning of a common law right of privacy is generally traced back to an 1890 law review article co-authored by Louis Brandeis.[2] The article advocated a need to protect an individual's personal and private information from being disclosed to the public. This new tort was based upon the idea that an individual had a right to be left alone.

During the next seventy years, the law of privacy continued to develop. In 1960, William Prosser summarized the status of the right of privacy in a law review article.[3] Prosser identified four distinct kinds of privacy:

- intrusion upon the plaintiff's seclusion or solitude, or into private affairs,
- public disclosure of embarrassing private facts about the plaintiff,
- publicity which places the plaintiff in a false light in the public eye, and
- appropriation, for the defendant's advantage, of the plaintiff's name or likeness.[4]

Interestingly, Prosser noted that, although these causes of action were lumped together under a common name, they had almost nothing in common except each represents, to a certain degree, a plaintiff's right to be left alone.[5]

Each of the four torts of privacy protects different interests. For example, the tort of "intrusion" deals with the unwanted invasion of a person's seclusion or solitude. This includes physical intrusions, such as intrusions into a person's home or hotel room and searches of a person's belongings. It also includes actions beyond physical intrusions, such as peeping toms and eavesdropping.[6] Each of these intrusions must be more than a mere annoyance, and the intrusion into the person's privacy must be objectionable to a reasonable person.

The tort of "disclosure" concerns the public revelation of embarrassing private facts about a person. This was the cause of action about which Warren and Brandeis wrote their law review article.

[Section 13:1]

[1]J. Thomas McCarthy, *The Rights of Publicity and Privacy* § 1.7 (2d ed. 2010).

[2]Samuel B. Warren and Louis B. Brandeis, *The Right to Privacy*, 4 Harv. L. Rev. 193 (1890).

[3]William L. Prosser, *Privacy*, 48 Calif. L. Rev. 383 (1960).

[4]*Prosser*, 48 Calif. L. Rev. at 389.

[5]*Prosser*, 48 Calif. L. Rev. at 389.

[6]*Prosser*, 48 Calif. L. Rev. at 390.

An early case espousing this cause of action upheld a woman's right to privacy against a movie-maker who exposed her past life as a prostitute.[7]

"False light" protects an individual's privacy from being presented to the public in an objectionable manner.[8] The action giving rise to a cause of action for false light is not necessarily, but often is, defamation. Consequently, both false light and defamation actions are often brought together.[9]

Finally, the tort of "appropriation" deals with the unauthorized use of an individual's identity, generally for commercial purposes, for the advantage of the unauthorized user.[10] By most accounts, the appropriation tort of privacy is the "immediate historical antecedent to the 'right of publicity'."[11]

The confusion caused by Prosser's inclusion of this fourth tort among the torts for invasion of privacy stems from the fact that persons seeking commercial exploitation of their name or likeness "do not seek the 'solitude and privacy' which" much of privacy law sought to protect.[12] Quite the contrary, these people exploit the publicity of their name or likeness for pecuniary gain. Thus, while it is important to understand the origin of the right of publicity as one of the four rights to privacy, it is equally important to recognize the fundamental differences between the right to publicity and the other three rights of privacy.

Judges have taken the term "privacy" at face value and denied celebrities recovery because they were already in the public eye and receiving publicity.[13] O'Brien v. Pabst Sales Co.[14] illustrates the confusion caused by the inclusion of the right of publicity among the rights of privacy. In O'Brien, a football player's photograph was used in a beer company's advertising calendar. The football player was upset by the use of his photograph in a beer advertisement. He was outspoken against the use of alcohol by young people, and he had refused beer endorsements on several occasions.[15] The court found that there was no cause of action for the football player against the beer company, because there was no express endorsement by the player and selling beer was a legitimate business. Furthermore, the court found that, because the football player was not a "private person," the publicity would not harm him because "the publicity he got was only

---

[7]*Prosser,* 48 Calif. L. Rev. at 392.

[8]*Prosser,* 48 Calif. L. Rev. at 398.

[9]*Prosser,* 48 Calif. L. Rev. at 400.

[10]*Prosser,* 48 Calif. L. Rev. at 401.

[11]*McCarthy* § 1.23.

[12]R. Nimmer, *The Right of Publicity,* 19 Law and Contemp. Prob. 203, 204 (1954).

[13]*McCarthy* § 1.25.

[14]O'Brien v. Pabst Sales Co., 124 F.2d 167 (C.C.A. 5th Cir. 1941).

[15]O'Brien, 124 F.2d at 169.

that which he had been constantly seeking and receiving."[16]

§ 13:2 Evolution of the right of publicity—The right of publicity

Research References

West's Key Number Digest, Torts ⊱384

The recognition of the value of an individual's right of publicity was first expressly acknowledged in *Haelan Laboratories, Inc. v. Topps Chewing Gum, Inc.*[1] The case involved a claim for intentional interference with contractual relations relating to the exclusive right to use baseball players' photographs for baseball cards. The plaintiff, engaged in selling chewing gum, made a contract with a baseball player giving plaintiff the exclusive right to use the baseball player's photograph in connection with sales of plaintiff's chewing gum. Defendant, a rival chewing gum manufacturer, deliberately induced the baseball player to give defendant the right to use the player's photograph in connection with the sales of defendant's chewing gum.[2]

Defendant argued that plaintiff was claiming a privacy right which was personal and not transferable. Therefore, plaintiff's exclusive contract right amounted to nothing more than a release from suit by the baseball player for use of his photo. Defendant also argued that, absent the release, plaintiff would be invading the player's right of privacy under New York Civil Rights Law. This privacy right is personal, not assignable, and therefore, plaintiff's contract vested in plaintiff no property right or other legal interest which defendant's conduct invaded.[3]

The court rejected defendant's argument. The court held that, in addition to, and independent of, the right of privacy derived from statute, a person "has a right in the publicity value of his [or her] photograph, i.e., the right to grant the exclusive privilege of publishing his [or her] picture * * * This right might be called a 'right of publicity.' "[4] Consequently, the "Right of Publicity" found legitimacy and recognition through the highly respected Court of Appeals for the Second Circuit.[5]

Soon after the right of publicity was recognized by courts, commentators pointed out that the importance of this right was the

---

[16]O'Brien, 124 F.2d at 170.

[Section 13:2]

[1]Haelan Laboratories, Inc. v. Topps Chewing Gum, Inc., 202 F.2d 866, 868 (2d Cir. 1953).

[2]Haelan Laboratories, 202 F.2d

at 867.

[3]Haelan Laboratories, 202 F.2d at 867.

[4]Haelan Laboratories, 202 F.2d at 867.

[5]Nimmer, 19 Law and Contemp. Prob. at 220.

acknowledgement of the economic reality of the pecuniary value inherent in publicity.[6] The value of privacy had been connected with whether a person's identity had been appropriated and used in an offensive manner. Consequently, the various privacy theories did not provide adequate protection for those who had their name or likeness appropriated. A specific tort for the right of publicity finally recognized the right of each person to control and profit from the publicity created by them.[7]

Among the shortcomings of the privacy theories used prior to the right of publicity was the fact that privacy rights are personal rights, and as such, are not capable of assignment and subsequent enforcement by the assignee. For the most part, the right of publicity is a property right, not a personal one. Thus, the right can be transferred and enforced by parties other than the actual one whose name or likeness is appropriated.[8]

Courts have continued to struggle with the difference between the commercial property right in identity and the traditional human dignity interests found in the right of privacy. Having resolved the existence of a right of publicity, various important issues, such as when does the right come into existence and when does the right end in relation to the life of the individual, continue to be tested in the courts.

Generally, right of publicity claims are not preempted by the Copyright Act because (1) a persona cannot be said to constitute a "writing" of an "author," and thus is not a "work of authorship" under the Copyright Act, and (2) names and likenesses do not become "works of authorship" merely by being embodied in copyrightable works such as photographs.[9]

§ 13:3 Policy behind the right of publicity

Research References

West's Key Number Digest, Torts ☞383

Several theories have been advanced to justify a right of publicity. One theory asserts a self-evident, natural property right.[1] *Pavesich* recognized that a business, in creating an advertisement, had no greater right to display an individual's likeness than it would to compel the person to take part in the

---

[6]Nimmer, 19 Law and Contemp. Prob. at 215.

[7]Nimmer, 19 Law and Contemp. Prob. at 216.

[8]Nimmer, 19 Law and Contemp. Prob. at 216.

[9]KNB Enterprises v. Matthews, 78 Cal. App. 4th 362, 92 Cal. Rptr. 2d 713, 28 Media L. Rep. (BNA) 1435, 53 U.S.P.Q.2d 1885 (2d Dist. 2000).

[Section 13:3]

[1]Pavesich v. New England Life Ins. Co., 122 Ga. 190, 50 S.E. 68 (1905).

advertisement.[2] This justification is premised on the view that an individual's identifiable aspects are legally recognizable property interests.

Another theory advances an incentive to promote socially desirable activities that require entry into the public scene.[3] This theory finds support in *Zacchini v. Scripps-Howard Broadcasting Co.*,[4] where the Supreme Court noted that Ohio's decision to protect a performer's right of publicity was based not only on the theory of compensation for time and effort, but also on the theory that individuals should be economically enticed to create public performances of interest.[5]

Additionally, an economic efficiency theory has been advanced.[6] According to the economic theory, in a free market, by granting an exclusive property right to a person's identity, the best and most efficient use of that identity will result. Simply stated, the party to whom the identity is most important will purchase a right to use it.

Finally, a "falsity" theory of the right of publicity has also been advanced. This theory views the right of publicity as a means to prevent false representations of product endorsement or commercial tie-ins.[7] However, some commentators have been critical of this theory. Falsity is the basis for other legal theories under state and federal law, such as the Lanham Act's false advertising provision, so under the falsity theory, the right of publicity appears redundant. Also, falsity is not an element to a right of publicity claim; a representation may be entirely true, yet still invade a person's right of publicity.[8]

Whatever theory is used to justify the right of publicity, it is clear that the right of publicity has been recognized by courts and legislatures. Although the right of publicity continues to develop and differs from state to state, it has found general acceptance as a cause of action.

§ 13:4 Enforcing the right of publicity—Common law claims

Research References

[2]*McCarthy* § 2.2 (*citing* Pavesich, 50 S.E. at 79).

[3]*McCarthy* § 2.6.

[4]Zacchini v. Scripps-Howard Broadcasting Co., 433 U.S. 562, 97 S. Ct. 2849, 2 Media L. Rep. (BNA) 2089, 205 U.S.P.Q. 741 (1977).

[5]*McCarthy* § 2.2.

[6]R. Posner, *Right of Privacy*, 12 Ga. L.Rev. 393, 411 (1978); *see also* R. Posner, *Economic Analysis of Law*, § 3.3 (4th ed.1992); *see also McCarthy* § 2.7.

[7]Fletcher & Ruben, *Privacy, Publicity and the Portrayal of Real People by the Media*, 88 Yale L.J. 1577, 1600 (1979).

[8]*McCarthy* § 2.8.

West's Key Number Digest, Torts ⚲386

After the right of publicity was recognized in *Haelan Laboratories*, it continued to develop in the common law of various states. Not surprisingly, the most significant cases arose in New York and California, where the entertainment industry is centered.

In the common law, the right of publicity continued to develop as a cause of action giving a plaintiff recourse when another person appropriates the plaintiff's name or likeness for commercial advantage. The cause of action is not personal in the sense of causing injury to the plaintiff's feelings or emotions. Instead, it focuses attention on whether the defendant reaped an economic windfall from plaintiff's enterprise to which the plaintiff is rightly entitled.[1]

One early California case to recognize a common law cause of action for the right of publicity was *Motschenbacher v. R.J. Reynolds Tobacco Co.*[2] In this case, the defendants used a photograph of a famous professional race car driver to sell Winston cigarettes. In finding for the plaintiff, the court stated that:

> So far as we can determine, California has no case on point; the state's appropriation cases uniformly appear to have involved only the "injury to personal feelings" aspect of the tort. Nevertheless, from our review of the relevant authorities, we conclude that the California appellate courts would, in a case such as this one, afford legal protection to an individual's proprietary interest in his own identity. We need not decide whether they would do so under the rubric of "privacy," "property," or "publicity"; we only determine that they would recognize such an interest and protect it.[3]

Eventually, the California courts formally adopted this interest as the right of publicity. A common law action under the right of publicity for appropriation of name or likeness may be brought in California by alleging:

- defendant's use of the plaintiff's identity,
- appropriation of plaintiff's name or likeness to defendant's advantage, commercially or otherwise,
- lack of consent, and

[Section 13:4]

[1]Lugosi v. Universal Pictures, 25 Cal. 3d 813, 834, 160 Cal. Rptr. 323, 335, 603 P.2d 425, 437, 5 Media L. Rep. (BNA) 2185, 205 U.S.P.Q. 1090, 10 A.L.R.4th 1150 (1979).

[2]Motschenbacher v. R. J. Reynolds Tobacco Co., 498 F.2d 821, 826 (9th Cir. 1974).

[3]Motschenbacher, 498 F.2d at 825-26 (footnotes omitted).

• resulting injury.[4]

California's common law cause of action for right of publicity is representative of common law claims available in other states that recognize this cause of action.

However, the first sale doctrine limits a right of publicity or commercial appropriation invasion of privacy claim. As a result, the lawful owner of an article including a celebrity's likeness may resell that article without being exposed to liability under a right of publicity claim.[5]

§ 13:5 Enforcing the right of publicity—State statutory claims

Research References

West's Key Number Digest, Torts ☞326

In addition to developing the common law, California was one of the states that adopted a statute codifying the right of publicity. California Civil Code § 3344 prohibits the use of another's name, voice, signature, photograph, or likeness for advertising or selling or soliciting purposes:

> Any person who knowingly uses another's name, voice, signature, photograph or likeness, in any manner, on or in products, merchandise, or goods, or for purposes of advertising or selling, or soliciting purchases of, products, merchandise, goods or services, without such person's prior consent, * * * shall be liable for any damages sustained by the person or persons injured as a result thereof.[1]

Unlike the common law cause of action, under the California statute, a plaintiff must show that the defendant *knowingly* used another's name for purposes of solicitation of purchases of products without such person's prior consent. Further, in addition to the explicit requirements of the statute, a plaintiff must also show a direct connection between the alleged use and the commercial purpose.[2] The statute was then changed in 1984 to no longer require a commercial use.[3]

Despite differences between the statute and the common law,

---

[4]Eastwood v. Superior Court, 149 Cal. App. 3d 409, 417, 198 Cal. Rptr. 342, 347, 10 Media L. Rep. (BNA) 1073 (2d Dist. 1983) (superseded by statute in Cal. Civ. Code § 3344).

[5]Allison v. Vintage Sports Plaques, 136 F.3d 1443, 46 U.S.P.Q.2d 1138 (11th Cir. 1998).

[Section 13:5]

[1]Cal. Civ. Code § 3344 (2014).

[2]Johnson v. Harcourt, Brace, Jovanovich, Inc., 43 Cal. App. 3d 880, 895, 118 Cal. Rptr. 370, 381 (2d Dist. 1974).

[3]KNB Enterprises v. Matthews, 78 Cal. App. 4th 362, 92 Cal. Rptr. 2d 713, 28 Media L. Rep. (BNA) 1435, 53 U.S.P.Q.2d 1885 (2d Dist. 2000).

it is clear that California Civil Code § 3344 complements the common law right of publicity. It is not a strict codification that replaces the common law claim.[4] California Civil Code § 3344(g) specifically provides that the remedies provided for in the statute are cumulative, so they are in addition to any remedies provided for by the common law. Thus, some have theorized that the common law action is actually a better option to plead, because it is less restrictive than the § 3344 cause of action since it does not require knowledge by the defendant.[5]

However, it is also clear that recovery under the common law may be available even when there is a failure to qualify under the statutory right.[6] Consequently, there does not appear to be any disadvantage to pleading both a common law and a statutory cause of action.

New York's statute covering the right of publicity is found in § 50 of its Civil Rights Law:

> A person, firm or corporation that uses for advertising purposes, or for the purposes of trade, the name, portrait or picture of any living person without having first obtained the written consent of such person, or if a minor of his or her parent or guardian, is guilty of a misdemeanor.[7]

The next statute, § 51, provides the right to bring a civil action to enforce § 50.

Sections 50 and 51 have their origin in the 1902 decision of *Roberson v. Rochester Folding Box Co.*[8] *Roberson* held that a young woman whose picture had been used by the defendant on flour advertisements without her consent could not recover for a violation of her right to privacy because no such right existed at common law. Dissatisfied, the Legislature responded to the court's decision the following year by amending the Civil Rights Law to establish a statutory "right to privacy." Since the adoption of these statutes, New York courts have repeatedly held that the right of privacy is governed entirely by this statute in New York.[9]

Since *Roberson* and the subsequent legislation in response to

---

[4]Eastwood, 198 Cal. Rptr. at 347 n.6.

[5]*See McCarthy* § 6.46.

[6]White v. Samsung Electronics America, Inc., 971 F.2d 1395, 20 Media L. Rep. (BNA) 1457, 23 U.S.P.Q.2d 1583 (9th Cir. 1992), as amended, (Aug. 19, 1992).

[7]N.Y. Civ. Rights Law § 50 (2014).

[8]Roberson v. Rochester Folding Box Co., 171 N.Y. 538, 64 N.E. 442 (1902) (disapproved of by, Vanderbilt v. Mitchell, 72 N.J. Eq. 910, 67 A. 97 (Ct. Err. & App. 1907)) (cited in Shamsky v. Garan, Inc., 167 Misc. 2d 149, 632 N.Y.S.2d 930 (Sup. 1995)).

[9]Shamsky, 632 N.Y.S.2d at 933.

it, New York courts have stayed faithful to the legislative begin-
nings of the right of publicity. Thus, unlike California, which recognizes both a common law and statutory right of publicity, New
York courts have held that the " 'right of publicity' is encompassed
under the Civil Rights Law as an aspect of the right of privacy,
which, as noted, is exclusively statutory in this State, [a] * * *
plaintiff cannot claim an independent common-law right of
publicity."[10] Consequently, a right of publicity action in New York
can only be pleaded under §§ 50 and 51 of the New York Civil
Rights Law, and cannot be pleaded under the common law.

Under § 50, a violation of the right of publicity consists of two
elements: the commercial use of a persons's name or photograph
and the failure to procure the person's written consent for such
use.[11] New York courts look to the statute's underlying purpose,
rather than adhering to its exact letter, and seek to protect an individual against "selfish, commercial exploitation" by another.[12]

§ 13:6 Proving infringement of the right of publicity—
Elements of a claim

Research References

West's Key Number Digest, Torts ☞410

Establishing an action for infringement of the right of publicity
typically involves proving the following elements:

- appropriation of plaintiff's identity, name or likeness,
- for defendant's commercial advantage,
- without plaintiff's consent, and
- resulting in injury.[1]

While the actual elements involved in a right of publicity action
will vary from state to state, most of the issues raised in these
elements will be central to any right of publicity claim.

§ 13:7 Proving infringement of the right of publicity—
Appropriation of plaintiff's identity, name or
likeness

Research References

---

[10]Stephano v. News Group
Publications, Inc., 64 N.Y.2d 174, 183,
485 N.Y.S.2d 220, 223, 474 N.E.2d 580,
583, 11 Media L. Rep. (BNA) 1303
(1984).

[11]Brinkley v. Casablancas, 80
A.D.2d 428, 432, 438 N.Y.S.2d 1004,
1012, 7 Media L. Rep. (BNA) 1457, 212
U.S.P.Q. 783 (1st Dep't 1981).

[12]Shamsky, 632 N.Y.S.2d at 933
(citing Rand v. Hearst Corp., 31 A.D.2d
406, 408–409, 298 N.Y.S.2d 405 (1st
Dep't 1969), order aff'd, 26 N.Y.2d 806,
309 N.Y.S.2d 348, 257 N.E.2d 895
(1970)).

[Section 13:6]

[1]31 Causes of Action 2d § 121
(2012).

West's Key Number Digest, Torts ⚖385

Whether a defendant is using the identity of another may seem fairly straightforward. However, defendants are often creative in their appropriation of a plaintiff's identity. For example, in one case, defendants produced and televised a commercial utilizing a color photograph depicting a professional racing driver's car. Although plaintiff was the driver, his facial features were not visible. Further, in producing the commercial, defendants slightly altered the photograph by changing the numbers on plaintiff's car from "11" to "71," attaching a wing-like spoiler to plaintiff's car, and adding the word "Winston" to that spoiler.[1] However, they made no other changes. The familiar white pinstriping, the oval medallion, and the red color of plaintiff's car were retained. The commercial was subsequently broadcast nationally on network television.

Several of plaintiff's witnesses who had seen the commercial on television had immediately recognized plaintiff's car and had inferred that it was sponsored by defendant's cigarettes. In reversing the district court's grant of summary judgement for defendants, the Court of Appeals for the Ninth Circuit ruled that defendants did use plaintiff's identity. The Court of Appeals agreed with the district court that the "likeness" of plaintiff was itself unrecognizable. However, the Court of Appeals disagreed that the driver is not identifiable. "[T]he [district] court's further conclusion of law to the effect that the driver is not identifiable as plaintiff is erroneous in that it wholly fails to attribute proper significance to the distinctive decorations appearing on the car. As pointed out earlier, these markings were not only peculiar to the plaintiff's cars, but they caused some persons to think the car in question was plaintiff's and to infer that the person driving the car was the plaintiff."[2]

In another case involving the creative appropriation of a person's identity, Ford Motor Company commissioned an impersonator to record a song from a 1973 Bette Midler album and to "sound as much as possible like the Bette Midler record."[3] In reversing the district court's granting of summary judgement for defendant, the Ninth Circuit held that there is a violation of a person's right of publicity when a distinctive voice of a professional singer is widely known and is deliberately imitated in or-

---

[Section 13:7]

[1]Motschenbacher, 498 F.2d at 822.

[2]Motschenbacher, 498 F.2d at 827.

[3]Midler v. Ford Motor Co., 849 F.2d 460, 461, 15 Media L. Rep. (BNA) 1620, 7 U.S.P.Q.2d 1398, 1399 (9th Cir. 1988).

der to sell a product.[4] Consequently, while using a person's picture to sell a product will certainly satisfy the "appropriation of identity" element, acts falling short of such blatant use may satisfy the requirement as well.

However, federal Copyright laws may preempt a right of publicity claim if the alleged misappropriation occurs with respect to copyrighted material. In 1981, Debra Laws recorded the song "Very Special" with Elektra/Asylum Records. Elektra copyrighted the song and, under the recording agreement, had "the exclusive worldwide right in perpetuity . . . to lease, license, convey or otherwise use or dispose of" the copyrighted master recordings. In 2002, Elektra entered into an agreement to grant Sony Music Entertainment, Inc., a nonexclusive license to use a sample of "Very Special" in the song "All I Have" by Jennifer Lopez and L.L. Cool J. Laws brought suit against Sony, alleging that Sony violated her common law right to privacy and statutory right of publicity by sampling her voice without her consent. The Court of Appeals for the Ninth Circuit affirmed the district court's decision that because the entirety of the allegedly misappropriated vocal performance was contained within a copyrighted medium, Laws' claims for violation of her common law right to privacy and her statutory right of publicity were preempted by the Copyright Act.[5]

§ 13:8   Proving infringement of the right of publicity— For defendant's commercial advantage

Research References

West's Key Number Digest, Torts ⊕392

Infringement of a person's right to publicity requires that defendant's use be commercial. There is no cause of action for infringement of a person's right of publicity based on news coverage or artistic criticism. Use of a person's name or likeness in connection with "any news, public affairs, or sports broadcast or account, or any political campaign" is not an infringement of a person's right to publicity.[1] This defense is similar to the fair use defense found in copyright and trademark law. It prevents celebrities from using their right of publicity to prevent legitimate news reporting or to shield themselves from criticism.

California courts have adopted a three-part test for determining whether a particular event or publication meets the criteria

---

[4]Midler, 849 F.2d at 462.

[5]Laws v. Sony Music Entertainment, Inc., 448 F.3d 1134, 1141, 78 U.S.P.Q.2d 1910, 1916 (9th Cir. 2006),

cert. denied, 549 U.S. 1252, 127 S. Ct. 1371 (2007).

[Section 13:8]

[1]Cal. Civ. Code § 3344(d).

for news-worthiness: the social value of the facts published, the depth of the intrusion into ostensibly private affairs and the extent to which an individual voluntarily acceded to a position of public notoriety.[2] One case employing this test involved a "legendary figure in surfing," Mickey Dora, who sued the producers of a documentary featuring him and other well-known surfers from the 1950s.[3] Explaining that he simply wished to be left alone, Dora brought a right of publicity claim and alleged that defendant's program did not meet *Maheu's* criteria for newsworthiness.[4]

In ruling against Dora, the court found that the program did have a public interest giving it social value, and that there was little, if anything, of a private nature that the program disclosed about Dora.[5] Although the court recognized that Dora "seems to have spent a good deal of energy avoiding the limelight," it found that sometimes those who do not seek the public eye are nevertheless sought out by it. The court, influenced by the fact that nearly all the program's footage of Dora was recorded at a public beach, stated that "[o]ne's voluntary action in a public place waives one's right of privacy as 'there can be no privacy in that which is already public.' "[6]

Many news programs and newspapers are commercial ventures that contain commercial advertisements. Simply because a commercial newspaper or television program makes use of a person's likeness does not mean that the use is commercial. Rather, whether a specific use is commercial is "a question of fact [as to] whether or not the use of the person's name, voice, signature, photograph, or likeness was so directly connected with the commercial sponsorship or with the paid advertising as to constitute a use for which consent is required."[7]

§ 13:9 Proving infringement of the right of publicity— Without plaintiff's consent

Research References

West's Key Number Digest, Torts ⚷395

The right of publicity may not be used to subvert other legitimate property rights. For example, a celebrity cannot prevent

---

[2]Maheu v. CBS, Inc., 201 Cal. App. 3d 662, 675, 247 Cal. Rptr. 304, 311, 15 Media L. Rep. (BNA) 1548, 7 U.S.P.Q.2d 1238 (2d Dist. 1988).

[3]Dora v. Frontline Video, Inc., 15 Cal. App. 4th 536, 18 Cal. Rptr. 2d 790, 21 Media L. Rep. (BNA) 1398, 26 U.S.P.Q.2d 1705 (2d Dist. 1993).

[4]Dora, 18 Cal. Rptr. 2d at 791.

[5]Dora, 18 Cal. Rptr. 2d at 792.

[6]Dora, 18 Cal. Rptr. 2d at 792 (quoting Gill v. Hearst Pub. Co., 40 Cal. 2d 224, 230, 253 P.2d 441, 444 (1953)).

[7]Cal. Civ. Code § 3344(e).

someone from using or selling copyrighted material that they properly own. Nor can it be used to prohibit someone from selling or transferring any materials containing the celebrity's name or likeness. Note, however, that this rule is similar to the "first sale" doctrine in copyright and trademark law. A celebrity cannot prevent downstream sale or use of a lawfully obtained article containing the name or likeness of the celebrity.[1] However, that is different from using the article as an advertisement. For example, the right of publicity cannot be used to stop someone from selling a photograph of a celebrity that the person owns lawfully. However, it can be used to prevent the person from reproducing the photograph in a magazine advertisement for a product the celebrity does not endorse.

If the person claiming a right of publicity is a minor, then the consent must be obtained from his or her parent or legal guardian.[2]

§ 13:10 Proving infringement of the right of publicity— Resulting in injury

Research References
West's Key Number Digest, Torts ☞385

As in most intellectual property cases, injury is presumed in right of publicity cases.[1]

§ 13:11 Right of publicity surviving the death of a celebrity

Research References
West's Key Number Digest, Abatement and Revival ☞52; Torts ☞384
C.J.S., Abatement and Revival §§ 130 to 141, 146, 148, 151 to 154; Right of Privacy and Publicity § 41

Soon after the right of publicity became recognized as a cause of action, the issue arose whether that cause of action could be brought by the descendants of the celebrity. In California, the courts decided that the right to exploit one's name and likeness is personal to the artist and must be exercised, if at all, during the

---

[Section 13:9]

[1]*See, e.g.,* Allison v. Vintage Sports Plaques, 136 F.3d 1443, 46 U.S.P.Q.2d 1138 (11th Cir. 1998) (first sale doctrine applies to prevent athletes from controlling resale of clocks and plaques that incorporated licensed sports trading cards).

[2]Cal. Civ. Code § 3344(a).

[Section 13:10]

[1]Agassi Enterprises, Inc. v. Target Corp., 2007 WL 4441195 (D. Nev. 2007) (*citing McCarthy* § 11:22).

lifetime of the artist.[1] In so deciding, the court reasoned that the right of publicity "is embraced in the law of privacy and is protectable during one's lifetime but does not survive death * * * ."[2]

Recognizing the distinct differences of the right of publicity from the law of privacy, the California legislature responded to the *Lugosi* decision by enacting California Civil Code § 3344.1. This legislation effectively overruled the *Lugosi* decision:

> Any person who uses a deceased personality's name, voice, signature, photograph, or likeness, in any manner, on or in products, merchandise, or goods, or for purposes of advertising or selling, or soliciting purchases of, products, merchandise, goods, or services, without prior consent from the person or persons specified in subdivision (c), shall be liable for any damages sustained by the person or persons injured as a result thereof.[3]

However, unlike in California, in New York the right of publicity is a privacy claim that is personal to an individual, is nontransferable, and is extinguished upon the individual's death.[4]

§ 13:12   Statute of limitations—Duration for bringing action

Research References

West's Key Number Digest, Torts ⚷413

In those places where the right of publicity is a property interest that may be enforced by a celebrity's heirs, the appropriate statute of limitations is often significant. One New Jersey court applied a six-year statute of limitations to a right of publicity claim. Its decision was based on the theory that appropriation of this right is injury to property. That is, defendant's action infringes a specific property interest in the right of publicity; it is not an injury to a person.[1] In California, the two-year statute of limitations period applied to property rights was also applied to right of publicity actions.[2]

§ 13:13   Statute of limitations—Tolling of statute

[Section 13:11]

[1]Lugosi v. Universal Pictures, 25 Cal. 3d 813, 160 Cal. Rptr. 323, 603 P.2d 425, 5 Media L. Rep. (BNA) 2185, 205 U.S.P.Q. 1090, 10 A.L.R.4th 1150 (1979).

[2]Lugosi, 25 Cal. 3d at 819, 160 Cal. Rptr. at 326, 603 P.2d at 428.

[3]Cal. Civ. Code, § 3344.1(a)(1).

[4]Smith v. Long Island Jewish-Hillside Medical Center, 118 A.D.2d 553, 499 N.Y.S.2d 167 (2d Dep't 1986).

[Section 13:12]

[1]Canessa v. J. I. Kislak, Inc., 97 N.J. Super. 327, 340, 235 A.2d 62, 70 (Law Div. 1967).

[2]Christoff v. Nestle USA, Inc., 62 Cal. Rptr. 3d 122, 140, 35 Media L. Rep. (BNA) 2002 (Cal. App. 2d Dist. 2007), as modified on denial of reh'g, (July 24, 2007) and review granted and opinion superseded, 67 Cal. Rptr. 3d 468, 169 P.3d 888 (Cal. 2007).

Research References
West's Key Number Digest, Limitation of Actions ☞55(1)
C.J.S., Limitations of Actions §§ 164, 167 to 170

Where a defendant's infringement of a plaintiff's right of publicity is continuing, each separate act gives rise to a separate cause
of action for purposes of the statute of limitations. A plaintiff is
not barred from bringing an action as long as there has been an
act of infringement by the defendant within the period of time
specified by the statute of limitations.

However, where the conduct constituting the infringement is
founded upon a one-time publication, such as a newspaper, book,
or magazine article, the "single publication rule" typically applies.
For example, California has codified the Uniform Single Publication Act.[1] This provides that the cause of action accrues upon the
date of the first publication.[2] Under such a scheme, successive
publication of CD-ROM containing copyrighted photographs was
held to be a single publication.[3]

§ 13:14 Remedies—Injunctions

Research References
West's Key Number Digest, Injunction ☞96, 138.75
C.J.S., Injunctions §§ 253, 255, 257

Injunctions are routine in right of publicity cases. Right of
publicity statutes all explicitly provide for injunctive relief. Under
the common law, right of publicity cases are viewed as equitable
actions, and a successful plaintiff is entitled to an injunction. The
more difficult issue is whether a plaintiff is entitled to damages.[1]

§ 13:15 Remedies—Damages

Research References
West's Key Number Digest, Damages ☞114

California law provides that plaintiff's damages comprise all of
defendant's profits attributable to the exploitation of defendant's

---

[Section 13:13]

[1]Cal. Civ. Code § 3425.3.

[2]*McCarthy* § 11.39.

[3]Auscape Intern. v. National
Geographic Soc., 461 F. Supp. 2d 174,
186–187, 35 Media L. Rep. (BNA) 1017
(S.D. N.Y. 2006), certification granted,

2007 WL 426731 (S.D. N.Y. 2007) and
judgment aff'd, 282 Fed. Appx. 890 (2d
Cir. 2008) (*citing* Belli v. Roberts Bros.
Furs, 240 Cal. App. 2d 284, 49 Cal.
Rptr. 625 (1st Dist. 1966)).

[Section 13:14]

[1]*McCarthy* § 11.22.

name and likeness.[1] Plaintiff has the burden of proving defendant's gross revenue attributable to the use and commercial exploitation of plaintiff's name and likeness, while defendant has the burden of proving all costs associated therewith. Statutory damages are also available.

Plaintiff is entitled to the fair market value of the services that defendant has appropriated.[2] Furthermore, plaintiff is entitled to the market value of the use of plaintiff's identity in the commercial setting in which defendant has used it.[3] Although some courts require a plaintiff to prove that his or her identity has value to meet the commercial advantage element of a claim for "right of publicity," the Colorado Supreme Court has found that the common law application of the tort does not require the plaintiff to prove the value of his or her identity where the damages sought are for mental anguish, not for recovery of commercial interests.[4]

Additionally, some states allow plaintiffs to recover additional damages, such as punitive damages for cases of oppression, fraud, or malice, and compensatory damages for both non-economic harms, including injuries to "peace, happiness, and feelings," and harms to a plaintiff's goodwill.[5]

§ 13:16 Remedies—Attorney's fees

Research References

West's Key Number Digest, Costs ☞194.28
C.J.S., Costs § 125

The prevailing party in any action is entitled to attorney's fees and costs. The grant of attorney's fees and costs is not discretionary under the California statute.[1] Fees and costs shall be awarded to a prevailing party. Note also that this provision applies to whomever prevails in the suit, plaintiff or defendant. Thus, an

[Section 13:15]

[1]Cal. Civ. Code § 3334(a).

[2]Hoffman v. Capital Cities/ABC, Inc., 33 F. Supp. 2d 867, 27 Media L. Rep. (BNA) 1527, 50 U.S.P.Q.2d 1195 (C.D. Cal. 1999), judgment rev'd on other grounds, 255 F.3d 1180, 29 Media L. Rep. (BNA) 1993, 59 U.S.P.Q.2d 1363 (9th Cir. 2001).

[3]Alonso v. Parfet, 253 Ga. 749, 325 S.E.2d 152, 52 A.L.R.4th 151 (1985).

[4]Joe Dickerson & Associates, LLC v. Dittmar, 34 P.3d 995, 29 Media L. Rep. (BNA) 2618 (Colo. 2001).

[5]Waits v. Frito-Lay, Inc., 978 F.2d 1093, 1103–1106 (9th Cir. 1992) (rejected on other grounds by, Conte Bros. Automotive, Inc. v. Quaker State-Slick 50, Inc., 165 F.3d 221, 49 U.S.P.Q.2d 1321, 1999-1 Trade Cas. (CCH) ¶ 72383 (3d Cir. 1998)) and (abrogated on other grounds by, Lexmark Intern., Inc. v. Static Control Components, Inc., 134 S. Ct. 1377, 188 L. Ed. 2d 392, 109 U.S.P.Q.2d 2061, 2014-1 Trade Cas. (CCH) ¶ 78716 (2014)).

[Section 13:16]

[1]Cal. Civ. Code § 3334(a).

unsuccessful plaintiff will not only fail to recover any damages of his or her own, but will be required to pay for defendant's attorney's fees.

§ 13:17   Defenses—First Amendment

First Amendment free speech rights do not automatically confer a defense to a right of publicity action.[1] The First Amendment may, however, provide a defense in certain circumstances. The Eighth Circuit has held that First Amendment rights may supersede a right to publicity even if a person's liceness is being used for a commercial benefit.[2] In that case, the defendant was using the names and performance and biographical data of actual major league baseball players to operate a website offering fantasy baseball games. Because that information was already in the public domain and is in the public interest, and because baseball players are already compensated for their performances, the court held that the right of publicity must give way to First Amendment considerations. Conversely, the Ninth Circuit held that a videogame developer's use of the likeness of college athletes was not "reporting" or publication of facts, and was therefore not, as a matter of law, protected by the First Amendment.[3]

[Section 13:17]

[1]Zacchini v. Scripps-Howard Broadcasting Co., 433 U.S. 562, 579, 97 S. Ct. 2849, 2 Media L. Rep. (BNA) 2089, 205 U.S.P.Q. 741 (1977).

[2]C.B.C. Distribution and Marketing, Inc. v. Major League Baseball Advanced Media, L.P., 505 F.3d 818,

823, 35 Media L. Rep. (BNA) 2473, 84 U.S.P.Q.2d 1328 (8th Cir. 2007), cert. denied, 128 S. Ct. 2872 (2008).

[3]In re NCAA Student-Athlete Name & Likeness Licensing Litigation, 724 F.3d 1268, 107 U.S.P.Q.2d 1629 (9th Cir. 2013), cert. dismissed, 135 S. Ct. 42, 189 L. Ed. 2d 894 (2014).

Chapter 14

Transferring, Licensing and Securing Intellectual Property Rights

---

KeyCite®: Cases and other legal materials listed in KeyCite Scope can be researched through the KeyCite service on Westlaw®. Use KeyCite to check citations for form, parallel references, prior and later history, and comprehensive citator information, including citations to other decisions and secondary materials.

---

§ 14:1   Assignments—Distinguishing between assignments and licenses

Research References

West's Key Number Digest, Copyrights and Intellectual Property ☞43, 48; Patents ☞193 to 213; Trademarks ☞1198, 1203
C.J.S., Copyrights and Intellectual Property §§ 27, 33, 93; Patents §§ 225 to 232, 316 to 338, 340 to 348, 350 to 355

An assignment results from a transfer of substantially all commercial rights in intellectual property. The transfer of anything less than substantially all commercial rights is a license.[1] When characterizing a transfer as a license or an assignment, courts look not only at the labels and terms used in the agreement, but also to the purpose and substance of the agreement as a whole.[2]

An assignment of intellectual property passes title in the intellectual property from an assignor to an assignee. The assignment enables the assignee to assert rights arising from holding title to the intellectual property. With a license, on the other hand, title remains with the licensor and the licensee obtains the right to use the intellectual property in the manner specified in the license agreement(s).

Examples of assignments of patents, trademarks, and copyrights can be found in Appendices U to W.

Examples of license agreements for patents, trademarks, and copyrights can also be found in Appendices X to Z.

§ 14:2   Assignments—Structure of assignments

Research References

[Section 14:1]

[1]Waterman v. Mackenzie, 138 U.S. 252, 11 S. Ct. 334 (1891).

[2]Jones v. Pepsi-Cola Co., 223 F. Supp. 650, 142 U.S.P.Q. 212 (D. Neb. 1963).

West's Key Number Digest, Copyrights and Intellectual Property ⚷43;
Patents ⚷196; Trademarks ⚷1199
C.J.S., Copyrights and Intellectual Property §§ 27, 33, 93; Patents
§§ 326 to 330, 340 to 341

In Writing. Assignment of intellectual property rights based
on federal statutes, such as patents, trademarks, and copyrights,
must be in writing.[1] Assignments of intellectual property that are
not governed by federal law, such as common law trademarks
and trade secrets, must conform with applicable state laws, such
as the Statue of Frauds.

Title. The title of the agreement should be relatively simple
and consistently referenced in capital letters to distinguish the
agreement from other agreements that may exist between the
parties. Generally, a title such as "ASSIGNMENT" will suffice.
However, when there are several assignments between the parties, a more specific title, such as "COPYRIGHT ASSIGNMENT"
or "ASSIGNMENT OF U.S. PATENT NUMBER 9,876,543,"
should be used.

Parties. Identify the parties to the agreement by reciting:

- Legal names of the parties,
- States of incorporation (for corporate entities) and
- Addresses of the portions of a corporation involved with the
  subject matter of the agreement.

After the parties' names are recited, the assignment should
identify each party with a short name that is used throughout
the remainder of the assignment. For simple assignments, the
names ASSIGNOR and ASSIGNEE will suffice. For complex assignments, short names derived from the legal names of the parties should be used.

Grant. The grant clause is the portion of the assignment that
sets forth exactly what type or types of intellectual property are
being assigned, as well as the terms of the assignment. The grant
clause should be drafted to unambiguously identify the intellectual property that is being transferred. While assignments are
conventionally thought to convey the entire interest in the intellectual property, the assignment may also convey an undivided
part interest in the intellectual property.[2] Therefore, the grant
clause should clearly state the amount of interest that is being
transferred.

Each form of intellectual property has its own unique restric-

---

[Section 14:2]

[1]35 U.S.C.A. § 261 (patents); 15
U.S.C.A. § 1060 (trademarks); 17
U.S.C.A. § 204 (copyrights).

[2]Site Microsurgical Systems, Inc.
v. Cooper Companies, Inc., 797 F.
Supp. 333, 24 U.S.P.Q.2d 1463 (D. Del.
1992).

tions that will affect drafting of the grant clause. For instance, a valid patent assignment requires agreement transfer of the rights to make, use, and sell the inventions set forth in all of the claims in the patent, as well as the right to prevent others from infringing the claims in the patent. If rights to less than all of the claims are transferred, the agreement is construed as a license.[3]

When assigning a trademark, the assignment must include the goodwill associated with the trademark.[4] A trademark is merely a symbol of goodwill and has no significance apart from the goodwill the trademark symbolizes. Because of this, a trademark cannot be transferred apart from the goodwill it symbolizes.[5] A person or business may not assign a trademark that does not have its goodwill attached to it. Since a trademark that has not been used cannot have any goodwill associated with it, a trademark that is the subject of an intent-to-use application may not be assigned other than to a successor until the applicant files a verified statement of use.[6]

With respect to a copyright, the owner need not transfer all exclusive rights[7] to maintain a valid assignment. The assignor is also free to impose geographic limits on the assignment of one or more exclusive rights without converting the assignment into a license, so long as the transfer is otherwise unrestricted.

When assigning trade secrets, the grant clause should only describe the trade secrets in general terms. It should not describe the trade secrets in specific terms because the assignment may be recorded with a federal or state agency. Since such recordation makes the assignment open for public inspection, disclosure of the trade secrets in the grant clause would destroy the trade secrets. The grant clause should also require that the assignor maintain the confidentiality of the information, so that the value of the trade secrets is not diminished.[8]

Compensation. When negotiating the compensation aspect of an assignment, the parties should analyze both the present value of the intellectual property and the future value of the intellectual property. Methods of valuing the intellectual property include determining how the intellectual property will make goods less expensive to manufacture or more appealing to

---

[3]Pope Mfg. Co. v. Gormully & Jeffery Mfg. Co., 144 U.S. 238, 12 S. Ct. 637 (1892).

[4]Memorylink Corp. v. Motorola Solutions, Inc., Motorola Mobility, Inc., 773 F.3d 1266, 1269, 113 U.S.P.Q.2d 1088 (Fed. Cir. 2014).

[5]Marshak v. Green, 746 F.2d 927,

223 U.S.P.Q. 1099 (2d Cir.1984).

[6]15 U.S.C.A. § 1060.

[7]17 U.S.C.A. § 201(d)(1).

[8]E.I. Du Pont De Nemours & Co. v. U.S., 153 Ct. Cl. 274, 288 F.2d 904, 129 U.S.P.Q. 473, 61-1 U.S. Tax Cas. (CCH) P 9359, 7 A.F.T.R.2d 1107 (1961).

consumers. It also includes a determination of the market for the products protected by the intellectual property.

One form of compensation involves a single payment of a fixed amount for the intellectual property rights set forth in the assignment. This form of compensation is commonly referred to as a lump sum payment because the fixed amount is typically paid in full when the assignment is executed. The lump sum payment may be desirable in fields where the assignor and the assignee do not need to have a working relationship after the initial transfer of the intellectual property. As an alternative to paying a fixed amount when the assignment is executed, the parties may agree to a payment of the fixed amount in a series of installments.

Another common compensation system involves payment of a royalty. The basis for the royalty and the amount of the royalty are commonly the most heavily negotiated aspects of an assignment. The royalty may be based on a specified amount for each item sold or a percentage of gross or net sales. To encourage an assignee to exploit the licensed intellectual property, the assignment may include a minimum royalty provision. The minimum royalty obligates the assignee to pay a specified amount regardless of whether the intellectual property is used. Another option to encourage the assignee to exploit the intellectual property is a regressive royalty. With a regressive royalty, the royalty rate proportionately decreases as the assignee's usage of the intellectual property increases.

A combination of a lump sum payment with periodic royalty payments is sometimes used as an alternative. The lump sum payment provides the assignor with immediate compensation for the assigned intellectual property and encourages the assignee to begin using the assigned intellectual property. The periodic royalty payments allow the parties to share the risks and rewards associated with the success of the assigned intellectual property.

In many instances, nominal consideration is received for an assignment. When examining the consideration aspect of assignments, courts typically do not inquire into the adequacy of consideration as long as the assignment specifies some type of consideration.[9] The identification of consideration as "good and valuable" along with a nominal payment can be sufficient for a valid assignment.[10]

Duration of Assignment. For patent and copyright assignments, the term of the assignment is the duration of the patent

---

[9]Transparent-Wrap Mach. Corp. v. Stokes & Smith Co., 329 U.S. 637, 67 S. Ct. 610, 72 U.S.P.Q. 148 (1947).

[10]Money Store v. Harriscorp Finance, Inc., 689 F.2d 666, 216 U.S.P.Q. 11 (7th Cir.1982).

or copyright, unless the assignment provides otherwise.[11] In certain circumstances, it may be desirable to include termination provisions in the assignment. For example, the assignor may desire to terminate the assignment if the assignee fails to complete payment obligations for the assignment or if the assignee fails to pay maintenance fees.

In contrast to patent and copyright assignments, trademark assignments must have a perpetual duration. If the duration is anything less than perpetual, the purported assignment is a license. In spite of this restriction, an assignor may retain the right to cancel the assignment upon the occurrence of a specified event, such as the liquidation of the assignee.[12]

Warranties. An assignment alone does not give the assignee the absolute right to produce or market the items associated with the intellectual property. There is always the risk that the products associated with the assigned intellectual property are protected by other intellectual property retained by the assignor.

In addition, a product may be covered by several patents. The assignment of one of these patents does not give the assignee the right to make or sell the product because the other patents can be used to prohibit such actions on the part of the assignee. One mechanism for protecting the assignee is an express warranty of noninfringement, where the assignor agrees to indemnify the assignee for any expenses relating to infringement of other intellectual property. As further protection, the assignee can also conduct a search for intellectual property that may be infringed by the assigned intellectual property. However, such searches are generally not feasible for copyrights or trade secrets.

Geographic Restrictions. A patent assignment may be limited in geographical scope to a portion of the United States.[13] Through such a transaction, the assignee obtains the right to enforce the patent within the specified geographical region. When assigning patents for specified geographic regions, care must be exercised to ensure that the assignment does not violate antitrust laws. It is also possible to assign trademarks for a portion of the United States using a territorial assignment.[14] A copyright assignment may be limited to certain geographic regions as long as the assignee is given the right to enforce the copyright within the

---

[11]Viacom Intern. Inc. v. Tandem Productions, Inc., 368 F. Supp. 1264, 181 U.S.P.Q. 749, 1974-1 Trade Cas. (CCH) ¶ 74866 (S.D.N.Y. 1974), judgment aff'd, 526 F.2d 593, 1975-2 Trade Cas. (CCH) ¶ 60636 (2d Cir. 1975).

[12]American Dirigold Corp. v. Dirigold Metals Corp., 125 F.2d 446, 52 U.S.P.Q. 510 (C.C.A. 6th Cir. 1942).

[13]35 U.S.C.A. § 261.

[14]Houlihan v. Parliament Import Co., 921 F.2d 1258, 17 U.S.P.Q.2d 1208 (Fed. Cir. 1990).

specified geographic region.[15]

Payment of Expenses. An assignment should address which party has the responsibility of obtaining and maintaining the intellectual property. For example, it should identify who is responsible for prosecuting a patent application or defending validity of an issued patent, either in court or before the U.S. Patent and Trademark Office (USPTO).

Assignment of Related Rights. When the assignment relates to a patent or a patent application, the assignment should address whether the assignment includes other related patents or patent applications, such as continuations, continuations-in-part, or reissues. The assignment should also address whether any foreign patents or patent applications corresponding to the U.S. patent or patent application are also within the scope of the assignment.

Prior Licenses and Other Encumbrances. When a patent or trademark is assigned, the assignee takes the patent or trademark subject to all prior licenses, even if the licenses were not recorded and the assignee did not have notice of the licenses. However, if the assignor represented that there were no prior licenses, the assignee would have a cause of action against the assignor for breach of warranty.

Recovery for Infringement. Assignment of intellectual property conveys with it the right to prevent others from infringing the intellectual property. However, without express provision to the contrary, an assignee only has the right to collect damages for infringement occurring after the execution of the assignment.[16] One excaption where courts have interpreted an assignment to include existing causes of action is in conjunction with the sale of an entire business.[17]

Assignment of Royalty Rights. Similar to the right to collect damages for infringement prior to an assignment, courts have held that an assignee only enjoys the right to collect royalties that accrue after the execution of the assignment unless the assignment expressly indicates otherwise.[18]

Signature. A valid assignment only needs to be executed by the assignor. While there are procedural advantages to having an assignment notarized or witnessed, these actions are not required for a valid assignment.

---

[15]17 U.S.C.A. § 201(d).

[16]Crown Die & Tool Co. v. Nye Tool & Machine Works, 261 U.S. 24, 43 S. Ct. 254 (1923).

[17]George W. Luft Co. v. Zande Cosmetic Co., 142 F.2d 536, 61 U.S.P.Q.

424 (C.C.A. 2d Cir. 1944).

[18]Chemical Foundation v. E.I. Du Pont de Nemours & Co., 29 F.2d 597 (D. Del. 1928), aff'd, 39 F.2d 366, 4 U.S.P.Q. 352 (C.C.A. 3d Cir. 1930), aff'd, 283 U.S. 152, 51 S. Ct. 403, 9 U.S.P.Q. 31 (1931).

§ 14:3   Assignments—Recording requirements

Research References

West's Key Number Digest, Copyrights and Intellectual Property ⑤46;
  Patents ⑤199; Trademarks ⑤1199
C.J.S., Copyrights and Intellectual Property §§ 27, 93; Patents §§ 326,
  328, 330

The patent statutes[1] and the trademark statutes[2] provide that assignments of patents, patent applications, federal trademark registrations, and federal trademark applications may be recorded with the USPTO. Recording patent and trademark assignments within three months of execution or prior to a subsequent transfer by the assignor protects the assignee by providing constructive notice of the transfer to subsequent transferees. The copyright statutes contain recording provisions that are similar to the patent and trademark recording provision. However, copyright assignments must be recorded within one month of execution or before the recordation of a subsequent transfer to take advantage of the constructive notice benefits.[3]

§ 14:4   Assignments—Prohibited assignment practices

Research References

West's Key Number Digest, Copyrights and Intellectual Property ⑤44;
  Patents ⑤129, 193; Trademarks ⑤1198
C.J.S., Copyrights and Intellectual Property §§ 27, 93; Patents §§ 225 to
  232, 316 to 319, 331

Intellectual property assignments must comply with antitrust laws. While an intellectual property owner is generally free to decide whether to assign intellectual property as well as to set the terms on which the intellectual property will be assigned, there are certain areas in which the transfer is restrained. One area that raises the potential for violating the antitrust laws is patent pooling. With patent pooling, members of the pool assign all patents into the pool so that other members of the pool can freely use the patented technology. Generally, patent pools are permissible as long as the pool is not enacted for predatory purposes and the pool does not impose restraints on the marketing of products by companies in the pool.

Another prohibition is that the assignor and the assignee of an assigned patent are estopped from challenging the validity of the

---

[Section 14:3]   [2]15 U.S.C.A. § 1060.
  [1]35 U.S.C.A. § 261.   [3]17 U.S.C.A. § 205.

patent.[1] This doctrine prohibits the assignor from representing that he or she is selling something of value and then challenging the validity of the transferred property.[2]

Additional prohibitions may apply to joint owners of a patent. Joint owners of a patent are free to make, use, offer to sell, or sell the patented invention without the consent of the other owners.[3] However, joint owners may only assign the portion of the patent to which they hold rights. Thus, assignment by a joint inventor or joint owner renders the assignee a partial assignee. The partial assignee would be similarly limited in assignment rights.

§ 14:5 Assignments—Termination of assignment

Research References

West's Key Number Digest, Copyrights and Intellectual Property ☞47; Patents ☞202(1); Trademarks ☞1200
C.J.S., Copyrights and Intellectual Property §§ 27, 33, 93; Patents § 332

While the issue of termination primarily arises with licenses, it is possible that termination may occur in the context of assignments. The parties can include provisions in the assignment that specify the conditions under which the parties may terminate the assignment as well as the process for terminating the assignment.

§ 14:6 Assignments—Arbitration

Research References

West's Key Number Digest, Alternative Dispute Resolution ☞142

Arbitration has become a popular mechanism for resolving many types of intellectual property disputes in a cost-effective manner. An arbitration clause should address how an arbitration proceeding can be initiated, how an arbitrator will be selected, and what rules will govern the arbitration. The arbitration clause should also specify any other important guidelines that govern the arbitration, such as whether the arbitration is binding on the parties and what type of relief may be obtained through the arbitration.

It is important to note that courts have held that subsequent transfers of intellectual property do not necessarily include all encumbrances from a previous license or assignment, including

---

[Section 14:4]

[1]Sybron Transition Corp. v. Nixon, Hargrave, Devans & Doyle, 770 F. Supp. 803, 21 U.S.P.Q.2d 1515 (W.D. N.Y. 1991).

[2]Diamond Scientific Co. v. Ambico, Inc., 848 F.2d 1220, 1225, 6 U.S.P.Q.2d 2028, 2031 (Fed. Cir. 1988).

[3]35 U.S.C.A. § 262 (Joint owners).

the duty to arbitrate.[1] The duty to arbitrate requires consent and must be signed by the party invoking it.[2] If a party to the previous license or assignment wishes to include such encumbrances in the subsequent assignments, it is suggested that any restrictions or encumbrances from previous agreements be explicitly included in the subsequent agreement.

§ 14:7 Assignments—Right to remedy a breach

Research References

West's Key Number Digest, Copyrights and Intellectual Property ☞47; Patents ☞203; Trademarks ☞1200

C.J.S., Copyrights and Intellectual Property §§ 27, 33, 93; Patents §§ 334 to 338

To encourage the parties to work through minor disputes that arise during the pendency of an assignment, the assignment may contain provisions for remedying these disputes prior to terminating the assignment. The provisions may include notifying the deficient party and allowing the deficient party a specified time period to correct the deficiencies.

§ 14:8 Assignments—Non-default

Research References

West's Key Number Digest, Copyrights and Intellectual Property ☞47; Patents ☞202(1); Trademarks ☞1200

C.J.S., Copyrights and Intellectual Property §§ 27, 33, 93; Patents § 332

The assignment may include provisions that delineate the obligations of the parties when occurrences beyond the control of the parties arise. Typically, these provisions specify that the affected party has an obligation to mitigate damages and that the failure of either party to perform its obligations after the occurrences does not constitute a breach to the extent that the damages could not be mitigated.

§ 14:9 Assignments—No implied continuing waiver

Research References

West's Key Number Digest, Copyrights and Intellectual Property ☞47; Patents ☞202(1); Trademarks ☞1200

C.J.S., Copyrights and Intellectual Property §§ 27, 33, 93; Patents § 332

In certain circumstances, it has been held that a party's failure

---

[Section 14:6]

[1]Datatreasury Corp. v. Wells Fargo & Co., 522 F.3d 1368, 86 U.S.P.

Q.2d 1440 (Fed. Cir. 2008).

[2]Datatreasury, 522 F.3d at 1373.

to assert its rights in response to a breach of the assignment constitutes a waiver of the right to object to the breach.[1] To prevent the waiver from being implied, the parties can include a provision in the assignment stating that no action or lack of action shall be construed as a waiver of any of the rights under the assignment.

§ 14:10 Assignments—Choice of law

Research References

West's Key Number Digest, Contracts ⊘129(1)
C.J.S., Contracts §§ 229 to 230, 238 to 240

Intellectual property assignments are governed by state law unless state law is preempted by federal law, such as for patent, trademarks, and copyrights. Choice of law provisions are typically desirable and generally enforceable as a long as the state selected has a logical relationship to the parties and the assignment.

§ 14:11 Assignments—Choice of forum

Research References

West's Key Number Digest, Contracts ⊘127(4)
C.J.S., Contracts §§ 236 to 237

Similar to choice of law provisions, courts generally enforce choice of forum provisions in assignments as long as the forum has a logical relationship to the parties and the assignment. Including a choice of forum provision in an assignment is often advisable in intellectual property assignments because it allows the parties to negotiate this as part of the initial agreement. It also reduces the chance that one of the parties will file a lawsuit before settlement negotiations are exhausted simply to gain an advantage in racing to file in a preferred forum.

§ 14:12 Licenses—Types of licenses

Research References

West's Key Number Digest, Copyrights and Intellectual Property ⊘48; Patents ⊘206 to 213; Trademarks ⊘1203
C.J.S., Copyrights and Intellectual Property §§ 27, 33, 93; Patents §§ 225 to 232, 342 to 348, 350 to 355

Licenses may arise in several different contexts, the most com-

---

[Section 14:9]

[1]Specialties Development Corp. v. C-O-Two Fire Equipment Co., 207 F.2d 753, 99 U.S.P.Q. 301 (3d Cir. 1953).

mon being in the form of an express agreement. An express license results from either oral or written agreements between a licensor and a licensee. An express license is typically what is meant by the common usage of the term "license."

A license may also be implied. Implied licenses arise by operation of law, in view of some objective manifestations of the parties. One situation where courts are likely to find an implied license is where an express license relates to a first patent and use of an invention in a second patent owned by the licensor is necessary for the licensee to enjoy the benefits of the express license.[1] Conversely, courts are generally reluctant to find an implied license where there is an express agreement between the parties regarding the general subject matter. Naturally, this is true where the implied license would be contrary to the express license.

A shop right is one form of implied license. It is a royalty-free, nonexclusive, and nonassignable license that is implied to enable a business to use intellectual property that was created using the business's resources or facilities.[2] The scope of the shop right depends on the nature of the invention, the business, the conduct of the parties, and other circumstances surrounding the creation of the intellectual property.[3]

§ 14:13 Licenses—Structure of license

Research References

West's Key Number Digest, Copyrights and Intellectual Property ⚖48; Patents ⚖208 to 211; Trademarks ⚖1204
C.J.S., Copyrights and Intellectual Property §§ 27, 33, 93; Patents §§ 225 to 232, 344 to 348, 350

While many licenses contain a common structure, details in the license make each license unique. Care should be taken when drafting a license to ensure that each of the provisions is appropriate for the particular license and that the terms of the license are sufficiently definite to enable a court to construe and enforce the license.

Title. The title of the agreement should be relatively simple and consistently referenced in capital letters to distinguish the agreement from other agreements that may exist between the parties. Generally, a title such as "AGREEMENT" or "LICENSE

[Section 14:12]

[1]Lever Bros. Co. v. Procter & Gamble Distributing Co., 668 F. Supp. 924, 5 U.S.P.Q.2d 1239 (D.N.J. 1987).

[2]Hazeltine Research Corporation

v. Freed-Eisemann Radio Corporation, 3 F.2d 172 (E.D.N.Y. 1924).

[3]Mitchell v. Hawley, 83 U.S. 544, 1872 WL 15359 (1872).

AGREEMENT" will suffice. However, when there are several licenses between the parties, a more specific title, such as "COPYRIGHT LICENSE" or "LICENSE OF U.S. TRADEMARK REGISTRATION NUMBER 98/765,432," should be used.

Parties. Identify the parties to the agreement by reciting:

- Legal names of the parties,
- States of incorporation (for corporate entities) and
- Addresses of the parties, including corporate addresses.

After the parties' legal names are initially recited, the license should set forth short names that are used to identify the parties throughout the remainder of the license. For simple licenses, LICENSOR and LICENSEE will suffice. For complex licenses, such as cross-licenses, short names derived from the legal names of the parties should be used.

Recitals. Traditionally, licenses have included a number of "WHEREAS" clauses that establish the environment and conditions that make entering into the agreement desirable for all parties. These clauses generally recite that a first party owns certain intellectual property, and a second party is interested in licensing the intellectual property. A "NOW, THEREFORE" clause is usually recited after the last "WHEREAS" clause to establish that the parties desire to enter into the licensing agreement.

Example:

WHEREAS, LICENSOR is the owner of certain PATENT RIGHTS (defined hereinafter) claiming DEVICES and/or METHODS (defined hereinafter);

WHEREAS, LICENSEE is a manufacturer of various equipment and desires to manufacture/employ the DEVICES/METHODS protected by PATENT RIGHTS; and

WHEREAS, LICENSEE would like to receive and LICENSOR is willing to grant a license under the PATENT RIGHTS.

NOW, THEREFORE, in consideration of the premises and mutual covenants contained herein, the parties agree as follows:

However, traditional "WHEREAS" and "NOW, THEREFORE" clauses are usually not necessary. Often, the facts stated in these clauses are obvious in light of the existence of the agreement itself. In addition, where a recital is included, the modern trend is to drop the capitalized "WHEREAS" and "NOW, THEREFORE" phrases, and draft the recital as a simple narrative, without the phraseology recited above.

While traditional recitals such as those shown above can often be eliminated with little harm, other recitals can serve a variety of purposes. An attorney drafting a licensing agreement should first decide whether a recital is necessary, and if so, should carefully draft the recital to achieve the ends desired.

For example, a recital can serve as an abstract or summary of the agreement, setting out in broad terms the basic elements of the agreement. This can be valuable if the agreement is exceptionally complex, and the executives signing the agreement are not in a position to understand every detail. In addition, such recitals are convenient for anyone who must manage a large number of unrelated agreements.

Since the recital may include an abstract or summary, and a series of broad admissions, it may be desirable to include a statement that the recital is provided for the convenience of the parties, and is not to be used in the interpretation or construction of license terms.

Example:

ABC is the owner of U.S. Patent No. 9,876,543 claiming DEVICES, and XYZ is a manufacturer desiring to manufacture the DEVICES protected by U.S. Patent No. 9,876,543. ABC is willing to grant a license under U.S. Patent No. 9,876,543.

Accordingly, the parties have entered into this LICENSE AGREEMENT, in which ABC grants to XYZ a license to manufacture DEVICES claimed by U.S. Patent No. 9,876,543.

The parties both regard U.S. Patent No. 9,876,543 as valid. Further, both parties envision that XYZ will be the sole manufacturer and seller of DEVICES in the United States of America and its Territories.

This recital is provided for the convenience of the parties and shall not be used in the interpretation or construction of this LICENSE AGREEMENT.

Definitions. It is important that key terms be defined within the licensing agreement. It is common practice to capitalize or boldface the defined terms wherever they appear in the body of the agreement.

Example:

LICENSED PATENTS shall mean U.S. Patent No. 9,876,543, and any reissue, divisional, continuation, or continuation-in-part applications filed thereon and patents issuing therefrom. In addition, LICENSED PATENTS shall include any corresponding patents or patent applications filed in any foreign country, or any reissue, divisional, continuation, or continuation-in-part applications filed in such foreign countries and patents issuing therefrom.

DEVICE shall mean any apparatus sold by LICENSEE that is claimed by any of the claims of LICENSED PATENTS.

METHOD shall mean any METHOD performed by any apparatus or used to manufacture any apparatus sold by LICENSEE that is claimed by any of the claims of LICENSED PATENTS.

NET SALES PRICE shall mean the price at which a DEVICE is invoiced in an arm's length transaction, less any royalties agreed to hereunder, discounts, sales taxes, excise taxes, or freight charges that are included in such invoice price.

TERM shall mean the period from the EFFECTIVE DATE to the date of cancellation by one of the parties under paragraph (Paragraph Number) hereof, or the last expiration date of LICENSED PATENTS, whichever occurs first.

AFFILIATE shall mean any entity that is controlled by LICENSEE or LICENSOR through ownership of at least 50% of the voting stock of such entity.

IMPROVEMENTS shall mean all modifications, variations, revisions, and new models of products manufactured and equipment employed under this LICENSE AGREEMENT, and all modifications, variations, and revisions to processes and methods used under this LICENSE AGREEMENT, that LICENSOR or LICENSEE may conceive, develop, or otherwise acquire.

Grant Clause. The grant clause is one of the most important clauses in a license. In the grant clause the parties set forth the type or types of intellectual property rights being licensed as well as the terms of the license.

The intellectual property rights transferred must be identified with particularity to minimize disputes relating to the scope of the license. For example, when licensing patents it is advisable to list the patent number, the title, the inventor's names, and the issue date. In addition, if only one of many rights associated with the intellectual property is being licensed, the grant clause should specifically indicate that right. For example, when the license includes the transfer of rights under a patent and only some of the claims in the patent are being licensed, the license should identify which claims are being licensed.

A licensor can limit the scope of the licensed intellectual property through a restricted license. Restricted licenses are permissible as long as the limitations do not violate any of the prohibited licensing practices, which are described later in this section. Examples of potential restrictions include: duration; manufacture, use or sale; field of use; geography; and quantity.

Improvements. When patent rights are licensed, the license should address the rights and responsibilities of the parties with respect to improvements in the patented subject matter. The improvements section should define what constitutes an improvement, address how the improvement will be protected, and set forth the parties' rights with respect to the improvement.

Defining what constitutes an improvement or a new invention is difficult because it encompasses subject matter that has not yet been conceived. The uncertainty relating to the nature of the improvement also makes it difficult to determine what type of intellectual property protection is best suited for the improvement.

One method of setting forth the parties' rights to the improvement is through a grant back clause. A grant back is a particular type of cross-license where the licensee's intellectual property comes into existence after the license is executed. A grant back clause gives the licensor access to improvements developed by the licensee.

Alternatively, the parties may include a clause that states that improvements in the licensed technology are the sole property of the party that makes the improvements. This type of winner-take-all clause can also be modified to grant each party a right of first refusal to acquire rights to the improvements.

Compensation. When negotiating the compensation aspect of a license, the parties should analyze both the present and future value of the intellectual property. Methods of valuing the intellectual property include determining how the intellectual property will make goods less expensive to manufacture or more appealing to consumers, as well as the expected market for the goods associated with the intellectual property.

One form of compensation involves the payment of a fixed amount at the beginning of the license. This type of compensation is commonly referred to as a lump sum payment because the fixed amount is typically paid in full when the license is executed. The lump sum payment may be desirable in fields where the licensor and the licensee do not need to have a working relationship after the initial transfer of the intellectual property. A potential drawback of the lump sum payment is that it is difficult to estimate the potential value of the license where the license lasts for an extended period of time.

As an alternative to paying the entire amount at the execution of the license, the parties may agree to payment of the fixed amount in a series of installments. While the installments do not account for variations in the commercial success of the intellectual property, they do give the licensee a greater period of time in which to raise money for the license.

Another method for paying the amount owed under a license is through periodic royalty payments. In many situations, periodic royalties are believed to provide a fair method of compensating the licensor for the licensed intellectual property because the licensee's payments are directly related to the success of the licensed intellectual property. For example, if the intellectual property relates to a market that is not established, the parties may find that the payment of periodic royalties provides the most equitable means of compensation.

Selection of the basis for the royalty and the amount of the royalty are heavily negotiated aspects of a license. The royalty may be based on a variety of factors, such as a fixed amount for each item sold under the license or a percentage of gross or net sales. An alternative compensation system involves a combination of a lump sum payment with periodic royalty payments. The lump sum payment provides the licensor with immediate compensation for the licensed intellectual property and encourages the licensee to begin using the licensed intellectual property. The periodic royalty payments allow the parties to share the risks and rewards associated with the intellectual property.

To encourage a licensee to exploit the licensed intellectual property, the license may include a minimum royalty provision or a regressive royalty. The minimum royalty obligates the licensee to pay a specified amount regardless of whether the intellectual property is used. A regressive royalty has a royalty rate that decreases as the licensee's usage of the intellectual property increases.

Other Compensation-Related Issues. A "most favored licensee" clause keeps the licensor from granting licenses to others on more favorable terms than negotiated with the licensee. If the licensor gives more favorable terms to a different licensee, the first licensee may elect to include those favorable terms into its license. Typically, however, the licensee must consent to all of the operative terms of the later license, even those that are less favorable than those set forth in the original license.

A common method for providing compensation in a license is through a cross-license. In a cross-license, each of the parties grants the other party some rights arising from an intellectual property asset. Cross-licensing is commonly seen where one party owns intellectual property and the other party owns improvements to the intellectual property. However, cross-licensing can also arise when both parties have large amounts of intellectual property that they are willing to license to gain access to other intellectual property rights.

In both cross-licensing and cash compensated licensing, the parties may be licensing more than one form of intellectual property. Since all forms of intellectual property can expire, it is important that such licenses detail the relationship between the compensation and the forms of intellectual property found in the license. For instance, if the license includes cash compensation for the right to use a trade secret and a related patent, the license should describe the amount of compensation that will be paid if one of these assets expires. This can be accomplished by assigning portions of the total compensation to each of the intellectual property assets or by indicating that the total compensation will be decreased by a fixed amount each time one of the assets expires.

In compensation systems involving royalty payments, the licensor often wants the ability to audit the licensee's operation so that the licensor can verify they are being appropriately compensated. To accommodate this desire, the parties can set forth an orderly process of preparation and disclosure of documents relating to the licensee's manufacture and sale of goods or services. In some situations it might also be necessary for the licensor to periodically monitor the licensee's operations to confirm that the licensee is honestly reporting its use of the licensed intellectual property. This process is typically set forth in a records and audit clause.

The licensor may also want some form of assurance that the licensee will use its best efforts to exploit the licensed intellectual property. This is especially true in exclusive licenses where the licensor is precluded from licensing the intellectual property to other parties and therefore dependent on a single licensee for revenue from the intellectual property. One form of assurance is a "best efforts" clause where the licensee agrees to exploit the intellectual property to the fullest extent possible. An alternative to a best efforts clause is a minimum royalty provision where the licensor receives a minimum royalty whether or not the licensee uses the intellectual property.

Licensing agreements often arise in the context of an infringement settlement where an infringer agrees to enter a license to avoid the expense of defending an infringement lawsuit. In such situations, the licensee wants the right to use the intellectual property but also wants a release for any past infringement. The release is important because a cause of action for infringement accrues to the intellectual property owner when its intellectual property rights are infringed. The later act of using the intellectual property under a license does not by itself exonerate the licensee for previously infringing the intellectual property.

Warranties. When licensing intellectual property, there is always the risk that practicing the licensed intellectual property may infringe intellectual property owned by other parties. The license should address how this burden is allocated. One mechanism for protecting the licensee is an express warranty of noninfringement where the licensor agrees to indemnify the licensee for any expenses relating to infringement of intellectual property owned by other parties. To provide additional protection to the licensee, the licensee may conduct a search for intellectual property that is infringed by the licensed intellectual property.

Confidentiality. A confidentiality clause protects the licensor when the subject matter of the license is not publicly known. Confidentiality clauses can vary greatly in scope. For example, a confidentiality clause may require the licensee to take extensive actions to limit disclosure of the licensed intellectual property, such as only disclosing the licensed intellectual property to a designated group of employees.

Mutual Disclaimers. In certain circumstances, it has been held that parties to a license become agents to each other so that the parties become liable for the debts, liabilities, or obligations of the other party.[1] To prevent this relationship from being implied between the parties, the license may contain explicit provisions to the contrary.

Supercession. To prevent statements made during the negotiations leading up to the execution of a license from impacting the terms set forth in the license, the license typically includes a clause that prevents the license from being modified by previous oral or written negotiations, representations, or agreements between the parties.

Alterations. Parties to a license typically find it desirable to explicitly state that the license cannot be altered, changed, supplemented or amended, except by a written agreement that is signed by each of the parties.

Transfer Restrictions. Without an express agreement to the contrary, an intellectual property license cannot be assigned or transferred. In spite of this implied restriction, parties to a license typically include provisions that expressly prohibit transfer of the license.

Right to Sublicense. Without an express agreement to the contrary, a licensee cannot grant sublicenses of an intellectual property license.[2] In spite of this implied restriction, parties to a license typically include provisions that expressly prohibit sublicensing.

Patent Marking. Failure to mark patented goods with a proper patent marking may preclude the licensor from recovering for infringement by a third party who has no knowledge of the patent. As a result, it is advisable for the licensor to insist that the licensee mark any goods that utilize patented technology.

Obligation to Prevent or Stop Infringement. Without a provision to the contrary, an intellectual property license does not include an obligation for the licensor to prevent others from infringing the licensed intellectual property. To overcome this

---

[Section 14:13]

[1]*See* Wood v. Holiday Inns, Inc., 508 F.2d 167, 176 (5th Cir. 1975) ("an agency relationship may arise from acts and appearances which lead others to believe that such a relationship has been created"); *but see* L.A. Gear, Inc. v. E.S. Originals, Inc., 859 F. Supp. 1294, 1299–1300, 32 U.S.P.Q.2d 1613 (C.D. Cal. 1994) (trademark license agreements do not in and of themselves create an agency relationship).

[2]PPG Industries, Inc. v. Guardian Industries Corp., 597 F.2d 1090, 13 Ohio Op. 3d 260, 202 U.S.P.Q. 95, 49 A.L.R. Fed. 878 (6th Cir. 1979).

presumption, licenses may include provisions that obligate the licensor to affirmatively act to prevent or stop infringement of the licensed intellectual property.

Signature Block. A license should be executed by both the licensor and the licensee to bind each of the parties to the terms of the license. While there are procedural advantages to notarizing and witnessing a license, these actions are not required for a valid license.

§ 14:14 Licenses—Prohibited licensing practices

Research References

West's Key Number Digest, Copyrights and Intellectual Property ⚷48; Patents ⚷208.1; Trademarks ⚷1203
C.J.S., Copyrights and Intellectual Property §§ 27, 33, 93; Patents § 344

Intellectual property licenses must comply with antitrust laws. A licensor cannot tie the licensing of a desired product to another product if the tying is involved in monopolization. Also, the licensor cannot condition the use of a licensed item on the licensee's promise to refrain from utilizing it in connection with items from competitors.

Another area that raises the potential for violating the antitrust laws is patent pooling. With patent pooling, members of the pool assign or license all patents into the pool so that other members of the pool can freely use the patented technology. Patent pools are permissible as long as they do not impose restraints on the marketing of products by companies in the pool and they are not enacted for predatory purposes, such as monopolization.

In addition, a patent license cannot require the payment of royalties beyond the term of the licensed patent even if the patent was not in existence at the time the license was executed.[1] However, if a patent license also includes trade secret aspects, royalties relating to the trade secret may be collected after the patent expires as long as the license includes an allocation of royalties distinguishing between the patent aspects and the trade secret aspects.

Licensees are free to challenge the validity of patents they license,[2] and contractual restrictions of a licensee's ability to challenge patent validity are generally not enforceable.[3] However, these restrictions may be enforceable where the licensing agree-

---

[Section 14:14]

[1]Brulotte v. Thys Co., 379 U.S. 29, 85 S. Ct. 176, 143 U.S.P.Q. 264, 3 A.L.R.3d 761 (1964).

[2]Lear, Inc. v. Adkins, 395 U.S. 653, 89 S. Ct. 1902, 23 L. Ed. 2d 610, 162 U.S.P.Q. 1 (1969).

[3]Rates Technology Inc. v. Speakeasy, Inc., 685 F.3d 163, 103 U.S.P.Q.2d 1462 (2d Cir. 2012), cert.

ment was created between parties after litigation commenced.[4]

§ 14:15 Licenses—Termination of agreement

Research References

West's Key Number Digest, Copyrights and Intellectual Property ⊙48; Patents ⊙214; Trademarks ⊙1206
C.J.S., Copyrights and Intellectual Property §§ 27, 33, 93; Patents §§ 356 to 363

The license should set forth the rights and responsibilities of the parties regarding unforeseen changes in the scope of any licensed intellectual property which may occur. For example, with respect to patent licenses, the license might set forth the rights and responsibilities of the parties in the event of cancellation of claims, invalidation, an interference proceeding, or a reexamination proceeding. In addition, the license should specify which party has the responsibility of defending the patents in a reexamination or interference proceeding, or in litigation. If the licensee is a relatively large entity and the licensing agreement provides an exclusive license to the licensee, it may be desirable to assign the duty to defend any licensed patents to the licensee. An area that raises some concern with respect to termination is that the "actual controversy" requirement of the Declaratory Judgment Act does not require that a licensee breach its licensing agreement by refusing to pay royalties prior to alleging either patent invalidity or non-infringement.[1] This is important to keep in mind when drafting the license agreement. For example, a licensor may want to consider adding a clause that allows the licensor to terminate the license agreement if the licensee challenges the validity of the patent, that specifies venue for validity challenges, or that shifts costs for an unsuccessful validity challenge, among other possibilities.

§ 14:16 Licenses—Arbitration

Research References
West's Key Number Digest, Alternative Dispute Resolution ⊙142

Arbitration has become a popular mechanism for resolving

---

denied, 133 S. Ct. 932, 184 L. Ed. 2d 724 (2013).

[4]Flex-Foot, Inc. v. CRP, Inc., 238 F.3d 1362, 57 U.S.P.Q.2d 1635 (Fed. Cir. 2001).

[Section 14:15]

[1]MedImmune, Inc. v. Genentech, Inc., 549 U.S. 118, 127 S. Ct. 764, 166

L. Ed. 2d 604, 81 U.S.P.Q.2d 1225, 2007-1 Trade Cas. (CCH) ¶ 75543 (2007).

licensing disputes in a cost effective manner. An arbitration clause should address how an arbitration proceeding can be initiated, how an arbitrator will be selected, and what rules will govern the arbitration. The arbitration clause should also specify any other important guidelines that should govern the arbitration, such as whether the arbitration is binding on the parties and what type of relief may be obtained through the arbitration.

It is important to note that courts have held that subsequent transfers of intellectual property do not necessarily include all encumbrances from a previous license or assignment, including the duty to arbitrate.[1] The duty to arbitrate requires consent and must be signed by the party invoking it.[2] If a party to the previous license or assignment wishes to include such encumbrances in the subsequent assignments, it is suggested that any restrictions or encumbrances from previous agreements be explicitly included in the subsequent agreement.

§ 14:17 Licenses—Right to remedy a breach

Research References

West's Key Number Digest, Copyrights and Intellectual Property ⚖48; Patents ⚖212; Trademarks ⚖1205

C.J.S., Copyrights and Intellectual Property §§ 27, 33, 93; Patents §§ 352 to 355

To encourage the parties to work through minor disputes that arise during the pendency of a license, the license may contain provisions for remedying disputes prior to terminating the license. The provisions may include notifying the deficient party and allowing the deficient party a specified time period to correct the deficiencies.

§ 14:18 Licenses—Non-default

Research References

West's Key Number Digest, Copyrights and Intellectual Property ⚖48; Patents ⚖212; Trademarks ⚖1205

C.J.S., Copyrights and Intellectual Property §§ 27, 33, 93; Patents §§ 352 to 355

A license may include provisions that delineate the obligations of the parties when events beyond the control of the parties arise. Typically, these provisions specify that the affected party has an obligation to mitigate damages and that the failure of either

---

[Section 14:16]

[1]Datatreasury Corp. v. Wells Fargo & Co., 522 F.3d 1368, 86 U.S.P.

Q.2d 1440 (Fed. Cir. 2008).

[2]Datatreasury, 522 F.3d at 1373.

party to perform its obligations after such an event does not constitute a breach to the extent that the damages could not be mitigated.

§ 14:19 Licenses—No implied continuing waiver

Research References

West's Key Number Digest, Copyrights and Intellectual Property ☞48; Patents ☞212; Trademarks ☞1205

C.J.S., Copyrights and Intellectual Property §§ 27, 33, 93; Patents §§ 352 to 355

In certain circumstances, it has been held that a party's failure to assert its rights in response to a breach of a license constitutes a waiver of the ability to object to the breach at a later time.[1] To prevent the waiver from being implied, the parties may include a provision in the license stating that no action or lack of action shall be construed as a waiver of any of the rights under the license.

§ 14:20 Licenses—Choice of law

Research References

West's Key Number Digest, Contracts ☞129(1)
C.J.S., Contracts §§ 229 to 230, 238 to 240

Intellectual property licenses are governed by state law unless state law is preempted by federal law, such as for patents, trademarks, and copyrights. Choice of law provisions are typically found in licenses because they provide some certainty regarding the construction and enforcement of the license provisions. Choice-of-law provisions are generally enforceable as a long as the state selected has a logical relationship to the parties and the license.

§ 14:21 Licenses—Choice of forum

Research References

West's Key Number Digest, Contracts ☞127(4)
C.J.S., Contracts §§ 236 to 237

Similar to choice of law provisions, courts generally enforce choice of forum provisions in license agreements as long as the forum has a logical relationship to the parties and the license. Including a choice of forum provision in a license is often advisable in intellectual property licenses because it reduces the

---

[Section 14:19]

[1]Trace Minerals Research, L.C.

v. Mineral Resources Intern., Inc., 505 F. Supp. 2d 1233, 1243 (D. Utah 2007).

chance that one of the parties will file suit before negotiations are exhausted simply to gain their choice of forum.

§ 14:22   Security interests—Creation of a security interest

Research References

West's Key Number Digest, Secured Transactions ⊙5
C.J.S., Secured Transactions §§ 2 to 6

A security interest is created by a written agreement (the "security agreement") signed by the debtor, expressing an intent to create a security interest, and describing the collateral subject to the security interest.[1] The security interest is perfected by filing a financing statement for the security agreement.[2] The collateral may be "goods"[3] or "general intangibles."[4] The classification of collateral as "goods" or "general intangibles" affects both the rights acquired in the collateral, as well as the method of perfecting the security interest. Therefore, it is extremely important that collateral be correctly classified.

Intellectual property, including patents, trademarks, service marks, copyrights, mask work registrations, trade secrets, know-how, etc., are classified as "general intangibles" rather than "goods."[5] "Goods," as used in the UCC, includes products, such as copies of printed books, as opposed to the right to make or distribute copies of the books. "General intangibles," as used in the UCC, include the right to use trade secrets and know-how, the right to print or distribute books, the right to modify software, and the right to manufacture products. The distinction is subtle, but important: If computer programs or products are identified as goods in the security agreement, the secured party or purchaser at foreclosure acquires no right to produce the product or modify the software. They only acquire the computer programs or the products that exist at the time of the foreclosure.

In *Kingsrow Enterprises, Inc. v. Metromedia, Inc.*,[6] the judgment-sale purchase of television broadcast tapes identified as "goods" did not include the right to broadcast the tapes under the copyright. Also, in *U.S. v. Antenna Systems, Inc.*,[7] a security agreement for "goods" did not include blueprints of product designs because they were research materials concerning

---

[Section 14:22]

[1]U.C.C. §§ 9-203(1)(a), 9-203(b)(3)(A).

[2]U.C.C. § 9-310(a).

[3]U.C.C. §§ 9-105(1)(h), 9-102(a)(44).

[4]U.C.C. §§ 9-106, 9-102(a)(42).

[5]U.C.C. §§ 9-106, 9-102 cmt. 5.d.

[6]Kingsrow Enterprises, Inc. v. Metromedia, Inc., 203 U.S.P.Q. 489, 1978 WL 952 (S.D.N.Y. 1978).

[7]U.S. v. Antenna Systems, Inc., 251 F. Supp. 1013, 3 U.C.C. Rep. Serv. 258 (D.N.H. 1966).

"intangible" trade secrets.

The distinction is particularly delicate with computer programs. The UCC identifies a computer program as a "good" if the computer program is embedded in a good and is customarily considered part of the good, or if, by becoming the owner of the good, a person acquires a right to use the computer program in connection with the good.[8] An example of this situation involves hardware drivers embedded in computers. The drivers are computer programs that are considered part of the computer goods, and are treated as goods in a security agreement. In contrast, however, the term "goods" does not include computer programs embedded in products that consist solely of the medium in which the program is embedded, such as computer programs embedded on disks.[9] Computer programs in this latter category are identified as "software" by the UCC and are treated as "general intangibles."[10]

§ 14:23 Security interests—Perfecting the security interest—Perfecting under the UCC

Research References

West's Key Number Digest, Secured Transactions ⚷81; States ⚷18.87
C.J.S., Copyrights and Intellectual Property § 8; Monopolies § 20; Secured Transactions §§ 2, 50 to 51, 53 to 54, 62

As a general rule, a security interest in both goods and general intangibles (such as intellectual property) is perfected by filing a financing statement in the jurisdiction of the principal place of business or residence of the debtor.[1] However, there is an important exception to this rule that affects intellectual property. UCC filing is not necessary or effective if the property is subject to a federal statute, regulation, or treaty of the United States, and if the federal statute, regulation, or treaty establishes a separate system of filing the security interest.[2] In such a case, UCC filing is preempted by the federal statute, regulation, or treaty, and is ineffective.[3]

§ 14:24 Security interests—Perfecting the security interest—Preemption of UCC filing

Research References

---

[8]U.C.C. § 9-102(a)(44).

[9]U.C.C. § 9-102(a)(44).

[10]U.C.C. §§ 9-102(a)(75), 9-102 cmt. 4.a., 9-102 cmt. 25.

[Section 14:23]

[1]U.C.C. §§ 9-103(3), 9-301(1),

9-301 cmt. 4, 9-307, 9-310(a).

[2]U.C.C. §§ 9-302(3), 9-310(b)(3), 9-311(a)(1).

[3]U.C.C. §§ 9-104(a), 9-109(c)(1), 9-109 cmt. 8.

West's Key Number Digest, Secured Transactions ⊕81; States ⊕18.87
C.J.S., Copyrights and Intellectual Property § 8; Monopolies § 20;
  Secured Transactions §§ 2, 50 to 51, 53 to 54, 62

Security interests are accepted for recording by the U.S. Patent
and Trademark Office (patents, patent applications, federal
trademark registrations, and federal trademark applications),
the U.S. Copyright Office (copyright, vessel hull designs, and
semiconductor mask work registrations) and the Plant Variety
Office (plant variety certificates). Whether recording the security
interest at the federal level is necessary, and whether UCC filing
is preempted by federal recording statutes, however, are two different questions which must be addressed separately for different
types of intellectual property.

Preemption under the Supremacy Clause of the U.S. Constitution invalidates state laws that interfere with or are contrary to
federal law.[1] Preemption generally falls into three categories:
express preemption, field preemption, and conflict preemption.[2]
Express preemption occurs where Congress expressly and clearly
states that UCC filing is preempted.[3] Even if Congress does not
expressly preempt the UCC, field preemption occurs when the
federal regulation is sufficiently comprehensive to infer that
Congress left no room for supplementary state regulation.[4]
Finally, conflict preemption occurs when it is impossible to comply
with both the UCC and federal law, or if the UCC obstructs
Congress' purposes and objectives.[5]

UCC § 9-109(c)(1) recognizes that Article 9 of the UCC does not
apply if preempted by a federal statute, regulation, or treaty.
Therefore, if UCC filing is preempted, only recording under the
federal statute will perfect the security interest.[6] State filing
under the UCC will have no force or effect.

§ 14:25 Security interests—Perfecting the security
interest—Copyrights and mask works

Research References

West's Key Number Digest, Copyrights and Intellectual Property ⊕46;
  Secured Transactions ⊕81; States ⊕18.87
C.J.S., Copyrights and Intellectual Property §§ 8, 27, 93; Monopolies
  § 20; Secured Transactions §§ 2, 50 to 51, 53 to 54, 62

[Section 14:24]

[1]U.S. Const. Art. VI, cl. 2.

[2]In re Cybernetic Services, Inc., 252 F.3d 1039, 1045, 59 U.S.P.Q.2d 1097, 44 U.C.C. Rep. Serv. 2d 639 (9th Cir. 2001).

[3]In re Cybernetic Services, 252 F.3d at 1046.

[4]In re Cybernetic Services, 252 F.3d at 1045.

[5]In re Cybernetic Services, 252 F.3d at 1045.

[6]U.C.C. §§ 9-109(c)(1), 9-311.

The leading case on preemption is *In re Peregrine Entertainment, Ltd.*,[1] which held that the copyright recording statute[2] and its implementing regulation[3] preempt UCC filing for recording security interests in *registered* copyrights. In addressing the appropriate location for recording a security interest in a registered copyright, the *Peregrine* court reasoned that dual recording under both the UCC and the Copyright Act would undermine the ability of an interested party to search a specific location to determine whether a particular interest had been transferred or encumbered, and undermine the priority scheme intended by Congress with respect to registered copyrights. Therefore, security interests in registered copyrights can only be perfected by recording the security agreement with the Copyright Office.

The *Peregrine* decision did not address whether preemption applied to unregistered copyrights. However, the Ninth Circuit Court of Appeals in California, while affirming *Peregrine* with respect to *registered* copyrights, held that the UCC is not preempted by the Copyright Act for *unregistered* copyrights.[4] No other circuit has contradicted the Ninth Circuit with respect to preemption of UCC recording requirements for unregistered copyrights. Nevertheless, a creditor holding a security interest in an unregistered copyright should record the security interest both at the State level under the UCC and with the Copyright Office. In addition, the creditor should require the copyright claimant or debtor to register the copyright as a condition of the security agreement. The reason for this is that an instrument that affects unregistered copyrights and which is recorded with the Copyright Office gives constructive notice to third parties effective as of the date of subsequent registration of the copyright.[5] However, the creditor may not have standing to register the copyright, even ofter granting of the security interest. Only a copyright claimant or holder of exclusive rights has standing under § 101 of the Copyright Act.

A mask work is a two- or three-dimensional layout of an integrated circuit. The Semiconductor Chip Protection Act includes a recording statute for mask works[6] similar to the copyright recording statute and an implementing regulation[7] that incorporates the copyright implementing regulation. In light of

---

[Section 14:25]

[1]In re Peregrine Entertainment, Ltd., 116 B.R. 194, 203, 16 U.S.P.Q.2d 1017, 11 U.C.C. Rep. Serv. 2d 1025 (C.D. Cal. 1990).

[2]17 U.S.C.A. § 205(a).

[3]37 C.F.R. § 201.4.

[4]In re World Auxiliary Power Co., 303 F.3d 1120, 40 Bankr. Ct. Dec.

(CRR) 36, 49 Collier Bankr. Cas. 2d (MB) 518, 64 U.S.P.Q.2d 1433, 48 U.C.C. Rep. Serv. 2d 447 (9th Cir. 2002).

[5]2 Melville B. Nimmer & David Nimmer, The Law Of Copyright § 7.16[E] (1991).

[6]17 U.S.C.A. § 903(c).

[7]37 C.F.R. § 211.2.

the *Peregrine* decision, it is probable that a court would find that the UCC filing requirements are preempted by the mask work recording statute and that security interests in mask work registrations must be recorded with the Copyright Office to be perfected.

§ 14:26   Security interests—Perfecting the security interest—Patents and plant variety certificates

Research References

West's Key Number Digest, Patents ⊕199; Secured Transactions ⊕81; States ⊕18.87

C.J.S., Copyrights and Intellectual Property § 8; Monopolies § 20; Patents §§ 326, 328, 330; Secured Transactions §§ 2, 50 to 51, 53 to 54, 62

The *Peregrine* decision considered two earlier cases that addressed recording of security interests in patents.[1] Both cases held that, unlike licenses and assignment, security interests in patents could be recorded at the state level pursuant to the UCC, and the patent recording statute[2] and its implementing regulation[3] protect only subsequent purchasers and mortgagees, not lien creditors of the type intended to be protected by the UCC Similarly, in *In re Cybernetic Services, Inc.*[4], a bankruptcy appellant panel for the Ninth Circuit held that a UCC financing statement filed with the California Secretary of State rather than the USPTO was sufficient to perfect a security interest in a patent. Unlike the Federal Copyright Act, the Patent Act does not preempt state law because the Patent Act is not sufficiently comprehensive to exclude state requirements for perfecting security interests in patents.

Nonetheless, it is unclear if recording in the USPTO is even effective to perfect the security interests. The Tenth Circuit Court of Appeals, in a nonprecedential decision, held that because the Patent Act does not preempt the UCC, filing a security agreement with the USPTO alone, without meeting the UCC perfection requirements, fails to perfect a security interest.[5] Pursuant to this reasoning, only filing a financing statement pursuant to the applicable state implementation of the UCC would perfect

---

[Section 14:26]

[1]*See* In re Transportation Design and Technology, Inc., 48 B.R. 635, 226 U.S.P.Q. 424, 40 U.C.C. Rep. Serv. 1393 (Bankr. S.D. Cal. 1985) and City Bank and Trust Co. v. Otto Fabric, Inc., 83 B.R. 780, 7 U.S.P.Q.2d 1719, 5 U.C.C. Rep. Serv. 2d 1459 (D. Kan. 1988) (both rejected by In re Peregrine Entertainment, Ltd., 116 B.R. 194, 16

U.S.P.Q.2d 1017, 11 U.C.C. Rep. Serv. 2d 1025 (C.D. Cal. 1990)).

[2]35 U.S.C.A. § 261.

[3]37 C.F.R. § 1.331.

[4]In re Cybernetic Services, 252 F.3d at 1052.

[5]In re Tower Tech, Inc., 67 Fed. Appx. 521, 50 U.C.C. Rep. Serv. 2d 923 (10th Cir. 2003).

the security interest.

The Plant Variety Act includes provisions for recording plant variety certificates that are similar to the patent recording statute.[6] The supporting regulations implementing the plant variety recording statute are similar to the regulations implementing the patent recording statute.[7] Therefore, it is probable that UCC filing provisions are not preempted by the plant variety recording statute as to Plant Variety Certificates and that security interests in Plant Variety Certificates can be recorded either with the Plant Variety Office or under state UCC filings.

§ 14:27 Security interests—Perfecting the security interest—Federally registered trademarks and goodwill

Research References

West's Key Number Digest, Secured Transactions ⊚81; States ⊚18.87; Trademarks ⊚1200

C.J.S., Copyrights and Intellectual Property § 8; Monopolies § 20; Secured Transactions §§ 2, 50 to 51, 53 to 54, 62

The federal statutory basis for recording interests in federal trademark registrations is limited to actual transfers of title and does not include security interests.[1] The implementing regulation indicates that assignments must be recorded by the Commissioner, but other instruments may be recorded at the discretion of the Commissioner.[2] Based on this discretion, the USPTO has adopted the practice of accepting security interests in federally registered trademarks and applications for trademarks if the security interest includes the goodwill of the business with which the mark is associated.

Nevertheless, courts have consistently held that because the federal trademark statute and implementing regulation are limited to recording of assignments and outright transfers, security interests in federally registered trademarks should be filed under the UCC.[3] The court in *In re 199Z, Inc.*[4] relied on *Peregrine* in holding that federal trademark law does not preempt the UCC provisions for perfection of security interests. The court drew a distinction between the Copyright Act that "provides expressly

---

[6]7 U.S.C.A. § 2531.

[7]7 C.F.R. § 180.130.

[Section 14:27]

[1]35 U.S.C.A. § 1060.

[2]37 C.F.R. § 2.185.

[3]Matter of Roman Cleanser Co., 43 B.R. 940, 944, 225 U.S.P.Q. 140, 39 U.C.C. Rep. Serv. 1770 (Bankr. E.D. Mich. 1984); In re TR-3 Industries, 41 B.R. 128, 131, 39 U.C.C. Rep. Serv. 279 (Bankr. C.D. Cal. 1984).

[4]In re 199Z, Inc., 137 B.R. 778, 781-82, 17 U.C.C. Rep. Serv. 2d 598 (Bankr. C.D. Cal. 1992).

for the filing of any 'mortgage' or 'hypothecation' of a copyright"
and the Lanham Act that "provides expressly only for the filing of
an assignment of a trademark."[5] Since an assignment is distinct
from a security interest, the Lanham Act does not apply. Thus,
the UCC is not preempted.[6]

Debtors should be particularly careful where a trademark is
the subject of a security interest. Banks ordinarily require a security interest in the form of an assignment of the trademark application and registration, with a promise to re-assign the same
to the debtor upon repayment of the loan. This poses several
problems unique to trademarks. First, by what right can the
debtor continue to use the trademark assigned to the bank? It is
likely that the nature of the transaction would be viewed as at
least a tacit license back to the debtor. Second, if such a license
exists, how are the quality measures required for trademark licenses governed? It is likely that the quality would be that which
the debtor adopted in the first place, and therefore continues to
govern. The more serious issues arise where only the owner can
do some act, or where the statute expressly prohibits some action.
For example, if the trademark is subject to a federal registration,
the owner can renew the registration or make a use declaration
required by § 8 and § 15 of the Lanham Act. Thus, where the
trademark and registration is the subject of a security interest,
care must be taken when preparing a use declaration or renewal
application. Additionally, if the trademark is the subject of an
intent-to-use application, a security interest in the form of an assignment might be deemed an illegal assignment under § 10 of
the Lanham Act.[7]

§ 14:28 Security interests—Perfecting the security
interest—Trade secrets, know-how, rights of
publicity, and other intellectual property created
by state law

Research References
West's Key Number Digest, Secured Transactions ☞84
C.J.S., Secured Transactions § 54

Other forms of intellectual property, such as state trade secrets,
know-how, inventions not the subject of patents or patent applications, unregistered mask works, state trademark registrations, common law trademarks, rights of publicity, etc. are not affected by UCC § 9-311(a)(1). Accordingly, security interests in

---

[5]In re 199Z, Inc., 137 B.R. at 782.   Bank, 40 U.S.P.Q.2d 1098, 1104, 1996
[6]In re 199Z, Inc., 137 B.R. at 782.   WL 579826 (T.T.A.B. 1996).
[7]The Clorox Co. v. Chemical

these forms of intellectual property should be perfected under the UCC as general intangibles.[1]

§ 14:29 Security interests—Perfecting the security interest—Dual filing

Research References

West's Key Number Digest, Secured Transactions ⇔81
C.J.S., Secured Transactions §§ 2, 50 to 51, 53 to 54, 62

In the case of intellectual property created by federal statute, such as patents, patent applications, federal trademark registrations, federal trademark applications, copyrights, and registered mask works, it may be prudent to record security interests at both the federal and state levels. Dual filing increases the likelihood that third parties affected by the security interest will have actual knowledge of it, and therefore that the security agreement may be effective against such third parties even though the security interest may have been misfiled.

§ 14:30 Security interests—Description of intellectual property in security agreements

Research References

West's Key Number Digest, Secured Transactions ⇔43
C.J.S., Secured Transactions § 46

Intellectual property should be described in security agreements with as much specificity as possible. Patents and patent applications should be identified by the patent number or serial number, date of grant or filing, title of the invention as recited in the patent or application, and the full names of the inventors as they appear in the patent or application.[1]

Federal trademark registrations should be identified by a description of the mark (including facsimiles, if appropriate), the registration number, and grant date if the mark is registered, or by the serial number and filing date if the application is pending.[2] If the mark is not registered, also identify the types of goods or services to which the mark is applied.

Copyrights should be identified by the title of the work, author, type of work (book, play, speech, audio-visual, software, etc.), and whether the work is published or unpublished. If the copyright is

---

[Section 14:28]   [2]37 C.F.R. § 2.185.
  [1]U.C.C. § 9-301(2).
[Section 14:30]
  [1]37 C.F.R. § 1.331.

registered, include the registration number and grant date.

Mask work registrations should be identified by the title of the semiconductor chip (as it appears on the registration), name of the owner, registration number and grant date.

Plant variety certificates and plant variety applications should be identified by number, date, name of the owner, and name of the plant variety.

Trade secrets should be identified, but details should not be revealed. The agreement may refer to blueprints, specifications, deposits in escrow, or the like. The identification or description of trade secrets should not reveal the actual proprietary information because the security agreement will be a public document, and disclosure of a trade secret in a public document is likely to destroy any trade secret protection.

A security interest in a trademark or service mark must include the goodwill of the business with which the mark is associated.[3] Transfer of a trademark or service mark without goodwill is tantamount to a naked assignment and confers no rights to the recipient.[4] Because goodwill includes the standard of quality associated with the mark, include in the collateral all the tools, know-how and other physical and intangible assets (including specifications, trademark use manuals, etc.) necessary to make the products and/or perform the services associated with the mark to ensure their quality.

Where service marks are used in connection with personal services involving specific people, such as entertainment services (e.g., names of recording groups and personal names of entertainers), the goodwill and the "tools" necessary to ensure quality of the services often reside in the persons themselves. Since persons are not collateral to which a security interest may attach, it may be desirable to obtain a security interest in the right of publicity of the group or entertainer, as well as in the service mark. Thus, the security interest would attach to the name and likeness of the entertainer or group in connection with merchandizing rights. Trademark rights of the group or entertainer in certain merchandise may also be subject to a security interest.

The security agreement can include all rights for damages due to past infringement of the intellectual property, including the right to sue third parties for such infringement. This is important because at the time the security interest is created, the infringing action of third parties might not be known or have yet to take place.

---

[3]Matter of Roman Cleanser Co., 802 F.2d at 210.

[4]Mister Donut of America, Inc. v. Mr. Donut, Inc., 418 F.2d 838, 842, 164 U.S.P.Q. 67 (9th Cir. 1969).

Where the debtor is a business having ongoing research and development, the security agreement can include future inventions and know-how, future patent applications, and future patents as after-acquired collateral pursuant to UCC § 9-204(a). The security agreement can also include procedures to identify and attach after-acquired collateral as it comes into existence or is acquired by the debtor. If the security interest in after-acquired collateral must be perfected by federal recording as outlined above, be certain that mechanisms are in place to complete the recordings with adequate identification of the patents, copyrights, mask work registrations, plant variety certificates, etc.

§ 14:31 Security interests—Priority

Research References

West's Key Number Digest, Secured Transactions ☞138
C.J.S., Secured Transactions §§ 88, 90, 106 to 107

Priority of conflicting claims to patents, copyrights, mask work registrations, and plant variety certificates that are the subject of a security interest perfected under the federal recording statute may differ from the priority established under the UCC More-over, the priority scheme is not consistent between the several federal recording statutes. For example, the patent recording statute establishes priority over subsequent purchasers and mortgagees, whereas the copyright statute establishes priority over subsequent transferees. A judicial lien creditor may be a subsequent transferee under the Copyright Act but not a subsequent purchaser or mortgagee under the Patent Act.[1]

§ 14:32 Security interests—Right of debtor to use the secured property

Research References

West's Key Number Digest, Secured Transactions ☞165
C.J.S., Secured Transactions §§ 113 to 117

Where a security agreement includes an assignment of a trademark and the goodwill of a business to a creditor during a period of indebtedness, the agreement should provide for continued use and enforcement of the trademark by the debtor. For instance, the agreement can give the debtor a license to use the trademark and goodwill during the term of the indebtedness. Such a license will keep the trademark active relative to the business and thus maintain its integrity. Both parties should

---

[Section 14:31]
[1]In re Cybernetic Services, 252

F.3d at 1054-1055; In re Peregrine Entertainment, 116 B.R. at 204.

avoid a naked license to the debtor that could have the effect of destroying rights in the trademark.

§ 14:33 Security interests—Effects of bankruptcy

Research References
West's Key Number Digest, Bankruptcy ☞3106
C.J.S., Bankruptcy §§ 217 to 220

Under the Bankruptcy Act, a trustee may repudiate executory contracts of a bankrupt debtor.[1] An executory contract is a contract where both parties have yet to perform one or more of their obligations under the contract. For instance, if the parties agreed to a sale of goods but neither the goods nor the cash for the goods had been exchanged, the contract would be executory. If one party has completed their obligations under the contract, the contract is not executory even though the other party has yet to perform. Generally, the trustee has considerable latitude in rejecting a contract, although the trustee must use sound business judgment when making the rejection. The trustee must balance the interests of and damage to the other party to the contract on one hand and the unsecured creditors on the other hand.[2] Cases have been directed at balancing equities.[3]

Executory contracts can be found in both assignments and licenses of intellectual property. However, executory contracts rarely arise in the context of an assignment because one or both of the parties tend to perform their obligations soon after the contract is signed. This is not true of intellectual property licenses where both parties tend to have on-going obligations. For instance, the licensee typically must continue to make royalty payments on a periodic basis and the licensor must take steps to maintain the integrity of the intellectual property over the life of the license.

In *Lubrizol Enterprises, Inc. v. Richmond Metal Finishers, Inc.*,[4]

[Section 14:33]

[1]11 U.S.C.A. § 365(a).

[2]*See* In re Chi-Feng Huang, 23 B.R. 798, 803, 9 Bankr. Ct. Dec. (CRR) 972, 7 Collier Bankr. Cas. 2d (MB) 639 (B.A.P. 9th Cir. 1982) (refusing rejection where the estate was solvent); In re Petur U.S.A. Instrument Co., Inc., 35 B.R. 561, 563, 9 Collier Bankr. Cas. 2d (MB) 1363 (Bankr. W.D. Wash. 1983) (rejection of a license agreement not permitted where it would put the licensee out of business).

[3]*See* In re Monarch Tool & Mfg. Co., 114 B.R. 134, 137, Bankr. L. Rep. (CCH) P 73377 (Bankr. S.D. Ohio 1990); In re Blackstone Potato Chip Co., Inc., 109 B.R. 557, 560-61 (Bankr. D. R.I. 1990); *Contra*, In re Logical Software, Inc., 66 B.R. 683, 686-87, Bankr. L. Rep. (CCH) P 71639 (Bankr. D. Mass. 1986) (questioning balancing of equities).

[4]Lubrizol Enterprises, Inc. v. Richmond Metal Finishers, Inc., 756 F.2d 1043, 12 Bankr. Ct. Dec. (CRR) 1281, 12 Collier Bankr. Cas. 2d (MB)

a bankrupt debtor had granted a license under its patent, and had undertaken to (1) notify the licensee of additional licenses under the patent at more favorable royalty rates; (2) notify the licensee of any litigation affecting the patent; and (3) receive and inspect royalty reports from the licensee. Thus, the licensee was obligated to pay future royalties and the licensor was obligated to provide future notification to the licensee. In light of these future obligations, the court sustained the trustee's repudiation of the license as an executory contract. The *Lubrizol* decision illustrates how minimal the activities must be for a contract to be executory.

Three years after *Lubrizol*, Congress amended the Bankruptcy Act by adding § 365(n). Pursuant to § 365(n), the licensee of "intellectual property" may, upon repudiation by the trustee, either treat the contract as terminated or retain its rights under the license agreement. If the licensee elects to retain its rights under the agreement, the licensee must pay all royalties due during the duration of the license, must waive all rights of setoff with respect to the agreement and must waive all rights to administrative costs under 11 U.S.C.A. § 503(b) arising from the performance of the contract.[5]

For purposes of § 365(n), "intellectual property" is defined in 11 U.S.C.A. § 101(35A) as trade secrets, patents and patent applications, plant varieties, copyrights, and mask works. If the property comprises trademarks, trade names, rights of publicity, or other intellectual property rights not specifically recited in § 101(35A), the licensee's election under § 365(n) is not available, and the rights of the parties are governed by *Lubrizol* and pre-1988 law.[6]

There is a presumption in favor of the trustee's rejection of executory contracts.[7] Therefore, when making an election under § 365(n), the licensee must strictly follow the procedures of that section to enforce the contract. In *EI Int'l*, the bankrupt party failed to deliver certain custom software to the Canadian licensee as required by the contract. The contract included a provision for liquidated damages. The licensee did not elect to retain rights under § 365(n), but instead urged that Canadian law should be applied since the contract was to be performed and governed by the laws of Canada. The Bankruptcy Court held that since the licensee did not elect under § 365(n), the contract was validly rejected by the trustee. Moreover, since the entirety of the

---

310, 226 U.S.P.Q. 961, Bankr. L. Rep. (CCH) P 70311 (4th Cir. 1985).

[5]11 U.S.C.A. § 365(n); In re Centura Software Corp., 281 B.R. 660, 668-69, 39 Bankr. Ct. Dec. (CRR) 249 (Bankr. N.D. Cal. 2002).

[6]In re Centura Software, 281 B.R. at 669-70.

[7]In re EI Int'l, 123 B.R. 64, 68, 18 U.S.P.Q.2d 2045 (Bankr. D. Idaho 1991).

contract was rejected, the provisions of the contract no longer applied, including those dealing with breach and liquidated damages. Since the licensee did not elect to retain rights under the contract, it could not receive liquidated damages, under the contract or otherwise.

Section 365(n) is effective only to licensees seeking to maintain their license rights. It does not apply to licensors seeking to enforce the contract against a bankrupt licensee. The licensor cannot elect to maintain the contract under 11 U.S.C.A. § 365(n), but instead is limited to a position of an unsecured creditor as to any past due royalties. Consequently, where the licensee is the bankrupt party, the trustee may reject the contract as executory under 11 U.S.C.A. § 365(n), and the licensor may not seek to enforce the contract. By termination, the trustee terminates all executory obligations, including future royalties, minimum royalties, and noncompete restrictions.[8] Since the entire contract is terminated, the trustee cannot continue to make licensed products or do things that the bankrupt licensee was permitted to do under the license agreement.[9]

The trustee may elect to maintain the license, in which case future obligations, including breach, are governed by nonbankruptcy law. However, if the contract is personal to the debtor/licensee, an assignment for the benefit of creditors may be a breach.[10] Thus, bankruptcy of the licensee may be a breach of the agreement permitting the licensor to terminate. However, this is not always the case.

For trademarks, trade names, rights of publicity, or other intellectual property rights not protected under § 365(n), protection should be considered when negotiating a transfer of rights. An assignment, as opposed to a license, can prevent repudiation because assignments are not executory contracts. When assignments are not available, licensees should consider other protections. One option is to require a separate entity hold the rights (e.g., trademarks), with additional conditions such as bankruptcy consent rights for the licensee. Another option is to include an explicit provision in the agreement stating that the parties do not intend for the agreement to be an executory contract. Alternatively, licensees can secure their interest in the trademark to dissuade a trustee from repudiating the licensing agreement, though that technique is rarely used in practice. Finally, licensees

---

[8]Matter of Golconda, Inc., 56 B.R. 136, 137 (Bankr. M.D. Fla. 1985) (licensee discharged from a noncompete clause).

[9]Matter of Golconda, 56 B.R. at 137.

[10]*See* 11 U.S.C.A. § 365(c)(1); In re Alltech Plastics Inc., 5 U.S.P.Q.2d 1806, 1987 WL 123991 (Bankr. W.D. Tenn. 1987) (distinguishing personal patent licenses from shop rights).

should consider stipulating that royalties are paid over the term of the license, as opposed to an up-front lump sum. A trustee is less likely to reject a license that provides future income, though there are trade-offs in terms of audit or accounting burdens with regard to ongoing royalty payments.

§ 14:34 Mergers and acquisitions—Letter of intent and confidentiality agreement

Research References
West's Key Number Digest, Corporations ☞585
C.J.S., Corporations §§ 802, 804 to 806

The parties to friendly transactions, such as negotiated acquisitions and mergers, usually disclose to each other details concerning the businesses being acquired or merged so that each party may evaluate the businesses, their condition, and whether the businesses meet their respective business objectives. The negotiations begin with a letter of intent that provides the framework for the transfer of the property, and hence the conduct of the "due diligence" phase of the transaction. While it is common to recite that assets will be transferred free of liens and encumbrances, such language may not be accurate when applied to intellectual property. For a variety of reasons, the seller may not be in a position to transfer full rights to the intellectual property. For example, licenses may exist that encumber the full or free exercise of patents (e.g., licenses to third parties permitting them to compete with the business).

Also, key intellectual property might be licensed from third parties under agreements that restrict the ability of the business to fully use, protect, or enforce the property rights. Moreover, license rights might not be transferable (an important consideration in an asset purchase), or they may be terminable upon a change of ownership or control of the licensee (an important consideration in both stock and asset purchases). Therefore, language dealing with liens and encumbrances should be carefully drafted to reflect the accuracy of the transaction as well as to avoid possible allegations of bad faith negotiation or misrepresentation.

The second preliminary document is a nondisclosure agreement or confidentiality agreement. This document should make clear that each party will not use the other party's confidential information for any purpose other than evaluation for the contemplated merger or acquisition. This agreement is an important tool to protect the confidentiality of sensitive and confidential information exchanged during the "due diligence" phase of the transaction. This agreement should survive any

termination of the transaction and should provide that all copies
of materials containing or reflecting confidential information or
the condition of assets will be returned or destroyed upon conclusion of the negotiations. The "confidential information" covered
by the agreement should include trade secrets, confidential business and financial records, customer lists, advertising and
marketing programs, contemplated research programs, pending
patent application and similar information.

§ 14:35   Mergers and acquisitions—Identifying the assets

Research References
West's Key Number Digest, Corporations ⇒585
C.J.S., Corporations §§ 802, 804 to 806

With the letter of intent and the nondisclosure or confidentiality agreement in place, the next step is to locate the assets of the
target company, and evaluate their condition (the so-called "due
diligence" phase). Depending upon the business of the target
company, the purchaser's attorney might conduct searches of the
official records of domestic and foreign patent and trademark offices, the U.S. Copyright Office, the U.S. Department of Agricul-
ture, the Food and Drug Administration, the Federal Communications Commission, the Securities and Exchange Commission
(SEC), various Secretaries of State, corporate and insurance agencies, and/or the designated filing offices of UCC documents
(particularly in the jurisdiction of the seller's principal places of
business). The purchaser's attorney might review SEC filings, annual reports, and various databases dealing with patents,
trademarks, copyrights, and litigation.

Early in the due diligence phase, the purchaser's attorney
should also identify the trademarks of the target company, and
conduct availability searches as if the trademarks were being
adopted for the first time. This will provide the purchaser with
information as to the likelihood of third party objections to the
continued use of the marks, as well as to the likelihood that the
purchaser will be able to keep third parties from using similar
marks or from trading on the reputation of the target company.

In the case of a friendly acquisition, a due diligence letter
should be sent from the purchaser to the seller requesting information and copies of intellectual property documents, employee
records relating to intellectual property, information concerning
litigation, claims and disputes concerning intellectual property,
liens and security interests affecting intellectual property, present and contemplated research and development, marketing
plans and plant security procedures affecting trade secrets.

After the assets being acquired have been identified, they

should be evaluated. While evaluation of assets is often left to the business executives, an intellectual property attorney can provide valuable insight and guidance. The purchaser's intellectual property attorney can review the intellectual property portfolio of the subject company to determine the strength of the company's patent, copyright, and trademark portfolio.

The value of the acquired business will be greater to the purchaser if the purchaser can use intellectual property rights to fend off competition. The purchaser's attorney can also evaluate third party intellectual property rights to determine if significant infringement claims might arise that will affect the purchaser's ability to continue to manufacture and market products through the subject company. The value of the acquired business will be reduced to the purchaser if the purchaser is enjoined from making or marketing the product or has to pay royalties to third parties to continue operating the business.

§ 14:36 Mergers and acquisitions—Stock purchase agreement

Research References

West's Key Number Digest, Corporations ☞585
C.J.S., Corporations §§ 802, 804 to 806

In a stock purchase transaction, schedules of assets should be developed, including patents, trademarks, copyrights, licenses, lawsuits, trade secrets, and all other matters discovered during the due diligence phase of the transaction. Licenses and other agreements necessary to the transaction should be prepared, including technical assistance agreements, general patent and/or copyright cross-licenses, noncompetition agreements and licenses under untransferred property, such as patents, trademarks, (e.g., housemarks used in the business) and copyrights (e.g., software).

The seller's representations and warranties should be prepared, addressing the condition of liens, encumbrances, mortgages, licenses, and litigation. The representations and warranties should extend to confidentiality agreements and indemnities to third parties concerning the exercise of rights granted by the seller. The seller's representations and warranties might include:

- That the seller's files reveal no information concerning infringement of third party rights by the practice of the acquired intellectual property or the continuation of the business,
- That third parties are not infringing the seller's rights,
- That the intellectual property transferred and licensed represents all the intellectual property necessary for the purchaser to conduct the business in the manner conducted

by the seller,

- That the purchaser may use the intellectual property after the sale to the same extent that the seller used the property before the sale (recognize, however, that licenses may exist that are not transferrable with the business, so some modification of this representation may be necessary),
- That the conduct of the business will not infringe the rights of any third party, both known and unknown,
- That the continued use of the intellectual property by the purchaser will not conflict with any agreement to which the seller is a party,
- That the seller has not defaulted in any contract, and
- That the seller has not entered into any agreement that in any way limits the use of the intellectual property to compete with third parties.

Representations and warranties represent significant liability to the seller, particularly where the representations and warranties extend to matters beyond the seller's actual knowledge (e.g., noninfringement of third party rights, noninfringement by third parties). Although the representations and warranties may provide some degree of comfort to the purchaser, the purchaser should be concerned about the value of the representations and warranties (i.e., whether the seller will be in a position to correct any breach after the transaction). If the agreement includes a ceiling on damages due to breach, the purchaser should consider the adequacy of the ceiling in the event of an injunction shutting down the business. The purchaser should also consider excluding the ceiling on damages for certain breaches, such as on infringement claims reflected in the seller's files which are not identified on the schedules to the agreement.

During the negotiations, the seller may not wish to pay expenses concerning intellectual property of the business, such as expenses incurred for filing and prosecuting patent and trademark applications or payment of maintenance fees. One approach to avoiding loss of rights during this period of time is to include a covenant in the letter of intent requiring the seller to maintain the portfolio and take no action (in its sound business judgment) that would adversely affect existing or potential rights in intellectual property. In addition, it may be desirable to establish interim procedures such as transferring responsibility for these matters to an independent outside counsel.

§ 14:37 Mergers and acquisitions—Asset purchase agreement

Research References

West's Key Number Digest, Corporations ⚖585

C.J.S., Corporations §§ 802, 804 to 806

The asset purchase agreement is similar to the stock purchase agreement except that the company holding the assets is not sold. Therefore, additional agreements will be necessary to transfer the intellectual properties (patents, trademarks, copyrights, etc.) to the purchaser.

These agreements should be drafted as stand-alone documents appended to asset purchase agreements as an exhibit or an addendum. This allows the assignment of the intellectual property rights to be recorded apart from the general asset purchase documents. This practice avoids such issues as having to record long and cumbersome asset purchase agreements or having to authorize a stand-alone assignment after an execution of the original purchase agreement.

These documents should be in forms which are recordable with domestic and foreign patent and trademark offices. An assignment of licenses from one organization to the other may be required, and consent for the assignment must be secured if required. Care should be taken in preparing these documents to avoid later problems.

§ 14:38 Mergers and acquisitions—Hostile takeovers

Research References

West's Key Number Digest, Corporations ⟜585
C.J.S., Corporations §§ 802, 804 to 806

In the case of a hostile takeover, the purchaser does not have the luxury of due diligence or negotiated agreements found in friendly transactions. Therefore, it is important to independently review all available sources to determine the extent and value of the assets before initiating the hostile takeover. The above section on identifying the assets will provide some guidance on this subject.

§ 14:39 Mergers and acquisitions—After the transaction

License agreements should be recorded with government authorities as necessary. This includes trademark licenses and registered user agreements concerning trademarks registered in foreign countries (particularly important in Commonwealth countries, especially Canada). The parties should record assignments with the proper authorities, both domestic and foreign.

Chapter 15

Intellectual Property Rights in Foreign Countries

KeyCite®: Cases and other legal materials listed in KeyCite Scope can be researched through the KeyCite service on Westlaw®. Use KeyCite to check citations for form, parallel references, prior and later history, and comprehensive citator information, including citations to other decisions and secondary materials.

---

§ 15:1   International treaties—Reciprocity

Research References

West's Key Number Digest, Copyrights and Intellectual Property ⬥34; Patents ⬥189; Trademarks ⬥1236; Treaties ⬥1

C.J.S., Copyrights and Intellectual Property §§ 21, 92; Patents §§ 314, 349; Treaties § 2

The concept of granting intellectual property rights to did not originate in the United States. In fact, intellectual property was recognized in other parts of the world long before the establishment of the United States as a country. As early as 1068, China limited the public's ability to copy some printed materials, and by 1474 a Venetian law granted ten year privileges to inventors of new arts and machines.[1]

However, the idea of granting intellectual property rights to foreigners is relatively new. Before the 1800s, most countries only protected the intellectual property rights of their own citizens. For nationalistic reasons, they refused to grant protection to foreigners. For instance, between 1793 and 1800 the United States only granted patents to U.S. citizens; it did not allow aliens to file for U.S. patent protection.[2]

Gradually, this nationalistic view of intellectual property changed. Today, instead of merely protecting the intellectual property rights of their own citizens, most nations of the world protect the intellectual property rights of both foreign and domestic citizens. However, granting this protection is not entirely altruistic. The rights granted to foreigners are usually made contingent on other nations providing similar rights and privileges to foreigners.

Such contingent rights are often based on reciprocity. Under reciprocity, nations match the protection their citizens receive in other nations. If nation A protects the rights of nation B's citizens, nation B will protect the rights of nation A's citizens. The amount of protection that a reciprocal nation grants to aliens is the lesser of the amount of protection it grants its own citizens and the amount of protection its citizens receive abroad.

The fact that an alien's intellectual property rights depend on the laws of its own country makes reciprocity difficult to implement. A reciprocal nation must keep track of the intellectual property laws of every nation of the world. If one nation changes its laws to limit or expand the intellectual property rights of aliens, the reciprocal nation must change its laws to match. This places a significant burden on the reciprocal nation. It also places a burden on the citizens of the reciprocal nation because it makes it very difficult for average citizens to predict the scope of protection that a foreign applicant will be awarded.

[Section 15:1]

[1]W.R. Cornish, *World Intellectual Property Guidebook—United Kingdom* at 72, n. 8 (1990).

[2]The first patent act of the United States allowed any person to apply for letters patent. Patent Act of 1790, 1 Stat. 118, 118 (1790) (a patent shall be granted "upon the petition of any person or persons"). The Patent Act of 1790 was replaced three years later, and a citizenship requirement was added. Patent Act of 1793, 1 Stat. 318, 318 (1793) (stating that "any person or persons, being a citizen or citizens of the United States" is entitled to a patent, provided they meet certain additional requirements). In 1800, the citizenship requirement was removed, and has not been reinstated. Act of April 17, 1800, 2 Stat. 37 (1800).

§ 15:2 International treaties—Bilateral agreements

Research References

West's Key Number Digest, Copyrights and Intellectual Property ⊙34; Patents ⊙189; Trademarks ⊙1236; Treaties ⊙1

C.J.S., Copyrights and Intellectual Property §§ 21, 92; Patents §§ 314, 349; Treaties § 2

In light of these difficulties, some nations have entered into bilateral agreements that set out the procedures, protections, and remedies that two nations will provide to each other's citizens. The two nations do not have to monitor each other's intellectual property laws to determine the rights they will grant to each other's citizens. They merely have to look to the agreement. This greatly simplifies the task of awarding rights to citizens from the other signatory country.

The benefits of bilateral agreements induced some nations to enter into several different bilateral agreements with several different nations. Because the different agreements usually have different standards of protection, applicants from different nations usually enjoy different rights. Thus, even with bilateral agreements, it is sometimes difficult to anticipate the amount of protection a particular work will receive.

§ 15:3 International treaties—Multilateral agreements

Research References

West's Key Number Digest, Copyrights and Intellectual Property ⊙34; Patents ⊙189; Trademarks ⊙1236; Treaties ⊙1

C.J.S., Copyrights and Intellectual Property §§ 21, 92; Patents §§ 314, 349; Treaties § 2

In an effort to further reduce this burden while ensuring access to foreign rights, some nations have entered into multilateral agreements. Today, there are three major multilateral agreements: the Paris Convention for the Protection of Industrial Property (Paris Convention),[1] the Berne Convention for the Protection of Literary and Artistic Works (Berne Convention),[2] and the World Trade Organization (WTO) Agreement.[3] The Paris Convention and the Berne Convention were formed in the late

---

[Section 15:3]

[1]Paris Convention for the Protection of Industrial Property, July 12, 1967, S. Treaty Doc. No. 91-1(B), 21 U.S.T. 1583, 28 U.N.T.S. 305.

[2]Berne Convention for the Protection of Literary and Artistic Works,

Sept. 9, 1886, as revised at Paris on July 24, 1971 and amended in 1979, S. Treaty Doc. No. 99-27, 1161 U.N.T.S. 3.

[3]Marrakesh Agreement Establishing the World Trade Organization, April 15, 1994, 1867 U.N.T.S. 3, 33 I.L.M. 1125.

1800s. The intellectual property aspects of the WTO Agreement were added by the Trade Related Aspects of Intellectual Property (TRIPS) Agreement during the Uruguay Round of negotiations that ended in 1993.[4] Under TRIPS, each WTO country accepts the provisions for protecting intellectual property that are found in the Paris and Berne Conventions. These include the basic protections for patents, trademarks, and unfair competition avoidance found in the Paris Convention as well as the basic copyright protections found in the Berne Convention. In addition, TRIPS includes requirements for protecting trade secrets, a form of intellectual property that is not found in either the Paris or Berne Conventions.

The signatory nations to each of these treaties agree to provide three basic privileges to foreign applicants: national treatment, minimum levels of protection, and a right of priority for foreign acts. The "national treatment" provisions require that each nation grant intellectual property rights to the citizens of other signatory nations on the same basis as they would grant those rights to their own citizens. National treatment does not mean that each nation follows one set of intellectual property laws. Each nation may still have its own requirements, definitions, and remedies. However, the requirements, definitions, and remedies a nation makes available to its own citizens must be identical to those the nation makes available to the citizens of other signatory nations.

However, the signatory nations are not completely free to set their own definitions and requirements. Under all three multilateral agreements each signatory nation must provide certain basic levels of protection for certain forms of intellectual property. For instance, the Berne convention requires that each nation provide a term of copyright protection that lasts at least fifty years after the death of the author. One of the significant features of TRIPS is that it generally provides a level of protection that is higher than the minimum levels found in either the Paris Convention or the Berne Convention.

The multilateral agreements also provide for a right of priority based on actions taken in other signatory nations. In most cases, the right of priority does not last indefinitely; a claim to the right must be made within a certain time period after the foreign act. For instance, the trademark right of priority under the Paris Convention must be claimed within six months of the first filing. The provisions for priority greatly simplify the task of obtaining protection in multiple countries because applicants can reserve

---

[4]Agreement on Trade-Related Aspects of Intellectual Property Rights, Apr. 15, 1994, 1869 U.N.T.S. 299, 33 I.L.M. 1197.

rights in a number of countries simply by filing in their home country.

In addition to these three basic provisions, the Paris and Berne Conventions provide that their members may make additional agreements with other member nations. Two such special agreements, made by some members of the Paris Convention, play a significant role in international intellectual property protection. The first is the Patent Cooperation Treaty (PCT).[5] The PCT is a patent filing provision that defers filing in foreign countries while an international search and examination are performed on the invention. The international search and examination are performed by a national patent office under the control of an international bureau called the World Intellectual Property Organization (WIPO). After the search and examination are complete, the applicant can file in one or more PCT member nations. Such filings are treated as if they had been filed in each chosen member country on the day the original PCT application was filed. This deferred filing system allows applicants to better evaluate the patentability of their inventions before spending large amounts of money on filing fees and drafting costs for filing in multiple foreign countries.

The second significant special arrangement under the Paris Convention is the Madrid system, which includes the Madrid Agreement[6] and the Madrid Protocol.[7] Under these special agreements, applicants may file a trademark application with an International Bureau and designate one or more of the member countries for protection. Each designated country then has twelve months to oppose registration of the mark within its country. In each nation that does not oppose the mark, the owner is afforded national protection without having to file a separate application.

Outside of the Paris Convention, the Berne Convention, and TRIPS are several international agreements that also have an effect on international intellectual property. For instance, several European nations signed the European Patent Convention,[8] creating a simplified patent filing system similar to the simplified trademark registration provided by the Madrid Agreement. Under the European Patent Convention, applicants may file a single application that designates one or more member nations.

---

[5]Patent Cooperation Treaty, June 19, 1970, 28 U.S.T. 7645, 1160 U.N.T.S. 231.

[6]Madrid Agreement Concerning the International Registration of Marks, 828 U.N.T.S. 389.

[7]Protocol Relating to Madrid Agreement Concerning International Registration of Marks, June 27, 1989, S. Treaty Doc. No. 106-41, 1997 U.K.T.S. No. 3 (Cmnd. 3505).

[8]Convention on the Grant of European Patents, 1065 U.N.T.S. 199.

The application is filed with and examined by the European Patent Office (EPO). If the EPO determines that the invention is patentable, the applicant is awarded patent protection in each designated country. Unlike the Madrid Agreement's treatment of trademarks, the individual countries of the European Patent Convention are not given the opportunity to examine the patent before it takes force. Each patent that issues from the EPO is separate from all of the other patents that issued from the same EPO application. Thus, if an EPO based patent is later invalidated in France it will not affect a German patent that came from the same EPO application.

The European Union (EU) has passed a proposal for unitary patent protection, which will extend the concept of international examination and international grant to a broader level. Under these agreements, the EU will have a single examination process that will lead to the grant of a single unitary patent. Unitary patents would have force in all EU countries. Moreover, if a unitary patent is invalidated in one EU country, it will be invalid in all EU countries. The regulations entered into force in 2013, but they will only apply from the date of entry into force of the Agreement on a Unified Patent Court. This Agreement, which has yet to be ratified by the necessary number of states, will create a specialized patent court with exclusive jurisdiction for litigation relating to EU patents, including unitary patents. The EU also maintains a community trademark system which is analogous to the unitary patent system. Applications are currently being accepted for EU community trademarks.

Other important treaties affecting intellectual property in the Unites States are the Universal Copyright Convention (UCC),[9] the Convention on Literary and Artistic Copyrights (Buenos Aires Convention),[10] and the North American Free Trade Agreement (NAFTA).[11] The UCC and Buenos Aives Convention are, like the Berne Convention, primarily copyright treaties; NAFTA is similar to TRIPS, but on a smaller scale.

Even with the large number of multinational treaties that are now in effect, nations continue to differ dramatically in the requirements, definitions, and remedies they provide for protecting intellectual property. The differences are so great that it is beyond this chapter to discuss all the forms of protection available in each country. Instead, this chapter highlights aspects of

---

[9]Universal Copyright Convention, Sept. 6, 1952, 6 U.S.T. 2731, 216 U.N.T.S. 132 (Geneva Act); Universal Copyright Convention, July 10, 1974, 25 U.S.T. 1341, 943 U.N.T.S. 178 (Paris Act).

[10]Convention on Literary and Artistic Copyright, Apr. 9, 1908, 38 Stat. 1785, Pan-Am. T.S. No. 22, at 36.

[11]North American Free Trade Agreement, ch. 17, Dec. 17, 1992, 32 I.L.M. 605, 670.

protecting intellectual property that are found in foreign nations but not in the United States. In addition, the chapter discusses the basic operation of the various international agreements including the Paris Convention, the Berne Convention, TRIPS, and the European Patent Convention.

§ 15:4 Patents—Foreign protection

Research References
West's Key Number Digest, Patents ☞97, 189
C.J.S., Patents §§ 135 to 138, 145, 178, 314, 349

Almost all nations of the world provide some form of patent protection for new inventions. However, as discussed in the introduction, most nations will only provide patent protection to a foreign applicant under an agreement with the applicant's home country. Although these agreements usually require some minimum patent protection, they generally leave most of the specific requirements to the discretion of the individual nations. The specific requirements adopted by these nations vary considerably. However, there are some common elements found in nearly every nation, including the United States.

For instance, most countries insist that any patent application filed in the country be filed by a registered agent of that country. This means that if a U.S. company wishes to apply for a patent in a foreign country it will usually have to hire a foreign associate. In addition, most countries require that the application be written in its language. This usually means that a U.S. based applicant must have its application translated into the foreign country's language. In practice, the U.S. application is usually sent to the foreign associate who translates the application into the local language and modifies the application so that it meets the particular requirements of that nation.

Every nation charges a fee when an applicant files for patent protection. In addition, some nations charge an examination fee that is separate from the filing fee. Even after the patent is issued, most countries continue to assess fees to maintain the patent. If the patent owner does not pay the fees, the patent is eventually terminated by the granting nation. In some countries the maintenance fees are charged annually; in others they are charged three or four times during the life of the patent. In nearly every country, the maintenance fees increase as the patent ages. This is done to create an incentive for patent owners to release their inventions to the public.

As in the United States, most nations also require marking of patented products in order to receive full damages for infringement. Naturally, each country expects that the marking will be in its native language. For instance, in Cuba products must be marked with the word "Registrado."

Another aspect of patent protection that is found in nearly every country of the world is that patent owners must enforce their own patents. Few governments will enforce patent owners' rights. For U.S. based owners of foreign patent rights, this means litigating in a foreign country. Such litigation is costly and logistically complex.

The requirements listed above are familiar to most U.S. patent owners because they are found in the U.S. system. However, there are many things that are common to foreign patent protection that are different from practice in the United States. For example, deferred examination is permitted and routinely used in many nations. With deferred examination, a filed patent application is not examined until the applicant requests examination. The advantage of deferred examination is that the applicant can defer the costs of examination without losing the application's priority date. This gives applicants additional time to evaluate the marketability of their inventions before spending money on the examination process. This system also reduces the number of applications which the country's patent office must examine for patentability. One of the more notable countries that utilize deferred examination is Japan, where applicants can defer examination for up to three years.

In the United States and most foreign patent systems, patent applications are typically published shortly after 18 months from the earliest priority date.[1] In the United States, however, an applicant who avers, in a nonpublication request, that it has not and will not file any corresponding foreign applications can have its U.S. application held in secrecy until the patent issues.[2] Such a nonpublication request must be submitted with the U.S. patent application upon filing. If an applicant files a nonpublication request but then decides to file a corresponding foreign application, the applicant must file a rescindment of the nonpublication request and a notice of the foreign filing with the USPTO within 45 days of the foreign application filing date. Failure to timely rescind the nonpublication request and to provide a notice of the foreign filing leads to abandonment of the U.S. application.[3]

Early publication is designed to help reduce many of the negative effects created by the delays associated with patent examination. First, early publication eliminates "submarine" patents. Submarine patents are patents that issue after a very long examination, sometimes as long as ten or twenty years,

---

[Section 15:4]   [2]37 C.F.R. § 1.213.
   [1]37 C.F.R. § 1.211.   [3]35 U.S.C.A. § 122.

without any warning to the applicable industry. Submarine patents are dangerous because they are held in secrecy until they issue. When they do issue, they surprise the general public, which may have come to believe that the invention was open to public use. Often, submarine patents surprise entire industries that have adopted the invention without knowing that it would someday be protected by a patent.

With early publication, the public is notified that an inventor claims rights in the particular technology. In fact, in some nations, including the U.S., if the inventor makes a third party aware of the fact that a patent application has been published, the inventor can receive damages from infringement of the invention from the date the inventor made the third party aware of the publication, instead of from the later date of patent grant.[4] Early publication also gives the public earlier access to inventions that may otherwise remain secret during the patent application process. By giving third parties earlier access to the technology, early publication is thought to quicken the progress of science.

Early publication is thought to produce stronger patents because it gives the general public an opportunity to comment and oppose the patentability of an invention. By obtaining the comments of competitors prior to or during the examination of the patent, it is hoped that the patents that are granted will be much stronger than those that issue only on the basis of an Examiner's knowledge of the prior art.

The unfortunate aspect of early publication is that it discourages some inventors from filing for patent protection. In an early publication system, inventions are disclosed to the public before patent protection is guaranteed. If the invention is a trade secret, publication destroys the secrecy of the invention and thereby destroys its trade secret status. This means that in early publication systems, inventors are sometimes forced to give up their trade secrets before they have been assured patent protection. In light of the disastrous effect early publication has on trade secrets, some inventors simply do not file for patent protection. They believe any patent protection would be too limited to risk the loss of valuable trade secrets.

Another difference between the United States and most countries is the standard used for determining patentability. The United States has moved from a first-to-invent system to a first-to-file system, but maintains a narrow one year grace period exception for certain disclosures made by an inventor before filing a patent application. In this sense, the Unites States has moved from requiring only relative novelty to something closer to

---

[4]35 U.S.C.A. § 154(d).

absolute novelty. In most other countries, an invention must have absolute novelty. With absolute novelty, any disclosure of the invention to the public prior to filing a patent application in that country bars patentability for the invention. This includes disclosures made in other countries and in other languages. This differs from relative novelty because relative novelty allows some disclosure of the invention for set periods of time before the application's filing date.

Even in those countries that purport to have absolute novelty requirements, there are situations in which the country will grant a patent for an invention that was disclosed prior to the filing date. Examples include publications or patent applications that were made without the inventor's consent, disclosures to certain government departments, disclosures made at certain exhibitions certified by the state, publications in a "learned" society's journal, and public disclosures made during reasonable experimentation. In addition, a very small number of countries make an exception if the only prior art affecting novelty is more than fifty years old.[5] In these countries, such prior art is considered to have passed into antiquity and its rediscovery is considered inventive.

Unlike the United States, many nations revoke or diminish patent rights if a patent owner does not exploit the patented invention within that country. This is often referred to as "revocation for nonworking." This type of revocation is designed to make sure that the public enjoys the technical advances that the inventor has made. It keeps the inventor from securing rights to technology that he or she does not intend to use. In many countries, the patent owner is given three to five years after the filing date to "work" the invention.[6] "Working" usually involves making a product claimed in a patent or practicing a patented process within the country. It usually does not include merely importing patented products into the country.

Failure to work a product can result in either revocation or compulsory licensing of the patent. Under compulsory licensing, the patent owner must grant a license to anyone who requests one. If the parties cannot agree on a royalty rate for the license, a court will set a reasonable rate.

---

[5]Countries within the British Empire only examined patents from the prior 50 or 100 years. Falk, Originality or Novelty in Cases of Misappropriation of Ideas, 33 J. Pat. & Trademark Off. Soc'y 888, 901 n. 60 (1951). This practice was eliminated with the signing of the European Patent Convention and other treaties which defined prior art more broadly.

[6]For example, the Paris Convention permits for compulsory licensing four years from the date of filing of a patent or three years from its grant, whichever is later. Paris Convention for the Protection of Industrial Property, July 12, 1967, 21 U.S.T. 1583, 28 U.N.T.S. 305, at Art. 5.

Even if a patent owner does not work his invention, there are ways for a patent owner to avoid a finding of nonworking. In some countries, a patent owner may overcome nonworking by "nominal working" of the invention, a procedure that consists of inserting advertisements in suitable trade journals offering to sell the patent or offering to grant licenses. In some other nations, the patent owner is given an opportunity to justify his nonworking by providing legitimate reasons for it.

Inventors can also be forced into compulsory licensing for certain types of inventions. Specifically, some countries require compulsory licensing for foods, medicines, and surgical or curative devices. In some countries the compulsory licensing is required immediately after grant while others provide for compulsory licensing only after a number of years have passed. As with other compulsory licensing, if the parties cannot agree on a royalty rate, a court will set a reasonable royalty rate.

Another feature common to foreign patent systems but not found in the United States is a "License of Right." A License of Right is a pledge by the patent owner to license anyone who asks. In exchange for this pledge, the owner receives a reduction in annuity fees charged by the state. The reduction is often substantial, amounting to half the annuity fees. If the patent owner and a potential licensee cannot agree on a rate for the license, a licensee can ask the court to set a reasonable royalty rate.

Patent enforcement also varies from country to country. In some countries certain forms of patent infringement are considered a crime. For example, in Germany, deliberate infringement of a patent is punishable by up to five years in jail.[7] This differs from the United States where, at most, deliberate infringement results in treble damages.

It is important to note that even though a foreign nation may allow a U.S. inventor to file for patent protection, the law of the foreign nation is not the only law that can affect the inventor's ability to file abroad. Under U.S. law, all U.S. inventors must obtain permission from the U.S. Government to file for patent protection in a foreign county. Filing a U.S. patent application constitutes a request for a foreign filing license and a grant is usually indicated on a filing receipt mailed to the applicant. A foreign filing license is required if a foreign application is to be filed prior to a U.S. application or before the six month anniversary of U.S. filing. This requirement is designed to maintain the secrecy of inventions related to U.S. national defense and U.S. atomic development.

---

[7]Patentgesetz [Patent Law], July 31, 2009, Bundesgesetzblatt [BGBl] at   2521 (Ger.).

§ 15:5   Patents—Foreign filing under the Paris Convention

Under the Paris Convention, member nations must provide patent protection to the citizens of other member nations. The protection a nation provides to the citizens of other member nations must be identical to the protection it provides to its own citizens. For the purposes of patent protection, a foreign patent applicant or owner must be treated as if he or she were a citizen of the nation providing protection; this requirement is known as national treatment.

In addition, the Paris Convention requires that each nation provide certain minimum levels of protection. For instance, the convention places limits on the penalties for not working an invention. Under the Paris Convention, countries may not revoke a patent for nonworking; they may only institute compulsory licensing.[1] In addition, the Paris Convention insists that applicants receive a grace period of at least six months in which to file late maintenance fees.[2] The Paris Convention also requires that each patent remain independent of the patents obtained for the same invention in other countries.[3] The revocation of a patent in one Paris Convention country can not automatically result in the revocation of patents in other member countries. Other than these minimum protections, the individual laws of a member nation determine the rights and requirements associated with filing in that nation. As long as it gives national treatment to applicants of other Paris Convention countries, a Paris Convention country may establish any rights or requirements beyond the minimums established by the Convention.

Each Paris Convention nation must also recognize certain claims of priority made by foreign applicants. Under the Convention, an inventor from a member nation has a limited right to claim priority to his or her invention in other member countries. To make such a claim, the invention must be adequately disclosed in an application filed in a member country. In addition, the claim of priority must be made no more than twelve months after the filing date used to establish priority.[4]

Member nations must use the priority date as the filing date

[Section 15:5]

[1]Paris Convention for the Protection of Industrial Property, July 12, 1977, 21 U.S.T. 1583, 28 U.N.T.S. 305 at art. 5.

[2]Paris Convention for the Protection of Industrial Property, July 12, 1967, 21 U.S.T. 1583, 28 U.N.T.S. 305

at art. 5bis.

[3]Paris Convention for the Protection of Industrial Property, July 12, 1967, 21 U.S.T. 1583, 28 U.N.T.S. 305 at art. 4bis.

[4]Paris Convention for the Protection of Industrial Property, July 12, 1967, 21 U.S.T. 1583, 28 U.N.T.S. 305 at art. 4(C).

for determining patentability. However, member nations may not use the priority date to reduce the term of a patent. For instance, countries that have a patent term that ends twenty years after the filing date may not use the priority date to determine when that term ends. The term must be determined from the actual filing date although patentability is determined from the priority date.

§ 15:6 Patents—Foreign filing under the WTO Agreement

The TRIPS Agreement of the WTO Agreement includes many of the provisions of the Paris Convention. However, there are some differences. For instance, the Paris Convention does not require a minimum patent term. The TRIPS Agreement, however, requires a minimum term of twenty years from the date of filing.[1] In addition, the TRIPS Agreement requires that the patent's disclosure describe the invention in such clear and concise terms that those skilled in the art could make and use the invention after reading the disclosure. Under TRIPS, each nation must provide the patentee with the right to exclude others from making, using, selling, offering for sale or importing infringing products or processes.[2] Other than these differences, the protection provided by TRIPS are the same as the protection provided under the Paris Convention: national treatment, minimum protection, and rights of priority.

§ 15:7 Patents—PCT filing as entry into foreign nations

As discussed above, many foreign countries require absolute novelty as the standard of patentability. Under that standard, any public disclosure of an invention renders the invention unpatentable. The longer an inventor waits to file for patent protection, the more likely it is that the invention will have been publicly disclosed. The absolute novelty standard forces inventors who want protection in many countries to file quickly in each desired country. Otherwise, they run the risk of losing patent rights in one or more countries because of some public disclosure. Essentially, the absolute novelty standard encourages inventors to apply simultaneously and promptly in multiple countries.

However, filing simultaneously in each desired country is expensive. Furthermore, this is financially risky because the inventor generally knows very little about the scope of protection

---

[Section 15:6]

[1]Agreement on Trade-Related Aspects of Intellectual Property Rights, Apr. 15, 1994, 1869 U.N.T.S. 299, 33 I.L.M. 1197, at art. 33.

[2]Agreement on Trade-Related Aspects of Intellectual Property Rights, Apr. 15, 1994, 1869 U.N.T.S. 299, 33 I.L.M. 1197 at art. 28.

that is available for the invention at the time of the multiple filings or about the value of the invention in the market place. The applicant may spend a large amount of money on applications that have little chance of being granted.

To make it easier for applicants to secure patent protection in different countries, some member nations of the Paris Convention have developed an international patent filing system under the terms of the Patent Cooperation Treaty (PCT). Under the PCT, an applicant files a single international application. The international application is checked for formalities and an international search is performed to find prior art relevant to the invention. The prior art is included in a search report that is sent to the applicant.

The International Search Report (ISR) is accompanied by a Written Opinion (WO) by an Examiner of the International Searching Authority (ISA). The Examiner issues the WO after reviewing the application for general patentability. This includes comparing the application against the prior art to determine if the invention is novel and if it involves an "inventive step" over the prior art. The WO is not binding on the application or on any of the elected states. After issuance of the WO and by the end of 19 months from the priority date, the applicant may choose to enter either Chapter I or Chapter II of the PCT process. In both Chapters I and II, an International Preliminary Report on Patentability (IPRP) is forwarded to the designated national offices.

If the applicant does nothing, the applicant enters Chapter I by default. With Chapter I, the IPRP is the WO. Chapter I does not allow the applicant to conduct a dialogue with the Examiner or make amendments to the application before the IPRP/WO is sent to the designated offices. The applicant may wait until the end of 30 months from the priority date before entering the national stage of examination in most countries. In Luxembourg the applicant must enter the national stage before the end of 20 months from the priority date. In Uganda and the United Republic of Tanzania the applicant must enter the national stage before the end of 21 months from the priority date.

An applicant chooses Chapter II by filing a "demand" for an International Preliminary Examination Report (IPER). With the filing of the demand, the applicant may make amendments to the application and conduct a dialogue with the Examiner in light of the WO. In response to the applicant's amendments and arguments, the Examiner issues the IPER, which serves as the IPRP in Chapter II. The IPRP/IPER is then forwarded to the applicant and the designated national offices. Thus, while there is some additional cost associated with the demand and amendments, Chapter II allows an applicant to better place an application in patentable condition before entry into the national phase.

Both Chapters I and II of the PCT process end thirty or thirty-one months after the priority filing date of the PCT application, depending on the designated country (except for Chapter I in those countries with a 20 or 21 month time limit). If the applicant has not entered the national phase by the 30 or 31 month date, the PCT application and any priority it provided are abandoned.[1] The applicant enters the national phase by filing an application in one or more of the designated countries along with an appropriate translation of the international application. Each national or regional patent office then examines the application for patentability under its own laws.

Entering the national stage from PCT Chapter I or Chapter II is similar to directly filing in each designated or elected nation with two exceptions. First, each designated and elected nation recognizes the filing date of the PCT application as a constructive filing date. Under the PCT, each designated or elected nation must treat a national stage application as being filed in that nation on the priority date of the PCT application. This means that the applicant gains additional time in which to evaluate the market for his or her invention without losing the right of priority and without having to pay for multiple filings or examinations. Second, each nation gains the benefit of the information found in the international search and international examination. Although the search and examination reports are not binding, they help focus the national examinations. They also give applicants a clearer idea of the amount of protection that may be available for their inventions. Based on that information, an applicant can decide whether it is financially prudent to pursue patent protection in all of the designated countries.

A PCT filing may base priority on a home country application under the Paris Convention. Thus, a PCT application may be filed up to twelve months after the home country application and still receive the home country's filing date. In addition, any national stage applications filed from such a PCT application gain the benefit of the priority date the PCT application gained from the earlier home country filing.

A PCT application may also designate the applicant's home country. Thus, an applicant may choose to enter the examination process in his or her own country through the PCT process instead of through direct filing. Filing through the PCT gives the applicant more time to evaluate the invention but also increases the cost of filing in the applicant's home country.

[Section 15:7]

[1]Some nations, but not all, will accept late-filed national-phase applications if good cause is shown.

§ 15:8   Patents—Filing under the European Patent Convention

The European Patent Convention is a treaty designed to simplify the procedure for filing identical patent applications in multiple European nations. The European Patent Convention was signed by many European countries and creates a single filing and examination process that can produce patent protection in several European nations from just one application. The treaty created a special patent office, the EPO, to handle the examination and grant of these European patents. Under the European Patent Convention, an applicant files a single European patent application that designates one or more European Patent Convention nations in which the applicant wants patent protection. The applicant need not designate the nations when they file the application. The applicant must designate the nations, however, no later than six months after the application is published.

A European patent application is examined by the EPO, which makes a determination of patentability.[1] If granted, the patent becomes enforceable in each designated country for a term of twenty years from the filing date of the European patent application. For example, if an applicant designates Sweden and Germany on an European patent application, separate patents can be received in Germany and Sweden with only a single examination and grant in the EPO. Although European patent applications can be filed in any European language, some countries require that the applicant file a translation of the European patent within a certain time after its grant. If a required translation is not received, that country can revoke the national patent grant that issued from the European patent. Such a revocation does not affect other national patents because the granted patents are separate and each may be transferred, abandoned, or revoked independently of the other patents granted from the same European patent application.

Due to the independent nature of national patents granted under the EPO, the invalidation of one national patent does not automatically invalidate a national patent held in a different European country under the EPO. For example, if the inventor obtains patents in France and Germany through the EPO, the later invalidation of the French patent would not necessarily invalidate the German patent. The same concept applies to

---

[Section 15:8]

[1]European Patent Convention, European Patent Office, art. 52 § 1, Oct. 5, 1973, 1065 U.N.T.S. 199 (15th Edition, Oct. 2013) ("European patents shall be granted for any inventions, in all fields of technology, provided that they are new, involve an inventive step and are susceptible of industrial application.").

infringement. Just because one national patent is being infringed, does not mean other national patents granted under the EPO are infringed. This means that patent owners must very carefully draft warning letters to potential infringers—only those national patents identified in the letter will be at issue. The same is true when there are later legal battles in court. For instance, if the patent owner obtained national patents in Turkey and Germany through the EPO, but only issued a warning letter claiming infringement of the Turkish patent, then the German patent is not at issue in the ensuing litigation.[2]

In addition, the rights conferred by each national patent are determined by the laws of each country. For instance, a German patent may confer different rights than a Swedish patent even though they originate from the same European patent. The scope of the granted patent rights and the requirements for enforcing those rights are determined by looking to the particular nations designated in the European patent application. This includes looking to each designated nation to determine annuity fees that must be paid to keep the national patent from lapsing. Such fees are not paid to the EPO but directly to each nation.

The fee for an European patent application is considerably higher than the fee charged by most countries for direct national filing. Combined with the translation costs for each designated country and the continued need to pay annuity fees in each designated country when the European patent is granted, the cost of obtaining and maintaining a European patent can be quite high. Nonetheless, a European patent is generally more cost effective than filing separately in two or more European countries.

The EPO will continue to operate in this manner, granting national patents through this system, as the EU moves towards the implementation of the unitary patent system. The unitary patent system, which will not be in full force until the ratification of the Unified Patent Court by at least 13 EU countries, will offer a singular European patent option for the EU. The European "patent with unitary effect" will be a European patent granted through the EPO which will have uniform effect and validity throughout the 25 member nations once it is granted by the EPO. These patents will be valid and enforceable throughout all member nations. However, if a unitary patent is later proved invalid, it will be invalid in all member nations. The unitary patent could also simplify infringement suits, as the patent owner would only need to reference one patent (the unitary patent) in a warning letter to encompass infringement in any European member

___

[2]Order of the Higher Regional 8/14 (March 20, 2014).
Court Düsseldorf, docket no. I-2 W

nation. The unitary patent system is under development in the EU.

§ 15:9   Trademarks—Foreign trademark registrations

Research References

West's Key Number Digest, Trademarks ☞1236

As with patent protection, most nations only provide trademark protection on a reciprocal basis or as agreed to in a trademark treaty. Today, there are several international trademark treaties, most of which provide for access to foreign registration, minimum standards of registrability, and minimum protections for trademarks. Some treaties have even eliminated the need for separate national filings. These treaties provide for a single filing that is effective in all of the nations designated by the applicant.

Most, but not all nations of the world provide some sort of trademark protection. Some provide trademark protection without examination. However, most nations have a formal examination process for determining whether a trademark may be registered. That process commonly requires the applicant to file an application along with several prints of the mark, a certified copy of any national registration used to claim priority, and a specific claim of priority if applicable. In addition, most nations publish trademarks for opposition before registering them.

The requirements for registration are important because the rights a business has to a trademark come from registration. Once a mark is registered within a nation's borders, the owner of the mark is usually given the right to sue in order to prohibit others from using the mark. This right typically does not arise from simply using the mark in the foreign nation. In fact, the United States is one of a handful of nations that recognizes rights to a trademark based on use of the mark. In nearly every other country, use of the mark only gives the user the right to oppose the registration of the mark to another person. It does not give the user the right to stop others from using the mark. Thus, a mark that has been used for twenty years in a country cannot be enforced against a new user unless it has been registered.

In most nations, an applicant does not need to use a mark in order to register the mark. For most nations, a mere intent-to-use the mark is sufficient for an applicant to be awarded a trademark registration. The intent does not have to be very definite; a moderate intent to distribute a product on which the mark may be used is usually sufficient intent-to-use. In the United States, a mark must generally be used in commerce as a condition to registration.[1]

Even among countries that permit initial registration without use, there are differences as to how much use is required to maintain the registration. In most countries, the registered owner must use the mark sometime after registration in order to keep the registration. If the registered owner does not use the mark for a period of time, a third party may request cancellation of the mark. Typically, cancellation is triggered by five consecutive years of nonuse.

Sometimes a registered owner may avoid a finding of nonuse even though it did not use the trademark during the relevant period. In some countries, the owner can accomplish this by giving reasons for the nonuse, by proving that a licensee used the mark during the relevant period, or by proving use in another country.

In addition, many countries recognize nonuse registrations for certain types of marks. In most countries, these nonuse registrations are limited to defensive registrations used to protect famous trademarks from dilution. A defensive trademark is one that is filed in connection with one class of goods to keep people from using a mark that is famous for a different class of goods. The idea behind defensive marks is that the fame of a mark can cause consumers to believe that any goods carrying the mark are produced by the famous mark's owner. For instance, consumers may believe that PEPSI cigarettes come from the same people who make PEPSI soft drinks even though cigarettes and soft drinks are different types of goods. This form of registration is not available to all applicants; it is only available to applicants who show they own rights to a mark in connection with a class of goods, that the mark has become famous in connection with those goods and that defensive registration of the mark in other classes of goods is necessary to prevent consumer confusion. By allowing registration of defensive marks, some countries believe they can lessen consumer confusion and trademark dilution.

A few countries will not cancel a trademark for nonuse. For instance, Chile will register a trademark without use and continue to recognize the registration even though the owner

---

[Section 15:9]

[1]Intent to use marks are available, but are not recorded on the principal register or enforceable until actual use. 15 U.S.C.A. § 1051(b). One exception is for marks registered abroad which are then registered in this country by treaty. Such marks are registrable in the United States without a showing of use, but the registrant must submit a showing of use in a section 8 or section 15 affidavit to keep the registration. 15 U.S.C.A. § 1126.

never uses the trademark.[2] This means that anyone with a filing fee can secure rights to a trademark and prevent others from using the trademark in Chile. The ability to "corner the market" on certain trademarks has not eluded some enterprising individuals in Chile. These individuals have secured rights to trademarks that they never intended to use, but that they believed other businesses would want to use. Commonly, these individuals have secured rights to marks that have been used abroad but have yet to be introduced into Chile. By grabbing marks that they know others will want, these individuals can extract large licensing fees from manufacturers who use the same mark elsewhere in the world and who want to expand into Chile.

Some countries also permit a registered trademark owner to nominate a registered user that will use the mark instead of, or in addition to, the registered trademark owner. Most nations that recognize registered users do not grant registrations to applicants unless the applicant has a present intent to use the mark. Applicants who merely intend to license the mark to a registered user can only receive a registration if they show they have the right to control the registered user's behavior in connection with the goods and services associated with the mark.

Similar to the United States, many nations limit the types of words that may be used as trademarks. Because of cultural differences between nations, these limits differ from nation to nation. In Greece, the words "the academy," "academic" or "national" can not be used as trademarks; the image of a shamrock or the word "shamrock" may not be used on goods in Ireland unless the goods were made in Ireland; and Iraq does not permit registration of trademarks that indicate that the proprietor has been privileged with distinguished patronage. Other examples of marks that may not be registered include marks that are confusingly similar with other marks found anywhere in the world and marks that include images of medals, badges of honor, coins, or bank notes. In the Province of Quebec, Canada, if a trademark is of English-language origin it must be used with a French-language equivalent. Some nations are extremely adamant about not using certain items as trademarks. For instance, in Saudi Arabia, it is a crime to use any mark that is contrary to religious rites or contrary to morality.

Lastly, in most countries, a local agent must apply for trademark registrations. In addition, many countries require that marks be translated or transliterated into the country's native language for examination, even if the mark will only appear in the foreign version. For instance, in Saudi Arabia, all foreign

---

[2]Law No. 19,039, Septiembre 30,   1991, Diario Oficial [D.O.] (Chile).

words in a trademark must be translated into Arabic and the applicant must indicate the pronunciation of foreign words using Arabic letters, even if the Arabic version will not be used in Saudi Arabia.

§ 15:10 Trademarks—Foreign filing under the Paris Convention

The Paris Convention modifies national trademark practices in three basic ways. It provides that each member nation should treat foreigners in the same fashion that it treats its own citizens; it requires certain basic levels of registrability and protection for trademarks; and it provides for a right of priority between member nations.

The national treatment created under the Paris Convention for trademarks is identical to that created for patents. This means that the registration process and the enforceability of a trademark in a Paris Convention nation is the same for all Paris Convention applicants. This does not mean that all nations of the Convention have the same requirements for registration and enforcement of trademark rights. The nations may differ in their trademark laws to some extent, as long as they provide equal protection to national applicants and foreign applicants. In addition, trademark registration in one member country is independent of trademark registration in other member countries. The invalidation of a trademark registration in one country does not necessarily force the invalidation of a trademark in other member countries. One exception to the independence of national trademarks registered under the Paris Convention is the Convention's treatment of well-known, or famous, marks. Under the Paris Convention, each member country must refuse registration or revoke registration for any mark that is confusingly similar to a well-known mark used elsewhere within the Paris Convention Union.

The Paris Convention provides for basic trademark protection in all member countries. The Paris convention requires that trademarks not be invalidated unless: they infringe third parties' rights; they are devoid of distinctive character (generic or descriptive); or they are contrary to morality or public order. The definitions of morality and public order cannot be read so broadly as to include all foreign marks or all marks that are merely suggestive. Nonetheless, the definition of morality and public order may vary from country to country. The Paris Convention also requires that member nations refuse registration of any marks that include the flags, emblems, or names of member countries.

The Paris Convention includes two enforcement provisions. First, the Paris Convention requires that all member countries seize goods with infringing marks at the time of their importation into the country. Second, the Paris Convention requires that member countries seize goods having a false indication of source, including a false indication of country, region or producer.

The priority provided by the Paris Convention gives trademark applicants a six-month right of priority. An applicant's filing date in one member country can be used to establish priority to the mark in any other Paris Convention country if an application for the trademark is filed in the other country within six months of the first filing.

§ 15:11 Trademarks—Foreign trademark filing under TRIPS

Under the TRIPS Agreement of the WTO Agreement, each WTO nation must provide the level of trademark protection created by the Paris Convention: national treatment for citizens of other WTO nations, minimum levels of protection, and a six-month right of priority. In addition, TRIPS includes certain minimum levels of protection that are not found in the Paris Convention.

TRIPS requires that each nation allow applicants to file for registration prior to actually using the trademark in commerce. Nations do not have to actually register trademarks before use; they must only allow for the filing of trademark applications before use. If the applicant has not commercially used the trademark within three years after filing the application, each nation is permitted to deny registration of the mark.

TRIPS also requires a trademark term of at least seven years and prohibits compulsory licensing of trademarks. Additionally, TRIPS prohibits cancellation of trademark registrations for lack of use unless there have been at least three continuous years of nonuse. TRIPS also incorporates the Paris Convention's six month right of priority, allowing applicants to use earlier filed marks in other member countries to establish their effective trademark filing date.[1]

One of the major aspects of TRIPS (insisted upon by France) is a prohibition against false geographic indications for wine.[2] Before TRIPS, wine makers were able to indicate that their wine was similar to a regional wine of France by including the French region's name on the bottles. The regional indicator was allowed as long as the label clearly indicated that the wine did not come

[Section 15:11]

[1]Agreement on Trade-Related Aspects of Intellectual Property Rights, Apr. 15, 1994, 1869 U.N.T.S. 299, 33 I.L.M. 1197, at Art. 4.C.

[2]Agreement on Trade-Related Aspects of Intellectual Property Rights, Apr. 15, 1994, 1869 U.N.T.S. 299, 33 I.L.M. 1197, at art. 23.

from France. Under TRIPS, however, new wine labels cannot include a specific wine region unless the wine actually comes from that region. Thus, California wineries can no longer refer to their new wines as being types of burgundy or champagne since Burgundy and Champagne are regions in France. This provision does not apply to existing wine labels and only affects wine labeling that first appeared after January 1, 1996.

§ 15:12   Trademarks—Foreign filing under the Madrid System

The first treaty of the Madrid System is the Madrid Agreement Concerning the International Registration of Marks (the Madrid Agreement), which is a special agreement under the Paris Convention that creates a form of international trademark for its signatory nations.[1] The United States is not a signatory nation. However, U.S. industries and individuals may take advantage of the Madrid Agreement if they are either domiciled in a member nation or have an industrial facility in a member nation. A U.S. company's foreign subsidiary located in a member nation may take advantage of the Madrid Agreement. However, any trademarks issued to the foreign subsidiary would be the property of the subsidiary. If the subsidiary is taken over by another company, the mark could be lost to the purchaser. Members of the Madrid Agreement include, among others, most of the countries of Europe, North Korea, Mongolia and portions of the former Soviet Union.

Before an applicant files for international trademark protection under the Madrid Agreement, it must register its trademark in its home country. An applicant's home country can be any country in which the applicant is a citizen, is domiciled, or has an industrial facility as long as that country is a member of the Madrid Union. After the mark is registered in the applicant's home country, the applicant may file an International Trademark application with the International Bureau in Switzerland. The International application must be written in French and must designate one or more Madrid Union countries where trademark protection is desired. The International Bureau does not examine the application for registrability. Instead, the International Bureau alerts each designated country to the fact that an international application has been filed for the mark. After this notification, each designated country has twelve months in which to reject national protection for the mark. If a country does not reject the mark during this one-year period, the Trademark

---

[Section 15:12]

[1]Madrid Agreement Concerning   the International Registration of Marks, 828 U.N.T.S. 389.

becomes registered in that country.

The national registrations formed through this process are separate and distinct from each other. With one exception, the later invalidation of one nation's registration does not affect the registrations in the other designated states. The one exception involves the invalidation of the trademark registration in the country of origin. The country of origin is the country in which the applicant filed for trademark registration before filing the international registration. If the country of origin invalidates the national trademark registration within five years of the international registration, all of the national registrations based on the international trademark are invalidated. This is referred to as a "central attack" on the international registration.

The first term of the international registration may be ten or twenty years, at the discretion of the applicant. All renewal terms are for periods of twenty years. Because the Madrid Agreement only produces a bundle of national trademark registrations, it cannot be thought of as creating a true international trademark.

The second treaty of the Madrid System is The Protocol Relating to the Madrid Agreement Concerning the International Registration of Marks (the Madrid Protocol).[2] Although the Madrid Protocol is separate from the Agreement, it is similar in structure and operation. Countries can be signatories to either or both treaties. The United States is signatory to the Madrid Protocol. Therefore, U.S. trademark owners can file applications under the Madrid Protocol directly, without having to apply through a foreign subsidiary in an Agreement country.

The operating provisions of the Madrid Protocol are similar to those of the Agreement, but with the following notable differences. With the Madrid Protocol, each national office can extend the time period for refusing registrations to 18 months. English is accepted in addition to French as the language of the application. Moreover, international registrations can be transformed into individual national registrations to prevent invalidation by a central attack; the transformed national registrations maintain the original filing date. The Madrid Protocol does not require the trademark owner to obtain a registration from its home country before it can request an extension of protection. Instead, the trademark holder only needs to have applied for a registration with its home office. A Madrid Protocol registration, along with all of its extensions to any member country, regardless of when each extension was obtained, is renewable every ten years.

---

[2]Protocol Relating to Madrid Agreement Concerning International Registration of Marks, June 27, 1989, S. Treaty Doc. No. 106-41, 1997 U.K.T.S. No. 3 (Cmnd. 3505).

Thus, the Madrid Protocol allows for a more comprehensive international trademark filing system. Notably, however, most South American countries and Canada are not members of the Agreement or the Madrid Protocol.

§ 15:13   Trademarks—The European Community Trademark

Applicants may file for a European Community Trademark (CTM). This is a true international trademark, because it does not have a separate existence in each nation; it only has one existence across the entire European Union. If it is registered, canceled or assigned in one EU country, the registration, cancellation or assignment is effective in all EU states.

An applicant may file for a European CTM if the applicant is a citizen of a EU nation or a citizen of a Paris Convention nation. The application may be filed in any national trademark office in the EU or in the Office for Harmonization in the Internal Market (OHIM) located in Alicante, Spain. The application may be made in any of the official languages of the EU but must also include a translation into one of the working languages of OHIM (English, French, German, Italian or Spanish).

OHIM examines each application for distinctiveness and deceptiveness. If the mark is considered distinct and nondeceptive, OHIM publishes the mark in the European Community Trademark Journal.

In addition, OHIM searches registered European CTM's for marks that are similar to the proposed trademark. If OHIM finds a European CTM that is similar to the proposed mark, OHIM notifies the owner of the existing European CTM. In the notification, OHIM describes the proposed mark and gives the existing owner the opportunity to oppose registration of the mark.

OHIM does not search for European national trademarks that are similar to the proposed mark. The only notice given to owners of European national trademarks is the publication found in the European Community Trademark Journal. An owner of a European national mark who becomes aware of a similar proposed mark may file an opposition with OHIM. OHIM will not reject a registration simply because it conflicts with an existing European CTM or European national trademark unless the registered owner of the conflicting mark files an opposition. The period for filing such an opposition ends three months after the proposed mark is published in the European Community Trademark Journal.

Infringement actions may be brought in any of the EU countries. A judgement in one European Community country is enforceable throughout the European Community. Revocation of a European CTM in one European Community country results in revocation in all European Community countries.

One of the great advantages of the European CTM is that use of the mark in one EU country is recognized by the rest of the European Union. This means that a European CTM can not be revoked if it is being used in at least one EU country. EU countries must respect and enforce a European CTM even though the mark is not being used in a particular country, if it is being used somewhere in the European Union.

§ 15:14 Copyright—Foreign copyright protection

Research References

West's Key Number Digest, Copyrights and Intellectual Property ⊙⊷34
C.J.S., Copyrights and Intellectual Property §§ 21, 92

As with other forms of Intellectual Property, not all nations recognize copyrights. Those that do recognize copyrights do not provide copyright protection to foreigners unless it is on a reciprocal basis or in accordance with a treaty. The three most significant treaties that relate to copyright are the Berne Convention,[1] TRIPS,[2] and the UCC.[3]

The nations that recognize copyright protection generally conform to standards and definitions used throughout the world. The term of copyright protection is usually the life of the author plus at least fifty years. Protection is generally available for literary and scientific works, including books, plays, movies, architecture and sculpture. There are usually few, if any, formalities required to receive copyright protection and as long as the work is in a tangible form within the country, it is generally protected by copyright.

One of the ways in which the United States differs from most of the world is in the definition of joint authorship. In the United States, a work may be considered a product of joint authorship if the contributions of each author are inseparable *or* interdependent.[4] However, most other countries do not recognize joint authorship if each author's contribution is separable, whether or not it is interdependent. For example, the lyrics and

---

[Section 15:14]

[1]Berne Convention for the Protection of Literary and Artistic Works, 1161 U.N.T.S. 3, S. Treaty Doc. No. 99-27 (1986).

[2]Agreement on Trade-Related Aspects of Intellectual Property Rights, Marrakesh Agreement Establishing the World Trade Organization,

Annex 1C, 1869 U.N.T.S. 299, 33 I.L.M. 1125, 1197.

[3]Universal Copyright Convention (Geneva Act), 6 U.S.T. 2731, 216 U.N.T.S. 132; Universal Copyright Convention (Paris Act), 25 U.S.T. 1341, 943 U.N.T.S. 178.

[4]17 U.S.C.A. § 101.

score of a song are interdependent, but separable. Therefore, a song may have joint authors in the United States, but not in most foreign jurisdictions.

The U.S. treatment of joint owners also differs from the treatment found in most foreign nations. In the United States, a joint owner may license its copyright independently of the other joint owners as long as the licensor makes an accounting to the other joint owners. In most foreign jurisdictions, a license is invalid if it is not signed by all joint owners. This means that a "licensee" in a foreign jurisdiction who received a license from only one of several joint owners will actually infringe the copyright of the other joint owners if the "licensee" performs acts restricted by the copyright laws of that jurisdiction. Thus, determining the identity of the authors and securing all of their signatures on a license is critical to avoiding copyright infringement in most foreign jurisdictions.

The copyright term in many nations ends fifty years after the author dies. However, there are nations with different terms than this norm. In light of these differences in term, some nations have adopted the rule of the shorter term. Under this rule, a foreign nation will only extend copyright protection for a term equal to the lesser of the term set in the foreign nation, the term set in the author's home nation, or the term set in the nation where the work was first published.

Some foreign nations also provide for compulsory licensing in copyright. Such licensing usually occurs when the copyrighted work does not exist in sufficient quantity within the country or does not exist in sufficient quantity in a translation that most of the country's citizens can understand. For instance, India will force licensing if copies of an edition are not available in India, or copies have not been put on sale in India for a period of six months.

§ 15:15 Copyright—Foreign copyright under the Berne Convention

In 1989, the United States joined the Berne Convention for the Protection of Literary and Artistic Works (Berne Convention). Accession to the Berne Convention is not retroactive and only those U.S. works first published after 1989 may use the Berne Convention for foreign protection. The Berne Convention has been in existence since 1886 and is the second largest copyright treaty in the world (in terms of the number of member nations).

The Berne Convention requires that all signatory nations provide protection to authors who are nationals of a member country or to any authors who first publish or simultaneously publish their works in a member country. The rule requiring protection for works simultaneously published in a member country was used by U.S. citizens to obtain protection through the Berne Convention even before the United States had become a member of the Berne Convention. This "back-door" entry into the Berne Convention was usually accomplished by simultaneously publishing in the United States and Canada. By using Canada's membership in the Berne Convention, the United States was able to take advantage of the foreign privileges provided by the Berne Convention without having to provide those privileges to foreign authors.

The Berne Convention provides national treatment, minimum levels of protection, and priority between nations for the protection of copyrights. Under national treatment, each signatory nation must give foreign artists, writers and architects the same copyright privileges that it awards to its own citizens. Under the minimum protections created by the Berne Convention, each nation must provide protection for many of the literary and artistic works protected by U.S. Copyright, including collections and derivative works. However, unlike the United States, the Berne Convention does not require copyright protection for computer programs or compilations of data. Member nations may protect computer programs with copyright, but they are not required to do so under the Berne Convention. Berne Convention nations are also not required to protect political speeches, which some nations believe must be kept open to the public to maintain open political dialogue. Under similar reasoning, the Berne Convention explicitly forbids protecting the news of the day. Wide dissemination of the news is thought to be more important than protecting the economic interests of the news gatherers.

One notable feature of the Berne Convention is that it forbids member nations from conditioning copyright protection on the fulfillment of formalities such as registration, fees, or deposits of copies of the work. Thus, under the Berne Convention, an author cannot be forced to file an application in order to receive copyright protection. This bar on formalities forced the United States to remove its notice requirement when it joined the Berne Convention in 1989. Today, the United States, like all Berne Convention nations, recognizes copyrights in a work as soon as the work is fixed in tangible form. However, with regards to American authors, the United States still requires the formality of registration with the federal government if the copyright holder wishes to enforce its copyright against an infringer in a court of law.

Another notable feature of the Berne Convention is that it recognizes authors' moral rights to their works. These moral rights extend beyond the author's economic rights and even after selling the economic rights, an author may object to any distortion, mutilation, or other modification which would prejudice the author's honor or reputation. In addition, an author's moral rights allow the author to object to works that are falsely attributed to them in any Berne Convention member country. Moral rights come from the civil law tradition in countries such as France and Canada, rather than the common law tradition of the United Kingdom and the United States. Countries which endorse moral rights generally do not allow such rights to be assigned, but are only vested in the author of the copyrighted work. The United States generally acknowledges moral rights as part of economic rights such as defamation or unfair competition, rather than as a distinct part of copyright law. The United States only explicitly acknowledges moral rights in the Visual Artists Rights Act.

The Berne Convention requires that copyright terms last at least fifty years after the author's death. Member nations may grant longer terms, but they may not grant shorter ones.

§ 15:16 Copyright—Copyright protection under the WTO Agreement

Under the TRIPS Agreement, all WTO nations agree to comply with most of the Articles of the Berne Convention. There are, however, several differences between the Berne Convention and TRIPS.

Most notably, TRIPS requires that each nation recognize copyright protection for computer programs and compilations of data. For computer programs, TRIPS allows for the copyright of the computer code itself rather than the program as a whole. In this way, TRIPS treats computer programs as if they were copyrightable literary works and only the verbatim "text" is copyrighted. TRIPS also allows for the copyright of data compilations where there has been selection or arrangement of the contents which required intellectual creation. This protection, however, only applies to the organization of the data, not the data itself. TRIPS further requires that each nation give authors the exclusive right to control the rental of computer programs and cinematographic works. Thus, TRIPS requires that video rental and computer game establishments in any WTO country acquire a license from the author or his assignees to rent movies and games to the public.

Although TRIPS does not add significantly to the Berne Convention, TRIPS has a significant impact on world copyright protection because TRIPS has many more signatory nations than the Berne Convention. This, coupled with the trade sanction enforcement powers found in the WTO Agreement, makes TRIPS a more powerful tool for enforcing basic copyrights throughout the world.

§ 15:17 Copyright—Copyright under the Universal Copyright Convention

Before becoming a member of the Berne Convention or TRIPS, the United States became a member of the UCC in 1955. The UCC is still in effect and can be used in connection with works published before or after the U.S. accession to the Berne Convention in 1989. While providing national treatment and minimum levels of protection like the Berne Convention, the UCC differs from the Berne Convention. Due to the number of WTO member countries, the passage of the TRIPS Agreement has reduced the significance of the UCC.

Under the UCC, each member nation only has to provide copyright protection for a minimum of twenty-five years after the author's death as opposed to the minimum of fifty years after the author's death found in the Berne Convention. In addition, the UCC provides that member nations may require compliance with certain formalities as a condition of copyright protection. Thus, UCC member nations may require that authors deposit copies of the work with the government, register the work with the government, or pay fees as conditions to receiving copyright protection. However, member nations must consider these requirements satisfied if a work is first published in another member country and all copies of the work include the symbol. Accompanied by the name of the copyright owner and the date of first publication. This differs from the Berne Convention where all formalities to protection are simply barred.

§ 15:18 Trade secrets

Trade secrets are one of the least recognized forms of intellectual property in the world. Many nations simply do not recognize a cause of action for appropriating another person's idea unless the idea is protected by a patent, trademark or copyright. Where trade secret laws exist, they are usually a creation of common law. However, under the TRIPS agreement, all member nations must protect "undisclosed information." Each nation must create laws to prevent the disclosure and use of information if that information is secret and reasonable steps were taken to maintain the information's secrecy. TRIPS also requires protection for chemical and pharmaceutical trade secrets when such products are submitted for Government approval. The incorporation of trade secrets into TRIPS has significantly affected the protection of trade secrets in its member nations throughout the world.

Chapter 16

Extra-Territorial Application of U.S. Intellectual Property Law

---

KeyCite®: Cases and other legal materials listed in KeyCite Scope can be researched through the KeyCite service on Westlaw®. Use KeyCite to check citations for form, parallel references, prior and later history, and comprehensive citator information, including citations to other decisions and secondary materials.

---

§ 16:1 Using American law against foreign infringers— U.S. Customs Service

Research References

West's Key Number Digest, Customs Duties ⟨⟩22
C.J.S., Customs Duties §§ 31 to 37

As discussed above, protection of intellectual property is generally a matter of national law. Each nation determines the amount of protection it will provide and the procedures it will require for enforcement of intellectual property rights. In most situations, owners of foreign intellectual property must work within the foreign nation's legal system to enforce their rights. The difficulties and uncertainties of working within a foreign nation's legal system often make enforcement unattractive to U.S. citizens. Therefore, many Americans do not aggressively enforce their intellectual property rights abroad. Fortunately, U.S. intellectual property owners have a number of mechanisms for using the American legal system to limit the activities of foreign infringers.

One strategy for stopping foreign manufacturers of infringing goods is to stop the importation of infringing goods into the United States. This can be accomplished by enlisting the aid of the U.S. Customs and Border Protection (CBP). CBP is an agency of the U.S. Department of Homeland Security that has designated intellectual property rights enforcement a priority trade issue. CBP is responsible for controlling the importation of articles into the United States and for assessing tariffs on imported articles. An intellectual property owner may enlist the aid of CBP in a number of ways.

CBP will take steps to stop the importation of articles that infringe registered trademarks and registered copyrights. Registered owners of U.S. trademarks and copyrights may request that CBP seize articles that appear to infringe the trademark or copyright.[1] Upon proof that the trademark or copyright is federally registered, CBP will add the mark to its own register. Registration of trademarks and copyrights with CBP is completely voluntary. This registration will last for a period of twenty years with the option to renew at the end of each twenty-year term. The registration is automatically canceled if the trademark or copyright is no longer enforceable in the United States.

To register a trademark with CBP, the owner must file an Intellectual Property Rights e-Recordation application. The application includes the name, complete business address, and citizenship of the trademark owner; places where goods bearing the recorded mark are manufactured; names and principal business addresses of each foreign person or business authorized to use the trademark; and the identity of any parent or subsidiary company or other foreign company under common ownership or control which uses the trademark abroad. In addition, the application must include a fee for each class of goods to be included in the U.S. Customs' Registration.[2]

Once registered, CBP will delay the importation of any product with a mark that is identical to or confusingly similar to the registered trademark. For trademarks that are not identical to but merely confusingly similar to a registered mark, CBP will detain the imported articles and issue a Notice of Detention to the importer. The importer is then given the opportunity to establish a right to import the items. This can be accomplished by showing that the trademark owner has given consent to the importation or by obliterating the confusingly similar mark on the imported articles. If the importer does not establish a right to import within thirty days, the goods are seized and forfeiture proceedings are started.

For marks that are identical to the registered trademark, CBP immediately seizes the imported articles as counterfeits. CBP then notifies the trademark owner, but not the importer. The

---

[Section 16:1]   [2]19 C.F.R. § 133.2, § 133.3.
   [1]19 C.F.R. §§ 133.21, 133.31.

trademark owner is given thirty days in which to consent to the importation. If the owner does not, forfeiture proceedings are started.

During forfeiture proceedings, the importer is given the opportunity to petition for relief from the forfeiture. If the petition is unsuccessful, CBP distributes the imported goods after obliterating the counterfeit marks. CBP is allowed to distribute the goods by giving them to government agencies that establish a need for the imported articles, giving the imported articles to charity, or selling the imported articles to the general public.

Copyrighted works may also be registered with CBP if they have first been registered with the Library of Congress.[3] To register a copyrighted work with CBP, the owner must file an application that includes: any foreign titles of the work, if they are different from the U.S. title; names of foreign entities authorized to use the copyright; names of countries from which genuine articles will be imported; and five photographic likenesses of the copyrighted item.

After a copyrighted work is registered, CBP will seize infringing items that are imported into the United States. Upon seizure, CBP gives the importer thirty days to deny that the imports infringe a copyright. If the importer denies infringement, the copyright owner must assert infringement and post a bond. The importer and copyright owner are then given thirty days to submit evidence supporting their claims. If the Commissioner of Customs finds that the copyright is valid and infringed, the imported articles are seized and forfeiture proceedings are begun. All such forfeited articles are destroyed because the infringing articles generally cannot be modified to avoid further infringement. If the Commissioner of Customs does not find infringement, the bond posted by the copyright owner is given to the importer.

It is not possible to register a U.S. patent with customs or to ask customs directly to seize imported articles that infringe a U.S. patent. However, such seizures by customs can be accomplished by filing a complaint with the U.S. International Trade Commission (USITC).

§ 16:2 Using American law against foreign infringers—U.S. International Trade Commission

Research References

West's Key Number Digest, Customs Duties ⚷22
C.J.S., Customs Duties §§ 31 to 37

---

[3]19 C.F.R. § 133.31.

Under § 337 of the Tariff Act of 1930, it is unlawful to import articles into the United States that infringe a valid U.S. patent, a registered U.S. copyright or a registered U.S. trademark, or articles that misappropriate trade secrets.[1] Intellectual property owners may file a complaint based on such unlawful importation with the U.S. International Trade Commission (USITC). The USITC is a federal administrative agency that includes administrative law judges who handle the investigation of claims of illegal importation. The investigation is controlled by rules of procedure and evidence that are modeled after the Federal Rules of Civil Procedure and the Federal Rules of Evidence. Decisions by the USITC are appealable to the Court of Appeals for the Federal Circuit.

In order to bring an action under § 337 to prevent importation of accused articles, the intellectual property owner must show that a domestic industry exists or is in the process of being established. A domestic industry shall be considered to exist if there is in the United States significant investment in plant and equipment; significant employment of labor or capital; or substantial investment in its exploitation, including engineering, research and development, or licensing with respect to the protected articles.[2] Following recent decisions of the USITC and the Court of Appeals for the Federal Circuit, non-practicing entities (NPEs) can satisfy the domestic industry requirement with licensing activities.[3]

The enforcement of trade secrets under the ITC is unique. To establish misappropriation, the intellectual property holder must show: the existence of a process that is protectable as a trade secret, that the complainant is the owner of the trade secret, that the respondent wrongfully took the trade secret by unfair means or the complainant disclosed the trade secret to the respondent while in a confidential relationship, and that the respondent has used or disclosed the trade secret causing injury to the complainant.[4] To show these elements, the trade secret owner must consistently be vigilant at protecting that trade secret. If

---

[Section 16:2]

[1]19 U.S.C.A. § 1337.

[2]19 U.S.C.A. § 1337(a)(3); *E.g.*, Lelo Inc. v. International Trade Com'n, 786 F.3d 879, 37 Int'l Trade Rep. (BNA) 1689, 114 U.S.P.Q.2d 1840 (Fed. Cir. 2015) (holding that 19 U.S.C. § 1337(a)(3) requires a quantitative, instead of qualitative, analysis of the impact on domestic investment and employment in order to determine the existence of a domestic industry).

[3]Certain Coaxial Cable Connectors and Components Thereof, Inv. No. 337-TA-650 (2011); InterDigital Communications, LLC v. International Trade Com'n, 707 F.3d 1295, 1303-1304, 34 Int'l Trade Rep. (BNA) 2393, 105 U.S.P.Q.2d 1581 (Fed. Cir. 2013).

[4]In the Matter of Certain Rubber Resins & Processes for Mfg. Same Comm'n Opinion, U.S.I.T.C. Inv. No. 337-TA-849, 2014 WL 7497801 (Int'l Trade Comm'n 2014).

the trade secret owner tries to enforce their right at the ITC, they must also show a concrete injury and a domestic industry, just as the owners of other types of intellectual property must do. Their available remedies are also the same.

As part of its request for an investigation, the intellectual property owner may include a request to prevent the importation of the accused articles during the investigation of the complaint. This is the equivalent of a preliminary injunction. Within ninety days of the Commissioner's public announcement of the complaint, the USITC must decide if it will exclude the suspected articles during the investigation.

If, after the investigation, the Commission finds that the intellectual property is valid and that it is infringed by the imported articles, the Commissioner will issue an order to prevent entry of the articles. This order is passed to the Secretary of Treasury and implemented by the U.S. Customs Service. The exclusion order from the USITC continues until the intellectual property is no longer enforceable or until the imported articles no longer infringe.

Instead of excluding the articles, or in addition to excluding the articles, the USITC may issue a cease and desist order to the importer. Violation of the cease and desist order results in fines for each day of continued importation, sale for importation, or sale after importation. The fines can be quite large, but are not to exceed the greater of $100,000 a day or twice the value of the articles imported in a day.

Because the USITC's ruling can have a significant effect on international trade, the President of the United States is given final review of USITC decisions that find violations of § 337. The President of the United States has vetoed an USITC decision only six times, with the most recent occurring in 2013 involving a dispute between Samsung and Apple. In response to an exclusion order issued by the USITC in favor of Samsung, President Obama overrode the USITC's decision to prevent import of Apple products into the United States.[5] Coincidentally, on the same day that the USITC issued its decision on *Samsung v. Apple*, the White House announced the creation of the Task Force on High-Tech Patent Issues which included a legislative recommendation to "change the ITC standard for obtaining an injunction to better align it with the traditional four-factor test in *eBay v. MercExchange*, to enhance consistency in the standards applied at the

---

[5]Exclusion Order in Samsung-Apple ITC case, Inv. No. 337-TA-794, p. 114 (basing disapproval of the ITC's exclusion order on policy considerations as they relate to the enforce-ment of standard-essential patents, competitive conditions in the U.S. economy, and effects on U.S. consumers).

ITC and the district courts."[6]

§ 16:3 Using American law against foreign infringers—Extra-territorial application of U.S. trademark and copyright law

Research References

West's Key Number Digest, Copyrights and Intellectual Property ⊕36; Trademarks ⊕1559

C.J.S., Copyrights and Intellectual Property §§ 10, 40 to 41, 97

Under certain circumstances, a U.S. company may obtain relief in a U.S. court for trademark infringement, copyright infringement, and unfair competition that take place in other countries. Obtaining relief in the United States requires that a U.S. court be able to obtain subject matter jurisdiction over the foreign infringement and personal jurisdiction over the foreign infringer.

The Lanham Act incorporates the substantive provisions of the Paris Convention.[1] The Paris Convention provides that signatory countries must protect individuals from unfair competition. The broad concept of unfair competition set out in the Paris Convention is not premised upon the narrow meaning of "unfair competition" as it is understood in American common law, but adopts the more liberal construction of European countries: "Any act of competition contrary to honest practices in industrial or commercial matters constitutes an act of unfair competition."[2]

The leading case applying U.S. trademark law to foreign infringement is *Steele v. Bulova Watch Co.*[3] Bulova owned a U.S. trademark registration for "BULOVA" for watches. The defendant, Steele, was a U.S. citizen who exported watch parts to Mexico from the United States; built watches from the parts; stamped the watches with the word "BULOVA" and sold the watches in Mexico. Steele never sold the watches in the United States. Nevertheless, Bulova sued Steele for trademark infringement in U.S. District Court.

The case eventually reached the Supreme Court, which developed a three part test to determine if the Lanham Act could

---

[6]White House Task Force on High-Tech Patent Issues, The White House—Office of the Press Secretary (June 4, 2013) (*available at* http://www.whitehouse.gov/the-press-office/2013/06/04/fact-sheet-white-house-task-force-high-tech-patent-issue).

[Section 16:3]

[1]General Motors Corp. v. Ignacio Lopez de Arriortua, 948 F. Supp. 684,

688-90, 41 U.S.P.Q.2d 1490 (E.D. Mich. 1996).

[2]Paris Convention for the Protection of Industrial Property art. 10bis, *done* July 14, 1967, 21 U.S.T. 1583, 838 U.N.T.S. 303.

[3]Steele v. Bulova Watch Co., 344 U.S. 280, 73 S. Ct. 252, 95 U.S.P.Q. 391 (1952).

be applied to infringement that took place in foreign nations. The Court held that the Lanham Act could be given extra-territorial effect if all of the following were true:

1. The foreign activity had an effect on the commerce of the United States, either between states in the Union or between a state and a foreign country;
2. The defendant was a citizen of the United States; and
3. Application of the Lanham Act did not conflict with or interfere with the laws of the foreign country.

By far the most difficult part of applying the Bulova three-part test is determining whether a foreign act of infringement had "some effect" on U.S. commerce. In some cases the determination is straight forward. For instance, if the plaintiff loses U.S. sales because of the foreign infringement, courts commonly find that the foreign acts affected U.S. commerce.[4]

In other cases, the effect on U.S. commerce is not as clear. For example, in *Scotch Whiskey Ass'n v. Barton Distilling Co.*[5] the defendant was an American company which supplied a Panamanian company with labels and bottles shipped from the United States. The Panamanian company mixed Scotch malts with locally produced spirits and sold the mixed product in the bottles with labels provided by the defendant.

The defendant argued that because the goods bearing the label were produced in Panama and placed into commerce in Panama, they only affected foreign and not U.S. commerce. However, the Court disagreed, finding that "the 'commerce' involved began with the defendants' acts in the United States and continued to the ultimate distribution of the whiskey."[6]

One court has gone so far as to find that U.S. commerce may be affected even though all of the infringing activity took place outside of the United States and no sales filtered into the United States.[7] In *American Rice*, the plaintiff sold rice in Saudi Arabia under the trademark "ABU BINT" (which roughly translates to "Girl Brand") in red, yellow and black packaging. The defendant, an American company, sold rice in Saudi Arabia under the trademark "ABU BINTEN" ("Twin Girl") also in red, yellow and black packaging. Despite the fact that all of the infringing activity took place in Saudi Arabia and none of the defendant's products found their way back into the United States, the court

---

[4]*See, e.g.,* Calvin Klein Industries, Inc. v. BFK Hong Kong, Ltd., 714 F. Supp. 78, 11 U.S.P.Q.2d 1730 (S.D. N.Y. 1989).

[5]Scotch Whiskey Ass'n v. Barton Distilling Co., 489 F.2d 809, 179

U.S.P.Q. 712 (7th Cir.1973).

[6]Scotch Whiskey Ass'n, 489 F.2d at 812, 179 U.S.P.Q. at 713.

[7]American Rice, Inc. v. Arkansas Rice Growers Co-op. Ass'n, 701 F.2d 408, 218 U.S.P.Q. 489 (5th Cir. 1983).

held that there was still "some" effect on commerce in the United States. It found that because the defendant was an American corporation, each of the defendant's activities affected U.S. commerce even though the final sales only took place in Saudi Arabia.[8]

In addition to achieving subject matter jurisdiction, U.S. courts also need personal jurisdiction over the defendant. When the defendant is an American citizen, there is no question that a United States court has authority to enjoin its activities abroad. However, courts are very reluctant to enjoin foreign companies for acts that take place in a foreign country. "[T]he Lanham act should not be applied to a foreign citizen allegedly committing infringing acts in his or her home country."[9]

It is also essential that extraterritorial exercise of the Lanham Act not conflict with the law of a foreign nation. The most common example of such a conflict is when a defendant has a valid trademark registration in a foreign country. In such a situation, the court will almost always decline jurisdiction.[10]

However, a foreign country's indifference to a defendant's infringing activities is not sufficient to create a conflict with foreign law. If the trademark is not protected in the foreign country and the foreign country has not asserted that the mark is in the public domain, U.S. courts may exert jurisdiction over foreign acts of infringement.

As a general rule, United States copyright laws have no extraterritorial effect.[11] Consequently, infringing actions which take place outside the United States are not actionable in a United States district court.[12] However, if some acts of copyright infringement take place in the United States, then the court has subject matter jurisdiction, and a plaintiff may recover the extraterritorial profits derived from those infringing acts.[13]

However, a copyright plaintiff cannot secure damages for foreign infringement if the defendant's U.S. acts only constitute an "integral part" of a foreign infringement. Thus, a defendant was not liable for damages in a United States court for Canadian performances of "Jesus Christ Superstar," even though all the necessary elements for the performances in Canada were as-

---

[8]American Rice, 701 F.2d at 415, 218 U.S.P.Q. at 495.

[9]C-Cure Chemical Co., Inc. v. Secure Adhesives Corp., 571 F. Supp. 808, 821, 220 U.S.P.Q. 545, 555 (W.D. N.Y. 1983).

[10]Vanity Fair Mills, Inc. v. T. Eaton Co., 234 F.2d 633, 109 U.S.P.Q. 438 (2d Cir. 1956).

[11]Subafilms, Ltd. v. MGM-Pathe Communications Co., 24 F.3d 1088, 1095-1096, 30 U.S.P.Q.2d 1746 (9th Cir. 1994).

[12]Subafilms, 24 F.3d at 1098.

[13]Fantasy, Inc. v. Fogerty, 984 F.2d 1524, 27 U.S.P.Q.2d 1039 (9th Cir. 1993), judgment rev'd on other grounds, 510 U.S. 517, 114 S. Ct. 1023, 127 L. Ed. 2d 455, 29 U.S.P.Q.2d 1881 (1994).

sembled and arranged in the United States, and the defendant simply travelled to Canada to complete the performances.[14]

§ 16:4 Using American law against foreign infringers—Extraterritorial application of U.S. patent law

Research References

West's Key Number Digest, Patents ☜258, 259(3)
C.J.S., Patents §§ 406 to 407, 427 to 430

Historically, U.S. patent law limited liability for infringement to activities that took place within the United States. For example, in *Deepsouth Packing Co. v. Laitram Corp.*,[1] the Supreme Court held that manufacturers could avoid liability for infringement by manufacturing unassembled components of patented products in the United States and then shipping them outside the United States for assembly. This created a perceived loophole in patent law, which Congress addressed by amending § 271.[2] Specifically, § 271(f) and § 271(g) extended the scope of U.S. patent protection to include foreign activities that result in infringement of a U.S. patent.

Section 271(f) prevents an infringer from supplying components of patented inventions in or from the United States when the components will be combined outside the United States in a manner that would infringe had the assembly taken place in the United States.[3] Thus, Congress gave U.S. courts jurisdiction over parties who exported components of patent inventions, even though the components themselves do not infringe the patent until combined. The statute requires a domestic activity, which is the supplying from the United States, and a foreign aspect, which is an inducement to combine the components supplied in a manner that would infringe a U.S. patent if the combination had occurred within the United States.

Offers for sale may also infringe the patent right.[4] In 2011, the Federal Circuit addressed where the location of an offer for sale occurs.[5] In that decision, the Federal Circuit held that an offer made in Norway by an alleged infringer, a United States

---

[14]Robert Stigwood Group Ltd. v. O'Reilly, 530 F.2d 1096, 1100-01, 189 U.S.P.Q. 453, 457 (2d Cir. 1976).

[Section 16:4]

[1]Deepsouth Packing Co. v. Laitram Corp., 406 U.S. 518, 92 S. Ct. 1700, 173 U.S.P.Q. 769 (1972).

[2]Pellegrini v. Analog Devices, Inc., 375 F.3d 1113, 1116, 71 U.S.P.Q.2d 1630 (Fed. Cir. 2004).

[3]35 U.S.C.A. § 271(f).

[4]35 U.S.C.A. § 271(a) ("Except as otherwise provided in this title, whoever without authority . . . offers to sell . . . within the United States . . . any patented invention during the term of the patent therefor, infringes the patent.").

[5]Transocean Offshore Deepwater Drilling, Inc. v. Maersk Contractors USA, Inc., 617 F.3d 1296, 96 U.S.P.

company, to another Unites States company to sell a drilling rig within the United States, for delivery and use within the United States, constituted an offer to sell within the United States under the statute defining infringing conduct as including an offer to sell a patented invention within the United States.[6] In doing so, the Federal Circuit determined that offers for sale occur at the location of delivery of infringing goods, regardless of whether anything is ever in fact delivered. Thus, acts wholly outside the United States may infringe the United States Patent Act.

Courts have interpreted the scope of 35 U.S.C.A. § 271(f) narrowly, determining that the "whoever without authority supplies or causes to be supplied" language does not apply to parties' design or instructions for manufacture which originates in the United States.[7] The Supreme Court has stated that a master disk used to make copies of software is not a component. Software alone without a physical embodiment is not a component amenable to combination as required by 35 U.S.C.A. § 271(f). A copy of software made from a master disk and installed on a machine in a foreign jurisdiction is not a component, as it is not the copy but rather the master disk that is supplied. The Court was reluctant to give an expansive view of what "component" means due to a presumption against giving extraterritorial effect to United States law.[8]

The Federal Circuit further limited the scope of § 271(f) by finding that it does not apply to method or process patents.[9] The components in a method patent are the intangible steps that comprise the method.[10] Because the ordinary meanings of "supply" imply the transfer of a physical object, "[s]upplying an intangible step is thus a physical impossibility."[11] Therefore, because § 271(f) specifically requires that the components of a patented invention be supplied, and intangible steps cannot be supplied, method patents are not within the scope of § 271(f).[12]

Section 271(g) prohibits importation into the United States, or sales within the United States, of a product made by a process patented in the United States without the patent holders

---

Q.2d 1104 (Fed. Cir. 2010).

[6]Transocean Offshore Deepwater Drilling, Inc. v. Maersk Contractors USA, Inc., 617 F.3d 1296, 1309, 96 U.S.P.Q.2d 1104, 1112 (Fed. Cir. 2010).

[7]Pellegrini, 375 F.3d at 1118.

[8]Microsoft Corp. v. AT&T Corp., 550 U.S. 437, 127 S. Ct. 1746, 167 L. Ed. 2d 737, 82 U.S.P.Q.2d 1400, 33 A.L.R. Fed. 2d 745 (2007).

[9]Cardiac Pacemakers, Inc. v. St. Jude Medical, Inc., 576 F.3d 1348, 1364, 91 U.S.P.Q.2d 1898 (Fed. Cir. 2009), cert. denied, 130 S. Ct. 1088 (2010).

[10]Cardiac Pacemakers, 576 F.3d at 1363.

[11]Cardiac Pacemakers, 576 F.3d at 1364.

[12]Cardiac Pacemakers, 576 F.3d at 1364.

authority.[13] "Without authority" in § 271(g) does not prohibit importation into the United States of goods produced abroad with permission from the patent holder, such as import of goods under a license from a patent holder.[14] Specifically exempted from this law are products materially changed by subsequent processes, or a part that becomes a trivial or nonessential component of another product.[15] Whether a product is materially changed by a subsequent process is a question of fact.[16]

The courts have taken a narrow view as to what is "made by a process." Specifically, the Federal Circuit has determined that the term "made" is synonymous with "manufacture" and thus § 271(g) only applies to manufactured physical products.[17] This means that information obtained from a process is not covered, even if it is used to determine what to manufacture.[18] Liability for selling or using products under § 271(g) requires that a patent be issued and in force at the time the process is practiced and the tangible product is made.[19] Although given a narrow interpretation, patent holders may still be able to prevent the importation of goods through the USITC pursuant to 19 U.S.C.A. § 1337(c) as discussed in § 14:20 supra.

The Federal Circuit has also applied § 271(a) extraterritorially to claims covering systems. Evidence of foreign activities is relevant to infringement by imported goods accused of infringing a U.S. Patent.[20] Further, in NTP v. Research in Motion, the court determined that even though a component of the invention was located outside the United States, infringement existed because the use and control of the system was within the United States.[21] Infringement of a system occurs at "the place at which the system as a whole is put into service, i.e., the place where the control of

---

[13]35 U.S.C.A. § 271(g).

[14]Ajinomoto Co., Inc. v. Archer-Daniels-Midland Co., 228 F.3d 1338, 1348, 56 U.S.P.Q.2d 1332 (Fed. Cir. 2000).

[15]35 U.S.C.A. § 271(g).

[16]Biotec Biologische Naturverpackungen GmbH & Co. KG v. Biocorp, Inc., 249 F.3d 1341, 1352, 58 U.S.P.Q.2d 1737, 184 A.L.R. Fed. 669 (Fed. Cir. 2001).

[17]Bayer AG v. Housey Pharmaceuticals, Inc., 340 F.3d 1367, 1372, 25 Int'l Trade Rep. (BNA) 1769, 68 U.S.P.Q.2d 1001 (Fed. Cir. 2003); see also ClearCorrect Operating, LLC v. International Trade Com'n, 810 F.3d 1283, 1299, 37 Int'l Trade Rep. (BNA) 2457, 116 U.S.P.Q.2d 1883 (Fed. Cir.

2015) ("[T]he unambiguously expressed intent of Congress is that 'articles' means 'material things' and does not extend to electronically transmitted digital data.").

[18]Bayer AG v. Housey Pharmaceuticals, Inc., 340 F.3d at 1378.

[19]Mycogen Plant Science, Inc. v. Monsanto Co., 252 F.3d 1306, 1319, 58 U.S.P.Q.2d 1891 (Fed. Cir. 2001) (cert. granted, judgment vacated, 535 U.S. 1109, 122 S. Ct. 2324 (2002) (vacated for further consideration in light of Festo Corp., 533 U.S. 722)).

[20]Biotec, 249 F.3d at 1350.

[21]NTP, Inc. v. Research In Motion, Ltd., 418 F.3d 1282, 75 U.S.P.Q.2d 1763 (Fed. Cir. 2005).

the system is exercised and beneficial use of the system is obtained."[22] However, in relationship to method claims, "use" is fundamentally different than that of system claims. Method claims lack a corresponding "whole operable assembly" of a system, and "use" of a method is a sequence of steps. Infringement of method claims cannot be found in the United States unless each step is performed within this country.[23]

Additionally, in response to USITC rulings applying patent infringement under § 271(b) and § 271(c), the Federal Circuit has applied induced and contributory infringement extraterritorially as well. In *Suprema, Inc. v. International Trade Commission*, the Federal Circuit sitting *en banc* determined that the USITC has the power to make a determination of induced infringement under § 271(b), even if the imported products themselves are not infringing.[24] Additionally, the court in *Suprema* found the USITC has the power to make a determination of contributory infringement under § 271(c) by making the distinction that "[u]nder §§ 271(a) and (c), it is not articles that infringe, but actions that infringe."[25]

However, the Federal Circuit declared in *Halo Electroncis, Inc. v. Pulse Electronics., Inc.*[26] that U.S. patent laws do not apply to units sold internationally even if negotiations for foreign sale occurred in the U.S. In this case, Halo Electronics owned a series of patents relating to electronic packages containing transformers for mounting on a printed circuit board inside electronic devices such as internet routers or computers. Halo Electronics sued Pulse Electronics, an electronic parts distributor, for infringement of these patents. However, Pulse Electronics' sales contracts and performance occurred outside of the United States—only pricing negotiations occurred domestically. The court determined that, where substantial activities of a sales transaction, including the final formation of the contract for sale and the performance of that sale, occur outside the United States, then the presence of pricing and contract negotiations within the United States do not make the sale a "sale within the U.S." for purposes of 35 U.S.C.A. § 271(a). In order for a there to be an infringement, the offer to sell must contemplate a sale in the U.S.

---

[22]NTP, Inc., 418 F.3d at 1317.

[23]NTP, Inc., 418 F.3d at 1317-18.

[24]Suprema, Inc. v. International Trade Com'n, 796 F.3d 1338, 37 Int'l Trade Rep. (BNA) 1877, 116 U.S.P. Q.2d 1177 (Fed. Cir. 2015) (en banc) (holding ITC has power to stop infringing imports if those imports are going to be used to induce infringement of a

patented method of use).

[25]*Suprema*, 796 F.3d at 1347.

[26]Halo Electronics, Inc. v. Pulse Electronics, Inc., 769 F.3d 1371, 112 U.S.P.Q.2d 1739 (Fed. Cir. 2014), vacated in part on other grounds and remanded, 136 S. Ct. 1923 (2016), on remand, 2016 WL 4151239 (Fed. Cir. 2016).

§ 16:5 Gray market goods

Research References

West's Key Number Digest, Customs Duties ⊶22; Trademarks ⊶1433
C.J.S., Customs Duties §§ 31 to 37

One area where trademark owners have had difficulty controlling the importation of articles possessing their mark is gray market goods. Gray market goods arise when a manufacturer has foreign and U.S. protection for the same trademark. Because the foreign manufacturer is selling goods abroad, it is possible for someone to buy the goods and ship them into the U.S. for sale. When the goods are imported without the manufacturer's consent, the goods are known as gray market goods. The goods have the genuine mark of the manufacturer and in fact were made by the manufacturer. Therefore, the marks are not deceptive as to origin.[1]

Foreign manufacturers and their exclusive U.S. licensees find it difficult to stop the importation of these goods because U.S. Customs refuses to stop the importation of gray market goods unless ordered by a court. Some courts have ordered the exclusion of some gray market goods under § 42 of the Lanham Act. This Act bars importation of goods with marks that "copy or simulate registered marks." Those courts reason that if the gray market goods physically differ from the authorized imports, they are a copy or simulation of the authorized imports. Thus, even though they may originate from the same manufacturer as the authorized imports, they can be barred under § 42 of the Lanham Act as copies or simulations.[2] Most courts, however, have ruled that since gray market goods are genuine, they cannot "copy or simulate" the mark and therefore they cannot be barred under § 42.[3] Additionally, the Supreme Court has held that the first sale doc-

---

[Section 16:5]

[1]However, failure to designate a product as foreign made may constitute a violation of § 43(a) of the Lanham Act. A consumer encountering goods with no marking as to the country of origin will assume that they are American-made, thus creating a likelihood of confusion with goods that are actually made in America. Alto Products Corp. v. Ratek Industries Ltd., 40 U.S.P.Q.2d 1738, 1743, 1996-2 Trade Cas. (CCH) ¶ 71601, 1996 WL 497027 (S.D. N.Y. 1996).

[2]Societe Des Produits Nestle, S.A. v. Casa Helvetia, Inc., 982 F.2d 633, 638, 25 U.S.P.Q.2d 1256 (1st Cir. 1992) ("[T]he unauthorized importation and sale of materially different merchandise violates [the Lanham Act] because a difference in products bearing the same name confuses consumers and impinges on the local trademark holder's goodwill."); Lever Bros. Co. v. U.S., 981 F.2d 1330, 15 Int'l Trade Rep. (BNA) 1065, 25 U.S.P.Q.2d 1579 (D.C. Cir. 1993).

[3]Weil Ceramics and Glass, Inc. v. Dash, 878 F.2d 659, 11 Int'l Trade Rep. (BNA) 1293, 11 U.S.P.Q.2d 1001 (3d Cir. 1989).

trine, as codified in the Copyright Act,[4] applies to copies of copyrighted works lawfully made abroad, therefore allowing resale of gray market goods without permission from a publisher.[5]

---

[4]17 U.S.C.A. § 109(a).

[5]Kirtsaeng v. John Wiley & Sons,

Inc., 133 S. Ct. 1351, 106 U.S.P.Q.2d 1001 (2013).

Chapter 17

Advising a Business About Intellectual Property

KeyCite®: Cases and other legal materials listed in KeyCite Scope can be researched through the KeyCite service on Westlaw®. Use KeyCite to check citations for form, parallel references, prior and later history, and comprehensive citator information, including citations to other decisions and secondary materials.

---

§ 17:1 Introduction

Most clients would never think of opening a business without limiting liability by forming a corporation. Yet, many products (meaning both goods or services) are introduced into commerce every day without consideration of intellectual property liability. To make matters worse, many products are introduced that intentionally mirror a competitor's products to trade off of that competitor's success. Frequently, this is done without regard for or knowledge of the vast array of legal rights surrounding a product in the marketplace. Many products, as well as their packaging, are eligible for protection under some combination of patent, trademark, copyright and trade dress rights. Without understanding how these rights work and knowing where to look for them, a company may unknowingly infringe a competitor's intellectual property rights. Or, perhaps even worse, the company might give away valuable intellectual property rights it could have protected.

Given the increasing value and importance of intellectual property, more and more clients expect their attorneys to be familiar with intellectual property rights. Accordingly, the most significant intellectual property issue for attorneys and their clients is education. From the perspective of a business lawyer, the most important point about intellectual property law is being able to recognize intellectual property issues when they arise. An attorney must be able to recognize intellectual property opportunities for his or her clients, while guiding those clients away from trouble.

A client must be made aware of competitors' intellectual property, so that the client can avoid infringing the rights of others. In addition, the client must recognize its own intellectual property rights and take the proper steps to secure those rights. Not all intellectual property problems are immediately recognizable as such. An attorney who is knowledgeable about intellectual property issues can identify problems while they are still small, and can identify a client's rights while they are still proprietary.

Making sure that a client is knowledgeable about intellectual property maximizes the client's resources and minimizes its liability. A client that has knowledge of intellectual property will avoid wasting resources on potential products and services that infringe another's rights. Accordingly, being aware of intellectual property rights of competitors can avoid very costly and embarrassing situations in which a company must recall products from the market or pay damages to a competitor.

A client's knowledge of intellectual property will also maximize its resources by enabling the client to protect its own ingenuity and hard work. A sophisticated client may design its products and services in a manner that virtually ensures that the product or service will be protectable. A client's knowledge of intellectual property also allows it to gain valuable insight into its competitor's direction, enabling the client to compete more effectively.

§ 17:2 Attorneys must learn about their client's intellectual property—Identify an intellectual property contact person

Corporate clients are both an institution and an individual.

While counsel must know who the client is on the institutional level, they must also know who the client is on an individual level and where that person fits into the framework of the institution. Before a business attorney begins analyzing the intellectual property needs of his or her client, he or she must understand the client's business. Of course, this process begins with the recognition that every client is unique and, when presented with a legal problem or opportunity, the same legal solution or response does not fit the needs of every client.

One vital task is to identify which person in the company has an interest in the company's intellectual property. Communicating with the wrong decision maker can lead to poor decisions, while communicating with non-decision makers can lead to no decisions at all. Accordingly, counsel should determine who is the best intellectual property decision maker and make efforts to communicate with that person.

In some instances, this decision maker can be an individual or even a team of people. A team of people is frequently desirable for larger clients since each team member can be responsible for different types of intellectual property matters (e.g., patent, trademark, etc.) or different technology areas. In any case, care should be taken to communicate with the appropriate persons to get the information and authorization needed to deal with a particular situation.

In larger organizations, the contact person may be an Intellectual Property Director or a Research & Development Director. In this case, the task of counseling on intellectual property related issues is easier, since that individual will typically have some background and familiarity with intellectual property issues. In some instances, the contact person is a product designer or marketing employee. While this contact may lack some authority on all intellectual property decisions, he or she frequently has the best grasp of practical aspects of a product or service.

§ 17:3 Attorneys must learn about their client's intellectual property—Identify how intellectual property is created

No matter what the client makes or sells, it typically will produce a good or service protectable as intellectual property. The key to applying an intellectual property framework to the product is to identify an aspect of the product, and then match it with the appropriate intellectual property right. For instance, patent rights frequently protect the structure of the manufactured article or the process for producing the article. In the case of design patents, ornamental features of the appearance of a product can be protected. Trademark rights protect the source identifier of the product or service while trade dress rights protect the appearance and packaging of the product. Copyright may protect the product itself or advertising about the product. Copyright may also protect material used in making the product, such as computer software developed to manufacture the product, or in delivering services to a customer, such as supportive data or instructions. Virtually every good or service can invoke at least one form of intellectual property.

Each client will also possess its own way of developing products and services. Some companies have developed their products and services through the genius of a single inventor. In these cases, keeping track of product and service developments can be easier if this single person is identified and trained to recognize intellectual property opportunities and potential intellectual property problems.

For some clients, an organized research and development ("R & D") effort paves the way for new products and services. In addition to creating new products and services, an organized R & D effort can generate intellectual property rights, whether or not the ideas and products ever make it to market. These rights become part of that client's portfolio of intellectual property rights. Building an intellectual property portfolio can provide enormous value to a client, such as positioning the client for cross licensing or sale of intellectual property rights to competitors. A business lawyer needs to be aware of how the client's R & D efforts work. The attorney must ensure that he or she stays apprised of new developments by the client. In particular, care should be taken that the R & D team implements a system for capturing intellectual property rights and converting that information into intellectual property assets as often as possible.

Since many markets are driven by customer demand, the client may create new products or services from customer suggestions. In these cases, counsel must stay abreast of how the client receives this information. In particular, the client must have a policy for dealing with products that are based on customer suggestions. Many companies have the policy that the customer relinquishes any claim to the idea upon submitting the idea to the company. However, in some instances a more flexible approach can be taken in view of a highly valuable suggestion. In any case, counsel should be careful that the client protects itself from future claims of theft of a customer idea.

Some clients may not be market leaders, but market followers. Many companies have been successful in lawfully copying other companies' products. Copying is not necessarily bad, provided that the things copied are not protectable intellectual property. The key is to recognize which aspects of competitors' products or services are protectable (and must not be copied) and which aspects are not protectable (and may be freely copied). Here, counsel's knowledge of intellectual property will serve the client by recognizing when and how copying a competitor's product can create problems.

Clients can be counseled on how to design around a competitor's intellectual property rights, but intentionally infringing another's intellectual property rights can have grave consequences. Willful infringement can result in enhanced damages. A competent legal opinion that the client does not infringe another's intellectual property rights is usually very helpful in avoiding any enhanced damages in a subsequent infringement action.

Some clients may make and sell their products under a license. In these instances, resolution of intellectual property issues will typically be at the forefront of the relationship. However, counsel should always watch for hidden issues. For example, if the client licenses a trademark, counsel should determine whether the license invokes franchise laws. Since the scope of these franchise laws is quite broad, the simplest of licensing arrangements may be covered by franchise law.

All that is required for a franchise to exist is the payment of a fee (either a flat fee or a royalty), the licensing or permission to use a trademark, and quality controls in excess of the quality controls for a one-time trademark license. If these elements exist, the client may have a franchise problem requiring preregistration before any sales or promotional activity begins.

§ 17:4 Attorneys must learn about their client's intellectual property—Identify how products are marketed

Another question to consider is how the client sells its products and services. For example, counsel should be aware that several bodies of law govern intellectual property rights in advertising, not merely trademarks and copyrights. A whole body of administrative rules govern fair play in advertising. Accordingly, counsel should examine a client's advertising, not only to determine whether the client uses a trade name or trademark that too closely resembles that of a competitor, or whether the client's brochure too closely resembles information created by a competitor, but also to consider the foundation for any product claims or comparative statements made by the client.

While many other advertising and marketing scenarios that raise intellectual property issues can be discussed, the key point to remember is that advertising and marketing affect intellectual property rights, the client's rights, competitors' rights, and the public's right to be free from false and misleading advertising. Attorneys should also identify the sales and distribution networks used in offering products and services. Counsel should consider the environment in which the client sells its goods, such as wholesale, retail, mail-order, or custom order. The question of how and where customers are buying the client's products can matter a great deal with respect to intellectual property matters. For example, a client may successfully fend off a complaint of trademark infringement if the client's products are sold in a channel of trade that is distinct from the channel of trade in which the complaining trademark owner sells its products.

The client will also have customers or suppliers that can either be individuals, companies or government institutions at the federal, state and local level. Each of these customers or vendors has different demands for obtaining products from suppliers, which can implicate the patent rights of the supplier. For example, if the client is a company that obtains government funding, then the federal government may have rights in a patent or other intellectual property covering technology embodied in the product. Thus, the nature of the customer/supplier relationship can raise a whole host of issues including whether a license is necessary to obtain or make the product, whether a nondisclosure agreement is necessary to transact business with the customer/supplier and whether the client's customers may need licenses to use a product.

§ 17:5   Attorneys must learn about their client's intellectual property—Identify the industry and competitors

Identifying competitors can be critical in recognizing intellectual property problems and opportunities. The initial inquiry is to consider whether the competitors are old or new. Old competitors in the market will likely have some intellectual property rights via patent, trademark, trade secret or some combination of them. With an older competitor it is usually easier to determine what rights the competitor has, and thus how the client should treat this competitor in the marketplace. On the other hand, if the competition includes new competitors, evaluating their rights and directions in the field can be riskier, since less will be known about the intellectual property rights of the competitors.

This inquiry can also be applied to the client. Is the client a new entrant in the field? If so, counsel should determine whether the client's products will be protectable, so that counsel can assess the likelihood that the client can obtain a desired market share for their newly introduced product. If the client is an old competitor in the field, counsel should focus on assessing what intellectual property rights the client already has and how they have been protected. Counsel should also consider how future rights will be recognized and protected.

The role that intellectual property will play for the client will depend heavily on the climate in the client's field of competition. Some industries have a long and active history of intellectual property litigation. In these instances, every product introduced by the client must be carefully scrutinized to make sure that the product does not infringe the intellectual property rights of the competition. Even after such internal scrutiny, new product introductions must be accompanied with an awareness that litigation may ensue despite an internal conclusion that the product does not infringe a competitor's rights.

A number of industries, particularly those in the computer, software and portable electronics fields, can attract a number of other parties into the competition for intellectual property rights. Some of these non-practicing entities have been known to purchase patents and pending patent applications and then attempt to enforce patents against successful businesses and products in an attempt to collect license fees. Thus, the client and its counsel should be aware not only of the activities and litigation tendencies of potential competitors, but they should also investigate and evaluate the likelihood of litigation coming from those outside the industry.

Other industries, while being very active in acquiring patents, are slow to attack competitors that infringe their patents. In these industries, many patents are sold or cross-licensed so that the industry as a whole can benefit from the various contributions amongst the major competitors.

Nothing attracts unlawful copiers faster than a successful product or service. Accordingly, in addition to being concerned about whether the client is infringing anyone's rights, counsel should consider the likelihood that a competitor will infringe the client's intellectual property rights. If the industry is very combative, then counsel should advise the client to be vigilant in examining its competitors' products, trademarks, and advertising. Indeed, the level of resources and policing required in a given industry may determine whether the client will enter that market, depending upon the client's preferences for allocating resources to policing efforts. While the cost of policing can be high, the rewards can be substantial. The costs of not doing so can be even higher.

A related inquiry is whether there is substantial research and development in the client's industry. If so, intellectual property rights are typically the main method for protecting the heavy capital expenditure for product introduction. In fact, many companies could not afford to devote substantial resources to research and development unless they were assured of protecting their investment through intellectual property rights. Pharmaceutical companies are prime examples of companies that would not even consider developing a new drug without some guarantee of exclusivity in the marketplace provided by patents. In the absence of intellectual property rights, these companies would never devote the time and money needed to develop new drugs.

Counsel should also determine technology life cycles in the client's market. If the technology life cycles are short (like in the computer field), then the client must be very diligent about seeking intellectual property protection from the inception of the product. The technology life cycle can expire before intellectual property rights are permanently secured if there is delay in seeking protection.

Alternatively, some types of products have long technology life cycles for a number of reasons, such as requirements of government approval before the product can enter the market. For example, medical products, such as pharmacenticeds and medical devices, require approval from the Federal Food and Drug Administration (FDA). This approval process can last many years. In this situation, the client could obtain patent protection on a medical product several years before the drug or product is approved for sale by the FDA In the meantime, the period during which the client can enforce their patent continues to elapse while waiting for FDA approval. The good news is that there are statutory provisions that remedy this situation by extending the term of the patent. However, the lesson is that counsel must be aware of events (e.g., FDA approval) that affect the life cycle of sales of the product and how the client's intellectual property rights can be affected by these events.

Counsel should consider how the client learns about the competition. Currently, most U.S. and foreign patent applications are published eighteen months after their effective filing date. Patents and published applications can provide a wealth of information about the state of the art in a particular industry. However, in evaluating these publicly available documents, one must keep in mind that the information in the patents and published patent applications may be indicative of the state of the art when those documents were filed, about two years earlier. Accordingly, when the client evaluates intellectual property, counsel must keep an eye to the future.

Not only must counsel evaluate what the client's direct competitors are doing, but counsel should be aware of what others are doing in related fields or what major suppliers in the field are doing. The field of computer software provides a good example. Computer application software developers must be aware of not only what their direct competitors are doing, but must be concerned with what Microsoft is doing in the area of operating systems and ancillary software support, with what IBM and Apple are doing in computer hardware and user interfaces, and with what other more amorphous environments are doing, such as the Internet and the World Wide Web. Moreover, in addition to evaluating the current products and services offered by competitors, counsel must assist the client in looking to what these entities will be doing in the next generation of products.

§ 17:6 Attorneys must learn about their client's intellectual property—Identify ways to systematically protect intellectual property

After recognizing the role intellectual property may play in the client's industry, counsel should next consider how the client is recognizing and protecting its own intellectual property rights. A starting place for most clients is whether the client has an employee agreement that obligates employees to assign their rights in any intellectual property to the client as the employer. These agreements are commonly referred to as employee invention agreements. These agreements typically require the employee to assign to the employer any rights in patents, trademarks, copyrights or other confidential information created by the employee relating to the job.

The client should require employees to regularly document and report their creative activities. It also can be helpful to have a system in place to encourage employees to cooperate in documenting and reporting their creative work. At least one person with working knowledge of intellectual property should be designated and responsible for periodically reviewing and evaluating these reports, which can then be used by counsel to determine an appropriate intellectual property strategy. One example commonly used by companies is to provide bonus compensation for useful ideas submitted to the company. The success with which these systems work depends on a company's demonstrated commitment to promoting, rewarding, and capitalizing on employee-generated ideas.

A related document that is frequently used in protecting intellectual property rights is a nondisclosure agreement, which requires that the employee not disclose the company's confidential information. This agreement serves to inhibit the loss of trade secrets and confidential information. It can be effective in retaining a trade secret even where there has been an unauthorized disclosure, provided that other safeguards are in place. Accordingly, counsel should determine whether the client has a policy of using nondisclosure agreements as a part of an overall security system.

Nondisclosure agreements can also be effective in protecting intellectual property in dealings with third parties, particularly suppliers. A nondisclosure agreement can obligate both the supplier and client not to disclose confidential information that is exchanged in the course of doing business together.

A very important aspect of this information security system is how the client interacts with its intellectual property counsel. Regular communication with intellectual property counsel, either directly or through a general counsel, is critical to spotting and evaluating issues. Relevant information about intellectual property can come from many different levels in a client's company. Accordingly, regular interaction is required between intellectual property counsel and employees, supervisors, top management, and general counsel. Therefore, counsel should evaluate the client's current method of communicating intellectual property-related issues and suggest a regular system of intellectual property issue spotting and evaluation. This issue-spotting system should include consideration of intellectual property issues each time any change in corporate structure takes place. These events frequently raise ownership issues regarding intellectual property as well as issues concerning the value and status of intellectual property rights.

Two areas of procedural concern for protecting intellectual property are avoiding inadvertent loss of currently owned intellectual property and ensuring early identification of newly developed intellectual property.

Techniques for avoiding loss depend largely on the type of intellectual property to be protected. For example, publishing information about an invention or selling a product embodying an invention can erase foreign and U.S. patent rights. Accordingly, counsel should determine whether the client is quick to publish new product developments and should identify the possible directions in which the company may go, since these publications and communications can adversely affect the ability to acquire intellectual property rights. In such instances, counsel should advise the client to consider intellectual property issues prior to indiscriminately publishing information about new developments. This issue can be illustrated by the pressure faced by a university or university professor who must "publish or perish" within the academic community. While publishing new developments may be the life blood of the academic world, it can be harmful if done before securing intellectual property rights.

The challenge of creating early protection for intellectual property can be made easier by providing techniques to identify potential intellectual property rights before any product reaches the marketplace. For instance, many companies with regular research and development efforts have their employees regularly document their contributions in product development. Regular reviews of employee ideas can filter out problematic developments while harnessing contributions expected to enhance the company's product or service lines.

Similarly, providing public access to internal client information can destroy possible trade secrets. Counsel should focus on the ways in which the client interacts with the public and identify how those interactions can impact intellectual property rights. Upon recognition of how these contacts occur, counsel should ensure that the client takes appropriate steps to protect potential intellectual property rights before any public contact is made.

This challenge of excluding information from the public can be met in simple, nonsophisticated ways. For example, the client's business should have at least some areas of restricted access (both physical restrictions and electronic data access restrictions). This protects the client from claims that its information is not confidential or not a trade secret because of uncontrolled access to company information. Similar protection includes only providing information on a "need to know" basis and regularly marking appropriate documents as "confidential." In short, counsel must ensure that the client acts as if it wants to protect its information in order for the client to ensure its safety.

§ 17:7 Attorneys must learn about their client's intellectual property—Identify the role of intellectual property

Industries sometimes go through fast-growth phases featuring newly-developed and currently emerging technology. In such industries, it is particularly important to use intellectual property rights to establish a competitive position to ensure that the client may have market exclusivity and to avoid being locked out of competition because of a competitor's intellectual property rights. In newly-emerging technologies, a key patent can mean the difference between being an industry leader or a peripheral player in a market.

An intellectual property portfolio can be useful for cross-licensing, particularly in fast-growth industries in which each competitor may excel in developing a niche aspect of a product or line of products. By cross-licensing, each competitor can share in an advance while allowing the industry to grow as a whole.

Mature industries may see only incremental growth in new technologies. In these cases, the boundaries of a competitor's intellectual property rights are often well established. This can be cause for both celebration and concern. While the more established rights lend certainty to what the client can and cannot do, these established rights can form a barrier to entry into a market. Accordingly, dealing with the intellectual property rights of existing competitors can be very challenging in an existing market. For example, if the client is contemplating entering an industry crowded with generic products, then acquiring or developing trademark or trade dress rights while steering clear of existing trademarks and trade dress can be quite difficult.

Counsel also should consider whether the client's industry is cyclical or seasonal. Cyclical industries probably will not affect the type of intellectual property rights that are prevalent, but may greatly affect the time at which those intellectual property rights should be acquired, licensed, or enforced. For example, a client should seek patent protection or trademark protection prior to a trade show season for that industry to ensure that its rights are protected before its new products are exposed to competitors. Being aware of these cyclical product or sales cycles can also be important in preserving the client's rights from self destruction.

For example, patent rights in most foreign countries will be forfeited if the client publicly divulges or sells an invention before filing a patent application. Thus it is important to identify the locations in which a client conducts its business. In the United States, a client has historically been given one year from a first offer for sale, public use, or publication of the invention to file a patent application and preserve its rights. The America Invents Act (AIA) has made several changes to U.S. law with respect to this one-year time period, many of which take effect for patent applications that are first filed in the United States on or after March 16, 2013.

Determining where the client conducts its business involves several components, including where the client makes its goods, where the client sells its goods, where the client's competition makes its goods, and where the competition's products are sold. The client may be located locally, nationally, or internationally. Similarly, the client's goods may be sold in a single location, statewide, nationally, or internationally. Knowing the boundaries of the client's presence in the marketplace is very important. Also, it is important to know the countries in which the client does business so that appropriate steps can be taken to secure intellectual property rights in those countries. Similarly, this knowledge is crucial in avoiding infringement of a competitor's rights in other countries.

While many countries protect similar aspects of intellectual property rights, each country has its own set of legal rules with its own unique interpretation. Moreover, some countries do a much better job of enforcing intellectual property rights than others. Counsel should learn which of the countries in which the client does business have meaningful systems for both acquiring and enforcing intellectual property rights.

Because different rights exist in different states and countries, counsel should know whether the client's products are manufactured in one country and sold in another as well as where the competitors' products are made, marketed and sold. In situations in which competition is international, the client will have to contend with products shipped into the client's market.

Intellectual property rights can be used as a means to exclude others and achieve market exclusivity. This can result in supranormal profits or a greater market share. Some clients may want to create an income stream based on licensing their products or services to others or licensing others to make or sell the product. A patent or trademark frequently provides the necessary leverage to make a licensing program effective. On the other hand, offering a product without intellectual property rights can often make it difficult to convince a potential licensee that the client has something of value and something protectable to make the price of a license worthwhile. Accordingly, knowing that the client wants to make money by licensing should alert counsel to recognize opportunities for licensing intellectual property.

A client may want to make money but may not want to actually make or sell anything. In some instances, intellectual property rights alone can be valuable enough that the outright sale or license of a patent, even in the absence of a developed product, can generate a substantial return on the client's research and development efforts.

Many clients have a larger goal in mind such as to enhance the value of the company, to raise shareholder equity, or to position the company for future acquisition. This is important for counsel to know since building a well-rounded portfolio of intellectual property rights is a recognized way to achieve such goals.

Some clients have altruistic and charitable goals to be achieved. Knowledge about intellectual property can help the client no matter what its motivation for selling a product or providing a service. If the client is interested in altruistic goals, intellectual property rights still have a key role to play. Without some intellectual property protection (such as its own trademark or copyright) and without assurance of avoiding the rights of others, the client could be frustrated from meeting its altruistic goals. For example, many charities need a protectable trademark to compete effectively in the competition for consumer dollars. Without a protectable trademark, a charity will have trouble fending off scam artists using similar names. A protectable trademark can serve as a guarantee to the donor that the money donated will be used for charitable purposes. Accordingly, even charitable institutions have a reason to be mindful of intellectual property rights.

§ 17:8   Educating the client about intellectual property— Creating awareness of the benefits of intellectual property

Most companies have the goal of maximizing their use of available resources. They strive to obtain the greatest value for each dollar spent and to provide the best value for each dollar received. By doing so, the company hopes to build and maintain a successful and prosperous business. Yet many of those same companies fail to maximize the value of what may be their greatest asset: the intellectual property generated by the hard work, creativity and ingenuity of their employees.

A client's failure to maximize the value of its intellectual property is rarely intentional. Rather, the failure occurs because the client is not aware that it possesses intellectual property, not aware of how to protect its intellectual property, or not aware of the opportunities its intellectual property could provide if properly harnessed. All of these potential failures to take advantage of intellectual property can be addressed by an attorney who properly educates and advises the client.

Once an attorney is educated about his or her client, it is time to educate and advise the client about the opportunities that intellectual property presents. The level of sophistication a client requires with respect to intellectual property will vary. Some clients will need only a rudimentary understanding of what intellectual property encompasses, while others will need to become rather sophisticated about what intellectual property is and how it can be used. But every client should understand the opportunities intellectual property provides if properly harnessed, and every client must be made aware of the dangers that intellectual property presents if ignored.

The greatest benefit that intellectual property can provide—if properly protected and utilized—is a competitive advantage. Many clients originally started their business because they could provide a better product or service than those businesses already in existence, or because they had an idea that was not being exploited in the marketplace. Their "secret to success" may be a better design, an improved method of doing business, a client list compiled at great cost, or a particularly gifted employee.

Unless the client effectively protects the elements of its business that allow it to be successful, its ability to remain in business may be compromised. Properly protected intellectual property can allow a client to be the sole provider of a particular product or service, and can prevent competitors from copying the client's achievements. Nothing attracts copying more than success. If the client intends to be successful it must prevent, or at least inhibit, its competitors' ability to copy those elements that allow the client to be successful.

In addition to providing the client with a competitive advantage, properly protected intellectual property can add greatly to the value of the client's business. The increase in value is, of course, at least in part related to the competitive advantage provided by intellectual property. A competitive advantage typically translates to market share, increased profitability and an increased business valuation.

The client may also have intellectual property that does not provide a significant competitive advantage, but still increases the value of the client's business. For example, in the course of developing new products or improving existing products, the client may come up with ideas and knowledge that it is not fully able or willing to exploit. The inability or unwillingness to exploit such new ideas may be due to a lack of available capital, an insufficient market or inadequate expertise within the business. However, just because the client is unable to immediately use or profit from its intellectual property does not mean that the intellectual property is without value.

If the client has invested limited resources in developing intellectual property, it makes sense to protect all of the fruits of that labor, even if the ideas and products never make it to the market via the client's business. By developing a portfolio of intellectual property, the client positions itself for cross-licensing or selling intellectual property rights, while simultaneously building additional assets for the business. Patents, trade secrets or know-how that the client owns but cannot fully exploit may be a significant portion of the total value of the client's business.

§17:9 Educating the client about intellectual property— Creating awareness of the dangers of ignoring intellectual property

Just as intellectual property can afford valuable opportunities to the client by providing a competitive advantage and increasing the value of the client's business, ignorance or neglect of intellectual property can present dangers to the health of the client's enterprise. By ignoring or neglecting its intellectual property, the client fails to take full advantage of its assets. It may even give ground to its competitors by inadvertently making its intellectual property public, thereby providing the competition with an unearned and uncompensated benefit. It is unlikely that any business would intentionally "give away the store," but that is exactly what many businesses do by neglecting their intellectual property.

The most common danger of ignoring intellectual property is the loss of business opportunities. When a client neglects its intellectual property, it is passing up business opportunities without careful consideration as to whether those opportunities are worth pursuing. The client may be passing up a new product, limiting access to a new market or losing the ability to cross-license its intellectual property with competitors. The client is often not even aware that a business opportunity was presented and lost, and goes on with business as usual. However, the result is a business which must work harder to compete.

Usually, if a client neglects its own intellectual property, it also neglects its competitors' intellectual property. Infringing the intellectual property rights of others may result in many problems: resources wasted on products which must be pulled from the market; legal costs which could have been avoided; and loss of customers. The consequences of infringing the intellectual property rights of others can be a major inconvenience at best and a devastating blow at worst.

In today's fast-paced business world, businesses are forced to act quickly and decisively if they are to remain competitive. In this situation, it is easy to imagine a client that leaps before it looks. Imagine a client who manufactures health and fitness equipment for sale to the public, and wants to capitalize on the recent boom in equipment used for toning and developing a user's abdominal muscles. There are many such products already on the market, each with a unique combination of features. The client hires a team of researchers to test and evaluate each existing product, rating the effectiveness of the various features and selecting the features that prove to be most effective. The research team provides the results to a group of engineers who set out designing a new machine that combines those features. Several prototypes are built and taken to an industry trade show, where the response is overwhelming. The client's sales staff returns with advance orders for thousands of the machine. Immediately, custom production tooling is developed, manufacturing lines are set up, orders are placed with suppliers for raw materials and the marketing people begin an expensive advertising campaign for the "ABSolutely Great" machine. The warehouses are soon full and the product is being shipped out the door. The client is pleased because it has identified a lucrative market and acted quickly to introduce a popular product to that market. This is clearly going to be a profit-making venture for the client.

Not long after production is in full swing and orders are flowing in, a letter from Competitor X arrives on the client's desk, informing the client that the ABSolutely Great machine infringes a patent owned by Competitor X. The letter states that if the client does not immediately stop producing and selling the ABSolutely Great machine, Competitor X will sue for patent infringement. In addition, Competitor X demands that all ABSolutely Great machines currently in inventory be destroyed.

A review of the patent shows that one of the popular features of the ABSolutely Great machine is indeed covered by Competitor X's patent. The production line is shut down and all orders are placed on hold. The client immediately calls in the engineers, in an attempt to design around the patent. The engineers propose several ingenious options that will avoid infringement of the patent, including several new and completely unique machines. Introducing an entirely new machine is far too expensive, but a relatively minor alteration is made in the design of the ABSolutely Great machine that avoids infringing the patent. The new design will in fact provide an improved abdominal workout.

Unfortunately, the "minor alteration" in the design of the ABSolutely Great machine necessitates a complete retooling of the production line, and renders the existing ABSolutely Great machines worthless because they cannot be altered to avoid infringing Competitor X's patent. A large investment in production equipment and costly inventory has instantly become worthless. The client swallows hard, invests in new tooling for the production line, and destroys the old ABSolutely Great machines. Soon, production of the "new and improved" ABSolutely Great machine is under way.

Interestingly, the design change required to get around Competitor X's patent makes the ABSolutely Great machine even more popular. Sales of the new machine are soaring. Having learned its lesson the hard way, the client recognizes the value of protecting a good idea, and decides to quickly seek patent protection for the improved design. A patent application is filed in the United States. At the same time, the client notices that sales to foreign countries have been increasing rapidly, to the point that foreign sales are overtaking sales in the United States. The client decides obtaining foreign patent protection is also a good idea. Unfortunately, the prior public sale of the improved ABSolutely Great machine has foreclosed the option of obtaining patent protection in most foreign countries.

Not long after this, Competitor Y starts selling exact copies of the ABSolutely Great machine overseas, at a large discount to the client's product. Competitor Y can afford to undercut the client's price, since it invested very little in research and development of the product. There is nothing the client can do to stop the copycat products, and foreign sales of the ABSolutely Great machine plummet. The client is forced to slash prices in an attempt to maintain its market share, and revenues plunge as a result. Foreign sales are now only a break-even proposition. Competitor Y soon captures the foreign market (which continues to grow) with its cheap copycat design.

The client eventually obtains a U.S. Patent on the improved ABSolutely Great machine. Total sales of the machine are steady and provide an acceptable profit. Unfortunately, as the fickle and trendy U.S. market looks for new products, sales of the ABSolutely Great machine are expected to decline. The main competition to the ABSolutely Great machine is a new abdominal exercise machine introduced by Competitor Z called the ABSolutely Best machine. The new machine is different from anything currently on the market, and looks strangely familiar to the client. Upon further investigation, the client discovers that the ABSolutely Best machine is in fact a design developed (and discarded) during the redesign of the ABSolutely Great machine. The engineer who developed the design left the employment of the client and went to work for Competitor Z several months ago. In the frantic attempt to redesign the ABSolutely Great machine, no efforts were undertaken to protect the ideas that emerged from the redesign effort. Further, the seemingly luckless client never required that its employees assign their new inventions to the business. As it also turned out, the client never required its engineers to sign a robust nondisclosure agreement, which also could have discouraged the engineer in question from disclosing the client's designs and proprietary data to Company Z.

While the preceding example may seem to exaggerate the problems that can occur when intellectual property is ignored, such events can and do happen every day. Two important lessons can be drawn from the example. First, ignoring or neglecting intellectual property, whether it be your own or someone else's, can result in a plethora of problems that are often expensive, embarrassing and avoidable. It is far too easy to blunder into a significant intellectual property problem, and more often than not, it is neither easy nor inexpensive for a client to extricate itself from the situation. Second, the client needs to be made aware of intellectual property considerations before undertaking a business venture, rather than after the problems arise. It is much easier (and less costly) to take a proactive role with respect to intellectual property matters, rather than reacting to the issues as they arise.

§ 17:10 Creating a system for protecting intellectual property—Identifying existing intellectual property

Once the client is aware that intellectual property affords many opportunities, and the client is also aware that paying attention to intellectual property can avoid expensive problems, counsel is well on his or her way to properly educating and advising the client about intellectual property matters. The next step is to create a system to effectively identify intellectual property issues.

Before any meaningful actions can be taken to capture and protect the client's intellectual property, an intellectual property management structure within the client's business must be created or identified. Specifically, the individual or group of individuals who will be making the final decisions on intellectual property matters must be identified. This individual or group of individuals will be responsible for implementing and maintaining the procedures and systems for protecting the client's intellectual property portfolio. To be effective, the effort must be coordinated and comprehensive. For this reason, it is best to identify one individual who is ultimately responsible for the client's intellectual property protection.

However, in some situations the final intellectual property decision maker may lack the time or expertise to be fully involved in all aspects of the client's intellectual property management. In such cases, an alternative contact should be identified to facilitate the day-to-day communication between the client and outside counsel. In the event a subordinate contact is used, that person should have the ability to collect and disseminate all necessary information both within the company and to outside counsel. After an intellectual property management structure has been identified, an intellectual property protection program can be put in place to capture and secure the client's intellectual property rights.

The first step in implementing an intellectual property protection program requires identifying and protecting those intellectual property rights that the client already possesses. This includes patents, trademarks, copyrights, trade secrets and trade dress. To identify all of the client's intellectual property rights, each of the client's products or services should be dissected to match various aspects of the product or service to the appropriate intellectual property right. For example, the structure of the product may be protectable by a patent, the name of the product protectable by a trademark, and the method of producing the product protectable by a trade secret. Copyrights may protect the product itself, literature that accompanies the product, the packaging for the product, or advertising for the product. Every product or service manufactured or provided by the client should be examined to ensure all intellectual property rights are identified.

Of course, just because it is possible to protect a particular

piece of intellectual property does not mean it is always necessary or desirable to do so. After the products and services of the
client are matched with the appropriate intellectual property
protection, the client can perform a cost-benefit analysis to
determine whether securing and maintaining intellectual property protection for each of the identified pieces of intellectual
property is warranted.

§ 17:11   Creating a system for protecting intellectual property—Protecting new intellectual property

Once all existing intellectual property has been identified and
appropriately protected, a system for capturing new intellectual
property rights developed by the client can be put in place. Such
a system will have many facets. The types of intellectual property created by the client will dictate exactly what types of intellectual property protection procedures should be used. However,
there are several systems and procedures that nearly every client
should use to protect its intellectual property.

If the client does not already have employee agreements
obligating employees to assign their rights in intellectual property to the client, such an agreement should be implemented
immediately. The agreement should require employees to assign
their rights in patents, trademarks, copyrights or other confidential information created by the employee in the course of their
employment to the client. An example of an employment agreement containing an assignment provision is found in Appendix Q.
Implementing an employee invention assignment agreement for
new employees is relatively easy. However, implementing a new
invention assignment agreement for existing employees may
require some additional consideration on the part of the employer
in exchange for the employee's acceptance of the agreement.

A document related to the employee invention assignment
agreement is a confidential nondisclosure agreement. The
confidential nondisclosure agreement inhibits the loss of intellectual property such as trade secrets and know-how, which derive their value from not being readily available and are not
otherwise protected. Employees who have access to trade secrets
and confidential information should be required to sign a
nondisclosure agreement, as should third parties such as suppliers or large customers who may have access to trade secrets and
confidential information through the course of doing business. A
sample nondisclosure agreement is provided in Appendix P.

Security should be put in place to protect the client's intellectual property from access by individuals who do not have the
authority or a need to know the information. The client must
treat the information as secret or confidential if a court is to

regard it as such. The type of security will obviously depend upon the form the information is in, and may include both physical and electronic restricted access. Filing cabinets containing confidential information should be locked. Access to computer files with such information should have limited access. Access to a manufacturing facility should be limited if a trade secret could be discerned by an observer. In short, secret or confidential information should be provided on a need to know basis and documents containing sensitive information should be marked as confidential.

An organized invention documentation program should be implemented to encourage all employees to regularly document their inventive activities. The program should clearly set forth the type of information to be preserved (dates, inventors, drawings, etc.), and the manner in which the information should be recorded. For example, an invention disclosure form can be developed so that all of the disclosures contain the necessary information. A sample invention disclosure form is provided in Appendix BB. The documentation program should make the creation of written invention disclosures a part of the regular routine of every employee who is involved in research and development of new products or services. For those employees who may not be regularly involved in research and development efforts, the client may wish to provide bonus compensation for useful ideas submitted to the company. The written disclosures should be periodically collected for review and evaluation.

A regular review should be conducted of all documents that may contain secret or confidential information, or which may lead to inadvertent public disclosure of intellectual property that is not otherwise protected. For example, all company publications, distribution agreements, supplier agreements and license agreements should be reviewed. Company publications should be reviewed to ensure that new and valuable developments are not inadvertently disclosed to the public prior to obtaining protection. Distribution and license agreements should be reviewed to ensure that intellectual property rights are adequately protected through nondisclosure agreements and that the agreement does not create an unregistered franchise.

In addition, an employee education plan should be created to educate the client's employees about intellectual property. The information disseminated to employees should include an explanation of the importance of intellectual property to the client's business (and the employee's livelihood) and a description of the measures the client is taking to protect its intellectual property. Of course, not all of the employees will have a need to be educated about the same intellectual property issues, so it may be useful to identify various employee types, and then tailor the training to each of those employee groups.

For example, the client's employees may include an engineering staff, a marketing group, a sales and distribution force, and other administrative employees. Each of these employee groups have different concerns with respect to the client's intellectual property rights. For example, engineers or designers should be counseled about patents, trade secrets, copyrights, and employee agreements that require assignment of inventions to their employer. The marketing staff should be apprised of various trademark, copyright, advertising, and trade secret issues that affect the ability to market and advertise a new product. The sales and distribution force must be made aware of trade secret issues and perhaps franchising and advertising issues. The administrative force employed by the company should also be made aware of trade secret issues so that sensitive business information is not inadvertently released to the public.

§ 17:12   Creating a system for protecting intellectual property—Enforcing intellectual property rights

Before embarking on a suit to enforce a client's intellectual property rights, it is crucial that the client understand the nature of the suit and what will be expected of the client. Intellectual property cases (especially patent infringement cases) are notoriously long and expensive. In 2015, the median cost of a patent infringement case (through trial) ranged from $600,000, for cases where less than $1 million was at risk, up to $5 million, for cases where over $25 million was at risk. Over the same scale of dollars at risk, the median cost for trademark infringement cases ranged from $325,000 to $1.6 million. For copyright infringement cases, the median cost ranged from $250,000 to $1.2 million; for trade secret misappropriation, the median cost ranged from $500,000 to about $2.6 million.[1] Therefore, the cost of even a "small" intellectual property case can be quite significant. It is crucial that the client be made aware of this fact at the outset of the case and that the client be committed to seeing the case through.

While patent, trademark and copyright infringement cases differ in detail, the basic pleading and discovery is similar. For purposes of this brief overview, a patent infringement case is a good example.

Drafting the complaint is relatively simple. The more difficult task is the pre-filing investigation. For example, in patent cases,

---

[Section 17:12]   Law Association, *Report of the*
[1]American Intellectual Property   *Economic Survey* 37–39 (2015).

it is important to become familiar with the patent and the infringing products before drafting the complaint. It is also crucial to review the patent file history and relevant prior art in order to anticipate any problems with the validity of the patent. Similar investigation is necessary for trademark and copyright infringement cases.

Most jurisdictions now require each party to make an "initial disclosure." This means that the patent owner must voluntarily provide documents relating to the development of the patent and its products, as well as identifying those persons involved with the patent and products relating to the patent. The alleged infringer is also required to make an initial disclosure. This usually involves all documents relating to the development of the products charged with infringement, and all documents relating to the patent owner, its products and its patent.

The next step is to take depositions. Typically, the patent owner will want to depose someone who can testify as to the sales of the alleged infringer's product, any people involved in development, design and marketing of the allegedly infringing product, and anyone who had knowledge of the patent owner's product or patent. The alleged infringer will typically depose the inventor and anyone involved in deciding to develop and market the patent owner's product. An alleged infringer will also probably depose the attorneys who prepared and prosecuted the patent. Also, if there are any significant invalidity defenses, both parties will want to depose people who have information about the prior art.

Most patent cases have at least two expert witnesses: a technical expert to explain the patent and testify on infringement; and a financial expert to testify on damages. Experts are usually retained early during the discovery process because experts are often very helpful in focusing discovery and help make sure that sufficient documents are disclosed.

Most intellectual property cases involve substantial motion practice. In addition to discovery motions, preliminary injunction motions are increasingly important in patent cases, and routine in trademark and copyright cases. In addition, summary judgment motions are not unusual. Particularly in patent cases, where issues such as claim interpretation and some validity defenses are questions of law, the chances of winning summary judgment (at least on some issues) is fairly high. Even if the case is not disposed of, the issues for trial are often narrowed.

As with most civil cases, very few intellectual property cases actually go to trial. The conventional wisdom today is that a patent owner should seek a jury trial. Juries tend to be impressed with patents and are hesitant to second-guess the U.S. Patent and Trademark Office. This is in contrast to the conventional wisdom of many years ago, when most lawyers believed that patent cases were too complicated for juries to understand, and that judges were more likely to favor the patent owner. Jury trials, of course, are significantly more expensive than bench trials.

After all of that expense, what are the chances of recovering significant damages? In patent and copyright cases, the chances are very good. The damages statutes provide attractive measures of damages, and, if infringement is proven, judges and juries tend to be generous. Trademark and trade dress cases are a different story. Trademark law has its basis in equity, and there is substantial case law that requires actual confusion or intentional infringement before awarding trademark damages. Therefore, most trademark cases are injunction cases; they settle if the alleged infringer is willing to agree to an injunction. An award of substantial damages is not likely in a trademark case, although there are always exceptions.

The patent, trademark, and copyright statutes all provide for awards of enhanced damages and attorney's fees in unusual cases. Typically, some sort of intentional infringement is required before the court will consider enhancing damages or awarding attorney's fees. Findings of willful infringement are unusual, but not unheard of. Generally, if the defendant has obtained an opinion of counsel that it was not infringing, this is sufficient to avoid a finding of willful infringement. However, an opinion is not a complete shield to a finding of willfulness. Clients can find themselves liable for willful infringement if they withhold information from the attorney who is giving the opinion if the opinion is held to be insufficient or lacking in some regard, or if they do not follow the advice given in the opinion. Full disclosure of information to counsel is always crucial.

§ 17:13 Avoiding infringement of intellectual property rights of others

In addition to protecting its own intellectual property, the client must be careful to avoid infringing the intellectual property rights of others. As noted earlier, infringement of someone else's intellectual property can have potentially disastrous results. Fortunately, there are several steps a client can take to minimize the possibility of infringing another party's intellectual property rights.

In the realm of patent law, the best way to avoid infringing another party's patent(s) depends upon many factors such as the client's industry, the number of patents in the subject area, and the number of competitors. One method of avoiding patent infringement is to consistently monitor what the client's competitors and others in the field are doing. If the client stays abreast of current developments in the industry (as most do), it is likely to be aware of what intellectual property is protected and thus avoid infringement of those patents. By reviewing the competitors' patents on a regular basis, it is possible not only to avoid infringing a particular patent, but also to determine the direction and strategy of the competition. In addition, the client's competitors are most likely to notice and raise infringement issues, so reviewing the patents of those competitors can head off the bulk of any infringement problems at the earliest possible opportunity. This method of avoiding patent infringement is most successful in well-established industries having only a few competitors and a relatively small number of new patents.

Another method to avoid patent infringement is for the client to undertake a "freedom to operate" or "clearance" study to determine whether a proposed product would infringe another party's patent. Ideally, the study is conducted before the product is sold or offered for sale. A freedom to operate study should generally begin with a search to locate any patents that would cover the proposed device. For complex devices, it is helpful to identify and search each individual component or feature of the device separately. When conducting such a search, it is important to have an understanding of what the client wishes to produce. If the search is conducted during the preliminary design of the client's product, the search may need to be updated as more product definition develops or as features of the product change. If the freedom to operate study locates a patent that may potentially be infringed by the proposed product, a detailed analysis of the patent to determine whether the patent would be infringed and/or if the patent is valid may be undertaken. Where the proposed product is determined to be noninfringing or the patent is determined to be invalid, the client may wish to obtain an oral or written opinion from an attorney to that effect.

The need for a detailed infringement study will probably be dictated by the level of investment the client proposes for a particular venture. As the potential investment (and risk) increases, greater attention should be focused on avoiding infringement of another party's patent. A benefit of conducting a freedom to operate study early in the product development cycle is that the opportunity exists to conduct a redesign at relatively low cost. In addition, a freedom to operate study will generally help the client identify those features of its own product which are protectable in their own right. In fact, a sophisticated client can use a freedom to operate study to design a product or process that is likely to be protectable. Of course, if it is not possible or cost-effective to design around a competitor's protected intellectual property, the client is afforded the opportunity, early in the product development process, to abandon the project or potentially license the required technology at a relatively low cost.

Similar to patents, a trademark infringement study can avoid infringement of another party's trademark, and should be performed before a client begins using a mark. A trademark infringement study can vary in degree from a preliminary search to a complete or full search. A preliminary search involves a quick search of a trademark database to locate any trademark registrations or applications similar to the proposed trademark. A full search covers not only federal registration, but also state registrations, and common law usages found in trade directories, telephone books, and lists of company names. Trademark practitioners are often able to provide same-day reports on whether a particular mark or corporate name will face a trademark infringement problem.

The need for a complete or full trademark infringement search will probably be dictated by the level of investment the client proposes for a particular venture. Similar to patents, as the potential investment (and risk) increases, greater attention should be focused on avoiding infringement of another party's trademark. The cost of a full trademark infringement search is insignificant compared to possible infringement charges, wasted production time, and wasted materials bearing an unusable mark.

Copyright infringement involves prior knowledge of the copyrighted work, and occurs by copying the work of another. Unlike patent law, independent creation precludes copyright infringement liability. Therefore, the best way to avoid copyright infringement is to ensure that copying does not occur, which can involve training employees, monitoring activities, and developing sound procedural guidelines. Documentation and retention of records related to creative works may also be helpful in proving independent creation.

The marketing efforts of a client may also create trademark and copyright infringement issues. A regular review of marketing efforts should be instituted to monitor for such issues. Advertisements, promotional materials, and product packaging should be reviewed to determined whether there are any potential trademark, copyright, or trade dress problems. In particular, the client's trademarks, written material, and trade dress should be compared to those of the competition to determine if any unacceptable similarities exist. Often, copyright infringement by promotional materials can be avoided by asking the people who created the materials how they came up with their ideas. If it appears that an infringement issue may exist, a more detailed analysis can be conducted.

§ 17:14 Intellectual property due diligence considerations

Due diligence is a process undertaken in conjunction with mergers, acquisitions, or other activities requiring asset valuation or risk assessment. Frequently, general corporate and finance due diligence is conducted at the same time as intellectual property due diligence. Intellectual property due diligence is essentially an assessment of the nature and value of intellectual property. The goal is to ensure that the client (purchaser) knows about the rights and liabilities associated with the ownership and use of the intellectual property in question. Thus, a few of the key determinations that due diligence should provide include the scope of the intellectual property rights involved, whether the intellectual property is encumbered in any way, an accurate assessment of the value of the intellectual property rights, and whether the intellectual property is currently being litigated or carries a litigation risk.[1]

Prior to beginning due diligence, it is advisable to plan the scope of the search based on budget, time, personnel, and the complexity and breadth of the target's intellectual property. A due diligence checklist could be created for the target, establishing the goals of due diligence and the procedure that will be taken to accomplish those goals. The client should specify how documents and information regarding the target's intellectual property assets need to be prepared and organized.

Another important consideration in due diligence strategy for publicly traded companies is compliance with reporting requirements in the Sarbanes-Oxley Act (SOX).[2] SOX § 302 requires a number of internal procedures meant to ensure accurate financial disclosure.[3] This implicitly includes fair and accurate valuation of intellectual property assets. As a result, the scope of intellectual property due diligence needs to ensure that once the client acquires new intellectual property assets, the client will still be able to accurately disclose their financial status under SOX.

SOX § 404 imposes additional requirements of documentation and certification of internal financial reporting procedures and controls.[4] This includes self-assessments of business risks, such as likelihood of litigation issues with intellectual property assets.

[Section 17:14]

[1]For a detailed list of potential issues for due diligence, *see* Assets & Finance: Audits and Valuation of Intellectual Property § 1:2 (2010 ed.). *See also* Klein, Intellectual Property in Mergers and Acquisitions § 4:1 et seq. (2012 ed.).

[2]Sarbanes-Oxley Act of 2002, Pub. L. 107-204, 116 Stat. 745 (July 30, 2002) (codified as scattered 29 U.S.C.A. §§ 11, 15, 18, 28).

[3]*See* Sarbanes-Oxley § 302 (codified at 15 U.S.C.A. § 7241).

[4]*See* Sarbanes-Oxley § 404 (codified at 15 U.S.C.A. § 7262).

Therefore, it is crucial that the due diligence search includes a review of the target's internal financial control standards used to assess intellectual property assets. This will allow the client to compare its own internal financial controls with that of the target in order to account for any discrepancies after the target's intellectual property assets have been acquired.[5] In light of SOX, due diligence now needs to be conducted not only with the goal of determining the scope, value, and risks associated with acquiring intellectual property assets, but also with the goal of complying with the reporting requirements in SOX.

---

[5]For more specifics regarding compliance with Sarbanes-Oxley requirements in an intellectual property context *see* Brownlee, *Assets & Finance: Audits and Valuation of Intellectual Property* §§ 1:24 to 1.31 (2010 ed.).

APPENDICES

APPENDIX A

United States Utility Patent and Published Application

US007766010B2

(12) **United States Patent**
Jagger et al.

(10) Patent No.: **US 7,766,010 B2**
(45) **Date of Patent:** **Aug. 3, 2010**

(54) **METHOD OF CONTROLLING THE RATE OF OXYGEN PRODUCED BY AN OXYGEN CONCENTRATOR**

(75) Inventors: **Theodore W. Jagger**, White Bear Lake, MN (US); **Nicholas P. Van Brunt**, White Bear Lake, MN (US); **John A. Kivisto**, Oak Grove, MN (US); **Perry B. Lonnes**, White Bear Lake, MN (US)

(73) Assignee: **VBOX, Incorporated**, White Bear Lake, MN (US)

(*) Notice: Subject to any disclaimer, the term of this patent is extended or adjusted under 35 U.S.C. 154(b) by 220 days.

(21) Appl. No.: **11/054,342**

(22) Filed: **Feb. 9, 2005**

(65) **Prior Publication Data**

US 2006/0174882 A1 Aug. 10, 2006

(51) **Int. Cl.**
A61M 15/06 (2006.01)
B01D 59/26 (2006.01)
B01D 19/00 (2006.01)
(52) **U.S. Cl.** 128/202.21; 95/96; 95/97; 95/98; 95/99; 95/100; 95/101; 95/102; 95/103; 96/121; 96/130; 96/133; 96/157
(58) **Field of Classification Search** 96/121, 96/130, 133, 157; 95/96–103; 128/202.21
See application file for complete search history.

(56) **References Cited**

U.S. PATENT DOCUMENTS

4,194,890 A	*	3/1980	McCombs et al.	.... 95/23
4,449,990 A	*	5/1984	Tedford, Jr.	.... 95/26
4,472,177 A	*	9/1984	Sircar	.... 95/11
4,491,459 A		1/1985	Pinkerton	
4,648,888 A		3/1987	Rowland	
4,813,977 A		3/1989	Schmidt et al.	
4,826,510 A		5/1989	McCombs	
4,925,464 A		5/1990	Rabenau et al.	
4,971,609 A	*	11/1990	Pawlos	.... 96/128
5,084,075 A		1/1992	Sircar et al.	
5,114,440 A	*	5/1992	Reiss	.... 95/96

(Continued)

FOREIGN PATENT DOCUMENTS

EP 0 860 646 A2 2/1998

(Continued)

OTHER PUBLICATIONS

Recommendations of the Fifth Oxygen Consensus Conference, 1999.

(Continued)

Primary Examiner—Loan H Thanh
Assistant Examiner—Nihir Patel
(74) *Attorney, Agent, or Firm*—Kinney & Lange, P.A.

(57) **ABSTRACT**

A method of providing concentrated oxygen product gas to a patient. The method comprises producing product gas by a vacuum swing adsorption (VSA) process with an oxygen concentrator comprising a plurality of separation columns connected to a vacuum source driven by a motor. Separated product gas is then pumped to a product reservoir. The pressure of the reservoir is monitored and used to adjust the speed of the motor based on the reservoir pressure. The separated gas is then delivered to the patient.

21 Claims, 19 Drawing Sheets

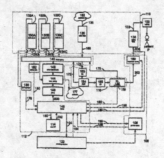

US 7,766,010 B2
Page 2

U.S. PATENT DOCUMENTS

5,366,541 A	11/1994	Hill et al.	
5,429,666 A	7/1995	Agrawal et al.	
RE35,099 E	11/1995	Hill	
5,531,807 A	7/1996	McCombs	
5,593,478 A	1/1997	Hill et al.	
5,656,066 A	8/1997	Reiss et al.	
5,730,778 A	3/1998	Hill et al.	
5,827,358 A	10/1998	Kulish et al.	
5,858,062 A	1/1999	McCulloh et al.	
5,893,275 A	4/1999	Henry	
5,893,944 A	4/1999	Dong	
5,928,189 A	7/1999	Phillips et al.	
5,979,440 A	11/1999	Honkonen et al.	
6,010,555 A	1/2000	Smolarek et al.	
6,162,283 A	12/2000	Conrad et al.	
6,212,904 B1	4/2001	Arkharov et al.	
6,217,635 B1	4/2001	Conrad et al.	
6,287,366 B1	9/2001	Derive et al.	
6,302,107 B1	10/2001	Richey, II et al.	
6,311,719 B1	11/2001	Hill et al.	
6,314,957 B1	11/2001	Boissin et al.	
6,344,069 B2	2/2002	Smolarek et al.	
6,346,139 B1	2/2002	Czabala	
6,446,630 B1	9/2002	Todd, Jr.	
6,457,485 B2	10/2002	Hill et al.	
6,471,744 B1 *	10/2002	Hill	95/19
6,478,857 B2	11/2002	Czabala	
6,511,526 B2	1/2003	Jagger et al.	
6,520,176 B1	2/2003	Dubois et al.	
6,544,318 B2 *	4/2003	Dee et al.	95/96
6,551,384 B1	4/2003	Ackley et al.	
6,629,525 B2	10/2003	Hill et al.	
6,641,644 B2	11/2003	Jagger et al.	
6,651,653 B1	11/2003	Honkonen et al.	
6,651,658 B1 *	11/2003	Hill et al.	128/204.23
6,681,764 B1	1/2004	Honkonen et al.	
6,691,702 B2	2/2004	Appel et al.	
6,698,423 B1	3/2004	Honkonen et al.	
6,712,087 B2	3/2004	Hill et al.	
6,712,886 B2 *	3/2004	Kim	96/111
6,764,534 B2	7/2004	McCombs et al.	
6,802,889 B2	10/2004	Graham et al.	
6,805,729 B2	10/2004	Lim et al.	
6,811,590 B2	11/2004	Lee et al.	
6,866,041 B2	3/2005	Hardy, Jr. et al.	
7,066,985 B2	6/2006	Deane et al.	
7,135,059 B2 *	11/2006	Deane et al.	96/115
2002/0053286 A1	5/2002	Czabala	
2002/0127442 A1	9/2002	Connor et al.	
2004/0020366 A1	2/2004	Walker et al.	
2004/0149133 A1	8/2004	McCombs et al.	
2005/0072426 A1	4/2005	Deane et al.	
2005/0081713 A1 *	4/2005	Lee et al.	95/96

FOREIGN PATENT DOCUMENTS

WO	WO 98/58219	12/1998
WO	WO 03/092817	11/2003

OTHER PUBLICATIONS

"AirSep lowers boom.", www.hmenews.com/2004.12/depts/vendors/vendors1.htm.

* cited by examiner

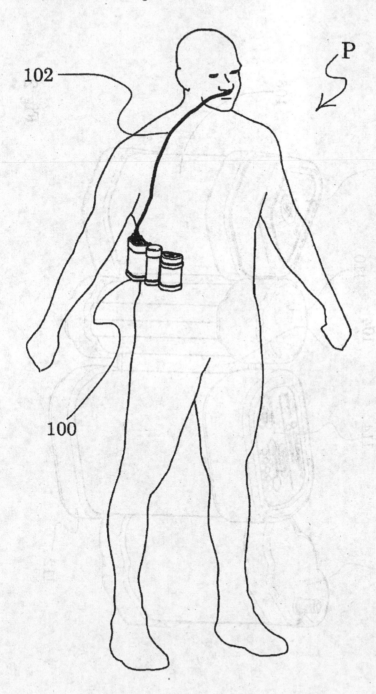

P

102

100

Fig 1

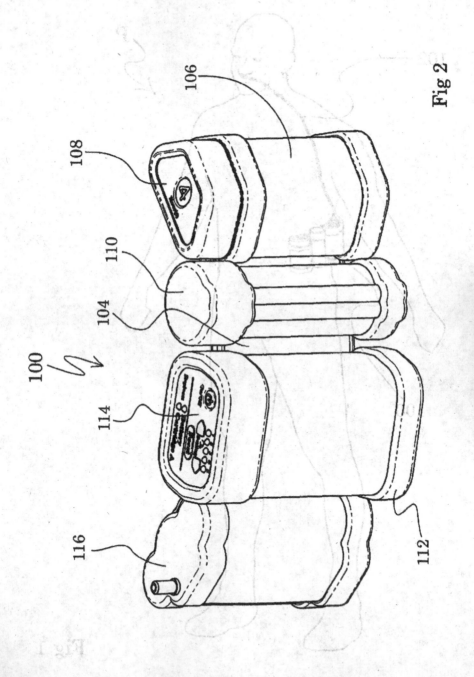

Fig 2

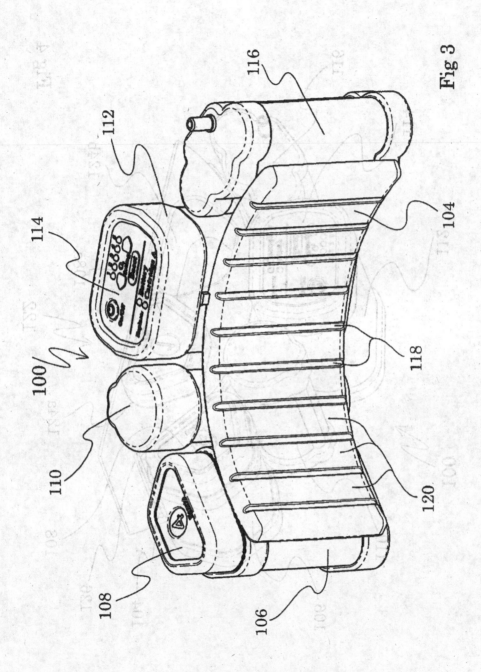

Fig 3

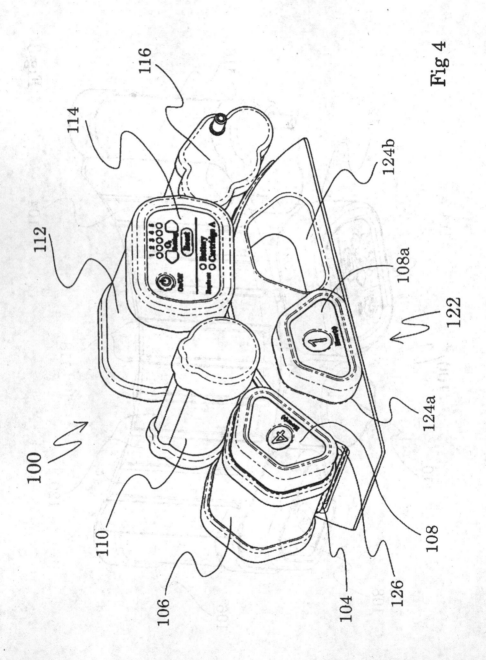

Fig 4

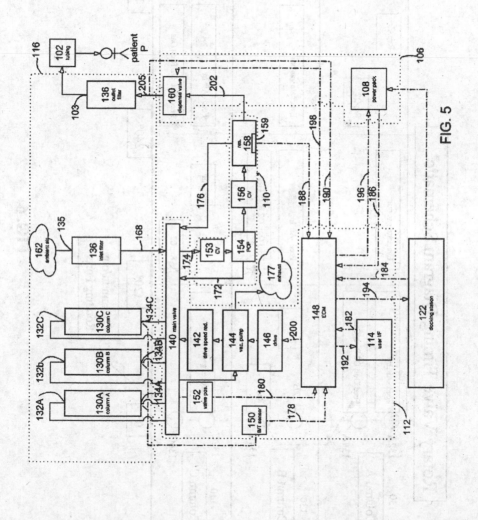

FIG. 5

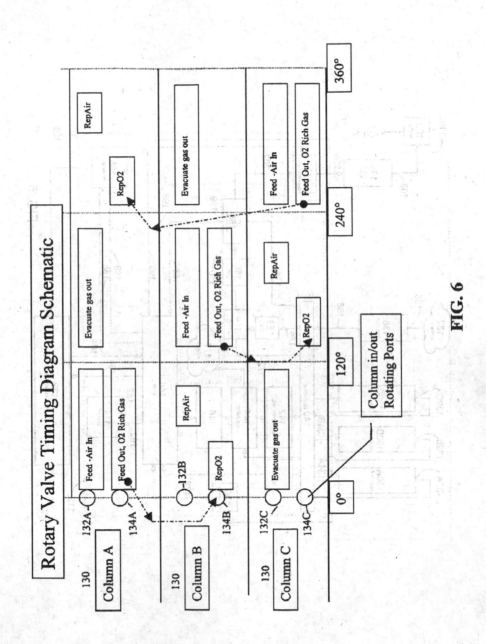

FIG. 6

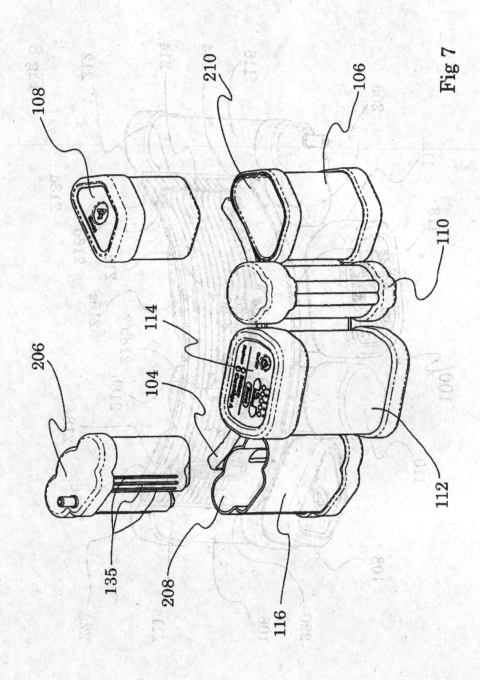

Fig 7

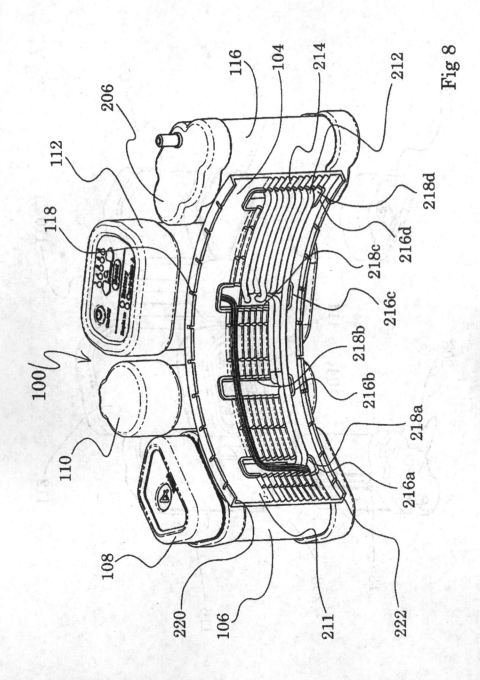

Fig 8

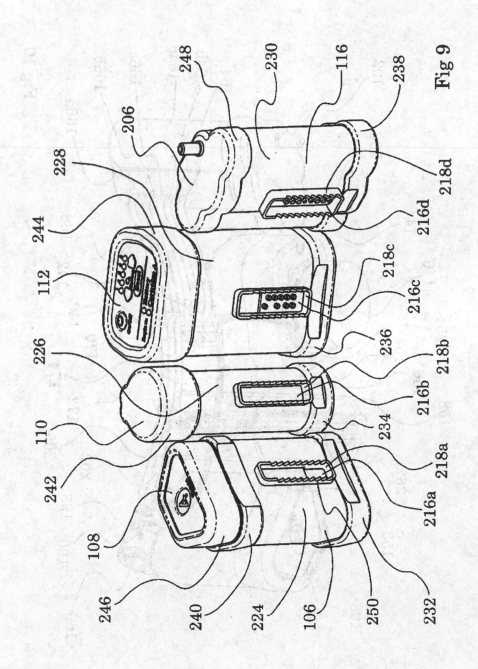

Fig 9

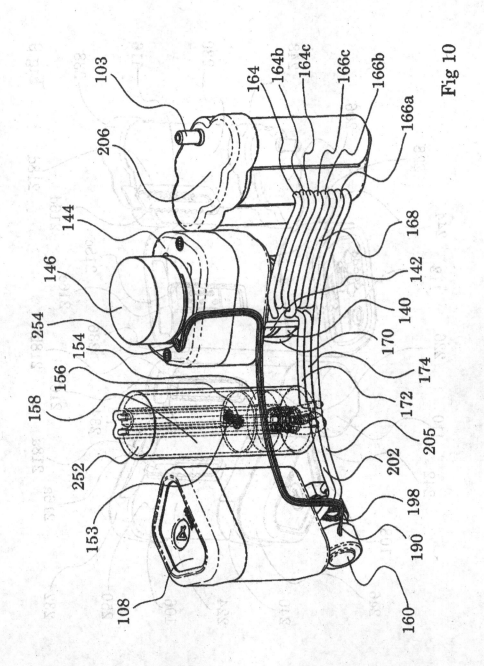

Fig 10

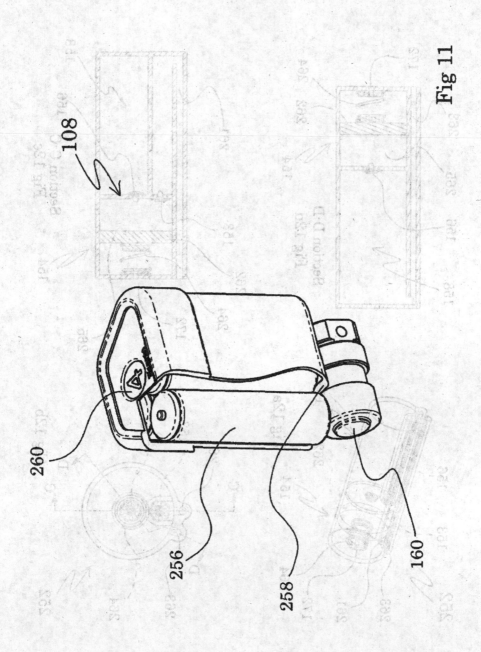

Fig 11

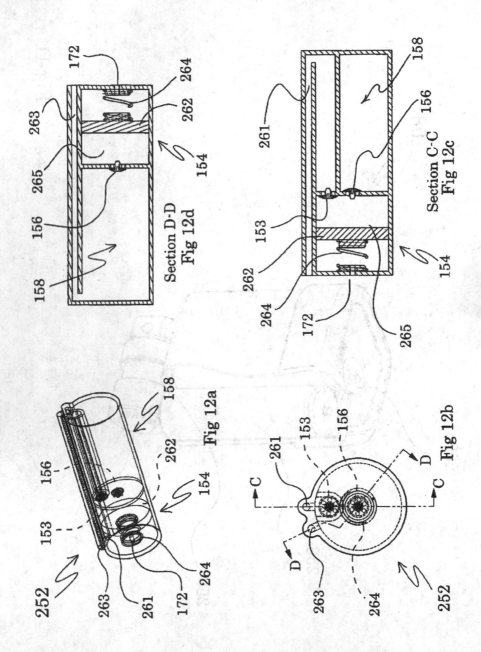

Section D-D
Fig 12d

Section C-C
Fig 12c

Fig 12a

Fig 12b

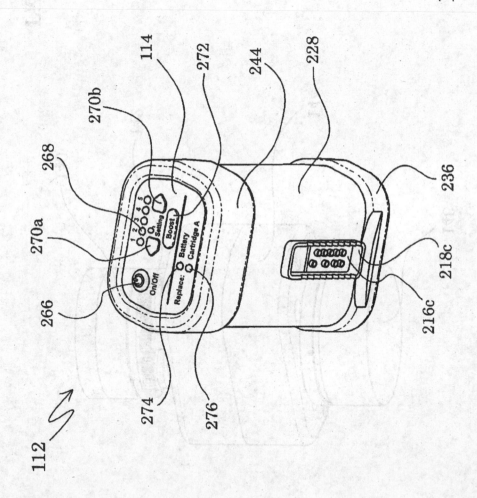

Fig 13

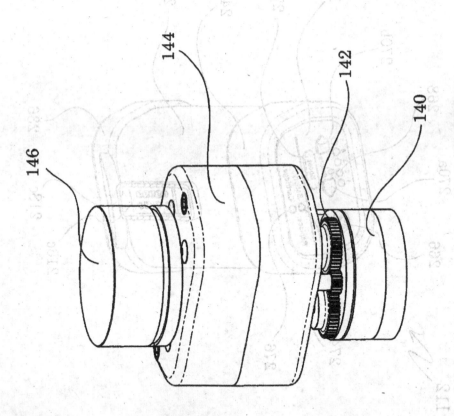

Fig 14

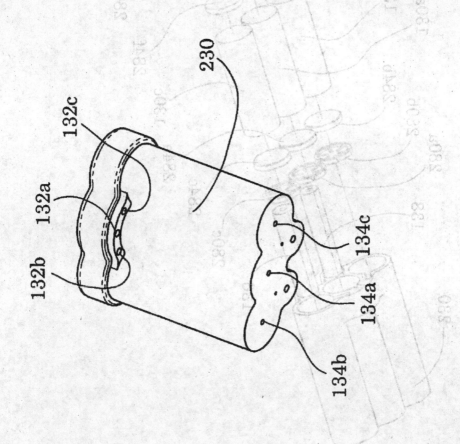

Fig 15

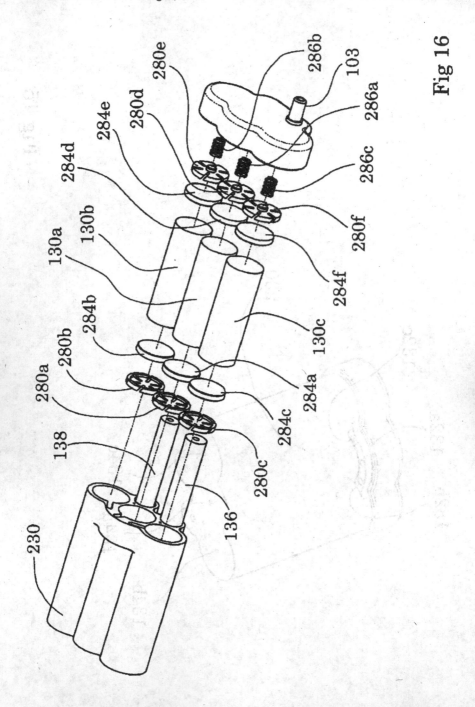

Fig 16

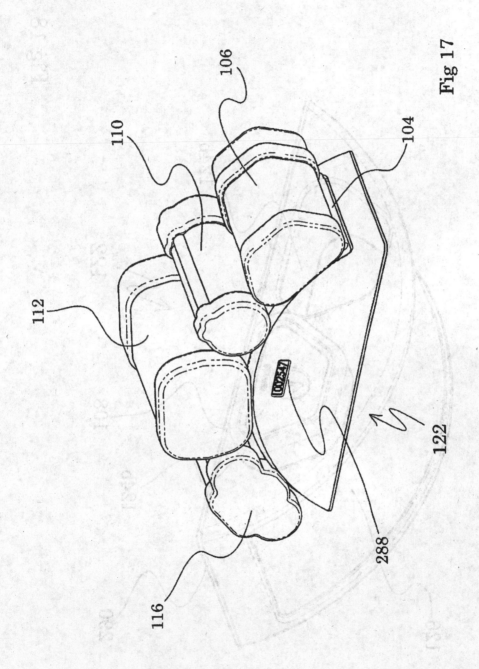

Fig 17

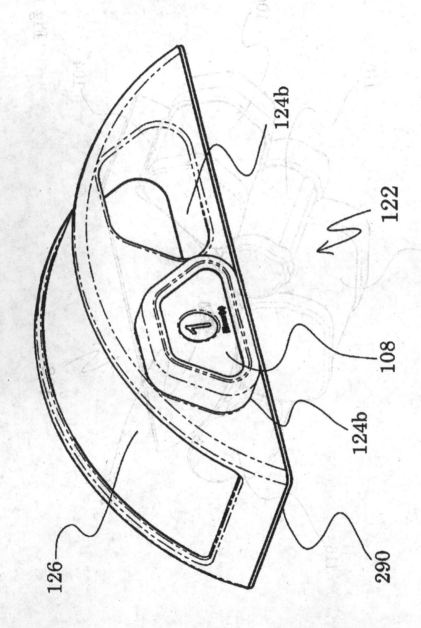

Fig 18

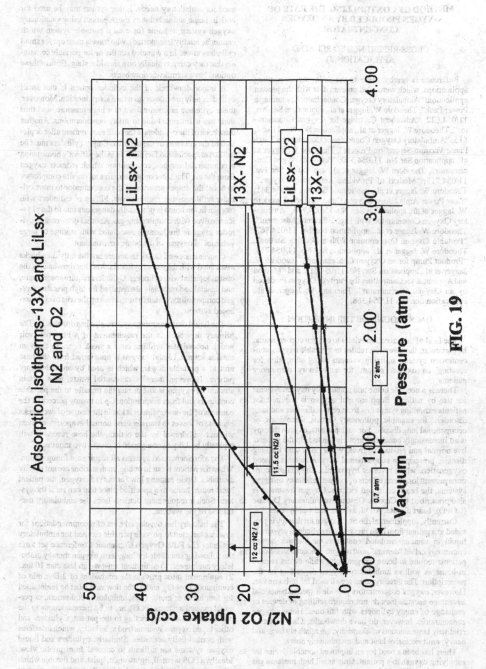

FIG. 19

US 7,766,010 B2

1

METHOD OF CONTROLLING THE RATE OF OXYGEN PRODUCED BY AN OXYGEN CONCENTRATOR

CROSS-REFERENCE TO RELATED APPLICATION(S)

Reference is hereby made to the following co-pending applications, which were filed on even date with the present application: "Ambulatory Oxygen Concentrator Containing a Power Pack", Theodore W. Jagger et al., application Ser. No. 11/054,622; "Adsorbent Cartridge for Oxygen Concentrator", Theodore W. Jagger et al., application Ser. No. 11/054,615; "Ambulatory Oxygen Concentrator Containing a Three Phase Vacuum Separation Process", Theodore W. Jagger et al., application Ser. No. 11/054,340; "Personal Oxygen Concentrator", Theodore W. Jagger et al., application Ser. No. 11/054,713; "Method of Providing Ambulatory Oxygen", Theodore W. Jagger et al., application Ser. No. 11/054,341; "Low Power Ambulatory Oxygen Concentrator", Theodore W. Jagger et al., application Ser. No. 11/054,716; "Ambulatory Oxygen Concentrator With High Efficiency Adsorbent", Theodore W. Jagger et al., application Ser. No. 11/054,367; "Portable Oxygen Concentrator With a Docking Station", Theodore W. Jagger et al., application Ser. No. 11/054,714; "Product Pump for an Oxygen Concentrator", Theodore W. Jagger et al., application Ser. No. 11/054,512; and "Method and Apparatus for Controlling the Purity of Oxygen Produced by an Oxygen Concentrator", Theodore W. Jagger et al., application Ser. No. 11/054,368.

BACKGROUND OF THE INVENTION

The field of this invention relates to oxygen concentrators. In particular, the invention relates to wearable oxygen concentration systems utilizing vacuum swing adsorption for creating an oxygen stream for ambulatory respiratory patients.

There is a need for home and ambulatory oxygen systems for use by patients. Supplemental oxygen is required for patients exhibiting symptoms from certain diseases and lung disorders; for example, pulmonary fibrosis, sarcoidosis, or occupational lung disease. For such patients, oxygen therapy is an increasingly beneficial prescription to help the patients live normal and productive lives. While not a cure for lung disease, prescriptive supplemental oxygen increases blood oxygenation, which reverses hypoxemia. Oxygen prescriptions prevent long-term effects of oxygen deficiency on organ systems, the heart, brain and kidneys. Oxygen treatment is also prescribed for Chronic Obstructive Pulmonary Disease (COPD), heart disease, AIDS, asthma, and emphysema.

Currently, supplemental medical oxygen for therapy is provided to a patient from high pressure gas cylinders; cryogenic liquid in vacuum-insulated containers or thermos bottles commonly called "dewars", and oxygen concentrators. Some patients require in-home oxygen only, while others require in-home as well as ambulatory oxygen depending on the prescription. The three systems are all used for in-home use. However, oxygen concentrators provide a special beneficial advantage because they do not require refilling of dewars or exchange of empty cylinders with full ones. Home oxygen concentrators, however, do have drawbacks. They consume relatively large amounts of electricity; are relatively large and heavy; emit excessive heat and are relatively noisy.

There has been a need for an improved portable device for supplying oxygen to a patient. Only small high pressure gas bottles and small liquid dewars are truly portable enough to be

2

used for ambulatory needs. Either system may be used for both in-home and ambulatory use. A patient using a stationary oxygen system at home (or even a portable system which cannot be readily transported), who travels must opt for small cylinders towed in a wheeled stroller or for portable containers that they carry, typically on a shoulder sling. Both of these options have significant drawbacks.

A major drawback of the cylinder option is that small cylinders only provide oxygen for a short duration. Moreover, these cylinders are maintained at a high pressure, and thus their use is restricted due to safety considerations. Another drawback of the cylinders is the refill requirement after depletion of the contents of the cylinder. Empty cylinders must be refilled at specialized facilities, or in the patient's home using a commercial oxygen concentrator which extracts oxygen from the air. The latter option requires an on-site compressor to boost the output pressure of the concentrator to meet cylinder refill pressure requirements. Filling of cylinders with oxygen in the home is potentially dangerous due to the physics involved with compressing gas. Another detriment to cylinder usage is fire hazards associated with storage of large volumes of oxygen in the home environment.

Convenience and safety issues are not the only drawbacks associated with the use of cylinders. Another drawback is the cost associated with cylinders. Cylinders require special care, and specialized materials are required for high pressure oxygen compatibility, which in turn drives up the cost of cylinder-based systems.

The liquid oxygen storage system also has drawbacks. The primary drawback is the requirement of a base reservoir which necessitates refilling once a week or more from an outside source. Liquid oxygen is transferred from the base unit to a portable dewar, which is used by an ambulatory patient. However, there is substantial waste, as a certain amount of oxygen is lost during the transfer to the portable containers and from evaporation. Up to twenty percent of the contents of the base cylinder is lost in the course of two weeks because of losses in transfers and normal evaporation. Even without withdrawal by the patient, the base reservoir will typically boil dry over a period of one to two months.

The aforementioned systems all require are filling station. When the patient is out in public, such stations are not readily available. Upon running low (or out) of oxygen, the patient must return home to a specified place that can refill the system. Such a requirement detracts from the ambulatory usefulness of the systems.

The industry has developed a set of recommendations for systems targeted to provide portable oxygen for ambulatory patients. The Fifth Oxygen Consensus Conference set forth the following standards for long-term oxygen therapy ambulatory equipment: 1) equipment must weigh less than 10 lbs., 2) equipment must provide the equivalent of 2 liter/min of continuous flow O_2, and 3) the flow rate must be maintained for four hours or more. Thus, ambulatory equipment, or personal oxygen systems (POS), are to be inconspicuous to the public as well as unrestricting to the patient. Cylinders and other liquid oxygen systems tend to be bulky, which interferes with normal daily activities. Similarly, cylinders and liquid oxygen systems are difficult to conceal from public view. Ideally, a POS is small, lightweight, quiet, and flexible which allows the device to be concealed from the public. The present

3

invention, whereby oxygen rich gas is provided to a patient from a wearable oxygen concentrator, meets and exceeds these standards.

BRIEF SUMMARY OF THE INVENTION

A method of providing concentrated oxygen product gas to a patient comprises producing product gas by a vacuum swing adsorption (VSA) process through a plurality of separation columns connected to a vacuum source driven by a motor. Separated product gas is then pumped to a reservoir in which the pressure is monitored and used to adjust the speed of the motor based on that pressure. The separated gas is then delivered to the patient.

BRIEF DESCRIPTION OF THE DRAWINGS

FIG. 1 is a front view of a patient carrying the oxygen concentrator of the present invention.

FIG. 2 is a front perspective view of the oxygen concentrator.

FIG. 3 is a rear perspective view of the oxygen concentrator.

FIG. 4 is a front perspective view of the oxygen concentrator and a docking station.

FIG. 5 is a block diagram showing the components and connections of the oxygen concentrator.

FIG. 6 is a diagram showing rotary valve timing.

FIG. 7 is an exploded view of the oxygen concentrator in which the power pack and the adsorbent cartridge have been removed.

FIG. 8 is a perspective view of the oxygen concentrator with a portion of the belt removed.

FIG. 9 is a perspective view of the components of the oxygen concentrator without the belt.

FIG. 10 is a perspective view of the components contained within the case portions of the modules and their associated pneumatic and electrical connections of the oxygen concentrator.

FIG. 11 is a perspective view of the components contained within a battery module.

FIG. 12a is a perspective view of an accumulator.

FIG. 12b is a top view of the accumulator.

FIG. 12c is a sectional view of the accumulator.

FIG. 12d is another sectional view of the accumulator.

FIG. 13 is a perspective view of a control module.

FIG. 14 is a front view of the interior components of the control module.

FIG. 15 is a perspective view of the cartridge contained within a cartridge module.

FIG. 16 is an exploded view of columns and filters within the cartridge.

FIG. 17 is a rear perspective view of the oxygen concentrator and the docking station.

FIG. 18 is a front perspective view of the docking station.

FIG. 19 is a chart showing the adsorption isotherms for two different adsorbent materials.

DETAILED DESCRIPTION

The current invention relates to separation of gases using vacuum swing adsorption. Specifically, disclosed is an oxygen concentrator for a patient who requires a source of oxygen. The present invention is further explained with reference to the drawn figures in which like structures are referred to by like numerals throughout the several views.

4

Overview—Oxygen Concentrator 100 (FIGS. 1-4)

FIG. 1 is a front view showing patient P with oxygen concentrator 100 and oxygen delivery tube 102. Oxygen concentrator 100 is a small unit which utilizes vacuum swing adsorption to separate oxygen from the ambient air around patient P. Oxygen concentrator 100 is compact and light so as not to interfere with the ambulatory movement of patient P, and can produce a product stream of gas containing a range of eighty-five to ninety-five percent oxygen.

Oxygen delivery tube 102 is a polymer tube or similar oxidation resistant structure, which extends from oxygen concentrator 100 to the nose, mouth, or port into the upper airway of patient P. Tube 102 allows delivery of oxygen to patient P for inhalation. In FIG. 1, patient P is about six foot tall to illustrate an approximation of the relative size of oxygen concentrator 100.

FIG. 2 is a perspective view of oxygen concentrator 100. Oxygen concentrator 100 is comprised of belt 104, power module 106 containing power pack 108, reservoir module 110, control module 112 containing user interface 114, and separation cartridge module 116. Oxygen concentrator 100 is a portable oxygen separator used to provide an oxygen rich gas stream to patient P. Belt 104 connects and carries the modules 106, 110, 112, and 116 of oxygen concentrator 100. Belt 104 may contain belt loops (not illustrated), clips, or a pair of straps that contain a buckle and holes or like fastening device for securing oxygen concentrator 100 to patient P. Alternatively, oxygen concentrator 100 may be placed in a purse, fannypack, or similar personal carrying device for transport with patient P.

Power module 106 provides the necessary power to operate the systems of oxygen concentrator 100. In the embodiment illustrated, power module 106 contains replaceable power pack 108. Reservoir module 110 stores oxygen rich gas that has been separated from ambient air by cartridge module 116. Control module 112 pilots and regulates the interaction of the power module 106, reservoir module 110, and separation cartridge module 116 of oxygen concentrator 100. User interface 114 on control module 112 is a console which allows patient P to adjust and monitor oxygen concentrator 100.

FIG. 3 is a perspective view of the opposite side of oxygen concentrator 100 as shown in FIG. 2. Illustrated in FIG. 3 are belt 104, power module 106, reservoir module 110, control module 112, and separation cartridge module 116. Belt 104 is constructed to contain belt segments 120 formed by serrations 118. This allows the belt 104 to be flexible and conform to patient P's body while wearing oxygen concentrator 100. Belt 104 is fabricated from a flexible material, such as textile or plastic and contains an inner padding such as foam. Belt 104 also houses the electrical and pneumatic connections of oxygen concentrator 100.

FIG. 4 is a perspective view of the front side of the oxygen concentrator 100 on docking station 122. Illustrated are oxygen concentrator 100 comprising belt 104, power module 106, reservoir module 110, control module 112, and separation cartridge module 116, along with docking station 122 containing power pack chargers 124a and 124b. Belt 104 is flexible and thus rests on the arc shaped docking station 122. Docking station 122 contains power pack chargers 124a (with power pack 108a inserted therein) and 124b, as well as concentrator dock 126 which supports the oxygen concentrator 100 while on the docking station 122. Docking station 122 converts AC power to recharge power packs 108.

5

Oxygen Concentrator 100 System Components and Connections (FIG. 5)

FIG. 5 is a block diagram of oxygen concentrator 100 illustrating power module 106, reservoir module 110, control module 112, and separation cartridge module 116, along with docking station 122 and showing the components and connections among the modules and docking station 122. Oxygen concentrator 100 components includes product gas outlet port 103, adsorbent columns 130a-130c (each containing a respective inlet port 132a-132c and a respective outlet port 134a-134c), air inlet port 135, air inlet filter 136, product gas final filter 138, main valve 140, drive reducer 142, vacuum pump 144, drive 146, electric control module (ECM) 148, breakthrough flow sensor 150, valve position sensor 152, product control pump 154, check valve 156, main storage reservoir 158 containing pressure sensor 159, dispensing valve 160, as well as previously identified components tubing 102, power pack 108, user interface 114, and docking station 122.

As shown in FIG. 5, adsorbent cartridge module 116 includes adsorbent columns 130a-130c each containing respective inlet ports 132a-132c and outlet ports 134a-134c, air inlet filter 136, and product gas final filter 138. Ambient air enters air inlet port 135, passes through air inlet filter 136, and enters valve 140 for distribution to adsorbent columns 130a-130c. Product gas passes through final filter 138 and product gas outlet port 103 into tubing 102 for delivery to patient P. Inlet ports 132a-132c of adsorbent columns 130a-130c connect to valve 140 through inlet lines 164a-164c. Similarly, outlet ports 134a-134c connect to valve 140 through outlet lines 166a-166c.

Control module 112 houses main valve 140, drive reducer 142, vacuum pump 144, drive 146, electric control module (ECM) 148, breakthrough flow sensor 150, valve position sensor 152, and contains user interface 114. Main valve 140 is pneumatically connected to adsorbent columns 130a-130c, as well as inlet filter 136 via inlet line 168, vacuum pump 144 via vacuum inlet line 170, product control pump 154 via vacuum line 172 and product gas line 174, and main reservoir 158 via product gas line 176. Valve 140 is actuated by drive 146 through a motor speed reducer 142. Also, valve 140 connects to breakthrough flow sensor 150 and valve position sensor 152 which send electrical inputs 178 and 180 to ECM 148.

ECM 148 is a logic control, such as a PLC (programmable logic controller), microprocessor, or similar structure which controls operation of oxygen concentrator 100. ECM 148 contains the set of inputs and outputs associated with the modules for regulating oxygen concentrator 100. ECM 148 also receives control setting inputs 182 and 184 from user interface 114, and docking station 122, respectively, power pack management input 186 from power pack 108, reservoir pressure input 188 from pressure sensor 159 in main reservoir 158, and nasal pressure input 190 from dispensing valve 160. ECM 148 provides interface output 192 to the user interface 114, interface output 194 to docking station 122, power management output 196 to power pack 108, dispensing valve time open output 198 to dispensing valve 160, and motor drive output 200 to drive 146.

User interface 114 contains physical controls such as dials, toggle switches, push button switches, and similar controls, for operating oxygen concentrator 100. The physical controls provide electrical control settings to ECM 148. ECM 148 reads these settings as inputs 182 and provides output 192 to the user interface 114. The status is converted from electric signals to physical output by indicator lights, status display, and similar structures of user interface 114.

6

Power pack management input 186 and output 196 control the charge and discharge of voltage from power pack 108 to drive 146 via ECM 148. Drive 146 will activate vacuum pump 144, valve 140 through drive speed reducer 142, and any other systems requiring power. Power pack management output 196 will also supply power to indicator lights, status display, audible alarm (if included), and other passive electrical system requirements on user interface 114 through ECM 148.

ECM 148 controls and coordinates the steps of the vacuum swing adsorption cycle through its inputs and outputs. In one embodiment, breakthrough flow sensor 150 provides an input 178 into ECM 148 by measuring air flow rates. The position of valve 140 is detected by valve position sensor 152 to produce input 180. Reservoir 158 contains a sensor to produce reservoir pressure input 188. Dispensing valve 160 also contains a pressure sensor which provides nasal pressure input 190 in response to differential pressure. ECM 148 reads these inputs to control the cycle by changing outputs, such as motor drive output 200 for drive 146. Drive 146 propels vacuum pump 144. Vacuum pump 144 creates a vacuum that is communicated to valve 140 through vacuum input line 170, while dispelling nitrogen rich gas as exhaust 177. Another output 198 controls the time that dispensing valve 160 is open. In this embodiment, the inputs and outputs are connected to a PLC within ECM 148 which is programmed to control the cycle of oxygen concentrator 100.

Contained within reservoir module 110 is an oxygen-rich gas accumulator comprising reservoir 158, check valve 156, product control pump 154, and check valve 153. Reservoir 158 receives oxygen-rich gas produced by oxygen concentrator 100 and stores it at a low pressure above ambient until it is required for use. A portion of the stored oxygen-rich gas is delivered back to valve 140 by product gas line 176 for use in ordering the nitrogen content in adsorbent columns 130a-130c by moving much of the residual nitrogen held after evacuation near the outlets 134a-134c toward inlets 132a-132c of the columns 130a-130c. Reservoir 158 is in communication with dispensing valve 160 through product gas line 202. Check valve 156 opens to allow oxygen into reservoir 158 and closes to prevent backflow of oxygen upon reaching the desired pressure in reservoir 158.

Product control pump 154 is driven by vacuum provided by the vacuum pump 144 through valve 140 via vacuum line 172. Product line 174 is in communication from separation cartridge module 116 to check valve 153, which opens to allow product control pump 154 to transport separated oxygen-rich gas to reservoir 158. Product control pump 154 delivers the product gas to main reservoir 158 through check valve 156.

Dispensing valve 160 and power pack 108 are contained within power module 106. Dispensing valve 160 is used to feed the flow of oxygen-rich gas to the patient P by delivery of the product gas through final product gas line 205 to product final filter 138. The product gas is obtained from the main reservoir 158 through product gas line 202. Power pack 108 provides the power supply for oxygen concentrator 100 as previously described. Power pack 108 is rechargeable through docking station 122 as represented by power connection 204.

Vacuum Swing Adsorption (VSA) Process—Overview

Oxygen concentrator 100 operates using a vacuum swing adsorption process, which involves a series of cycles that include a feed step or phase, an evacuation step or phase, and a repressurization step or phase. Each of these three phases takes place in one of the three columns 130a-130c at any given time. Each column 130a-130c is in a different phase. For purposes of explanation, the VSA process will be

US 7,766,010 B2

7

described in reference to "column 130", which is representative of each of the three columns 130a-130c.

In the feed phase, a gas stream of ambient air 162 enters inlet end 132 of column 130 while product gas containing concentrated oxygen is delivered from outlet end 134 of column 130. The slight vacuum in column 130 draws air 162 into column 130 and through an adsorbent material (typically a zeolite) which preferentially retains specific components of air (nitrogen), allowing the desired product (oxygen) to pass through. A mass transfer zone (MTZ), which is a small region in which nitrogen is being adsorbed, is passing through the adsorbent material. The MTZ divides the column 130 into two segments: a nitrogen-rich segment where the MTZ has passed through, and an oxygen-rich segment ahead of the moving MTZ. The MTZ forms at the inlet 132 at the start of the process and gradually moves through the column to the outlet 134 as the process proceeds. Outlet end 134 of column 130 is connected to main reservoir 158 through main valve 140, check valve 153, and product control pump 154, so that oxygen-rich product gas from column 130 is pumped into reservoir 158.

In the evacuation phase, column 130 is brought to a stronger vacuum by vacuum pump 144, causing the adsorbed component, i.e. nitrogen, to be desorbed. The nitrogen is evacuated from column 130 through main valve 140, and is discharged by vacuum pump 144 as waste exhaust 177.

In the repressurization phase, the previously evacuated column 130 is returned to near 1 atm. Ambient air 162 enters column 130 through inlet end 132, and recycled product gas from product line 176 enters column 130 through outlet end 134. The gases replace the vacuum that was previously drawn in column 130 during the evacuation phase. Just prior to column 130 reaching about 1 atm, the repressurization phase ends and the feed phase of the cycle begins again.

This constitutes the general principles of vacuum swing adsorption (VSA) for gas separation. All phases can be accomplished with a single column, or with a plurality of columns. If a plurality of columns are used, it is preferable to have a multiple of three (illustrated as 130a-130c in FIG. 5) that are sequenced out of phase for the different cycle phases in order to maintain constant product flow.

The Feed Phase—Breakthrough Detection

During the feed phase of the separation cycle, the position of the MTZ within adsorbent column 130 is monitored, determined, and beneficially used to control the termination of the feed phase. The control results in improvements in product purity and recovery with concomitant decrease in energy consumed, as well as system size and system weight for a given volume of product produced.

Breakthrough is defined as the point when the MTZ reaches outlet 134 of adsorbent column 130. At this point, feed gas begins to flow into the separated product gas stream. This is undesirable because the purity of the product stream is reduced by the feed stream gas if the feed is allowed to continue past this point. Conversely, if the feed phase is terminated before the MTZ nears outlet 134 of column 130, product recovery will be reduced because product gas contained in column 130 between the MTZ and outlet 134 of column 130 will be subjected to the evacuation phase that follows the feed phase in the separation cycle, and much of this remaining product gas will be lost with the desorbed gas in the waste stream.

For a particular column geometry, temperature, adsorbent type and condition, and cycle vacuum levels, there is an optimal time during the feed phase of the cycle to terminate the feed—before purity requirements are compromised, but

8

after the maximum possible product has been recovered from column 130. This optimal time is determined by the detection of the passage of the mass transfer zone through a specific position relative to outlet end 134 of column 130.

For some combinations of system variables, the optimum feed termination time corresponds to the beginning of breakthrough when the leading edge of the MTZ has just reached outlet end 134 of column 130. This event can be detected by monitoring either or both of the gas flow rates at inlet 132 or outlet 134 to column 130. Before breakthrough, the outlet flow rate is less than the inlet flow rate by an amount equal to the rate of nitrogen gas adsorption of column 130 from the feed gas flow. After breakthrough, column 130 is no longer adsorbing nitrogen from the feed gas, so the inflow and outflow rates of column 130 become equal. Any method of measuring gas flow rates to determine the point in time when these flow rates begin the transition toward equality can be used to detect this beginning of breakthrough.

It has been determined that if the inflow rate of air to column 130 is maintained constant, a simple detection of a significant rise in slope of the outflow rate marks breakthrough. Conversely, if the outflow rate is held fairly steady, then a falling slope of the inflow rate marks the breakthrough. Monitoring the ratio of flow for the inlet and outlet and detecting a significant change in the ratio of flows toward a ratio of 1:1 can mark breakthrough in systems where inflow or outflow may not be steady enough to detect breakthrough by monitoring just one of the flow rates.

For other combinations of system variables, the optimum feed termination time may correspond to the MTZ position prior to breakthrough. In these cases, it is beneficial for a specific amount of product to be intentionally left in column 130 at the end of a feed phase. Detecting the position of the MTZ before breakthrough can be accomplished by additional methods.

One method used determines the volume of gas passed into or out of adsorbent column 130 up to the point of breakthrough by integrating the flow rate during the time interval between an initial feed and breakthrough while using some breakthrough detection method as previously described. Volume of flow may also be directly measured by physical equivalent methods using displacements of known volumes. Once the volume of gas that passes the column up to the point of breakthrough is determined, the volume of gas flow can be monitored during subsequent feed phases and the feed terminated when the volume reaches a specific value less than that for breakthrough. At anytime during the feed phase, the volume of gas passed through column 130 since the beginning of feed divided by the volume of gas at breakthrough will be the same ratio as the position of the mass transfer zone divided by the length of column 130 (assuming a constant cross sectional area along the length). Using this relationship, the position of the MTZ within column 130 can be adequately determined during the feed phase.

The components of oxygen concentrator 100 as previously described are used to complete the cyclical phases of VSA to separate gases. The feed phase operates at a slight vacuum just below ambient (in the range of 0.9 to 1 atm). This provides just enough driving force to pull ambient air 162 into adsorbent column 130 through inlet filter 136. The vacuum is caused by product control pump 154, which is driven by the vacuum drawn by vacuum pump 144. Product control pump 154 is a piston pump or similar structure that meters a volume of gas. Product control pump 154 connects with a volume much greater than the piston displacement volume, such as main reservoir 158.

9
10

The feed phase is allowed to proceed until breakthrough is detected. Up to this point, the outflow gas from adsorbent column 130 has been a high purity oxygen/argon, low percent nitrogen mixture. The MTZ position is controlled to minimize nitrogen into the product gas mixture. The MTZ position is monitored by breakthrough flow sensor 150, which detects a large increase in flow rate associated with breakthrough when the nitrogen no longer is preferentially adsorbed by adsorbent column 130. Breakthrough flow sensor is located near the column inlet 132, column outlet 134, or similar place where the flow rate being measured is accessible. When the increase MTZ flow is detected, a signal is sent to ECM 148, which also receives valve position signal 180 from the valve position sensor 152. The ECM 148 compares the timing of the MTZ breakthrough signal and the valve position signal and makes a minor adjustment to motor speed 200 based on lead, lag, or on-time status to keep the breakthrough time near the end of each feed phase. Alternately, ECM 148 receives a signal from breakthrough flow sensor 150 and immediately terminates the current feed phase in column 130 by signaling valve 140 to rotate to start the next phase. In yet another embodiment, the separation system contains a shut off valve that is signaled to close the feed of ambient air 162 into column 130, or the delivery of product gas from the column upon breakthrough detection.

In another embodiment, the method for determining the position of the mass transfer zone prior to breakthrough is accomplished by placing a small amount of non-adsorbing material within adsorbent column 130 at a particular position. When the mass transfer zone passes through this position, a flow change is detectable as the adsorption of gas is briefly interrupted by the non-adsorbing segment of column 130. The resulting flow change is detectable using the same methods for breakthrough detection previously described.

With larger columns and slower feed phases, the position of the mass transfer zone has been established by measuring temperature rise at positions of interest within column 130. Significant temperature increases result from the heat of adsorption at the MTZ and can be detected by thermistors or similar devices placed within column 130.

The Evacuation Phase

The evacuation phase brings the gas in adsorbent column 130 that was just in the feed phase to a vacuum state. At the end of the feed phase, the adsorbent column 130 is in equilibrium with the air infeed mixture near 1 atm from column inlet 132 up to the MTZ. Hence, if the ending position of the MTZ is established, and the nitrogen, oxygen, and argon isotherms for the chosen adsorbent mass are known, then the quantity of these gases present in adsorbent column 130 at the end of each feed phase is known. Vacuum pump 144 draws a vacuum on adsorbent column 130. This vacuum level is determined and set to a state that will remove a large portion of the gas left in column 130. In one embodiment, this is 0.2 to 0.3 atm. By percentage, the vast majority of gas discharged is nitrogen. The evacuated gas is discharged as waste from exhaust 177 of vacuum pump 144. The preferred embodiment uses a fixed displacement type of vacuum pump 144. During each evacuation phase, the adsorbed gas in column 130 is expanded into a much larger volume made up of the column volume plus the fixed displacement volume of pump 144.

The evacuate phase creates a self regulating effect that compensates for reductions in the amount of nitrogen adsorbed by adsorbent column 130 as the adsorbent degrades (ages). If the adsorbent loses efficiency, less nitrogen will be present in column 130 at the end of the phase, but the volume of the pump that the nitrogen expands into remains the same.

A stronger vacuum will result that will remove more nitrogen and therefore allow more air to be fed during the next feed phase. A more constant breakthrough time results and provides a more robust product cycle.

The evacuation is provided by vacuum pump 144, which is controlled and activated by drive 146. The volume removed for each cycle of the vacuum pump 144 will remain constant, but the motor drive output 200 will be controlled by the rate of product gas used by patient P. The amount of oxygen used by patient P depends on the patient P's on-demand respiratory rate, which is sensed by the device and from a variable position switch which sends an input 192 from user interface 114 to ECM 148, which in turn provides motor drive output 200 to drive 146. This determines the speed of each successive phase and, therefore, the oxygen production rate.

In one embodiment, a purge is applied at the very end of an evacuation phase. While still in the evacuation phase, a purge of product gas (mostly oxygen) introduced through outlet 134 effectively drives out a portion of nitrogen in column 130 through inlet 132. Adding the purge gas of high purity oxygen/argon through outlet 134 desorbs more nitrogen from outlet 134 of column 130, and pushes the nitrogen toward inlet 132 of adsorbent column 130 and creates an ordering of the gases. The purge volume is a function of vacuum level and adsorbent characteristics. A purge portion of the evacuation phase is not a necessary phase for a functioning device, but allows high oxygen purity to be maintained with weaker vacuum levels.

The Repressurization Phase

The repressurization phase brings adsorbent column 130 (just previously evacuated and purged) to the feed pressure. In one embodiment, the gas used for repressurization is from both the infeed ambient air 162 and a counter stream from the (oxygen-rich) product gas line 176 from the main reservoir 158. Alternately, the repressurization of product gas can be accomplished through valve design negating the need for a separate line. The product gas is dispensed from a stream of product gas from the adsorbent column that is in the feed phase through a vacuum break valve used during repressurization. Repressurization with product gas can be done before, simultaneously, or after partial pressurization with ambient air. Repressurization with product gas is done at the opposite end of column 130 as repressurization with ambient air 162.

The effect of adding the repressurization gas of high purity oxygen/argon through outlet 134 creates a cleaning zone at outlet 134 of adsorbent column 130 where, during the feed phase that follows next, any stray nitrogen can be preferentially adsorbed and not discharged as product gas. This improves the ordering of gases in the adsorbent column 130. By repeating this phase during successive cycles, the purity will continue to increase in the product output. Weaker vacuums require more oxygen volume returned to column 130 during repressurization if high purity is desired. That is, a stronger vacuum must be drawn on the column 130 to effectuate the same purity of oxygen absent the use of oxygen-rich gas as aback flush for repressurization at the outlet 134 of column 130. At the end of repressurization, the feed phase will proceed.

Valve 140 Timing (FIG. 6)

The VSA cycle comprises three phases: evacuation, repressurization, and feed, which occur sequentially in each column 130a-130c. For clarity, only column 130a will be discussed, although each phase is performed (at different times during a complete cycle) in each of columns 130a-130c.

11

Starting with the evacuation phase of the cycle, a small amount of oxygen (not illustrated) may flow into outlet 134a of adsorption column 130a to purge adsorption column 130a, while vacuum pump 144 withdraws gas present at inlet 134a of the column, i.e. nitrogen-rich gas.

During the repressurization phase, an amount of previously separated oxygen flows into outlet 134a of adsorption column 130a for a short time, and then air is allowed to enter inlet 132a of column 130a that has been previously evacuated. There may be a slight overlap of the oxygen flow into outlet 134a of adsorption column 130a and the air flow in the opposite direction into inlet 132a. Air freely flows into inlet 132a of adsorption column 130a upon opening of valve 140 as adsorption column 130a has been previously evacuated during the evacuation phase.

During the feed phase, air continues to flow into inlet 132a of adsorption column 130a while oxygen is removed from outlet 134a of column 130a by a pressure differential created by product control pump 154. As the MTZ passes through the adsorption column and reaches a position at or near outlet 134a, vacuum pump 144 will again begin to evacuate adsorbent column 130a and restart with the evacuation phase. In the embodiment illustrated in FIG. 6, these phases are controlled by main valve 140.

FIG. 6 is a diagram showing timing for main valve 140, which is a rotary valve that moves 360°(one full revolution about a central axis) for each complete cycle of the VSA process. In the embodiment with three columns 130a-130c, the timing for each phase of the cycle is 120°. Each column 130a-130c is present in a different phase for each 120° of rotation of valve 140 that is different from the other two columns to obtain a sequence that creates a steady flow of oxygen as valve 140 keeps rotating.

As shown in the timing diagram, adsorption column 130a is in the feed phase of the cycle at a start point of zero degrees. Air is being let in through inlet filter 136 and column inlet 132a while separated gas consisting of highly concentrated oxygen is being removed through column outlet 134a. A portion of the oxygen-rich product gas is used in the repressurization of column 130b. Adsorption column 130b is in the repressurization phase at a point of rotary valve 140 being in initial position zero degrees. As valve 140 is turned, column outlet 134b is fed with the oxygen-rich gas for a portion of the valve's rotation, preferably less than 120°. After the flow of oxygen-rich gas enters column 130b through the column outlet 134b, air repressurization through the opening of column inlet 132b begins. In the embodiment shown, this takes place at a point after valve 140 has begun its rotation and ends before it reaches a third of its rotation, or a 120° rotation.

While column 130a is in feed phase and column 130b is in the repressurization phase, column 130c is in the evacuation phase. During the evacuation phase, a vacuum is drawn to remove adsorbed gas through inlet 132c, thereby regenerating it for the following feed phase.

In the embodiment shown, each column 130a, 130b, and 130c, is in a different phase of the cycle as one moves vertically down the diagram in FIG. 6. During the first one hundred twenty degrees of rotation of the rotary valve, column 130a is in the feed phase. Simultaneously, from zero to one hundred twenty degrees of rotation, column 130b is being repressurized, while column 130c is being evacuated.

For the next one hundred twenty degrees of rotation of valve 140 (i.e., from 120° to 240°), adsorption column 130a is in the evacuation phase. At this same time, column 130b is in the feed phase, and column 130c is in the repressurization phase.

12

Moving horizontally across the diagram for column 130a, during the final one hundred twenty degrees of rotation of valve 140 (i.e., from 240° to 360°), column 130a is repressurized first using separated gas, and then ambient air. Separated gas and ambient air are introduced to the column 130a through column inlet 132a and column outlet 174a at opposite ends of column 130a. During the final one hundred twenty degrees of rotation (i.e. from 240° to 360°) of main valve 140, column 130b is in the evacuation phase, and column 130c is in the feed phase. Upon reaching three hundred sixty degrees, valve 140 is back at its starting position (zero degrees), and the cycles for each column 130a-130c restart from the zero degree position.

Oxygen Concentrator 100 Physical Components (FIGS. 7-16)

FIG. 7 shows an exploded view of the oxygen concentrator 100, which includes belt 104, power module 106 containing removable power pack 108, reservoir module 110, control module 112, and separation cartridge module 116 containing adsorbent cartridge 206. Power pack 108 has been removed from receptacle 210 of power module 106. Adsorbent cartridge 206 has been removed from receptacle 208 of cartridge module 116. Adsorbent cartridge 206 and power pack 108 are easily removable to facilitate replacement.

In this embodiment, power pack 108 is a rechargeable battery. Receptacle 210 contains electrical contacts (not illustrated) for connection to power pack 108. Cartridge 206 contains a quick-connect attachment (not illustrated) for inlet lines 164a-164c, outlet lines 166a-166c, inlet air line 168, and final product gas line 205 (not illustrated) within receptacle 208. Also present on cartridge 206 are air inlet ports 135 which receive ambient air 162 for separation. Adsorbent cartridge 206 contains adsorbent material that deteriorates in efficiency as it is used and ages.

FIG. 8 is a perspective view of oxygen concentrator 100. A portion of belt 104 has been removed revealing back interior surface 211 and inner connections amongst the modules, including utility tubes 212, tube pathways 214, module apertures 216a-216d, and module sockets 218a-218d.

Utility tubes 212 run between the adjacent modules and contain either electrical wiring or pneumatic lines, or comprise pneumatic lines and electrical wiring and associated connections. Tubes 212 are constructed to be flexible and bend as belt 104 is manipulated. If the tubes 212 contain electrical lines, the tubes are constructed from a dielectric material to insulate electrical wires, or similar material commonly used in electrical connections. If the tubes 212 comprise pneumatic lines, they may be air tight, small diameter polyvinyl or PVC tubes to connect the various gas input, gas separation, and gas removal systems of the oxygen concentrator 100. Tubes 212 contain openings or connections as required for electrical and pneumatic communication with each module. The back interior surface 211 of belt 104 contains tube pathways 214. Pathways 214 fabricated on the interior surface 211 of belt 104 allow the utility tubes 212 to extend between the modules 106, 110, 112, and 116. Tube pathways 214 create a semi-partitioned area on back interior surface 211 of belt 104 which support tubes 212.

Belt 104 is fabricated to contain apertures 216a-216d which allow modules 106, 110, 112, and 116 to connect utility tubes 212 of belt 104 through sockets 218a-218d. Apertures 216a-216d and sockets 218a-218d are fabricated as part of modules 106, 110, 112, and 116. Serrations 118 can be seen between the upper and lower edges 220 and 222 of belt 104. When fabrication of belt 104 is completed, padding will be inserted between edges 220 and 222, and material will be

US 7,766,010 B2

13

wrapped around creating serrations 118 and belt segments 120 to complete belt 104 as illustrated in FIG. 3. The padding is fabricated over the top of tubes 212 and tube pathways 214, or separately fabricated and fastened to back interior surface 211 during assembly of belt 104. Individual modules allow the device to flex when mounted about a curved surface, such as a belt around patient P's waist. The construction of belt 104 with tubes 212 allows patient P to manipulate the oxygen concentrator 100, such as by bending belt 104 to wear around the waist, place on docking station 122, or folding concentrator 100 in half for transport in a carryall.

FIG. 9 is a perspective view of modules 106, 110, 112, and 116 of oxygen concentrator 100. In this view, belt 104 has been removed to illustrate the positions of sockets 218a-218d containing apertures 216a-216d on each respective module 106, 110, 112, and 116. Each respective module 106, 110, 112, and 116 is constructed from a thermoplastic material such as acrylanitrile butadine styrene (ABS) or high density polyethylene (HDPE), or a lightweight metal or a similar rigid material that is oxidation resistant.

Each module 106, 110, 112, and 116, comprises a case portion 224, 226, 228, and 230, defining the outer volume of each respectively. Bottom padding 232, 234, 236, and 238, covers the lower base portion of each module 106, 110, 112, and 116, respectively. Similarly, top padding 240 extends around the top perimeter of power module 106, while top padding 242 and 244 covers the top portions of modules 110 and 112. Power pack top padding 246 covers the top portion of power pack 108 and cartridge top padding 248 covers the top of separation cartridge 206. Padding 222-248 is a foam or similar lightweight material that adds protection to the modules as well as acts to reduce vibration of oxygen concentrator 100 felt by patient P. Alternately, oxygen concentrator 100 is enclosed in soft, flexible material to further increase comfort and maintain flexibility. In one embodiment, padding 232-248 is fabricated separately from the modules 106, 110, 112, and 116, power pack 108 and cartridge 206. In assembling the oxygen concentrator 100, padding 232-248 and case portions 224, 226, 228, and 230, are merged and secured either using fasteners, adhesives, or a manufacturing process such as ultrasonic welding.

Case portions 224, 226, 228, and 230, of each of the modules 106, 110, 112, and 116, contain sockets 218a-218d fabricated on the surface that contacts belt 104. Socket 218a-218d for each module is constructed to have support paths 250 for electrical wiring and pneumatic tubing similar to those contained within belt 104 represented by tube pathways 214. Sockets 218a-218d are constructed so that support paths 250 on sockets 218a-218d align with tube pathways 214 in belt 104 when each individual module 106, 110, 112, and 116, is connected to belt 104. In one embodiment, sockets 218a-218d are constructed to allow each individual module 106, 110, 112, and 116, to snap onto belt 104 or attach in a similar quick connect fashion. Utility tubes 212 comprise quick connects at module apertures 216a-216d. Apertures 216a-216d are openings in the case portions 224, 226, 228, and 230, provided for connection of utility tubes 212 to components contained within each module 106, 110, 112, and 116. This allows for removal of a single module 106, 110, 112, or 116 should a specific component require maintenance or replacement. Sockets 218a-218d are constructed from the same material as the case portions 224, 226, 228, and 230.

FIG. 10 is a perspective view of the components contained within modules 106, 110, 112, and 116, and the associated pneumatic and electrical connections of oxygen concentrator 100. Illustrated are power pack 108, valve 140, drive reducer 142, vacuum pump 144, drive 146, oxygen accumulator 252

14

(comprising product control pump 154, check valves 153 and 156, and reservoir 158), dispensing valve 160 connected to nasal pressure sensor line 190 and dispensing valve open line 198, column inlet lines 164a-164c, column outlet lines 166a-166c, product control pump vacuum line 172, product control pump inlet line 174, product gas line 202, final product gas line 205, adsorbent cartridge 206, and main electrical cable 254.

Main electrical cable 254 contains a set of electrical wires that carry inputs 178, 180, 182, 188, and 190, outputs 192 and 198, and power lines 186, 198, and 200 shown in FIG. 5. Main electrical cable 254 extends from power pack 108 to ECM 148 (not visible in FIG. 10). Dispensing valve time open output 198 and nasal pressure sensor input 190 are wires that extend between ECM 148 and dispensing valve 160. Similarly, the other inputs and outputs are wired to the appropriate system components as illustrated in FIG. 5 (although not specifically illustrated in FIG. 10.)

Product gas line 202 connects dispensing valve 160 with reservoir 158 of accumulator 252. Final product gas line 205 connects dispensing valve 160 to product gas outlet port 103 for connection to delivery tube 102 after passing through final filter 136 located in adsorbent cartridge 206 to provide patient P with oxygen rich product gas. Product control pump inlet line 174 extends from main valve 140 to product control pump 154, which pumps separated oxygen rich gas into reservoir 158. Vacuum line 172 connects product control pump 154 through valve 140 to a vacuum drawn by vacuum pump 144, and provides the actuation for product control pump 154. Column inlet lines 164a-164c and column outlet lines 166a-166c connect main valve 140 with column inlet ports 132a-132c and column outlet ports 134a-134c of columns 130a-130c, respectively (not illustrated). Inlet air line 168 transports ambient air 162 from separation cartridge 206 to main valve 140, while vacuum inlet line 170 connects vacuum pump 144 to main valve 140. All lines 164a-164c, 166a-166c, 168, 170, 172, 174, 176, 202, and 205, are pneumatic lines or similar structures that allow for the isolated flow of gases between system components.

FIG. 11 is a perspective view of the components contained within power module 106: power pack 108 (comprising cells 256, outer wall 258, and power pack life indicator 260) and dispensing valve 160. In the embodiment illustrated, power pack 108 is a lithium-ion battery pack comprised of five cells 256. Individual cells 256 are contained within outer wall 258, part of which has been removed to show cell 256. Power pack 108 is a battery that is rechargeable and removable from power module 106. Although illustrated as a trapezoid containing five cylindrical cells, the shape and number of cells will vary depending on the shape of power module 106 and power requirements of oxygen concentrator 100.

Power pack 108 is a lithium based battery pack capable of being recharged in a recharging socket or station that connects to an external power supply. Alternatively, power pack 108 comprises a battery or fuel cell. In one embodiment, power pack 108 is a lithium ion battery pack that is constructed from several interconnected lithium-ion batteries. Oxygen concentrator 100 uses a maximum of fifteen watts of power. This results in a battery weight of less than 0.7 pounds (0.3 kg). In this embodiment, patient P taking twenty breaths per minute at a setting of 2 liters per minute equivalent can use oxygen concentrator 100 for a minimum of four hours on a fully charged battery. Power pack 108 is easily exchanged with another similar battery pack, and can be removed with a simple pulling or tugging motion. In another embodiment (not illustrated), oxygen concentrator 100 contains a jack for receiving a power cord which can then be plugged into either a 110 volt wall outlet or a 12 volt power supply system (such as a car utility plug) so that power pack 108 can be charged in place in oxygen concentrator 100.

Power pack life indicator 260 displays the amount of time left that the power pack will operate the oxygen concentrator 100. As illustrated, power pack life indicator 260 is a display, such as a liquid-crystal display (LCD) or light emitting diode (LED) screen, with numeric output of expected life in hours. The LCD or LED screen may also contain a series of bars that act as indicators. Alternately, power pack life indicator 260 is a light or series of lights.

Dispensing valve 160 is contained within power module 106 and is used to feed the flow of oxygen to patient P. Dispensing valve 160 is a valve activated by a change in pressure, such as that caused when a person is inhaling. A sensor in the dispensing valve circuit monitors pressure, and opens dispensing valve 160 when a drop in pressure is sensed. ECM 148 communicates with dispensing valve 160 through input 190 and output 198 (see FIG. 5). Dispensing valve 160 is in communication with reservoir 158 through product gas line 202. Reservoir 158 is kept at a slight pressure above ambient. Thus, when dispensing valve 160 is opened, oxygen rich gas will flow from reservoir 158 through final product gas line 205, final product filter 138, and product gas outlet port 103 for delivery to patient P through tubing 102. The flow of gas is further assisted by the pressure drop created by patient P's inhaling. Dispensing valve 160 can be set to deliver oxygen rich gas to patient P for the beginning portion of a breath when patient P first inhales rather than the whole breath.

Dispensing valve 160 provides for operating oxygen concentrator 100 in one of two possible modes: pulse flow or continuous flow. When patient P is using the oxygen concentrator 100 in the pulse flow mode, dispensing valve 160 will open intermittently in response to inhalation and will stay open for a pulse time according to the setting of the controls as set by patient P. If continuous flow is desired, dispensing valve 160 is maintained at an open or partially opened state. The product is dispensed to patient P though oxygen delivery tube 102 at a continuous rate, typically in the range of 1-1.5 lpm (liters per minute). The pressure difference corresponding to a dispensing orifice in delivery tube 102 will accommodate the flow rate from the reservoir 158.

FIGS. 12a-12d are various views of components contained inside of reservoir module 110. FIG. 12a is a perspective view of accumulator 252. FIG. 12b is a top view of accumulator 12b. FIGS. 12c and 12d are sectional views corresponding to the section lines in 12b. Contained within reservoir module 110 is oxygen accumulator 252 (comprising reservoir 158, check valves 153 and 156, and product control pump 154), inlet port 261, and outlet port 263. Accumulator 252 receives separated product gas through inlet port 261. Product inlet line 174 (shown in FIG. 10) is connected to inlet port 261 and links product control pump 154 to separation cartridge 206 through main valve 140 to transport oxygen rich gas separated by cartridge 206. Inlet port 261 connects to check valve 153 which allows product gas into product control pump 154.

Product control pump 154 includes piston 262, actuated by spring 264 within pump chamber 265, which pushes separated oxygen-rich product gas into reservoir 158. Check valve 156 opens to allow oxygen into the reservoir 158 and closes to prevent back flow of oxygen-rich gas when the desired pressure in reservoir 158 is attained. The low pressure of reservoir 158 exerts a force on check valve 156 to keep valve 156 closed. Reservoir 158 takes oxygen-rich gas produced by oxygen concentrator 100 and stores it at a low pressure above ambient until the product is required for use by patient P.

Product control pump 154 is driven by vacuum. Product control pump vacuum line 174 is connected to the vacuum drawn by vacuum pump 144 through main valve 140. When a vacuum is drawn, the force draws piston 262 down to compress spring 264 which expands pump chamber 265, and causes check valve 153 to open. Oxygen-rich gas from separation cartridge 206 flows through check valve 153 and enters pump chamber 265 in the volume created by the displacement of piston 262. At the appropriate time in the cycle, valve 140 will interrupt the vacuum to product control pump 154, and spring 264 will force piston 262 upwards. The movement of piston 262 will force oxygen rich gas in pump chamber 265 through check valve 156 and into reservoir 158. At the same time, check valve 153 closes to prevent more gas from entering pump 154. With this embodiment, no additional drive (other than the vacuum to pull piston 262 down and the spring force to move it up) is required for product control pump 154 which adds to the overall efficiency of the system.

In one embodiment, reservoir 158 has a capacity that is about four times larger than the size of the largest pulse provided by oxygen concentrator 100. In one embodiment, extra volume is included to account for separated oxygen used as a back flow in adsorbent columns 130a-130c. Specifically, main storage reservoir 158 for oxygen concentrator 100 can be designed according to the flow rates listed in Table 1. Storage reservoir 158 is 100 cc (cubic centimeters) to 400 cc in volume. Main storage reservoir 158 is maintained at a low pressure to provide delivery of the product gas to patient P through outlet 263 which is connected to final product dispensing line 202. In one embodiment, the pressure is between 1 atm (ambient) and 1.5 atm. Also acceptable are pressures less than eight psi (55,158 Pa), with a pressure of two and one half to five psi (17,236 to 34,473 Pa) preferred. The low pressure of reservoir 158 allows oxygen concentrator 100 to be used in most areas where high pressure oxygen is banned. Also, low pressure requires less energy to fill reservoir 158, which adds to the efficiency of the system by requiring a simpler pressurizing mechanism compared to high pressure systems.

Reservoir 158 contains pressure sensor 159 (such as a piezoresistive or capacitive sensor) that sends reservoir pressure signal 188 to ECM 148 (see FIG. 5). ECM 148 adjusts the speed of the motor of drive 146 based on reservoir pressure signal 188 in combination with the current settings on user interface 114. As patient P's respiratory rate increases for the current setting, more oxygen-rich gas from reservoir 158 is dispensed thus lowering the pressure of reservoir 158. The drop in pressure is sensed and the system will react by increasing the production of product gas. Similarly, a decrease in the respiratory rate of patient P at the current setting of oxygen concentrator 100 raises the pressure in reservoir 158. The rise in pressure is sensed and ECM 148 adjusts drive 146 accordingly to maintain a preset pressure range in reservoir 158. Thus, only the amount of oxygen used by patient P is produced by oxygen concentrator 100.

FIG. 13 is a perspective view of the control module 112. Illustrated are the case 228 containing aperture 216c and socket 218c, and padding 236 and 234. Control module 112 contains user interface 114 comprising power switch 266, flow level indicator lights 268, flow setting switches 270a and 270b, boost switch 272, and indicator lights 274 and 276. Power switch 266 is an ordinary toggle or push button switch capable of turning oxygen concentrator 100 on and off.

Flow settings are dually controlled by patient P utilizing flow setting switches 270. First, continuous or pulse mode is selected by patient P. In a continuous flow mode, oxygen is dispensed at a continuous flow rate such as one to one and a

US 7,766,010 B2

<table>
<tr><td>17</td><td>18</td></tr>
</table>

half liters per minute. If oxygen concentrator **100** is set in a pulse mode for controlling flow, oxygen concentrator **100** utilizes dispensing valve **160** to provide pulse dispensing of product gas. The pulse mode is set to meet patient P's needs for the equivalent of one to five liters per minute of continuous oxygen flow. In one embodiment, a dial containing settings of one to five is utilized. In the embodiment illustrated in FIG. 13, flow setting switches are used to adjust the flow rate between various stepped levels. Each setting corresponds to the specific value for continuous flow, or a corresponding pulse volume. For example, settings for a pulse mode are contained in the table below.

TABLE 1

Set-ting	Total Volume Pulse Range (cc/pulse)	Trigger Time (sec)	Pulse Flow Ramp Rate (sec)	Pulse Duration Max (sec)	Peak Pulse Flow (LPM)
1	10 to 12	.001 to .02	.03 to .07	.15	14
2	20 to 24	.001 to .02	.03 to .07	.20	14
3	30 to 36	.001 to .02	.03 to .07	.25	15
4	40 to 48	.001 to .02	.03 to .07	.30	16
5	50 to 60	.001 to .02	.03 to .07	.35	17

When the unit is set in pulse mode, product gas is dispensed only at the beginning of inhalation. In one embodiment, product dispensing valve **160** is only opened between zero and 0.4 seconds of the beginning of a breath of patient P. This controls the amount of oxygen removed from reservoir **158**. In another embodiment, oxygen concentrator **100** is shut off if no pressure drop is sensed by nasal pressure sensor **190** for a set amount of time, such as two minutes, which in turn closes dispensing valve **160**.

Patient P can temporarily increase (or "boost") the flow rate of oxygen by actuating boost control switch **272** on user interface **114**. When boost switch **272** is activated, oxygen concentrator **100** increases the flow rate of oxygen for a set period of time, such as 10 minutes. After timing out, oxygen concentrator **100** returns to the previous setting. The boost function will not work if oxygen concentrator **100** is already operating at the maximum flow rate.

Indicator light **274** indicates power pack **108** is running low. Indicator light **276** indicates that there is a problem with separation cartridge **206**, such as a bad connection with receptacle **208**. In one embodiment, oxygen concentrator **100** contains three different colored lights: red, yellow, and green. The green light indicates that there are no problems detected with oxygen concentrator **100**. A yellow flashing light or a yellow non-flashing light indicates a condition has been sensed that should be addressed. An example of such a condition is a low battery. A red flashing light indicates that a condition has been detected that requires an immediate response. A red non-flashing light indicates that oxygen concentrator **100** has failed, and has shut down. For example, if oxygen concentrator **100** fails to produce a stream of separated gas of eighty-five percent oxygen, oxygen concentrator **100** will detect this problem via breakthrough flow sensor **150**. ECM **148** shuts off main valve **140** so no ambient air **162** is being submitted to the gas separation cartridge **206**. Product gas is no longer being supplied to reservoir **158**. After a few breaths, reservoir **158** will empty, triggering reservoir pressure sensor output **188** (shown in FIG. 5), which communicates to ECM **148** to shut down oxygen concentrator **100**, and display the red warning light. This signals patient P that maintenance is needed. In addition to the aforementioned indicator lights, the unit may also contain a boost indicator

light to indicate when a boost function is in operation. Similarly, an audible alarm may be included in oxygen concentrator **100** to indicate failure.

FIG. 14 is a front view of the interior components of control module **112**. Illustrated are drive **146**, vacuum pump **144**, drive speed reducer **142**, and valve **140**. Drive **146** includes a DC motor, driven by battery power pack **108**, which supplies the necessary power to operate vacuum pump **144**. The motor draws a maximum of 15 watts of power. Vacuum pump **144** is a positive displacement pump. In this embodiment, drive **146** runs both vacuum pump **144** and valve **140**. Vacuum pump **144** is run by the motor at one speed, while valve **140** is run off the same motor but at a reduced speed. The reduction in speed is accomplished with gears that comprise drive speed reducer **142** between the motor of drive **146** and valve **140**.

Valve **140** is a valve containing a minimum number of ports equal to two times the number of adsorbent beds (columns) in separation cartridge **206**. Additionally, main valve **140** contains other ports for the inlet of ambient air **162**, vacuum provided by vacuum pump **144**, and recycling of product gas used to purge columns **130a-130c** during repressurization. In the preferred embodiment, valve **140** is a rotary valve, but may also be a solenoid valve, directional control valve, or series of individual valves in communication with each other and each connected to an adsorbent column **130a-130c**.

In an alternate embodiment, drive **146** may contain an independent motor for operating valve **140**. If valve **140** is run by an independent motor, that motor is powered by power pack **108** and synchronized with the other motor(s) of drive **146** by ECM **148**. As illustrated, drive **146** contains a single motor and valve **140** is connected to a system of gears that comprise drive speed reducer **142**. Alternately, drive speed reducer **142** can be any common power transmission components such as pulley and belts, or gears and sprockets.

FIG. 15 is a perspective view of separation cartridge **206** contained within separation cartridge module **116**. Illustrated are inlet ports **132a-132c**, outlet ports **134a-134c**, and casing **230**. In the embodiment illustrated, three adsorption columns are contained within casing **230** with one inlet port **132a-132c**, and one outlet port **134a-134c**, for each adsorption column **130a-130c**. Each adsorption column **130a-130c** is a hermetically sealed container containing a bed of adsorption material, preferably a zeolite capable of adsorbing nitrogen gas, such as lithium low silica 13X zeolite. Each bed contains between five and twenty-five cubic centimeters of material, and in one embodiment contains fifteen (plus or minus one) cubic centimeters of material. The adsorbent bead size is a thirty by sixty mesh, wherein thirty mesh is equal to 0.0234 inches (0.0594 cm) and sixty mesh is equal to 0.01 inches (0.0254 cm).

Column inlet ports **132a-134c** are connected to receive either ambient air **162** or vacuum, while outlet ports **134a-134c** expel product gas or receive purge gas. This arrangement promotes ordering of gases within the columns **130a-130c** by having oxygen rich gas always present at one end of the column. This results in improved efficiency as air flow through the columns **130a-130c** creates an oxygen rich zone continuously at one end, which allows the vacuum to evacuate and desorb the previously adsorbed nitrogen where it is contained in the greatest concentration.

FIG. 16 is a perspective view of the columns **130a-130c** and the filters **136** and **138** within casing **230** of separation cartridge **206**. Illustrated are final product filter **138** connected to product gas outlet port **103** which connects to tubing **102**, inlet air filter **136**, and adsorbent columns **130a-130c** each comprising spin inducers **280a-280f**, adsorbent material **282a-282c**, porous filters **284a-284f**, and springs **286a-286c**.

Springs 286a-286c are coil springs that hold each adsorbent column in compression 130a-130c in place within casing 230 of separation cartridge 206 to prevent movement of adsorbent beads. Spin inducers 280a-280f help force even distribution of gases through columns 130a-130c, which helps to keep the MTZ well defined for more accurate detection.

Adsorbent material 282a-282c is the same as that previously described. Filters 136 and 138 are constructed of common filtering materials and are used to remove dust and other large particulate matter from the air streams to assure that the flow of oxygen out to patient P is free of such materials. Porous filters 284a-284f are a small section of material commonly used as a particle filter provided at each end of columns 130a-130c. Porous filters 284a-284 fact to prevent adsorbent particles from contacting the mechanisms and valving of concentrator 100.

Docking Station 122 (FIGS. 17-18)

FIG. 17 is a perspective view of the back side of oxygen concentrator 100 on docking station 122. Illustrated are oxygen concentrator 100 comprising power module 106, reservoir module 110, control module 112, and separation cartridge module 116, belt 104, and docking station 122 containing status display 288. Status display 288 is an LED, LCD, or similar digital display used to provide information to patient P such as time of day, time the concentrator has been used, time of recharging for power pack 108, or similar information. Additionally, docking station 122 may contain other controls (not illustrated) including a boost setting while the concentrator is docked, a mode switch for switching between pulse and continuous flow of oxygen, and indicator lights to show expected battery life, adsorbent column life, gas input, gas output, or gas separation system malfunctions, or other similar items that were previously described as part of user interface 114.

FIG. 18 is a perspective view of the docking station 122 with oxygen concentrator 100 removed. Concentrator dock 126 is visible on docking station 122 with oxygen concentrator 100 removed. Concentrator dock 126 may optionally contain electrical connections (not illustrated) to charge power pack 108 contained within power module 106 while oxygen concentrator 100 is docked. Additionally, docking station 122 contains a power cord (not illustrated) available to connect to a wall socket or other power source such as a car utility plug. Docking station 122 uses power provided through the power cord to operate oxygen concentrator 100 and/or recharge power packs 108. Docking station 122 contains a flat bottom 290 to rest on a level surface and allow oxygen concentrator 100 to be in the docking station without moving. Alternately, docking station 122 is mountable to a wall in one embodiment, and is a free standing device that is set on a generally flat surface in another embodiment.

In one embodiment, docking station 122 comprises indicator lights and control power switch (not illustrated) in addition to status display 288, power pack chargers 124a and 124b, and concentrator dock 126. Indicator lights provide information to patient P utilizing oxygen concentrator 100. Indicator lights will indicate if oxygen concentrator 100 is functioning properly, requires maintenance, or has failed. Control switch is a master switch for supplying or terminating power or controlling the setting of flow for oxygen concentrator 100. Status display 128 is an LED, LCD or similar digital display that can be used to indicate various information to patient P such as time of day, time oxygen concentrator 100 has been docked, time of recharging for the power pack, or similar information.

Docking station 122 also contains power pack chargers 124a and 124b and concentrator dock 126. Docking station 122 contains a power cord (not illustrated) available to plug into a wall socket or a similar power pack. Docking station 122 converts AC power to recharge power pack 108 in power pack chargers 124a and 124b. Power pack chargers 124a and 124b contain contacts that are used to transfer power to power pack 108 while recharging. Alternatively, a power pack 108 placed in charger 124a or 124b is inductively coupled to recharge the power pack 108. Similarly, power is provided to oxygen concentrator 100 itself while on docking station 122, and to recharge of the power pack 108 (see FIG. 4) still attached to the oxygen concentrator 100. Concentrator dock 126 is shaped to provide a place to set oxygen concentrator 100 while docked, as well as facilitate easy removal of oxygen concentrator 100 for ambulatory use.

In one embodiment, docking station 122 performs several functions with oxygen concentrator 100 docked. First, oxygen concentrator 100 is allowed to run without utilizing power pack 108 while it is docked. Second, a boost setting is available to increase the delivery rate of oxygen while oxygen concentrator 100 is docked. Boost switch 272 is located on user interface 114 (See FIG. 13). In an alternate embodiment, a boost switch is located on docking station 122. Upon removal of oxygen concentrator 100 from docking station 122, the boost setting is removed and oxygen concentrator 100 operates at a set delivery rate in either a continuous or pulse mode.

Oxygen concentrator 100 contains flow setting switch 270 (FIG. 13), and a mode switch (not illustrated). The mode switch allows patient P to select continuous or pulse flow. In one embodiment, patient P is allowed to adjust the setting of oxygen concentrator 100 only while docked. That is, patient P can reprogram by changing a pulse setting (e.g., from 2 to 3), or continuous flow mode (e.g., from 1.0 to 1.5 liters per minute), only while oxygen concentrator 100 is on docking station 122. Patient P wishing to adjust settings will be required to hold the control switch while adjusting the flow setting dial or mode switch. In another embodiment, docking station 122 contains a switch automatically activated by placing oxygen concentrator 100 in docking station 122 which allows patient P to adjust flow setting. The requirement that settings can only be changed during docking prevents accidental switching of the flow mode of oxygen concentrator 100 during ambulatory use. For example, there is no change in flow if flow setting switch 130 is bumped, which would normally increase oxygen flow. If oxygen concentrator 100 can only be reprogrammed in docking station 122, oxygen concentrator 100 will remain in the preset mode set at docking station 122 and will not increase or decrease flow by a change of the setting. In one embodiment, the flow setting switch and mode switch are located on a user interface located directly on docking station 122.

Another function of docking station 122 is to provide diagnostic features of the system. Docking station 122 may indicate expected battery life, adsorbent column life, or pump malfunctions through the use of indicator lights, or status display 128, or a combination of both. Alternatively, these items are located on user interface 114, or at a combination of locations of user interface 114 and docking station 122. For example, battery life indicator 142 is located directly on power pack 108 that comprises the battery itself, and battery problem warning light 274 is on user interface 114 also. Similarly, adsorbent cartridge warning light 276 is located on user interface 114, but may also be on either the cartridge module 116 or docking station 122 as well.

US 7,766,010 B2

21

Concentrator Efficiency

Oxygen concentrator **100** can produce a stream of product gas containing a range of 85-95 percent oxygen which provides up to 5 liters per minute pulsed equivalent of product gas. By utilizing vacuum swing adsorption, the separation process phases are all performed at less than 1 atm.

Utilizing a vacuum to exhaust unwanted gas from adsorbent columns **130a-130c** improves efficiency of the oxygen concentrator **100**. Less power is required than pressure swing adsorption (PSA) or vacuum-pressure swing adsorption (VPSA), which results in a smaller battery and thus a lighter weight product. Oxygen concentrator **100** as disclosed weighs less than 3 pounds (1.4 kg) and occupies less than 1 liter of volume. Also, the efficiency of the system allows for oxygen concentrator **100** to operate for at least three hours while producing up to 5 liters per minute pulsed equivalent of product gas without requiring patient P to attend to the unit, e.g. changing the battery. Further, the low energy consumption causes less heat transfer. The product gas is discharged from the separation system at a temperature of ± six degrees Celsius from that of the ambient air. This eliminates the need for heat exchangers which add to the overall weight and reduces system efficiency. The amount of heat generated causes no discomfort to patient P wearing and utilizing the oxygen concentrator **100**. Also, upon starting oxygen concentrator **100**, the flow of product gas will increase from 21 percent oxygen (ambient) to 85 percent or more oxygen in under two minutes.

Improvements over the prior art are attained by regulating the device to only separate the amount of oxygen needed by patient P at any given time. The prior art separates a flow of oxygen and delivers that rate to patient P as a steady flow. Patient P is only inhaling this oxygen during about ⅓ of the normal breathing cycle. Within the inhalation portion of the breathing cycle, the volume of gas inhaled last stays in the dead space of the airways and is not presented to the alveoli. Therefore if oxygen is dispensed to patient P only during the early part of inhalation, less than ⅓ the steady flow is actually required. Moreover, prior art devices do not adjust the flow based on a patient P's needs, but operate at the same steady flow. The present concentrator slows down its entire cycle rate producing only the amount of oxygen needed. Thus, oxygen concentrator **100** retains a high oxygen recovery percentage at all product flow rates while minimizing energy consumption and maximizing adsorbent life. Patient P's actual needs vary with real time changes in activity. This causes a corresponding variation in breathing rate. Oxygen concentrator **100** tracks patient P's breathing rate and adjusts oxygen separation and delivery rates proportionally. In combination, these two features allow oxygen concentrator **100** to separate oxygen only at the rate it is being consumed, resulting in a reduction in the amount of oxygen needing to be separated for patient P.

Another improvement over the prior art involves reducing the waste of separated oxygen in the various adsorb and desorb cycle phases. This is typically referred to as maximizing product recovery. The primary system components become larger or smaller as the amount of oxygen separated increases or decreases. Therefore, a dramatic reduction in size and weight of the concentrator requires use of as much separated oxygen as possible by delivering it to patient P rather than losing it to the waste stream. The prior art works by using the Skarstrom cycle well known to those skilled in the art.

During one phase of the Skarstrom cycle in PSA or VPSA, air is pumped into one end of a column of adsorbent pressurizing it above atmospheric pressure while oxygen is flowing out of the opposing end. Nitrogen is being adsorbed as the

22

MTZ propagates toward the oxygen outlet end of the column. This phase is terminated before the MTZ breaks through into the oxygen stream so that oxygen purity is not diluted by the nitrogen rich air trailing the MTZ. If it is terminated earlier than necessary to maintain purity there will be substantial separated oxygen left in the column in front of the MTZ that is not passed to the patient. During the next cycle phase the column pressure is reduced to a lower cycle pressure desorbing the nitrogen that was adsorbed during the separation phase and it is passed to the waste stream. Some of the oxygen left in the column at higher pressure will also be passed to the waste stream as gas flows from the column when pressure is reduced. Recovery of separated oxygen can therefore be maximized by stopping the previous separation phase just short of breakthrough, leaving minimal oxygen in the column to be lost to the waste stream during the reduced pressure evacuation phase. The position of the MTZ needs to be accurately known to terminate the separation phase for optimal recovery without compromising purity. This position cannot be accurately estimated because its propagation rate is a function of many variables including product oxygen flow rate, high and low cycle pressures, temperature, adsorbent water content and the amount of other contaminants accumulated in the adsorbent. Prior art systems stop the separation phase well short of breakthrough to encompass worst case operating conditions without sacrificing purity and thereby waste separated oxygen in the evacuation phases during most typical non-worst case operating conditions.

Oxygen concentrator **100** determines the position of the MTZ just prior to breakthrough and terminates the flow from outlet **134** for the remainder of the feed phase or adjusts the motor speed, as previously described. Additional oxygen is left in the column at the end of a feed phase and is wasted during the evacuation phases. This is oxygen adsorbed by the adsorbent combined with oxygen present in the interstitial and dead spaces of the adsorbent and column. All adsorbents used in oxygen separators adsorb nitrogen, and also oxygen to some extent. The adsorbent used in oxygen concentrator **100** presents a very high ratio of adsorbed nitrogen to adsorbed oxygen. As the amount of oxygen adsorbed is minimized through the choice of an adsorbent with a low affinity for oxygen, the amount of adsorbent needed to separate a given amount of nitrogen during a separation phase will decrease as its affinity for nitrogen increases. The less adsorbent needed to adsorb a given amount of nitrogen, the less adsorbent there is to adsorb oxygen and the smaller the column can be with less interstitial and dead space.

For example, a LiLSX adsorbent referred to as Oxysiv MDX from UOP Corporation has a very high ratio of adsorbed nitrogen to adsorbed oxygen in the operating pressure range of oxygen concentrator **100**. The Skarstrom cycle of the prior art uses a purge phase in which separated oxygen is fed back into the product end of the column while nitrogen rich gas is passing out of the opposing end of the column into the waste stream as the pressure transitions to the lower cycle pressure. While this purge can enhance product purity, some of the purge oxygen passes all the way through the column and is lost to the waste stream. Oxygen concentrator **100** using VSA achieves a measured 60% oxygen recovery rate, compared to a typical recovery rate of 30% for the prior art utilizing PSA.

Another improvement over the prior art concerns the choice of adsorbent and operating pressure range. The energy required by the separation process directly defines the weight and size of major components such as the battery, motor and gas pump of a concentrator. Minimizing the amount of adsorbent minimizes the amount of energy needed to separate a given amount of oxygen. Each adsorbent has a characteristic pair of isotherms that show the amount of oxygen and nitrogen a given mass of adsorbent will hold at equilibrium over a range of pressures and vacuums for these gasses at a constant temperature. The cycle phases of the system necessarily include the pumping of gas contained in volumes of adsorbent to produce a change in nitrogen partial pressure between a chosen higher pressure and a chosen lower pressure. The pneumatic energy a pump must deliver in the process of cycling a given volume of gas between a higher and a lower level is in direct proportion to the volume of gas pumped multiplied by the difference between the high and low vacuum levels. The isotherms for various adsorbent candidates specify the amount of nitrogen contained in a fixed mass of adsorbent at a fixed temperature as a function of nitrogen partial pressure.

An example of the isotherm for the LiLSX adsorbent Oxysiv MDX along with the isotherm for a typical 13X type adsorbent used in the prior art is shown in FIG. 19. Having minimized the amount of oxygen needed to be separated from air and having maximized the recovery percent of oxygen as previously disclosed, along with knowing the percentage of oxygen present in air prescribes a specific minimum amount of air that must be moved into the system to produce the needed oxygen. This minimum amount of air minus the maximized separated oxygen must pass out of the system as a minimized volume of waste gas. Oxygen concentrator **100** acts to minimize the flow rates of the air feed stream and the waste stream. This flow must be pumped across a pressure difference defined by the choice of high and low operating pressures requiring a pumping energy that is proportional to both the flow rate and the pressure difference. The gas streams are pumped into or out of the adsorbent during each complete cycle to produce the needed swing in pressure between high and low cycle pressure levels allowing the separation of nitrogen from oxygen. Minimizing the amount of gas being pumped through the system reduces the pumping energy in proportion to reductions in the difference between chosen high and low pressure points that the gas must be pumped across. The isotherm for nitrogen shows that nitrogen is transferred in or out of the adsorbent with the smallest change in pressure where the slope of the isotherm is the steepest. Using typical PSA, a ratio of high to low pressure levels in these systems needs to be 3:1 or greater to maintain the desired oxygen purity. Lower pressure ranges, i.e. sub-atmospheric or vacuum ranges used in VSA, allow this ratio to be maintained with less total difference between the high and low pressure levels.

For example, prior art operates between 1 and 3 atmospheres for a 3:1 ratio and a pressure difference between high and low levels of 2 atmospheres. Oxygen concentrator **100** using VSA operates between 0.3 atmospheres and 1 atmosphere. A ratio of about 3.3:1 is achieved with a pressure difference of only 0.7 atmospheres. Operating on this range of the isotherm as seen in FIG. **19** allows just as much nitrogen to be passed in and out of the LiLSX adsorbent with a 0.7 atmosphere pressure range as a PSA system does with 13X adsorbent and a 2.0 atmosphere pressure range. The LiLSX adsorbent allows a cycle pressure range that is nearly ⅓ that of a PSA system with a proportional reduction in pumping energy.

Oxygen concentrator **100** is a quiet device. When oxygen concentrator **100** is running, it produces a noise level in the range often to thirty decibels. Further, with the compact size of the parts, vacuum pump **144** is running continuously and there is very little vibration to affect a person using it docked or wearing it as an ambulatory device. The device of the present invention with the described components weighs less than three pounds (1.36 kg). The compact size (less than about 61 cu. in. (1000 cc)) allows for easy portability. Similarly, the small size does not disrupt counter space or storage when used at home. The device does give off some heat, however the outer case is less than 6 degrees Celsius higher than ambient when oxygen concentrator **100** is running on battery power. The device may emit more heat while it is docked and operating on AC power to charge the power pack **108**, but is still less than 15 degrees Celsius above ambient.

Based on the foregoing embodiments, the efficiency of the concentrator can be determined. One measure of efficiency is the ratio of oxygen produced to the amount of adsorbent material used to obtain the oxygen, represented by the following:

Qp=Liter/min O$_2$ produced
Madsorbent=Kg of Adsorbent Material

for example, the disclosed embodiments include adsorbent columns **130a-130c**, with each column containing 15 cubic centimeters (cc) of adsorbent material with a density of 0.66 gm/cc. That is:

$$(3\text{columns})\left(\frac{15 \text{ cc}}{\text{column}}\right)\left(\frac{0.66 \text{ gm}}{\text{cc}}\right) = 30 \text{ gms for the system.}$$

The following flow rates (Qp) were obtained by the above disclosed concentrator:

Qp max=1.5 L/min
Qp min=0.14 L/min
This results in a range for kilograms of adsorbent material to oxygen flow rate of:

$$0.020 < \frac{Madsorbent}{Qp} < 0.214$$

Similarly, flow rates (Qp) were determined for a system that contains three adsorption columns, each column containing 15 cc of adsorbent material. The separation completed in a range of 0.3 atm to 0.95 atm. Values were calculated for breakthrough time, work, battery life, and flow rate. The volume of gas contained in a column at the end of a feed phase was 150 cc. These constants were used to determine the following measures of efficiency:

Work per evacuation cycle or pneumatic power requirements were determined based on the following calculations:

$$\text{W(work)=(volume moved)*(vacuum differences);}$$

The vacuum differences are calculated as the vacuum pump is continuously changing gas out, and as vacuum progresses to end point. From this:

V_H=Vacuum upper level
V_L=Vacuum lower level
Vol=Volume of gas in the column at end of feed phase

$$W=\text{Vol}*(V_H - V_L)*(1+(V_H/(V_H - V_L))*\ln(V_L/V_H)+\ln(V_H/V_L))$$

Inserting the above constants and converting to joules (multiply by 100.32 to get L*atm to joules) yields:
W=4.81 joules

Thus, 4.81 joules is required to evacuate the gas which desorbs during the evacuation phase. From experimentation, the following flow rates (LPM is liters per minute) and cycle times were recorded:

US 7,766,010 B2

25

Qp (flow rate)	Low = .14 LPM
	Med = .720 LPM
	High = 1.5 LPM
Cycle time	Low = 5.6 sec.
	Med = 1.12 sec.
	High = .54 sec.

Power consumption can be determined by calculating work divided by the time of the cycle.

Low flow power=4.81 joule/5.6 sec=0.85 watts

Medium Flow power=4.81 joule/1.12 sec=4.29 watts

High flow power=4.81 joule/0.54 sec=8.9 watts

From the above, a measure of energy consumed to the flow rate can be made and used as an indicator of the system efficiency:

$$\text{Low:} \frac{.85 \text{ w}}{.14 \text{ LPM}} = 6.07 \text{ w/LPM}$$

$$\text{Medium:} \frac{4.29 \text{ w}}{.72 \text{ LPM}} = 5.95 \text{ w/LPM}$$

$$\text{High:} \frac{8.9 \text{ w}}{1.5 \text{ LPM}} = 5.93 \text{ w/LPM}$$

Another measure of efficiency is the ratio of mass of the power pack (Mpowerpack) compared to the amount of oxygen produced (Qp) over time:

$$\frac{Mpowerpack}{QpT(time)}$$

The following constants are used in the calculation: the battery cell is a type 18650 lithium ion battery with 7.4 watts-hrs, measuring 42 g; motor efficiency is 90 percent; and vacuum pump efficiency is 80 percent.

Pneumatic work = 6 W/L/min. Thus,

$$\text{Electric power} = \frac{6 \text{ W/LPM}}{(.9)(.8)} = 8.3 \text{ W/LPM}$$

Battery mass compared to energy consumption is:

$$\frac{42g}{7.4 \text{ (watt)(hr)}}\left(\frac{1 \text{ Kg}}{1000 \text{ g}}\right)\frac{8.3 \text{ watt}}{\text{LPM}} = .047\frac{Kg}{\text{LPM } (HR)}$$

Total battery mass for the power pack can be determined from this equation. For example, if a patient requires the concentrator to run for four hours at setting of "3" and takes 20 breaths per minute (the medium flow rate):

$$(4 \text{ hr}) * \frac{.047 \text{ kg}}{\text{LPM (hr)}}.72 \text{ LPM} = .135 \text{ kg}$$

26

The mass of the batteries needed is 0.135 Kg. Assuming each battery cell is 42 g as previously stated, the number of batteries for the power pack can be calculated:

$$.135 \text{ kg}\left(\frac{1000 \text{ g}}{1 \text{ kg}}\right)\frac{\text{battery cell}}{42 \text{ g}} = 3.2 \text{ battery cells}$$

Although the present invention has been described with reference to preferred embodiments, workers skilled in the art will recognize that changes may be made in form and detail without departing from the spirit and scope of the invention. For example, larger flow rates may be achieved by scaling the concentrator components to achieve desired flow rates at the disclosed efficiencies.

The invention claimed is:

1. A method of providing concentrated oxygen product gas to a patient, the method comprising:
   producing product gas by a vacuum swing adsorption (VSA) process with an oxygen concentrator comprising a plurality of separation columns connected to a vacuum source driven by a motor, wherein the VSA process comprises:
   (a) introducing ambient air at atmospheric pressure into a first end of a column containing an adsorbent material that preferentially adsorbs nitrogen and removes oxygen-rich product gas out a second end of the column;
   (b) evacuating the column through the first end to remove adsorbed gas from the column;
   (c) repressurizing the column by introducing ambient air into the first end of the column until pressure within the column is near 1.0 atm; and
   (d) repeating steps (a)-(c);
   pumping product gas separated by the concentrator to a product reservoir;
   sensing the pressure of the product gas in the reservoir;
   controlling the speed of the motor based on the sensed pressure in the reservoir to control a rate of which product gas is produced by the VSA process; and
   delivering product gas to the patient.

2. The method of claim 1 and further comprising:
   introducing product gas into the column through the second end during a portion of step (c).

3. The method of claim 2 wherein introducing product gas occurs during an initial portion of step (c).

4. The method of claim 1 and further comprising:
   terminating step (a) based upon a position of a mass transfer zone to prevent breakthrough of nitrogen-rich gas out the second end of the column.

5. The method of claim 1 wherein delivering the product gas to the patient occurs during a portion of the patient's inhalation.

6. An oxygen concentrator comprising:
   an oxygen reservoir;
   a plurality of adsorbent columns, each having an inlet, an outlet and a bed of adsorbent material;
   a vacuum pump for removing separated nitrogen rich gas from the column inlets;
   a product control pump for pumping oxygen rich gas from the column outlets to the oxygen reservoir, wherein the product control pump is run by the vacuum pump;
   a control valve for controlling flow of fluids in and out of the columns;

27

a motor for driving the vacuum pump and control valve to produce vacuum swing adsorption (VSA) cycles in which oxygen-rich product gas is separated and accumulated in the reservoir;

a pressure sensor for providing a signal as a function of gas pressure in the oxygen reservoir; and

an electric control module (ECM) that receives a signal from the pressure sensor, and adjusts the speed of the motor based on the signal to control a rate at which oxygen rich gas is produced by the VSA cycles.

7. The oxygen concentrator of claim 6 wherein the oxygen concentrator has a volume of less than 1.0 liter.

8. The oxygen concentrator of claim 6 wherein the oxygen concentrator has a mass of less than 2.3 kg.

9. The oxygen concentrator of claim 6 wherein the oxygen concentrator has a mass of less than 1.4 kg.

10. The oxygen concentrator of claim 6 further comprising:

a rechargeable power source for actuating the control valve, motor, and ECM.

11. The oxygen concentrator of claim 6 wherein the adsorbent material comprises a zeolite which preferentially adsorbs nitrogen.

12. The oxygen concentrator of claim 6 wherein the control valve comprises a rotary valve.

13. The oxygen concentrator of claim further comprising an oxygen conserver connected to the oxygen reservoir.

14. An oxygen concentrator comprising:

an oxygen gas separator for producing oxygen-rich product gas from air by a vacuum swing adsorption (VSA) process, the process running between approximately 0.1 atm and 1.0 atm;

28

a reservoir for storing product gas from the separator;

a delivery system for delivering product gas from the reservoir to a patient;

a pressure sensor for providing a reservoir pressure signal as a function of product gas pressure in the reservoir;

a motor configured to drive the separator; and

a control for controlling a rate of production of product gas by the separator as a function of product gas delivered from the reservoir by adjusting the speed of the motor.

15. The oxygen concentrator of claim 14 further comprising:

an oxygen conserver connected to the reservoir.

16. The oxygen concentrator of claim 14 wherein the oxygen gas separator utilizes vacuum swing adsorption to produce the oxygen-rich product gas.

17. The oxygen concentrator of claim 14 wherein the oxygen concentrator has a volume of less than 1.0 liter.

18. The oxygen concentrator of claim 14 wherein the oxygen concentrator has a mass of less then 2.3 kg.

19. The oxygen concentrator of claim 14 wherein the oxygen concentrator has a mass of less then 1.4 kg.

20. The oxygen concentrator of claim 14 wherein the oxygen gas separator comprises a plurality of gas separation columns, each column including a first filter, a bed of adsorbent material, and a second filter encased within the column.

21. The oxygen concentrator of claim 20 wherein the bed of adsorbent material comprises a zeolite that preferentially adsorbs nitrogen.

* * * * *

US 20060174882A1

(19) **United States**

(12) **Patent Application Publication**   (10) Pub. No.: **US 2006/0174882 A1**

Jagger et al.   (43) **Pub. Date:**   **Aug. 10, 2006**

(54) **METHOD OF CONTROLLING THE RATE OF OXYGEN PRODUCED BY AN OXYGEN CONCENTRATOR**

(75) Inventors: **Theodore W. Jagger**, White Bear Lake, MN (US); **Nicholas P. Van Brunt**, White Bear Lake, MN (US); **John A. Kivisto**, Oak Grove, MN (US); **Perry B. Lonnes**, White Bear Lake, MN (US)

Correspondence Address:
KINNEY & LANGE, P.A.
THE KINNEY & LANGE BUILDING
312 SOUTH THIRD STREET
MINNEAPOLIS, MN 55415-1002 (US)

(73) Assignee: **Vbox, Incorporated**

(21) Appl. No.: **11/054,342**

(22) Filed: **Feb. 9, 2005**

Publication Classification

(51) Int. Cl.
   A62B *7/10*   (2006.01)
   A62B *7/00*   (2006.01)
(52) U.S. Cl. 128/201.25; 128/205.11; 128/205.18; 128/202.26

(57)   **ABSTRACT**

A method of providing concentrated oxygen product gas to a patient. The method comprises producing product gas by a vacuum swing adsorption (VSA) process with an oxygen concentrator comprising a plurality of separation columns connected to a vacuum source driven by a motor. Separated product gas is then pumped to a product reservoir. The pressure of the reservoir is monitored and used to adjust the speed of the motor based on the reservoir pressure. The separated gas is then delivered to the patient.

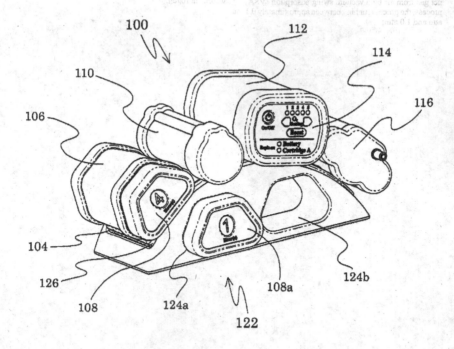

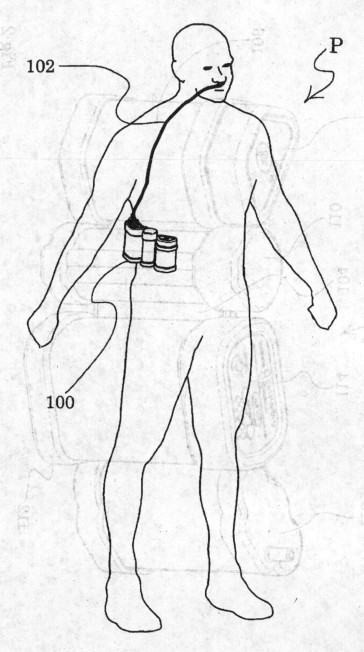

Fig 1

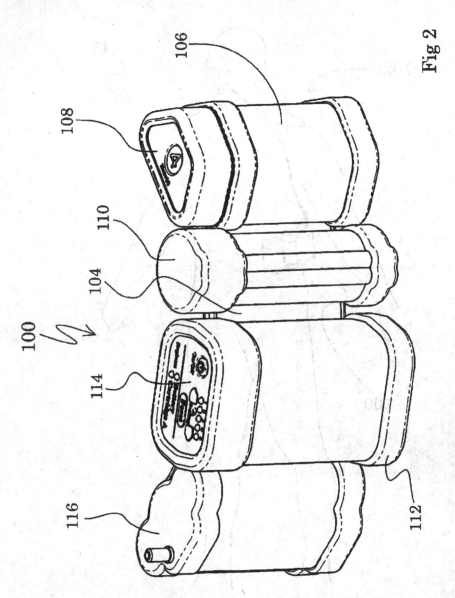

Fig 2

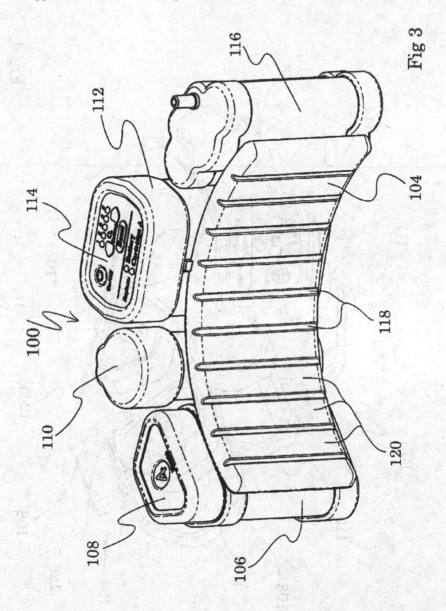

Fig 3

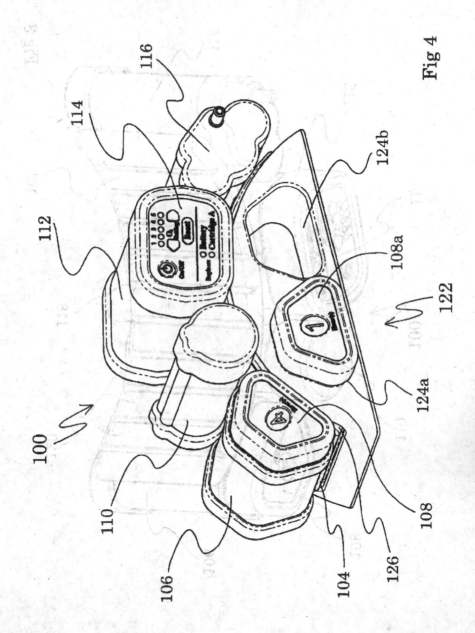

Fig 4

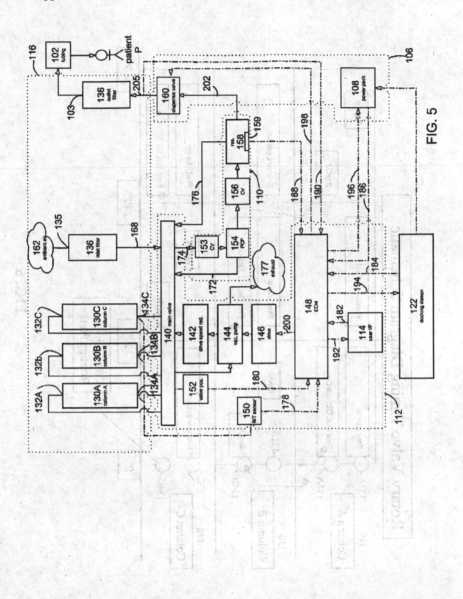

FIG. 5

743

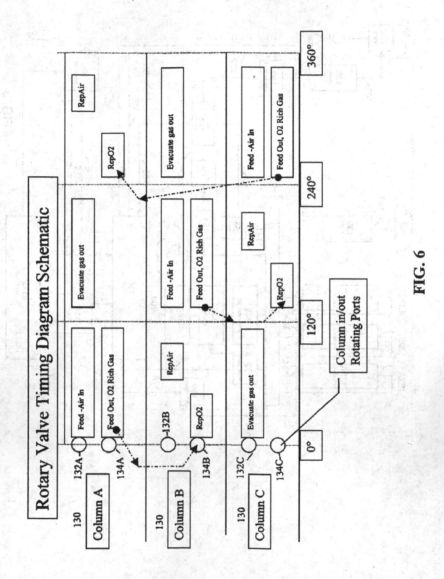

Rotary Valve Timing Diagram Schematic

FIG. 6

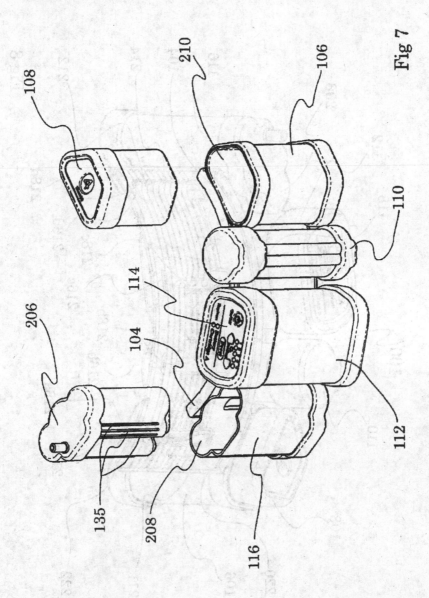

Fig 7

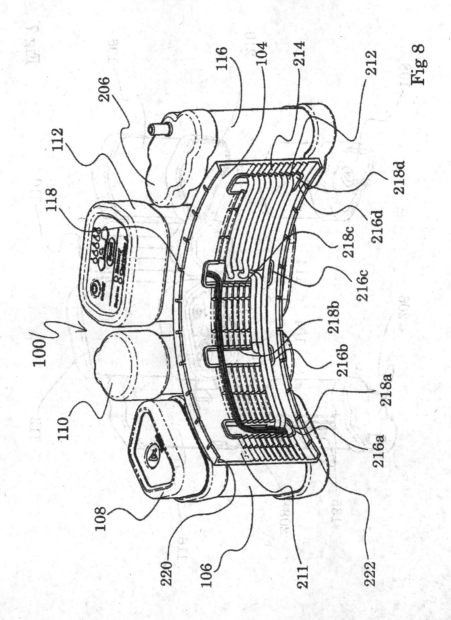

Fig 8

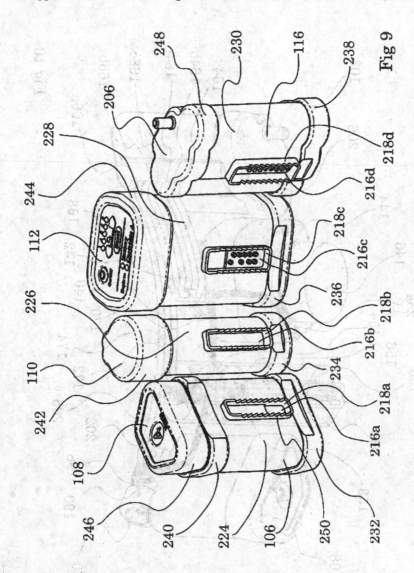

Fig 9

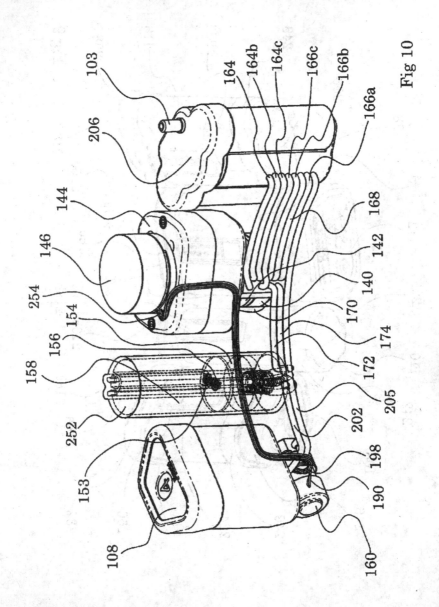

Fig 10

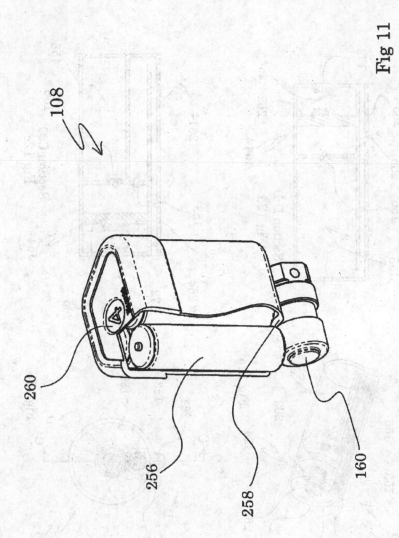

Fig 11

108

260

256

258

160

Section D-D
Fig 12d

Section C-C
Fig 12c

Fig 12a

Fig 12b

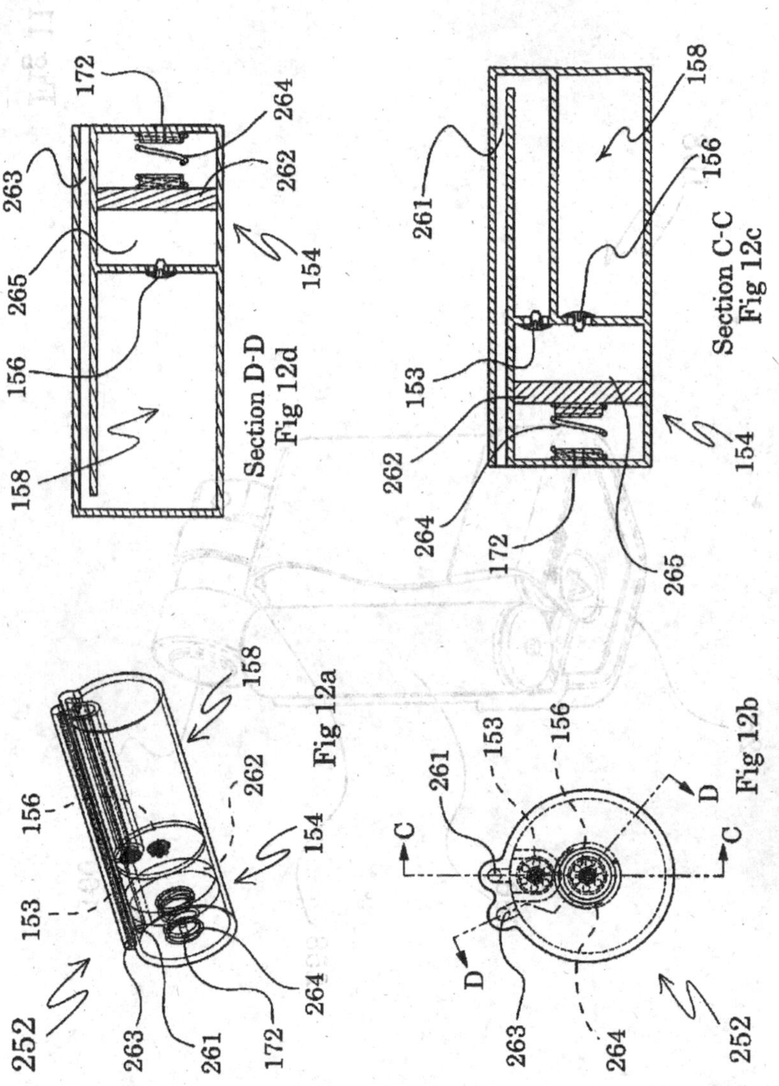

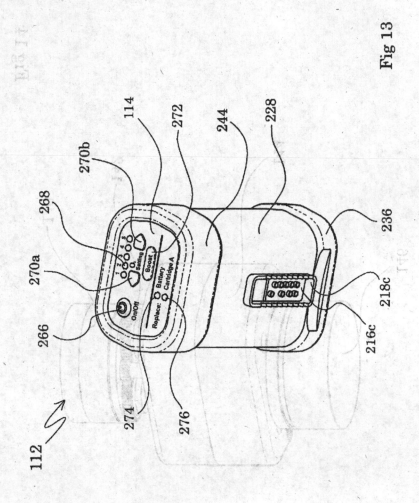

Fig 13

112
266
270a
268
270b
114
272
244
228
236
274
276
216c
218c
On/Off
Replace:
Battery
Cartridge A
Setting
Boost

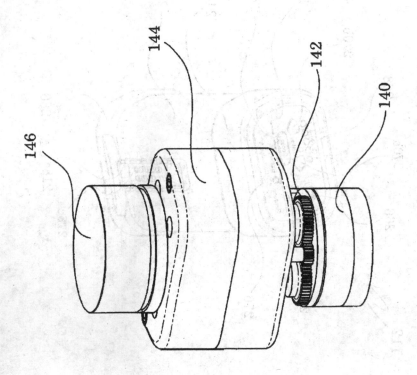

Fig 14

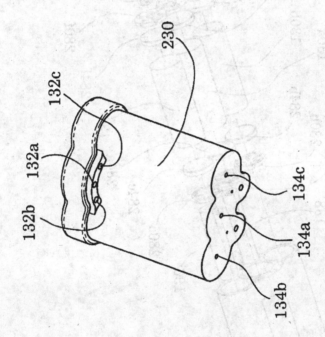

Fig 15

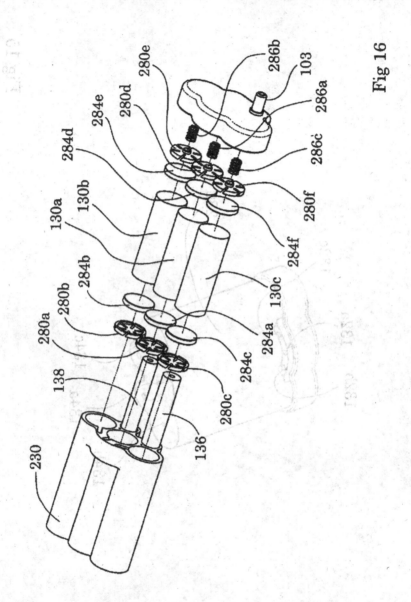

Fig 16

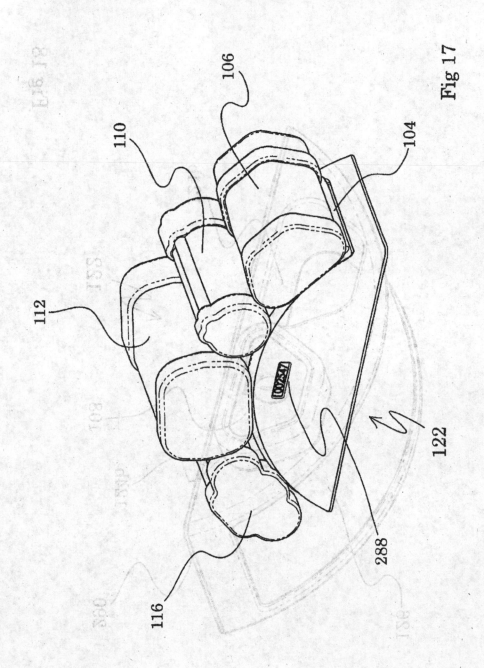

Fig 17

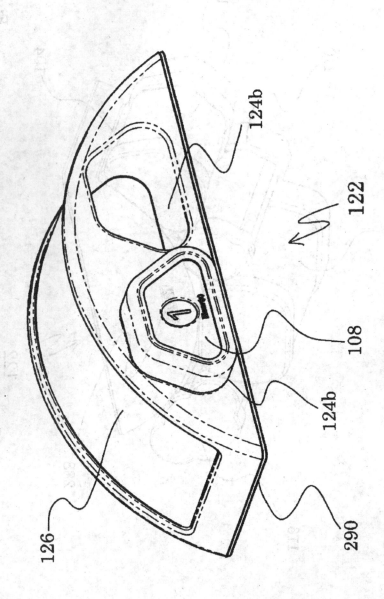

Fig 18

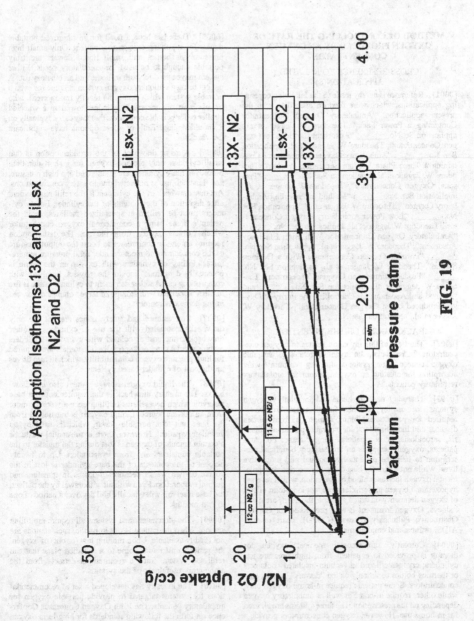

Adsorption Isotherms-13X and LiLsx
N2 and O2

LiLsx- N2

13X- N2

LiLsx- O2

13X- O2

N2/ O2 Uptake cc/g

Pressure (atm)

Vacuum

2 atm

0.7 atm

11.5 cc N2/ g

12 cc N2/ g

FIG. 19

METHOD OF CONTROLLING THE RATE OF OXYGEN PRODUCED BY AN OXYGEN CONCENTRATOR

CROSS-REFERENCE TO RELATED APPLICATION(S)

[0001] Reference is hereby made to the following copending applications, which were filed on even date with the present application: "Ambulatory Oxygen Concentrator Containing a Power Pack", Theodore W. Jagger et al., application Se. No. _____; "Adsorbent Cartridge for Oxygen Concentrator", Theodore W. Jagger et al., application Ser. No. _____; "Ambulatory Oxygen Concentrator Containing a Three Phase Vacuum Separation Process", Theodore W. Jagger et al., application Ser. No. _____; "Personal Oxygen Concentrator", Theodore W. Jagger et al., application Ser. No. _____; "Method of Providing Ambulatory Oxygen", Theodore W. Jagger et al., application Ser. No. _____; "Low Power Ambulatory Oxygen Concentrator", Theodore W. Jagger et al., application Ser. No._____; "Ambulatory Oxygen Concentrator With High Efficiency Adsorbent", Theodore W. Jagger et al., application Ser. No. _____; "Portable Oxygen Concentrator With a Docking Station", Theodore W. Jagger et al., application Ser. No. _____; "Product Pump for an Oxygen Concentrator", Theodore W. Jagger et al., application Ser. No. _____; and "Method and Apparatus for Controlling the Purity of Oxygen Produced by an Oxygen Concentrator", Theodore W. Jagger et al., application Ser. No. _____.

BACKGROUND OF THE INVENTION

[0002] The field of this invention relates to oxygen concentrators. In particular, the invention relates to wearable oxygen concentration systems utilizing vacuum swing adsorption for creating an oxygen stream for ambulatory respiratory patients.

[0003] There is a need for home and ambulatory oxygen systems for use by patients. Supplemental oxygen is required for patients exhibiting symptoms from certain diseases and lung disorders; for example, pulmonary fibrosis, sarcoidosis, or occupational lung disease. For such patients, oxygen therapy is an increasingly beneficial prescription to help the patients live normal and productive lives. While not a cure for lung disease, prescriptive supplemental oxygen increases blood oxygenation, which reverses hypoxemia. Oxygen prescriptions prevent long-term effects of oxygen deficiency on organ systems, the heart, brain and kidneys. Oxygen treatment is also prescribed for Chronic Obstructive Pulmonary Disease (COPD), heart disease, AIDS, asthma, and emphysema.

[0004] Currently, supplemental medical oxygen for therapy is provided to a patient from high pressure gas cylinders; cryogenic liquid in vacuum-insulated containers or thermos bottles commonly called "dewars", and oxygen concentrators. Some patients require in-home oxygen only, while others require in-home as well as ambulatory oxygen depending on the prescription. The three systems are all used for in-home use. However, oxygen concentrators provide a special beneficial advantage because they do not require refilling of dewars or exchange of empty cylinders with full ones. Home oxygen concentrators, however, do have drawbacks. They consume relatively large amounts of electricity; are relatively large and heavy; emit excessive heat and are relatively noisy.

[0005] There has been a need for an improved portable device for supplying oxygen to a patient. Only small high pressure gas bottles and small liquid dewars are truly portable enough to be used for ambulatory needs. Either system maybe used for both in-home and ambulatory use. A patient using a stationary oxygen system at home (or even a portable system which cannot be readily transported), who travels must opt for small cylinders towed in a wheeled stroller or for portable containers that they carry, typically on a shoulder sling. Both of these options have significant drawbacks.

[0006] A major drawback of the cylinder option is that small cylinders only provide oxygen for a short duration. Moreover, these cylinders are maintained at a high pressure, and thus their use is restricted due to safety considerations. Another drawback of the cylinders is the refill requirement after depletion of the contents of the cylinder. Empty cylinders must be refilled at specialized facilities, or in the patient's home using a commercial oxygen concentrator which extracts oxygen from the air. The latter option requires an on-site compressor to boost the output pressure of the concentrator to meet cylinder refill pressure requirements. Filling of cylinders with oxygen in the home is potentially dangerous due to the physics involved with compressing gas. Another detriment to cylinder usage is fire hazards associated with storage of large volumes of oxygen in the home environment.

[0007] Convenience and safety issues are not the only drawbacks associated with the use of cylinders. Another drawback is the cost associated with cylinders. Cylinders require special care, and specialized materials are required for high pressure oxygen compatibility, which in turn drives up the cost of cylinder-based systems.

[0008] The liquid oxygen storage system also has drawbacks. The primary drawback is the requirement of a base reservoir which necessitates refilling once a week or more from an outside source. Liquid oxygen is transferred from the base unit to a portable dewar, which is used by an ambulatory patient. However, there is substantial waste, as a certain amount of oxygen is lost during the transfer to the portable containers and from evaporation. Up to twenty percent of the contents of the base cylinder is lost in the course of two weeks because of losses in transfers and normal evaporation. Even without withdrawal by the patient, the base reservoir will typically boil dry over a period of one to two months.

[0009] The aforementioned systems all require are filling station. When the patient is out in public, such stations are not readily available. Upon running low (or out) of oxygen, the patient must return home to a specified place that can refill the system. Such a requirement detracts from the ambulatory usefulness of the systems.

[0010] The industry has developed a set of recommendations for systems targeted to provide portable oxygen for ambulatory patients. The Fifth Oxygen Consensus Conference set forth the following standards for long-term oxygen therapy ambulatory equipment: 1) equipment must weigh less than 10 lbs., 2) equipment must provide the equivalent of 2 liter/min of continuous flow O_2, and 3) the flow rate must be maintained for four hours or more. Thus, ambulatory equipment, or personal oxygen systems (POS), are to be inconspicuous to the public as well as unrestricting to the patient. Cylinders and other liquid oxygen systems tend to be bulky, which interferes with normal daily activities. Similarly, cylinders and liquid oxygen systems are difficult to conceal from public view. Ideally, a POS is small, lightweight, quiet, and flexible which allows the device to be concealed from the public. The present invention, whereby oxygen rich gas is provided to a patient from a wearable oxygen concentrator, meets and exceeds these standards.

BRIEF SUMMARY OF THE INVENTION

[0011] A method of providing concentrated oxygen product gas to a patient comprises producing product gas by a vacuum swing adsorption (VSA) process through a plurality of separation columns connected to a vacuum source driven by a motor. Separated product gas is then pumped to a reservoir in which the pressure is monitored and used to adjust the speed of the motor based on that pressure. The separated gas is then delivered to the patient.

BRIEF DESCRIPTION OF THE DRAWINGS

[0012] FIG. 1 is a front view of a patient carrying the oxygen concentrator of the present invention.

[0013] FIG. 2 is a front perspective view of the oxygen concentrator.

[0014] FIG. 3 is a rear perspective view of the oxygen concentrator.

[0015] FIG. 4 is a front perspective view of the oxygen concentrator and a docking station.

[0016] FIG. 5 is a block diagram showing the components and connections of the oxygen concentrator.

[0017] FIG. 6 is a diagram showing rotary valve timing.

[0018] FIG. 7 is an exploded view of the oxygen concentrator in which the power pack and the adsorbent cartridge have been removed.

[0019] FIG. 8 is a perspective view of the oxygen concentrator with a portion of the belt removed.

[0020] FIG. 9 is a perspective view of the components of the oxygen concentrator without the belt.

[0021] FIG. 10 is a perspective view of the components contained within the case portions of the modules and their associated pneumatic and electrical connections of the oxygen concentrator.

[0022] FIG. 11 is a perspective view of the components contained within a battery module.

[0023] FIG. 12a is a perspective view of an accumulator.

[0024] FIG. 12b is a top view of the accumulator.

[0025] FIG. 12c is a sectional view of the accumulator.

[0026] FIG. 12d is another sectional view of the accumulator.

[0027] FIG. 13 is a perspective view of a control module.

[0028] FIG. 14 is a front view of the interior components of the control module.

[0029] FIG. 15 is a perspective view of the cartridge contained within a cartridge module.

[0030] FIG. 16 is an exploded view of columns and filters within the cartridge.

[0031] FIG. 17 is a rear perspective view of the oxygen concentrator and the docking station.

[0032] FIG. 18 is a front perspective view of the docking station.

[0033] FIG. 19 is a chart showing the adsorption isotherms for two different adsorbent materials.

DETAILED DESCRIPTION

[0034] The current invention relates to separation of gases using vacuum swing adsorption. Specifically, disclosed is an oxygen concentrator for a patient who requires a source of oxygen. The present invention is further explained with reference to the drawn figures in which like structures are referred to by like numerals throughout the several views.

Overview—Oxygen Concentrator 100 (FIGS. 1-4)

[0035] FIG. 1 is a front view showing patient P with oxygen concentrator 100 and oxygen delivery tube 102. Oxygen concentrator 100 is a small unit which utilizes vacuum swing adsorption to separate oxygen from the ambient air around patient P. Oxygen concentrator 100 is compact and light so as not to interfere with the ambulatory movement of patient P, and can produce a product stream of gas containing a range of eighty-five to ninety-five percent oxygen.

[0036] Oxygen delivery tube 102 is a polymer tube or similar oxidation resistant structure, which extends from oxygen concentrator 100 to the nose, mouth, or port into the upper airway of patient P. Tube 102 allows delivery of oxygen to patient P for inhalation. In FIG. 1, patient P is about six foot tall to illustrate an approximation of the relative size of oxygen concentrator 100.

[0037] FIG. 2 is a perspective view of oxygen concentrator 100. Oxygen concentrator 100 is comprised of belt 104, power module 106 containing power pack 108, reservoir module 110, control module 112 containing user interface 114, and separation cartridge module 116. Oxygen concentrator 100 is a portable oxygen separator used to provide an oxygen rich gas stream to patient P. Belt 104 connects and carries the modules 106, 110, 112, and 16 of oxygen concentrator 100. Belt 104 may contain belt loops (not illustrated), clips, or a pair of straps that contain a buckle and holes or like fastening device for securing oxygen concentrator 100 to patient P. Alternatively, oxygen concentrator 100 maybe placed in a purse, fannypack, or similar personal carrying device for transport with patient P.

[0038] Power module 106 provides the necessary power to operate the systems of oxygen concentrator 100. In the embodiment illustrated, power module 106 contains replaceable power pack 108. Reservoir module 110 stores oxygen rich gas that has been separated from ambient air by cartridge module 116. Control module 112 pilots and regulates the interaction of the power module 106, reservoir module 110, and separation cartridge module 116 of oxygen concentrator 100. User interface 114 on control module 112 is a console which allows patient P to adjust and monitor oxygen concentrator 100.

[0039] FIG. 3 is a perspective view of the opposite side of oxygen concentrator 100 as shown in FIG. 2. Illustrated in

FIG. 3 are belt 104, power module 106, reservoir module 110, control module 112, and separation cartridge module 116. Belt 104 is constructed to contain belt segments 120 formed by serrations 118. This allows the belt 104 to be flexible and conform to patient P's body while wearing oxygen concentrator 100. Belt 104 is fabricated from a flexible material, such as textile or plastic and contains an inner padding such as foam. Belt 104 also houses the electrical and pneumatic connections of oxygen concentrator 100.

[0040] FIG. 4 is a perspective view of the front side of the oxygen concentrator 100 on docking station 122. Illustrated are oxygen concentrator 100 comprising belt 104, power module 106, reservoir module 110, control module 112, and separation cartridge module 116, along with docking station 122 containing power pack chargers 124a and 124b. Belt 104 is flexible and thus rests on the arc shaped docking station 122. Docking station 122 contains power pack chargers 124a (with power pack 108a inserted therein) and 124b, as well as concentrator dock 126 which supports the oxygen concentrator 100 while on the docking station 122. Docking station 122 converts AC power to recharge power packs 108.

Oxygen Concentrator 100 System Components and Connections (FIG. 5)

[0041] FIG. 5 is a block diagram of oxygen concentrator 100 illustrating power module 106, reservoir module 110, control module 112, and separation cartridge module 116, along with docking station 122 and showing the components and connections among the modules and docking station 122. Oxygen concentrator 100 components includes product gas outlet port 103, adsorbent columns 130a-130c (each containing a respective inlet port 132a-132c and a respective outlet port 134a-134c), air inlet port 135, air inlet filter 136, product gas final filter 138, main valve 140, drive reducer 142, vacuum pump 144, drive 146, electric control module (ECM) 148, breakthrough flow sensor 150, valve position sensor 152, product control pump 154, check valve 156, main storage reservoir 158 containing pressure sensor 159, dispensing valve 160, as well as previously identified components tubing 102, power pack 108, user interface 114, and docking station 122.

[0042] As shown in FIG. 5, adsorbent cartridge module 116 includes adsorbent columns 130a-130c each containing respective inlet ports 132a-132c and outlet ports 134a-134c, air inlet filter 136, and product gas final filter 138. Ambient air enters air inlet port 135, passes through air inlet filter 136, and enters valve 140 for distribution to adsorbent columns 130a-130c. Product gas passes through final filter 138 and product gas outlet port 103 into tubing 102 for delivery to patient P. Inlet ports 132a-132c of adsorbent columns 130a-130c connect to valve 140 through inlet lines 164a-164c. Similarly, outlet ports 134a-134c connect to valve 140 through outlet lines 166a-166c.

[0043] Control module 112 houses main valve 140, drive reducer 142, vacuum pump 144, drive 146, electric control module (ECM) 148, breakthrough flow sensor 150, valve position sensor 152, and contains user interface 114. Main valve 140 is pneumatically connected to adsorbent columns 130a-130c, as well as inlet filter 136 via inlet line 168, vacuum pump 144 via vacuum inlet line 170, product control pump 154 via vacuum line 172 and product gas line 174, and main reservoir 158 via product gas line 176. Valve

140 is actuated by drive 146 through a motor speed reducer 142. Also, valve 140 connects to breakthrough flow sensor 150 and valve position sensor 152 which send electrical inputs 178 and 180 to ECM 148.

[0044] ECM 148 is a logic control, such as a PLC (programmable logic controller), microprocessor, or similar structure which controls operation of oxygen concentrator 100. ECM 148 contains the set of inputs and outputs associated with the modules for regulating oxygen concentrator 100. ECM 148 also receives control setting inputs 182 and 184 from user interface 114, and docking station 122, respectively, power pack management input 186 from power pack 108, reservoir pressure input 188 from pressure sensor 159 in main reservoir 158, and nasal pressure input 190 from dispensing valve 160. ECM 148 provides interface output 192 to the user interface 114, interface output 194 to docking station 122, power management output 196 to power pack 108, dispensing valve time open output 198 to dispensing valve 160, and motor drive output 200 to drive 146.

[0045] User interface 114 contains physical controls such as dials, toggle switches, push button switches, and similar controls, for operating oxygen concentrator 100. The physical controls provide electrical control settings to ECM 148. ECM 148 reads these settings as inputs 182 and provides output 192 to the user interface 114. The status is converted from electric signals to physical output by indicator lights, status display, and similar structures of user interface 114.

[0046] Power pack management input 186 and output 196 control the charge and discharge of voltage from power pack 108 to drive 146 via ECM 148. Drive 146 will activate vacuum pump 144, valve 140 through drive speed reducer 142, and any other systems requiring power. Power pack management output 196 will also supply power to indicator lights, status display, audible alarm (if included), and other passive electrical system requirements on user interface 114 through ECM 148.

[0047] ECM 148 controls and coordinates the steps of the vacuum swing adsorption cycle through its inputs and outputs. In one embodiment, breakthrough flow sensor 150 provides an input 178 into ECM 148 by measuring air flow rates. The position of valve 140 is detected by valve position sensor 152 to produce input 180. Reservoir 158 contains a sensor to produce reservoir pressure input 188. Dispensing valve 160 also contains a pressure sensor which provides nasal pressure input 190 in response to differential pressure. ECM 148 reads these inputs to control the cycle by changing outputs, such as motor drive output 200 for drive 146. Drive 146 propels vacuum pump 144. Vacuum pump 144 creates a vacuum that is communicated to valve 140 through vacuum input line 170, while dispelling nitrogen rich gas as exhaust 177. Another output 198 controls the time that dispensing valve 160 is open. In this embodiment, the inputs and outputs are connected to a PLC within ECM 148 which is programmed to control the cycle of oxygen concentrator 100.

[0048] Contained within reservoir module 110 is an oxygen-rich gas accumulator comprising reservoir 158, check valve 156, product control pump 154, and check valve 153. Reservoir 158 receives oxygen-rich gas produced by oxygen concentrator 100 and stores it at a low pressure above ambient until it is required for use. A portion of the stored oxygen-rich gas is delivered back to valve 140 by product gas line 176 for use in ordering the nitrogen content in adsorbent columns 130a-130c by moving much of the residual nitrogen held after evacuation near the outlets 134a-134c toward inlets 132a-132c of the columns 130a-130c. Reservoir 158 is in communication with dispensing valve 160 through product gas line 202. Check valve 156 opens to allow oxygen into reservoir 158 and closes to prevent backflow of oxygen upon reaching the desired pressure in reservoir 158.

[0049] Product control pump 154 is driven by vacuum provided by the vacuum pump 144 through valve 140 via vacuum line 172. Product line 174 is in communication from separation cartridge module 116 to check valve 153, which opens to allow product control pump 154 to transport separated oxygen-rich gas to reservoir 158. Product control pump 154 delivers the product gas to main reservoir 158 through check valve 156.

[0050] Dispensing valve 160 and power pack 108 are contained within power module 106. Dispensing valve 160 is used to feed the flow of oxygen-rich gas to the patient P by delivery of the product gas through final product gas line 205 to product final filter 138. The product gas is obtained from the main reservoir 158 through product gas line 202. Power pack 108 provides the power supply for oxygen concentrator 100 as previously described. Power pack 108 is rechargeable through docking station 122 as represented by power connection 204.

Vacuum Swing Adsorption (VSA) Process—Overview

[0051] Oxygen concentrator 100 operates using a vacuum swing adsorption process, which involves a series of cycles that include a feed step or phase, an evacuation step or phase, and a repressurization step or phase. Each of these three phases takes place in one of the three columns 130a-130c at any given time. Each column 130a-130c is in a different phase. For purposes of explanation, the VSA process will be described in reference to "column 130", which is representative of each of the three columns 130a-130c.

[0052] In the feed phase, a gas stream of ambient air 162 enters inlet end 132 of column 130 while product gas containing concentrated oxygen is delivered from outlet end 134 of column 130. The slight vacuum in column 130 draws air 162 into column 130 and through an adsorbent material (typically a zeolite) which preferentially retains specific components of air (nitrogen), allowing the desired product (oxygen) to pass through. A mass transfer zone (MTZ), which is a small region in which nitrogen is being adsorbed, is passing through the adsorbent material. The MTZ divides the column 130 into two segments: a nitrogen-rich segment where the MTZ has passed through, and an oxygen-rich segment ahead of the moving MTZ. The MTZ forms at the inlet 132 at the start of the process and gradually moves through the column to the outlet 134 as the process proceeds. Outlet end 134 of column 130 is connected to main reservoir 158 through main valve 140, check valve 153, and product control pump 154, so that oxygen-rich product gas from column 130 is pumped into reservoir 158.

[0053] In the evacuation phase, column 130 is brought to a stronger vacuum by vacuum pump 144, causing the adsorbed component, i.e. nitrogen, to be desorbed. The nitrogen is evacuated from column 130 through main valve 140, and is discharged by vacuum pump 144 as waste exhaust 177.

[0054] In the repressurization phase, the previously evacuated column 130 is returned to near 1 atm. Ambient air 162 enters column 130 through inlet end 132, and recycled product gas from product line 176 enters column 130 through outlet end 134. The gases replace the vacuum that was previously drawn in column 130 during the evacuation phase. Just prior to column 130 reaching about 1 atm, the repressurization phase ends and the feed phase of the cycle begins again.

[0055] This constitutes the general principles of vacuum swing adsorption (VSA) for gas separation. All phases can be accomplished with a single column, or with a plurality of columns. If a plurality of columns are used, it is preferable to have a multiple of three (illustrated as 130a-130c in FIG. 5) that are sequenced out of phase for the different cycle phases in order to maintain constant product flow.

The Feed Phase—Breakthrough Detection

[0056] During the feed phase of the separation cycle, the position of the MTZ within adsorbent column 130 is monitored, determined, and beneficially used to control the termination of the feed phase. The control results in improvements in product purity and recovery with concomitant decrease in energy consumed, as well as system size and system weight for a given volume of product produced.

[0057] Breakthrough is defined as the point when the MTZ reaches outlet 134 of adsorbent column 130. At this point, feed gas begins to flow into the separated product gas stream. This is undesirable because the purity of the product stream is reduced by the feed stream gas if the feed is allowed to continue past this point. Conversely, if the feed phase is terminated before the MTZ nears outlet 134 of column 130, product recovery will be reduced because product gas contained in column 130 between the MTZ and outlet 134 of column 130 will be subjected to the evacuation phase that follows the feed phase in the separation cycle, and much of this remaining product gas will be lost with the desorbed gas in the waste stream.

[0058] For a particular column geometry, temperature, adsorbent type and condition, and cycle vacuum levels, there is an optimal time during the feed phase of the cycle to terminate the feed—before purity requirements are compromised, but after the maximum possible product has been recovered from column 130. This optimal time is determined by the detection of the passage of the mass transfer zone through a specific position relative to outlet end 134 of column 130.

[0059] For some combinations of system variables, the optimum feed termination time corresponds to the beginning of breakthrough when the leading edge of the MTZ has just reached outlet end 134 of column 130. This event can be detected by monitoring either or both of the gas flow rates at inlet 132 or outlet 134 to column 130. Before breakthrough, the outlet flow rate is less than the inlet flow rate by an amount equal to the rate of nitrogen gas adsorption of column 130 from the feed gas flow. After breakthrough, column 130 is no longer adsorbing nitrogen from the feed gas, so the inflow and outflow rates of column 130 become equal. Any method of measuring gas flow rates to determine the point in time when these flow rates begin the transition toward equality can be used to detect this beginning of breakthrough.

[0060] It has been determined that if the inflow rate of air to column 130 is maintained constant, a simple detection of a significant rise in slope of the outflow rate marks break-through. Conversely, if the outflow rate is held fairly steady, then a falling slope of the inflow rate marks the break-through. Monitoring the ratio of flow for the inlet and outlet and detecting a significant change in the ratio of flows toward a ratio of 1:1 can mark breakthrough in systems where inflow or outflow may not be steady enough to detect breakthrough by monitoring just one of the flow rates.

[0061] For other combinations of system variables, the optimum feed termination time may correspond to the MTZ position prior to breakthrough. In these cases, it is beneficial for a specific amount of product to be intentionally left in column 130 at the end of a feed phase. Detecting the position of the MTZ before breakthrough can be accomplished by additional methods.

[0062] One method used determines the volume of gas passed into or out of adsorbent column 130 up to the point of breakthrough by integrating the flow rate during the time interval between an initial feed and breakthrough while using some breakthrough detection method as previously described. Volume of flow may also be directly measured by physical equivalent methods using displacements of known volumes. Once the volume of gas that passes the column up to the point of breakthrough is determined, the volume of gas flow can be monitored during subsequent feed phases and the feed terminated when the volume reaches a specific value less than that for breakthrough. At anytime during the feed phase, the volume of gas passed through column 130 since the beginning of feed divided by the volume of gas at breakthrough will be the same ratio as the position of the mass transfer zone divided by the length of column 130 (assuming a constant cross sectional area along the length). Using this relationship, the position of the MTZ within column 130 can be adequately determined during the feed phase.

[0063] The components of oxygen concentrator 100 as previously described are used to complete the cyclical phases of VSA to separate gases. The feed phase operates at a slight vacuum just below ambient (in the range of 0.9 to 1 atm). This provides just enough driving force to pull ambient air 162 into adsorbent column 130 through inlet filter 136. The vacuum is caused byproduct control pump 154, which is driven by the vacuum drawn by vacuum pump 144. Product control pump 154 is a piston pump or similar structure that meters a volume of gas. Product control pump 154 connects with a volume much greater than the piston displacement volume, such as main reservoir 158.

[0064] The feed phase is allowed to proceed until break-through is detected. Up to this point, the outflow gas from adsorbent column 130 has been a high purity oxygen/argon, low percent nitrogen mixture. The MTZ position is con-trolled to minimize nitrogen into the product gas mixture. The MTZ position is monitored by breakthrough flow sensor 150, which detects a large increase in flow rate associated with breakthrough when the nitrogen no longer is preferen-tially adsorbed by adsorbent column 130. Breakthrough flow sensor is located near the column inlet 132, column outlet 134, or similar place where the flow rate being measured is accessible. When the increase MTZ flow is detected, a signal is sent to ECM 148, which also receives valve position

signal 180 from the valve position sensor 152. The ECM 148 compares the timing of the MTZ breakthrough signal and the valve position signal and makes a minor adjustment to motor speed 200 based on lead, lag, or on-time status to keep the breakthrough time near the end of each feed phase. Alternately, ECM 148 receives a signal from breakthrough flow sensor 150 and immediately terminates the current feed phase in column 130 by signaling valve 140 to rotate to start the next phase. In yet another embodiment, the separation system contains a shut off valve that is signaled to close the feed of ambient air 162 into column 130, or the delivery of product gas from the column upon breakthrough detection.

[0065] In another embodiment, the method for determin-ing the position of the mass transfer zone prior to break-through is accomplished by placing a small amount of non-adsorbing material within adsorbent column 130 at a particular position. When the mass transfer zone passes through this position, a flow change is detectable as the adsorption of gas is briefly interrupted by the non-adsorbing segment of column 130. The resulting flow change is detectable using the same methods for breakthrough detec-tion previously described.

[0066] With larger columns and slower feed phases, the position of the mass transfer zone has been established by measuring temperature rise at positions of interest within column 130. Significant temperature increases result from the heat of adsorption at the MTZ and can be detected by thermistors or similar devices placed within column 130.

The Evacuation Phase

[0067] The evacuation phase brings the gas in adsorbent column 130 that was just in the feed phase to a vacuum state. At the end of the feed phase, the adsorbent column 130 is in equilibrium with the air infeed mixture near 1 atm from column inlet 132 up to the MTZ. Hence, if the ending position of the MTZ is established, and the nitrogen, oxygen, and argon isotherms for the chosen adsorbent mass are known, then the quantity of these gases present in adsorbent column 130 at the end of each feed phase is known. Vacuum pump 144 draws a vacuum on adsorbent column 130. This vacuum level is determined and set to a state that will remove a large portion of the gas left in column 130. In one embodiment, this is 0.2 to 0.3 atm. By percentage, the vast majority of gas discharged is nitrogen. The evacuated gas is discharged as waste from exhaust 177 of vacuum pump 144. The preferred embodiment uses a fixed displacement type of vacuum pump 144. During each evacuation phase, the adsorbed gas in column 130 is expanded into a much larger volume made up of the column volume plus the fixed displacement volume of pump 144.

[0068] The evacuate phase creates a self regulating effect that compensates for reductions in the amount of nitrogen adsorbed by adsorbent column 130 as the adsorbent degrades (ages). If the adsorbent loses efficiency, less nitro-gen will be present in column 130 at the end of the phase, but the volume of the pump that the nitrogen expands into remains the same. A stronger vacuum will result that will remove more nitrogen and therefore allow more air to be fed during the next feed phase. A more constant breakthrough time results and provides a more robust product cycle.

[0069] The evacuation is provided by vacuum pump 144, which is controlled and activated by drive 146. The volume removed for each cycle of the vacuum pump 144 will remain constant, but the motor drive output 200 will be controlled by the rate of product gas used by patient P. The amount of oxygen used by patient P depends on the patient P's on-demand respiratory rate, which is sensed by the device and from a variable position switch which sends an input 192 from user interface 114 to ECM 148, which in turn provides motor drive output 200 to drive 146. This determines the speed of each successive phase and, therefore, the oxygen production rate.

[0070] In one embodiment, a purge is applied at the very end of an evacuation phase. While still in the evacuation phase, a purge of product gas (mostly oxygen) introduced through outlet 134 effectively drives out a portion of nitrogen in column 130 through inlet 132. Adding the purge gas of high purity oxygen/argon through outlet 134 desorbs more nitrogen from outlet 134 of column 130, and pushes the nitrogen toward inlet 132 of adsorbent column 130 and creates an ordering of the gases. The purge volume is a function of vacuum level and adsorbent characteristics. A purge portion of the evacuation phase is not a necessary phase for a functioning device, but allows high oxygen purity to be maintained with weaker vacuum levels.

The Repressurization Phase

[0071] The repressurization phase brings adsorbent column 130 (just previously evacuated and purged) up to the feed pressure. In one embodiment, the gas used for repressurization is from both the infeed ambient air 162 and a counter stream from the (oxygen-rich) product gas line 176 from the main reservoir 158. Alternately, the repressurization of product gas can be accomplished through valve design negating the need for a separate line. The product gas is dispensed from a stream of product gas from the adsorbent column that is in the feed phase through a vacuum break valve used during repressurization. Repressurization with product gas can be done before, simultaneously, or after partial pressurization with ambient air. Repressurization with product gas is done at the opposite end of column 130 as repressurization with ambient air 162.

[0072] The effect of adding the repressurization gas of high purity oxygen/argon through outlet 134 creates a cleaning zone at outlet 134 of adsorbent column 130 where, during the feed phase that follows next, any stray nitrogen can be preferentially adsorbed and not discharged as product gas. This improves the ordering of gases in the adsorbent column 130. By repeating this phase during successive cycles, the purity will continue to increase in the product output. Weaker vacuums require more oxygen volume returned to column 130 during repressurization if high purity is desired. That is, a stronger vacuum must be drawn on the column 130 to effectuate the same purity of oxygen absent the use of oxygen-rich gas as aback flush for repressurization at the outlet 134 of column 130. At the end of repressurization, the feed phase will proceed.

Valve 140 Timing (FIG. 6)

[0073] The VSA cycle comprises three phases: evacuation, repressurization, and feed, which occur sequentially in each column 130a-130c. For clarity, only column 130a will be discussed, although each phase is performed (at different times during a complete cycle) in each of columns 130a-130c.

[0074] Starting with the evacuation phase of the cycle, a small amount of oxygen (not illustrated) may flow into outlet 134a of adsorption column 130a to purge adsorption column 130a, while vacuum pump 144 withdraws gas present at inlet 134a of the column, i.e. nitrogen-rich gas.

[0075] During the repressurization phase, an amount of previously separated oxygen flows into outlet 134a of adsorption column 130a for a short time, and then air is allowed to enter inlet 132a of column 130a that has been previously evacuated. There maybe a slight overlap of the oxygen flow into outlet 134a of adsorption column 130a and the air flow in the opposite direction into inlet 132a. Air freely flows into inlet 132a of adsorption column 130a upon opening of valve 140 as adsorption column 130a has been previously evacuated during the evacuation phase.

[0076] During the feed phase, air continues to flow into inlet 132a of adsorption column 130a while oxygen is removed from outlet 134a of column 130a by a pressure differential created by product control pump 154. As the MTZ passes through the adsorption column and reaches a position at or near outlet 134a, vacuum pump 144 will again begin to evacuate adsorbent column 130a and restart with the evacuation phase. In the embodiment illustrated in FIG. 6, these phases are controlled by main valve 140.

[0077] FIG. 6 is a diagram showing timing for main valve 140, which is a rotary valve that moves 360°(one full revolution about a central axis) for each complete cycle of the VSA process. In the embodiment with three columns 130a-130c, the timing for each phase of the cycle is 120°. Each column 130a-130c is present in a different phase for each 120° of rotation of valve 140 that is different from the other two columns to obtain a sequence that creates a steady flow of oxygen as valve 140 keeps rotating.

[0078] As shown in the timing diagram, adsorption column 130a is in the feed phase of the cycle at a start point of zero degrees. Air is being let in through inlet filter 136 and column inlet 132a while separated gas consisting of highly concentrated oxygen is being removed through column outlet 134a. A portion of the oxygen-rich product gas is used in the repressurization of column 130b. Adsorption column 130b is in the repressurization phase at a point of rotary valve 140 being in initial position zero degrees. As valve 140 is turned, column outlet 134b is fed with the oxygen-rich gas for a portion of the valve's rotation, preferably less than 120°. After the flow of oxygen-rich gas enters column 130b through the column outlet 134b, air repressurization through the opening of column inlet 132b begins. In the embodiment shown, this takes place at a point after valve 140 has begun its rotation and ends before it reaches a third of its rotation, or a 120° rotation.

[0079] While column 130a is in feed phase and column 130b is in the repressurization phase, column 130c is in the evacuation phase. During the evacuation phase, a vacuum is drawn to remove adsorbed gas through inlet 132c, thereby regenerating it for the following feed phase.

[0080] In the embodiment shown, each column 130a, 130b, and 130c, is in a different phase of the cycle as one moves vertically down the diagram in FIG. 6. During the first one hundred twenty degrees of rotation of the rotary valve, column 130a is in the feed phase. Simultaneously, from zero to one hundred twenty degrees of rotation, column 130b is being repressurized, while column 130c is being evacuated.

[0081] For the next one hundred twenty degrees of rotation of valve 140 (ie., from 120° to 240°), adsorption column 130*a* is in the evacuation phase. At this same time, column 130*b* is in the feed phase, and column 130*c* is in the repressurization phase.

[0082] Moving horizontally across the diagram for column 130*a*, during the final one hundred twenty degrees of rotation of valve 140 (i.e., from 240° to 360°), column 130*a* is repressurized first using separated gas, and then ambient air. Separated gas and ambient air are introduced to the column 130*a* through column inlet 132*a* and column outlet 174*a* at opposite ends of column 130*a*. During the final one hundred twenty degrees of rotation (i.e. from 240° to 360°) of main valve 140, column 130*b* is in the evacuation phase, and column 130*c* is in the feed phase. Upon reaching three hundred sixty degrees, valve 140 is back at its starting position (zero degrees), and the cycles for each column 130*a*-130*c* restart from the zero degree position.

Oxygen Concentrator 100 Physical Components (**FIGS. 7-16**)

[0083] FIG. 7 shows an exploded view of the oxygen concentrator 100, which includes belt 104, power module 106 containing removable power pack 108, reservoir module 110, control module 112, and separation cartridge module 116 containing adsorbent cartridge 206. Power pack 108 has been removed from receptacle 210 of power module 106. Adsorbent cartridge 206 has been removed from receptacle 208 of cartridge module 116. Adsorbent cartridge 206 and power pack 108 are easily removable to facilitate replacement.

[0084] In this embodiment, power pack 108 is a rechargeable battery. Receptacle 210 contains electrical contacts (not illustrated) for connection to power pack 108. Cartridge 206 contains a quick-connect attachment (not illustrated) for inlet lines 164*a*-164*c*, outlet lines 166*a*-166*c*, inlet air line 168, and final product gas line 205 (not illustrated) within receptacle 208. Also present on cartridge 206 are air inlet ports 135 which receive ambient air 162 for separation. Adsorbent cartridge 206 contains adsorbent material that deteriorates in efficiency as it is used and ages.

[0085] FIG. 8 is a perspective view of oxygen concentrator 100. A portion of belt 104 has been removed revealing back interior surface 211 and inner connections amongst the modules, including utility tubes 212, tube pathways 214, module apertures 216*a*-216*d*, and module sockets 218*a*-218*d*.

[0086] Utility tubes 212 run between the adjacent modules and contain either electrical wiring or pneumatic lines, or comprise pneumatic lines and electrical wiring and associated connections. Tubes 212 are constructed to be flexible and bend as belt 104 is manipulated. If the tubes 212 contain electrical lines, the tubes are constructed from a dielectric material to insulate electrical wires, or similar material commonly used in electrical connections. If the tubes 212 comprise pneumatic lines, they may be air tight, small diameter polyvinyl or PVC tubes to connect the various gas input, gas separation, and gas removal systems of the oxygen concentrator 100. Tubes 212 contain openings or connections as required for electrical and pneumatic communication with each module. The back interior surface 211 of belt 104 contains tube pathways 214. Pathways 214

fabricated on the interior surface 211 of belt 104 allow the utility tubes 212 to extend between the modules 106, 110, 112, and 116. Tube pathways 214 create a semi-partitioned area on back interior surface 211 of belt 104 which support tubes 212.

[0087] Belt 104 is fabricated to contain apertures 216*a*-216*d* which allow modules 106, 110, 112, and 116 to connect utility tubes 212 of belt 104 through sockets 218*a*-218*d*. Apertures 216*a*-216*d* and sockets 218*a*-218*d* are fabricated as part of modules 106, 110, 112, and 116. Serrations 118 can be seen between the upper and lower edges 220 and 222 of belt 104. When fabrication of belt 104 is completed, padding will be inserted between edges 220 and 222, and material will be wrapped around creating serrations 118 and belt segments 120 to complete belt 104 as illustrated in FIG. 3. The padding is fabricated over the top of tubes 212 and tube pathways 214, or separately fabricated and fastened to back interior surface 211 during assembly of belt 104. Individual modules allow the device to flex when mounted about a curved surface, such as a belt around patient P's waist. The construction of belt 104 with tubes 212 allows patient P to manipulate the oxygen concentrator 100, such as by bending belt 104 to wear around the waist, place on docking station 122, or folding concentrator 100 in half for transport in a carryall.

[0088] FIG. 9 is a perspective view of modules 106, 110, 112, and 116 of oxygen concentrator 100. In this view, belt 104 has been removed to illustrate the positions of sockets 218*a*-218*d* containing apertures 216*a*-216*d* on each respective module 106, 110, 112, and 116. Each respective module 106, 110, 112, and 116 is constructed from a thermoplastic material such as acrylanitrile butadine styrene (ABS) or high density polyethylene (HDPE), or a lightweight metal or a similar rigid material that is oxidation resistant.

[0089] Each module 106, 110, 112, and 116, comprises a case portion 224, 226, 228, and 230, defining the outer volume of each respectively. Bottom padding 232, 234, 236, and 238, covers the lower base portion of each module 106, 110, 112, and 116, respectively. Similarly, top padding 240 extends around the top perimeter of power module 106, while top padding 242 and 244 covers the top portions of modules 110 and 112. Power pack top padding 246 covers the top portion of power pack 108 and cartridge top padding 248 covers the top of separation cartridge 206. Padding 222-248 is a foam or similar lightweight material that adds protection to the modules as well as acts to reduce vibration of oxygen concentrator 100 felt by patient P. Alternately, oxygen concentrator 100 is enclosed in soft, flexible material to further increase comfort and maintain flexibility. In one embodiment, padding 232-248 is fabricated separately from the modules 106, 110, 112, and 116, power pack 108 and cartridge 206. In assembling the oxygen concentrator 100, padding 232-248 and case portions 224, 226, 228, and 230, are merged and secured either using fasteners, adhesives, or a manufacturing process such as ultrasonic welding.

[0090] Case portions 224, 226, 228, and 230, of each of the modules 106, 110, 112, and 116, contain sockets 218*a*-218*d* fabricated on the surface that contacts belt 104. Socket 218*a*-218*d* for each module is constructed to have support paths 250 for electrical wiring and pneumatic tubing similar to those contained within belt 104 represented by tube pathways 214. Sockets 218a-218d are constructed so that support paths 250 on sockets 218a-218d align with tube pathways 214 in belt 104 when each individual module 106, 110, 112, and 116, is connected to belt 104. In one embodiment, sockets 218a-218d are constructed to allow each individual module 106, 110, 112, and 116, to snap onto belt 104 or attach in a similar quick connect fashion. Utility tubes 212 comprise quick connects at module apertures 216a-216d. Apertures 216a-216d are openings in the case portions 224, 226, 228, and 230, provided for connection of utility tubes 212 to components contained within each module 106, 110, 112, and 116. This allows for removal of a single module 106, 110, 112, or 116 should a specific component require maintenance or replacement. Sockets 218a-218d are constructed from the same material as the case portions 224, 226, 228, and 230.

[0091] FIG. 10 is a perspective view of the components contained within modules 106, 110, 112, and 116, and the associated pneumatic and electrical connections of oxygen concentrator 100. Illustrated are power pack 108, valve 140, drive reducer 142, vacuum pump 144, drive 146, oxygen accumulator 252 (comprising product control pump 154, check valves 153 and 156, and reservoir 158), dispensing valve 160 connected to nasal pressure sensor line 190 and dispensing valve open line 198, column inlet lines 164a-164c, column outlet lines 166a-166c, product control pump vacuum line 172, product control pump inlet line 174, product gas line 202, final product gas line 205, adsorbent cartridge 206, and main electrical cable 254.

[0092] Main electrical cable 254 contains a set of electrical wires that carry inputs 178, 180, 182, 188, and 190, outputs 192 and 198, and power lines 186, 198, and 200 shown in FIG. 5. Main electrical cable 254 extends from power pack 108 to ECM 148 (not visible in FIG. 10). Dispensing valve time open output 198 and nasal pressure sensor input 190 are wires that extend between ECM 148 and dispensing valve 160. Similarly, the other inputs and outputs are wired to the appropriate system components as illustrated in FIG. 5 (although not specifically illustrated in FIG. 10.)

[0093] Product gas line 202 connects dispensing valve 160 with reservoir 158 of accumulator 252. Final product gas line 205 connects dispensing valve 160 to product gas outlet port 103 for connection to delivery tube 102 after passing through final filter 136 located in adsorbent cartridge 206 to provide patient P with oxygen rich product gas. Product control pump inlet line 174 extends from main valve 140 to product control pump 154, which pumps separated oxygen rich gas into reservoir 158. Vacuum line 172 connects product control pump 154 through valve 140 to a vacuum drawn by vacuum pump 144, and provides the actuation for product control pump 154. Column inlet lines 164a-164c and column outlet lines 166a-166c connect main valve 140 with column inlet ports 132a-132c and column outlet ports 134a-134c of columns 130a-130c, respectively (not illustrated). Inlet air line 168 transports ambient air 162 from separation cartridge 206 to main valve 140, while vacuum inlet line 170 connects vacuum pump 144 to main valve 140. All lines 164a-164c, 166a-166c, 168, 170, 172, 174, 176, 202, and 205, are pneumatic lines or similar structures that allow for the isolated flow of gases between system components.

[0094] FIG. 11 is a perspective view of the components contained within power module 106: power pack 108 (comprising cells 256, outer wall 258, and power pack life indicator 260) and dispensing valve 160. In the embodiment illustrated, power pack 108 is a lithium-ion battery pack comprised of five cells 256. Individual cells 256 are contained within outer wall 258, part of which has been removed to show cell 256. Power pack 108 is a battery that is rechargeable and removable from power module 106. Although illustrated as a trapezoid containing five cylindrical cells, the shape and number of cells will vary depending on the shape of power module 106 and power requirements of oxygen concentrator 100.

[0095] Power pack 108 is a lithium based battery pack capable of being recharged in a recharging socket or station that connects to an external power supply. Alternatively, power pack 108 comprises a battery or fuel cell. In one embodiment, power pack 108 is a lithium ion battery pack that is constructed from several interconnected lithium-ion batteries. Oxygen concentrator 100 uses a maximum of fifteen watts of power. This results in a battery weight of less than 0.7 pounds (0.3 kg). In this embodiment, patient P taking twenty breaths per minute at a setting of 2 liters per minute equivalent can use oxygen concentrator 100 for a minimum of four hours on a fully charged battery. Power pack 108 is easily exchanged with another similar battery pack, and can be removed with a simple pulling or tugging motion. In another embodiment (not illustrated), oxygen concentrator 100 contains a jack for receiving a power cord which can then be plugged into either a 110 volt wall outlet or a 12 volt power supply system (such as a car utility plug) so that power pack 108 can be charged in place in oxygen concentrator 100.

[0096] Power pack life indicator 260 displays the amount of time left that the power pack will operate the oxygen concentrator 100. As illustrated, power pack life indicator 260 is a display, such as a liquid-crystal display (LCD) or light emitting diode (LED) screen, with numeric output of expected life in hours. The LCD or LED screen may also contain a series of bars that act as indicators. Alternately, power pack life indicator 260 is a light or series of lights.

[0097] Dispensing valve 160 is contained within power module 106 and is used to feed the flow of oxygen to patient P. Dispensing valve 160 is a valve activated by a change in pressure, such as that caused when a person is inhaling. A sensor in the dispensing valve circuit monitors pressure, and opens dispensing valve 160 when a drop in pressure is sensed. ECM 148 communicates with dispensing valve 160 through input 190 and output 198 (see FIG. 5). Dispensing valve 160 is in communication with reservoir 158 through product gas line 202. Reservoir 158 is kept at a slight pressure above ambient. Thus, when dispensing valve 160 is opened, oxygen rich gas will flow from reservoir 158 through final product gas line 205, final product filter 138, and product gas outlet port 103 for delivery to patient P through tubing 102. The flow of gas is further assisted by the pressure drop created by patient P's inhaling. Dispensing valve 160 can be set to deliver oxygen rich gas to patient P for the beginning portion of a breath when patient P first inhales rather than the whole breath.

[0098]   Dispensing valve **160** provides for operating oxygen concentrator **100** in one of two possible modes: pulse flow or continuous flow. When patient P is using the oxygen concentrator **100** in the pulse flow mode, dispensing valve **160** will open intermittently in response to inhalation and will stay open for a pulse time according to the setting of the controls as set by patient P. If continuous flow is desired, dispensing valve **160** is maintained at an open or partially opened state. The product is dispensed to patient P though oxygen delivery tube **102** at a continuous rate, typically in the range of 1-1.5 lpm (liters per minute). The pressure difference corresponding to a dispensing orifice in delivery tube **102** will accommodate the flow rate from the reservoir **158**.

[0099]   FIGS. **12a-12d** are various views of components contained inside of reservoir module **110**. FIG. **12a** is a perspective view of accumulator **252**. FIG. **12b** is a top view of accumulator **12b**. FIGS. **12c** and **12d** are sectional views corresponding to the section lines in **12b**. Contained within reservoir module **110** is oxygen accumulator **252** (comprising reservoir **158**, check valves **153** and **156**, and product control pump **154**), inlet port **261**, and outlet port **263**. Accumulator **252** receives separated product gas through inlet port **261**. Product inlet line **174** (shown in FIG. **10**) is connected to inlet port **261** and links product control pump **154** to separation cartridge **206** through main valve **140** to transport oxygen rich gas separated by cartridge **206**. Inlet port **261** connects to check valve **153** which allows product gas into product control pump **154**.

[0100]   Product control pump **154** includes piston **262**, actuated by spring **264** within pump chamber **265**, which pushes separated oxygen-rich product gas into reservoir **158**. Check valve **156** opens to allow oxygen into the reservoir **158** and closes to prevent back flow of oxygen-rich gas when the desired pressure in reservoir **158** is attained. The low pressure of reservoir **158** exerts a force on check valve **156** to keep valve **156** closed. Reservoir **158** takes oxygen-rich gas produced by oxygen concentrator **100** and stores it at a low pressure above ambient until the product is required for use by patient P.

[0101]   Product control pump **154** is driven by vacuum. Product control pump vacuum line **174** is connected to the vacuum drawn by vacuum pump **144** through main valve **140**. When a vacuum is drawn, the force draws piston **262** down to compress spring **264** which expands pump chamber **265**, and causes check valve **153** to open. Oxygen-rich gas from separation cartridge **206** flows through check valve **153** and enters pump chamber **265** in the volume created by the displacement of piston **262**. At the appropriate time in the cycle, valve **140** will interrupt the vacuum to product control pump **154**, and spring **264** will force piston **262** upwards. The movement of piston **262** will force oxygen rich gas in pump chamber **265** through check valve **156** and into reservoir **158**. At the same time, check valve **153** closes to prevent more gas from entering pump **154**. With this embodiment, no additional drive (other than the vacuum to pull piston **262** down and the spring force to move it up) is required for product control pump **154** which adds to the overall efficiency of the system.

[0102]   In one embodiment, reservoir **158** has a capacity that is about four times larger than the size of the largest pulse provided by oxygen concentrator **100**. In one embodiment, extra volume is included to account for separated oxygen used as a back flow in adsorbent columns **130a**-**130c**. Specifically, main storage reservoir **158** for oxygen concentrator **100** can be designed according to the flow rates listed in Table 1. Storage reservoir **158** is 100 cc (cubic centimeters) to 400 cc in volume. Main storage reservoir **158** is maintained at a low pressure to provide delivery of the product gas to patient P through outlet **263** which is connected to final product dispensing line **202**. In one embodiment, the pressure is between 1 atm (ambient) and 1.5 atm. Also acceptable are pressures less than eight psi (55,158 Pa), with a pressure of two and one half to five psi (17,236 to 34,473 Pa) preferred. The low pressure of reservoir **158** allows oxygen concentrator **100** to be used in most areas where high pressure oxygen is banned. Also, low pressure requires less energy to fill reservoir **158**, which adds to the efficiency of the system by requiring a simpler pressurizing mechanism compared to high pressure systems.

[0103]   Reservoir **158** contains pressure sensor **159** (such as a piezoresistive or capacitive sensor) that sends reservoir pressure signal **188** to ECM **148** (see FIG. 5). ECM **148** adjusts the speed of the motor of drive **146** based on reservoir pressure signal **188** in combination with the current settings on user interface **114**. As patient P's respiratory rate increases for the current setting, more oxygen-rich gas from reservoir **158** is dispensed thus lowering the pressure of reservoir **158**. The drop in pressure is sensed and the system will react by increasing the production of product gas. Similarly, a decrease in the respiratory rate of patient P at the current setting of oxygen concentrator **100** raises the pressure in reservoir **158**. The rise in pressure is sensed and ECM **148** adjusts drive **146** accordingly to maintain a preset pressure range in reservoir **158**. Thus, only the amount of oxygen used by patient P is produced by oxygen concentrator **100**.

[0104]   FIG. 13 is a perspective view of the control module **112**. Illustrated are the case **228** containing aperture **216c** and socket **218c**, and padding **236** and **234**. Control module **112** contains user interface **114** comprising power switch **266**, flow level indicator lights **268**, flow setting switches **270a** and **270b**, boost switch **272**, and indicator lights **274** and **276**. Power switch **266** is an ordinary toggle or push button switch capable of turning oxygen concentrator **100** on and off.

[0105]   Flow settings are dually controlled by patient P utilizing flow setting switches **270**. First, continuous or pulse mode is selected by patient P. In a continuous flow mode, oxygen is dispensed at a continuous flow rate such as one to one and a half liters per minute. If oxygen concentrator **100** is set in a pulse mode for controlling flow, oxygen concentrator **100** utilizes dispensing valve **160** to provide pulse dispensing of product gas. The pulse mode is set to meet patient P's needs for the equivalent of one to five liters per minute of continuous oxygen flow. In one embodiment, a dial containing settings of one to five is utilized. In the embodiment illustrated in FIG. 13, flow setting switches are used to adjust the flow rate between various stepped levels. Each setting corresponds to the specific value for continuous flow, or a corresponding pulse volume. For example, settings for a pulse mode are contained in the table below.

TABLE 1

Set-ting	Total Volume Pulse Range (cc/pulse)	Trigger Time (sec)	Pulse Flow Ramp Rate (sec)	Pulse Duration Max (sec)	Peak Pulse Flow (LPM)
1	10 to 12	.001 to .02	.03 to .07	.15	14
2	20 to 24	.001 to .02	.03 to .07	.20	14
3	30 to 36	.001 to .02	.03 to .07	.25	15
4	40 to 48	.001 to .02	.03 to .07	.30	16
5	50 to 60	.001 to .02	.03 to .07	.35	17

[0106] When the unit is set in pulse mode, product gas is dispensed only at the beginning of inhalation. In one embodiment, product dispensing valve 160 is only opened between zero and 0.4 seconds of the beginning of a breath of patient P. This controls the amount of oxygen removed from reservoir 158. In another embodiment, oxygen concentrator 100 is shut off if no pressure drop is sensed by nasal pressure sensor 190 for a set amount of time, such as two minutes, which in turn closes dispensing valve 160.

[0107] Patient P can temporarily increase (or "boost") the flow rate of oxygen by actuating boost control switch 272 on user interface 114. When boost switch 272 is activated, oxygen concentrator 100 increases the flow rate of oxygen for a set period of time, such as 10 minutes. After timing out, oxygen concentrator 100 returns to the previous setting. The boost function will not work if oxygen concentrator 100 is already operating at the maximum flow rate.

[0108] Indicator light 274 indicates power pack 108 is running low. Indicator light 276 indicates that there is a problem with separation cartridge 206, such as a bad connection with receptacle 208. In one embodiment, oxygen concentrator 100 contains three different colored lights: red, yellow, and green. The green light indicates that there are no problems detected with oxygen concentrator 100. A yellow flashing light or a yellow non-flashing light indicates a condition has been sensed that should be addressed. An example of such a condition is a low battery. A red flashing light indicates that a condition has been detected that requires an immediate response. A red non-flashing light indicates that oxygen concentrator 100 has failed, and has shut down. For example, if oxygen concentrator 100 fails to produce a stream of separated gas of eighty-five percent oxygen, oxygen concentrator 100 will detect this problem via breakthrough flow sensor 150. ECM 148 shuts off main valve 140 so no ambient air 162 is being submitted to the gas separation cartridge 206. Product gas is no longer being supplied to reservoir 158. After a few breaths, reservoir 158 will empty, triggering reservoir pressure sensor output 188 (shown in FIG. 5), which communicates to ECM 148 to shut down oxygen concentrator 100, and display the red warning light. This signals patient P that maintenance is needed. In addition to the aforementioned indicator lights, the unit may also contain a boost indicator light to indicate when a boost function is in operation. Similarly, an audible alarm maybe included in oxygen concentrator 100 to indicate failure.

[0109] FIG. 14 is a front view of the interior components of control module 112. Illustrated are drive 146, vacuum pump 144, drive speed reducer 142, and valve 140. Drive 146 includes a DC motor, driven by battery power pack 108, which supplies the necessary power to operate vacuum pump 144. The motor draws a maximum of 15 watts of power. Vacuum pump 144 is a positive displacement pump. In this embodiment, drive 146 runs both vacuum pump 144

and valve 140. Vacuum pump 144 is run by the motor at one speed, while valve 140 is run off the same motor but at a reduced speed. The reduction in speed is accomplished with gears that comprise drive speed reducer 142 between the motor of drive 146 and valve 140.

[0110] Valve 140 is a valve containing a minimum number of ports equal to two times the number of adsorbent beds (columns) in separation cartridge 206. Additionally, main valve 140 contains other ports for the inlet of ambient air 162, vacuum provided by vacuum pump 144, and recycling of product gas used to purge columns 130a-130c during repressurization. In the preferred embodiment, valve 140 is a rotary valve, but may also be a solenoid valve, directional control valve, or series of individual valves in communication with each other and each connected to an adsorbent column 130a-130c.

[0111] In an alternate embodiment, drive 146 may contain an independent motor for operating valve 140. If valve 140 is run by an independent motor, that motor is powered by power pack 108 and synchronized with the other motor(s) of drive 146 by ECM 148. As illustrated, drive 146 contains a single motor and valve 140 is connected to a system of gears that comprise drive speed reducer 142. Alternately, drive speed reducer 142 can be any common power transmission components such as pulley and belts, or gears and sprockets.

[0112] FIG. 15 is a perspective view of separation cartridge 206 contained within separation cartridge module 116. Illustrated are inlet ports 132a-132c, outlet ports 134a-134c, and casing 230. In the embodiment illustrated, three adsorption columns are contained within casing 230 with one inlet port 132a-132c, and one outlet port 134a-134c, for each adsorption column 130a-130c. Each adsorption column 130a-130c is a hermetically sealed container containing a bed of adsorption material, preferably a zeolite capable of adsorbing nitrogen gas, such as lithium low silica 13X zeolite. Each bed contains between five and twenty-five cubic centimeters of material, and in one embodiment contains fifteen (plus or minus one) cubic centimeters of material. The adsorbent bead size is a thirty by sixty mesh, wherein thirty mesh is equal to 0.0234 inches (0.0594 cm) and sixty mesh is equal to 0.01 inches (0.0254 cm).

[0113] Column inlet ports 132a-134c are connected to receive either ambient air 162 or vacuum, while outlet ports 134a-134c expel product gas or receive purge gas. This arrangement promotes ordering of gases within the columns 130a-130c by having oxygen rich gas always present at one end of the column. This results in improved efficiency as air flow through the columns 130a-130c creates an oxygen rich zone continuously at one end, which allows the vacuum to evacuate and desorb the previously adsorbed nitrogen where it is contained in the greatest concentration.

[0114] FIG. 16 is a perspective view of the columns 130a-130c and the filters 136 and 138 within casing 230 of separation cartridge 206. Illustrated are final product filter 138 connected to product gas outlet port 103 which connects to tubing 102, inlet air filter 136, and adsorbent columns 130a-130c each comprising spin inducers 280a-280f, adsorbent material 282a-282c, porous filters 284a-284f, and springs 286a-286c. Springs 286a-286c are coil springs that hold each adsorbent column in compression 130a-130c in place within casing 230 of separation cartridge 206 to prevent movement of adsorbent beads. Spin inducers 280a-280f help force even distribution of gases through columns 130a-130c, which helps to keep the MTZ well defined for more accurate detection.

[0115]   Adsorbent material 282a-282c is the same as that previously described. Filters 136 and 138 are constructed of common filtering materials and are used to remove dust and other large particulate matter from the air streams to assure that the flow of oxygen out to patient P is free of such materials. Porous filters 284a-284f are a small section of material commonly used as a particle filter provided at each end of columns 130a-130c. Porous filters 284a-284 fact to prevent adsorbent particles from contacting the mechanisms and valving of concentrator 100.

Docking Station 122 (FIGS. 17-18)

[0116]   FIG. 17 is a perspective view of the back side of oxygen concentrator 100 on docking station 122. Illustrated are oxygen concentrator 100 comprising power module 106, reservoir module 110, control module 112, and separation cartridge module 116, belt 104, and docking station 122 containing status display 288. Status display 288 is an LED, LCD, or similar digital display used to provide information to patient P such as time of day, time the concentrator has been used, time of recharging for power pack 108, or similar information. Additionally, docking station 122 may contain other controls (not illustrated) including a boost setting while the concentrator is docked, a mode switch for switching between pulse and continuous flow of oxygen, and indicator lights to show expected battery life, adsorbent column life, gas input, gas output, or gas separation system malfunctions, or other similar items that were previously described as part of user interface 114.

[0117]   FIG. 18 is a perspective view of the docking station 122 with oxygen concentrator 100 removed. Concentrator dock 126 is visible on docking station 122 with oxygen concentrator 100 removed. Concentrator dock 126 may optionally contain electrical connections (not illustrated) to charge power pack 108 contained within power module 106 while oxygen concentrator 100 is docked. Additionally, docking station 122 contains a power cord (not illustrated) available to connect to a wall socket or other power source such as a car utility plug. Docking station 122 uses power provided through the power cord to operate oxygen concentrator 100 and/or recharge power packs 108. Docking station 122 contains a flat bottom 290 to rest on a level surface and allow oxygen concentrator 100 to be in the docking station without moving. Alternately, docking station 122 is mountable to a wall in one embodiment, and is a free standing device that is set on a generally flat surface in another embodiment.

[0118]   In one embodiment, docking station 122 comprises indicator lights and control power switch (not illustrated) in addition to status display 288, power pack chargers 124a and 124b, and concentrator dock 126. Indicator lights provide information to patient P utilizing oxygen concentrator 100. Indicator lights will indicate if oxygen concentrator 100 is functioning properly, requires maintenance, or has failed. Control switch is a master switch for supplying or terminating power or controlling the setting of flow for oxygen concentrator 100. Status display 128 is an LED, LCD or similar digital display that can be used to indicate various information to patient P such as time of day, time oxygen concentrator 100 has been docked, time of recharging for the power pack, or similar information.

[0119]   Docking station 122 also contains power pack chargers 124a and 124b and concentrator dock 126. Docking station 122 contains a power cord (not illustrated) available to plug into a wall socket or a similar power pack. Docking station 122 converts AC power to recharge power pack 108

in power pack chargers 124a and 124b. Power pack chargers 124a and 124b contain contacts that are used to transfer power to power pack 108 while recharging. Alternatively, a power pack 108 placed in charger 124a or 124b is inductively coupled to recharge the power pack 108. Similarly, power is provided to oxygen concentrator 100 itself while on docking station 122, and to recharge of the power pack 108 (see FIG. 4) still attached to the oxygen concentrator 100. Concentrator dock 126 is shaped to provide a place to set oxygen concentrator 100 while docked, as well as facilitate easy removal of oxygen concentrator 100 for ambulatory use.

[0120]   In one embodiment, docking station 122 performs several functions with oxygen concentrator 100 docked. First, oxygen concentrator 100 is allowed to run without utilizing power pack 108 while it is docked. Second, a boost setting is available to increase the delivery rate of oxygen while oxygen concentrator 100 is docked. Boost switch 272 is located on user interface 114 (See FIG. 13). In an alternate embodiment, a boost switch is located on docking station 122. Upon removal of oxygen concentrator 100 from docking station 122, the boost setting is removed and oxygen concentrator 100 operates at a set delivery rate in either a continuous or pulse mode.

[0121]   Oxygen concentrator 100 contains flow setting switch 270 (FIG. 13), and a mode switch (not illustrated). The mode switch allows patient P to select continuous or pulse flow. In one embodiment, patient P is allowed to adjust the setting of oxygen concentrator 100 only while docked. That is, patient P can reprogram by changing a pulse setting (e.g., from 2 to 3), or continuous flow mode (e.g., from 1.0 to 1.5 liters per minute), only while oxygen concentrator 100 is on docking station 122. Patient P wishing to adjust settings will be required to hold the control switch while adjusting the flow setting dial or mode switch. In another embodiment, docking station 122 contains a switch automatically activated by placing oxygen concentrator 100 in docking station 122 which allows patient P to adjust flow setting. The requirement that settings can only be changed during docking prevents accidental switching of the flow mode of oxygen concentrator 100 during ambulatory use. For example, there is no change in flow if flow setting switch 130 is bumped, which would normally increase oxygen flow. If oxygen concentrator 100 can only be reprogrammed in docking station 122, oxygen concentrator 100 will remain in the preset mode set at docking station 122 and will not increase or decrease flow by a change of the setting. In one embodiment, the flow setting switch and mode switch are located on a user interface located directly on docking station 122.

[0122]   Another function of docking station 122 is to provide diagnostic features of the system. Docking station 122 may indicate expected battery life, adsorbent column life, or pump malfunctions through the use of indicator lights, or status display 128, or a combination of both. Alternatively, these items are located on user interface 114, or at a combination of locations of user interface 114 and docking station 122. For example, battery life indicator 142 is located directly on power pack 108 that comprises the battery itself, and battery problem warning light 274 is on user interface 114 also. Similarly, adsorbent cartridge warning light 276 is located on user interface 114, but may also be on either the cartridge module 116 or docking station 122 as well.

Concentrator Efficiency

[0123] Oxygen concentrator 100 can produce a stream of product gas containing a range of 85-95 percent oxygen which provides up to 5 liters per minute pulsed equivalent of product gas. By utilizing vacuum swing adsorption, the separation process phases are all performed at less than 1 atm.

[0124] Utilizing a vacuum to exhaust unwanted gas from adsorbent columns 130a-130c improves efficiency of the oxygen concentrator 100. Less power is required than pressure swing adsorption (PSA) or vacuum-pressure swing adsorption (VPSA), which results in a smaller battery and thus a lighter weight product. Oxygen concentrator 100 as disclosed weighs less than 3 pounds (1.4 kg) and occupies less than 1 liter of volume. Also, the efficiency of the system allows for oxygen concentrator 100 to operate for at least three hours while producing up to 5 liters per minute pulsed equivalent of product gas without requiring patient P to attend to the unit, e.g. changing the battery. Further, the low energy consumption causes less heat transfer. The product gas is discharged from the separation system at a temperature of ± six degrees Celsius from that of the ambient air. This eliminates the need for heat exchangers which add to the overall weight and reduces system efficiency. The amount of heat generated causes no discomfort to patient P wearing and utilizing the oxygen concentrator 100. Also, upon starting oxygen concentrator 100, the flow of product gas will increase from 21 percent oxygen (ambient) to 85 percent or more oxygen in under two minutes.

[0125] Improvements over the prior art are attained by regulating the device to only separate the amount of oxygen needed by patient P at any given time. The prior art separates a flow of oxygen and delivers that rate to patient P as a steady flow. Patient P is only inhaling this oxygen during about ⅓ of the normal breathing cycle. Within the inhalation portion of the breathing cycle, the volume of gas inhaled last stays in the dead space of the airways and is not presented to the alveoli. Therefore if oxygen is dispensed to patient P only during the early part of inhalation, less than ⅓ the steady flow is actually required. Moreover, prior art devices do not adjust the flow based on a patient P's needs, but operate at the same steady flow. The present concentrator slows down its entire cycle rate producing only the amount of oxygen needed. Thus, oxygen concentrator 100 retains a high oxygen recovery percentage at all product flow rates while minimizing energy consumption and maximizing adsorbent life. Patient P's actual needs vary with real time changes in activity. This causes a corresponding variation in breathing rate. Oxygen concentrator 100 tracks patient P's breathing rate and adjusts oxygen separation and delivery rates proportionally. In combination, these two features allow oxygen concentrator 100 to separate oxygen only at the rate it is being consumed, resulting in a reduction in the amount of oxygen needing to be separated for patient P.

[0126] Another improvement over the prior art involves reducing the waste of separated oxygen in the various adsorb and desorb cycle phases. This is typically referred to as maximizing product recovery. The primary system components become larger or smaller as the amount of oxygen separated increases or decreases. Therefore, a dramatic reduction in size and weight of the concentrator requires use of as much separated oxygen as possible by delivering it to

patient P rather than losing it to the waste stream. The prior art works by using the Skarstrom cycle well known to those skilled in the art.

[0127] During one phase of the Skarstrom cycle in PSA or VPSA, air is pumped into one end of a column of adsorbent pressurizing it above atmospheric pressure while oxygen is flowing out of the opposing end. Nitrogen is being adsorbed as the MTZ propagates toward the oxygen outlet end of the column. This phase is terminated before the MTZ breaks through into the oxygen stream so that oxygen purity is not diluted by the nitrogen rich air trailing the MTZ. If it is terminated earlier than necessary to maintain purity there will be substantial separated oxygen left in the column in front of the MTZ that is not passed to the patient. During the next cycle phase the column pressure is reduced to a lower cycle pressure desorbing the nitrogen that was adsorbed during the separation phase and it is passed to the waste stream. Some of the oxygen left in the column at higher pressure will also be passed to the waste stream as gas flows from the column when pressure is reduced. Recovery of separated oxygen can therefore be maximized by stopping the previous separation phase just short of breakthrough, leaving minimal oxygen in the column to be lost to the waste stream during the reduced pressure evacuation phase. The position of the MTZ needs to be accurately known to terminate the separation phase for optimal recovery without compromising purity. This position cannot be accurately estimated because its propagation rate is a function of many variables including product oxygen flow rate, high and low cycle pressures, temperature, adsorbent water content and the amount of other contaminants accumulated in the adsorbent. Prior art systems stop the separation phase well short of breakthrough to encompass worst case operating conditions without sacrificing purity and thereby waste separated oxygen in the evacuation phases during most typical non-worst case operating conditions.

[0128] Oxygen concentrator 100 determines the position of the MTZ just prior to breakthrough and terminates the flow from outlet 134 for the remainder of the feed phase or adjusts the motor speed, as previously described. Additional oxygen is left in the column at the end of a feed phase and is wasted during the evacuation phases. This is oxygen adsorbed by the adsorbent combined with oxygen present in the interstitial and dead spaces of the adsorbent and column. All adsorbents used in oxygen separators adsorb nitrogen, and also oxygen to some extent. The adsorbent used in oxygen concentrator 100 presents a very high ratio of adsorbed nitrogen to adsorbed oxygen. As the amount of oxygen adsorbed is minimized through the choice of an adsorbent with a low affinity for oxygen, the amount of adsorbent needed to separate a given amount of nitrogen during a separation phase will decrease as its affinity for nitrogen increases. The less adsorbent needed to adsorb a given amount of nitrogen, the less adsorbent there is to adsorb oxygen and the smaller the column can be with less interstitial and dead space.

[0129] For example, a LiLSX adsorbent referred to as Oxysiv MDX from UOP Corporation has a very high ratio of adsorbed nitrogen to adsorbed oxygen in the operating pressure range of oxygen concentrator 100. The Skarstrom cycle of the prior art uses a purge phase in which separated oxygen is fed back into the product end of the column while nitrogen rich gas is passing out of the opposing end of the column into the waste stream as the pressure transitions to the lower cycle pressure. While this purge can enhance product purity, some of the purge oxygen passes all the way through the column and is lost to the waste stream. Oxygen concentrator **100** using VSA achieves a measured 60% oxygen recovery rate, compared to a typical recovery rate of 30% for the prior art utilizing PSA.

[0130] Another improvement over the prior art concerns the choice of adsorbent and operating pressure range. The energy required by the separation process directly defines the weight and size of major components such as the battery, motor and gas pump of a concentrator. Minimizing the amount of adsorbent minimizes the amount of energy needed to separate a given amount of oxygen. Each adsorbent has a characteristic pair of isotherms that show the amount of oxygen and nitrogen a given mass of adsorbent will hold at equilibrium over a range of pressures and vacuums for these gasses at a constant temperature. The cycle phases of the system necessarily include the pumping of gas contained in volumes of adsorbent to produce a change in nitrogen partial pressure between a chosen higher pressure and a chosen lower pressure. The pneumatic energy a pump must deliver in the process of cycling a given volume of gas between a higher and a lower level is in direct proportion to the volume of gas pumped multiplied by the difference between the high and low vacuum levels. The isotherms for various adsorbent candidates specify the amount of nitrogen contained in a fixed mass of adsorbent at a fixed temperature as a function of nitrogen partial pressure.

[0131] An example of the isotherm for the LiLSX adsorbent Oxysiv MDX along with the isotherm for a typical 13X type adsorbent used in the prior art is shown in **FIG. 19**. Having minimized the amount of oxygen needed to be separated from air and having maximized the recovery percent of oxygen as previously disclosed, along with knowing the percentage of oxygen present in air prescribes a specific minimum amount of air that must be moved into the system to produce the needed oxygen. This minimum amount of air minus the maximized separated oxygen must pass out of the system as a minimized volume of waste gas. Oxygen concentrator **100** acts to minimize the flow rates of the air feed stream and the waste stream. This flow must be pumped across a pressure difference defined by the choice of high and low operating pressures requiring a pumping energy that is proportional to both the flow rate and the pressure difference. The gas streams are pumped into or out of the adsorbent during each complete cycle to produce the needed swing in pressure between high and low cycle pressure levels allowing the separation of nitrogen from oxygen. Minimizing the amount of gas being pumped through the system reduces the pumping energy in proportion to reductions in the difference between chosen high and low pressure points that the gas must be pumped across. The isotherm for nitrogen shows that nitrogen is transferred in or out of the adsorbent with the smallest change in pressure where the slope of the isotherm is the steepest. Using typical PSA, a ratio of high to low pressure levels in these systems needs to be 3:1 or greater to maintain the desired oxygen purity. Lower pressure ranges, i.e. sub-atmospheric or vacuum ranges used in VSA, allow this ratio to be maintained with less total difference between the high and low pressure levels.

[0132] For example, prior art operates between 1 and 3 atmospheres for a 3:1 ratio and a pressure difference between high and low levels of 2 atmospheres. Oxygen concentrator **100** using VSA operates between 0.3 atmo-

spheres and 1 atmosphere. A ratio of about 3.3:1 is achieved with a pressure difference of only 0.7 atmospheres. Operating on this range of the isotherm as seen in **FIG. 19** allows just as much nitrogen to be passed in and out of the LiLSX adsorbent with a 0.7 atmosphere pressure range as a PSA system does with 13X adsorbent and a 2.0 atmosphere pressure range. The LiLSX adsorbent allows a cycle pressure range that is nearly ⅓ that of a PSA system with a proportional reduction in pumping energy.

[0133] Oxygen concentrator **100** is a quiet device. When oxygen concentrator **100** is running, it produces a noise level in the range often to thirty decibels. Further, with the compact size of the parts, vacuum pump **144** is running continuously and there is very little vibration to affect a person using it docked or wearing it as an ambulatory device. The device of the present invention with the described components weighs less than three pounds (1.36 kg). The compact size (less than about 61 cu. in. (1000 cc)) allows for easy portability. Similarly, the small size does not disrupt counter space or storage when used at home. The device does give off some heat, however the outer case is less than 6 degrees Celsius higher than ambient when oxygen concentrator **100** is running on battery power. The device may emit more heat while it is docked and operating on AC power to charge the power pack **108**, but is still less than 15 degrees Celsius above ambient.

[0134] Based on the foregoing embodiments, the efficiency of the concentrator can be determined. One measure of efficiency is the ratio of oxygen produced to the amount of adsorbent material used to obtain the oxygen, represented by the following:

$$Qp = \text{Liter/min } O_2 \text{ produced}$$
$$Madsorbent = \text{Kg of Adsorbent Material}$$

for example, the disclosed embodiments include adsorbent columns **130a-130c**, with each column containing 15 cubic centimeters (cc) of adsorbent material with a density of 0.66 gm/cc. That is:

$$(3 \text{columns})\left(\frac{15cc}{\text{column}}\right)\left(\frac{0.66gm}{cc}\right) = 30gms \text{ for the system.}$$

The following flow rates (Qp) were obtained by the above disclosed concentrator:

$$Qpmax = 1.5 \text{ L/min}$$
$$Qpmin = 0.14 \text{ L/min}$$

[0135] This results in a range for kilograms of adsorbent material to oxygen flow rate of:

$$0.020 < \frac{Madsorbent}{Qp} < 0.214$$

[0136] Similarly, flow rates (Qp) were determined for a system that contains three adsorption columns, each column containing 15 cc of adsorbent material. The separation completed in a range of 0.3 atm to 0.95 atm. Values were calculated for breakthrough time, work, battery life, and flow rate. The volume of gas contained in a column at the end of a feed phase was 150 cc. These constants were used to determine the following measures of efficiency:

[0137] Work per evacuation cycle or pneumatic power requirements were determined based on the following calculations:

$$W(\text{work}) = (\text{volume moved}) * (\text{vacuum differences});$$

[0138] The vacuum differences are calculated as the vacuum pump is continuously changing gas out, and as vacuum progresses to end point. From this:

[0139] V_H=Vacuum upper level

[0140] V_L=Vacuum lower level

[0141] Vol=Volume of gas in the column at end of feed phase

$$W = Vol*(V_H - V_L)*(1 + (V_H/(V_H - V_L))*\ln(V_L/V_H) + \ln(V_H/V_L))$$

Inserting the above constants and converting to joules (multiply by 100.32 to get L*atm to joules) yields:

[0142] W=4.81 joules

[0143] Thus, 4.81 joules is required to evacuate the gas which desorbs during the evacuation phase. From experimentation, the following flow rates (LPM is liters per minute) and cycle times were recorded:

Qp (flow rate)	Low = .14 LPM
	Med = .720 LPM
	High = 1.5 LPM
Cycle time	Low = 5.6 sec.
	Med = 1.12 sec.
	High = .54 sec.

Power consumption can be determined by calculating work divided by the time of the cycle.

Low flow power=4.81 joule/5.6 sec=0.85 watts

Medium Flow power=4.81 joule/1.12 sec=4.29 watts

High flow power=4.81 joule/0.54 sec=8.9 watts

From the above, a measure of energy consumed to the flow rate can be made and used as an indicator of the system efficiency:

$$\text{Low: } \frac{.85w}{.14LPM} = 6.07w/LPM$$

$$\text{Medium: } \frac{4.29w}{.72LPM} = 5.95w/LPM$$

$$\text{High: } \frac{8.9w}{1.5LPM} = 5.93w/LPM$$

[0144] Another measure of efficiency is the ratio of mass of the power pack (Mpowerpack) compared to the amount of oxygen produced (Qp) over time:

$$\frac{Mpowerpack}{QpT(\text{time})}$$

The following constants are used in the calculation: the battery cell is a type **18650** lithium ion battery with 7.4

watts-hrs, measuring 42 g; motor efficiency is 90 percent; and vacuum pump efficiency is 80 percent.

Pneumatic work = 6W/L/min. Thus,

$$\text{Electric power} = \frac{6W/LPM}{(.9)(.8)} = 8.3W/LPM$$

Battery mass compared to energy consumption is:

$$\frac{42g}{7.4(\text{watt})(hr)}\left(\frac{1Kg}{1000g}\right)\frac{8.3\text{watt}}{LPM} = .047\frac{Kg}{LPM(HR)}$$

Total battery mass for the power pack can be determined from this equation. For example, if a patient requires the concentrator to run for four hours at setting of "3" and takes 20 breaths per minute (the medium flow rate):

$$(4hr) * \frac{.047kg}{LPM(hr)} .72LPM = .135kg$$

The mass of the batteries needed is 0.135 Kg. Assuming each battery cell is **42g** as previously stated, the number of batteries for the power pack can be calculated:

$$.135kg\left(\frac{1000g}{1kg}\right)\frac{\text{battery cell}}{42g} = 3.2\text{battery cells}$$

[0145] Although the present invention has been described with reference to preferred embodiments, workers skilled in the art will recognize that changes maybe made in form and detail without departing from the spirit and scope of the invention. For example, larger flow rates maybe achieved by scaling the concentrator components to achieve desired flow rates at the disclosed efficiencies.

1. A method of providing concentrated oxygen product gas to a patient, the method comprising:

producing product gas by a vacuum swing adsorption (VSA) process with an oxygen concentrator comprising a plurality of separation columns connected to a vacuum source driven by a motor;

pumping product gas separated by the concentrator to a product reservoir;

sensing the pressure of the product reservoir;

controlling the speed of the motor based on the sensed pressure;

delivering product gas to the patient.

2. The method of claim 1 wherein the VSA process comprises:

(a) introducing ambient air at atmospheric pressure into a first end of a column containing an adsorbent material that preferentially adsorbs nitrogen and removes oxygen-rich product gas out a second end of the column;

(b) evacuating the column through the first end to remove adsorbed gas from the column;

(c) repressurizing the column by introducing ambient air into the first end of the column until pressure within the column is near 1.0 atm; and

(d) repeating steps (a)-(c).

3. The method of claim 2 and further comprising:

introducing product gas into the column through the second end during a portion of step (c).

4. The method of claim 3 wherein introducing product gas occurs during an initial portion of step (c).

5. The method of claim 2 and further comprising:

terminating step (a) based upon a position of a mass transfer zone to prevent breakthrough of nitrogen-rich gas out the second end of the column.

5. The method of claim 1 wherein delivering the product gas to the patient occurs during a portion of the patients inhalation.

6. An oxygen concentrator comprising:

an oxygen reservoir;

a plurality of adsorbent columns, each having an inlet, an outlet and a bed of adsorbent material;

a vacuum pump for removing separated nitrogen rich gas from the column inlets;

a product control pump for pumping oxygen rich gas from the column outlets to the oxygen reservoir;

a control valve for controlling flow of fluids in and out of the columns;

a motor for driving the vacuum pump and control valve to produce vacuum swing adsorption (VSA) cycles in which oxygen-rich product gas is separated and accumulated in the reservoir;

a pressure sensor for providing a signal as a function of gas pressure in the oxygen reservoir; and

an electric control module (ECM) that receives a signal from the pressure sensor, and adjusts the speed of the motor based on the signal.

7. The oxygen concentrator of claim 6 wherein the oxygen concentrator has a volume of less than 1.0 liter.

8. The oxygen concentrator of claim 6 wherein the oxygen concentrator has a mass of less than 2.3 kg.

9. The oxygen concentrator of claim 6 wherein the oxygen concentrator has a mass of less than 1.4 kg.

10. The oxygen concentrator of claim 6 further comprising:

a rechargeable power source for actuating the control valve, motor, and ECM.

11. The oxygen concentrator of claim 6 wherein the adsorbent material comprises a zeolite which preferentially adsorbs nitrogen.

12. The oxygen concentrator of claim 6 wherein the control valve comprises a rotary valve.

13. The oxygen concentrator of claim 6 further comprising an oxygen conserver connected to the oxygen reservoir.

14. An oxygen concentrator comprising:

an oxygen gas separator for producing oxygen-rich product gas from air;

a reservoir for storing product gas from the separator;

a delivery system for delivering product gas from the reservoir to a patient; and

a control for controlling production of product gas by the separator as a function of product gas delivered from the reservoir.

15. The oxygen concentrator of claim 14 further comprising:

an oxygen conserver connected to the reservoir.

16. The oxygen concentrator of claim 14 wherein the oxygen gas separator utilizes vacuum swing adsorption to produce the oxygen-rich product gas.

17. The oxygen concentrator of claim 14 wherein the oxygen concentrator has a volume of less than 1.0 liter.

18. The oxygen concentrator of claim 14 wherein the oxygen concentrator has a mass of less then 2.3 kg.

19. The oxygen concentrator of claim 14 wherein the oxygen concentrator has a mass of less then 1.4 kg.

20. The oxygen concentrator of claim 14 wherein the oxygen gas separator comprises a plurality of gas separation columns, each column including a first filter, a bed of adsorbent material, and a second filter encased within the column.

21. The oxygen concentrator of claim 20 wherein the bed of adsorbent material comprises a zeolite that preferentially adsorbs nitrogen.

22. The oxygen concentrator of claim 14 and further comprising:

a pressure sensor for providing a reservoir pressure signal as a function of product gas pressure in the reservoir; and

wherein the control controls production of product gas as a function of product gas delivered based on the reservoir pressure signal.

* * * * *

APPENDIX B

United States Design Patent

(12) **United States Design Patent**
Fosse et al.

(10) Patent No.: **US D626,014 S**
(45) Date of Patent: ** Oct. 26, 2010

---

(54) **EGG CLAMSHELL CONTAINER**

(75) Inventors: **David B. Fosse**, Saint Francis, MN (US);
Daniel K. Fosse, Cambridge, MN (US)

(73) Assignee: **Lindar Corporation**, Baxter, MN (US)

(**) Term: **14 Years**

(21) Appl. No.: **29/348,863**

(22) Filed: **Feb. 16, 2010**

(51) LOC (9) Cl. **09–03**
(52) U.S. Cl. **D9/757**; D9/762
(58) **Field of Classification Search** D9/762,
D9/757, 737, 761, 420, 425, 426, 456; D7/611;
206/521, 521.1, 521.3, 521.4, 521.6, 521.8,
206/521.9, 564; 220/508; 229/406
See application file for complete search history.

(56) **References Cited**

U.S. PATENT DOCUMENTS

D385,780 S	*	11/1997	Krupa et al. D9/757
D466,802 S	*	12/2002	Davkovski D9/757
D484,796 S	*	1/2004	Buckley D9/757
D491,463 S	*	6/2004	Zelina et al. D9/757
D506,932 S	*	7/2005	Ramirez D9/737
D514,954 S	*	2/2006	Kim D9/757
D520,377 S	*	5/2006	Beese et al. D9/762
D606,421 S	*	12/2009	Krummenacher D9/757

* cited by examiner

Primary Examiner—Mark A Goodwin
(74) *Attorney, Agent, or Firm*—Kinney & Lange, P.A.

(57) **CLAIM**

The ornamental design for an egg clamshell container, as shown and described.

DESCRIPTION

FIG. 1 is an isometric view of an egg clamshell container in an open position;

FIG. 2 is a right side view of the egg clamshell container in an open position;

FIG. 3 is a left side view of the egg clamshell container in an open position;

FIG. 4 is a front view of the egg clamshell container in an open position;

FIG. 5 is a rear view of the egg clamshell container in an open position;

FIG. 6 is a top view of the egg clamshell container in an open position;

FIG. 7 is a bottom view of the egg clamshell container in an open position;

FIG. 8 is an isometric view of the egg clamshell container in a closed position;

FIG. 9 is a right side view of the egg clamshell container in a closed position;

FIG. 10 is a left side view of the egg clamshell container in a closed position;

FIG. 11 is a front view of the egg clamshell container in a closed position;

FIG. 12 is a rear view of the egg clamshell container in a closed position;

FIG. 13 is a top view of the egg clamshell container in a closed position; and,

FIG. 14 is a bottom view of the egg clamshell container in a closed position.

1 Claim, 9 Drawing Sheets

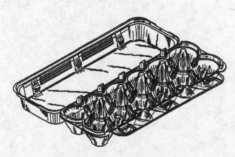

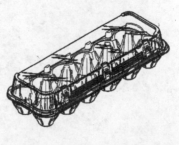

773

IP LAW FOR BUSINESS LAWYERS

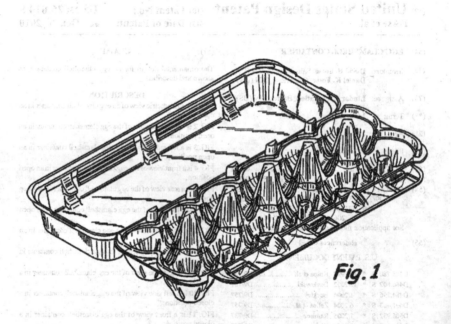

Fig. 1

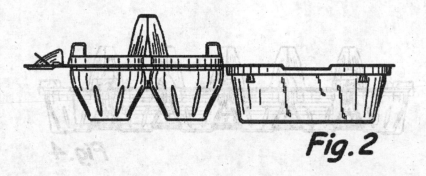

Fig.2

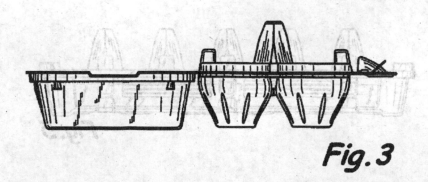

Fig.3

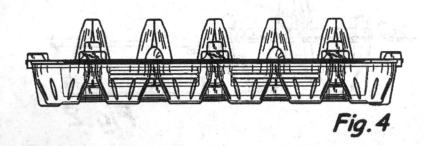

Fig. 4

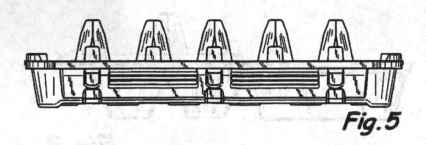

Fig. 5

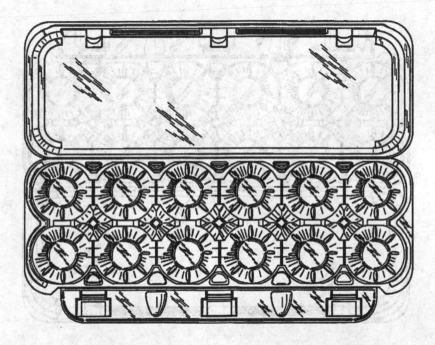

Fig.6

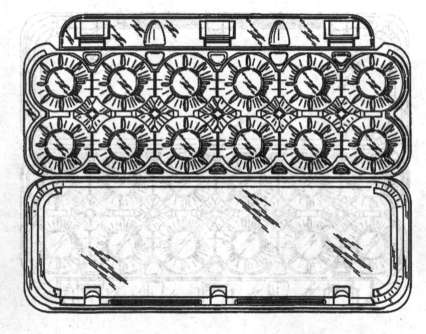

Fig.7

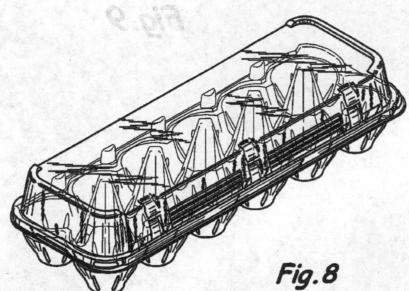

Fig.8

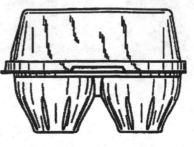

Fig.9

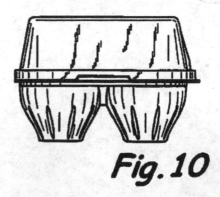

Fig.10

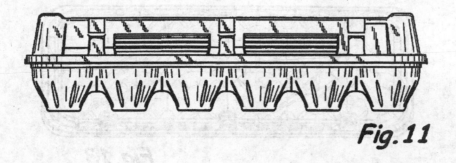

Fig. 11

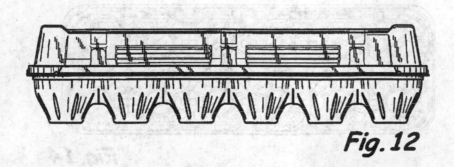

Fig. 12

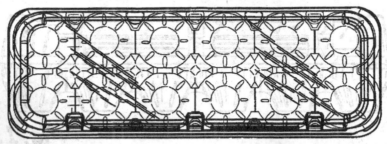

Fig. 13

Fig. 14

APPENDIX C

United States Plant Patent

(12) **United States Plant Patent**
Luby et al.

(10) Patent No.: **US PP16,478 P3**
(45) **Date of Patent:** **Apr. 25, 2006**

(54) **GRAPE PLANT NAMED 'FRONTENAC GRIS'**

(50) Latin Name: *Vitis* spp hybrid
Varietal Denomination: Frontenac gris

(75) Inventors: **James Luby**, St. Paul, MN (US); **Peter Hemstad**, Edina, MN (US)

(73) Assignee: **Regents of the University of Minnesota**, Minneapolis, MN (US)

(*) Notice: Subject to any disclaimer, the term of this patent is extended or adjusted under 35 U.S.C. 154(b) by 214 days.

(21) Appl. No.: **10/775,435**

(22) Filed: **Feb. 10, 2004**

(65) **Prior Publication Data**

US 2004/0237158 P1 Nov. 25, 2004

Related U.S. Application Data

(60) Provisional application No. 60/446,660, filed on Feb. 11, 2003.

(51) **Int. Cl.**
A01H 5/00 (2006.01)

(52) **U.S. Cl.** **Plt./205**
(58) **Field of Classification Search** Plt./205
See application file for complete search history.

Primary Examiner—Anne Marie Grunberg
(74) *Attorney, Agent, or Firm*—Penny J. Aguirre

(57) **ABSTRACT**

The invention is a new and distinct variety of grape plant designated 'Frontenac gris', which produces gray colored fruit suitable for white wine production, and has a combination of high wine quality, excellent cold hardiness and disease resistance, and very good productivity.

4 Drawing Sheets

1

Botanical classification: *Vitis* spp hybrid.
Variety denomination: 'Frontenac gris'.

BACKGROUND OF THE INVENTION

Most grape varieties used for production of high quality wines around the world are of the species *Vitis vinifera*. These *V. vinifera* varieties, when cultivated in northern regions of the United States with a continental climate, are often subject to serious injury or death from low temperatures during winter. Although several wild *Vitis* species occur in colder regions of North America and eastern Asia, the wine made from these species generally has serious defects. Thus, there is a need for grape varieties that are winter hardy, yet produce fruit capable of yielding high quality wine. A grape breeding program at the University of Minnesota has been engaged in developing such varieties since the early 1980s.

BRIEF SUMMARY OF THE INVENTION

'Frontenac gris' is a variety of grape (*Vitis* hybrid) with gray (or gris, in French) colored fruit suitable for white wine production, and is well adapted to the Upper Midwest climate of the United States. 'Frontenac gris' has an unusual combination of high wine quality, excellent cold hardiness and disease resistance, and very good productivity. 'Frontenac gris' was originally identified as a sport of 'Frontenac' (unpatented), a variety of grape of hybrid origin with bluish black colored fruit with red juice suitable for red wine production that was introduced in 1996 by the grape breeding program at the University of Minnesota Horticultural Research Center (HRC) in Carver County, Minn.

'Frontenac gris' propagates readily from hardwood cuttings, with young vines quick to become established, and all 'Frontenac gris' plants propagated in this manner have been genetically stable, producing only gray colored fruit with clear juice. As grown in east central Minnesota, the plants of 'Frontenac gris' are vigorous, productive, and

2

winter hardy. The vines of 'Frontenac gris' have relatively few tendrils and an open growth habit well suited to upper cordon training systems. The budbreak and bloom of 'Frontenac gris' are early to midseason, and its flowers are perfect and self-fertile. 'Frontenac gris' vines typically set a moderate to heavy crop. The fruit of 'Frontenac gris' is borne on medium sized clusters that are usually somewhat loose, and the berries are small and gray with a waxy bloom at maturity. Berry splitting and bunch rots have rarely been observed, even under wet conditions in the autumn harvest season. In some years, over-cropping may occur and cluster thinning may be required. In east central Minnesota, the fruit typically ripens around September 29, about three days after fruit of the 'Seyval' variety (unpatented), and at harvest is usually relatively high in both sugar and acidity. When grown in Minnesota, the fruit of 'Frontenac gris' has a high titratable acidity which usually requires either malolactic fermentation or residual sugar in order to produce a well balanced wine, and when grown in regions experiencing greater degree day accumulations, the acidity has been substantially lower.

The fruit of 'Frontenac gris' can be fermented to produce either white table wine or dessert wine, and such wines have been well received in various tastings. The wine tends to have good body and pleasant aromas, with very little of the herbaceous qualities associated with *V. riparia* and many interspecific grape hybrids. 'Foxy aromas' derived from *V. labrusca* have not been detected. The most common aroma component identified by tasters has been peach, but apricot, citrus, and tropical fruit aromas have also been noted. At times the wine may exhibit a slightly pink or peach coloration derived from the lightly pigmented skin of the fruit.

'Frontenac gris', like 'Frontenac', has exhibited resistance to several important diseases in evaluations. Even under conditions of high disease pressure, 'Frontenac gris' is highly resistant to downy mildew (*Plasmopara viticola*) on both the foliage and the fruit. 'Frontenac gris' is moderately

US PP16,478 P3

<table>
<tr><td>3</td><td>4</td></tr>
</table>

resistant to powdery mildew (*Uncinula necator*), which has been observed frequently at low levels on the foliage, but has not been seen on the fruit. 'Frontenac gris' is moderately resistant to black rot (*Guignardia bidwellii*), which has been observed sporadically and at low levels on the foliage and the fruit. Anthracnose (*Elsinoe ampelina*) has rarely been observed on the foliage and fruit of 'Frontenac gris'. 'Frontenac gris' is susceptible to the foliar form of grape phylloxera (*Daktulosphaira vitifoliae*) while tolerant to the root form of this disease. 'Frontenac gris' is tolerant to the adverse effects of phenoxy herbicide drift.

'Frontenac gris' has proven to be sufficiently cold hardy for consistent production in east central Minnesota where temperatures frequently reach –35° C. during the winter season. Field tests have shown 'Frontenac gris' to be at least as cold hardy as the 'Marachal Foch' variety (unpatented), and substantially cold hardier than the 'Seyval' variety and most other presently available grape cultivars used for wine production.

BRIEF DESCRIPTION OF THE FIGURES

The accompanying color photographs were taken in mid September and represent typical mature berry clusters and vines of 'Frontenac gris' and 'Frontenac' as grown under standard field conditions in Excelsior, Minn.

The Photograph in FIG. 1 is a close-up view of clusters of berries of 'Frontenac gris'.

The photographs in FIG. 1 and FIG. 3 provide a comparison between the berry clusters of 'Frontenac gris' (FIG. 2) and 'Frontenac' (FIG. 3).

FIG. 4 and FIG. 5 are photographs comparing mature vines of 'Frontenac gris' and 'Frontenac', respectively.

FIG. 6 is a drawing taken from Dettweiler E., 1991, 'Preliminary Minimal Descriptor List for Grapevine Varieties', Institut fur Rebenzüchtung, Geilweilerhof, Germany: N1 is the length along the primary vein (midrib) from the tip of the blade to the petiole sinus, N2 is the length of the vein from the tip of the first major lobe of the blade to the petiole sinus, N3 is the length of the vein from the tip of the second major lobe of the blade to the petiole sinus, N4 is the length of the vein from the tip of the third major lobe of the blade to where it joins the vein measured in N3, N5 in the length of the vein from the tip of the first tooth proximal to the petiole sinus to where it joins the vein measured in N4.

The colors in the photographs are as close as possible with the photographic and printing technology utilized. The color values cited in the detailed botanical description accurately describe the colors of the new grape.

DETAILED BOTANICAL DESCRIPTION

'Frontenac gris' arose from the spontaneous mutation of the 'Frontenac' variety in 1992. 'Frontenac' arose from a controlled cross as part of the grape breeding program at the University of Minnesota Horticultural Research Center (HRC) in Carver County, Minn., and originated from the cross designated GE 7828 and made in 1978 between the French hybrid variety 'Landot 4511' (unpatented) and the University of Minnesota *Vitis riparia* clone #89 found growing wild near Jordan, Minn. The 'Frontenac' parental variety was originally tested as MN 1047 and is described in *The Brooks and Olmo Register of New Fruit and Nut Varieties*, Third Edition, 1997, p. 265.

'Frontenac gris' originated as a single cane sport bearing gray colored fruit on a plant of the bluish black fruited 'Frontenac' variety growing at location Block 10 Row 16 Panel 7 at the HRC in 1992. When ripe, the berries of 'Frontenac gris' are gray and contain only slight amounts of anthocyanin pigment, whereas the 'Frontenac' parental variety produces highly pigmented dark bluish black berries. A total of 8 vines of 'Frontenac gris' were asexually propagated by hardwood cuttings from this original cane and planted at the HRC as follows: 2 plants were planted in 1995 in Block 10 Row 17 Panel 11; 3 plants were planted in 1996 in Block 18 Row 8 Panel 3; and 3 plants were planted in 1999 in Block 18 Row 11 Panel 5. These plants were observed through 2002, including their flowers and fruit, and were indistinguishable in appearance from the original 'Frontenac gris' cane. Therefore, the asexual progeny of 'Frontenac gris' are stable and reproduced true to type in successive generations.

The following data pertain to vines grown at the University of Minnesota Horticultural Research Center in Carver County, Minn. near Excelsior. For comparison purposes, data were collected for certain morphological descriptors from fruit of the variety 'Seyval', a grape variety commonly grown in Minnesota and the eastern United States for the production of white wine. Alphanumeric color designations refer to values based on the 1995 R.H.S. Colour Chart published by The Royal Horticultural Society, London, England. Many of the descriptors are based on those set forth by the International Board for Plant Genetic Resources in collaboration with the Office Internationale de la Vigne et du Vin (OIV) and the International Union for the Protection of New Varieties of Plants.

When dimensions, sizes, colors and other characteristics are given, it is to be understood that such characteristics are approximations set forth as accurately as possible. Variations of the usual magnitude incident to climatic factors, fertilization, pruning, pest control and other cultural practices are to be expected.

A) Mature Canes

The values presented are the means (with ranges in parentheses) of 10 canes observed from the 2002 growing season.

1. Color of canes: Striated, reddish brown. RHS colors 166A, 166C.
2. Internode length at base: 2.4 cm (2.1–3.0).
3. Internode length at midpoint: 9.3 cm (7.5–12.2).
4. Lenticels present: Yes (very small).
5. Lenticel color: 200A.
6. Cane cross-section shape: Elliptical.
7. Density of hairs on mature cane: None.
8. Tendril pattern on shoot: 2, 0, 2, 0 etc. (two nodes with a tendril followed by one node without).
9. Tendrils forked: Yes.
10. Tendril texture: Striated.
11. Tendril length: 15 cm (11–20).
12. Tendril color: 166C.
13. Bud width: 3.8 mm (3.1–5.0).
14. Bud shape: Triangular.
15. Bud color: 166B.

B) Trunk

The observations presented are from the 2002 growing season.

1. Bark texture: Somewhat flaky, small vertical segments approx. 1–2 cm.×4–6 cm.
2. Bark color: Silver-gray. RHS colors 201B, 201C.

5

6

C) Mature Leaves

Ten representative mature leaves from above the clusters in the middle third of the shoot were examined. The leaves were pressed and dried for later analysis. The values presented below are means (with ranges in parentheses) from collections in September 2000. Descriptors of mature leaves, including the designations N1 through N5, relate to "OIV—Code Numbers 065–093" of *Preliminary Minimal Descriptor List for Grapevine Varieties* (Dettweiler E., 1991, Instit üt fur Rebenzüchtung, Geilweilerhof, Germany).

		'Frontenac gris'
1.	Length of blade:	15.3 cm (13.3–18.3)
2.	Width of blade:	15.5 cm (12.5–18.2)
3.	Shape of blade:	circular-kidney shaped
4.	Number of lobes:	4.4 (3–5)
5.	Length of vein N1:	12.6 cm (10.5–15.0)
6.	Length of vein N2:	11.5 cm (9.7–13.5)
7.	Length of vein N3:	8.5 cm (7.3–9.3)
8.	Length of vein N5:	4.2 cm (2.9–5.5)
9.	Length of N2 teeth:	13.3 mm (10–16)
10.	Width of N2 teeth:	14.0 mm(11–16)
11.	Length/width ratio of N2 teeth:	0.96 (0.71–1.1)
12.	Length of N4 teeth:	8.2 mm (7–9)
13.	Width of N4 teeth:	11.9 mm (10–18)
14.	Length/width ratio of N4 teeth:	0.71 (0.5–0.9)
15.	Shape of teeth:	rectilinear-convex
16.	Shape of petiolar sinus:	wide open
17.	Shape of base of petiolar sinus:	u-shaped
18.	Depth of petiolar sinus:	22.4 mm (17–29)
19.	Width of petiolar sinus:	48.6 mm (39–61)
20.	Length of petioles:	7.2 cm (4.7–9.6)
21.	Shape of upper sinuses:	open
22.	Shape of base of upper sinuses:	u-shaped
23.	Pubescence on adaxial surface:	none
24.	Pubescence on abaxial surface:	very sparse on main veins and at petiolar junction
25.	Color of adaxial leaf surface:	146B, yellow-green
26.	Color of abaxial leaf surface:	146C, yellow-green
27.	Color of leaf Petiole	59C, red-purple

D) Young Shoots

The observations presented are from the 2002 growing season.

		'Frontenac gris'
1.	Form of shoot tip:	closed by small leaves
2.	Density of prostate hairs on tip:	none
3.	Density of erect hairs on tip:	very sparse
4.	Petiole pigmentation:	dark red on adaxial, light red on abaxial
5.	Shoot pigmentation:	adaxial striped to solid purple, abaxial striped

E) Flowers

1. Fragrance: Moderately fragrant.
2. Mean time of flowering: June 14 when grown in Excelsior, Minn.
3. Color of petal: 145A, yellow-green.
4. Color of sepal: 144A, yellow-green.

5. Color of pollen: 4B, yellow.
6. Petal number: 5, fused in calyptra.
7. Petal shape: Cohering at summit and separating at base: 2.5 mm long; 1 mm wide at fused end; reflexed after dehiscence from flower.
8. Shape of cluster: Somewhat conical, typically with one shoulder.
9. Size of cluster: 14.5 cm long (range 10.1–19.8); 6.3 cm wide (range 3.6–11.1).
10. Number of flowers per cluster: 190 (range 111–278).
11. Size of individual entire flower: 5.6 mm long; 4.1 mm wide.
12. Pollen fertility: Yes, based on use in controlled pollinations.
13. Color of stamen: Anther: 162C, grayed-yellow. Filament: 155A, white.
14. Stamen number: 4.9 (range 4–6).
15. Pistil number: 1 per flower.
16. Pistil length: 2.5 mm.
17. Color of pistil: 144A, yellow-green.

F) Fruit

The values presented below are means (with ranges in parentheses) from fruit observed in the 2000 growing season, except for those traits indicated (**), which are means from the 2000–2003 growing seasons for 'Frontenac gris' and from the 1995 and 1999–2002 growing seasons for 'Seyval'.

		'Frontenac gris'	'Seyval'
1.	Cluster length:	17.4 cm (14.7–22.4)	12.1 cm (9.0–15.1)
2.	Cluster weight**	137.1 g (88–193)	162.4 g (92–298)
3.	Cluster density:	loose-medium	medium
4.	Berry weight:**	1.13 g (1.02–1.09)	1.90 g (1.59–2.22)
5.	Berry length:	11.4 mm (10.2–12.1)	13.8 mm (12.2–15.4)
6.	Berry diameter at equator:	11.3 mm (10.1–12.2)	13.3 mm (12.1–15.3)
7.	Berry shape:	roundish	roundish
8.	Berry cross-section:	circular	circular
9.	Berry, color of skin:	gray-golden RHS color 151A Intermediate between 199C and 201C.	yellow-green
10.	Berry, color of flesh:	light green RHS colors 160A, 160B	light green RHS color 150D
11.	Berry, particular flavor:	lightly fruity (peach, kiwi)	neutral
12.	Length of pedicel:	5.7 mm	6.2 mm
13.	Berry, separation from pedicel:	difficult	difficult
14.	Berry, presence of seeds:	fully developed	fully developed
15.	Seed number/berry:	2.4 (2–4)	2.2 (1–4)
16.	Seed length:	0.53 mm (0.50–0.55)	0.59 mm (0.54–0.65)
17.	Seed width:	0.33 mm (0.31–0.36)	0.39 mm (0.35–0.46)
18.	Seed length/width ratio:	1.61	1.51
19.	Seed weight:	0.023 g	0.031 g
20.	Seed color:	RHS color 165A	RHS color 177A

G) Harvest Parameters

Values represent the means (with ranges in parentheses) for fruit harvested over four growing seasons (1999–2003) for 'Frontenac gris' and six growing seasons (1995, 1996, 1999–2002) for 'Seyval'.

US PP16,478 P3

7

	'Frontenac gris'	'Seyval'
1. Harvest date:	9/29 (9/18–10/5)	9/26 (9/16–10/6)
2. Brix:	26.30° (24.6°-26.8°)	20.9°(18.6°–23.2°)
3. pH:	3.06 (2.85–3.18)	3.11 (2.91–3.41)
4. % titratable acidity:	1.22% (1.06–1.41%)	0.86% (0.72–1.02%)

H) Vineyard Performance

Based on observations compiled over four years (1999–2003).

1. Susceptibility to powdery mildew (*Uncinula necator*): Moderate.
2. Susceptibility to downy mildew (*Plasmopara viticola*): Very low.
3. Susceptibility to black rot (*Guignardia bidwellii*): Low-moderate.
4. Susceptibility to bunch rot (*Botrytis*, etc): Very low.
5. Susceptibility to foliar phylloxera (*Daktulosphaira vitifoliae*): Moderate-severe.
6. Susceptibility to crown gall (*Agrobacterium tumefaciens*): No natural infection observed.

8

7. Susceptibility to phenoxy herbicide drift (e.g., 2,4-D): Low.
8. Berry splitting: Low.
9. Berry shelling: Low.
10. Vigor level: High.
11. Winter hardiness: High, trunks have survived –38° C.
12. Wood ripening: Very good.

I) Wine Quality

Descriptions below are compiled from observations on wine made from 'Frontenac gris' fruit harvested during the 1999–2003 growing seasons.

1. Flavors and aromas: Peach, apricot, citrus, tropical fruit; no 'hybrid', herbaceous, or labrusca aromas.
2. Balance: Good body, well balanced when finished with residual sugar or put through malolactic fermentation.
3. Color: Attractive light pink/peach unless filtered or fined.
4. Propensity for oxidation: Low.
5. Overall quality: Very good.

What is claimed is:

1. A new and distinct variety of grape plant designated 'Frontenac gris' as described and illustrated herein.

* * * * *

Figure One

Figure Two

Figure Three

Figure Four

Figure Five

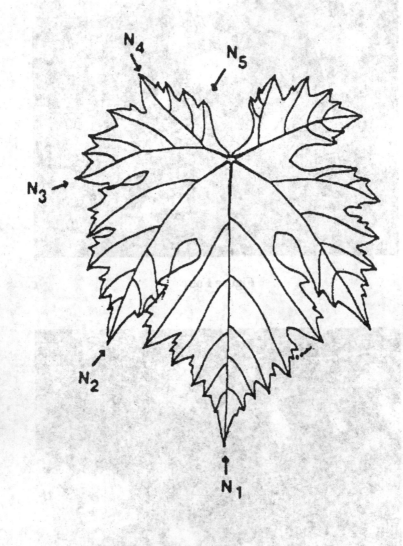

Figure Six

APPENDIX D

Comparison of Post-Grant Patent Proceedings

	Reissue	Supplemental Examination	*Ex Parte* Reexamination	*Inter Partes* Review	Post-Grant Review	Covered Business Method Review
Initiator	Patent owner	Patent owner	Patent owner or third party	Third party	Third party	Infringement defendant
Grounds	Patent is wholly or partly inoperative or invalid, or overly broad or narrow in scope	Any information relevant to patentability (e.g. new art)	§ 102 and 103 invalidity based on patents and printed publications	§ 102 and 103 invalidity based on patents and printed publications	Any grounds	Any grounds, with some prior art limitations for pre-AIA cases.
Threshold Standard	Wholly or partially inoperative or invalid through error	Substantial new question of patentability	Substantial new question of patentability	Substantial likelihood of success with respect to at least one challenged claim	More likely than not that at least one challenged claim is unpatenatable	More likely than not that at least one challenged claim is unpatenatable
Filing window	During lifetime of patent, but broadening reissue must be filed within 2 years of grant	During lifetime of patent	During enforceability of patent (typically life + 6 years)	Later of 9 months after issuance or after termination of Post-Grant Review	Within 9 months of issuance	Before September 16, 2020 and after lawsuit commenced
Estoppel	None	None	None	Real party in interest; grounds that were raised and considered, or could have been raised, in the proceeding	Real party in interest; grounds that were raised and considered, or could have been raised, in the proceeding	Real party in interest; grounds that were raised and considered.
Adjudicator	Original examiner, if available	Original examiner, if available	Examiner from central reexam unit	Patent Trial and Appeal Board	Patent Trial and Appeal Board	Patent Trial and Appeal Board

APPENDIX E

Patent Infringement Complaint

UNITED STATES DISTRICT COURT
FOR THE DISTRICT OF MINNESOTA

)	
)	
)	Civil Action No. _____
)	
Horton, Inc.,)	
)	
Plaintiff,)	
)	**COMPLAINT FOR**
v.)	**PATENT INFRINGEMENT**
)	
)	
Kit Masters Inc.,)	
)	
Defendant.)	
)	(JURY TRIAL DEMANDED)
)	
)	

Plaintiff, Horton, Inc. ("Horton"), for its complaint against Defendant, Kit Masters

Inc. ("Kit Masters"), alleges as follows:

THE PARTIES

1.   Plaintiff Horton is a domestic corporation organized under the laws of the

state of Minnesota having a principal place of business at 2565 Walnut Street, Roseville,

MN 55113.

2.   Upon information and belief, Defendant Kit Masters is a corporation

organized under the laws of the state of Minnesota having a principal place of business at

825 1st Street NE, Perham, MN 56573.

- 1 -

JURISDICTION AND VENUE

3.   This is an action for patent infringement under the patent laws of the United States, 35 U.S.C. §1 *et seq.*, and particularly 35 U.S.C. §271.

4.   This court has subject matter jurisdiction under 28 U.S.C. §§1331 and 1338(a).

5.   Upon information and belief, defendant Kit Masters transacts and has transacted business throughout the United States, and has committed tortious acts within the State of Minnesota, causing injury to Horton in the State of Minnesota, thereby establishing sufficient minimum contacts. This Court has personal jurisdiction over Kit Masters by reason of its presence within the State of Minnesota as well as by reason of committing acts of infringement, inducement to infringe and/or contributory infringement within the State of Minnesota and this judicial district.

6.   Venue in the United States District Court for the District of Minnesota is proper pursuant to 28 U.S.C. §§1391(c) and 1400(b) because Kit Masters is a corporation over which the Court has personal jurisdiction, and because Kit Masters has an established place of business in that judicial district.

COUNT I: INFRINGEMENT OF U.S. PATENT NO. 5,636,719

7.   Horton incorporates and re-alleges paragraphs 1 through 6.

8.   On June 10, 1997, U.S. Patent No. 5,636,719 entitled "Rotational Control Apparatus" ("the '719 patent") was duly and legally issued to assignee Horton. A true and correct copy of the '719 patent is attached as Exhibit A to the Complaint.

-2-

9.   Horton is the owner by assignment of the entire right, title, and interest in and to the '719 patent with the right to sue for past, present, and future infringement of the '719 patent.

10.   Upon information and belief, Kit Masters has been and is making, using, selling, offering for sale, and/or importing, without license or authority from Horton, in this district and elsewhere in the United States, clutch components that embody the invention(s) claimed in the '719 patent, and has been and is infringing the '719 patent under 35 U.S.C. §271.

11.   Attached as Exhibit B is a true and correct copy of a Kit Masters promotional flyer entitled "Kit Masters 2-Speed Conversion Kits" distributed in 2008 that depicts at least one clutch product that infringes the '719 patent.

12.   Upon information and belief, Kit Masters will continue to directly infringe, contributorily infringe, and/or induce infringement of the '719 patent unless enjoined by the Court.

13.   Upon information and belief, Horton has been damaged by Kit Masters' infringement of the '719 patent, and will continue to be damaged by that infringement unless enjoined by this court.

14.   Upon information and belief, Kit Masters has actual knowledge of the full contents of the '719 patent, and its prior and continuing infringement of the '719 patent was and is willful and deliberate.

PRAYER FOR RELIEF

WHEREFORE, Plaintiff, Horton, prays for the following relief:

a.   That Kit Masters, its officers, agents, servants, employees and attorneys, and all persons in active concert or participation with them be found to have infringed the valid U.S. Patent No. 5,636,719, and be enjoined, preliminarily and permanently, from making, using, selling, offering for sale or importing into the United States products and components which infringe U.S. Patent No. 5,636,719;

b.   That Horton be compensated by Kit Masters for the damages caused by Kit Masters' infringement of U.S. Patent No. 5,636,719 under 35 U.S.C. §284, in an amount to be determined by an accounting, but not less than a reasonable royalty, plus interest;

c.   That the award of damages for infringement of U.S. Patent No. 5,636,719 be trebled as provided for by 35 U.S.C. §284 for willful infringement by Kit Masters;

d.   That Horton be awarded its costs and attorneys' fees incurred in prosecuting this exceptional case, as provided for by 35 U.S.C. §285, plus interest; and

e.   That Horton be awarded such other relief as the Court deems just and proper.

-4-

JURY DEMAND

Horton demands a jury trial on all issues so triable.

Dated: 4/20/09　　　　　　　By: _David R. Fairbairn signature_

David R. Fairbairn (28,125)
Alan M. Koenck (268,926)
Austen P. Zuege (330,267)
KINNEY & LANGE, P.A.
The Kinney & Lange Building
312 South Third Street
Minneapolis, MN 55415-1002
(612) 339-1863

**ATTORNEYS FOR PLAINTIFF
HORTON, INC.**

APPENDIX F

Patent Infringement Answer and Counterclaim

IN THE UNITED STATES DISTRICT COURT
FOR THE WESTERN DISTRICT OF WISCONSIN

MUELLER SPORTS MEDICINE, INC. A Wisconsin corporation,	)))	**Civil Action No. 02 C 0445 C – BBC/SLC**
Plaintiff,	))	
v.	)))	
CORE PRODUCTS INTERNATIONAL, INC. A Minnesota corporation,	))))	
Defendant.	)))	

ANSWER AND COUNTERCLAIMS

Defendant Core Products International, Inc. ("Core Products"), for its answer to plaintiff's

Complaint, states as follows:

GENERAL DENIAL

Core Products denies each and every allegation in the Complaint, unless the allegation is

specifically or otherwise pleaded.

SPECIFIC RESPONSE TO ALLEGATIONS

1. Core Products admits to paragraph 1 of the complaint.

2. Core Products admits to paragraph 2 of the complaint.

3. Core Products admits that this Court has subject matter jurisdiction over the

alleged causes of action and that venue is proper in this district. Core Products denies that it has

committed acts of infringement in this or any other district.

4. Upon information and belief, Core Products admits the first two sentences of

paragraph 4. Core Products is without sufficient knowledge or information to admit or deny the

allegations set forth in the last sentence of paragraph 4.

5.   Core Products denies each and every allegation of paragraph 5.

6.   Core Products reincorporates its responses to paragraphs 1-5.

7.   Core Products denies each and every allegation of paragraph 7.

DEFENSES

1.   United States Patent No. 5,814,002 is not infringed by Core Products.

2.   United States Patent No. 5,814,002 is invalid under the U.S. patent laws,

35 U.S.C. § 1 et seq.

COUNTERCLAIMS

Defendant Core Products International, Inc., for counterclaims against Plaintiff, Mueller

Sports Medicine, Inc., alleges as follows:

1.   Core Products reincorporates Mueller's allegations in the Complaint as to the

identity of the parties.

2.   This Court also has subject matter jurisdiction under 28 U.S.C. §§ 1331 and 1338

(a), this being an action arising under the patent laws of the United States.

3.   This counterclaim is an action for declaratory judgment under 28 U.S.C. § 2201,

which arises from an actual controversy between Core Products and Mueller Sports Medicine,

Inc. as to the validity and infringement of U.S. Patent No. 5,814,002.

4.   Core Products reincorporates Mueller's allegations as to ownership of

U.S. Patent No. 5,814,002.

-2-

5.   Mueller has alleged that products made, used and sold by Core Products infringe U.S. Patent No. 5,814,002.

FIRST COUNTERCLAIM

6.   This is a counterclaim for declaratory judgment of non-infringement of U.S. Patent No. 5, 814, 002. Core Products does not infringe, contribute to the infringement, or induce the infringement of U.S. Patent No. 5,814,002, nor has it ever done so, and Core Products is entitled to a declaration of non-infringement.

SECOND COUNTERCLAIM

7.   This is a counterclaim for declaratory judgment of invalidity of U.S. Patent No. 5,814,002.

8.   U.S. Patent No. 5,814,002 is invalid under the U.S. patent laws, 35 U.S.C. § 1 et seq., and Core Products is entitled to a declaration of invalidity.

PRAYER FOR RELIEF

WHEREFORE, Defendant Core Products prays for the following relief:

A.   A declaration that Core Products has not, and does not, infringe any of the claims of U.S. Patent No. 5,814,002;

B.   A declaration that U.S. Patent No. 5, 814, 002 is invalid;

C.   Dismissal of all counts listed in Plaintiff's complaint;

D.   An award to Core Products of its costs and attorneys' fees incurred in defending this action and in prosecuting its counterclaims, plus interest, as provided for by 35 U.S.C. § 285; and

-3-

801

E.   Such other and further relief as the Court deems just and equitable.

CORE PRODUCTS INTERNATIONAL, INC.

Dated: _____   By:_____

Gayle A. Bush, Member No. 1036104
Sherri L. Sowinski
KINNEY & LANGE, P.A.
312 South Third Street
Minneapolis MN 55415-1002
(612) 339-1863
(612) 339-6580 (Facsimile)

ATTORNEYS FOR DEFENDANT

-4-

APPENDIX G

Protective Order

FORM 6 STIPULATION FOR PROTECTIVE ORDER

UNITED STATES DISTRICT COURT
DISTRICT OF MINNESOTA

[NAME OF PARTY],	)	Case No. _____
	)	
Plaintiff,	)	
	)	STIPULATION FOR
v.	)	PROTECTIVE ORDER
	)	
[NAME OF PARTY],	)	
	)	
Defendant.	)	
_____	)	

Upon stipulation of the parties for an order pursuant to Fed. R.Civ. P. 26(c) that confidential information be disclosed only in designated ways:

1.   As used in the Protective Order, these terms have the following meanings:

"Attorneys" means counsel of record;

"Confidential" documents are documents designated pursuant to paragraph 2;

"Documents" are all materials within the scope of Fed. R. Civ. P. 34;

"Outside Vendors" means messenger, copy, coding, and other clerical-services vendors not employed by a party or its Attorneys; and

"Written Assurance" means an executed document in the form attached as Exhibit A.

2.   A Party may designate a document "Confidential", to protect information within the scope of Fed. R. Civ. P. 26(c).

3.   All Confidential documents, along with the information contained in the documents, shall be used solely for the purpose of this action, and no person receiving

803

such documents shall, directly or indirectly, use, transfer, disclose, or communicate in any way the documents or their contents to any person other than those specified in paragraph. Any other use is prohibited.

4.   Access to any Confidential document shall be limited to:

    (a)   the Court and its staff;

    (b)   Attorneys, their law firms, and their Outside Vendors;

    (c)   persons shown on the face of the document to have authored or received it;

    (d)   court reporters retained to transcribe testimony;

    (e)   the parties;

    (f)   outside independent persons (i.e., persons not currently or formerly employed by, consulting with, or otherwise associated with any party) who are retained by a party or its Attorneys to provide assistance as mock jurors or focus group members or the like, or to furnish technical or expert services, and/or to give testimony in this action.

5.   Third parties producing documents in the course of this action may also designate documents as "Confidential", subject to the same protections and constraints as the parties to the action. A copy of the Protective Order shall be served along with any subpoena served in connection with this action. All documents produced by such third parties shall be treated as "Confidential" for a period of 14 days from the date of their production, and during that period any party may designate such documents as "Confidential" pursuant to the terms of the Protective Order.

6.   Each person appropriately designated pursuant to paragraphs 4(f) to receive

Confidential information shall execute a "Written Assurance" in the form attached as

Exhibit A. Opposing counsel shall be notified at least 14 days prior to disclosure to any

such person who is known to be an employee or agent of, or consultant to, any

competitor of the party whose designated documents are sought to be disclosed. Such

notice shall provide a reasonable description of the outside independent person to

whom disclosure is sought sufficient to permit objection to be made. If a party objects in

writing to such disclosure within 14 days after receipt of notice, no disclosure shall be

made until the party seeking disclosure obtains the prior approval of the Court or the

objecting party.

7.   All depositions or portions of depositions taken in this action that contain

confidential information may be designated "Confidential" and thereby obtain the

protections accorded other "Confidential" documents. Confidentiality designations for

depositions shall be made either on the record or by written notice to the other party

within 14 days of receipt of the transcript. Unless otherwise agreed, depositions shall

be treated as "Confidential" during the 14-day period following receipt of the transcript.

The deposition of any witness (or any portion of such deposition) that encompasses

Confidential information shall be taken only in the presence of persons who are qualified

to have access to such information.

8.   Any party who inadvertently fails to identify documents as "Confidential" shall,

promptly upon discovery of its oversight, provide written notice of the error and

substitute appropriately-designated documents. Any party receiving such improperly-

designated documents shall retrieve such documents from persons not entitled to receive those documents and, upon receipt of the substitute documents, shall return or destroy the improperly-designated documents.

9.   If a party files a document containing Confidential information with the Court, it shall do so in compliance with the Electronic Case Filing Procedures for the District of Minnesota. Prior to disclosure at trial or a hearing of materials or information designated "Confidential", the parties may seek further protections against public disclosure from the Court.

10.   Any party may request a change in the designation of any information designated "Confidential". Any such document shall be treated as designated until the change is completed. If the requested change in designation is not agreed to, the party seeking the change may move the Court for appropriate relief, providing notice to any third party whose designation of produced documents as "Confidential" in the action may be affected. The party asserting that the material is Confidential shall have the burden of proving that the information in question is within the scope of protection afforded by Fed. R. Civ. P. 26(c).

11.   Within 60 days of the termination of this action, including any appeals, each party shall either destroy or return to the opposing party all documents designated by the opposing party as "Confidential", and all copies of such documents, and shall destroy all extracts and/or data taken from such documents. Each party shall provide a certification as to such return or destruction within the 60-day period. However, Attorneys shall be entitled to retain a set of all documents filed with the Court and all correspondence generated in connection with the action.

12.   Any party may apply to the Court for a modification of the Protective Order, and

nothing in this Protective Order shall be construed to prevent a party from seeking such

further provisions enhancing or limiting confidentiality as may be appropriate.

13.   No action taken in accordance with the Protective Order shall be construed as a

waiver of any claim or defense in the action or of any position as to discoverability or

admissibility of evidence.

14.   The obligations imposed by the Protective Order shall survive the termination of

this action.

Stipulated to:

Date: _____   By: _____

Date: _____   By: _____

EXHIBIT A

WRITTEN ASSURANCE

_____ declares that:

I reside at _____ in the City of

_____, County of _____, State of _____ .

My telephone number is _____.

I am currently employed by _____, located

at _____, and my current

job title is _____.

I have read and I understand the terms of the Protective Order dated

_____, filed in Case No. _____, pending in the United States

District Court for the District of Minnesota. I agree to comply with and be bound by the

provisions of the Protective Order. I understand that any violation of the Protective

Order may subject me to sanctions by the Court.

I shall not divulge any documents, or copies of documents, designated

"Confidential" obtained pursuant to such Protective Order, or the contents of such

documents, to any person other than those specifically authorized by the Protective

Order. I shall not copy or use such documents except for the purposes of this action

and pursuant to the terms of the Protective Order.

As soon as practical, but no later than 30 days after final termination of this

action, I shall return to the attorney from whom I have received them, any documents in

my possession designated "Confidential", and all copies, excerpts, summaries, notes,

digests, abstracts, and indices relating to such documents.

I submit myself to the jurisdiction of the United States District Court for the District of Minnesota for the purpose of enforcing or otherwise providing relief relating to the Protective Order.

Executed on _____   _____
                    (Date)   (Signature)

APPENDIX H

Consent Judgment

UNITED STATES DISTRICT COURT
DISTRICT OF MINNESOTA

DataCard Corporation, d/b/a Datacard Group,	)))	
Plaintiff,	))	Civil Action No. 02-1366 DWF/SRN
v.	))	**CONSENT JUDGMENT**
Zebra Technologies Corporation,	))	
Defendant.	))	

The parties, having agreed to settlement of the matters in issue before them, and to the entry of this Consent Judgment, it is ordered, adjudged and decreed that:

1.   This Court has personal jurisdiction over Plaintiff DataCard Corporation ("Datacard Group") and Defendant Zebra Technologies Corporation. This Court has jurisdiction over the subject matter in issue.

2.   Datacard Group is the owner by Assignment of the entire right, title, and interest in and to U.S. Patent No. 5,762,431 entitled "THERMAL PRINTER AND METHOD FOR USING." Zebra Technologies admits that the '431 patent is valid.

3.   Zebra Technologies infringed the '431 patent by making, using and/or selling those thermal printers known as the current Eltron® P205 and P210 card printers and associated OEM printers including but not limited to, J210 and J205 to NBS, C210 and C205 to CIM, and Polaroid (all hereafter "Subject Printers") which embody one or more of the inventions claimed in the '431 patent. The Subject Printers are described in detail in Datacard Group's supporting papers for its motion for Preliminary Junction, which are attached hereto as Exhibit A.

4.   Zebra Technologies, its officers, agents, servants, employees, attorneys and those

in active concert with them are permanently enjoined from making, using or selling in the United

States the Subject Printers and any device which infringes any claim of the '431 patent.

5.   Each party shall bear its own costs and attorneys fees in this action.

6.   With entry of this judgment, the case is dismissed with prejudice.

7.   The clerk is directed to enter this judgment forthwith.

DATACARD CORPORATION
d/b/a DATACARD GROUP

Dated:_____   By: _____

Donovan W. Frank, US District Court Judge

AGREED AND CONSENTED TO BY:

Dated: _____   By: _____

David R. Fairbairn (No. 28,125)
Paul P. Kempf (No. 239,215)
KINNEY & LANGE, P.A.
Kinney & Lange Building
312 South Third Street
Minneapolis, MN 55415
(612) 339-1863

ATTORNEYS FOR PLAINTIFF
DATACARD CORPORATION
d/b/a DATACARD GROUP

2

Dated: _____   By: _____

Jerry Podkopacz
LEONARD, STREET AND DEINARD
150 South Fifth Street, Suite 2300
Minneapolis, MN 55402
(612) 335-1756

**ATTORNEYS FOR DEFENDANT
ZEBRA TECHNOLOGIES
CORPORATION**

Dated: _____   By: _____

Daniel P. Albers
BARNES & THORNBURG
2600 Chase Plaza
10 South LaSalle Street
Chicago, Illinois 60606
(312) 357-1313

**ATTORNEYS FOR DEFENDANT
ZEBRA TECHNOLOGIES
CORPORATION**

3

APPENDIX I

Copyright Application Form TX

 Form TX

Detach and read these instructions before completing this form.
Make sure all applicable spaces have been filled in before you return this form.

When to Use This Form: Use Form TX for registration of published or unpublished nondramatic literary works, excluding periodicals or serial issues. This class includes a wide variety of works: fiction, nonfiction, poetry, textbooks, reference works, directories, catalogs, advertising copy, compilations of information, and computer programs. For periodicals and serials, use Form SE.

Deposit to Accompany Application: An application for copyright registration must be accompanied by a deposit consisting of copies or phonorecords representing the entire work for which registration is to be made. The following are the general deposit requirements as set forth in the statute:

Unpublished Work: Deposit one complete copy (or phonorecord).

Published Work: Deposit two complete copies (or one phonorecord) of the best edition.

Work First Published Outside the United States: Deposit one complete copy (or phonorecord) of the first foreign edition.

Contribution to a Collective Work: Deposit one complete copy (or phonorecord) of the best edition of the collective work.

The Copyright Notice: Before March 1, 1989, the use of copyright notice was mandatory on all published works, and any work first published

before that date should have carried a notice. For works first published on and after March 1, 1989, use of the copyright notice is optional. For more information about copyright notice, see Circular 3, *Copyright Notice.*

For Further Information: To speak to a Copyright Office staff member, call (202) 707-3000 or 1-877-476-0778 (toll free). Recorded information is available 24 hours a day. Order forms and other publications from the address in space 9 or call the Forms and Publications Hotline at (202) 707-9100. Access and download circulars, certain forms, and other information from the Copyright Office website at *www.copyright.gov.*

Please type or print using black ink. The form is used to produce the certificate.

1 SPACE 1: Title

Title of This Work: Every work submitted for copyright registration must be given a title to identify that particular work. If the copies or phonorecords of the work bear a title or an identifying phrase that could serve as a title, transcribe that wording *completely* and *exactly* on the application. Indexing of the registration and future identification of the work will depend on the information you give here.

Previous or Alternative Titles: Complete this space if there are any additional titles for the work under which someone searching for the registration might be likely to look or under which a document pertaining to the work might be recorded.

Publication as a Contribution: If the work being registered is a contribution to a periodical, serial, or collection, give the title of the contribution in the "Title of This Work" space. Then, in the line headed "Publication as a Contribution," give information about the collective work in which the contribution appeared.

2 SPACE 2: Author(s)

General Instructions: After reading these instructions, decide who are the "authors" of this work for copyright purposes. Then, unless the work is a "collective work," give the requested information about every "author" who contributed any appreciable amount of copyrightable matter to this version of the work. If you need further space, request Continuation Sheets. In the case of a collective work, such as an anthology, collection of essays, or encyclopedia, give information about the author of the collective work as a whole.

Name of Author: The fullest form of the author's name should be given. Unless the work was "made for hire," the individual who actually

created the work is its "author." In the case of a work made for hire, the statute provides that "the employer or other person for whom the work was prepared is considered the author."

What Is a "Work Made for Hire"? A "work made for hire" is defined as (1) "a work prepared by an employee within the scope of his or her employment"; or (2) "a work specially ordered or commissioned for use as a contribution to a collective work, as a part of a motion picture or other audiovisual work, as a translation, as a supplementary work, as a compilation, as an instructional text, as a test, as answer material for a test, or as an atlas, if the parties expressly agree in a written instrument signed by them that the works shall be considered a work made for hire." If you have checked "Yes" to indicate that the work was "made for hire," you must give the full legal name of the employer (or other person for whom the work was prepared). You may also include the name of the employee along with the name of the employer (for example: "Elster Publishing Co., employer for hire of John Ferguson").

"Anonymous" or "Pseudonymous" Work: An author's contribution to a work is "anonymous" if that author is not identified on the copies or phonorecords of the work. An author's contribution to a work is "pseudonymous" if that author is identified on the copies or phonorecords under a fictitious name. If the work is "anonymous" you may: (1) leave the line blank; or (2) state "anonymous" on the line; or (3) reveal the author's identity. If the work is "pseudonymous" you may: (1) leave the line blank; or (2) give the pseudonym and identify it as such (for example: "Huntley Haverstock, pseudonym"); or (3) reveal the author's name, making clear which is the real name and which is the pseudonym (for example, "Judith Barton, whose pseudonym is Madeline Elster"). However, the citizenship or domicile of the author *must* be given in all cases.

Dates of Birth and Death: If the author is dead, the statute requires that the year of death be included in the application unless the work is anonymous or pseudonymous. The author's birth date is optional but is

815

useful as a form of identification. Leave this space blank if the author's contribution was a "work made for hire."

Author's Nationality or Domicile: Give the country of which the author is a citizen or the country in which the author is domiciled. Nationality or domicile *must* be given in all cases.

Nature of Authorship: After the words "Nature of Authorship," give a brief general statement of the nature of this particular author's contribution to the work. Examples: "Entire text"; "Coauthor of entire text"; "Computer program"; "Editorial revisions"; "Compilation and English translation"; "New text."

3 SPACE 3: Creation and Publication

General Instructions: Do not confuse "creation" with "publication." Every application for copyright registration must state "the year in which creation of the work was completed." Give the date and nation of first publication only if the work has been published.

Creation: Under the statute, a work is "created" when it is fixed in a copy or phonorecord for the first time. Where a work has been prepared over a period of time, the part of the work existing in fixed form on a particular date constitutes the created work on that date. The date you give here should be the year in which the author completed the particular version for which registration is now being sought, even if other versions exist or if further changes or additions are planned.

Publication: The statute defines "publication" as "the distribution of copies or phonorecords of a work to the public by sale or other transfer of ownership, or by rental, lease, or lending." A work is also "published" if there has been an "offering to distribute copies or phonorecords to a group of persons for purposes of further distribution, public performance, or public display." Give the full date (month, day, year) when, and the country where, publication first occurred. If first publication took place simultaneously in the United States and other countries, it is sufficient to state "U.S.A."

4 SPACE 4: Claimant(s)

Name(s) and Address(es) of Copyright Claimant(s): Give the name(s) and address(es) of the copyright claimant(s) in this work even if the claimant is the same as the author. Copyright in a work belongs initially to the author of the work (including, in the case of a work made for hire, the employer or other person for whom the work was prepared). The copyright claimant is either the author of the work or a person or organization to whom the copyright initially belonging to the author has been transferred.

Transfer: The statute provides that, if the copyright claimant is not the author, the application for registration must contain "a brief statement of how the claimant obtained ownership of the copyright." If any copyright claimant named in space 4 is not an author named in space 2, give a brief statement explaining how the claimant(s) obtained ownership of the copyright. Examples: "By written contract"; "Transfer of all rights by author"; "Assignment"; "By will." Do not attach transfer documents or other attachments or riders.

5 SPACE 5: Previous Registration

General Instructions: The questions in space 5 are intended to show whether an earlier registration has been made for this work and, if so, whether there is any basis for a new registration. As a general rule, only one basic copyright registration can be made for the same version of a particular work.

Same Version: If this version is substantially the same as the work covered by a previous registration, a second registration is not generally possible

unless: (1) the work has been registered in unpublished form and a second registration is now being sought to cover this first published edition; or (2) someone other than the author is identified as copyright claimant in the earlier registration, and the author is now seeking registration in his or her own name. If either of these two exceptions applies, check the appropriate box and give the earlier registration number and date. Otherwise, do not submit Form TX. Instead, write the Copyright Office for information about supplementary registration or recordation of transfers of copyright ownership.

Changed Version: If the work has been changed and you are now seeking registration to cover the additions or revisions, check the last box in space 5, give the earlier registration number and date, and complete both parts of space 6 in accordance with the instructions below.

Previous Registration Number and Date: If more than one previous registration has been made for the work, give the number and date of the latest registration.

6 SPACE 6: Derivative Work or Compilation

General Instructions: Complete space 6 if this work is a "changed version," "compilation," or "derivative work" and if it incorporates one or more earlier works that have already been published or registered for copyright or that have fallen into the public domain. A "compilation" is defined as "a work formed by the collection and assembling of preexisting materials or of data that are selected, coordinated, or arranged in such a way that the resulting work as a whole constitutes an original work of authorship." A "derivative work" is "a work based on one or more preexisting works." Examples of derivative works include translations, fictionalizations, abridgments, condensations, or "any other form in which a work may be recast, transformed, or adapted." Derivative works also include works "consisting of editorial revisions, annotations, or other modifications" if these changes, as a whole, represent an original work of authorship.

Preexisting Material (space 6a): For derivative works, complete this space and space 6b. In space 6a identify the preexisting work that has been recast, transformed, or adapted. The preexisting work may be material that has been previously published, previously registered, or that is in the public domain. An example of preexisting material might be: "Russian version of Goncharov's 'Oblomov.'"

Material Added to This Work (space 6b): Give a brief, general statement of the new material covered by the copyright claim for which registration is sought. *Derivative work* examples include: "Foreword, editing, critical annotations"; "Translation"; "Chapters 11–17." If the work is a *compilation*, describe both the compilation itself and the material that has been compiled. Example: "Compilation of certain 1917 speeches by Woodrow Wilson." A work may be both a derivative work and compilation, in which case a sample statement might be: "Compilation and additional new material."

7,8,9 SPACE 7,8,9: Fee, Correspondence, Certification, Return Address

Deposit Account: If you maintain a Deposit Account in the Copyright Office, identify it in space 7a. Otherwise leave the space blank and send the fee with your application and deposit.

Correspondence (space 7b): Give the name, address, area code, telephone number, fax number, and email address (if available) of the person to be consulted if correspondence about this application becomes necessary.

Certification (space 8): The application cannot be accepted unless it bears the date and the *handwritten signature* of the author or other copyright claimant, or of the owner of exclusive right(s), or of the duly authorized agent of author, claimant, or owner of exclusive right(s).

Address for Return of Certificate (space 9): The address box must be completed legibly because the certificate will be returned in a window envelope.

Copyright Office fees are subject to change. For current fees, check the Copyright Office website at www.copyright.gov, write the Copyright Office, or call (202) 707-3000.

Privacy Act Notice: Sections 408-410 of title 17 of the *United States Code* authorize the Copyright Office to collect the personally identifying information requested on this form in order to process the application for copyright registration. By providing this information you are agreeing to routine uses of the information that include publication to give legal notice of your copyright claim as required by 17 U.S.C. §705. It will appear in the Office's online catalog. If you do not provide the information requested, registration may be refused or delayed, and you may not be entitled to certain relief, remedies, and benefits under the copyright law.

Form TX
For a Nondramatic Literary Work
UNITED STATES COPYRIGHT OFFICE

REGISTRATION NUMBER

TX   TXU

EFFECTIVE DATE OF REGISTRATION

Month   Day   Year

DO NOT WRITE ABOVE THIS LINE. IF YOU NEED MORE SPACE, USE A SEPARATE CONTINUATION SHEET.

1 TITLE OF THIS WORK ▼

PREVIOUS OR ALTERNATIVE TITLES ▼

PUBLICATION AS A CONTRIBUTION If this work was published as a contribution to a periodical, serial, or collection, give information about the collective work in which the contribution appeared.   **Title of Collective Work ▼**

If published in a periodical or serial give: Volume ▼   Number ▼   Issue Date ▼   On Pages ▼

2 a NAME OF AUTHOR ▼

DATES OF BIRTH AND DEATH
Year Born ▼   Year Died ▼

Was this contribution to the work a "work made for hire"?
☐ Yes
☐ No

AUTHOR'S NATIONALITY OR DOMICILE
Name of Country
OR { Citizen of _____
     { Domiciled in _____

WAS THIS AUTHOR'S CONTRIBUTION TO THE WORK
Anonymous?   ☐ Yes ☐ No
Pseudonymous?   ☐ Yes ☐ No
If the answer to either of these questions is "Yes," see detailed instructions.

NOTE
Under the law, the "author" of a "work made for hire" is generally the employer, not the employee (see instructions). For any part of this work that was "made for hire" check "Yes" in the space provided, give the employer (or other person for whom the work was prepared) as "Author" of that part, and leave the space for dates of birth and death blank.

NATURE OF AUTHORSHIP Briefly describe nature of material created by this author in which copyright is claimed. ▼

b NAME OF AUTHOR ▼

DATES OF BIRTH AND DEATH
Year Born ▼   Year Died ▼

Was this contribution to the work a "work made for hire"?
☐ Yes
☐ No

AUTHOR'S NATIONALITY OR DOMICILE
Name of Country
OR { Citizen of _____
     { Domiciled in _____

WAS THIS AUTHOR'S CONTRIBUTION TO THE WORK
Anonymous?   ☐ Yes ☐ No
Pseudonymous?   ☐ Yes ☐ No
If the answer to either of these questions is "Yes," see detailed instructions.

NATURE OF AUTHORSHIP Briefly describe nature of material created by this author in which copyright is claimed. ▼

c NAME OF AUTHOR ▼

DATES OF BIRTH AND DEATH
Year Born ▼   Year Died ▼

Was this contribution to the work a "work made for hire"?
☐ Yes
☐ No

AUTHOR'S NATIONALITY OR DOMICILE
Name of Country
OR { Citizen of _____
     { Domiciled in _____

WAS THIS AUTHOR'S CONTRIBUTION TO THE WORK
Anonymous?   ☐ Yes ☐ No
Pseudonymous?   ☐ Yes ☐ No
If the answer to either of these questions is "Yes," see detailed instructions.

NATURE OF AUTHORSHIP Briefly describe nature of material created by this author in which copyright is claimed. ▼

3 a YEAR IN WHICH CREATION OF THIS WORK WAS COMPLETED
This information must be given in all cases.
Year

b DATE AND NATION OF FIRST PUBLICATION OF THIS PARTICULAR WORK
Complete this information ONLY if this work has been published.
Month _____ Day _____ Year _____
_____ Nation

4 COPYRIGHT CLAIMANT(S) Name and address must be given even if the claimant is the same as the author given in space 2. ▼

See instructions before completing this space.

TRANSFER If the claimant(s) named here in space 4 is (are) different from the author(s) named in space 2, give a brief statement of how the claimant(s) obtained ownership of the copyright. ▼

APPLICATION RECEIVED

ONE DEPOSIT RECEIVED

TWO DEPOSITS RECEIVED

FUNDS RECEIVED

DO NOT WRITE HERE
OFFICE USE ONLY

MORE ON BACK ▶
• Complete all applicable spaces (numbers 5-9) on the reverse side of this page.
• See detailed instructions.
• Sign the form at line 8.

DO NOT WRITE HERE
Page 1 of _____ pages

EXAMINED BY	FORM TX
CHECKED BY	

☐ CORRESPONDENCE
Yes

FOR
COPYRIGHT
OFFICE
USE
ONLY

DO NOT WRITE ABOVE THIS LINE. IF YOU NEED MORE SPACE, USE A SEPARATE CONTINUATION SHEET.

PREVIOUS REGISTRATION Has registration for this work, or for an earlier version of this work, already been made in the Copyright Office?

☐ Yes ☐ No If your answer is "Yes," why is another registration being sought? (Check appropriate box.) ▼

a. ☐ This is the first published edition of a work previously registered in unpublished form.

b. ☐ This is the first application submitted by this author as copyright claimant.

c. ☐ This is a changed version of the work, as shown by space 6 on this application.

If your answer is "Yes," give: **Previous Registration Number** ▶   **Year of Registration** ▶

5

DERIVATIVE WORK OR COMPILATION

Preexisting Material Identify any preexisting work or works that this work is based on or incorporates. ▼

a

6

See instructions
before completing
this space.

Material Added to This Work Give a brief, general statement of the material that has been added to this work and in which copyright is claimed. ▼

b

DEPOSIT ACCOUNT If the registration fee is to be charged to a deposit account established in the Copyright Office, give name and number of account.

Name ▼   **Account Number** ▼

a

7

CORRESPONDENCE Give name and address to which correspondence about this application should be sent.   Name/Address/Apt/City/State/Zip ▼

b

Area code and daytime telephone number ▶   Fax number ▶

Email ▶

CERTIFICATION* I, the undersigned, hereby certify that I am the

Check only one ▶

☐ author
☐ other copyright claimant
☐ owner of exclusive right(s)
☐ authorized agent of _____

of the work identified in this application and that the statements made
by me in this application are correct to the best of my knowledge.

Name of author or other copyright claimant, or owner of exclusive right(s) ▲

8

Typed or printed name and date ▼ If this application gives a date of publication in space 3, do not sign and submit it before that date.

_____ Date ▶

Handwritten signature ▼

_____

Certificate
will be
mailed in
window
envelope
to this
address:

Name ▼

Number/Street/Apt ▼

City/State/Zip ▼

YOU MUST:
· Complete all necessary spaces
· Sign your application in space 8

**SEND ALL 3 ELEMENTS
IN THE SAME PACKAGE:**
1. Application form
2. Nonrefundable filing fee in check or money
   order payable to Register of Copyrights
3. Deposit material

MAIL TO:
Library of Congress
Copyright Office-TX
101 Independence Avenue SE
Washington, DC 20559

9

---

*17 U.S.C. §506(e): Any person who knowingly makes a false representation of a material fact in the application for copyright registration provided for by section 409, or in any written statement filed in connection with the application, shall be fined not more than $2,500.

APPENDIX J

Copyright Registration

Certificate of Registration

This Certificate issued under the seal of the Copyright
Office in accordance with title 17, *United States Code*,
attests that registration has been made for the work
identified below. The information on this certificate has
been made a part of the Copyright Office records.

Marybeth Peters

Register of Copyrights, United States of America

Registration Number:

TXu 1-578-596

Effective date of
registration:

September 24, 2007

Title

Title of Work: Vision Training System

Completion/ Publication

Year of Completion: 2007

Author

- Author: Ted Kopren

Author Created: entire work

Work made for hire: No

Citizen of: United States

Year Born: 1951

Anonymous: No   Pseudonymous: No

Copyright claimant

Copyright Claimant: Ted Kopren

433 3rd Avenue NE, Osseo, MN 55369

Limitation of copyright claim

Previously registered: No

Certification

Name: David R. Fairbairn

Date: September 24, 2007

Page 1 of 1

APPENDIX K

Copyright Infringement Complaint

UNITED STATES DISTRICT COURT
DISTRICT OF MINNESOTA

R.H. NAGEL DISTRIBUTING COMPANY, INC.	)	
Plaintiff,	)	**COMPLAINT FOR**
	)	**COPYRIGHT INFRINGEMENT**
v.	)	
	)	
KELLER MONUMENT	)	**[JURY TRIAL DEMANDED]**
Defendant	)	

Plaintiff R.H. Nagel Distributing Company, Inc. ("Nagel"), for its complaint against

Defendant Keller Monument ("Keller"), states and alleges as follows:

PARTIES

1.   Plaintiff R.H. Nagel Distributing Company, Inc. is a Minnesota corporation with a

principal place of business at P.O. Box 26, Little Falls, Minnesota 56345.

2.   Upon information and belief, Defendant Keller Monument is a Minnesota

corporation with a principal place of business at 20100 Hardwood Road N.E., Miltona,

Minnesota 56354.

JURISDICTION AND VENUE

3.   This Court has subject matter jurisdiction under the copyright law of the United

States, Title 17 U.S.C.A. §§ 101 *et seq.*, and Title 28 U.S.C.A. §§ 1331 and 1338.

4.   This Court has personal jurisdiction under the Minnesota Long-Arm Statute,

Minn. Stat. 543.19, because Defendant has transacted business in this District.

5.   Venue in this District is proper under 28 U.S.C.A. §§ 1391(c) and 1400(a).

COUNT I

COPYRIGHT INFRINGEMENT

6.   Nagel realleges and incorporates by reference as is fully set forth herein the allegations contained in Paragraphs 1-5 above.

7.   Plaintiff Nagel is a retailer of funeral products including monuments. Nagel has developed and utilized an original book of line drawings called "A Picture is Worth a Thousand Words."

8.   Nagel registered its rights to the revised and updated book, "A Picture is Worth a Thousand Words", and obtained from the Registrar of Copyrights, Certificates of Copyright Registration Nos. VA 1-032-503 dated February 29, 2000 and VA 1-098-427 dated June 11, 2001. Copies of U.S. Certificate of Copyright Registration Nos. VA 1-032-503 and VA 1-098-427 are attached as Exhibits A and B, respectively.

9.   Nagel has been and is the sole owner of all rights, title, and interest in and to U.S. Copyright Registration Nos. VA 1-032-503 and VA 1-098-427.

10.   Since the effective date of its Copyright Registrations, Nagel has offered for sale to the public monuments engraved with its copyrighted line drawings.

11.   On July 8, 2002, Nagel provided a customer with a layout for a monument, which contained copyrighted line drawings. The bottom right corner of the layout clearly stated, "This drawing is the property of R.H. Nagel Distributing. No portion of this work may be displayed or duplicated without permission." A copy of the layout provided by Nagel is attached as Exhibit C.

12.   By October, 2002, Keller installed a monument in a cemetery. A copy of a picture of that monument is attached as Exhibit D. The monument of Exhibit D is engraved with line drawings that are substantially similar to Nagel's copyrighted line drawings contained in the

layout of Exhibit C. The preparation, reproduction, and distribution of a derivative work by

Keller based on Nagel's copyrighted work had been done without license from Nagel, contrary to

the desires of Nagel, and without Nagel's consent.

13. Upon information and belief, by the acts alleged herein, Defendant has directly

infringed Nagel's copyright.

14. Nagel formally notified Defendant that it infringed Nagel's rights in a letter dated

December 12, 2002, and demanded that Keller cease any future infringing activity and pay Nagel

reasonable damages for past infringement. Keller has failed to pay damages.

15. Defendant's infringement of Nagel's copyright has caused irreparable injury and

damages.

PRAYER FOR RELIEF

WHEREFORE, Plaintiff Nagel demands judgment against Defendant as follows:

A. That Defendant, its officers, agents, servants, employees, and attorneys, and all

persons in active concert or participation with any of them, be enjoined from infringing

Plaintiff's copyrights pursuant to 17 U.S.C.A. § 502.

B. That Defendant be required to pay Plaintiff such damages and profits as provided

in 17 U.S.C.A. § 504 including statutory damages, or actual damages suffered by Plaintiff, or

Defendant's profits attributable to its infringement.

C. That Defendant be required to pay Plaintiff the costs and disbursements of this

action, together with reasonable attorneys fees, as provided by 17 U.S.C.A. § 505.

D. Awarding Plaintiff all such other relief including exemplary damages or statutory

damages as this Court will deem just in this action.

JURY DEMAND

Plaintiff Nagel demands a trial by jury of issues triable by jury.

R.H. NAGEL DISTRIBUTING COMPANY, INC.

Dated:_____, 20___   By:_____
                                       David R. Fairbairn (No. 28,125)
                                       Catherine J. Benson (No. 317,172)
                                       KINNEY & LANGE, P.A.
                                       312 South Third Street
                                       Minneapolis, MN 55415-1002
                                       (612) 339-1863 (telephone)
                                       (612) 339-6580 (facsimile)
                                       Attorneys for Plaintiff

APPENDIX L

Trademark Registration

United States of America
United States Patent and Trademark Office

GRIND GUARD

Reg. No. 4,655,574

Registered Dec. 16, 2014

ARCHTEK, INC. (COLORADO CORPORATION)
12105 WEST CEDAR DRIVE
LAKEWOOD, CO 80228

Int. Cl.: 10

FOR: THERMOFORMED DENTAL TRAYS FOR PROTECTING TEETH DURING SLEEP, IN CLASS 10 (U.S. CLS. 26, 39 AND 44).

TRADEMARK

FIRST USE 12-11-2007; IN COMMERCE 12-11-2007.

PRINCIPAL REGISTER

THE MARK CONSISTS OF STANDARD CHARACTERS WITHOUT CLAIM TO ANY PARTICULAR FONT, STYLE, SIZE, OR COLOR.

NO CLAIM IS MADE TO THE EXCLUSIVE RIGHT TO USE "GRIND", APART FROM THE MARK AS SHOWN.

SER. NO. 86-217,963, FILED 3-11-2014.

ARETHA SOMERVILLE, EXAMINING ATTORNEY

Michelle K. Lee
Deputy Director of the United States
Patent and Trademark Office

REQUIREMENTS TO MAINTAIN YOUR FEDERAL
TRADEMARK REGISTRATION

WARNING: YOUR REGISTRATION WILL BE CANCELLED IF YOU DO NOT FILE THE DOCUMENTS BELOW DURING THE SPECIFIED TIME PERIODS.

Requirements in the First Ten Years*
What and When to File:

> ***First Filing Deadline:*** You must file a Declaration of Use (or Excusable Nonuse) between the 5th and 6th years after the registration date. *See* 15 U.S.C. §§1058, 1141k. If the declaration is accepted, the registration will continue in force for the remainder of the ten-year period, calculated from the registration date, unless cancelled by an order of the Commissioner for Trademarks or a federal court.

> ***Second Filing Deadline:*** You must file a Declaration of Use (or Excusable Nonuse) **and** an Application for Renewal between the 9th and 10th years after the registration date.* *See* 15 U.S.C. §1059.

Requirements in Successive Ten-Year Periods*
What and When to File:

> You must file a Declaration of Use (or Excusable Nonuse) **and** an Application for Renewal between every 9th and 10th-year period, calculated from the registration date.*

Grace Period Filings*

The above documents will be accepted as timely if filed within six months after the deadlines listed above with the payment of an additional fee.

The United States Patent and Trademark Office (USPTO) will NOT send you any future notice or reminder of these filing requirements.

*ATTENTION MADRID PROTOCOL REGISTRANTS: The holder of an international registration with an extension of protection to the United States under the Madrid Protocol must timely file the Declarations of Use (or Excusable Nonuse) referenced above directly with the USPTO. The time periods for filing are based on the U.S. registration date (not the international registration date). The deadlines and grace periods for the Declarations of Use (or Excusable Nonuse) are identical to those for nationally issued registrations. *See* 15 U.S.C. §§1058, 1141k. However, owners of international registrations do not file renewal applications at the USPTO. Instead, the holder must file a renewal of the underlying international registration at the International Bureau of the World Intellectual Property Organization, under Article 7 of the Madrid Protocol, before the expiration of each ten-year term of protection, calculated from the date of the international registration. *See* 15 U.S.C. §1141j. For more information and renewal forms for the international registration, see http://www.wipo.int/madrid/en/.

NOTE: Fees and requirements for maintaining registrations are subject to change. Please check the USPTO website for further information. With the exception of renewal applications for registered extensions of protection, you can file the registration maintenance documents referenced above online at http://www.uspto.gov.

APPENDIX M

Trademark Notice of Opposition

IN THE UNITED STATES PATENT AND TRADEMARK OFFICE

BEFORE THE TRADEMARK TRIAL AND APPEAL BOARD

Louis E. Kemp	Opposition No. _____
Opposer,	Serial No. 76/454,734
v.	Published: December 16, 2003
Bumble Bee Seafoods, Inc.	TM Page: 59, 60
Applicant	

NOTICE OF OPPOSITION

Commissioner for Trademarks
P.O. Box 1451
Alexandria, VA 22315-1451

Opposer Louis E. Kemp, believes that he will be damaged by the registration of LOUIS KEMP SEAFOOD CO. in application Serial No. 76/454,734, in International Classes 029 and 030, and opposes the same under the provision of 15 U.S.C. 1063.

As grounds of opposition, Opposer alleges:

1.   Opposer, Louis E. Kemp, is an individual, with his principal place of residence at 9440 Cresta Drive, Los Angeles, California 90035.

4.   The Kemp family has been engaged in the wholesale and retail sale of fish and seafood since 1930. In 1985, Opposer started Kemp Foods, Inc., a company that made and sold artificial seafood products made from surimi, which is commonly defined as a minced, processed fish product made from inexpensive whitefish often processed to resemble more expensive seafood such as crabmeat.

5.   On March 30, 1987, Opposer sold his surimi business to Oscar Mayer Foods Corporation ("Oscar Mayer") pursuant to a Stock Acquisition Agreement ("the Agreement").

Opposer continued to operate numerous other businesses involving fish and seafood under various names and marks including names and marks containing the name KEMP.

        6.   As part of the Agreement, Opposer transferred all of the trademarks used in connection with the surimi business, including KEMP, KEMP's, KEMP's & Design, to Oscar Mayer. The Agreement also defined Opposer's right to use marks containing his family name in the future. These restrictions, embodied in sections 7.5, 7.6 and 7.7 of the Agreement, provide:

> 7.5   Seller represents and warrants that Seller or any entity in which Seller has an interest (except for Company) has never engaged and is not presently engaged in marketing, selling, or otherwise distributing at retail any product bearing the name KEMP, KEMP'S, KEMP'S & Design or any variation thereof except as disclosed and described in Exhibit 35 attached hereto. Seller agrees that neither Seller, nor any entity in which Seller has an interest, shall in the future market, sell or otherwise distribute any product except as provided in Section 7.6 and 7.7 or any other food or any other food or beverage product either at wholesale or retail bearing the name KEMP, KEMP'S, KEMP'S & Design or any variation thereof.

> 7.6   Seller agrees that within nine months, Seller or any entity in which Seller has an interest, shall cease all use of the name KEMP, KEMP'S and KEMP'S & Design in connection with the marketing, selling or otherwise distributing of any products.

> 7.7   It is agreed that Seller or any entity in which Seller has an interest, may market, sell or otherwise distribute those products identified on Exhibit 36 attached hereto, bearing a composite trademark consisting of the word KEMP or KEMP'S and preceded by one or more additional words the selection of which shall be approved in advance in writing by Buyer. The terms of said Exhibit 36 may not be changed or modified except with the approval by Buyer, such approval not to be unreasonably withheld, and by an instrument in writing duly signed on behalf of Buyer and Seller. It is the intention of the parties to avoid any likelihood of confusion among consumer resulting from the use of the respective marks of Seller and Buyer. It is further agreed that the

companies described in Exhibit 37 as indicated in Exhibit 37 attached hereto for all purposes except in connection with marketing, selling or distribution of products.

7. Approximately six months after the parties finalized the Agreement, Lee Scheele, Oscar Mayer Vice-President, asked Opposer if Oscar Mayer could use Opposer's personal name, "Louis Kemp", to market its surimi based seafood products. This was the first time either party had discussed using "Louis Kemp" in connection with the sale of surimi based products. Oscar Mayer desired to use Opposer's personal name because the company had achieved significant success in the past by using the first and last names of individuals as trademarks, such as "Oscar Mayer" and "Louis Rich" for certain of its processed food products. Opposer granted Mr. Scheele's request to use his name on surimi based seafood products as a favor and for no additional consideration.

8. Thereafter, the parties entered negotiations to amend the 1987 Agreement and put the in writing the oral agreement regarding the use of "Louis Kemp". During negotiations, Oscar Mayer initially requested the right to use "Louis Kemp" on all products. This request was rejected by Opposer, who stated that he had only given Oscar Mayer the limited right to use "Louis Kemp" on surimi based products.

9. Counsel for Oscar Mayer also attempted to get Opposer to agree to a provision which would have contractually precluded Opposer from using "Louis Kemp" to sell food products of any type. Opposer refused to agree to this unlimited blanket preclusion.

10. On June 23, 1989, the parties entered into Amendment No. 1 to the 1987 Agreement ("the Amendment"). Section 7.8 of that Amendment provides, in its entirety:

> Seller grants to Buyer (a) the right to use and register the mark LOUIS KEMP, any design marks incorporating LOUIS KEMP and/or LOUIS KEMP SEAFOOD COMPANY in the United States and elsewhere for **surimi based seafood products and such other seafood and fish accessory products within the natural zone of product line expansion**; and (b) the right to adopt, use and register the name LOUIS KEMP SEAFOOD COMPANY in the United States and elsewhere as trade name or as the corporate, firm or business title of any business, operating division or subsidiary of Buyer for the sale

of surimi based seafood products and such other seafood and fish accessory products within the natural zone of product line expansion. Seller hereby agrees to reasonably cooperate with Buyer in obtaining trademark registrations, corporate, firm or business title recordals and/or trade name recordals that involve or include the name described in this section 7.8 and shall execute, at not expense to Seller, all consents and documents reasonably necessary for said registrations and recordals. Seller further agrees that it shall not attack or assist another in attacking the validity of the trademark LOUIS KEMP or any design marks incorporating LOUIS KEMP or any registration thereof permitting hereunder or the trade name LOUIS KEMP SEAFOOD COMPANY or any recordals thereof owned by Buyer in the United States or elsewhere. (Emphasis added.)

11.   The language of the Amendment in general, and specifically the emphasized portion, was drafted by Oscar Mayer's attorneys.

12.   The language of the Amendment was specifically requested by Oscar Mayer to cover packaging concerns in which Oscar Mayer had wanted to sell cocktail and tartar sauces with surimi based seafood in the same package. Therefore, "such other seafood and fish accessory products within the natural zone of product line expansion" was intended to permit accessory products such as cocktail and tartar sauces that could be included as an accessory to "surimi based seafood products" and sold in the same package.

13.   Opposer signed the Amendment as a consent to the use of his name for surimi based seafood products and "such other seafood and fish accessory products within the natural zone of product line expansion." Opposer has never signed a consent or agreed to the use or registration by Bumble Bee or its predecessors of the LOUIS KEMP marks for any products beyond those specifically listed in the Amendment.

14.   On August 25, 1992, Oscar Mayer, through its parent corporation Kraft General Foods ("Kraft"), sold its surimi seafood business to Tyson Foods, Inc., ("Tyson").

15.   Kraft assigned its rights, privileges and obligations of the LOUIS KEMP marks in its sale of the surimi seafood business to Tyson.

16.   During the sales negotiations between Kraft and Tyson, Opposer called John Tyson, president of Tyson, to inform him that Kraft did not have the right to transfer the LOUIS KEMP marks because the Agreement contained a right of first refusal clause and a non-assignment clause. Opposer also informed Mr. Tyson that there were usage restrictions on the LOUIS KEMP trademarks limiting use of the mark to "surimi based seafood products and such other seafood and fish accessory products within the natural zone of product line expansion", i.e. surimi alone or in the same package as cocktail and tartar sauces.

17.   Tyson continued with the purchase fully aware of the trademark issues involved with the LOUIS KEMP marks.

18.   Tyson has since sold its rights to the LOUIS KEMP marks to Applicant Bumble Bee.

19.   Bumble Bee has engaged in litigation in an attempt to block Opposer from using his name in connection with products outside the scope of consent granted in the Amendment. The Memorandum Opinion and Order in Civil No. 96-173 (District of Minnesota) dated March 31, 2001 is attached as Exhibit A, and the Findings of Fact, Conclusions of Law and Order for Judgment in Civil No. 5-96-173 (District of Minnesota) dated September 30, 2002 is attached as Exhibit B.

20.   Bumble Bee has attempted to expand its use of the LOUIS KEMP mark to products outside of the scope of consent given by Opposer, such as smoked salmon. In a letter from its attorneys Bumble Bee stated "Smoked salmon is a type of processed fish and, therefore, falls within the scope of goods permitted to be sold under our client's (Bumble Bee) LOUIS KEMP mark". Bumble Bee's letter dated May 29, 2001 is attached as Exhibit C.

21.   Bumble Bee is also attempting to further improperly expand use of the LOUIS KEMP marks to other products outside of the scope of consent given by Opposer. Bumble Bee's attempt to expand its use of the LOUIS KEMP mark is contrary to the Court's ruling in the Memorandum Opinion and Order dated March 31, 2001 (Ex. A) in which the Court stated that "it is clear that defendants (Tyson and Bumble Bee) acquired only a limited right to use and register LOUIS KEMP and LOUIS KEMP SEAFOOD COMPANY in connection with surimi based products and related products."

22.   Bumble Bee filed two trademark applications, U.S. Application Serial Nos. 76-454609 on October 1, 2002 and 76-454734, on October 2, 2002 which further expands the scope of the LOUIS KEMP and LOUIS KEMP SEAFOOD COMPANY marks outside the scope of consent to "frozen, prepared and refrigerated meals and entrees consisting primarily of seafood or imitation seafood; shellfish; seafood-based dips and seafood-based cocktails" and "sauces and marinades". Bumble Bee has indicated that it intends to further expand its use of the marks containing Opposer's name to all sorts of other food products.

23.   At the time that the two trademark applications were filed, Bumble Bee was fully aware of Judge Tunheim's Orders (Ex. A and B) limiting Bumble Bee's use of and right to register the LOUIS KEMP marks to only "surimi based seafood and related products".

24.   Opposer has been damaged and will continue to be damaged if U.S. Application Serial No. 76-454734 registered for the reasons set forth above.

Opposer, Louis E. Kemp, believes that he will be damaged by registration of the alleged mark LOUIS KEMP SEAFOOD CO., and requests that registration on application Serial No. 76/454,734 be refused, that no registration be issued to Applicant, and that this Opposition be sustained in favor of Opposer.

Enclosed is two checks for $300.00 for this Opposition.

This Notice of Opposition is being filed in triplicate.

The Commissioner is authorized to charge any additional fees associated with this application or credit any overpayment to Deposit Account 11-0982. A duplicate copy of this communication is enclosed.

All correspondence should be addressed to David R. Fairbairn, Kinney & Lange, P.A., THE KINNEY & LANGE BUILDING, 312 South Third Street, Minneapolis, Minnesota 55415-1002.

Respectfully submitted,

LOUIS E. KEMP

Dated: _____   By:_____
                                       David R. Fairbairn
                                       THE KINNEY & LANGE BUILDING
                                       312 South Third Street
                                       Minneapolis, MN 55415-1002
                                       Telephone: (612) 339-1863
                                       Fax: (612) 339-6580

DRF:ks
K335.28-0001

CERTIFICATE OF MAILING

      I hereby certify that this correspondence is being deposited with the United States Postal Service with sufficient postage as first class mail in an envelope addressed to: Commissioner for Trademarks, P.O. Box 1451, Alexandria, Virginia 22313-1451 on this _____ day of _____, 200 .

_____
                        Attorney

APPENDIX N

Trademark Petition for Cancellation

IN THE UNITED STATES PATENT AND TRADEMARK OFFICE

BEFORE THE TRADEMARK TRIAL AND APPEAL BOARD

In the matter of Trademark Registration No. 1,859,815 for LOUIS KEMP, Registered October 25, 1994:

Louis E. Kemp, 　　　　　Petitioner v. Bumble Bee Seafoods, Inc., 　　　　　Registrant.	Cancellation No. _____ RE: Reg. No. 1,859,815 Issued: October 25, 1994

PETITION FOR CANCELLATION

Commissioner for Trademarks
P.O. Box 1451
Alexandria, VA 22313-1451

Sir:

In the matter of Trademark Registration No. 1,859,815, issued October 25, 1994, Bumble Bee Seafoods, Inc, (hereinafter "Bumble Bee") for the mark LOUIS KEMP, the Petitioner Louis E. Kemp believes that it will be damaged by the continued registration thereof, and hereby petitions to cancel the same.

As grounds for cancellation, Petitioner alleges:

1. The Petitioner, Louis E. Kemp, is an individual, with his principal place of residence at 9440 Cresta Drive, Los Angeles, California 90035.

2. The Kemp family has been engaged in the wholesale and retail sale of seafood since 1930. In 1985, Louis Kemp ("Mr. Kemp") started Kemp Foods, Inc., a company that made and sold artificial crab products made from surimi, a low-fat process fish product.

3. On March 30, 1987, Mr. Kemp sold his surimi-seafood business to Oscar Mayer Foods Corporation ("Oscar Mayer") pursuant to a Stock Acquisition Agreement ("the

Agreement").

4.   As part of the Agreement, Mr. Kemp transferred all of the trademarks used in connection with that business, including KEMP, KEMP's, KEMP's & Design, to Oscar Mayer. The Agreement also placed contractual restrictions on Mr. Kemp's right to use the marks in the future. These restrictions, embodies in sections 7.5, 7.6 and 7.7 of the Agreement, provide:

7.5   Seller represents and warrants that Seller or any entity in which Seller has an interest (except for Company) has never engaged and is not presently engaged in marketing, selling, or otherwise distributing at retail any product bearing the name KEMP, KEMP'S, KEMP'S & Design or any variation thereof except as disclosed and described in Exhibit 35 attached hereto. Seller agrees that neither Seller, nor any entity in which Seller has an interest, shall in the future market, sell or otherwise distribute any product except as provided in Section 7.6 and 7.7 or any other food or any other food or beverage product either at wholesale or retail bearing the name KEMP, KEMP'S, KEMP'S & Design or any variation thereof.

7.6   Seller agrees that within nine months, Seller or any entity in which Seller has an interest, shall cease all use of the name KEMP, KEMP'S and KEMP'S & Design in connection with the marketing, selling or otherwise distributing of any products.

7.7   It is agreed that Seller or any entity in which Seller has an interest, may market, sell or otherwise distribute those products identified on Exhibit 36 attached hereto, bearing a composite trademark consisting of the word KEMP or KEMP'S and preceded by one or more additional words the selection of which shall be approved in advance in writing by Buyer. The terms of said Exhibit 36 may not be changed or modified except with the approval by Buyer, such approval not to be unreasonably withheld, and by an instrument in writing duly signed on behalf of Buyer and Seller. It is the intention of the parties to avoid any likelihood of confusion among consumer resulting from the use of the respective marks of Seller and Buyer. It is further agreed that the companies described in Exhibit 37 as indicated in Exhibit 37

attached hereto for all purposes except in connection with
marketing, selling or distribution of products.

5.   Approximately six months after the parties finalized the Agreement, Lee
Scheele, Oscar Mayer Vice-President, asked Mr. Kemp if Oscar Mayer could use Mr. Kemp's
personal name, Louis Kemp, to market its surimi-based seafood products. This was the first time
anyone had contemplated using Louis Kemp in connection with the sale of Kemp products. Oscar
Mayer desired to use Mr. Kemp's full name because the company had achieved significant success
in the past by using the first and last names of individuals as trademarks, such as Oscar Mayer and
Louis Rich for certain of its processed food products. Mr. Kemp granted Mr. Scheele's request to
use his name on surimi seafood products as a favor and for no additional consideration. Oscar Mayer
then expended considerable capital marketing the Louis Kemp mark.

6.   Thereafter, the parties entered negotiations to amend the 1987 Agreement and
put the oral agreement in writing. During negotiations, Kraft initially requested the right to use
Louis Kemp on all products. This request was rejected by Mr. Kemp, who stated that he had only
given Oscar Mayer the limited right to use the mark on surimi products.

7.   Counsel for Kraft also attempted to get Mr. Kemp to agree to a provision
which would have contractually precluded Mr. Kemp from using Louis Kemp to sell food products.
Mr. Kemp refused to agree to this unlimited blanket preclusion.

8.   Another draft version of the amendment contained a clause which expressly
reserved Mr. Kemp's right to use Louis Kemp on other products. This language, however, did not
end up in the final version.

9.   On June 23, 1989, the parties entered into Amendment 1 to the 1987
Agreement ("the Amendment"). Section 7.8 of that Amendment provides, in its entirety:

> Seller grants to Buyer (a) the right to use and register the mark
> LOUIS KEMP, any design marks incorporating LOUIS KEMP
> and/or LOUIS KEMP SEAFOOD COMPANY in the United States
> and elsewhere for surimi-based seafood products and such other
> seafood and fish accessory products within the natural zone of
> product expansion; and (b) the right to adopt, use and register the
> name LOUIS KEMP SEAFOOD COMPANY in the United States

-4-

and elsewhere as trade name or as the corporate, firm or business title of any business, operating division or subsidiary of Buyer for the sale of surimi-based seafood products as such other seafood and fish accessory products within the natural zone of product expansion. Seller hereby agrees to reasonably cooperate with Buyer in obtaining trademark registrations, corporate, firm or business title recordals and/or trade name recordals that involve or include the name described in this section 7.8 and shall execute, at not expense to Seller, all consents and documents reasonably necessary for said registrations and recordals. Seller further agrees that it shall not attach or assist another in attacking the validity of the trademark LOUIS KEMP or any design marks incorporating LOUIS KEMP or any registration thereof permitting hereunder or the trade name LOUIS KEMP SEAFOOD COMPANY or any recordals thereof owned by Buyer in the United States or elsewhere.

10.   The Amendment also deleted and inserted a revised version of section 7.7, which provides, in relevant part:

It is agreed that Seller, or any entity in which Seller has an interest, may utilize a composite trademark consisting of the word KEMP or KEMP'S and preceded or followed by one or more additional words the selection of which shall be approved in advance in writing by Buyer in connection with the marketing, selling or distribution of those products identified in Exhibit 36.

The Amendment expressly provides that "except as hereinabove amended, all other provisions of the Agreement shall remain in full force and effect."

11.   On August 25, 1992, Oscar Mayer, through its parent corporation Kraft General Foods ("Kraft"), sold its surimi-seafood business to Tyson Foods, Inc., ("Tyson").

12.   Kraft assigned its rights, privileges and obligations to the LOUIS KEMP marks in its sale of the surimi-seafood business to Tyson.

13.   Paragraph 16.4 of the Stock Acquisition Agreement states that "No party hereto may make an assignment of its rights, privileges or obligations" under the Stock Acquisition Agreement. Kraft did not have authority to transfer any rights to the LOUIS KEMP trademark to Tyson.

14. During the sales negotiations between Kraft and Tyson, Mr. Kemp called John Tyson, president of Tyson, to inform that Kraft did not have the right to transfer the LOUIS KEMP marks including LOUIS KEMP Mr. Kemp also informed Mr. Tyson that there were usage restrictions on the LOUIS KEMP trademarks limiting use of the mark to "surimi-based seafood products and such other seafood and fish accessory products within the natural zone of product expansion".

15. Tyson continued with the purchase fully aware of the trademark issues involved with the LOUIS KEMP marks.

16. During prosecution of the trademark application that resulted in this registration, Registration No. 1,859,815, Tyson represented to the U.S. Patent and Trademark Office that Tyson had Mr. Kemp's consent to register his name as a trademark.

17. Mr. Kemp had never consented to allowing Tyson to register his name as a trademark, and Tyson did not have Mr. Kemp's consent to register his name as a trademark.

18. Additionally, during the prosecution of trademark application for LOUIS KEMP, Tyson listed under the goods and/or services section listed "surimi seafood, processed fish or imitation seafood". This exceeded the scope of use that Mr. Kemp had consented to in the Agreement, which was "surimi-based seafood products and such other seafood and fish accessory products within the natural zone of product expansion".

19. Tyson misrepresented to the U.S. Patent and Trademark Office that it had consent from Mr. Kemp to register the LOUIS KEMP mark, specifically for the goods "processed fish or imitation seafood".

20. Tyson obtained these registrations by fraud and deceit.

21. Tyson has since sold its rights to the LOUIS KEMP mark to Bumble Bee, which was in turn acquired by Con Agra Foods ("Con Agra").

22. Bumble Bee is now using the registered mark, obtained by fraud, to misrepresent the source of Bumble Bee's goods.

23. Bumble Bee has continued to improperly use the LOUIS KEMP SEAFOOD CO. mark on products outside of the scope of consent given by Mr. Kemp.

-6-

24.   Bumble Bee is also attempting to further improperly expand use the LOUIS KEMP SEAFOOD CO. mark to other products outside of the scope of consent given by Mr. Kemp.

25.   Bumble Bee filed a trademark application, U.S. Application 76-454609, on October 2, 2002 which further expands the scope of the LOUIS KEMP mark to "frozen, prepared and refrigerated meals" and "sauces and marinades".

26.   Bumble Bee has gone beyond the scope of what Mr. Kemp consented to in the original agreement by selling products outside the scope of surimi seafood products and accessories. Bumble Bee is attempting to and has indicated that it intends to further expand its improper use of the LOUIS KEMP mark to all sorts of other food products.

27.   Louis Kemp has been damaged and will continue to be damaged if U.S. Trademark Registration No. 1,879,815 is allowed to remain on the Register for the reasons set forth above.

WHEREFORE, Petitioner, Louis Kemp believes and avers that he is being and will be continued to be damaged by said registration and requests cancellation of Registration No. 1,859,815.

The filing fee for this Petition for Cancellation in the amount of $300.00 is enclosed. The Commissioner if hereby authorized to charge payment of any additional fees associated with this communication or credit any overpayment to Deposit Account No. 11-0982. An original and two copies of this Petition for Cancellation are enclosed.

All correspondence should be addressed to **David R. Fairbairn, Esq.**

Respectfully submitted,

LOUIS E. KEMP

Date: _____   By:_____

                            David R. Fairbairn
                            THE KINNEY & LANGE BUILDING
                            312 South Third Street
                            Minneapolis, MN 55415-1002
                            Telephone: (612) 339-1863
                            Fax: (612) 339-6580

DRF:HLN:mep

CERTIFICATE OF MAILING

     I hereby certify that this correspondence is being deposited with the United States Postal Service with sufficient postage as first class mail in an envelope addressed to: Commissioner for Trademarks, P.O. Box 1451, Alexandria, VA 22313-1451 on this _____ day of _____, 200___.

_____
Attorney

APPENDIX O

Trademark Infringement Complaint

UNITED STATES DISTRICT COURT
DISTRICT OF MINNESOTA

Suburban Taxi, Corp.,)	
)	
Plaintiff,)	Civil Action No. _____
)	
v.)	**COMPLAINT FOR TRADEMARK**
)	**INFRINGEMENT, UNFAIR**
Ali and Rasoul Houshyar, d/b/a)	**COMPETITION AND DECEPTIVE**
Aspen Travel Taxi & Limo - Suburban)	**TRADE PRACTICES.**
Airport Taxi Service and)	
Suburban Airport Taxi Service)	
)	
Defendants.)	
)	

Plaintiff Suburban Taxi, Corp. ("Suburban Taxi"), for its claims for relief against defendants

Ali and Rasoul Houshyar, d/b/a Aspen Travel Taxi & Limo - Suburban Airport Taxi Service and

Suburban Airport Taxi Service ("Suburban Airport Taxi"), alleges as follows:

<u>JURISDICTION</u>

1.   Suburban Taxi is a Minnesota corporation with a principal place of business in

Minneapolis, MN. Suburban Taxi is engaged in providing taxi services in interstate commerce,

primarily throughout the metropolitan area of Minneapolis and St. Paul, Minnesota and including

parts of western Wisconsin.

2.   Suburban Airport Taxi, upon information and belief, is an assumed name of Defendants

Ali and Rasoul Houshyar having a principle place of business at 185 Beaumont Circle, Apple

Valley, Minnesota. Upon information and belief, Suburban Airport Taxi is engaged in providing

taxi services in interstate commerce.

843

3.   This is an action for trademark infringement under the trademark laws of the United States

(15 U.S.C. §1051 et seq.); Federal Unfair competition under §43(a) of the Lanham Act (15

U.S.C. §1125(a)); and Deceptive Trade Practices under the laws of the state of Minnesota (Minn.

Stat. §325D.43 et seq.).

4.   This court has subject matter jurisdiction over the claims under 15 U.S.C. §1121(a), 28

U.S.C. §1331 and 28 U.S.C. §1338. This court has personal jurisdiction over the defendant

under Minnesota Statute §543.19.

5.   Venue in this district is proper under 38 U.S.C. §1391.

COUNT I

(Trademark Infringement)

6.   Count one arises under the trademark laws of the United States, 15 U.S.C. §1051 et seq.

7.   Suburban Taxi has been and is now engaged in providing taxi services in interstate

commerce. Since as earlier as 1982, Suburban Taxi has used the service mark "SUBURBAN" in

association with providing paid transportation services and with marketing in interstate

commerce. Suburban Taxi has used the service marks to distinguish its transportation services

from all other services of the same class, and Suburban Taxi has acquired substantial goodwill

through the use of its service mark. Exhibit A shows an example of Suburban Taxi's use of its

"SUBURBAN" service mark.

8.   Suburban Taxi is owner of U.S. Trademark Registration No. 1,519,233 for

"SUBURBAN" in class 39 for taxi services, which has been duly and legal issued by the United

States Patent and Trademark Office. A copy of the registration is attached as Exhibit B.

2

9. Since the date of issuance of this registration, Suburban Taxi has continued to use the service mark in interstate commerce.

10. Since the date of issuance of this registration, Suburban Taxi has been and still is the owner of the service mark.

11. Since the issuance of this service mark registration, Suburban Taxi has given notice to the public that the mark is a registered service mark by affixing notice as provided for in 15 U.S.C. §1111.

12. The Patent and Trademark Office has accepted Suburban Taxi's request to the incontestable right of Suburban Taxi to use the service mark "SUBURBAN" for taxi services. A copy of the acceptance of Suburban Taxi's incontestability request is attached as Exhibit C.

13. Subsequent to the issuance of Suburban Taxi's service mark registration, Suburban Airport Taxi, without consent or license from Suburban Taxi, infringed the service mark by reproducing, counterfeiting, copying and colorably imitating this service mark and applying the reproductions, counterfeits, copies and imitations to advertisements for providing taxi services in interstate commerce. Suburban Airport Taxi's use of "SUBURBAN AIRPORT TAXI SERVICE" is likely to cause confusion, mistake and deception and will continue to cause confusion, mistake and deception in violation of 15 U.S.C. §1114. An example of Suburban Airport Taxi's infringing use is attached as Exhibit D.

14. Suburban Taxi's use of the service mark preceded by many years Suburban Airport Taxi's adoption of their imitation marks.

3

15.   Prior to filing this Complaint, Suburban Taxi contacted Suburban Airport Taxi and requested that it cease and desist its infringement. A copy of the correspondence to Suburban Airport Taxi is attached as Exhibit E.

16.   Suburban Airport Taxi did not respond to Suburban Taxi's requests and as of June 1999 is still committing infringing acts.

17.   Upon information and belief, Suburban Airport Taxi will continue to infringe Suburban Taxi's service marks unless enjoined by this court.

18.   Upon information and belief, Suburban Airport Taxi was fully aware of Suburban Taxi's service marks and the registrations thereof when it committed its acts of infringement in willful and flagrant disregard of Suburban Taxi's lawful rights.

19.   Upon information and belief, Suburban Airport Taxi intended to cause confusion and mistake and intended to deceive the buyers of Suburban Airport Taxi's services into believing that they were buying services provided by Suburban Taxi.

20.   As a result of Suburban Airport Taxi's unlawful conduct, Suburban Taxi has been and continues to be substantially and irreparably harmed. If Suburban Airport Taxi's infringement is permitted to continue, further damage and irreparable injury will be sustained by Suburban Taxi, and others will be encouraged or induced to infringe upon Suburban Taxi's service marks. Through infringement of its service mark, the value of Suburban Taxi's service mark will be destroyed, for which Suburban Taxi cannot be adequately compensated at law.

21.   Suburban Airport Taxi has derived unlawful gains and profits from its infringement of Suburban Taxi's service mark, and Suburban Taxi thereby has been caused loss and damage. As a proximate result of Suburban Airport Taxi's infringement, Suburban Taxi has suffered injury to

4

its business, goodwill, reputation and profits, all to its damage and in an amount not yet fully

ascertained.

22.   This is an exceptional case of trademark infringement to Suburban Taxi's service mark.

Suburban Taxi is entitled to recover reasonable attorneys fees and three times its actual damages

pursuant to 15 U.S.C. §1117.

COUNT II

(Violation of Section 43(a) of the Lanham Act)

23.   Suburban Taxi re-alleges and incorporates by reference paragraphs 1 through 22.

24.   Count two arises under §43(a) of the Federal Trademark Act of 1946 as amended (15

U.S.C. §1125(a)).

25.   For many years, Suburban Taxi has used the service mark "SUBURBAN" and the trade

name "Suburban Taxi" in association with taxi services provided by it and marketed in interstate

commerce.

26.   Suburban Taxi has used its service mark and trade name to distinguish its products from

all other services of the same class, and Suburban Taxi has acquired substantial goodwill through

the use of its service mark.

27.   Suburban Taxi's service mark and trade name have acquired secondary meaning to the

public indicating Suburban Taxi as the source of its taxi services.

28.   Suburban Taxi's use of its service mark and trade name preceded by many years

Suburban Airport Taxi's adoption of its imitation marks.

29.   Suburban Airport Taxi's use of the mark "SUBURBAN AIRPORT TAXI SERVICE"

constitute acts in violation of 15 U.S.C. §1125(a) in that such use falsely describes Suburban

5

Taxi as the source of Suburban Airport Taxi's services, and falsely represents that Suburban

Airport Taxi's services are provided by, marketed by, sponsored by, approved of or licensed by

Suburban Taxi.

30.   As a proximate result of Suburban Airport Taxi's acts, Suburban Taxi has suffered great

detriment to its business, goodwill, reputation and profits, all to its damage in an amount as yet

not fully ascertained.

31.   This is an exceptional case and Suburban Taxi is entitled to recover three times its

damages plus recover attorneys fees pursuant to 15 U.S.C. §1117.

<u>COUNT III</u>

(Violation of Uniform Deceptive Trade Practices Act)

32.   Suburban Taxi re-alleges and incorporates by reference paragraphs 1- 31.

33.   Count three arises under the Uniform Deceptive Trade Practices Act, Minn. Stat.

§325D.43-48.

34.   Suburban Airport Taxi's use of the mark "SUBURBAN AIRPORT TAXI SERVICE"

constitute acts in violation of Minn. Stat. §325D.44.

35.   Upon information and belief, Suburban Airport Taxi's deceptive trade practices have

been willful.

36.   Suburban Taxi is entitled to recover its costs and attorneys fees pursuant to Minn. Stat.

§325D.45, Subd.2.

    WHEREOF, Plaintiff Suburban Taxi Corp. demands with respect to each of its claims:

a.   That Defendant, its agents, servants, employees, officers, attorneys, successors and

assigns, and all those persons in active concert or participation with each or any of them, be

6

enjoined, during the pendency of this action and permanently, from directly or indirectly

infringing the service mark of the Plaintiff in any manner.

b.   That Defendant be required to pay Plaintiff such damages as Plaintiff has sustained as a

result of Defendant's infringement of said service marks, and to account for all gains, profits and

advantages derived by said Defendant from its infringement of Plaintiff's service marks, together

with interest on such damages as the court deems appropriate.

c.   That Defendant be required to pay to Plaintiff three times its actual damages sustained as

a result of Defendant's infringement of said service marks, pursuant to 15 U.S.C. §1117.

d.   That Defendant pay to Plaintiff the costs and disbursements of this action, together with

reasonable attorneys fees as provided by 15 U.S.C. §1117 and Minn. Stat. §325D.45.

e.   Such other and further relief as the court deems just and proper.

JURY DEMAND

Suburban Taxi demands a jury trial on all issues so triable.

Respectfully submitted,

Dated: 6/23/99   By: _____

David R. Fairbairn (No. 28,125)
Michael Pape (No. 26,989X)
KINNEY & LANGE, P.A.
312 South Third Street
Minneapolis, MN 55414-1659
(612) 339-1863

**ATTORNEYS FOR PLAINTIFF
SUBURBAN TAXI, CORP.**

7

849

GO WITH GREEN AND WHITE

SUBURBAN TAXI CORP.

9614 HUMBOLDT AVE. SO.
BLOOMINGTON, MN 55431
(612) 888-9199
Gary Tournier, President

SUBURBAN
TAXI CORPORATION
(612) 888-9199

9614 HUMBOLDT AVE. SO. H. WILLIAMS
BLOOMINGTON, MN 55431 FLEET OPERATIONS MANAGER

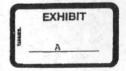

EXHIBIT

A

Int. Cl.: 39

Prior U.S. Cl.: 105

United States Patent and Trademark Office

Reg. No. 1,519,233
Registered Jan. 3, 1989

SERVICE MARK
PRINCIPAL REGISTER

SUBURBAN

SUBURBAN TAXI CORP. (MINNESOTA COR-
PORATION)
9614 HUMBOLDT AVENUE SOUTH
BLOOMINGTON, MN 55431

FIRST USE 7-0-1982; IN COMMERCE
7-0-1982.

SER. NO. 731,180, FILED 5-27-1988.

FOR: TAXI SERVICES, IN CLASS 39 (U.S. CL.
105).

ALICE SUE CARRUTHERS, EXAMINING AT-
TORNEY

UNITED STATES DEPARTMENT OF COMMERCE
Patent and Trademark Office
ASSISTANT SECRETARY AND COMMISSIONER
OF PATENTS AND TRADEMARKS
Washington, D.C. 20231

REGISTRATION NO. 1519233   SERIAL NO. 73/731180   PAPER NO.
                                                MAILING DATE: 08/15/94
MARK: SUBURBAN   542022-1

REGISTRANT: SUBURBAN TAXI CORP.

CORRESPONDENCE ADDRESS:
JO M. FAIRBAIRN
KINNEY & LANGE, P.A.
SUITE 1500
625 FOURTH AVENUE SOUTH
MINNEAPOLIS, MN 55415

Please furnish the following
in all correspondence:

1. Your phone number and zip code.
2. Mailing date of this action.
3. Affidavit-Renewal Examiner's name.
4. The address of all correspondence
   not containing fees should include
   the words "Box 5"
5. Registration No.

RECEIPT IS ACKNOWLEDGED OF THE SUBMITTED REQUEST UNDER:

SECTION 8 OF THE TRADEMARK STATUTE AND 37 CFR SECS. 2.161-2.166.

SECTION 15 OF THE TRADEMARK STATUTE AND 37 CFR SECS. 2.167-2.168.

YOUR REQUEST FULFILLS THE STATUTORY REQUIREMENTS AND HAS BEEN ACCEPTED.

Wye Jean Smith

WYE JEAN SMITH
AFFIDAVIT-RENEWAL EXAMINER
TRADEMARK EXAMINING OPERATION
(703) 308-9500   EXT. 38

AUG 1 5 1994

EXHIBIT
C

1-27-1999 5:00PM   FROM TRANSPORTATION GROUP 612 338 2000

USA
ⵣⵓ USC380
cial Sponsor of the
U.S. Olympic Team

Minneapolis
and Surrounding Area
January 1999/2000

Area Codes 612/651
See last page and inside back cover for
map and prefix listings by area code.

USWEST Dex®

Your Directory Expert

The Yellow Pages

Audio Information
Look for this symbol for free
24-hour audio information

http://uswestdex.com
Visit uswestdex.com to get the most
accurate business information for your area

Complete Listings
Listings for all local telephone companies including:
U S WEST, MCI, Ovation Communications
See page one for details.

New!   **Updated Area Codes**
All listings now include updated area codes

EXHIBIT

D

New! Internet Guid
See the Internet Products & S
heading in the Yellow Pa

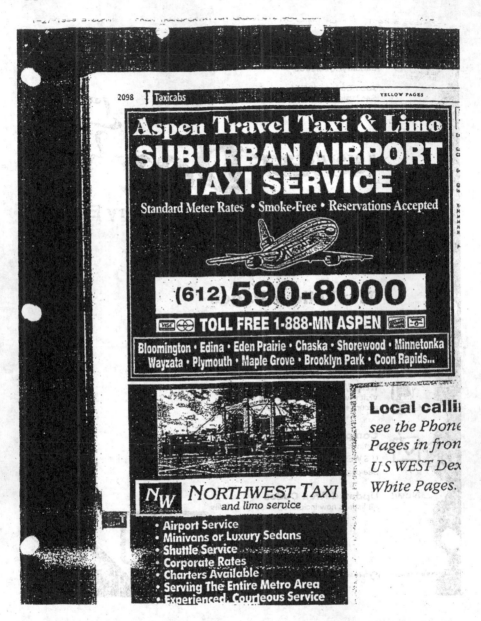

PATENT, TRADEMARK,
COPYRIGHT, AND RELATED
INTELLECTUAL PROPERTY L

INFO@KINNEY.COM
FACSIMILE (612) 339-6580
TELEPHONE (612) 339-1863

February 18, 1999

CERTIFIED MAIL
RETURN RECEIPT REQUESTED

Rasoul Houshyar
Ali Houshyar
Aspen Travel Taxi & Limo
185 Beaumont Circle
Apple Valley, MN 55124

Re: Suburban Taxi, Corp. v. Aspen Travel Taxi & Limo
       Infringement of "SUBURBAN" Service Mark
       U.S. Registration No.1,519,233
       Our File   :   S420.27-0001

Gentlemen:

    We represent Suburban Taxi, Corp., the holder of United States Service Mark Registration
No. 1,519,233 "SUBURBAN" for taxi services. A copy of this registration is enclosed for your
reference. The registered mark has become "incontestable" under the federal trademark laws, and
thereby gives my client the highest level of protection.

    It has come to my client's attention that you are using the mark SUBURBAN AIRPORT
TAXI SERVICE in the latest Minneapolis Yellow Pages. A copy of your advertisement is enclosed.
Your use of the mark SUBURBAN AIRPORT TAXI SERVICE is likely to confuse potential
customers into believing that you are associated, affiliated, or otherwise sponsored or related to my
client, Suburban Taxi, Corp.

    Your use of the mark is likely to cause confusion in the marketplace and constitutes an
infringement of our client's exclusive rights to the trademark "SUBURBAN". This is a violation
of federal as well as state trademark, service mark and unfair competition laws.

EXHIBIT

E

Chief Executive Officer
Page 2
February 18, 1999

    We must insist, therefore, on your immediate assurance that you have ceased all acts of infringement of our client's mark. Once we have received this assurance, we will be willing to discuss with you the damages that have been incurred by our client as a result of your infringement.

    We will expect to receive a written response to this letter within ten days of the date of this letter.

Very truly yours,

David R. Fairbairn

DRF:jmf
Encls.
cc: Gary Tournier, President
       Suburban Taxi, Corp.

Int. Cl.: 39

Prior U.S. Cl.: 105

Reg. No. 1,519,233

United States Patent and Trademark Office   Registered Jan. 3, 1989

SERVICE MARK
PRINCIPAL REGISTER

SUBURBAN

SUBURBAN TAXI CORP. (MINNESOTA COR-
PORATION)
9614 HUMBOLDT AVENUE SOUTH
BLOOMINGTON, MN 55431

FOR: TAXI SERVICES, IN CLASS 39 (U.S. CL. 105).

FIRST USE 7-0-1982; IN COMMERCE 7-0-1982.

SER. NO. 731,180, FILED 5-27-1988.

ALICE SUE CARRUTHERS, EXAMINING AT-
TORNEY

APPENDIX P

Confidentiality and Non-Disclosure Agreement

This Confidentiality and Nondisclosure Agreement (the "Agreement") is entered into this [Day] day of [Month], [Year] by and between [Company/Individual Name], a(n) corporation/individual with its principal office/residence at [Address] ("Disclosing Party"), and [Company Name], a corporation with principal office located at [Address] ("Receiving Party"), for the purpose of preventing the unauthorized disclosure of Confidential Information as defined below. The parties agree to enter into a confidential relationship with respect to the disclosure of certain proprietary and confidential information ("Confidential Information").

WHEREAS, Disclosing Party is willing to give Receiving Party access to certain Confidential Information in order for Receiving Party to provide certain services to Disclosing Party.

NOW THEREFORE, in consideration of the promises contained in this Agreement and for other good and valuable consideration, the adequacy and sufficiency of which are hereby acknowledged, the parties agree as follows:

1. **Definition of Confidential Information.** For purposes of this Agreement, "Confidential Information" shall include all information or material that has or could have commercial value or other utility in the business in which Disclosing Party is engaged, including, but not limited to, technical data, trade secrets, know-how, product plans, products, devices, database information, compilations, programs, methods, techniques, processes, inventions, developments, technology, designs, formula, pattern, engineering data, hardware configuration information, marketing materials and marketing information, financial information, customer lists, business plans, business strategies or other business information.

2. **Exclusions from Confidential Information.** Receiving Party's obligations under this Agreement do not extend to information that is:

   (2a) publicly known at the time of disclosure or subsequently becomes publicly known through no fault of the Receiving Party;

   (2b) discovered or created by the Receiving Party before

859

disclosure by Disclosing Party;

(2c) learned by the Receiving Party through legitimate means other than from the Disclosing Party or Disclosing Party's representatives; or

(2d) is disclosed by Receiving Party with Disclosing Party's prior written approval.

3. **Obligations of Receiving Party.** Receiving Party shall hold and maintain the Confidential Information in strictest confidence for the sole and exclusive benefit of the Disclosing Party. Receiving Party agrees to take all steps reasonably necessary to protect the secrecy of the Confidential Information, and to prevent the Confidential Information from falling into the public domain or into the possession of unauthorized persons. Receiving Party shall carefully restrict access to Confidential Information to employees, contractors, and third parties as is necessary and reasonably required for authorized use of the Confidential Information, and shall require any such non-employee persons receiving the Confidential Information to sign nondisclosure restrictions at least as protective as those in this Agreement. Receiving Party shall not, without prior written approval of Disclosing Party, use for Receiving Party's own benefit, publish, copy, or otherwise disclose to others, or permit the use by others for their benefit or to the detriment of Disclosing Party, any Confidential Information. Receiving Party shall return to Disclosing Party any and all records, notes, and other written, printed, or tangible materials in its possession pertaining to Confidential Information immediately if Disclosing Party so requests in writing.

4. **Ownership.** All Confidential Information shall remain the property of the Disclosing Party, and the Disclosing Party may use Confidential Information for any purpose without obligation to the Receiving Party. Nothing contained herein shall be construed as granting or implying any transfer of rights to the Receiving Party in the Confidential Information, or any patents or other intellectual property protecting or relating to the Confidential Information.

5. **Time Periods.** The nondisclosure provisions of this Agreement shall survive the termination of this Agreement and Receiving Party's duty to hold Confidential Information in confidence shall remain in effect until the Confidential Information no longer qualifies as a trade secret or until Disclosing Party sends Receiving Party written notice releasing Receiving Party from this Agreement, whichever occurs first, but no longer than [Number] years.

6. **Relationships.** Nothing contained in this Agreement shall be deemed to constitute either party a partner, joint venturer or

employee of the other party for any purpose.

7. **Severability.** If a court finds any provision of this Agreement invalid or unenforceable, the remainder of this Agreement shall be interpreted so as best to effect the intent of the parties.

8. **Waiver.** The failure to exercise any right provided in this Agreement shall not be a waiver of prior or subsequent rights.

9. **Merger.** This Agreement expresses the complete understanding of the parties with respect to the subject matter and supersedes all prior proposals, agreements, representations, and understandings. This Agreement may not be amended except in a writing signed by both parties.

10. **Choice of Law.** This Agreement shall be governed by [State] law without regard to conflict of law principles.

11. **Venue.** Disputes arising under or involving this Agreement shall be venued in [State].

This Agreement and each party's obligations shall be binding on the representatives, assigns, and successors of such party. Each party has signed this Agreement through its authorized representative.

Disclosing Party   Receiving Party
By: _____   By: _____
Printed Name: _____   Printed Name: _____
Title: _____   Title: _____
Dated: _____   Dated: _____

APPENDIX Q

Employment Agreement

EMPLOYEE AGREEMENT

Employee's Last Name	First Name	Middle Initial

In order for EMPLOYER to maintain a competitive edge, EMPLOYER must protect its inventions, discoveries, works, of authorship and its proprietary technical and business information.

Therefore, every new employee is required to sign this Agreement as a condition of employment with EMPLOYER.

By signing this Agreement, I agree:

1. As they are used in this Agreement, the term "inventions" includes inventions, improvements and discoveries, (whether or not they are patentable); and the term "works of authorship" includes writings, drawings, software, semiconductor mask works, and other works of authorship (whether or not they are copyrightable).

2. I will promptly disclose to EMPLOYER in writing, all inventions and works of authorship which are conceived, made, discovered, written or created by me alone or jointly with someone else on EMPLOYER'S time or on my own time, while I am employed by EMPLOYER and for one year after termination of my employment; and I assign all rights to these inventions and works of authorship to EMPLOYER.

3. I will give EMPLOYER all assistance it reasonably requires to perfect, protect, and use its rights to inventions and works of authorship. In particular, I will sign all documents, do all things, and supply all information that EMPLOYER considers necessary or desirable to transfer or record the transfer of my entire right, title and interest in inventions and works of authorship; and to enable EMPLOYER to obtain patent, copyright, or other legal protection for inventions and works of authorship. Any out-of-pocket expenses will be paid by EMPLOYER.

4. NOTICE: Minnesota law exempts from this Agreement "AN INVENTION FOR WHICH NO EQUIPMENT, SUPPLIES, FACILITY OR TRADE SECRET INFORMATION OF THE EMPLOYER WAS USED AND WHICH WAS DEVELOPED

ENTIRELY ON THE EMPLOYEE'S TIME, AND (1) WHICH DOES NOT RELATE (a) DIRECTLY TO THE BUSINESS OF THE EMPLOYER OR (b) TO THE EMPLOYER'S ACTUAL OR DEMONSTRABLY ANTICIPATED RESEARCH OR DEVELOPMENT, OR (2) WHICH DOES NOT RESULT FROM ANY WORK PERFORMED BY THE EMPLOYEE FOR THE EMPLOYER.

5. Also excluded from this Agreement are the following inventions and works of authorship which I own or control and WHICH WERE CONCEIVED, MADE, WRITTEN, OR CREATED by me PRIOR TO EMPLOYMENT WITH EMPLOYER, although they would be useful to EMPLOYER, its subsidiaries or affiliates.

   (1) _____
   (2) _____
   (3) _____

Other than these, I do not claim to own or control rights in any inventions or works of authorship and will not assert any rights against EMPLOYER.

6. I understand that if I possess proprietary information of another person or company as a result of prior employment, EMPLOYER expects me to honor any legal obligation I have with that person or company with respect to that proprietary information.

7. I will never divulge or use any of the proprietary technical and business information of EMPLOYER for my or another's benefit, unless authorized in writing by EMPLOYER. Nor will I accept any employment which would inherently involve the use or disclosure by me of proprietary information of EMPLOYER.

8. All documents and other tangible property relating in any way to the business of EMPLOYER are the exclusive property of EMPLOYER (even if I authored or created them). I agree to return all such documents and tangible property to EMPLOYER upon termination of employment or at such earlier time as EMPLOYER may request me to do so.

9. During my employment, I will not plan, organize or engage in any business competitive with any product or service marketed or planned for marketing by EMPLOYER or conspire with others to do so, and will not engage in any other activity which may create a conflict of interest with EMPLOYER.

10. For a period of two years after termination of my employment with EMPLOYER (the "Noncompetition Period"):

    (a) I will inform my new employer, prior to accepting employment, of the existence of this Employee Agreement and provide such employer with a copy thereof.

(b) I will inform EMPLOYER in writing of any successive employment obtained after termination of my employment with EMPLOYER.

(c) If I have been or am employed by EMPLOYER in a sales capacity, I will not render services in the United States, directly or indirectly, to any Conflicting Organization in connection with the development, manufacture, marketing, sale, merchandising, leasing, servicing or promotion of any Conflicting Product to any person or organization upon whom I called, or whose account I supervised on behalf of EMPLOYER, at any time during the last three years of my employment by EMPLOYER.

(d) If I have been or am employed by EMPLOYER in a nonsales capacity, I will not render, to any Conflicting Organization, services, directly or indirectly, in the United States, or in any country in which EMPLOYER has a plant for manufacturing a product upon which I worked during my employment by EMPLOYER or in which EMPLOYER provides a service, in which I participate during my employment by EMPLOYER, except that I may accept employment with a large Conflicting Organization whose business is diversified (and which as to part of its business is not a Conflicting Organization), provided EMPLOYER, prior to my accepting such employment, shall receive separate written assurances satisfactory to EMPLOYER from such Conflicting Organization and from me, that I will not render services directly or indirectly in connection with any Conflicting Product.

(e) Without limiting the generality of the foregoing, during the Noncompetition Period, I agree I will not, directly or indirectly, for my benefit or for the benefit of any other person, firm or entity, solicit the employment or services of any person who is at any time during the Noncompetition period an employee of or consultant to EMPLOYER.

(f) If I am unable to obtain employment consistent with my abilities and education, within one month after termination of my employment with EMPLOYER, solely because of provisions of this paragraph 10, such provisions shall thereafter continue to bind me only as long as EMPLOYER shall make payments to me equal to my monthly base pay at termination (exclusive of extra compensation, bonus or employee benefits) for each month of such unemployment, commencing with the second month after termination of my employment with EMPLOYER.

I agree that I will, during each month of such unemployment, make conscientious and aggressive efforts to find employment; and I will, within ten days after the end of each calendar

865

month, give EMPLOYER a detailed written account of my efforts to obtain employment. Such account will include a statement by me that although I aggressively sought employment, I was unable to obtain it solely because of the provisions of this paragraph 10.

It is understood that EMPLOYER shall, at its option, be relieved of making a monthly payment to me for any month during which I failed to seek employment conscientiously and aggressively, and to account to EMPLOYER, as provided for above.

EMPLOYER is obligated to make such payments to me, upon my fulfillment of the conditions set forth above, for twenty-three consecutive months unless EMPLOYER gives me written permission to accept available employment, or gives me a written release from the obligations of paragraph 10.

EMPLOYER's obligation to make such monthly payments shall terminate upon my death or upon my obtaining employment. I agree that I will give prompt written notice of such employment to EMPLOYER.

EMPLOYER shall not be liable, under this Agreement, or in any action relating thereto, for any amount greater than the equivalent of twenty-three such monthly payments, less amounts paid to me by EMPLOYER pursuant to this Agreement; EMPLOYER not being obligated to make a payment to me for the first month of such employment.

(g) If, after termination of my employment with EMPLOYER, I obtain other employment but because of the provisions of paragraph 10, my position is such that my gross monthly income will be less than that which I last received from EMPLOYER as monthly base pay at termination, then EMPLOYER's obligations to make payments to me for the period specified in paragraph 10(f) will be limited to the difference between my monthly base pay at EMPLOYER, at termination, and the gross monthly income I will receive in my subsequent employment.

(h) CONFLICTING PRODUCT, as used in this agreement, means any product, method or process, system or service of any person or organization other than EMPLOYER, in existence or under development, which is the same as or similar to or competes with, or has a usage allied to, a product, method or process, system or service upon which I work (in either a sales or a nonsales capacity) during the last three years of my employment by EMPLOYER, or about which I acquire Confidential Information.

(i) CONFLICTING ORGANIZATION, as used in this agreement, means any person or organization which is engaged in or about to become engaged in, research on or development, production, marketing, leasing, selling or servicing of a Conflicting Product.

11. I will comply with all EMPLOYER guidelines, policies and procedures.

12. I will participate in an exit interview at the time of termination of employment with EMPLOYER, and will sign a statement that I have returned to EMPLOYER all documents and tangible property, and that I acknowledge my continuing obligations under this Employee Agreement.

13. I acknowledge that all of the provisions of this Agreement are fair and necessary to protect the interests of EMPLOYER. However, if a provision of this Agreement is held invalid by a court of competent jurisdiction, the remaining provisions will nonetheless be enforceable according to their terms. Further, if any provision is held to be overbroad as written, that provision should be considered to be amended to narrow its application to the extent necessary to make the provision enforceable according to applicable law and enforced as amended.

14. I understand that even if EMPLOYER waives or fails to enforce the terms, covenants or agreements contained in this Agreement or any similar agreement in one instance, that will not constitute a waiver or acquiescence by EMPLOYER of rights with respect to other violations of this or any other agreement.

15. This Agreement will be binding on my heirs, assigns and legal representatives, and it may be transferred by EMPLOYER to it successors and assigns.

16. This Agreement shall be interpreted and construed in accordance with the laws of the State of Minnesota, without regard to choice of law principles.

_____
Date

_____
Signature of Employee

_____
Address

_____

Accepted by EMPLOYER, INCORPORATED

_____
Date

_____
By

Title

APPENDIX R

Citations to State Deceptive Trade Practices Acts

Alabama: Ala. Code § 8-19-1 et seq.

Alaska: Alaska Stat. § 45.50.471 et seq.

Arizona: Ariz. Rev. Stat. § 44-1521 et seq.

Arkansas: Ark. Code Ann. § 4-88-107 et seq.

California: Cal. Civ. Code § 17500 et seq.

Colorado: Colo. Rev. Stat. § 6-1-101 et seq.

Connecticut: Conn. Gen. Stat. § 42-110a et seq.

Delaware: Del. Code Ann. tit. 6, § 2531 et seq.

District of Columbia: D.C. Code Ann. § 28-3901 et seq.

Florida: Fla. Stat. Ann. § 501.201 et seq.

Georgia: Ga. Code Ann. § 10-1-370 et seq.

Hawaii: Haw. Rev. Stat. § 481A-1 to 481A-5

Idaho: Idaho Code § 48-601 et seq.

Illinois: 815 Ill. Comp. Stat. 510/1 et seq.

Indiana: Ind. Code § 24-5-0.5-1 et seq.

Iowa: Iowa Code Ann. § 714.16

Kansas: Kan. Stat. Ann. § 50-623 et seq.

Kentucky: Ky. Rev. Stat. Ann. § 367.110 et seq.

Louisiana: La. Rev. Stat. Ann. § 51:1401 et seq.

Maine: Me. Rev. Stat. Ann. tit. 5, § 206 et seq.; tit. 10, § 1211 et seq.

Maryland: Md. Code Ann., Com. Law § 13-101 et seq.

Massachusetts: Mass. Gen. Laws. ch. 93A, § 1 et seq.

Michigan: Mich. Comp. Laws Ann. § 445.901 et seq.

Minnesota: Minn. Stat. Ann. § 325D.43 et seq.

Mississippi: Miss. Code Ann. § 75-24-1 et seq.

Missouri: Mo. Rev. Stat. § 407.010 et seq.

Montana: Mont. Code Ann. § 30-14-101 et seq.

Nebraska: Neb. Rev. Stat. § 87-301 et seq.

Nevada: Nev. Rev. Stat. ch. 598

New Hampshire: N.H. Rev. Stat. Ann. § 358-A et seq.

New Jersey: N.J. Rev. Stat. § 56:8-1 et seq.

New Mexico: N.M. Stat. Ann. § 57-12-1 et seq.

New York: N.Y. Gen. Bus. Law § 349 et seq.

North Carolina: N.C. Gen. Stat. § 75-1 et seq.

North Dakota: N.D. Cent. Code § 51-10-01 et seq.

Ohio: Ohio Rev. Code Ann. § 1345.01 et seq.

Oklahoma: Okla. Stat. Ann. tit. 78, § 51 et seq.

Oregon: Or. Rev. Stat. § 646.605 et seq.

Pennsylvania: 73 P.S. § 201-1 et seq.

Rhode Island: R.I. Gen. Laws §§ 6-13.1-1 to -13.1-11

South Carolina: S.C. Code Ann. § 39-5-10 et seq.

South Dakota: S.D. Codified Laws § 37-24-1 et seq.

Tennessee: Tenn. Code Ann. § 47-18-101 et seq.

Texas: Tex. Bus. & Com. Code Ann. § 17.41 et seq.

Utah: Utah Code Ann. § 13-11-1 et seq.

Vermont: Vt. Stat. Ann. tit. 9, § 2451 et seq.

Virginia: Va. Code Ann. § 59.1-196 et seq.

Washington: Wash. Rev. Code § 19.86.010 et seq.

West Virginia: W. Va. Code Ann. § 46A-6-101 et seq.

Wisconsin: Wis. Stat. Ann. § 421 to 427

Wyoming: Wyo. Stat. Ann. § 40-12-101 et seq.

APPENDIX S

Citations to State Unfair Business Practices Acts

Alabama: Ala. Code § 8-10-1 et seq.

Arizona: Ariz. Rev. Stat. Ann. § 44-1521 et seq. (provides competitor standing)

Arkansas: Ark. Code Ann. § 4-75-101 et seq.

California: Cal. Bus. & Prof. Code § 17000 et seq. (provides competitor standing)

Colorado: Colo. Rev. Stat. § 6-2-101 et seq. (provides competitor standing)

Connecticut: Conn. Gen. Stat. § 42-110a et seq. (provides competitor standing)

Delaware: Del. Code Ann. tit. 6, § 2511 et seq.

District of Columbia: D.C. Code Ann. § 28-3901 et seq.

Florida: Fla. Stat. ch. 501 (provides competitor standing)

Georgia: Ga. Code Ann. § 10-1-390 et seq. (provides competitor standing)

Hawaii: Haw. Rev. Stat. § 480-1 et seq. (provides competitor standing)

Idaho: Idaho Code § 48-601 et seq.

Illinois: 815 Ill. Comp. Stat. 505/1 et seq. (provides competitor standing for damages)

Kansas: Kan. Stat. Ann. § 50-623 et seq.

Kentucky: Ky. Rev. Stat. Ann. ch. 367

Louisiana: La. Rev. Stat. Ann. § 51:1401 et seq. (provides competitor standing)

Maine: Me. Rev. Stat. Ann. tit. 5, § 206 et seq., tit. 10, § 1211 et seq.

Maryland: Md. Code Ann., Com. Law § 13-301

Massachusetts: Mass. Gen. Laws Ann. ch. 93A, § 1 et seq. (provides competitor standing)

Michigan: Mich. Comp. Laws Ann. § 445.901 et seq. (provides competitor standing)

Minnesota: Minn. Stat. Ann. chs. 325D, 325E, 325F and 325G (provides competitor standing)

Mississippi: Miss. Code Ann. § 75-24-1 et seq.

Missouri: Mo. Rev. Stat. § 407.010 et seq.

Montana: Mont. Code Ann. § 30-14-101 et seq.

Nebraska: Neb. Rev. Stat. § 59-1601 et seq. (provides competitor standing)

Nevada: Nev. Rev. Stat. § 598A.010 et seq.

New Jersey: N.J. Stat. Ann. § 56:8-1 et seq. (provides competitor standing)

New Mexico: N.M. Stat. Ann. § 57-12-2 et seq. (provides competitor standing)

New Hampshire: N.H. Rev. Stat. Ann. § 358-A:1 et seq.

New York: N.Y. Gen. Bus. Law § 349 et seq.

North Carolina: N.C. Gen. Stat. § 75-1.1 (provides competitor standing)

North Dakota: N.D. Cent. Code § 51-10-01 et seq. (provides competitor standing)

Ohio: Ohio Rev. Code Ann. § 1345.01 et seq.

Oklahoma: Okla. Stat. Ann. tit. 15, § 751 et seq.

Pennsylvania: 73 P.S. § 201-1 et seq.

Puerto Rico: P.R. Laws Ann. tit. 10, § 257 et seq. (provides competitor standing)

South Carolina: S.C. Code Ann. § 39-5-10 et seq. (provides competitor standing)

South Dakota: S.D. Codified Laws Ann. § 37-24-6 et seq. (provides competitor standing)

Tennessee: Tenn. Code Ann. § 47-18-101 et seq. (provides competitor standing for injunctions)

Texas: Tex. Bus. & Com. Code Ann. § 17.41 et seq.

Utah: Utah Code Ann. § 13-5-1 et seq. (provides competitor standing)

Vermont: Vt. Stat. Ann. tit. 9, § 2451 et seq.

Virginia: Va. Code Ann. § 59.1-196 et seq.

Washington: Wash. Rev. Code § 19.86.010 et seq. (provides competitor standing)

West Virginia: W.Va. Code § 46A-6-101 et seq.

Wisconsin: Wis. Stat. § 100.20

Wyoming: Wyo. Stat. § 40-12-101 et seq.

APPENDIX T

Citations to State False Advertising Acts

Alabama: Ala. Code § 13A-9-42

Alaska: Alaska Stat. § 45.50.471 et seq.

Arizona: Ariz. Rev. Stat. Ann. § 44-1481

Arkansas: Ark. Code Ann. § 5-37-515

California: Cal. Bus. & Prof. Code § 17500 et seq. (provides competitor standing)

Colorado: Colo. Rev. Stat. § 6-1-101 et seq. and 18-5-301 (provides competitor standing)

Delaware: Del. Code Ann. tit. 6, § 2532

District of Columbia: D.C. Code Ann. § 22-1511 et seq.

Florida: Fla. Stat. §§ 817.06 and 817.40 et seq.

Georgia: Ga. Code Ann. § 10-1-420 et seq. (provides competitor standing)

Hawaii: Haw. Rev. Stat. § 708-871

Idaho: Idaho Code § 48-412 (provides competitor standing)

Illinois: 720 Ill. Comp. Stat. 5/17-5.7 et seq.

Indiana: Ind. Code § 35-43-5-3(a)(9)

Iowa: Iowa Code § 714.16(2)(a)

Kansas: Kan. Stat. Ann. § 50-626

Kentucky: Ky. Rev. Stat. Ann. § 517.030

Louisiana: La. Rev. Stat. Ann. § 51:411 et seq.

Maine: Me. Rev. Stat. Ann. tit. 17-A, § 901(1)(G)

Maryland: Md. Code Ann. Com. Law § 11-701 et seq.

Massachusetts: Mass. Gen. Laws Ann. ch. 266, § 91 (provides competitor standing)

Michigan: Mich. Comp. Laws Ann. § 290.626, 445.315, and 445.1525

Minnesota: Minn. Stat. Ann. § 325F.67 (provides competitor standing)

Mississippi: Miss. Code Ann. § 97-23-1 and 97-23-3

Missouri: Mo. Rev. Stat. § 407.010 et seq.

Montana: Mont. Code Ann. § 32-5-309

Nebraska: Neb. Rev. Stat. § 87-302

Nevada: Nev. Rev. Stat. § 207.170 et seq.

New Hampshire: N.H. Rev. Stat. Ann. § 358-A:2

New Jersey: N.J. Rev. Stat. § 56:8-2

New Mexico: N.M. Stat. Ann. § 57-15-1 et seq.

New York: N.Y. Gen. Bus. Law §§ 350, 350-A

North Carolina: N.C. Gen. Stat. §§ 75-1.1, 75-29, and 75-42

North Dakota: N.D. Cent. Code § 51-12-01 et seq.

Ohio: Ohio Rev. Code Ann. § 4165.02

Oklahoma: Okla. Stat. Ann. tit. 21, § 1502

Oregon: Or. Rev. Stat. § 646.608

Pennsylvania: 73 P.S. §§ 201-3, 201-4

Puerto Rico: P.R. Laws Ann. tit. 10, §§ 311 et seq.

Rhode Island: R.I. Gen. Laws § 6-13.1-1

South Carolina: S.C. Code Ann. § 39-1-20

South Dakota: S.D. Codified Laws Ann. § 37-24-6

Tennessee: Tenn. Code Ann. §§ 39-14-127 and 47-18-104 et seq.

Texas: Tex. Bus. & Com. Code Ann. § 17.46

Utah: Utah Code Ann. § 13-11a-1 et seq. (provides competitor standing)

Vermont: Vt. Stat. Ann. tit. 13, § 2005

Virginia: Va. Code Ann. § 18.2-216 (provides competitor standing)

Washington: Wash. Rev. Code § 9.04.010 et seq.

West Virginia: W.Va. Code §§ 32A-1-2, 46A-6-102(7) and 46A-6-104 (provides competitor standing)

Wisconsin: Wis. Stat. § 100.18 (provides competitor standing)

Wyoming: Wyo. Stat. § 6-3-611

APPENDIX U

Citations to State Right of Publicity Acts

California: Cal. Civ. Code § 3344
Florida: Fla. Stat. ch. 540.08
Illinois: 765 Ill. Comp. Stat. 1075/1 et seq.
Indiana: Ind. Code § 32-36-1-1 et seq.
Kentucky: Ky. Rev. Stat. Ann. § 391.170
Massachusetts: Mass. Ann. Laws ch. 214, § 3A
Nebraska: Neb. Rev. Stat. § 20-202
Nevada: Nev. Rev. Stat. § 597.770 et seq.
New York: N.Y. Civ. Rights Law § 50 et seq.
Ohio: Ohio Rev. Code Ann. § 2741.01 et seq.
Oklahoma: Okla. Stat. Ann. tit. 21, §§ 839.1 to 839.3 and Okla.
Stat. Ann. tit. 12, §§ 1448 to 1449
Pennsylvania: 42 Pa. Cons. Stat. Ann. § 8316
Rhode Island: R.I. Gen. Laws §§ 9-1-28 and 9-1-28.1
Tennessee: Tenn. Code Ann. § 47-25-1101 et seq.
Texas: Tex. Prop. Code Ann. § 26.001 et seq.
Utah: Utah Code Ann. § 45-3-1 et seq.
Virginia: Va. Code Ann. § 8.01-40
Washington: Wash. Rev. Code Ann. § 63.60.010 et seq.
Wisconsin: Wis. Stat. § 995.50

APPENDIX V
Patent Assignment

ASSIGNMENT	Attorney Docket No.

First Named Inventor   :

Title   :

     WHEREAS, we, _____, of _____, ___, U.S.A.; _____, of _____, ___, U.S.A.; _____, of _____, ___, U.S.A.; and _____, of _____, ___, U.S.A. have invented certain new and useful improvements as described in an application entitled _____ for Letters Patent of the United States, the application being identifiable by its title and named inventors listed above, and/or being identifiable in the United States Patent and Trademark Office by Application No. _____, filed _____; and

     WHEREAS, _____, a corporation organized and existing under the laws of the State of___, and having offices at _____, ("Assignee") is desirous of acquiring the entire right, title and interest in and to the invention, the application, and any and all Letters Patent or similar legal protection, foreign or domestic, to be obtained therefor;

     NOW, THEREFORE, for good and valuable consideration, the receipt and adequacy of which is hereby acknowledged, I transfer to Assignee, its successors and assigns, my entire right, title and interest in and to the invention, the above-identified application, corresponding domestic and foreign applications, all Letters Patent or similar legal protection issuing thereon, and all rights and benefits under any applicable treaty or convention; and I authorize the Commissioner of Patents and Trademarks of the United States or foreign equivalent thereof to issue the Letters Patent or similar legal protection to the Assignee.

     I authorize the Assignee, its successors and assigns, to insert in this instrument the filing date and application number of the application when ascertained.

     I authorize the Assignee, its successors and assigns, or anyone it may properly designate, to apply for Letters Patent or similar legal protection, in its own name if desired, in any and all foreign countries.

     I represent to the Assignee, its successors and assigns, that I have not and shall not execute any writing or do any act whatsoever conflicting with this Assignment. I, my executors or administrators, will at any time upon request, without additional consideration, but at the expense of the Assignee, its successors and assigns, execute such additional writings and do such additional acts as the Assignee, its successors and assigns, may deem desirable to perfect its enjoyment of this grant, and render all assistance in making application for and obtaining, maintaining, and enforcing the Letters Patent or similar legal protection on the invention in any and all countries.

_____

STATE OF   )
) ss.
COUNTY OF   )

     Subscribed and sworn to before me, a Notary Public, this ____ day of _____, 200__.

_____
Notary Public

(SEAL)

Page 1 of 3 Pages

877

STATE OF   )
) ss.
COUNTY OF   )

         Subscribed and sworn to before me, a Notary Public, this ____ day of _____, 200__.

_____
                    Notary Public

(SEAL)

STATE OF   )
) ss.
COUNTY OF   )

         Subscribed and sworn to before me, a Notary Public, this ____ day of _____, 200__.

_____
                    Notary Public

(SEAL)

Page 2 of 3 Pages

_____

STATE OF   )
) ss.
COUNTY OF   )

        Subscribed and sworn to before me, a Notary Public, this ____ day of _____, 200__.

_____
                Notary Public

(SEAL)

APPENDIX W

Trademark Assignment

TRADEMARK ASSIGNMENT

Amalgamated Breathing Crystals Inc. has an office and principal place of business at 1000 Rose Street, Minneapolis, Minnesota, a Delaware corporation (herein "Assignor"), and has adopted and is using the mark SUPER CRYSTALS for which the Assignor has obtained registration in the United States Patent and Trademark Office, Reg. No. 1,234,456, granted January 10, 2004.

Xenocrystic Yellow Zircon Company has an office and principal place of business at 1001 Rose Street, Minneapolis, Minnesota, a Minnesota corporation (herein "Assignee") and desires to acquire the Assignor's entire right, title and interest in and to the mark and the above-identified registration.

For good and valuable consideration, the receipt and adequacy of which are acknowledged, the Assignor assigns to the Assignee the Assignor's entire right, title and interest in and to the mark, together with the good will of the business associated with the mark, and the above-identified registration.

AMALGAMATED BREATHING CRYSTALS INC.

By: _____   Date: _____
    Thomas Jones
    President

STATE OF MINNESOTA   )
)   ss.
COUNTY OF HENNEPIN)

Subscribed and sworn to before me, a Notary Public, this 10th day of January, 2004.

_____

Notary Public

(SEAL)

APPENDIX W

Trademark Assignment

TRADEMARK ASSIGNMENT

APPENDIX X

Copyright Assignment

COPYRIGHT ASSIGNMENT

WHEREAS, ASSIGNOR, a corporation organized and existing under and by virtue of the laws of the State of STATE with offices at ADDRESS, is, by operation of law, the owner of the entire right, title and interest in, to and under the Copyrights and Copyright Registrations and applications identified on Schedule 1.04 hereto; and

WHEREAS, ASSIGNEE, a corporation organized and existing under and by virtue of the laws of the State of STATE with offices at ADDRESS is desirous of acquiring the entire right, title and interest in, to and under the aforesaid Copyrights and Copyright Registrations.

NOW, THEREFORE, for and in consideration of One Dollar ($1.00) and other good and valuable consideration, the receipt and adequacy of which is hereby acknowledged, ASSIGNOR hereby assigns, sells and transfers unto ASSIGNEE its entire right, title and interest in, to and under the Copyrights and Copyright Registrations identified on Schedule 1.04, including all rights of recovery for past infringement thereof, to have and to hold for its own use and enjoyment, and for the use and enjoyment of its successors and assigns, as fully and completely as the same would have been held by ASSIGNOR had this assignment and sale not been made.

ASSIGNOR

By _____

OFFICER OF ASSIGNOR

State of STATE   )
)
County of COUNTY)

      Subscribed and sworn to before me this _____ day of _____, 2004.

_____
Notary Public

APPENDIX X

Copyright Assignment

[COPYRIGHT ASSIGNMENT]

STATE OF ____

COUNTY OF ____

Subscribed and sworn to before me this ____ day of ____, 2004

Notary Public

APPENDIX Y

Patent License

PATENT LICENSE

LICENSE OF U.S. PATENT NO. X,XXX,XXX

This agreement, entered into as of this 25th day of April, 2004, by and between Amalgamated Breathing Crystals Inc., a corporation of Delaware with offices at 1000 Rose Street, Minneapolis, Minnesota 55413, hereinafter referred to as LICENSOR, and Xenocrystic Yellow Zircon Company, a corporation of Minnesota with offices at 1001 Rose Street, Minneapolis, Minnesota 55413, hereinafter referred to as LICENSEE.

Recitals

WHEREAS, LICENSOR is the owner of certain PATENT RIGHTS (hereinafter defined) covering DEVICES (hereinafter defined).

WHEREAS, LICENSEE is a manufacturer of various equipment and desires to manufacture and sell DEVICES.

WHEREAS, LICENSEE would like to receive and LICENSOR is willing to grant a non-exclusive license under the PATENT RIGHTS.

NOW, THEREFORE, in consideration of the promises and mutual covenants hereinafter contained the parties hereto agree as follows:

ARTICLE I

DEFINITIONS

1.1 PATENT RIGHTS

PATENT RIGHTS shall mean U.S. Patent No. X,XXX,XXX, any corresponding patents or patent applications filed in other countries, any reissue applications, continuation application, and continuation-in-part applications filed thereon in the United States or any foreign country and any patents issuing thereon.

1.2 DEVICES

DEVICES shall mean any apparatus sold by LICENSEE that is covered by any of the claims of the PATENT RIGHTS.

1.3 NET SALES PRICE

NET SALES PRICE shall mean the price at which a DEVICE is invoiced in an arms length transaction less any royalties hereunder, discounts, sales taxes, excise taxes, or freight charges which are included in such invoice price.

1.4 EFFECTIVE DATE

>EFFECTIVE DATE shall mean the date upon which the last of the parties hereto signs this LICENSE AGREEMENT FOR PATENT X,XXX,XXX.

1.5 TERM

>TERM shall mean the period from the EFFECTIVE DATE to the date of cancellation by one of the parties under ARTICLE V hereof or the expiration date of U.S. Patent No. X,XXX,XXX or any reissue, continuation, or continuation-in-part thereof whichever occurs first.

1.6 AFFILIATE

>AFFILIATE shall mean any entity that is controlled by LICENSEE through ownership of at least 50% of the voting stock of such entity.

ARTICLE II

GRANT

2.1 LICENSOR hereby grants to LICENSEE and its AFFILIATES an irrevocable, worldwide, non-exclusive license during the TERM to make, have made, use, lease and sell DEVICES, and components and parts therefore under the PATENT RIGHTS.

2.2 LICENSOR and LICENSEE understand and agree that LICENSEE receives no licenses or rights whatsoever, by implication or otherwise, under any other patents or applications owned or controlled by LICENSOR, except those specifically granted to LICENSEE by the terms of this LICENSE AGREEMENT FOR PATENT X,XXX,XXX.

2.3 This LICENSE AGREEMENT FOR PATENT X,XXX,XXX shall be binding upon and shall inure to the benefit of any corporation, company or entity into which either LICENSOR or LICENSEE may be merged or consolidated and the rights and obligations of the parties shall be assignable to any purchaser of that part of the assets of such party to which this LICENSE AGREEMENT FOR PATENT X,XXX,XXX relates.

2.4 In the event LICENSOR grants another license under the PATENT RIGHTS on more favorable terms than those set forth in this LICENSE AGREEMENT FOR PATENT X,XXX,XXX, LICENSEE may elect to include such more favorable terms herein provided that LICENSEE also includes any terms from such other license that are less favorable than those herein.

2.5 LICENSEE agrees for itself and its AFFILIATES that no sublicenses shall be granted to any third party under the PATENT RIGHTS except to the extent that licenses are implied with the sale of DEVICES under the Uniform Commercial Code.

ARTICLE III

CONSIDERATION

3.1 Down Payment

Within thirty (30) days after the EFFECTIVE DATE, LICENSEE shall pay to LICENSOR the sum of One Thousand Dollars ($1,000.00).

3.2 Royalty Payment

During the TERM, LICENSEE shall pay to LICENSOR a royalty of five percent (5%) of the NET SALES PRICE of all DEVICES sold by LICENSEE.

3.3 Reports and Payments

Each calendar quarter after the EFFECTIVE DATE there shall be an accounting period (a fractional initial or terminal period to be regarded as an accounting period) and LICENSEE shall within sixty (60) days after the end of each and every such accounting period, report in writing to LICENSOR the total number of DEVICES sold by LICENSEE during such accounting period. Each such report shall also include the total NET SELLING PRICE of the DEVICES. LICENSEE shall send to LICENSOR with each such report a check to the order of LICENSOR in U.S. Dollars in payment of the amount, if any, due to LICENSOR under this LICENSE AGREEMENT FOR PATENT X,XXX,XXX, for said accounting period.

3.4 Release for Past Infringement

LICENSOR hereby releases LICENSEE for any infringement of the PATENT RIGHTS that may have arisen before the EFFECTIVE DATE of this LICENSE AGREEMENT FOR PATENT X,XXX,XXX.

ARTICLE IV

WARRANTIES

4.1 LICENSOR warrants that it is the owner of the entire right, title and interest in the PATENT RIGHTS.

4.2 LICENSOR warrants that it has the sole right to grant licenses under the PATENT RIGHTS and has not heretofore granted any rights thereunder which would interfere with any rights granted LICENSEE under this LICENSE AGREEMENT FOR PATENT X,XXX,XXX.

4.3 LICENSOR warrants that it agrees to prosecute all substantial claims of infringement of the PATENT RIGHTS at its own expense.

ARTICLE V

RIGHTS OF CANCELLATION

5.1 In the event that LICENSEE defaults in making a payment or report hereunder, or shall commit any other breach of covenant herein contained, then LICENSOR may, at its option, cancel and terminate this LICENSE AGREEMENT FOR PATENT X,XXX,XXX and rights under the PATENT RIGHTS, by giving LICENSEE thirty (30) days written notice. Provided however, that if LICENSEE shall correct the default within thirty (30) days after such notice, then said notice shall cease to be operative and this LICENSE AGREEMENT FOR PATENT X,XXX,XXX shall continue in full force and effect as if such default had not occurred. Cancellation of this LICENSE AGREEMENT FOR PATENT X,XXX,XXX under this Article shall not prejudice the right of LICENSOR to recover any sum due it at the time such cancellation becomes effective and shall not prejudice any cause of action or claim of LICENSOR accrued or to accrue on account of any breach or default by LICENSEE.

5.2 LICENSOR shall have the right to cancel this LICENSE AGREEMENT FOR PATENT X,XXX,XXX at any time effective at the conclusion of thirty (30) days written notice to LICENSEE. Such cancellation shall not relieve LICENSEE of its obligation to pay LICENSOR any sums then due it under this LICENSE AGREEMENT FOR PATENT X,XXX,XXX. LICENSEE may elect in its notice of cancellation to have the right to sell those DEVICES it has on hand and that would have been subject to the terms of this LICENSE AGREEMENT FOR PATENT X,XXX,XXX had this LICENSE AGREEMENT FOR PATENT X,XXX,XXX remained in force by agreeing to pay the royalties as set forth herein, provided that such right on the part of LICENSEE shall terminate upon the expiration of one year from the effective date of such cancellation.

5.3 Any and all disputes arising in connection with this LICENSE AGREEMENT that cannot be settled by negotiation between the parties hereto, shall at the request of either or both parties be referred to and finally settled under the then prevailing Rules of the American Arbitration Association by one or more arbitrators appointed in accordance with said Rules. Notwithstanding any provisions of the Rules of the American Arbitration Association or any applicable state or federal law, the parties agree that the Arbitration cannot award exemplary or punitive damages. Judgement upon the award rendered may be entered in any court having jurisdiction, or application may be made to the court for judicial acceptance of the award and an order of enforcement as the case may be. All arbitration proceedings shall take place in Minneapolis, Minnesota.

ARTICLE VI

RECORDS AND AUDIT

6.1 LICENSEE shall keep and cause its AFFILIATES to keep true and accurate records relating to DEVICES sold under this LICENSE AGREEMENT FOR PATENT X,XXX,XXX to the extent necessary for making the reports and payments provided for herein. Such records shall be open for inspection by LICENSOR through an independent Certified Public Accountant appointed by it or for inspection by any other person to whom LICENSEE has no objection in order to permit LICENSOR to determine the accuracy of reports and payments hereunder. It is the intent of the parties that the person making such inspection shall not disclose to LICENSOR or others any business details that may be found in LICENSEE's records which are not necessary in determining the accuracy of the reports and payments. The inspection provided for herein shall be made during business hours and not more often than once each calendar year.

ARTICLE VII

CHANGES IN STATUS OF CLAIMS

7.1 If, during the life of this LICENSE AGREEMENT FOR PATENT X,XXX,XXX any claim included in the PATENT RIGHTS is disclaimed or becomes canceled or of no force or effect by operation of law (as through an adverse interference judgement or otherwise), then such claims shall be considered as no longer included in said PATENT RIGHTS unless and until it becomes reinstated, beginning with the date of such disclaimer or cancellation or the date it becomes of no force or effect.

7.2 If, during the TERM, a claim of the PATENT RIGHTS shall be construed or held invalid by a court of competent jurisdiction from whose decision no appeal is taken, then for the purpose of this LICENSE AGREEMENT FOR PATENT X,XXX,XXX the construction placed upon such claim shall thereafter be followed and any claims so held invalid shall be ignored.

IN WITNESS THEREOF, the parties have caused this agreement to be executed by their respective officers thereunto duly authorized as of the dates respectively indicated.

Amalgamated Breathing.   Xenocrystic Yellow
Crystals Inc   Zircon Company

By _____   By _____

Dated _____   Dated _____

APPENDIX Z

Trademark License

TRADEMARK LICENSE AGREEMENT

AGREEMENT by and between [Licensor], a corporation organized and existing under the laws of the State of [State], having its principal place of business in [City, State], (hereinafter referred to as LICENSOR); and [Licensee], a corporation organized and existing under the laws of the State of [State], having its principal place of business in [City, State], (hereinafter referred to as LICENSEE). This AGREEMENT is to provide a license from LICENSOR to LICENSEE to use the mark [Trademark] in advertisements for, and on packages used with [Product]. LICENSOR and LICENSEE, in consideration of the mutual covenants hereinafter set forth, represent, warrant, covenant and agree under this AGREEMENT only as follows:

1.0 TERM

1.1 The term (hereinafter referred to as "TERM") of this AGREEMENT shall begin on or before [Date], and shall expire [Date], unless extended by LICENSOR and LICENSEE together in writing, or unless earlier terminated in accordance with the provisions of Section 4.0 of this AGREEMENT. LICENSEE shall have the right after sixty (60) days prior to the end of the TERM to request of LICENSOR a two (2) year extension of this AGREEMENT.

2.0 TRADEMARK LICENSE

2.1 LICENSEE acknowledges that LICENSOR is the owner of the trademark [Trademark] and agrees that all use by LICENSEE of such trademark, in any manner whatsoever, shall inure to the benefit of LICENSOR. No right, title, or interest in this trademark is transferred to LICENSEE except the right to use it in the manner and subject to the terms and conditions set forth herein.

2.2 LICENSOR hereby licenses and authorizes LICENSEE to use during the TERM and thereafter the trademark [Trademark] in the United States of America upon or in relation to [Products] provide [Products] are manufactured strictly in accordance with the standards of LICENSOR, and any drawings, specifications, data, directions and information approved by LICENSOR which meet the necessary standards of quality satisfactory to LICENSOR as established by LICENSOR from time to time to protect its good name, good will and trademarks. LICENSEE shall display the trademark in all advertisements for such goods at least once.

2.3 LICENSEE agrees to notify LICENSOR, in writing, of any conflicting uses of the trademark [Trademark], any application for registration of any of it by anyone other than LICENSOR and any acts of infringement or act of unfair competition involving the trademark in the United States of America or Canada, promptly after such matters are brought to its attention, or it has knowledge thereof. In the event that LICENSOR is concerned as to a substantial amount of infringement in these countries and notifies LICENSEE to this effect, LICENSOR shall consult with LICENSEE with respect to the protection of their respective interests and shall take such steps to this end as may be reasonable under the circumstances.

2.4 LICENSEE shall include in all advertisements, specification sheets and other sales and promotional material, in which the trademark [Trademark] is used, a notice stating that it is LICENSOR's trademark, or other words of similar import. In such advertisements, specification sheets and other sales and promotional material, there shall also be given the name of LICENSEE and, in addition, notice shall be given therein that the goods are manufactured by LICENSEE as a licensee, or words of similar import.

2.5 All [Products] manufactured by LICENSEE, or packages therefor if not feasible on the

891

[Product], must carry a notice that the trademark [Trademark] thereon is the trademark or trade name of LICENSOR, or words of similar import. Also, LICENSEE shall indicate on such [Products], or packages therefor, it's name and, in addition, notice shall be given thereon that they are manufactured by LICENSEE as a licensee, or words of similar import. LICENSEE shall at all times comply with the trademark and trade name marking laws, regulations and requirements of the United States of America and Canada in which use of the trademark is occurring.

2.6 Nothing herein shall be construed as prohibiting or limiting the right of LICENSEE to use the trademark [Trademark] independently of and concurrently with LICENSOR.

2.7 Nothing herein shall be construed as prohibiting or limiting the adoption or use of other designations, trademarks or trade names by LICENSEE; provided, however, that LICENSEE shall not adopt or use as one of its own trademarks or trade names, a trademark or trade name which includes or is confusingly similar to the trademark [Trademark], nor shall LICENSEE combine any other name or trademark with that trademark or otherwise modify or alter that trademark. LICENSEE agrees that whenever its attention is called by LICENSOR to any confusion or risk of confusion, it will accept any reasonable suggestion which may be made by LICENSOR for avoiding such confusion.

2.8 LICENSEE undertakes and agrees that in the use of the trademark [Trademark] and the promotion and sale of [Products] and in all other matters affecting the [Products], it will conduct its business in a manner which will uphold and enhance the reputation of the trademark in the market place, and that it will not engage in or permit any commercial or other practices which may tend to injure or impair the value of the trademark and LICENSEE agrees that it will accept any reasonable suggestions made by LICENSOR for change of any practices by LICENSEE or others under its control which, in LICENSOR's opinion, are harmful to the trademark or to the good will which it represents.

2.9 LICENSEE shall also execute a Registered User Application at the time of the execution of this AGREEMENT or, at the choice of LICENSOR, thereafter promptly upon a written request to do so for the purpose of applying at the expense of LICENSEE for the recording of LICENSEE as a Registered User of the trademark in Canada if LICENSEE makes efforts toward, or actually uses, the trademark in Canada.

2.10 LICENSOR has the right to call upon LICENSEE at reasonable intervals to provide to it reasonable numbers of samples of the [Products] so that LICENSOR can conduct quality control testing thereon.

2.11 The duly authorized representatives of LICENSOR shall have the right upon reasonable notice to enter the business premises of LICENSEE during normal business hours to inspect the methods of manufacture of the [Products] so as to determine that LICENSEE is adhering to the specifications and directions for manufacture and the standards of quality for the [Products] given, laid down or agreed upon by LICENSOR.

3.0 FEES

3.1 In consideration of the rights granted to LICENSEE by LICENSOR under this AGREEMENT for the use of the trademark [Trademark] by LICENSEE, LICENSEE agrees to pay to LICENSOR a royalty equal to one percent (1%) of Net Sales of all [Products under Trademark] sold by LICENSEE during the continuance of this AGREEMENT.

3.2 As used in the AGREEMENT, the term "Net Sales" shall mean the total selling price of any Products for which customers are billed, or otherwise charged for by LICENSEE in the usual course of business excluding (i) sales taxes, excise taxes and other taxes levied in respect to such sales, (ii) return sales, (iii) trade or quantity discounts, (iv) bona fide price adjustments, and (v) transportation and insurance costs. Any out-of-payment-period credit adjustments for return sales or other bona fide price adjustments which exceed royalties payable for any period will be accrued and offset against royalties which accrue to LICENSOR in subsequent payment periods.

3.3 A royalty payment shall accrue when any Product is sold in any form or combination by LICENSEE whether or not payment therefor is actually received by LICENSEE.

3.4 LICENSEE shall keep full, clear and accurate records, with respect to the sale of all Products and the selling prices thereof. LICENSOR shall at its own expense have a right with respect to LICENSEE, through an independent certified public accountant selected by LICENSOR, to examine and audit, not more than twice a year, and during normal business hours, all such records and such other records and accounts as may, under recognized accounting practices, contain information bearing upon the amount of royalty payment due to LICENSOR from LICENSEE under this AGREEMENT. Prompt adjustment shall be made to compensate for any errors or omissions disclosed by such an examination or audit. Neither such right to examine or audit nor the right to receive such adjustment shall be affected by any statement to the contrary appearing on checks or otherwise, unless such statement appears in a letter signed by both parties hereto.

3.5 Within forty-five (45) days after the end of each quarterly period ending on March 31, June 30, September 30 or December 31, commencing with the quarterly period in which the beginning of the TERM occurs, and continuing thereafter until all the royalties payable hereunder shall have been reported and paid, LICENSEE shall furnish LICENSOR a statement signed by a duly authorized officer of LICENSEE showing all Products which were sold during such quarterly period and the prices at which they were sold, and the amount of the royalty payable thereon. If no Products subject to royalty have been sold, that fact shall be set forth in such a statement. The royalties stated to be payable in each such quarterly statement shall also be paid within forty-five (45) days after the end of that quarter in which they accrue. All payments hereunder shall be in United States Dollars.

3.6 Sales of Products in Canadian Dollars by LICENSEE, for the purposes of calculating royalty payments, will be converted by LICENSEE to United States Dollars based on the rate of exchange for such currencies as set forth in the *Wall Street Journal* (Eastern Edition) on the day that LICENSEE sends invoices or bills to its customers, or otherwise charges them. In the event of a misprint in the rate of exchange for Canadian Dollars in the *Wall Street Journal*, the rate of exchange for such currency shall be the published rate for the date prior to the misprint.

3.7 LICENSEE shall bear the cost of all taxes, duties and assessments payable in the United States of America or Canada or in any political subdivision thereof on the royalties due hereunder and use of the molds hereunder and on any other charges payable to LICENSOR hereunder; provided, however, that should LICENSOR be entitled to take advantage of any existing or future tax treaty wherein it would be allowed a tax credit for taxes paid in Canada, LICENSEE may deduct such creditable tax amounts from the amounts payable to LICENSOR, pay such deducted amounts on behalf of LICENSOR, and provide LICENSOR with all required proof of payment there for.

4.0 TERMINATION

4.1 Prior to the satisfaction by LICENSEE of all royalty obligations to LICENSOR under Section 3.0 hereof, and without prejudice to other rights of termination by either party, LICENSOR may terminate this AGREEMENT if LICENSEE is in material breach or default in keeping, observing, or performing any of the obligations imposed pursuant to this AGREEMENT, and upon such termination the licenses granted hereunder shall terminate and LICENSEE shall cease using the trademark [Trademark] except as set out in subparagraph 4.3. The obligation of LICENSEE to pay accrued royalties, however, shall not terminate and shall continue until they have been paid in full to LICENSOR.

4.2 Termination under provisions of subparagraph 4.1 above shall be effective only upon fifteen (15) days written notice by LICENSOR to LICENSEE specifying the reasons therefor, and if LICENSEE corrects the breach or default within such fifteen (15) days, then this AGREEMENT and the licenses hereunder shall remain in force.

4.3 Upon termination of this AGREEMENT, all further rights by LICENSEE to use the trademark [Trademark] licensed by LICENSOR hereunder shall cease, and all further rights by LICENSEE to use the that trademark, whether they be based upon this AGREEMENT or otherwise, shall cease, except with respect to Products which were manufactured and marked with the trademark prior to the date of termination. LICENSEE agrees that the ownership of the trademark and the good will relating thereto shall always remain vested in the trademark owner, both during the period of this AGREEMENT and thereafter, and LICENSEE further agrees never to challenge, contest, or call into question the validity or ownership of the trademark or its registration in the United States of America or Canada or elsewhere, and never to contest the owner's right to use such trademark in the United States of America or Canada or elsewhere. LICENSEE agrees to execute any acknowledgements or waivers that may be required to establish LICENSOR as the sole and exclusive owner of the trademark in the United States of America or Canada.

4.4 Any licenses granted hereunder shall be immediately terminated by LICENSOR should LICENSEE become bankrupt or insolvent, or if the business of LICENSEE is given over to, or operated by, a receiver or trustee in bankruptcy, or if LICENSEE participates in the transaction for the benefit of creditors such as an assignment thereto.

5.0 NOTICES

5.1 Any notice or other communication or delivery to LICENSOR from LICENSEE related to this AGREEMENT shall be in writing and addressed to:

LICENSOR

[Address]

5.2. Any notice or other communication or delivery to LICENSEE from LICENSOR related to this AGREEMENT shall be in writing and addressed to:

LICENSEE

[Address]

5.3 On thirty (30) days written notice to the other, a party may change the address at which it is to receive notices or other communications or deliveries from that address set out immediately above.

6.0 INDEPENDENT CONTRACTORS

6.1 The parties hereto are independent contractors, and in no event shall either party or its employees be agents, employees, or consultants of the other.

6.2 This AGREEMENT shall not establish a joint venture, partnership, franchise, or other like relationship between the parties.

7.0 FREEDOM OF AND SUCCESSION OF THE PARTIES

7.1 LICENSOR and LICENSEE each represent that it is not under any obligation which will prevent or substantially interfere with the performance of this AGREEMENT, and that each agrees that it will not undertake any such obligations during its performance under this AGREEMENT.

7.2 Neither party shall assign any of its rights or privileges hereunder without prior written consent of the other party, except that LICENSOR may assign such rights as part of a sale of its entire business relating to the Products. Any attempted assignment in derogation of the foregoing shall be null and void.

7.3 This AGREEMENT shall be binding upon LICENSOR and upon LICENSEE and upon the successors of each, if any, and upon the assigns of each to the extent such are permitted.

8.0 CONSTRUCTION OF AGREEMENT PROVISIONS

8.1 Nothing in this AGREEMENT shall be construed with respect to either LICENSOR or LICENSEE as:

(a) a warranty or representation that anything sold or leased or otherwise disposed of under any licenses granted under this AGREEMENT is or will be free from infringement of trademarks belonging to any person or business organization not involved in this AGREEMENT, and neither LICENSOR nor LICENSEE shall indemnify against, nor be responsible in any manner whatsoever for, infringement claimed by any such person or business organization; or

(b) a requirement that either LICENSOR or LICENSEE shall file any trademark registration application, or that LICENSOR or LICENSEE shall provide any license under its trademarks other than those obtained specifically under this AGREEMENT, or under the trademarks of others if empowered to do so; or

(c) an obligation by either LICENSOR or LICENSEE to bring or prosecute actions or suits against others for infringement; or

(d) conferring any authorization of either LICENSOR or LICENSEE to act as agent of the other for any purpose including representing or obligating the other in any manner; or

(e) the assumption of any debt, liability or other obligation to someone other than LICENSOR or LICENSEE.

8.2 Neither LICENSOR nor LICENSEE make any representation, extends any warranty of any kind, either express or implied, nor assumes any responsibility whatsoever with respect to the use, sale, lease, or other disposition by the other, or the other's vendees or the other's transferees, of Products marked with the trademark [Trademark] licensed under this AGREEMENT, and in no event under this AGREEMENT shall either LICENSOR or LICENSEE be liable for any special, incidental or consequential damages resulting from its performance or failure to perform pursuant to the terms and conditions of this AGREEMENT or for the use, sale, lease or other disposition by the other, or the other's vendees or the other's transferees, of products marked with the trademark.

8.3 This AGREEMENT and its performance shall be construed under the laws of the State of Minnesota.

9.0 LAWS, REGULATIONS, APPROVALS, EXPORTS

9.1 This AGREEMENT is subject to all applicable laws and regulations of the Governments of Canada and the United States of America.

9.2 This AGREEMENT is subject to all laws and regulations of the Government of the United States of America relating to exports and to all administrative acts of that Government pursuant to such laws and regulations.

9.3 No export, sale, transfer or other disposition of Products is authorized to any country outside the territory where manufacture or sale is herein licensed.

10.0 ENTIRETY OF AGREEMENT

10.1 This AGREEMENT shall constitute the entire AGREEMENT and understanding of LICENSOR and LICENSEE with reference to its subject matter. No representation, promise, modification nor amendment shall be binding upon either LICENSOR or LICENSEE unless in writing and unless signed by a duly authorized representative of each, and the AGREEMENT shall not be modified, supplemented, or qualified or interpreted by any trade, usage or prior course of dealing not specifically made part of this AGREEMENT.

IN WITNESS WHEREOF, LICENSOR AND LICENSEE have executed this AGREEMENT in duplicate:

LICENSOR   LICENSEE

By _____   By _____

Title _____   Title _____

Date _____   Date _____

APPENDIX AA

Copyright License

COPYRIGHT LICENSE

This Agreement is between [Author] of [Address], and [Licensee] of [Address].

[Author] has prepared [Description of Works] and provided them to [Licensee] under the terms of this Agreement. As consideration, [Licensee] has paid to [Author] [Amount], receipt of which is acknowledged by [Author].

[Author] agrees that [Licensee] has a paid-up *exclusive*, world-wide license to reproduce [Author]'s Works for use in connection with the Licensed Products listed in attached Exhibit A, and to manufacture, sell, offer for sale, advertise, promote and distribute such products bearing the Works. [Licensee]'s license rights to the Works are nontransferable,

except to a successor to [Licensee]'s entire business to which this Agreement relates, without the prior written consent of [Author], which consent will not be unreasonably withheld. This Agreement will inure to the benefit of, and be binding upon, the parties, their lawful successors and permitted transferees.

[Author] agrees not to compete with [Licensee] in the manufacture and sale of Licensed Products bearing the Works, and [Author] agrees to maintain as confidential information provided to her by[Licensee] about his business in connection with the Licensed Products. It is understood that [Author] may continue to make and sell original renderings of any of the Works except for all the Licensed Products which are represented on Exhibit A. It is understood that all other rights in the Works, including specifically copyright rights, are reserved by [Author].

[Author] has provided original artwork for each Work to [Licensee]. [Licensee] agrees to make, or to allow [Author] to make, fine color reproductions of the Works at [Author]'s request, and at [Author]'s expense.

As [Author]'s exclusive licensee, [Licensee] has the right to enforce his rights against third parties through settlement or by instituting a legal action for copyright infringement in his own name. If [Licensee] institutes any such legal action, [Author] agrees to assist and fully cooperate as necessary, and to join in such an action if required by the court. All proceeds of such a settlement or legal action shall belong to [Licensee], who shall also bear any costs and attorneys fees associated therewith.

[Licensee] agrees to defend, indemnify and hold [Author] harmless against any claims, demands, causes of action and judgments arising out of [Licensee]'s manufacture, sale, offering for sale, distribution, promotion and/or advertising of products under this Agreement.

This Agreement shall be governed by the laws of the State of Minnesota.

This Agreement represents the entire understanding between the parties hereto with respect to the subject matter hereof and this Agreement supersedes all prior representations, understandings or agreements, oral or written, between the parties with respect to the subject matter hereof and cannot be modified except in writing signed by [Licensee] and [Author].

By their signatures below, the parties hereto have agreed to all of the terms and conditions of this Agreement, effective on the last date listed below.

[Author]

Date _____

[Licensee]

Date _____

_____

APPENDIX BB

Invention Disclosure

INVENTION DISCLOSURE--CONFIDENTIAL

TITLE OF INVENTION: _____

1. **DESCRIPTION OF THE INVENTION AND BACKGROUND - attach additional sheets as needed**
    ( ) Check if additional sheets are attached

    A. Please describe the background of the technology field and/or problem(s) being solved with the invention (include any technical references and patents [pat. numbers only] that you believe are relevant to the invention):

    B. Please describe the invention in detail, and describe how it works. Include sketches, CAD drawings, flow charts (for computer algorithms), and other visual aides to assist in the description. Clearly define parts/features in sketches, CAD drawings, etc., and document how the parts/features connect and interact (avoid using code names and acronyms, unless defined):

    C. Please identify the features that are considered to be changes or improvements:

    D. Please describe the advantages of the identified changes or improvements:

Page 1 of 4

CONFIDENTIAL

2.   **WRITTEN DOCUMENTATION AND REDUCTION TO PRACTICE**

    A.   When was the invention first disclosed? _____ To whom? _____

    B.   When was the invention first present in writing? _____
        (please attach evidence of work on this invention, e.g., copies of log book pages and presentation slides)

    C.   Has the invention been built?   Yes ( )   No ( )
        a.   Date Completed _____   Not completed as of this date ( )
        b.   Date first successfully tested _____   Not tested as of this date ( )
        c.   Names of persons with knowledge of testing:_____

    D.   What the invention developed under a government contract? Yes ( ) No ( )
        If yes, list contracting agency and contract numbers: _____

3.   **PUBLICLICATIONS, SALES, OFFERS FOR SALE, AND USES OF THE INVENTION**

Please indicate whether any of the following events have occurred relative to the invention, and if so, the earliest date of such occurrence. If any event will probably occur in the future, identify the estimated date(s).

		Yes	No	Date Occurred or Expected
A.	Has it been demonstrated to any person (including dealers) outside the company?	( )	( )	_____
B.	Has it been exhibited at any trade show or exhibition?	( )	( )	_____
C.	Has it been described orally or in writing to any person outside of the company?	( )	( )	_____
D.	Has it been offered for sale?	( )	( )	_____
E.	Has it been sold?	( )	( )	_____
F.	Has it been advertised or otherwise described in any publication?	( )	( )	_____
G.	Has it been released to production?	( )	( )	_____
H.	Has it been commercially used?	( )	( )	_____
I.	Has the invention been made available to the public in any way?	( )	( )	_____

CONFIDENTIAL

5.   INVENTOR INFORMATION

Name and Residence Address of Inventors – Include as inventor, everyone who contributed to conception of invention (attach additional sheets as necessary):

Inventor A:

| (Name) | First | Middle | Last | Citizenship |

| (Home Address) | Street | City | State | ZIP |

| (Company Contact Information) Telephone number | Email address |

| (Inventor A Signature) | Date |

Inventor B:

| (Name) | First | Middle | Last | Citizenship |

| (Home Address) | Street | City | State | ZIP |

| (Company Contact Information) Telephone number | Email address |

| (Inventor B Signature) | Date |

SEEN AND UNDERSTOOD BY ME

Witness 1

| (Witness 1 Signature) | Date |

| (Witness 1 printed name) |

CONFIDENTIAL

Witness 2

_____
(Witness 2 Signature)   Date

_____
(Witness 2 printed name)

_____

FOR MANAGEMENT USE ONLY:

A. Is invention/product central to Company's present business?   Y( ) N( )
B. Is invention/product central to Company's future business?   Y( ) N( )
C. Can invention be used/sold without competitors gaining knowledge of invention?   Y( ) N( )
D. How important is invention toward sales, as viewed by consumer? Very important 1 2 3 4 5 Insignificant
E. Estimate yearly sales of invention/product: Units _____ Dollars _____
F. Estimate duration of market for invention/product: _____ Years _____

Table of Laws and Rules

UNITED STATES CONSTITUTION

AMERICA INVENTS ACT

COPYRIGHT ACT

DIGITAL MILLENNIUM COPYRIGHT ACT

INTERNAL REVENUE CODE

LANHAM ACT

Sec.	Sec.	Sec.	Sec.
1	10:12	36	11:14
2	10:38	42	16:5
2(a)	10:28	43(a)	9:16; 9:23; 10:39; 11:5; 11:8; 11:10; 11:11 n.11; 11:14; 11:15; 11:35 n.1; 11:36; 11:37; 11:38 n.28; 11:39; 11:40; 16:5 n.1
8	10:41; 14:27		
10	14:27		
13	10:38	43(c)	11:5
15	10:1; 14:27	44	10:12
32	11:5	44(d)	10:9 n.1
35	11:15	44(e)	10:10 n.1

SARBANES-OXLEY ACT

Sec.	Sec.	Sec.	Sec.
302	17:14	404	17:14

TARIFF ACT OF 1930

Sec.	Sec.
337	16:2

UNITED STATES CODE ANNOTATED

7 U.S.C.A. Sec.	Sec.	15 U.S.C.A. Sec.	Sec.
2531	14:26 n.6	1051(b)(2)	10:17 n.1
		1051(c)	10:23
9 U.S.C.A. Sec.	**Sec.**	1051(d)	10:23 n.3
1 et seq.	11:34 n.23	1052 to 1056	10:36
		1052.	10:4 n.1; 10:10; 10:24 n.1; 10:31 n.8
11 U.S.C.A. Sec.	**Sec.**		
101(35A)	14:33	1052(a)	10:26 n.1; 10:27 n.1; 10:28 n.1
365(a)	14:33 n.1		
365(c)(1)	14:33 n.10	1052(b)	10:29 n.1
365(n)	14:33 n.5	1052(c)	10:29 n.10, 11
503(b)	14:33	1052(d)	10:25 n.1
		1052(e)(1)	10:30 n.1
		1052(e)(2)	10:31 n.1, 2
15 U.S.C.A. Sec.	**Sec.**	1052(e)(3)	9:17 n.6
1051 et seq.	10:2; 11:35 n.2	1052(e)(4)	10:32 n.1
1051	10:14 n.2; 10:16 n.2	1052(f)	9:11 n.7; 9:17 n.6; 10:4 n.3; 10:30 n.1, 4; 10:31 n.1, 2; 10:32 n.1; 10:33 n.1, 5
1051(a)	10:7 n.1		
1051(a)(1)	10:20 n.1		
1051(a)(2)	10:17 n.1	1056(a)	10:35 n.4
1051(b)	10:8 n.1; 15:9 n.1	1056(b)	10:35 n.7
1051(b)(1)	10:20 n.1	1057(b)	10:1 n.3; 11:8 n.1; 11:16 n.5

UNITED STATES CODE ANNOTATED—Continued

15 U.S.C.A. Sec.	Sec.
1057(c)	9:21 n.2
1058	10:41 n.1, 2, 3
1059	10:41 n.5
1060	14:2 n.1, 6; 14:3 n.2
1062	10:34 n.1
1062(b)	10:34 n.6, 7, 9
1063	10:37 n.2; 10:38 n.1, 3
1063(a)	10:38 n.12
1064	10:39 n.1, 8
1064(3)	9:10 n.4, 5; 9:26 n.9, 10, 11
1065	10:1 n.5, 6, 7; 11:8
1068	10:39 n.11
1070	10:36 n.1
1072	10:1 n.1, 2; 11:19
1091	10:4 n.1; 10:36
1092	10:37 n.3; 10:39 n.2, 10
1096	10:4 n.2
1111	9:28 n.1, 2; 10:1 n.8, 9
1112	10:5 n.1
1114	9:4 n.3
1114(1)	11:1 n.1; 11:5 n.1
1114(1)(a)	11:7 n.1
1115(b)	11:8 n.3; 11:19
1115(b)(4)	9:9 n.5; 11:17 n.2, 7; 11:28 n.16
1115(a),(b)	10:38 n.10
1116(a)	11:14 n.1
1117	11:31 n.1; 11:34 n.15
1117(a)	11:15 n.1, 2, 8, 10, 15
1117(e)	11:15 n.14; 11:31 n.2
1118	11:14
1124	10:1 n.10
1125	9:4 n.4
1125(1)	11:7 n.1
1125(a)	9:16; 9:23 n.1
1125(a)(1)	11:38 n.26
1125(a)(3)	9:16 n.13
1125(c)	9:4 n.1; 10:38 n.12; 10:39 n.8; 11:27 n.2
1125(c)(1)	11:26 n.2; 11:30 n.1; 11:32 n.6; 11:33 n.9
1125(c)(2)(A)	11:5 n.4
1125(c)(2)(B)	11:26 n.4; 11:29 n.7
1125(c)(2)(C)	11:26 n.5; 11:29 n.11
1125(c)(3)	11:26 n.10
1125(c)(4)(A)	11:28 n.16
1125(d)	9:4 n.5
1125(d)(1)(A)	11:34 n.4
1125(d)(1)(B)	11:34 n.5

15 U.S.C.A. Sec.	Sec.
1125(d)(1)(C)	11:34 n.14
1125(d)(2)	11:34 n.1
1125(d)(2)(C)	11:34 n.2
1126	10:16 n.2; 15:9 n.1
1126(b)	10:9 n.2
1126(d)	10:9 n.1, 3
1126(e)	10:10 n.1
1127	9:1 n.1; 9:3 n.1; 9:21 n.1, 4, 5, 6, 7; 9:24 n.1, 3; 9:27 n.1; 10:3 n.1, 3, 5, 7, 8; 10:7 n.3, 4, 5, 6; 10:8 n.2; 10:14 n.1; 10:24 n.2; 10:31 n.15; 11:16 n.3, 19; 11:19; 11:26 n.3
1141e(a)	10:12 n.2
1141f(a)	10:12 n.8; 10:16
1141f(b)	10:12 n.4
1141h(a)(4)	10:12 n.7
1141i(a)	10:12 n.10, 11
1141j	10:12 n.12
1225(d)(1)(B)(ii)	11:34 n.7
7241	17:14 n.3
7262	17:14 n.4

17 U.S.C.A. Sec.	Sec.
101 et seq	6:1 n.2
101	6:3 n.1, 4, 12, 13, 24, 28, 32, 36, 39, 41; 6:4 n.1, 2; 6:7 n.1; 6:8 n.2; 6:13 n.3; 6:16 n.1, 2; 6:17 n.1, 2; 6:19 n.1; 7:2 n.1; 7:12 n.5, 6; 15:14 n.4
102	8:5
102(a)	6:2 n.1; 6:4 n.3; 7:1 n.1
102(b)	6:18 n.2; 8:16 n.16; 12:1 n.2
103	6:3 n.44; 8:5
103(b)	6:3 n.37
104	6:1 n.4
104(b)	6:25 n.1
104(d)	6:25 n.1
104A	6:3 n.47
104A(h)	6:25 n.2
105	6:5 n.21
106	6:11; 6:13 n.1; 8:4; 8:7; 8:12 n.1
106(1)	6:13 n.2
106(3)	6:15 n.1
106A	11:37 n.5
106A(a)(2)	6:28 n.1
106A(a)(3)	6:28 n.4
106A(c)	6:28 n.3
107	6:22 n.1, 2; 8:18 n.6

UNITED STATES CODE ANNOTATED—Continued

UNITED STATES CODE ANNOTATED—Continued

UNITED STATES CODE ANNOTATED—Continued

UNITED STATES CODE ANNOTATED—Continued

UNITED STATES PUBLIC LAWS

CODE OF FEDERAL REGULATIONS

CODE OF FEDERAL REGULATIONS—Continued

CODE OF FEDERAL REGULATIONS—Continued

CODE OF FEDERAL REGULATIONS—Continued

FEDERAL RULES OF CIVIL PROCEDURE

PATENT TRADEMARK OFFICE TRADEMARK MANUAL OF EXAMINING PROCEDURE

PATENT TRADEMARK OFFICE TRADEMARK MANUAL OF EXAMINING PROCEDURE—Continued

PATENT TRADEMARK OFFICE TRADEMARK TRIAL AND APPEAL BOARD MANUAL OF PROCEDURE

FEDERAL REGISTER

CONGRESSIONAL RECORD

Vol.	Sec.
157, p. S1370	2:32 n.4

HOUSE REPORTS

No.	Sec.	No.	Sec.
94-1476	8:18 n.7	94-1476	7:2 n.2

SENATE REPORTS

Sec.	Sec.	Sec.	Sec.
82-1979	5:11 n.2	94-473	8:18 n.7, 30

ALABAMA CODE

Sec.	Sec.	Sec.	Sec.
8-12-17	11:25 n.2	8-19-10(a)	11:39 n.3
8-13-1	11:41 n.3	8-27-1 to 8-27-6	12:1 n.17

ALASKA STATUTES

Sec.	Sec.
45.50.910 to 45.50.945	12:1 n.17

ARIZONA STATUTES

Sec.	Sec.
44-401 to 44-407	12:1 n.17

ARKANSAS CODE ANNOTATED

Sec.	Sec.
4-75-601 to 4-75-607	12:1 n.17

DISTRICT OF COLUMBIA CODE

Sec.	Sec.
36-401 to 36-410	12:1 n.17

FLORIDA STATUTES

Sec.	Sec.	Sec.	Sec.
495.151	11:25 n.3	817.41	11:41 n.2
Ch 688.001 to 688.009	12:1 n.17		

GEORGIA CODE

Sec.	Sec.	Sec.	Sec.
10-1-760 to 10-1-767	12:1 n.17	16-8-13	12:37 n.2
10-1-766	12:22 n.3	26-2-152(b)	11:41 n.5

HAWAII REVISED STATUTES

Sec.	Sec.
482B-1 to 482B-9	12:1 n.17

IDAHO CODE

Sec.	Sec.
48-801 to 48-807	12:1 n.17

ILLINOIS COMPILED STATUTES

765 Ill. Comp. Stat.	Sec.	765 Ill. Comp. Stat.	Sec.
1036	11:25 n.3	1065/1 to 1065/9	12:1 n.17
1060/2	12:12 n.17		

INDIANA CODE

Sec.	Sec.
24-2-3-1 to 24-2-3-8	12:1 n.17

IOWA CODE

Sec.	Sec.
550.1 to 550.8	12:1 n.17

KANSAS STATUTES

Sec.	Sec.	Sec.	Sec.
44-130	12:12 n.17	60-3320 to 60-3330	12:1 n.17

KENTUCKY REVISED STATUTES

Sec.	Sec.
365.880 to 365.900	12:1 n.17

LOUISIANA REVISED STATUTES ANNOTATED

Sec.	Sec.
51:1431 to 51:1439	12:1 n.17

MAINE REVISED STATUTES ANNOTATED

10 M.R.S.A. Sec.	Sec.	10 M.R.S.A. Sec.	Sec.
1541 to 1548	12:1 n.17	1547	12:22 n.4

MARYLAND CODE, COMMERCIAL LAW (I, II)

Sec.	Sec.
11-1201 to 11-1209	12:1 n.17

MICHIGAN COMPILED LAWS ANNOTATED

Sec.	Sec.
445. 1901 to 445.1910	12:1 n.17

MINNESOTA STATUTES

MISSISSIPPI CODE ANNOTATED

MISSOURI STATUTES

MONTANA CODE

NEBRASKA REVISED STATUTES

NEVADA REVISED STATUTES

NEW HAMPSHIRE REVISED STATUTES

NEW JERSEY STATUTES

Sec.	Sec.
56:15-1 to 56:15-9	12:1 n.17

NEW MEXICO STATUTES

Sec.	Sec.
57-3A-1 to 57-3A-7	12:1 n.17

NEW YORK CIVIL RIGHTS LAW

Sec.	Sec.	Sec.	Sec.
50	13:5 n.7	50 and 51	13:5
51	13:5		

NORTH CAROLINA GENERAL STATUTES

Sec.	Sec.	Sec.	Sec.
66-57.1	12:12 n.17	66-152 to 66-157	12:1 n.17

NORTH DAKOTA CENTURY CODE

Sec.	Sec.
47-25.1-01 to 47-25.1-08	12:1 n.17

OHIO REVISED CODE

Sec.	Sec.	Sec.	Sec.
1333.61 to 1333.69	12:1 n.17	1333.66	12:22 n.4

OKLAHOMA STATUTES

12 Okla. Stat. Sec.	Sec.	78 Okla. Stat. Sec.	Sec.
1449(A)	11:18	85 to 94	12:1 n.17

OREGON REVISED STATUTES

Sec.	Sec.	Sec.	Sec.
646.461 to 646.475	12:1 n.17	646.885(2)	11:41 n.4
646.885(1)	11:41 n.1		

PENNSYLVANIA CONSOLIDATED STATUTES

12 Pa. Cons. Stat. Sec.	Sec.
5301 to 5308	12:1 n.17

PUERTO RICO LAWS

10 P.R. Laws Sec.	Sec.
4131 to 4141	12:1 n.17

RHODE ISLAND GENERAL LAWS

Sec.	Sec.
6-41-1 to 6-41-11	12:1 n.17

SOUTH CAROLINA CODE

Sec.	Sec.
39-8-10 to 39-8-130	12:1 n.17

SOUTH DAKOTA CODIFIED LAWS

Sec.	Sec.	Sec.	Sec.
15-7-2(2)	11:2 n.3	37-29-1 to 37-29-11	12:1 n.17

TENNESSEE CODE

Sec.	Sec.
47-25-1701 to 47-25-1709	12:1 n.17

TEXAS BUSINESS AND COMMERCE CODE ANNOTATED

TEXAS CIVIL PRACTICE AND REMEDIES CODE ANNOTATED

UTAH CODE

VERMONT STATUTES

VIRGINIA CODE

VIRGIN ISLANDS CODE

WASHINGTON REVISED CODE

RESTATEMENT THIRD, UNFAIR COMPETITION

RESTATEMENT FIRST, TORTS

EXEC-US-COLC-COMP3 NOT IN FORMAT TABLE

Table of Cases

Agassi Enterprises, Inc. v. Target Corp., 2007 WL 4441195 (D. Nev. 2007)—§ 13:10 n.1

A. H. Emery Co. v. Marcan Products Corp., 389 F.2d 11, 11 Fed. R. Serv. 2d 377 (2d Cir. 1968)—§ 12:19 n.10

Ajinomoto Co., Inc. v. Archer-Daniels-Midland Co., 228 F.3d 1338 (Fed. Cir. 2000)—§ 16:4 n.14

Akamai Technologies, Inc. v. Limelight Networks, Inc., 797 F.3d 1020 (Fed. Cir. 2015)—§ 5:10 n.7

Akamai Technologies, Inc v. Limelight Networks, Inc., 786 F.3d 899 (Fed. Cir. 2015)—§ 5:10 n.6

Akro Corp. v. Luker, 45 F.3d 1541 (Fed. Cir. 1995)—§ 11:2 n.10

Aktiebolag v. E.J. Co., 121 F.3d 669 (Fed. Cir. 1997)—§ 5:10 n.3

Aktiebolaget Karlstads Mekaniska Werkstad v. U.S. Intern. Trade Com'n, 1 Fed. Cir. (T) 21, 705 F.2d 1565 (1983)—§ 5:33 n.6

Akzona Inc. v. E.I. du Pont de Nemours & Co., 662 F. Supp. 603 (D. Del. 1987)—§ 5:9 n.2

Al-Site Corp. v. VSI Intern., Inc., 174 F.3d 1308 (Fed. Cir. 1999)—§ 5:15 n.11

Alden v. Maine, 527 U.S. 706, 119 S. Ct. 2240, 144 L. Ed. 2d 636 (1999)—§ 11:7 n.8

Alice Corp. Pty. Ltd. v. CLS Bank Intern., 134 S. Ct. 2347, 189 L. Ed. 2d 296 (2014)—§§ 3:20 n.4, 5, 6, 7; 5:34 n.5

Aliotti v. R. Dakin & Co., 831 F.2d 898 (9th Cir. 1987)—§ 8:15 n.12

Alk Associates, Inc. v. Multimodal Applied Systems, Inc., 276 N.J. Super. 310, 647 A.2d 1359 (App. Div. 1994)—§§ 12:21 n.13; 12:25 n.8

Allen v. Men's World Outlet, Inc., 679 F. Supp. 360 (S.D. N.Y. 1988)—§ 11:36 n.2

Allen v. National Video, Inc., 610 F. Supp. 612 (S.D. N.Y. 1985)—§ 11:36 n.1

Allied Maintenance Corp. v. Allied Mechanical Trades, Inc., 42 N.Y.2d 538, 399 N.Y.S.2d 628, 369 N.E.2d 1162 (1977)—§ 11:29 n.5

Allison v. Vintage Sports Plaques, 136 F.3d 1443 (11th Cir. 1998)—§§ 13:4 n.5; 13:9 n.1

Alltech Plastics Inc., In re, 5 U.S.P.Q.2d 1806, 1987 WL 123991 (Bankr. W.D. Tenn. 1987)—§ 14:33 n.10

Alonso v. Parfet, 253 Ga. 749, 325 S.E.2d 152, 52 A.L.R.4th 151 (1985)—§ 13:15 n.3

Alpo Petfoods, Inc. v. Ralston Purina Co., 720 F. Supp. 194 (D.D.C. 1989)—§ 11:38 n.22

ALS Scan, Inc. v. Digital Service Consultants, Inc., 293 F.3d 707, 52 Fed. R. Serv. 3d 1121 (4th Cir. 2002)—§§ 8:2 n.10; 11:2 n.14

Altiris, Inc. v. Symantec Corp., 318 F.3d 1363 (Fed. Cir. 2003)—§ 5:15 n.7

Alto Products Corp. v. Ratek Industries Ltd., 40 U.S.P.Q.2d 1738, 1996-2 Trade Cas. (CCH) ¶ 71601, 1996 WL 497027 (S.D. N.Y. 1996)—§ 16:5 n.1

AmBrit, Inc. v. Kraft, Inc., 812 F.2d 1531 (11th Cir. 1986)—§§ 11:8 n.15; 11:16 n.8

American Dairy Queen Corp. v. RTO, Inc., 16 U.S.P.Q.2d 1077, 1990 WL 103649 (N.D. Ill. 1990)—§ 11:28 n.70

§ 10:31 n.8, 9

Calvin Klein Cosmetics Corp. v. Lenox Laboratories, Inc., 815 F.2d 500 (8th Cir. 1987)—§ 11:9 n.7

Calvin Klein Industries, Inc. v. BFK Hong Kong, Ltd., 714 F. Supp. 78 (S.D. N.Y. 1989)—§ 16:3 n.4

Campbell v. Acuff-Rose Music, Inc., 510 U.S. 569, 114 S. Ct. 1164, 127 L. Ed. 2d 500 (1994)—§§ 6:23 n.1; 8:18 n.1; 11:18 n.6

Campbell Soup Co. v. Giles, 47 F.3d 467 (1st Cir. 1995)—§ 12:31 n.8

Canada Dry Ginger Ale, In re, 86 F.2d 830 (C.C.P.A. 1936)—§ 10:31 n.5

Canessa v. J. I. Kislak, Inc., 97 N.J. Super. 327, 235 A.2d 62 (Law Div. 1967)—§ 13:12 n.1

Capital Speakers Inc. v. Capital Speakers Club of Washington D.C. Inc., 41 U.S.P.Q.2d 1030, 1996 WL 754043 (T.T.A.B. 1996)—§ 10:3 n.4

Car-Freshner Corp. v. Scentex, Inc., 12 U.S.P.Q.2d 1361, 1989 WL 47373 (N.D. N.Y. 1989)—§ 9:16 n.17

Cardiac Pacemakers, Inc. v. St. Jude Medical, Inc., 576 F.3d 1348 (Fed. Cir. 2009)—§§ 5:12 n.7; 16:4 n.9

Cardinal Chemical Co. v. Morton Intern., Inc., 508 U.S. 83, 113 S. Ct. 1967, 124 L. Ed. 2d 1 (1993)—§ 5:9 n.3

Card Technology Corp. v. DataCard Corp., 2007 WL 2156320 (D. Minn. 2007)—§ 5:8 n.5

Cardtoons, L.C. v. Major League Baseball Players Ass'n, 95 F.3d 959 (10th Cir. 1996)—§ 11:18 n.33

Carl Schenck, A.G. v. Nortron Corp., 713 F.2d 782 (Fed. Cir. 1983)— § 1:1 n.1

Carl Zeiss Stiftung v. V. E. B. Carl Zeiss, Jena, 293 F. Supp. 892 (S.D. N.Y. 1968)—§ 11:21 n.12

Carol Barnhart Inc. v. Economy Cover Corp., 773 F.2d 411 (2d Cir. 1985)—§ 6:3 n.23

Carter v. Helmsley-Spear, Inc., 71 F.3d 77, 138 A.L.R. Fed. 711 (2d Cir. 1995)—§ 6:28 n.6

Castrol, Inc. v. Quaker State Corp., 977 F.2d 57 (2d Cir. 1992)—§ 11:38 n.25

Catalina Lighting, Inc. v. Lamps Plus, Inc., 295 F.3d 1277 (Fed. Cir. 2002)—§ 5:32 n.4

Caveney, In re, 761 F.2d 671 (Fed. Cir. 1985)—§§ 2:33 n.28; 5:36 n.9

C.B.C. Distribution and Marketing, Inc. v. Major League Baseball Advanced Media, L.P., 505 F.3d 818 (8th Cir. 2007)—§ 13:17 n.2

CBS, Inc. v. Gusto Records, Inc., 403 F. Supp. 447 (M.D. Tenn. 1974)— § 11:38 n.7

CBS Inc. v. Liederman, 866 F. Supp. 763 (S.D. N.Y. 1994)—§ 11:28 n.68

Celebrity Service Intern. Inc. v. Celebrity World Inc., 9 U.S.P.Q.2d 1673, 1988 WL 1091944 (S.D. N.Y. 1988)—§ 11:15 n.13

Celeritas Technologies, Ltd. v. Rockwell Intern. Corp., 150 F.3d 1354 (Fed. Cir. 1998)—§ 12:8 n.10

Centaur Communications, Ltd. v. A/S/M Communications, Inc., 830 F.2d 1217 (2d Cir. 1987)—§ 11:10 n.1

Centura Software Corp., In re, 281 B.R. 660 (Bankr. N.D. Cal. 2002)— § 14:33 n.5

Century 21 Real Estate Corp. v. Lendingtree, Inc., 425 F.3d 211 (3d Cir.

H

Hamilton Pharmaceuticals Ltd., In re, 27 U.S.P.Q.2d 1939, 1993 WL
368803 (T.T.A.B. 1993)—§§ 9:17 n.11; 10:32 n.2

Hana Financial, Inc. v. Hana Bank, 135 S. Ct. 907, 190 L. Ed. 2d 800
(2015)—§ 9:25 n.11, 12

Harley-Davidson Motor Co. v. Iron Eagle of Cent. Florida, Inc., 973 F.
Supp. 1421 (M.D. Fla. 1997)—§ 11:32 n.4

Harold F. Ritchie, Inc. v. Chesebrough-Pond's, Inc., 281 F.2d 755 (2d Cir.
1960)—§ 11:9 n.12

Harper & Row Publishers, Inc. v. Nation Enterprises, 471 U.S. 539, 105
S. Ct. 2218, 85 L. Ed. 2d 588 (1985)—§§ 6:22 n.3; 8:18 n.3

Harper & Row, Publishers, Inc. v. Nation Enterprises, 501 F. Supp. 848
(S.D. N.Y. 1980)—§ 8:5 n.2

Harper House, Inc. v. Thomas Nelson, Inc., 889 F.2d 197 (9th Cir.
1989)—§§ 6:5 n.16; 11:38 n.33

Harris v. Emus Records Corp., 734 F.2d 1329 (9th Cir. 1984)—§ 8:21 n.7

Hartford House, Ltd. v. Hallmark Cards, Inc., 846 F.2d 1268 (10th Cir.
1988)—§ 11:8 n.16

Hasbro, Inc. v. Clue Computing, Inc., 66 F. Supp. 2d 117 (D. Mass.
1999)—§ 11:27 n.5

Haughton Elevator Company v. Seeberger (Otis Elevator Company
Substituted), 85 U.S.P.Q. 80, 1950 WL 4178 (Comm'r Pat. &
Trademarks 1950)—§ 9:26 n.3

Hazeltine Research Corporation v. Freed-Eisemann Radio Corporation,
3 F.2d 172 (E.D. N.Y. 1924)—§ 14:12 n.2

HBP, Inc. v. American Marine Holdings, Inc., 290 F. Supp. 2d 1320
(M.D. Fla. 2003)—§ 11:28 n.55

Helferich Patent Licensing, LLC v. New York Times Co., 778 F.3d 1293
(Fed. Cir. 2015)—§ 5:47 n.6

Helsinn Healthcare S.A. v. Dr. Reddy's Laboratories Ltd., 2016 WL
832089 (D.N.J. 2016)—§ 5:36 n.6

Herbaceuticals, Inc. v. Xel Herbaceuticals, Inc., 86 U.S.P.Q.2d 1572,
2008 WL 618623 (T.T.A.B. 2008)—§ 10:19 n.4

Herbert Rosenthal Jewelry Corp. v. Kalpakian, 446 F.2d 738 (9th Cir.
1971)—§ 6:18 n.3

Hercules, Inc. v. Exxon Corp., 434 F. Supp. 136, 24 Fed. R. Serv. 2d 1343
(D. Del. 1977)—§ 5:19 n.6

Herman Miller, Inc. v. Palazzetti Imports and Exports, Inc., 270 F.3d
298 (6th Cir. 2001)—§ 11:17 n.3

Herrick v. Garvey, 298 F.3d 1184, 59 Fed. R. Evid. Serv. 472 (10th Cir.
2002)—§ 12:5 n.2

Hershey, In re, 6 U.S.P.Q.2d 1470, 1988 WL 252485 (T.T.A.B. 1988)—
§ 10:26 n.9

Hester Industries, Inc. v. Tyson Foods, Inc., 16 U.S.P.Q.2d 1275, 1990
WL 88645 (N.D. N.Y. 1990)—§ 11:28 n.51

Hewlett-Packard Co. v. Repeat-O-Type Stencil Mfg. Corp., Inc., 123 F.3d
1445 (Fed. Cir. 1997)—§ 5:10 n.4

H.H. Robertson, Co. v. United Steel Deck, Inc., 820 F.2d 384 (Fed. Cir.
1987)—§ 5:25 n.4

Hiland Potato Chip Co. v. Culbro Snack Foods, Inc., 720 F.2d 981 (8th

I

J

L

N

O

1990 WL 120945 (N.D. N.Y. 1990)—§ 11:28 n.47

Robbins Co. v. Lawrence Mfg. Co., 482 F.2d 426, 25 A.L.R. Fed. 473 (9th Cir. 1973)—§ 2:33 n.43

Roberson v. Rochester Folding Box Co., 171 N.Y. 538, 64 N.E. 442 (1902)—§ 13:5 n.8

Robert Bosch, LLC v. Snap-On Inc., 769 F.3d 1094 (Fed. Cir. 2014)— § 5:15 n.5

Robert R. Jones Associates, Inc. v. Nino Homes, 858 F.2d 274, 26 Fed. R. Evid. Serv. 1245, 100 A.L.R. Fed. 241 (6th Cir. 1988)—§ 6:3 n.33

Robert Stigwood Group Ltd. v. O'Reilly, 530 F.2d 1096 (2d Cir. 1976)— § 16:3 n.14

Roboserve, Ltd. v. Tom's Foods, Inc., 940 F.2d 1441, 16 U.C.C. Rep. Serv. 2d 987 (11th Cir. 1991)—§ 12:15 n.2

Rockland Mortg. Corp. v. Shareholders Funding, Inc., 835 F. Supp. 182 (D. Del. 1993)—§ 9:5 n.3

Rogers v. Grimaldi, 875 F.2d 994 (2d Cir. 1989)—§ 11:36 n.13

Roley v. New World Pictures, Ltd., 19 F.3d 479, 140 A.L.R. Fed. 813 (9th Cir. 1994)—§ 8:23 n.3, 4

Rolley, Inc. v. Younghusband, 204 F.2d 209 (9th Cir. 1953)—§ 10:1 n.4

Roman Cleanser Co., Matter of, 43 B.R. 940, 39 U.C.C. Rep. Serv. 1770 (Bankr. E.D. Mich. 1984)—§ 14:27 n.3

Rosetta Stone Ltd. v. Google, Inc., 676 F.3d 144 (4th Cir. 2012)—§ 11:27 n.1

Ross, Brovins & Oehmke, P.C. v. Lexis Nexis Group, a Div. of Reed Elsevier Group, PLC, 463 F.3d 478, 2006 FED App. 0358P (6th Cir. 2006)—§ 6:5 n.13

Rototron Corp. v. Lake Shore Burial Vault Co., Inc., 712 F.2d 1214 (7th Cir. 1983)—§ 12:16 n.1

Roulo v. Russ Berrie & Co., Inc., 886 F.2d 931 (7th Cir. 1989)—§ 11:15 n.17

Rubbermaid Commercial Products, Inc. v. Contico Intern., Inc., 836 F. Supp. 1247 (W.D. Va. 1993)—§ 9:16 n.27

Russ Berrie & Co., Inc. v. Jerry Elsner Co., Inc., 482 F. Supp. 980 (S.D. N.Y. 1980)—§ 8:21 n.2

S

Safeway Stores, Inc. v. Safeway Quality Foods, Inc., 433 F.2d 99 (7th Cir. 1970)—§ 11:21 n.4

Sage Products, Inc. v. Devon Industries, Inc., 45 F.3d 1575 (Fed. Cir. 1995)—§ 5:50 n.6

Salazar v. Procter & Gamble Co., 414 F.3d 1342 (Fed. Cir. 2005)—§ 3:32 n.3

Sally Gee, Inc. v. Myra Hogan, Inc., 699 F.2d 621 (2d Cir. 1983)—§ 11:22 n.6

Salsbury Laboratories, Inc. v. Merieux Laboratories, Inc., 908 F.2d 706 (11th Cir. 1990)—§ 12:1 n.9

Sanda Hosiery Mills, In re, 154 U.S.P.Q. 631, 1967 WL 11667 (T.T.A.B. 1967)—§ 9:12 n.19

Sandberg and Sikorski Corp. v. Andin International Inc., 51 U.S.P.Q.2d 1574, 1999 WL 628076 (S.D. N.Y. 1999)—§ 7:1 n.6

T

U

X

Index